Lecture Notes in Computer Science 2239
Edited by G. Goos, J. Hartmanis, and J. van Leeuwen

Springer
Berlin
Heidelberg
New York
Barcelona
Hong Kong
London
Milan
Paris
Tokyo

Toby Walsh (Ed.)

Principles and Practice of Constraint Programming – CP 2001

7th International Conference, CP 2001
Paphos, Cyprus, November 26 – December 1, 2001
Proceedings

Springer

Series Editors

Gerhard Goos, Karlsruhe University, Germany
Juris Hartmanis, Cornell University, NY, USA
Jan van Leeuwen, Utrecht University, The Netherlands

Volume Editor

Toby Walsh
The University of York, Department of Computer Science
Heslington, York, YO10 5DD, UK
E-mail: tw@cs.york.ac.uk

Cataloging-in-Publication Data applied for

Die Deutsche Bibliothek - CIP-Einheitsaufnahme

Principles and practice of constraint programming : 7th international conference ; proceedings / CP 2001, Paphos, Cyprus, November 26 – December 1, 2001. Toby Walsh (ed.). - Berlin ; Heidelberg ; New York ; Barcelona ; Hong Kong ; London ; Milan ; Paris ; Tokyo : Springer, 2001
(Lecture notes in computer science ; Vol. 2239)
ISBN 3-540-42863-1

CR Subject Classification (1998): D.1, D.3.2-3, I.2.3-4, F.3.2, F.4.1, I.2.8

ISSN 0302-9743
ISBN 3-540-42863-1 Springer-Verlag Berlin Heidelberg New York

Springer-Verlag Berlin Heidelberg New York
a member of BertelsmannSpringer Science+Business Media GmbH

http://www.springer.de

Printed in Germany

Typesetting: Camera-ready by author, data conversion by PTP-Berlin, Stefan Sossna
Printed on acid-free paper SPIN: 10845842 06/3142 5 4 3 2 1 0

Preface

The Seventh International Conference on Principles and Practice of Constraint Programming (CP 2001) provided an international forum for cutting edge research into constraints. There were several important innovations at the conference this year. Most important of these were the Innovative Applications program, the Doctoral Program, and co-location with the 17th International Conference on Logic Programming (ICLP 2001).

The Innovative Applications (IA) Program showcased the very best applications of constraint technology. It provided a forum for practitioners and end users, and an interface between them and academic researchers. It took over the task previously performed by the Conference on the Practical Application of Constraint Technologies and Logic Programming (PACLP). I am especially gratefully to Edward Tsang, who was to be Chair of PACLP 2001, for chairing this section of the conference.

The second innovation, the Doctoral Program allowed PhD students to present their work and to receive feedback from more senior members of the community. I am especially grateful to Francesca Rossi who chaired this section of the conference, and who raised enough sponsorship to support the participation of over two dozen students.

This volume contains the papers accepted for presentation at CP 2001. The conference attracted a record number of 135 submissions. Of these, 37 papers were accepted for presentation in the Technical Program. A further 9 papers were accepted into the Innovative Applications Program. In addition, 14 papers were accepted as short papers and presented as posters during the Technical Program.

We were privileged to have three distinguished invited speakers this year: Peter van Beek (University of Waterloo), Eugene Freuder (Cork Constraint Computation Center), and Moshe Vardi (Rice University). We also had a large number of workshops and tutorials organized by Thomas Schiex, the Workshop and Tutorial Chair.

Finally, I would like to thank Antonis Kakas, the Local Chair who did a great job organizing both CP 2001 and ICLP 2001. I would also like to thank again Edward Tsang and Francesca Rossi, as well as Thomas Schiex, and last but not least Ian Miguel, the Publicity Chair.

September 2001 Toby Walsh

Conference Organization

Conference Chair:	Toby Walsh (University of York, UK)
Local Chair:	Antonis Kakas (University of Cyprus, Cyprus)
Chair of IA Program:	Edward Tsang (University of Essex, UK)
Chair of Doctoral Program:	Francesca Rossi (University of Padova, Italy)
Workshop and Tutorial Chair:	Thomas Schiex (INRA, France)
Publicity Chair:	Ian Miguel (University of York, UK)

Program Committee

Fahiem Bacchus
Christian Bessiere
Philippe Codognet
Boi Faltings
Thom Fruehwirth
Georg Gottlob
Pascal Van Hentenryck
Peter Jonsson
Helene Kirchner
Manolis Koubarakis
Francois Laburthe
Javier Larrosa
Joao Marques-Silva
Pedro Meseguer
Michela Milano
Jean-Charles Regin
Christian Schulte
Peter Stuckey
Benjamin Wah
Roland Yap
Makoto Yokoo

Prizes

Best Paper (Technical Program)
Hybrid Benders Decomposition Algorithms in Constraint Logic Programming, Andrew Eremin and Mark Wallace.
Branch-and-Check: A Hybrid Framework Integrating Mixed Integer Programming and Constraint Logic Programming, Erlendur S. Thorsteinsson.

Best Paper (Innovative Applications Program)
Fast Optimal Instruction Scheduling for Single-Issue Processors with Arbitrary Latencies, Peter van Beek and Kent Wilken.

Sponsors

AAAI
ALP
CP Organizing Committee
Cyprus Telecommunications Authority
IBM
ILOG Inc.
SINTEF
UK Constraints Network (EPSRC)
University of Cyprus

Additional Referees

Ola Angelsmark
Alessandro Armando
Philippe Baptiste
Pedro Barahona
Oskar Bartenstein
Nicolas Beldiceanu
Frédéric Benhamou
Thierry Benoist
Stefano Bistarelli
Christian Bliek
Alexander Bockmayr
James Borrett
Eric Bourreau
Stéphane Bressan
Ken Brown
Marco Cadoli
Carlos Castro
Amedeo Cesta
Yixin Chen
Berthe Choueiry
Dave Cohen
James Cussens
Romuald Debruyne
Rina Dechter
Yves Deville
Clare Dixon
Sylvain Durand
Francois Fages
Torsten Fahle
Filippo Focacci
Alan Frisch
Vincent Furnon
Rosella Gennari
Ian Gent
Carmen Gervet
Ulrich Geske
Vineet Gupta
Warwick Harvey
Martin Henz
Miki Hermann
Luc Hernandez
Pat Hill
Katsutoshi Hirayama
Petra Hofstedt
Kazuhoshi Honda
Peter Jeavons
Ulrich Junker
Kalev Kask
Thomas Kasper
Michael Kohlhase
Phokion Kolaitis
Alvin Kwan
Jimmy Lee
Nicola Leone
Claude LePape
Jordi Levy
Olivier Lhomme
Gerard Ligozat
Andrew Lim
Carsten Lutz
Ines Lynce
Iain McDonald
Arnold Maestre
Kazuhisa Makino
Vasco Manquinho
Michael Marte
Laurent Michel
Philippe Michelon
Ian Miguel
Patrick Mills
Eric Monfroy
Pierre-Etienne Moreau
Tobias Müller
Bertrand Neveu
Greger Ottoson
Catuscia Palamidessi
Jordi Pereira
Thierry Petit
Nicolai Pisaruk
Dimitrios Plexousakis
Patrick Prosser
Jean-Francois Puget
Minglun Qian
Philippe Refalo
Jochen Renz
Nadine Richard
Christophe Rigotti
Christophe Ringeissen
Andrea Roli
Nicolas Romero
Francesca Rossi
Benoit Rottembourg
Abhik Roychoudhury
Michel Rueher
Michael Rusinowitch
Djamila Sam-Haroud
Marti Sanchez
Frederic Saubion
Francesco Scarcello
Thomas Schiex
Eddie Schwalb
Yi Shang
Paul Shaw
Qiang Shen
Marius-Calin Silaghi
Nikos Skarmeas
Spiros Skiadopoulos
Wolfgang Slany
John Slaney
Oscar Slotosch
Francis Sourd
Kostas Stergiou
Terrance Swift
Vincent Tam
Jose Teixeira de Sousa
Sven Thiel
Erlendur Thorsteinsson
Carme Torras
Marc Torrens
Andrew Verden
Gérard Verfaillie
Laurent Vigneron
Marie Vilarem
Chris Voudris
Mark Wallace
Richard Wallace
Joachim Walser
Armin Wolf
Franz Wotawa
Weixiong Zhang

Table of Contents

Hybrid Benders Decomposition Algorithms in Constraint Logic Programming

Andrew Eremin and Mark Wallace

IC-Parc
London, UK
{a.eremin, mgw}@icparc.ic.ac.uk

Abstract. Benders Decomposition is a form of hybridisation that allows linear programming to be combined with other kinds of algorithms. It extracts new constraints for one subproblem from the dual values of the other subproblem. This paper describes an implementation of Benders Decomposition, in the ECLiPSe language, that enables it to be used within a constraint programming framework. The programmer is spared from having to write down the dual form of any subproblem, because it is derived by the system. Examples are used to show how problem constraints can be modelled in an undecomposed form. The programmer need only specify which variables belong to which subproblems, and the Benders Decomposition is extracted automatically. A class of minimal perturbation problems is used to illustrate how different kinds of algorithms can be used for the different subproblems. The implementation is tested on a set of minimal perturbation benchmarks, and the results are analysed.

1 Introduction

1.1 Forms of Hybridisation

In recent years, research on combinatorial problem solving has begun to address real world problems which arise in industry and commerce [1,2,3]. These problems are often large scale, complex, optimisation (LSCO) problems and are best addressed by decomposing them into multiple subproblems. The optimal solutions of the different subproblems are invariably incompatible with each other, so researchers are now exploring ways of solving the subproblems in a way that ensures the solutions are compatible with each another - i.e. globally consistent. This research topic belongs to the area of "hybrid algorithms" [4,5], but more specifically it addresses ways of making different solvers cooperate with each other. Following [6] we shall talk about "forms of hybridisation".

An early form of hybridisation is the communication between global constraints in constraint programming, via the finite domains of the shared variables. Different subproblems are handled by different global constraints (for example a scheduling subproblem by a cumulative constraint and a TSP subproblem by a cycle constraint [7]), and they act independently on the different subproblems

T. Walsh (Ed.): CP 2001, LNCS 2239, pp. 1–15, 2001.

yielding domain reductions. This is a clean and sound hybridisation form because a domain reduction which is correct for a subproblem is necessarily correct for any larger problem in which the subproblem is contained.

1.2 Hybridisation Forms for Linear Programming

Master Problems and other Subproblems. LSCO problems involve a cost function, and for performance reasons it is important to find solutions quickly that are not only feasible but also of low cost. Usually these cost functions are linear, or can be approximated by a linear or piecewise linear function. Linear programming offers efficient constraint solvers which can quickly return optimal solutions to problems whose cost function and constraints can be expressed using only linear expressions. Consequently most industrial LSCO problems involve one or more linear subproblems which are addressed using linear programming as available in commercial products such as XPRESS [8] and CPLEX [9].

Whilst global constraints classically return information excluding certain assignments from any possible solution, linear solvers classically return just a single optimal solution. In contrast with global constraints, the information returned by a linear solver for a subproblem does not necessarily remain true for any larger problem in which it is embedded. Thus linear solvers cannot easily be hybridised in the same way as global constraints.

Nevertheless several hybridisation forms have been developed for linear solvers, based on the concept of a "master" problem, for which the optimal solution is found, and other subproblems which interact with the master problem. In the simplest case this interaction is as follows. The subproblem examines the last optimal solution produced for the master problem, and determines whether this solution violates any of the constraints of the subproblem. If so the subproblem returns to the master problem one or more alternative linear constraints which could be added to the master problem to prevent this violation occurring again. One of these constraints is added to the master problem and a new optimal solution is found. To prove *global* optimality each of the alternatives are added to the master problem on different branches of a search tree. These alternatives should cover all possible ways of fixing the violation.

A generalisation of this form of hybridisation is "row generation" [10], where a new set of constraints ("rows") are added to the master problem at each node of the search tree. Unimodular probing [11] is an integration of a form of row generation into constraint programming.

Column Generation. Another form of hybridisation for linear programming is *column generation* [12]. In this case the master problem is to find the optimal combination of "pieces" where each piece is itself a solution of another subproblem. A typical application of column generation is to crew scheduling: the assignment of crew to a bus or flight schedule over a day or a month. There are complex constraints on the sequence of activities that can be undertaken by a single crew, and these constraints are handled in a subproblem whose solutions are complete tours which can be covered by a single crew over the time period. The master problem is the optimal combination of such tours. The master problem constraints enforce that each scheduled bus trip or flight must belong to one tour. Each tour is represented in the master problem by a variable, which corresponds to a column in the matrix representing the problem.

In the general case, each call to another subproblem returns a solution which has the potential to improve on the current optimum for the master problem. Each call to a subproblem adds a column to the master problem, and hence the name "column generation".

A number of applications of column generation have been reported in which the subproblem is solved by constraint programming [13,14]. A column generation library has been implemented in the ECLiPSe constraint logic programming system, which allows both subproblem, communication of solutions and search to be specified and controlled from the constraint program.

While column generation utilises the *dual values* returned from convex solvers to form the optimisation function of a subproblem, a closely related technique exploits them to approximate subproblem constraints within the optimisation function of the master problem. This technique is known as *Lagrangian relaxation* and has been used for hybridising constraint programming and convex optimisation by Sellmann and Fahle [15] and Benoist et. al. [16] in[17].

Other Hybridisation Forms. Besides optimal solutions, linear solvers can return several kinds of information about the solution. *Reduced costs* are the changes in the cost which would result from changes in the values of specific variables. These are, in fact, underestimates so if the reduced cost is "-10" the actual increase in cost will be greater than or equal to 10. In case the variable has finite domain, these reduced costs can be used to prune values from the domain in the usual style of a global constraint. (A value is pruned from the domain if the associated reduced cost is so bad it would produce a solution worse than the current optimum). In this way linear programming can be hybridised with other solvers in the usual manner of constraint programming. Indeed the technique has been used very successfully [18].

1.3 Benders Decomposition

Benders Decomposition is a hybridisation form based on the master problem/subproblem relationship. It makes use of an important and elegant aspect of mathematical programming, the dual problem [19]. Benders Decomposition is applicable when some of the constraints and part of the optimisation function exhibit duality. The master problem need not use mathematical programming at all. The subproblems return information which can be extracted by solving the dual. The new constraints that are added to the master problem are extracted from the dual values of the subproblems.

We have implemented Benders Decomposition in ECLiPSe and used it to tackle several commercial applications in transportation and telecommunications. The technique has proved very successful and has outperformed all other hybridisation forms in these applications.

For the purposes of this paper we have also used Benders Decomposition to tackle a set of benchmarks originally designed to test another hybridisation form, Unimodular Probing [11]. Whilst our results on these benchmarks have not been so striking as the applications mentioned above, they nicely illustrate the use of Benders Decomposition and the combination of linear programming with a simple propagation algorithm for the master problem. From these benchmarks we also make some observations about the kinds of problems and decompositions that are most suited to the hybrid form of Benders Decomposition.

1.4 Contents

In the following section we introduce Benders Decomposition, explain and justify it, and present the generic Benders Decomposition algorithm. In section 3 we show how it is embedded in constraint programming. We describe the user interface, and how one models a problem to use Benders Decomposition in ECLiPSe. We also describe how it is implemented in ECLiPSe. In section 4 we present the application of Benders Decomposition to a "minimal perturbation" problem, its definition, explanation and results on a set of benchmarks. Section 5 concludes and discusses the next application, further work on modeling and integration, and open issues.

2 Benders Decomposition

Benders decomposition is a cut or row generation technique for the solution of specially structured mixed integer linear programs that was introduced in the OR literature in [20]. Given a problem $\mathbf{P}$ over a set of variables V, if a subset X of the variables can be identified for which fixing their values results in one or more disconnected *SubProblems* ($\mathbf{SP_i}$) over the variable sets $Y_i : \bigcup_i Y_i = V - X$ which are easily soluble — normally due to some structural property of the resulting constraints — it may be beneficial to solve the problem by a two stage iterative procedure.
At each iteration k a *Relaxed Master Problem* ($\mathbf{RMP^k}$) in the complicating or connecting variables X is first solved and the solution assignment $X = X^k$ used to construct the subproblems $\mathbf{SP^k_i}$; these subproblems are then solved and the solutions used to tighten the relaxation of the master problem by introducing *Benders Cuts*, $\beta^k_i(X)$.
The subproblems optimise over reduced dimensionality subspaces $\mathcal{D}^k_{Y_i}$ of the original problem solution space obtained by fixing the variables $X = X^k$, while the master problem optimises over the optimal solutions of these subspaces augmented by X^k guided by the cuts generated.
In classical Benders Decomposition both the master and subproblems are linear and are solved by MILP algorithms, while the cuts are derived from Duality

theory. In general however, we are free to use any appropriate solution methods for master and subproblems — all that is required is an assignment of the master problem variables $X = X^k$ to construct convex subproblems, and a procedure for generating valid cuts from subproblem solutions. The most naive such scheme would merely result in the master problem enumerating all assignments of X, while more informative cuts can result in substantial pruning of the master problem search space.

2.1 Classical Benders Decomposition

Consider the linear program $\mathbf{P}$ given by:

$$\begin{aligned}\mathbf{P}: \min \ & \mathbf{f^T x} + \sum_{i=1}^{I} \mathbf{c_i^T y_i} \\ \text{subject to} \quad & \mathbf{G_i x} + \mathbf{A_i y_i} \geq \mathbf{b_i} \qquad \forall i \\ & \mathbf{x} \in \mathcal{D}_X \\ & \mathbf{y_i} \geq \mathbf{0} \qquad \forall i\end{aligned} \tag{1}$$

When $\mathbf{x}$ is fixed to some value $\mathbf{x^k}$ we have linear programs in $\mathbf{y_i}$ which may be specially structured or easy to solve, prompting us to partition the problem as follows:

$$\begin{aligned}\mathbf{P}: \quad & \min_{\mathbf{x} \in \mathcal{D}_X} \left\{ \mathbf{f^T x} + \sum_{i=1}^{I} \left(\min \left\{ \mathbf{c_i^T y_i} : \mathbf{A_i y_i} \geq \mathbf{b_i} - \mathbf{G_i x}, \mathbf{y_i} \geq \mathbf{0} \right\} \right) \right\} \\ = \ & \min_{\mathbf{x} \in \mathcal{D}_X} \left\{ \mathbf{f^T x} + \sum_{i=1}^{I} \left(\max \left\{ \mathbf{u_i}(\mathbf{b_i} - \mathbf{G_i x}) : \mathbf{u_i A_i} \leq \mathbf{c_i}, \mathbf{u_i} \geq \mathbf{0} \right\} \right) \right\}\end{aligned} \tag{2}$$

where the inner optimizations have been dualised. Given that $U_i = \{\mathbf{u_i} : \mathbf{u_i A_i} \leq \mathbf{c_i}, \mathbf{u_i} \geq \mathbf{0}\}$ is non-empty for each i either there is an extreme point optimal solution to each inner optimization or it is unbounded along an extreme ray; letting $\mathbf{u_i^1}, \ldots, \mathbf{u_i^{t_i}}$ and $\mathbf{d_i^1}, \ldots, \mathbf{d_i^{s_i}}$ be respectively the extreme points and directions of U_i we can rewrite (2) as the mixed integer *Master Problem* **MP**:

$$\begin{aligned}\mathbf{MP}: \min \ & z = \mathbf{f^T x} + \sum_{i=1}^{I} \beta_i \\ \text{subject to} \quad & \beta_i \geq \mathbf{u_i^k}(\mathbf{b_i} - \mathbf{G_i x}) \qquad \forall i \quad \forall k \\ & 0 \geq \mathbf{d_i^l}(\mathbf{b_i} - \mathbf{G_i x}) \qquad \forall i \quad \forall l \\ & \mathbf{x} \in \mathcal{D}_X\end{aligned} \tag{3}$$

Since there will typically be very many extreme points and directions of each U_i and thus constraints in (3) we solve relaxed master problems containing a subset of the constraints. If for some relaxed master problem $\mathbf{RMP^k}$ the optimal relaxed solution $(z^k, \mathbf{x^k})$ satisfies all the constraints of (3), then $(z^k, \mathbf{x^k}, \mathbf{y_1^k}, \ldots, \mathbf{y_I^k})$ is an optimal solution of (1); otherwise there exists some constraint or *Benders*

Cut in (3) which is violated for $\mathbf{x} = \mathbf{x^k}$ which we add to $\mathbf{RMP^k}$ to form $\mathbf{RMP^{k+1}}$ and iterate.
To determine such a cut or prove optimality we obtain the optimal solution $(\beta_i^k, \mathbf{u_i^k})$ of the *Subproblems* $\mathbf{SP_i^k}$ formed by fixing $\mathbf{x} = \mathbf{x^k}$ in (2):

$$\begin{array}{ll} \mathbf{SP_i^k} : \max\ \beta_i^k = \mathbf{u_i}(\mathbf{b_i} - \mathbf{G_i x^k}) & \\ \text{subject to} \quad \mathbf{u_i A_i} \le \mathbf{c_i} & \\ \qquad\qquad\quad \mathbf{u_i} \ge \mathbf{0} & \end{array} \tag{4}$$

If any subproblem $\mathbf{SP_i^k}$ has an unbounded optimal solution for some $\mathbf{x^k}$ then the primal of the subproblem is infeasible for $\mathbf{x^k}$; if any subproblem $\mathbf{SP_i^k}$ is infeasible for some $\mathbf{x^k}$ then it is infeasible (and the primal of the subproblem is infeasible or unbounded) for any $\mathbf{x}$ since the (empty) feasible region U_i is independent of $\mathbf{x}$. In either case we proceed by considering the *Homogeneous Dual* of the primal of the subproblem:

$$\begin{array}{l} \max\ \mathbf{u_i}(\mathbf{b_i} - \mathbf{G_i x^k}) \\ \text{subject to} \quad \mathbf{u_i A_i} \le \mathbf{0} \\ \qquad\qquad\quad \mathbf{u_i} \ge \mathbf{0} \end{array} \tag{5}$$

This problem is always feasible ($\mathbf{u_i} = \mathbf{0}$ is a solution), having an unbounded optimum precisely when the primal is infeasible and a finite optimal solution when the primal is feasible. In the unbounded case we can obtain a cut

$$\mathbf{u_i^k}(\mathbf{b_i} - \mathbf{G_i x}) \le 0$$

corresponding to an extreme direction of $U_i' = \{\mathbf{u_i} : \mathbf{u_i A_i} \le \mathbf{0}, \mathbf{u_i} \ge \mathbf{0}\}$. The complete Benders decomposition algorithm proceeds as follows:

Algorithm 1 *The Benders Decomposition Algorithm*

1. Initialisation step: From the original linear program $\mathbf{P}$ (1) construct the *relaxed master problem* $\mathbf{RMP^0}$ (3) with the initial constraint set $\mathbf{x} \in \mathcal{D}_X$ and set $k = 0$.
2. Iterative step: From the current relaxed master problem $\mathbf{RMP^k}$ with optimal solution $(z^k, \mathbf{x^k})$ construct $\mathbf{RMP^{k+1}}$ with optimal solution $(z^{k+1}, \mathbf{x^{k+1}})$: fix $\mathbf{x} = \mathbf{x^k}$ in $\mathbf{P}$, and solve the resulting *subproblems* $\mathbf{SP_i^k}$ (4); there are three cases to consider:
   a) $\mathbf{SP_i^k}$ is primal unbounded for some i — halt with the original problem having unbounded solution.
   b) $\mathbf{y_i^k}, \mathbf{u_i^k}$ are respectively primal and dual optimal solutions of subproblem $\mathbf{SP_i^k}$ with objective values β_i^k for each i — there are two cases to consider:
      i. $\sum_{i=1}^{I} \beta_i^k = z^k$ halt with $(z^k, \mathbf{x^k}, \mathbf{y_1^k}, \ldots, \mathbf{y_I^k})$ as the optimal solution to the original problem.
      ii. $\sum_{i=1}^{I} \beta_i^k > z^k$ add the *Benders Cuts* $\beta_i \ge \mathbf{u_i^k}(\mathbf{b_i} - \mathbf{G_i x})$ to $\mathbf{RMP^k}$ to form the new relaxed master problem $\mathbf{RMP^{k+1}}$ set $k = k+1$ and return to (2).
   c) $\mathbf{SP_i^k}$ is dual unbounded or both primal and dual infeasible for some i — find an extreme direction $\mathbf{d_i^k}$ of the homogeneous dual leading to unboundedness; add the cut $\mathbf{d_i^k}(\mathbf{b_i} - \mathbf{G_i x}) \le 0$ to $\mathbf{RMP^k}$ to form the new relaxed master problem $\mathbf{RMP^{k+1}}$ set $k = k+1$ and return to (2).

2.2 Hybrid Benders Decomposition

The classical linear Benders Decomposition can be generalised to cover problems in which the constraints and objective function are nonlinear, using any appropriate solution method for $\mathbf{RMP^k}$ and $\mathbf{SP_i^k}$ — we require only a procedure for generating valid lower bounds $\beta_i^k(x)$ from the solutions of $\mathbf{SP_i^k}$. In its most general form we have the original problem:

$$\begin{array}{rll} \mathbf{P}: \min & f(f_1(\mathbf{x},\mathbf{y_1}),\ldots,f_I(\mathbf{x},\mathbf{y_I})) & \\ \text{subject to} & g_i(\mathbf{x},\mathbf{y_i}) \geq \mathbf{b_i} & \forall i \\ & \mathbf{x} \in \mathcal{D}_X & \\ & \mathbf{y_i} \in \mathcal{D}_Y & \forall i \end{array} \tag{6}$$

which we decompose into the master problem:

$$\begin{array}{rll} \mathbf{MP}: \min & z = f(\mathbf{x},\beta_1\ldots,\beta_I) & \\ \text{subject to} & \beta_i \geq \beta_i^k(\mathbf{x}) & \forall i\ \forall k \\ & 0 \geq \beta_i^l(\mathbf{x}) & \forall i\ \forall l \\ & \mathbf{x} \in \mathcal{D}_X & \end{array} \tag{7}$$

and subproblems:

$$\begin{array}{rl} \mathbf{SP_i^k}: \min & f_i(\mathbf{x^k},\mathbf{y_i}) \\ \text{subject to} & g_i(\mathbf{x^k},\mathbf{y_i}) \geq \mathbf{b_i} \\ & \mathbf{y_i} \in \mathcal{D}_Y \end{array} \tag{8}$$

In particular when we can identify one or more distinct sets of variables in which the problem constraints and objective function are linear and a complicating set of variables, it will be useful to decompose the problem into a nonlinear relaxed master problem and linear subproblems.

3 Embedding Benders Decomposition in Constraint Programming

In this section we discuss the implementation of Benders Decomposition in ECLiPSe . In designing the structure of the implementation two important considerations were to maintain the flexibility of the approach and to ensure ease of use for non-mathematicians.

The flexibility of hybrid Benders Decomposition algorithms is due in large part to the possibility of using arbitrary solution methods for master and subproblems; in order to allow appropriate solvers to be simply slotted in to the framework it is essential to cleanly separate the method of solution of master and subproblems from the communication of solutions between them.

As many users of the solver may be unfamiliar with the intricacies of linear programming and duality theory, it is important to provide a user interface that allows for problems to be modeled in a natural and straightforward formulation. All constraints are therefore input in their original formulation — i.e. without having been decomposed and dualised and containing both master and subproblem variables. The sets of variables occurring solely in the subproblems are specified when the optimisation is performed, and the original problem constraints automatically decomposed into master and subproblem constraints and the subproblems dualised.

3.1 ECLiPSe Implementation

The implementation of Benders Decomposition in ECLiPSe uses the same features of the language that are used to implement finite domain and other constraints. These are demons, variable attributes, waking conditions, and priorities.

A demon is a procedure which, on completing its processing, suspends itself. It can be woken repeatedly, each time re-suspending on completion, until killed by an explicit command. Demons are typically used to implement constraint propagation. For Benders Decomposition a demon is used to implement the solver for the master problem, with separate demons for each subproblem.

A variable attribute is used to hold information about a variable, such as its finite domain. Programmers can add further attributes, and for Benders decomposition an attribute is used to hold a *tentative* value for each of the variables in the master problem. Each time the master problem is solved, the tentative values of all the variables are updated to record the new solution.

When the waking conditions for a demon are satisfied, it wakes. For a finite domain constraint this is typically a reduction in the domain of any of the variables in the constraint. For the subproblems in Benders Decomposition the waking condition is a change in the tentative values of any variable linking the subproblem to the master problem. Thus each time the master problem is solved any subproblem whose linking variables now have a new value is woken, and solved again. The master problem is woken whenever a new constraint (in the form of a *Benders cut*) is passed to the solver. Thus processing stops at some iteration either if after solving the master problem no subproblems are woken, or if after solving all the subproblems no new cuts are produced.

Priorities are used in ECLiPSe to ensure that when several demons are woken they are executed in order of priority. For finite domain propagation this is used to ensure that simple constraints, such as inequalities, are handled before expensive global constraints. By setting the subproblems at a higher priority than the master problem, it is ensured that all the subproblems are solved and the resulting Benders cuts are all added to the master problem, before the master problem itself is solved again. While it is possible to wake the master problem early with only some cuts added by setting lower priorities for subproblems, this proved ineffective in practice.

4 Benders Decomposition for Scheduling Problems

4.1 Minimal Perturbation in Dynamic Scheduling with Time Windows

The minimal perturbation dynamic scheduling problem with time windows and side constraints is a variant of the classic scheduling problem with time windows:

given a current schedule for a set of n possibly variable duration tasks with time windows on their start and end time points, a set $\mathcal{C}$ of unary and binary side constraints over these time points and a reduced number of resources r we are required to produce a new schedule feasible to the existing time windows and constraints and the new resource constraint that is minimally different from the current schedule.
The user enters these problems in a simple form that is automatically translated into a set of constraints that can be passed to the `bd` library. For the purposes of this paper, in the next section we give the full model generated by the translator. The subsequent section reports how this model is split into a master/subproblem form for Benders Decomposition

4.2 The Constraints Modeling Minimal Perturbation

For each task T_i in the current schedule with current start and end times t_{s_i}, t_{e_i} respectively there are:

Time point variables for the start and end of the task s_i, e_i and **task duration constraints**

$$(s_i, e_i) \in \mathcal{L}_i \tag{9}$$

where $\mathcal{D}_i = \{(s,e)\colon e - s \geq l_i,\ e - s \leq u_i,\ l_{s_i} \leq s \leq u_{s_i},\ l_{e_i} \leq e \leq u_{e_i}\}$ and $l_{s_i}, u_{s_i}, l_{e_i}, u_{e_i}, l_i, u_i$ are derived from the time windows of the task start and end points and any constraints on these time points in $\mathcal{C}$.

Perturbation cost variables c_{s_i}, c_{e_i} and **perturbation cost constraints**

$$(c_{s_i}, s_i, c_{e_i}, e_i) \in \mathcal{P}_i \tag{10}$$

where $\mathcal{P}_i = \{(c_s, s, c_e, e) : c_s \geq s - t_{s_i},\ c_s \geq t_{s_i} - s,\ c_e \geq e - t_{e_i},\ c_e \geq t_{e_i} - e\}$ so that $c_{s_i} \geq |s_i - t_{s_i}|, c_{e_i} \geq |e_i - t_{e_i}|$

For each pair of tasks T_i, T_j there are:

Binary non-overlap variables $Pre_{ij}, Post_{ij}$ for each task $T_j \neq T_i$ which take the value 1 iff task i starts before the start of task j and after the end of task j respectively, so that we have

$$Pre_{ij} = \begin{cases} 1 \text{ if } s_i < s_j \\ 0 \text{ if } s_i \geq s_j \end{cases} \qquad Post_{ij} = \begin{cases} 1 \text{ if } s_i \geq e_j \\ 0 \text{ if } s_i < e_j \end{cases}$$

and the distances between the time points s_i and s_j, e_j are bounded by

$$\begin{aligned} s_i - s_j &\geq \left(l_{s_i} - u_{s_j}\right) Pre_{ij} \\ s_i - s_j &\leq \left(l_{s_j} - u_{s_i} - 1\right) Pre_{ij} + \left(u_{s_i} - l_{s_j}\right) \\ s_i - e_j &\geq \left(u_{e_j} - l_{s_i}\right) Post_{ij} + \left(l_{s_i} - u_{e_j}\right) \\ s_i - e_j &\leq \left(u_{s_i} - l_{e_j} + 1\right) Post_{ij} - 1 \end{aligned} \tag{11}$$

The resource feasibility constraint that the start time point s_i overlaps with at most r other tasks

$$\sum_{j \neq i} (Pre_{ij} + Post_{ij}) \geq n - r - 1 \tag{12}$$

Time point distance constraints between s_i, e_i and all other time points. Since for each task $T_j \neq T_i$ we have the distance bounds (11) between s_i and T_j and between s_j and T_i of which at most half can be binding, we combine them with the binary constraints

$$\begin{array}{ll} s_i \geq s_j + b_{ij} & \quad e_j \geq s_i + b_{u_{ij}} \\ s_i \geq e_j + b_{l_{ij}} & \quad e_i \geq e_j + b_{e_{ij}} \end{array}$$

appearing in the constraint set $\mathcal{C}$ to give the distance constraints

$$\begin{array}{c} (s_i, e_i, s_j, e_j, B_{ij}, L_{ij}, U_{ij}) \in \mathcal{D}_{ij} \\ (s_i, e_i, s_j, e_j, B_{ij}, L_{ij}, U_{ij}, Pre_{ij}, Pre_{ji}, Post_{ij}) \in \mathcal{O}_{ij} \end{array} \tag{13}$$

where

$$\begin{aligned} \mathcal{D}_{ij} = \{ & (s_i, e_i, s_j, e_j, B, L, U) : \\ & s_i - s_j \geq B, s_i - e_j \geq L, -s_i + e_j \geq U, e_i - e_j \geq b_{e_{ij}} \} \\ \mathcal{O}_{ij} = \{ & (s_i, e_i, s_j, e_j, B, L, U, Pre_{ij}, Pre_{ji}, Post_{ij}) : \\ & B \geq b_{ij}, L \geq b_{l_{ij}}, U \geq b_{u_{ij}}, \\ & B \geq \left(l_{s_i} - u_{s_j}\right) Pre_{ij}, B \geq \left(u_{s_j} - l_{s_i} + 1\right) Pre_{ji} + \left(l_{s_i} - u_{s_j}\right), \\ & L \geq \left(u_{e_j} - l_{s_i}\right) Post_{ij} + \left(l_{s_i} - u_{e_j}\right), \\ & U \geq \left(l_{e_j} - u_{s_i} - 1\right) Post_{ij} + 1 \} \end{aligned}$$

Valid ordering constraints for each task $T_j \neq T_i$ there are many additional constraints that we may choose to introduce restricting the binary variables to represent a valid ordering. These constraints are not necessary for the correctness of the algorithm as invalid orderings will be infeasible to the subproblem, but may improve its efficiency as fewer iterations will be needed.

The complete MILP problem formulation is then

$$\mathbf{P} : \min \sum_{i=1}^{n} (c_{s_i} + c_{e_i})$$

subject to

$$\left.\begin{array}{rcl} (c_{s_i}, s_i, c_{e_i}, e_i) & \in & \mathcal{P}_i \\ (s_i, e_i) & \in & \mathcal{L}_i \\ \left.\begin{array}{r} (s_i, e_i, s_j, e_j, B_{ij}, L_{ij}, U_{ij}) \\ (s_i, e_i, s_j, e_j, B_{ij}, L_{ij}, U_{ij}, Pre_{ij}, Pre_{ji}, Post_{ij}) \end{array}\right. & \begin{array}{c} \in \\ \in \end{array} & \left.\begin{array}{l} \mathcal{D}_{ij} \\ \mathcal{O}_{ij} \end{array}\right\} \forall j \neq i \\ \sum_{j \neq i} (Pre_{ij} + Post_{ij}) & \geq & n - r - 1 \end{array}\right\} \forall i \tag{14}$$

4.3 Benders Decomposition Model for Minimal Perturbation

Master Problem.

$$\begin{array}{l}\mathbf{MP}: \min\ z\\ \text{subject to}\\ \begin{array}{rcll}\beta^k(\mathbf{B},\mathbf{L},\mathbf{U}) & \le & z & \forall k\\ \beta^l(\mathbf{B},\mathbf{L},\mathbf{U}) & \le & 0 & \forall l\\ \left.\begin{array}{r}(s_i,e_i,s_j,e_j,B_{ij},L_{ij},U_{ij},Pre_{ij},Pre_{ji},Post_{ij})\\ \sum_{j\neq i}(Pre_{ij}+Post_{ij})\end{array}\right. & \begin{array}{c}\in\\ \ge\end{array} & \left.\begin{array}{l}\mathcal{O}_{ij}\ \forall j\neq i\\ n-r-1\end{array}\right\} & \forall i\end{array}\end{array} \tag{15}$$

Subproblem. There is a single subproblem with primal formulation

$$\begin{array}{l}\mathbf{LP^k}: \min \displaystyle\sum_{i=1}^{n}(c_{s_i}+c_{e_i})\\ \text{subject to}\\ \left.\begin{array}{r}(c_{s_i},s_i,c_{e_i},e_i)\in\mathcal{P}_i\\ (s_i,e_i)\in\mathcal{L}_i\\ (s_i,e_i,s_j,e_j,B_{ij},L_{ij},U_{ij})\in\mathcal{D}_{ij}\ \forall j\neq i\end{array}\right\}\forall i\end{array} \tag{16}$$

The Benders Decomposition library in ECLiPSe automatically extracts a dual formulation of the subproblem. For the current subproblem $\mathbf{LP^k}$, the dual has the form:

$$\begin{array}{l}\mathbf{SP^k}: \max \displaystyle\sum_{i=1}^{n}\left(\alpha_i+\sum_{j\neq i}\left(B_{ij}w_{B_{ij}}+L_{ij}w_{L_{ij}}+U_{ij}w_{U_{ij}}\right)\right)\\ \text{subject to}\ \left.\begin{array}{r}\sum_{j\neq i}\left(w_{B_{ij}}+w_{L_{ij}}-w_{U_{ij}}-w_{B_{ji}}\right)\\ +w_{t_{s_i}}-w_{l_i}+w_{u_i}+w_{l_{s_i}}-w_{u_{s_i}}\le 0\\ \\ \sum_{j\neq i}\left(w_{b_{e_{ij}}}-w_{L_{ji}}-w_{U_{ji}}-w_{b_{e_{ji}}}\right)\\ +w_{t_{e_i}}+w_{l_i}-w_{u_i}+w_{l_{e_i}}-w_{u_{e_i}}\le 0\\ w_{t_{s_i}},w_{t_{e_i}}\ge -1\\ w_{t_{s_i}},w_{t_{e_i}}\le 1\\ w_{l_i},w_{u_i},w_{l_{s_i}},w_{u_{s_i}},w_{l_{e_i}},w_{u_{e_i}}\ge 0\\ w_{B_{ij}},w_{L_{ij}},w_{U_{ij}},w_{b_{e_{ij}}}\ge 0\ \forall j\neq i\end{array}\right\}\forall i\end{array} \tag{17}$$

where

$$\begin{aligned}\alpha_i = {} & t_{s_i}w_{t_{s_i}}+t_{e_i}w_{t_{e_i}}+l_iw_{l_i}+u_iw_{u_i}+\textstyle\sum_{j\neq i}b_{e_{ij}}w_{b_{e_{ij}}}+\\ & l_{s_i}w_{l_{s_i}}-u_{s_i}w_{u_{s_i}}+l_{e_i}w_{l_{e_i}}-u_{e_i}w_{u_{e_i}}\end{aligned}$$

Solutions to $\mathbf{SP^k}$ produce cuts of the form $z\ge\beta^k(\mathbf{B},\mathbf{L},\mathbf{U})$ which exclude orderings with worse cost from further relaxed master problems when the subproblem is feasible, or $\beta^k(\mathbf{B},\mathbf{L},\mathbf{U})\le 0$ which exclude orderings infeasible to the start windows and durations of the tasks when the subproblem is infeasible, where

$$\beta^k(\mathbf{B},\mathbf{L},\mathbf{U})=\sum_{i=1}^{I}\left(\alpha_i^k+\sum_{j\neq i}\left(w^k_{B_{ij}}B_{ij}+w^k_{L_{ij}}L_{ij}+w^k_{U_{ij}}U_{ij}\right)\right)$$

All coefficients $\mathbf{w^k}$ and constants α_i^k in the cuts are integral since the subproblems are totally unimodular.

4.4 Results and Discussion

Summary. We ran this model on 100 minimal perturbation problem instances. The number of variables in the problem model was around 900, and there were some 1400 constraints in the master problem and around 20 in the subproblem. Most problems were solved within 10 iterations between master and subproblem, though a few notched up hundreds of iterations.

The time and number of iterations for each problem are given in Table 1. The bulk of the time was spent in the finite domain search used to solve the master problem. Typically, for the feasible instances, the optimal solution was found early in the search, and much time was wasted in generating further solutions to the master problem which were not better in the context of the full problem.

Correct and optimal solutions to all the problems were returned, but the performance was an order of magnitude slower than the specially designed algorithm presented in [11].

Analysis. Minimal perturbation can be decomposed into a master and subproblem for the Benders Decomposition approach, but the size of the problems is very disparate. The behaviour of the algorithm on the benchmark problem reflect the number of constraints - the subproblems are trivial and almost all the time is spent in the master problem. The imbalance is probably an indication that this algorithm is better suited to problems with larger or more complex subproblems.

Nevertheless it is not always the *number* of constraints that make a problem hard, but the difficulty of handling these constraints. It may be that the master problem constraints, while numerous, are easy to handle if the right algorithm is used.

Currently the algorithm used to solve the master problem is a two-phase finite domain labelling routine. In the first phase a single step lookahead is used to instantiate binary variables that cannot take one of their values. In the second step all the binary variables are labelled, choosing first the variables at the bottleneck of the minimal perturbation scheduling problem. This is not only a relatively naive search method, but it also lacks any active handling of the optimisation function. Linear programming does offer an active handling of the optimisation function. Thus, using a hybrid algorithm to tackle the master problem within a larger Benders Decomposition hybridisation form, could be very effective on these minimal perturbation problems.

Benders Decomposition has proven to be a very efficient and scalable approach in case the problem breaks down into a master problem and multiple subproblems. The minimal perturbation problems benchmarked in this paper involve a single kind of resource. These problems do not have an apparent decomposition with multiple subproblems. This is a second reason why our benchmark results do not compete with the best current approach, on this class of problems. Minimal perturbation problems involving different kinds of resources might, by contrast, prove to be very amenable to the Benders Decomposition form of hybridisation.

Table 1. Number of iterations and total solution time for Benders Decomposition on RFP benchmark data

Problem	Iterations	Time	Problem	Iterations	Time	Problem	Iterations	Time
1	11	4.92	35	4	1.09	69	26	39.48
2	12	3.16	36	20	7.06	70	13	4.86
3	10	2.40	37	22	20.91	71	-	>200
4	15	11.30	38	36	67.48	72	-	>200
5	16	7.93	39	59	184.57	73	-	>200
6	58	109.22	40	13	5.66	74	26	18.72
7	25	19.82	41	28	27.05	75	91	154.00
8	10	3.27	42	9	5.86	76	12	3.49
9	32	16.25	43	39	21.02	77	54	111.17
10	107	151.01	44	25	9.43	78	35	37.52
11	-	>200	45	11	5.20	79	44	38.00
12	-	>200	46	-	>200	80	10	3.56
13	44	96.77	47	5	1.37	81	28	12.69
14	29	18.30	48	51	51.75	82	8	2.01
15	70	83.87	49	9	2.06	83	16	14.52
16	20	30.96	50	18	8.80	84	32	22.24
17	23	11.65	51	30	19.44	85	20	4.94
18	18	15.16	52	43	119.66	86	-	>200
19	14	4.94	53	28	26.10	87	18	9.56
20	21	8.17	54	33	17.32	88	12	4.72
21	19	5.01	55	14	6.01	89	7	2.26
22	60	180.47	56	14	9.95	90	43	42.51
23	20	8.46	57	45	100.94	91	8	2.12
24	39	82.93	58	4	0.88	92	54	111.5
25	13	2.74	59	8	2.45	93	-	>200
26	3	0.71	60	-	>200	94	25	8.08
27	10	7.14	61	19	9.41	95	8	2.99
28	22	12.23	62	24	11.48	96	22	10.97
29	27	13.24	63	-	>200	97	5	1.59
30	-	>200	64	46	95.07	98	6	2.37
31	42	36.69	65	30	18.62	99	15	4.82
32	15	4.48	66	14	5.57	100	19	47.61
33	15	8.77	67	10	3.10			
34	20	23.70	68	62	132.87			

5 Conclusion

This paper has investigated hybridisation forms for problems that admit a decomposition. A variety of hybridisation forms can be used in case one or more subproblems are handled by linear programming. We aim to make them all available in the ECLiPSe language in a way that allows users to experiment easily with the different alternatives so as to quickly find the best hybrid algorithm for the problem at hand.

Benders Decomposition is a technique that has not, to date, been applied to many real problems within the CP community. Publications on this technique have described a few pedagogical examples and "academic" problem classes such as satisfiability [20,21]. This paper presents the first application of Benders Decomposition to a set of minimal perturbation problems which have immediate application in the real world. Indeed the benchmarks were based on an industrial application to airline scheduling.

The significance of Benders Decomposition in comparison with other master/subproblem forms of hybridisation (such as row and column generation) is that it takes advantage of linear duality theory. The Benders Decomposition library in ECLiPSe harnesses the power of the dual problem for constraint programmers who may not find the formulation and application of the linear dual either easy or natural.

Moreover the implementation of Benders Decomposition in ECLiPSe has been proven both efficient and scalable. Indeed its results on the minimal perturbation benchmark problems compare reasonably well even against an algorithm specially developed for problems of this class. However the Benders Decomposition for minimal perturbation problems comprises a master problem and a single trivial subproblem. Our experience with this technique has shown that this hybridisation form is more suitable to applications where the decomposition introduces many or complex subproblems.

This paper was initially motivated by a network application where Benders Decomposition has proven to be the best hybridisation form after considerable experimentation with other algorithms. We plan to report on the application of this technique to a problem brought to us by an industrial partner in a forthcoming paper.

There remains further work to support fine control over the iteration between the master and subproblems in Benders Decomposition. The importance of such fine control has been clearly evidenced from our ECLiPSe implementation of another hybridisation form - column generation - applied to mixed integer problems. In particular we will seek to implement early stopping, and more control over the number of Benders cuts returned at an iteration.

References

1. Chic-2 - creating hybrid algorithms for industry and commerce. ESPRIT PROJECT 22165: http://www.icparc.ic.ac.uk/chic2/, 1999.

2. Parrot - parallel crew rostering. ESPRIT PROJECT 24 960: http://www.uni-paderborn.de/ parrot/, 2000.
3. Liscos - large scale integrated supply chain optimisation software. http://www.dash.co.uk/liscosweb/, 2001.
4. *CP98 Workshop on Large Scale Combinatorial Optimisation and Constraints*, volume 1, Pisa, Italy, 1999. http://www.elsevier.nl/gej-ng/31/29/24/25/23/show/Products/notes/index.htt.
5. *CP99 Workshop on Large Scale Combinatorial Optimisation and Constraints*, volume 4, Alexandra, Virginia, USA, 2000. http://www.elsevier.nl/gej-ng/31/29/24/29/23/show/Products/notes/index.htt.
6. H. H. El Sakkout. *Improving Backtrack Search: Three Case Studies of Localized Dynamic Hybridization.* PhD thesis, Imperial College, London University, 1999.
7. N. Beldiceanu and E. Contjean. Introducing global constraints in CHIP. *Mathematical and Computer Modelling*, 12:97–123, 1994.
8. XPRESS-MP. http://www.dash.co.uk/, 2000.
9. CPLEX. http://www.ilog.com/products/cplex/, 2000.
10. R. E. Gomory. An algorithm for integer solutions to linear programs. In R. L. Graves and P. Wolfe, editors, *Recent Advances in Mathematical Programming*, pages 269–302. McGraw-Hill, 1963.
11. H. H. El Sakkout and M. G. Wallace. Probe backtrack search for minimal perturbation in dynamic scheduling. *Constraints*, 5(4):359–388, 2000.
12. L. H. Appelgren. A column generation algorithm for a ship scheduling problem. *Transportation Science*, 3:53–68, 1969.
13. U. Junker, S. E. Karisch, N. Kohl, B. Vaaben, T. Fahle, and M. Sellmann. A framework for constraint programming based column generation. In *Proceedings of the 5th International Conference on Principles and Practice of Constraint Programming - LNCS 1713*, pages 261–274. Springer-Verlag, 1999.
14. T. H. Yunes, A. V. Moura, and C. C. de Souza. A hybrid approach for solving large scale crew scheduling problems. In *Proceedings of the Second International Workshop on Practical Aspects of Declarative Languages (PADL'00)*, pages 293–307, Boston, MA, USA, 2000.
15. M. Sellmann and T. Fahle. Cp-based lagrangian relaxation for a multimedia application. In *[17]*, 2001.
16. T. Benoist, F. Laburthe, and B. Rottembourg. Lagrange relaxation and constraint programming collaborative schemes for travelling tournament problems. In *[17]*, 2001.
17. *CP-AI-OR01 Workshop on Integration of AI and OR Techniques in Constraint Programming for Combinatorial Optimization Problems*, Wye, Kent, UK, 2001. http://www.icparc.ic.ac.uk/cpAIOR01/.
18. F. Focacci, A. Lodi, and M. Milano. Embedding relaxations in global constraints for solving TSP and its time constrained variant. *Annals of Mathematics and Artificial Intelligence*, Special issue on Large Scale Combinatorial Optimization, 2001.
19. G. B. Dantzig. *Linear Programming and Extensions.* Princeton University Press, 1963.
20. J. F. Benders. Partitioning procedures for solving mixed variables programming problems. *Numerische Mathematik*, 4:238–252, 1962.
21. J. N. Hooker and G. Ottosson. Logic-based benders decomposition. http://ba.gsia.cmu.edu/jnh/papers.html, 1999.

Branch-and-Check: A Hybrid Framework Integrating Mixed Integer Programming and Constraint Logic Programming

Erlendur S. Thorsteinsson

Graduate School of Industrial Administration; Carnegie Mellon University;
Schenley Park; Pittsburgh, PA 15213–3890; U.S.A.
esth@erlendur.com

Abstract. We present Branch-and-Check, a hybrid framework integrating Mixed Integer Programming and Constraint Logic Programming, which encapsulates the traditional Benders Decomposition and Branch-and-Bound as special cases. In particular we describe its relation to Benders and the use of nogoods and linear relaxations. We give two examples of how problems can be modelled and solved using Branch-and-Check and present computational results demonstrating more than order-of-magnitude speedup compared to previous approaches. We also mention important future research issues such as hierarchical, dynamic and adjustable linear relaxations.

1 Introduction

The first goal of this paper is to propose a modeller/solver framework, Branch-and-Check, that not only encompasses both the traditional Benders Decomposition and Branch-and-Bound schemes of Mixed Integer Programming (MIP) as special cases of a spectrum of solution methods, but also adds an extra dimension by allowing the integration of Constraint Logic Programming (CLP) in a MIP style branching search.

In this framework we model a problem in a mixture of CLP and MIP. The CLP part of the model then adds a relaxation of itself to the MIP part (or it is added explicitely). If the two parts do not use the same variables then the model should include mapping relations between them (*shadowed* variables). The solution method is then a branching search, solving the LP relaxation of the MIP part at every node and branching on the discrete variables, but only solving the CLP part at the nodes of the branching tree where it is advantageous (or necessary), e.g., based on how difficult/large the MIP part is compared to the CLP part or how easy it is to strengthen the MIP part using the CLP solution and on the quality of those cuts.

The second goal of this paper is to identify one of the key elements for the integration of CLP and MIP that has still not been adequately addressed and to propose it as a pertinent and pressing research topic in the area of integration: *Dynamic* linear relaxations of global constraints. We will present computational results that indicate that for efficient communication between the different parts of a hybrid model some double modelling is required, i.e., the same constraint or parts of the model must be present in both CLP and MIP form. It is also vital that the different forms of the same constraint

T. Walsh (Ed.): CP 2001, LNCS 2239, pp. 16–30, 2001.

communicate (intra-constraint communication). This is what we have previously termed *mixed* propagation of *mixed* CLP–MIP global constraints [20,21,24].

This holds regardless of the scheme used, be it (Tight) Cooperation [2,22], Mixed Logical/Linear Programming (MLLP) [15,16,20,21,24], Branch-and-Check (see Sec. 3) or some other integration approach [3,6,7,18,23]. This double modelling could be explicit, but most preferably it should be implicit, i.e., mixed global constraints should post and dynamically update a linear relaxation of themselves, in addition to the classical CLP propagation on their discrete parts and mixed propagation between the discrete and continuous parts.

This extends the idea proposed by Beringer and De Backer in [2]. They argued that the standard CLP architecture is not optimal because cooperation between different solvers is only done by value propagation. In addition, they proposed, solvers, e.g., CLP and MIP solvers, should be able to communicate by exchanging information through variable bounds. Variable bounds are only a special type of linear constraints, so linear relaxations take this idea a step further and open up many more possibilities in CLP–MIP integration.

We will exemplify this based on our experiences when developing the Branch-and-Check framework and also based on our previous line of research [15,16,20,21,24]. The paper is organised as follows. This section outlined the focus of this research. Section 2 reviews the history of efforts in integrating CLP and MIP along with two classical MIP techniques, Benders Decomposition and Branch-and-Bound. In Sec. 3 we introduce the Branch-and-Check framework, discuss how it generalises Benders and Branch-and-Bound, and show how CLP can be integrated. Section 4 then gives two examples, Scheduling with Dissimilar Parallel Machines and Capacitated Vehicle Routing with Time Windows, and presents computational results demonstrating more than order-of-magnitude speedup compared to previous approaches.

2 Background

2.1 Classical MIP Techniques

Branch-and-Bound: We will assume that the reader is familiar with the classical Branch-and-Bound approach for solving MIPs. Due to different vocabulary in the two fields, however, we would like to note that this is the technique that is sometimes referred to as Branch-and-Relax [3].

Benders Decomposition: Classical Benders Decomposition exploits the fact that in some problems, fixing the values of certain difficult variables simplifies the problem tremendously. By enumerating those difficult variables, solving each resulting *subproblem* and selecting the best subproblem solution found, the original problem can be solved. Benders' method [1] is more ingenious. It solves a *master problem* to assign values to the difficult variables. Each solution to the subproblem then generates a Benders cut that is added to the master problem before resolving it. Thus each solution to the master problem must satisfy all the Benders cuts obtained so far, avoiding searching similar regions of the solutions space again. This is similar to the role nogoods play in CLP.

Classical Benders Decomposition applies if the problem can be written

$$\begin{aligned} \min \quad & cx + fy \\ \text{s.t.} \quad & Ax + Gy \geq b, \\ & x \in D,\ y \in \mathbb{R}^n_+. \end{aligned} \tag{1}$$

If x^* denotes the solution to the master problem then the subproblem is an LP,

$$\begin{aligned} \min \quad & cx^* + fy \\ \text{s.t.} \quad & Gy \geq b - Ax^*, \\ & y \in \mathbb{R}^n_+, \end{aligned} \tag{2}$$

which is easily solved. The procedure is iterative, interleaving solving the master problem to optimality and the resulting subproblem. By applying duality theory to the solution of the subproblem, cuts can be generated that are added to the master problem

$$\begin{aligned} \min \quad & z \\ \text{s.t.} \quad & z \geq u_q^* (b - Ax) + cx, && q \in Q_1, && (3) \\ & u_q^* (b - Ax) \leq 0, && q \in Q_2, && (4) \\ & x \in D, \end{aligned}$$

where u_q^* is the dual solution to the subproblem when the subproblem is feasible in iterations $q \in Q_1$, and infeasible in iterations $q \in Q_2$, before resolving the master problem in the next iteration. A more detailed description of Benders Decomposition can be found in [1,8,11,14,17].

2.2 Previous Integration Schemes

Properties of a number of different problems were considered by Darby-Dowman and Little in [4,5] and their effect on the performance of CLP and MIP approaches were presented. They reported experimental results that illustrate some key properties of the techniques: MIP is very efficient for problems with good relaxations, but it suffers when the relaxation is weak or when its restricted modelling framework results in large models. CLP, with its more expressive constraints, has smaller models that are closer to the problem description and behaves well for highly constrained problems, but it lacks the "global perspective" of relaxations.

(Tight) Cooperation: Beringer and De Backer proposed in [2] that CLP and MIP solvers can be coupled together with common (or shadowed) variables in a double modelling framework using two way communication: The MIP solver sends the CLP solver the values of the common variables that are fixed, which relies on the MIP solver being able to detect implied inequalities, and the CLP solver sends the MIP solver strengthened bounds for the common variables. They compared solving a multi-knapsack problem as a pure CLP or a pure MIP against using the cooperation of the two solvers, and obtained favourable results.

Refalo proposed an extension to this framework in [22], where the MIP model is dynamic; it is restated when variable bounds are tightened or variables are fixed, by the CLP solver.

Mixed Logical/Linear Programming (MLLP): Hooker et al. proposed a new modelling paradigm to efficiently integrate CLP and MIP in [12,13,15,16]. In that framework, constraints are in the form of conditionals that link the discrete and continuous elements of the problem. An MLLP model has the form

$$\begin{aligned} \min \quad & cx \\ \text{s.t.} \quad & h_i(y) \rightarrow A^i x \geq b^i, \quad i \in I, \\ & y \in D, \ x \in \mathbb{R}^n. \end{aligned} \tag{5}$$

The antecedents $h_i(y)$ of the conditionals are constraints that can be treated with CLP techniques. The consequents are linear inequality systems that form an LP relaxation.

An MLLP problem is solved by branching on the discrete variables. The conditionals assign roles to CLP and LP: CLP is applied to the discrete constraints to reduce the search and help determine when partial assignments satisfy the antecedents. At each node of the branching tree an LP solver minimises cx subject to the inequalities $A^i x \geq b^i$ for which $h_i(y)$ is determined to be true. This delayed posting of inequalities leads to small and lean LP problems that can be solved efficiently.

Ottosson, Thorsteinsson and Hooker, and Ottosson and Thorsteinsson extended MLLP in [21,24] by proposing adding *mixed* global constraints that have both discrete and continuous elements within them. A mixed global constraint has a dynamically stated linear relaxation that becomes a part of the continuous part and propagates information between the discrete and continuous parts of the model. In that framework the mixed global constraints serve both as a modelling tool and a way to exploit structure in the solution process. Mixed global constraints can be written in the form (5) as conditionals, analogous to global constraints in CLP, but improve the solution process by improving the propagation.

Hybrid Decomposition: Jain and Grossmann, and Harjunkoski, Jain and Grossmann presented a scheme in [9,18] where the problem is decomposed into two sub-parts, one handled by MIP and the other by CLP. This is demonstrated using a multi-machine scheduling problem where the assignment of tasks to machines is modelled as a MIP and the sequencing of the tasks on the assigned machines is handled using CLP. The search scheme is an iterative procedure where the assignment problem is first solved to optimality, identifying which machine to use for each task, and then a CLP feasibility problem is solved trying to sequence according to this assignment. If the sequencing fails, cutting planes are added to the MIP problem to forbid this (and subsumed) assignments and the process is iterated. This approach has many similarities to Benders and in fact, in [11] it is shown how this problem can be written for Benders.

Other Approaches: Bockmayr and Kasper proposed an interesting framework in [3] for combining CLP and MIP, in which several approaches to integration or synergy are possible, by dividing the constraints for both CLP and MIP into two different categories, primitive and non-primitive. Primitive constraints are those for which there exists a polynomial time solution algorithm and non-primitive constraints are those for which this is not true.

Rodošek et al. presented in [23] a systematic approach for transforming a CLP model into a corresponding MIP model. CLP is then used along with linear relaxations in a single search tree to prune domains and establish bounds. The downside of this approach is that the systematic procedure that creates the shadow MIP model for the original CLP model includes reified arithmetic constraints, big-M constraints. A translation involving numerous big-M constraints may result in a poor MIP model, i.e., with a poor linear relaxation.

3 Branch-and-Check

3.1 Description of the General Method

Branch-and-Check builds to a certain extent on Benders Decomposition. The basic idea is to identify a part of the problem that is *basic* and a part that is *delayed*. The solution process is a branching search on the basic part where the delayed part is checked (e.g., for feasibility) as late or as seldom as possible. The rationale is that while the delayed part is necessary to check for the correctness of the solution, it may be large and computationally expensive to include in every step of the calculations and thus we want to delay looking at it as long as possible. We are going to refer to the basic part as the master problem and the delayed part as the subproblem.

This strategy can be applied to a problem of this general form:

$$\begin{aligned} \min \quad & cx + f(y) && (6)\\ \text{s.t.} \quad & Ax \le b, && (7)\\ & H(x, y), && (8) \end{aligned}$$

where the problem is naturally split into a mixed integer linear part (7) and a non-linear part (8), e.g., (mixed) global constraints such as the `piecewise-linear` and `alldifferent` constraints. The constraints of master problems are in the top part and the constraints of the subproblems are in the lower part. The non-linear part can also include linear constraints or mappings between the x and y variables. Thus the following would be examples of problem forms this strategy can be applied to:

$$\begin{array}{ll} \min & cx + f(y) \\ \text{s.t.} & Ax \le b, \\ & H(x, y), \end{array} \qquad \begin{array}{ll} \min & cx + dy \\ \text{s.t.} & A^1 x \le b^1, \\ & A^2 y \le b^2, \end{array} \qquad \begin{array}{ll} \min & cx + f(y) \\ \text{s.t.} & Ax \le b, \\ & x \sim y, \\ & F(y). \end{array}$$

In the third form, $x \sim y$ represents that there is a mapping between the values of the variables x and y, e.g., a one-to-one mapping between two variables or between a variable and a set of variables such as $y \in \{1, \ldots, n\}$, $x_1, \ldots, x_n \in \{0, 1\}$ and $x_y = 1$. This second mapping is a common mapping between CLP and MIP.

Since the master problem is a relaxation of the original problem, when a solution to the master problem is found in the branching search it is not guaranteed that the solution is truly feasible nor that the objective value is correct. At those nodes in the branching tree, i.e., where all the variables in the master problem have been instantiated and the branching search is about to fathom the subtree, we solve the subproblem as well to determine if the overall solution is feasible and then what its correct objective function value is. We can solve the subproblem more often, but how often to consult the subproblem is a matter of how large or computationally expensive the subproblem is compared to the master problem.

Completely ignoring the subproblem for most of the solution process, only solving it at selected nodes, is not going to work, however, so we augment the master problem with a relaxation of the subproblem: A simpler and computationally less expensive representation of the subproblem that focuses the master problem on good candidate solutions with respect to the subproblem. For example, for the third form, the master problem would become

$$\begin{array}{ll} \min & cx + \mathcal{L}_{f(y)}(x) \\ \text{s.t.} & Ax \leq b, \\ & \mathcal{L}_{F(y)}(x). \end{array}$$

The relaxation should be hierarchical if possible, e.g., if the subproblem is a CLP then the whole relaxation should preferably be the union of the relaxations of the individual global constraints that comprise the subproblem. It should also be dynamic, i.e., as the solution process progresses it should be updated, e.g., when variables are fixed; and adjustable, i.e, it should be possible to efficiently make incremental changes, rather than have to recompute it at every node.

Whenever the subproblem is solved, cuts are added to the master problem. We add a lower bounding cut if the subproblem is feasible, bounding the objective function from below, or an infeasibility cut (a *nogood*) if the subproblem is infeasible, disallowing this solution and others similar to it. For example, for the third form, the master problem would become

$$\begin{array}{ll} \min & cx + z \\ \text{s.t.} & Ax \leq b, \\ & \mathcal{L}_{F(y)}(x), \\ & z \geq \mathcal{L}_{f(y)}(x), \\ & z \geq L(x), \\ & N(x). \end{array}$$

The subproblem in this case will be

$$\begin{array}{ll} \min & f(y) \\ \text{s.t.} & F(y), \end{array}$$

given the mapping $x \sim y$ between the variables in the master and subproblems, i.e., some of the variables in the subproblem may be fixed or have restricted values based on the current solution of the master problem. In the examples we will look at in Sec. 4, the solution to the master problem will determine how the subproblem decomposes.

The master problem for the general form (6)–(8) is

$$\begin{aligned} \min \quad & cx + z && (9)\\ \text{s.t.} \quad & Ax \le b, && (10)\\ & \mathcal{L}_{H(x,y)}(x), && (11)\\ & z \ge \mathcal{L}_{f(y)}(x), && (12)\\ & z \ge L(x), && (13)\\ & N(x), && (14) \end{aligned}$$

and the corresponding subproblem is

$$\begin{aligned} \min \quad & cx^* + f(y) && (15)\\ \text{s.t.} \quad & H(x^*, y), && (16) \end{aligned}$$

where x^* is the solution to the master problem.

3.2 Special Cases

Benders Decomposition: The correspondence to the Branch-and-Check framework is that a problem solved using classical Benders has an *empty* basic part (see (10)) and no relaxation of the subproblem (see (11)–(12)). It only has general (i.e., non-problem specific) lower bounding cuts (3) (see (13)) and nogoods (4) (see (14)) that are derived using LP duality theory.

Branch-and-Bound: Classical Branch-and-Bound,

$$\begin{aligned} \min \quad & cx \\ \text{s.t.} \quad & Ax \le b, && (17)\\ & x \in \mathbb{R}^n, \text{ some } x_i \in \mathbb{Z}, \end{aligned}$$

is at the other extreme, it has an *empty* delayed part, and hence no relaxation of the subproblem, no lower bounding cuts and no nogoods or only the trivial nogoods that are implicit in the branching and fathoming scheme (see (11)–(16)). It only has a basic part (17) (see (10)).

3.3 Integrating MIP and CLP

It is immediately obvious that a spectrum of techniques exist between classical Benders Decomposition and Branch-and-Bound. In particular:

- In Benders the solution process might be accelerated by adding some cuts or valid inequalities a priori, i.e., adding a linear relaxation of the subproblem (11)–(12), instead of starting with an empty master problem and waiting for the Benders cuts to accumulate and start guiding the process (in the master problem) to promising candidate solutions.

– Instead of looking at the entire problem at every node of the Branch-and-Bound search tree, a part of the set of variables/constraints can be delayed and only examined when need arises. This will result in smaller problems being solved at each node, which although more nodes may be needed, may still result in overall savings.

We note, however, that in addition to this merger of Benders and Branch-and-Bound, the Branch-and-Check framework also allows for an additional dimension of flexibility. The subproblem can be of almost any form, in particular MIP and CLP can be integrated by using CLP to model and solve the subproblems. The MIP search in the master problem is still guided by the subproblem, via the relaxation (11)–(12) and the lower bounds and nogoods (13)–(14).

It is true that if the subproblem is not an LP, or more accurately if duality theory is not available, more work has to be put into deriving the lower bounds and nogoods. A survey of different duality concepts for a variety of problem classes can be found in [14]. It is not uncommon in CLP and MIP, however, to have to tailor methods for specific structures. For example, global constraints in CLP require that propagation algorithms be designed for each one and in MIP, problem specific cutting planes are widely used. In a similar fashion, when integrating CLP and MIP, work has to be put into deriving linear relaxations of mixed global constraints.

3.4 Relation to Previous Work on Decomposition Methods and Nogoods

The first key idea for extensions to the classical Benders framework was due to Jeroslow and Wang [19]. They envisioned the dual of a problem (in the case of classical Benders, an LP) as an inference problem, by showing that when LP demonstrates the unsatisfiability of a set of Horn clauses in propositional logic, the dual solution contains information about a unit resolution proof of unsatisfiability.

Hooker defined the general inference dual in [10], which was then used by Hooker and Yan in [17] for a logic-based Benders scheme in the context of logic circuit verification. There are many similarities between that paper and the paper of Jain and Grossmann [18], except that Hooker and Yan used a specialised inference algorithm rather than a general CLP package for the subproblem, and the problem was logic circuit verification rather than machine scheduling.

Benders Decomposition for Branching, generating Benders cuts from an LP subproblem while *in* the process of solving the master problem, was described by Hooker in [11]. This is the essence of Branch-and-Check, in the context of classical Benders; the examples there do not solve the subproblem with CLP. We go a step further by using a CLP solver to get the cuts for Branch-and-Check, and in addition, we give the first computational results for Branch-and-Check in a Benders context. Branch-and-Check as defined here is a form of Generalised Benders (it partitions the variables and only uses some of them in the master problem, which is the core of Benders) that generates cuts in the process of solving the master problem once.

The idea of using nogoods in branching is a standard AI technique. Branch-and-Check is different in that only a *relaxation* of the problem, rather than the full problem, is solved at each node. The full problem is consulted at only a few nodes, and nogoods generated accordingly. In classical AI, the *full* problem would generally be checked at every node. The optimisation community has apparently never used nogoods in branching search and the constraint satisfaction community has apparently never used generalised Benders as a means to generate nogoods, although Beringer and De Backer have done related work. The integration of Benders and CLP could give new life to the idea of a nogood, which has received limited attention in practical optimisation algorithms.

4 Examples

In this next section, we will examine two problems, Scheduling with Dissimilar Parallel Machines (SDPM) and Capacitated Vehicle Routing with Time Windows (CVRTW), that benefit from using CLP to model and solve the subproblems, and demonstrate some of the issues that arise.

4.1 Scheduling with Dissimilar Parallel Machines

This problem and a decompositional method to solve it was first presented by Jain and Grossmann in [18]. The problem is described as follows: The least cost schedule has to be derived for processing a set of orders with release and due dates using a set of dissimilar parallel machines. The machines are dissimilar in the sense that there is different cost and processing time associated with each order–machine pair, but all the machines perform the same job. Jain and Grossmann modelled the problem thus:

$$\min \quad \sum_{i\in I}\sum_{m\in M} C_{im}x_{im} \tag{18}$$

$$\text{s.t.} \quad ts_i \le d_i - \sum_{m\in M} p_{im}x_{im}, \quad ts_i \ge r_i, \qquad \forall i \in I, \tag{19}$$

$$\sum_{m\in M} x_{im} = 1, \qquad \forall i \in I, \tag{20}$$

$$\sum_{i\in I} p_{im}x_{im} \le \max_i\{d_i\} - \min_i\{r_i\}, \qquad \forall m \in M, \tag{21}$$

$$\text{if } (x_{im} = 1) \text{ then } (z_i = m), \qquad \forall i \in I, \forall m \in M, \tag{22}$$

$$i.\text{start} \le d_i - p_{z_i}, \quad i.\text{start} \ge r_i, \qquad \forall i \in I, \tag{23}$$

$$i.\text{duration} = p_{z_i}, \qquad \forall i \in I, \tag{24}$$

$$i \text{ requires } t_{z_i}, \qquad \forall i \in I. \tag{25}$$

They also presented a decompositional method that solves this class of MIP problems, i.e., in which only a subset of the variables appears in the objective function. The problem decomposes into an optimisation problem (18)–(20) that is suitable for MIP (has all of the variables of the objective function and a tight relaxation), and into a feasibility problem (23)–(25) that can be solved efficiently using CLP. The variables of the two parts are linked using the mapping (22). The constraints (21) are not necessary for the correctness of the problem, but are valid inequalities for the overall problem that are added to the MIP part.

Table 1. Results for 5×23 problems using Jain & Grossmann's approach.

Problem	Model Size		Find and Prove Opt. Solution			
Number	Mach.	Jobs	Iter.	Nogoods	MIP sec	CLP sec
1	5	23	33	71	42.10	0.54
2	5	23	16	15	0.93	0.37
3	5	23	33	76	9.15	0.47
4	5	23	43	104	14.05	0.60
5	5	23	57	72	13.07	1.01

Table 2. Results for 5×23 problems using Branch-and-Check.

Problem	Model Size		Find Opt. Solution				Prove Opt. Thereafter			
Number	Mach.	Jobs	Iter.	Nog.	MIP sec	CLP sec	Iter.	Nog.	MIP sec	CLP sec
1	5	23	8	20	2.99	0.07	7	18	6.62	0.12
2	5	23	3	2	0.09	0.07	0	0	0.00	0.00
3	5	23	19	51	3.78	0.20	0	0	0.00	0.00
4	5	23	19	55	4.05	0.19	0	0	0.00	0.00
5	5	23	17	25	1.79	0.21	6	8	1.12	0.14

The solution process then alternates between solving the optimisation problem to optimality and the resulting feasibility problems. If all the feasibility problems are feasible then the solution is optimal, if not then cuts are added to the optimisation problem to exclude that solution and others similar to it.

This approach bears a striking resemblance to Benders Decomposition. In fact, Hooker showed in [11] how this problem can be written for Benders. It was while studying this result that the idea of Branch-and-Check took form. We note that the correspondence with Branch-and-Check is that the function f, the subproblem part of the objective function, is identically zero (see (6)), there are no lower bounding cuts (see (12)), there is a simple relaxation of the subproblem (21) in the master problem (see (11)), and the problem is solved using multiple search trees by adding nogoods (see (14)) of the form:

$$\sum_{i \in I} a_{im}^j x_{im} \leq \sum_{i \in I} a_{im}^j - 1, \; \forall m \in M.$$

Jain and Grossmann presented very nice computational result in their paper [18], comparing against pure CLP and MIP approaches. While studying the CVRTW problem and how Branch-and-Check could be applied to that problem, we wondered what was the power of this method. First we were looking at the nogoods, but it turns out that the real power of this method lies in the linear relaxation (21). If it is removed from the formulation, problems that are solved in a matter of seconds with the relaxation, can be run for more than 24 hours without making any progress. This indicates that further research into linear relaxations of the global CLP constraints, i.e., *mixed* global constraints [21,24], is very important.

A further study of the results also revealed a significant difference in the time it took to solve the MIPs vs. the CLPs, up to a factor of 30 times more solving the MIPs.

Table 3. Results for 7 × 30 problems using Jain & Grossmann's approach.

Problem	Model Size		Find and Prove Opt. Solution			
Number	Mach.	Jobs	Iter.	Nogoods	MIP sec	CLP sec
1	7	30	36	80	15.15	1.06
2	7	30	96	206	90.66	2.78
3	7	30	115	225	116.87	3.42
4	7	30	71	112	34.94	2.25
5	7	30	58	97	28.25	1.92

Table 4. Results for 7 × 30 problems using Branch-and-Check.

Problem	Model Size		Find Opt. Solution				Prove Opt. Thereafter			
Number	Mach.	Jobs	Iter.	Nog.	MIP sec	CLP sec	Iter.	Nog.	MIP sec	CLP sec
1	7	30	10	11	0.83	0.36	0	0	0.00	0.00
2	7	30	32	62	9.92	0.98	0	0	0.00	0.00
3	7	30	8	11	0.73	0.27	0	0	0.00	0.00
4	7	30	16	27	2.55	0.46	0	0	0.00	0.00
5	7	30	8	13	0.94	0.24	0	0	0.00	0.00

This indicated, and is verified by our results, see Tables 1–4, that the master problem should not necessarily be solved to optimality, instead the CLP subproblems should be solved regularly throughout the tree. This result is very intuitive, as we note that the CLP subproblem decomposes into problems for each individual machine and hence are rather small, compared to the larger MIP master problem that considers all the machines at the same time. We also compared our approach on the original data given by Jain and Grossmann in [18] and obtained very favourable results. Most of those instances are, however, trivially solved using either method, so we do not include them here.

We implemented the Branch-and-Check approach for this problem thus, using OPL and OPL Script [25]: We halted the MIP master problem when a feasible solution was found and solved the CLP subproblems. If any of them were infeasible, we added nogoods to the master problem and re-solved. If all were feasible, we recorded that as a new "current-best-solution", constrained the objective function of the master problem and re-solved. This process was iterated until the master problem was infeasible, indicating that no further solutions could be found given the current bound on the objective function and the nogoods posted.

There is significant overhead with this implementation and redundant calculations: We re-start the master problem after adding cuts, instead of continuing from where we left off, and thus resolve many similar nodes of the search tree repeatedly. A better tool that would allow dynamic modifications of the master problem at each node of the search tree would obtain substantially better results.

4.2 Capacitated Vehicle Routing with Time Windows

This problem is one of visiting a set of customers using vehicles stationed at a central depot; respecting constraints such as the *capacity* of the trucks, a *time window* promised to each customer, *precedence* constraints on the customers, etc. The goal is to produce a low cost routing plan, specifying for each vehicle what customers they should visit and in what order. Cost is generally proportional to the number of vehicles, the maximum time or the total travel time.

We note that this problem decomposes. Given an assignment of trucks to routes that assigns each customer to a specific truck and obeys the capacity constraints, we have to sequence each truck by solving a Travelling Salesman Problem with Time Windows that satisfies the time window and precedence constraints and minimises our objective for each one.

Using the global `cumulative` and `count` constraints and variable index sets we can state the problem as follows for Branch-and-Check, minimising the cost of the trucks:

$$\min \sum_{i \in T} c_i y_i \tag{26}$$

$$\text{s.t. } t_j \geq R_j,\ t_j + D_j \leq S_j, \qquad \forall j \in C, \tag{27}$$

$$\sum_{j \mid (z_j = i)} w_j \leq L_i, \qquad \forall i \in T, \tag{28}$$

$$(y_i = 0) \Rightarrow \texttt{count}(i, [z_1, \dots, z_n], =, 0), \qquad \forall i \in T, \tag{29}$$

$$\texttt{cumulative}((j \mid (z_j = i)), t_k, R_k, S_k, D_k, [d_{k_1 k_2}], \mathbf{1}, 1), \qquad \forall i \in T. \tag{30}$$

Equations (27) are the time windows, (28) are the capacity constraints and (29) ensure that if a truck is not being used, then no customers are assigned to it. The cumulative constraint (30) is imposed for each truck and schedules the customers assigned to it. The parameters are the customers assigned to the truck, the start time variables, time windows and durations of service, the transition times between all pairs of customers, a vector of all ones indicating that each customer requires one truck, and finally that there is one truck available. If z has been fixed to z^* then the subproblem for each truck i is:

$$\texttt{cumulative}((j \mid (z_j^* = i)), t'_k, R_k, S_k, D_k, [d_{k_1 k_2}], \mathbf{1}, 1), \tag{31}$$

$$t'_j \geq R_j,\ t'_j + D_j \leq S_j, \qquad \forall j \mid (z_j^* = i). \tag{32}$$

If the subproblem is infeasible then nogoods can be generated to avoid that assignment and added to the master problem. Call the accumulated set of those nogoods in the l-th iteration $N_l(x_{ij})$. Then we can write the master problem thus as a MIP:

$$\min \sum_{i \in T} c_i y_i \tag{33}$$

$$\text{s.t. } t_j \geq R_j,\ t_j + D_j \leq S_j, \qquad \forall j \in C, \tag{34}$$

$$\sum_{j \in C} w_j x_{ij} \leq L_i, \qquad \forall i \in T, \tag{35}$$

$$x_{ij} \leq y_i, \qquad \forall i \in T,\ j \in C, \tag{36}$$

$$\sum_{i \in T} x_{ij} = 1, \qquad \forall j \in C, \tag{37}$$

$$N_l(x_{ij}). \tag{38}$$

We note that the 0–1 variables x_{ij} and (37) correspond to the general integer variables z_j and the index sets $\{j \mid (z_j = i)\}$.

We add a dynamic relaxation of the subproblem to the master problem by approximating the total travel time as follows: A truck will have to travel to each customer from somewhere. Thus if for each customer we find the nearest neighbour, the sum of those distances and the services times for the customers assigned to a truck is a lower bound on the actual travel time. While solving the master problem some customers will be assigned to a particular truck, through the branching. When that happens we can update the lower bound, noting that the nearest neighbour can not be among those that have been assigned to other trucks. For truck i, let A_i be the set of customers that have been assigned to truck i and let A_0 be the set of unassigned customers. For truck $i \in T$ we add

$$\sum_{j \in C} \left(D_j + \left(\min_{q \in (A_0 \cup A_i) \setminus \{j\}} d_{qj} \right) x_{ij} \right) \leq \max_{q \in A_0 \cup A_i} S_q - \min_{q \in A_0 \cup A_i} R_q.$$

to the master problem. The sets A_i and the relaxation can be updated based on what x_{ij}'s have been fixed to 1:

Set propagation: All customers start in A_0. When x_{pq} is fixed to 1, then customer q moves from A_0 to A_p and x_{pj}, $j \neq q$, can be fixed to 0.

Relaxation propagation: We calculate the $n \times n$ table of shortest distances and sort each list, before solving, so that for each customer there is a list of length $n-1$ of the other customers in increasing distance order. We then build graph of nearest neighbours. Each node has one outgoing arc, the nearest neighbour, and some incoming arcs from the nodes that consider it to be their nearest neighbour. The trigger for the propagation is when customer q moves from A_0 to A_p:

Outgoing arc propagation: Customer q may have to revise its choice for nearest neighbour q^*. If q^* is in A_k, $k \neq 0, p$, then q must look at its list and find the first customer after q^* that is in A_0 or A_p.

Incoming arc propagation: Node q must notify the nodes that consider it to be their nearest neighbour. Every such node in A_k, $k \neq 0, p$, must perform outgoing arc propagation, revising its choice for nearest neighbour by looking for the first customer on its list after q that is in A_0 or A_k.

In addition we can add various other valid inequalities to the master problem, such as symmetry breaking constraints if the trucks are identical (i.e., same cost and capacity). We can require that the first stop assigned truck i be less than or equal to the first stop assigned truck $i+1$. This can be stated in inequality form as

$$x_{i+1,n} \leq \sum_{j=1}^{m} x_{ij}, \quad \forall m, n \text{ with } n \leq m, \ \forall i \in T.$$

We can also order the trucks by adding constraints of the form $y_i \leq y_{i+1}$ (if the number of trucks is variable).

5 Conclusion

CLP and MIP are approaches that have the potential for integration to benefit the solution of combinatorial optimisation problems. In this paper we proposed a modeller/solver framework, Branch-and-Check, that encompasses both the traditional Benders and Branch-and-Bound schemes of MIP as special cases of a spectrum of solution methods and adds an extra dimension by allowing the integration of CLP in a MIP style branching search. In particular we have described the relationship between Branch-and-Check and Benders.

We have presented the intuition behind Branch-and-Check, to delay parts of the problem, and verified with computational experiments. We have also addressed one of the key elements for the integration of CLP and MIP: Dynamic linear relaxations of global constraints. The computational results indicate that efficient communication between the different parts of a hybrid model requires some double modelling, i.e., the same constraint must be present in both CLP and MIP form. Most preferably this double modelling should be implicit, i.e., mixed global constraints should post and dynamically update a linear relaxation of themselves. This relaxation should be adjustable, i.e, it should be possible to efficiently make incremental changes, rather than recompute it at every node.

Indirectly, we have also mentioned the issue of the availability of flexible tools for testing integration ideas, of the lack thereof. We conclude that there is pressing need in this community to have access to a branching solver that is efficient but also highly customisable to allow for customisation of how each node of the search tree is processed, solved and propagated, and how the problem is modified at each node both when branching and backtracking.

Acknowledgements. We would like to thank Prof. John N. Hooker for his helpful comments on this paper.

References

[1] J. F. Benders. Partitioning procedures for solving mixed-variables programming problems. *Numer. Math.*, 4:238–252, 1962.

[2] H. Beringer and B. De Backer. Combinatorial problem solving in constraint logic programming with cooperating solvers. In C. Beierle and L. Plümer, editors, *Logic Programming: Formal Methods and Practical Applications*, Studies in Computer Science and Artificial Intelligence, chapter 8, pages 245–272. Elsevier, 1995.

[3] A. Bockmayr and T. Kasper. Branch-and-infer: A unifying framework for integer and finite domain constraint programming. *INFORMS Journal on Computing*, 10(3):287–300, 1998.

[4] K. Darby-Dowman and J. Little. The significance of constraint logic programming to operational research. *Operational Research Tutorial Papers*, pages 20–45, 1995.

[5] K. Darby-Dowman and J. Little. Properties of some combinatorial optimization problems and their effect on the performance of integer programming and constraint logic programming. *INFORMS Journal on Computing*, 10(3):276–286, Summer 1998.

[6] I. R. de Farias, E. L. Johnson, and G. L. Nemhauser. A branch-and-cut approach without binary variables to combinatorial optimization problems with continuous variables and combinatorial constraints. *Knowledge Engineering Review, special issue on AI/OR, submitted*, 1999.

[7] F. Focacci, A. Lodi, and M. Milano. Cutting planes in constraint programming: An hybrid approach. In *CP-AI-OR'00 Workshop on Integration of AI and OR techniques in Constraint Programming for Combinatorial Optimization Problems*, March 2000.

[8] A. M. Geoffrion. Generalized Benders decomposition. *Journal of Optimization theory and Applications*, 10:237–260, 1972.

[9] I. Harjunkoski, V. Jain, and I.E. Grossmann. Hybrid mixed-integer/constraint logic programming strategies for solving scheduling and combinatorial optimization problems. *Computers and Chemical Engineering*, 24:337–343, 2000.

[10] J. N. Hooker. Logic-based methods for optimization. In Alan Borning, editor, *Principles and Practice of Constraint Programming*, volume 874 of *Lecture Notes in Computer Science*. Springer, May 1994. (PPCP'94: Second International Workshop, Orcas Island, Seattle, USA).

[11] J. N. Hooker. *Logic-Based Methods for Optimization*. Wiley, New York, 2000.

[12] J. N. Hooker and M. A. Osorio. Mixed logical/linear programming. *Discrete Applied Mathematics*, 96–97(1–3):395–442, 1999.

[13] John N. Hooker, Hak-Jin Kim, and Greger Ottosson. A declarative modeling framework that integrates solution methods. *Annals of Operations Research, Special Issue on Modeling Languages and Approaches, to appear*, 1998.

[14] John N. Hooker and Greger Ottosson. Logic-based Benders decomposition. *Mathematical Programming*, 2000. Submitted.

[15] John N. Hooker, Greger Ottosson, Erlendur S. Thorsteinsson, and Hak-Jin Kim. On integrating constraint propagation and linear programming for combinatorial optimization. In *Proceedings of the Sixteenth National Conference on Artificial Intelligence (AAAI-99)*, pages 136–141. AAAI, The AAAI Press/The MIT Press, July 1999.

[16] John N. Hooker, Greger Ottosson, Erlendur S. Thorsteinsson, and Hak-Jin Kim. A scheme for unifying optimization and constraint satisfaction methods. *Knowledge Engineering Review, Special Issue on Artifical Intelligence and Operations Research*, 15(1):11–30, 2000.

[17] John N. Hooker and Hong Yan. Logic circuit verification by Benders decomposition. In V. Saraswat and P. Van Hentenryck, editors, *Principles and Practice of Constraint Programming: The Newport Papers*, pages 267–288. MIT Press, 1995.

[18] V. Jain and I.E. Grossmann. Algorithms for hybrid MILP/CP models for a class of optimization problems. INFORMS, 2000. Presented at INFORMS Salt Lake City, paper SD32.1.

[19] R.G. Jeroslow and J. Wang. Dynamic programming, integral polyhedra, and horn clause knowledge bases. *ORSA Journal on Computing*, 1(1):7–19, 1988.

[20] Michela Milano, Greger Ottosson, Philippe Refalo, and Erlendur S. Thorsteinsson. Global constraints: When constraint programming meets operation research. *INFORMS Journal on Computing, Special Issue on the Merging of Mathematical Programming and Constraint Programming*, March 2001. Submitted.

[21] Greger Ottosson, Erlendur S. Thorsteinsson, and John N. Hooker. Mixed global constraints and inference in hybrid CLP–IP solvers. *Annals of Mathematics and Artificial Intelligence, Special Issue on Large Scale Combinatorial Optimisation and Constraints*, March 2001. Accepted for publication.

[22] Philippe Refalo. Tight cooperation and its application in piecewise linear optimization. In Joxan Jaffar, editor, *Principles and Practice of Constraint Programming*, volume 1713 of *Lecture Notes in Computer Science*. Springer, October 1999.

[23] Robert Rodošek, Mark Wallace, and Mozafar Hajian. A new approach to integrating mixed integer programming and constraint logic programming. *Annals of Operations Research, Advances in Combinatorial Optimization*, 86:63–87, 1999.

[24] Erlendur S. Thorsteinsson and Greger Ottosson. Linear relaxations and reduced-cost based propagation of continuous variable subscripts. *Annals of Operations Research, Special Issue on Integration of Constraint Programming, Artificial Intelligence and Operations Research Methods*, January 2001. Submitted.

[25] P. Van Hentenryck. *The OPL Optimization Programming Language*. MIT Press, 1999.

Towards Inductive Constraint Solving

Slim Abdennadher[1] and Christophe Rigotti[2]*

[1] Computer Science Department, University of Munich
Oettingenstr. 67, 80538 München, Germany
Slim.Abdennadher@informatik.uni-muenchen.de

[2] Laboratoire d'Ingénierie des Systèmes d'Information
Bâtiment 501, INSA Lyon, 69621 Villeurbanne Cedex, France
Christophe.Rigotti@insa-lyon.fr

Abstract. A difficulty that arises frequently when writing a constraint solver is to determine the constraint propagation and simplification algorithm. In previous work, different methods for automatic generation of propagation rules [5,17,3] and simplification rules [4] for constraints defined over finite domains have been proposed. In this paper, we present a method for generating rule-based solvers for constraint predicates defined by means of a constraint logic program, even when the constraint domain is infinite. This approach can be seen as a concrete step towards *Inductive Constraint Solving.*

1 Introduction

Inductive Logic Programming (ILP) is a machine learning technique that has emerged in the beginning of the 90's [12]. ILP has been defined as the intersection of inductive learning and logic programming. It aims at inducing hypotheses from examples, where the hypothesis language is the first order logic restricted to Horn clauses. To handle numerical knowledge, an inductive framework, called *Inductive Constraint Logic Programming* (ICLP), similar to that of ILP but based on constraint logic programming schemes have been proposed [13]. ICLP extends ideas and results from ILP to the learning of constraint logic programs.

In this paper, we propose a method to *learn* rule-based constraint solvers from the definitions of the constraint predicates. We call this approach *Inductive Constraint Solving* (ICS). It extends previous works [5,17,3] where different methods for automatic generation of propagation rules for constraints defined over finite domains have been proposed.

In rule-based constraint programming, the solving process of constraints consists of a repeated application of rules. In general, we distinguish two kinds of rules: simplification and propagation rules. Simplification rules rewrite constraints to simpler constraints while preserving logical equivalence, e.g. $X{\leq}Y \wedge Y{\leq}X \Leftrightarrow X{=}Y$. Propagation rules add new constraints which are logically redundant but may cause further simplification, e.g. $X{\leq}Y \wedge Y{\leq}Z \Rightarrow X{\leq}Z$.

* The research reported in this paper has been supported by the Bavarian-French Hochschulzentrum.

T. Walsh (Ed.): CP 2001, LNCS 2239, pp. 31–45, 2001.

In this paper, we present an algorithm, called PropMiner, that can be used to generate propagation rules for constraint predicates defined by means of a constraint logic program, even when the constraint domain is infinite. The PropMiner algorithm can be completed with the algorithm presented in [4] to transform some propagation rules into simplification rules improving both the time and space behavior of constraint solving.

The combination of these techniques can be seen as a true ICS tool. Using this tool, the user only has to determine the semantics of the constraints of interest by means of their intentional definitions (a constraint logic program), and to specify the admissible syntactic form of the rules he wants to obtain.

Example 1. Consider the following constraint logic program, where $min(A, B, C)$ means that C is the minimum of A and B:

$$min(A, B, C) \leftarrow A{\leq}B \wedge C{=}A.$$
$$min(A, B, C) \leftarrow B{\leq}A \wedge C{=}B.$$

For the predicate min, our algorithm PropMiner described in Section 2 generates the following propagation rules if the user specifies that the left hand side of the rules may consist of min constraints and equality constraints:

$$min(A, B, C) \Rightarrow C{\leq}A \wedge C{\leq}B.$$
$$min(A, B, C) \wedge A{=}B \Rightarrow A{=}C.$$

For example, the second rule means that the constraint $min(A, B, C)$ when it is known that the input arguments A and B are equal can propagate the constraint that the output C must be equal to the input arguments.

If the user additionally allows disequality and less-or-equal constraints on the left hand side of the rules, the algorithm generates the following rules:

$$min(A, B, C) \wedge C{\neq}B \Rightarrow C{=}A.$$
$$min(A, B, C) \wedge C{\neq}A \Rightarrow C{=}B.$$
$$min(A, B, C) \wedge B{\leq}A \Rightarrow C{=}B.$$
$$min(A, B, C) \wedge A{\leq}B \Rightarrow C{=}A.$$

Using the algorithm presented in [4] some propagation rules can be transformed into simplification rules and we obtain the following rule-based constraint solver for min:

$$min(A, B, C) \Rightarrow C{\leq}A \wedge C{\leq}B.$$
$$min(A, A, C) \Leftrightarrow A{=}C.$$
$$min(A, B, C) \wedge C{\neq}B \Rightarrow C{=}A.$$
$$min(A, B, C) \wedge C{\neq}A \Rightarrow C{=}B.$$
$$min(A, B, C) \wedge B{\leq}A \Leftrightarrow C{=}B \wedge B{\leq}A.$$
$$min(A, B, C) \wedge A{\leq}B \Leftrightarrow C{=}A \wedge A{\leq}B.$$

For example, the goal $min(A, B, B)$ will be transformed into $B{\leq}A$ using the first propagation rule and then the second last simplification rule. □

The generated rules can be directly encoded in a rule-based programming language, e.g. Constraint Handling Rules (CHR) [6] to provide a running constraint solver. The Inductive Constraint Solving tool presented in this paper can also be simply used as a software engineering tool to help solver developers to find out propagation and simplification rules.

The paper is organized as follows. In Section 2, we present an algorithm to generate propagation rules for constraint predicates defined by a constraint logic program. In Section 3, we give more examples for the use of our algorithm. We discuss in Section 4 how recursive programs can be handled. Finally, we conclude with a summary and compare the proposed approach with related work.

2 Generation of Propagation Rules

In this section, we present an algorithm, called PropMiner, to generate propagation rules for constraints using the intensional definitions of the constraint predicates. These definitions are given by means of a program in a constraint logic programming (CLP) language. We assume some familiarity with constraint logic programming as defined by Jaffar and Maher in [9] and follow their definitions and terminology when applicable.

The CLP programs are parameterized by a constraint system defined by a 4-tuple $\langle \Sigma, \mathcal{D}, \mathcal{L}, \mathcal{T} \rangle$ and a signature Π determining the predicate symbols defined by a program. Σ is a signature determining the predefined predicate and function symbols, $\mathcal{D}$ is a Σ-structure (the domain of computation), $\mathcal{L}$ is a class of Σ-formulas closed by conjunction and called constraints, and $\mathcal{T}$ is a first-order Σ-theory that is an axiomatization of the properties of $\mathcal{D}$.

We require that $\mathcal{D}$ is a model of $\mathcal{T}$ and that $\mathcal{T}$ is satisfaction complete with respect to $\mathcal{L}$, that is, for every constraint $c \in \mathcal{L}$ either $\mathcal{T} \models \tilde{\exists} c$ or $\mathcal{T} \models \neg\tilde{\exists} c$, where $\tilde{\exists}(\phi)$ denotes the existential closure of ϕ. Note that these requirements are fulfilled by most commonly used CLP languages.

In the rest of this paper, we use the following terminology.

Definition 1. A *constrained clause* is a rule of the form

$$H \leftarrow B_1 \wedge \ldots \wedge B_n \wedge C_1 \wedge \ldots \wedge C_m$$

where $H, B_1, \ldots, B_n$ are atoms over Π and $C_1, \ldots, C_m$ are constraints. A *goal* is a set of atoms over Π and constraints, interpreted as their conjunction. An *answer* is a set of constraints also interpreted as their conjunction. A *CLP program* is a finite set of constrained clauses. The logical semantics of a CLP program P is its Clark's completion and is denoted by P^*.

In programs, goals and answers, when clear from the context, we use upper case letters (resp. lower case and numbers) to denote variables (resp. constants).

2.1 Rules of Interest

A *propagation pattern* is a set of constraints and of atoms over Π, interpreted as their conjunction.

A *propagation rule* is a rule of the form $C_1 \Rightarrow C_2$ or of the form $C_1 \Rightarrow false$, where C_1 is a propagation pattern and C_2 is a set of constraints (also interpreted as their conjunction). C_1 is called the *left hand side* (lhs) and C_2 the *right hand side* (rhs) of the rule. A rule of the form $C_1 \Rightarrow false$ is called *failure rule.* To formulate the logical semantics of these rules, we use the following notation: let $\mathcal{V}$ be a set of variables then $\exists_{-\mathcal{V}}(\phi)$ denotes the existential closure of ϕ except for the variable in $\mathcal{V}$.

Definition 2. A propagation rule $\{c_1, \ldots, c_n\} \Rightarrow \{d_1, \ldots, d_m\}$ is *valid*[1] wrt. the constraint theory $\mathcal{T}$ and the CLP program P iff $P^*, \mathcal{T} \models \bigwedge_i c_i \rightarrow \exists_{-\mathcal{V}}(\bigwedge_j d_j)$, where $\mathcal{V}$ is the set of variables appearing in $\{c_1, \ldots, c_n\}$.
A failure rule $\{c_1, \ldots, c_n\} \Rightarrow false$ is *valid* wrt. $\mathcal{T}$ and P if and only if $P^*, \mathcal{T} \models \neg\tilde{\exists}(\bigwedge_i c_i)$.

To reduce the number of rules which are uninteresting to build a solver, we restrict with a syntactic bias the generation to a particular set of rules called *relevant propagation rules.* These rules must contain in their lhs atoms corresponding to the predicates on which we want to propagate information, and all elements in this lhs must be connected by common variables. This is defined more precisely by the notion of *interesting pattern.*

Definition 3. A propagation pattern $\mathcal{A}$ is an *interesting pattern* wrt. a propagation pattern $Base_{lhs}$ if and only if the following conditions are satisfied:

1. $Base_{lhs} \subseteq \mathcal{A}$.
2. the graph defined by the relation $join_{\mathcal{A}}$ is connected, where $join_{\mathcal{A}}$ is a binary relation that holds for pairs of elements in $\mathcal{A}$ that share at least one variable, i.e., $join_{\mathcal{A}} = \{\langle c_1, c_2\rangle \mid c_1 \in \mathcal{A}, c_2 \in \mathcal{A}, Var(\{c_1\}) \cap Var(\{c_2\}) \neq \emptyset\}$, where $Var(\{c_1\})$ and $Var(\{c_2\})$ denote the variables appearing in c_1 and c_2, respectively.

A *relevant propagation rule* wrt. $Base_{lhs}$ is a propagation rule such that its lhs is an interesting pattern wrt. $Base_{lhs}$.

2.2 The PropMiner Algorithm

In this section, we describe the PropMiner algorithm to generate propagation rules from a program P expressed in a CLP language determined by $\langle \Sigma, \mathcal{D}, \mathcal{L}, \mathcal{T}\rangle$.

The algorithm takes as input the program P, a propagation pattern $Base_{lhs}$ and a set of constraints $Cand_{lhs}$ (for which we already have a built-in solver). It generates propagation rules that are valid wrt. $\mathcal{T}$ and P, relevant wrt. $Base_{lhs}$ and such that their lhs are subsets of $Base_{lhs} \cup Cand_{lhs}$.

[1] The requirement made on CLP programs that $\mathcal{T}$ must be satisfaction complete is not sufficient to ensure the decidability of the propagation rule validity. However, it should be noticed that the soundness of the algorithm proposed in Section 2.2 is not based on such a decidability property.

```
begin

    Let R be an empty set of rules.
    Let L be a list containing all non-empty subsets
    of Base_lhs ∪ Cand_lhs in any order.

    Remove from L any element C which is not an interesting pattern wrt. Base_lhs.
    Order L with any total ordering compatible with the subset partial ordering
    (i.e., for all C1 in L if C2 is after C1 in L then C2 ⊄ C1).

    while L is not empty do
        Let C_lhs be the first element of L and then remove C_lhs from L.
        Let A be the set of answers for the goal C_lhs wrt. the program P.
        if A is empty then
            add the failure rule (C_lhs ⇒ false) to R
            and remove from L each element C such that C_lhs ⊂ C.
        else
            if A is finite then
                compute the set of constraints C_rhs
                as the least general generalization (lgg) of A
                if C_rhs is not empty then
                    add the rule (C_lhs ⇒ C_rhs) to R
                endif
            endif
        endif
    endwhile

    output R

end
```

Fig. 1. The PROPMINER Algorithm

Principle. From an abstract point of view, the algorithm enumerates each possible lhs subset of $Base_{lhs} \cup Cand_{lhs}$ (denoted by C_{lhs}). For each C_{lhs} it computes a set of constraints noted C_{rhs} such that $C_{lhs} \Rightarrow C_{rhs}$ is valid wrt. $\mathcal{T}$ and P and relevant wrt. $Base_{lhs}$.

For each C_{lhs}, the algorithm PROPMINER determines C_{rhs} by calling the CLP system to execute C_{lhs} as a goal and then

1. if C_{lhs} has no answer then it produces the failure rule $C_{lhs} \Rightarrow false$.
2. if C_{lhs} has a finite number of answers $\{Ans_1, \ldots, Ans_n\}$ then let C_{rhs} be the *least general generalization* (lgg) of $\{Ans_1, \ldots, Ans_n\}$ as defined by [15]. C_{rhs} is then in some sense the strongest constraint common to all answers as

illustrated below (see Example 2). If C_{rhs} is not empty then the algorithm produces the rule $C_{lhs} \Rightarrow C_{rhs}$.

It is clear that these two criteria can be used only if all answers can be collected in finite time. The application of the algorithm to handle recursive programs leading to non-terminating executions is discussed in Section 4.

The algorithm is given in Figure 2.2. To simplify its presentation, we consider that all possible lhs are stored in a list. For efficiency reasons the concrete implementation is based on a tree and unnecessary candidates are not materialized. More details on the implementation are given in Section 2.4.

A particular ordering is used to enumerate the lhs candidates so that the more general lhs are tried before the more specific ones. Then, we use the following pruning criterion which improves greatly the efficiency of the algorithm: if a rule $C_{lhs} \Rightarrow false$ is generated then there is no need to consider any superset of C_{lhs} to form other rule lhs.

We now illustrate on the following example the basic behavior of the algorithm PROPMINER. More uses of the algorithm are given in Section 3.

Example 2. Consider the following CLP program defining p and q:

$$\begin{aligned} p(X,Y,Z) &\leftarrow q(X,Y,Z). \\ p(X,Y,Z) &\leftarrow X{\leq}W \ \wedge \ Y{=}W \ \wedge \ X{>}Z. \\ q(X,Y,Z) &\leftarrow X{\leq}a \ \wedge \ Y{=}a \ \wedge \ Z{\neq}b. \end{aligned}$$

We use the algorithm to find rules to propagate constraints over propagation patterns involving p. Let $Base_{lhs} = \{p(X,Y,Z)\}$ and let for example $Cand_{lhs}$ be the set $\{X{\leq}Z,\ Y{=}a,\ Z{=}b\}$.

When the while loop is entered for the first time we have

$$\begin{aligned} L = \{\ &\{p(X,Y,Z)\},\ \{p(X,Y,Z),\ X{\leq}Z\},\ \{p(X,Y,Z),\ Y{=}a\}, \\ &\{p(X,Y,Z),\ Z{=}b\},\ \{p(X,Y,Z),\ X{\leq}Z,\ Y{=}a\},\ \{p(X,Y,Z),\ X{\leq}Z,\ Z{=}b\}, \\ &\{p(X,Y,Z),\ Y{=}a,\ Z{=}b\},\ \{p(X,Y,Z),\ X{\leq}Z,\ Y{=}a,\ Z{=}b\}\ \} \end{aligned}$$

Each element in L is executed in turn as a goal and the corresponding answers are collected and used to build a rule rhs. For example, $\{p(X,Y,Z),\ Z{=}b\}$ leads to a single answer $Ans_1 = \{X{\leq}W,\ Y{=}W,\ X{>}Z,\ Z{=}b\}$. The lgg is simply Ans_1 itself and we have the propagation rule $\{p(X,Y,Z),\ Z{=}b\} \Rightarrow \{X{\leq}W,\ Y{=}W,\ X{>}Z,\ Z{=}b\}$. For $\{p(X,Y,Z), X{\leq}Z\}$ we have again a single answer $\{X{\leq}a, Y{=}a, Z{\neq}b, X{\leq}Z\}$ and thus also a trivial lgg producing the rule $\{p(X,Y,Z), X{\leq}Z\} \Rightarrow X{\leq}a, Y{=}a, Z{\neq}b, X{\leq}Z\}$.

For the goal $\{p(X,Y,Z),\ \ Y{=}a\}$, the situation is different since we have the two following answers $Ans_1 = \{X{\leq}a, Y{=}a, Z{\neq}b\}$ and $Ans_2 = \{X{\leq}a, Y{=}a, X{>}Z\}$. The lgg which is based on a syntactical generalization is $\{X{\leq}a, Y{=}a\}$ and we have the rule $\{p(X,Y,Z), Y{=}a\} \Rightarrow \{X{\leq}a, Y{=}a\}$.

The situation may be more tricky. For example, the goal $\{p(X,Y,Z)\}$ have two answers $Ans_1 = \{X{\leq}a,\ Y{=}a,\ Z{\neq}b\}$ and $Ans_2 = \{X{\leq}W,\ Y{=}W,\ X{>}Z\}$

having no common element. Fortunately, the lgg corresponds in some sense to the least upper bound of $\{Ans_1, Ans_2\}$ wrt. the θ-subsumption ordering [15] (more precisely it represents the equivalence class of constraints that corresponds to this least upper bound). Thus, the lgg of $\{Ans_1, Ans_2\}$ is $\{X{\leq}E,\ Y{=}E\}$, where E is a new variable, and the algorithm produces the rule $\{p(X,Y,Z)\} \Rightarrow \{X{\leq}E, Y{=}E\}$. However, it should be noticed that the notion of lgg is not based on the semantics of the constraints in the set of answers. Thus, two sets of answers that are equivalent wrt. the constraint theory but not identical from a syntactic point of view will lead in general to different lgg's. As shown in sections 2.3 and 3, the user can partially overcome this difficulty by providing ad hoc propagation rules to take into account the constraint semantics.

The effect of the pruning criterion is straightforward. The goal $G = \{p(X,Y,Z),\ X{\leq}Z,\ Z{=}b\}$ has no answer and leads to the rule $\{p(X,Y,Z),\ X{\leq}Z,\ Z{=}b\} \Rightarrow false$. Then the element $\{p(X,Y,Z),\ X{\leq}Z,\ Y{=}a,\ Z{=}b\}$ that is a super set of G is simply removed from L and will not be considered to generate any rule.

Properties. It is straightforward to see that the algorithm is complete in the sense that if $C_{lhs} \subseteq Base_{lhs} \cup Cand_{lhs}$ is an interesting pattern wrt. $Base_{lhs}$ and there is no $C \subset C_{lhs}$ such that $C \Rightarrow false$ is valid, then C_{lhs} is considered by the algorithm as a candidate to form the lhs of a rule.

To establish the soundness of the algorithm, we need the following results presented in [9].

Theorem 1. Let P be a program in the CLP language determined by $\langle \Sigma, \mathcal{D}, \mathcal{L}, \mathcal{T} \rangle$, where $\mathcal{D}$ is a model of $\mathcal{T}$. Suppose that $\mathcal{T}$ is satisfaction complete wrt. $\mathcal{L}$, and that P is executed on a CLP system for this language. Then:

1. If a goal G has a finite computation tree, with answers $c_1, \ldots, c_n$ then $P^*, \mathcal{T} \models G \leftrightarrow \exists_{-\mathcal{V}}(c_1 \vee \ldots \vee c_n)$, where $\mathcal{V}$ is the set of variables appearing in G.
2. If a goal G is finitely failed for P then $P^*, \mathcal{T} \models \neg G$.

The soundness of PropMiner is stated by the following theorem.

Theorem 2 (Soundness). The PropMiner algorithm produces propagation rules that are relevant wrt. $Base_{lhs}$ and valid wrt. $\mathcal{T}$ and P.

Proof. All C_{lhs} considered are interesting pattern wrt. $Base_{lhs}$, thus only relevant rules can be generated. If a rule of the form $C_{lhs} \Rightarrow false$ is produced then by property 2 in Theorem 1 this rule is valid. Suppose a rule of the form $C_{lhs} \Rightarrow C_{rhs}$ is generated. Then C_{rhs} is the lgg of a finite set of answers $\{Ans_1, \ldots, Ans_n\}$ obtained by the execution of the goal C_{lhs} on the program P.

By property 1 in Theorem 1, we have $P^*, \mathcal{T} \models C_{lhs} \leftrightarrow \exists_{-\mathcal{V}}(Ans_1 \vee \ldots \vee Ans_n)$, where $\mathcal{V}$ is the set of variables appearing in C_{lhs}. Since C_{rhs} is the lgg of $\{Ans_1, \ldots, Ans_n\}$ then by [15] we know that $Ans_1 \vee \ldots \vee Ans_n \rightarrow C_{rhs}$. Thus $P^*, \mathcal{T} \models C_{lhs} \rightarrow \exists_{-\mathcal{V}}\ C_{rhs}$, i.e. $C_{lhs} \Rightarrow C_{rhs}$ is valid wrt. $\mathcal{T}$ and P. □

2.3 Interesting Rules for Constraint Solvers

The basic form of the PROPMINER algorithm given in Figure 2.2 produces a very large set of rules. Most of these rules are redundant (partly or completely) or propagates too weak constraints or on the contrary propagates too many stronger constraints (inflating considerably the constraint store at runtime) and thus may be of little interest to built a constraint solver.

We present in this section mandatory complementary processing that is integrated in the basic algorithm in order to generate rules of practical interest wrt. solver construction.

Consider again the CLP program of example 2. Let $Base_{lhs} = \{p(X,Y,Z)\}$ and let us use a richer set of constraints to form the lhs of the rules $Cand_{lhs} = \{X{\leq}Z,\ Y{\leq}X,\ X{=}Z, Y{=}Z,\ X{=}b,\ Y{=}a,\ Z{=}b\}$.

Among the rules generated by the basic algorithm PROPMINER, we have:

$$\{p(X,Y,Z)\} \Rightarrow \{X{\leq}E,\ Y{=}E\}. \tag{1}$$
$$\{p(X,Y,Z),\ X{\leq}Z\} \Rightarrow \{X{\leq}a,\ Y{=}a,\ Z{\neq}b,\ X{\leq}Z\}. \tag{2}$$
$$\{p(X,Y,Z),\ Y{\leq}X\} \Rightarrow \{X{\leq}E,\ Y{=}E,\ Y{\leq}X\}. \tag{3}$$
$$\{p(X,Y,Z),\ X{=}Z\} \Rightarrow \{X{\leq}a,\ Y{=}a,\ Z{\neq}b,\ X{=}Z\}. \tag{4}$$
$$\{p(X,Y,Z),\ Y{=}Z\} \Rightarrow \{X{\leq}a,\ Y{=}a,\ Z{\neq}b,\ Y{=}Z\}. \tag{5}$$
$$\{p(X,Y,Z),\ X{=}b\} \Rightarrow \{X{\leq}E,\ Y{=}E,\ X{=}b\}. \tag{6}$$
$$\{p(X,Y,Z),\ Y{=}a\} \Rightarrow \{X{\leq}E,\ Y{=}E,\ Y{=}a\}. \tag{7}$$
$$\{p(X,Y,Z),\ Z{=}b\} \Rightarrow \{X{\leq}W,\ Y{=}W,\ X{>}Z,\ Z{=}b\}. \tag{8}$$
$$\{p(X,Y,Z),\ X{\leq}Z,\ Z{=}b\} \Rightarrow false. \tag{9}$$

Since the algorithm only imposes that the exploration ordering is a total ordering compatible with the subset ordering on the lhs, the real order of the rules generated may be slightly different according to implementation choices (see Section 2.4). However, the specific processing presented in this section can still be applied.

Removing redundancy. The key idea of the simplification is to remove from the rhs of a rule R all constraints that can be derived from the lhs of R using the built-in solvers and the rules already generated. If the remaining rhs is empty then the whole rule can be suppressed.

For example, according to this process rule (6) is removed because its rhs is fully redundant wrt. its lhs and wrt. rule (1). For rule (2) only the rhs is modified and becomes $\{X{\leq}a,\ Y{=}a,\ Z{\neq}b\}$, since $X{\leq}Z$ is trivially entailed by the lhs of the rule.

Depending on the behavior of the built-in solvers, rule (4) may be only transformed into $\{p(X,Y,Z),\ X{=}Z\} \Rightarrow \{X{\leq}a,\ Y{=}a,\ Z{\neq}b\}$ while if we know the semantics of $\leq$ we may use rule (2) to derive the same constraints. If the built-in solver does not allow to discover this redundancy, then in our implementation (see Section 2.4) the user can add in a simple way propagation rules to derive explicitely logical consequences of the built-in constraints. In this example, one of the complementary rules that can be provided by the user is $\{X{=}Z\} \Rightarrow \{X{\leq}Z\}$ which allows to find that rule (4) is then fully redundant wrt. rule (2).

This simplification process also applies to failure rules. Suppose that the built-in solver is able to detect that $Z{=}b \wedge Z{\neq}b$ is inconsistent, then the rule (9) is removed since it is redundant wrt. rule (2).

Generating stronger rhs. If we consider rule (6) $\{p(X,Y,Z), X{=}b\} \Rightarrow \{X{\leq}E,\ Y{=}E, X{=}b\}$ the rhs constructed from the least general generalization of the answers obtained for the goal $\{p(X,Y,Z),\ \ X{=}b\}$ is in some sense too general. The execution of the goal gives two answers. One containing $\{Z{\neq}b\}$ and the other $\{X{>}Z,\ X{=}b\}$. From a semantical point of view, this leads clearly to $Z{\neq}b$ in both cases, but the least general generalization is mainly syntactical and do not retains this information.

If we want a richer rhs (containing $Z{\neq}b$) then we must have at hand a (built-in) solver that propagates $\{Z{\neq}b\}$ also in the second answer. If we do not have such a solver, then here again the user can provide himself complementary propagation rules (in this example the single rule $\{X{>}Y\} \Rightarrow \{X{\neq}Y\}$) to produce this piece of information.

Projecting variables. For efficiency reasons in constraint solving it is particularly important to limit the number of variables.

Then a rule like $\{p(X,Y,Z)\} \Rightarrow \{X{\leq}E,\ \ Y{=}E\}$ should be avoided since it will create a new variable each time it is fired.

So, we simply project out such useless variables in the following way. We consider in turn each equality in the rhs of a rule. If this equality is of the form $E{=}F$ or $F{=}E$ where E and F are variables and E does not appear in the lhs of the rule, then we suppress this equality from the rhs and we apply the substitution transforming E into F to the whole remaining rhs.

More subtle situations may arise. Suppose that the second clause of the program given in example 2 was $p(X,Y,Z) \leftarrow X{\leq}W \wedge Y{=}W \wedge Z{\neq}a$. Then, the first rule generated would have been $\{p(X,Y,Z)\} \Rightarrow \{X{\leq}E,\ Y{=}E,\ Z{\neq}F\}$. And then projecting out E would transform it into $\{p(X,Y,Z)\} \Rightarrow \{X{\leq}Y,\ Z{\neq}F\}$. Then, during constraint solving the application of this rule will add to the store the constraint $Z{\neq}F$, where F is a new variable. This phenomena leads in general to a rather inefficient solving process. So, we propose the following optional treatment: When all other previous processing has been performed (simplification, additional propagation and projection of variable in equalities) the user can choose to apply a strict *range restriction* criteria: all constraints in the rhs containing a variable that does not appear in the lhs is removed (e.g., $Z{\neq}F$ in the previous rule). This range restriction criteria is applied in all examples presented in this paper. However, it should be noticed that this process remains optional since this simplification criteria is purely syntactic and does not guarantee that the constraints removed from the rhs are semantically redundant, and thus may produce weaker rules (although still valid).

2.4 Implementation Issues

The key aspects of our implementation of the PropMiner algorithm are presented in this section. The prototype has been developed under SICStus Prolog 3.7.1. It is written in Prolog and takes advantage of the rule-based programming language Constraint Handling Rules (CHR) [6] supported in this environment.

Using CHR. The CHR language facilitates in two ways the implementation of the important processing described in Section 2.3. Firstly, we can use the rules generated as CHR rules and then run CHR to decide if a rule propagates new constraints wrt. the rules we have already. Secondly, the user can directly add new rules to perform complementary propagations wrt. the built-in solvers as mentioned in Section 2.3.

Clause encoding. It should be noticed that in this environment the equality $=$ is reserved to specify unification. So in practice, we use another binary predicate to denote the equality constraint. Moreover, the bindings of the variables due to the resolution steps are not handled explicitely as equalities in the store. Suppose that the third clause of the program given in example 2 was written under the form $q(X, a, Z) \leftarrow X{\leq}a{\wedge}Z{\neq}b$. Then, for the goal $\{p(X, Y, Z),\ X{\leq}Z\}$ we may have not collected the constraint $Y{=}a$ explicitely and thus $Y{=}a$ will not appear in the rhs of rule (2). Thus, we simply preprocess the clauses so that the atom in the head of a clause does not contain functors (including constants) and coreferences. The corresponding functors and coreferences are simply encoded by equality constraints in the body of the clause. For example a head of the form $p(X, a, X)$ will be transformed into $p(X, Y, Z)$ and $X{=}Z \wedge Y{=}a$ will be added to the body.

Enumeration of lhs. The PropMiner algorithm enumerates the possible lhs (the elements in L). The implementation of this enumeration is based on the exploration of a tree corresponding to the lhs search space. This tree is explored using a depth first strategy. As in [3], the branches are expanded using a partial ordering on the lhs candidates such that the more general lhs are examined before more specialized ones. The partial ordering used in our implementation is the θ-subsumption ordering [15].

3 Practical Uses of PropMiner

In this section, we show on examples that a practical application of our approach lies in solver development. All the set of rules presented in this section have been generated in a few seconds on a PC Pentium 3 with 128 MBytes of memory and a 500 MHZ processor.

For convenience, we introduce the following notation. Let c be a constraint symbol of arity 2 and D_1 and D_2 be two sets of terms. We define $atomic(c, D_1, D_2)$ as the set of all constraints built from c over $D_1 \times D_2$. More precisely,
$atomic(c, D_1, D_2) = \{c(\alpha, \beta) \mid \alpha \in D_1 \text{ and } \beta \in D_2\}$.

Example 3. For the minimum predicate $min(A, B, C)$ defined by the CLP program of Example 1, the PROPMINER algorithm with the following input

$$\begin{aligned} Base_{lhs} &= \{min(A, B, C)\} \\ Cand_{lhs} &= atomic(=, \{A, B, C\}, \{A, B, C\}) \cup \\ &\quad atomic(\neq, \{A, B, C\}, \{A, B, C\}) \cup \\ &\quad atomic(\leq, \{A, B, C\}, \{A, B, C\}) \end{aligned}$$

generates the 6 propagation rules presented in Example 1.

It should be noticed that to be able to generate the first rule, the following rules for equality and less-or-equal constraints have to be present in the built-in solver to ensure the generation of stronger rhs (as illustrated in Section 2.3):

$$\begin{aligned} X{\leq}Y \wedge Y{\leq}Z &\Rightarrow X{\leq}Z. \\ X{=}Y &\Rightarrow X{\leq}Y. \end{aligned}$$

If these rules are not already in the built-in solver, in our implementation the user can provide them very easily by means of CHR rules (see Section 2.4). Moreover, using this possibility, PROPMINER can incorporate additional knowledge given by the user about the predicate of interest. For example, the user can express the symmetry of min with respect to the the first and second arguments by the rule:

$$min(A, B, C) \Rightarrow min(B, A, C).$$

If this rule is provided by the user as a CHR rule, it completes the built-in solver and then the PROPMINER algorithm generates only the following simplified set of 4 rules:

$$\begin{aligned} min(A, B, C) &\Rightarrow C{\leq}A \wedge C{\leq}B. \\ min(A, B, C) \wedge A{=}B &\Rightarrow A{=}C. \\ min(A, B, C) \wedge C{\neq}B &\Rightarrow C{=}A. \\ min(A, B, C) \wedge B{\leq}A &\Rightarrow C{=}B. \end{aligned}$$

Example 4. If we consider the maximum predicate max, a set of rules similar to the rules for min is generated by PROPMINER. Then the user has the possibility to add these two sets of rules to the built-in solver and to execute PROPMINER to generate interaction rules between min and max. This execution is performed with the following input

$$\begin{aligned} Base_{lhs} &= \{min(A, B, C) \wedge max(D, E, F)\} \\ Cand_{lhs} &= atomic(\neq, \{A, B, C\}, \{D, E, F\}) \end{aligned}$$

and a CLP program consisting of the definitions of min and max. Since the propagation rules specific to min and max alone have been added to the built-in solver, PropMiner takes advantage of these rules to simplify many redundancies. Thus only 10 propagation rules specific to the conjunction of *min* with *max* are generated. Examples of rules are:

$$min(A,B,C) \wedge max(D,E,F) \wedge C{\neq}E \wedge C{\neq}D \Rightarrow F{\neq}C.$$
$$min(A,B,C) \wedge max(D,E,F) \wedge B{\neq}D \wedge A{\neq}D \Rightarrow D{\neq}C.$$
$$min(A,B,C) \wedge max(D,E,F) \wedge C{\neq}E \wedge B{\neq}D \wedge A{\neq}F \Rightarrow F{\neq}C.$$
$$min(A,B,C) \wedge max(D,E,F) \wedge C{\neq}D \wedge B{\neq}F \wedge A{\neq}E \Rightarrow F{\neq}C.$$

4 Handling Recursive Constraint Definitions

In this section, we show informally that the algorithm PropMiner can be applied when the CLP program P defining the constraint predicates is recursive and may lead to non-terminating executions.

As presented in Figure 2.2, for each possible rule lhs in L (denoted by C_{lhs}) the algorithm needs to collect in finite time all answers to the goal C_{lhs} wrt. the program P. In general, we cannot guarantee such a termination property, but we can use standard Logic Programming solutions developed to handle recursive clauses. For example, we can prefer a resolution based on the OLDT [19] scheme that ensures finite refutations more often than a resolution following the SLD principle (e.g., with the OLDT resolution the execution always terminates for Datalog programs).

We can also decide to bound the depth of the resolution to stop the execution of a goal that may cause non-termination. In this case, if the execution of goal C_{lhs} has a resolution depth exceeding a given threshold, we interrupt this execution and proceed with the next possible lhs in L. Of course this strategy may be too restrictive, in the sense that it may stop too early some terminating executions and thus may avoid the generation of some interesting rules.

Example 5. Consider the well-known ternary *append* predicate for lists, which holds if its third argument is a concatenation of the first and the second argument. It is usually implemented by these two clauses:

$$append(X,Y,Z) \leftarrow X{=}[] \wedge Y{=}Z.$$
$$append(X,Y,Z) \leftarrow X{=}[H|X1] \wedge Z{=}[H|Z1] \wedge append(X1,Y,Z1).$$

Then, if we bound the resolution depth to discard non-terminating executions, the algorithm PropMiner terminates and using the appropriate input produces, among others, the following rules:

$$append(A,B,C) \wedge A{=}B \wedge C{=}[D] \Rightarrow false.$$
$$append(A,B,C) \wedge B{=}C \wedge C{=}[D] \Rightarrow A{=}[].$$
$$append(A,B,C) \wedge C{=}[] \Rightarrow B{=}[] \wedge A{=}[].$$
$$append(A,B,C) \wedge A{=}[] \Rightarrow B{=}C.$$

5 Conclusion and Related Work

We have presented an approach to generate rule-based constraint solvers from the intentional definition of the constraint predicates given by means of a CLP program. The generation is performed in two steps. In a first step, it produces propagation rules using the algorithm PropMiner described in Section 2, and in a second step it transforms some of these rules into simplification rules using the method proposed in [4].

Now, we briefly compare our work to other approaches and give directions for future work.

- In [5,17,3] first steps towards automatic generation of propagation rules have been done. In these approaches the constraints are defined extensionally over finite domains by e.g. a truth table or their solution tuples. Thus, this paper can be seen as an extension of these previous works towards constraints defined intensionally over infinite domains. Over finite domains the algorithm PropMiner, can be used to generate the rules produces by the other methods.

  Example 6. For the boolean negation $neg(X,Y)$, the algorithm PropMiner and the algorithm described in [3] generate the same rules:

$$\begin{aligned} neg(X,X) &\Rightarrow false. \\ neg(X,1) &\Rightarrow X{=}0. \\ neg(X,0) &\Rightarrow X{=}1. \\ neg(1,Y) &\Rightarrow Y{=}0. \\ neg(0,Y) &\Rightarrow Y{=}1. \end{aligned}$$

- *Generalized Constraint Propagation* [16] extends the propagation mechanism from finite domains to arbitrary domains. The idea is to find and propagate a simple *approximation* constraint that is a kind of least upper bound of a set of computed answers to a goal. In contrast to our approach where the generation of rules is done once at compile time, generalized propagation is performed at runtime.
- *Constructive Disjunction* [8,20] is a way to extract common information from disjunctions of constraints over finite domains. We are currently investigating how constructive disjunction can be used in our case to enhance the computation of the least upper bound of set of answers in the case of constraints over finite domains. One advantage is that this approach can collect more information since it takes into account the semantics of the arithmetic operators, comparison predicates, and interval constraints.
- In ILP [12] and ICLP [13,11,10,18], the user is interested to find out logic programs and CLP programs from examples. In our case, we generate constraint solvers in the form of propagation and simplification rules, using the

definition of the constraint predicates given by means of a CLP program. We used techniques also used in ILP and ICLP (e.g., [15]), and it is important to consider which of the works done in these fields may be used for the generation of constraint solvers.

To our knowledge, the work done on Generalized Constraint Propagation, Constructive Disjunction, and in the fields of ILP and ICLP have not previously been adapted or applied to the generation of rule-based constraint solvers.

Future work includes the extension of the algorithm PropMiner to generate more information to be propagated in the right hand side of the rules. In the current algorithm, the computation of the least upper bound of set of answers is based on [15] which does not rely on the semantics of the constraints in the answers. As illustrated in Section 2.3 and Section 3, the user can provide by hand propagation rules to take into account (partially) this semantics, but, as it has been pointed out to us, approaches like [14] can be used to embed this semantics in a more general way and directly in the computation of the least upper bound. Another complementary aspect that needs to be investigated is the completeness of the solvers generated. It is clear that in general this property cannot be guaranteed, but in some cases it may be possible to check it, or at least to characterize the kind of consistency the solver can ensure.

Acknowledgments. We would like to thank Thom Frühwirth for helpful discussions. We also grateful to the anonymous referees for many helpful suggestions which undoubtedly improved the paper.

References

1. S. Abdennadher. Operational semantics and confluence of constraint propagation rules. In *Proc. of the third International Conference on Principles and Practice of Constraint Programming, CP'97*, LNCS 1330, pages 252–266. Springer-Verlag, November 1997.
2. S. Abdennadher, T. Frühwirth, and H. Meuss. Confluence and semantics of constraint simplification rules. *Constraints Journal, Special Issue on the Second International Conference on Principles and Practice of Constraint Programming*, 4(2):133–165, May 1999.
3. S. Abdennadher and C. Rigotti. Automatic generation of propagation rules for finite domains. In *Proc. of the 6th International Conference on Principles and Practice of Constraint Programming, CP'00*, LNCS 1894, pages 18–34. Springer-Verlag, September 2000.
4. S. Abdennadher and C. Rigotti. Using confluence to generate rule-based constraint solvers. In *Proc. of the third International Conference on Principles and Practice of Declarative Programming.* ACM Press, September 2001. To appear.
5. K. Apt and E. Monfroy. Automatic generation of constraint propagation algorithms for small finite domains. In *Proc. of the 5th International Conference on Principles and Practice of Constraint Programming, CP'99*, LNCS 1713, pages 58–72. Springer-Verlag, October 1999.

6. T. Frühwirth. Theory and practice of constraint handling rules, special issue on constraint logic programming. *Journal of Logic Programming*, 37(1-3):95–138, October 1998.
7. T. Frühwirth. Proving termination of constraint solver programs. In *New Trends in Constraints*, pages 298–317. LNAI 1865, 2000.
8. P. V. Hentenryck, V. Saraswat, and Y. Deville. Desing, implementation, and evaluation of the constraint language cc(FD). *Journal of Logic Programming*, 37(1-3):139–164, 1998.
9. J. Jaffar and M. J. Maher. Constraint logic programming: A survey. *Journal of Logic Programming*, 19-20:503–581, 1994.
10. L. Martin and C. Vrain. Induction of constraint logic programs. In *Proc. of the International Conference on Algorithms and Learning Theory*, LNCS 1160, pages 169–176. Springer-Verlag, October 1996.
11. F. Mizoguchi and H. Ohwada. Constrained relative least general generalization for inducing constraint logic programs. *New Generation Computing*, 13:335–368, 1995.
12. S. Muggleton and L. De Raedt. Inductive Logic Programming : theory and methods. *Journal of Logic Programming*, 19,20:629–679, 1994.
13. S. Padmanabhuni and A. K. Ghose. Inductive constraint logic programming: An overview. In *Learning and reasoning with complex representations*, LNCS 1359, pages 1–8. Springer-Verlag, 1998.
14. C. Page and A. Frisch. Generalization and learnability: a study of constrained atoms. In *Inductive Logic Programming*, pages 29–61. London: Academic Press, 1992.
15. G. Plotkin. A note on inductive generalization. In *Machine Intelligence*, volume 5, pages 153–163. Edinburgh University Press, 1970.
16. T. L. Provost and M. Wallace. Generalized constraint propagation over the CLP scheme. *Journal of Logic Programming*, 16(3):319–359, 1993.
17. C. Ringeissen and E. Monfroy. Generating propagation rules for finite domains: A mixed approach. In *New Trends in Constraints*, pages 150–172. LNAI 1865, 2000.
18. M. Sebag and C. Rouveirol. Constraint inductive logic programming. In *Advances in ILP*, pages 277–294. IOS Press, 1996.
19. H. Tamaki and T. Sato. OLD resolution with tabulation. In *Proc. of the 3rd International Conference on Logic Programming*, LNCS 225, pages 84–98. Springer-Verlag, 1986.
20. J. Würtz and T. Müller. Constructive disjunction revisited. In *Proc. of the 20th German Annual Conference on Artificial Intelligence*, LNAI 1137, pages 377–386. Springer-Verlag, 1996.

Collaborative Learning for Constraint Solving

Susan L. Epstein[1] and Eugene C. Freuder[2]

[1] Department of Computer Science, Hunter College and The Graduate School of The City University of New York, New York, NY 10021, USA
susan.epstein@hunter.cuny.edu

[2] Cork Constraint Computation Centre, University College Cork, Cork, Ireland*
e.freuder@4c.ucc.ie

Abstract. Although constraint programming offers a wealth of strong, general-purpose methods, in practice a complex, real application demands a person who selects, combines, and refines various available techniques for constraint satisfaction and optimization. Although such tuning produces efficient code, the scarcity of human experts slows commercialization. The necessary expertise is of two forms: constraint programming expertise and problem-domain expertise. The former is in short supply, and even experts can be reduced to trial and error prototyping; the latter is difficult to extract. The project described here seeks to automate both the application of constraint programming expertise and the extraction of domain-specific expertise. It applies FORR, an architecture for learning and problem-solving, to constraint solving. FORR develops expertise from multiple heuristics. A successful case study is presented on coloring problems.

1 Introduction

Difficult constraint programming problems require human experts to select, combine and refine the various techniques currently available for constraint satisfaction and optimization. These people "tune" the solver to fit the problems efficiently, but the scarcity of such experts slows commercialization of this successful technology. The few initial efforts to automate the production of specialized software have thus far focused on choosing among methods or constructing special purpose algorithms [1-4].

Although a properly-touted advantage of constraint programming is its wealth of good, general-purpose methods, at some point complex, real applications require human expertise to produce a practical program. This expertise is of two forms: constraint programming expertise and problem domain expertise. The former is in short supply, and even experts can be reduced to trial and error prototyping; the latter is difficult to extract. This project seeks to automate both the application of constraint programming expertise and the extraction of domain-specific expertise.

Our goal is to automate the construction of problem-specific or problem-class-specific constraint solvers with a system called *ACE* (Adaptive Constraint Engine). ACE is intended to support the automated construction of such constraint solvers in a number of different problem domains. Each solver will incorporate a learned, collabo-

* This work was performed while this author was at the University of New Hampshire.

T. Walsh (Ed.): CP 2001, LNCS 2239, pp. 46-60, 2001.

rative "community" of heuristics appropriate for their problem or problem class. Both the way in which they collaborate and some of the heuristics themselves will be learned.

This paper reports initial steps toward that goal in the form of a case study that applies FORR, a well-tested, collaborative, problem-solving architecture, to a subset of constraint programming: graph coloring. The FORR architecture permits swift establishment of a well-provisioned base camp from which to explore this research frontier more deeply. Section 2 presents some minimal background, including a description of FORR. Section 3 presents the initial, successful case study. Section 4 outlines further opportunities and challenges. Section 5 is a brief conclusion.

2 The Problem

We provide here some minimal background information on CSP's and on the *FORR* (FOr the Right Reasons) architecture. Further details will be provided on a need-to-know basis during our description of the case study.

2.1 CSP

Constraint satisfaction problems involve a set of variables, a *domain* of values for each variable, and a set of *constraints* that specify which combinations of values are allowed [5-8]. A *solution* is a value for each variable, such that all the constraints are satisfied. For example, graph coloring problems are CSP's: the variables are the graph vertices, the values are the available colors, and the constraints specify that neighboring vertices cannot have the same color. The basic CSP paradigm can be extended in various directions, for example to encompass optimization or uncertainty. Solution methods generally involve some form of search, often interleaved with some form of inference.

Many practical problems – such as resource allocation, scheduling, configuration, design, and diagnosis – can be modeled as constraint satisfaction problems. The technology has been widely commercialized, in Europe even more so than in the U.S. This is, of course, an NP-hard problem area, but there are powerful methods for solving difficult problems. Artificial intelligence, operations research, and algorithmics all have made contributions. There is considerable interest in constraint programming languages. Although we take an artificial intelligence approach, we expect our results to have implications for constraint programming generally.

Constraint satisfaction problem classes can be defined by "structural" or "semantic" features of the problem. These parameterize the problem and establish a multidimensional problem space. We will seek to synthesize specialized solvers that operate efficiently in different portions of that space.

2.2 FORR

FORR is a problem-solving and learning architecture for the development of expertise from multiple heuristics. It is a *mixture of experts* decision maker, a system that combines the opinions of a set of procedures called *experts* to make a decision [9, 10]. This approach is supported by evidence that people integrate a variety of strategies to accomplish problem solving [11-13].

A FORR-based artifact is constructed for a particular set of related tasks called a *domain*, such as path finding in mazes [14] or game playing [15]. A FORR-based program develops expertise during repeated solution attempts within a *problem class*, a set of problems in its domain (e.g., contests at the same game or trips with different starting and ending points in the same maze).

FORR-based applications have produced expert-level results after as few as 20 experiences in a problem class. Learning is relatively fast because a FORR-based application begins with prespecified, domain-specific knowledge. To some extent, a FORR-based application resembles a person who already has substantial general expertise in a domain, and then develops expertise for a new problem class. Such a person is already aware of general principles that may support expert behavior, and also recognizes what is important to learn about a new class, how to acquire that information, and how to apply it. In FORR, that information is called *useful knowledge,* and the decision principles are called *Advisors.* FORR learns *weights* to reflect the reliability and utility of Advisors.

Useful knowledge is knowledge that is possibly reusable and probably correct. In path finding, for example, a dead-end is a particular kind of useful knowledge, an *item.* Each item of useful knowledge is expected to be relevant to every class in the domain. The *values* for a particular useful knowledge item, however, are not known in advance; dead-ends, for example, must be learned, and they will vary from one maze to another. This is what is meant by *problem-class-specific* useful knowledge.

A FORR-based program learns when it attempts to solve a problem, or when it observes an external expert solve one. The program is provided in advance with a set of useful knowledge items. Each item has a name (e.g., "dead-end"), a learning algorithm (e.g., "detect backing out"), and a trigger (e.g., "learn after each trip"). A learning trigger may be set for after a decision, after a solution attempt, or after a sequence of solution attempts. When a useful knowledge item triggers, its learning algorithm executes, and the program acquires problem-class-specific useful knowledge. Note that there is no uniform learning method for useful knowledge items — in this sense, FORR truly supports multi-strategy learning.

FORR organizes Advisors into a hierarchy of tiers (see Figure 1), based upon their correctness and the nature of their response. A FORR-based program begins with a set of prespecified Advisors intended to be *problem-class-independent*, that is, relevant to most classes in the domain. Each Advisor represents some domain-specific principle likely to support expert behavior.

Each Advisor is represented as a time-limited procedure that accepts as input the current problem-solving state, the legal actions from that state, and any useful knowledge that the program has acquired about the problem class. Each Advisor produces as output its opinion on any number of the current legal actions. An opinion is represented as a *comment*, of the form *<strength, action, Advisor>* where *strength* is an integer in [0, 10]. A comment expresses an Advisor's support for (strength > 5), or opposition to (strength < 5), a particular action. Comments may vary in their strength, but an Advisor may not comment more than once on any action in the current state.

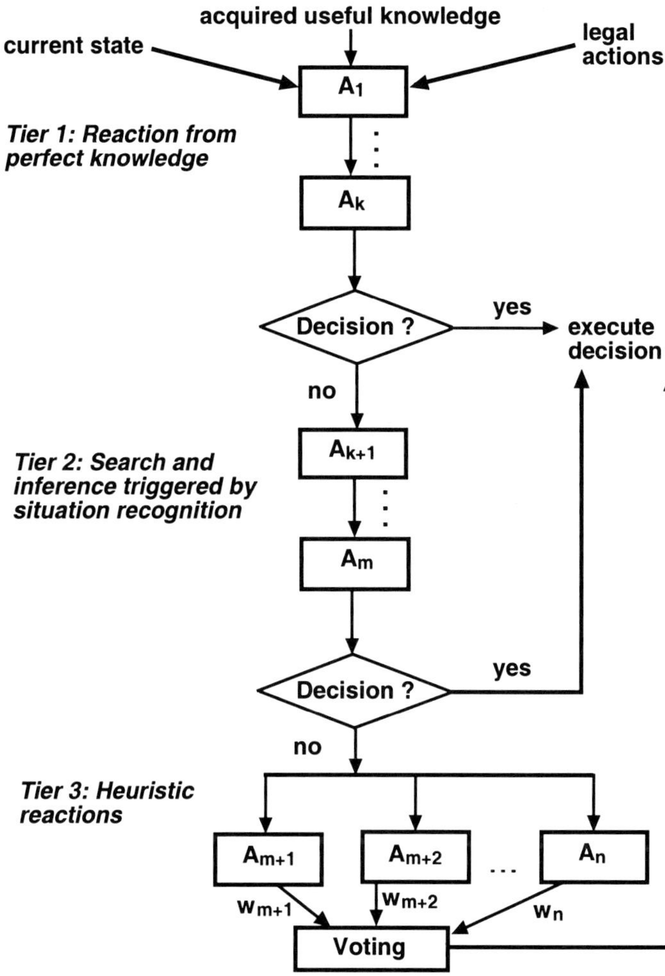

Fig. 1. How the FORR architecture organizes and manages Advisors to make a decision. PWL produces the weights applied for voting.

Our work applies FORR to CSP. To apply FORR to a particular application domain, one codes definitions of problem classes and useful knowledge items, along with algorithms to learn the useful knowledge. In addition, one postulates Advisors, assigns them to tiers, and codes them as well. Effective application of the architecture requires a domain expert to provide such insights. The feasibility study of the next section was generated relatively quickly, within the framework of Figure 1. The future work outlined in Section 4, however, is expected to require substantial changes to FORR.

3 Case Study

This case study on graph coloring is provided to introduce the basic approach we are pursuing, and to demonstrate its potential. We understand that there is a vast literature on graph coloring; we do not wish to give the erroneous impression that we believe that this study makes a serious contribution to it.

3.1 GC, the Graph Colorer

Graph Colorer (*GC*) is a FORR-based program for the specific CSP problem domain of graph coloring. We developed it as a proof of concept demonstration that the FORR architecture is a suitable basis for a research program aimed at learning collaborative algorithms attuned to classes of similar problems. GC includes only a few Advisors and learns only weights, but its results are quite promising. For GC, a problem class is the number of vertices and edges in a *c*-colorable graph, and a problem is an instance of such a graph. For example, a problem class might be specified as 4-colorable on 20 vertices with 10% *edge density*. ("Percentage edge density" here actually refers to percentage of possible edges above a minimal n-1, in this case 10% edge density means 19 + 17 = 36 edges.) A problem in that class would be a particular 4-colorable graph on 20 vertices with 36 edges. Problems are randomly generated, and are guaranteed to have at least one solution. There are, of course, a great many potential graphs in any given problem class.

GC basically simulates a standard CSP algorithm, *forward checking*. A world state for GC is a legally, partially (or fully) colored graph. On each iteration, GC either selects a vertex to color or, if a vertex has already been selected, colors it. Color selection is random. Our objective was to have GC learn an efficient way to select the vertices. In CSP terms, we wanted to acquire an efficient variable ordering heuristic [16-19]. After a color is chosen for a vertex, that color is removed from the domain of neighboring vertices. If after a coloring iteration, some vertex is left without any legal colors, then the state is automatically transformed by retracting that coloring and removing it from the legal colors that vertex may subsequently assume. If necessary, vertices can be "uncolored" to simulate backtracking. Thus, given enough time and space, GC is *complete*, that is, is capable of finding a solution.

Figure 2 shows how FORR has been applied to produce GC. GC has two tier-1 Advisors. In *tier 1*, FORR maintains a presequenced list of prespecified, always correct Advisors, denoted by A_1... A_k in Figure 1. A FORR-based artifact begins the decision making process there, with the current position, the legal actions from it, and any useful knowledge thus far acquired about the problem class. When a tier-1 Advisor comments positively on an action, no subsequent Advisors are consulted, and the action is executed. When a tier-1 Advisor comments negatively on an action, that action is eliminated from consideration, and no subsequent Advisor may support it. If the set of possible actions is thereby reduced to a single action, that action is executed.

GC's two tier-1 Advisors are Victory and Later. If only a single vertex remains uncolored and that vertex has been selected and has at least one legal coloring, *Victory* colors it. If an iteration is for vertex selection, *Later* opposes coloring any vertex whose degree is less than the number of colors that could legally be applied to it, on the theory that consideration of such a vertex can be delayed. Typically with FORR,

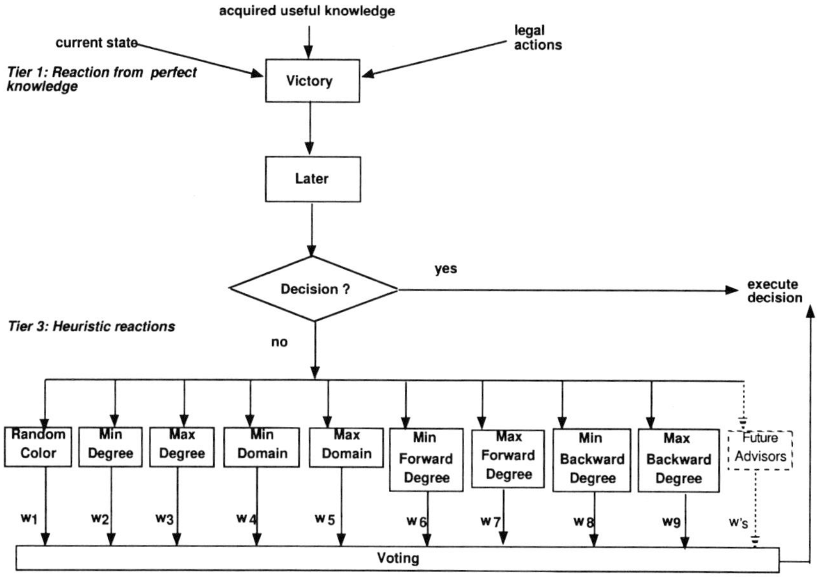

Fig. 2. GC's decision structure is a version of Figure 1. Additional tier-3 Advisors may be added where indicated.

the first tier does not identify an action, and control passes to *tier 2*, denoted by $A_{k+1}...A_m$ in Figure 1. Tier-2 Advisors plan, and may recommend sequences of actions, instead of a single action. GC does not yet incorporate tier-2 Advisors.

If neither the first nor the second tier produces a decision, control passes to *tier 3*, denoted by $A_{m+1}...A_n$ in Figure 1. In FORR, all tier-3 Advisors are heuristic and consulted in parallel. A decision is reached by combining their comments in a process called *voting*. When control resorts to tier 3, the action that receives the most support during voting is executed, with ties broken at random. Originally, voting was simply a tally of the comment strengths. Because that process makes tacit assumptions that are not always correct, voting can also be weighted.

GC has nine tier-3 Advisors, eight of which encapsulate a single primitive, naive approach to selecting a vertex. *Random Color* is the only coloring Advisor, so GC always selects a legal color for a selected vertex at random. Each of the remaining tier-3 Advisors simply tries to minimize or maximize a basic vertex property. *Min Degree* supports the selection of uncolored vertices in increasing degree order with comment strengths from 10 down. *Max Degree* is its dual, rating in decreasing degree order. *Min Domain* supports the selection of uncolored vertices in increasing order of the number of their current legal colors, again with strengths descending from 10. *Max Domain* is its dual. *Min Forward Degree* supports the selection of uncolored vertices in increasing order of their fewest uncolored neighbors, with strengths from 10 down. *Max Forward Degree* is its dual. *Min Backward Degree* supports the selection of uncolored vertices in increasing order of their fewest colored neighbors, with strengths from 10 down. *Max Backward Degree* is its dual. The use of such heuristic, rather than absolutely correct, rationales in decision making is supported by evidence that people *satisfice*, that is, they make decisions that are good enough [20]. Although satisficing solutions are not always optimal, they can achieve a high level of expertise. See, for example, [21].

Arguably these eight properties are simply the most obvious properties one could ascribe to vertices during the coloring process, making it all the more remarkable that the experiments we carried out were able to use them to such good effect. They also correspond naturally to properties of the "constraint graph" and "search tree" associated with general CSP's, providing additional resonance to the case study. Of course, a skeptical reader might be concerned that, consciously or not, we have "biased" our set of Advisors here. Even if that were so, we would respond that it is still up to FORR to learn how to use the Advisors appropriately, and that the ability to incorporate our expertise into the FORR architecture by specifying appropriate Advisors is a feature, not a bug.

Although a FORR-based program begins with a set of problem-class-independent, tier-3 Advisors, there is no reason to believe that they are all of equal significance or reliability in a particular problem class. Therefore, FORR uses a weight-learning algorithm called *PWL* (*Probabilistic Weight Learning*) to learn problem-class-specific weights for its tier-3 Advisors. The premise behind PWL is that the past reliability of an Advisor is predictive of its future reliability.

Initially, every Advisor has a weight of .05 and a *discount factor* of .1. Each time an Advisor comments, its discount factor is increased by .1, until, after 10 sets of comments, the discount factor reaches 1.0, where it remains. Early in an Advisor's use, its weight is the product of its learned weight and its discount factor; after 10 sets of comments, its learned weight alone is referenced. In tier 3 with PWL, a FORR-based program chooses the action with the greatest support:

$$\underset{j}{argmax}\left\{\sum_i \omega_i w_i s_{ij}\right\} \text{ where } \left\{\begin{array}{l} d = \text{number of opinions } i \text{ has generated} \\ \omega_i = \begin{cases} 0.1^*d \text{ if } d < 10 \\ 1 \text{ otherwise} \end{cases} \end{array}\right.$$

If an Advisor is correct, its wisdom will gradually be incorporated. If an Advisor is incorrect, its weight will diminish as its opinions are gradually introduced, so that it has little negative impact in a dynamic environment.

During testing, PWL drops Advisors whose weights are no better than random guessing. This threshold is provided by a non-voting tier-3 Advisor called *Anything*. Anything comments only for weight learning, that is, it never actually participates in a decision. Anything comments on one action 50% of the time, on two actions 25% of the time, and in general on n actions $(0.5)^n$% of the time. Each of Anything's comments has a randomly-generated strength in {0, 1, 2, 3, 4, 6, 7, 8, 9, 10}. An Advisor's weight must be at least .01 greater than Anything's weight to be consulted during testing. During testing, provisional status is also eliminated (i.e., ω_i is set to 1), to permit infrequently applicable but correct Advisors to comment at full strength. In summary, PWL fits a FORR-based program to correct decisions, learning to what extent each of its tier-3 Advisors reflects expertise. Because problem-class-specific Advisors can also be acquired during learning, PWL is essential to robust performance.

To get some sense of how GC behaves, consider the partially 3-colored graph in Figure 3(a). (The graph was used in a different context in [22].) Six of the vertices are

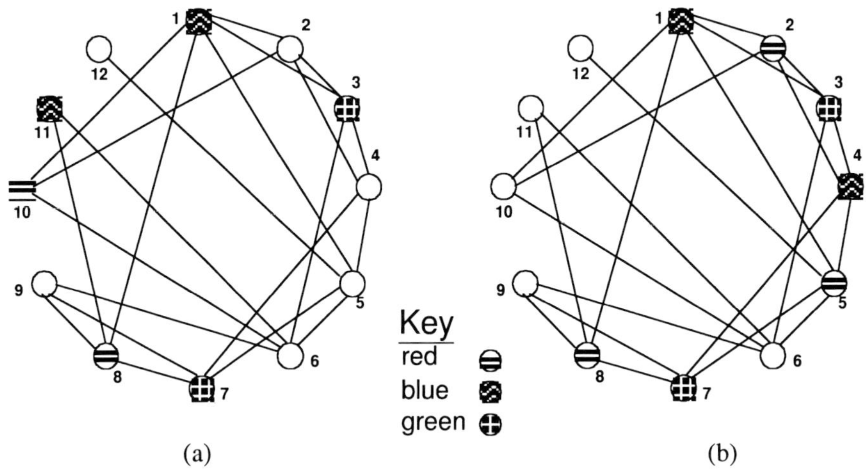

Fig. 3. Two partially 3-colored graphs.

colored, and the next vertex should now be selected for coloring. Since vertex 6 has no legal color, however, the most recently selected vertex will be uncolored. Now consider the partially colored graph in Figure 3(b). Since the number of possible colors for vertex 12 is 2, Later will eliminate vertex 12 as an immediate choice for coloring, and the remaining uncolored vertices will be considered by tier 3. For example, Min Degree would support the selection of vertex 11 with a strength of 10, and the selection of vertices 9 and 10 with a strength of 9. Similarly, Max Backward Degree would support the selection of vertices 9 and 10 with a strength of 10, and vertices 6 and 11 with a strength of 9. When the comments from all the tier-3 Advisors are tallied without weights, vertices 6 and 11 would receive maximum support, so GC would choose one of them at random to color. If GC were using PWL, however, the strengths would be multiplied by the weights learned for the Advisors before tallying them.

3.2 Experimental Design and Results

Performance in an experiment with GC was averaged over 10 runs. Each *run* consisted of a learning phase and a testing phase. In the *learning phase*, GC learned weights while it attempted to color each of 100 problems from the specified problem class. In the *testing phase*, weight-learning was turned off, and GC tried to color 10 additional graphs from the same class. Multiple runs were used because GC learning can get stuck in a "blind alley," where there are no successes from which to learn. Thus a fair evaluation averages behavior over several runs. This is actually conservative, as we argue below that one could reasonably utilize the best result from multiple runs.

Problems were generated at random, for both learning and testing. Although there is no guarantee that any particular set of graphs was distinct, given the size of the problem classes the probability that a testing problem was also a training problem is extremely small. The fact that the training set varied from one run to another is, as we shall see, an advantage.

We ran experiments on five different problem classes: 4-colorable graphs on 20 vertices with edge densities of 10%, 20%, and 30%, and 4-colorable graphs on 50 vertices with edge densities of 10% and 20%. (Edge densities were kept relatively low so that enough 4-colorable graphs could be readily produced by our CSP problem generator. Those classes contain 36, 53, 70, 167, and 285 undirected edges, respectively.) To speed data collection, during both learning and testing, GC was permitted no more than 1000 task steps for the 20-vertex graphs, and 2000 task steps for the 50-vertex graphs. (A *task step* is either the selection of a vertex, the selection of a color, or the retraction of a color.)

We evaluated GC on the percentage of testing problems it was able to solve, and on the time it required to solve them. As a baseline, we also had GC attempt to color 100 graphs in each problem class without weight-learning. These results appear in Table 1 as "no learning." As Table 1 shows, weight learning ("yes" in Table 1) substantially improved GC's performance in all but the largest graphs. With weight learning, GC solved more problems and generally solved them faster. With weight learning, the program also did far less backtracking and required 32%-72% fewer steps per task.

An unanticipated difficulty was that, in the 50-vertex-20%-density class, GC was unable to solve any problem within the 2000-step limit, and therefore could not train its weights and improve. We therefore adapted the program so that it could learn in two other environments. With *transfer* learning, GC learned on small graphs but tested on larger graphs of the same density. With *bootstrap* learning, GC learned first on 50 small graphs of a given density, then learned on 50 larger graphs of the same density, and then tested on the larger graphs. Table 1 reports the result of both bootstrap learning and transfer learning between 20-vertex and 50-vertex-classes of the same density (e.g., from 20-vertex-20%-density to 50-vertex-20%-density).

Table 1. A comparison of GC's performance, averaged over 10 runs. Time is in seconds per solved problem; retractions is number of backtracking steps per solved or unsolved problem.

Vertices	Edges	Learning	Solutions	Time	Retractions
20	10%	no	95%	0.22	22.28
20	10%	yes	100%	0.11	0.00
20	20%	no	35%	1.11	418.16
20	20%	yes	83%	0.48	79.63
20	30%	no	12%	1.40	631.60
20	30%	yes	41%	1.43	427.05
50	10%	no	1%	3.23	815.82
50	10%	yes	46%	1.02	414.29
50	10%	transfer	32%	4.16	428.54
50	10%	bootstrap	40%	3.62	382.18
50	20%	no	0%	—	—
50	20%	yes	0%	—	—
50	20%	transfer	26%	5.09	486.61
50	20%	bootstrap	20%	4.51	519.89

3.3 Discussion

The most interesting results from our case study are reflected in the resultant learned weights. In the 20-vertex-10%-density experiment, where every test graph was colored correctly, on every run only the Advisors Max Degree, Min Domain, and Min Backward Degree had weights high enough to qualify them for use during testing. Inspection indicated that in the remaining experiments, runs were either *successful* (able to color correctly at least 5 of the 10 test graphs), or *unsuccessful* (able to color correctly no more than 2 test graphs). The 8 successful runs in the 20-vertex 20%-density experiment solved 95% of their test problems. In the 20-vertex-30%-density experiment, the 6 successful runs solved 65% of their test problems. On the 50-vertex-10%-density graphs, the 6 successful runs colored 76.7% of their test graphs. Inspection indicates that a run either starts well and goes on to succeed, or goes off in a futile direction. Rather than wait for learning to recover, multiple runs are an effective alternative. As used here then, GC can be thought of as a restart algorithm: if one run does not result in an effective algorithm for the problem class, another is likely to do so.

For each problem class, the Advisors on which GC relied during testing in successful runs appear in Table 2. Together with their weights, these Advisors constitute an algorithm for vertex selection while coloring in the problem class. Observe that different classes succeed with different weights; most significantly the sparsest graphs prefer the opposite Backward Degree heuristic to that preferred by the others.

The differences among ordinary GC learning on 50-vertex-10%-density graphs, and transfer and bootstrap learning from them with 20-vertex-10%-density graphs, are statistically significant at the 95% confidence level: ordinary learning produces the best results, followed by bootstrap learning (where weights learned for the smaller graphs are tuned), followed by transfer learning (where weights for the smaller graphs are simply used). This further indicates that 20-vertex-10%-density graphs and 50-vertex-10%-density graphs lie in different classes with regard to appropriate heuristics. Although solution of 50-vertex-20%-density graphs was only possible with with transfer or bootstrap learning, these are not our only recourses. We could also extend the number of steps permitted during a solution attempt substantially, on the theory that we can afford to devote extended training time to produce efficient "production" algorithms.

In this study, we attempted to "seed" GC with an "impartial" set of alternative vertex characteristics. Two factors previously considered individually by constraint researchers in a general CSP context as variable ordering heuristics, minimal domain size and maximal degree, were selected in all successful runs. Moreover, the combination of the two is consistent with the evidence presented in [23] that minimizing domain-size/degree is a superior CSP ordering heuristic to either minimizing domain

Table 2. Learned weights for those GC vertex-selection Advisors active during testing, averaged across successful runs in five different experiments. 50-vertex values are from bootstrap learning.

Advisor	20-10%	20-20%	20-30%	50-10%	50-20%
Max Degree	0.678	0.678	0.743	0.547	0.678
Min Domain	0.931	0.841	0.713	0.841	0.723
Min Backward Degree	0.943	—	—	—	—
Max Backward Degree	—	0.862	0.724	0.852	0.716

size or maximizing degree alone. Given the relatively recent vintage of this insight, its "rediscovery" by FORR is impressive. Min Backward Degree corresponds to the "minimal width" CSP variable ordering heuristic, and again FORR was arguably insightful in weighting this so heavily for the 20-10 case, since it can guarantee a backtrack-free search for tree-structured problems [24]. The success of Max Backward Degree for the other classes may well reflect its correlation with both Min Domain (the domain will be reduced for each differently colored neighbor) and Max Degree.

In a final experiment we implemented the classic Brelaz heuristic for graph coloring within FORR by simply eliminating any vertex that does not have minimum domain in tier 1 and then voting for vertices with maximum forward degree in tier 3. Table 3 shows the results. Note that GC, learning from experience, does considerably better.

4 Future Work

GC is a feasibility study for our planned Adaptive Constraint Engine (ACE). ACE will support the automated construction of problem-class-specific constraint solvers in a number of different problem domains. Automating constraint solving as a learned collaboration among heuristics presents a number of specific opportunities and challenges. FORR offers a concrete approach to these opportunities and challenges; in turn, ACE provides new opportunities and challenges to extend the FORR architecture.

4.1 Opportunities

We anticipate a range of opportunities along four dimensions:

• **Algorithms:** Algorithmic devices known to the CSP community can be specified as individual Advisors for ACE. Advisors can represent varying degrees of local search or different search methods (e.g., backjumping), and they can represent heuristic devices for variable ordering or color selection. ACE could be modified to employ other search paradigms, including stochastic search.

• **Domains:** ACE will facilitate the addition of domain-specific expertise at varying degrees of generality, and in various fields. For example, we might discover variable ordering heuristics for a class of graphs or general graphs, for employee scheduling problems or general scheduling problems.

Table 3. A performance comparison of GC with the Brelaz heuristic. "GC best" is the top-performing runs with GC. Brelaz comment frequencies are provided for Min Domain (MD) and Max Forward Degree (MFD).

		Number of solutions			Time in seconds		Comment frequency	
Vertices	**Density**	**Brelaz**	**GC**	**GC best**	**Brelaz**	**GC**	**MD**	**MFD**
20	10%	86%	100%	100.0%	0.33	0.11	15.99	34.01
20	20%	26%	83%	95.0%	1.19	0.48	3.77	64.41
50	10%	0%	46%	76.7%	1.71	1.23	11.27	13.11

• **Change:** We will begin by learning good algorithms for a static problem or problem class, that is, good weights for a set of prespecified Advisors. In practice, however, problems change. For example, a product configuration problem changes when a new product model is introduced. ACE will offer opportunities to adapt to such change. Furthermore, ACE should be able to adapt to changing conditions during a single problem-solving episode. (The FORR architecture has proved resilient in other dynamic domains.)
• **Discovery:** We can select among standard techniques, for example, minimal domain variable ordering. We can combine these techniques, through a variety of weighting and voting schemes. Most exciting, we can learn new techniques, in the form of useful knowledge and new Advisors. These will include planners at the tier-2 level. Some preliminary work on learning new Advisors based on relative values of graph properties (Later is an example of such an Advisor, albeit prespecified here) has shown both improved solution rates and considerable speedup.

4.2 Challenges

Exploring these opportunities will require progress in several areas. Basically, we need to provide the elements of a collaborative learning environment. FORR permits us to begin addressing this challenge quickly and concretely.
• **Advice:** Many interesting issues arise in appropriately combining advice. With variable ordering heuristics, for example, we can now move beyond using secondary heuristics to break ties, or combining heuristics in crude mathematical combinations. Ordering advice can be considered in a more flexible and subtle manner. The challenge lies in using this new power intelligently and appropriately. In particular, this may require new voting schemes, such as partitioning FORR's tier 3 into prioritized subsets. Such higher order control could be learned.
• **Reinforcement:** Opportunities to learn can come from experience or from expert advice. ACE will provide a mechanism to generalize experience computed from exhaustive analysis or random testing. It will also provide a mechanism for knowledge acquisition from constraint programming experts and domain experts. In particular, we expect that ACE will be able to extract, from domain expert decisions, knowledge that the experts could not impart directly in a realizable form, thereby addressing the knowledge acquisition problem for constraint programming. Specific reinforcement schemes, analysis, and experimental protocols are required to accomplish this. For example, what is the proper definition of an "optimal" variable ordering choice, and what forms of experiment or experience will come closest to modeling optimality?
• **Modeling:** We need languages for expressing general constraint solving knowledge and domain specific expertise. Such languages will support discovery of useful knowledge and new Advisors. They will enable us to learn the context in which tools are to be brought to bear. For example, a grammar has been formulated for a language that compares relative values (e.g., <, =) of vertex properties (e.g., degree, number of colored neighbors); this grammar can be used to formulate learned Advisors.

Modeling constraint solving and domain knowledge to facilitate discovery presents perhaps the most exciting combination of opportunity and challenge. The feasibility study already gives us a glimpse of this capability. The features we used, involving domain size and degree, are basic features of a constraint graph model of a problem, and of the coloring domain in particular. We simply described possible variations on those features, and let GC "discover" which ones most effectively contributed to control of variable ordering during search.

More broadly, we envision modeling constraint satisfaction search as movement through a space of sets of potential solutions (the power set of the Cartesian product of the variable domains). Conventional algorithms may be viewed as special cases of movement through that space. Backtrack search operates by fixing one value at a time and moving to the Cartesian product of the remaining (pruned) domains. Hill climbing operates by moving from one singleton set to another. ACE can explore the vast realm of intermediate algorithms. We envision expanding FORR to operate with sets of possible states, an extension of the architecture that would facilitate exploration of algorithms modeled in this manner.

In FORR, not all Advisors are prespecified. Given a language from which to develop them, and a learning method, a FORR-based program can acquire and integrate new, problem-class-specific Advisors into tier 3. For example, *Hoyle*, the FORR-based game player, has learned two different kinds of game-specific Advisors from perceptual data [25]. The Advisors Hoyle learns provide insight into the nature of a game, extend its representational ability, and substantially improve the program's performance. The mechanism for learning new Advisors is sketched in [26] and detailed in [25].

This work will motivate numerous enhancements to FORR. For example, we hope to learn to sequence the tier-1 Advisors, rather than prespecify their order. We will also work on collaborative planning in tier 2. We intend to add some generic, resource-bounded versions of forward search. We will partition tier 3 based upon learned weights, and then prioritize the allocation of resources accordingly. Finally, we expect to explore weight-learning algorithms that are more domain-specific. In that context, we expect to consider non-linear voting algorithms, including pairs of Advisors as in WINNOW [27].

5 Conclusions

The combination of constraint programming and Advisor-based collaborative learning is an innovative approach toward making constraint software more effective and more widely available. Our Adaptive Constraint Engine will provide a comprehensive architecture for acquiring and controlling collaborative and adaptive constraint solving methods.

The FORR architecture supports this frontier CSP research by transforming amorphous objectives ("reinforce success") into concrete ones ("reward Advisors"). The CSP research will in turn motivate major extensions of FORR facilities. A case study has demonstrated the potential of our project; it constructed different algorithms for different classes of graphs, "rediscovered" some constraint solving insights, and outperformed the Brelaz heuristic.

Acknowledgements. This work was supported in part by NSF grant IIS-9907385 and by NASA. We thank Richard Wallace for his assistance in generating test problems, and the referees for their constructive comments. A preliminary version of this paper appeared in the working notes of the workshop on Modeling an Solving Problems with Constraints at IJCAI-2001. Professor Freuder is supported by a Principal Investigator Award from Science Foundation Ireland.

References

1. Borrett, J., Tsang, E.P.K., Walsh, N.R. Adaptive constraint satisfaction: the quickest first principle. In Proceedings of the 12th European Conference on AI. Budapest, Hungary. (1996) 160-164
2. Caseau, Y., Laburthe, F., Silverstein, G.: A Meta-Heuristic Factory for Vehicle Routing Problems. Principles and Practice of Constraint Programming – CP'99. Springer, Berlin (1999)
3. Minton, S., Automatically Configuring Constraint Satisfaction Programs: A Case Study. Constraints. **1** (1996)
4. Smith, D.R.: KIDS: A Knowledge-based Software Development System. In: M.R. Lowry and R.D. McCartney (eds.): Automating Software Design. AAAI Press (1991)
5. Saraswat, V.J., Van Hentenryck, P., Constraint Programming. ACM Computing Surveys, Special Issue on Strategic Directions in Computing Research. **28** (1996)
6. Freuder, E., Wallace, M., eds.): Special Issue on Constraints. IEEE Intelligent Systems, ed. Series , 15:1 (2000)
7. Freuder, E., Mackworth, A., eds.): Constraint-Based Reasoning. , ed. Series . MIT Press, Cambridge, MA (1992)
8. Tsang, E.P.K.: Foundations of Constraint Satisfaction. Academic Press, London (1993)
9. Chatterjee, S., Chatterjee, S., On Combining Expert Opinions. American journal of Mathematical and Management Sciences. **7** (1987) 271-295
10. Jacobs, R.A., Methods for Combining Experts' Probability Assessments. Neural Computation. **7** (1995) 867-888
11. Biswas, G., Goldman, S., Fisher, D., Bhuva, B., Glewwe, G.: Assessing Design Activity in Complex CMOS Circuit Design. In: P. Nichols, S. Chipman, and R. Brennan (eds.): Cognitively Diagnostic Assessment. Lawrence Erlbaum, Hillsdale, NJ (1995)
12. Crowley, K., Siegler, R.S., Flexible Strategy Use in Young Children's Tic-Tac-Toe. Cognitive Science. **17** (1993) 531-561
13. Ratterman, M.J., Epstein, S.L. Skilled like a Person: A Comparison of Human and Computer Game Playing. In Proceedings of the Seventeenth Annual Conference of the Cognitive Science Society. Pittsburgh: Lawrence Erlbaum Associates. (1995) 709-714
14. Epstein, S.L. On Heuristic Reasoning, Reactivity, and Search. In Proceedings of the Fourteenth International Joint Conference on Artificial Intelligence. Montreal: Morgan Kaufmann. (1995) 454-461
15. Epstein, S.L., Prior Knowledge Strengthens Learning to Control Search in Weak Theory Domains. International Journal of Intelligent Systems. **7** (1992) 547-586
16. Kiziltan, Z., Flener, P., Hnich, B. Towards Inferring Labelling Heuristics for CSP Application Domains. In Proceedings of the KI'01: Springer-Verlag. (2001)
17. Sadeh, N., Fox, M.S., Variable and value ordering heuristics for the job shop scheduling constraint satisfaction problem. Artificial Intelligence. **86** (1996) 1-41
18. Nadel, B., Consistent labeling problems and their algorithms: expected complexities and theory-based heuristics. Artificial Intelligence. **21** (1983) 135-178
19. Gent, I., MacIntyre, E., Prosser, P., Smith, B., Walsh, T. An empirical study of dynamic variable ordering heuristics for the constraint satisfaction problem. In Proceedings of the CP-96. (1996) 179-193
20. Simon, H.A.: The Sciences of the Artificial. second edn. MIT Press, Cambridge, MA (1981)

21. Keim, G.A., Shazeer, N.M., Littman, M.L., Agarwal, S., Cheves, C.M., Fitzgerald, J., Grosland, J., Jiang, F., Pollard, S., Weinmeister, K. PROVERB: The Probabilistic Cruciverbalist. In Proceedings of the Sixteenth National Conference on Artificial Intelligence. Orlando: AAAI Press. (1999) 710-717
22. Smith, B.M.: The Brélaz Heuristic and Optimal Static Orderings. Principles and Practice of Constraint Programming – CP'99,. Springer, Berlin (1999) 405-418
23. Bessiere, C., Regin, J.-C.: MAC and combined heuristics: Two reasons to forsake FC (and CBJ?) on hard problems. In: E.C. Freuder (ed. Principles and Practice of Constraint Programming - CP96, LNCS 1118. Springer-Verlag (1996) 61-75
24. Freuder, E.C., A sufficient condition for backtrack-free search. Journal of the ACM. **29** (1982) 24-32
25. Epstein, S.L., Perceptually-Supported Learning. (Submitted for publication)
26. Epstein, S.L., Gelfand, J., Lock, E.T., Learning Game-Specific Spatially-Oriented Heuristics. Constraints. **3** (1998) 239-253
27. Littlestone, N., Warmuth, M.K., The Weighted Majority Algorithm. Information and Computation. **108** (1994) 212-261

Towards Stochastic Constraint Programming: A Study of Online Multi-choice Knapsack with Deadlines

Thierry Benoist, Eric Bourreau, Yves Caseau, and Benoît Rottembourg

Bouygues e-lab, 1 av. Eugène Freyssinet,
78061 St Quentin en Yvelines Cedex, France
{tbenoist,ebourreau,ycs,brottembourg}@bouygues.com

Abstract. Constraint Programming (CP) is a very general programming paradigm that proved its efficiency on solving complex industrial problems. Most real-life problems are stochastic in nature, which is usually taken into account through different compromises, such as applying a deterministic algorithm to the average values of the input, or performing multiple runs of simulation. Our goal in this paper is to analyze different techniques taken either from practical CP applications or from stochastic optimization approaches. We propose a benchmark issued from our industrial experience, which may be described as an Online Multi-choice Knapsack with Deadlines. This benchmark is used to test a framework with four different dynamic strategies that utilize a different combination of the stochastic and combinatorial aspects of the problem. To evaluate the expected future state of the reservations at the time horizon, we either use simulation, average values, systematic study of the most probable scenarios, or yield management techniques.

1 Introduction

One of Constraint Programming (CP) major claims to success has been its application to solving complex industrial application problems. The strength of CP is its ability to represent complex domain-dependent constraints, which yield interesting modeling abilities, that have been completed, over the previous years, with resolution techniques such as meta-heuristics [CLS99]. Interestingly, most industrial combinatorial problems are stochastic in nature, due to the uncertainty that is characteristic of real world situations. Our own experience with industrial problems include construction planning, call center scheduling, equipment inventory management or TV advertisement booking, to name a few. In all these situations, the resolution of a static problem is only a compromise, since the data that is given to the algorithm only reflects the situation that is expected in the future. As a consequence, the algorithm needs to be run often and incrementally, to adjust to real-time events that modify the validity of the solution. When the future is widely unpredictable, this may be the wisest thing to do, but most often, probabilistic information is available (mean, standard deviation and distribution characterization), that should be used to derive more robust solutions.

T. Walsh (Ed.): CP 2001, LNCS 2239, pp. 61-76, 2001.

When confronted with this challenge, practitioners of constraint programming have often developed and used ad hoc techniques. There is a large lore of practical advise available in the community, but very little of it has been formalized. Three strategies may be observed:

1. The simplest is to use a static combinatorial algorithm using the expected values (means) as the input.
2. Another simple approach is to use simulation to compare possible decisions, making multiple runs of the algorithm using different sets of input data that are generated following the probability information that is available. This is easy to implement but places a heavy burden on the run time.
3. Hybrid approaches may be developed, that try to introduce the stochastic nature into the general design of the algorithm. For instance, a strategy that was reported to the authors in the field of industrial process control is to couple a CP solver that solves a resource-constrained scheduling problem with a stochastic generator that produces "ghost" orders in the future and with a matching algorithm that links upcoming orders with ghosts when appropriate. Thus the scheduler runs continuously (and incrementally) on a flow of tasks that contains both real and predicted orders.

The nearby field of stochastic optimization has produced over the last 30 years a wealth of impressive results, some of which being very relevant to this issue ([BL97] for a survey). These results both cover the stochastic behavior of classical combinatorial algorithm or heuristics (such as the WSPT rule from W. Smith) or the definition of new, stochastic, algorithms [HSS+96,ABC+99]. However, these results rely both on the relative simplicity of the static algorithm that is analyzed stochastically, and many independence hypotheses about the input data that are required to make the analysis work.

The combination of NP-hard problems and stochastic input data has been studied under the field of *online algorithms* [FW97]. Competitive analysis has provided some upper bounds for the *competitive ratio*, which is the ratio between the worst-case behavior of the online algorithm and the optimal solution given a complete knowledge of the input. However, there are few practical results and fewer practical good heuristics available for these problems. The consequence is that *simulation* is required for answering most of the characterization questions that we may have, as soon as the problem becomes too difficult. For instance, finding the probability that the makespan of a simple scheduling problem with precedence (that would be solved statically with a PERT) is higher than a given value is achieved with a Monte-Carlo simulation (more precisely, with a pseudo-MC simulation [AW96]). The scheduling problems that we address in our industrial applications are NP-hard (contrary to the PERT problem) and the stochastic characterization of the complex branch-and-bound algorithms that are used to solve them is an open issue.

Our goal with this paper is to propose a first contribution that creates a bridge between the two communities. On the one hand, we want to address combinatorial problems with complex constraints while taking the stochastic nature into account. On the other hand, we want to follow a scientific approach, using public benchmarks, and a survey of different techniques that either come from the field of stochastic programming or from the experience of CP practitioners. Thus our goal is threefold:

1. Compare the relative strengths of different techniques that we have used in the past on different problems, as well as methods that we have been referred to by researchers from the stochastic programming community, including "Yield Management". YM has been popularized by the airline industry and is finding its way into many industrial domains.
2. Propose directions that may lead to better algorithms, either through the stochastic characterization of complex CO techniques or through the introduction of "combinatorial insights" into stochastic methods.
3. Publish a benchmark problem that is representative of our industrial problems and holds a strong combinatorial component, yet that is simple enough so that many other methods can be applied and compared.

The experience that we have proposed as a benchmark comes from an online reservation system. It has been simplified and can be described as a multi-choice knapsack with deadlines. It represents the reservation problem faced by a tour operator that operates a set of sites and receives reservation requests, as well as cancellations, for groups of tourists. The goal is to maximize the final occupancy of the hotels (at a given deadline), given a penalty that is given for overbooking. The algorithm that needs to be built receives the stream of reservation/cancellation events and is required to accept or decline each reservation.

The paper is organized as follows. The next section gives a detailed presentation of our benchmark problem and an associated best-fit dynamic algorithm that will be used as a reference. The algorithms presented in this paper are dynamic algorithms that computes, each time they are called, an expected valuation of the current state with and without the incoming reservation. The difference between the various approaches is the technique that is used to make this valuation. Section 3 presents a set of approaches that are based on simulation, using a reasonably simple strategy to fill the hotels (bins). Section 4 presents on the contrary an approach that uses a more sophisticated filling algorithm but that is only applied to mean values. Section 5 presents a technique that is based on the characterization of the most representative scenarios of demand/cancellation and then solves heuristically the problem for each scenario. Section 6 presents a Yield Management approach, which is based on the characterization of the expected marginal revenue over the duration of the scenario. The last section gives a preliminary comparison of the results of these different approaches.

2 Problem Description

2.1 Mathematical Description

Let b_1, b_2, ... b_N, be N bins of respective capacities C_1, C_2,...C_N and consider K types of items of sizes w_1, w_2, .. w_K, and values v_1, v_2, .. v_K. The numbers of items of each type are positive integer random variables In_k. The arrivals of these items are distributed into T periods indexed from 0 to T-1, according to a common repartition function $f(t)$. During each period, previously arrived items have a probability q_k to leave.

A state of the packing is an N x K matrix P of positive integers, such that $P[n,k]$ is the number of items of type k present in bin b_n. A strategy is a function $s(P,k,t)$ returning an integer in [0,N], denoting in what bin an item of type k arriving at date t should be put (0 standing for refusal).

All bins are initially empty. At each date $t \in [0,T-1]$, a list of events is presented one after another, in random order. These events can be :

- The departure of an item of type k (that was present at date t) from bin n: then P[n,k] is decreased by one
- The arrival of an item of type k: then if $s(P,k,t)$ is non null, P[$s(P,k,t)$,k] is increased by one.

The objective of the strategy is to maximize the expected value of the following function at the end of the process:

$$F=\sum_{n=1}^{N}\left(\sum_{k=1}^{K} v_k P_{n,k} - \alpha \times \max\left(0, \sum_{k=1}^{K} w_k P_{n,k} - C\right)\right) \quad \textbf{(1)}$$

where α is a penalty coefficient.

2.2 Corresponding Situation

This problem could be that of a travel agency, filling holiday centers with school groups, in presence of stochastic demand and cancellation. In this case, bins and items would be respectively holiday centers and stays of school groups. We consider the optimization of the filling during a specific week (say Christmas week). Stays are booked by school academies, each of them characterized by the size of the groups it organizes (deterministic) and the price it pays for each group (not necessarily related to the group size). Until Christmas, these academies can book stays for this festive week, but they *cannot* specify in which holiday center they would like to go. On the other hand, when the agency accepts to book a stay, it informs the group of its destination, and cannot modify it later. School academies can also cancel previously booked stays (with no penalty). The goal of the agency is to maximize its final profit under the following overload constraint: for each holiday center, each supernumerary person must be accommodated in a nearby hotel at fix cost α.

2.3 Scenarios

In all considered scenarios, bins have identical capacities (normalized to 100) the repartition function $f(t)$ is uniform and arrivals follow simple integer distributions (binomial). Experiments were conducted on more than 20 scenarios, based on a "master" scenario detailed below:

- 5 bins, 10 periods, 5 types of items.
- sizes of items are respectively (17,20,25,30,33)
- values are respectively (13,26,21,26,39)
- Overload penalty α=10 (see equation (**1**))
- For all k: q_k=0.066967 (→initial leaving probability = 0.5) and $In_k = \mathcal{B}_{12,\frac{8}{12}}$ (→average=8)

2.4 Naïve Strategies and Far-Seeing Strategies

Some strategies do not take into account the stochastic aspects of the problem. For instance the First-Fit (also named First-Come First-Serve) consists in putting arriving requests in the first possible bin (if any). Otherwise it is refused (no overbooking). The Best-Fit strategy is a refinement of the First-Fit: the arriving item is put in the possible bin with the smallest current remaining size. This Best-Fit strategy (BF) will be used in the following to normalize results on different scenarios.

A far-seeing or clairvoyant strategy is a strategy that knows exactly what will happen in the future, and deals therefore with a deterministic problem. Hence it is *not* a feasible strategy but only a hypothetic one that can be useful to compute upper bounds. In our case a far-seeing strategy knows exactly what requests will arrive, at which dates, and when they will be cancelled. Then it can extract the number of requests of each type that will not be cancelled before the final date T. Hence the associated deterministic problem is a *multi-choice knapsack*. This deterministic problem can be optimally solved using integer programming (less than 5 mn with XPRESS-MP).

3 Forward Sampling (FS)

As explained in the introduction, our dynamic algorithms are based on state evaluation. When a request arrives, each possible decision leads to a different state. After evaluating all states with a certain method, the decision leading to the best state is chosen.

A simple idea to evaluate a state is to generate scenarios from the current date to the end (date T), or more precisely from the beginning of the next period to the end of the final one (period T-1). Hence the evaluation of a state will be an aggregation (usually the average) of the evaluations of "many" generated scenarios (Monte-Carlo simulations).

To generate these scenarios, it is necessary to compute the conditional distribution of the remaining number of arrivals of each type. Several methods can be used to evaluate a scenario: we can simulate the behavior of a Best-Fit strategy on this scenario, or the behavior of a far-seeing strategy (exact or greedy approximation), or the behavior of any other "slave" strategy (for instance other strategies described in this paper).

These first experiments tend to reveal that the results of this strategy are not so dependent on the quality of the slave algorithm. For instance, evaluating with a Best-Fit or with a far-seeing algorithm lead to very similar results, whereas the former is a pessimistic evaluation (the final gain is significantly higher in general) and the latter is an optimistic evaluation (it gives an upper bound that cannot be reached). Besides, using an evaluation with the strategy described in the next section does not improve the results, whereas the behavior of this strategy is very similar to that of Forward Sampling. Moreover, forgetting to take into account the possibility for items already present to be cancelled caused a surprisingly small deterioration of results. Finally, since what is important is the sensitivity of this algorithm used for comparisons, a greedy heuristic similar to C1 in Section 4 seems to be a good slave strategy.

On the contrary, Table 1 shows that the number of samples has a great influence on the average gain: even if 8 samples are sufficient to get better results than the Best-Fit (1.67 %), increasing this number up to 1000 leads to an average gain of 8.23%.

Table 1. Influence of the number of samples (1000 runs on the "master" problem)

Number of samples	*8*	*10*	*20*	*50*	*100*	*1000*
average gain (%)	1.67	2.8	6.85	7.89	7.95	8.23

4 Using Expected Values and Combinatorial Optimization (EV)

This second approach is similar to the previous one in its global principle, but uses a precise resolution of a combinatorial problem that is generated from the expected values of the departures/arrival as an oracle of what may happen. To evaluate a current state, we try to compute the mean of the optimal "far-seeing" (a posteriori) filling of the bins. If we designate by C an algorithm to solve this multi-choice knapsack problem, and by C* an optimal algorithm, we can say that we want to use E(C*) as the expected value to guide our decision.

In the previous section we used $\frac{1}{n}\times\sum_{i=1}^{i=n} C(S_i)$ to evaluate E(C*), making use of a simple heuristic C to fill the bins. Here we will use a better algorithm C^+ but we will run it only once, over the mean values of the *a posteriori* problem, yielding $C^+(E(S))$. One can say that the goal of this paper is to evaluate different strategies to produce an estimate of E(C*), and this section deals with the C*(E) approach, where C* is approximated by C+.

This points out to another, more complex but possibly better suited, direction for producing online algorithms. When we evaluate the future, we use an optimal a posteriori strategy, whereas it would be more interesting to use recursively the strategy that is being defined. This type of recursive definition, where the optimal decision at date t is defined using the future decisions at time $t + \delta_i$, may be solved (numerically) using differential equations when the problem is simple enough, but is, to our knowledge, too difficult for this present problem.

However, it is clear that we cannot evaluate the expected penalty for overbooking using an a posteriori strategy: in the *a posteriori* scenario, we decide to simply ignore those reservations that we do not consume for our optimal filling. To take the penalty into account, we add a simple lower bound estimate of the penalty that is expected based on the current balance and the expected cancellation rate. Note that this lower bound is only "exact" if we were to refuse all future incoming reservations, which shows that there is an opportunity for a better analysis and a more precise algorithm.

Thus, we can summarize the online algorithm as follows:

1. Compute expected reservations and reservations from date to deadline
2. Produce average deadline scenario S and compute reference value $V = C+(S)$

3. For each bin *b*,
   compute v = C+(S) + ExpectedPenalty(current state) with *item* added to *b*
   pick *b* that maximizes v using balance(*b*) to break ties
4. If v >= V, accept *item* and place it into bin *b,* otherwise refuse *item*

As noticed in the previous section, the algorithm is not very sensitive to the quality of the cancellation prediction, although it is important to use a conservative estimate.

The combinatorial algorithm is a constraint propagation algorithm that uses a limited form of branching with a LDS scheme [HG95]. The branching strategy is to pick which kind of items should be inserted into the current solution and then to branch on all possible bins. To evaluate which bin to pick, we measure the difference in the maximal expected value for the bin before and after the insertion. This maximal value is the solution of the single knapsack problem for the bin, applied to all incoming reservation. We use a LDS scheme, and decide to branch on which bin to pick when there are two bins for which the difference between the two valuations is small enough. The single knapsack is solved with another LDS algorithm that is very similar but much simpler since the value of an insertion is simply the current value of the bin.

The next table addresses the importance of the quality of the C+ algorithm. We give here the results obtained respectively with a naïve greedy heuristic (C1), with a smarter algorithm with one level of branching (C2) and last with our complete algorithm presented here (C+). In this table, we have included the standard deviation to substantiate our claims about the statistical relevance of the experiment, thus each cell in the table is a tuple (average, standard deviation).

Table 2. Comparison of C1,C2 and C+

Problem	*BF*	*C1*	*C2*	*C+*
Master	454, 27.7	481, 32.9	484, 33.6	487, 34.8
Pb1	454, 29.1	489, 30.2	492, 31.6	494, 32.7
Pb2	469, 28.9	496, 34.5	499, 34.0	504, 34.8
Pb3	431, 47.4	448, 49.4,	444, 34.9	449, 49.9
Pb4	82, 18.1	83, 17.6	83, 17.6,	83, 17.6
Pb5	453, 29.9	481, 34.1	484, 34.9	487, 35.6
Pb6	11782, 797.6	12852, 1023.7	12935, 1024.3	12951, 1034.6
Pb7	938, 51.5	906, 53.4	922, 56.2	938, 51.4
Pb8	458, 26.5	519, 29.6	528, 30.5	538, 30.4
Pb9	421, 48.5	418, 50.4	419, 49.1	420, 48.7

A more traditional approach in the field of stochastic programming is to concentrate on whether a new request should be accepted, using a stochastic evaluation, and then simply use a best-fit algorithm to pick which bin must be used. This is for instance the case for most "Yield Management" approaches, including the one that will be presented in Section 6. Therefore, we have conducted the following experiment, where the decision of which bin to pick is left to a best–first heuristic, but we use the same analysis (C+(E) with or without the new reservation) to decide whether to accept or refuse the reservation.

One may see that the impact of the combinatorial choice between the bins depends on the type of problem. This table is useful when comparing with results obtained with

our preliminary implementation of the Yield Management approach in Section 6, since it is similar to the binary approach presented here.
Although this approach presented in this section produces satisfactory results, it still ignores the true stochastic nature of the problem. To remedy this drawback, there are two possible directions:

Table 3. Full exploration vs. binary strategy

Problem	*Full exploration*	*Binary (simpler) strategy*
Master	487, 34.8	481, 39.5
Pb 1	494, 32.7	433, 64.1
Pb 2	504, 34.8	493, 39.5,
Pb 3	449, 49.9	388, 60.2

1. Develop techniques borrowed from stochastic optimization to better characterize E(C). This is the approach that we plan to investigate in the future. Because the algorithm C+ is fairly complex and uses various heuristics, it may actually be easier to characterize C*, that is the optimal resolution of the combinatorial problem and derive information that also applies to C+.
2. Characterize the stochastic nature of the problem, either with a segmentation, which will be developed in the next section, or through cutting rules, which will be shown at the end of Section 6.

5 Combinatorial Analysis (CA)

5.1 Related Markov Decision Processes

MDP is the model of choice [H60, P94] to build optimal policies for stochastic decision problems. Under the assumptions that the arrival laws (In_k) and departure laws (q_k) are time-independent and non correlated, the online Multi-choice Knapsack Problem can be modelled as a fully observable MDP, with an obviously large number of states.

Classic techniques for solving MDPs like Linear Programming [D63], policy iteration [H60] or value iteration [B57] are not suitable in the case of large state space and advocate the development of MDP-decomposition methods. Various approaches have been proposed for the latter, among which: adaptative aggregation [BC89], Dantzig-Wolfe Decomposition [KC74] or, for planning problems, [BDG95, DL95, BT96]. More recently, new decomposition schemes have been developed that exploit the "weakly coupled structure" of some MDP that occur in online resource allocation: policy caches [P98], dynamic MDP merging [SC98] or Markov Task Decomposition [MHK+98].

Our approach consists in a crude implementation of an event-aggregation strategy, focussing on regions of final states of the MDP.

5.2 Combinatorial Sampling

A particularity of our stochastic optimization problem relies in the fact that the revenue is evaluated at the very end of the process. In a sense, the ordering of the incoming events has little importance as no immediate reward or holding cost influence the revenue, provided that the strategy is efficient. The method in this Section takes advantage of this context and is based upon the following property holding for the deterministic case: at time t, if all external events (incoming items, departing items) are known in advance, an optimal strategy consists in choosing for the item the bin that maximizes the revenue of the Multi-choice Deterministic Knapsack Problem for which:

- All already accepted items that will not be cancelled are forced into the solution.
- All incoming items that will not be cancelled are possible candidates for filling the bins.

Though NP-hard, the afore-mentioned combinatorial optimization problem can be solved with on-the-shelf MIP tools (see [MT90] for a deep description of knapsack-like problems). Let $F^*(P[n,k],j,t)$ denote the optimal Deterministic Knapsack value over all possible choices for an item of type j arriving at t. We refer the reader to [WB92] or [PRK95] for discrete and continuous markovian models related to online knapsack and perishable asset revenue management problems. The solution produced by the MIP is the best (in terms of revenue) valid "state" that is reachable from the current state of the system taking corresponding decisions of acceptations and reject.

For the non-deterministic case, our evaluation strategy would ideally aim at enumerating all possible event sets, compute their occurrence probability together with the Deterministic Knapsack revenue, hence deduce the overall expected value of each possible choice of bin for item j: $E[F^*]$.

Not surprisingly, an obvious drawback of this strategy is its computational time. In order to estimate the revenue of each possible final state of the process that are reachable from $P[n,k]$ taking into account the choice at stake, one has to generate all possible pairs $((n^T_1,\ldots,n^T_k),P^T(n,k))$ where:

- N^T_i is the number of items of type i arrived after t and remaining at T if accepted
- $P^T(n,k)$ is the number of remaining items of type k, already present in bin n before t and still present in bin n at T.

with a computational cost of $O(P^{kn} \,.\, (D/K)^k)$, if P denotes the maximum number of items of the same type present in the bins at t, and D the maximum number of items that can enter the system between t and T. Thus we limited our final states study to the most probable states, above a given threshold, restraining ourselves to typically 10000 states at all. Finally, since evaluating each final state by computing the best MIP solution can potentially require a couple of minutes, we use the C1 heuristic instead (described in section 4).

The experimental results not surprisingly indicate that this "combinatorial" sampling offer results that are close to the forward sampling strategy of section 3.

6 Yield Management (YM)

Yield Management techniques analytically estimate impact on the expected final revenue. As with thresholds principle [GR99], at each new arrival is computed expected final revenue and the item is accepted if its marginal revenue improved it.

In a first step, we will describe the computation of the final total balance (FTB) and the final total revenue ($\widetilde{F}$) in a deterministic vision. In a second step, we extend these notions for the stochastic case (probability and penalties) and deduce the stochastic expected final revenue with penalties (ϕ).

Finally, we observe that YM results are better than those of the naïve Best-Fit (BF) strategy in most of the cases. Limitations are two fold: multi choice blindness (the multi bin aspect wasn't involved in the formulas) and packing blindness (the major limitation). The influence of this last combinatorial dimension is illustrated on some special instances.

6.1 Deterministic Case

Let us start with the simple relaxation defined by using only one bin with capacity C.N and one demand type with size $\overline{w}$ (average of real sizes). Since in this case, maximizing the revenue means maximizing the balance, we compute the Final Total Balance (FTB) witch is the sum of all arrivals. As total arrival exceeds C.N, the first intuition, to remove overloading penalty, is to adjust it with a p_{accept} ratio. We have that $\left(\overline{w}\sum_{k=0}^{K} In^k(1-Out^k_{In})\right)p_{accept}$ is equal to exactly C.N when refusing arrivals with a $(1-p_{accept})$ probability. A way to increase revenue, instead of refusing every item with a fixed probability, consists in applying price *segregation* whilst refusing only low price items and accepting good ones. In order to compute a threshold between *low* price and *good* price, we sort items types (re-numbered $\widetilde{k}$) by decreasing marginal revenue ($v_{\widetilde{k}}/w_{\widetilde{k}}$) and incrementally compute the FTB by aggregating all accepted items. We find $\widetilde{k}*$ such that $\widetilde{B}_{\widetilde{k}*}=\sum_{i=1}^{\widetilde{k}*} In_i(1-Out_{In_i,i})w_i$ just exceeds C.N. For this item type, we apply a p_{accept} ratio. Thus, expected revenue become:

$$\widetilde{F}=\sum_{k=1}^{\widetilde{k}*-1} v_k In_k(1-Out_{In_k,k})+v_{\widetilde{k}*}In_{\widetilde{k}*}(1-Out_{In_{\widetilde{k}*},\widetilde{k}*})\left(\frac{C.N-\widetilde{B}_{\widetilde{k}*-1}}{\widetilde{B}_{\widetilde{k}*}-\widetilde{B}_{\widetilde{k}*-1}}\right) \tag{2}$$

6.2 Stochastic Case

To take into account the distribution of possible arrivals, let us focus now on the computation of the final revenue, which is a combination of expected stochastic revenue

(ER) decremented by expected stochastic penalty (EP). This stochastic revenue $\phi = ER - EP$ is computed with the aggregated request volume, on all the items that will not be cancelled: $p_{In}(x)$.

$$\phi = \left(\frac{\overline{v}}{\overline{w}} \sum_{x=0}^{\infty} p_{In}(x)[x.\overline{w}] \right) - \alpha \left(\sum_{x=\left\lceil \frac{CN}{\hat{w}} \right\rceil}^{\infty} p_{In}(x)[x.\overline{w} - C.N] \right) \tag{3}$$

To understand the threshold idea, we can describe graphically ϕ as shown on next figure according to the level of arrival still controlled by our p_{accept} ratio. In the beginning of the dashed line, the revenue for each new accepted arrival does not yield a penalty probability. There is a linear progression of revenue depending on amount of arrivals, with a rate a_R. At a certain level C_1, a small part of the arrival distribution overloads the capacity C.N. The cost function penalty (EP) starts to reduce the amount of additional revenue in ϕ. At level C_2, all the additional arrivals become penalty. In this last portion, we have a linear behavior for the revenue with rate a_R-αa_P. Now, in the full line, if we cumulate the price segregation with this stochastic estimation of revenue, we apply the same strategy on incremental computation based on ϕ by accepting every item until the final expected revenue decreases: this is the desired threshold item $\tilde{k}^*$ with his threshold revenue r^*. As illustrated on the next figure (where a_{ri} is the ith best marginal revenue), the price segregation offers a better revenue than the one-item vision.

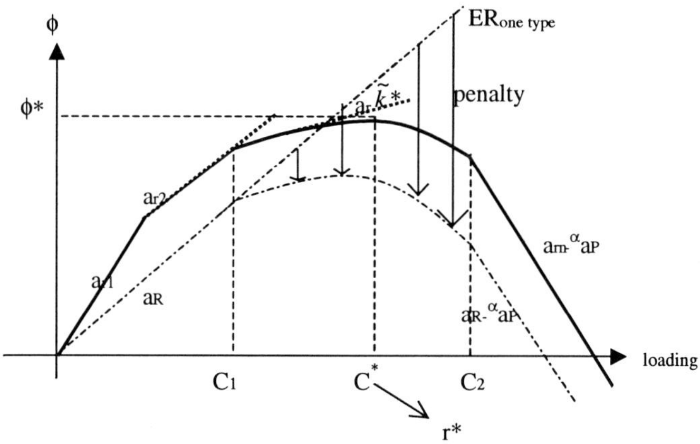

Fig. 1. Revenue as a function of the current balance

As described in the introduction of this part, we dynamically recompute the r* threshold values to decide if we accept arrivals (hence the p_{accept} ratio is no longer needed).

6.3 Limitations and Extensions

The YM strategy results presented in the next section exhibit a better behavior than BF on almost all instances. The disappointing results (compared to other approaches) illustrate clearly the weakness of our current approach from a combinatorial perspective (for instance, on pb3 which packs at most 2 items by bin).

In order to illustrate this last limitation, we have extended the master characteristics by only increasing the average number of item in a bin. Clearly the combinatorial packing aspect (master benchmark: at most 5 items by bin) is smoothed when this number increased.

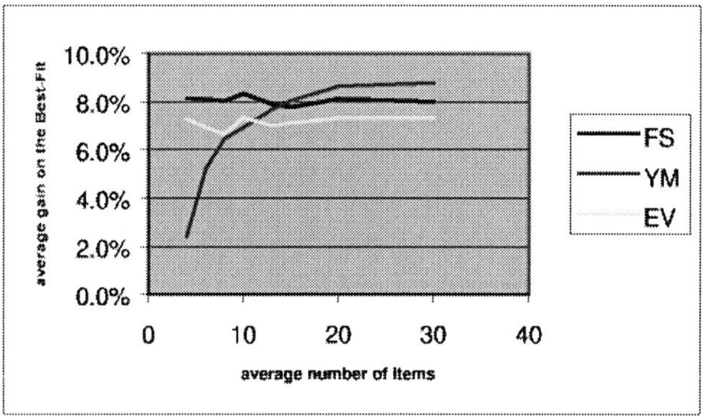

Fig. 2. Influence of the average number of item by bin

Although it may appear from this preliminary experiment that the YM approach is too difficult to tune for this type of combinatorial problems, this is not the case. For instance, we may use the YM analysis to generate simple cut-off rules that will prevent from accepting the lowest value/size ratio during the X first periods. Embedding these rules to EV (section 4) leads to a revenue 7.93% better than BF on the master problem (compared to 7.19% without these rules).

7 Comparisons

This paper is clearly a first step towards an ambitious goal and, therefore, suffers from many limitations. For instance, we plan to extend the experience to stochastic sizes of groups (with an associated probability distribution). Last, we have limited our first experiments to a size that is well suited to analysis, but larger experiments are also required.

7.1 Results

The following table compares the efficiency of our four algorithms: FS (with 1000 samples), EV, CA and YM (respectively in sections 3,4,5 and 6). BF designs the Best-Fit and XMP the optimal far-seeing method quoted in 2.4 (→competitive ratios on the master: FS=90.6% vs. BF=83.8%).

These results are the average results on 1000 runs so that the half width of the confidence interval at 95% is typically 0.7 %. The final column gives the average gain of the best algorithm (bold underlined results) against the BF.

One may notice that run-times vary considerably from one approach to the other. We designed these algorithms to be usable in a human-interaction context, with a response time of around one second (thus 60s for a complete iteration is acceptable). Obviously some online problem would require a faster approach such as YM or EV.

Table 4. Comparative results

Prob-lem	Comment	BF	FS	EV	CA	YM	best gain (%)	*XMP*
Master		454	**491**	487	489	465	8.2	*542*
Pb1	smaller penalty	454	**500**	494	498	485	10	*542*
Pb2	various q_k	469	**510**	504	509	482	8.7	*556*
Pb3	bigger items	431	**459**	449	458	380	6.5	*508*
Pb4	single knapsack	82	86	83	**87**	60	5.8	*101*
Pb6	value = size^2 (convex)	11782	13175	12951	**13232**	12630	12	*14439*
Pb7	value =10size$^{1/2}$ (concave)	910	**948**	938	**948**	901	4.2	-
Pb8	huge arrival volume : 300%	458	533	**538**	513	511	17	*587*
Pb9	small arrival volume: 120%	421	425	420	**426**	393	1.2	-
Pb10	no departures	469	**542**	533	524	514	15	-
Pb11	Small items more frequent	442	**488**	483	487	465	10	-
Pb12	Big items more frequent	464	**504**	**504**	499	472	8.5	-
Pb17	Large standard deviation: 35%	452	**486**	479	-	464	7.6	-
Pb18	Small standard deviation: 12%	453	**495**	486	481	458	9.2	-
Pb19	No deviation and no departure (only the order change)	468	542	536	**548**	481	17	-
CPU	Run time (s) for 1 scenario master	0.01	20	0.5	60	0.02		

Although this is a preliminary report, these results *show the interest of mixing insights from the stochastic and the combinatorial optimization field.* For instance, we showed that using a better CO algorithm in the EV method pays off. On the other hand, there is balance to be found and using a sophisticated optimization technique is easily wasted if the level of stochastic analysis is too low. Another illustration of our central claim is that YM techniques used without using combinatorial insights do not seem competitive, but for "fluid" instances (cf. 6.3), whereas YM filters may improve significantly a combinatorial method.

7.2 Robustness

In all scenarios tested in 7.1, events are generated according to the distributions that are known to the algorithms. On the contrary, this section evaluates the robustness of our approaches, when based on a slightly erroneous estimation of the input distribution (as in real life): wrong law (Table 5) or wrong average (Table 6).

Facing non-regular distributions, our strategies become very sensible to the standard deviation (especially CA). Estimation errors on the input average have less influence (except for YM) but in both cases, the most robust behavior consists in focusing on average values.

Table 5. Non-regular distributions

Problem	Comment	BF	FS	EV	CA	YM	best gain (%)
Pb29	non-regular distribution (avg:8.08409, stdev:1.87479)	454	**<u>492</u>**	484	490	463	8.2
Pb30	"Very" non-regular distribution (avg:8.01173, stdev:3.12526)	453	444	454	-	**<u>457</u>**	0.9

Table 6. Influence of estimation errors on the input distribution

estimation error in %	*-25*	*-12.5*	*0*	*+12.5*	*+25*
average gain of FS (%)	3.83	**<u>6.85</u>**	**<u>8.23</u>**	**<u>8.45</u>**	6.93
average gain of EV (%)	**<u>6.15</u>**	6.63	6.34	7.40	**<u>7.71</u>**
average gain of YM (%)	**<u>-8</u>**	-3.7	2.4	1	**<u>-1.7</u>**

8 Conclusions

We have presented different algorithms that try to solve an online combinatorial optimization problem through different techniques that borrow from different fields. Although we report preliminary results, they are stable enough to confirm the need for combining insights from combinatorial and stochastic programming. We argue that constraint programming is a relevant technique for such problems for two reasons:

1. On the one hand, many problems for which CP is well suited because of its expressive power (its ability to capture situations that are difficult to model) have a stochastic nature
2. On the other hand, two of the algorithms presented here can be easily adapted to a CP approach for a given problem: the simulation approach (FS) and the expected value approach (EV)

We have identified different topics that must be investigated before we may develop a generic method for solving stochastic combinatorial optimization problems with constraints:

1. How does one obtain stochastic indicators about a lower or upper bound that is computed by a (limited) branch-and-bound algorithm?
2. How can an abstract search space be abstracted from a stochastic description, onto which a combinatorial approach may be found?
3. How does one develop fast, incremental CP simulation engines, which is a request that is also found when developing hybrid methods that combine CP and meta-heuristics such as stochastic methods?

In this last question, we see that the combination of CP and stochastic has been mostly studied so far with the angle of introducing stochastic methods (such as randomized algorithms) as opposed to solving stochastic problems. For instance, one may notice the difference with the proposal of Probabilistic Constraint Programming (PCP [DW00]), where probabilities are assigned to constraints as opposed to data. However, we plan to investigate how PCP could be used to solve this type of online problems.

Last, we want to emphasize the availability of our benchmark problem (www.e-lab.bouygues.com/adhoc/prototypes/stokp), which we hope to see attempted by other teams with other methods.

References

[ABC+99] F. Afrati, E. Bampis, C. Chekuri, D. Karger, C. Kenyon, S. Khanna, I. Milis, M. Queyranne, M. Skutella, C. Stein, and M. Sviridenko: *Approximation schemes for minimizing average weighted completion time with release dates*. Proc. of the 1999 Symposium on Foundations of Computer Science (FOCS99), 1999.

[AW96] A.N. Avramidis, J. R. Wilson : *Integrated variance reduction strategies for simulation*. Operations Research 44 (2): 327-346, 1996.

[B57] R. Bellman. *Dynamic Programming*. Princeton University Press, 1957.

[BC89] D. P. Bertsekas, D.A. Castanon. *Adaptative aggregation for infinite horizon dynamic programming*. IEEE Transactions on Automatic Control, 34(6):589-598, 1989.

[BDG95] C. Boutilier, R. Dearden, M. Goldszmidt: *Exploiting structure in policy construction*. In Proceedings of the 1995 international joint conference on artificial intelligence, 1995.

[BL 97] J. Birge, F. Louveaux,: *Introduction to Stochastic Programming*
Springer Series in Operations Research, 1997.

[BT96] D. P. Bertsekas, J. N. Tsitsiklis: *Neuro-dynamic Programming*. Athena, Belmont, MA, 1996.

[CSL99] Y. Caseau, G. Silverstein. F. Laburthe, *A Meta-Heuristic Factory for Vehicle Routing Problems*, Proc. of the 5th Int. Conference on Principles and Practice of Constraint Programming CP'99, LNCS 1713, Springer, 1999.

[D63] F. D'Epenoux. *A probabilistic production and inventory problem*. Management Science: 10:98-108, 1963.

[DL95] T. Dean, S. H. Lin. *Decomposition techniques for planning in stochastic domains*, In Proceedings of the 1995 international joint conference on artificial intelligence, 1995.

[DW00] A. Di Pierro, H. Wiklicky: *Randomised Algorithms and Probabilistic Constraint Programming* Proc. of the ERCIM/Compulog Workshop on Constraints, 19-21 June, Padova, Italy, 2000.

[FW97] A. Fiat, G.J. Woeginger: *Online Algorithms* Lecture Notes in Computer Science, vol. 1442.

[GR99] J.I. McGuill, G.J. Van Ryzin *Revenue Management: research overview and prospects* Transportation science vol.33 n°2, may 99.

[H60] R.A.Howard: *Dynamic programming and markov Chains*. MIT Press. Cambridge, 1960.

[HG95] W. Harvey, M. Ginsberg : *Limited Discrepancy Search*. Proceedings of the 14th IJCAI, p. 607-615, Morgan Kaufmann, 1995.

[HSS+96] L. Hall, A. S. Schulz, D. Shmoys, J. Wein: *Scheduling to Minimize Average Completion Time: Off-line and On-line Approximation Algorithms*. Proc of SODA: ACM-SIAM Symposium on Discrete Algorithms, 1996.

[KC74] H. J. Kushner, C. H. Chen: *Decomposition of systems governed by Markov chains*. IEEE transactions on Automatic Control, AC-19(5):501-507, 1974.

[MHK+98] N. Meuleau, M. Hauskrecht, K.-E. Kim, L. Peshkin, L.P. Kaelbling, T. dean, C. Boutilier. *Solving Very Large Weakly Coupled Markov Decision Processes*. American Association for Artificial Intelligence, 1998.

[MT90] S. Martello, P. Toth, *Knapsack problems. Algorithms and computer implementations*. John Wiley and Sons, West Sussex, England, 1990.

[P98] R. Parr. *Flexible Decompostion Algorithms for weakly coupled Markov Decision Problems.* Uncertainty in Artificial Intelligence. Madison, Wisconsin, USA, 1998

[P94] M. L. Puterman. Markov Decision Processes: *Discrete Stochastic Dynamic Programming.* Wiley, New York, 1994.

[PRK95] J. Papastavrou, S. Rajagopalan, A. Kleywegt : *The Dynamic and Stochastic Knapsack Problem with Deadlines.* Technical report, School of Industrial Engineering, Purdue University, West Lafayette, April 1995.

[SC98] S. P. Singh, D. Cohn. *How to dynamically merge Markov Decision Processes.* In M. Mozer, M. Jordan and T. Petsche eds, NIPS-11. MIT Press, Cambridge, 1998.

[WB92] L.R. Weatherford, S.E. Bodily: *A Taxonomy and Research Overview of Perishable-Asset Revenue Managment : Yield Managment, Overbooking and Pricing.* Operations Research 40:831-844, 1992

Global Cut Framework for Removing Symmetries

Filippo Focacci[1] and Michaela Milano[2]

[1] ILOG S.A., 9 rue de Verdun, BP 85, F-94253 Gentilly France
ffocacci@ilog.fr
[2] DEIS University of Bologna, V.le Risorgimento, 2. 40136 Italy
mmilano@deis.unibo.it

Abstract. In this paper, we propose a general technique for removing symmetries in CSPs during search. The idea is to record *no-goods*, during the exploration of the search tree, whose symmetric counterpart (if any) should be removed. The no-good, called *Global Cut Seed* (GCS), is used to generate *Symmetry Removal Cuts* (SRCs), i.e., constraints that are dynamically generated during search and hold in the entire search tree. The propagation of SRCs removes symmetric configurations with respect to already visited states. We present a general, correct and complete filtering algorithm for SRCs. The main advantages of the proposed approach are that it is not intrusive in the problem-dependent search strategy, treats symmetries in an additive way since GCSs are symmetry independent, and enables to write filtering algorithms which handle families of symmetries together. Finally, we show that many relevant previous approaches can be seen as special cases of our framework.

1 Introduction

Constraint Satisfaction Problems (CSPs) occur widely in Artificial Intelligence and are used for solving many real life applications. In this paper, we focus on symmetric CSPs. A CSP is symmetric when a mapping exists that transforms a state in another equivalent to the first. Symmetries [12] have been identified as a source of inefficiency since much time is spent in visiting equivalent states.

In recent years, symmetry removal methods have interested many researchers; three main approaches have been identified to remove symmetries. The first imposes additional constraints to the model of the CSP; the work by Puget [12] defines valid reductions for the original problem obtained by imposing additional constraints, e.g., ordering constraints among variables, that enable to avoid permutations. If a valid reduction of a given CSP is proven to be unsatisfiable, the original CSP is unsatisfiable as well. This approach seems appealing, but presents two drawbacks: first, it is not always simple to find proper symmetry-breaking constraints in case of general symmetries; second, the search strategy can be influenced by the additional constraints.

The second approach starts from a different idea: constraints able to prune symmetric states are introduced during search. In this setting, [7] and [2] use

T. Walsh (Ed.): CP 2001, LNCS 2239, pp. 77–92, 2001.

respectively the notion of *conditional constraints* and *entailment* to avoid searching in branches leading to symmetric solutions. They add constraints to nodes of the search tree and consider the constraints valid globally in order to remove symmetric configurations upon backtracking. In [13] the authors detect and exploit *intensional permutation* symmetries. Then, each time they detect a failure, they use this information by removing the value causing the failure from the domain of permutable variables. In [9], a similar pruning after failure filtering algorithm is proposed. Similar approaches are based on general notions of interchangeble values [5] and syntactical symmetries [3] which partition variable domains in equivalence classes: when a failure is detected for a given value, all values belonging to the same equivalence class are removed since they also lead to a failure.

A third way of coping with symmetries is to define a search strategy that breaks symmetries as soon as possible. In [9] and [10], the authors propose a symmetry breaking strategy that selects first variables involved in the greatest number of local symmetries. The problem dependent search strategy is affected, but this approach can be very effective if symmetries are the prevailing feature of the problem.

We focus on the second approach and propose a general framework for coping with symmetries. We collect information during search, called Global Cut Seeds (GCSs), representing states whose symmetric counterpart, if any, should be removed. GCSs are *no-goods*. F. Bacchus in [1] provided a uniform view of backtracking algorithms based on no-goods. A no-good $\mathcal{A}$ is a set of assignments which cannot appear in any unenumerated solution. The notion of no-good depends only on the not yet explored search space. Thus, as soon as a solution is found, it becomes a no-good and is treated uniformly with other no-goods.

In backtracking algorithms, no-goods are used for many purposes: to avoid searching subtrees, to prune domain values, to backtrack and to save constraint checks. In a symmetric problem, all these tasks can be done as well, but we can do something more. If a no-good is detected, its symmetric counterparts are no-goods as well. However, while in general backtracking algorithms no-goods are forgotten on backtracking, as soon as the no-good is "broken", in our symmetry removal framework they are used to impose non backtrackable constraints, called Symmetry Removal Cuts (SRCs), that act in the unexplored part of the search tree. Unfortunately, the number of SRCs could be exponential. Thus, we need to limit their number. An interesting property of GCSs is that they are symmetry independent, while SRCs depend on it. Thus, many SRCs, one for each symmetry, can be generated independently in an additive way starting from the same GCS or can be considered all together in a global constraint tailored for a family of symmetries. We propose a method for inferring GCSs during search, a general filtering algorithm for SRCs that prunes symmetric configurations, and several specializations. We show that many relevant previous approaches can be seen as specialization of the framework proposed.

2 Symmetric CSPs

In this section, we provide preliminary notions on symmetric CSPs. A CSP is a triple (V, D, C) where V is a list of variables $X_1, \ldots, X_n$ ranging respectively on finite domains $D(X_1), \ldots, D(X_n)$. A constraint $c_i(X_{i_1}, \ldots X_{i_k})$ defines a subset S_i of the cartesian product of $D(X_{i_1}) \times \ldots \times D(X_{i_k})$, containing those configurations of assignments *allowed* by the constraint. An element $\tau = (v_1, \ldots, v_k)$ of $D(X_{i_1}), \ldots, D(X_{i_k})$ is called *tuple.* A tuple is consistent with the constraint if it belongs to S_i. The negative counterpart of consistency is the concept of *no-good.* A no-good $\mathcal{A}$ is a set of assignments which cannot appear in any unenumerated solution (see e.g. [1]). Thus, solutions and failures are uniformly treated.

CSPs may exhibit symmetries; if two or more states are symmetric, they represent equivalent states. Thus, only one of them should be visited, while the others discarded. According to [9], a symmetry σ is a sequence of bijective mappings $\sigma_0, \sigma_1, ..., \sigma_n$, where $\sigma_0 : V \to V$ and $\sigma_i : D(X_i) \to D(\sigma_0(X_i))$ that preserves constraints. Preserving constraints means that by applying the symmetry to the variables involved in the constraint, if a tuple τ is consistent with the constraints, also $\sigma(\tau)$ is consistent. Thus, if a tuple τ is a no-good, also $\sigma(\tau)$ is a no-good[1]. Note that when σ_i is the identity function for every i, then σ is a symmetry on variables. When σ_0 is the identity function, then σ is a symmetry on values. In the general case considered in this paper, σ can be a symmetry on both variables and values.

3 Global Cut Seeds and Symmetry Removal Cuts

The general framework proposed is based on no-goods called *Global Cut Seeds* (GCSs). Intuitively, a GCS represents a set of states whose symmetric counterpart, if any, should be removed. Consider a CSP P, and suppose a feasible solution s has been found for P. Since we aim at removing all solutions symmetric to s, s should be "part" of the GCS. Similarly, given a state $\bar{s}$ infeasible for P, configuration of values symmetric to $\bar{s}$ represent infeasible states as well. Therefore $\bar{s}$ should also be "part" of a GCS. Formally, a GCS is defined as follows:

Definition 1 (Global Cut Seed) *Given a CSP P with n variables, a Global Cut Seed is a n-tuple $\Delta = (\delta_1, \delta_2, ..., \delta_n)$, where each δ_i is a non empty set of values, such that each n-tuple $(v_1, \ldots, v_n)$, $v_1 \in \delta_1, ..., v_n \in \delta_n$ is either an already found solution or an infeasible state for the original problem P.*

The definition of GCS uniformly treats already found solutions and infeasible configuration for P, as happens for no-goods. Indeed, the definition of GCS is nothing more than a reformulation of the definition of no-good proposed in [1] that is better suited to be used in the setting of symmetry removals.

[1] A symmetry σ applied to a tuple $\tau = (v_1, \ldots, v_n)$ is defined as follows: for each $v_i \in \tau$ its symmetrical counterpart is $\sigma_i(v_{idx(\sigma_0(X_i))})$.

Starting from GCSs, we propose a general algorithm for pruning symmetric configurations based on the use of *Symmetry Removal Cuts* (SRCs), i.e., constraints deduced during search that hold in the remaining part of the search tree. Intuitively, during search, we collect GCSs (independent from the problem symmetries), that will be used for generating SRCs. SRCs exploit the GCS collected at node N for pruning symmetric configurations w.r.t. the one in N.

Definition 2 (Symmetry Removal Cut) *Given a CSP on variables* $V = X_1, ..., X_n$*, a Global Cut Seed* $\Delta = (\delta_1, ..., \delta_n)$ *and a symmetry* σ*, a Symmetry Removal Cut is the constraint* $remove\_symmetric(\Delta, V, \sigma)$ *imposing that configuration symmetric to* Δ *with respect to* σ *are not explored in the remaining search tree. Declaratively,* $remove\_symmetric(\Delta, V, \sigma)$ *holds iff* $\exists X_i \in V |\ \sigma_i(X_{idx(\sigma_0(X_i))}) \not\subseteq \delta_i$ *where* $i = idx(X_i)$ *is the index of variable* X_i.

Note that constraints $remove\_symmetric(\Delta, V, \sigma)$ are defined as *cuts* since they are globally valid. Each time a GCS Δ is found, a symmetry removal constraint $remove\_symmetric(\Delta, V, \sigma)$ is imposed removing all configurations symmetric to Δ. Hence, $remove\_symmetric(\Delta, V, \sigma)$ is a global non backtrackable constraint. Similarly, in Mathematical Programming, Branch and Cut (see e.g. [11]) algorithms deduce, during search linear inequalities (cutting planes) valid for the original problem.

The gap between the definition of GCS and SRC, and a practically useful symmetry removal filtering algorithm is huge, and several problems need to be considered. How to find GCSs ? How to limit their number ? How to efficiently use GCSs for filtering? We will answer all these questions in the rest of the paper.

4 Filtering Algorithm for Pruning Symmetries

Let $V = \{X_1, \ldots, X_n\}$ be the set of variables of a CSP P. A branching strategy partitions problem $P(N)$ in a given node N by imposing additional constraints. With no loss of generality, we suppose that at each node of the search tree the problem is partitioned in two subproblems (binary branching), that the branching strategy imposes on the left branch a *positive* constraint c, and on the right branch a *negative* constraint $\neg c$, and that the left branch is explored before the right branch[2]. All constraints imposed from the root node to a node N are called *branching constraints BC*.

A node N is described by a triple (D_{old}, D_{new}, BC), where D_{old} is a set of domains prior to propagation, D_{new} is the set of domains (possibly) shrunk due to constraint propagation after the application of the branching constraint, and BC is the set of branching constraints imposed to reach the node. Let $f(N)$ be the father node of N, D_{old} of N corresponds to D_{new} in $f(N)$. At the root node, D_{old} is the set of initial domains. If one domain in D_{new} is empty, a failure is detected and a backtracking forced.

[2] We assume that the positive branching constraint the constraint is explored first, and we build the search tree with the positive constraint on the left branch

We define a general filtering algorithm for SRCs. Given a GCS $\Delta = (\delta_1, \ldots, \delta_n)$, we have to remove from variable domains all configurations of assignments that are symmetric w.r.t. values contained in the GCS. The filtering algorithm is based on this simple idea. Given a GCS $\Delta = (\delta_1, \ldots, \delta_n)$, we transform it by applying the symmetry to each value belonging to each δ_i[3]. Let $i = idx(X_i)$ be the index of variable X_i. At each node N of the search tree, if there exists a subset $M_j = V \setminus \{X_j\}$ of variables V whose cardinality is $n-1$ such that for each pair $(X_i, \delta_{idx(\sigma_0(X_i))})$, $i = 1, \ldots, n$, $i \neq j$, $D_{new}(X_i) \subseteq \sigma_i(\delta_{idx(\sigma_0(X_i))})$, we can remove from the domain of the free variable X_j all values $v_k \in \sigma_j(\delta_{idx(\sigma_0(X_j))})$. Note that if the subset of variables for which the condition holds has cardinality equal to n, the search fails and backtracks. It is easy to see that larger δ_i in GCSs allow more powerful filtering. The filtering algorithm has a time complexity of $O(n * maxD)$, where $maxD$ is the size of the largest initial domain.

As a simple example, consider a problem where we have three variables subject to a constraint of difference. Their initial domain is $D(X_1) = D(X_2) = D(X_3) = I = [1, 2, 3, 4]$ and they are subject to permutation symmetries. Now suppose we find the first feasible solution $S1 = \{X_1 = 1, X_2 = 2, X_3 = 3\}$, which represents a GCS by definition. Proceeding depth first, we find the second solution $S2 = \{X_1 = 1, X_2 = 2, X_3 = 4\}$ (see the search tree in figure 1). Therefore, $\Delta = (\{1\}, \{2\}, \{3, 4\})$ is a GCS. Consider the symmetry σ_0 which maps X_1 in itself, X_2 in X_3 and vice-versa. Upon backtracking, we find a node where variable $X_1 = 1$, $X_2 = 3$ and the domain of variable X_3 contains values $\{2, 4\}$. Thus, we can find a matching of size $n - 1 = 2$ which maps X_1 in $\delta_1 = \{1\}$ since $D_{new}(X_1) \subseteq \delta_1$ and X_2 in $\delta_3 = \{3, 4\}$, since $D_{new}(X_2) \subseteq \delta_3$. The domain of the free variable X_3 (for which $D_{new}(X_3) \nsubseteq \delta_2$) can be pruned by removing all values belonging to $\delta_2 = \{2\}$. In this way we have removed the symmetrical solution $S3 = \{X_1 = 1, X_2 = 3, X_3 = 2\}$.

Proposition 1 (Correctness) *The filtering algorithm is sound, i.e., it does not remove any configuration which is not symmetric with respect to a previously found configuration in* $\Delta = \{\delta_1, \ldots, \delta_n\}$. **Proof:** *see [4].*

Proposition 2 (Completeness) *The filtering algorithm is complete, i.e., it removes all configurations symmetric with respect to a previously found configuration.* **Proof:** *see [4].*

5 Building Global Cut Seeds during Search

We have shown that GCS can be used to filter values that would otherwise lead either to symmetric solutions or to failures. We still need to show how cut seeds can be built during search. Failures and already found solutions are treated uniformly as dead-ends. In fact, no-goods refer to the unexplored part of the search space.

[3] The application of a symmetry to a set $\delta_i = \{v_1, \ldots, v_m\}$ is $\sigma_i(\delta_i) = \{\sigma_i(v_1), \ldots, \sigma_i(v_m)\}$.

At a given node N, infeasibility is detected when the problem $P(N)$, derived from P by the application of the sequence of branching constraint, is inconsistent. From the definition of GCSs, we are looking for configurations of assignments that are inconsistent for the original problem P. Therefore, we need to find a way to distinguish between configurations of values that are inconsistent with P and those inconsistent with $P(N)$, but consistent with P.

This distinction can be easily done if every branching constraint c can be solved in one propagation step. In other words, after one run of the propagation algorithm associated with c, c can be safely removed from the constraint store. This is the case of unary branching constraints that split the domain of a single variable (branching variable) in two. A unary constraint c on variable X_k can be defined by a set of values S_k that are removed from the domain of variable X_k as soon as c is posted. Note that under this hypothesis, at any node N of the search tree, any combination of values $(v_1, \ldots, v_n)$ with $v_i \in D_{old}(X_i)$, $i = 1, \ldots, n$ is consistent with the set of branching constraints $BC(N)$.

We focus now on dead-end nodes, i.e., nodes where a failure has been detected or forced after a solution has been found. In a dead-end node N only one no-good can be built $\Delta^{(N)} = \{\delta_1^{(N)}, \ldots, \delta_n^{(N)}\}$. Let X_k be the branching variable and S_k be the set of values removed by $D_{old}(X_k)$ by the branching constraint at node N. It is easy to prove that each combination of assignments taken from $\delta_k^{(N)} = D_{old}(X_k) \setminus S_k$ and $\delta_i^{(N)} = D_{old}(X_i)$ for all $i = 1..n$, $i \neq k$ is a no-good, thus a GCS $\Delta^{(N)}$, because it is inconsistent with the original problem P. We will refer to these seeds as *simple dead-end seeds.*

In [4] this result is extended, and it is shown that no-goods can also be generated by reasoning on values removed by constraint propagation. In particular, at each node of the search tree, we can derive at most n no-goods (one for each variable with $D_{old} \neq D_{new}$) each involving n variables. Nevertheless, in practice we only use no-goods derived at dead-end nodes.

We can improve these seeds. As seen in Section 4, seeds composed by larger sets δ_j lead to better pruning of the search space. If N is a dead-end node and it is reached by applying branching constraints $BC(N)$ to the original problem P, it means that $P(N) = P \cup BC(N)$ is infeasible. Since branching constraints remove from the domain of each variable X_i a set of values S_i, $P(N)$ is derived from P by removing from the initial domain I_i of each variable X_i the set S_i. Thus, we define a *dead-end global cut seed* or simply dead-end seed:

Definition 3 (Dead-end global cut seed) *Let $V = \{X_1, \ldots, X_n\}$ be the set of variables of a CSP. Let N be a dead-end node. Let S_i be the set of values removed by the application of all branching constraints of $BC(N)$ on variable X_i from the root node to the current node*[4]*. Then, at node N, a dead-end seed $\Delta^{(N)}$ can be defined as follows: $\Delta^{(N)} = \{(I_1 \setminus S_1), \ldots, (I_n \setminus S_n)\}$ where I_i is the initial domain of each variable.*

[4] If a variable X_j has not been involved in a branching constraints, the corresponding S_j is empty.

Proposition 3 (A dead-end seed is a global cut seed) *In a dead end node N, the dead-end seed associated to N is a global cut seed if branching constraints are unary.* **Proof:** *see [4].*

It is worth noting that such a dead-end seed subsumes all dead-end seeds that could (eventually) be found in children nodes of N. The dead-end seeds can be maintained in a list, and every time a new dead-end seed is generated at node N, all node seeds corresponding to children nodes of N can be removed from the list.

A further improvement to these cut seeds can be done. The idea is that whenever a right branch is selected (a negative branching constraint is imposed) the right branch has already been explored and has lead to a failure[5].

Definition 4 (Extended dead-end seed) *Let $V = \{X_1, \ldots, X_n\}$ be the set of variables of a CSP. Let N be a dead-end node. Let $SP^{(N)} = \{SP_1, \ldots, SP_n\}$ be the set containing, for each SP_i, the set of values removed by the application of all positive branching constraints (i.e. the left branches constraints) in $BC(N)$ on variable X_i from the root node to the current node. Then, at node N, an extended dead-end seed $\Delta^{(N)}$ can be defined as follows: $\Delta^{(N)} = \{(I_1 \setminus SP_1), \ldots, (I_n \setminus SP_n)\}$ where I_i is the initial domain of each variable.*

Proposition 4 (An extended dead-end seed is a global cut seed) *In a dead end node N, the extended dead-end seed associated to N is a GCS if branching constraints are unary.* **Proof:** *see [4].*

Proposition 5 (Extended dead-end seeds are limited) *If the tree is explored depth first, the number of non-subsumed extended dead-end seeds is less or equal to the depth of the search tree.* **Proof:** *see [4].*

Note that our approach is independent from the search strategy used. It is applicable on *discrepancy based* tree exploration methods (see e.g., Limited Discrepancy Search [8], Depth-bounded Discrepancy Search [15]) as well as Best First strategies.

Although some classes of problems (for example scheduling problems) typically do not rely on unary constraints, in most CSP applications (as well as Integer Linear Programming) the search strategy is defined by imposing unary constraints on the problem variables. Note that if hypothesis on unary branching constraints is relaxed, the cut seeds can be built as well. However, they become *Local Cut Seeds* since they are not valid for the entire search space. Local Cut Seeds are subject of current research.

---

[5] In this setting, also solutions are considered since a failure is forced to find other solutions upon backtracking.

6 Example

Now consider a simple example on how to build GCS and on the pruning achieved. We have three variables subject to a constraint of difference. Their initial domain is $D(X_1) = D(X_2) = D(X_3) = I = [1, 2, 3, 4]$ and they are subject to permutation symmetries. In figure 1 part of the problem search space is depicted.

We first find the first solution (node A) $X_1 = 1$, $X_2 = 2$ and $X_3 = 3$. Then, a failure is forced. Upon backtracking we build $GCS1$. Different types of GCSs can be built: the simple dead-end seed that records the solution found (i.e., domains at node A), the global dead end seed that considers initial domains I_i and removes only values pruned by the unary branching constraints, referred in section 5 to as S_i. Thus, the set δ_2, corresponding to X_2, is equal to $I_2 \setminus S_2$. S_2 contains values deleted by the branching constraint $X_2 = 2$. Note that value 1 has been deleted by problem constraint propagation before the branching constraint on X_2 is posted. As a consequence, S_2 contains only values 3 and 4. Thus, 1 belongs to the GCS. The extended global cut seed in this case is equal to the global one since no negative branching constraints have been posted.

$GCS2$ is generated after backtracking from node B (after the second solution found). The simple dead end seed corresponds to the domains of node B. The global dead-end seed instead considers for variable X_2 the same set as for $GCS1$. The interesting part here is δ_3. In fact, since in node B variable X_3 has not been involved in any branching decision, the corresponding S_3 is empty and δ_3 is equal to the whole initial domain. Again, the extended dead-end seed is equal to the global one since no negative branching constraints have been posted. Having generated $GCS2$, we can remove (in node D) value 2 from the domain of X_3. In fact, the following mapping exists: $D(X_1) \subseteq \delta_1$, $D(X_2) \subseteq \delta_3$. Thus, we can remove from $D(X_3)$ values belonging to δ_2, i.e., values 1 and 2. In this way, we avoid computing a symmetric solution with respect to the two solutions found.

$GCS3$ is generated upon backtracking from the third solution. The simple dead end seed corresponds again to the solution. The global dead end seed instead contains values from the initial domain minus those removed by the branching constraints, i.e., $S_1 = \{2, 3, 4\}$, $S_2 = \{2, 4\}$ (again value 1 was previously pruned by constraint propagation) and S_3 is empty. The interesting case here is the extended dead-end seed, and in particular the set δ_2. On X_2 a negative branching constraint has been posted, but we remove only values pruned by its positive counterpart, i.e., $SP_2 = \{2\}$. The generation of the $GCS3$ lead to prune the subtree corresponding to $X_2 = 4$ since it leads to symmetric solutions.

Simple, global and extended dead-end seed have an increasing filtering power since they involve larger sets δ_i.

7 Specialization of the Filtering Algorithm and Related Approaches

We will now describe some specializations of the general filtering algorithm. Some of these specialization lead to new symmetry removal algorithms; some

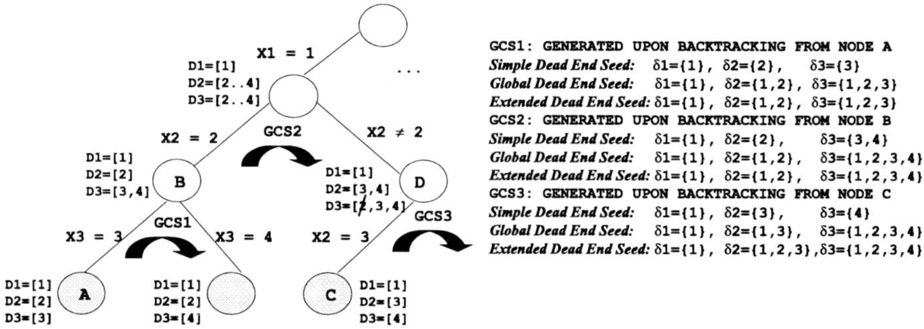

Fig. 1. Example

others instead show that already known results can be seen as special cases of the general algorithm given in Section 4.

7.1 First Specialization (CUTS1)

The first specialization considers problems having a set of variables subject to permutation symmetries. Without loss of generality, we suppose that the entire set of variables is subject to permutation symmetries, and that all symmetric variables have the same initial domain. In this specialization, we suppose that the branching strategy chooses a variable and a value for the variable. In this case, the filtering algorithm outlined in section 4 can be easily implemented.

Intuitively, we can see that if a value *val* for a given variable X_i is infeasible, being all variables symmetric, *val* will also be infeasible for any other variable X_j. Thus, upon backtracking on the branching choice $X_i = val$, we can remove *val* from the domain of any other variable not yet bound by branching.

This algorithm is a special case of the general filtering algorithm proposed. Consider a node h, on which a failure is generated by the assignment $X_i = val$. Being *Selected* the set of the k variables already assigned by branching, and being X_i the current branching variable, the node h has the following extended dead-end seed: $\Delta^{(h)} = \{\delta_1^{(h)}, \ldots, \delta_n^{(h)}\}$ where for each $s \in Selected$, $\delta_s^{(h)} = \{v_s\}$; for each $j \notin Selected$, $\delta_j^{(h)} = I \setminus SP_j^{(h)} = I$, being I the initial domain of all variables; finally $\delta_i^{(h)} = \{val\}$.

At father node $f(h)$, $D_{new}(X_s) = \{v_s\}$ for $s \in Selected$. There exist exactly $n-k$ different matchings M_l (for each $l \notin Selected$) of cardinality $n-1$ between the GCS and the domain set. Each matching M_l allows to remove $\delta_i^{(h)} = \{val\}$ from $D_{new}(X_l)$. This pruning can be done for each $l \notin Selected$. Using different arguments, Roy and Pachet [13] found this same algorithm for pruning in case of permutation symmetries. Here we deduce the algorithm from the general one described in Section 4.

An extension of this algorithm for removing (local) symmetries is that described in [9]. It is based on the idea that if the instantiation $X_i = val$ is tried without success, we can remove $\sigma_i(val)$ from the domain of $\sigma_0(X_i)$. In fact, given the same extended dead-end seed as before[6], we can find in node $f(h)$ only one mapping M_l of size $n-1$ where $l = idx(\sigma_0(X_i))$. Thus, we can remove from the domain of $\sigma_0(X_i)$ the symmetrical of val.

7.2 Second Specialization (CUTS2)

The second specialization still considers the same problems and permutation symmetries as for CUTS1. Here we suppose that the branching constraints are unary constraints (e.g., $X < val$, $X \geq val$, $X \neq val$). We are, in a way, generalizing the results presented in [13].

Given $\Delta^{(h)} = \{(I \backslash SP_1^{(h)}), \ldots, (I \backslash SP_n^{(h)})\}$ generated after a failure at node h, the domain of variables can be reduced if there exists a matching of cardinality $n-1$ between the set of domains and $\Delta^{(h)}$. The left subtree of node $f(h)$ is the fail node h. In the right subtree of node $f(h)$, for each $i \neq k$, we have $D_{new}(X_i) \subseteq \delta_i^{(h)}$. Thus, for each j such that $D_{new}(X_k) \subseteq \delta_j^{(h)}$, a matching M_j of cardinality $n-1$ exists, and $\delta_k^{(h)}$ can be removed from $D_{new}(X_j)$.

Whenever a new GCS $\Delta^{(h)}$ is inserted into the pool, the filtering algorithm checks for each j if $D_{new}(X_k) \subseteq \delta_j^{(h)}$. At most $sizeOf(I)$ values are removed from $D_{new}(X_j)$. Therefore, the initial propagation of each GCS can be obtained in $O(n\, sizeOf(I)^2)$. For each variable there are at most $sizeOf(I)$ cuts to be considered, if all the instantiations of different values to a variable provide a non-subsumed GCS. Whenever a set of values is removed from a domain of a variable, at most n checks should be performed for each cut. Each time a check $D_{new}(X_k) \subseteq \delta_j^{(h)}$ is successful, at most $sizeOf(I)$ values are removed from $D_{new}(X_j)$. Therefore, the worst case complexity of the filtering algorithm on a single cut **for the entire set of permutation symmetries** is $O(n\, sizeOf(I))$; computational results show that the mean case complexity is lower.

7.3 Third Specialization (CUTS3)

We now give a specialization of the algorithm for symmetries defined by interchangeable values [5]. Let consider a CSP with n variables having interchangeable values. Given n variables $X_1, \ldots X_n$, with initial domain I_i, suppose I_i can be partitioned in k_i subset of values $S_1^i, \ldots, S_{k_i}^i$ such that for any couple of values belonging to the same partition, $va \in S_j^i, vb \in S_j^i$ any two solutions $(v_1, \ldots, v_{i-1}, va, v_{i+1}, \ldots, v_n)$ and $(v_1, \ldots, v_{i-1}, vb, v_{i+1}, \ldots, v_n)$ are equivalent.

GCSs can be built at each failure, leading to $\Delta^{(h)} = \{(I_1 \setminus SP_1^{(h)}), \ldots, (I_n \setminus SP_n^{(h)})\}$ at node h. $SP_i^{(h)}$ is the set of values removed from variable X_i by positive branching constraints. Let X_k be the branching variable at node $f(h)$. In the right subtree defined by node $f(h)$, for each $i, i \neq k, D_{new}(X_i) \subseteq \delta_i^{(h)}$. Thus, a matching of cardinality $n-1$ exists with $\delta_k^{(h)}$ and $D_{new}(X_k)$ unmatched.

[6] The dead-end seed is in fact independent from the symmetry considered.

Therefore, for each value $v* \in \delta_k^{(h)}$ all values v such that v and $v*$ belong to the same partition of the domain I_k can be removed from $D_{new}(X_k)$.

In [3], the concept of interchangeable values is extended to cycle of symmetries where values are symmetrical two by two. Therefore, if a value participates to no solution, all symmetrical values can be removed as well. Our approach applies also in this case, by defining cycle symmetries instead of simple interchangeable values.

7.4 Forth Specialization (CUTS4)

One of the first general filtering algorithm for removing symmetries was given in [7]. The authors propose an algorithm, called SBDS, that, under the hypothesis that branching decisions are of type $Var = val$ as opposed to $Var \neq val$, is able to remove a given symmetry σ. We show that SBDS can be reinterpreted as a specialization of our filtering algorithm.

Let A be the set of already assigned variables at node N ($X_i = v_i \forall X_i \in A$); and $\{\sigma_0, \sigma_1, \ldots, \sigma_n\}$ be the symmetry handled by SBDS. If X_k is the current branching variable at node N, the left branch imposes the constraint $X_k = val$. In [7], the authors show that the following constraints can be added in the right branch in order to remove symmetric solutions w.r.t $\{\sigma_0, \sigma_1, \ldots, \sigma_n\}$:

$\forall X_i \in A(X_i = v_i, \sigma_0(X_i) = \sigma_i(\{v_i\}) \wedge X_k \neq val \Rightarrow \sigma_0(X_k) \neq \sigma_k(\{val\})$

This constraint is a special case of the filtering algorithm proposed in Section 4. To prove that, let $I_i, i = 1, \ldots, n$ be the initial domain for variables X_i involved in the symmetry σ. By definition of symmetry, $I_i = \sigma_i(I_{idx(\sigma_0(X_i))}), i = 1, \ldots, n$.

Let now consider the GCS generated by the failure and backtracking from the left branch of node N. $\Delta = \{\delta_1, \ldots, \delta_n\}$ where $\delta_i = \{v_i\}$ $\forall i | X_i \in A$, $\delta_k = val$, $\delta_j = (I_j \setminus SP_j)$ $\forall j | X_j \notin A, j \neq k$, where I_j is the initial domain of variable X_j. Positive branching constraints have been applied only to variables in A. Thus $SP_j = \emptyset$ $\forall j | X_j \notin A$. Then, $\delta_j = I_j$ $\forall j | X_j \notin A, j \neq k$.

We show that when the left hand side of the implication is true, then the propagation algorithm in Section 4 imposes the right hand side to be true as well. Let consider the left hand side $(X_i = v_i, \sigma_0(X_i) = \sigma_i(\{v_i\}) \forall X_i \in A) \wedge X_k \neq val$ to be true. Then the following matching of cardinality $n-1$ exists: $(D_{new}(X_l), \delta_i), \forall l | X_l = \sigma_0(X_i)$, with $X_i \in A$, in fact $D_{new}(X_l) = \sigma_i(\{v_i\})$, and $\delta_i = \{v_i\}$.

All $\delta_j, | X_j \notin A, j \neq k$ contain the whole initial domain of the corresponding variable ($\delta_j = I_j \forall j | X_j \notin A, j \neq k$), and therefore they also find a match.

Finally, $\delta_k = \{val\}$, and $D_{new}(X_h) | \sigma_0(X_h) = X_k$ are unmatched. Therefore, the algorithm removes $\sigma_h(\delta_k)$ from X_h. This corresponds exactly to the pruning performed by SBDS, i.e., $\sigma(X_k \neq val)$. In the same way, it is easy to see that when the right hand side of the implication is false, then the left hand side must be false as well or a failure will be triggered.

A similar way of coping with symmetries is that of [2], which applies for any search strategy. When the branching strategy considers unary constraints on branching variables, our approach can again be seen as a generalization of that of [2]. However, when the hypothesis does not apply, their approach is more general provided that they are able to define the symmetrical counterpart for a general branching constraint. We are currently studying the extension of our approach to the case of non-unary branching constraints leading to the generation of *Local Cut Seeds* instead of Global ones.

7.5 Removing Families of Symmetries

A very common characteristic of symmetric combinatorial problems is that they present a very large (often exponential) number of symmetries. Consider, for example, a problem with permutation symmetries. Since there are $n!$ different permutations (i.e., $n!$ different symmetries), it is clearly impractical to remove all symmetries of the problem one by one. In case of exponential number of symmetries, in [7] the authors propose to remove only subsets of symmetries using conditional constraints. With our framework, we can either consider a subset of symmetries or a family of symmetries at a time. We believe that the separation between GCSs, and SRCs provides the basis for more sophisticated reasoning on *families of symmetries*. We can easily develop (as shown in Section 7.1) a specific cut generator for removing permutation symmetries, and the corresponding SRC. Using this *family of symmetry removal cut* we are able to efficiently remove *all* permutation symmetries together. We are currently developing other specific cuts for removing the value-permutation family of symmetry and rotation family of symmetry. Similarly to the introduction of global constraints in CP, we believe that the development of symmetry dependent cuts dedicated to families of symmetries could greatly increase the performance of CP in symmetric combinatorial problems.

8 Using the Framework

In this section, we will try to close the gap between the theoretical study of Section 3 and 4, and the practical use of our framework. We have implemented the framework by using ILOG solver. Symmetric values are pruned through SRCs which exploit the information contained in particular no-goods called GCSs. Global Cut Seeds (extended dead-end seeds) are created during tree search by a cut seed manager. The cut seed manager contains the set of problem variables and is informed of the application of the positive and negative branching constraints. Positive branching constraints are stored, while negative branching constraints trigger the generation of a new global cut seed.

A symmetry σ can be defined by a function returning, for each pair variable-value (X_i, v_h), a pair (X_j, v_k) such that $X_j = \sigma_0(X_i)$ and $v_k = \sigma_i(v_h)$. We built a cut generator responsible for generating a symmetry removal cut for a general symmetry σ for each GCS in the cut seed manager.

Once the cut seed manager and the cut generator have been provided, any type of symmetry can be easily handled by simply defining the function describing the symmetry itself, and passing it to the cut generator.

9 Computational Results

Although the main focus of this paper is to provide a general framework for removing symmetries, we show some computational results on well known symmetric CSP. The approach was tested on four problems: the n-Queen problem, the pigeonhole problem, the Ramsey problem, and the golfer problem. All tests run on a Pentium III 600 MHz.

The n-Queen problem has 7 rotational and mirror symmetries corresponding to the symmetries of a chessboard. The all-solutions n-Queen problem has been previously solved by [7] using the SBDS method. The use of the extended dead-end global cut seeds enables to detect symmetric configurations earlier than SBDS. In fact, on this problem, we reduce the number of fails obtained in [7]. Nevertheless, the conditional constraints used in SBDS are "lighter" than our symmetry removal cuts, and therefore the run time of our approach is higher than the one presented in [6]. The results for the 10 and 12 queens problems are shown in table 1 with and without symmetry removal cuts. On this problem, the only advantage of the cut generation technique w.r.t. SBDS lies on the fact that we are not forced to use a labeling strategy.

Table 1. Experimental Results on n-Queen problem

Problem	sym remov			symmetric		
	Nb Sol	Time	Fail	Nb Sol	Time	Fail
n-Queen 10	92	0.52	868	724	0.71	5451
n-Queen 12	1787	12	17427	14200	15	107797

The pigeonhole problem is a classical benchmark for methods aiming at removing symmetries. This problem has an exponential number of symmetries, being all possible permutations of variables. We built a symmetry removal cut able to effectively handle the family of permutation symmetries together. We tested the approach on problems of size 9 and 10, using a domain splitting branching strategy, and a labeling branching strategy. We compare our approach with the one proposed in [12], where symmetry breaking constraints were used. The results show that our approach is competitive with the one proposed in [12] where ordering constraints were added to the model. The results for the 12 pigeons problem are reported in table 2, where the first line uses a labeling strategy, while the second one uses a domain splitting branching strategy.

Table 2. Experimental Results on the 12 pigeon problem

Strategy	sym rem cut		sym break cst	
	Time	Fail	Time	Fail
labeling	0.1	1024	0.07	1280
dom split	0.7	7888	0.5	13531

The Ramsey problem is another well known symmetric problem. For its definition and CP model we refer to [12]. For $N < 17$ the problem is feasible and contains a large number of symmetrical solutions; for $N = 17$ the problem is infeasible. We have used the same model proposed by Puget in [12] and previously studied in [7].

The golfer problem was proposed by W. Harvey and can be found in the CSPLib. The problem states as follows: *G golfers want to play in Gr groups of W weeks each, in such a way that any two golfers play in the same group at most once. How many week can they do this for?.* An instance is described as $golfer(Gr, G, W)$[7].

To the best of our knowledge, all methods used to solve these problems [14] add symmetry breaking constraints to the model plus other methods (like SBDS). Although our objective is to remove all symmetries using symmetry removal cuts, we also add symmetry breaking constraints and symmetry removal cuts. On both problems we used GCSs to remove variable permutation type of symmetries and symmetry breaking constraint to remove other types of symmetries. The results for the Ramsey problem are comparable with the ones in [12] and the results for the golfer problem improve the ones published in [14]. However, the improvement w.r.t. [14] is mainly due to a different model of the problem. The important point here is the proof that the generation of GCSs, and the pruning of global cuts do not penalize the run time obtained with symmetry breaking constraint.

Table 3 shows the results for three Ramsey problems (*R6-All*, *R7-All* and *R17*), and for two golfer problems. Problems *R6-All* and *R7-All* find all solutions for problems with 6 and 7 nodes. *R17* is infeasible and the results refer to the proof of infeasibility. In the Ramsey problems only node permutation symmetries were removed using our method while color symmetries were handled as in [12]; combined symmetries on nodes and colors are not handled. Note that using a global symmetry removal constraint (removing all node permutations) we are able to reduce the number of symmetric solutions found w.r.t. the approach proposed in [12], and in [7]. Results on *golfer(4,3,4)* refer to the run time and number of fails to find all solutions. Results for the infeasible problem *golfer(4,3,5)* refer to the run time and number of fails to prove infeasibility. The task of removing all symmetries in these two problems is subject of current work.

10 Conclusions and Future Work

In this paper we propose a method to collect information during search and a general filtering algorithm able to use the collected information to prune the search space in symmetric CSPs. The method proposed does not interfere with problem dependent heuristics, and can be easily implemented in Constraint Programming when commonly verified hypothesis on branching constraint are respected. The general filtering algorithm can be, in practice, very easily special-

[7] The $golfer(4, 3, 4)$ has a large number of symmetric solutions while $golfer(4, 3, 5)$ has no solutions.

Table 3. Experimental Results on the Ramsey problem and Golfer problem

Problem	sym rem cut			sym break cst		
	Sol	Time	Fail	Sol	Time	Fail
R6-all	1161	0.43	864	7697	0.9	27
R7-all	20054	8.1	14367	252325	29.5	135
R17	0	0.4	181	0	0.2	636
golfer(4,3,4)	16	2.9	1235	16	1.6	1235
golfer(4,3,5)	0	3.0	1078	0	1.7	1473

ized to obtain constraints able to remove a given set of symmetries, and we show that many relevant previous approaches can be reinterpreted as specialization of the filtering algorithm proposed. Finally, the separation between the symmetry independent GCS data structure and the filtering algorithm allows to treat families of symmetry together. We are currently extending this framework to the case of non-unary branching constraints, developing symmetry removal cuts for other families of symmetries (permutations of values, rotations, etc.), and applying global cut seeds ideas in "quasi-symmetric" problems such as job-shop scheduling problems.

References

1. F. Bacchus. A uniform view of backtracking. In *Unpublished manuscript*, 2000. http://www.cs.toronto.edu/f̃bacchus/on-line.
2. R. Backofen and S. Will. Excluding symmetries in constraint based search. In *Proceedings CP'99*, pages 400–405, 1999.
3. B. Benhamou. Study of symmetries in constraint satisfaction problems. In *Proceedings of PPCP'94*, LNCS - Springer Verlag, 1994.
4. F. Focacci. *Solving Combinatorial Optimization Problems in Constraint Programming*. PhD thesis, Fac. Ingegneria, Universita' di Ferrara, Italy, 2001. http://www-lia.deis.unibo.it/Research/TechReport/lia01005.zip.
5. E. Freuder. Eliminating interchangeble values in constraint satisfaction problems. In *Proceedings AAAI'91*, pages 227–233, 1991.
6. I.P. Gent and B. Smith. Symmetry breaking during search in constraint programming. In *TR 99.02 School of Computer Studies*, 1999.
7. I.P. Gent and B. Smith. Symmetry breaking during search in constraint programming. In W.Horn, editor, *Proceedings ECAI2000*, pages 599–603, 2000.
8. W. Harvey and M. Ginsberg. Limited discrepancy search. In *Proceedings of the 14th International Joint Conference on Artificial Intelligence - IJCAI*, pages 607–615. Morgan Kaufmann, 1995.
9. P. Meseguer and C. Torras. Solving strategies for highly symmetric csps. In *Proceedings IJCAI'99*, pages 400–405, 1999.
10. P. Meseguer and C. Torras. Exploiting symmetries within constraint satisfaction search. *Journal of Artificial Intelligence*, 129:133–163, 2001.
11. M Padberg and G Rinaldi. Optimization of a 532-symmetric traveling salesman problem. *Operations Research Letters*, 6:1–8, 1987.
12. J. F. Puget. On the satisfiability of symmetrical constraint satisfaction problems. In *Proceedings ISMIS'93*, pages 350–361, 1993.

13. P. Roy and F. Pachet. Using symmetry of global constraints to speed up the resolution of constraint satisfaction problems. In *Proceedings of ECAI98 Workshop on Non Binary Constraints*, pages 27–33, 1998.
14. B. Smith. Reducing symmetries in a combinatorial design problem. In *Proceedings CPAIOR01*, 2001.
15. T. Walsh. Depth-bounded discrepancy search. In *Proceedings of the 15th International Joint Conference on Artificial Intelligence - IJCAI*. Morgan Kaufmann, 1997.

Symmetry Breaking*

Torsten Fahle, Stefan Schamberger, and Meinolf Sellmann

University of Paderborn
Department of Mathematics and Computer Science
Fürstenallee 11, D-33102 Paderborn
{tef,schaum,sello}@uni-paderborn.de

Abstract. Symmetries in constraint satisfaction or combinatorial optimization problems can cause considerable difficulties for exact solvers. One way to overcome the problem is to employ sophisticated models with no or at least less symmetries. However, this often requires a lot of experience from the user who is carrying out the modeling. Moreover, some problems even contain inherent symmetries that cannot be broken by remodeling. We present an approach that detects symmetric choice points during the search. It enables the user to find solutions for complex problems with minimal effort spent on modeling.

Keywords. symmetry breaking during search, graph partitioning, n-queens problem, golfer problem

1 Introduction

Symmetries can give rise to severe problems for solution algorithms as equivalent search regions are unnecessarily being explored more than just once. There are several ways of handling symmetries. One is to model the problem in such a way that no or at least less symmetries remain. This may also imply the adding of constraints which will only be satisfied by one assignment in each equivalence class. The major disadvantage of this approach is that it requires the user to have a certain level of experience, and sometimes it is even not possible to remove symmetries from a problem formulation as they are inherent to the given problem. Another way to break symmetries is to add constraints during the search for a solution. Those constraints can e.g. be derived from functions mapping single assignments to their symmetric versions.

We refer to all methods that avoid the exploration of symmetric parts of the search space as symmetry breaking strategies. However, there is of course a difference between approaches adding constraints to the model either statically or dynamically, and pruning/propagation approaches like the one we describe in this paper. Whenever a complete search is performed, all those methods have the same effect in that they do not expand symmetric choice points. Note, that

* This work was partly supported by the German Science Foundation (DFG) project SFB-376, and by the IST Programme of the EU under contract number IST-1999-14186 (ALCOM-FT).

T. Walsh (Ed.): CP 2001, LNCS 2239, pp. 93–107, 2001.

for incomplete searches, the approach presented here may be used as well, but requires caution with respect to the handling of previously visited search nodes (see Section 2.2).

1.1 State of the Art

Whereas model reformulations have been used successfully for quite a few specific problems in combinatorial optimization or constraint satisfaction, only very little research has been carried out on the topic of breaking symmetries systematically. In [7], Rothberg presents ways to remove symmetries from mixed integer problems (MIPs) by using cuts. Sherali and J.C. Smith discuss the effectiveness of adding constraints to a basic model in a number of case studies [10]. In [4], Gent and B. Smith develop a generic approach called SBDS. In every choice point, SBDS may extend the model dynamically by adding symmetry breaking constraints. For a combinatorial design problem, this approach has been shown to be efficient in combination with refined problem formulations which are used to remove symmetries already in the model [11]. As the number of symmetries in the given problem is enormous, the approach presented is not able to detect all of them and thus also gives non-unique solutions. In [6], Meseguer and Torras introduce a symmetry avoiding approach that works by adapting the search strategy.

We introduce a method that detects symmetric choice points within the search procedure. Every time the search algorithm generates a new choice point, we check if it is equivalent to or dominated by a node that has been expanded earlier. If so, the current choice point can be pruned. If not, it is processed normally. By checking whether a value assignment to a variable yields a symmetric search node, we can also use symmetries to shrink the domains of variables. However, that propagation can be very costly and thus is not suited in all cases. As the method is based on the detection of dominance relations between subtrees, we call it *Symmetry Breaking via Dominance Detection (SBDD).*

The remaining part of the paper is structured as follows: In Section 2, we formally introduce the SBDD approach. In the Sections 3, 4, and 5, it is applied to three different examples from combinatorial optimization and combinatorial design. Numerical results are given that circumstantiate the effectiveness of the approach.

2 Breaking Symmetries

The goal of breaking symmetries is to avoid the exploration of a search space $\triangle$ that can be mapped into a previously considered part $\square$ via a symmetry function. Because if $\square$ does not contain any solution, nor does $\triangle$. And otherwise, all solutions in $\triangle$ are symmetric to those already computed during the investigation of $\square$. Thus, symmetries can be used to prune the search tree, and also to remove values from variable domains that would yield the search to a symmetric part of the search space.

Before we outline the concept more formally, first we introduce some helpful definitions.

Definition 1. *Let* $\mathcal{X} = \{x_1 \dots x_n\}$ *denote the set of variables of the model to solve,* $D(x)$ *denote the domain of variable* $x \in \mathcal{X}$.

The tuple $P^c = (D^c(x_1), \dots, D^c(x_n))$ *denotes the current state in choice point* c. *We refer to the representation* P^c *as a* pattern.

Definition 2. *Let* $P^c = (D^c(x_1), \dots, D^c(x_n))$, $P^{c'} = (D^{c'}(x_1), \dots, D^{c'}(x_n))$.

- *We say that* $P^{c'}$ includes P^c ($P^c \subseteq P^{c'}$), *iff* $\forall\, x \in \mathcal{X} : D^c(x) \subseteq D^{c'}(x)$.
- *We set* $\mathcal{MD}^c := D^c(x_1) \times \dots \times D^c(x_n)$.
- *Given a* symmetry mapping function $\varphi : \mathcal{MD}^c \to \mathcal{MD}^c$, *we say that* $P^{c'}$ dominates P^c *(under the symmetry* φ*), iff* $\varphi(P^c) \subseteq P^{c'}$. *Then, we write* $P^c \sqsubseteq P^{c'}$.

Property 1. Given two choice points c and c', where c' is a successor of c in the search tree. Then it holds: $P^{c'} \sqsubseteq P^c$.

To ease the presentation, in the following we assume that the partitioning of the search space is achieved by using unary branching constraints. However, the concept can be generalized by adding information on the branching constraints active in a search node to the definition of a pattern that is used to reflect the current situation in the search. Then, the definitions of symmetry mapping functions etc. have to be adapted accordingly.

The approach we suggest for the pruning of symmetric parts of the search space is based on the following ingredients:

- A database $\mathcal{T}$ that stores information on the search space already explored.
- A problem specific function $\Phi : (P^\triangle, P^\square) \longrightarrow \{false, true\}$ that yields *true* iff the pattern $P^\triangle$ is dominated by $P^\square$ under some symmetry function φ.
- If symmetries shall also be used for propagation, a similar function is needed that, for all variables x, removes all values b from the domain of x for which $\Phi(P^\triangle[x = b], P^\square) = true$.

In every choice point, we check whether the current pattern $P^\triangle$ is dominated by some pattern in $\mathcal{T}$. And if so, the current node is pruned. Otherwise, we can use the function Φ for propagation. Thus, we perform Symmetry Breaking via Dominance Detection (SBDD). Figure 1 visualizes the general procedure. White nodes are still active, black nodes have been fully expanded already. Boxes represent patterns in $\mathcal{T}$, circles are patterns not or no longer contained in $\mathcal{T}$. Finally, $\triangle$ marks the current node. Originally, a pattern $\triangle$ must be checked against all fully expanded nodes (see Figure (1a)).

Obviously, it is problematic if we are to store all expanded nodes in $\mathcal{T}$. In the next Section, we describe how to handle $\mathcal{T}$ efficiently for depth first search (DFS). Then, we generalize the result to arbitrary search strategies.

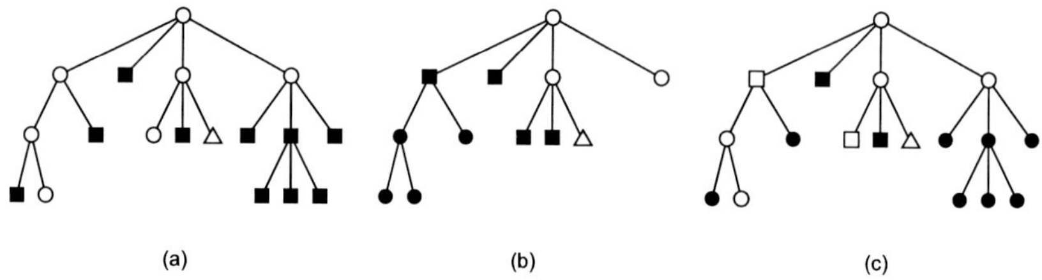

Fig. 1. The concept of SBDD

2.1 Efficient Realization in a Depth First Search

The key for an efficient realization of the general SBDD concept as described above is the observation that, within a DFS, we do not need to keep the information of all previously expanded nodes in the search tree. Instead, we can merge sibling entries in $\mathcal{T}$ on backtracking, thus summarizing and compressing the information gathered.

Lemma 1. *Let c be a choice point with state*

$$P^c = (D^c(x_1), \ldots, D^c(x_i), \ldots, D^c(x_n)),$$

where i is the index of the branching variable in c, and $D^c(x_i) = \{v_1, \ldots, v_l\} \subseteq D(x_i)$. Further, denote with $P^{c_k} = (D^{c_k}(x_1), \ldots, \{v_k\}, \ldots, D^{c_k}(x_n)) \; \forall\, 1 \leq k \leq l$ the states of the children $c_1, \ldots, c_n$ of c. Finally, let $P^{c'}$ the state in choice point c' with $P^{c'} \sqsubseteq P^{c_k}$ for some $1 \leq k \leq l$. Then, it holds $P^{c'} \sqsubseteq P^c$.

Proof. For all $x \in \mathcal{X}$ it holds that $D^{c_k}(x) \subseteq D^c(x)$. Thus, $\varphi(P^{c'}) \subseteq P^{c_k} \subseteq P^c$.

Using Lemma 1, SBDD in combination with DFS can now be realized efficiently: We start with $\mathcal{T} = \emptyset$ and process each choice point as follows:

---

1. Check the pattern P^c of the current choice point c against all patterns in $\mathcal{T}$. If $\exists\, P \in \mathcal{T} : \Phi(P^c, P)$ then fail. (Alternatively encapsulate this function in a constraint and use it for propagation as well.)
2. (normal processing within the choice point)
3. on backtracking: if there are more siblings to be expanded, then add the current pattern to $\mathcal{T}$, else delete all patterns of the other siblings from $\mathcal{T}$.

To subsume, when using DFS the current pattern needs only be compared with patterns left-adjacent to the path from the root to $\triangle$ (see Figure (1b)). Notice, that step 2 refers to the normal processing of a choice point that also takes place when no additional symmetry breaking framework is utilized, including the choice of a branching variable and the exploration of the children.

The efficiency of the approach mainly depends on the number of patterns that have to be checked. The number of patterns is at most as large as the depth of the search tree times the cardinality of the largest domain.

2.2 Arbitrary Search Strategies

Referring to the discussion on the size of $\mathcal{T}$, it seems to be impractical to combine SBDD with search strategies other than DFS, because the number of previously expanded nodes, and thus the size of $\mathcal{T}$ may be enormous. Or, the method becomes ineffective, because many nodes are closed late, as it is the case for breadth first search, for instance.

Nevertheless, with a slight modification, it is possible to cope with general search strategies. Let c be the current choice point, and P^c the corresponding pattern. The idea now is to check whether a symmetry function maps P^c to a pattern of a choice point c' that would have been processed *before* c *if DFS would have been applied* on a statical variable ordering (see Figure (1c)). If so, c is rejected, otherwise we proceed normally. Like that, we prune the tree because we detect that the work has either been carried out already or because we decide to do it later. Notice, that the current path in the search tree contains all information necessary to identify the patterns that are relevant for checking. The assumption of a statical variable ordering defines an ordering of all choice points. The approach rejects the current choice point iff a dominating pattern exists left of it in a DFS tree, i.e. iff the current choice point is *greater* than one that already has been or will be explored later. As an exhaustive search eventually will consider the leftmost nodes as well, we can be sure not to miss a solution.

Notice, that the search strategy is slightly affected by this procedure, because the exploration of choice points can be postponed by the symmetry breaking algorithm. However, one might expect a reasonable search strategy to rate symmetric parts of the search tree as equally important. In that case, the expanding of the current choice point is only postponed formally, but in fact is carried out next in a symmetric version.

After having outlined the general approach, in the following Sections we apply it to three different applications in the field of combinatorial optimization and constraint satisfaction.

3 Graph Partitioning

The first application of the method described in Section 2 is the graph bipartitioning problem. Given an undirected graph $G = (V, E)$, the graph bipartitioning problem asks for a set $V' \subset V$ such that the number of nodes in V' and $V \setminus V'$, differs at most by one, and the number of edges between both sets is minimal. This optimal number is often referred to as the *bisection width* of the graph. Graph bipartitioning is known to be NP-hard, exact solutions can only be computed for small graphs, i.e. $|V| < 200$. Interestingly, graph bipartitioning alone already induces a symmetry as the sets V' and $V \setminus V'$ can be exchanged.

An obvious symmetry breaking strategy in this case is the assignment of node 0 to set V'. Unfortunately, if graph G itself introduce symmetries, such an assignment does not break the resulting combined symmetries.

In parallel computing, connection networks are typically nicely structured and their symmetries are known. Graphs of the hypercube family have been studied intensively (see [1,5]). One popular network is the so-called *de Bruijn network* which is defined as follows:

Definition 3 (de Bruijn Network DB(k)). *The* de Bruijn Network of di- *mension k is a directed graph $DB(k) = (V_k, E_k)$. The edge set can be described best by associating the nodes with their corresponding binary representation, i.e. $V_k = \{(b_0 \dots b_{k-1}) \in \{0,1\}^k\}$. Then,*

$$E_k = \left\{(b\alpha, \alpha b),\ (b\alpha, \alpha\overline{b}) \,|\, \alpha \in \{0,1\}^{k-1},\ b \in \{0,1\}\right\}$$

where $\overline{b}$ denotes inverting bit b, i.e. $\overline{b} = 1 - b$.

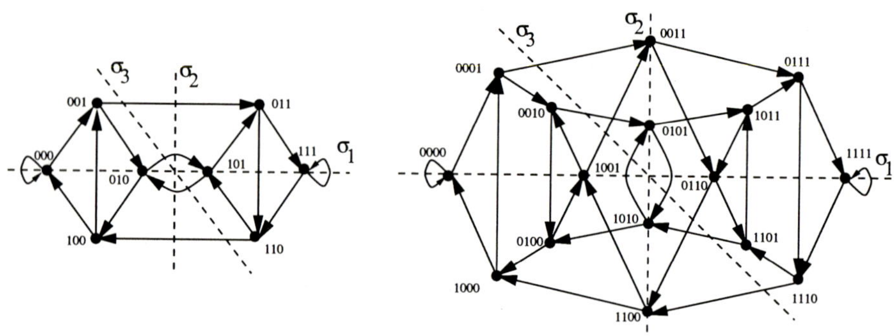

Fig. 2. de Bruijn networks of dimension 3 (left) and 4 (right). A node is marked by the binary string corresponding to its number. The dashed lines mark the symmetries of the de Bruijn network.

DB(k) contains 2^k nodes, each having degree 4, and 2^{k+1} edges. Furthermore, DB(k) contains 3 symmetries described by the following automorphisms:

$$\begin{aligned}
\sigma_1 &: V \to V,\ (b_0, b_1, \dots, b_{k-1}) \mapsto (b_{k-1}, b_{k-2}, \dots, b_0) \\
\sigma_2 &: V \to V,\ (b_0, b_1, \dots, b_{k-1}) \mapsto (\overline{b_0}, \overline{b_1}, \dots, \overline{b_{k-1}}) \\
\sigma_3 &: V \to V,\ (b_0, b_1, \dots, b_{k-1}) \mapsto (\overline{b_{k-1}}, \overline{b_{k-2}}, \dots, \overline{b_0})
\end{aligned}$$

Symmetries σ_1, σ_2 and σ_3 are visualized in Figure 2, where DB(3) and DB(4) are shown.

In the following, for the graph partitioning problem we will interpret any directed arc of DB(k) as an undirected edge.

3.1 Bisection Width of the de Bruijn Graph

It can be shown that the bisection width of DB(k) is $\Theta(\frac{2^k}{k})$, but there are only few results for concrete graphs. In [3], an optimal bisection width of 30 for DB(7) has been computed. At the time that paper was written, the algorithm based on LP bounds ran for about two weeks. To our knowledge, no exact bisection widths for bigger de Bruijn networks were known at that time.

Recently, Sensen [9] improved the well known bound based on clique embeddings (equivalent to 1-1 multi-commodity flows) by introducing variable multi-commodity flows. Using interior point methods for the resulting linear programs, he was able to prove an exact bisection width of 54 for DB(8). The symmetry detection routine described in Section 2 was used to avoid the consideration of symmetric parts of the search space. We refer to [9] for details on the overall approach. Here, we concentrate on the symmetry breaking. We use this example to show an easy application of SBDD rather than to underline its efficiency. For comparisons with SBDS we refer to Sections 4 and 5.

3.2 Symmetry Breaking for Graph Partitioning

When bipartitioning de Bruijn networks, seven symmetries have to be encoded in Φ. They stem from the three automorphisms of the network itself, the exchange of V' against $V \setminus V'$ and the combination of these symmetries.

For the graph bipartitioning problem, a pattern is implemented as an n-tuple $p \in \{0,1,*\}^n$. $p_i = 0$ ($p_i = 1$) means, that node $i \in V'$ ($i \in V \setminus V'$). $p_i = *$ means, that node i has not been assigned yet. The symmetry functions $\varphi_1, \ldots, \varphi_7$ permute the nodes according to σ_1, σ_2 or σ_3 and/or invert the entries. A pattern $P^{\triangle}$ is dominated by $P^{\square}$ iff there is a symmetry function φ_k, $1 \leq k \leq 7$ such that for all $0 \leq i < n$ it holds $\varphi_k(P^{\square})_i = *$ or $P_i^{\triangle} = \varphi_k(P^{\square})_i$.

It is also possible to use pattern information for propagation. Assume that there is a symmetry function φ_k and an index j, $0 \leq j < n$, such that $\varphi_k(P^{\square})_i = *$ or $P_i^{\triangle} = \varphi_k(P^{\square})_i$ $\forall 1 \leq i < n, i \neq j$ and $p_j^{\triangle} = *$. Let $\varphi_k(p^{\square})_j = 0$ (or $\varphi_k(p^{\square})_j = 1$). Then we can force that node j is in $V \setminus V'$ (or V', respectively).

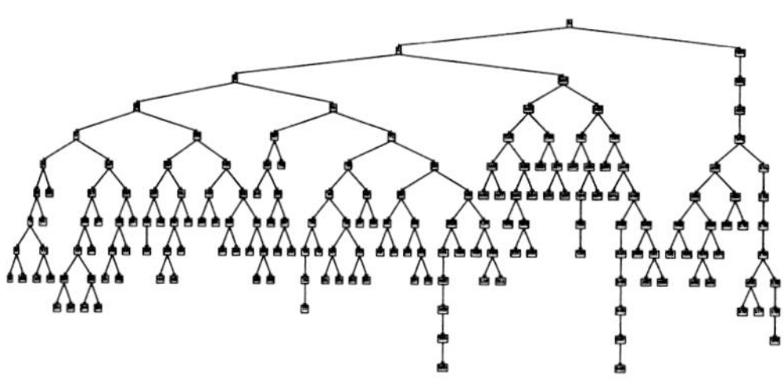

Fig. 3. The search tree for DB(8) bipartitioning when breaking all possible symmetries. Notice, that chains of choice points with only one successor result from detecting symmetric parts that are not explored.

Figure 3 and 4 show the different branching trees resulting from a computation of DB(8) with and without breaking symmetries. As expected, the search tree is much smaller in the first case. Notice, that huge parts of the solution

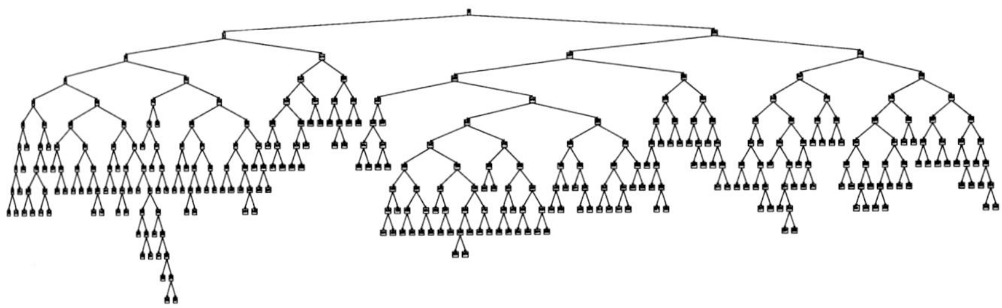

Fig. 4. The search tree for DB(8) bipartitioning without breaking any symmetries.

space are cut off by lower bound information. Thus, many symmetric subtrees are pruned early, thereby diminishing the effect of symmetry breaking. However, since in this approach the effort per choice point is very high due to expensive bound computations ($\approx$ 14 minutes per choice point), any reduction of the tree size reduces the overall cpu time consumption significantly. Thus, for the computation of the bisection width of DB(8), the breaking of symmetries was able to reduce the running time by roughly 2 days, whereby the remaining overall computation time then took 37.5 hours.

4 The Golfer Problem

We also applied SBDD to find solutions for the *Golfer Problem* (Problem 10 in CSPLib [2]) which is:

> *32 golfers want to play in 8 groups of 4 each week, in such way that any two golfers play in the same group at most once. How many weeks can they do this for?* [1]

This problem can be generalized by parameterizing it to w weeks and g groups of s players each, written as g-s-w from now on. In case of $(s-1)w = gs-1$, we achieve a specification where every player must play with every other exactly once. This problem is also known as the *Schoolgirl Problem* (see Section 4.3).

4.1 Symmetries in the Golfer Problem

Obviously, there is a lot of symmetry in the problem. First, players can be placed at any position within a group (φ_P), groups can be exchanged within their week (φ_G), and also the weeks can be ordered arbitrarily (φ_W). Furthermore, the players can be permuted (φ_X).

Following the idea that symmetry detection should also work well in combination with simple models, we have chosen a straightforward one that can be

[1] In the original problem it is clear that the golfers cannot play for more than 10 weeks. On the other hand, a solution for 5 weeks can be found easily without backtracking by always choosing the first possible player for a group in each week.

implemented with little effort using the ILOG Solver environment. The groups are modeled as sets of players with the cardinality of each set fixed to s. Each week contains g such sets, and the full pattern covers w weeks. To shrink the search space, we fix all players in the first week in increasing order. Additionally, we insert the first s players into the first s groups for all weeks thereafter. Finally, the first group of the second week is filled with the smallest players possible. All these assignments can be made without increasing the complexity of the model nor losing unique solutions.

4.2 Breaking Symmetries

By using set variables for each group, the model does not contain symmetry φ_P anymore. To detect the domination of patterns with respect to the other symmetries, we describe three symmetry detection functions Φ_G, $\Phi_{W,G}$ and $\Phi_{W,G,X}$, that are used during the search. Function $\Phi_{W,G}$ includes checks performed by Φ_G, and $\Phi_{W,G,X}$ includes those done by $\Phi_{W,G}$.

Φ_G Given two week indices $1 \leq i, j \leq w$, Φ_G is used to check if a week i of pattern $P^{\square}$ dominates week j of pattern $P^{\triangle}$ with respect to symmetry φ_G. This is done by checking whether all groups of week i of pattern $P^{\square}$ can be mapped to groups in week j of pattern $P^{\triangle}$. In the example shown in Figure 5, week 2 of pattern $P^{\square}$ cannot be mapped to week 1 of pattern $P^{\triangle}$, because players 1 ans 2 are in the same group in pattern $P^{\triangle}$, but are in different groups in pattern $P^{\square}$. A similar reasoning for players 2 and 3 prevents mapping week 3 of pattern $P^{\square}$ to week 2 of pattern $P^{\triangle}$. However, week 2 of pattern $P^{\square}$ can be mapped to week 2 of pattern $P^{\triangle}$, as the latter is just a specialization of the first.

$\Phi_{W,G}$ To break symmetries φ_W and φ_G, function $\Phi_{W,G}$ constructs a bipartite graph G containing a node for each week of $P^{\square}$ and $P^{\triangle}$. An edge is inserted, iff a week of $P^{\square}$ dominates a week of $P^{\triangle}$, which is determined using φ_G. If G contains a matching of cardinality w, $P^{\square}$ dominates $P^{\triangle}$. Again, Figure 5 shows an example.

$\Phi_{W,G,X}$ Incorporating also the last symmetry φ_X results in a huge computational effort, as $\Phi_{W,G}$ has to be applied for $(g \cdot s)!$ different permutations. To reduce the cost of this check, we use the fact that the first week of a pattern is always complete due to the fixed entries. Since it has to be matched to some other week, "only" $w \cdot (s!)^g \cdot g!$ possibilities are left. However, the test remains expensive. Therefore, we tried some variations reducing the frequency when $\Phi_{W,G,X}$ is applied. A parameter q can be set to restrict full symmetry checks to every q-th level of the search tree. Optionally, it can be limited to be performed on full patterns, i.e. leaves, only, which is the default.

4.3 Numerical Results

The model described has been implemented in ILOG Solver 5.0 and run for different configurations on a Sun Enterprise 450 (400 MHz UltraSparc-II). Tables 1

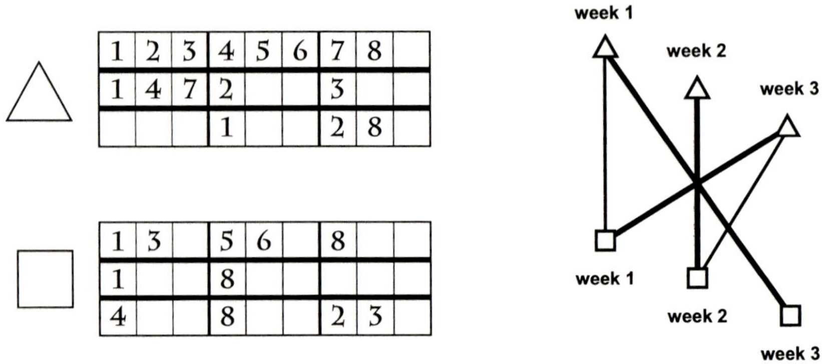

Fig. 5. The left hand side shows two patterns $P^{\triangle}$ and $P^{\square}$. Each pattern consists of three weeks (horizontal) of three groups of three players. Unbounded variables are left empty. On the right hand side, the corresponding bipartite graph is shown, containing a node for each week of both patterns. Since a matching of cardinality 3 exists (bold edges), $P^{\triangle}$ is dominated by $P^{\square}$.

and 2 show the results of the experiments. Apart from the time (in seconds) needed to find the first solution (t_1) and the time to find all solutions (t_{all}), the number of calls to the symmetry detection functions $\Phi_{W,G}$ and $\Phi_{W,G,X}$ is given. In the *sym*-section, $\Phi_{W,G}$ is applied to check for symmetries φ_W and φ_G in each node of the search tree. Since symmetries φ_X are not detected, there are many non-unique solutions found. In the *nosym*-section, $\Phi_{W,G}$ is also applied in every node of the search tree, and additionally $\Phi_{W,G,X}$ is applied in leaves preventing symmetric solutions from being written out. The Tables continue with the number of detected symmetries (*symmetries*), the number of choice points (*cp*), and the number of fails. Since we are using a very simple model for the problem, an approach that does not prevent the exploration of symmetric parts of the search tree is not applicable in practice as shown in [11]. Therefore, a comparison with such an approach is left out here.

Since invoking the symmetry detection function $\Phi_{W,G,X}$ is computationally very expensive, applying it in every search node does not improve the overall runtime, although the number of choice points is reduced. Thus, there is a trade-off between the reduction of choice points and the effort spent for the detection of symmetries. We have tested a scheme that applies $\Phi_{W,G,X}$ not only in leaves but also performs additional checks for all symmetries in every node in the q-th level of the search tree. Table 3 shows that invoking $\Phi_{W,G,X}$ too often rather increases the overall runtime, but applying it too rarely (e.g., only in leaves) is not the best choice, either. For the 4-4-4 problem, an invocation in about every 8-th level has shown to be the best. Similar observations have been made for other instances as well. Table 4 shows the improved running times for the 4-4-X problem.

Table 1. Results of the golfer 4-3-X problem.

problem	*solutions*	t_1	t_{all}	$\Phi_{W,G}$	$\Phi_{W,G,X}$	*symmetries*	*cp*	*fails*
				sym				
4-3-2	48	0.00	0.03	226	0	0	195	148
4-3-3	2688	0.02	6.09	99454	0	0	28299	25612
4-3-4	1968	0.05	26.70	382120	0	2808	94845	92878
4-3-5	0	0.00	36.34	412456	0	3120	100389	200390
				nosym				
4-3-2	1	0.00	0.04	226	47	47	195	194
4-3-3	4	0.01	10.00	99454	2687	2684	28299	28296
4-3-4	3	0.04	29.18	382120	1967	4773	94845	94843
4-3-5	0	0.00	36.28	412456	0	3120	100389	200390

Table 2. Results of the golfer 4-4-X problem.

problem	*solutions*	t_1	t_{all}	$\Phi_{W,G}$	$\Phi_{W,G,X}$	*symmetries*	*cp*	*fails*
				sym				
4-4-2	216	0.00	0.09	735	0	0	555	340
4-4-3	5184	0.01	8.71	74175	0	0	43755	38572
4-4-4	1296	0.01	20.53	140595	0	1296	82635	81340
4-4-5	432	0.01	25.90	132531	0	2160	75723	75292
4-4-6	0	0.00	30.76	114027	0	0	72267	72268
				nosym				
4-4-2	1	0.01	0.17	735	215	215	555	555
4-4-3	2	0.01	136.31	74175	5183	5182	43755	43754
4-4-4	1	0.01	22.09	140595	1295	2591	82635	82634
4-4-5	1	0.02	26.51	132531	431	2591	75723	75723
4-4-6	0	0.00	30.71	114027	0	0	72267	72268

Table 3. Results of the golfer 4-4-4 problem performing additional checks for symmetry φ_X in search tree nodes of every q-th depth.

level of $\Phi_{W,G,X}$	*solutions*	t_1	t_{all}	$\Phi_{W,G}$	$\Phi_{W,G,X}$	*symmetries*	*cp*	*fails*
				nosym				
1	1	0.01	698.51	0	26	18	82	82
2	1	0.02	271.35	29	27	24	123	123
4	1	0.02	101.26	156	79	79	339	339
8	1	0.01	14.51	5292	1296	1296	4730	4730
leaves	1	0.01	22.09	140595	1295	2591	82635	82634

Table 4. Improved results of the golfer 4-4-X performing additional checks for symmetry φ_X in search tree nodes of every 8-th depth.

problem	*solutions*	t_1	t_{all}	$\Phi_{W,G}$	$\Phi_{W,G,X}$	*symmetries*	*cp*	*fails*
			nosym, level of $\Phi_{W,G,X} = 8$					
4-4-2	1	0.00	0.17	735	215	215	555	555
4-4-3	2	0.01	134.10	5283	1298	1297	6492	2891
4-4-4	1	0.01	14.51	5292	1296	1296	4730	4730
4-4-5	1	0.02	15.68	5291	1295	1296	4722	4722
4-4-6	0	0.00	17.16	5290	1295	1295	4714	4715

SBDS versus SBDD. In [11], an SBDS approach is developed for the golfer problem. As has been mentioned before, to break symmetries SBDS inserts additional constraints to the model during the search, and hands them over to the solver. Even in combination with complex models, due to the large amount of symmetries in the golfer problem, the approach presented is not able to add all constraints necessary to break all symmetries. However, SBDS allows ro reduce the number of search nodes significantly.

When using SBDD for the golfer problem, it is possible to find unique solutions only, even in combination with a very simple model. Obviously, the performance of the approach presented here can be further improved by using more sophisticated problem formulations. However, the focus in this paper was not to develop a most efficient approach for the golfer problem, but to present a method for symmetry breaking that can be used efficiently also by inexperienced users and in combination with simple models.

We are currently working on an approach combining SBDD and a refined model for the golfer problem, that is able to solve the so called schoolgirl problem.

In 1850, Thomas Kirkman stated the following problem, which in fact is equivalent to the golfer 5-3-7 problem:

> *How can 15 schoolgirls walk in 5 rows of 3 each for 7 days so that no girl walks with any other girl in the same triplet more than once?*

Preliminary experimentation shows that this approach is able to compute all 7 unique solutions to the schoolgirl problem in less than 2 hours.

5 The n-Queens Problem

Finally, we consider the classical n-queens problem. It consists of placing n queens on a $n \times n$ chessboard such that no two queens can capture each other. That is, no two queens are allowed to be placed on the same row, the same column, or the same diagonal.

Nowadays it is possible to find *one* solution using CP for 1 000-queens in a few seconds. Asking for *all non-symmetric* solutions of n-queens requires some more effort. In the following, we describe the SBDS approach of Gent and Smith [4] on the n-queens problem and compare it to SBDD.

5.1 Breaking Symmetries in n-Queens

It is easy to see that the n-queens problem incorporates seven symmetries, namely reflections in the horizontal and vertical axis, reflections in the main diagonals, and rotations through $90°, 180°, 270°$.

SBDS. In [4], SBDS is introduced first and tested on a variety of problems. The approach is general and compatible with different search strategies. A user of the concept only needs to provide symmetry functions mapping a single assignment to its symetric version.

In a choice point where we assign, $x = v$ on the left and $x \neq v$ on the right branch, SBDS adds all constraints that are necessary to prevent the solver from exploring a subtree symmetric to an already investigated one. By keeping track of all already broken symmetries, only necessary constraints are posted, thus keeping the overhead small.

SBDD. For the n-queens problem, a pattern p is an n-tuple where p_i is the column number in which the queen covering row i is placed, or, in case the position of the queen in row i has not been set yet, $p_i = *$. E.g., the pattern corresponding to the first chessboard in Figure 6 is $p = (0, 4, 1, 5, 2, 6, 3)$.

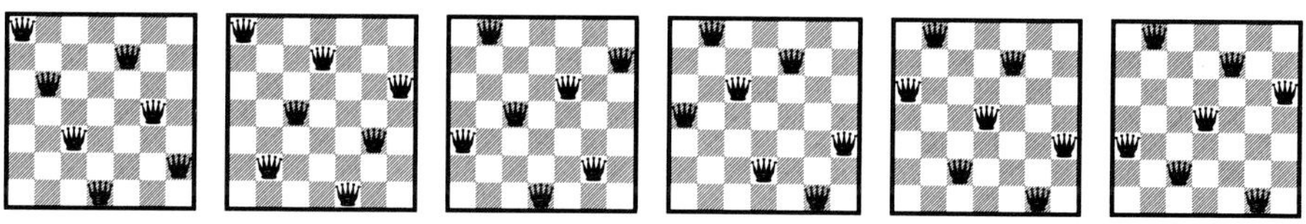

Fig. 6. Six out of forty solutions of 7-queens are unique

5.2 Experimental Evaluation

For our experiments, we used the following standard model for n-queens:

- Each row $i = 0, \ldots, n-1$ is represented by an integer variable x_i. Assigning $x_i = j$ corresponds to placing a queen in row i and column j.
- Additional integer variables y_i and w_i, $i = 0, \ldots, n-1$, are used to check the diagonals of the chessboard. We post the constraints $y_i = x_i + i$, $w_i = x_i - i$.
- The domains are $x \in \{0, \ldots, n-1\}$, $y \in \{0, \ldots, 2n\}$, $w \in \{-n, \ldots, n\}$.
- AllDiff constraints on x, y, and w ensure that no two queens can capture each other.

In contrast to the algorithm we developed for the golfer problems, here we use symmetry also for propagation. A constraint is posted to the model that keeps track of the current situation in the search. As propagation turned out to

Table 5. Solving n-queens without breaking symmetries (*sym*), with breaking symmetries via *SBDS*, and by avoiding them via *SBDD*. Computing times are given in seconds.

	sym			*SBDS*			*SBDD*	
n	*solutions*	*fails*	*time*	*solutions*	*fails*	*time*	*fails*	*time*
4	2	4	0.01	1	3	0.00	6	0.00
5	10	4	0.00	2	4	0.00	13	0.00
6	4	35	0.01	1	11	0.02	31	0.01
7	40	69	0.02	6	19	0.01	56	0.02
8	92	289	0.04	12	63	0.01	130	0.03
9	352	1111	0.16	46	216	0.04	397	0.08
10	724	5072	0.57	92	851	0.13	1464	0.29
11	2680	22124	2.49	341	3808	0.53	5991	1.26
12	14200	103956	11.88	1787	17673	2.52	27731	6.27
13	73712	531401	61.56	9233	89534	12.55	140348	33.11
14	365596	2932626	337.00	45752	483214	69.62	746530	189.07
15	2279184	16920396	1946.07	285053	2784876	403.16	4391877	1213.36
16	14772512	105445065	12154.60	1846955	17277508	2608.51	27153758	7463.62

be rather expensive, we limited the number of calls to the propagation routine to one.

We also implemented a version of SBDS and tested it on the model described above. Both codes were running on the same Sun Enterprise as the program for the golfers problem in Section 4.

Table 5 compares the number of solutions, the number of fails, and the computation time for calculating *all* solutions (*sym*), calculating only *unique* solutions via SBDS, and *unique* solutions using SBDD, respectively. We omit the number of solutions for *SBDD* as it is identical to *SBDS*. The results given for SBDS are similar to those given in [4]. Only the number of fails slightly differs, which we expect to be caused by small variations in the implementation and the different CP engines used (Solver 4.3 vs. Solver 5.0).

Obviously, SBDD does not perform as well as SBDS on the n-queens problem. The reason for this is, that the number of symmetries is rather small (compared to the golfer problem), which makes the application of different additional symmetry breaking constraints on backtracking favorable.

6 Conclusion

We have suggested an approach for breaking symmetries that is based on the detection of dominance relations between choice points. The method is generally applicable and works in combination with all exhaustive search strategies while it may overrule strategies other than DFS. Moreover, it removes symmetric parts of the search tree efficiently in combination with any model. Thus, it can also be used easily by inexperienced users on straightforward models that do not break symmetries themselves.

The ease of use mainly results from the fact that it is only necessary to define the pattern structure and a function that checks if one pattern dominates another. This algorithmic approach allows somewhat more flexibility than a model that breaks symmetries itself, as has been demonstrated for the golfer problem when adapting the frequency of certain symmetry considerations.

The method has shown to be easily applicable without causing a big implementation overhead on three very different applications from combinatorial optimization and constraint satisfaction. Moreover, it worked efficiently even in combination with very easy models and also on highly symmetric problems.

As a disadvantage, the use of patterns appears to be less efficient on transparent and – with respect to symmetry considerations – manageable problems such as the n-queens problem. There, the dynamic adding of constraints in an SBDS fashion is clearly favorable.

Acknowledgment. We would like to thank Barbara Smith, Warwick Harway, and three anonymous referees for helpful comments.

References

1. J.C. Bermond and C. Peyrat. De bruijn and kautz networks: a competitor for the hypercube? *Proc. of the 1st Europ. Workshop on Hypercubes and Distributed Computers*, pp. 279–293, North-Holland, 1989.
2. *CSPLib: a problem library for constraints*, maintained by I.P. Gent, T. Walsh, B. Selman, `http://www-users.cs.york.ac.uk/~tw/csplib/`
3. R. Feldmann, B. Monien, P. Mysliwietz, and S. Tschöke. A Better Upper Bound on the Bisection Width of de Bruijn Networks. Tech. Report University of Paderborn. short version: *Proc. of STACS'97*, Springer LNCS 1200:511-522, 1997.
4. I.P. Gent and B. Smith. Symmetry Breaking During Search in Constraint Programming. *Proc. of ECAI'2000*, Berlin, pp. 599–603, 2000.
5. F.T. Leighton. *Introduction to Parallel Algorithms and Architectures: Arrays, Trees, Hypercubes.* Morgan Kaufmann Publishers, 1992.
6. P. Meseguer and C. Torras. Exploiting symmetries within constraint satisfaction search. *Artificial Intelligence*, 129 (1–2) pp. 133–163, 2001.
7. E. Rothberg. Using Cuts to Remove Symmetry. *ISMP'00*, Atlanta, 2000.
8. ILOG. ILOG SOLVER. Reference manual and user manual. V5.0, ILOG, 2000.
9. N. Sensen. Lower Bounds and Exact Algorithms for the Graph Partitioning Problem using Multicommodity Flows. *Europ. Symp. on Algorithms, ESA'01*, 2001.
10. H.D. Sherali and J. Cole Smith. Improving Discrete Model Representation Via Symmetry Considerations. *ISMP'00*, Atlanta, 2000.
11. B. Smith. Reducing Symmetry in a Combinatorial Design Problem. *Proc. of CPAIOR'01*, Wye/UK, pp. 351–360, April 2001.

The Non-existence of (3,1,2)-Conjugate Orthogonal Idempotent Latin Square of Order 10*

Olivier Dubois[1] and Gilles Dequen[2]

[1] LIP6, CNRS-Université Paris 6
4 place Jussieu, 75252 Paris cedex 05, France.
Olivier.Dubois@lip6.fr
[2] LaRIA, Université de Picardie Jules Verne
CURI, 5 Rue du moulin neuf, 80000 Amiens, France.
dequen@laria.u-picardie.fr

Abstract. To denote a (3,1,2)-conjugate orthogonal idempotent latin square of order n, the usual acronym is (3,1,2)-COILS(n). Up to now, existence of a (3,1,2)-COILS(n) had been proved for every positive integer n except $n = 2, 3, 4, 6$, for which the problem was answered in the negative, and $n = 10$, for which it remained open. In this paper, we use a computer program to prove that a (3,1,2)-COILS(10) does not exist. Following along the lines of recent studies which led to the solution, by means of computer programs, of many open latin square problems, we use a constraint satisfaction technique combining an economical representation of (3,1,2)-COILS with a drastic reduction of the search space. In this way, resolution time is improved by a ratio of 10^4, as compared with current computer programs. Thanks to this improvement in performance, we are able to prove the non-existence of a (3,1,2)-COILS(10).

1 Background and Notations

Over the last decade, it has become apparent that the field of finite algebra could largely benefit from computational techniques. Particularly in the area of latin squares, theorem-proving or constraint-satisfaction techniques have led to the solution of many open problems [6,7,11,3,5]. A quite extensive recent survey on the latin square is provided by F. E. Bennett and L Zhu [1]. A latin square may be defined as an $n \times n$ grid with each integer $0, 1, \ldots, n-1$ appearing exactly once in each row and column. Such a grid can be viewed as defining a binary operation, say $*$, on the set $S = 0, 1, \ldots, n-1$; and the above property means that S with $*$ is a *quasigroup*, i.e. equations are uniquely solvable: for $a, b \in S$ there is a unique $x \in S$ such that $a * x = b$, and a unique $y \in S$ such that $y * a = b$. The operation of a quasigroup is often written multiplicatively and referred to as a product; note, however, that associativity is *not* assumed. Henceforth we shall consider only quasigroups with S as underlying set. The quasigroups $Q_1 =< S, * >$ and

* This work was supported by Advanced Micro Devices Inc.

T. Walsh (Ed.): CP 2001, LNCS 2239, pp. 108–120, 2001.

$Q_2 =< S, \circ >$, with binary operations $*$ and $\circ$, are *isomorphic* iff there is a permutation g of S such that for all a, b, $g(a * b) = g(a) \circ g(b)$. A property much studied over many decades, especially because of statistical applications, is the orthogonality of two quasigroups. $Q_1 =< S, * >$ and $Q_2 =< S, \circ >$ are said to be *orthogonal* iff for all $a, b, c \in S$, $a * b = c * d$ and $a \circ b = c \circ d$ together imply that $a = c$ and $b = d$. In other words, when superimposing the multiplication tables of $Q_1 =< S, * >$ and $Q_2 =< S, \circ >$, every ordered pair of integers occurs exactly once among the n^2 pairs $(a, b) \in S^2$ thus formed. Noteworthy special orthogonal quasigroup pairs are the so-called *conjugate orthogonal quasigroups*. A *conjugate* Q_2 of a quasigroup Q_1 is obtained by carrying out a given permutation on the three elements of the multiplication table: index of row, index of column, and value of the product. That is for example, given $Q_1 =< S, * >$, for any $a, b, c \in S$ such that $a * b = c$, the so-called 312-conjugate is the quasigroup denoted by $Q_2 =< S, *_{312} >$ such that $c *_{312} a = b$. Thus from a quasigroup $< Q, * >$, six conjugate quasigroups can be obtained, corresponding to the six permutations of three elements. These conjugate quasigroups are denoted in a self-explanatory way: $< Q, *_{123} >$, $< Q, *_{132} >$, $< Q, *_{213} >$, $< Q, *_{231} >$, $< Q, *_{312} >$, $< Q, *_{321} >$. In a conjugate pair (Q_1, Q_2) with *specified* permutation σ, Q_2 is redundant, so for brevity we talk of the σ-conjugate latin square Q_1. An additional quasigroup property is often considered, namely *idempotence*. A quasigroup is idempotent iff for every $a \in S$, $a * a = a$. The conjunction of all quasigroup properties just introduced is indicated by the acronym COILS, and thus the symbol (i,j,k)-COILS(n) used throughout this paper means '(i,j,k)-Conjugate Orthogonal Idempotent Latin Square'. The existence of (i,j,k)-COILSs and of related structures has been intensively studied, and a list of open problems appears in [1]. Very many open problems have yielded to the use of powerful model generators. A by now well-established nomenclature, introduced in [5,10], sees the existence or non-existence problems for (2,1,3)-COILS, (3,2,1)-COILS, and (3,1,2)-COILS as respectively QG0, QG1, and QG2. The notation QG$i(n)$ with $i = 0, 1, 2$ is used where the order n of the quasigroup has to be made explicit. Other quasigroup problems are listed in Table 1. Among the open

Table 1. Constraints of QGi ($i \in \{3, ..7\}$)

code name	constraint to be satisfied
QG3	$(a * b) * (b * a) = a$
QG4	$(b * a) * (a * b) = a$
QG5	$((b * a) * b) * b = a$
QG6	$(a * b) * b = a * (a * b)$
QG7	$(b * a) * b = a * (b * a)$

problems solved by means of model generators let us mention that first solutions, for example the QG5(9) were obtained using J. Zhang's *FALCON* [16]. For several quasigroups (and several orders) solutions of QG2, QG3, QG4, QG5, QG6,

QG7 [9] were obtained by the model generators *MGTP*, *DDPP*, *FINDER*, due respectively to M. Fujita et al., M. Stickel, J. Slaney [4,15,8]. Similarly, solutions were found for several quasigroups (and several orders) of QG2, QG5, and QG6 [14] with H. Zhang's *SATO* [12]. Finally, let us also mention that the model generator *SEM* by J. Zhang and H. Zhang [17] has solved new open problems of types QG5, QG7, QG8, QG9.

In this paper we are concerned with quasigroups of type QG2. In 1992 the situation was as follows. The existence of quasigroups QG2(n) had been proved for any integer n except $n = 2, 3, 4, 6$ for which it had been proved that no quasigroup QG2 of such orders existed, and $n = 10, 12, 14, 15$ for which the answer was unknown. In 1995 M. Stickel gave a solution for the QG2(12) using DDPP, then in 1996 H. Zhang et al. gave a (non-idempotent) solution of a QG2(14) and a QG2(15) [14]. In order to completely solve the problem QG2, there remained to find an answer for the QG2(10). Solving the QG2(10) had been noted as particularly difficult in [9,14]. We developed a specific model generator, *qgs*, which we present in this paper, to solve the QG2(10). *qgs* allows us to conclude that there exists no quasigroup of type QG2 and order 10. *qgs* is a model generator along the lines of existing ones. The essential innovation in *qgs* is to provide an effective resolution strategy for exploring a huge search space when there is no solution. The efficiency of *qgs* resides essentially in two things:

- a representation of the constraints inherent in the quasigroup and in the orthogonality property, which offers an economical treatment of the elementary operations concerned with search space exploration,
- A drastic reduction of the search space by eliminating redundant isomorphic subspaces.

These two points are explained in detail in Sections 2 and 3 below. We then give the ensuing conclusion as to non-existence. For information, the last section gives performance comparisons of *qgs* vs. *FINDER*, *SATO*, and *SEM* on type-QG1, and QG2 quasigroup resolution.

2 Encoding the Constraints Inherent in the Quasigroup of Type QG2

Using the notations of the foregoing section, $< Q, * >$ denotes a quasigroup on the set $S = 0, 1, \ldots, n-1$, n being the order of the quasigroup, and $*$ the associated binary operation.

There are essentially two types of constraints that a quasigroup of type QG2 and order n has to satisfy:

- the constraints related to the existence of the quasigroup itself, demanding that any integer $i \in S$ appear just once in every line and column of the multiplication table of the quasigroup.
- the constraints related to the orthogonality property, demanding that for any $i, j, k, l \in S$, the two pairs $(i * j, i *_{312} j)$ and $(k * l, k *_{312} l)$ be distinct.

Two options are available for the treatment of these constraints. They may be expressed as propositional clauses. In this case the treatment will consist in investigating the existence of a truth value assignment to the propositional variables so as to satisfy all clauses. Or, the constraints may be expressed as first order predicates. In this case, the treatment will consist in searching for an assignment of values to the variables within their respective domains, so as to satisfy the predicates. The main existing model generators, such as *DDPP*, *FINDER*, and *SATO*, treat the constraints as propositional clauses. This choice made by the authors of these model generators, seems to stem from the intention to build general-purpose model generators, i.e. ones able to handle all problems pertaining to quasigroups and related structures, and beyond that, other finite algebra problems if necessary. Indeed, when the constraints of the problem under consideration are expressed as propositional clauses, the resolution strategy is independent of the original problem. The specificity of the latter is taken account of at the level of the translation of the constraints into propositional clauses. If, on the other hand, the choice is made to represent the constraints as predicates, then efficiency requires that the treatment within the model generator be specifically designed for these particular constraints. Every new type of problem then calls for a specific model generator. These two ways of handling the constraints entail different resolution strategies. For example, regarding quasigroups, propositional constraints allow a propositional variable to be associated with the value of a *cell* in the multiplication table. A heuristic will therefore be able to make decisions at the level of the value of a cell. By contrast, constraints expressed as predicates only allow a variable to be associated with a cell in the multiplication table, not with its values. For the reasons just mentioned, namely generality of purpose of the model generator's treatment, and subtlety of the resolution strategy, the choice of propositional clauses to model the constraints is justified. However, we show in the sequel that the cost of treatment of the propositional clauses for the quasigroups of type QG2 is exorbitant. Besides, this problem was clearly raised in [13] in connection with *SATO*.

We developed a model generator *qgs* specifically for the resolution of quasigroup problems of type QG2. In *qgs* the constraints are treated in the classical form of CSPs. Thus, to each cell of the multiplication table to be constructed for a quasigroup, i.e. to every $i, j \in S = 0, 1, \ldots, n-1$, we associate a variable $X(i,j)$ with domain $DX(i,j) = S$. Similarly, to each cell of the multiplication table of the (3,1,2)-conjugate, a variable $Y(i,j)$ is associated with domain $DY(i,j) = S$. Finally, to each pair $(u,v) \in S^2$, we associate a variable $Z(u,v)$ whose domain is $0, 1$. All variables $Z(u,v)$ have the value 0 initially, and $Z(u,v)$ takes the value 1 as soon as a pair has appeared in the quasigroup and its conjugate such that $X(i,j) = u$ and $Y(i,j) = v$. In *qgs*, resolution treatment consists in developing a search tree by assigning the variables $X(i,j)$ admissible values within their domains. A value is admissible for a variable $X(i,j)$ if it complies with the quasigroup constraint, i.e. if no variable $X(i,k)$ or $X(k,j)$ (for some $k \in S$) has already been assigned the same value; and with the orthogonality constraint, i.e., pairing it with the value in the conjugate's homologous cell does not produce a pair already giving the associated variable Z the value 1.

qgs and existing model generators dealing with propositional constraints explore the search space by means of similar elementary operations. Particularly two are:

- assigning a variable a value, with the ensuing propagations;
- the backtracking process, which consists in reconstructing a previous state of the data structures.

We did a performance comparison of these two types of operations in *qgs* as against *SATO*, which happened to be the most convenient for such a study. Tables 2 and 3 give mean treatment times for each operation, performed 500,000 times by both *SATO* and *qgs* in the course of processing problems from QG2(8) to QG2(15) (without, of course, the aim to solve them).

Table 2. Mean time (on first 500,000 calls to the branch function) to assign a value to a cell with *qgs* and *SATO*

Quasigroup Problem	*SATO* (in μseconds)	*qgs* (in μseconds)
QG2(8)	1239.5	10.2
QG2(9)	2458.4	11.1
QG2(10)	4863.9	13.5
QG2(11)	8578.9	15.6
QG2(12)	12996.1	17.9
QG2(13)	21447.8	19.4
QG2(14)	34666.9	22.1
QG2(15)	57362.1	24.2

Table 3. Mean time (on first 500,000 calls to the backtrack function) to rebuilt a cell with *qgs* and *SATO*

Quasigroup Problem	*SATO* (in μseconds)	*qgs* (in μseconds)
QG2(8)	139.7	0.8
QG2(9)	319.5	1.0
QG2(10)	685.9	1.1
QG2(11)	1276.9	1.1
QG2(12)	2096.3	1.1
QG2(13)	3244.6	1.2
QG2(14)	4634.6	1.2
QG2(15)	6119.1	1.3

Tables 2 and 3 show that mean processing times for *SATO* are 100 to 1000 higher than those of *qgs*. Figure 1 allows the comparative evolution of these

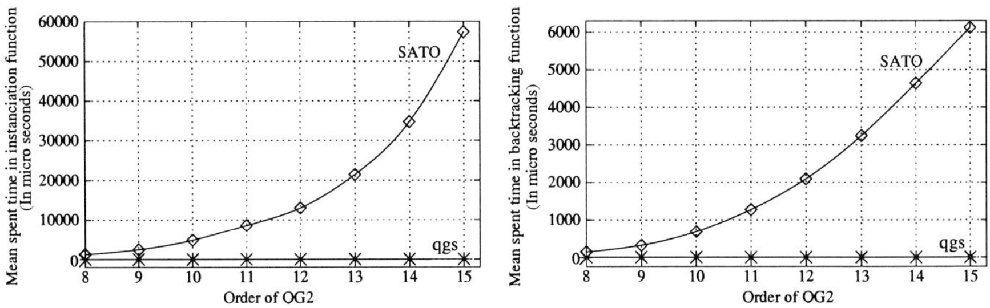

Fig. 1. Mean time (on first 500,000 calls to the functions) to compute the next node and rebuilt it with *SATO* and *qgs*

times, as a function of quasigroup order, to be visualized for both generators. The curves linking the points corresponding to the values in Tables 2 and 3 only serve for visual appreciation, they obviously have no reality since the order of a quasigroup is an integer. Such substantial differences in processing time for similar operations in *SATO* and *qgs* are explained by the size of the structures handled by *SATO*. For an order n QG2 quasigroup, *SATO* is known to generate clauses containing exactly n^3 variables. The clauses generated to express the orthogonality constraint have 4 literals, and their number is in $O(n^6)$, lending itself to reduction to $O(n^4)$ [13]. The clauses generated to express the quasigroup constraints have 2 literals, and their number is in $O(n^2)$. Table 4 gives, for

Table 4. Number of variables, clauses of size 4 and 2 in the cnf formulae generated by *SATO*

Quasigroup Problem	number of 4-Clauses	number of 2-Clauses	number of propositionnal variables
QG2(6)	1550	970	216
QG2(7)	5781	2002	343
QG2(8)	17775	3696	512
QG2(9)	46096	6288	729
QG2(10)	105187	10050	1000
QG2(11)	217561	15290	1331
QG2(12)	416366	22352	1728

problems QG2(6) to QG2(12), the exact numbers of generated clauses for both the orthogonality and the quasigroup constraints. As for *qgs*, the number of variables is $O(n^2)$, the orthogonality constraint translates into a test of the form $Z(u,v) \leq 1$ for every $u, v \in S$, and the quasigroup constraints translate into a domain update for the variables $X(i,j)$ et $Y(i,j)$, together with a test on domain size for $X(i,j)$.

The question may be raised as to whether the computation time ratios between *SATO* and *qgs*, as shown in Tables 2 and 3, carry over to their respective global resolution times when effectively solving QG2 quasigroups. Table 5 gives these resolution times, which do not provide a definite answer. Apart from

Table 5. Run time of *qgs* and *SATO* on some orders of QG2 problems

Quasigroup Problem	*SATO* (in seconds)	*qgs* (in seconds)
QG2(6)	0.00s	0.00s
QG2(7)	0.02s	0.00s
QG2(8)	8.72s	17.15s
QG2(9)	319.09s	0.25s

QG2(6) which has no solution but for which the processing time is too short, for the other QG2s which have a solution, the time depends essentially not on the time taken to explore the search space, but of the speed at which the solution is found. In the next section, search space exploration times will be compared on subproblems of QG2(10), which has no solution.

To conclude, for solving the problem QG2(10), and thus to possibly explore in its entirely the search space for this quasigroup, the computation time ratios in the above test make it reasonable to assume that it is more efficient to treat QG2 quasigroup constraints in the CSP form rather than in the propositional clauses form.

3 Reducing the Search Space by Eliminating Redundant Isomorphic Quasigroups

To make the resolution of QG2(10) possible, space search reduction is essential. In [5], M. Fujita *et al.* have defined a rule, called *Least Number Heuristic* (*LNH*) by J. Zhang in [16], aimed at eliminating some subspaces isomorphic to ones already searched. Recall that two quasigroups $Q_1 =< S, * >$ and $Q_2 =< S, \circ >$ are isomorphic if there exists a permutation g on the n integers of S, such that for all $i,j \in S$, $g(i*j) = g(i) \circ g(j)$. This property of isomorphism between quasigroups is crucial for search space reduction. The rule defined by M. Fujita et al. is used in the model generators *FALCON*, *MGTP*, *DDPP*, *FINDER*, *SATO*, and *SEM* for solving quasigroups. Applied to the first row of a quasigroup multiplication table, this rule permits the search space of idempotent QG2(10) quasigroups to be reduced to quasigroups whose first row is one of the 21 listed in the first column of Table 6, labelled L1 to L21. However, the search space reduction thus attained is still quite insufficient for solving QG2(10). A first remark makes it

Table 6. The 21 first rows produced by *lnh* reduced to 8 rows by isomorphisme

configurations of first lines in $QG2(10)$ *value of cells: (0,0),(0,1),...,(0,9)*		Permutations to apply	Configuration obtain after permutation
L1:	0, 2, 3, 1, 5, 6, 4, 8, 9, 7	none	–
L2:	0, 2, 1, 4, 3, 6, 5, 8, 9, 7	none	–
L3:	0, 2, 1, 4, 3, 6, 7, 8, 9, 5	none	–
L4:	0, 2, 1, 4, 5, 3, 7, 8, 9, 6	none	–
L5:	0, 2, 3, 4, 1, 6, 7, 8, 9, 5	none	–
L6:	0, 2, 3, 1, 5, 6, 7, 8, 9, 4	none	–
L7:	0, 2, 1, 4, 5, 6, 7, 8, 9, 3	none	–
L8:	0, 2, 3, 4, 5, 6, 7, 8, 9, 1	none	–
L9:	0, 2, 1, 4, 3, 6, 7, 5, 9, 8	0, 1, 2, 3, 4, 7, 8, 9, 5, 6	L2
L10:	0, 2, 1, 4, 5, 3, 7, 6, 9, 8	0, 1, 2, 7, 8, 9, 3, 4, 5, 6	L2
L11:	0, 2, 3, 1, 5, 4, 7, 6, 9, 8	0, 7, 8, 9, 1, 2, 3, 4, 5, 6	L2
L12:	0, 2, 1, 4, 5, 6, 7, 3, 9, 8	0, 1, 2, 5, 6, 7, 8, 9, 3, 4	L3
L13:	0, 2, 3, 1, 5, 4, 7, 6, 9, 8	0, 5, 6, 7, 8, 9, 1, 2, 3, 4	L3
L14:	0, 2, 1, 4, 5, 6, 3, 8, 9, 7	0, 1, 2, 6, 7, 8, 9, 3, 4, 5	L4
L15:	0, 2, 3, 1, 5, 4, 7, 8, 9, 6	0, 3, 4, 5, 1, 2, 6, 7, 8, 9	L4
L16:	0, 2, 3, 1, 5, 6, 7, 4, 9, 8	0, 3, 4, 5, 6, 7, 8, 9, 1, 2	L4
L17:	0, 2, 3, 4, 1, 6, 5, 8, 9, 7	0, 6, 7, 8, 9, 1, 2, 3, 4, 5	L4
L18:	0, 2, 3, 4, 1, 6, 7, 5, 9, 8	0, 6, 7, 8, 9, 3, 4, 5, 1, 2	L4
L19:	0, 2, 3, 4, 5, 1, 7, 8, 9, 6	0, 5, 6, 7, 8, 9, 1, 2, 3, 4	L5
L20:	0, 2, 3, 4, 5, 6, 1, 8, 9, 7	0, 4, 5, 6, 7, 8, 9, 1, 2, 3	L6
L21:	0, 2, 3, 4, 5, 6, 7, 1, 9, 8	0, 3, 4, 5, 6, 7, 8, 9, 1, 2	L7

possible to further enhance the space search reduction resulting from the rule of M. Fujita et al. For each of rows L9 to L21, there exists a permutation of the (ordered) integer sequence $0, 1, 2, \ldots, 10$ into an integer sequence appearing in the 2nd column of Table 6, such that, applying it to 0 and to the integers $j, k \in S$ in the binary operation $0*j = k$ associated with each of rows L9 to L21, a binary operation $g(0) * g(j) = 0 * g(j) = g(k)$ is obtained which actually corresponds to one of those associated to the first 8 rows, L1 to L8. The row labels associated by permutation to rows L9 to L21 are listed as the 3rd column. As a result of this observation, the search for QG2(10) quasigroups may be restricted to those whose first row is among those labelled L1 to L8. This shrinks the search space by a ratio of nearly 3. In spite of this additional search space reduction, we were not able using *qgs* to complete the processing of QG2(10) for one of the rows L1 to L8. We therefore sought to enlarge the configuration of a row for which isomorphisms between quasigroups could be checked on a computer. Two configurations were studied: **(a)** first row and second row denoted RR, **(b)** first row and first column denoted RC.

(a) Configuration of type RR.
A computer program was used to enumerate a set of 69,411 configurations of type RR, denoted c_i, with $i = 1, 2, \ldots 69411$, for an idempotent QG2(10) quasigroup,

such that no permutation g exists which, when applied to the binary operation associated with an arbitrary RR configuration of an idempotent QG2(10), returns a binary operation associated with one of the configurations c_i. In other words, the configurations *not* belonging to the c_i's are such that there exists a permutation g of the integers of S with $g(0) = 0$ and $g(1) = 1$ which, when applied to the integers $j, k, m, p \in S$ of the binary operation defined by $0 * j = k$ and $1 * m = p$ associated with each of these configurations, produces a binary operation $0 * g(j) = g(k)$ and $1 * g(m) = g(p)$ associated to one of the configurations c_i. A quasigroup with such a configuration corresponding by a permutation to one of the configurations c_i, is isomorphic to one of the quasigroups having the latter configuration. It may therefore be rejected. To enumerate the configurations c_i, we first selected the first row configurations liable to belonging to the configurations c_i, in order to limit the combinatorial enumeration. We found 17 such first rows. We then enumerated all possible second row configurations compatible with one of these 17 first rows. All in all, 69,411 configurations of type RR were found to conform to the above conditions. The time required to carry out these enumerations was $1h53mn$.

(b) Configuration of type RC.
A similar enumeration to the above was accomplished, substituting the first column for the second row. In this case, the permutations g considered only satisfy the relation $g(0) = 0$, and not $g(1) = 1$ as previously. It was possible in this case to carry out the enumeration directly from the first 8 rows $L1, \ldots, L8$. Moreover, the admissible permutations are those which, when applied to Li for $i = 1, \ldots, 8$, return Li identically. We call them identity permutations. Table 7 gives the number of these unit permutations for each row Li. Then, enumerating all possible column configurations compatible with each of the rows Li, we obtained a total of 16,085 configurations of type RC. The time required to carry out these enumerations was $21s$. Table 7 gives the detail of configuration numbers for the first 8 rows. It may be observed that, as expected, the number of retained configurations increases as the number of unit permutations decreases.

Table 7. Non-isomorphic RC configurations produced

configurations of first lines in $QG2(10)$	Number of identity permutations	Number of non isomorphic RC configurations
L1	161	290
L2	143	318
L3	39	1094
L4	23	1820
L5	19	2178
L6	17	2442
L7	13	3100
L8	8	4843

The number of *RC* configurations is seen to be inferior to that of *RR* configurations by a factor of more than 4. This result was predictable since globally a maximum of 8!2! permutations can be applied to the set of *RR* configurations, as against a higher maximum of 9! for the set of *RC* configurations.

The choice between the two types *RR* and *RC* of configurations for solving QG2(10) was determined by the shortest processing time that could be expected from either type. Table 8 gives the mean resolution time with *qgs* on samples of 100 randomly drawn configurations. Configurations of type *RC* are also seen

Table 8. Mean nodes and mean time to solve 100 randomly drawn configurations based on 8 first rows of QG2(10)

Algorithm	*RC*		*RR*	
	mean #nodes (std dev.)	mean time (std dev.)	mean #nodes (std dev.)	mean time (std dev.)
SATO	$12.6\ 10^6$ ($3.2\ 10^6$)	3 days, 19h (1 day, 16h)	-	> 7 days
qgs	$22.1\ 10^6$ ($7.4\ 10^6$)	11m 38s (3m 55s)	$115.4\ 10^6$ ($43.5\ 10^6$)	59m 31s (22m 21s)

to have a mean resolution time smaller than those of type *RR* by a factor of 5. This a priori hard to predict result may be understood by examining Figure 2. For *RC* configurations, the number of pairs formed by combining values in the multiplication table of the quasigroup and that of its conjugate is 10, as against 4 for *RR* configurations. If we assume the orthogonality constraint to be paramount in determining resolution time, it is normal that this time should be smaller for *RC* than for *RR* configurations.

Finally, the 16,085 *RC* configurations were solved with *qgs* on PCs equipped with AMD Athlons running at 1GHz under a Linux operating system. No QG2(10) was found, enabling us to conclude to the non-existence of a QG2(10). The total cumulative processing time was 137 days, 4 hours, and 20 minutes. The total number of branches of the trees developed by *qgs* was 387,732,916,219. The mean processing time of an *RC* configuration was 736 seconds, with a standard deviation of 256 seconds. The mean number of branches of the search tree for an *RC* configuration was 24,105,000, with a standard deviation of 8,115,000. We have attempted, on the other hand, to provide an estimate of *SATO*'s processing time on this problem, to be compared with that of 2^{25} workdays $\sim$ 30643 years given in [14]. We ran *SATO* on a sample of 100 *RC* configurations. The mean time was 3 days 19 hours, with a standard deviation of 1 day 16 hours. From this mean time, *SATO*'s total processing time to solve the 16,085 *RC* configurations can be estimated as about 167 years. The time ratio with respect to *qgs* is seen to be about 440, in absolute coherence with those indicated for elementary operations (for QG2(10)) in Section 2, Table 2 and Table 3. Turning now to *SATO*'s habitual working conditions, i.e. without using *RC* configurations to reduce the search space, an estimate of total resolution time for QG2(10) is 9240 years,

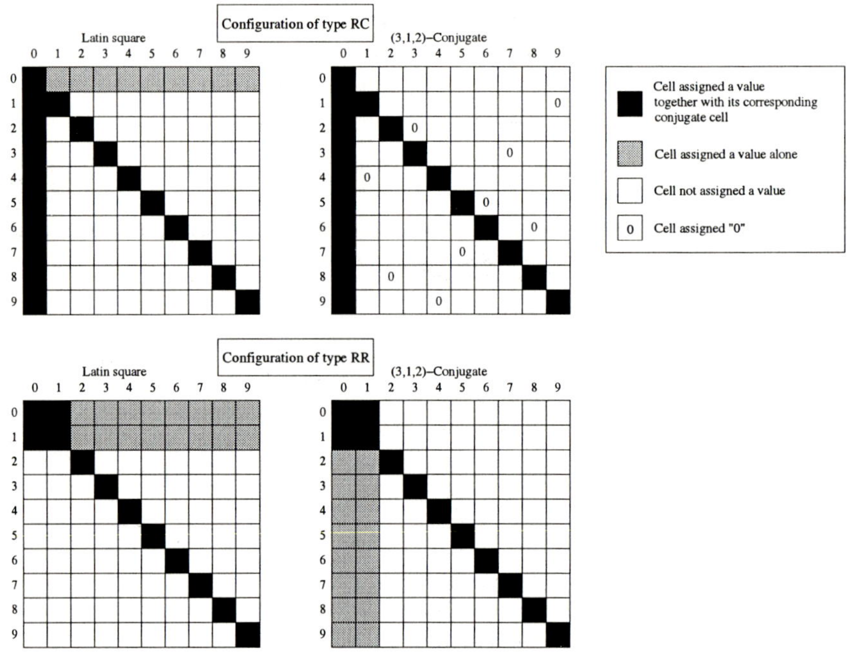

Fig. 2. Orthogonality on the configurations "*RR*" and "*RC*"

which may be viewed as of similar order of magnitude to that of 30,643 years given by its author in [14].

4 Further Results

For the reader's information, *qgs*'s performance on quasigroups of type QG1 and QG2 is compared to that of the main model generators, namely *SATO*, *FINDER*, *SEM*, and, as a reference point, the 'general' SAT solver *posit* [2]. As regards *qgs*, we applied the same strategy of elimination of isomorphic subspaces as in the resolution of QG2(10). Table 9 lists resolution tree sizes for *posit*, *SATO*, and *qgs* in terms of nodes developed. *FINDER* and *SEM* do not appear in Table 9, since they do not provide explicit branch numbers on each of their runs.

It should be noted that *qgs* develops trees of significant size, much larger for instance than those developed by *SATO* (by a factor of up to 50). These differences have an explanation. Almost all quasigroups in this test have a solution. *qgs*, contrary to *SATO*, specializes in search space exploration and not in solution finding. In terms of computing time, in Table 10 *qgs* is seen the fastest (beyond order 7 we were unable to give computation time for *FINDER* and *SEM* which are tricky to use, especially in the phase of problem description using first order logic).

Table 9. Number of nodes developed in the search tree of *posit*, *SATO* and *qgs* for QG1 and QG2 of order from 6 to 9

Quasigroup Problem	model exist ?	*posit* in #nodes	*SATO* in #nodes	*qgs* in #nodes
QG1(6)	no	1	7	63
QG1(7)	yes	4	15	106
QG1(8)	yes	198	84313	18091
QG1(9)	yes	–	4.51 10^5	229 10^5
QG2(6)	no	0	6	23
QG2(7)	yes	16	8	6
QG2(8)	yes	21	11173	15453
QG2(9)	yes	240 10^5	1.83 10^5	110 10^5

Table 10. Computation time of *posit*, *SEM*, *FINDER*, *SATO* and *qgs* to prove existence or non-existence of QG1 and QG2 of order from 6 to 9

Quasigroup Problem	model exist ?	*posit* run time in seconds	*SEM* run time in seconds	*FINDER* run time in seconds	*SATO* run time in seconds	*qgs* run time in seconds
QG1(6)	no	0.01s	0.20s	0.03s	0.01s	0.00s
QG1(7)	yes	0.00s	4.57s	0.27s	0.03s	0.01s
QG1(8)	yes	0.20s	–	–	107.02s	0.70s
QG1(9)	yes	> 7 days	–	–	1170.59s	632.98s
QG2(6)	no	0.00s	0.63s	0.03s	0.00s	0.00s
QG2(7)	yes	0.00s	0.72s	0.23s	0.02s	0.01s
QG2(8)	yes	0.04s	–	–	8.72s	1.75s
QG2(9)	yes	59451.00s	–	–	319.09s	227.79s

5 Conclusion

The last few years have been very rich in respect of quasigroup resolution. Computer programs developed to this effect have made possible the resolution of many open problems about quasigroup existence or non-existence. For QG2, solely the order 10 remained open and unattainable by current computer programs, irrespective of whether the approach was sequential or parallel. With the aim of solving QG2(10), we have presented a new solver, *qgs*, specialized in the resolution of quasigroups of type QG2. *qgs* achieves a very significant reduction of the search space, allied with economical processing. We were thus able to disprove the existence of QG2(10) in 140 days of sequential computation. This leads to the conclusion that designing specialized model generators can increase the likelihood of solving further open problems.

References

1. Bennett, F., Zhu, L.: Conjugate-orthogonal Latin squares and related structures. In: J. H. Dinitz & D. R. Stinson (eds): Contemporary Design Theory: A Collection of Surveys. John Willey & Sons 1992
2. Freeman, J. W.: Hard random 3-SAT Problems and the Davis-Putnam Procedure. Artificial Intelligence **81**, no 1–2, (1996) 183–198
3. Fujita, H., Hasegawa, R.: A Model Generation Theorem Prover in KL1 Using Ramified-Stack Algorithm. In: Proc. of ICLP-91 (1991) 535–548
4. Fujita, M., Hasegawa, R., Koshimura, M., Fujita, H.: Model Generation Theorem Provers on A Parallel Inference Machine. In: Proc. of FGCS-92 (1992)
5. Fujita, M., Slaney, J., Bennett, F.: Automatic generation of some results in finite algebra. In: Proc. of Int. Joint Conference on Artificial Intelligence (1993) 52–57
6. Lam, C. W. H., Thiel, L., Swierck, S.: The non-existence of Finite Projective Planes of Order 10. Canadian Journal of Mathematics (1989) 1117–1123
7. McCune, W.: OTTER 2.0. In: Proc. of CADE-10 (1990) 663–664
8. Slaney, J.: FINDER: Finite Domain Enumerator. In: Version 3.0 Notes and Guide (1993) 1–22
9. Slaney, J., Fujita, M., Stickel, M.: Automated reasoning and exhaustive search: Quasigroup existence problems. In: Computers and Mathematics with Applications (1995) 115–132
10. Stickel, M., Zhang, H.: First results of studying quasigroup identities by rewriting techniques. In: Proc. of Workshop on Automated Theorem Proving (1994)
11. Stickel, M. E.: A Prolog Technology Theorem Prover: Implementation by an Extended Prolog Compiler. Journal of Automated Reasoning (1998) 353–380
12. Zhang, H.: SATO: A decision procedure for propositional logic. Association for Automated Reasoning Newsletter (1993) 1–3
13. Zhang, H: Specifying Latin squares in propositional logic. In: Association for Automated reasoning Newsletter, Essays in honor of Larry Wos, Chapter 6,. MIT Press 1997
14. Zhang, H., Bonacina, M. P., Hsiang H.: PSATO: a distributed propositional prover and its application to quasigroup problems. Journal of Symbolic Computation (1996) 543–560
15. Zhang, H., Stickel, M.: Implementing the Davis-Putnam Method. Journal of Automated Reasonning **24**, no 1/2 (2000) 277–296
16. Zhang, J.: Constructing finite algebras with FALCON. Journal of Automated Reasoning (1996) 1–22
17. Zhang, J., Zhang, H.: SEM: a System for enumerating Models. In: Proc. of International Joint Conference on Artificial Intelligence (1995) 11–18

Random 3-SAT and BDDs: The Plot Thickens Further

Alfonso San Miguel Aguirre[1*] and Moshe Y. Vardi[2**]

[1] Dept. of Computer Science
Instituto Tecnologico Autonomo de Mexico
Rio Hondo 1, 01000 Mexico City, Mexico
[2] Department of Computer Science
Rice University
6100 S. Main St MS 132
Houston TX 77005-1892,USA

Abstract. This paper contains an experimental study of the impact of the construction strategy of reduced, ordered binary decision diagrams (ROBDDs) on the average-case computational complexity of random 3-SAT, using the CUDD package. We study the variation of median running times for a large collection of random 3-SAT problems as a function of the density as well as the order (number of variables) of the instances. We used ROBDD-based pure SAT-solving algorithms, which we obtained by an aggressive application of existential quantification, augmented by several heuristic optimizations. Our main finding is that our algorithms display an "*easy-hard-less-hard*" pattern that is quite similar to that observed earlier for search-based solvers. When we start with low-density instances and then increase the density, we go from a region of polynomial running time, to a region of exponential running time, where the exponent first increases and then decreases as a function of the density. The locations of both transitions, from polynomial to exponential and from increasing to decreasing exponent, are algorithm dependent. In particular, the running time peak is quite independent from the crossover density of 4.26 (where the probability of satisfiability declines precipitously); it occurs at density 3.8 for one algorithm and at density 2.3 for for another, demonstrating that the correlation between the crossover density and computational hardness is algorithm dependent.

1 Introduction

The last decade has seen an intense focus on the complexity of randomly generated combinatorial problems. This interest was stimulated by the discovery of a fascinating connection between the *density* of combinatorial problems and their computational complexity, see [11,31]. A problem that has received a lot of attention in this area is the *3-satisfiability problem* (3-SAT), which is a paradigmatic combinatorial problem,

---

* Part of this work was done while this author was on sabbatical at Rice University, funded in part by CONACyT grant 145502.

** Work partially supported by NSF grants IIS-9908435, IIS-9978135, CCR-9988322, and EIA-0086264, and by a grant from the Intel Corporation.

T. Walsh (Ed.): CP 2001, LNCS 2239, pp. 121–136, 2001.

and also important for its own sake. An instance of 3-SAT consists of a conjunction of clauses, each one a disjunction of three literals. The goal is to find a truth assignment that satisfies all clauses. The density of a 3-SAT instance is the ratio of the number of clauses to the number of Boolean variables (we refer to the latter number as the *order* of the instance). Clearly, a low density suggests that the instance is under-constrained, and therefore is likely to be satisfiable, while a high density suggests that the instance is over-constrained and is unlikely to be satisfiable. Experimental research [15,31] has shown that for ratio below (roughly) 4.26, the probability of satisfiability goes to 1 as the order increases, while for ratio above 4.26 the probability goes to 0. At 4.26, the probability of satisfiability is 0.5. We call this density the *crossover density*. Formally establishing the crossover density is known to be quite difficult, and is the subject of continuing research, cf. [18,17,1].

The experiments in [15,31], which applied algorithms based on the so-called *Davis-Logemann-Loveland method* (abbr., DLL method) (a depth-first search with unit propagation [16]), also show that the density of a 3-SAT instance is intimately related to its computational complexity. Intuitively, it seems that under-constrained instances are easy to solve, as a satisfying assignment can be found fast, and over-constrained instances are also easy to solve, as all branches of the search terminate quickly. Indeed, the data displayed in [15,31] show how the running time increases with increasing density until the crossover density and then declines with increasing density, with a marked running-time peak essentially at the crossover density. What we see at the crossover density is in essence a *phase transition*, viz., a marked qualitative change in the structural properties of the problem. This pattern of behavior with a running-time peak at the crossover density is called the *easy-hard-easy* pattern and is the subject of extensive research, cf. [30].

In [13] it was pointed out that this picture is quite simplistic for various reasons. First, it is not clear where the boundaries between the "easy", "hard", and "easy" regions are. Second, the terms "easy" and "hard" do not carry any rigorous meaning. The computational complexity of a problem is typically studied on an infinite collection of instances, and is specified as a function of problem size or order. The easy-hard-easy pattern, however, is observed when the order is fixed while the density varies, but once the order is fixed, there are only finitely many possible instances. For that reason, theoretical analyses of the random 3-SAT problem focus on collections of fixed-density instances, rather than on collections of fixed-order instances.[1] Third, in the context of a concrete application, e.g., bounded model checking [4], it is typically the order that tends to grow while the density stays fixed, for example, as we search for longer and longer counterexamples in bounded model checking. Thus, the easy-hard-easy pattern tells us little about the complexity of 3-SAT in such settings. Until recently, however, there was little experimental work that studies how the running time of a SAT solver varies as a function of the order for fixed-density instances. Finally, the experiments reported in [31,15] are focused solely on DLL-based algorithms. While these are indeed the most popular algorithms for the satisfiability problem, one cannot jump to conclusions about

[1] For example, it is known that in the high-density region, above density 5.2, the DLL method is provably exponential [12]; see also [3].

the inherent and practical complexity of random 3-SAT based solely on experiments using these algorithms.

The goal of the research reported in [13] was to determine how the average-case complexity of random 3-SAT, understood as a function of the order for fixed density instances, depends on the density for a variety of SAT solvers. Is there a phase transition in which the complexity shifts from polynomial to exponential? Is such a transition dependent or independent of the solver? To explore these questions, Coarfa et el. [13] set out to obtain a good coverage of an initial quadrangle of the two-dimensional $d \times n$ quadrant, where d is the density and n is the order, exploring the range $0 \leq d \leq 15$ using three different SAT solvers, embodying different underlying algorithms: GRASP, which is based on the DLL method [27], the CPLEX MIP Solver, which is a commercial optimizer for integer-programming problems, and CUDD[2], which implements functions to manipulate Reduced Ordered Binary Decision Diagrams (ROBDDs), providing an efficient representation for Boolean functions [7].[3]

The findings in [13] show that for GRASP and CPLEX the easy-hard-easy pattern is better described as an *easy-hard-less-hard* pattern, where, as is the standard usage in computational complexity theory, "easy" means *polynomial time* and "hard" means *exponential time*. When we start with low-density instances and then increase the density, we go from a region of polynomial running time to a region of exponential running time, where the exponent first increases and then decreases as a function of the density. Thus, one observes at least *two* phase transitions as the density is increased: a transition at about density 3.8 from polynomial to exponential running time and a transition at about density 4.26 (the crossover density) from an increasing exponent to a decreasing exponent.[4] The region between 3.8 and 4.26 is also characterized by the prevalence of very hard instances, the so called "heavy-tail phenomenon", cf. [23,28,30].

A very different picture emerged in [13] for CUDD (described in Section 3). Here the algorithm is exponential (in both time and space) for densities between 0.5 and 15. There is, however, no running-time peak near the crossover density and no heavy-tail phenomenon was observed. A peak, however, is observed in the size of the final ROBDDs constructed by the algorithm at about density 2, indicating a phase transition at about this density. At a very low density (0.1), a polynomial (cubic) behavior is observed, which suggests that another phase transition is "lurking" between densities 0.1 and 0.5. Thus, unlike earlier predictions (cf. [26]), phase-transition phenomena related to random 3-SAT are not solver independent.

Our interest in studying ROBDD-based algorithms is motivated by the fact that ROBDDs have proven to be very effective in the context of hardware verification [9,25] and they are very different from standard search-based SAT solving methods. Uribe and Stickel [35] compared ROBDDs with the DLL method for SAT solving, concluding that the methods are incomparable, and that ROBDDs dominate the DLL method on many examples. Recent work by Groote and Zantema formally proved the incomparability of

[2] `http://bessie.colorado.edu/~fabio/CUDD`

[3] We use ROBDDs to represent Boolean functions. This is different than the usage in [10] of (zero-suppressed) ROBDDs to represent compactly sets of clauses.

[4] The polynomial to exponential phase transition, preceding the crossover point, was discovered independently by Cocco and Monasson [14].

ROBDDs and resolution (which is the proof system underlying the DLL method) [22]. The comparison in [13] between GRASP and CPLEX, on one hand, and CUDD, on the other hand, is, however, somewhat unenlightening. Unlike GRASP and CPLEX, CUDD does not search for a single satisfying truth assignment. Rather, it constructs a compact symbolic representation of the set of *all* satisfying truth assignments and then checks whether this set is nonempty. (Note, however, that for extremely sparse formula, the ROBDD-based algorithm is polynomial in spite of the fact that we have exponentially many satisfying truth assignments, due to the compactness of the representation.) In this paper we study the behavior of *pure* ROBDD-based SAT solvers. A pure SAT solver has to simply decide for a given propositional formula whether or not it is satisfiable; unlike search-based SAT solvers, it need not return a satisfying truth assignment.[5] The key step in constructing an ROBDD-based pure SAT solver is an aggressive application of existential quantification. (We describe the algorithm later on.) Once we have the basic algorithm, we can apply several heuristic optimizations, resulting in rather dramatic improvement in running time.

Our aim, however, is not to directly compare the performance of the different algorithms in order to see which one has the "best" performance, but rather to understand their behavior in the $d \times n$ quadrant in order to make qualitative observations on how the complexity of random 3-SAT is viewed from different algorithmic perspectives. It is important to note that the algorithms we used do not explicitly refer to the density of the input instances. Thus, a qualitative change in the behavior of the algorithm, as a result of changing the density, indicates a genuine structural change in the SAT instances from the perspective of the algorithm.

Our main finding is that the optimized ROBDD-based pure SAT-solving algorithms display *easy-hard-less-hard* pattern that is quite similar to that observed for GRASP and CPLEX in [13]. When we start with low-density instances and then increase the density, we go from a region of polynomial running time, to a region of exponential running time, where the exponent first increases and then decreases as a function of the density. Thus, one again observes at least *two* phase transitions as the density is increased: a transition from polynomial to exponential running time, accompanied by a heavy-tail phenomenon, and a transition from an increasing exponent to a decreasing exponent. Surprisingly, however, the location of both phase transitions is algorithm dependent. Unlike what has been observed so far in numerous papers, the transition from increasing to decreasing exponent, which corresponds to the running-time peak as one increase the density for a fixed order, does not occur at the crossover density of density 4.26. For one algorithm this transition occurs at density 3.8 and for the other at density 2.3.

Our findings provide further experimental evidence for the following two hypotheses. First, the running-time peak can change with the choice of solver not only in a minor way, as noted in [28], but in quite a major way, moving quite dramatically from the crossover density. This demonstrates that the correlation between the crossover density and computational hardness is algorithm-dependent, challenging the widely-held belief that the "hard problems" are always located at the crossover density [11]. Second, as

[5] Note, however, that by successively assigning truth values to the variables we can use a pure SAT solver to find a satisfying truth assignment, increasing the running time only by a linear multiplicative factor. This means that SAT enjoyes self-reducibility [2].

observed in [13], the density-order quadrant contains several phase transitions; in fact, the region between density 0 and density 4.26 seems to be rife with phase transitions, which are also solver dependent. In essence, each solver provides us with a different tool with which to study the complexity of random 3-SAT. This is analogous to astronomers observing the sky using telescopes that operate at different wave lengths. While our results are purely empirical, as the lack of success with formally proving a sharp threshold at the crossover density indicates (cf. [18,17,1]), providing rigorous proof for our qualitative observations may be a rather difficult task.

2 Experimental Setup

Our experimental setup is identical to that of [15,31,13]. We generate dn clauses, each by picking three distinct variables at random and choosing their polarity uniformly. For each studied point in the $d \times n$ quadrant we generate at least 100 random instances and apply a solver. Our experiments were run on Sun Ultra 1 machines, with a 167MHZ UltraSPARC processor and 256MB RAM. The CUDD package has been used through the GLU C–interface [34], a set of low-level utilities to access BDD packages. It is well known that the size of the ROBDD for a given function depends on the variable order chosen for that function. We have used automatic dynamic reordering during the tests with the default method for automatic reordering of CUDD (except in Section 6, where we used a certain fixed order).

As in [31], we chose to focus on median running time rather than mean running time. The difficulty of completing the runs on very hard instances makes it less practical to measure the mean. Furthermore, the median and the mean are typically quite close to each other, except for the regions that display heavy-tail phenomena, where the median and the mean diverge dramatically [20,30,13]. It would be interesting to analyze our data at percentiles other than the 50th percentile (the median) (cf. [30]), though a meaningful analysis for high percentiles would require many more sample points than we have in our experiments.

For the statistical analysis and plotting of data, we used MATLAB [6], which is an integrated technical computing environment that combines numeric computation, advanced graphics and visualization, and a high-level programming language. The MATLAB functions we used for statistical analysis were:

- *polyfit*, for computing the best fit to a set of data using polynomial regression, and
- *corrcoef*, for computing r^2, the square of correlation (r^2 is the fraction of the variance of one variable that is explained by regression on the other variable).

For all the results reported in this paper, r^2 exceeded 0.98. This establishes high confidence in the validity of the fit of the curve to the data points.

3 Random 3-SAT and CUDD

In this section we review the results of [13] regarding Random 3-SAT and CUDD. CUDD [32] is a package that provides functions for the manipulation of Boolean functions, based

[6] http://www.mathworks.com

on the reduced, ordered, binary decision diagram (ROBDD) representation [7]. A binary decision diagram (BDD) is a rooted directed acyclic graph that has only two terminal nodes labeled 0 and 1. Every non-terminal node is labeled with a Boolean variable and has two outgoing edges labeled 0 and 1. An ordered binary decision diagram (OBDD) is a BDD with the constraint that the input variables are ordered and every path in the OBDD visits the variables in ascending order. An ROBDD is an OBDD where every node represents a distinct logic function. The *support set* of an ROBDD is the set of variables labeling its internal nodes.

CUDD constructs a compact representation of the set of satisfying truth assignments. The input formula φ is a conjunction $c_1 \wedge \ldots \wedge c_m$ of 3-clauses, where $m = dn$. Our algorithm constructs an ROBDD A_i for each clause c_i. (Note that A_i has to represent only the seven satisfying truth assignments of c_i.) An ROBDD for the set of satisfying truth assignment is then constructed incrementally; B_1 is A_1, while B_{i+1} is the result of $\textsc{apply}(B_i, A_i, \wedge)$, where $\textsc{apply}(A, B, \circ)$ is the result of applying a Boolean operator $\circ$ to two ROBDDs A and B. Finally, the resulting ROBDD B_m is compared against the predefined constant 0 (the empty ROBDD) in order to find if an instance is (un)satisfiable. We call this the BDD algorithm.

The goal of the experiments was to evaluate CUDD's performance on an initial quadrangle of the $d \times n$ quadrant. Densities 0.1, 0.5, and 1 to 15 were explored in [13]. In Figure 1 the median running time is shown on a logarithmic (base 2) scale. Note the absence of a peak; the running-time curve flattens roughly at density 2. The explanation for the lack of running-time peak is that the running time of ROBDD-based algorithms is determined mostly by the size of the manipulated ROBDDs. Our algorithm involves $m = dn$ conjunction operations between the possibly large ROBDD B_i and the small ROBDD A_i. Thus, the running time of our algorithm is determined by the largest intermediate ROBDD B_i constructed. As shown in [13], the peak in ROBDD size is attained after processing about $2n$ clauses, which explains the flattening of the running-time plot at density 2, and suggests that a phase transition in terms of ROBDD size occurs at about this density.

The median running time was analyzed as a function of the order for fixed-density instances. At densities 0.5 and above, the median running time of CUDD is exponential in the order, i.e., it behaves as $2^{\alpha n}$. In contrast, at density 0.1 the running time is cubic. This is explained by the fact that ROBDDs can represent very large sets quite compactly, which is why the method is quite effective for very low-densities instances, where the number of satisfying truth assignments is very large. Unlike what is observed for search-based algorithms, the BDD algorithms does not exhibit a heavy-tail phenomenon.

4 Existential Quantification of Variables

CUDD enables us to apply existential quantification to an ROBDD B:

$$(\exists x)B = \textsc{apply}(B|_{x \leftarrow 1}, B|_{x \leftarrow 0}, \vee),$$

where $B|_{x \leftarrow c}$ restricts B to truth assignments that assign the value c to the variable x. Note that quantifying x existentially eliminates it from the support set of B. We now see how we can take advantage of existential quantification.

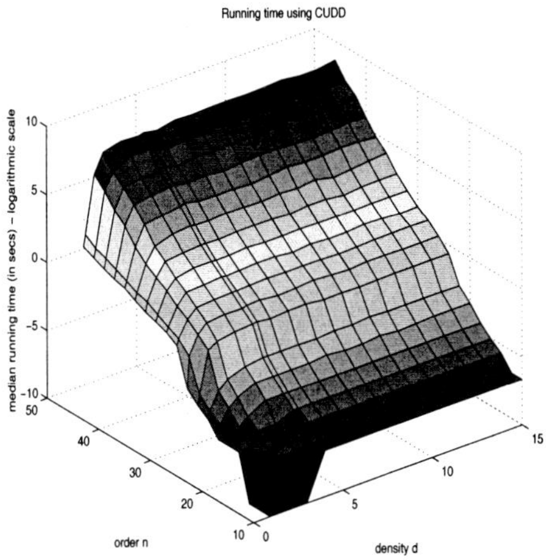

Fig. 1. BDD – 3-D Plot of median running time

The satisfiability problem is to determine whether a given formula $c_1 \wedge \ldots \wedge c_m$ is satisfiable. In other words, the problem is to determine whether the existential formula $(\exists x_1) \ldots (\exists x_n)(c_1 \wedge \ldots \wedge c_m)$ is true. Since checking whether the final ROBDD B_m is equal to 0 can be done by CUDD in constant time, it makes little sense, however, to apply existential quantification to B_m. Suppose, however, that a variable x_j does not occur in the clauses $c_{i+1}, \ldots, c_m$. Then the existential formula can be rewritten as

$$(\exists x_1) \ldots (\exists x_{j-1})(\exists x_{j+1}) \ldots (\exists x_n)((\exists x_j)(c_1 \wedge \ldots \wedge c_i) \wedge (c_{i+1} \wedge \ldots \wedge c_m)).$$

This means that after constructing the ROBDD B_i, we can existentially quantify x_j before conjuncting B_i with $A_{i+1}, \ldots, A_m$.

This suggests the following modification of our algorithm: after constructing the ROBDD B_i, quantify existentially variables that do not occur in the clauses $c_{i+1}, \ldots, c_m$. In this case we say that the variable x has been *quantified out*. The computational advantage of quantifying out stems from the fact that reducing the size of the support set of an ROBDD typically (though not necessarily) results in a reduction of its size; that is, the size of $(\exists x)B$ is typically smaller than that of B. This method is call the *early quantification method*, and proposed first in the context of symbolic model checking [8]. Early quantification was applied to SAT solving in [21] (under the name of *hiding functions*) and tried on random 3-SAT instances, but without a systematic study of the complexity of random 3-SAT. Our implementation adds the slight improvement of stopping the construction as soon as we construct a B_i that is equal to 0; this is called *early termination*. We will call this algorithm, i.e., early quantification with early termination, BDD(Q).

Figure 2 (left) shows the median running time of BDD(Q) on a logarithmic (base 2) scale. The median running time has decreased with respect to the BDD algorithm. At order 46, for densities less than or equal to two we got an order of magnitude improvement (10X) in running time. For greater densities, the improvement is only between 5% to 15%.

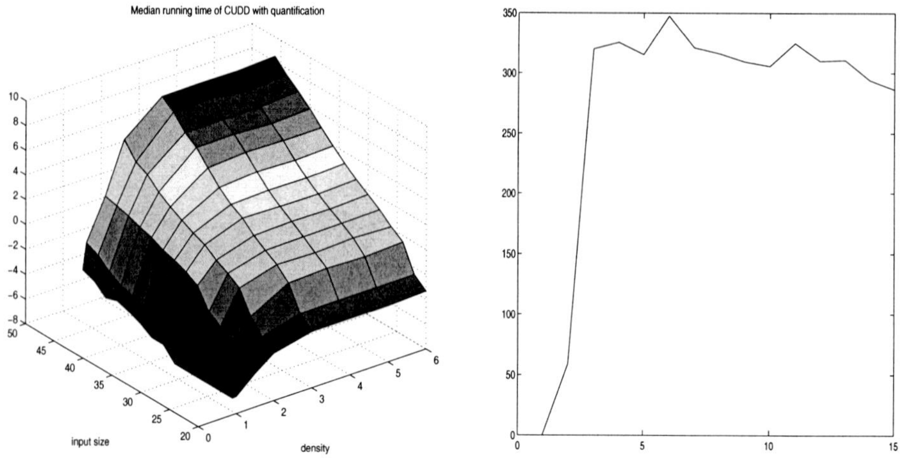

Fig. 2. BDD(Q) – (left) 3-D Plot of median running time, and (right) median running time as a function of the density for order 46

The overall shape of the running-time surface is somewhat similar to that observed in Section 3; the running time increases with density and then seems to flatten. The flattening, however, occurs at about density 4, rather than density 2. Note that once we have processed $i = 4.3n$ clauses, the conjunction $c_1 \wedge \ldots \wedge c_i$ is with very high probability unsatisfiable, which means that B_i is with high probability equal to 0. Thus, BDD(Q) typically terminates by the time $5n$ clauses have been processed, which explains the flattening of the run-time surface for densities over 5. In Figure 2 (right) median running times are shown as a function of the density, for order 46.

An interesting difference between the BDD and BDD(Q) algorithms is that the transition from polynomial to exponential has shifted to the right. Our results indicate a quadratic-time behavior at density 0.5—see Figure 3 (left)—while at densities 1 and above the median running time is exponential in the order, see Figure 3 (right) for median running times for instances of density 1, on a logarithmic (base 2) scale. It should also be noted that BDD(Q) also does not exhibit a heavy-tail phenomenon.

5 Reordering the Clauses

BDD(Q) processes the clauses of the input formula in a linear fashion. Since the main point of early quantification is to quantify variables out as early as possible, reordering the clauses may enable us to do more aggressive early quantification. That is, instead of processing the clauses in the order $c_1, \ldots, c_m$, we can apply a permutation π and process the clauses in the order $c_{\pi(1)}, \ldots, c_{\pi(m)}$. The permutation π should be chosen so as to minimize the number of variables in the support sets of the intermediates ROBDDs. This observation was first made in the context of symbolic model checking, cf. [8,19,24, 5]. Unfortunately, finding an optimal permutation π is by itself a difficult optimization

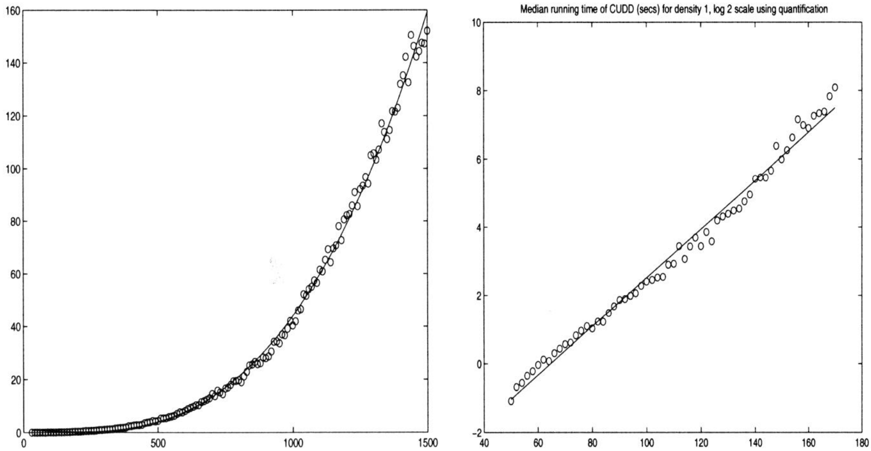

Fig. 3. BDD(Q) – (left) median running time for density 0.5 as a function of the order of the instances; a quadratic function fits these points better than an exponential function, and (right) median running time for density 1 (log scale)

problem, motivating a *greedy* approach: searching at each step for the clause that would result in the maximum number of variables to be quantified out.

Our proposed algorithm searches for a clause with the maximum number of variables with only one occurrence in the remaining clauses. If more than one clause is a possible candidate then a second criterion is applied; from the candidate clauses, the algorithm looks for one that shares least variables with the remaining clauses. (This is as opposed to [19], where the algorithm looks for a candidate that shares most variables with the remaining clauses. We have tried this latter heuristic, and the results are not as good as using our heuristic.) The rationale of our heuristic is trying to quantify out variables as soon as possible. We will call this algorithm BDD(Q,R).

Figure 4 shows median running time using our algorithm. The median running time has decreased quite dramatically with respect to the BDD algorithm. The improvements are most dramatic at low and high densities. For example, for order 46, for density 1 we get a 30X improvement (i.e., the running time of BDD(Q,R) is about 0.03 times that of that of BDD) and for densities 9 and above we get a 100X improvement, while for density 4 we get a 6X improvement. Most interestingly, the shape of the running-time surface is now similar to the shape of the running-time surface for search-based algorithms (GRASP and CPLEX) in [13].

Unlike what we saw in [13], where the running-time peak roughly occurs at the crossover density, running-time peak for BDD(Q,R) seems to occur at about density 3.8. In Figure 5, we plot the median running time in the "hard" zone, for 40 and 46 variables, respectively, with 1000 experiments per point. It is interesting to note that density 3.8 is where the transition from polynomial to exponential running time for search-based solvers was observed in [13].

Another interesting development is a further shift to the right of the transition from polynomial to exponential median running time. At density 1 our data indicate a quadratic

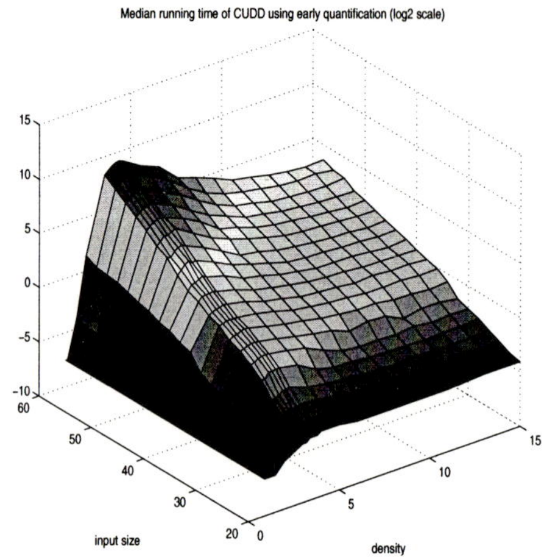

Fig. 4. BDD(Q,R) – 3-D Plot of median running time

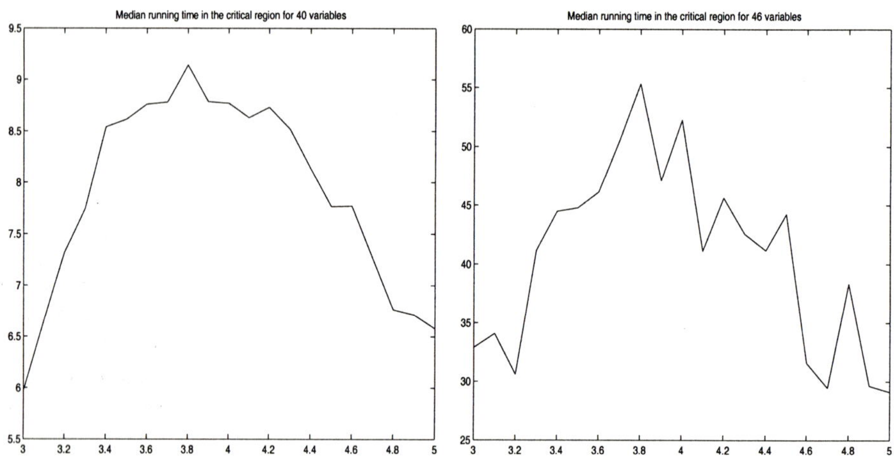

Fig. 5. BDD(Q,R) – median running time in the hard region, for order 40 (left) and 46 (right)

running time. See Figure 6 (left) for median running times for instances of density 1, with 200 instances per point. For densities 1.5 and above the running time is exponential. See Figure 6 (right) for median running times for instances of density 1.5 on a logarithmic (base 2) scale. Thus, the transition occurs between densities 1 and 1.5. Recall that, in contrast, the transition for the BDD algorithm occurs between densities 0.1 and 0.5, while for BDD(Q) it occurs between densities 0.5 and 1. Thus, the improvement in the algorithm is not merely quantitative, it is also qualitative, as it expands the region in which the algorithm is feasible.

As with GRASP and CPLEX [13], the transition from polynomial to exponential behavior of BDD(Q,R) is accompanied by a "heavy-tail phenomenon", which is a preva-

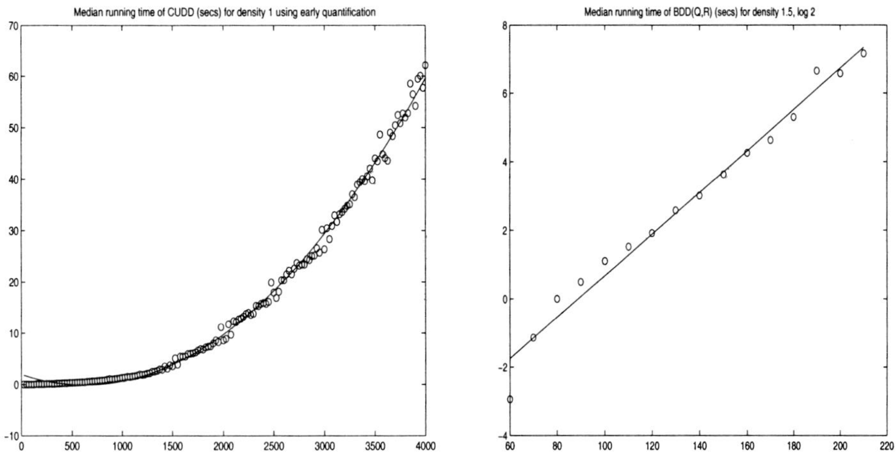

Fig. 6. BDD(Q,R) – (left) median running time for density 1 as a function of the order of the instances; a quadratic function fits these points better than an exponential function, and (right) median running time for density 1.5 (log scale)

lence of *outliers*, i.e., instances on which the actual running time is at least an order of magnitude (10X) larger than the median running time, as well as a divergence of the mean and the median. See Figure 7, where we plot the mean to median ratio and the proportion of outliers as a function of the density. Thus, in spite of the incomparability of search-based solvers and ROBDD-based solvers [35,22], we see a significant similarity between the qualitative results in [13] and here. For both GRASP, CPLEX, and BDD(Q,R). For low densities, the algorithms are polynomial. As the density increases, we see a transition from polynomial to exponential behavior, accompanied by a heavy-tail phenomenon. As the density increases further, the exponent first increases and then decreases. BDD(Q,R) differs, however, in the location of the running-time peak, which is roughly at the crossover density for GRASP and CPLEX, and markedly to its left for BDD(Q,R).

A further improvement of early quantification and reordering was proposed in the context of symbolic model checking in [29]. In this approach, the clauses are not processed one at a time, but several clauses are first *clustered* together without being processed. Once the *size* (number of clauses) of a cluster C attains a pre-established bound, then we first apply conjunction to all the ROBDDs of the clauses in the C to obtain an ROBDD B_C and we then combine B_C with the ROBDD B_i (which corresponds to all the clauses processed earlier) and apply early quantification. Obviously, setting higher limits in the cluster size leads to fewer clusters, but a larger cluster C results in a larger OBDD B_C. To quote [29]: "as the size of the clusters is raised, the number of iterations is reduced, while the BDD sizes of the formula increase. In the beginning, the reduction in the number of iterations offsets the increase in BDD sizes. Hence initially, runtime is reduced as the cluster size increases. But later, the BDD computation time starts to dominate and the running time increases".

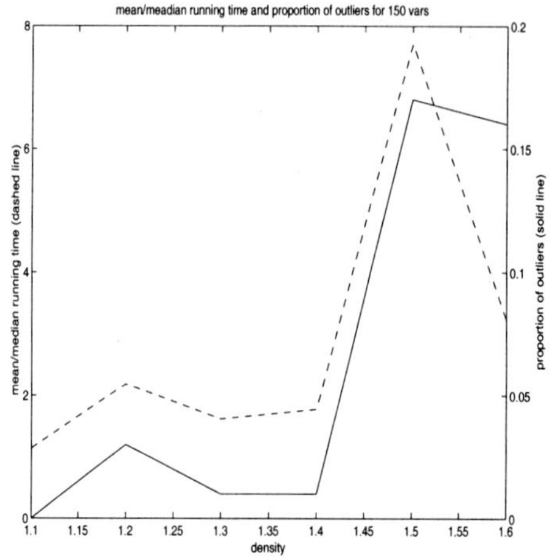

Fig. 7. BDD(Q,R) – ratio of mean to median running time and proportion of outliers

We implemented clustering on top of BDD(Q,R) (that is, we order the clauses as in BDD(Q,R) before clustering). We will call this algorithm BDD(Q,R,C). Experimentation showed that the best results are obtained when cluster size is set to the "magic number" 20. We found out that BDD(Q,R,C) performs badly at low densities, but yields an improvement of 10%-30% for densities above 3. The qualitative behavior of BDD(Q,R,C) is, however, quite similar to that of BDD(Q,R): we observe a transition from polynomial to exponential, accompanied by a heavy-tail phenomenon, between densities 1.0 and 1.5, and the exponent then rises and declines, peaking at about density 3.8.

6 Variable Ordering

The previous ROBDD-based methods focused on the processing of the input clauses, while at the same time letting CUDD handle the critical issue of variable ordering (including dynamic reordering). Inspired by work of Bouquet [6], we studied an ROBDD-based algorithm using variable ordering based on a graph representation of the input formula. As we shall see, by using knowledge about the structure of the input formula, we can obtain dramatic improvement in running time.

The graph associated with a CNF formula $\varphi = \bigwedge_i c_i$ is $G_\varphi = (V, E)$, where V is the set of variables in φ and an edge $\{x_i, x_j\}$ is in E if there exists a clause c_k such that x_i and x_j occur in c_k. To extract variable order from G_φ. Bouquet uses the "maximum cardinality search" (MCS) of [33]. Let n be the number of vertices of G_φ. MCS numbers the vertices from 1 to n in the following way: As the next vertex to number, select the vertex adjacent to the largest number of previously numbered vertices, breaking ties arbitrarily. It is this variable ordering that we now provide to CUDD (turning off dynamic reordering).

Bouquet then uses the variable order to cluster the clauses. Let the *rank* of a clause $c = \{l_1, l_2, l_3\}$ be $rank(c) = \max(order(x_1), order(x_2), order(x_3))$, where x_i is the variable of the literal l_i. The clusters are the equivalent classes of the relation $\sim$ defined by: $c \sim c'$ iff $rank(c) = rank(c')$. For each cluster $C_j = \{c_{j_1}, \ldots, c_{j_k}\}$, we then construct an ROBDD A_{C_j} by applying conjunction to the ROBDDs $A_{j_1}, \ldots, A_{j_k}$. The rank of a cluster is the rank of its clauses (by definition, all the clauses in a cluster have the same rank).

In [6], the final ROBDD is constructed by applying conjunction to the ROBDDs A_{C_j}'s of the clusters. We have combined Bouquet's method with the method of early quantification. We process the clusters in ascending rank order and quantify variables out as early as possible. We observed that early quantification plays an important role in the low densities, where satisfying truth assignments abound. We denote the combined method by BDD(B,Q,C). For densities 2 or above, BDD(B,Q,C) is significantly faster than BDD(Q,R,C). At order 46 we saw improvement between 5X and 10X (for lower densities BDD(B,Q,C) is about 30% slower). More interestingly, the shape of the running-time surface is quite different for BDD(B,Q,C). Figure 8 shows the median running time of BDD(B,Q,C) on a logarithmic (base 2) scale. As we can see, the interesting region has moved to the left. The running-time peak now seems to occur at about density 2.3. Figure 8 shows median running times for order 60.

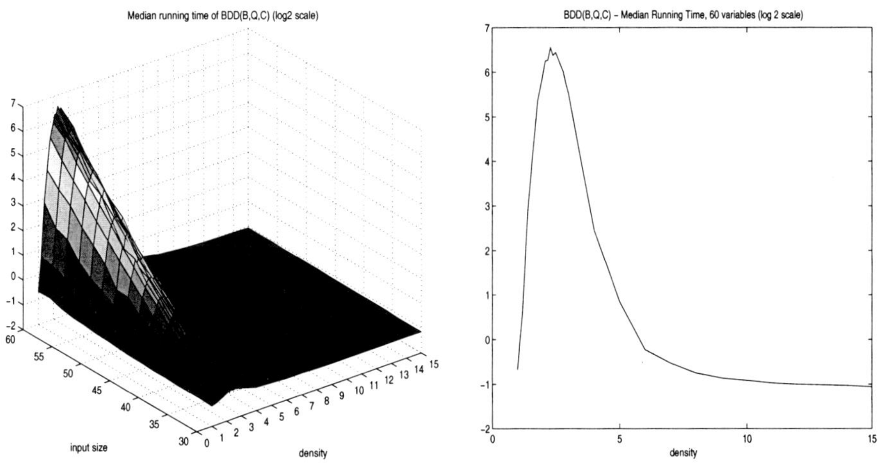

Fig. 8. BDD(B,Q,C) – (left) 3-D Plot of median running time, and (right) median running times as a function of the density for order 60

We again see a transition from polynomial to exponential behavior before the running-time peak, between densities 0.2 and 1 (to the left of the analogous transition for BDD(Q,R)). For very low densities (0.2 or below) our data indicate a cubic running time. See Figure 9 (left) for median running times for instances of density 0.2. For densities 1 and above the median running time of BDD(B,Q,C) is exponential (but see remark below). See Figure 9 (right) for median running time for instances of density 1 on a logarithmic (base 2) scale. The transition from polynomial to exponential behavior is again accompanied by a heavy-tail phenomenon. The pattern of that phenomenon is significantly more complex than that observed for BDD(Q,R) and we have not yet been able to characterize it.

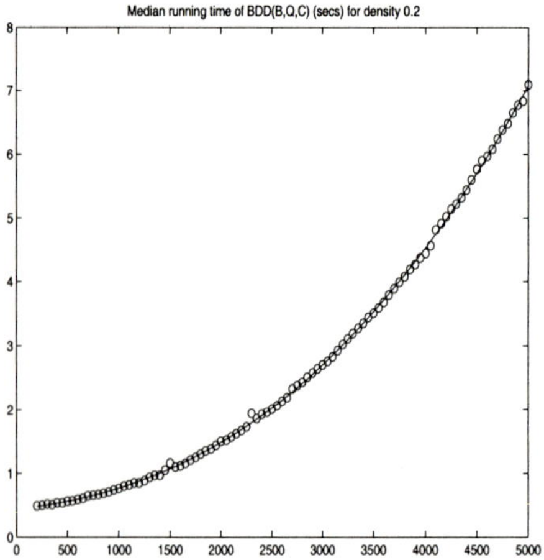

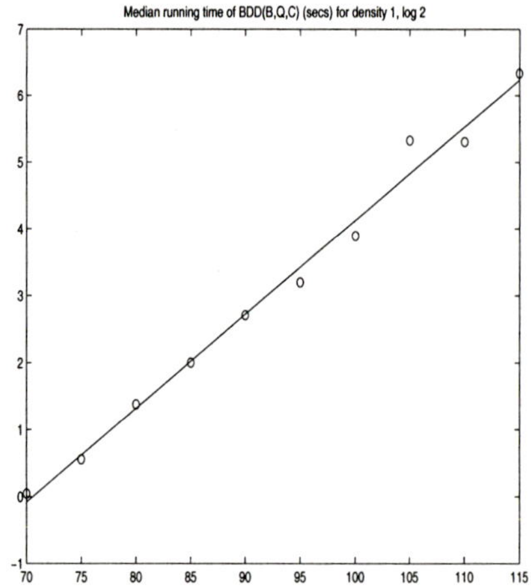

Fig. 9. BDD(B,Q,C) – (left) median running time for density 0.2 as a function of the order of the instances; a quadratic function fits these points better than an exponential function, and (right) median running time for density 1 (log scale)

Remark: Note that the running time decreased quite dramatically with increasing densities above 2.3. Is it possible that at high enough density we see again polynomial behavior? Our data is inconclusive. For example, at density 20 our data fit cubic and exponential curves almost equally well. This issue requires further investigation.

7 Discussion

In this paper we studied the complexity of random 3-SAT experimentally using ROBBD-based pure SAT solvers. Our main finding is that these solvers display *easy-hard-less-hard* pattern that is quite similar to that observed for search-based solvers in [13]. When we start with low-density instances and then increase the density, we go from a region of polynomial running time, to a region of exponential running time, where the exponent first increases and then decreases as a function of the density. The location of both transitions, from polynomial to exponential and from increasing to decreasing exponent, are algorithm dependent. In particular, the running time peak is quite independent than the crossover density, challenging the widely-held belief that the "hard problems" are always located near the crossover density [11].

These findings should be contrasted with those of [13], which revealed a marked difference between solvers like GRASP and CPLEX, which are search based and display interesting similarities in the shapes of the median running time surface despite their different underlying algorithmic techniques, and ROBDD-based solvers, like CUDD, which are based on compactly representing all satisfying truth assignments. By developing here ROBDD-based *pure* SAT solvers, we showed that certain qualitative features of the complexity of random 3-SAT do seem to be algorithm independent. Explaining these common features is a challenging research problem.

References

1. D. Achlioptas. Setting two variables at a time yields a new lower bound for random 3-SAT. In *Proc. 32th ACM Symp. on Theory of Computing*, pages 28–37, 2000.
2. J. Balcazar. Self-reducibility. *Journal of Computer and System Sciences*, 41(3):367–388, 1990.
3. P. Beame, R. M. Karp, T. Pitassi, and M. E. Saks. On the complexity of unsatisfiability proofs for random k-CNF formulas. In *Proc. 30th ACM Symp. on Theory of Computing*, pages 561–571, 1998.
4. A. Biere, A. Cimatti, E. M. Clarke, M. Fujita, and Y. Zhu. Symbolic model checking using SAT procedures instead of BDDs. In *Proc. 36th Conf. on Design Automation*, pages 317–320, 1999.
5. M. Block, C. Gröpl, H. Preuß, H. L. Proömel, and A. Srivastav. Efficient ordering of state variables and transition relation partitions in symbolic model checking. Technical report, Institute of Informatics, Humboldt University of Berlin, 1997.
6. F. Bouquet. *Gestion de la dynamicité et énumération d'implicants premiers: une approche fondée sur les Diagrammes de Décision Binaire*. PhD thesis, Université de Provence, France, 1999.
7. R. E. Bryant. Graph-based algorithms for Boolean function manipulation. *IEEE Trans. on Computers*, 35(8):677–691, 1986.
8. J. R. Burch, E. M. Clarke, and D. E. Long. Symbolic model checking with partitioned transition relations. In *Proc. IFIP TC10/WG 10.5 Int'l Conf. on Very Large Scale Integration, Edinburgh, Scotland (VLSI'91)*, pages 49–58, 1991.
9. J.R. Burch, E.M. Clarke, K.L. McMillan, D.L. Dill, and L.J. Hwang. Symbolic model checking: 10^{20} states and beyond. *Information and Computation*, 98(2):142–170, June 1992.
10. P. Chatalic and L. Simon. The old Davis-Putnam procedure meets ZBDDs. In D. McAllester, editor, *17th Int'l Conf. on Automated Deduction (CADE'17)*, volume 1831 of *Lecture Notes in Artificial Intelligence*, pages 449–454, 2000.
11. P. Cheeseman, B. Kanefsky, and W. M. Taylor. Where the really hard problems are. In *Proc. 12th Int'l Joint Conf. on Artificial Intelligence (IJCAI '91)*, pages 331–337, 1991.
12. V. Chvátal and E. Szemerédi. Many hard examples for resolution. *J. of the ACM*, 35(4):759–768, 1988.
13. C. Coarfa, D.D. Demopolous, A. San Miguel Aguirre, D. Subramanian, and M.Y. Vardi. Random 3-SAT: The plot thickens. In R. Dechter, editor, *Proc. Principles and Practice of Constraint Programming (CP'2000)*, Lecture Notes in Computer Science 1894, pages 143–159, 2000.
14. S. Cocco and R. Monasson. Trajectories in phase diagrams, growth processes and computational complexity: how search algorithms solve the 3-Satisfiability problem. *Phys. Rev. Lett.*, 86:1654–1657, 2001.
15. J. M. Crawford and L. D. Auton. Experimental results on the crossover point in random 3-SAT. *Artificial Intelligence*, 81(1-2):31–57, 1996.
16. M. Davis, G. Logemann, and D. Loveland. A machine program for theorem proving. *Comm. of the ACM*, 5:394–397, 1962.

17. O. Dubois, Y. Boufkhad, and J. Mandler. Typical random 3-SAT formulae and the satisfiability threshold. In *Proc. 11th Annual ACM-SIAM Symp. on Discrete Algorithms*, pages 126–127, 2000.
18. E. Friedgut. Necessary and sufficient conditions for sharp threshold of graph properties and the k-SAT problem. *J. Amer. Math. Soc.*, 12:1017–1054, 1999.
19. D. Geist and H. Beer. Efficient model checking by automated ordering of transition relation partitions. In *Proc. 6th Int'l Conf. on Computer Aided Verification (CAV '94)*, pages 299–310, 1994.
20. I. P. Gent and T. Walsh. Easy problems are sometimes hard. *Artificial Intelligence*, 70(1-2):335–345, 1994.
21. J. F. Groote. Hiding propositional constants in BDDs. *Formal Methods in System Design*, 8:91–96, 1996.
22. J.F. Groote and H. Zantema. Resolution and binary decision diagrams cannot simulate each other polynomially. Technical report, Department of Computer Science, Utrecht University, 2000. Technical Report UU-CS-2000-14.
23. T. Hogg and C. P. Williams. The hardest constraint problems: A double phase transition. *Artificial Intelligence*, 69(1-2):359–377, 1994.
24. R. Hojati, S. C. Krishnan, and R. K. Brayton. Early quantification and partitioned transition relations. In *Proc. 1996 Int'l Conf. on Computer Design*, pages 12–19, 1996.
25. S. Jha, Y. Lu, M. Minea, and E.M. Clarke. Equivalence checking using abstract BDDs. In *Proc. Int'l Conf. on Computer Design (ICCD'97)*, pages 332–337, 1997.
26. T. Larrabee and Y. Tsuji. Evidence for a satisfiability threshold for random 3CNF formulas. In *Working Notes of AAAI 1993 Spring Symposium: AI and NP-Hard Problems*, pages 112–118, 1993.
27. J. P. Marques Silva and K. A. Sakallah. GRASP–A search algorithm for propositional satisfiability. *IEEE Trans. on Computers*, 48(5):506–521, 1999.
28. D. G. Mitchell and H. J. Levesque. Some pitfalls for experimenters with random SAT. *Artificial Intelligence*, 81(1-2):111–125, 1996.
29. R. K. Ranjan, A. A. Aziz, R. K. Brayton, B. Plessier, and C. Pixley. Efficient formal design verification: Data structure + algorithms. Technical report, University of California at Berkeley, 1994. Tech. Rep. UCB/ERL M94/100.
30. B. Selman and S. Kirkpatrick. Critical behavior in the computational cost of satisfiability testing. *Artificial Intelligence*, 81(1-2):273–295, 1996.
31. B. Selman, D. G. Mitchell, and H. J. Levesque. Generating hard satisfiability problems. *Artificial Intelligence*, 81(1-2):17–29, 1996.
32. F. Somenzi. CUDD: CU Decision Diagram package. release 2.3.0., 1998. Dept. of Electrical and Computer Engineering. University of Colorado at Boulder.
33. R. E. Tarjan and M. Yannakakis. Simple linear-time algorithms to tests chordiality of graphs, tests acyclicity of hypergraphs, and selectively reduce acyclic hypergraphs. *SIAM J. on Computing*, 13(3):566–579, 1984.
34. The VIS Group. VIS: A system for verification and synthesis. In *Proc. 8th Int'l Conf. on Computer Aided Verification (CAV '96)*, pages 428–432, 1996. LNCS 1102. Ed. by R. Alur and T. Henziger.
35. T. E. Uribe and M. E. Stickel. Ordered binary decision diagrams and the Davis-Putnam procedure. In *First Int'l Conf. on Constraints in Computational Logics*, volume 845 of *Lecture Notes in Computer Science*, pages 34–49, Munich, September 1994. Springer-Verlag.

Capturing Structure with Satisfiability

Ramón Béjar[1], Alba Cabiscol[2], Cèsar Fernàndez[2], Felip Manyà[2], and Carla Gomes[1]

[1] Dept. of Comp. Science, Cornell University, Ithaca, NY 14853, USA
{bejar,gomes}@cs.cornell.edu

[2] Dept. of Comp. Science, Universitat de Lleida, Jaume II 69, 25001 Lleida, Spain
{alba,cesar,felip}@eup.udl.es

Abstract. We present Regular-SAT, an extension of Boolean Satisfiability based on a class of many-valued CNF formulas. Regular-SAT shares many properties with Boolean SAT, which allows us to generalize some of the best known SAT results and apply them to Regular-SAT. In addition, Regular-SAT has a number of advantages over Boolean SAT. Most importantly, it produces more compact encodings that capture problem structure more naturally. Furthermore, its simplicity allows us to develop Regular-SAT solvers that are competitive with SAT and CSP procedures. We present a detailed performance analysis of Regular-SAT on several benchmark domains. These results show a clear computational advantage of using a Regular-SAT approach over a pure Boolean SAT or CSP approach, at least on the domains under consideration. We therefore believe that an approach based on Regular-SAT provides a compelling intermediate approach between SAT and CSPs, bringing together some of the best features of each paradigm.

1 Introduction

In the last few years, the tremendous advance in the state of the art of SAT solvers, combined with progress in hardware design, has led to the development of very fast SAT solvers. As a consequence, SAT encodings have become competitive with specialized CSP encodings in several domains. However, there is a tradeoff between using a uniform encoding, such as SAT, and a more structured encoding, as found in the CSP paradigm.

In general, CSP-based encodings capture problem structure in a more natural way than SAT encodings. CSP encodings therefore allow in principle for highly efficient solution strategies that exploit inherent problem structure. However, in order to take full advantage of the CSP approach, the user may be required to develop specialized propagation and search techniques that may be difficult to implement efficiently. In a SAT formulation, some of the intricate problem structure may be lost, but the availability of highly optimized general SAT solvers can often compensate for not directly exploiting inherent problem structure.

Our goal is to provide an encoding paradigm that is sufficiently uniform, so that we can develop general solvers, and at the same time allows us to recover the problem structure in a more straightforward manner. Our approach is based

T. Walsh (Ed.): CP 2001, LNCS 2239, pp. 137–152, 2001.

on using so-called Regular-SAT encodings. Regular-SAT retains the uniformity and simplicity of Boolean SAT but in addition captures problem structure in a more straightforward manner. Regular-SAT is an extension of Boolean Satisfiability based on a special class of many-valued CNF formulas, called regular CNF formulas [14,15]. These clausal forms have their origin in the many-valued logic community [3] and are similar to Boolean CNF formulas, except that they use a generalized notion of literal. A literal now is an expression of the form $S:p$, where p is a propositional variable and S is a subset of truth values having a particular structure.

Although more general than SAT, Regular-SAT has many properties in common with traditional Boolean SAT. For example, we have tractable cases such as Regular 2-SAT [18] and Regular Horn-SAT [15], and there exist well-defined phase transitions boundaries in random formula ensembles [5].

Our results show that we can solve certain combinatorial problems more efficiently by using Regular-SAT encodings, compared to approaches based on state-of-the-art SAT or CSP approaches. We present results for both local search and systematic search. Moreover, we show that the Regular-SAT encodings nicely preserve certain structural properties of the original problem domain. In particular, we consider the so-called backbone structure of the problem domain. Phase-transition properties of backbone structure are properly preserved in a Regular-SAT encoding; in a Boolean SAT approach, on the other hand, the phase transition structure in the backbone is not directly recoverable.

The paper is structured as follows. We begin by formally defining the satisfiability problem of Regular CNF formulas (Section 2). In the next section, we describe Regular-DP and Regular-WalkSAT, which are generalizations of the so called Davis-Putnam procedure (though it is actually due to Davis, Logemann and Loveland [9]) and WalkSAT [22]. In Section 4, we present a detailed evaluation of the performance of Regular-SAT procedures. In Section 5, we compare Boolean SAT and Regular SAT w.r.t. capturing problem structure. Section 6 gives overall conclusions.

2 The SAT Problem of Regular CNF Formulas

Regular-SAT is the problem of deciding the satisfiability of regular CNF formulas. A *regular CNF formula* is a classical propositional conjunctive clause form based on a generalized notion of literal, called *regular literal.* Given a truth value set T ($|T| \geq 2$) equipped with a total ordering $\leq$, a *regular literal* is an expression of the form $S:p$, where p is a propositional variable and S is a subset of T which is either of the form $\uparrow i = \{j \in T \mid j \geq i\}$ or of the form $\downarrow i = \{j \in T \mid j \leq i\}$ for some $i \in T$. The informal meaning of $S:p$ is "p is constrained to the values in S", and one can consider the language of regular CNF formulas as a constraint programming language between SAT and CSP.

Definition 1. *A* truth value set *is a non-empty set* $T = \{i_1, i_2, \dots, i_n\}$, *equipped with a total ordering* $\leq$. *A* sign *is a set* $S \subseteq T$ *of truth values. For each element* i *of the truth value set* T, *let* $\uparrow i$ *denote the sign* $\{j \in T \mid j \geq i\}$, *and let* $\downarrow i$ *denote the sign* $\{j \in T \mid j \leq i\}$. *A sign* S *is* regular *if it is identical to* $\uparrow i$ *or to* $\downarrow i$ *for some* $i \in T$.

Definition 2. *A* regular literal *is an expression of the form* $S : p$, *where* S *is a regular sign and* p *is a propositional variable. The complementary literal of* $S : p$ *is* $(T \setminus S) : p$. *A regular literal* $S : p$ *is of* positive *(*negative*)* polarity *if* S *is of the form* $\uparrow i$ $(\downarrow i)$ *for some* $i \in T$. *A* regular clause *is a finite set of regular literals. A* regular CNF formula *is a finite set of regular clauses.*

Example 1. Let T be the set $\{0, 1, 2\}$ with the standard order on natural numbers. An example of regular CNF formula is

$$(\downarrow 0 : p_1 \vee \downarrow 1 : p_2 \vee \uparrow 2 : p_3) \wedge (\uparrow 1 : p_1 \vee \downarrow 0 : p_2).$$

Definition 3. *An* interpretation *is a mapping that assigns to every propositional variable an element of the truth value set. An interpretation* I *satisfies a regular literal* $S : p$ *iff* $I(p) \in S$. *An interpretation satisfies a regular clause iff it satisfies at least one of its regular literals. A regular CNF formula* Γ *is* satisfiable *iff there exists at least one interpretation that satisfies all the regular clauses in* Γ. *A regular CNF formula that is not satisfiable is* unsatisfiable. *The empty regular clause, denoted by* $\Box$, *is always unsatisfiable and the empty regular CNF formula is always satisfiable.*

Regular-SAT has advantages over SAT, as well as interesting computational properties:

- SAT is a special case of Regular-SAT: any SAT instance can be transformed into a logically equivalent Regular-SAT instance of the same size by taking $T = \{0, 1\}$ and replacing every literal p $(\neg p)$ with $\uparrow 1 : p$ $(\downarrow 0 : p)$.
- Regular CNF formulas are a more expressive representation formalism than classical CNF formulas, and give rise to more compact encodings (less clauses, variables, etc.) for many combinatorial problems.
- Classical proof methods like resolution, and satisfiability algorithms like Davis-Putnam, GSAT and WalkSAT can be generalized to deal with regular CNF formulas in a natural way. As we will see, the good properties of the classical algorithms remain in regular algorithms, and one does not have to start from scratch when designing algorithms and heuristics.
- Regular-SAT, like SAT, is one of the syntactically and conceptually simplest NP-complete problems. The design, implementation and analysis of algorithms for Regular-SAT tend to be easier than for other CSP algorithms.
- Using regular signs instead of arbitrary subset of truth values as signs has clear advantages. For instance, 2-SAT is solvable in polynomial-time when signs are regular while it is NP-complete for arbitrary signs [18]. Horn CNF formulas admit a natural generalization because regular signs have polarity and Regular Horn-SAT is solvable in polynomial-time.

3 Regular-SAT Algorithms

In this section we first describe Regular-DP and then Regular-WalkSAT, which are generalizations of the Davis-Putnam procedure and WalkSAT. Regular-DP is based on the following rules:

Regular one-literal rule: given a regular CNF formula Γ containing a regular unit clause $\{S:p\}$,

1. remove all clauses containing a literal subsumed by $\{S:p\}$; i.e., all clauses containing a literal $S':p$ such that $S \subseteq S'$;
2. delete all occurrences of literals $S'':p$ such that $S \cap S'' = \emptyset$.

Regular branching rule: reduce the problem of determining whether a regular CNF formula Γ is satisfiable to the problem of determining whether $\Gamma \cup \{S:p\}$ is satisfiable or $\Gamma \cup \{(T \setminus S):p\}$ is satisfiable, where $S:p$ is a regular literal occurring in Γ and the regular literal $(T \setminus S):p$ is its complement.

The pseudo-code of Regular-DP is shown in Figure 1. It returns true (false) if the input regular CNF formula Γ is satisfiable (unsatisfiable). First, it applies repeatedly the regular one-literal rule and derives a simplified formula Γ'. Once the formula cannot be further simplified, it selects a regular literal $S:p$ of Γ', applies the branching rule and solves recursively the problem of deciding whether $\Gamma' \cup \{S:p\}$ is satisfiable or $\Gamma' \cup \{(T \setminus S):p\}$ is satisfiable. In the pseudo-code, $\Gamma_{S:p}$ denotes the formula obtained after applying the regular one-literal rule to a regular CNF formula Γ using the regular unit clause $\{S:p\}$.

Observe that the Davis-Putnam procedure is a particular case of Regular-DP. Our implementation of Regular-DP incorporates two branching heuristics which are extensions of the two-sided Jeroslow-Wang rule [15,6]. Given a regular CNF formula Γ, such heuristics select a regular literal L occurring in Γ that

procedure Regular-DP

Input: a regular CNF formula Γ
Output: `true` if Γ is satisfiable and `false` if Γ is unsatisfiable

```
begin
  if Γ = ∅ then return true;
  if □ ∈ Γ then return false;
  /* regular one-literal rule*/
  if Γ contains a unit clause {S':p} then Regular-DP(Γ_{S':p});
  let S:p be a regular literal occurring in Γ;
  /* regular branching rule */
  if Regular-DP(Γ_{S:p}) then return true;
  else return Regular-DP(Γ_{(T\S):p});
end
```

Fig. 1. The Regular-DP procedure

maximizes $J(L) + J(\overline{L})$, where $J(L)$ can be defined either as in Equation 1 or as in Equation 2:

$$J(L) = \sum_{\substack{\exists L' : L' \subseteq L \\ L' \in C \in \Gamma}} 2^{-|C|} \quad (1) \qquad J(L) = \sum_{\substack{\exists L' : L' \subseteq L \\ L' \in C \in \Gamma}} \left(\prod_{S:p \in C} \frac{|T| - |S|}{2(|T| - 1)} \right) \quad (2)$$

where $\overline{L}$ denotes the complement of literal L, $L' \subseteq L$ denotes that literal L' subsumes literal L, $|C|$ denotes the number of literals in clause C, and $|S|$ the number of truth values in sign S.

Equation 1 assigns a larger value to those regular literals L subsumed by regular literals L' that appear in many small clauses. This way, when Regular-DP branches on $\overline{L}$, the probability of deriving new regular unit clauses is larger. Equation 2, that was used in our experiments, takes into account the length of regular signs as well. This fact is important because regular literals with small signs have a larger probability of being eliminated during the application of the regular one-literal rule. Observe that in the case that $|T| = 2$ we get the same equation.

Regular-WalkSAT, whose pseudo-code is shown in Figure 2, tries to find a satisfying interpretation for a regular CNF formula Γ performing a greedily biased walk through the space of possible interpretations. It starts with a randomly generated interpretation I. If I does not satisfy Γ, it proceeds as follows: (i) it randomly chooses an unsatisfied clause C, (ii) it chooses — using function select-WalkSAT — a variable-value pair (p', k') from the set S of pairs (p, k) such that C is satisfied by the current interpretation I if the truth value that I assigns to p is changed to k, and (iii) it creates a new interpretation I' that is identical to I except that $I'(p') = k'$. Such changes are repeated until either

```
procedure Regular-WalkSAT

Input: a regular CNF formula Γ, MaxChanges, MaxTries and ω
Output: a satisfying interpretation of Γ, if found
 begin
  for i := 1 to MaxTries
    I := a randomly generated interpretation for Γ;
    for j := 1 to MaxChanges
      if I satisfies Γ then return I;
      Pick one unsatisfied clause C from Γ;
      S := { (p,k) | S' : p ∈ C, k ∈ S' };
      (p',k') := select-WalkSAT( S, Γ, ω );
      I := I with the truth assignment of p' changed to k';
  return "no satisfying interpretation found";
 end
```

Fig. 2. The Regular-WalkSAT procedure

a satisfying interpretation is found or a pre-set maximum number of changes (MaxChanges) is reached. This process is repeated as needed, up to a maximum of MaxTries times.

Function select-WalkSAT calculates, for each pair $(p, k) \in S$, the number of broken clauses; i.e. the number of clauses that are satisfied by I but that would become unsatisfied if the assignment of p is changed to k. If the minimum number of broken clauses found (u) is greater than zero then either it randomly chooses, with probability ω, a pair (p', k') from S or it randomly chooses, with probability $1 - \omega$, a pair (p', k') from those pairs for which the number of broken clauses is u. If $u = 0$, then it randomly chooses a pair from those pairs for which $u = 0$.

To our best knowledge, the first implementations of local search algorithms for non-Boolean satisfiability were Regular-GSAT [6] and Regular-WalkSAT [7]. In our experiments we used the last available version (10.0) of Regular-WalkSAT, which is faster than the previous ones. Recently, Frisch and Peugeniez [10] have considered a class of non-Boolean formulas where the signs of literals are singletons, and have implemented an efficient local search algorithm for this kind of formulas. Their results show that using non-Boolean satisfiability encodings and solvers is a competitive generic problem solving approach. The reader is invited to consult [3] for related many-valued satisfiability problems and algorithms.

4 Performance Evaluation

A key question regarding Regular-WalkSAT and Regular-DP is how their performance compares to standard WalkSAT and DP. In this section, we consider four benchmark domains. Our results show that there is a concrete computational advantage to using the Regular-SAT procedures, at least on these domains. This suggests that the more compact Regular-SAT encodings, which also preserve more of the problem structure, allow for a more efficient, yet general, solution strategy.

This section is divided in two parts. The first part summarizes our results on three benchmarks, graph coloring, round robin scheduling, and all interval series. These results were obtained as part of the first author's Ph.D. dissertation [4]. Here we only present a summary of the main results. We refer to the thesis for a detailed description of the problem encodings and more detailed run time data.

The second part gives a more detailed evaluation of our Regular-WalkSAT strategy on the quasigroup domain, which provides a structured benchmark with fine control of problem hardness.

4.1 Graph Coloring, Round Robin, and All Interval Series

Our problem domains are graph coloring (flat graphs [8] and DIMACS benchmark instances), round robin scheduling [19], and all interval series (`ais`) [16]. The problems were selected not because of their inherent hardness per se, but because they are known to be hard to solve with SAT algorithms.

For local search algorithms, we observed that the mean cost needed to solve an instance with Regular-WalkSAT is smaller than with WalkSAT in the three problems. This was true in terms of both number of flips and time, although the difference in the time needed was not as significant as in the number of flips[1]. It was shown in [4] that the performance for the round robin problem is slightly better with Regular-WalkSAT, and is considerably better for the other two problems.

Figure 3 shows the mean number of flips and mean time needed to solve instances of the ais problem of different size. The number of flips varies from 7 times to 10 times smaller with Regular-WalkSAT and the time is always about 2 times smaller with Regular-WalkSAT.

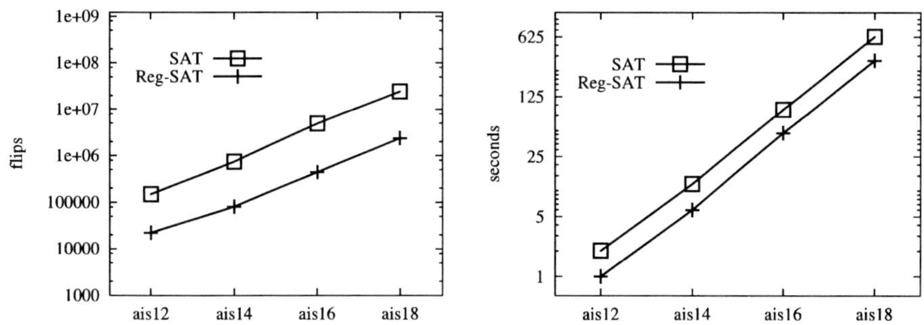

Fig. 3. Scaling behaviour of Regular-SAT and SAT on the ais problem

Local search algorithms for Regular-SAT are better in terms of the mean cost, but also in terms of the cost distribution as a whole. In fact, the cost distribution for Regular-SAT on a particular instance dominates the cost distribution for SAT on the same instance. In other words, the probability of finding a solution in less than x flips is always greater with Regular-WalkSAT for each x. Moreover, we observed that the computational cost follows an exponential distribution, at least when solving the instances with approximately optimal noise. This was observed before for local search algorithms for SAT [16]. Figure 4 shows the distribution for the number of flips (RLD) for both algorithms when solving the DIMACS graph coloring instance `DSJC125.5.col`. The figure also shows the exponential distributions (EDs) that were found to best approximate the empirical distributions. The expression for the cumulative form of the EDs is $ed[m](x) = 1 - 2^{-x/m}$, where m is the median of the distribution. The approximations were derived using the Marquart-Levenberg algorithm.

For systematic search, we compared the performance of Regular-DP with the performance of DP when solving Regular-SAT and SAT encodings, respectively, of flat graph problem instances. When we say DP we mean our implementation of Regular-DP but working with $T = \{0, 1\}$. In order to study only the benefits of the encodings, both algorithms used the function of Equation 2 in the branching heuristic. Table 1 shows the mean cost needed to solve a flat graph instance

[1] However, we cannot consider our current version of Regular-WalkSAT (10.0) as optimized as the current one of WalkSAT (35.0).

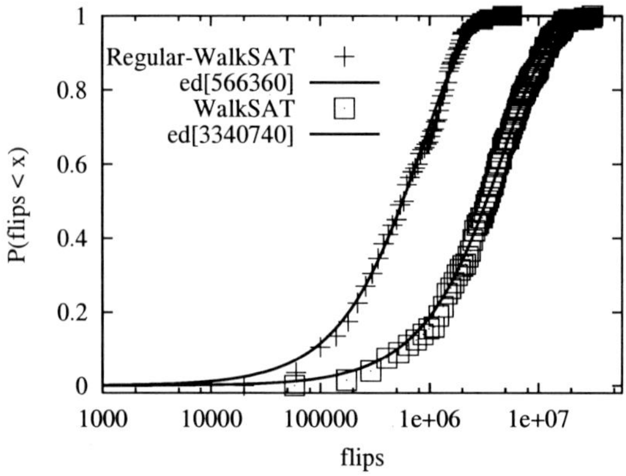

Fig. 4. RLDs for Regular-SAT and SAT on instance `DSJC125.5.col`

with both approaches, as well as the coefficient of variation (CV) that is the ratio between the standard deviation and the mean of the cost. The table shows results for sets of instances obtained with different values for the number of vertices and the number of colors used. For 4 colours and 150 vertices, only 10% of instances were solved with DP, and 85% of instances were solved with Regular-DP; in both cases we used a cutoff of 4 hours, and the results shown correspond to the instances successfully solved by both approaches. Observe that even if the number of nodes in Regular-DP is not smaller in all the cases, the time is always smaller. The likely explanation for this phenomenon is that the number of unit propagations per node is sufficiently small to compensate for a larger number of backtrack nodes. These results indicate that Regular-DP, using our simple branching heuristic, is more effective on the Regular-SAT encoding. In fact, the information contained in the regular literals may help the heuristic to make better decisions. We expect that by incorporating more sophisticated heuristics in Regular-DP (e.g. extensions of look-ahead [17] and look-back [2] heuristics) we will extend the range and size of instances that Regular-DP can solve faster than state-of-the-art SAT solvers.

4.2 Quasigroup Domain

The quasigroup with holes problem (QWH) was recently introduced in [1]. This problem considers randomly generated instances of the quasigroup (or Latin square) completion problem (QCP) [13], and all instances are satisfiable and thus well-suited for evaluating local search methods. The structure of QWH is similar to that found in real-world domains; for example timetabling, routing, and scheduling. Instances are generated by first randomly generating a complete quasigroup, and then erasing some of the colors of the quasigroup (punching "holes"). The hardness of completing a QWH instance can be finely controlled by the number of holes punched. With relatively few holes, a completion is easy because the problem is highly constrained; similarly, instances with a large frac-

Table 1. Results of DP and Regular-DP on flat graph instances

colors		**vertices = 100** **Encoding** classical mean	CV	regular mean	CV	**vertices = 150** **Encoding** classical mean	CV	regular mean	CV
3	nodes	349	1.05	89	0.88	6182	1.71	597	1.12
	time (sec)	0.70	1.04	0.075	0.90	19	1.57	0.80	1.05
4	nodes	133572	1.96	156303	1.97	2457689	1.5	3861096	1.95
	time (sec)	470	1.91	191	1.88	9955	1.3	5920	1.83

tion of holes are relatively easy to solve, since the instances are under-constrained and many possible completions exists. In [1], it is shown that there is a region of very hard completion problems in between these two extremes. The hard instances arise in the vicinity of a phase transition threshold in the average size of the so-called backbone [1]. The backbone of an instance measures the amount of shared structure among solutions [20,1]. In Section 5, we show that Regular-SAT captures the backbone in a natural way.

Encoding. We have encoded this problem using similar SAT and Regular-SAT encoding schemas. In the SAT encoding, each variable represents a color assigned to a particular cell, so if n is the order (or size) of the quasigroup, we have n^3 variables (n^2 cells with n colors each). Then, we generate clauses that encode the following constraints:

1. Some color must be assigned to each cell.
2. No color is assigned to two cells in the same row.
3. No color is assigned to two cells in the same column.

The first constraint generates clauses of length n with positive literals, and the second and third ones generate binary clauses with negative literals. The total number of clauses generated is $O(n^4)$.

In the Regular-SAT encoding, each variable represents a cell of the quasigroup and the truth value assigned to it represents the color of the cell, so we have $O(n^2)$ variables and n truth values. Then, we generate clauses that encode the same constraints as in the SAT encoding, except for the first constraint. This constraint does not need to be stated explicitly in the Regular-SAT encoding, because a many-valued interpretation to the variables of the formula ensures that each cell receives exactly one color. For encoding the constraint that a particular color i cannot be assigned to two different cells $c1$ and $c2$ of the same row (or column) we generate a regular clause of the form

$$(\downarrow i-1 : c_1 \vee \uparrow i+1 : c_1 \vee \downarrow i-1 : c_2 \vee \uparrow i+1 : c_2).$$

By repeating this clause for all the possible colors, we ensure that $c1$ and $c2$ do not receive the same color. The total number of clauses generated is also $O(n^4)$.

Local search results. In order to compare the typical performance of the Boolean SAT with the Regular-SAT approach, we solved hard QWH instances (*i.e.*, at the phase transition boundary in the backbone) of different orders. For each order, we considered 100 instances and solved the SAT and Regular-SAT encodings using WalkSAT [22] and Regular-WalkSAT [4], respectively. Every instance was solved 100 times with both algorithms. The implementation of WalkSAT used is the one available in the SATLIB and the implementation of Regular-WalkSAT is the one used in [4] (implemented in C++).

Table 2. Median cost for SAT, Regular-SAT and CSP when solving hard QWH instances of different order (at the phase transition)

order	flips		time (seconds)		
	SAT	Regular-SAT	SAT	Regular-SAT	CSP
27	964,849	168,455	2.1	1.5	1.7
30	2,985,105	525,884	7.2	4.8	6.9
33	11,123,065	1,520,667	27.1	16.2	57.1
36	30,972,407	5,099,701	70.8	53.9	1422.3

Table 2 shows the median cost, in time and flips, of all the test-sets used. The cost for a particular instance is defined as the mean time and mean number of flips needed to find a solution. We have also included results for the median time when using a CSP-based systematic search algorithm implemented with the constraint programming library ILOG and that uses the all-different constraint and the *R-brelaz-R* randomized branching strategy [12,21,23]. The results show that the median cost is smaller for the Regular-SAT approach, although between SAT and Regular-SAT the difference is more significant in terms of the number of flips. The greater difference in the number of flips can be in part attributed to the fact that the Regular-SAT encoding is more compact in terms of the number of variables. However, this difference does not directly translate in an equivalent difference in overall run time because the flip rate (flips per second) in Regular-WalkSAT is lower than in WalkSAT. At least some of this difference can be attributed to a higher level of optimization of the WalkSAT code. Despite that our implementation of Regular-WalkSAT is not so optimized, Table 2 still shows that Regular-WalkSAT also outperforms the other approaches in overall run time.

Figure 5 shows graphically the scaling bevahior in time and flips when we increase the order of the QWH instances. We see that the relative good performance of Regular-SAT scales up nicely with the order of the quasigroup. These results are consistent with the experimental results obtained with the other problem domains tested in [4] and summarized in Section 4.1.

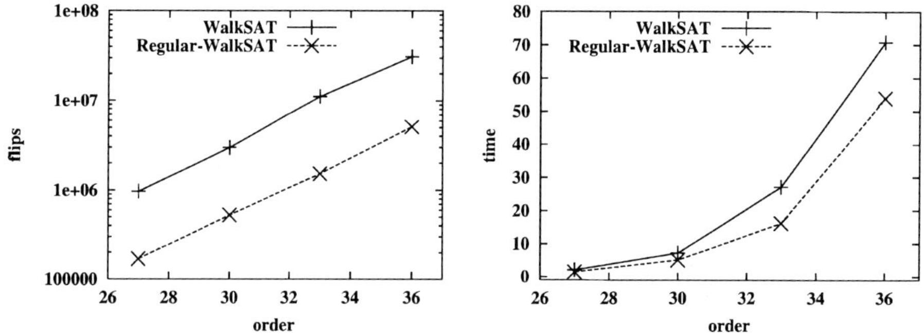

Fig. 5. Scaling behaviour of the median hardness for Regular-SAT and SAT on QWH instances

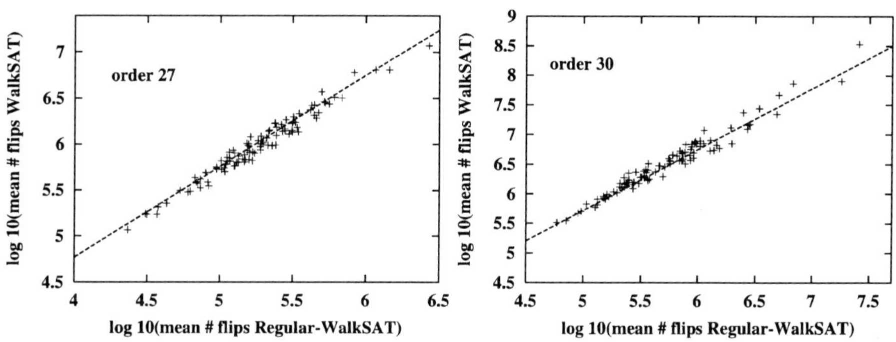

Fig. 6. Correlation between mean cost with Regular-SAT and SAT for order 27 ($a = 0.99, b = 0.81$ and $R_a^2 = 0.97$) and order 30 ($a = 1.03, b = 0.57$ and $R_a^2 = 0.96$).

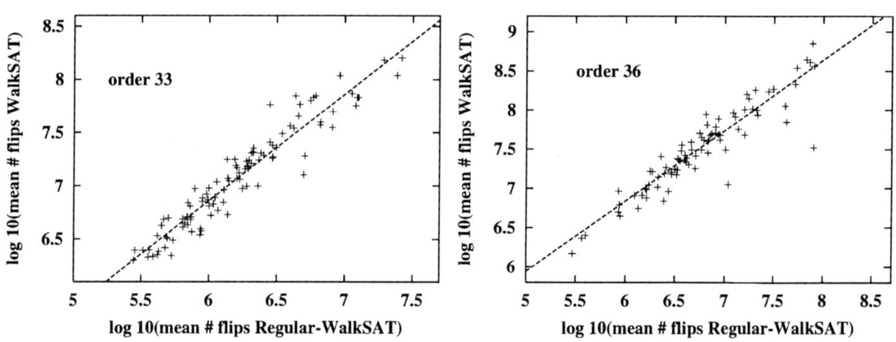

Fig. 7. Correlation between mean cost with Regular-SAT and SAT for order 33 ($a = 1.00, b = 0.86$ and $R_a^2 = 0.91$) and order 36 ($a = 0.90, b = 1.44$ and $R_a^2 = 0.86$)

We have also performed a regression analysis to study the relation between the computational cost of the two different approaches for all the instances of a given test-set. This kind of analysis allows us to investigate to what extent the superior performance observed for the median instance is also observed for any randomly obtained instance within the test-set. Figure 6 (left) shows the results of the regression analysis performed with the instances of order 27. A least-mean-squares (lms) regression analysis of the logarithm of the cost was performed. The figure shows the scatter plot, where each data point (x, y) represents the logarithm, in base 10, of the mean number of flips performed by Regular-WalkSAT (x value) and the same quantity for WalkSAT (y value) when solving a particular instance. The figure also shows the linear equation obtained by the regression analysis ($log_{10}(y) = a \log_{10}(x) + b$) and the adjusted coefficient of determination (R^2_{a}) that quantifies to what extent the model obtained fits the experimental data. Observe that by working with the logarithm of the data the actual functional relation we are fitting is $y = (10^b) \cdot x^a$. We see that, for order 27, a is close to 1 while 10^b is about 6.45. So, the relative performance increase for Regular-SAT holds uniformly for both easy, medium, and hard instances within the test-set.

Figures 6 (right) and 7 give the correlation analysis results for orders 30, 33, and 36. Observe that the fit of the experimental data is better for the smaller orders. A possible explanation is that as the order increases, the variability in the hardness of QWH instances increases. To properly model the correlation between instance hardness and relative performance may require a more complex regression model. Nevertheless, our analysis still suggests that the increase in performance of Regular-SAT holds fairly uniformly across each test-set.

Although the average complexity of solving instances from a problem domain distribution gives us a valuable information about the difficulty of the problem, the complexity of solving individual instances obtained with the same parameters can vary drastically from instance to instance. So, a more detailed analysis requires a study of the complexity of solving individual instances. To do so, we have constructed empirical Run-time distributions (RTDs) and Run-length (number of flips needed) distributions (RLDs) for both local search algorithms when solving the same instance. The methodology followed has been the one used in [16]. We have focused our attention on the median instance and the hardest instance of a given test-set. Here we present results for the test-set of quasigroups of order 33. Figure 8 shows the RLDs and RTDs for Regular-SAT and SAT on the median instance and also the RTD for CSP on the same instance. These empirical RLDs, in the cumulative form shown, give the probability that the algorithm finds a solution for the instance in less than the number of flips of the $x-$axis (similarly in the RTDs). We observe that Regular-SAT strictly dominates SAT; *i.e.*, the probability of finding a solution with Regular-SAT in less than x flips is always greater than the probability of finding a solution with SAT. Regular-SAT dominates the CSP approach even more significantly than SAT in the run time. Figure 9 shows the same results but for the hardest instance of the same test-set. We observe a similar relative difference between the run time performance of the three approaches.

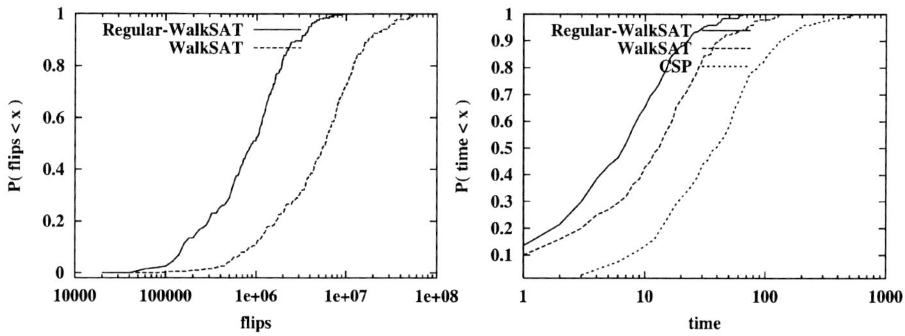

Fig. 8. RLDs (left) and RTDs (right) on the median instance for order 33

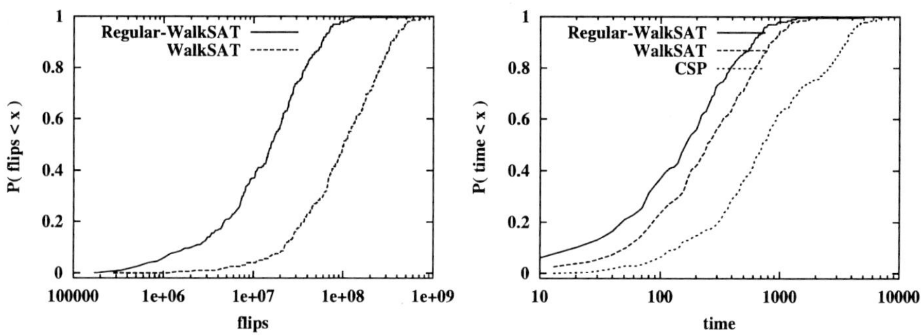

Fig. 9. RLDs (left) and RTDs (right) on the hardest instance for order 33

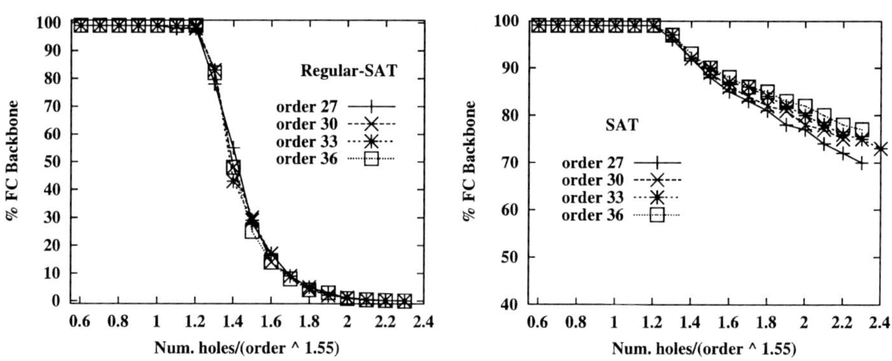

Fig. 10. The average forward-checing backbone for Regular-SAT (left) and SAT (right) on QWH instances

5 The Backbone Structure

We now consider the structure of the backbone in the QWH problem. Informally speaking, the backbone measures the amount of shared structure among the set of all solutions to a given problem instance [20]. The size of the backbone is measured in terms of the percentage of variables that have the same value in all solutions. Achlioptas *et al.* [1] observed a transition from a phase where the size of the backbone is almost 100% to a phase with a backbone size close to 0%. The transition is sudden and coincides with the hardest problem instances both for incomplete and complete search methods.

For efficiency purposes, Achlioptas *et al.* also propose a slightly weaker version of the backbone, which is computed by only using forward-checking (FC) to find shared variable settings in the solution set. They show that this backbone is qualitatively similar to the original notion of backbone. We adapted the notion of SAT FC backbone for Regular-SAT, which is obtained by applying the one-literal rule to every regular literal of the formula and computing the fraction of the total number of variables that becomes constrained to a single truth value.

The left panel of Figure 10 shows the FC backbone for QWH instances of different orders and with a different number of holes for the Regular-SAT encoding. We observe a phase transition in the fraction of backbone variables for the Regular-SAT encoding. In contrast, the right panel of Figure 10 displays the FC backbone structure for the Boolean SAT encoding. As we see from the figure, the SAT encoding does *not* properly preserve the phase transition properties of the backbone structure.[2] The Regular-SAT encoding can capture a structural property such as the backbone more faithfully than the Boolean SAT encoding.

6 Conclusions

We have shown that Regular-SAT provides an attractive approach for encoding and solving combinatorial problems. The formulation provides an intermediate alternative to the SAT and CSP approaches, and combines many of the good properties of each paradigm. Its similarity to SAT allows us to extend existing SAT algorithms to Regular-SAT without incurring excessive overhead in terms of computational cost. We have shown, using a range of benchmark problems, that Regular-SAT offers practical computational advantages for solving combinatorial problems. In addition, Regular-SAT maintains more of the original problem structure compared to Boolean SAT encodings. By providing more powerful search heuristics and optimizing the data structures, we expect to further extend the reach of the Regular-SAT approach.

Acknowledgements. We would like to thank Bart Selman for useful comments and discussions that helped to improve the paper. This research was partially

[2] This phenomenon was initially observed by [1,11]. One can still recover the phase transition of the backbone for the SAT encoding by restricting the backbone count to include only the variables set positively, as done in [1].

funded by the DARPA contracts F30602-00-2-0530 and F30602-00-2-0596, and project CICYT TIC96-1038-C04-03. The fourth author was supported by the "Secretaría de Estado de Educación y Universidades". This research was also partially funded by the Intelligent Information Systems Institute, Cornell University, funded by AFRL/AFOSR (F49620-01-1).

References

1. D. Achlioptas, C. P. Gomes, H. Kautz, and B. Selman. Generating satisfiable problem instances. In *Proc. of AAAI-2000*, pages 256–261, 2000.
2. R. J. Bayardo and R. C. Schrag. Using CSP look-back techniques to solve real-world SAT instances. In *Proc. of AAAI'97*, pages 203–208, 1997.
3. B. Beckert, R. Hähnle and F. Manyà. The SAT problem of signed CNF formulas. In *Labelled Deduction*, pages 61–82, Kluwer, 2000.
4. R. Béjar. *Systematic and Local Search Algorithms for Regular-SAT*. PhD thesis, Universitat Autònoma de Barcelona, 2000.
5. R. Béjar and F. Manyà. Phase transitions in the regular random 3-SAT problem. In *Proc. of ISMIS'99*, pages 292–300. LNAI 1609, 1999.
6. R. Béjar and F. Manyà. A comparison of systematic and local search algorithms for regular CNF formulas. In *Proc. of ECSQARU'99*, pages 22–31. LNAI 1638, 1999.
7. R. Béjar and F. Manyà. Solving combinatorial problems with regular local search algorithms. In *Proc. of LPAR'99*, pages 33–43. LNAI 1705, 1999.
8. J. C. Culberson and F. Luo. Exploring the k-colorable landscape with iterated greedy. In *Cliques, Coloring and Satisfiability*, volume 26 of *DIMACS Series in Discrete Mathematics and Theoretical Computer Science*. 1996.
9. M. Davis, G. Logemann, and D. Loveland. A machine program for theorem-proving. *Communications of the ACM*, 5:394–397, 1962.
10. A.M. Frisch and T.J. Peugniez. Solving non-Boolean satisfiability problems with stochastic local search. In *Proc. of IJCAI'01*, pages 282–288, 2001.
11. C. Gomes, H. Kautz, and Y. Ruan. QWH - A structured benchmark domain for local search. *Technical Report, Intelligent Information Systems Institute (IISI), Cornell University*, 2001.
12. C. Gomes, B. Selman, and N. Crato. Heavy-tailed distributions in combinatorial search. In *Proc. of CP'97*, pages 121–135. Springer LNCS 1330, 1997.
13. C. P. Gomes and B. Selman. Problem structure in the presence of perturbations. In *Proc. of AAAI'97*, pages 221–226, 1997.
14. R. Hähnle. Short conjunctive normal forms in finitely-valued logics. *Journal of Logic and Computation*, 4(6):905–927, 1994.
15. R. Hähnle. Exploiting data dependencies in many-valued logics. *Journal of Applied Non-Classical Logics*, 6:49–69, 1996.
16. H. Hoos and T. Stützle. Local search algorithms for SAT: An empirical evaluation. *Journal of Automated Reasoning*, 24(4):421–481, 2000.
17. C. M. Li and Anbulagan. Look-ahead versus look-back for satisfiability problems. In *Proc. of CP'97*, pages 341–355. LNCS 1330, 1997.
18. F. Manyà. The 2-SAT problem in signed CNF formulas. *Multiple-Valued Logic. An International Journal*, 5(4):307–325, 2000.
19. K. McAloon, C. Tretkoff, and G. Wetzel. Sports league scheduling. In *Proc. of ILOG International Users Meeting*, 1997.

20. R. Monasson, R. Zecchina, S. Kirkpatrick, B. Selman, and L. Troyansky. Determining computational complexity from characteristic 'phase transitions'. *Nature*, 400(8), 1999.
21. J.-C. Régin. A filtering algorithm for constraints of difference in CSPs. In *Proc. of AAAI'94*, pages 362–367, 1994.
22. B. Selman, H. A. Kautz, and B. Cohen. Noise strategies for improving local search. In *Proc. of AAAI'94*, pages 337–343, 1994.
23. K. Stergiou and T. Walsh. The difference all-difference makes. In *Proc. of IJCAI'99*, 1999.

Phase Transitions and Backbones of 3-SAT and Maximum 3-SAT

Weixiong Zhang

Department of Computer Science
Washington University
Campus Box 1045
One Brookings Drive
St. Louis, MO 63130
zhang@cs.wustl.edu

Abstract. Many real-world problems involve constraints that cannot be all satisfied. Solving an overconstrained problem then means to find solutions minimizing the number of constraints violated, which is an optimization problem. In this research, we study the behavior of the phase transitions and backbones of constraint optimization problems. We first investigate the relationship between the phase transitions of Boolean satisfiability, or precisely 3-SAT (a well-studied NP-complete decision problem), and the phase transitions of MAX 3-SAT (an NP-hard optimization problem). To bridge the gap between the easy-hard-easy phase transitions of 3-SAT and the easy-hard transitions of MAX 3-SAT, we analyze bounded 3-SAT, in which solutions of bounded quality, e.g., solutions with at most a constant number of constraints violated, are sufficient. We show that phase transitions are persistent in bounded 3-SAT and are similar to that of 3-SAT. We then study backbones of MAX 3-SAT, which are critically constrained variables that have fixed values in all optimal solutions. Our experimental results show that backbones of MAX 3-SAT emerge abruptly and experience sharp transitions from nonexistence when underconstrained to almost complete when overconstrained. More interestingly, the phase transitions of MAX 3-SAT backbones seem to concur with the phase transitions of satisfiability of 3-SAT. The backbone of MAX 3-SAT with size 0.5 approximately collocates with the 0.5 satisfiability of 3-SAT, and the backbone and satisfiability seems to follow a linear correlation near this 0.5-0.5 collocation.

1 Introduction and Overview

Understanding phase transition phenomena in complex systems and combinatorial problems [3,11,12,13,15,16,23,24] has been an active research focus for more than a decade. It is now well known that Boolean satisfaction problems typically exhibit easy-hard-easy phase transitions [3,16]. Specifically, the computational complexity of 3-SAT, a Boolean satisfaction problem in a conjunctive normal form with three literals (variable or its negation) per clause, experiences dramatic transitions from easy to difficult and then from difficult back to easy

T. Walsh (Ed.): CP 2001, LNCS 2239, pp. 153–167, 2001.

when the ratio of the number of clauses to the number of variables increases. Note that 3-SAT is a decision problem, which gives a solution when the problem is satisfiable or an answer NO when it is unsatisfiable.

On the other hand, it has also been shown that the expected complexity of finding optimal solutions of tree search problems, which include many of those combinatorial optimization problems that are solved by branch-and-bound methods, goes through easy to difficult transitions when the underlying heuristic functions degenerate [13,15,23,24].

In short, the phase transitions of some NP-complete decision problems have easy-hard-easy patterns and the phase transitions of some NP-hard optimization problems follow easy-hard patterns. These phase transition results exhibit a discrepancy between the phase transitions of decision and optimization problems.

An example of such a discrepancy is explicitly shown in two independent experimental study of phase transitions of the Traveling Salesman Problem (TSP) [10,25]. It was shown that there exists a rapid transition between soluble and insoluble instances of the decision problem of two-dimensional Euclidean TSP, and hard instances are associated with this transition, showing an easy-hard-easy pattern [10]. On the other hand, it was shown that the complexity of finding optimal solutions to the TSP displays an easy-hard pattern [25].

Phase transitions of different problems have different control or order parameters that may be adjusted to alter the phases of the problems. For instance, an order parameter for 3-SAT is the ratio of the number of clauses to the number of variables [3,16] and the number of distinct values of intercity distances is an order parameter for the TSP [25].

A more profound concept related to phase transitions is that of the backbone, which has been suggested as a more pertinent order parameter to characterize a complex problem. For examples, a *backbone* of a Boolean formula is the set of literals that are true in every model [17]; and a backbone of a k-coloring problem is defined to be the set of pairs of nodes each of which has the same color in every possible k coloring [5]. In other words, backbone variables are extremely constrained. A violation to a backbone variable rules out all optimal solutions.

This research was first motivated by the fact that there are numerous real-world constraint problems for which not all constraints can be satisfied. Such problems can be found in application areas such as scheduling, multi-agent cooperation and coordination, and pattern recognition [2,4,7]. Given such an overconstrained problem, the task of finding an solution to minimize the total number of violated constraints is an optimization problem or *constraint optimization problem.*

We are also motivated to understand the relationship between the phase transitions of decision problems and that of their optimization counterparts. In this study, we will focus our investigation on 3-SAT, which is a decision problem, and MAX 3-SAT, which is an optimization problem that requires the optimal solutions minimizing the total number of unsatisfied constraints.

Furthermore, We are motivated to investigate the backbones of optimization problems, particularly the backbone of MAX 3-SAT. Our goal is to understand the characteristics of all optimal solutions and the behavior of algorithms for finding them.

The paper is organized as follows. After a brief review of 3-SAT and MAX 3-SAT, we examine the phase transitions of 3-SAT and MAX 3-SAT by showing their different phase transition patterns (Section 2.2). We then generalize the notion of satisfiability to different decision problems with various bounds on decision quality (Section 2.3). We then study the backbone of MAX 3-SAT (Section 3). We discuss related work in Section 4 and conclude in Section 5.

2 Decision vs. Optimization Phase Transitions

In this section, we experimentally analyze the relationship between the phase transitions of decision problems and that of optimization problems using 3-SAT and MAX 3-SAT.

In our experiments on 3-SAT and MAX 3-SAT, we used 25 variables and varied the number of clauses to generate random problem instances. We restricted ourselves to this set of relatively small problems because of the following reasons. First, as we will see in the rest of the paper, MAX 3-SAT is much more difficult to solve than 3-SAT. Second, to find the backbones of these problems, we need to find all optimal solutions, which is substantially more difficult than finding just one solution. Third, this study is a statistical, experimental investigation so that we need to collect data from a relatively large pool of problem instances. Nevertheless, we have done experiments on 50 variable problems using a few dozen instances, and observed similar phenomena reported here.

In generating a clause, a randomly chosen variable has a 50 percent chance to be negated. No duplicate clause is allowed in a problem instance. We varied the clause/variable ratio from 1 to 20, with an increment of 0.2. For each clause/variable ratio, we generated 1,000 problem instances. We collected the median value or computed an averaged value of the results on these instances as needed.

In this study, we used the well-known Davis-Putman-Loveland (DPL) method, a backtracking method with unit resolution [6]. This algorithm is a special case of depth-first branch-and-bound where one variable is instantiated at each step. We extended the method to handle both 3-SAT and MAX 3-SAT. Due to space limit, we leave the detail of our extension to another report of the research.

2.1 3-SAT and MAX 3-SAT Problems

A *Boolean satisfiability*, or *SAT* for short, is a constraint satisfaction problem (CSP) that involves a Boolean formula consisting of a set of Boolean variables and a conjunction of a set of disjunctive clauses of literals, which are variables and their negations. A clause is satisfied if a literal within it takes a true value, and a Boolean formula is satisfied if all the clauses are satisfied. The conjunction defines constraints on the possible combinations of variable assignments. A *3-SAT* is a special Boolean satisfiability where each clause has three literals. 3-SAT is NP-complete and it is unlikely to have a polynomial algorithm for the problem [8]. Many practical problems can be cast as SAT [7,22].

Furthermore, there are also practical SAT problem in which no variable assignments can be found which does not violate a constraint [7]. In this case, it is required to find an assignment such that the total number of satisfied clauses is maximized. This is called *maximum 3-Sat.*

2.2 Discrepancy of Phase Transitions

As discussed in Section 1, there is a discrepancy between the phase transitions of decision problems and the phase transitions of their corresponding optimization versions. We investigate this discrepancy in detail.

We first consider 3-SAT. Figure 1 shows two types of phase transitions, a transition between satisfiability and unsatisfiability and easy-hard-easy transitions of computation cost. The order parameter that determines the phase transitions is the ratio of the number of clauses to the number of variables. The critical value of this order parameter for 3-SAT is around 4.13 [16]. A 3-SAT is almost always satisfiable when the clause/variable ratio is below this critical value and is almost always unsatisfiable when the ratio is beyond the critical value, making a sharp transition from satisfiability to unsatisfiability. Furthermore, the computational complexity required to decide the satisfiability is low when the probability of satisfiability is close to one or zero; while the complexity is the highest when this probability is 0.5, a value taken when the clause/variable ratio is around 4.13.

We now consider MAX 3-SAT. The only property we need to consider is its computational complexity, since an optimal solution is required throughout the whole spectrum of consideration so that there is no notion of satisfiability for the problem. Figure 2 shows the complexity of solving random MAX 3-SAT with 25 variables and various numbers of clauses. The problem instances used in Figure 2 are the same as that in Figure 1. To contrast the result with 3-SAT, we also include the complexity curve for 3-SAT. Figure 2 shows that starting at point A in the figure, MAX 3-SAT follows 3-SAT to enter computationally difficult region. However, MAX 3-SAT becomes more and more difficult when the clause/variable ratio increases even when 3-SAT enters its second easy region. In other words, the complexity of MAX 3-SAT follows an easy-hard pattern as the clause/variable ratio increases.

The discrepancy between the different patterns of the complexity phase transitions of 3-SAT and MAX 3-SAT indicates that optimizing is more difficult than making decision. The optimal solution to a MAX 3-SAT can be obviously used to answer the question if the corresponding 3-SAT is satisfiable or not. Thus a MAX 3-SAT, an optimal problem, is at least as hard as its corresponding 3-SAT, a decision problem. This discrepancy also indicates that constraints play different roles in an optimization problem and in its decision counterpart. When a problem instance is satisfiable, deciding if it is satisfiable is to find a variable

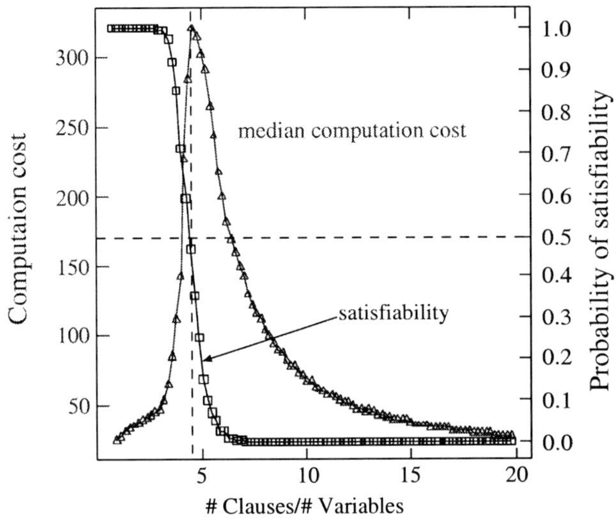

Fig. 1. Phase transitions of 3-SAT.

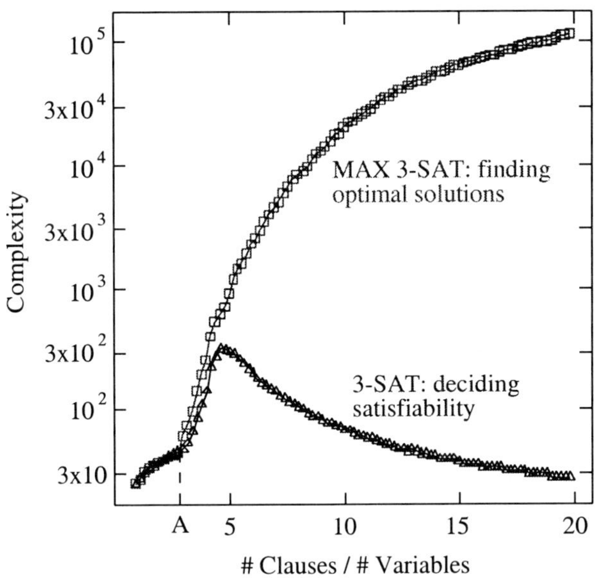

Fig. 2. Phase transitions of MAX 3-SAT.

assignment satisfying all the constraints, which is also an optimal solution to the optimization version of the problem. When a constraint problem is overconstrained, a small subset of the problem is very likely to be overconstrained as well, so that the problem can be declared unsatisfiable when such an overconstrained subproblem is detected unsatisfiable. The more constrained the problem is, the more quickly the decision process can conclude that no solution exists. However, in an overconstrained case, finding an optimal solution to minimize the total number of violated constraints is typically hard since every possible variable assignment can be a candidate of a optimal solution.

2.3 Quality-Bounded Decision Problems

The discrepancy between the two different phase transition patterns of 3-SAT and MAX 3-SAT has motivated us to investigate the relationship of the phase transitions of these two closely related problems.

In between a decision problem and its optimization counterpart there are many middle grounds that consist of decision problems with different decision objectives and quality. Such a decision problem may ask if there exists a variable assignment that violates no more than B constraints for an integer bound B. We call such a general decision problem *quality-bounded decision problem*, or *bounded decision problems* for short, and note it as 3-SAT(B). A 3-SAT(B) is satisfied if an assignment that violates no more than B constraints exists. It takes 3-SAT and MAX 3-SAT as special cases. When $B = 0$ it is 3-SAT; when B is the optimal solution cost, it is equivalent to MAX 3-SAT.

Are the phase transition properties of 3-SAT reserved under the general notion of satisfiability? Specifically, are there still a sharp transition from satisfiability to unsatisfiability and easy-hard-easy complexity transitions in 3-SAT(B) when the clause/variable ratio increases?

Figures 3 and 4 show our experimental results that answer these questions. Figure 3 shows the probability of satisfiability of 3-SAT(0), 3-SAT(5), 3-SAT(10), 3-SAT(15), and 3-SAT(20). The figure shows that 3-SAT(B) still has a sharp transition from satisfiable to unsatisfiable as the clause/variable ratio increases. The location of the transition for a given clause/variable ratio depend on B, however. The larger B is, the more problem instances are satisfiable. Similar to the unsettled issue of the exact location of the satisfiable to unsatisfiable transition of 3-SAT, it remains an interesting open problem to analytically determine the transition location of 3-SAT(B) with a non-zero integer bound B.

Figure 4 shows the computational complexity of an extended Davis-Putman-Loveland (DPL) algorithm on 3-SAT(0), 3-SAT(5), 3-SAT(10), 3-SAT(15), 3-SAT(20), and MAX 3-SAT. Note that the vertical axis is in a logarithmic scale. As the curves in the figure show, although the complexity of 3-SAT(B) still follows an easy-hard-easy transition pattern, the second easy region where problem instances are overconstrained becomes no longer very easy comparing to the first easy region where the problems are underconstrained. The larger B is, the computationally more difficult the second easy region becomes.

In short, a profound feature of phase transitions on computational complexity of 3-SAT(B) is that the transition from the first easy region to the difficult region is very sharp. In the first easy region, the computational complexity of 3-SAT(B) is relatively constant regardless the actual value of B. Whenever the complexity enters the difficult region, the complexity increases exponentially.

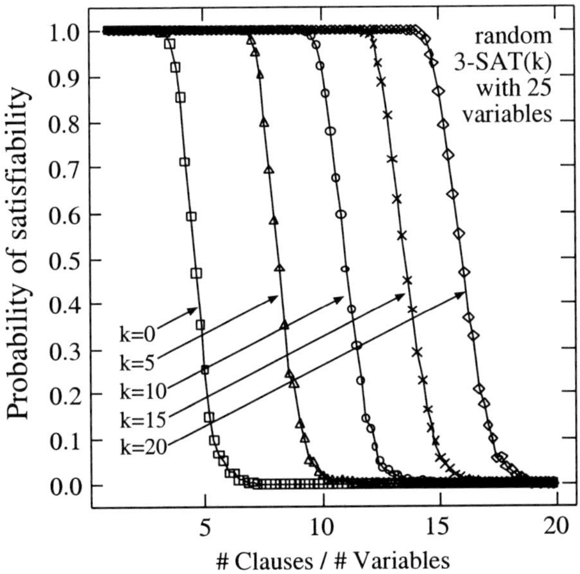

Fig. 3. Satisfiability phase transitions of 3-SAT(B).

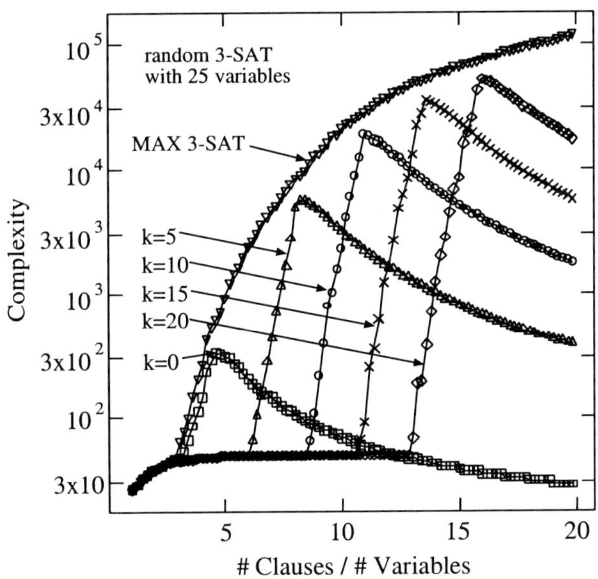

Fig. 4. Complexity phase transitions of 3-SAT(B).

More importantly, Figure 4 shows that the complexity curve of MAX 3-SAT is an upper envelop of the complexity curve of 3-SAT(B). Furthermore, the peak of the complexity of 3-SAT(B) is at the location where the quality bound B is near the the optimal solution cost of MAX 3-SAT, and this peak is close to the complexity of the corresponding MAX 3-SAT.

3 Phase Transitions and Backbones

We now study the phase transitions and backbones of decision and optimization problems. We investigate in particular various phase transition behavior and backbones of optimal solutions of 3-SAT and MAX 3-SAT.

In our experiments, we used the same set of randomly generated problem instances as for the experiments in the previous section. Specifically, we used 25 variables and varied the number of clauses by changing the clause/variable ratio from 1 to 20, with an increment of 0.2. For each clause/variable ratio, we generated 1,000 problem instances. We collected the median value or computed an averaged value of the results on these instances as needed. We also used the same extended DPL algorithm in these experiments.

3.1 Phase Transitions Related to Optimal Solutions

It is known that there are a large number of satisfying solutions whenever 3-SAT is underconstrained, which are credited for the low computation cost in the underconstrained region. These satisfying solutions are also optimal solutions to MAX 3-SAT. When 3-SAT is overconstrained, however, a satisfiable solution is unlikely to exist. What is the total number of optimal solutions when MAX 3-SAT is overconstrained? How will the other two important characteristics, the cost of optimal solutions and the computational cost of finding all optimal solutions, behave?

Figure 5 shows the median number of optimal solutions of 3-SAT and MAX 3-SAT with 25 variables in terms of clause/variable ratio. The dotted line in the figure is where the 50 percent satisfiability of 3-SAT occurs. The vertical axis is in a logarithmic scale. As Figure 5 shows, the curve of the average number of optimal solutions can be divided into two segments. In the underconstrained region, where the satisfiable instances dominate, the average number of solutions decreases *exponentially* as the clause/variable ratio increase. In the overconstrained region, the number of solutions is less than a dozen, and decreases approximately linearly with the clause/variable ratio.

Another characteristic factor associated with finding all solutions is the cost of optimal solutions, which is shown in Figure 6. The cost curve also has two segments, separated again by the 50 percent satisfiability line, the dotted line in the figure. In the underconstrained region, the median number of violated clauses remains zero; while in the overconstrained region, the cost increases linearly with the clause/variable ratio.

We now examine the computational costs of finding all optimal solutions. Figure 7 shows the experimental results. The median computational costs are shown in a logarithmic scale along the vertical axis. The overall computational curve is again separated by the 50 percent satisfiability point of 3-SAT, which

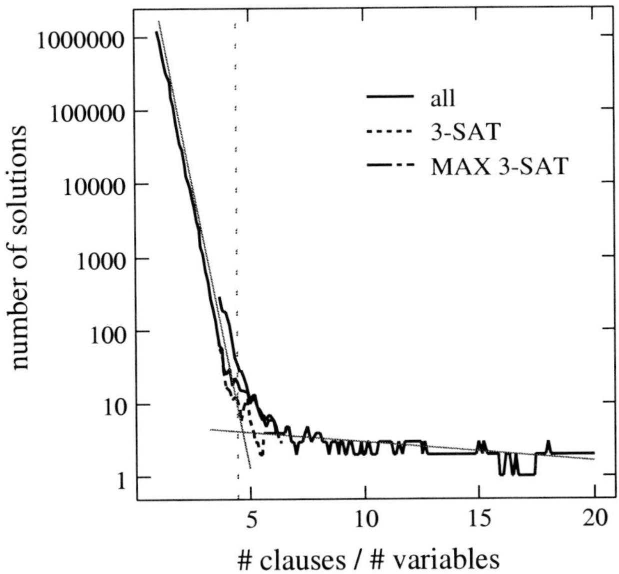

Fig. 5. Number of optimal solutions of 3-SAT and MAX 3-SAT.

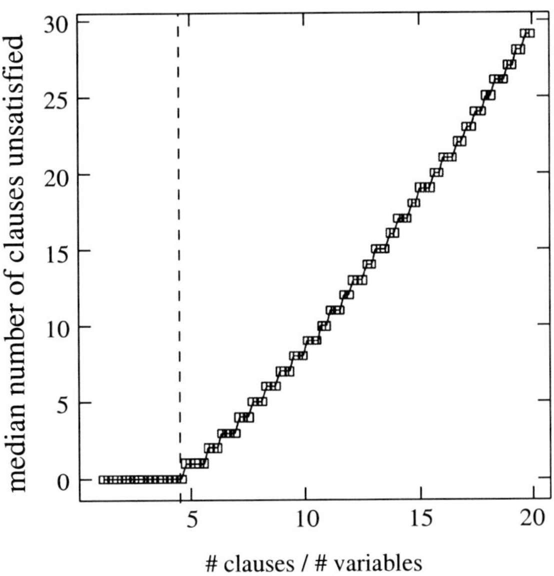

Fig. 6. Cost of optimal solutions of MAX 3-SAT.

is shown by the vertical dotted line in Figure 7. The major trend of the curve in the underconstrained region is an exponential drop. This differs significantly from the low, increasing computational cost for finding one satisfiable solution of

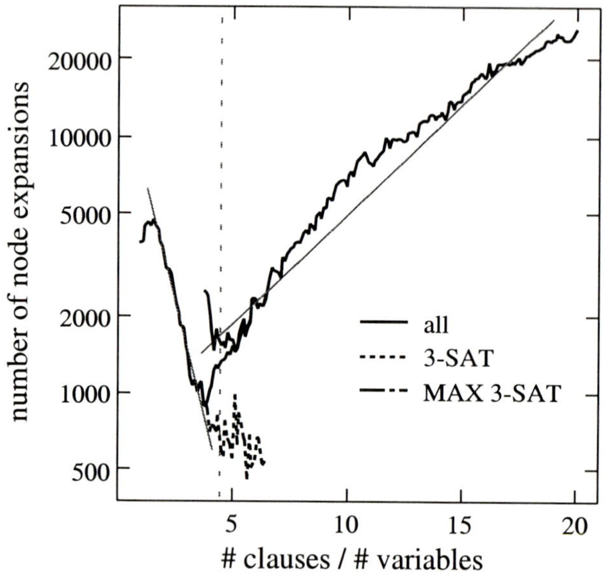

Fig. 7. Computational cost of 3-SAT and MAX 3-SAT.

3-SAT in this region as shown in Figure 1. The higher computational cost when the ratio is smaller is mostly due to enumerating the large number of optimal solutions (cf. Figure 5). When the clause/variable ratio passes through the 50 percent satisfiability separation point, the computational cost steadily increases exponentially.

If finding a single satisfiable solution to a 3-SAT at the 50 percent satisfiability point is considered difficult (cf. Figure 1), then finding all solutions of 3-SAT and MAX 3-SAT is a much harder problem. Based on Figure 7, the cost for finding all solutions around the 50 percent satisfiability point is near the lowest.

In summary, the three main features associated with finding all optimal solutions of 3-SAT and MAX 3-SAT, the number of optimal solutions, the computational cost and the cost of optimal solutions, are segmented by the 50 percent satisfiability point of 3-SAT, and follow different patterns in the underconstrained and overconstrained regions.

3.2 Backbone Phase Transitions

A backbone of a 3-SAT is a fraction of literals that have fixed values in all satisfying solutions [17]. In parallel, a backbone of a MAX 3-SAT is the fraction of literals that have fixed values in all optimal solutions. In short, backbone variables are critically constrained. A violation to any of these variables will rule out any optimal solution.

The size of a backbone can be normalized to a real number ranging from 0 to 1. A normalized backbone of 0 means that no variable is a backbone variable;

while a normalized backbone of size 1 means that all variables are backbone variables.

Our study of MAX 3-SAT backbones revealed two interesting results. First, there exist phase transitions of the backbones, shown in Figure 8, where the normalized median backbone sizes of 1,000 3-SAT and MAX 3-SAT problem instances are included. As the figure shows, backbones emerge abruptly as the clause/variable ratio increases. When the clause/variable ratio is less than 3.6, backbones almost do not exist. When the ratio is more than 3.6, backbones emerge quickly. Before the clause/variable ratio gets to 6, the median backbone size grows to more than 0.7, and reaches more than 0.9 when the ratio is 11. The first also shows that the backbone size of 3-SAT grows faster than that of MAX 3-SAT as the clause/variable ratio increases.

The second interesting, and a little bit surprising, result is that the backbone phase transitions of MAX 3-SAT are coincident with the satisfiability phase transitions of the corresponding 3-SAT. This is shown in Figure 9. The location where the backbone of MAX 3-SAT is 0.5 concurs approximately with the location where the corresponding 3-SAT has a probability 0.5 to be satisfiable. Within the vicinity near this 0.5-0.5 collocation (the dotted square within Figure 9), the backbone of MAX 3-SAT and the satisfiability of 3-SAT seem to be linearly correlated. An increase in backbone will cause the probability of satisfiability to drop proportionally, and vice versa.

There are only a few optimal solutions when the clause/variable ratio is very large, as shown by Figure 5. The backbone size is large when the clause/variable

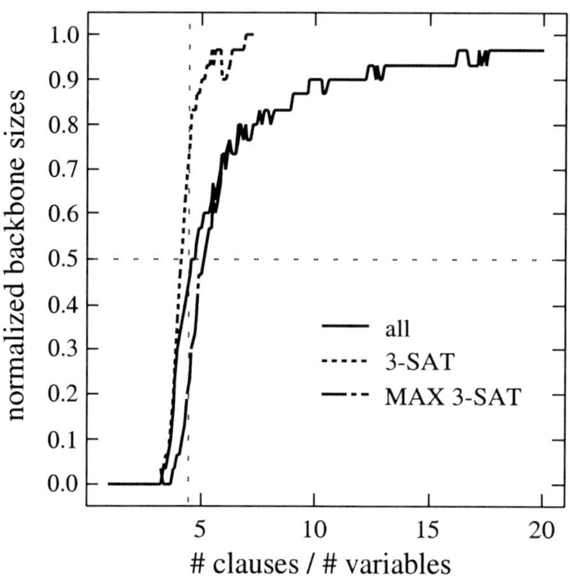

Fig. 8. Phase transitions of 3-SAT and MAX 3-SAT backbones.

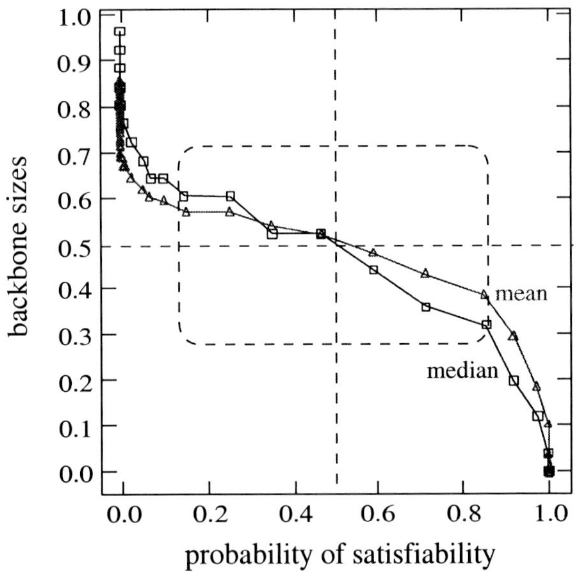

Fig. 9. Collocation of 0.5-0.5 transition points and near linear relation.

ratio is large, as shown in Figure 8. The combination of these two factors indicates that a handful of optimal solutions are clustered in a small neighborhood. Therefore, searching for any one of the clustered optimal solutions is difficult when backbone is large, since it is more likely to make a mistake of not setting a backbone variable to its correct value. On the other hand, when there exists no backbone variable, an arbitrary variable assignment may be an optimal solution. Therefore, finding such an optimal solution is easy.

4 Related Work

Huberman and Hogg discussed and argued that phase transitions are a universal feature of complex systems and problems [12]. Cheeseman et. al. [3] first experimentally demonstrated the existence of phase transitions in many combinatorial decision problems, including Boolean satisfiability, the Traveling Salesman Problem and graph coloring. The phase transitions of 3-SAT were extensively examined by Mitchell et. al. [16] and many other authors. This line of work concentrated mainly on decision problems. One of the main results is that the average computational complexity of decision problems follows an easy-hard-easy pattern.

The study of phase transitions of optimization problems probably started with Karp and Pearl's work of best-first search on a special random tree [13]. This random tree is an abstract model of many combinatorial search problems and state-space search algorithms, including best-first search and depth-first branch-and-bound. This work was extended to a more general tree by McDiarmid [15].

Zhang and Korf expanded the work to various linear space search algorithms, including depth-first branch-and-bound and iterative deepening [23,24]. A main conclusion of this line of research is that the expected computational complexity of optimization problems typically exhibits an easy-hard pattern.

The discrepancy between the easy-hard-easy phase transitions of decision problems and the easy-hard transitions of optimization problems has inspired us to investigate the relationship of these two types of problems and their phase transitions closely in this research. This complements the previous research on phase transitions of decision and optimization problems [20,9]. One of the results of this research reconciles the relationship between the phase transitions of these two types of combinatorial problems, especially 3-SAT and MAX 3-SAT. In addition, we also show that the curves of the computational cost of bounded 3-SATs are upper bounded by the curve of computational cost of MAX 3-SAT.

Backbone seems to be an old concept, studied by Kirkpatrick and Toulouse on the Traveling Salesman Problem [14], and attracting much attention recently. Monasson et. al., investigated the backbones of 3-SAT and (2+p)-SAT and suggested backbone as an order parameter for the decision problems [17]. Culberson and Gent extended the concept of backbones to graph coloring [5]. Achiloptas also considered the backbones of quasigroup complete problems [1]. Slaney and Walsh studied the backbones of many combinatorial optimization and approximation problems, such as graph coloring, the Traveling Salesman Problem, number partitioning and blocks world planning [21]. The relationship between backbone and local search on 3-SAT was studied by Parkes [18] and Singer et. al. [19].

Compared to the existing work on backbone, we made two main contributions in this research. The first is the result of the collocation of the 0.5 backbone of MAX 3-SAT (an optimization problem) and the 0.5 satisfiability of 3-SAT (a decision problem). The second is the result of the near linear correlation between these two phase transitions of two different but closely related problems.

5 Conclusions

We draw two conclusions from this research on constraint satisfaction and constraint optimization problems. First, phase transitions are persistent in bounded 3-SAT (3-SAT(B)) in which up to B constraints may be violated. We showed that deciding if there exists a variable assignment with no more than B constraints unsatisfied exhibits similar phase transitions as that in 3-SAT, i.e., dramatic satisfiable to unsatisfiable transitions and easy-hard-easy computational complexity phase transitions. However, the difficulty of the second computationally easy phase in 3-SAT(B) increases with the quality bound B. Furthermore, the computational cost of MAX 3-SAT envelops the computational cost peaks of 3-SAT(B).

Second, the backbones of 3-SAT MAX 3-SAT also experience phase transitions. A backbone is almost not existent in the underconstrained region, abruptly emerges when moving toward the critically constrained region, and quickly increases to almost a full size in the overconstrained region. The backbone of MAX 3-SAT with size 0.5 appears approximately at the location where 3-SAT is satisfiable with probability 0.5. Near this 0.5-0.5 phase transition collocation, the backbone of MAX 3-SAT and the satisfiability of 3-SAT seems to be linearly correlated.

This research makes two contributions. First, it reconciles the relationship between the phase transitions of decision and optimization problems, which were discovered different problem domains, bridging the gap of the previous phase transition results on these two types of problems. Second, it suggests that backbone in the solutions of optimization problems is an order parameter for the problems.

This work also gives rise to many interesting open questions for future research. For instance, where is the exact phase transition location of bounded 3-SAT(B)? Why does the backbone of MAX 3-SAT with size 0.5 collocate with 50 percent satisfiability of 3-SAT? Why does the backbone appear to have a linear correlation with the satisfiability?

Acknowledgment. This author was funded in part by NSF Grants #IRI-9619554, #IIS-0196057 and #ITR-0113618, and in part by DARPA Cooperative Agreements F30602-00-2-0531 and F33615-01-C-1897. Thanks to the anonymous reviewers for suggestions and comments that improved the quality of the paper.

References

1. D. Achlioptas, C. Gomes, H. Kautz, and B. Selman. Generating satisfiable problem instances. In *Proceedings of the 17th National Conference on Artificial Intelligence (AAAI-00)*, pages 256–261, Austin, Texas, July-August 2000.
2. J. C. Beck and M. S. Fox. A generic framework for constraint-directed search and scheduling. *AI Magazine*, 19(4):101–130, 1998.
3. P. Cheeseman, B. Kanefsky, and W. M. Taylor. Where the really hard problems are. In *Proceedings of the 12th International Joint Conference on Artificial Intelligence, (IJCAI-91)*, pages 331–337, Sydney, Australia, August 1991.
4. P. Codognet and F. Rossi. Notes for the ECAI2000 tutorial on Solving and Programming with Soft Constraints: Theory and Practice. Available at http://www.math.unipd.it/ frossi/papers.html.
5. Joseph Culberson and Ian P. Gent. Frozen development in graph coloring. *Theoretical Computer Science*, page to appear, 2001.
6. M. Davis, G. Logemann, and D. Loveland. A machine program for theorem proving. *Communications of ACM*, 5:394–397, 1962.
7. E. C. Freuder and R. J. Wallace. Partial constraint satisfaction. *Artificial Intelligence*, 58:21–70, 1992.
8. M. R. Garey and D. S. Johnson. *Computers and Intractability: A Guide to the Theory of NP-Completeness.* Freeman, New York, NY, 1979.
9. I. Gent and T. Walsh. Phase transitions and annealed theories: Number partitioning as a case stud,. In *ECAI-96*, pages 170–174, 1996.
10. I. P. Gent and T. Walsh. The TSP phase transition. *Artificial Intelligence*, 88:349–358, 1996.

11. T. Hogg, B. A. Huberman, and C. Williams. Phase transitions and the search problem. *Artificial Intelligence*, 81:1–15, 1996.
12. B. A. Huberman and T. Hogg. Phase transitions in artificial intelligence systems. *Artificial Intelligence*, 33:155–171, 1987.
13. R. M. Karp and J. Pearl. Searching for an optimal path in a tree with random costs. *Artificial Intelligence*, 21:99–117, 1983.
14. S. Kirkpatrick and G.Toulouse. Configuration space analysis of traveling salesman problems. *J. de Physique*, 46:1277–1292, 1985.
15. C. J. H. McDiarmid. Probabilistic analysis of tree search. In G. R. Gummett and D. J. A. Welsh, editors, *Disorder in Physical Systems*, pages 249–260. Oxford Science, 1990.
16. D. Mitchell, B. Selman, and H. Levesque. Hard and easy distributions of SAT problems. In *Proceedings of the 10th National Conference on Artificial Intelligence (AAAI-92)*, pages 459–465, San Jose, CA, July 1992.
17. R. Monasson, R. Zecchina, S. Kirkpatrick, B. Selman, and L. Troyansky. Determining computational complexity from characteristic 'phase transitions'. *Nature*, 400:133–137, 1999.
18. A. J. Parkes. Clustering at the phase transition. In *Proceedings of the 14th National Conference on Artificial Intelligence (AAAI-97)*, pages 340–245, Providence, RI, July, 1997.
19. J. Singer, I. P. Gent, and A. Smaill. Backbone fragility and the local search cost peak. *J. Artificial Intelligence Research*, 12:235–270, 2000.
20. J. Slaney and S. Thiebaux. On the hardness of decision and optimisation problems. In *Proceedings of ECAI-98*, pages 224–248, 1998.
21. J. Slaney and T. Walsh. Backbones in optimization and approximation. In *Proceedings of the 17th International Joint Conference on Artificial Intelligence, (IJCAI-01)*, page to appear, Seattle, WA, August 2001.
22. E. Tsang. *Foundations of Constraint Satisfaction.* Academic Press, London, 1993.
23. W. Zhang. *State-Space Search: Algorithms, Complexity, Extensions, and Applications.* Springer, New York, NY, 1999.
24. W. Zhang and R. E. Korf. Performance of linear-space search algorithms. *Artificial Intelligence*, 79:241–292, 1995.
25. W. Zhang and R. E. Korf. A study of complexity transitions on the asymmetric Traveling Salesman Problem. *Artificial Intelligence*, 81:223–239, 1996.

Solving Non-binary CSPs Using the Hidden Variable Encoding

Nikos Mamoulis[1] and Kostas Stergiou[2]

[1] CWI, Kruislaan 413, 1098 SJ Amsterdam, The Netherlands
nikos@cwi.nl,

[2] University of Glasgow, Department of Computer Science, Scotland
kostas@dcs.gla.ac.uk

Abstract. Non-binary constraint satisfaction problems (CSPs) can be solved in two different ways. We can either translate the problem into an equivalent binary one and solve it using well-established binary CSP techniques or use extended versions of binary techniques directly on the non-binary problem. Recently, it has been shown that the hidden variable encoding is a promising method of translating non-binary CSPs into binary ones. In this paper we make a theoretical and empirical investigation of arc consistency and search algorithms for the hidden variable encoding. We analyze the potential benefits of applying arc consistency on the hidden encoding compared to generalized arc consistency on the non-binary representation. We also show that search algorithms for non-binary constraints can be emulated by corresponding binary algorithms that operate on the hidden variable encoding and only instantiate original variables. Empirical results on various implementations of such algorithms reveal that the hidden variable is competitive and in many cases better than the non-binary representation for certain classes of non-binary constraints.

1 Introduction

The majority of the research on constraint satisfaction problems (CSPs) has focused on algorithms and heuristics that are applied on binary problems. The main reason for this is that any problem that contains constraints of an arbitrary arity can be transformed to an equivalent binary problem [11]. In the past, research on non-binary CSPs has mainly dealt with filtering algorithms. Recently, it is being recognized that more research on other non-binary issues is also required. As a result, search algorithms for binary CSPs have been extended for non-binary ones ([3]) and the efficiency of binary encodings has been investigated ([1,12,7]).

The most popular binary translations are the dual graph encoding and the hidden variable encoding. It is not clear which of the two is the best. However, the hidden variable encoding has some nice theoretical properties which make it a promising technique in many cases [12,13]. First, arc consistency (AC) on this

T. Walsh (Ed.): CP 2001, LNCS 2239, pp. 168–182, 2001.

binary representation achieves the same consistency level as generalized arc consistency (GAC) on the non-binary problem. This means that MAC (i.e., *maintaining arc consistency*) applied on the hidden variable encoding of a non-binary CSP visits the same search tree nodes as MGAC (i.e., *maintaining generalized arc consistency*) on the non-binary representation. Second, enforcing AC on an arbitrary encoded non-binary constraint takes the same number of consistency checks in the worst-case as GAC on its non-binary representation. These theoretical results, indicate that the hidden variable encoding is a promising way of solving non-binary CSPs with MAC. In practice, we can only use the hidden variable encoding on CSPs that have tight constraints. For CSPs with a large number of loose constraints it is reasonable to assume that the hidden variable encoding will be inefficient due to the large space requirements. It has also been shown experimentally that solving the binary encoding of a non-binary CSP can be less efficient than applying a non-binary version of some search algorithm, and vice versa, depending on the tightness of the constraints [1,12].

In this paper we take a closer look on arc consistency and search algorithms for the hidden variable encoding. The difference between an arc consistency algorithm on the encoding and a generalized arc consistency algorithm is the fact that the former has to update the domains of the hidden variables as well as the original ones. We show that this can lead to an arc consistency algorithm that runs on the encoding and, for any arc consistent graph, performs exactly the same number of consistency checks as the corresponding generalized arc consistency algorithm. For arc inconsistent graphs we show that the AC on the encoding can detect the inconsistency earlier and thus perform fewer checks than GAC. In a special case, the algorithms are equivalent not only in consistency checks but also in all the primitive operations they perform (e.g. domain lookups and deletions). In general, there is a trade-off between the binary and non-binary algorithms in the amount of primitive operations they perform. We also show that, like MGAC, the generalizations of forward checking to non-binary CSPs can be simulated by a corresponding binary forward checking algorithm on the hidden variable encoding that only instantiates original variables, resulting in the same node visits. We make an empirical comparison of different implementations of binary and generalized algorithms which reveals that the hidden variable encoding can be competitive and often better than the non-binary representation in certain classes of tight non-binary CSPs.

2 Background

A *constraint satisfaction problem* (CSP) $\mathcal{P}$ is defined by a triple $(\mathcal{X}, \mathcal{D}, \mathcal{C})$. $\mathcal{X}$ is a set of n variables. Each variable $x_i \in \mathcal{X}$ takes values from a domain $D_i \in \mathcal{D}$. $\mathcal{C}$ is a set of e constraints. Each k-ary constraint is defined over an ordered set of variables $\{x_1, \ldots, x_k\}$ by a subset of the Cartesian product $D_1 \times \ldots \times D_k$ that specifies the set of allowed value combinations (tuples). A constraint can be defined either extensionally by the set of allowed tuples or intensionally by a predicate or arithmetic function. In the following we will assume that all non-binary constraints are defined extensionally by nature, or can be represented extensionally without excessive space requirements. We also assume that there is at most one constraint per variable combination.[1]

A value a in the domain D of variable x is *consistent* with a constraint c if x is not included in the variables of the constraint, or if it is included and there exists a valid tuple τ in c where $x = a$. In the latter case we say that τ is a *support* for a in c. Checking whether a tuple is a support for a variable value pair (x, a) is called a *consistency check*. A variable x is *consistent* with a constraint c if $D \neq \emptyset$ and all its values are consistent with c. A constraint c is *arc consistent* (AC) if $\forall x_i \in \mathcal{X}$, x_i is consistent with c. A binary CSP is arc consistent if all its constraints are arc consistent. A CSP is *singleton arc consistent* (SAC) iff it has non-empty domains and for any instantiation of a variable, the problem can be made arc consistent. We call the generalizations of AC and SAC to non-binary CSPs GAC and SGAC respectively. Finally, a solution to a CSP is an assignment of values to variables which are consistent with all constraints.

Following [8], we call a local consistency property A *stronger* than B iff for any problem A deletes at least the same values as B, and *strictly stronger* iff it is stronger and for at least one problem A deletes more values than B. We call A *equivalent* to B iff they delete the same values for all problems. Similarly, we call a search algorithm A stronger than an algorithm B iff for every problem A visits at most the same search tree nodes as B, and strictly stronger iff it is stronger and for at least one problem A visits less nodes than B. A is equivalent to B iff they visit the same nodes for all problems.

2.1 Hidden Variable Encoding

The *hidden variable encoding* [11] is a well-known method for transforming a non-binary CSP to a binary one. It encodes the non-binary constraints to variables (called "hidden" variables) that have as domain the valid tuples of the constraint. For each tuple in the domain of the hidden variable v_c, the encoding introduces compatibility constraints between v_c and each original variable x_i in the constraint c. Each constraint specifies that the tuple assigned to v_c is consistent with the value assigned to x_i. Consider the following example with six variables with 0,1 domains, and four constraints: $x_1+x_2+x_6 = 1$, $x_1-x_3+x_4 = 1$, $x_4 + x_5 - x_6 \geq 1$, and $x_2 + x_5 - x_6 = 0$. In the hidden variable encoding (Figure 1) there are, in addition to the original six variables, four hidden variables. The domains of these hidden variables are the tuples that satisfy the respective constraint. For example, the hidden variable associated with the third constraint v_3 has the domain $\{(0,1,0),(1,0,0),(1,1,0),(1,1,1)\}$, as these are the tuples of values for (x_4, x_5, x_6) which satisfy $x_4+x_5-x_6 \geq 1$. There are now compatibility constraints between v_3 and x_2, between v_3 and x_5 and between v_3 and x_6, as these are the variables mentioned in the third constraint.

[1] Multiple constraints on the same set of variables can be reduced to a single constraint in the extensional representation.

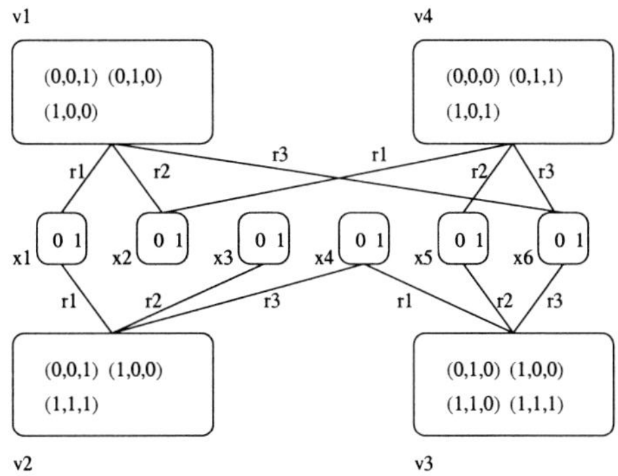

Fig. 1. Hidden variable encoding of a non-binary CSP. The binary constraint ri applies to a tuple and a value and is true iff the ith element of the tuple equals the value.

3 Arc Consistency

In this section we study the relationship between AC on the hidden variable encoding and GAC in more detail by examining the benefits of revising the domains of hidden variables. We will show that these revisions can help an AC algorithm on the encoding to identify inconsistencies earlier than the corresponding GAC algorithm.

3.1 GAC Algorithms

GAC-4 [10] is designed for constraints represented in extension by their allowed tuples. Each time a value a is deleted from a variable x, the tuples that include this variable-value pair are also deleted from the lists of allowed tuples. The deletion of these tuples may trigger the deletion of further values that lose their support, and so on. We can view this algorithm as a binary algorithm that runs on the hidden variable encoding. The only modification we need to make is to consider a constraint c as a hidden variable h_c and the set of allowed tuples of c as the domain of h_c. The propagation of deletions can then be done in exactly the same way resulting in the same primitive operations as in the non-binary case.[2] By *primitive operation* we mean a domain lookup (i.e, check if a value is in the domain of a variable), a deletion of a value (or a tuple), a consistency check, and any other check in a list or other data structure.

GAC-3 is an extension of the well-known AC-3 algorithm to non-binary CSPs. When a value is deleted from a variable, GAC-3 adds to a stack all constraints that involve that variable. Then, constraints are removed from the stack and are "revised". Revising a constraint means searching for a new supporting tuple for the values of all variables in the constraint. Checking whether an variable-value assignment is consistent with respect to a constraint $c = (x_1, \ldots, x_k)$ involves

[2] This equivalence has been pointed out by Christian Bessière at CP'99.

finding all tuples $< a_1, \ldots, a_k >$ in c that contain this assignment and checking if values $a_1, \ldots, a_k$ are still in the domains of variables $x_1, \ldots, x_k$. The reason for this is that GAC-3 like algorithms, in their standard implementation, do not make updates in the lists of allowed tuples like GAC-4 does when a value is deleted. So, they cannot check directly if tuple $< a_1, \ldots a_k >$ is still valid. This results in extra operations compared to GAC-4, but on the other hand GAC-3 like algorithms avoid updating the usually large sets of allowed tuples (i.e., hidden variable domains) and require less space. Like GAC-4, a GAC-3 algorithm that updates the lists of allowed tuples can be viewed as a binary algorithm that operates on the hidden variable encoding. GAC-schema [5] is another GAC algorithm that does not update the allowed tuples but instead looks for supports in a similar, but more sophisticated, way as GAC-3.

Recently, the binary AC-3 algorithm has been modified to yield an algorithm with optimal worst-case time complexity [6,14]. What makes the new AC-3 algorithms optimal is the use of a pointer $currentSupport_{x,a,c_{xy}}$ for each value a of a variable x involved in a constraint c between x and y. This pointer records the current value in the domain of y that was found to be a support of a. After a value deletion, if we look for a new support for a in y, we first check if the value where $currentSupport_{x,a,c_{xy}}$ points is still in the domain of y. If not, we search for a new support starting from the value immediately after the current support. Assuming that the domains are ordered, [6,14] prove that the new algorithm is optimal. This algorithm can be extended to non-binary constraints in a straightforward way. Again, we can use a pointer $currentSupport_{x,a,c}$ that points to the last tuple (assuming an ordering of the tuples) in constraint c that supported value a of variable x, where x is a variable involved in c. A sketch of the main functions of the algorithm, omitting the initialization phase, is shown in Figure 2. We now briefly discuss the complexity of this algorithm.

Like GAC-3, when a variable-value pair (x, a) is deleted, each constraint involving x is pushed on the stack. Then, constraints are popped from the stack and revised. Each $k-$ary constraint can be revised at most kd times, one for every deletion of a value from the domain of one of the k variables. Since we use the pointers $currentSupport_{x,a,c}$, for each variable-value pair (x, a) we can check at most d^{k-1} subtuples to find a support.[3] This results in $O(kdd^{k-1})$ checks for one constraint in the worst-case. For e constraints the worst-case complexity, measured in consistency checks, becomes $O(ekd^k)$. To check if a tuple is valid, in lines 3 and 4, we have to check if the values in the tuple are present in the domains of the corresponding variables. If one of these values has been deleted then the tuple is not valid.

3.2 AC on the Hidden Variable Encoding

As discussed, the worst-case cost of AC on the hidden variable encoding, measured in consistency checks, is the same as GAC on the non-binary representa-

[3] In fact, $\min\{d^{k-1}, |T|\}$ subtuples, where $|T|$ is the number of allowed tuples in the constraint. See [6,14] for details.

function *Propagation*
  While Q is not empty
    pick c from Q
    for each uninstantiated $x_i \in c$
      if $Revise(x_i, c) = TRUE$ *then*
        if domain of x_i is empty **then return** INCONSISTENCY
1   put in Q all constraints that involve x_i
  Return CONSISTENCY
function $Revise(x_i, c)$
  DELETION $\leftarrow$ FALSE
    for each value a in the domain of x_i
2   **if** $currentSupport_{x_i,a,c}$ is not *valid* **then**
3   **if** $\exists\ \tau(\in\ c) > currentSupport_{x_i,a,c}$, τ includes (x_i, a) and τ is *valid*
          then $currentSupport_{x_i,a,c} \leftarrow \tau$
4   **else** remove a from the domain of x_i
        DELETION $\leftarrow$ TRUE
  Return DELETION

Fig. 2. The algorithm of [6,14] for non-binary CSPs.

tion. When GAC-4 and its equivalent in the encoding are used, we can also get exactly the same number of primitive operations. We now analyze the difference between the extended GAC-3 algorithm and its equivalent on the encoding. To get the hidden variable equivalent of the GAC-3 algorithm shown in Figure 2 we need to make 3 changes. First, any references to constraints are substituted by references to hidden variables. For example, line 1 in Figure 2 will read: "put in Q all hidden variables that involve x_i". Second, after a value is removed from the domain of an original variable (line 4), all tuples that include that value are removed from the domains of the corresponding hidden variables. Third, checking if a tuple is *valid* is done in a different way than in the non-binary case. If a tuple is not valid then one of its values has been removed from the domain of the corresponding variable. This means that the tuple has also be removed from the domain of the hidden variable. Therefore, to check the validity of a tuple we only need to look in the domain of the hidden variable and check if the tuple is present.

We will now show that the GAC algorithm of Figure 2 and its corresponding AC algorithm on the encoding will perform the same number of consistency checks when applied on a problem that is GAC. Consider that if no domain wipeout in any variable (original or hidden) occurs then the two algorithms will add constraints (hidden variables) to the stack and remove them for revision in exactly the same order. The difference is that the binary version will revise domains of hidden variables as an extra step. However, this does not involve any consistency checks. Therefore, we only need to show that if a value is deleted from a variable during the revision of a constraint or finds a new support in the constraint then these operations will require the same number of checks in both representations. Assume that in the non-binary version of the algorithm value a

is deleted from variable x because it has no support in constraint c. If $|T|$ is the number of allowed tuples in c then this will require $|T| - currentSupport_{x,a,c}$ checks, one for each of the tuples in c that have not been checked yet. If the value is not deleted but finds a new support τ, with $\tau > currentSupport_{x,a,c}$, then $\tau - currentSupport_{x,a,c}$ checks will be performed. In the hidden variable encoding, x will be processed in the same order as in the non-binary version and we will require $|T| - currentSupport_{x,a,h_c}$ or $\tau - currentSupport_{x,a,h_c}$ checks depending on the case. h_c represents the hidden variable corresponding to c. Obviously, both supports are the same, since a tuple in c corresponds to a value in h_c, and the same number of checks will be performed in both representations.

On the other hand, on a problem that is not GAC, the AC algorithm on the encoding can perform less checks than the GAC algorithm. Consider a problem that includes variables x_1, x_2, x_3, x_4 with domains $\{0,1\}$, $\{0,1\}$, $\{0,\ldots,9\}$, and $\{0,1\}$, respectively. There are two constraints, c and c', over variables (x_1, x_2, x_3) and (x_1, x_2, x_4) respectively. Value 0 of x_2 is supported in c by tuples that include the variable-value pair $(x_1, 1)$. Value 0 of x_1 is supported in c' by tuples that include the variable-value pair $(x_2, 0)$. Values $0,\ldots,9$ of x_3 are supported in c by tuples that include $(x_2, 0)$ and by tuples that include $(x_2, 1)$. Assume that variable x_1 is instantiated to 0, which means that the deletion of 1 from x_1 must be propagated. In the encoding, we will first delete all tuples that include the value $(x_1, 1)$ from hidden variables h_c and $h_{c'}$. Then, we revise all original variables connected to hidden variables h_c and $h_{c'}$. Assuming that h_c is processed first, value 0 of x_2 will have no support in h_c so it will be deleted. As a result, we will delete all tuples from hidden variable $h_{c'}$ that include the pair $(x_2, 0)$. This means that the domain of $h_{c'}$ will be wiped out. In the non-binary representation, after the deletion of 0 from x_2, we will find that value 1 of x_2 and all values of x_3 have supports in c. This will involve checks that are avoided in the encoding. The inconsistency will be discovered when we process constraint c' and find out that value 1 of x_2 has no support in c' resulting in the domain wipeout of x_2.

We have demonstrated that AC in the hidden variable encoding can detect an inconsistency with fewer checks than GAC in the non-binary representation, while on graphs that are AC both algorithms will perform the same checks. This does not mean that algorithms on the encoding will always be more efficient in run times because the run time of an algorithm depends on the total number of primitive operations it will perform. There is a trade-off in the operations that the GAC algorithm performs in the non-binary version compared to the binary one. Assuming there are k_p past (instantiated) and k_f future variables in a constraint with $|T|$ allowed tuples then the binary GAC-3 algorithm will, in the worst case, perform $O(k_f d^{k_f})$ checks + $O(|T|)$ updates in the domain of the hidden variable, when applied on the encoding. That is, the worst-case complexity in the number of primitive operations is $O(k_f d^{k_f} + |T|)$. The non-binary GAC-3 will perform $O(k k_f d^{k_f})$ operations in the worst case. That is, for every check, the algorithm will have to make $O(k)$ domain checks to make sure that the checked tuple is valid.

4 Search Algorithms

Like GAC algorithms, non-binary search algorithms can be simulated by equivalent algorithms that run on the hidden variable encoding. For example, it has been shown that the MGAC algorithm on a non-binary CSP is equivalent to MAC on the hidden variable encoding of the CSP when only original variables are instantiated and similar branching heuristics are used [12]. We now show that similar results hold for generalized versions of forward checking (FC).

According to the simplest generalization of FC, forward checking is performed only after k-1 variables of an k-ary constraint have been instantiated. This algorithms is called nFC0 in [3]. More, and stronger, generalizations of FC to non-binary constraints were introduced in [3]. These generalizations differ between them in the extent of look-ahead they perform after each variable instantiation. For example, algorithm nFC5, which is the strongest version, tries to make the set of constraints involving at least one past variable and at least one future variable GAC. All the generalizations reduce to simple FC when applied to binary constraints.

Here we will show that the various versions of nFC are equivalent, in terms of visited nodes, to binary versions of FC that run on the hidden variable encoding of the problem. As mentioned, this holds under the assumption that the binary algorithms only instantiate original variables and they use similar branching heuristics as their non-binary counterparts. We call these binary algorithms hFC0–hFC5. Each binary algorithm performs the same amount of propagation as the corresponding non-binary algorithm. For example, hFC5 will enforce AC on the set of hidden variables, and original variables connected to them, such that each hidden variable is connected to at least one past original variable and at least one future original variable. The equivalence between nFC1 and an algorithm called FC+ in [1] has already been proven in [3].

Proposition 1. *In any non-binary CSP, algorithms nFC0–nFC5 are equivalent to binary forward checking algorithms hFC0–hFC5 that operate on the hidden variable encoding of the problem resulting in the same node visits.*

Proof. We prove this for nFC5, the strongest among the generalized FC algorithms. Proofs for the other versions are similar. We only need to prove that at each node of the search tree algorithms nFC5 and hFC5 will delete exactly the same values from original variables. Assume that at some node, after instantiating the current variable, nFC5 deletes value a from a future variable x because it found no support in a constraint c that has at least one instantiated variable. hFC5 will also delete this value from x because it will find no consistent tuple in the corresponding hidden variable h_c. This is due to the fact that the current domain of h_c will contain only valid tuples with respect to the current variable domains of the original variables, since inconsistent ones will have been deleted either in a previous run of AC, or after the instantiation of the current variable (recall that h_c contains at least one instantiated variable). Now in the opposite case, if hFC5 deletes value a from an original variable x it means that all tuples including that assignment are not present in the domains of a hidden variable

h_c that include x and at least one past variable. In other words, there is no consistent tuple in c, with respect to the current variable domains, that contains the assignment $x = a$. As a result, nFC5 will remove a from the domain of x. □

Therefore, if we never instantiate hidden variables in the binary representation and apply algorithms hFC0–hFC5 we will end up with the same node visits as the respective nFC0–nFC5 algorithms in the non-binary representation. Note that in [1] experimental results show differences between FC on the hidden variable encoding and non-binary FC. However, the algorithms compared there were FC+ and nFC0 which are not equivalent. We have also experimented with a stronger version of hFC5, which we call hFC5b, that visits fewer nodes than nFC5 and hFC5 but may perform more operations at each node. hFC5b is a FC algorithm that operates exactly like hFC5 in that no original variable involved in constraints that contain only future variables is revised. If however a value is deleted from some future variable x because of a constraint between x and past variables then all hidden variables connected to x are revised, including hidden variables that are only connected to future originals. Observe that there is no equivalent to hFC5b that applies on the non-binary representation. In general, the hidden variable encoding is a flexible representation that allows for the definition of algorithms that maintain more refined consistency levels depending on which hidden variables are updated.

5 Instantiating Hidden Variables

So far we have shown that solving an extensionally defined CSP by using the non-binary representation is in many ways equivalent to solving it using the hidden variable encoding, assuming that only original variables are instantiated. A natural question is whether search techniques which are inapplicable in the non-binary case can be applied on the encoding. The answer is the ability of a search algorithm that operates on the encoding to select and instantiate hidden variables. In the equivalent non-binary representation this would imply instantiating values of variables simultaneously. To implement such an algorithm we would have to modify standard search algorithms and heuristics or devise new ones. On the other hand, in the hidden variable encoding an algorithm that instantiates hidden variables can be easily implemented using a standard search algorithm and branching heuristic. Note, that if we only instantiate original variables then the hidden variables will be instantiated implicitly. That is, when all the original variables connected to a hidden are instantiated then the domain of the hidden variable is reduced to a singleton (i.e., it is instantiated). As the next section shows, by instantiating hidden variables in the encoding we can also achieve higher levels of consistency than in the non-binary representation.

5.1 Singleton Consistencies

We know that enforcing AC in the hidden variable encoding is equivalent to enforcing GAC in the original problem. Here we prove that when we move up to the consistency level of SAC then enforcing it on the hidden variable encoding is strictly stronger than enforcing SGAC on the original problem. This is derived from the ability of SAC to istantiate hidden variables and check their consistency. We denote by $P_{D_i=\{a\}}$ the CSP obtained by restricting the domain of variable x_i to $\{a\}$ in a CSP P.

Proposition 2. *Achieving singleton arc consistency on the hidden variable encoding of a non-binary problem is strictly stronger than achieving singleton generalized arc consistency on the variables in the original problem.*

Proof. We have to prove that if a value a of a variable x_i in a CSP P is not SGAC then SAC on the encoding of P will prune that value. From [12] we know that if a value b of variable x_j is not GAC in $P|_{D_i=\{a\}}$ then it is also arc inconsistent in the encoding of $P|_{D_i=\{a\}}$. For SGAC to remove value a, all values in a variable x_j must be deleted when a is assigned to x_i. According to the above, all such values will also be deleted from the domain of x_i in the hidden variable encoding of $P|_{D_i=\{a\}}$. Therefore, value a will be singleton arc inconsistent in the hidden variable encoding. To show strictness, consider a problem with five variables $\{x_1, x_2, x_3, x_4, x_5\}$, all of them with domain $\{0, 1\}$, and the following ternary constraints: A constraint over $\{x_1, x_2, x_3\}$ with allowed tuples $\{< 0,0,1 >, < 0,1,0 >, < 1,0,0 >, < 1,1,1 >\}$, a constraint over $\{x_1, x_2, x_4\}$ with allowed tuples $\{< 0,0,1 >, < 0,1,0 >, < 1,0,0 >, < 1,1,1 >\}$, and a constraint over $\{x_1, x_2, x_5\}$ with allowed tuples $\{< 0,1,0 >, < 1,0,1 >\}$, Enforcing SGAC on this problem will make no deletions. However, enforcing SAC on the encoding will show that the problem is insoluble. If we take the hidden variable h_1 corresponding to the constraint over $\{x_1, x_2, x_3\}$, for example, enforcing SAC will delete all the tuples from its domain because they are all singleton arc inconsistent.

□

In [12] it is proved that all consistency levels between SAC and AC (e.g. path inverse consistency and restricted path consistency) collapse onto AC, in the hidden variable encoding. Also, neighborhood inverse consistency, which is incomparable to SAC collapses onto AC. Therefore, the weakest consistency level where we notice a gap between the amount of pruning achieved in the hidden encoding and the non-binary representation is SAC. In fact, to get the pruning achieved by SAC in the encoding we only need to consider the hidden variables. For example, if all tuples in a hidden variable that include the variable-value pair (x, a) are removed by SAC then so will the value a from x. However, the extra pruning achieved in the encoding incurs extra cost because of the (usually) large domain sizes of the hidden variables. If we restrict SAC on encoding to the original variables only then we get the same level of consistency as SGAC in the original problem. The proof is easy and is omitted due to space restrictions.

6 Experimental Results

In this section we study empirically the efficiency of algorithms that run on the hidden variable encoding compared to their non-binary counterparts. For the empirical investigation we use randomly generated problems and benchmark crossword puzzle generation problems. Both of these classes are naturally defined by an extensional representation of the constraints. In the case of crossword puzzles the constraints are by nature very tight. In the case of random problems we also focus our attention on tight instances. The reason being that the binary encoding can only be practical if the constraints are tight enough so that the domains of the hidden variables are not prohibitively large.

6.1 Random Problems

Random problems were generated using the extended model B as in [3]. Under this model, a random CSP is defined by five parameters $< n, d, k, p, q >$, where n is the number of variables, d the domain size, k the arity of the constraints, p the density of the generated graph, and q the looseness of the constraints. p and q are given as a % percentage of the constrained variable combinations and allowed tuples in these constraints, respectively. In this empirical comparison we included the following algorithms: MGAC, MHAC, which stands for MAC in the encoding that only instantiates original variables, nFC5, hFC5, and hFC5b. hFC5 and hFC5b also instantiate only original variables. All algorithms use the dom/deg heuristic for variable ordering [4] and lexicographic value ordering. The GAC and AC algorithms used are the ones described in Sections 3.1 and 3.2. We chose to use these algorithms because they have a good asymptotic complexity and they are easy to implement. We do not include results on algorithms that can instantiate hidden variables as well as original ones because experiments showed that such algorithms have very similar behavior to the corresponding algorithms that instantiate only original variables. The reason is that, because of the nature of the constraints, the dom/deg heuristic almost always selects original variables. In the rare cases where the heuristic selected hidden variables, this resulted in an increase in node visits. Table 1 shows the performance of the algorithms on four classes of randomly generated ternary CSPs. All classes are from the hard phase transition region. Classes 1 and 2 are sparse, 3 is very sparse, and 4 is again relatively sparse but denser than the others. We report node visits, CPU times, and consistency checks. A consistency check consists of two operations. 1) Checking if a tuple τ includes the value for which we search for support, and 2) checking if τ is valid.

From Table 1 we can see that algorithms that operate on the encoding and instantiate only original variables perform fewer checks in all classes than the corresponding non-binary algorithms. This is due to their ability of early domain wipeout detection at dead ends. CPU times are influenced not only by the number of checks but by the total number of primitive operations performed. We can see that MHAC performs better than MGAC on the sparser problems. However, the differences in classes 1 and 2 are marginal. In general, for all the 3-ary classes we tried with density less than $3\% - 4\%$ the relative performance of MHAC and MGAC (in run times) ranged from being equal to a 40% advantage for MHAC. The differences are more notable on the very sparse class 3. This is due to the fact that for sparse problems the hard region is located at

Table 1. Comparison of algorithms on sparse random classes. Classes 1 and 2 taken from [3]. CPU times are in seconds. For nodes and checks we give mean numbers for 50 instances at each class. "K" implies $\times 10^3$ and "M" implies $\times 10^6$

	nFC5	hFC5	hFC5b	MGAC	MHAC
class 1: $n = 30$, $d = 6$, $k = 3$, $p = 1.847$, $q = 50$					
nodes	4645	4645	4150	3430	3430
sec	1.47	1.65	1.90	2.08	1.90
checks	13M	11M	10M	20M	14M
class 2: $n = 75$, $d = 5$, $k = 3$, $p = 0.177$, $q = 41$					
nodes	21976	21976	16723	7501	7501
sec	5.67	6.90	5.63	4.09	3.41
checks	17M	16M	12M	24M	15M
class 3: $n = 50$, $d = 10$, $k = 5$, $p = 0.001$, $q = 0.5$					
nodes	21283	21283	20260	16496	16496
sec	58.56	22.25	27.73	74.72	22.53
checks	783M	643M	631M	847M	628M
class 4: $n = 20$, $d = 10$, $k = 3$, $p = 5$, $q = 40$					
nodes	5400	5400	5124	4834	4834
sec	4.19	5.19	7.78	5.75	8.15
checks	119M	99M	95M	151M	119M

low constraint tightnesses (i.e., small domains for hidden variables) where only a few operations are required for the revision of hidden variables. Another factor contributing to the dominance of the binary algorithms in class 5 is the arity of the constraints. The non-binary algorithms require more operations to check the validity of tuples when the tuples are of large arity, as explained in Section 3.1.

When the density of the graph increases (class 4), the overhead of revising the large domains of hidden variables and restoring them after failed instantiations slows down the binary algorithms, and as a result they are outperformed by the non-binary ones. For denser classes than the ones reported, the phase transition region is at a point where more than half of the tuples are allowed, and in such cases the non-binary algorithms perform even better.

6.2 Crossword Puzzles

Crossword puzzle generation problems have been used for the evaluation of search heuristics for CSPs [9,2] and binary encodings of non-binary problems [1,12]. Tables 2 and 3 show the performance of the tested algorithms for various crossword puzzles in running time and number of visited nodes. We used selected hard puzzles from [9] and 20 15×15 and 19×19 puzzles from [2]. Apart from algorithms that instantiate only original variable we tested versions of hFC5 and MAC which may also instantiate hidden variables. We call these algorithms hidFC5, hidFC5b, and hidMAC. Again, all algorithms use the dom/deg heuristic for variable ordering. An em-dash (—) is placed wherever some method did not manage to find a solution within 5 hours of cpu-time. **n** is the number of words and **m** is the number of blanks in each puzzle. Problems marked by (*) are insoluble.

We used the Unix dictionary for the allowed words in the puzzles. Four puzzles (15.06, 15.10, 19.03, 19.04) could not be solved by any of the algorithms within 5 hours of cpu time. Also two puzzles (19.05 and 19.10) were arc inconsistent. GAC discovered the inconsistency slower than HAC in both cases (around 3:1 time difference in 19.05 and 10:1 in 19.10) because the latter method discovered early the domain wipe-out of a hidden variable.

At the rest of the puzzles we can observe that MHAC usually performs better than MGAC on the hard instances. For the hard insoluble puzzles the difference is considerable, and so is the difference between hFC5 and nFC5. This is mainly due to the uniformly large arity of the constraints in these classes.[4] Another interesting observation is that there can be large differences between the performance of methods that instantiate hidden variables and those which instantiate only original ones. In many cases hidMAC managed to find a (different) solution than MHAC and MGAC earlier. This shows that we can benefit from a method that instantiates hidden variables. In puzzle 19.08 hidMAC managed to find a solution fast, while the other MAC algorithms thrashed. Note, that the FC algorithms also found a solution quickly, which means that in this case the propagation of MGAC and MHAC misguided the variable ordering heuristic. On the other hand, the hid* methods were also subject to thrashing in instances where other methods terminate. The fact that in all insoluble puzzles hidMAC did not do better than MHAC shows that its performance is largely due to the variable ordering scheme. When comparing MAC methods with equivalent FC5 ones, we see that in most cases maintaining full consistency is better for this class of problems. Also, the hFC5b and hidFC5b algorithms do not always pay-off.

Regarding node visits, observe that in many cases hidden variable instantiation methods visit less nodes than their original variable counterparts, but this does not reflect to the same time performance difference because when a hidden variable is instantiated hidMAC does more work than when an original one is. It has to instantiate automatically all original variables involved in the hidden and propagate these changes to all other hidden variables containing them. Note, that constraints in crosswords are much tighter than the constraints in random problems. For example, the tightness of a 6-ary constraint in a puzzle is 99,999988%. This is why the hid* methods can perform well on such problems. Consistent problems with such high tightnesses cannot be generated randomly.

In general, we believe that if we exploit better the potential of instantiating hidden variables (i.e., by a suitable variable ordering heuristic), methods that instantiate hidden variables can go down the search tree faster than ones that consider only original variables, because they can benefit from small hidden variable domains. Notice that hidMAC reduces to MHAC if it instantiates only original variables. Therefore, if employed with the optimal variable ordering it can never be worse than MHAC. We are currently working towards devising such ordering heuristics.

[4] Puzzles 6×6–10×10 correspond to square grids with no blank squares.

Table 2. Comparison (in cpu time) of algorithms on crossword puzzles. All times are in seconds except those followed by "m" (minutes).

puzzle	n	m	MGAC	MHAC	hidMAC	nFC5	hFC5	hidFC5	hFC5b	hidFC5b
15.01	78	189	8.5	7.9	4.4	11.5	15.4	5.3	10.1	4.2
15.02	80	191	24.5	26.9	—	77.8	138.7	—	61.1	—
15.03	78	189	4.2	4.6	2.3	21.2	30.6	2.3	30.9	2.81
15.04*	76	193	290	295	218	24.5	29.8	979	243	791
15.05	78	181	3	3.1	2.2	3.7	3.8	3.3	4.8	2.5
15.07	74	193	670	335	376m	48.3	39.4	482m	465m	367m
15.08	84	186	2.32	2.27	2.89	3.22	3.37	3.52	3.27	3.1
15.09	82	187	2.24	2.3	2.45	1.92	1.81	—	2.43	—
19.01	128	301	7.6	7.3	6.9	—	—	4.56	—	4.8
19.02	118	296	198	204	—	—	—	—	495	—
19.06	128	287	5.9	4.7	5.8	4.1	4.9	4.6	5	—
19.07	134	291	3.4	3.4	4.4	4.1	4.1	5.2	3.8	5.2
19.08	130	295	—	—	5.45	4	3.3	4.7	3.6	4.7
19.09	130	295	3.64	5	4.2	6.2	6.7	4.6	4.8	4.8
puzzleC	78	189	77.5	107	—	153	209	—	115	—
6×6	12	36	84	55	64	109	75	104	73	79
7×7*	14	49	120m	75m	96m	176m	107m	159m	120m	148m
8×8*	16	64	45m	29m	42m	58m	32m	57m	35m	59
9×9*	18	81	488	337	454	868	470	737	614	797
10×10*	20	100	117.7	77	93	534	331	363	192	217

Table 3. Comparison (in node visits) of algorithms on crossword puzzles. MGAC and MHAC visit the same number of nodes and this holds also for nFC5 and hFC5.

puzzle	n	m	MGAC,MHAC	hidMAC	nFC5,hFC5	hidFC5	hFC5b	hidFC5b
15.01	78	189	574	200	1607	398	1067	295
15.02	80	191	1312	—	15559	—	6029	—
15.03	78	189	338	126	4105	159	3364	183
15.04*	76	193	19667	18479	2869	75450	25202	63985
15.05	78	181	286	145	528	248	459	189
15.07	74	193	12733	568768	4180	1504450	2700150	744180
15.08	84	186	247	165	362	277	294	187
15.09	82	187	251	155	247	—	287	—
19.01	128	301	469	309	—	224	—	202
19.02	118	296	15764	—	—	—	33079	—
19.06	128	287	375	158	357	200	346	—
19.07	134	291	305	206	344	240	306	222
19.08	130	295	—	191	332	249	322	218
19.09	130	295	308	167	458	199	347	171
puzzleC	78	189	9827	—	26315	—	11820	—
6×6	12	36	2263	2097	7332	5735	5028	4259
7×7*	14	49	116082	138199	634858	455716	396791	303330
8×8*	16	64	31386	40037	231950	163527	108338	78076
9×9*	18	81	4972	5715	71020	35736	23279	14344
10×10*	20	100	1027	1120	35492	18922	13105	10438

7 Conclusion

In this paper, we performed a theoretical and empirical investigation of arc consistency and search algorithms for the hidden variable encoding of non-binary CSPs. We analyzed the potential benefits of using AC algorithms on the hidden encoding compared to GAC algorithms on the non-binary representation. We showed that FC algorithms for non-binary constraints can be emulated by corresponding binary algorithms that operate on the hidden variable encoding and only instantiate original variables. Empirical results on various implementations of search algorithms showed that the hidden variable is competitive and in many cases better than the non-binary representation for tight classes of non-binary constraints. A general conclusion from this study is that there is an interesting mapping between algorithms for non-binary constraints and corresponding algorithms for binary encodings, even in refined levels of implementation. For future work we plan to develop variable ordering heuristics more suitable to the hidden encoding. Also, we intend to investigate how lessons learned from this study apply to other GAC algorithms, like GAC-schema.

Acknowledgements. The second author is a member of the APES research group and would like to thank all other members. Especially, Peter van Beek, Ian Gent, Patrick Prosser and Toby Walsh. We would also like to thank Christian Bessière.

References

1. F. Bacchus and P. van Beek. On the Conversion between Non-Binary and Binary Constraint Satisfaction Problems. In *Proceedings of AAAI'98*, pages 310–318, 1998.
2. A. Beacham, X. Chen, J. Sillito and P. van Beek. Constraint programming lessons learned from crossword puzzles. In *Proceedings of the 14th Canadian AI Conf.*, 2001.
3. C. Bessière, P. Meseguer, E.C. Freuder, and J. Larrosa. On Forward Checking for Non-binary Constraint Satisfaction. In *Proceedings of CP'99*, pages 88–102, 1999.
4. C. Bessière and J.C. Régin. MAC and Combined Heuristics: Two Reasons to Forsake FC (and CBJ?) on Hard Problems. In *Proceedings of CP'96*, pages 61–75, 1996.
5. C. Bessière and J.C. Régin. Arc Consistency for General Constraint Networks: Preliminary Results. In *Proceedings of IJCAI'97*, pages 398–404, 1997.
6. C. Bessière and J.C. Régin. Refining the basic constraint propagation algorithm. In *Proceedings of IJCAI'2001.*
7. X. Chen. A Theoretical Comparison of Selected CSP Solving and Modeling Techniques. PhD thesis, University of Alberta, Canada, 2000.
8. R. Debruyne and C. Bessière. Some practicable filtering techniques for the constraint satisfaction problem. In *Proceedings of IJCAI'97*, pages 412–417, 1997.
9. M. Ginsberg, M. Frank, M. Halpin, and M. Torrance. Search lessons learned from crossword puzzles. In *Proceedings of AAAI-90*, pages 210–215, 1990.
10. R. Mohr and G. Masini. Good old discrete relaxation. In *Proceedings of ECAI'88*, pages 651–656, 1988.
11. F. Rossi, C. Petrie, and V. Dhar. On the equivalence of constraint satisfaction problems. In *Proceedings of ECAI'90*, pages 550–556, 1990.
12. K. Stergiou and T. Walsh. Encodings of Non-Binary Constraint Satisfaction Problems. In *Proceedings of AAAI'99*, pages 163–168, 1999.
13. K. Stergiou and T. Walsh. On the complexity of arc consistency in the hidden variable encoding of non-binary CSPs. *Submitted for publication.*
14. Y. Zhang and R. Yap. Making AC-3 an optimal algorithm. In *Proceedings of IJCAI'2001.*

A Filtering Algorithm for the Stretch Constraint

Gilles Pesant

Centre for Research on Transportation
Université de Montréal, C.P. 6128, succ. Centre-ville, Montreal, H3C 3J7, Canada
and
École Polytechnique de Montréal, Montreal, Canada
pesant@crt.umontreal.ca

Abstract. This paper describes a filtering algorithm for a type of constraint that often arises in rostering problems but that also has wider application. Defined on a sequence of variables, the stretch constraint restricts the number of consecutive identical values in the sequence. The algorithm mainly proceeds by determining intervals in which a given stretch must lie and then reasoning about them to filter out values. It is shown to have low time complexity and significant pruning capability as evidenced by experimental results.

Introduction

A number of global constraints introduced in the constraint programming literature have successfully encapsulated powerful filtering algorithms, often inspired from existing ones, while remaining sufficiently generic to ensure wide applicability (e.g. [7][2][8]). This paper proposes another such constraint that often arises in rostering problems, for example. Defined on a sequence of variables, the *stretch* constraint specifies lower and upper limits on the number of consecutive identical values in that sequence. These limits may also depend on the value. The filtering algorithm mainly proceeds by determining intervals in which a given stretch must lie and then reasoning about them to filter out values.

The rest of the paper is organized as follows. The next section briefly describes the usual context in which the constraint is found. Section 2 presents a formulation of the constraint while section 3 explains the filtering algorithm which is used to enforce it. Some experimental results are then reported in section 4 to assess the algorithm's efficiency. Section 5 discusses some consistency issues. Finally, section 6 presents concluding remarks on the applicability of such a constraint.

1 Rostering

Many industries and public services operate around the clock, seven days a week. In such a context, every day a number of work shifts must be covered by one or a team of workers. A workload requirement matrix is usually given or computed

T. Walsh (Ed.): CP 2001, LNCS 2239, pp. 183–195, 2001.

which specifies the number of (teams of) workers required for each type of shift of every day, either as a precise value or an interval. For shift work, it is often preferable to schedule work stretches of the same type of shift for individuals: it is easier on their internal body clock as well as on their family and social life [4].

Accordingly, restrictions on the length of a work stretch are usually given as part of the formulation of the problem. Work stretches will typically be constrained to span at least one or two shifts and at most six or seven. Such a restriction will rarely vary between shift types except maybe for days off. Permitted patterns of shift types are also usually given. As a special case of this, a common restriction is that between two consecutive work stretches, some minimum number of days off should be given. Other constraints are present too that do not concern us here.

1.1 Rotating Schedules

When the personnel is interchangeable, rotating schedules, a repeating pattern of sequences of work and rest days alternating over several weeks, are particularly well adapted. A schedule is given over a cycle of w weeks and the workforce is divided into w teams: initially the first team follows the schedule of week 1, the second one the schedule of week 2, and so forth. After the seventh day, each moves to the next week, the team on week w moving up to week 1. In effect, everyone has an identical schedule but that is out of phase with the other teams. This ensures that everybody is treated equally. An example of a rotating schedule is given in table 1.

Table 1. A simple rotating schedule. Symbols "D", "E", and "N" indicate day, evening, and night shifts respectively whereas "-" indicates a day off.

Week	Mon	Tue	Wed	Thu	Fri	Sat	Sun
1	-	-	-	D	D	D	D
2	-	-	E	E	E	-	-
3	D	D	D	-	-	E	E
4	E	E	-	-	N	N	N
5	N	N	N	N	-	-	-

That example features stretches of length four and three for day shifts; three and four for evening shifts; seven for night shifts; two, two, two, two, and six for days off.

1.2 Personalized Schedules

When members of the personnel have individual restrictions or preferences that must be taken into consideration, such as unavailabilities due to other activities, rotating schedules become inappropriate. Personalized schedules for each member of personnel are then elaborated. This is typical of some category of personnel such as physicians.

Instead of a cyclic schedule as before, many individual rosters need to be designed, spanning a given scheduling horizon. Constraints on the length of work stretches are still relevant in this context and may vary from one individual to another.

2 The Stretch Constraint

Let work shifts be numbered consecutively from 0 to $n-1$.[1] Consider a constraint programming model for the rostering problem in which a sequence of decision variables $s_0, s_1, \ldots, s_{n-1}$ stand for consecutive work shifts either representing the whole roster, in the case of rotating schedules, or one individual roster, in the case of personalized schedules. In the rest of the paper, we will take the point of view of rotating schedules, for which the sequence of shifts is cyclic — consequently indices will be computed modulo n. Let $\mathcal{D}_{s_i} \subseteq \mathcal{T}$ denote the domain of s_i, where $\mathcal{T} = \{\tau_1, \tau_2, \ldots, \tau_m\}$, the set of shift types , including one corresponding to a day off.

Definition 1. *Subsequence $s_i, s_{(i+1) \bmod n}, \ldots, s_j$ is called a* stretch *when $s_i = s_{(i+1) \bmod n} = \cdots = s_j$ but $s_{(i-1) \bmod n} \neq s_i$ and $s_{(j+1) \bmod n} \neq s_j$. The span of a stretch from indices i to j, denoted* span(i,j), *is defined as $1 + (j-i) \bmod n$.*

Definition 2. *We call* pattern *two contiguous work stretches of different types (e.g. $\tau_1, \tau_1, \tau_1, \tau_2, \tau_2$ denoted $\tau_1\tau_2$).*

As indicated before, instances of rostering problems often restrict which patterns may appear in a schedule. One sometimes meets slightly more complex prescribed arrangements of two work stretches of given types separated by a stretch of rest shifts (e.g. $\tau_1, \tau_1, \tau_m, \tau_2$). Though more elaborate patterns are conceivable, the previous two cases are sufficiently expressive for all real-life rostering instances encountered by the author so far.

Let $\check{\lambda}$ and $\hat{\lambda}$ be integer vectors of length m, Π be a set of patterns, and γ be a boolean value. The stretch constraint may then be formulated as

$$\texttt{stretch}(\langle s_0, s_1, \ldots, s_{n-1}\rangle, \check{\lambda}, \hat{\lambda}, \Pi, \gamma)$$

with the following semantics:

$$\forall\, 0 \leq i \leq n-1, \text{ the span of the stretch through } s_i \text{ lies between } \check{\lambda}_{s_i} \text{ and } \hat{\lambda}_{s_i}.$$

As $\check{\lambda}$ and $\hat{\lambda}$ respectively represent minimum and maximum lengths for stretches, the constraint is only well-defined when $\check{\lambda}_k \leq \hat{\lambda}_k \ \forall k$. Set Π represents the permitted patterns for the sequence — they are used to refine the

[1] We choose to start with 0 in order to simplify subsequent modulo expressions.

filtering but are not enforced by this constraint. The value *true* for γ indicates a cyclic schedule where s_{n-1}'s successor in the sequence is s_0; the value *false* indicates a sequence with no wrap around.

A similar constraint is the global sequencing constraint [8]. Defined on a sequence of variables as well, it is used to specify minimum and maximum numbers of appearances of each value within every subsequence of a given length. The main difference is that these values do not have to appear consecutively (i.e. in a stretch).

3 Its Filtering Algorithm

This section is devoted to the detailed description of the algorithm enforcing the semantics of `stretch`.

3.1 Determining Bounds on a Stretch

All the filterings described here are based on information about the possible beginning and end of a particular stretch. For any given shift s_i taking value τ_k, we wish to compute the tightest intervals $[\beta_{\min}, \beta_{\max}]$ and $[\epsilon_{\min}, \epsilon_{\max}]$ in which the beginning and the end of the stretch through that shift must lie, respectively, given the current domains of the s_j's. Figure 1 provides an example. The extremal values of the intervals are derived using the algorithms given below.

$\beta_{\max}$:

1. $j \leftarrow (i-1) \bmod n$;
2. **while** $s_j = \tau_k$ **do**
  a. $j \leftarrow (j-1) \bmod n$;
3. $\beta_{\max} \leftarrow (j+1) \bmod n$;

This first algorithm simply scans the shift variables backwards from index i until it reaches one that is not currently instantiated to τ_k. $\beta_{\max}$ is then set to the index following that (see figure 2). We do not reproduce the algorithm for $\epsilon_{\min}$ here as it is simply the mirror image of the previous one.

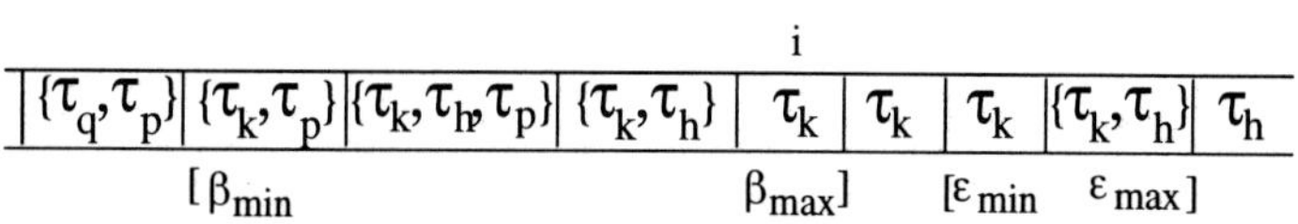

Fig. 1. Bounding a stretch of τ_k's on a sample fragment of a schedule.

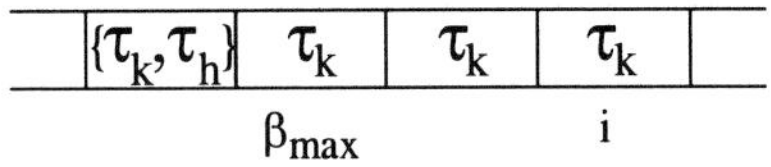

Fig. 2. Determining $\beta_{\max}$ on a sample fragment of a schedule.

$\beta_{\min}$:

```
1. if λ̂_k ≥ n then too_far ← (ε_min + 1) mod n;
2. else too_far ← (ε_min − λ̂_k) mod n;
3. j ← (β_max − 1) mod n;
4. done ← false;
5. while j ≠ too_far and not done do
   a. while τ_k ∈ D_{s_j} and |D_{s_j}| > 1 and j ≠too_far do
      i. j ← (j − 1) mod n;
   b. if τ_k ∉ D_{s_j} then
      i. β_min ← find-frontier(j, k, β_max);
      ii. done ← true;
   c. else if |D_{s_j}| = 1 then
      i. j' ← j;
      ii. while s_j = τ_k and j ≠ too_far do
            j ← (j − 1) mod n;
      iii. if s_j = τ_k then
            β_min ← find-frontier((j' + 1) mod n, k, β_max);
            done ← true;
6. if not done then β_min ← find-frontier(j, k, β_max);
```

The computation of $\beta_{\min}$ is more involved. In order to avoid unnecessary work a threshold value, *too_far*, is determined beyond which $\beta_{\min}$ cannot possibly lie. Step 1 deals with a special case whereas step 2 corresponds to the general case: the threshold is equal to the earliest position at which the stretch may end minus the longest it may run. In step 3, j is set to the position immediately preceding $\beta_{\max}$. Step 5 iterates until either $\beta_{\min}$ is determined or the threshold is reached. First, the shift variables are scanned backwards from j as long as the current variable has several values in its domain, including τ_k, and the threshold has not been reached (5a). If the scan was stopped because τ_k does not belong to the domain (5b), then $\beta_{\min}$ cannot lie beyond this point but its proper value is determined by the call to *find-frontier*, which we shall describe shortly, and then we are done (see figure 3). Failing that, if the scan was stopped because the shift variable is bound (5c), then it must be that $s_j = \tau_k$. If position j is included in the stretch then so must its immediate predecessor if it is also bound to τ_k, and so on, since a stretch clearly cannot be flanked by shifts of the very same type,

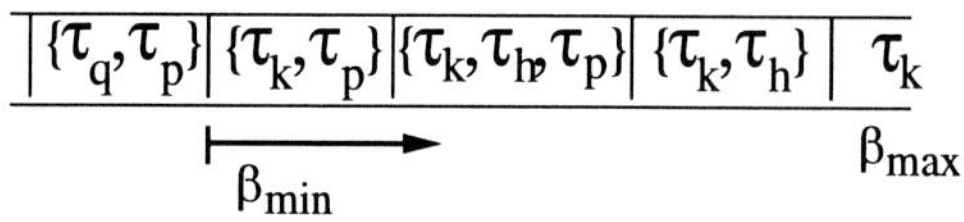

Fig. 3. Step 5b in determining $\beta_{\min}$ on a sample fragment of a schedule.

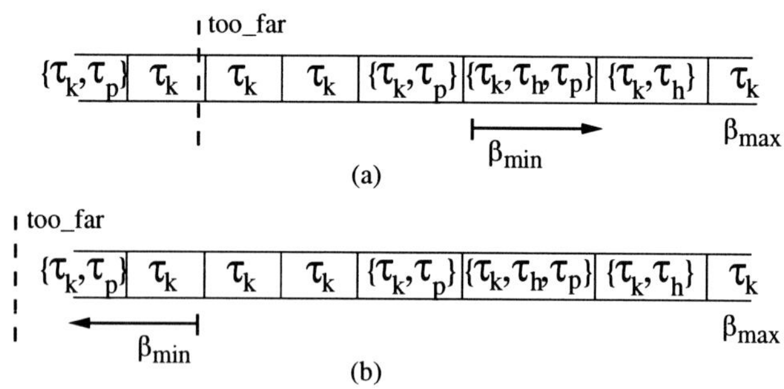

Fig. 4. Step 5c in determining $\beta_{\min}$ on a sample fragment of a schedule.

from its definition. So, the shift variables are scanned backwards until one that is not currently instantiated to τ_k is met or the threshold is reached (5cii). If at the threshold while still being instantiated to τ_k (5ciii), the stretch would be too long and so $\beta_{\min}$ must lie to the right of that run of bound variables, as determined by the call to *find-frontier*, and we are done (see figure 4a). Otherwise a new iteration of step 5 is begun (see figure 4b). Finally, if the threshold is reached without encountering any limitation to $\beta_{\min}$, *find-frontier* is called in order to determine $\beta_{\min}$ more precisely in light of what lies just beyond that threshold.

Just as for $\epsilon_{\min}$, the computation of $\epsilon_{\max}$ is not described since it proceeds similarly.

find-frontier(j, k, p):

> **1. while** $j \neq p$
> **a. for each** $\tau_\ell \in \mathcal{D}_{s_j}$ **such that** $\tau_\ell \tau_k \in \Pi$
> **i.** found $\leftarrow$ true;
> **ii. for** $i = 1$ **to** $\check{\lambda}_\ell - 1$
> **if** $\tau_\ell \notin \mathcal{D}_{s_{(j-i) \bmod n}}$ **then** found $\leftarrow$ false;
> **iii. if** found **then return** $(j+1) \bmod n$;
> **b.** $j \leftarrow (j+1) \bmod n$;
> **2. return** -1;

find-frontier ensures that on the immediate left of $\beta_{\min}$, enough variables have a common value in their domains to allow a valid neighbouring stretch. Step 1 scans the variables forward from j until a value τ_ℓ is found that lies in the domains of $s_j, s_{j-1}, \ldots, s_{j-\check{\lambda}_\ell}$ and that forms a permitted pattern of shift types with τ_k, at which time value $(j+1) \bmod n$ is returned. As an example, consider the fragment in figure 4a with $\check{\lambda}_p = 2$: $\beta_{\max} - 1$ will be returned. In step 2, if p is reached without any such value being found then -1 is returned. In the context of the computation of $\beta_{\min}$, the latter means that interval $[\beta_{\min}, \beta_{\max}]$ is empty, triggering one of the filtering rules in section 3.3.

The following confirms that our later reasoning based on those intervals will be sound:

Theorem 1. *Given the current domains of the sequence of variables, intervals $[\beta_{\min}, \beta_{\max}]$ and $[\epsilon_{\min}, \epsilon_{\max}]$ as computed above must respectively include the starting and the ending indices of the stretch through s_i.*

Proof. Clearly, the starting index cannot be larger than $\beta_{\max}$ since by construction of the latter this would mean that the stretch has a shift of the same type as its immediate left neighbour, contradicting its definition. The argument that the starting index cannot be smaller than $\beta_{\min}$ has already been given while describing the corresponding algorithm. Similar arguments can be made for $\epsilon_{\min}$ and $\epsilon_{\max}$, thus completing the proof. □

It is easy to see that all the algorithms given above, with the exception of the work performed in *find_frontier*, exhibit a worst-case time complexity that is linear in $\hat{\lambda}_k$, the maximum length of a stretch of type τ_k. Because of the three nested loops in *find_frontier*, its worst-case time complexity is in $\mathcal{O}(\hat{\lambda}_k \cdot m \cdot \max\{\check{\lambda}_i : 1 \le i \le m\})$. This is still low since in practice the number of shift types seldom exceeds four and the maximum length of stretches rarely exceeds eight.

Before proceeding further, we give a brief overview of the filtering algorithm. Two types of events are considered: when a value is removed from the domain of a shift variable, potentially breaking a stretch of the corresponding shift type, the possibility of a valid stretch of that type is verified on both sides of the variable; when a variable becomes bound, several filterings are applied based on where the beginning and end of the stretch through that variable may lie.

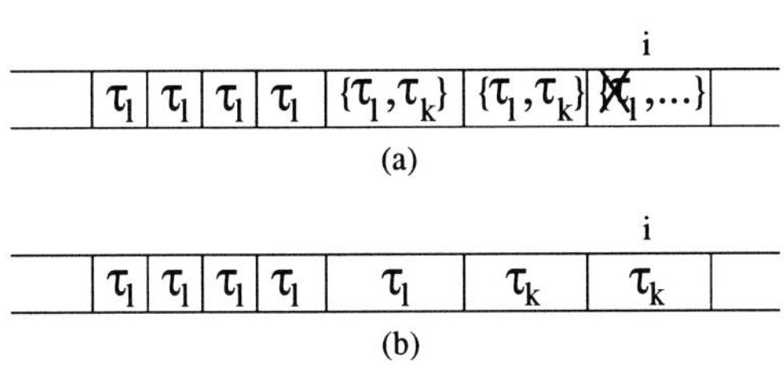

Fig. 5. Detecting a broken stretch (a); a possible fragment of the schedule (b).

3.2 Detecting Broken Stretches

Each time the domain of a shift variable s_i is modified, the following algorithm may be applied:

F1.

> **for each** τ_ℓ **just removed from** $\mathcal{D}_{s_i}$
>
> **1. if** $\tau_\ell \in \mathcal{D}_{s_{(i-1) \bmod n}}$
>
> **a.** $j \leftarrow$ computation of $\beta_{\min}$ for a potential stretch of τ_ℓ's ending at $(i-1) \bmod n$;
>
> **b. if** $\text{span}(j, (i-1) \bmod n) < \check{\lambda}_\ell$ **or** $j = -1$ **then**
>
> **i. remove** τ_ℓ **from** $\mathcal{D}_{s_{(i-1) \bmod n}}$;
>
> **2. if** $\tau_\ell \in \mathcal{D}_{s_{(i+1) \bmod n}}$
>
> **a.** $j \leftarrow$ computation of $\epsilon_{\max}$ for a potential stretch of τ_ℓ's starting at $(i+1) \bmod n$;
>
> **b. if** $\text{span}((i+1) \bmod n, j) < \check{\lambda}_\ell$ **or** $j = -1$ **then**
>
> **i. remove** τ_ℓ **from** $\mathcal{D}_{s_{(i+1) \bmod n}}$;

The algorithm considers in turn each value τ_ℓ removed from the domain of s_i. If a stretch of τ_ℓ's may appear on the immediate left of s_i, the left-hand side is examined (step 1). Step 1a determines the earliest beginning of such a stretch. If it cannot be long enough to be valid then value τ_ℓ is removed from the domain of $s_{(i-1) \bmod n}$. Note that, at this time, we may not remove that value for further neighbours to the left since it might prevent a stretch ending a little before. For example, consider figure 5a with $\check{\lambda}_\ell = 3$ and $\hat{\lambda}_\ell = 5$: value τ_ℓ will be removed from $\mathcal{D}_{s_{(i-1) \bmod n}}$ but τ_ℓ is still possible for $s_{(i-2) \bmod n}$, as shown in figure 5b. Nevertheless, that single removal in turn may trigger further deletions. The examination of the right-hand side (step 2) proceeds similarly.

The application of this algorithm guarantees that any value left in the domain of a shift variable has enough peers in neighbouring shift variables to make up a minimum length stretch. This property simplifies the algorithm for filtering rules F5 and F6 in section 3.3.

Since F1 features in the worst case $\mathcal{O}(m)$ computations of $\beta_{\min}$ which itself includes a call to *find-frontier*, its worst-case time complexity is in $\mathcal{O}(\hat{\lambda}_k \cdot m^2 \cdot \max\{\check{\lambda}_i : 1 \leq i \leq m\})$.

3.3 Reasoning on the Potential Extent of a Stretch

Once we have the intervals, a number of filtering rules may be applied each time a shift variable is instantiated to a value τ_k. First, a value of -1 may have been returned by a call to *find-frontier*:

F2. If $\beta_{\min} = -1$ or $\epsilon_{\max} = -1$ then the stretch constraint is violated.

We may also simply discover that the stretch is necessarily too long or too short:

F3. If span($\beta_{\max}, \epsilon_{\min}$) $> \hat{\lambda}_k$ then the stretch constraint is violated.
F4. If span($\beta_{\min}, \epsilon_{\max}$) $< \check{\lambda}_k$ then the stretch constraint is violated.

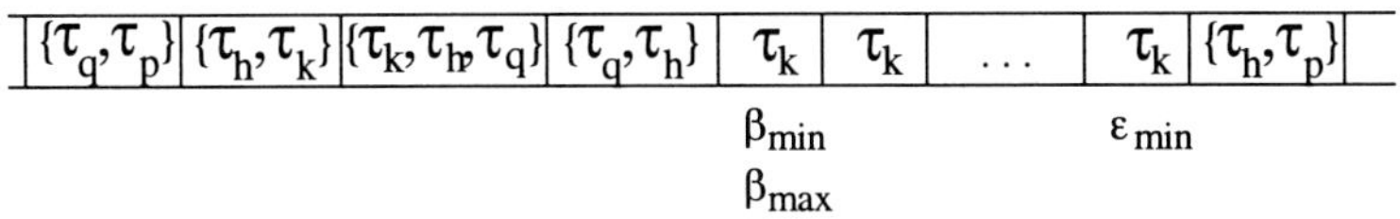

Fig. 6. Illustration of rule F5.

F5. If $\beta_{\max} = \beta_{\min}$ then we know precisely where the stretch begins. Value τ_k may thus be removed from preceding shift variables:

> **1.** $\lambda \leftarrow \infty$;
> **2. for each** $\tau_\ell \in \mathcal{D}_{s_{(\beta_{\max}-1) \bmod n}}$ **such that** $\tau_\ell \tau_k \in \Pi$
>   **a. if** $\check{\lambda}_\ell < \lambda$ **then** $\lambda \leftarrow \check{\lambda}_\ell$;
> **3. if** $\lambda \neq \infty$ **then for** $i = 1$ **to** λ
>   **a. remove** τ_k **from** $\mathcal{D}_{s_{(\beta_{\max}-i) \bmod n}}$;

Step 2 computes the length λ of the shortest feasible neighbouring stretch on the left so that step 3 may remove value τ_k from the λ shift variables immediately preceding the current stretch since those neighbours must necessarily be of a different type. For example in figure 6, suppose $\check{\lambda}_h = 3$ and $\check{\lambda}_q = 2$. So $\lambda = 2$ and τ_k may be removed from the domain of $s_{\beta_{\max}-2}$.

F6. If $\epsilon_{\max} = \epsilon_{\min}$ then we know precisely where the stretch ends. Value τ_k may thus be removed from following shift variables, using an algorithm that is the symmetric counterpart of the previous one.

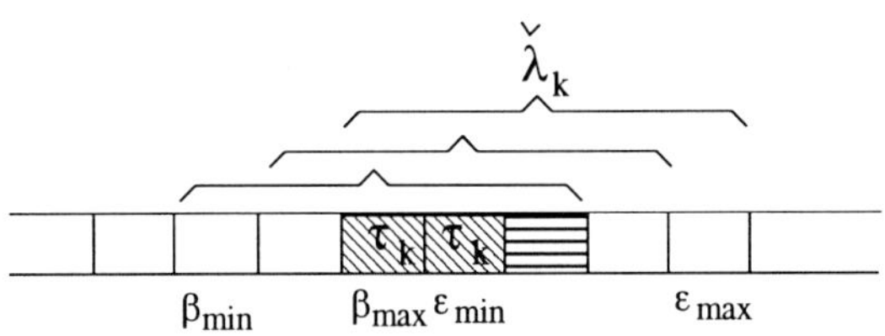

Fig. 7. The slots with diagonal stripes are already fixed. The horizontally striped one can also be fixed, from rule F7.

F7. Given the minimum length of the stretch, it may sometimes be the case that wherever it lies within the interval [$\beta_{\min}, \epsilon_{\max}$], a particular position is always covered by that stretch:

> **1. for** $i = 1$ **to** $\check{\lambda}_k - \text{span}(\beta_{\min}, \epsilon_{\min})$
>
> **a.** $s_{(\epsilon_{\min}+i) \bmod n} \leftarrow \tau_k$;
>
> **2. for** $i = 1$ **to** $\check{\lambda}_k - \text{span}(\beta_{\max}, \epsilon_{\max})$
>
> **a.** $s_{(\beta_{\max}-i) \bmod n} \leftarrow \tau_k$;

Step 1 fixes the variables beyond $\epsilon_{\min}$ which would be included in the shortest possible stretch (of length $\check{\lambda}_k$) starting at the earliest possible position ($\beta_{\min}$), if any, because these variables must be part of any valid stretch (see figure 7). Step 2 does the same from the other end.

The worst-case time complexity of the first three rules is in $\Theta(1)$, that of rules F5 and F6 is in $\mathcal{O}(m+\max\{\check{\lambda}_i : 1 \leq i \leq m\})$, and in $\mathcal{O}(\max\{\check{\lambda}_i : 1 \leq i \leq m\})$ for F7. This concludes our complexity analysis — note that the overall complexity of the algorithm is not related to n.

4 Experimental Results

In this section we propose to evaluate the efficiency of our algorithm both on realistic problems and on a larger set of generated benchmarks.

The stretch constraint as described in this paper was used to model and solve several real-life rotating schedule problem instances from the literature ([4][1][6][3]) using an algorithm described in [5]. Though it is far from being the only reason for the success of the algorithm since a few other global constraints are present and a specially tailored search strategy was devised, its impact on the overall efficiency is significant, as shown in table 2. Seven versions of the filtering algorithm were tested: a complete one, five versions leaving out one particular filtering component[2], and a naive version. Each time a shift variable is bound, the latter passively checks that the current stretch through that variable is not too long and that there is sufficient room to reach minimum length. For each version of the `stretch` constraint and each problem instance, the number of failures is reported.

Table 2. Number of failed branches for different versions of the algorithm applied to cyclic rostering problems from the literature.

version of `stretch`	alcan	horot	MOT	butler	laporte	hung	lau
complete	1004	16	0	2024	1	100	1
without F1	1491	67	0	11422	19	68	1
without F2	1004	16	0	2024	1	68	1
without F4	1004	16	0	2024	1	100	1
without F5,F6	1150	50	1	4631	1	100	48
without F7	1529	55	161	154685	121	100	1
naive	3578	176	204	-	457587	68	59

[2] F3 was not left out because it is necessary for the correctness of the algorithm.

A first observation is that every instance is easily solved by the complete version, but not so easily by the naive version. In fact, one instance (butler) could not be solved within one hour of computation. Of the individual filtering rules tested, F1 and F7 appear to be the most crucial while F2 and F4 have little effect. In fact, F4 is redundant with respect to F1 or F7.

Table 3. A comparison of the number of failed branches and computation time (in seconds on a SUN Ultra 5 at 400MHz) between the complete and naive versions over a range of generated benchmarks.

length	# values	mean gap	complete		naive	
			fails	time	fails	time
25	3	1	10.8	0.01	4970.6	0.74
		3	1.8	0.01	206.2	0.05
		5	1.9	0.02	401.8	0.04
	5	1	135.8	0.13	946310.0	212.52
		3	4.5	0.02	49323.9	3.33
		5	4.8	0.02	76988.1	8.92
	7	1	13.3	0.03	386865.0	73.14
		3	55.7	0.05	1.36×10^6	240.19
		5	23.0	0.03	179134.0	32.34
50	3	1	31.2	0.04	–	–
		3	5.7	0.04	–	–
		5	1.9	0.04	566220.0	105.36
	5	1	55.4	0.04	–	–
		3	158.6	0.11	–	–
		5	74.6	0.03	–	–
	7	1	914.7	0.38	–	–
		3	2532.2	0.77	–	–
		5	37114.3	1.97	–	–

For a more thorough assessment of the `stretch` constraint, a set of instances of the following benchmark problem were generated: given the length of a circular sequence, the set of values that may be used in the sequence, as well as minimum and maximum lengths for a stretch of each of those values, find a valid sequence. Here every juxtaposition of shift types constitutes a permitted pattern. Granted, this is not a difficult problem if we proceed sequentially and with a bit of planning but we further impose that the sequence should be filled in random order with values randomly selected from the current domain (the pseudo-random number generator used the same seed for both versions of the constraint). This not only makes the problem harder to solve but also approximates a more realistic context in which fragments of the sequence may be preassigned or fixed through the intervention of other constraints.

The first three columns of table 3 describe the parameters of the instances. The mean gap (column 3) refers to the difference between the minimum and maximum allowed stretch-lengths for a given value. In the following four columns, each entry corresponds to an average over ten instances. Entries left blank indicate that the corresponding instances could not be solved within one hour of computation.

It is difficult to notice a clear trend across the parameter space. With the exception of the occasional harder instance, it appears that the difficulty increases with the number of values allowed and, obviously, with the length of the sequence. The effect of the mean gap is unclear. More interestingly, the full version of the `stretch` constraint performs up to several orders of magnitude better than the naive version both in the size of the search tree and the computation time, even though more effort is expended during each call to the former. The smaller variance in the results of the full version is also noteworthy.

5 Discussion

Much of the filtering relies on the $[\beta_{\min}, \beta_{\max}]$ and $[\epsilon_{\min}, \epsilon_{\max}]$ intervals computed. Unfortunately these intervals are not necessarily the tightest possible as the following example witnesses.

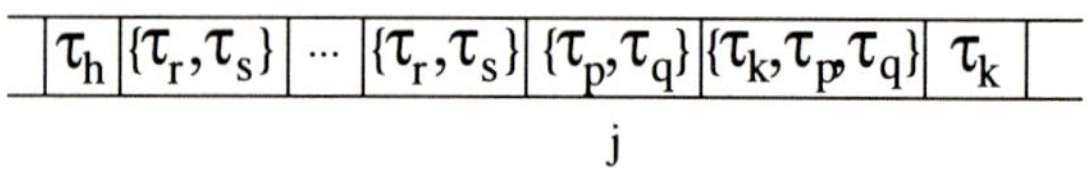

Fig. 8. An example of an interval that could be tighter.

The difficulty originates from *find_frontier*, in which permitted patterns are taken into account. Consider the situation depicted in figure 8 with $\check{\lambda}_p = 2$, $\check{\lambda}_q = 1$, and $\Pi = \{\ \tau_h\tau_r,\ \tau_r\tau_p,\ \tau_s\tau_q,\ \tau_p\tau_k,\ \tau_q\tau_k,\ \tau_k\tau_s,\ \tau_k\tau_h\}$. After fixing the rightmost shift of this fragment to τ_k, we wish to determine the corresponding $\beta_{\min}$. Eventually we reach step 5b and call *find_frontier* with j as indicated in the figure. Since a stretch of τ_q's may be as short as a single shift, $j+1$ is returned as the value of $\beta_{\min}$. However, closer inspection reveals that, several shifts back, a shift is fixed to τ_h and since neither $\tau_h\tau_s$ nor $\tau_r\tau_s$ belong to Π, τ_s cannot occur at $j-1$. This in turn means τ_q cannot occur at j (because $\tau_r\tau_q \notin \Pi$), which leaves τ_p. Since a stretch of τ_p's must include at least two shifts, $\beta_{\min}$ should rather be $j+2$. Ultimately, this difference could translate into an earlier detection of a violated constraint (for example, through rule **F4** in section 3.3).

Therefore a higher level of consistency could be achieved by examining a larger fraction of the sequence, potentially all of it, but at a higher computational cost as well since the complexity of the algorithm would then be related to n. A more efficient alternative would be to use the `stretch` constraint as described but in conjunction with a constraint for permitted patterns equipped with an appropriate filtering algorithm to prune the domains and thus avoid the situation depicted in figure 8. However this lies beyond the scope of the present paper.

6 Conclusion

This paper presented a new global constraint on a sequence of variables. It may be useful whenever limits are given on the number of consecutive identical values in the sequence. One immediate domain of application is rostering and several supporting experiments in that area were reported. The filtering algorithm used by the constraint was shown to have low complexity and significant pruning capability.

This constraint was successfully used in the multi-shift scheduling system described in [5] to model several of the constraints sometimes found in rostering problems: constraints on the length of work stretches of a given type or of mixed types, constraints on the length of stretches of days off, constraints on the number of consecutive weekends off, etc. It was also instrumental in constraining the number and spacing of stretches of each length, through a simple extension.

Acknowledgements. The author would like to thank Gilbert Laporte for introducing him to cyclic rostering, and the anonymous referees whose judicious comments were instrumental in improving this paper. This work was partially supported by the Canadian Natural Sciences and Engineering Research Council and the Fonds pour la Formation de Chercheurs et l'Aide à la Recherche under grants OGP0218028 and 01-ER-3254.

References

1. N. Balakrishnan and R.T. Wong. A Network Model for the Rotating Workforce Scheduling Problem. *Networks*, 20:25–42, 1990.
2. N. Beldiceanu and E. Contejean. Introducing Global Constraints in CHIP. *Mathematical and Computer Modelling*, 20:97–123, 1994.
3. R. Hung. A Multiple-Shift Workforce Scheduling Model under the 4-Day Workweek with Weekday and Weekend Labour Demands. *Journal of the Operational Research Society*, 45:1088–1092, 1994.
4. G. Laporte. The Art and Science of Designing Rotating Schedules. *Journal of the Operational Research Society*, 50:1011–1017, 1999.
5. G. Laporte and G. Pesant. A General Multi-Shift Scheduling System. Working paper, 2001.
6. H.C. Lau. Combinatorial Approaches for Hard Problems in Manpower Scheduling. *Journal of the Operations Research Society of Japan*, 39:88–98, 1996.
7. J.-C. Régin. A Filtering Algorithm for Constraints of Difference in CSPs. In *Proceedings of the Twelfth National Conference on Artificial Intelligence (AAAI-94)*, pages 362–367, 1994.
8. J.-C. Régin and J.-F. Puget. A Filtering Algorithm for Global Sequencing Constraints. In *Principles and Practice of Constraint Programming – CP97: Proceedings of the Third International Conference*, pages 32–46. Springer-Verlag LNCS 1330, 1997.

Network Flow Problems in Constraint Programming

Alexander Bockmayr[1], Nicolai Pisaruk[1], and Abderrahmane Aggoun[2]*

[1] Université Henri Poincaré, LORIA
B.P. 239, F-54506 Vandœuvre-lès-Nancy, France
{bockmayr|pisaruk}@loria.fr
[2] COSYTEC S.A., Parc Club Orsay Université
4, rue Jean Rostand, F-91893 Orsay, France
abderrahmane.aggoun@cosytec.com

Abstract. We introduce a new global constraint for modeling and solving network flow problems in constraint programming. We describe the declarative and operational semantics of the flow constraint and illustrate its use through a number of applications.

1 Introduction

Network flows are a fundamental concept in mathematics and computer science. They play an important role in various applications, e.g. in transportation, telecommunication, or supply chain optimization [2,8]. Many classical network models can be solved very quickly, they have naturally integer solutions, and they provide a modeling language for real world problems that is easier to understand than, e.g., the language of linear programming.

In spite of their importance, constraint programming systems normally do not provide special support to deal with network flows. We introduce here a new global constraint `flow` for modeling and solving network problems inside constraint programming. The `flow` constraint is complementary to existing global constraints. Typically, it is used together with other global constraints and all kind of side constraints. While pure network flow problems may be solved directly by specialized algorithms [2,8], our goal here is to handle efficiently problems in constraint programming that involve network flows as a subproblem.

Global constraints are a key concept of constraint programming. They were first introduced in the CHIP system [1,5]. Since that time, they have been continuously studied in the literature. Recent work on global constraints includes, e.g., [12,16,17]. A classification scheme for global constraints is presented in [4]. The role of global constraints for the integration of constraint programming and mathematical programming is discussed, among others, in [7,9,15,13,14].

There are two main benefits of global constraints. On the one hand, they provide high-level abstractions for modeling complex combinatorial problems in

* This work was partially supported by the European Commission, Growth Programme, Research Project LISCOS – Large Scale Integrated Supply Chain Optimisation Software, Contract No. G1RD-CT-1999-00034

T. Walsh (Ed.): CP 2001, LNCS 2239, pp. 196–210, 2001.

a natural and declarative way. They serve as building blocks for developing large applications. On the other hand, they make available efficient algorithms for solving specific combinatorial problems within a general-purpose solver. Typically, global constraints give much stronger propagation than equivalent formulations based on elementary constraints, provided such formulations exist at all.

The organization of this paper is as follows. We start in Sect. 2 with the declarative semantics of the new constraint. First we describe the underlying mathematical model, then we introduce the `flow` constraint in two different forms. A key feature of this constraint are the conversion nodes. They are particularly useful when modeling supply chain optimization problems. Sect. 3 discusses the operational semantics. We present a decomposition technique for generalized networks with conversion nodes and expose the main ideas used in propagation. Sect. 4 contains three applications of the `flow` constraint: maximum flow, production planning, and personnel scheduling. Finally, Sect. 5 briefly describes the current implementation of the `flow` constraint within the CHIP system.

2 A Global Constraint for Flow Problems

In this section, we introduce the new global constraint `flow`. We start by describing the underlying mathematical model.

2.1 Generalized Flow Networks

A *generalized flow network* $\mathcal{N} = (V = V^s \cup V^d \cup V^c, E; l, u, c; \gamma, d^-, d^+, q)$ is a directed network of n nodes and m arcs, where

- V is the set of nodes, which is partitioned into three subsets V^s, V^d, and V^c of *supply*, *demand*, and *conversion nodes* respectively;
- E is the set of directed arcs;
- $l, u : E \to \mathbb{R}$ are *lower* and *upper capacity* functions;
- $c : E \to \mathbb{R}$ is an *edge cost* function;
- $\gamma : E(V, V^c) \to \mathbb{R}$ is a *conversion* function;
- $q : V \to \mathbb{R}$ is a *node cost* function;
- $d^-, d^+ : V \to \mathbb{R}_+$ are *lower* and *upper demand* functions.

Here $E(X, Y)$, for $X, Y \subseteq V$, denotes the set $\{(v, w) \in E : \ v \in X, \ w \in Y\}$ of arcs leaving X and entering Y. An arc $(v, w) \in E(V, V^c)$ is called a *conversion arc*.

A *pseudoflow* in $\mathcal{N}$ is a function $f : \ E \to \mathbb{R}$ that satisfies the *capacity constraints*

$$l(v, w) \le f(v, w) \le u(v, w), \quad (v, w) \in E. \tag{1}$$

For a pseudoflow f, the *inflow*, *outflow*, and *excess* at node $v \in V$ are defined by

$$in_f(v) \stackrel{\text{def}}{=} \sum_{(w,v)\in E(V,v)} f(w,v),$$

$$out_f(v) \stackrel{\text{def}}{=} \sum_{(v,w)\in E(v,V)} f(v,w),$$

$$exc_f(v) \stackrel{\text{def}}{=} in_f(v) - out_f(v).$$

A *circulation* is a pseudoflow f in $\mathcal{N}$ with $exc_f(v) = 0$, for all $v \in V$.
A pseudoflow f is a *flow* if it satisfies the *balance constraints*

$$\begin{aligned} d^-(v) &\leq -exc_f(v) \leq d^+(v), & v \in V^s, \\ d^-(v) &\leq exc_f(v) \leq d^+(v), & v \in V^d, \\ d^-(w) &\leq out_f(w) \leq d^+(w), & w \in V^c, \end{aligned} \tag{2}$$

and the *flow conversion constraints*

$$f(v,w) = \gamma(v,w) \cdot out_f(w), \quad (v,w) \in E(V,w),\ w \in V^c. \tag{3}$$

Demand nodes have non-negative excess, supply nodes have non-positive excess (i.e., a deficit). Conversion nodes are a key feature of the generalized flow networks introduced in this paper. They are particularly useful when modeling production processes, see Sect. 4.2. The flow conversion constraints allow one to state, e.g., that in order to produce 1 unit of product P, we need 1 unit of raw material R_1 and two units of raw material R_2.

The *cost* of a pseudoflow f is the value

$$c(f) \stackrel{\text{def}}{=} \sum_{(v,w)\in E} c(v,w)\, f(v,w) + \sum_{v\in V\setminus V^c} q(v)\, exc_f(v) + \sum_{v\in V^c} q(v)\, out_f(v)\,.$$

Given a network $\mathcal{N}$, the goal is usually to find a flow of minimum cost, i.e., to solve a *minimum cost flow problem.*

2.2 The `Flow` Constraint

To handle flow problems on generalized networks within constraint programming, we introduce a global constraint `flow` of the following form:

`flow(NodeType, Edge, Conv, EdgeCost, NodeCost, Demand, Flow, FlowVal)`, (4)

where

- `NodeType`: a list $[s_1, \ldots, s_n]$ of values from the set {`supply`,`demand`,`conv`}; s_i specifies the type of node i, respectively, `supply`, `demand`, or `conversion`;
- `Edge`: a list of lists $[[t_1, h_1], \ldots, [t_m, h_m]]$ of values t_i, h_i from the set $V = \{1, \ldots, n\}$; t_i, h_i are the tail and head of arc i;

- `Conv`: a list $[\gamma_1, \dots, \gamma_m]$ of rational values γ_i or `-`; if defined, γ_i is the conversion factor of the conversion arc i;
- `EdgeCost`: a list $[c_1, \dots, c_m]$ of rational values c_i; c_i is the unit flow cost along arc i;
- `NodeCost`: a list $[q_1, \dots, q_n]$ of rational values q_i; q_i is the unit cost at node i;
- `Demand`: a list $[d_1, \dots, d_n]$ of variables d_i; d_i is the demand at node i and takes values from an interval $[d_i^-, d_i^+] \subset \mathbb{R}_+$;
- `Flow`: a list $[f_1, \dots, f_m]$ of variables f_i; f_i is the flow along arc i and takes values from an interval $[l_i, u_i] \subset \mathbb{R}_+$;
- `FlowVal`: a domain variable or a rational value.

In the context of finite domain constraint programming, we assume that all variables are defined over a finite domain of integer numbers. Note, however, that the algorithms described in this paper, can easily be extended to variables ranging over an interval of rational numbers. This is important when using the `flow` constraint within a hybrid CP/MIP solver. If the list `EdgeCost` (resp. `NodeCost`) is empty, the edge (resp. node) costs are assumed to be zero.

A `flow` constraint is *satisfiable* if, in the network $\mathcal{N}$ that is defined by its arguments, there exists a flow whose cost value is `FlowVal`.

For large networks, it may be preferable to define the `flow` constraint in the following equivalent form:

$$\texttt{flow}([\texttt{Node}_1, \dots, \texttt{Node}_n], \texttt{FlowVal}), \tag{5}$$

where, for $i = 1, \dots, n$, $\texttt{Node}_i$ is a list of the form

$$[[s_i, d_i, [v_{i,1}, l_{i,1}, u_{i,1}, c_{i,1}, f_{i,1}]], \dots, [s_{k(i)}, d_{k(i)}, [v_{i,k(i)}, l_{i,k(i)}, u_{i,k(i)}, c_{i,k(i)}, f_{i,k(i)}]]]$$

and

- s_i is a value from the set $\{\texttt{supply}, \texttt{demand}, \texttt{conv}_{\texttt{with}}, \texttt{conv}_{\texttt{without}}\}$, indicating whether node i is a supply node, a demand node, a conversion node with excess, or a conversion node without excess, respectively.
- d_i is a variable, the demand at node i; it takes values from an interval $[d_i^-, d_i^+] \subset \mathbb{R}_+$;
- for $j = 1, \dots, k(i)$,
  - $v_{i,j}$ is a value from $\{1, \dots, n\}$;
    $(v_{i,1}, i), \dots, (v_{i,k(i)}, i)$ are the arcs entering node i;
  - $c_{i,j}$ is a rational number, the cost of arc $(v_{i,j}, i)$;
  - $f_{i,j}$ is a variable, the flow along arc $(v_{i,j}, i)$;
    it takes values from an interval $[l_{i,j}, u_{i,j}] \subset \mathbb{R}_+$.

The interest of this alternative form of the `flow` constraint is that it can be constructed locally, i.e. by assembling separately data about the arcs entering each particular node v.

3 Operational Semantics

In this section, we present the operational semantics of the `flow` constraint. A key question is how to handle conversion nodes. First we show how a generalized flow network $\mathcal{N}$ with conversion nodes can be decomposed into smaller networks $\mathcal{N}_1, \dots, \mathcal{N}_k$ such that circulations in $\mathcal{N}_i$ yield flows in $\mathcal{N}$ and vice versa.

3.1 Decomposition into Subnetworks

Let $\mathcal{N} = (V = V^s \cup V^d \cup V^c, E; l, u, c; \gamma, d^-, d^+, q)$ be a generalized flow network as defined in Sect. 2.1. Let $G = (V, E)$ denote the graph of the network $\mathcal{N}$. Let $G_i = (\bar{V}_i, \bar{E}_i)$, $i = 1, \ldots, k$, be the weak components of the subgraph $G' = (V, E(V, V \setminus V^c))$. For $i = 1, \ldots, k$, we build the flow network $\mathcal{N}_i = (V_i, E_i, c^i, l^i, u^i)$ as follows. First we add a new node s_i, not previously in V, and set $V_i \stackrel{\text{def}}{=} \bar{V}_i \cup \{s_i\}$. Next, we extend the set of arcs $\bar{E}_i$ with two new families (see the example at the end of this section):

$$E_i \stackrel{\text{def}}{=} \bar{E}_i \cup D_i \cup H_i, \text{ where}$$
$$D_i \stackrel{\text{def}}{=} \{(s_i, v)\} : v \in \bar{V}_i \cap (V^s \cup V^c)\} \cup \{(v, s_i)\} : v \in \bar{V}_i \cap V^d\}, \text{ and}$$
$$H_i \stackrel{\text{def}}{=} \{(v, s_i)^w : (v, w) \in E(\bar{V}_i, V^c)\}.$$

For each supply and conversion node $v \in \bar{V}_i$ we include in D_i the arc (s_i, v), and for each demand node $v \in \bar{V}_i$ the arc (v, s_i). Arcs (v, w) in the original network $\mathcal{N}$ that lead from a node $v \in \bar{V}_i$ to a conversion node w are represented in G_i by an arc $(v, s_i) \in H_i$ that is labeled with the superscript "w". The cost function c^i and the capacity functions l^i, u^i on E_i are defined as follows:

$$\begin{array}{llll}
c^i(v,w) \stackrel{\text{def}}{=} c(v,w), & l^i(v,w) \stackrel{\text{def}}{=} l(v,w), & u^i(v,w) \stackrel{\text{def}}{=} u(v,w), & (v,w) \in \bar{E}_i \\
c^i(s_i,v) \stackrel{\text{def}}{=} q(v), & l^i(s_i,v) \stackrel{\text{def}}{=} d^-(v), & u^i(s_i,v) \stackrel{\text{def}}{=} d^+(v), & (s_i,v) \in D_i \\
c^i(v,s_i) \stackrel{\text{def}}{=} q(v), & l^i(v,s_i) \stackrel{\text{def}}{=} d^-(v), & u^i(v,s_i) \stackrel{\text{def}}{=} d^+(v), & (v,s_i) \in D_i \\
c^i(v,s_i)^w \stackrel{\text{def}}{=} c(v,w), & l^i(v,s_i)^w \stackrel{\text{def}}{=} l(v,w), & u^i(v,s_i)^w \stackrel{\text{def}}{=} u(v,w), & (v,s_i)^w \in H_i
\end{array}$$

For $i = 1, \ldots, k$, let f^i be a circulation in $\mathcal{N}_i$; if the collection $(f^1, \ldots, f^k)$ satisfies the constraints

$$f^i(v, s_i)^w = \gamma(v, w) f^j(s_j, w), \quad (v, w) \in E(\bar{V}_i \setminus V^c, \bar{V}_j \cap V_c), \tag{6}$$

then it determines in the network $\mathcal{N}$ a flow f which is defined by

$$f(v,w) = \begin{cases} f^i(v,w), & \text{if } (v,w) \in E(\bar{V}_i, \bar{V}_i), \\ f^i(v,s_i)^w, & \text{if } (v,w) \in E(\bar{V}_i, V \setminus \bar{V}_i). \end{cases} \tag{7}$$

Furthermore, the cost of the flow f is equal to the sum of the costs of the circulations $f^1, \ldots, f^k$, i.e.,

$$c(f) = \sum_{i=1}^{k} c^i(f^i), \tag{8}$$

where $c^i(f^i) \stackrel{\text{def}}{=} \sum_{(v,w) \in E_i} c^i(v,w) f^i(v,w)$.

Conversely, a flow f in $\mathcal{N}$ uniquely determines the collection of circulations $(f^1, \ldots, f^k)$ defined by (7) and

$$\begin{array}{rll}
f^i(s_i, v) = & -exc_f(v), & v \in \bar{V}_i \cap V^s, \\
f^i(s_i, v) = & out_f(v), & v \in \bar{V}_i \cap V^c, \\
f^i(v, s_i) = & exc_f(v), & v \in \bar{V}_i \cap V^d.
\end{array}$$

Example. Let us consider the generalized flow network $\mathcal{N}$ depicted in Fig. 1. The triples inside the nodes and near the arcs represent:

- $(q(v); d^-(v), d^+(v))$, for a node v;
- $(c(v,w); l(v,w), u(v,w))$, for a non-conversion arc (v,w);
- $(c(v,w); \alpha(v,w)/\beta(v,w))$, for a conversion arc (v,w), where $\gamma(v,w) = \frac{\alpha(v,w)}{\beta(v,w)}$.

Suppose that the conversion arcs have lower capacity 0 and upper capacity 10.

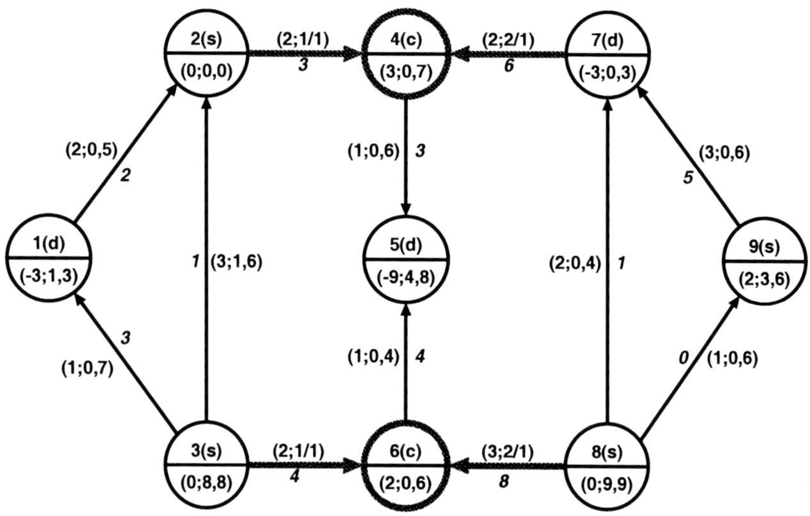

Fig. 1. Network $\mathcal{N}$

The decomposition of $\mathcal{N}$ into 3 subnetworks is presented in Fig. 2. The flow in network $\mathcal{N}$, represented by the italic numbers in Fig. 1, corresponds to the circulations depicted in Fig. 2.

3.2 Propagation

In the previous section we have shown that, to find a flow f in a generalized flow network $\mathcal{N}$, we can decompose $\mathcal{N}$ into smaller subnetworks $\mathcal{N}_1, \ldots, \mathcal{N}_k$ and then look for a collection of circulations $(f^1, \ldots, f^k)$ obeying the linear constraints (6). It remains to discuss propagation on these subnetworks. This is based on classical network algorithms. Due to lack of space, we can describe here only the main ideas.

For $i = 1, \ldots, k$, we verify whether there exists a circulation in every network $\mathcal{N}_i$; if, for some i, the answer is negative, then there is no flow in $\mathcal{N}$ and we are done. Otherwise, for each network $\mathcal{N}_i$, we apply two propagation subroutines to reduce the feasible intervals $[l(v,w), u(v,w)]$ for the flow variables $f(v,w)$. These subroutines are called recursively and in cooperation with a propagation procedure for the linear constraints (6) and (8).

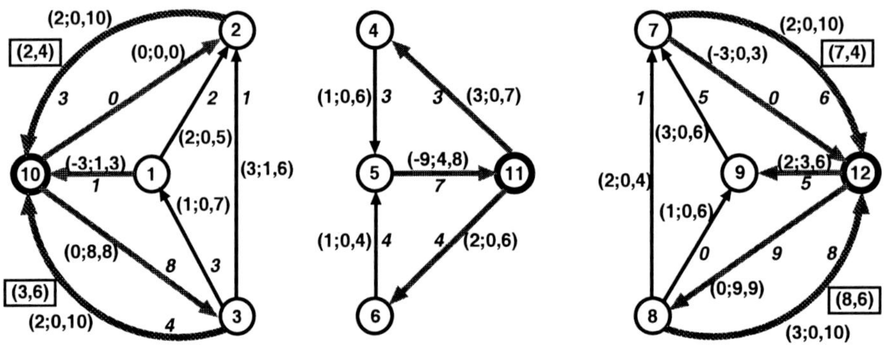

Fig. 2. Decomposition of network $\mathcal{N}$

Suppose that we are given a *circulation network*, i.e. a flow network of the form $\mathcal{CN} = (V, E; l, u, c)$, without γ, d^+, d^-, q. By Hoffman's theorem [10], there is a circulation in $\mathcal{CN}$ iff

$$\sum_{(v,w)\in E(X,V\setminus X)} l(v,w) \leq \sum_{(v,w)\in E(V\setminus X,X)} u(v,w), \quad \text{for all } X \subset V. \tag{9}$$

By a single maximum flow computation (see [2]), we can find either a circulation in $\mathcal{CN}$ or a subset X for which inequality (9) is most violated.

Our first propagation subroutine is based only on feasibility reasoning. For an arc $(v, w) \in E$, let $\alpha(v, w)$ (resp. $\beta(v, w)$) denote the maximum flow value from v to w (resp. from w to v) in the network $(V, E\setminus\{(v, w)\}; l, u)$. The recursive step of our first propagation subroutine calculates (or only estimates) for $(v, w) \in E$ the values $\alpha(v, w)$, $\beta(v, w)$, and then replaces $l(v, w)$ by $\max\{l(v, w), \alpha(v, w)\}$, and $u(v, w)$ by $\min\{u(v, w), \beta(v, w)\}$.

Our second subroutine is based on optimality reasoning. Let B be an upper bound on the cost of a minimal circulation. The subroutine first computes an optimal circulation f and an optimal *price function* $p : V \to \mathbb{R}$, i.e., such that the *complementary slackness condition* holds

$$\begin{array}{l} c_p(v,w) < 0 \Rightarrow f(v,w) = u(v,w), \\ c_p(v,w) > 0 \Rightarrow f(v,w) = l(v,w), \end{array} \tag{10}$$

where $c_p(v, w) \stackrel{\text{def}}{=} p(v) + c(v, w) - p(w)$ denotes the *reduced cost* of an arc (v, w) with respect to a price function p (see again [2]). Then it changes the lower and upper capacities according to the rule:

- if $c_p(v, w) < 0$ and $\epsilon = \dfrac{c(f) - B}{c_p(v, w)} < u(v, w) - l(v, w)$, then set $l(v, w) = u(v, w) - \epsilon$;
- if $c_p(v, w) > 0$ and $\delta = \dfrac{B - c(f)}{c_p(v, w)} < u(v, w) - l(v, w)$, then set $u(v, w) = l(v, w) + \delta$.

4 Some Applications

We present in this section a number of applications of the `flow` constraint. The list of examples given here is by no way exhaustive. We can illustrate here only some basic features of the `flow` constraint. More advanced applications would include, e.g., cyclic time tabling, multicommodity flows, network design, and flow problems with various side constraints, like the equal flow problem [3].

4.1 Maximum Flow

It is quite natural that the `flow` constraint can be used for solving most of the classical network problems. Here, we demonstrate this for the maximum flow problem.

Consider a network $(V, E; u, l, s, t)$, with $n = |V|$ nodes and $m = |E|$ arcs. $l, u : E \to \mathbb{R}$ are lower and upper capacity functions, $s \in V$ is a *source*, and $t \in V$ is a *sink*. The *maximum flow problem* consists in finding a flow f in G such that $exc_f(v) = 0$ for all $v \in V \setminus \{s, t\}$ and $exc_f(t) = -exc_f(s)$, the *value* of the flow f, is maximal.

As an example let us consider the instance of the maximum flow problem represented in Fig. 3. Here, the numbers in the parentheses are the arc capacities, the other numbers represent a maximum flow of value 15. This flow is obtained by the following simple solution strategy (see also Fig. 4):

- set up the list representation of the network;
- post one `flow` constraint and do propagation;
- fix the value of `Demand`[source] to its upper bound (this starts propagation again);
- in turn, fix each flow variable to any value from its current domain (followed each time by propagation).

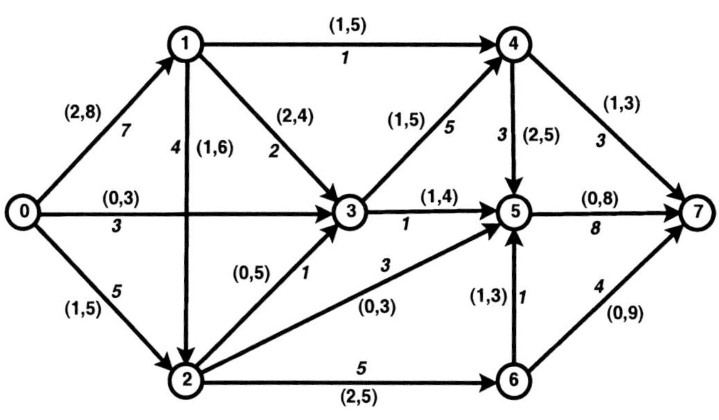

Fig. 3. Maximum flow: network

```
n = 8;    m = 16;    s = 0;    t = 7;
NodeType  = [supply,supply,supply,supply,supply,supply,demand];
Edge      = [[0,1],[0,2],[0,3],[1,2],[1,3],[1,4],[2,3],[2,5],[2,6],
             [3,4],[3,5],[4,5],[4,7],[5,7],[6,5],[6,7]];
LoCap     = [2,1,0,1,2,1,0,0,2,1,1,2,1,0,1,0];
UpCap     = [8,5,3,6,4,5,5,3,5,5,4,5,3,8,3,9];
Demand[v] = 0,   v ≠ s,t;
Demand[s] ∈ [0,16];
Demand[t] ∈ [0,16];
Flow[e]   ∈ [LoCap[e],UpCap[e]], e = 0,...,m − 1;
flow(NodeType,Edge,[],[],[],Demand,Flow,0).
Demand[s] ← max_val_in_domain(Demand[s]);
for (e = 0,...,m − 1)
  Flow[e] ← min_val_in_domain(Flow[e]);
```

Fig. 4. Maximum flow: model and solution procedure

4.2 Production Planning

Suppose there are two types of manufacturing facilities F_1, F_2 for producing a discrete product P. In both facilities, two raw materials R_1 and R_2 are used. Up to 400 units of R_1 and up to 700 units of R_2 are available. One unit of R_1 costs 5$, and one unit of R_2 costs 7$. Because of different technologies, the quantities of the raw materials used for producing one unit of product P are different in F_1 and F_2, see the following Tab. 1.

Table 1. Production planning: data

	R_1	R_2
P_1	1	2
P_2	1	3/2

	S_1	S_2	S_3
P_1	1	1	2
P_2	2	1	1

The production cost of one unit of product P is 12$ in facility F_1, and 10$ in facility F_2. The maximum capacities of facilities F_1 and F_2 are, respectively, 200 and 250 units of the product. Furthermore, at least 100 resp. 150 units of the product must be produced in the facilities F_1 resp. F_2. The demands for product P at the customer sites, S_1, S_2, and S_3, are 160, 70, 140 units respectively. The unit transportation costs for shipping units of products from facilities to customers can also be found in Tab. 1. The problem is to determine the production rates and the shipping patterns to meet all the demands at a minimum cost.

We formulate this problem as a generalized flow problem in the network given in Fig. 5. Nodes 0 and 1, respectively, represent the raw materials R_1 and R_2; nodes 2 and 3 are production facilities for product P_1 and P_2 respectively; nodes 4,5, and 6 are customers nodes that represent the sites S_1, S_2, and S_3. The numbers in parentheses at the nodes are the lower and upper demands. The numbers inside the circles are the costs, and the numbers inside the rectangles are the conversion factors. We define the upper capacity of an arc as the upper demand of its head node. All lower capacities are zero.

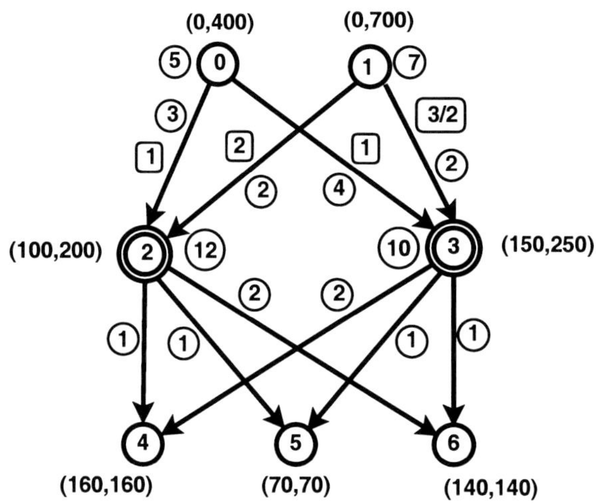

Fig. 5. Production planning: network

A complete model for this problem is given in Fig. 6. Labeling the demand variables and fixing the flow variables yields, after running the corresponding C implementation, an optimal flow $f(0,2) = 120$, $f(0,3) = 250$, $f(1,2) = 240$, $f(1,3) = 375$, $f(2,4) = 120$, $f(2,5) = f(2,6) = 0$, $f(3,4) = 40$, $f(3,5) = 70$, $f(3,6) = 140$, whose cost is 13095.

4.3 Personnel Scheduling

The telephone service of an airline operates around the clock. Tab. 2 indicates for 6 time periods of 4 hours the number of operators needed to answer the incoming calls.

Table 2. Personnel scheduling: data

Period	Time of day	Min. operator needed
0	3 a.m. to 7 a.m.	26
1	7 a.m. to 11 a.m.	52
2	11 a.m. to 3 p.m.	86
3	3 p.m. to 7 p.m.	120
4	7 p.m. to 11 p.m.	75
5	11 p.m. to 3 a.m.	35

```
n = 7;    m = 10;
NodeType = [supply,supply,conv,conv,demand,demand,demand];
Edge     = [[0,2],[0,3],[1,2],[1,3],[2,4],[2,5],[2,6],[3,4],[3,5],[3,6]];
Conv     = [1,1,2,3/2,-,-,-,-,-,-];
EdgeCost = [3,4,2,2,1,1,2,2,1,1];
NodeCost = [5,7,12,10,0,0,0];
LoDem    = [0,0,100,150,160,70,140];
UpDem    = [400,700,200,250,160,70,140];
UpCap    = [200,250,200,250,160,70,140,160,70,140];
Demand[v] ∈ [LoDem[v],UpDem[v]],  v = 0,... ,n − 1;
FlowCost ∈ [0,100000];
Flow[e]   ∈ [0,UpCap[e]], e = 0,... ,m − 1;
flow(NodeType,Edge,Conv,EdgeCost,NodeCost,Demand,Flow,FlowVal).
if (labeling(Demand)) {
  FlowVal = min_val_in_domain(FlowVal);
  for (e = 0,... ,m − 1)
    Flow[e] ← min_val_in_domain(Flow[e]); }
```

Fig. 6. Production planning: model and solution procedure

We assume that operators work for a consecutive periods of 8 hours. They can start to work at the beginning of any of the 6 periods. Let x_t denote the number of operators starting to work at the beginning of period t, $t = 0, \ldots, 5$. We need to find the optimum values for x_t to meet the requirements in all the periods, by employing the least number of operators.

Any feasible schedule $x = (x_0, x_1, x_2, x_3, x_4, x_5)$ that meets the requirements on the operators in the different time periods can be represented by a circulation f in the network depicted in Fig. 7.

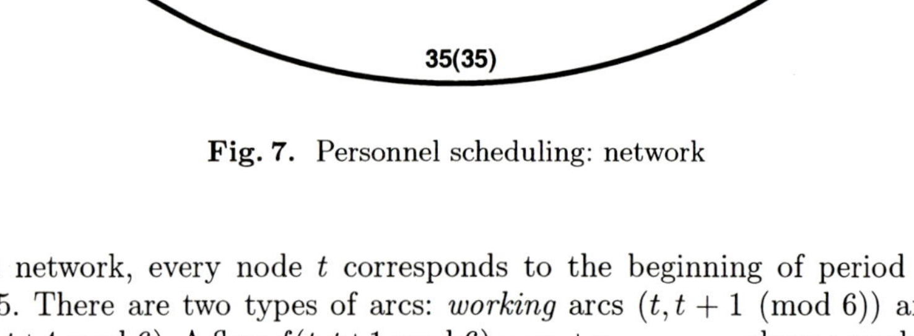

Fig. 7. Personnel scheduling: network

In this network, every node t corresponds to the beginning of period t, $t = 0, \ldots, 5$. There are two types of arcs: *working* arcs $(t, t+1 \pmod 6)$ and *free* arcs $(t, t{+}4 \bmod 6)$. A flow $f(t, t{+}1 \bmod 6) = x_t + x_{(t+5) \bmod 6}$ along a working arc $(t, t{+}1 \bmod 6)$ corresponds to the number of operators scheduled to work during period t; therefore, the lower capacity of this arc (number given in parentheses) is defined to be the number of operators needed during that period. A flow $f(t,(t+4) \bmod 6) = x_{(t+4)\bmod 6}$ along a free arc $(t,(t+4) \bmod 6)$ corresponds to the number of operators having free time during periods $t, t+1, t+2, t+3$; its lower capacity is zero. It can be easily checked that we can set the upper capacity of each arc to 120 (the maximal number of operators needed for one period).

The circulation represented by the numbers on the arcs in Fig. 7 yields a feasible schedule $x = (11, 41, 45, 75, 0, 35)$. In fact, this is even an optimal schedule. However, an arbitrary circulation does not always determine a feasible schedule. In general, it may violate the requirement that each operator works for a consecutive period of 8 hours. In other words, this means that the number of operators working during some period must be equal to the number of operators starting to work at the beginning of this period plus the number of operators finishing their work at the end of this period. To meet this condition, a *schedule-circulation* f must comply for $t = 0, \ldots, 5$ with the side constraints

$$f(t,(t+1) \bmod 6) = f((t-4) \bmod 6, t) + f((t+1) \bmod 6, (t+5) \bmod 6). \tag{11}$$

We define arc costs $c(t,(t+1) \bmod 6) = 1$ and $c(t, t+4 \bmod 6) = 0$, for $t = 0, \ldots, 5$. Since each operator works during two consecutive periods, the cost $c(f)$ of a circulation f is equal to twice the number of operators employed. If f is an optimal *schedule-circulation*, then the optimal values for x_t are defined by $x_t = f((t-4) \bmod 6, t)$, for $t = 0, \ldots, 5$.

The solution algorithm is very simple and given in Fig. 8. For `Flow` to be a circulation, we post one `flow` constraint. Since, for a circulation, the demand at any node is zero, we can set `NodeType[v]=supply` for every node `v`. To satisfy equations (11), we post n linear constraints. Finally, we solve the problem using the min_max procedure which labels variables `Flow` in order to minimize variable `FlowVal`.

```
n = 6;    m = 10;
OpNeeded = [26,52,86,120,75,35];
UpCap    = max_{0≤i<n} OpNeeded[i];
NodeType = [supply,supply,supply,supply,supply,supply];
Edge     = [[0,1],[1,2],[2,3],[3,4],[4,5],[5,0],[0,4],[1,5],[2,0],[3,1],[4,2],[5,3]];
EdgeCost = [1, 1, 1, 1, 1, 1, 0, 0, 0, 0, 0, 0];
Demand[v] = 0,   v = 0,... ,n − 1;
Flow[e]   ∈ [OpNeeded[e], UpCap], e = 0,... ,n − 1;
Flow[e]   ∈ [0, UpCap], e = n,... ,m − 1;
FlowVal   ∈ [0, UpCap · n];
flow(NodeType,Edge,[],EdgeCost,[],Demand,Flow,FlowVal).
for (i = 0,... ,n − 1)
  Flow[i] = Flow[n + ((i + 1) mod n)] + Flow[n + ((i + 2) mod n)];
min_max(labeling(Flow),FlowVal);
```

Fig. 8. Personnel scheduling: model and solution procedure

5 Implementation

The `flow` constraint has been implemented using the CHIP/C Library [6]. This gives us access to low-level primitives of the CHIP/C kernel in order to control the propagation mechanisms described in Sect. 3.2. The C++ layer on top of the C version of the `flow` constraint, which is needed for CHIP/C++, is currently under development.

```
void PersonnelScheduling(int* OperNeeded) {
const int n=6, m=12;
tagNodeType NodeType[ ] = {supply,supply,supply,supply,supply,supply};
int Tail[ ] = {0, 1, 2, 3, 4, 5, 0, 1, 2, 3, 4, 5};
int Head[ ] = {1, 2, 3, 4, 5, 0, 4, 5, 0, 1, 2, 3};
int EdgeCost[ ] = {1, 1, 1, 1, 1, 1, 0, 0, 0, 0, 0, 0};
DvarPtr Demand[6], Flow[12] , FlowVal;
int i, UpBound=0, Ones[ ] = {1,1};
DvarPtr* Var[2];
for (i=0; i < n; i++) {
   c_create_domain_array(Demand+i,1,0,0,INTERVAL);
   if (UpBound < OperNeeded[i]) UpBound =OperNeeded[i]; }
for (i=0; i < n; i++)
   c_create_domain_array(Flow+i,1,OperNeeded[i],UpBound,INTERVAL);
c_create_domain_array(Flow+n,n,0,UpBound,INTERVAL);
c_create_domain_array(&FlowVal,1,0,n*UpBound,INTERVAL);
for (i=0; i < n; i++) {
   Var[0]=Flow[n+(i+1)%n]; Var[1]=Flow[n+(i+2)%n];
   c_dom_linear_sum(Var,Ones,2,Flow[i]); }
Flow(n,m,NodeType,Tail,Head,NULL,Demand,0,NULL,
        Flow,m,NULL,1,NULL,EdgeCost,&FlowVal);
c_min_max(Flow,m,&FlowVal,1,METHOD_MAX_OF_MIN,NULL,NULL) ;
printf("Schedule: %d operators needed\n",c_domain_min(FlowVal)/2);
printf("Period : Starting work\n");
for (i=0; i < n; i++)
   printf(" %d %d\n",i,c_domain_min(Flow[n+(i+2)%n])); }
```

Fig. 9. Personnel scheduling: C implementation

There is an almost one-to-one correspondence between the parameters of the `flow` constraint described in Sect. 2.2 and the parameters of the C function `Flow` that implements the constraint. In Fig. 9, we present a C implementation of the procedure in Fig. 8, which solves the personnel scheduling problem described in Sect. 4.3. The procedure takes as input an integer array `OperNeeded` of size $n = 6$, where `OperNeeded[`i`]` is the number of operators needed during period i. We specify the graph of Fig. 7 using constant arrays `Tail` and `Head`. Furthermore, we are using the following CHIP/C primitives:

- `DvarPtr x`: defines a pointer `x` to a domain variable.
- `c_create_domain_array(array,n,min,max,INTERVAL)` : creates an array of n domain variables ranging over the interval `min` and `max`.

– `c_min_max(Flow,m,FlowVal,1,METHOD_MAX_OF_MIN)` : branch and bound method minimizing the domain variable `FlowVal` by enumerating variables of the array `Flow`, which contains m domain variables; the variable selection used is `METHOD_MAX_OF_MIN` (decreasing order of lower bounds).

6 Conclusion and Further Research

We have introduced in this paper a new global constraint `flow` for modeling and solving network flow problems in constraint programming. We have described the declarative and operational semantics and presented a number of illustrating examples.

Our work was motivated by problems in supply-chain optimization that we encountered through our participation in the LISCOS project (Large Scale Integrated Supply Chain Optimization Software based on Branch-and-Cut and Constraint Programming), funded by the European Community. We are currently studying how the `flow` constraint can be used in some large-scale supply chain optimization problems provided by our industrial partners. In particular, we are investigating models for batch processing problems occurring in the chemical industry, where nodes represent feeds (raw materials, intermediate products) and process operations, and arcs indicate the flow of the material. The `flow` constraint is complementary to the global constraints `cumulative` and `assignment` of CHIP. It allows us to handle in an efficient way the various constraints on stocks occurring in scheduling problems.

This paper has focussed on using the `flow` constraint within finite domain constraint programming. It is clear that the `flow` constraint can also be used as a mixed global constraint in a hybrid CP/MIP solver. This is another important topic for further research, see [11] for related work.

References

1. A. Aggoun and N. Beldiceanu. Extending CHIP in order to solve complex scheduling and placement problems. *Mathl. Comput. Modelling*, 17(7):57 – 73, 1993.
2. R. K. Ahuja, T. L. Magnanti, and J. B. Orlin. *Network flows : theory, algorithms and applications.* Prentice Hall, 1993.
3. R. K. Ahuja, J. B. Orlin, G. M. Sechi, and P. Zuddas. Algorithms for the simple equal flow problem. *Management Science*, 45(10):1440–1455, 1999.
4. N. Beldiceanu. Global constraints as graph properties on a structured network of elementary constraints of the same type. In *Principles and Practice of Constraint Programming, CP'2000, Singapore*, pages 52–66. Springer, LNCS 1894, 2000.
5. N. Beldiceanu and E. Contejean. Introducing global constraints in CHIP. *Mathl. Comput. Modelling*, 20(12):97 – 123, 1994.
6. N. Beldiceanu, H. Simonis, Ph. Kay, and P. Chan. The CHIP system, 1997. http://www.cosytec.fr/whitepapers/PDF/english/chip3.pdf.
7. A. Bockmayr and T. Kasper. Branch-and-infer: A unifying framework for integer and finite domain constraint programming. *INFORMS J. Computing*, 10(3):287 – 300, 1998.
8. H. A. Eiselt and C.-L. Sandblom. *Integer programming and network models.* Springer, 2000.

9. F. Focacci, A. Lodi, and M. Milano. Cutting planes in constraint programming: An hybrid approach. In *Principles and Practice of Constraint Programming, CP'2000, Singapore*, pages 187 – 201. Springer, LNCS 1894, 2000.
10. A. J. Hoffman. Some recent applications of the theory of linear inequalities to extremal combinatorial analysis. *Proceedings of Symposia on Applied Mathematics*, 10:113–127, 1960.
11. H. J. Kim and J. N. Hooker. Solving fixed-charge network flow problems with a hybrid optimization and constraint programming approach. GSIA, Carnegie Mellon University, January 2001.
12. K. Mehlhorn and S. Thiel. Faster algorithms for bound-consistency of the sortedness and the alldifferent constraint. In *Principles and Practice of Constraint Programming, CP'2000, Singapore*, pages 306–319. Springer, LNCS 1894, 2000.
13. M. Milano, G. Ottosson, P. Refalo, and E. S. Thorsteinsson. Global constraints: When constraint programming meets operation research. *INFORMS Journal on Computing, Special Issue on the Merging of Mathematical Programming and Constraint Programming*, March 2001. Submitted.
14. G. Ottosson, E. S. Thorsteinsson, and J. N. Hooker. Mixed global constraints and inference in hybrid CLP–IP solvers. *Annals of Mathematics and Artificial Intelligence, Special Issue on Large Scale Combinatorial Optimisation and Constraints*, March 2001. Accepted for publication.
15. P. Refalo. Linear formulation of constraint programming models and hybrid solvers. In *Principles and Practice of Constraint Programming, CP'2000, Singapore*, pages 369 – 383. Springer, LNCS 1894, 2000.
16. J.-C. Régin and M. Rueher. A global constraint combining a sum constraint and difference constraint. In *Principles and Practice of Constraint Programming, CP'2000, Singapore*, pages 384–395. Springer, LNCS 1894, 2000.
17. H. Simonis, A. Aggoun, N. Beldiceanu, and E. Bourreau. Complex constraint abstraction: Global constraint visualisation. In *Analysis and Visualization Tools for Constraint Programming*, pages 299–317. Springer, LNCS 1870, 2000.

Pruning for the *Minimum* Constraint Family and for the *Number of Distinct Values* Constraint Family

Nicolas Beldiceanu

SICS, Lägerhyddsvägen 18, SE-75237 Uppsala, Sweden
nicolas@sics.se

Abstract. The paper presents propagation rules that are common to the *minimum* constraint family and to the *number of distinct values* constraint family. One practical interest of the paper is to describe an implementation of the *number of distinct values* constraint. This is a quite common counting constraint that one encounters in many practical applications such as timetabling or frequency allocation problems. A second important contribution is to provide a pruning algorithm for the constraint "at most *n* distinct values for a set of variables". This can be considered as the counterpart of Regin's algorithm for the *alldifferent* constraint where one enforces having at least *n* distinct values for a given set of *n* variables.

1 Introduction

The purpose of this paper is to present propagation rules for the *minimum* constraint family as well as for the *number of distinct values* family that were introduced in [1]. The *minimum* constraint family has the form $\text{minimum}(M, r, \{V_1,..,V_n\})$ where M is a variable, r is an integer value ranging from 0 to $n-1$, and $\{V_1,..,V_n\}$ is a collection of variables. Variables take their value in a finite discrete set of items. The constraint holds if M corresponds to the item of rank r according to a given total ordering relation $\Re$ between the items assigned to variables $V_1,..,V_n$ [1]. For instance $\text{minimum}(4, 2, \{9,3,3,4\})$ fails since 4 is not the $(2+1)^{th}$ smallest distinct value of 9,3,3,4 while $\text{minimum}(9, 2, \{9,3,3,4\})$ succeeds. If there is no such item of rank r, M takes the maximum possible value over all items. Relation $\Re$ is defined in a procedural way by the following functions that will be used in order to make our propagation algorithms generic:

- min_item returns an item that corresponds to a value that is less or equal than all items that can be taken by variables $V_1,..,V_n$,
- max_item returns an item that corresponds to a value that is greater or equal than all items that can be taken by variables $V_1,..,V_n$,

---

[1] This is different from the problem of finding the $(r+1)^{th}$ smallest value [2, pages 185-191]: in our case all the variables that have the same value have the same rank and we want to find the $(r+1)^{th}$ smallest distinct value. For instance, the second smallest distinct value of 9,4,1,3,1,4 is equal to 3 (and not 1).

T. Walsh (Ed.): CP 2001, LNCS 2239, pp. 211-224, 2001.

- $I \prec J$ is true iff item I is less than item J,
- $I \succ J$ is true iff item I is greater than item J,
- next(I): if $I \neq$ max_item then returns the smallest item that is greater than item I,
- prev(I): if $I \neq$ min_item then returns the largest item that is smaller than item I,
- min(V) returns the minimum item that can be assigned to variable V,
- max(V) returns the maximum item that can be assigned to variable V,
- remove_val(V,I) removes item I from the feasible values of variable V,
- adjust_min(V,I) adjusts the minimum feasible value of variable V to item I,
- adjust_max(V,I) adjusts the maximum feasible value of variable V to item I.

Defining a member *C* of the *minimum* constraint family will be achieved by providing the previous set of functions for the total ordering relation $\mathfrak{R}$ that is specific to constraint *C*. This has the main advantage that one can introduce a new member of the family without having to reconsider all the propagation algorithms. The complexity results about the algorithms of this paper assume that all functions used for defining $\mathfrak{R}$ are performed in $O(1)$.
The *number of distinct values* family has the form $nclass(C, \{V_1,..,V_n\}, Eq)$ where C is a variable, $\{V_1,..,V_n\}$ is a collection of variables, and Eq an equivalence relation among the possible values of $\{V_1,..,V_n\}$. The constraint holds if C is the number of distinct equivalences classes taken by the values of variables $\{V_1,..,V_n\}$ according to the equivalence relation Eq.

The next section presents some instances of the *minimum* constraint family. Sect. 3 and 4 present two algorithms that are used several times by the different pruning algorithms. These algorithms provide a lower bound for the minimum number of distinct values and for the $(r+1)^{th}$ smallest distinct value. Sect. 5 shows how to reduce the domain of variable M, while Sect. 6 explains how to shrink domains of variables $V_1,..,V_n$. Finally, Sect. 7 indicates how to use the algorithms of this paper in order to implement the propagation for the *number of distinct values* constraint.

2 The *Minimum* Constraint Family

This section lists some instances of the *minimum* constraint family and provides the corresponding functions, which define the total ordering relation $\mathfrak{R}$, for two of the specified instances. Finally it gives one practical application within the domain of resource scheduling.

Examples of the *minimum* family are:
- minimum$(MIN, \{VAR_1,..,VAR_n\})$: MIN is the minimum value of $VAR_1,..,VAR_n$,
- maximum$(MAX, \{VAR_1,..,VAR_n\})$: MAX is the maximum value of $VAR_1,..,VAR_n$,
- min_n$(MIN, r, \{VAR_1,..,VAR_n\})$: MIN is the minimum of rank r of $VAR_1,..,VAR_n$, or max_item if there is no variable of rank r [2],

[2] Note that, removing value max_item from the possible values of variable MIN, will enforce the minimum of rank r to be defined.

- max_n$(MAX, r, \{VAR_1,..,VAR_n\})$: MAX is the maximum of rank r of $VAR_1,..,VAR_n$, or min_item if there is no variable of rank r,
- minimum_pair$(PAIR, \{PAIR_1,..,PAIR_n\})$: $PAIR$ is the minimum pair of $PAIR_1,..,PAIR_n$,
- maximum_pair$(PAIR, \{PAIR_1,..,PAIR_n\})$: $PAIR$ is the maximum pair of $PAIR_1,..,PAIR_n$.

Table 1. Functions associated to the *maximum* and *minimum_pair* constraints

function \ constraint	*maximum*	*minimum_pair*
min_item	MAXINT	(MININT,MININT)
max_item	MININT	(MAXINT,MAXINT)
$I \prec J$	$I > J$	$(I.x < J.x) \vee (I.x = J.x \wedge I.y < J.y)$
$I \succ J$	$I < J$	$(I.x > J.x) \vee (I.x = J.x \wedge I.y > J.y)$
next(I)	I -1	IF $I.y$ <MAX_Y THEN ($I.x$, $I.y$ +1) ELSE ($I.x$ +1,MIN_Y)
prev(I)	I +1	IF $I.y$ >MIN_Y THEN ($I.x$, $I.y$ -1) ELSE ($I.x$ -1,MAX_Y)
min(V)	max_var(V)	(min_var($V.x$),min_var($V.y$))
max(V)	min_var(V)	(max_var($V.x$),max_var($V.y$))
remove_val(V,I)	remove_val_var(V, I)	IF $V.x = I.x$ THEN[3] remove_val_var($V.y$, $I.y$) IF $V.y = I.y$ THEN[4] remove_val_var($V.x$, $I.x$)
adjust_min(V,I)	adjust_max_var(V, I)	adjust_min_var($V.x$, $I.x$) IF max_var($V.x$)= $I.x$ THEN[5] adjust_min_var($V.y$, $I.y$)
adjust_max(V,I)	adjust_min_var(V, I)	adjust_max_var($V.x$, $I.x$) IF min_var($V.x$)= $I.x$ THEN[6] adjust_max_var($V.y$, $I.y$)

In all the previous constraints, MIN, MAX and $VAR_1,..,VAR_n$ are domain variables[7], while $PAIR$ and $PAIR_1,..,PAIR_n$ are ordered pairs of domain variables. Table 1 gives

[3] For the if conditional statement we should generate the constraint: $V.x=I.x \Rightarrow V.y \neq I.y$.
[4] For the if conditional statement we should generate the constraint: $V.y=I.y \Rightarrow V.x \neq I.x$.
[5] For the if conditional statement we should generate the constraint: $V.x=I.x \Rightarrow V.y \geq I.y$.
[6] For the if conditional statement we should generate the constraint: $V.x=I.x \Rightarrow V.y \leq I.y$.
[7] A domain variable is a variable that ranges over a finite set of integers; min(V) and max(V) respectively denote the minimum and maximum values of variable V.

for the *maximum* and *minimum_pair* constraints the different functions introduced in the first section. For *minimum_pair* $.x$ and $.y$ indicate respectively the first and second attribute of a pair, while MIN_Y and MAX_Y are the minimum and maximum value for the $.y$ attribute. MININT and MAXINT correspond respectively to the minimum and maximum possible integers. min_var(V) (respectively max_var(V)) returns the minimum (respectively maximum) value of the domain variable V. remove_val_var(V , I) removes value I from variable V. adjust_min_var(V , I) (respectively adjust_max_var(V , I)) adjusts the minimum (respectively maximum) value of variable V to value I.

We finish Sect. 2 by providing a practical example of utilization of the $\text{min\_n}(MIN, r, \{VAR_1,..,VAR_n\})$ constraint for modeling a specific type of precedence constraint. Assume we have a set T of n tasks which all have a duration of one and which are in disjunction. Furthermore let $End_1,..,End_n$ be the end variables of the tasks of T, and let $Start$ be the start of one other task which should not start before the completion of at least m tasks of T. This generalized precedence constraint can be modeled by using the conjunction of the following constraints: $\text{min\_n}(S, m-1, \{End_1,..,End_n\})$ and $Start \geq S$. On one side this allows expressing directly the disjunctive constraint within the generalized precedence constraint. As a consequence this also leads to adjusting the minimum value of the $Start$ variable both according to the precedence constraint and to the fact that the tasks of T should not overlap.

3 Computing a Lower Bound of the Minimum Number of Distinct Values of a Sorted List of Variables

This section describes an algorithm that evaluates a lower bound of the minimum number of distinct values of a set of variables $\{U_1,..,U_n\}$ sorted on increasing minimum value. This lower bound depends on the minimum and maximum values of these variables. Note that this is similar to the problem of finding a lower bound on the number of vertices of the dominating set [5, page 190], [4] of the graph $G=(V,E)$ defined in the following way:

- to each variable of $\{U_1,..,U_n\}$ and to each possible value that can be taken by at least one variable of $\{U_1,..,U_n\}$ we associate a vertex of the set V,
- if a value v can be taken by a variable U_i $(1 \leq i \leq n)$ we create an edge that starts from v and ends at U_i; we also create an edge between each pair of values.

Fig. 1 shows the execution of the previous algorithm on a set of 9 variables $\{U_1,..,U_9\}$ with the respective domain 0..3, 0..1, 1..7, 1..6, 1..2, 3..4, 3..3, 4..6 and 4..5. Each variable corresponds to a given column and each value to a row. Values that do not belong to the domain of a variable are put in black, while intervals low..up that are produced by the algorithm (see lines 4,5) are dashed. In this example the computed minimum number of distinct values is equal to 3.

We now give the algorithm:

```
1  ndistinct:=1; reinit:=TRUE; i:=1;
2  WHILE i<n DO
3    IF NOT reinit THEN i:=i+1 ENDIF;
4    IF reinit OR low≺ min(U_i)[8] THEN low:= min(U_i) ENDIF;
5    IF reinit OR up ≻ max(U_i) THEN up := max(U_i) ENDIF;
6    reinit:=(low≻up);
7    IF reinit THEN ndistinct:=ndistinct+1 ENDIF;
8  ENDWHILE;
```

Alg. 1. Computing the minimum number of distinct values

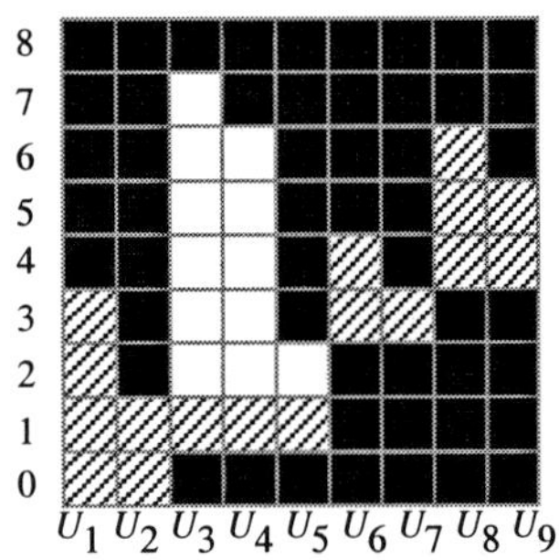

Fig. 1. Generated intervals

Algorithm 1 partitions the set of variables $\{U_1,..,U_n\}$ in `ndistinct` groups of consecutive variables by starting a new group each time `reinit` is set to value `TRUE` (see line 6). If for each group we consider the variable with the smallest maximum value and the largest minimum value in case of tie, then we have `ndistinct` pairwise non-intersecting[9] variables. From this fact we derive that we have a valid lower bound. In the example of Fig. 1 we have the three following groups U_1,U_2,U_3,U_4,U_5 and U_6,U_7 and U_8,U_9. The three pairwise non-intersecting variables are variables U_2, U_7 and U_9. The lower bound obtained by algorithm 1 is sharp when for each group of variables there is at least one value in common. This is for example the case when each domain variable consists of one single interval of consecutive values. Note that the same algorithm works also if the set of variables $\{U_1,..,U_n\}$ is sorted on decreasing maximum value. The algorithm[10] has a complexity $O(n)$ where n is the number of variables.

[8] Throughout the algorithms of this paper, the evaluation of boolean expressions is performed from left to right in a lazy way. This explains why `low` does not need to be initialized.

[9] Two domain variables are called *non-intersecting variables* when they don't have any value in common.

[10] We did not include the sorting phase of the variables within algorithm 1 since, in Sect. 5, we call this algorithm several times on different parts of a given array of variables sorted on their decreasing maximum value.

```
1  ndist:=1;
2  reinit:=TRUE;
3  i:=1;
4  start_previous_group:=1;
5  WHILE (reinit AND i≤n) OR ((NOT reinit) AND i+1≤n) DO
6    IF NOT reinit THEN i:=i+1 ENDIF;
7    IF reinit OR low≺ min(U_i) THEN low:= min(U_i) ENDIF;
8    IF reinit OR up ≻ max(U_i) THEN up := max(U_i) ENDIF;
9    reinit:=(low≻up);
10   IF reinit OR i=n THEN
11     kinf[ndist]:= min_item ; ksup[ndist]:= max_item ;
12     IF reinit THEN end_previous_group:=i-1
                  ELSE end_previous_group:=i   ENDIF;
13     FOR j:=start_previous_group TO end_previous_group DO
14       below_current_group:= (NOT reinit) OR max(U_j) ≺ min(U_i);
15       IF  below_current_group
         AND min(U_j) ≻ kinf[ndist] THEN kinf[ndist]:= min(U_j) ENDIF;
16       IF  max(U_j) ≺ ksup[ndist] THEN ksup[ndist]:= max(U_j) ENDIF;
17     ENDFOR;
18     start_previous_group:=i;
19   ENDIF;
20   IF reinit THEN ndist:=ndist+1 ENDIF;
21 ENDWHILE;
22 IF ndist>ndistinct THEN FAIL^11;
23 ELSE IF ndist=ndistinct THEN
24   adjust minimum values of U_1,..,U_n to kinf[1];
25   adjust maximum values of U_1,..,U_n to ksup[ndistinct];
26   FOR j:=1 TO ndistinct-1 DO
27   remove intervals of values ksup[j]+1..kinf[j+1]-1 from U_1,..,U_n ;
28   ENDFOR;
29 ENDIF;
```

Alg. 2. Pruning for avoiding to exceed the maximum number of allowed distinct values

Finally we make a remark that will be used later on, in order to shrink domains. Let $U_{i_1},..,U_{i_{ndistinct}}$ be a subset of variables $U_1,..,U_n$ such that intervals $\min(U_{i_1})..\max(U_{i_1})$, .. , $\min(U_{i_{ndistinct}})..\max(U_{i_{ndistinct}})$ do not pairwise intersect. If at least one variable of $U_1,..,U_n$ takes a value that does not belong to the union of intervals $\min(U_{i_1})..\max(U_{i_1})$, . . . , $\min(U_{i_{ndistinct}})..\max(U_{i_{ndistinct}})$, then the minimum number of distinct values in $U_1,..,U_n$ will be strictly greater than the quantity `ndistinct` returned by the algorithm. This is because we would get `ndistinct+1` pairwise non-intersecting variables: the "`ndistinct`" $U_{i_1},..,U_{i_{ndistinct}}$ variables, plus the

[11] `FAIL` indicates that the constraint cannot hold and that we therefore exit the procedure; for simplicity reason we omit the `FAIL` in lines 24, 25 and 27, but it should be understand that adjusting the minimum or the maximum value of a variable, or removing values from a variable could also generate a `FAIL`.

additional variable that we fix. In the example of Fig. 1, we can remove from variables $U_1,..,U_9$ all values that do not belong to
$\min(U_2)..\max(U_2)\cup\min(U_7)..\max(U_7)\cup\min(U_9)..\max(U_9)=\{0,1,3,4,5\}$, namely $\{2,6,7\}$ if we don't want to have more than three distinct values. But we can also remove all values that do not belong to
$\min(U_5)..\max(U_5)\cup\min(U_7)..\max(U_7)\cup\min(U_9)..\max(U_9)=\{1,2,3,4,5\}$, namely $\{0,6,7\}$. We show how to modify algorithm 1 in order to get the values to remove if one wants to avoid having more than `ndistinct` distinct values. The new algorithm uses two additional arrays `kinf[1..n]` and `ksup[1..n]` for recording the lower and upper limits of the intervals of values that we don't have to remove. These intervals will be called the kernel of $U_1,..,U_n$.

The complexity of lines 1 to 21 is still in $O(n)$, while the complexity of lines 22 to 29 is proportional to the number of values we remove from the domain of variables $U_1,..,U_n$. If we run algorithm 2 on the example of Fig. 1, we get three intervals `kinf[1]..ksup[1]`, `kinf[2]..ksup[2]` and `kinf[3]..ksup[3]` that respectively correspond to 1..1, 3..3 and 4..5. The lower and upper limits of interval 1..1 were respectively obtained by the minimum value of U_5 (see lines 14,15: U_5 is a variable for which $\max(U_5)<\min(U_6)=3$) and the maximum value of U_2 (see line 16). From this we deduce that, if we don't want to have more than three distinct values, all variables $U_1,..,U_9$ should be greater than or equal to 1, less than or equal to 5, and different from 2.

4 Computing a Lower Bound of the $(r+1)^{th}$ Smallest Distinct Value of a Set of Variables

When r is equal to 0 we scan the variables and return the associated minimum value. When r is greater than 0, we use the following greedy algorithm which successively produces the $r+1$ smallest distinct values by starting from the smallest possible value of a set of variables $\{U_1,..,U_n\}$. At each step of algorithm 3 we extract one variable from $\{U_1,..,U_n\}$ according to the following priority rule: we select the variable with the smallest minimum value and with the minimum largest value in case of tie (line 4). The key point is that at iteration `k` we consider the minimum value of all remaining variables to be at least equal to the `(k-1)`th smallest value `min` produced so far (or to min_item if `k=1`). This is achieved at line 4 of algorithm 3 by taking the maximum value between $\min(U)$ and `min`.

Table 2 shows for `r`=6 and for the set of variables $\{U_1,..,U_9\}$ with the respective domain 4..9, 5..6, 0..1, 3..4, 0..1, 0..1, 4..9, 5..6, 5..6 the state of `k`, U , `min` and `s` just before execution of the statement of line 10. From this we find out that the $(6+1)^{th}$ smallest distinct value is greater than or equal to 7.

```
1  min:= min_item ; SU := {U1,..,Un}; k:=1; s:=r;
2  DO
3    IF k>n THEN BREAK ENDIF;
4    U :=a variable of SU with the smallest value for
       maximum( min(U),min), and the smallest value for max(U)
       in case of tie;
5    SU := SU - {U};
6    IF k=1 OR min≺ max(U) THEN
7      IF k=1 OR min≺ min(U) THEN min:= min(U)
                                ELSE min:= next(min) ENDIF;
8      s:=s-1;
9    ENDIF;
10   k:=k+1;
11 WHILE s≥0;
12 IF s=-1 THEN RETURN min ELSE RETURN max_item ENDIF;
```

Alg. 3. Computing the $(r+1)^{th}$ smallest distinct value

Table 2. State of the main variables at the different iterations of algorithm 3

k	1	2	3	4	5	6	7	8	9
U	0..1	0..1	0..1	3..4	4..9	5..6	5..6	5..6	4..9
min	0	1	1	3	4	5	6	6	7
s	5	4	4	3	2	1	0	0	-1

In order to avoid the rescanning implied by line 4, and to have an overall complexity of $O(n.\lg n)$, we rewrite algorithm 3 by using a heap which contain variables $U_1,..,U_n$ sorted in increasing order of their maximum.

```
let S1,..,Sn be variables U1,..,Un sorted in increasing order
                                              of minimum value;
creates an empty heap; k:=1; s:=r;
DO
  extract from the heap all variables S for which:
                                     max(S)≺min ∨max(S)=min;
  IF k>n AND empty heap THEN BREAK ENDIF;
  IF empty heap THEN min:= min(Sk) ELSE min:= next(min) ENDIF;
  WHILE k≤n AND min(Sk)=min DO push Sk on the heap; k:=k+1; ENDWHILE;
  extract from the heap variable with smallest maximum value; s:=s-1;
WHILE s≥0;
IF s=-1 THEN RETURN min ELSE RETURN max_item ENDIF;
```

Alg. 4. Simplified version of Alg. 3 for computing the $(r+1)^{th}$ smallest distinct value

5 Pruning of M

The minimum value of M corresponds to the smallest $(r+1)^{th}$ item that can be generated from the values of variables $V_1,..,V_n$. Note that, since all variables that take the same value will have the same rank according to the ordering relation $\Re$, we have to find $r+1$ distinct values. For this purpose we use algorithm 4. Note that the previous algorithm will return max_item if there is no way to generate $r+1$ distinct values; since this is the biggest possible value, this will fix M to value max_item.

When r is equal to 0, the maximum value of M is equal to the smallest maximum value of variables $V_1,..,V_n$. When r is greater than 0, the maximum value of M is computed in the following way by the next three methods. We denote $\text{min\_nval}(U_1,..,U_m)$ a call to the algorithm that computes a lower bound of the minimum number of distinct values of a set of variables $\{U_1,..,U_m\}$ (see algorithm 1 of Sect. 3). We sort variables $V_1,..,V_n$ in decreasing order on their maximum value and perform the following points in that given order:

- if none of $V_1,..,V_n$ can take max_item as value, and if there are at least $r+1$ distinct values for variables $V_1,..,V_n$ (*i.e.* $\text{min\_nval}(V_1,..,V_n) \geq r+1$) then we are sure that the $(r+1)^{th}$ item will be always defined; so we update the maximum value of M to $\text{prev}(\text{max\_item})$.
- if the maximum value of M is less than max_item, we make a binary search (on $V_1,..,V_n$ sorted in decreasing order on their maximum value) of the largest suffix for which the minimum number of distinct values is equal to $r+1$; finally, we update the maximum value of M to the maximum value of the variables of the previous largest suffix. This is a valid upper bound for M, since taking a larger value for the smallest $(r+1)^{th}$ distinct value would lead to at least $r+2$ distinct values. Since algorithm 1 is called no more than $\lg n$ times, the overall complexity of this step is $O(n.\lg n)$.
- When the largest suffix founded at the previous step contains all variables $V_1,..,V_n$ we update the maximum value of M to the maximum value of the kernel of $V_1,..,V_n$. This is the value `ksup[ndist]` computed by algorithm 2. This is again a valid upper bound since taking a larger value for M would lead to $r+2$ distinct values: by definition of the kernel (see Sect. 3), all values that are not in the kernel lead to one additional distinct value.

Let us illustrate the pruning of the maximum value of M on the instance $\text{min\_n}(M, 1, \{V_1,..,V_9\})$, with $V_1,..,V_9$ having respectively the following domains 0..3, 0..1, 1..7, 1..6, 1..4, 3..4, 3..3, 4..6 and 4..5, and M having the domain 0..9. By sorting $V_1,..,V_9$ in decreasing order on their maximum value we obtain $V_3,V_4,V_8,V_9,V_5,V_6,V_1,V_7,V_2$. We then use a binary search that starts from interval 1..9 and produces the following sequence of queries:

- inf=1, sup=9, mid=5; $\text{min\_nval}(V_5,V_6,V_1,V_7,V_2)$ returns 2 that is less than or equal to $r+1=2$,
- inf=1, sup=5, mid=3; $\text{min\_nval}(V_8,V_9,V_5,V_6,V_1,V_7,V_2)$ returns 3 that is greater than $r+1=2$,
- inf=4, sup=5, mid=4; $\text{min\_nval}(V_9,V_5,V_6,V_1,V_7,V_2)$ returns 3 that is greater than $r+1=2$.

From this, we deduce that the maximum value of M is at most equal to the maximum value of variable V_5, namely 4.

Finally, since variable M will be equal to one of the variables $V_1,..,V_n$ or to value max_item, we must remove from M all values different from max_item, that do not belong to any variable of $V_1,..,V_n$. If only one single variable of $V_1,..,V_n$ has some values in common with M, and if M cannot take max_item as value, then this variable should be unified[12] with M.

6 Pruning of $V_1,..,V_n$

Pruning of variables $V_1,..,V_n$ is achieved by using the following deduction rules:

- Rule 1: If $n-r-1$ variables are greater than M then the remaining variables are less than or equal to M [13].
- Rule 2: If $M \prec$ max_item then we have at least $r+1$ distinct values for the variables of $V_1,..,V_n$ that are less than or equal to M.
- Rule 3: We have at most $r+1$ distinct values for the variables of $V_1,..,V_n$ that are less than or equal to M.
- Rule 4: If $M \prec$ max_item then we have at least r distinct values for the variables of $V_1,..,V_n$ that are less than M.
- Rule 5: We have at most r distinct values for the variables of $V_1,..,V_n$ that are less than M.

Rules 2 and 4 impose a condition on the minimum number of distinct values, while rules 3 and 5 enforce a restriction on the maximum number of distinct values. In order to implement the previous rules we consider the following subset of variables of $V_1,..,V_n$:

- $V_<$ is the set of variables V_i that are for sure less than M (*i.e.* $\max(V_i) < \min(M)$),
- $V_\leq$ is the set of variables V_i that are for sure less than or equal to M (*i.e.* $\max(V_i) \leq \min(M)$),
- $V_>$ is the set of variables V_i that are for sure greater than M (*i.e.* $\min(V_i) > \max(M)$),
- $\overline{V_>}$ is the set of variables V_i that may be less than or equal to M (*i.e.* $\min(V_i) \leq \max(M)$),
- $\overline{V_\geq}$ is the set of variables V_i that may be less than M (*i.e.* $\min(V_i) < \max(M)$),

---

12 Some languages such as Prolog for instance offer unification as a basic primitive. If this is not the case then one has to find a way to simulate it. This can be achieved by using equality constraints.

13 If there are not $r+1$ distinct values among variables $V_1,..,V_n$ then variable M takes by definition value max_item (see Sect. 2) and therefore all variables $V_1,..,V_n$ are less than or equal to M.

- $\overline{V_<}$ is the set of variables V_i that may be greater than or equal to M (*i.e.* $\max(V_i) \geq \min(M)$),
- $\overline{V_\leq}$ is the set of variables V_i that may be greater than M (*i.e.* $\max(V_i) > \min(M)$).

$|V_>|$ denotes the number of variables in $V_>$. We also introduce the four following algorithms that take a subset of variables V of $V_1,..,V_n$ and an integer value $vmax$ as arguments, and perform the respective following task:

- $\text{min\_nval}(\mathrm{V})$ is a lower bound of the minimum number of distinct values of the variables of V; it is computed with algorithm 1,
- $\text{min\_nval\_prune}(\mathrm{V}, vmin)$ removes from variables $V_1,..,V_n$ all values less than or equal to $vmin$ that do not belong to the kernel of V; it uses algorithm 2,
- $\text{max\_matching}(\mathrm{V}, vmax)$ is the size of the maximum matching of the following bipartite graph: the two classes of vertices correspond to the variables of V and to the union of values, less than or equal to a given limit $vmax$, of the variables of V; the edges are associated to the fact that a variable of V takes a given value that is less than or equal to $vmax$; when we consider only intervals for the variables of V, it can be computed in linear time in the number of variables of V with the algorithm given in [9].
- $\text{matching\_prune}(\mathrm{V}, vmax)$ removes from the bipartite graph associated to V and $vmax$ all edges that do not belong to any maximum matching (this includes values which are greater than $vmax$); for this purpose we use the algorithm given in [3] or [7].

We now restate the deduction rules in the following way:

Rule 1: IF $|V_>| = n - r - 1$ THEN $\forall V_i \in \overline{V_>} : \max(V_i) \prec \text{next}(\max(M))$

Rule 2: IF $\max(M) \prec \text{max\_item}$ AND $\text{max\_matching}(\overline{V_>}, \max(M)) < r + 1$ THEN fail
ELSE IF $\max(M) \prec \text{max\_item}$ AND $\text{max\_matching}(\overline{V_>}, \max(M)) = r + 1$ THEN $\text{matching\_prune}(\overline{V_>}, \max(M))$

Rule 3: IF $\text{min\_nval}(V_\leq) > r + 1$ THEN fail
ELSE IF $\text{min\_nval}(V_\leq) = r + 1$ THEN $\text{min\_nval\_prune}(V_\leq, \min(M))$

Rule 4: IF $\max(M) \prec \text{max\_item}$ AND $\text{max\_matching}(\overline{V_\geq}, \text{prev}(\max(M))) < r$ THEN fail
ELSE IF $\max(M) \prec \text{max\_item}$ AND $\text{max\_matching}(\overline{V_\geq}, \text{prev}(\max(M))) = r$ THEN $\text{matching\_prune}(\overline{V_\geq}, \text{prev}(\max(M)))$

Rule 5: IF $\text{min\_nval}(V_<) > r$ THEN fail
ELSE IF $\text{min\_nval}(V_<) = r$ THEN $\text{min\_nval\_prune}(V_<, \text{prev}(\min(M)))$

We give several examples of application of the previous deduction rules.

$\text{min\_n}(M:2..3, r:1, \{V_1:0..9, V_2:4..9, V_3:0..9\})$:

Rule 1: Since $V_> = \{V_2\}$ and $|V_>| = n - r - 1 = 3 - 1 - 1 = 1$, we have: $\begin{cases} \max(V_1) \le \max(M) = 3 \\ \max(V_3) \le \max(M) = 3 \end{cases}$.

$\text{min\_n}(M:4..6, r:3, \{V_1:3..4, V_2:3..4, V_3:3..4, V_4:6..9, V_5:7..9\})$:

Rule 2: No solution since $\overline{V_>} = \{V_1, V_2, V_3, V_4\}$ and $\text{max\_matching}(\overline{V_>}, 6) = 3 < r + 1 = 4$.

$\text{min\_n}(M:1..2, r:2, \{V_1:0..1, V_2:0..3, V_3:0..1, V_4:3..7\})$:

Rule 2: Since $\overline{V_>} = \{V_1, V_2, V_3\}$ and $\text{max\_matching}(\overline{V_>}, 2) = 3 = r + 1$, we have: $V_2 = 2$.

$\text{min\_n}(M:6..7, r:1, \{V_1:0..1, V_2:1..2, V_3:3..4, V_4:0..3, V_5:4..5, V_6:5..6, V_7:2..9\})$:

Rule 3: No solution since $V_\le = \{V_1, V_2, V_3, V_4, V_5, V_6\}$ and $\text{min\_nval}(V_\le) = 3 > r + 1 = 2$ ($\text{min\_nval}(V_\le)$ is equal to 3 since intervals $\min(V_1)..\max(V_1)$, $\min(V_3)..\max(V_3)$ and $\min(V_6)..\max(V_6)$ do not pairwise intersect).

$\text{min\_n}(M:6..7, r:2, \{V_1:0..1, V_2:1..2, V_3:3..4, V_4:0..3, V_5:4..5, V_6:5..6, V_7:2..9\})$:

Rule 3: Since $V_\le = \{V_1, V_2, V_3, V_4, V_5, V_6\}$ and $\text{min\_nval}(V_\le) = 3 = r + 1$ and because intervals $\min(V_1)..\max(V_1)$, $\min(V_3)..\max(V_3)$ and $\min(V_6)..\max(V_6)$ do not pairwise intersect, we can remove all values, less than or equal to $\min(M) = 6$, that do not belong to $\min(V_1)..\max(V_1) \cup \min(V_3)..\max(V_3) \cup \min(V_6)..\max(V_6) = \{0,1\} \cup \{3,4\} \cup \{5,6\}$; therefore we remove value 2 from V_2, V_4 and V_7.

$\text{min\_n}(M:4..6, r:3, \{V_1:1..2, V_2:1..2, V_3:1..2, V_4:6..9, V_5:7..9\})$:

Rule 4: No solution since $\overline{V_\ge} = \{V_1, V_2, V_3\}$ and $\text{max\_matching}(\overline{V_\ge}, 5) = 2 < r = 3$.

$\text{min\_n}(M:4..6, r:3, \{V_1:1..2, V_2:1..3, V_3:1..2, V_4:6..9, V_5:7..9\})$:

Rule 4: Since $\overline{V_\ge} = \{V_1, V_2, V_3\}$ and $\text{max\_matching}(\overline{V_\ge}, 5) = 3 = r$, we have: $V_2 = 3$.

$\text{min\_n}(M:5..6, r:1, \{V_1:0..1, V_2:1..2, V_3:3..4, V_4:5..9, V_5:0..9\})$:

Rule 5: No solution since $V_< = \{V_1, V_2, V_3\}$ and $\text{min\_nval}(V_<) = 2 > r = 1$ ($\text{min\_nval}(V_<)$ is equal to 2 since intervals $\min(V_1)..\max(V_1)$ and $\min(V_3)..\max(V_3)$ are disjoint).

$\text{min\_n}(M:5..6, r:2, \{V_1:0..1, V_2:1..2, V_3:3..4, V_4:5..9, V_5:0..9\})$:

Rule 5: Since $V_< = \{V_1, V_2, V_3\}$ and $\text{min\_nval}(V_<) = 2 = r$ and because the two intervals $\min(V_1)..\max(V_1)$ and $\min(V_3)..\max(V_3)$ are disjoint, we can remove all values, strictly less than $\min(M) = 5$, that do not belong to $\min(V_1)..\max(V_1) \cup \min(V_3)..\max(V_3) = \{0,1\} \cup \{3,4\}$; therefore we remove value 2 from V_2 and V_5. In addition, since the two intervals $\min(V_2)..\max(V_2)$ and $\min(V_3)..\max(V_3)$ are disjoint, we can also remove value 0 from V_1 and V_5.

7 The Number of Distinct Values Constraint

The *number of distinct values* constraint has the form $\text{nvalue}(D, \{V_1,..,V_n\})$ where D is a domain variable and $\{V_1,..,V_n\}$ is a collection of variables. The constraint holds if D is the number of distinct values taken by the variables $V_1,..,V_n$. This constraint was introduced in [6] and in [1], but a propagation algorithm for this constraint was not given. Note that the *nvalue* constraint can be broken up into two parts:

- at least $\min(D)$ distinct values must be taken,
- at most $\max(D)$ distinct values may be taken.

While the first part was already studied in [8, page 195], nothing was done for the second part. The *nvalue* constraint generalizes several more simple constraints like the *alldifferent* and the *notallequal*[14] constraints. The purpose of this section is to show how to reduce the minimum and maximum values of D and how to shrink the domains of $V_1,..,V_n$:

- since the minimum value of D is the minimum number of distinct values that will be taken by variables $V_1,..,V_n$, one can sort variables $V_1,..,V_n$ on increasing minimum value and use algorithm 1 in order to get a lower bound of the minimum number of distinct values. Then the minimum of D will be adjusted to the previous computed value.
- since the maximum value of D is the maximum number of distinct values that can be taken by variables $V_1,..,V_n$, one can use a maximum matching algorithm on the following bipartite graph: the two classes of vertices of the graph are the variables $V_1,..,V_n$ and the values that can be taken by the previous variables. There is an edge between a variable V_i $(1 \le i \le n)$ and a value *val* if V_i can take value *val*. The maximum value of D will be adjusted to the size of the maximum matching of the previous bipartite graph.
- the following rules, respectively similar to rules 2 and 3 of Sect. 6, are used in order to prune the domain of variables $V_1,..,V_n$:

  IF $\text{max\_matching}(V_1,...,V_n, \text{MAXINT}) = \min(D)$ THEN $\text{matching\_prune}(V_1,..,V_n, \text{MAXINT})$,

  IF $\text{min\_nval}(V_1,...,V_n) = \max(D)$ THEN $\text{min\_nval\_prune}(V_1,..,V_n, \text{MAXINT})$.

  The first rule enforces to have at least $\min(D)$ distinct values, while the second rule propagates in order to have at most $\max(D)$ distinct values.

Finally, we point out that one can generalize the *number of distinct values* constraint to the *number of distinct equivalence classes* constraint family by requiring to count the number of distinct equivalences classes taken by the values of variables $V_1,..,V_n$ according to a given equivalence relation.

---

[14] The $\text{notallequal}(\{V_1,..,V_n\})$ constraint holds if the variables $V_1,..,V_n$ are not all equal.

8 Conclusion

We have presented generic propagation rules for the *minimum* and *nvalue* constraints families and two algorithms that respectively compute a lower bound for the minimum number of distinct values and for the $(r+1)^{th}$ smallest distinct value. These algorithms produce a tight lower bound when each domain consists of one single interval of consecutive values. However there should be room for improving these algorithms in order to try to consider holes in the domains of variables. One should also provide for small values of r an algorithm for computing the rth smallest distinct value of a set of intervals for which the complexity depends of r. We did not address any incremental concern since it would involve other issues like maintaining a list of domain variables sorted on their minimum, or like regrouping all propagation rules together in order to factorize common parts.

Acknowledgements. Thanks to Mats Carlsson, Per Mildner and Emmanuel Poder for useful comments on an earlier draft of this paper. The author would also like to thank the anonymous referees for their insightful reviews.

References

1. Beldiceanu, N.: Global Constraints as Graph Properties on Structured Network of Elementary Constraints of the Same Type. SICS Technical Report T2000/01, (2000).
2. Cormen, T. H., Leiserson, C. E., Rivest R. L.: *Introduction to Algorithms*. The MIT Press, (1990).
3. Costa, M-C.: Persistency in maximum cardinality bipartite matchings. *Operation Research Letters* 15, 143-149, (1994).
4. Damaschke, P., Müller, H., Kratsch, D.: Domination in convex and chordal bipartite graphs. *Information Processing Letters* 36, 231-236, (1990).
5. Garey, M. R., Johnson, D. S.: *Computers and intractability. A guide to the Theory of NP-Completeness*. W. H. Freeman and Company, (1979).
6. Pachet, F., Roy, P.: Automatic Generation of Music Programs. In *Principles and Practice of Constraint Programming - CP'99, 5th International Conference*, Alexandria, Virginia, USA, (October 11-14, 1999), Proceedings. Lecture Notes in Computer Science, Vol. 1713, Springer, (1999).
7. Régin, J-C.: A filtering algorithm for constraints of difference in CSP. In *Proc. of the Twelfth National Conference on Artificial Intelligence (AAAI-94)*, 362-367, (1994).
8. Régin, J-C.: *Développement d'outils algorithmiques pour l'Intelligence Artificielle. Application à la chimie organique*, PhD Thesis of LIRMM, Montpellier, France, (1995). In French.
9. Steiner, G., Yeomans, J.S.: A Linear Time Algorithm for Maximum Matchings in Convex, Bipartite Graph. In *Computers Math. Applic.*, Vol. 31, No. 12, 91-96, (1996).

A Constraint Programming Approach to the Stable Marriage Problem*

Ian P. Gent[1], Robert W. Irving[2], David F. Manlove[2], Patrick Prosser[2], and Barbara M. Smith[3]

[1] School of Computer Science, University of St. Andrews, Scotland.
ipg@dcs.st-and.ac.uk

[2] Department of Computing Science, University of Glasgow, Scotland.
rwi/davidm/pat@dcs.gla.ac.uk

[3] School of Computing and Mathematics, University of Huddersfield, England.
b.m.smith@hud.ac.uk

Abstract. The Stable Marriage problem (SM) is an extensively-studied combinatorial problem with many practical applications. In this paper we present two encodings of an instance I of SM as an instance J of a Constraint Satisfaction Problem. We prove that, in a precise sense, establishing arc consistency in J is equivalent to the action of the established Extended Gale/Shapley algorithm for SM on I. As a consequence of this, the man-optimal and woman-optimal stable matchings can be derived immediately. Furthermore we show that, in both encodings, *all* solutions of I may be enumerated in a failure-free manner. Our results indicate the applicability of Constraint Programming to the domain of stable matching problems in general, many of which are NP-hard.

1 Introduction

An instance of the classical Stable Marriage problem (SM) [6] comprises n men and n women, and each person has a preference list in which they rank all members of the opposite sex in strict order. A matching M is a bijection between the men and women. A man m_i and woman w_j form a *blocking pair* for M if m_i prefers w_j to his partner in M and w_j prefers m_i to her partner in M. A matching that admits no blocking pair is said to be *stable*, otherwise the matching is *unstable*. SM arises in important practical applications, such as the annual match of graduating medical students to their first hospital appointments in a number of countries (see e.g. [12]).

Every instance of SM admits at least one stable matching, which can be found in time linear in the size of the problem instance, i.e. $O(n^2)$, using the Gale/Shapley (GS) algorithm [4]. An extended version of the GS algorithm – the Extended Gale/Shapley (EGS) algorithm [6, Section 1.2.4] – avoids some unnecessary steps by deleting from the preference lists certain (man,woman) pairs that cannot belong to a stable matching. The man-oriented version of the EGS

* This work was supported by EPSRC research grant GR/M90641.

T. Walsh (Ed.): CP 2001, LNCS 2239, pp. 225–239, 2001.

Men's lists	Women's lists
1: 1 3 6 2 4 5	1: 1 5 6 3 2 4
2: 4 6 1 2 5 3	2: 2 4 6 1 3 5
3: 1 4 5 3 6 2	3: 4 3 6 2 5 1
4: 6 5 3 4 2 1	4: 1 3 5 4 2 6
5: 2 3 1 4 5 6	5: 3 2 6 1 4 5
6: 3 1 2 6 5 4	6: 5 1 3 6 4 2

(a)

Men's lists	Women's lists
1: 1	1: 1
2: 2	2: 2
3: 4	3: 4 6
4: 6 5 3	4: 3
5: 5 6	5: 6 4 5
6: 3 6 5	6: 5 6 4

(b)

Fig. 1. (a) An SM instance with 6 men and 6 women; (b) the corresponding GS-lists.

algorithm involves a sequence of proposals from the men to women, provisional engagements between men and women, and deletions from the preference lists. At termination, the reduced preference lists are referred to as the *MGS-lists*. A similar proposal sequence from the women to the men (the woman-oriented version) produces the *WGS-lists*, and the intersection of the MGS-lists with the WGS-lists yields the *GS-lists* [6, p.16]. An important property of the GS-lists [6, Theorem 1.2.5] is that, if each man is given his first-choice partner (or equivalently, each woman is given her last-choice partner) in the GS-lists then we obtain a stable matching called the *man-optimal* stable matching. In the man-optimal (or equivalently, *woman-pessimal*) stable matching, each man has the best partner (according to his ranking) that he could obtain, whilst each woman has the worst partner that she need accept, in any stable matching. An analogous procedure, switching the roles of the men and women, gives the *woman-optimal* (or equivalently, *man-pessimal*) stable matching.

An example SM instance I is given in Figure 1, together with the GS-lists for I. (Throughout this paper, a person's preference list is ordered with his/her most-preferred partner leftmost.) There are three stable matchings for this instance: {(1,1), (2,2), (3,4), (4,6), (5,5), (6,3)} (the man-optimal stable matching); {(1,1), (2,2), (3,4), (4,3), (5,6), (6,5)} (the woman-optimal stable matching); and {(1,1), (2,2), (3,4), (4,5), (5,6), (6,3)}.

SMI is a generalisation of SM in which the preference lists of those involved can be incomplete. In this case, person p is *acceptable* to person q if p appears on the preference list of q, and *unacceptable* otherwise. A matching M in an instance I of SMI is a one-one correspondence between a subset of the men and a subset of the women, such that $(m, w) \in M$ implies that each of m and w is acceptable to the other. In this setting, a man m and woman w form a blocking pair for M if each is either unmatched in M and finds the other acceptable, or prefers the other to his/her partner in M. As in SM, a matching is stable if it admits no blocking pair. (It follows from this definition that, from the point of view of finding stable matchings, we may assume without loss of generality that p is acceptable to q if and only if q is acceptable to p.) A stable matching in I need not be a complete matching. However, all stable matchings in I involve exactly the same men and women [5]. It is straightforward to modify the Extended Gale/Shapley algorithm to cope with an SMI instance [6, Section 1.4.2]. A pseudocode description of the

```
assign each person to be free;
while some man m is free and m has a nonempty list loop
    w := first woman on m's list;   {m 'proposes' to w}
    if some man p is engaged to w then
        assign p to be free;
    end if;
    assign m and w to be engaged to each other;
    for each successor p of m on w's list loop
        delete the pair {p, w};
    end loop;
end loop;
```

Fig. 2. The man-oriented Extended Gale/Shapley algorithm for SMI.

man-oriented EGS algorithm for SMI is given in Figure 2 (the term *delete the pair* $\{p,w\}$ means that p should be deleted from w's list and vice versa.) The woman-oriented algorithm is analogous. Furthermore, the concept of GS-lists can be extended to SMI, with analogous properties.

The Stable Marriage problem has its roots as a combinatorial problem, but has also been the subject of much interest from the Game Theory and Economics community [13] and the Operations Research community [14]. In this paper we present two encodings of an instance I of SMI (and so of SM) as an instance J of a Constraint Satisfaction Problem (CSP). We show that Arc Consistency (AC) propagation [1] achieves the same results as the EGS algorithm in a certain sense. For the first encoding, we show that the GS-lists for I correspond to the domains remaining after establishing AC in J. The second encoding is more compact; although the arc consistent domains in J are supersets of the GS-lists, we can again obtain from them the man-optimal and woman-optimal stable matchings in I. We also show that, for both encodings, we are guaranteed a failure-free enumeration of all stable matchings in I using AC propagation (combined with a value-ordering heuristic in the case of the first encoding) in J.

Our results show that constraint propagation within a CSP formulation of SM captures the structure produced by the EGS algorithm. We have also demonstrated the applicability of constraint programming to the general domain of stable matching problems. Many variants of SM are NP-hard [11,10,8], and the encodings presented here could potentially be extended to these variants, giving a way of dealing with their complexity through existing CSP search algorithms.

The remainder of this paper is organised as follows. In Section 2 we present the first encoding, then prove the consequent relationship between AC propagation and the GS-lists in Section 3; the failure-free enumeration result for this encoding is presented in Section 4. A second encoding, using Boolean variables, is given in Section 5, and in Section 6 we show the relationship between AC propagation in this encoding and the man-optimal and woman-optimal stable matchings, together with the failure-free enumeration result. Section 7 contains some concluding remarks.

2 A First Encoding for SM and SMI

In this section we present an encoding of the Stable Marriage problem, and indeed more generally SMI, as a binary constraint satisfaction problem.

Suppose that we are given an SMI instance I involving men $m_1, m_2, \ldots, m_n$ and women $w_1, w_2, \ldots, w_n$ (it is not difficult to extend our encoding to the case that the numbers of men and women are not equal, but for simplicity we assume that they are equal). For any person q in I, $PL(q)$ (respectively $GS(q)$) denotes the set of persons contained in the original preference list (GS-list) of q in I. For the purposes of exposition, we introduce a dummy man m_{n+1} and a dummy woman w_{n+1} into the SMI instance, such that, for each i, m_i (respectively w_i) prefers all women (men) on his (her) preference list (if any) to w_{n+1} (m_{n+1}).

To define an encoding of I as a CSP instance J, we introduce variables $x_1, x_2, \ldots, x_n$ corresponding to the men, and $y_1, y_2, \ldots, y_n$ corresponding to the women. For each i ($1 \leq i \leq n$), we let $dom(x_i)$ denote the values in variable x_i's domain. Initially, $dom(x_i)$ is defined as follows:

$$dom(x_i) = \{j : w_j \in PL(m_i)\} \cup \{n+1\}.$$

For each j ($1 \leq j \leq n$), $dom(y_j)$ is defined similarly. For each i ($1 \leq i \leq n$), let $d_i^m = |dom(x_i)|$ and let $d_i^w = |dom(y_i)|$. Intuitively, for $1 \leq i, j \leq n$, the assignment $x_i = j$ corresponds to the case that man m_i marries woman w_j, and the constraints of our encoding will ensure that $x_i = j$ if and only if $y_j = i$. Similarly, for $1 \leq i \leq n$, the assignment $x_i = n+1$ (respectively $y_i = n+1$) corresponds to the case that m_i (w_i) is unmatched. It should be pointed out that, if the given SMI instance is an SM instance (i.e. every preference list is complete), then no variable will be assigned the value $n+1$ in its domain in any stable matching.

We now define the constraints between the variables to ensure that the solutions to the CSP correspond exactly to the stable marriages in I. Given any i and j ($1 \leq i, j \leq n$), the *stable marriage constraint* x_i/y_j involving x_i and y_j is a set of nogoods which we represent by a $d_i^m \times d_j^w$ conflict matrix C. To make the structure of the conflict matrix clear, we describe it using four possible values for the element $C_{k,l}$ of C, for any k, l ($k \in dom(x_i)$, $l \in dom(y_j)$), as follows. In a conventional conflict matrix, the values I and B are disallowed so would be 0, while the values A and S are allowed and so would be 1.

- A: $C_{k,l} =$ A when $k = j$ and $l = i$, which Allows $x_i = j$ (and $y_j = i$). At most one element in C can ever contain the value A.
- I: $C_{k,l} =$ I when *either* $k = j$ and $l \neq i$ *or* $l = i$ and $k \neq j$, i.e. the two pairings are Illegal, since *either* $x_i = j$ and $y_j = l \neq i$ *or* $y_j = i$ and $x_i = k \neq j$.
- B: $C_{k,l} =$ B when m_i prefers w_j to w_k and w_j prefers m_i to m_l. Any matching corresponding to the assignment $x_i = k$ and $y_j = l$ would admit a Blocking pair involving m_i and w_j.
- S: $C_{k,l} =$ S for all other entries that are not A, I or B. The simultaneous assignments of $x_i = k$ and $y_j = l$ are Supported.

The size of each conflict matrix is $O(n^2)$ and clearly there are $O(n^2)$ conflict matrices; consequently the overall size of the encoding is $O(n^4)$.

	2	4	6	1	3	5	7
1				I			
3				I			
6				I			
2	I	I	I	A	I	I	I
4				I	B	B	B
5				I	B	B	B
7				I	B	B	B

(a) x_1/y_2

	4	3	6	2	5	1	7
3	I	I	A	I	I	I	I
1			I	B	B	B	B
2			I	B	B	B	B
5			I	B	B	B	B
6			I	B	B	B	B
4			I	B	B	B	B
7			I	B	B	B	B

(b) x_6/y_3

	3	2	6	1	4	5	7
1	I						
4	I						
5	A	I	I	I	I	I	I
3	I	B	B	B	B	B	B
6	I	B	B	B	B	B	B
2	I	B	B	B	B	B	B
7	I	B	B	B	B	B	B

(c) x_3/y_5

Fig. 3. Conflict matrices for stable marriage constraints from the problem in Figure 1

Examples of different types of conflict matrices for stable marriage constraints x_i/y_j are shown in Figure 3 for the SM instance of Figure 1. In all cases, and henceforth in this paper, the values in x_i's (respectively y_j's) domain are listed in order down the rows (along the columns) according to m_i's (w_j's) preference list, and a blank entry represents an S. Another type of conflict matrix can occur in an SMI instance: the value A does not occur in a conflict matrix x_i/y_j if m_i and w_j are unacceptable to each other, and the matrix is then filled with S's.

Figure 3(a) shows the conflict matrix for the stable marriage constraint x_1/y_2. The row and column of I's, representing illegal marriages, intersect at the A entry, and the area to the right of and below A is filled with B's, representing nogood assignments to x_1 and y_2 which would lead to m_1 and w_2 being a blocking pair.

Figure 3(b) shows the conflict matrix for the stable marriage constraint x_6/y_3. Again the area with A at its top left corner is bounded by I's and filled with B's. However, the A is in the top row, since w_3 is at the top of m_6's preference list. Consequently all values in the domain of y_3 to the right of A are unsupported. Similarly, Figure 3(c) shows the conflict matrix for the stable marriage constraint x_3/y_5, where m_3 is at the top of w_5's preference list. The A entry is in the first column and all values in the domain of x_3 below the A are unsupported.

Enforcing AC on the instance of Figure 1 will delete the rows and columns from Figure 3(b) and (c) corresponding to unsupported values. As shown in the next section, these deletions are equivalent to those done by the EGS algorithm.

3 Arc Consistency and the GS-Lists

In this section we prove that, if I is an SMI instance and J is a CSP instance obtained from I using the encoding of Section 2, AC propagation in J essentially calculates the GS-lists of I.[1] The proof depends on two lemmas. The first shows

[1] Strictly speaking, we prove that, after AC propagation, for any i, j ($1 \leq i, j \leq n$), $w_j \in GS(m_i)$ iff $j \in dom(x_i)$, and similarly $m_i \in GS(w_j)$ iff $i \in dom(y_j)$.

that the domains remaining after AC propagation, apart from the dummy values, are subsets of the GS-lists. We prove this by showing that, when the EGS algorithm removes a value, so does the AC algorithm. The second proves that the GS-lists are subsets of the domains remaining after AC propagation. We do this by showing that the GS-lists correspond to arc consistent domains for the variables in J.

Lemma 1. *For a given variable x_i in J $(1 \leq i \leq n)$, after AC propagation,*

$$\{w_j : j \in dom(x_i) \backslash \{n+1\}\} \subseteq GS(m_i).$$

A similar result holds for each variable y_j $(1 \leq j \leq n)$.

Proof. The GS-lists for I are obtained from the original preference lists in I by deletions carried out by either the man-oriented or woman-oriented EGS algorithms. We show that the corresponding deletions would occur from the relevant variables' domains during AC propagation in J. The proof for deletions resulting from the man-oriented version is presented; the argument for deletions resulting from the woman-oriented version is similar.

We prove the following fact by induction on the number of proposals z during an execution E of the man-oriented EGS algorithm (see Figure 2) on I: for any deletion carried out in the same iteration of the while loop as the zth proposal, the corresponding deletion would be carried out during AC propagation. Clearly the result is true for $z = 0$. Now assume that $z = r > 0$ and the result is true for all $z < r$. Suppose that the rth proposal during E consists of man m_i proposing to woman w_j. At this point of E, we may use the induction hypothesis to deduce that, at some point during AC propagation, the conflict matrix for the stable marriage constraint x_i/y_j has a structure analogous to that of Figure 4(a), since w_j is at the top of m_i's list. Now suppose that in E, during the same iteration of the while loop as the rth proposal, the pair $\{m_k, w_j\}$ is deleted. Then in J, all values in y_j's domain to the right of the entry A (including k and $n+1$) are unsupported, and will be deleted when the constraint is revised during AC propagation. Subsequent revision of the constraint x_k/y_j will remove j from x_k's domain, since k is no longer in y_j's domain and therefore the jth row of the conflict matrix for x_k/y_j contains only I entries. Hence the inductive step is established.

Consequently, any deletion of a value from a preference list by the man-oriented EGS algorithm will be matched by a deletion of a value from the domain of the corresponding CSP variable when AC is enforced. The same is true for the woman-oriented EGS algorithm. The end result is that the domains remaining after AC propagation, omitting the dummy value, are subsets of the GS-lists. □

Lemma 2. *For each i $(1 \leq i \leq n)$, define a domain of values $dom(x_i)$ for the variable x_i as follows: if $GS(m_i) \neq \emptyset$, then $dom(x_i) = \{j : w_j \in GS(m_i)\}$; otherwise $dom(x_i) = \{n+1\}$. The domain for each y_j $(1 \leq j \leq n)$ is defined analogously. Then the domains so defined are arc consistent in J.*

	i					
j	I	I	A	I	I	I
	S	S	I	B	B	B
	S	S	I	B	B	B
	S	S	I	B	B	B
	S	S	I	B	B	B

(a)

					i
j	I	I	I	I	A
	S	S	S	S	I
	S	S	S	S	I
	S	S	S	S	I
	S	S	S	S	I
	S	S	S	S	I

(b)

	i					
	S	S	I	S	S	S
j	I	I	A	I	I	I
	S	S	I	B	B	B
	S	S	I	B	B	B
	S	S	I	B	B	B
	S	S	I	B	B	B

(c)

	S	S	S	S	S
	S	S	S	S	S
	S	S	S	S	S
	S	S	S	S	S
	S	S	S	S	S

(d)

Fig. 4. Four possible types of stable marriage constraints x_i/y_j

Proof. Suppose that the variables x_i $(1 \leq i \leq n)$ and y_j $(1 \leq j \leq n)$ are assigned the domains in the statement of the lemma. To show that these domains are arc consistent, we consider an arbitrary constraint x_i/y_j. There are six cases to consider:

- w_j is at the top of m_i's GS-list. Then m_i is at the bottom of w_j's GS-list. Hence the constraint x_i/y_j has a structure similar to that of Figure 4(b). Every row or column has at least one A or S and the constraint is arc consistent.
- w_j is at the bottom of m_i's GS-list. Then m_i is at the top of w_j's GS-list. Hence the constraint x_i/y_j has a structure similar to that of the transpose of Figure 4(b) and is arc consistent.
- w_j is in m_i's GS-list, but is not at the top or bottom of that list. Then the constraint x_i/y_j has a structure similar to that of Figure 4(c) (i.e. every row or column has at least one A or S), and is again arc consistent.
- $w_j \notin GS(m_i)$, but $w_j \in PL(m_i)$ and $GS(m_i) \neq \emptyset$. Then $m_i \notin GS(w_j)$. The pair $\{m_i, w_j\}$ were deleted from each other's original lists by either the man-oriented EGS algorithm (in which case all successors of m_i on w_j's original list were also deleted) or the woman-oriented EGS algorithm (in which case all successors of w_j on m_i's original list were also deleted). In either case, the constraint x_i/y_j has a structure similar to that of Figure 4(d) and is again arc consistent, since all A,B and I entries have been removed, leaving only S entries.
- $w_j \notin PL(m_i)$, so $w_j \notin GS(m_i)$, but $GS(m_i) \neq \emptyset$. Then it is straightforward to verify that the constraint x_i/y_j has a structure similar to that of Figure 4(d) and is arc consistent.
- $GS(m_i) = \emptyset$. Then the constraint x_i/y_j is a 1×1 conflict matrix with a single entry S and is arc consistent.

Hence no constraint yields an unsupported value for any variable, and the set of domains defined in the lemma is arc consistent. □

The following theorem follows immediately from the above lemmas, and the fact that AC algorithms find the unique maximal set of domains that are arc consistent.

Theorem 3 *Let I be an instance of SMI, and let J be a CSP instance obtained from I by the encoding of Section 2. Then the domains remaining after AC propagation in J are identical (in the sense of Footnote 1) to the GS-lists for I.*

Theorem 3 and the discussion of GS-lists in Section 1 show that we can find a solution to the CSP giving the man-optimal stable matching without search: we assign each x_i variable the most-preferred value[2] in its domain. Assigning the y_j variables in a similar fashion gives the woman-optimal stable matching. In the next section, we go further and show that the CSP yields all stable matchings without having to backtrack due to failure.

4 Failure-Free Enumeration

In this section we show that, if I is an SM (or more generally SMI) instance and J is a CSP instance obtained from I using the encoding of Section 2, then we may enumerate the solutions of I in a failure-free manner using AC propagation combined with a suitable value-ordering heuristic in J.

Theorem 4 *Let I be an instance of SMI and let J be a CSP instance obtained from I using the encoding of Section 2. Then the following search process enumerates all solutions in I without repetition and without ever failing due to an inconsistency:*

- *AC is established as a preprocessing step, and after each branching decision including the decision to remove a value from a domain;*
- *if all domains are arc consistent and some variable x_i has two or more values in its domain then search proceeds by setting x_i to the most-preferred value j in its domain. On backtracking, the value j is removed from x_i's domain;*
- *when a solution is found, it is reported and backtracking is forced.*

Proof. Let T be the search tree as defined above. We prove by induction on T that each node of T corresponds to a CSP instance J' with arc consistent domains; furthermore J' is equivalent to the GS-lists I' for an SMI instance derived from I, such that any stable matching in I' is also stable in I. Firstly we show that this is true for the root node of T, and then we assume that this is true at any branching node u of T and show that it is true for each of the two children of u.

The root node of T corresponds to the CSP instance J' with arc consistent domains, where J' is obtained from J by AC propagation. By Theorem 3, J' corresponds to the GS-lists in I, which we denote by I'. By standard properties of the GS-lists [6, Theorem 1.2.5], any stable matching in I' is stable in I.

Now suppose that we have reached a branching node u of T. By the induction hypothesis, u corresponds to a CSP instance J' with arc consistent domains, and

[2] Implicitly we assume that variable x_i inherits the corresponding preferences over the values in its domain from the preference list of man m_i.

also J' is equivalent to the GS-lists I' for an SMI instance derived from I such that any stable matching in I' is also stable in I. As u is a branching node of T, there is some i ($1 \leq i \leq n$) such that variable x_i's domain has size > 1. Hence in T, when branching from node u to its two children v_1 and v_2, two CSP instances J'_1 and J'_2 are derived from J' as follows. In J'_1, x_i is set to the most-preferred value j in its domain and y_j is set to i, and in J'_2, value j is removed from x_i's domain and value i is removed from y_j's domain.

We firstly consider instance J'_1. During arc consistency propagation in J'_1, revision of the constraint x_k/y_j, for any k such that w_j prefers m_k to m_i, forces l to be removed from the domain of x_k, for any l such that m_k prefers w_j to w_l (and similarly k is removed from the domain of y_l). Hence after such revisions, J'_1 corresponds to the SMI instance I'_1 obtained from I' by deleting pairs of the form $\{m_i, w_l\}$ (where $l \neq j$), $\{m_k, w_j\}$ (where $k \neq i$) and $\{m_k, w_l\}$ (where w_j prefers m_k to m_i and m_k prefers w_j to w_l). It is straightforward to verify that any stable matching in I'_1 is also stable in I', which is in turn stable in I by the induction hypothesis. At node v_1, AC is established in J'_1, giving the CSP instance J''_1 which we associate with this node. By Theorem 3, J''_1 corresponds to the GS-lists I''_1 of the SMI instance I'_1. By standard properties of the GS-lists [6, Section 1.2.5], any stable matching in I''_1 is also stable in I'_1, which is in turn stable in I by the preceding argument.

We now consider instance J'_2, which corresponds to the SMI instance I'_2 obtained from I' by deleting the pair $\{m_i, w_j\}$. It is straightforward to verify that any stable matching in I'_2 is also stable in I', which is in turn stable in I by the induction hypothesis. At node v_2, AC is established in J'_2, giving the CSP instance J''_2 which we associate with this node. The remainder of the argument for this case is identical to the corresponding part in the previous paragraph.

Hence the induction step holds, so that the result is true for all nodes of T. Therefore the branching process never fails due to an inconsistency, and it is straightforward to verify that no part of the search space is omitted, so that the search process lists all stable matchings in the SMI instance I. Finally we note that different complete solutions correspond to different stable matchings, so no stable matching is repeated. □

5 A Boolean Encoding of SM and SMI

In this section we give a less obvious but more compact encoding of an SMI instance as a CSP instance. As in Section 2, suppose that I is an SMI instance involving men $m_1, m_2, \ldots, m_n$ and women $w_1, w_2, \ldots, w_n$. For each i ($1 \leq i \leq n$) let l_i^m denote the length of man m_i's preference list, and define l_i^w similarly.

To define an encoding of I as a CSP instance J, we introduce $O(n^2)$ Boolean variables and $O(n^2)$ constraints. For each i, j ($1 \leq i, j \leq n$), the variables are labelled $x_{i,p}$ for $1 \leq p \leq l_i^m + 1$ and $y_{j,q}$ for $1 \leq q \leq l_j^w + 1$, and take only two values, namely T and F. The interpretation of these variables is:

- $x_{i,p} = T$ iff man m_i is matched to his p^{th} or worse choice woman or is unmatched, for $1 \leq p \leq l_i^m$;

Table 1. The constraints in a Boolean encoding of an SMI instance.

Constraint	Range
1. $x_{i,1} = T$	$(1 \le i \le n)$
2. $y_{j,1} = T$	$(1 \le j \le n)$
3. $x_{i,p} = F \rightarrow x_{i,p+1} = F$	$(1 \le i \le n, 2 \le p \le l_i^m)$
4. $y_{j,q} = F \rightarrow y_{j,q+1} = F$	$(1 \le j \le n, 2 \le q \le l_j^w)$
5. $x_{i,p} = T$ & $y_{j,q} = F \rightarrow x_{i,p+1} = T$	$(1 \le i, j \le n)$ (*)
6. $y_{j,q} = T$ & $x_{i,p} = F \rightarrow y_{j,q+1} = T$	$(1 \le i, j \le n)$ (*)
7. $x_{i,p} = T \rightarrow y_{j,q+1} = F$	$(1 \le i, j \le n)$ (*)
8. $y_{j,q} = T \rightarrow x_{i,p+1} = F$	$(1 \le i, j \le n)$ (*)

- $x_{i,p} = T$ iff man m_i is unmatched, for $p = l_i^m + 1$;
- $y_{j,q} = T$ iff woman w_j is matched to her q^{th} or worse choice man or is unmatched, for $1 \le q \le l_j^w$;
- $y_{j,q} = T$ iff woman w_j is unmatched, for $q = l_j^w + 1$.

The constraints are listed in Table 1. For each i and j $(1 \le i, j \le n)$, the constraints marked (*) are present if and only if m_i finds w_j acceptable; in this case p is the rank of w_j in m_i's list and q is the rank of m_i in w_j's list.

Constraints 1 and 2 are trivial, since each man and woman is either matched with some partner or is unmatched. Constraints 3 and 4 enforce monotonicity: if a man gets his $p - 1^{th}$ or better choice, he certainly gets his p^{th} or better choice. For Constraints 5-8, let i and j be arbitrary $(1 \le i, j \le n)$, and suppose that m_i finds w_j acceptable, where p is the rank of w_j in m_i's list and q is the rank of m_i in w_j's list. Constraints 5 and 6 are monogamy constraints; consider Constraint 5 (the explanation of Constraint 6 is similar). If m_i has a partner no better than w_j or is unmatched, and w_j has a partner she prefers to m_i, then m_i cannot be matched to w_j, so m_i has his $(p+1)$th-choice or worse partner, or is unmatched. Constraints 7 and 8 are stability constraints; consider Constraint 7 (the explanation of Constraint 8 is similar). If m_i has a partner no better than w_j or is unmatched, then w_j must have a partner no worse than m_i, for otherwise m_i and w_j would form a blocking pair.

The next section focuses on AC propagation in J.

6 Arc Consistency in the Boolean Encoding

In this section we consider the effect of AC propagation on a CSP instance J obtained from an SMI instance I by the encoding of Section 5. We show that, using AC propagation in J, we may recover the man-optimal and woman-optimal stable matchings in I, and moreover, we may enumerate *all* stable matchings in I in a failure-free manner.

Imposing AC in J corresponds (in a looser sense than with the first encoding) to the application of the EGS algorithm in I from both the men's and women's sides. Indeed, we can understand the variables in terms of proposals in the EGS algorithm. That is, $x_{i,p}$ being true corresponds to m_i's $p - 1^{th}$ choice woman

Men's lists	Women's lists
1: 1	1: 1
2: 2	2: 2
3: 4	3: 4 6
4: 6 5 3	4: 3
5: 5 6	5: 6 4 5
6: 3 6 5	6: 5 6 4

(a)

Men's lists	Women's lists
1: 1	1: 1
2: 2	2: 2
3: 4	3: 4 3 6
4: 6 5 3	4: 3
5: 5 6	5: 6 1 4 5
6: 3 1 2 6 5	6: 5 1 3 6 4

(b)

Fig. 5. (a) The GS-lists for the SM instance of Figure 1, and (b) the possible partners remaining after AC is applied in the Boolean encoding.

rejecting him after a proposal from a man she likes more. Consequently, the maximum value of p for which $x_{i,p}$ is true gives the best choice that will accept m_i, and the lowest value of p such that $x_{i,p+1}$ is false gives the worst choice that he need accept (and the same holds for the $y_{j,q}$ variables). In general, we will prove that, for a given person p in I, AC propagation in J yields a reduced preference list for p which we call the *Extended GS-list* or *XGS-list* – this contains all elements in p's preference list between the first and last entries of his/her GS-list (inclusive). For example, Figure 5(a) repeats the GS-lists from Figure 1, and (b) shows the XGS-lists after AC is enforced. Note that in general, the XGS-lists may include some values not in the GS-lists.

We now describe how we can use AC propagation in order to derive the XGS-lists for I. After we apply AC in J, the monotonicity constraints force the domains for the $x_{i,p}$ variables to follow a simple sequence, for $p = 1$ to $l_i^m + 1$. First, there is a sequence of domains $\{T\}$, then a sequence of domains which remain $\{T, F\}$, and a final sequence of domains $\{F\}$. The first sequence must be non-empty because $x_{i,1} = T$. If the middle sequence is empty then all variables associated with m_i are determined, while if the last sequence is empty it might still happen that m_i fails to find any partner at all. More formally, let π $(1 \leq \pi \leq l_i^m + 1)$ be the largest integer such that $dom(x_{i,\pi}) = \{T\}$, and let π' be the largest integer such that $T \in dom(x_{i,\pi'})$. We will prove that, if $\pi = l_i^m + 1$ then the XGS-list of m_i is empty; otherwise the XGS-list of m_i contains all people on m_i's original preference list between positions π and π' (inclusive). Hence, in the latter case, a man m_i's XGS-list consists of the women at position p in his original list, for each p such that $dom(x_{i,p}) = \{T, F\}$ after AC-propagation, together with the woman in position π in his original list. A similar correspondence exists between the women's XGS-lists and the $y_{j,q}$ variables.

As in Section 3, the proof of this result uses two lemmas. The first shows that the domains remaining after AC propagation correspond to subsets of the XGS-lists, whilst the second shows that the XGS-lists correspond to arc consistent domains.

Lemma 5. *For a given i $(1 \leq i \leq n)$, after AC propagation in J, let p be the largest integer such that $dom(x_{i,p}) = \{T\}$ and let p' be the largest integer such that $T \in dom(x_{i,p'})$. If $p < l_i^m + 1$ then all entries of m_i's preference list between* *positions p and p′ belong to the XGS-list of m_i. A similar correspondence holds for the women's lists.*

Proof. The first entry on a man m's XGS-list corresponds to the last woman (if any) to whom m proposed during an execution of the man-oriented EGS-algorithm. Similarly the last entry on a woman w's XGS-list corresponds to the last man (if any) who proposed to w during an execution of the man-oriented EGS-algorithm. A similar correspondence in terms of the woman-oriented EGS-algorithm yields the first entry on a woman's XGS-list and the last entry on a man's XGS-list. We prove that, if a person q is missing from a person p's XGS-list, then AC propagation reduces the domains of the variables relating to person p correspondingly. (We consider only the correspondences involving the man-oriented EGS-algorithm; the gender-reversed argument involving the woman-oriented EGS-algorithm yields the remaining cases.)

It suffices to prove the following result by induction on the number of proposals z during an execution E of the man-oriented EGS algorithm (see Figure 2) on I: if proposal z consists of man m_i proposing to woman w_j, then $x_{i,t} = T$ for $1 \leq t \leq p$ and $y_{j,t} = F$ for $q < t \leq l_j^w + 1$, where p denotes the rank of w_j in m_i's list and q denotes the rank of m_i in w_j's list.

Clearly the result is true for $z = 0$. Now assume that $z = a > 0$ and the result is true for all $z < a$. Suppose that the ath proposal during E consists of man m_i proposing to woman w_j. Suppose that p is the rank of w_j in m_i's list and q is the rank of m_i in w_j's list. Suppose firstly that $p = 1$. Then $x_{i,1} = T$ by Constraint 1, and $y_{j,t} = F$ for $q < t \leq l_j^w + 1$ by Constraints 7 and 4, since $x_{i,p}$'s value has been determined. Now suppose that $p > 1$. Then previously m_i proposed to w_k, his $p-1^{th}$-choice woman (since m_i proposes in his preference list order, starting with his most-preferred woman). By the induction hypothesis, $x_{i,t} = T$ for $1 \leq t \leq p-1$. Woman w_k rejected m_i because she received a proposal from some man m_l whom she prefers to m_i. Let r, s be the ranks of m_l, m_i in w_k's list respectively, so that $r < s$. By the induction hypothesis, $y_{k,t} = F$ for $t \geq r+1$. Thus in particular, $y_{k,s} = F$, so that by Constraint 5, $x_{i,p} = T$, since the values of $x_{i,p-1}$ and $y_{k,s}$ have been determined. Thus by Constraints 7 and 4, $y_{j,t} = F$ for $q < t \leq l_j^w + 1$, since $x_{i,p}$'s value has been determined. This completes the induction step.

Thus the proof of the lemma is established, so that the domains remaining after AC is enforced correspond to subsets of the XGS-lists. □

Lemma 6. *For each i ($1 \leq i \leq n$), define a domain of values $dom(x_{i,t})$ for the variables $x_{i,t}$ ($1 \leq t \leq l_i^m + 1$) as follows: if the XGS-list of m_i is empty, $dom(x_{i,t}) = \{T\}$ for $1 \leq t \leq l_i^m + 1$. Otherwise, let p and p' be the ranks (in m_i's preference list) of the first and last women on m_i's XGS-list respectively. $dom(x_{i,t}) = \{T\}$ for $1 \leq t \leq p$, $dom(x_{i,t}) = \{F\}$ for $p'+1 \leq t \leq l_i^m + 1$ and $dom(x_{i,t}) = \{T, F\}$ for $p < t \leq p'$. The domains for each variable $y_{j,t}$ ($1 \leq j \leq n$, $1 \leq t \leq l_j^w + 1$) are defined analogously. Then the domains so defined are arc consistent in J.*

Proof. The proof of this lemma is along similar lines to that of Lemma 2 and involves showing that Constraints 1 to 8 in Table 1 are arc consistent under the assignments defined above; we omit the details for space reasons. □

The following theorem follows immediately from the above lemmas, and the fact that AC algorithms find the unique maximal set of arc consistent domains.

Theorem 7 *Let I be an instance of SMI, and let J be a CSP instance obtained from I by the encoding of Section 5. Then the domains remaining after AC propagation in J are identical (in the sense described before Lemma 5) to the XGS-lists for I.*

Hence Theorem 7 shows that we may find solutions to the CSP giving the man-optimal and woman-optimal stable matchings in I without search.

We remark in passing that the SAT-based technique of unit propagation is strong enough for the same results to hold. This makes no theoretical difference to the cost of establishing AC, although in practice we would expect unit propagation to be cheaper. This observation implies that a SAT solver applying unit propagation exhaustively, e.g. a Davis-Putnam program [2], will perform essentially the same work as an AC-based algorithm.

As before, we show that solutions can be enumerated without failure. The results are better than before in two ways: first, maintenance of AC is much less expensive, and second, there is no need for a specific variable or value ordering.

Theorem 8 *Let I be an instance of SMI and let J be a CSP instance obtained from I using the encoding of Section 5. Then the following search process enumerates all solutions in I without repetition and without ever failing due to an inconsistency:*

- *AC is established as a preprocessing step, and after each branching decision including the decision to remove a value from a domain;*
- *if all domains are arc consistent and some variable v has two values in its domain, then search proceeds by setting v to T, and on backtracking, to F;*
- *when a solution is found, it is reported and backtracking is forced.*

Proof. This result can be proved by an inductive argument similar to that used in the proof of Theorem 4. The full details are omitted here for space reasons, but we indicate below the important points that are specific to this context.

An SMI instance is guaranteed to have a stable matching, though not necessarily a complete one [6, Section 1.4.2] so the initial establishing of AC in J cannot result in failure.

Branching decisions are only made when AC has been established, so Theorem 7 applies at branching points. If all domains are of size 1, we report the solution and terminate. Otherwise, we choose any variable with domain of size 2 and create two branches with the variable set to T and F respectively. If the variable represents a man, setting it to T excludes the man-optimal matching, but the man-pessimal matching remains possible so this branch still contains a solution. Conversely, setting the variable to F excludes the man-pessimal matching but leaves the man-optimal matching, so this branch also contains a solution.

The process of establishing AC never removes values which participate in any solution. As the branching process omits no part of the search space, the search process lists all solutions to the SMI instance. Finally we note that different complete solutions correspond to different stable matchings, so no stable matching is repeated. □

We conclude this section with a remark about the time complexities of AC propagation in both encodings. In general, AC can be established in $O(ed^r)$ time [1], where there are e constraints, each of arity r, and domain size is d. In the encoding of Section 5, $e = O(n^2)$, $d = 2$ and $r \leq 3$. Thus AC can be established in $O(n^2)$ time, which is linear in the size of the input. Hence this encoding of SM achieves the solution in $O(n^2)$ time, which is known to be optimal [9]. We find it remarkable that such a strong result can be obtained without any special-purpose consistency algorithms. Furthermore, this result contrasts with the time complexity of AC propagation in the encoding of Section 2: in this case, $e = O(n^2)$, $d = O(n)$ and $r = 2$, so that AC can be established in $O(n^4)$ time.

7 Conclusion

We have presented two ways of encoding the Stable Marriage problem and its variant SMI as a CSP. The first is a straightforward representation of the problem as a binary CSP. We show that enforcing AC in the CSP gives reduced domains which are equivalent to the GS-lists produced by the Extended Gale-Shapley algorithm, and from which the man-optimal and woman-optimal matchings can be immediately derived. Indeed, we show that all solutions can be found without failure, provided that values are assigned in preference-list order.

Enforcing AC using an algorithm such as AC-3 would be much more time-consuming than the EGS algorithm because of the number and size of the constraints. A constraint propagation algorithm tailored to the stable marriage constraint would do much better, but to get equivalent performance to EGS we should effectively have to embed EGS into our constraint solver.

Nevertheless, the fact that we can solve the CSP without search after AC has been achieved shows that this class of CSP is tractable. Previous tractability results have identified classes of constraint graph (e.g. [3]) or classes of constraint (e.g. [7]) which guarantee tractability. In the binary CSP encoding of SM, it is the combination of the structure of the constraints (a bipartite graph) and their type (the stable-marriage constraint) that ensures that we find solutions efficiently.

The second encoding we present is somewhat more contrived, but allows AC to be established, using a general algorithm, with time complexity equivalent to that of the EGS algorithm. Although the arc consistent domains do not exactly correspond to the GS-lists, we can again find man-optimal and woman-optimal matchings immediately, and all stable matchings without encountering failure during the search. Hence, this encoding yields a CSP-based method for solving SM and SMI which is equivalent in efficiency to EGS.

The practical application of this work is to those variants of SM and SMI which are NP-hard [11,10,8], or indeed to any situation in which additional constraints on the problem make the EGS algorithm inapplicable. If we can extend one of the encodings presented here to these variants, we then have tools to solve them, since we have ready-made search algorithms available for CSPs.

This paper provides a partial answer to a more general question: if we have a problem which can be expressed as a CSP, but for which a special-purpose algorithm is available, is it ever sensible to formulate the problem as a CSP? SM shows that it can be: provided that the encoding is carefully done, existing algorithms for simplifying and solving CSPs may give equivalent performance to the special-purpose algorithm, with the benefit of easy extension to variants of the original problem where the special-purpose algorithm might be inapplicable.

References

1. C. Bessière and J-C Régin. Arc consistency for general constraint networks: Preliminary results. In *Proceedings of IJCAI'97*, pages 398–404, 1997.
2. M. Davis, G. Logemann, and D. Loveland. A machine program for theorem-proving. *Communications of the ACM*, 5:394–397, 1962.
3. Eugene C. Freuder. A sufficient condition for backtrack-free search. *Journal of the ACM*, 29:24–32, 1982.
4. D. Gale and L.S. Shapley. College admissions and the stability of marriage. *American Mathematical Monthly*, 69:9–15, 1962.
5. D. Gale and M. Sotomayor. Some remarks on the stable matching problem. *Discrete Applied Mathematics*, 11:223–232, 1985.
6. D. Gusfield and R. W. Irving. *The Stable Marriage Problem: Structure and Algorithms*. The MIT Press, 1989.
7. P. Jeavons, D. Cohen, and M. Gyssens. A unifying framework for tractable constraints. In *Proceedings CP'95*, volume LNCS 976, pages 276–291. Springer, 1995.
8. D.F. Manlove, R.W. Irving, K. Iwama, S. Miyazaki, and Y. Morita. Hard variants of stable marriage. To appear in *Theoretical Computer Science*.
9. C. Ng and D.S. Hirschberg. Lower bounds for the stable marriage problem and its variants. *SIAM Journal on Computing*, 19:71–77, 1990.
10. C. Ng and D.S. Hirschberg. Three-dimensional stable matching problems. *SIAM Journal on Discrete Mathematics*, 4:245–252, 1991.
11. E. Ronn. NP-complete stable matching problems. *Journal of Algorithms*, 11:285–304, 1990.
12. A.E. Roth. The evolution of the labor market for medical interns and residents: a case study in game theory. *Journal of Political Economy*, 92(6):991–1016, 1984.
13. A.E. Roth and M.A.O. Sotomayor. *Two-sided matching: a study in game-theoretic modeling and analysis*, volume 18 of *Econometric Society Monographs*. Cambridge University Press, 1990.
14. J.E. Vande Vate. Linear programming brings marital bliss. *Operations Research Letters*, 1989.

Components for State Restoration in Tree Search

Chiu Wo Choi[1], Martin Henz[1], and Ka Boon Ng[2]

[1] School of Computing, National University Of Singapore, Singapore
{choichiu,henz}@comp.nus.edu.sg
[2] Honeywell Singapore Laboratory
kevin.ng@honeywell.com

Abstract. Constraint programming systems provide software architectures for the fruitful interaction of algorithms for constraint propagation, branching and exploration of search trees. Search requires the ability to restore the state of a constraint store. Today's systems use different state restoration policies. Upward restoration undoes changes using a trail, and downward restoration (recomputation) reinstalls information along a downward path in the search tree. In this paper, we present an architecture that isolates the state restoration policy as an orthogonal software component. Applications of the architecture include two novel state restoration policies, called lazy copying and batch recomputation, and a detailed comparison of these and existing restoration policies with "everything else being equal". The architecture allows the user to optimize the time and space consumption of applications by choosing existing and designing new state restoration policies in response to application-specific characteristics.

1 Introduction

Finite domain constraint programming (CP(FD)) systems are software systems designed for solving combinatorial search problems using tree search. The history of constraint programming systems shows an increasing emphasis on software design, reflecting user requirements for flexibility in performance debugging and application-specific customization of the algorithms involved.

A search tree is generated by branching algorithms, which at each node provide different choices that add new constraints to strengthen the store in the child nodes. Propagation algorithms strengthen the store according to the operational semantics of constraints in the store, and exploration algorithms decide on the order, in which search trees are explored.

Logic programming proved to be successful in providing elegant means of defining branching algorithms, reusing the built-in notion of choice points. Constraint programming systems like SICStus Prolog [Int00] and GNU Prolog [DC00] provide libraries for propagation algorithms and allow the programming of exploration algorithms on top of the built-in depth-first search (DFS) by using meta programming. To achieve a more modular architecture, recent

T. Walsh (Ed.): CP 2001, LNCS 2239, pp. 240–255, 2001.

systems moved away from the logic programming paradigm. The ILOG Solver library for constraint programming [ILO00] allows the user to implement propagation algorithms in C++. The user can implement exploration algorithms using objects that encapsulate the state of search. The language Claire [CJL99] allows for programming exploration algorithms using built-in primitives for state manipulation, and the language Oz provides a built-in data structure called space [Sch97b,Sch00] for implementing exploration algorithms.

At every node in the search tree, the state of variables and constraints is the result of constraint propagation of the constraints that were added along the path from the root to the node. During search, the nodes are visited in the order given by the exploration algorithm. In this paper, we address the question on how the state corresponding to a node is obtained or *restored*. Different systems currently provide different ways of restoring the state corresponding to the target node. All systems/languages except Oz are based on a state restoration policy (SRP) that records changes on the state in a data structure called trail. The trail is employed to restore the state back to an ancestor of the current node. Schulte [Sch97b,Sch00] presents several alternative SRPs based on copying and recomputation of states and evaluates their competitiveness conceptually and experimentally in [Sch99].

The best state restoration policy for a given application depends on the amount of propagation (state change), the exploration and the branching. The goal of this work is to identify software techniques that enable the employment of different SRPs in the same system without compromising the orthogonal development of other components such as propagation, branching and exploration. The architecture allows the user to optimize time and space consumption of applications by choosing existing or designing new SRPs in response to application-specific characteristics. We introduce two novel SRP, namely lazy copying and batch recomputation, and show experimentally that for many applications, they improve the time and/or space efficiency over existing SRPs. State restoration is an important aspect of tree search that deserves the attention of users and constraint programming systems designers.

We outline in Section 2 a software architecture for constraint programming systems that will form the base for further discussion. The components are designed and implemented in C++ using the Figaro library for constraint programming [HMN99,CHN00,Ng01]. The Figaro library is available at [Fig01]. In Section 3, we describe the two SRPs currently in use, namely trailing and recomputation. At the end of Section 3, we give an overview of the rest of the paper.

2 A Component Design for Search

In CP(FD), the constraint store represents a computational state, hosting finite-domain (FD) variables and constraints. A variable has a domain, which is the set of possible values it can take. A constraint maintains a relation among a set of variables by eliminating values, which are in conflict with the constraint,

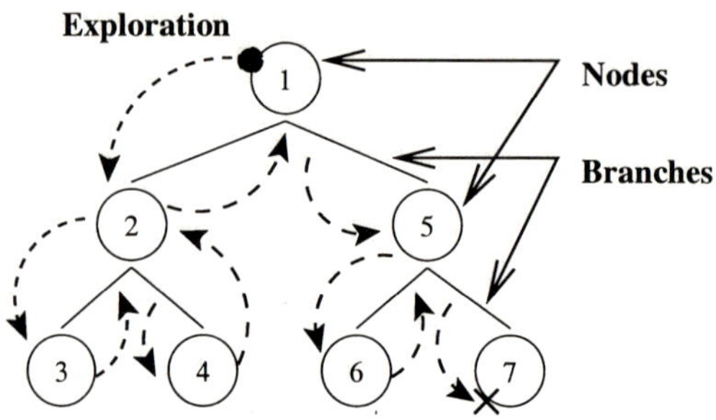

Fig. 1. Depth-First Tree Search

from variable domains according to the propagation algorithm. Each time a change is made to a constraint store, a propagation engine performs constraint propagation until it reaches a fix point, in which no constraint can eliminate any more values. In our framework, we represent a constraint store by a data structure called store [Ng01].

Usually, constraint propagation alone is insufficient to solve a problem. Therefore, we need tree search to find a solution. A search explores the tree in a top-down fashion. Nodes and branches build up the search tree. It is adequate to view search in terms of these components: branching, node and exploration. Figure 1 provides an illustration of tree search. Circles represent nodes, while lines connecting two nodes represent branches. The numbers inside the nodes give the order of exploration. The dashed arrows indicate DFS. For simplicity, we only consider binary search trees.

The branching describes the shape of the search tree. Common branching algorithms include a simple labeling procedure (naive enumeration of variables), variable ordering (such as first-fail), and domain splitting. For solving scheduling problems, more complex branching algorithms, such as resource serialization, are used. In our setting, branching coincides with the notion of a choice point. The class `Branching` shown in Program 1 has a method `choose` (line 5, for conciseness, we refer to C++ member functions as methods) which adds a constraint to the store based on the choice given and returns the branching (choice point) of the child node. `Branching` also defines methods to check whether it is done (line 3) or it has failed (line 4).

Program 1 Declaration of Branching

```
1  class Branching {
2  public:
3      bool done() const;
4      bool fail() const;
5      Branching* choose(store* s,int i) const;
6  };
```

Program 2 Declaration of Node

```
1  class Node {
2  protected:
3      store* cs;
4      Branching* branch;
5      Node* parent,left_child,right_child;
6  public:
7      Node(store* s,Branching* b);
8      bool isLeaf() const;
9      bool isFail() const;
10     Node* make_left_child();
11     Node* make_right_child();
12 };
```

A node represents a state in the search tree. The class Node shown in Program 2 contains a store, a branching, and pointers to parent and children nodes (line 3-4). The constructor (line 7) takes a store and a branching as arguments. The left and right children nodes are created by calling the method make_left_child and make_right_child respectively (line 10-11). Each time a child node is created, the branching adds a constraint to the store. To proceed to the next level of the search tree, constraint propagation must reach a fix point. Node also has methods to check if the node is a leaf node (line 8) or a failure node (line 9).

Figure 2 gives a graphical representation of nodes and branchings. The left side shows the design of nodes. A tree is linked bi-directionally, where the parent points to the children and vice versa. The right side shows the relation between nodes and branchings during the creation of children nodes. Solid arrows represent pointers, while labelled, dashed arrows represent the respective method calls. Calling the make_left_child or the make_right_child methods creates a child node, which, in turn, invokes the method choose of the current node branching that returns a branching for the child node.

The exploration specifies the tree traversal order. DFS is the most common exploration algorithm used in tree search for constraint programming. Program 3

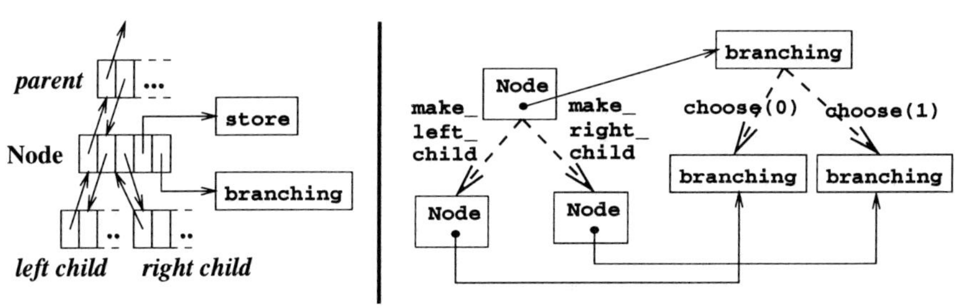

Fig. 2. Tree Node and Relation with Branching

Program 3 Exploration: Depth First Search

```
1   Node* DFS(Node* node) {
2       if (node->isLeaf()) return node;
3       if (node->isFail()) return NULL;
4       Node* result = DFS(node->make_left_child());
5       if (result != NULL) return result;
6       return DFS(node->make_right_child());
7   };
```

shows the implementation of DFS. Function DFS takes a node as an argument and tries to find the first solution using depth-first strategy. It returns the node containing the solution (line 2) or NULL if none is found (line 3). Otherwise, it recursively finds the solution on the left (line 4-5) and right (line 6) subtrees.

3 Restoration Policies

The problem of state restoration occurs in systems where a state results from a sequence of complex operations, and where the state corresponding to different (sub)sequences are requested over time. For example, in distributed systems, state restoration is used to recover from failure in a network node [NX95].

In constraint-based tree search, the dominant SRP has been trailing. This policy demands to record the changes done on the state in a data structure, called trail. To go from a node to its parent, the recorded changes are undone. The reason for this dominance lies in the historical fact that constraint programming evolved from logic programming, and that trailing is employed in all logic programming systems for state restoration. The combination of the general idea of trailing with constraint-programming specific modifications [AB90], was deemed sufficient for constraint programming.

Schulte [Sch00] shows that other SRPs have appealing advantages. Starting from the idea of copying an entire constraint store, he introduced several SRPs that trade space for time by recomputing the store from a copy made in an ancestor node instead of making a copy at every node [Sch99]. These SRPs have the advantage of not requiring the recording of changes in propagation algorithms, thereby considerably simplifying the design of CP(FD) systems.

In the design presented in Section 2, the SRP is determined by the definition of the methods `make_left_child` and `make_right_child` in the class `Node`. These methods need to create a new node together with its store and branching from the information present in the current node. This indicates that we may be able to arrive at different SRPs by providing different implementations of the `Node` class, without affecting other components such as branching and exploration. The next section shows that it is indeed possible.

By isolating the SRP in a separate component that is orthogonal to the other components, the development of new SRPs may be simplified, which may inspire the development of new SRPs. Indeed, we will present two new SRPs in Section 5, and 6. Trailing requires all operations to be search aware, and is not orthogonal to the rest of the system [Sch99]. Section 7 present a variant called coarse-grained trailing, which can be implemented as an orthogonal component. By having existing and new SRPs available in one system, we are able to conduct an experimental evaluation of them with "everything else being equal"; we report the results of this evaluation in Section 8.

4 Restoration Components

The previous section showed that the `Node` class is the component that decides the SRP. The aim, therefore, is to design different types of nodes for different SRPs, namely, `CopyingNode` for copying and `RecomputationNode` for recomputation. All these nodes inherit from the base class `Node`. Hence, we specify the restoration component of search by passing the correct node type as an argument.

The idea for `CopyingNode` and `RecomputationNode` is presented in [Sch97a] and it allows the Oz Explorer to have copying and recomputation as SRP for DFS exploration. We separate the SRP aspect of nodes from the exploration aspect by implementing SRP-specific extensions of the `Node` base class.

The `Node` base class is similar to the one introduced in Program 2 except that it does not contain a store anymore (remove line 3). Rather, the decision on whether to keep a store and on the type of store to keep is implemented in the subclasses.

The copying SRP requires each node of the search tree to keep a copy of the store. Hence, the class `CopyingNode` contains an additional attribute to keep the copy. As the store provides a method `clone` for creating a copy of itself, when a `CopyingNode` explores and creates a child node, it keeps a copy of the store and passes the other copy to the child node.

The recomputation SRP keeps stores for only some nodes, and recomputes the stores of other nodes from their ancestors. A parameter called maximum recomputation distance (MRD) of n, means that a copy of a store is kept at every n-th level of the tree. Figure 3 shows the difference between copying and recomputation with MRD of 2. Copies of the stores are kept only in shaded nodes. Copying can be viewed as recomputation with MRD of 1.

For `RecomputationNode`, we introduce four attributes: (1) a pointer to store; (2) an integer counter d to check, if we have reached the n-th level of the tree;

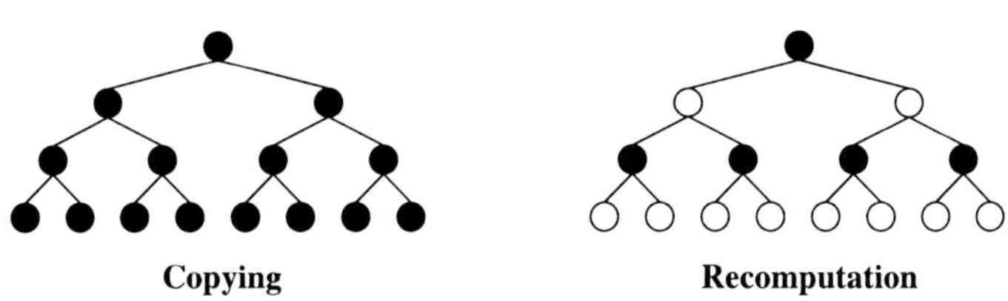

Fig. 3. Copying vs. Recomputation

Program 4 Recomputing Stores in Search Tree

```
1  Store* RecomputationNode::recompute(int i) {
2      Store* rs;
3      if (copy)
4          rs = cs->clone();
5      else
6          rs = parent->recompute(choice);
7      branch->choose(rs,i);
8      return rs;
9  };
```

(3) an integer `choice`, which indicates, if the node is the first or the second child of its parent; and (4) and a boolean flag `copy` to indicate the presence of a copy of a store. If d reaches the n-th level limit when creating a child node, a copy of the store is kept and `copy` is set to `true`. During the exploration of a node where recomputation of the store is needed (i. e. , no copy of store is kept), the method `recompute` shown in Program 4 recursively recomputes for the store from the ancestors, by committing each parent's store to the alternative given by `choice` (line 7).

Adaptive recomputation (AR) [Sch99] improves recomputation performance by keeping only a copy of the store at a depth equidistant from the depth of an existing copy (or root, if none exists) and the depth of the last-encountered failure. It is straightforward to implement AR by introducing another argument to the method `recompute` which counts the length of the recomputation path. The additional copy of the store is made when the counter reaches half the length.

During exploration, it is often clear that the store of a node is not needed any longer and can be safely passed to a child. For example in the case of DFS, we passed the store to the second child when the first child's subtree is fully explored. For such cases, nodes provide methods `create_last_right_child` and `create_last_left_child`. When a copy-holding node N is asked for its last child node A, the node N will pass its store to the child node A, which then becomes a copy-holding node. This optimization—described in [Sch00] as Last Alternative Optimization—saves space, and performs the recomputation step $N \to A$ only once.

Best solution search (for solving optimization problem) such as branch-and-bound requires the dynamic addition of constraint during search, which demand the next solution to be better than the currently best solution. The `Node` class has a method:

```
State post_constraint(BinaryFunction* BF,store* s);
```

to add this constraint to the store inside a node. This addition is similar to the injection of an computation in an Oz space [Sch97b]. The method takes in a binary function to enforce the order, and the best solution store. It returns `FAIL` if enforcing the order causes failure. However, care should be taken during recomputation, where not every node in the tree may contain a copy of the store. For that, we need to introduce extra attributes to keep the constraints, which will be added as recomputation is performed.

5 Lazy Copying

Lazy copying is essentially a copy-on-write technique, which maintains multiple references to an object. A copy is made only when we write to the object. Figure 4 shows the differences between copying and lazy copying.

Some operating systems use this technique for managing processes sharing the same virtual memory [MBKQ96]. In ACE [PGH95], a parallel implementation of Prolog, an incremental copying strategy reduces the amount of information transferred during its share operation. In Or-parallelism, sharing is used to pass work from one or-agent to another, and is similar to the lazy copying strategy.

In conventional CP(FD) systems, constraints have direct references (pointers) to the variables they use and/or vice versa. In such systems, lazy copying requires that every time an object (say O) is written to become N, every object that is pointing to O would need to be copied such that each new copy points to N while the old copies continue to point to O. This process needs to be executed recursively, until copies have been made for the entire connected sub-graph of the constraints and the variables. This requirement can be avoided through relative addressing [Ng01], where every reference to an object is an address (or index), called ID, into the vector of placeholders. This technique is implemented in Figaro, where constraint and variable objects are always referenced through the placeholders.

From a software engineering point of view, the technique allows us to provide the same concept for both copying and lazy copying. To support lazy copying, we introduce lazy-copying stores that possess the copy-on-write characteristics for the constraint and variable objects. Conceptually, a lazy copying store behaves like a copying store except that its internal implementation delays the copying until a write operation on the particular object. The implementation of `LazyCopyNode` is straightforward; we only need to replace the store in `CopyingNode` by a lazy copying store described above.

6 Batch Recomputation

Recomputation performs a sequence of constraint additions and fix point computations. At earlier fix point computations, the implicit knowledge of later constraints is not exploited. This means that work is done unnecessarily, since recomputation will never encounter failure. Thus, recomputation can be improved by accumulating the constraints to be added along the path and invoke the propagation engine for computing the fix point only once. Since recomputation constraints are added all at once, we call this technique batch recomputation.

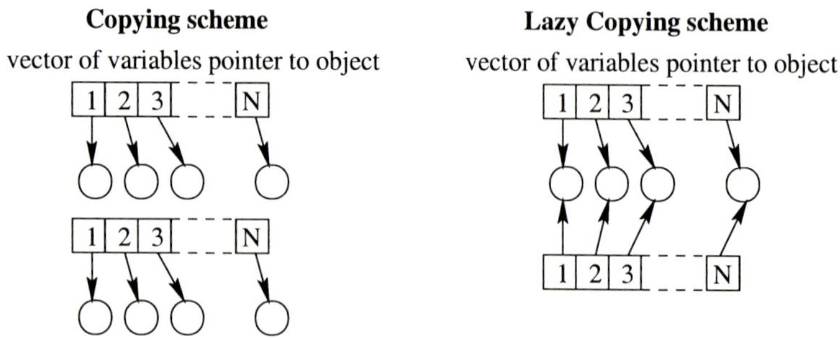

Fig. 4. Comparison between Copying and Lazy Copying

Batch recomputation is also applicable to adaptive recomputation, which we call batch adaptive recomputation.

Batch recomputation requires a data structure to record the branching decision during exploration. The recorded branching decision is useful to add the correct constraint in constant time along the recomputation path. Batch recomputation also requires a data structure to accumulate the added constraints along the recomputation path and the ability to control the propagation for performing propagation in a single batch. A condition for the correctness of batch recomputation is the monotonicity of constraints, meaning that different orders of constraint propagation must result in the same fix point.

The implementation of batch recomputation in our architecture is straightforward. The branching objects provide the facility to record the branching decisions during exploration. The method `choose` adds the correct constraint in constant time during recomputation. The store uses a propagation queue for accumulating the added constraints along the recomputation path and provides a feature to disable and invoke propagation explicitly.

In Mozart/Oz, the process of branching is achieved by communication between choice points and engines, which always run in separate threads. The communication insists on performing propagation to the fixpoint (in Oz terminology: until the space is stable), and thus precludes an implementation of batch recomputation in an Oz search engine in the current setup. On the other hand, it is conceivable that the branching primitive `choose` is wrapped in a mechanism that records the branching decisions, and that a data structure containing these decisions is made available to a batch recomputation engine. An alternative is to extend spaces by primitives to enable/disable stability enforcement.

7 Coarse-Grained Trailing

Coarse-grained trailing is an approximation of trailing as implemented in most CP(FD) systems. Instead of trailing updates of memory locations, we trail the complete variable object or constraint object when changes occur. As mentioned in Section 5, our architecture provides a relative addressing scheme and allows

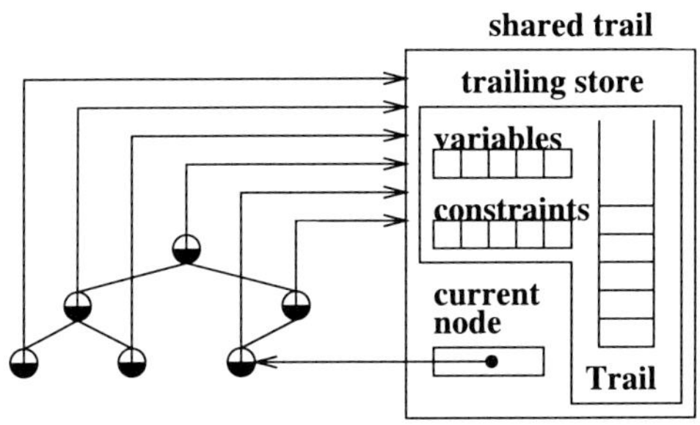

Fig. 5. Coarse-grained Trailing

to make copies of variables and constraints, which make the implementation simple.

Coarse-grained trailing only keeps a single store for the entire exploration. Figure 5 shows its implementation. A half-shaded node represents a trailing node and arrows represent pointers. A trailing node holds a pointer to a common shared trail. The shared trail contains a trailing store and a pointer to the current node where the store is defined. A trailing store is needed because of the strong dependency between the store and the actual trail.

Program 5 shows the declaration of the trailing node and shared trail. The class `TrailingNode` implements the coarse-grained trailing SRP. It contains an integer `mark`, which represents the trail marker for terminating backtracking (line 2). This corresponds to the time stamping technique [AB90]. The integer `i` (line 2) indicates whether the node is the first or second child of its parent. The constructor of the class `SharedTrail` takes a store and a pointer to the root node as argument (line 10). When exploring a node D, which is not pointed to by the current node, the method `jump` (line 12) changes the trailing store from the current node to the node D. First, `jump` computes the path leading to the common ancestor with method `computePath` (line 11), then backtracks to the common ancestor, and finally descends to node D by recomputation.

The implementations of trailing and lazy copying store are closely related, since both create a copy of the changed object before a state modification occurs. Compared to trailing, the coarse granularity imposes an overhead, which grows with the complexity of the constraints (global constraints). If the constraints contain large stateful data structures, trailing may record incremental changes as opposed to copying the whole data structure on the trail as it is done by coarse-grained trailing.

8 Experiments

This section compares and analyses the runtime and memory profile of the different SRPs. The experiments are run on a PC with 400 MHz Pentium II processor, 256MB main memory and 512MB swap memory, running Linux (RedHat

6.0 Kernel 2.2.17-14). All experiments are conducted using the current development version of the Figaro system [HMN99,CHN00,Ng01], a C++ library for constraint programming. The Figaro library is distributed under the Lesser GNU Public License [Fig01], and all benchmark programs are included in the distribution.

The SRPs are denoted by the following symbols: CP - Copying, TR - Coarse-grained Trailing, LC - Lazy copying, RE - Recomputation, AR - Adaptive recomputation, BR - Batch Recomputation, BAR - Batch Adaptive Recomputation. To facilitate the comparison, the maximal recomputation distance MRD for RE, AR, BR and BAR is computed using the formula: MRD $= \lceil depth \div 5 \rceil$ where *depth* is depth of the search tree. All benchmark timings (Time) are the average of 5 runs measured in seconds, and have been taken as wall clock time. The coefficient of variation is less than 5%. Memory requirements are measured in terms of maximum memory usage (Max) in kilobytes (KB). It refers to the memory used by the C++ runtime system rather than the actual memory usage because C++ allocates memory in chunks.

The set of benchmark problems are: The Alpha crypto-arithmetic puzzle, the Knights tour problem on an 18×18 chess board, the Magic Square puzzle of size 6, a round robin tournament scheduling problem with 7 teams and a resource constraint that requires fair distribution over courts (Larry), aligning for a Photo, a Hamiltonian path problem with 20 nodes, the ABZ6 Job shop scheduling benchmark, the Bridge scheduling benchmark with side constraints, and 100-S-Queens puzzle that uses three distinct (with offset) constraints.

Table 1 lists the characteristics of the problems. These benchmarks provide the evaluation of the different SRPs based on the following criteria: problem size, amount of propagation, search tree depth, and number of failures. Our comparison of the different SRPs are based on "everything else being equal", meaning all other elements such as store, branching, exploration, etc. are kept unchanged except the SRP.

Program 5 Shared Trail and Trailing Node

```
class TrailingNode : public Node {
protected:
    int i,mark; SharedTrail* trail;
public: // methods declaration...
};

class SharedTrail {
private:
    TrailingStore* ts; TrailingNode* current;
public:
    SharedTrail(Store* s,TrailingNode* tn);
    list<TrailingNode*> computePath(TrailingNode* tn);
    void jump(TrailingNode* tn);
};
```

Since different components of a CP(FD) system are dependent on one another, the performance may vary. For instance, the choice of FD representation has a significant effect on the performance. For these experiments, the FD representation is a lists of interval. Some problems may perform differently when a bit vector representation is used. Another remark is that the speed of copying between our system and Mozart is different for the following reasons: different FD representations, amount of data being copied, variable wake up scheme during propagation, and memory management (Mozart uses automatic garbage collection). Therefore, the results do not match exactly with Schulte [Sch99].

Table 1. Characteristics of Example Programs

example	search	choice	fail	soln	depth	var	constr
Alpha	all/naive	7435	7435	1	50	26	21
Knights	one/naive	266	12	1	265	7500	11205
Magic Square	one/split	46879	46829	1	72	37	15
Larry	one/naive	389	371	1	40	678	1183
Photo	best/naive	23911	23906	6	34	95	53
Hamilton	one/naive	7150	7145	1	66	288	195
ABZ6	best/rank	2409	2395	15	91	102	120
Bridge	best/rank	1268	1261	8	78	44	88
100-S-Queen	one/ff	115	22	1	97	100	3

Table 2. Runtime and Memory Performance of Copying

Example	Time	Max	Example	Time	Max
Alpha	19.200	1956	Hamilton	50.514	2176
Knights	22.086	330352	ABZ6	25.004	4936
Magic Square	160.360	2632	Bridge(10x)	8.582	2888
Larry	5.844	5712	100-S-Queen(10x)	8.444	7816
Photo	35.086	1912			

Table 2 gives the runtime and memory performance of copying. Figure 6 shows the comparison of coarse-grained trailing and recomputation. The numbers are obtained by dividing the performance of each SRP by the performance of copying. A value below 1 means better performance, while a value above 1 means worse performance than copying. This group of comparison confirms the following result of Schulte [Sch99]. Copying suffers from the problem of memory swapping for large problems with deep search trees such as Knights. Recomputation improves copying by trading space for time. Adaptive recomputation minimize the penalty in runtime of recomputation by using more space.

Coarse-grained trailing performs comparatively well to copying and other recomputation schemes. The memory peaks in Photo is probably due to STL library dynamic array memory allocation module which grows the array size by recursive doubling. Coarse-grained trailing provides us with an approximation for comparing the performance of trailing and recomputation.

Lazy copying aims at combining the advantages of both coarse-grained trailing and copying. Figure 7 shows its performance against both SRPs, the numbers are obtained by dividing lazy copying's numbers by copying's and coarse-grained trailing's numbers. Over the benchmark problems, in the worst case, lazy copying performs the same as copying, while for the cases with small amount of propagation, lazy copying can save memory and even time. Unfortunately, lazy copying still performs badly for large problems with deep search trees such as Knights, when compared to coarse-grained trailing. This is due to the extra accounting data we keep for lazy copying. However, lazy copying improves the runtime over coarse-grained trailing for problems like Magic Square, Larry and Bridge, where there are many failure nodes, because lazy copying can jump directly from one node to another upon backtracking, while coarse-grained trailing has to carry out the extra operation of undoing the changes.

Batch recomputation aims at improving the runtime performance of recomputation. The memory requirement is the same as recomputation. Figure 8 shows the runtime performance of batch recomputation versus recomputation and batch adaptive recomputation versus adaptive recomputation. Batch recomputation improves the runtime of recomputation for all cases. However, batch adaptive recomputation improve only little over adaptive recomputation except for Larry. This is due to the design of adaptive recomputation which makes a copy in the middle when a failure is encountered, which in turn, reduces the recomputation distance that batch recomputation can take advantage of.

Comparison with other constraint programming systems are needed in order to gauge the effect of the component architecture and the overhead for relative addressing. Initial results are reported in [Ng01].

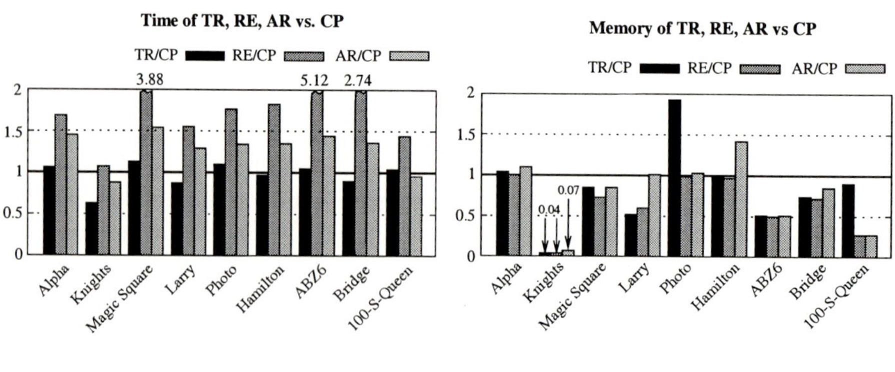

Fig. 6. Performance of Coarse-grained Trailing and Recomputation vs. Copying

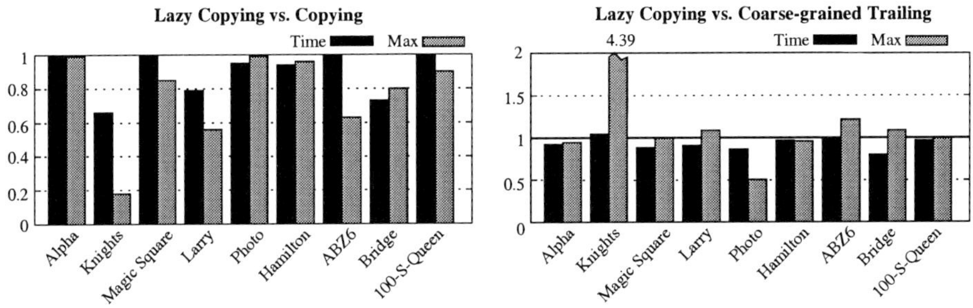

Fig. 7. Performance of Lazy Copying vs. Copying and Coarse-grained Trailing

9 Conclusion

We developed an architecture that allows us to isolate the state restoration policy (SRP) from other components of the system. Its main features are:

Relative addressing: Variable and constraint objects are referred to by IDs, which are mapped to actual pointers through store-specific vectors.

Branching objects: Search trees are defined by branching objects, which are recursive choice points.

Exploration algorithms: Exploration algorithms are defined in terms of a small number of operations on nodes.

SRPs are represented by different extensions of the base class `Node`. Apart from the existing copying and recomputation SRPs, we introduced the following two new SRPs.

Lazy copying uses a copy-on-write technique for variables and constraints and improves over or is equally good as copying on all benchmarks. Lazy copying benefits from a relative addressing implementation.

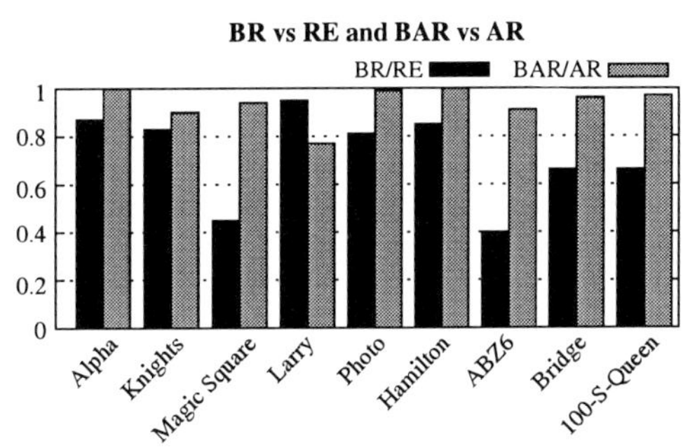

Fig. 8. Time of Batch Recomputation vs. Recomputation

Batch recomputation modifies recomputation by installing all constraints to be added to the ancestor at once and improves over Schulte's recomputation for all benchmarks.

The presented architecture allows the user to optimize time and space consumption of applications by choosing existing or designing new SRPs in response to application-specific characteristics. The SRP components are designed and implemented in C++ on the base of the Figaro library for constraint programming [HMN99,CHN00,Ng01], and evaluated on a set of benchmarks ranging from puzzles to realistic scheduling and timetabling problems. The library and benchmarks are distributed at [Fig01]. State restoration is an important aspect of tree search that deserves the attention of users and constraint programming systems designers. From the experiments, we concluded that SRP is problem dependent. It is interesting to study what kind of problem structure would benefit from what SRP, which leads to optimizing the time and space consumption of tree search.

Acknowledgements. We thank Tobias Müller and Christian Schulte for valuable feedback on this paper, Ong Kar Loon for continuous discussions and collaboration on the Figaro library, and Edgar Tan for comments.

References

[AB90] Abderrahamane Aggoun and Nicolas Beldiceanu. Time Stamps Techniques for the Trailed Data in Constraint Logic Programming Systems. In *Actes du Séminaire 1990–Programmation en Logique*, pages 487–509, Tregastel, France, May 1990. CNET.

[CHN00] Tee Yong Chew, Martin Henz, and Ka Boon Ng. A toolkit for constraint-based inference engines. In Enrico Pontelli and Vítor Santos Costa, editors, *Practical Aspects of Declarative Languages, Second International Workshop, PADL 2000*, Lecture Notes in Computer Science 1753, pages 185–199, Boston, MA, 2000. Springer-Verlag, Berlin.

[CJL99] Yves Caseau, François-Xavier Josset, and François Laburthe. CLAIRE: Combining sets, search and rules to better express algorithms. In Danny De Schreye, editor, *Proceedings of the International Conference on Logic Programming*, pages 245–259, Las Cruces, New Mexico, USA, 1999. The MIT Press, Cambridge, MA.

[DC00] Daniel Diaz and Philippe Codognet. The GNU prolog systems and its implementation. In *ACM Symposium on Applied Computing*, Como, Italy, 2000. Documentation and system available at `http://www.gnu.org/software/prolog`.

[Fig01] Fgaro library for constraint programming. Documentation and system available from `http://figaro.comp.nus.edu.sg`, Department of Computer Science, National University of Singapore, 2001.

[HMN99] Martin Henz, Tobias Müller, and Ka Boon Ng. Figaro: Yet another constraint programming library. In *Proceedings of the Workshop on Parallelism and Implementation Technology for Constraint Logic Programming*, Las Cruces, New Mexico, USA, 1999. held in conjunction with ICLP'99.

[ILO00] ILOG Inc., Mountain View, CA 94043, USA, `http://www.ilog.com`. *ILOG Solver 5.0, Reference Manual*, 2000.

[Int00] Intelligent Systems Laboratory. *SICStus Prolog User's Manual*. SICS Research Report, Swedish Institute of Computer Science, URL `http://www.sics.se/isl/sicstus.html`, 2000.

[MBKQ96] Marshall Kirk McKusick, Keith Bostic, Michael J. Karels, and John S. Quarterman. *The Design and Implementation of the 4.4BSD Operating System*. Addison-Wesley, Reading, MA, 1996.

[Ng01] Ka Boon Kevin Ng. *A Generic Software Framework For Finite Domain Constraint Programming*. Master's thesis, School of Computing, National University of Singapore, 2001.

[NX95] R. H. B. Netzer and J. Xu. Necessary and sufficient conditions for consistent global snapshots. *IEEE Transactions on Parallel and Distributed Systems*, (6):165–169, 1995.

[PGH95] Enrico Pontelli, Gopal Gupta, and Manuel Hermenegildo. &ACE: A high performance parallel prolog system. In *9th International Parallel Processing Symposium*, pages 564–571. IEEE Press, 1995.

[Sch97a] Christian Schulte. Oz Explorer: A visual constraint programming tool. In Lee Naish, editor, *Proceedings of the International Conference on Logic Programming*, pages 286–300, Leuven, Belgium, July 1997. The MIT Press, Cambridge, MA.

[Sch97b] Christian Schulte. Programming constraint inference engines. In Gert Smolka, editor, *Principles and Practice of Constraint Programming—CP97, Proceedings of the Third International Conference*, Lecture Notes in Computer Science 1330, pages 519–533, Schloss Hagenberg, Linz, Austria, October/November 1997. Springer-Verlag, Berlin.

[Sch99] Christian Schulte. Comparing trailing and copying for constraint programming. In Danny De Schreye, editor, *Proceedings of the International Conference on Logic Programming*, pages 275–289, Las Cruces, New Mexico, August 1999. The MIT Press, Cambridge, MA.

[Sch00] Christian Schulte. *Programming Constraint Services*. Doctoral dissertation, Universität des Saarlandes, Naturwissenschaftlich-Technische Fakultät I, Fachrichtung Informatik, Saarbrücken, Germany, 2000. To appear in Lecture Notes in Artificial Intelligence, Springer-Verlag.

Adaptive Constraint Handling with CHR in Java

Armin Wolf

Fraunhofer Gesellschaft
Institute for Computer Architecture and Software Technology (FIRST)
Kekuléstraße 7, D-12489 Berlin, Germany
Armin.Wolf@first.fraunhofer.de http://www.first.fraunhofer.de

Abstract. The most advanced implementation of adaptive constraint processing with Constraint Handling Rules (CHR) is introduced in the imperative object-oriented programming language Java. The presented Java implementation consists of a compiler and a run-time system, all implemented in Java. The run-time system implements data structures like sparse bit vectors, logical variables and terms as well as an adaptive unification and an adaptive entailment algorithm. Approved technologies like attributed variables for constraint storage and retrieval as well as code generation for each head constraint are used. Also implemented are theoretically sound algorithms for adapting of rule derivations and constraint stores after arbitrary constraint deletions. The presentation is rounded off with some novel applications of CHR in constraint processing: simulated annealing for the n queens problem and intelligent backtracking for some SAT benchmark problems.

1 Introduction

Java is a state-of-the-art, object-oriented programming language that is well-suited for interactive and/or distributed problem solving [2,5]. The development of graphical user interfaces is well supported by the JavaBeans concept and the graphical components of the Swing package (cf. [4]). There are several approaches using constraint technologies for (distributed) constraint solving that are based on Java (e.g. [3,14,15]). [14] in particular is a recent approach that integrates Constraint Handling Rules into Java. Constraint Handling Rules (CHR) are multi-headed, guarded rules used to propagate new or simplify given constraints [6,7]. However, this Java implementation of CHR only supports chronological backtracking for constraint deletions, similar to the implementations of CHR in ECLiPSe [8] and SICStus Prolog [11]. Arbitrary additions and deletions of constraints that may arise in interactive or even distributed problem solving environments are not directly supported. These restrictions have been removed by previous – mainly theoretical – work [18,19]. However, an implementation of a CHR system that allows arbitrary additions and deletions of constraints was not yet available.

This paper presents a first implementation of adaptive constraint handling with CHR (c.f. [18]). The implementation language is Java. This imperative

T. Walsh (Ed.): CP 2001, LNCS 2239, pp. 256–270, 2001.

programming language was chosen because of its properties (see above) and because it has no integrated, fixed add/delete mechanism for constraints like Prolog. This latest and advanced implementation of CHR improves the previous implementation in terms of flexibility and/or efficiency. For the user, this CHR implementation offers well-established aspects like

- no restriction of the number of heads in a rule
- compilation of rules in textual order
- constant time access to constraints
- code is compiled not interpreted

and opens up new application areas for CHR in constraint solving:

- local search
- back-jumping and dynamic backtracking
- adaptive solution of dynamic problems

There are several CHR examples in this paper. However, one example will guide us through the chapter on the system. This example is not a typical constraint handler, but it is small and still illustrates various considerations and stages during compilation and use of CHR in Java.

Example 1 (Primes). The sieve of Erathosthenes may be implemented as a kind of a "chemical abstract machine" (c.f. [11]): Assuming that for an integer $n > 2$, the constraints `prime(2)`, ..., `prime(`n`)` are generated. The CHR

```
prime(I) \ prime(J) <=> J mod I == 0 | true.
```

will filter out all non-prime "candidates". If the rule no longer applies, only the constraints `prime(`p`)`, where p is a prime number, are left. More specifically, if there is a constraint `prime(`i`)` and some other constraint `prime(`j`)` such that j `mod` $i = 0$ holds, then j is a multiple of i, i.e. j is non-prime. Thus, `prime(`i`)` is kept but `prime(`j`)` is removed. In addition, the empty body of the rule (`true`) is executed.

The paper is organized as follows. First, the syntax and operational semantics of CHR are briefly recapitulated. Then, the system's architecture, interfaces and performance are described. Specifically, the primes sieve is used as a benchmark to compare the runtime of the system with the recent implementation of CHR in SICStus Prolog. Some novel applications of CHR complete the presentation. The paper closes with some conclusions and a brief outline of future work.

2 The Syntax and Operational Semantics of CHR

Some familiarity with constraint logic programming is assumed (e.g. [13]). The presented CHR implementation supports a restricted set of built-in constraints, which are either syntactic equations or arithmetic relations over a predefined set of arithmetic terms (for details, see [18]). Arbitrary host language statements as in the SICStus implementation of CHR (see [11]) are not (yet) supported. One reason is that for every host language statement in the body of a CHR there must be an undo-statement, which is executed whenever applications of this rule are no longer valid.

2.1 Syntax

There are three kinds of CHR:

- *Simplification*: $H_1, \ldots, H_i \Leftrightarrow G_1, \ldots, G_j \mid B_1, \ldots, B_l$.
- *Propagation*: $H_1, \ldots, H_i \Rightarrow G_1, \ldots, G_j \mid B_1, \ldots, B_k$.
- *Simpagation*: $H_1, \ldots, H_m \backslash H_{m+1}, \ldots, H_i \Leftrightarrow G_1, \ldots, G_j \mid B_1, \ldots, B_k$.

The *head* $H_1, \ldots, H_i$ is a non-empty, finite sequence of CHR constraints, which are logical atoms. The *guard* $G_1, \ldots, G_j$ is a possibly empty, finite sequence of built-in constraints, which are either syntactic equations or arithmetic relations. If the guard is empty, it has the meaning of `true`. The *body* $B_1, \ldots, B_k$, is a possibly empty, finite sequence of built-in or CHR constraints. If the guard is empty, it has the meaning of `true`.

2.2 Operational Semantics

The operational semantics of CHR in the actual implementation (for details, see [18,19]) is compatible with the operational semantics given in [1,7]. Owing to lack of space, a repetition of the formal definitions is omitted, though an informal description of the operational behaviour of CHR is given, adopting the ideas presented in [11]: a CHR constraint is implemented as both *code* (a Java method) and *data* (a Java object), an entry in the constraint store. Whenever a CHR constraint is added (executed) or woken (re-executed), the applicability of those CHRs is checked that contain the executed constraint in their heads. Such a constraint is called *active*; all other constraints in the constraint store are called *passive*.

Head. The head constraints of a CHR serve as constraint patterns. If the active constraint matches a head constraint of a CHR, passive partner constraints are searched that match the other head constraints of this CHR. If matching partners are found for all head constraints, the guard is executed. Otherwise, the next CHR is tried.

Guard. After successful head matching, the guard must be entailed by the built-in constraints. Entailment means that all arithmetic calculations are defined, i.e. variables are bound to numerical values, arithmetic tests succeed and syntactical equations are entailed by the current constraint store, e.g. $\exists Y\ (X = f(g(Y)))$ is entailed by the equations $X = f(Z)$ and $Z = g(1)$. If the guard is entailed the CHR applies and the body is executed. Otherwise, either other matching partners are searched or, if no matching partners are found, the next CHR is tried.

Body. If the firing CHR is a simplification, all matched constraints (including the active one) are removed from the constraint store and the body constraints are executed. In the case of a simpagation, only the constraints that match the head constraints after the '\' are removed. In the case of a propagation, the body is executed without removing any constraints. It should be noted that a propagation will not fire again with the same matching constraints (in the same order). If the active constraint has not been removed, the next CHR is tried.

Suspension and Wakeup. If all CHR have been tried and the active constraint has not been removed, it suspends until a variable that occurs in it becomes more constrained by built-in constraints, i.e. is bound. Suspension means that the constraint is inserted in the constraint store as data. Wakeup means that the constraint is re-activated and re-executed as code.

3 The System

In the beginning, only the runtime system and the compiler are given. CHR handlers and applications are the responsibility of the user. The runtime system and the compiler contain the data structures that are required to define rule-based adaptive constraint solvers and to implement Java programs that apply these solvers to dynamic constraint problems. The definition of a rule-based constraint solver is quite simple: the CHRs that define the solver for a specific domain are coded in a so-called CHR handler. A CHR handler is a Java program that uses the compiler in a specific manner. Compiling and running a CHR handler generates a Java package containing Java code that implements the defined solver and its interface: the addition or deletion of user-defined constraints or syntactical equations, a consistency test and the explanation of inconsistencies. This problem-specific solver package may be used in any Java application. Figure 1 shows the components and their interactions.

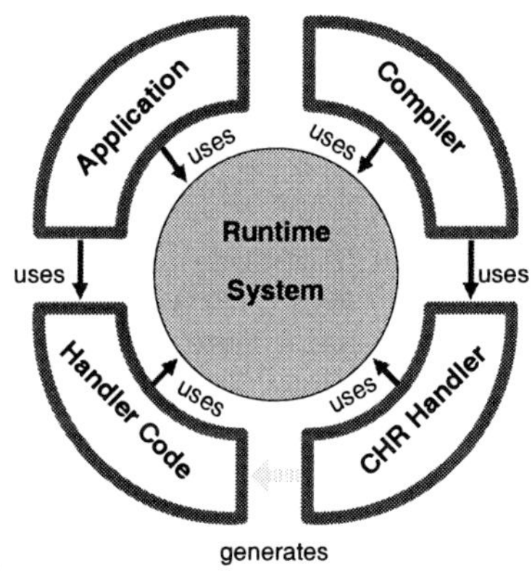

Fig. 1. The architecture of the adaptive CHR system.

3.1 The Runtime System

The core of the adaptive constraint-handling system is its runtime system. Among other things, it implements attributed logical variables (the subclass `Variable` of the class `Logical`) as presented in [10], logical terms (the subclass `Structure` of `Logical`) and data structures for CHR and built-in constraints. For dynamic constraint processing, constraints are justified by integer sets. These sets are implemented as sparse bit vectors (the class `SparseSet`, c.f. [18]). This implementation is much more storage- and runtime-efficient than the bit-sets in the Java API.[1] Based on these sets and the other data structures, an adaptive unification algorithm [17] and an adaptive entailment algorithm [16] is implemented. The runtime system is the common basis for

- the compiler
- the CHR handlers
- the generated handler packages
- the applications using the handlers

3.2 The Compiler and Its Interface

The compiler class is also written in Java. Logical term objects that represent CHR heads, guards and bodies may be added to a compiler object. Thus, a parsing phase that transfers CHR into an internal representation is unnecessary. All CHRs are represented in a canonical form, which allows uniform treatment of simplifications, propagations and simpagations (c.f. [11]). This form consists of

- a (*remove*) array of all head constraints that are removed when the rule is applied
- a (*keep*) array of all head constraints that are kept when the rule is applied
- an array of all guard conditions that have to be entailed
- an array of all body constraints that are added when the rule is applied

At most one of the two arrays of head constraints may be empty. To define a CHR-based constraint solver, the canonical form of the rules has to be added in a CHR handler to a compiler object.

Example 2 (Primes, continued). The canonical representation of the simpagation `prime(I) \ prime(J) <=> J mod I == 0 | true.` in Java is shown in the CHR handler for the primes sieve presented in Figure 2. The head variables are defined in lines 5 and 6. In line 7, the functor of the unary constraint `prime` is defined. In lines 8 and 9, the head constraints are constructed. The guard condition is constructed in lines 10–12, where the built-in modulo operator `mod_2` and the built-in predicate `identical_2` (the equivalent of Prolog's '==') are used. In lines 14–17, the canonical form of the rule is added to the compiler object.

When all rules have been added, the compilation has to be activated. The compiler method `compileAll()` that activates the translation phase is called (c.f. Figure 2, line 18). The generated methods for the active constraints

- match formal parameters to actual arguments of the active (head) constraint
- find and match passive partners for the remaining head constraints
- check the guards

[1] Experiments have shown that the improvement is at least one order of magnitude for randomly generated sparse sets.

```
import common.*; // import the runtime system
import compile.DJCHR; // import the compiler class
public class primeHandler {
    public static void main( String[] args ) {
        Variable i = new Variable("I");
        Variable j = new Variable("J");
        Functor prime_1 = new Functor("prime", 1);
        Structure prime_i = new Structure(prime_1, new Logical[]{ i });
        Structure prime_j = new Structure(prime_1, new Logical[]{ j });
        Structure cond = new Structure(DJCHR.identical_2, new Logical[] {
            new Structure (DJCHR.mod_2, new Logical[]{ j, i }),
            new ZZ(0) }); // j mod i == 0
        DJCHR djchr = new DJCHR("prime", new Structure[] { prime_1 });
        djchr.addRule(new Structure[] { prime_j },
                      new Structure[] { prime_i },
                      new Structure[] { cond },
                      null);
         djchr.compileAll();
    }
}
```

Fig. 2. The CHR handler for the sieve of Eratosthenes.

```
public boolean prime_1_0_0 (Constraint pc0, Logical[] args, SparseSet label) {
    pc0.lock();
    SolutionTriple etriple = new SolutionTriple(); etriple.addToLabel(label);
    Logical tmplogical; SparseSet tmplabel;
    primeVariable local0 = primeVariable.newLocal("J");
    local0.lbind(args[0], label);
    boolean applied = false;
    search: do {
        primeVariableTable.Stepper st1
            = primeVarTab.initIteration(new primeVariable[] {  }, 0);
        while (st1.hasNext()) {
            Constraint pc1 = st1.next();
            if (!pc1.isUsable()) continue;
            SparseSet plab1 = (SparseSet)pc1.getLabel();
            SolutionTriple.Point point1 = etriple.setPoint();
            etriple.addToLabel(plab1);
            primeVariable local1 = primeVariable.newLocal("I");
            local1.lbind(pc1.getArgs()[0], plab1);
            do {
                SparseSet guardLabel0 = new SparseSet();
                Logical logical0 = local0.deref(guardLabel0);
                Logical logical1 = local1.deref(guardLabel0);
                if ( ! (logical0 instanceof ZZ && logical1 instanceof ZZ &&
                        ((((ZZ)logical0).val % ((ZZ)logical1).val) == 0)) )
                            continue;
                etriple.addToLabel(guardLabel0);
                etriple.add(new Conditional(
                    new guard_0_0(new primeVariable[] {local0, local1}), guardLabel0));
                if (!etriple.getLabel().isEmpty())
                    derivation.add(
                        new RuleState_0(-1, new primeVariable[] {local0, local1},
                        new Constraint[] {pc0, pc1}, (SolutionTriple)etriple.clone()));
                primeVarTab.removeConstraint(pc0);
                applied = true;
                break search;
            } while (false);
            etriple.backToPoint(point1);
        } // end of iteration
    } while (false);
    pc0.unlock();
    return applied;
}
```

Fig. 3. Code generated for `prime(J)` in `prime(I)\prime(J)<=>J mod I==0|true`.

– remove matched constraints from the constraint store if required
– execute the bodies

Furthermore, for adaptations after constraint deletions, all constraints are justified by a set of integers. These justifications are used in the generated methods to perform truth maintenance. The generated methods additionally

– unite all justifications of all constraints that are necessary for successful head matching
– unite all justifications of all constraints that are necessary for guard entailment
– justify the executed body constraints with the union of the justifications for head matching and guard entailment
– store justifications and partners of the applied rules in rule state objects

For adaptation after deletions, a rule state class is generated for each CHR. Every rule state class contains a method that retries a previously applied rule if its present justification is no longer valid. If there is no alternative justification, the previous rule application is undone: removed head-matching constraints are re-inserted in the constraint store or re-executed and the consequences of the executed body constraints are erased.

Finding Partner Constraints. Like [11], we believe the real challenge in implementations of *multi-headed* CHRs is efficient computation of joins for partner constraints. A naive solution is to compute the cross-product of all potential partner constraints. However, if there are shared variables in the head constraints, only a subset of the cross-product has to be executed. If we consider, for instance, the transitivity rule `leq(X,Y), leq(Y,Z) ==> leq(X,Z)`, which has to be tried against all active constraints `leq(`u`, `v`)`, only `leq` constraints have to be considered as potential partners that have either v in their first argument position or u in their second. In order to (partially) apply this knowledge, the idea of *variable indexing* (c.f. [11]) is also implemented in our compiler. Thus, the partner search is better focused if the arguments of the active constraints are variables, e.g. if u and v are variables. The constraints in the store are therefore distributed over all variables that occur in these constraints. The constraints are attached to their variables as attribute values (c.f. [10]). The attributes are named after the constraints. For efficient $O(1)$ access to these constraints, the compiler generates for every CHR handler a subclass of variables to which the necessary attributes are added. All constraints defined in the handler must therefore be known by the compiler. This information is passed on when a compiler object is created (e.g. in line 13 in Figure 2). The name of the variable subclass accommodates this, receiving the handler's name as a prefix (e.g. `primeVariable` for the prime handler in Figure 2).

Unlike the SICStus Prolog implementation, the attribute values are not merged when a variable binding occurs. If there is a variable binding $X = f(\ldots Y \ldots)$ or $X = Y$ in SICStus Prolog, the attribute values stored under X

are added to the attribute values in Y because all variable occurrences of X in constraints are "substituted" by $f(\ldots Y \ldots)$ or Y, respectively. In our implementation however, only a "back pointer" $(X \leftarrow Y)$ from Y to X is established. The variables, together with these "back pointers", define graph structures; more precisely, rational trees[2] that are traversed to access all the attribute values, i.e. the constraints stored under an unbound variable. This design decision was made because variable bindings caused by built-in constraints might be arbitrarily deleted. In the case of a deletion of $X = f(\ldots Y \ldots)$ or $X = Y$, only the binding itself and the "back pointer" from Y to X have to be deleted. The connected attribute values of X and Y are automatically separated because the attribute values of X are no longer accessible from Y, the connecting link being removed. This approach is much simpler and more efficient than restoring the attribute values.

Example 3 (Primes, continued). The compiled method for the head constraint `prime(J)` in the CHR `prime(I) \ prime(J) <=> J mod I == 0 | true.` is presented in Figure 3. The formal parameter `J` (line 5) is matched to the actual argument `args[0]` (lines 1 and 6) of the active constraint `pc0`. To find a partner constraint matching `prime(I)`, an iteration over all stored constraints is activated until one is found that satisfies the guard condition (lines 9–38). Variable indexing is impossible because there are no common formal head parameters (the array of common `primeVariable` in line 10 is empty). The iteration continues with the next candidate if the current candidate is already being used (line 13). Otherwise, the formal parameter `I` is matched to the actual argument of the candidate `pc1.getArgs()[0]` (lines 17 and 18). Then, the guard is tested (lines 20-24) and the iteration continues with another candidate if the condition `J mod I == 0` is not satisfied (line 25). Otherwise, the rule is applicable and the rule body is normally executed. In this case, the body is empty (`true`) and so only the united justifications (lines 3, 16, 26) for head matching and guard entailment and the partners are stored for adaptation (lines 30–32) if necessary. No adaptation is necessary if the union of all justifications is empty, i.e. always true (c.f. line 29). Last, the active constraint is deleted (line 33) and a Boolean value is returned (line 41). It is true iff the rule was successfully applied and the active constraint was deactivated. This flag is used to prevent the method for the other head constraint `prime(I)` from being activated on `pc0`.

3.3 The Application Interface

During the translation phase for each head constraint of a CHR, a Java method is generated. Methods for constraints that have the same name and arity are subsumed under a method that is named after the constraints and their arities. Furthermore, for each constraint name and arity, there is a method for reading the corresponding constraints out of the constraint store. These methods form the "generic" part of the application interface of the generated constraint solver.

[2] Variable bindings like $X = f(Y)$ and $Y = g(X)$ are allowed, resulting in $X \leftrightarrows Y$.

They are complemented by "non-generic" methods to add syntactical equations to the constraint store, to delete all constraints with a specific justification, to test the consistency of the stored built-in constraints and to get an explanation (justification) for an inconsistency.

Example 4. The application interface generated for the CHR handler in Figure 2 comprises the following methods

- `public void prime_1(Logical[] args, SparseSet label)`
- `public ArrayList get_prime_1()`
- `public void equal(Logical lhs, Logical rhs, SparseSet lab)`
- `public void delete(SparseSet del)`
- `public boolean getStatus()`
- `public SparseSet getExplanation()`

of the class `prime`, the class of constraint stores that are processed by the CHR defined in the CHR handler. The variable subclass `primeVariable` of `Variable` is generated, too.[3]

The use of the interface is shown in the following program:

```
01   import common.*; // import the runtime system
02   import prime; // import the generated prime handler
03   public class primeTest {
04       public static void main( String[] args ) {
05           int n = Integer.parseInt( args[0] );
06           prime cs = new prime();
07           for (int i=2; i <= n; i++)
08               cs.prime_1(new Logical[] {new ZZ(i)}, new SparseSet(i));
09           cs.delete(new SparseSet(2));
10           cs.prime_1(new Logical[] {new ZZ(2)}, new SparseSet(2));
11       }
12   }
```

In lines 7–8, the constraints `prime(2)`, ..., `prime(`n`)` are executed, where n – a positive integer – is read from the command line (see line 5). In line 9, the constraint `prime(2)` (the only constraint justified by 2) is deleted and then re-added in line 10.

3.4 Runtime Comparisons

The sieve of Erathosthenes was used as a benchmark to compare the adaptive Java version with the recent SICStus Prolog implementation of CHR. In particular, the Java program presented in Example 4, which uses the compiled code of the handler in Figure 2, was compared to the following SICStus Prolog program

```
primetest(N) :-
    switch(Start,Phase), generate(3,N), runtime(End),
    Time is End-Start, print(Time), nl,
    Phase=delete, % causes backtracking and the deletion of prime(2)
    runtime(StartReAdd), prime(2), runtime(EndReAdd),
    ReAddTime is EndReAdd-StartReAdd, print(ReAddTime), nl.
switch(Time,process) :- runtime(Time), prime(2).
switch(Time,delete) :- runtime(Time).
runtime(Time) :- statistics(runtime, [_,Time])
generate(I,N) :- I > N, !.
generate(I,N) :- prime(I), J is I+1, generate(J,N).
```

[3] See Section 4.2 for the use of such a `Variable` subclass.

This program uses the SICStus CHR handler

```
handler prime.
constraints prime/1.
prime(I) \ prime(J) <=> J mod I =:= 0 | true.
```

runtime measurements were made on a Pentium III PC running SuSE Linux 6.2. For problem sizes $n = 1000, 2000, 4000, 8000$ and 16000, the constraints `prime(2)`, ..., `prime(`n`)` were generated and processed. Then, the constraint `prime(2)` and its consequences were deleted and the result was adapted/re-calculated. For this purpose, in the Java implementation the interface method `delete` was used, which is based on repair algorithms presented in [18,19]. This causes a re-insertion of all constraints on even numbers `prime(`$2k$`)` $2 \leq k \leq n/2$ and a re-removal of all these constraints except `prime(4)`. In the SICStus Prolog implementation however, chronological backtracking to the top level and re-processing of the constraints `prime(3)`, ..., `prime(`n`)` was forced, i.e. the equation `Phase=delete` causes a failure that causes backtracking to the second clause of `switch`. Then, after both kinds of adaptation, the constraint `prime(2)` was re-inserted. In both cases, this causes a removal of the previously re-inserted constraint `prime(4)`.

The runtimes for generation and processing show that the purely interpreted Java code is about 1.7 times slower than the consulted SICStus Prolog code and that the partially compiled Java code (Java version 1.3. in mixed mode) is about 2.9 times slower than the compiled SICStus Prolog code.

The runtimes for the deletion of `prime(2)` show the advantage of adaptation over recalculation: the purely interpreted Java code is about 2.6 times faster than the consulted SICStus Prolog code, and the partially compiled Java code is about 1.5 times faster than the compiled SICStus Prolog code.

The runtimes for re-addition of `prime(2)` show that the purely interpreted Java code is about 6 times slower than the consulted SICStus Prolog code, and that the partially compiled Java code is about 5.6 times slower than the compiled SICStus Prolog code.

Overall, the sums of the runtimes for all these operations are surprisingly comparable: Figure 4(a) shows that the performance of the interpreted/consulted code is nearly identical and that the compiled SICStus Prolog code is on the whole marginally faster than the Java code in mixed mode. However, a relative comparison of the two chosen adaptation strategies – “repair” and backtracking – with re-calculation from scratch is shown in Figure 4(b): in Java, the adaptation is 3–5 times faster than re-calculation; performance increases with problem size. Obviously, there is no performance improvement in the SICStus Prolog implementation.

A comparison of our Java implementation of CHR with the one presented in [14] was not considered further. For $n = 1000$, this implementation takes about 1 minute for the generation and processing phase. We assume that the interpretation of CHRs rather than their compilation is the reason for this runtime.

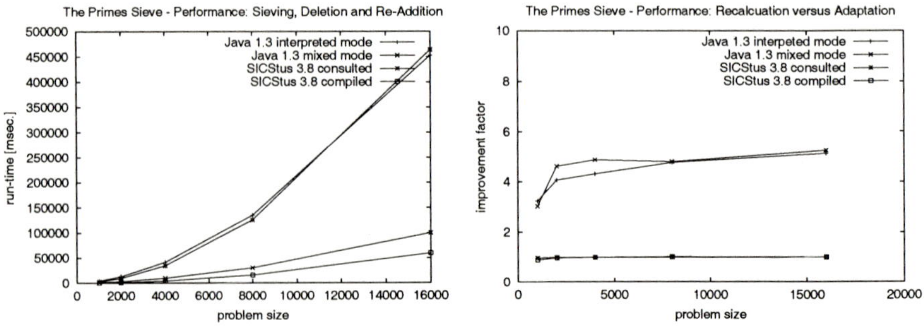

(a) Total Runtime (b) Recalculation versus Adaptation

Fig. 4. A benchmark comparison of the prime handler

4 Applications

The possibility of arbitrary constraint deletions opens up new application areas for CHR in constraint programming. One broad area is local search based on simulated annealing; another is back-jumping and dynamic backtracking. One application shows how CHR are used in a simple simulated-annealing approach to solve the well-known n queens problem. Another application compares chronological backtracking, back-jumping and dynamic backtracking in the solution of satisfiability problems.

4.1 Simulated Annealing for the n Queens Problem

The n queens problem is characterized as follows: place n queens on an $n \times n$ chessboard such that no queen is attacked by another. One simple solution of this problem is to place the n queens (one per row) randomly on the board until no queen is attacked. To detect an attack, the following CHR is sufficient:[4]

```
queen(I,J), queen(K,L) ==> I < K, (J == L ; K-I == abs(L-J))
                           | conflict(I, 1.0), conflict(K, 1.0).
```

The constraints conflict(i, 1.0) and conflict(k, 1.0) are derived whenever the queens in row/column i/j and k/l are attacking each other: They are either in the same column ($j = l$) or in the same diagonal ($|k - i| = |l - j|$). To detect the queens that are "in conflict with" the maximum number of other queens, the following CHR sums up these numbers:

```
conflict(I,R), conflict(I,S) <=> T is R+S | conflict(I, T).
```

The search algorithm to solve the n queens problem is based on a simple simulated-annealing approach. An initially given temperature is cooled down

[4] The semicolon ';' represents the logical "or" ($\vee$) in the guard of the CHR.

to minimize the total number C of conflicts: $T_k = T_0 \times \rho^k$ $(0 < \rho < 1)$. The search stops if either a solution is found or the temperature is below a predefined level $(T_k < T_{\min})$. While there are conflicts, a queen that is in conflict with the maximum number of other queens is chosen and placed at another randomly selected position, i.e. the corresponding constraint queen(i, j) is deleted and a new constraint queen(i, j') is inserted.[5] If, for the new number D of conflicts, it either holds that $D < C$ or $e^{-\frac{D-C}{T_k}} \geq \delta$, where $0 < \delta < 1$ is a random number, the search continues. Otherwise, the moved queen is placed in its original position. Using this simple simulated-annealing approach, solutions for 10, 20, 30, ..., 100 queens problems were easily found (0.5 sec. for 10 and 30 sec. for 100 queens).

The runtime performance of the implementation is rather poor; it is easily outperformed by other approaches. However, the aim of this example was to show that adaptive constraint handling with CHR can be used for rapid prototyping of local-search algorithms. These prototypes can be used for education or to examine and improve the search algorithm, e.g. the number of search steps required to find a solution.

4.2 Different Search Strategies for SAT Problems

The SICStus Prolog distribution[6] comes with several CHR handlers and example applications. One of these example applications is a SAT(isfiability) problem, called the Deussen problem ulm027r1. It is the conjunctive normal form of a propositional logic formula with 23 Boolean variables. The problem is to find a 0/1 assignment for all these variables such that the formula, a conjunction of Boolean constraints, is satisfied.

To solve such SAT problems, we coded and compiled the necessary CHRs that are part of the Boolean CHR handler in the SICStus Prolog distribution. These rules are:

```
or(0,X,Y) <=> Y=X.              or(X,Y,A) \ or(X,Y,B) <=> A=B.
or(X,0,Y) <=> Y=X.              or(X,Y,A) \ or(Y,X,B) <=> A=B.
or(X,Y,0) <=> X=0,Y=0.          neg(X,Y) \ neg(Y,Z) <=> X=Z.
or(1,X,Y) <=> Y=1.              neg(X,Y) \ neg(Z,Y) <=> X=Z.
or(X,1,Y) <=> Y=1.              neg(Y,X) \ neg(Y,Z) <=> X=Z.
or(X,X,Z) <=> X=Z.              neg(X,Y) \ or(X,Y,Z) <=> Z=1.
neg(0,X) <=> X=1.               neg(Y,X) \ or(X,Y,Z) <=> Z=1.
neg(X,0) <=> X=1.               neg(X,Z) , or(X,Y,Z) <=> X=0,Y=1,Z=1.
neg(1,X) <=> X=0.               neg(Z,X) , or(X,Y,Z) <=> X=0,Y=1,Z=1.
neg(X,1) <=> X=0.               neg(Y,Z) , or(X,Y,Z) <=> X=1,Y=0,Z=1.
neg(X,X) <=> fail.              neg(Z,Y) , or(X,Y,Z) <=> X=1,Y=0,Z=1.
```

We then implemented three different labelling algorithms to solve SAT problems. A labelling algorithm is a (systematic) search algorithm that assigns a possible value to an unassigned variable – the variable is labelled – until either

[5] From time to time the moved queen is arbitrarily chosen, avoiding starvation.

[6] See http://www.sics.se/sicstus.html.

all variables are assigned and the conjunction of all constraints is satisfied or some constraints are violated. If a violation occurs, a labelled variable that has an alternative value is selected. The selected variable is re-assigned an alternative value. If there is a violation but no labelled variable with an alternative value left, then the constraints are inconsistent, i.e. there is no assignment satisfying them.

The implemented labelling algorithms are based on chronological backtracking, back-jumping and dynamic backtracking. Search based on chronological backtracking and back-jumping assigns the variables systematically in a fixed order. In the case of a violation, the last labelled variable is re-assigned if it has an alternative value, otherwise the assignments of the some variables are "forgotten" (deleted). If the search is based on back-jumping, the recent variable assignment that justifies the violation and all the following assignments are forgotten; in the chronological case, e.g. if the justification is missing, only the last variable assignment is forgotten. The search "backtracks" or "back-jumps" until the violation is solved or there is no labelled variable left to backtrack or to jump to. In the latter case, the problem is unsolvable. During search with dynamic backtracking, neither the assignment nor the backtracking is in fixed order. If there is a violation and there is no alternative value for the last assigned variable, only the recent variable assignment is deleted, which justifies this "dead end" of the search process – all other assignments are untouched. A detailed, more formal description of all these algorithms is given in [9].

We implemented search procedures based on back-jumping (DJCHR BJ) and dynamic backtracking (DJCHR DBT) for SAT problems using the compiled Boolean CHR handler in Java 1.3. These implementations were compared with the search procedure, based on chronological backtracking, that comes with the Boolean CHR handler in the SICStus Prolog distribution (SICStus CBT). These three search procedures were used to solve the Deussen problem and some SAT problems that are available in the *Satisfiability Library* (SATLIB).[7] runtime measurements were made on a Pentium III PC using SICStus Prolog with consulted program code and Java 1.3 in mixed mode.

Table 1 shows the counted numbers of backtracking/back-jumping steps and the required runtime in milliseconds, used to find the (first) solution or to detect the unsatisfiability of the problem. These runtime experiments show that either back-jumping or dynamic backtracking requires less backtracking/back-jumping steps than chronological backtracking for the considered problems. Additionally, the improved search yields better absolute runtime performance of the Java implementations for nearly all the examined benchmarks.

This application impressively demonstrates the new possibilities offered by adaptive constraint handling with CHR: the existence of justifications for all derived constraints including false allows high-level implementations of sophisticated backtracking and search algorithms.

[7] The whole benchmark set is available online at `www.satlib.org`.

Table 1. Runtime comparison on SATLIB benchmark problems (except ulm027r1).

SATLIB benchmark problems	number of solutions	SICStus CBT steps	SICStus CBT msec.	DJCHR BJ steps	DJCHR BJ msec.	DJCHR DBT steps	DJCHR DBT msec.
Deussen ulm027r1	16	52	250	36	939	72	1524
The Pigeon Hole 6	0	14556	20950	3646	17837	1452121	19384972
aim-50-2_0-yes1-1	1	11110	61310	552	6062	5178	47850
aim-50-2_0-yes1-2	1	384	2000	154	2519	90	1805
aim-50-2_0-yes1-3	1	34088	168180	301	3340	978	15951
aim-50-2_0-yes1-4	1	302	2160	123	2540	167	3416
aim-50-2_0-no-1	0	906558	1706830	44492	429141	17697	184587
aim-50-2_0-no-2	0	70266	415340	944	13340	25528	418031
aim-50-2_0-no-3	0	172150	674910	46526	483830	295792	3817240
aim-50-2_0-no-4	0	53874	236130	198	4298	5689	85381

5 Conclusions and Future Work

The adaptive CHR system outlined in this paper was implemented over a six months period. The implemented system is the first system to combine recent developments in CHR implementation with dynamic constraint solving. More specifically, the number of constraints in CHR's heads is no longer limited to two, and rational trees of attributed variables are used to implement efficient access to the constraint store, especially during the partner search. Furthermore, arbitrary constraint additions and deletions are fully supported: constraint processing is automatically adapted. This opens up new areas in constraint programming for CHR. Three of these are now implemented: simulated annealing and adaptive search with back-jumping or dynamic backtracking. For the future, interactive diagrammatic reasoning with CHR is planned as well as the application of other "fancy backtracking" algorithms on harder SAT problems, e.g. all the AIM instances (c.f. [12]) will be examined and discussed.

Other future activities will concentrate on the compiler in order to produce highly optimized code. Besides general improvements like early guard evaluation and the avoidance of code generation and processing, there are improvements of the adaptation process. This will make it possible to avoid re-processing of constraints that are removed by rule applications and later re-activated by undoing these applications during adaptation. In some cases, it is correct and more efficient to put them directly back in the constraint store rather than activate them. This holds for removed constraints that would not have been re-activated by a later wake-up even if they would not have been removed.

Acknowledgement. The author wishes to thank Kathleen Steinhöfel for the crash course in simulated annealing and all the colleagues he met in Melbourne and who helped him with their valuable remarks and fruitful discussions. Special thanks go to Christian Holzbaur, Thom Frühwirth, Kim Marriott, Bernd Meyer and Peter Stuckey.

References

1. Slim Abdennadher. Operational semantics and confluence of Constraint Handling Rules. In *Proceedings of the Third International Conference on Principles and Practice of Constraint Programming – CP97*, number 1330 in Lecture Notes in Computer Science. Springer Verlag, 1997.
2. Ken Arnold, James Gosling, and David Holmes. *The Java Programming Language, Third Edition.* Addison-Wesley, June 2000.
3. Andy Hon Wai C. Constraint programming in Java with JSolver. In *Proceedings of PACLP99, The Practical Application of Constraint Technologies and Logic Programming*, London, April 1999.
4. David Flanagan. *Java Foundation Classes in a Nutshell.* O'Reilly, September 1999.
5. David Flanagan. *Java in a Nutshell.* O'Reilly, 3rd edition, November 1999.
6. Thom Frühwirth. Constraint Handling Rules. In Andreas Podelski, editor, *Constraint Programming: Basics and Trends*, number 910 in Lecture Notes in Computer Science, pages 90–107. Springer Verlag, March 1995.
7. Thom Frühwirth. Theory and practice of Constraint Handling Rules. *The Journal of Logic Programming*, 37:95–138, 1998.
8. Thom Frühwirth and Pascal Brisset. High-Level Implementations of Constraint Handling Rules. Technical report, ECRC, 1995.
9. Matthew L. Ginsberg. Dynamic backtracking. *Journal of Artificial Intelligence Research*, 1:25–46, 1993.
10. Christian Holzbaur. *Specification of Constraint Based Inference Mechanism through Extended Unification.* PhD thesis, Dept. of Medical Cybernetics & AI, University of Vienna, 1990.
11. Christian Holzbaur and Thom Frühwirth. A Prolog Constraint Handling Rules compiler and runtime system. *Applied Artificial Intelligence*, 14(4):369–388, April 2000.
12. K. Iwama, E. Miyano, and Y. Asahiro. Random generation of test instances with controlled attributes. In *Cliques, Coloring, and Satisfiability*, volume 26 of *DIMACS Series in Discrete Mathematics and Theoretical Computer Science*, pages 377–394. American Mathematical Society, 1996.
13. Kim Marriott and Peter J. Stuckey. *Programming with Constraints: An Introduction.* The MIT Press, 1998.
14. Matthias Schmauss. An implementation of CHR in Java. Master's thesis, Ludwig Maximilians Universität München, Institut für Informatik, May 1999.
15. Marc Torrens, Rainer Weigel, and Baoi Faltings. Java constraint library: Bringing constraint technology on the internet using java. In *Proceedings of the CP-97 Workshop on Constraint Reasoning on the Internet*, November 1997.
16. Armin Wolf. Adaptive entailment of equations over rational trees. In *Proceedings of the 13th Workshop on Logic Programming, WLP'98*, Technical Report 1843-1998-10, pages 25–33. Vienna University of Technology, October 1998.
17. Armin Wolf. Adaptive solving of equations over rational trees. In *Proceedings of the Fourth International Conference on Principles and Practice on Constraint Programming, CP'98, Poster Session*, number 1520 in Lecture Notes in Computer Science, page 475. Springer, 1998.
18. Armin Wolf. *Adaptive Constraintverarbeitung mit Constraint-Handling-Rules – Ein allgemeiner Ansatz zur Lösung dynamischer Constraint-Probleme*, volume 219 of *Disserationen zur Künstlichen Intelligenz (DISKI).* infix, November 1999.
19. Armin Wolf, Thomas Gruenhagen, and Ulrich Geske. On incremental adaptation of CHR derivations. *Applied Artificial Intelligence*, 14(4):389–416, April 2000.

Consistency Maintenance for ABT

Marius-Călin Silaghi, Djamila Sam-Haroud, and Boi Faltings

Swiss Federal Institute of Technology (EPFL)
EPFL, CH-1015, Switzerland
{Marius.Silaghi,Djamila.Haroud,Boi.Faltings}@epfl.ch

Abstract. One of the most powerful techniques for solving centralized constraint satisfaction problems (CSPs) consists of maintaining local consistency during backtrack search (e.g. [11]). Yet, no work has been reported on such a combination in asynchronous settings[1]. The difficulty in this case is that, in the usual algorithms, the instantiation and consistency enforcement steps must alternate sequentially. When brought to a distributed setting, a similar approach forces the search algorithm to be synchronous in order to benefit from consistency maintenance. Asynchronism [24,14] is highly desirable since it increases flexibility and parallelism, and makes the solving process robust against timing variations. One of the most well-known asynchronous search algorithms is Asynchronous Backtracking (ABT). This paper shows how an algorithm for maintaining consistency during distributed *asynchronous* search can be designed upon ABT. The proposed algorithm is complete and has polynomial-space complexity. Since the consistency propagation is optional, this algorithms generalizes forward checking as well as chronological backtracking. An additional advance over existing centralized algorithms is that it can exploit available backtracking-nogoods for increasing the strength of the maintained consistency. The experimental evaluation shows that it can bring substantial gains in computational power compared with existing asynchronous algorithms.

1 Introduction

Distributed constraint satisfaction problems (DisCSPs) arise when constraints and/or variables come from a set of independent but communicating agents. Successful centralized algorithms for solving CSPs combine search with local consistency. Most local consistency algorithms prune from the domains of variables the values that are locally inconsistent with the constraints, hence reducing the search space. When a DisCSP is solved by distributed search, it is desirable that this search exploits asynchronism as much as possible. Asynchronism gives the agents more freedom in the way they can contribute to search, allowing them to enforce individual policies (on privacy, computation, etc.). It also increases both parallelism and robustness. In particular, robustness is improved by the fact that the search can still detect unsatisfiability even in the presence of crashed agents. Existing work on asynchronous algorithms for distributed CSPs has focused on one of the following types of asynchronism:

[1] A preliminary version of this paper has been presented at the CP2000 Workshop on Distributed CSPs[15]

T. Walsh (Ed.): CP 2001, LNCS 2239, pp. 271–285, 2001.

a) *deciding instantiations* of variables by distinct agents. The agents can propose different instantiations asynchronously (e.g. Asynchronous Backtracking (ABT) [24]).
b) *enforcing consistency*. The distributed process of achieving "local" consistency on the global problem is asynchronous (e.g. Distributed Arc Consistency [25]).

Combining these two techniques is however not as easy as in the synchronous setting. A straightforward mapping of the existing combination scheme cannot preserve asynchronism of type a [21,4]. The contribution of this work is to consider consistency maintenance as a hierarchical nogood-based inference. This makes it possible to concurrently *i)* perform asynchronous search and *ii)* enforce the hierarchies of consistency, resulting in an *asynchronous* consistency maintenance algorithm. Since the consistency propagation is optional, this algorithms generalizes forward checking as well as chronological backtracking. More general than existing centralized algorithms, our approach can use any available backtracking nogoods to increase the strength of the maintained consistency. As expected from the sequential case, the experiments show that substantial gains in computational power can result from combining distributed search and distributed local consistency.

2 Related Work

The first complete asynchronous search algorithm for DisCSPs is the Asynchronous Backtracking (ABT) [23]. The approach in [23] considers that agents maintain distinct variables. Nogood removal was discussed in [8,14]. Other definitions of DisCSPs have considered the case where the interest on constraints is distributed among agents [25, 20,14,7,5]. [20] proposes algorithms that fit the structure of a real problem (the nurse transportation problem). The Asynchronous Aggregation Search (AAS) [14] family of protocols actually extends ABT to the case where the same variable can be instantiated by several agents (e.g. at different levels of abstraction [12,16]). An agent may also not know all constraint predicates relevant to its variables. AAS offers the possibility to aggregate several branches of the search. An aggregation technique for DisCSPs was then presented in [10] and allows for simple understanding of privacy/efficiency mechanisms, also discussed in [6]. The use of abstractions, [16], not only improves on efficiency but especially on privacy since the agents need to reveal less their details. A general polynomial space reordering protocol is described in [13] and several heuristics (e.g. weak commitment-like) are discussed in [18]. [3] explains how **add-link** messages can be avoided. A technique enabling parallelization and parallel proposals in asynchronous search is described in [19]. Several algorithms for achieving distributed arc consistency are presented in [9,25,2].

3 Preliminaries

In this paper we target problems with finite domains (we target problems with numeric domains in [12,16]). For simplicity, but here without loss of generality, we consider that each agent A_i can propose instantiations to exactly one distinct variable, x_i and knows all the constraints that involve x_i. Therefore each agent, A_i, knows a local CSP, **CSP($\mathbf{A_i}$)**,

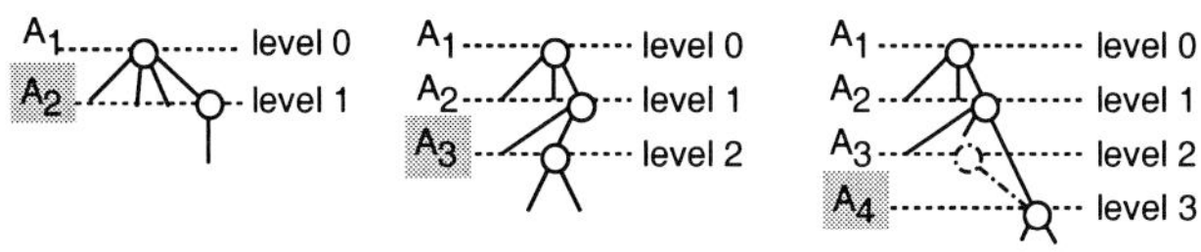

Fig. 1. *Distributed search trees in ABT: simultaneous views of distributed search seen by A_2, A_3, and A_4, respectively. Each arc corresponds to a proposal from A_i to A_j. Circles show the believed state of an agent. Dashed circle and line show known state that may have been changed.*

with variables **vars($\mathbf{A_i}$)**. We present the way in which our technique can be built on ABT, a simple instance of AAS for certain timings and agent strategies, but it can be easily adapted to more complex frameworks and extensions of AAS. ABT allows agents to asynchronously propose instantiations of variables. In order to guarantee completeness and termination, ABT uses a static order $\prec$ on agents. In the sequel of the paper, we assume that the agent A_i has position $i, i \geq 1$, when the agents are ordered according to $\prec$. If $i>j$ then A_i has a *lower priority* than A_j and A_j has a *higher priority* then A_i.[2] A_i is then a successor of A_j, and A_j a predecessor of A_i.

Asynchronous distributed consistency: Most centralized local-consistency algorithms prune from the domain of variables the values that are locally inconsistent with the constraints. Their distributed counterparts (e.g. [25]) work by exchanging messages on value elimination. The restricted domains resulting from such a pruning are called *labels*. In this paper we will only consider the local consistencies algorithms which work on labels for *individual* variables (e.g. arc-, bound-consistency). Let P be a Distributed CSP with the agents $A_i, i\in\{1..n\}$. We denote by $C(P)$ the CSP defined by $\cup_{i\in\{1..n\}}$CSP(A_i).[3] Let $\mathcal{A}$ be a centralized local consistency algorithm as just mentioned. We denote by DC($\mathcal{A}$) a distributed consistency algorithm that computes, by exchanging value eliminations, the same labels for P as $\mathcal{A}$ for $C(P)$. When DC($\mathcal{A}$) is run on P, we say that P becomes DC($\mathcal{A}$) consistent. Generic instances of DC($\mathcal{A}$) are denoted by DC. Typically with DC [25], the maximum number of generated messages is a^2vd and the maximum number of sequential messages is vd (v:number of variables, d:domain size, a:number of agents).

4 Asynchronous Consistency Maintenance

In the sequential/synchronous setting, the view of the search tree expanded by a consistency maintenance algorithm is unique. Each node at depth k, corresponds to assigning to the variable x_k a value v_i from its label. Initially the label of each variable is set to its full domain. After each assignment $x_k=v_i$, a local consistency algorithm is launched which computes for the future variables the labels resulting from this assignment.

[2] They can impose first eventual preferences they have on their values.

[3] The *union* of two CSPs, P_1 and P_2, is a CSP containing all the constraints and variables of P_1 and P_2.

In distributed search (e.g. ABT), each agent has its own perception of the distributed search tree. Its perception on this tree is determined by the proposals received from its predecessors. In Figure 1 is shown a simultaneous view of three agents. Only A_2 knows the fourth proposal of A_1. A_3 has not yet received the third proposal of A_2 consistent with the third proposal of A_1. However, A_4 knows that proposal of A_2. In Figure 1 we suppose that A_4 has not received anything valid from A_3 (e.g. after sending some nogood to A_3 which was not yet received). The term *level* in Figure 1 refers to the depth in the (distributed) search tree viewed by an agent.

Let P be a Distributed CSP with the agents $A_i, i \in \{1..n\}$, $\mathcal{A}$ be a centralized local consistency algorithm and DC($\mathcal{A}$) one of its distributed counterparts. Suppose that the instantiation order of the variables in $C(P)$ is determined by the order of the agents in P. In order to guarantee that with DC($\mathcal{A}$) one maintains for the variables of agents A_i of P the same labels, $\mathcal{L}$, than with $\mathcal{A}$ in $C(P)$, one can simply impose that:

1. Ai must have received the proposals of *all* its predecessors before launching DC($\mathcal{A}$),
2. Ai cannot make any proposal with values outside $\mathcal{L}$, computed by DC($\mathcal{A}$).

This approach [21,4] is synchronous. Alternatively, we propose to handle consistency maintenance as a hierarchical task. We show that A_i can then benefit from the value eliminations resulting from the proposals of *subsets* of its predecessors, as soon as available. More precisely, if A_i has received proposals from some of its k first predecessors, we say that it can benefit from value elimination (nogoods) of level k. Such nogoods are determined by instantiations of $x_t, t \leq k$ (known proposals), DC process at level k or inherited from DCs at previous levels along the same branch. A DC process of level k is a process which only takes into account the known proposals of the k first agents. The resulting labels are said to be of level k. When the nogoods defining labels are classified according to their corresponding levels, and when they are coherently managed by agents as shown here, the instantiation decisions and DCs of levels k can then be performed asynchronously for different k with polynomial space complexity and without loosing the inference power of DC($\mathcal{A}$). Moreover, backtrack-nogoods involving only proposals from agents $A_{i,i \leq k}$ can be used by DC at level k. Since the use of most nogoods is optional, many distinct algorithms result from the employment of different strategies by agents.

5 The DMAC-ABT Protocol

This section presents DMAC-ABT (Distributed Maintaining Asynchronously Consistency for ABT), a complete protocol for maintaining asynchronously consistency. Since it builds on ABT, we start by recalling the necessary background and definitions.

5.1 ABT

In asynchronous backtracking, the agents run concurrently and asynchronously. Each agent instantiates its variable and communicates the variable value to the relevant agents. As described for AAS [14], since we do not assume (generalized) FIFO channels, in the polynomial-space requirements description given here a **local counter**, $C^i_{x_i}$, in each agent A_i is incremented each time a new instantiation is chosen. The current value of $C^i_{x_i}$ **tags** each assignment made by A_i for x_i.

Definition 1 (Assignment). *An* assignment *for a variable x_i is a tuple $\langle x_i, v, c\rangle$ where v is a value from the domain of x_i and c is the* tag *value (value of $C^i_{x_i}$).*

Among two assignments for the same variable, the one with the higher *tag* (attached value of the counter) is the **newest**.

Rule 1 (Constraint-Evaluating-Agent) *Each constraint C is evaluated by the lowest priority agent whose variable is involved in C. This agent is denoted CEA(C).*

The set of constraints enforced by A_i are denoted **ECSP($\mathbf{A_i}$)** and the set of variables that are involved in ECSP(A_i) is denoted **evars($\mathbf{A_i}$)**, where $x_i \in$evars(A_i). Each agent holds a list of **outgoing links** represented by a set of agents. Links are associated with constraints. ABT assumes that every link is directed from the value sending agent to the constraint-evaluating-agent.

Definition 2 (Agent_View). *The* agent_view *of an agent, A_i, is a set, view(A_i), containing the* newest *assignments received by A_i for distinct variables.*

Based on their constraints, agents perform inferences concerning the assignments in their *agent_view*. By inference the agents generate new constraints called *nogoods*.

Definition 3 (Explicit Nogood). *An* explicit nogood *has the form $\neg N$ where N is a set of assignments for distinct variables.*

The following types of messages are exchanged in ABT:

- **ok?** message transporting an assignment is sent to a constraint-evaluating-agent to ask whether a chosen value is acceptable.
- **nogood** message transporting an *explicit nogood*. It is sent from the agent that infers an *explicit nogood* $\neg N$, to the constraint-evaluating-agent for $\neg N$.
- **add-link** message announcing A_i that the sender A_j owns constraints involving x_i. A_i inserts A_j in its *outgoing links* and answers with an **ok?**.

The agents start by instantiating their variables concurrently and send **ok?** messages to announce their assignment to all agents with lower priority in their *outgoing links*. The agents answer to received messages according to the Algorithm 1 (given in [13]).

Definition 4 (Valid assignment). *An assignment $\langle x, v_1, c_1\rangle$ known by an agent A_l is valid for A_l as long as no assignment $\langle x, v_2, c_2\rangle$, $c_2 > c_1$, is received.*

A **nogood is valid** if it contains only valid assignments. The next property is a consequence of the fact that ABT is an instance of AAS.

Property 1 *If only one valid nogood is stored for a value then ABT has polynomial space complexity in each agent, $O(dv)$, while maintaining its completeness and termination properties. d is the domain size and v is the number of variables.*

```
when received (ok?,⟨x_j, d_j, c_{x_j}⟩) do
    if(old c_{x_j}) return;
    add(x_j,d_j,c_{x_j}) to agent_view;
    eliminate invalidated nogoods;
    check_agent_view;
when received (nogood,A_j,¬N) do
    when any ⟨x, d, c⟩ in N is invalid (old c) then
        send (ok?,⟨x_i, current_value, C^i_{x_i}⟩) to A_j;
        return;
    when ⟨x_k, d_k, c_k⟩, where x_k is not connected, is contained in ¬N
        send add-link to A_k;
        add ⟨x_k, d_k, c_k⟩ to agent_view;
    when ⟨x_i, d, c⟩∈N, then put ¬N in nogood-list for x_i=d;
    add other new assignments to agent_view;
1.1 eliminate invalidated nogoods;
    old_value ← current_value;
    check_agent_view;
    when old_value = current_value
1.2     send (ok?,⟨x_i, current_value, C^i_{x_i}⟩) to A_j;
procedure check_agent_view do
    when agent_view and current_value are not consistent
        if no value in D_i is consistent with agent_view then
            backtrack;
        else
            select d ∈ D_i where agent_view and d are consistent;
            current_value ← d; C^i_{x_i}++;
            send (ok?,⟨x_i, d, C^i_{x_i}⟩) to lower priority agents in outgoing links;
procedure backtrack do
    nogoods ← {V | V = inconsistent subset of agent_view};
    when an empty set is an element of nogoods
        broadcast to other agents that there is no solution, terminate this algorithm;
    for every V ∈ nogoods;
        select (x_j,d_j,c) where x_j has the lowest priority in V;
        send (nogood,A_i,V) to A_j;
        eliminate invalidated explicit nogoods;
        remove (x_j,d_j,c) from agent_view;
    check_agent_view;
```

Algorithm 1: *Procedures of A_i for receiving messages in ABT with nogood removal.*

5.2 DMAC-ABT

Parts of the content of a message may become *invalid* due to newer available information. We require that messages arrive at destination in finite time after they are sent. The receiver can discard the invalid incoming information, or can reuse invalid nogoods with alternative semantics (e.g. as redundant constraints).

when received(propagate, A_j, k, $c^k_{x_v}(j)$, $V \rightarrow (x_v \notin l)$**) do**

2.1 **when** have higher tag $c^k_{x_v}(j,i) \geq c^k_{x_v}(j)$ **then** return;
$c^k_{x_v}(j,i) \leftarrow c^k_{x_v}(j)$; **when** any $\langle x, d, c\rangle$ in V is invalid (old c) **then** return;
when $\langle x_u, d_u, c_u\rangle$, where x_u is not connected, is contained in V
  send **add-link** to A_u; add $\langle x_u, d_u, c_u\rangle$ to *agent_view*;
2.2 add other new assignments in V to *agent_view*; eliminate invalidated nogoods;
$cn^k_{x_v}(i,j) \leftarrow \{V \rightarrow (x_v \notin l)\}$; **maintain_consistency**(minimal level that is modified);
check_agent_view; //only satisfies consistency nogoods of levels t, t<cL$_i$;

procedure maintain_consistency(*minT*) do

if (minT > cL$_i$) **then** return; //cL$_i$ is the current inconsistent level (initially i+1);
2.3 **for** (t←minT; t≤i; t++)
2.4   *new-cn* ← consistency nogood for x_i after local consistency on $P_i(t)$;
  when (domain wipe out by computing the explicit nogoods $\mathcal{N}$)
    for every $V \in \mathcal{N}$;
      select $\langle x_j, d_j, c_{x_j}\rangle$ where x_j has the lowest priority in V;
      send (**nogood**,A_i,V) to A_j; eliminate invalidated explicit nogoods;
      remove $\langle x_j, d_j, c_{x_j}\rangle$ from *agent_view*;
2.5   cL$_i$ ←t; **break**;
  when *new-cn* shrinks label of x_i (obtained from $\cup_{k \leq t} cn^k_{x_i}(i,i)$)
2.6 $cn^t_{x_i}(i,i) \leftarrow$ *new-cn*; $C^t_{x_i}$++;
    send (**propagate**,A_i,k,$C^t_{x_i}$,*new-cn*) to agents $A_j, j \geq t, x_i \in$ **evars**($\mathbf{A_j}$);

Algorithm 2: *Procedure of* A_i *for receiving* **propagate** *messages in DMAC-ABT.*

In addition to the messages of ABT, the agents in DMAC-ABT may exchange information about nogoods inferred by DCs. This is done using **propagate** messages as shown in Algorithm 2. Before making their first proposal as in ABT, cooperating agents can start with a call to **maintain_consistency**(0).

Definition 5 (Consistency nogood). *A consistency nogood for a level* k *and a variable* x *has the form* $V \rightarrow (x \in l^k_x)$ *or* $V \rightarrow \neg(x \in s \setminus l^k_x)$. V *is a set of assignments. Any assignment in* V *must have been proposed by* A_k *or its predecessors.* l^k_x *is a label,* $l^k_x \neq \emptyset$. s *is the initial domain of* x.[4]

The **propagate** messages for a level k are sent to all agents $A_i, i \geq k, x_i \in$ **evars**($\mathbf{A_i}$). They take as parameters the reference k of a level and a consistency nogood. Each consistency nogood for a variable x_i and a level k is **tagged** with the value of a counter $C^k_{x_i}$ maintained by the sender. The agents A_i use the most recent proposals of the agents $A_j, j \leq k$ when they compute DC consistent labels of level k. A_i may receive valid consistency nogoods of level k with assignments for the set of variables $\mathcal{V}$, $\mathcal{V}$ not in evars(A_i). A_i must then send **add-link** messages to all agents $A_{k'}, k' \leq k$ not yet linked to A_i and owning variables in $\mathcal{V}$. In order to achieve consistencies asynchronously, besides the structures of ABT, implementations can maintain at any agent A_i, for any level k, $k \leq i$:

– The set, V^i_k, of the newest valid assignments proposed by agents $A_j, j \leq k$, for each interesting variable.

[4] Or a previously known label of x (for AAS).

when received (**ok?**,$\langle x_j, d_j, c_{x_j}\rangle$) **do**
  if(old c_{x_j}) return;
3.1 add(x_j,d_j,c_{x_j}) to *agent_view*; eliminate invalidated nogoods;
  maintain_consistency(j);
  check_agent_view; //only satisfies consistency nogoods of levels t, t<cL$_i$;

procedure check_agent_view do
  when agent_view *and* current_value *are not consistent //cf. nogoods of levels t, t<cL$_i$*
    if *no value in* D_i *is consistent with* agent_view **then**
      backtrack;
    else
      select $d \in D_i$ where *agent_view* and d are consistent;
      current_value ← d; $C^i_{x_i}$++; **maintain_consistency**(i);
      send (**ok?**,$\langle x_i, d, C^i_{x_i}\rangle$) to lower priority agents in *outgoing links*;

Algorithm 3: *Procedures of A_i for receiving* **ok?** *messages in DMAC-ABT.*

- For each variable x, $x\in$vars(A_i), for each agent A_j, $j\geq k$, the last consistency nogood (with highest tag) sent by A_j for level k, denoted $cn^k_x(i,j)$. $cn^k_x(i,j)$ is stored only as long as it is valid. It has the form $V^k_{j,x}\rightarrow(x\in s^k_{j,x})$.

$\mathrm{NV_i}(\mathrm{V^i_k})$ is the constraint of coherence of A_i with the view V^i_k. Let $cn^k_x(i,.)$ be $(\cup^{t\leq k}_{t,j}V^t_{j,x})\rightarrow(x\in\cap^{t\leq k}_{t,j}s^t_{j,x})$. $P_i(k)$:= CSP(A_i) $\cup$ $(\cup_x cn^k_x(i,.))$ $\cup$ NV$_i$(V^i_k) $\cup$ CL^i_k. $C^k_{x_i}$ is incremented on each modification of $cn^k_{x_i}(i,i)$ (line 2.6).

On each modification of $P_i(k)$, $cn^k_{x_i}(i,i)$ is recomputed by inference (e.g. using local consistency techniques at line 2.4) for the problem $P_i(k)$. $cn^k_{x_i}(i,i)$ is initialized as an empty constraint set. CL^i_k is the set of all nogoods known by A_i and having the form $V\rightarrow C$ where $V\subseteq V^i_k$ and C is a constraint over variables in vars(A_i). $cn^k_{x_i}(i,i)$ is stored and sent to other agents by **propagate** messages iff its label shrinks and either CSP(A_i) or CL^i_k was used for its logical inference from $P_i(k)$. This is also the moment when $C^k_{x_i}$ is incremented. The procedure for receiving **propagate** messages is given in Algorithm 2.

We now prove the correctness, completeness and termination properties of DMAC-ABT. We only use DC techniques that terminate (e.g. [25,2]). By quiescence of a group of agents we mean that none of them will receive or generate any valid nogoods, new valid assignments, **propagate** or **add-link** messages.

Property 2 *In finite time t^i either a solution or failure is detected, or all the agents A_j, $0\leq j\leq i$ reach quiescence in a state where they are not refused a proposal satisfying* ECSP(A_j)$\cup$NV$_\mathrm{j}$(view(A_j)).

Proposition 1. *DMAC-ABT is correct, complete and terminates.*

The proof is given in Annexes. It remains to show the properties of the labels computed by DMAC-ABT at each level of the distributed search tree. If the agents, using DMAC-ABT, store all the valid consistency nogoods they receive, then DCs in DMAC-ABT converge and compute a local consistent global problem at each level (each pair initial_constraint-variable_label is checked by some agent). If on the contrary, the agents do not store all the valid consistency nogoods they receive but discard some of them after inferring the corresponding $cn_x^k(i,i)$, then some valid bounds or value eliminations can be lost when a $cn_x^k(i,i)$ is invalidated. Different labels are then obtained in different agents for the same variable. These differences have as result that the DC at the given level of DMAC-ABT can stop before the global problem is DC consistent at that level.

Among the consistency nogoods that an agent computes itself at level k from its constraints, $cn_x^k(i,i)$, let it store only the last one for each variable and only as long as it is valid. Let A_i also store only the last (with highest tag) consistency nogood, $cn_x^k(i,j)$, sent to it for each variable $x \in$vars(A_i) at each level k from any agent A_j. $cn_x^k(i,j)$ is also stored only as long as it is valid. Each agent stores the highest tag $c_x^k(j)$ for each variable x, level k and agent A_j that sends labels for x. Then:

Proposition 2. *DC($\mathcal{A}$) labels computed at quiescence at any level using* **propagate** *messages are equivalent to $\mathcal{A}$ labels when computed in a centralized manner on a processor. This is true whenever all the agents reveal consistency nogoods for all minimal labels, l_x^k, which they can compute* **and when $\mathrm{CL}_\mathrm{k}^\mathrm{i}$ are not used.**

Proof. In each sent **propagate** message, the consistency nogood for each variable is the same as the one maintained by the sender. By checking $c_{x_v}^k(j)$ at line 2.1, the stored consistency nogoods are coherent and are invalidated only when newer assignments are received (event that is coherent) at lines 1.1, 2.2, 3.1. Any assignment invalid in one agent will eventually become invalid for any agent. Therefore, any such nogood is discarded at any agent, iff it is also discarded at its sender. The labels known at different agents, being computed from the same consistency nogoods, are therefore identical and the distributed consistency will not stop at any level before the global problem is local consistent in each agent. □

Since consistency nogoods are not discarded when nogoods are sent to agents generating their assignments, asynchronism is ensured by temporarily disregarding those consistency nogoods. In Algorithm 3 we only satisfy consistency nogoods at levels lower than the current inconsistent level, cL$_i$ (see line 2.5 in Algorithm 2). Alternatively, such consistency nogoods could be discarded but then, to ensure coherence of labels, agents receiving any nogood should always broadcast assignments with new tags and many nogoods would be unnecessarily invalidated.

ABT may deal with problems that require privacy of domains. For such problems, agents may refuse to reveal labels for some variables, especially since the initial labels at level 0 are given by the initial domains. The strength of the maintained consistency is then function of how many such private domains are involved in the problem. The DisCSPs presenting only privacy on constraints, and the corresponding versions and extensions of ABT, suffer less of this problem.

Proposition 3. *The minimum space an agent needs with DMAC-ABT for ensuring maintenance of the highest degree of consistency achievable with DC is O($v^2(v+d)$). With bound consistency, the required space is $O(v^3)$.*

The proof is given in Annexes.

procedure maintain_consistency(*minT*) **do**
  if (minT > cL$_i$) **then** return;
4.1 **for** (t←minT; t≤i; t++)
    new-cns ← consistency nogoods for all vars(A_i) after local consistency on $P_i(t)$;
    when (domain wipe out by computing explicit nogoods *nogoods*)
      for every $V \in$ *nogoods*;
        select $\langle x_j, d_j, c_{x_j} \rangle$ where x_j has the lowest priority in V;
4.2   send (**nogood**,A_i,V) to A_j; eliminate invalidated explicit nogoods;
        cL$_i$ ←t; remove $\langle x_j, d_j, c_{x_j} \rangle$ from *agent_view*;
      break;
    forall *new-cn* ← consistency nogood for any variable x_u in *new-cns*
      when *new-cn* shrinks label of x_u (obtained from $\cup_{w,k \leq t} cn^k_{x_u}(i,w)$)
        $cn^t_{x_u}(i,i)$ ← *new-cn*; $c^t_{x_u}(i)$++;
        send (**propagate**,A_i,t,$c^t_{x_u}$,*new-cn*) to agents $A_j, j{\geq}t, x_u{\in}$**vars**($\mathbf{A_j}$);

Algorithm 4: *Procedure of* A_i *for receiving* **propagate** *messages in DMAC-ABT1.*

5.3 Using Available Valid Nogoods in $P_i(k)$ for Maintaining Consistency (DMAC-ABT1)

In Algorithm 2, an agent A_i only sends consistency nogoods for the variable x_i. However, when the local consistency is computed for $P_i(k)$, new labels are also computed for other variables known by A_i.

If in $P_i(k)$ we only use consistency nogoods and initial constraints, the final result of the consistency maintenance is coherent in the sense that at quiescence at any given level, each agent ends knowing the same label for each variable. Namely the new label obtained by A_i for some variable x_u will be computed and sent by A_u after receiving the other labels in consistency nogoods and instantiations that A_i knows and are related to x_u.

We propose that agents can use in their $P_i(k)$ valid explicit nogoods that they have received by **nogood** messages or old and invalidated consistency nogoods stored as redundant constraints. In this last case the labels obtained with Algorithm 2 are no longer minimal since an agent A_u does not know all constraints that can be used by A_i locally for computing its version of the label of x_u at level k.

In Algorithm 4 we present a version of DMAC-ABT that we call DMAC-ABT1. In DMAC-ABT1, A_i can send consistency nogoods for all variables found in CSP(A_i). The space complexity for storing the last tags for the consistency nogoods at all levels and coming from all other agents is now O(v^3) and for DMAC-ABT1 the space complexity is O($v^3(v+d)$). However, the power of DCs is increased since it can accommodate any available nogood. The number of sequential messages is also reduced since there is no need to wait for A_u to receive the label of x_i before reducing the label of x_u. Rather A_i propagates itself the label of x_u.

Proposition 4. *The minimum space an agent needs with DMAC-ABT1 for ensuring maintenance of the highest degree of consistency achievable with DC is O(*$v^3(v+d)$*). With bound consistency, the required space is O(*v^4*).*

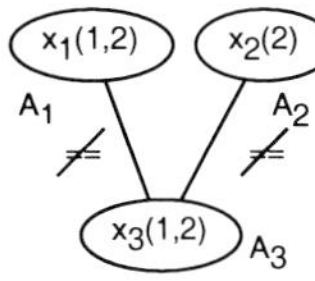

1: A_1 ——— **ok?**$\langle x_1, 1, 1\rangle$ ——→ A_3
2: A_2 —**propagate**(A_2,0,1,$x_3 \notin \{2\}$)→ A_1
3: A_2 —**propagate**(A_2,0,1,$x_3 \notin \{2\}$)→ A_3
4: A_2 ——— **ok?**$\langle x_2, 2, 1\rangle$ ——→ A_3
5: A_1 —**propagate**(A_1,0,1,$x_1 \notin \{1\}$)→ A_3
6: A_1 ——— **ok?**$\langle x_1, 2, 2\rangle$ ——→ A_3
7: A_3 —**propagate**(A_3,0,1,$x_1 \notin \{1\}$)→ A_1
8: A_3 ——— **nogood**$\neg(\langle x_1, 1, 1\rangle$→ A_1

Fig. 2. Simplified example for DMAC-ABT1. Function of the exact timing of the network, some of these messages are no longer generated. Only 2 messages are sequential (half round-trips). ABT needs 4 sequential messages (half round-trips) for the same example (see [23]).

The proof is given in Annexes. We denote by DMAC-ABT2 the version of DMAC-ABT where any agent A_i can compute, send and receive labels for variables constrained by their stored nogoods and redundant constraints but not found in **vars**($\mathbf{A_i}$).

6 Example

In Figure 2 we show a trace of DMAC-ABT1 for the example described in [23]. Before making its proposal, A_2 sends **propagate** messages to announce the consistency nogood $x_3 \notin \{2\}$ of level 0, tagged with $c^0_{x_3}(2) = 1$. These **propagate** messages are sent both to A_1 and A_3. A_1 sends an **ok?** message proposing a new instantiation.

A_3 (and A_1 when the domain of x_3 is public) compute both the consistency nogood $x_1 \notin \{1\}$ at level 0. A_3 computes an explicit nogood from consistency at level 1 and sends it to A_1. This nogood is invalid since A_1 has already changed its instantiation (and a small modification of DMAC-ABT1, for simplicity not given here, can avoid sending it). Then solution and quiescence are reached. The longest sequence of messages valid at their receivers (length 2) consists in messages 2,6. The worst case timing (slow communication channel from A_2 to A_1 or privacy for the domain of x_3) gives the longest sequence 3,7,6 (5 would not be generated). The fact that ABT (as well as any synchronous algorithm) would require at least 4 sequential messages illustrates the parallelism offered by asynchronous consistency maintenance.

7 Experiments

We have presented here DMAC-ABT1, an algorithm that allows to maintain consistency in ABT. ABT was chosen since it is simpler to present and explain. Recently we have presented an extension of ABT that allows several agents to propose modifications to the same variable and allows agents to aggregate values in domains. That extension is called Asynchronous Aggregation Search (AAS) [14]. In [14] is shown that the aggregations bring to ABT improvements of an order of magnitude for versions that maintain a polynomial number of nogoods. Here it is therefore appropriate to test the improvements that our technique for maintaining consistency brings to AAS. The version of DMAC-ABT1 for AAS is denoted DMAC.

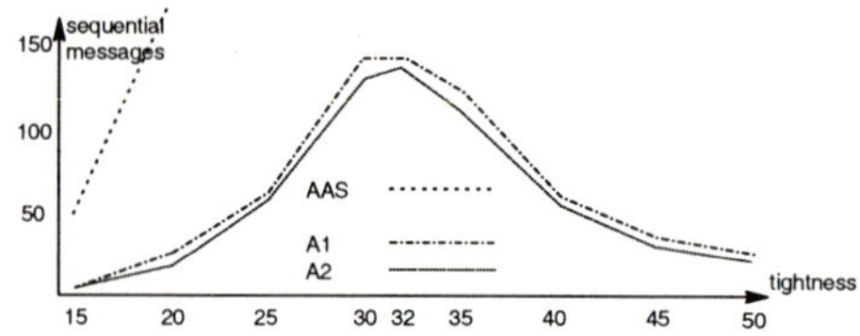

Fig. 3. *Results averaged over 500 problems per point.*

We have run our tests on a local network of SUN stations where agents are placed on distinct computers. We use a technique that enables agents to process with higher priority **propagate** and **ok?** messages for lower levels.

The DC used in our experimental evaluation maintains bound-consistency. In each agent, computation at lower levels is given priority over computations at higher levels. We generated randomly problems with 15 variables of 8 values and graph density of 20%. Their constraints were randomly distributed in 20 subproblems for 20 agents. Figure 3 shows their behavior for variable tightness (percentage of feasible tuples in constraints), averaged over 500 problems per point. We tested two versions of DMAC, A1 and A2. A1 asynchronously maintains bound consistency at all levels. A2 is a relaxation where agents only compute consistency at levels where they receive new labels or assignments, not after reduction inheritance between levels. A2 is obtained in Algorithm 4 by performing the cycle starting at line 4.1 only for $t = k$, where k is the level of the incoming **ok?** or **propagate** message triggering it. In both cases, the performance of DMAC is significantly improved compared to that of AAS. Even for the easy points where AAS requires less than 2000 sequential messages, DMAC proved to be more than 10 times better in average. A2 was slightly better than A1 on average (excepting at tightness 15%). In these experiments we have stored only the minimal number of nogoods. The nogoods are the main gain of parallelism in asynchronous distributed search. Storing additional nogoods was shown for AAS to strongly improve performance of asynchronous search. As future research topic, we foresee the study of new nogood storing heuristics [8,24, 22,18,6].

8 Conclusion

Consistency maintenance is one of the most powerful techniques for solving centralized CSPs. Bringing similar techniques to an asynchronous setting poses the problem of how search can be asynchronous when instantiation and consistency enforcement steps are combined. We present a solution to this problem. A distributed search protocol which allows for *asynchronously maintaining* distributed consistency with polynomial space complexity is proposed. DMAC-ABT builds on ABT, the basic asynchronous search technique. However, DMAC-ABT can be easily integrated into more complex versions of ABT (combining it with AAS and using abstractions [16], one can use complex splitting strategies [17] to deal efficiently with numeric DisCSPs [12]). Another original feature of DMAC is its capability of using backtrack nogoods to increase the strength of the maintained consistency.[5] The experiments show that the overall performance of asynchronous search with consistency maintenance is significantly improved compared to that of asynchronous search that does not maintain consistency.

Annexes (Proof)

Property 2 *In finite time t^i either a solution or failure is detected, or all the agents $A_j, 0 \leq j \leq i$ reach quiescence in a state where they are not refused a proposal satisfying* ECSP(A_j)∪NV$_j$(view(A_j)).

Proof. The proof is by induction on i. Let this be true for the agents $A_j, j<i$. Let τ be the maximum time taken by a message. After $t^{i-1}+\tau$, A_i no longer receives **ok?** messages. A_i receives the last valid **ok?** message at time $t_o^i \leq t^{i-1}+\tau$. $\exists t_v^i, t^{i-1}+\tau \geq t_v^i$ such that after t_v^i, view(A_i) and all $V_k^u, k<i$ of any agent A_u are no longer modified. The set of disabled tuples in CL$_k^u$, $k<i$ can contain only a bounded number of elements for each agent A_u and they cannot be invalidated after t_o^i. CL$_k^u$, $k<i$ cannot be invalidated after t_v^i. Since DCs were assumed to terminate, they terminate after each modification of a CL$_k^u$. Since the number of such modifications that can generate a new consistency nogood after t_v^i is bounded, after a finite time no consistency nogood is received any longer by A_i for levels $k<i$.
Since the domains are finite, A_i can make only a finite number of different proposals satisfying view(A_i). Once any of them is sent, the total number of consistency nogoods that can be received before the proposal is modified is finite (this results by induction to levels $k \leq i$ of the reasoning for $k<i$ in the previous paragraph since after $v\tau$, A_i can receive only valid nogoods: valid explicit nogoods trigger the modification of the instantiation of A_i so that they can arrive only in finite time; if valid explicit nogoods are not received and no instantiation modification is done in finite time, no **ok?** is sent any longer by A_i, and the number of valid consistency nogoods at level i is limited as in the previous paragraph).
Only one valid explicit nogood can be received for a proposal since the proposal is immediately changed on such an event. Invalid nogoods can be received only within $v\tau$ time delay after a proposal is made. Therefore, there is a finite number of nogoods that can be received by A_i for any of its proposals made after t_v^i (and after t_o^i).

1. If one of the proposals is not refused by incoming nogoods, and since the number of received nogoods is finite, the induction step is correct.

2. If all proposals that A_i can make after t_o^i are refused or if it cannot find any proposal, A_i has to send according to rules inherited from ABT a valid explicit nogood $\neg N$ to somebody. $\neg N$ is valid since all the assignments of $A_k, k<i$ were received at A_i before t_o^i.

2.a) If N is empty, failure is detected and the induction step is proved.

2.b) Otherwise $\neg N$ is sent to a predecessor $A_j, j<i$. Since $\neg N$ is valid, the proposal of A_j is refused, but due to the premise of the inference step, A_j either

2.b.i) finds an assignment and sends **ok?** messages or

[5] Since this paper was submitted, [1] presents an algorithm reusing some backtrack nogoods in MAC. That algorithm can be proven to behave as a centralized instance of DMAC.

2.b.ii) announces failure by computing an empty nogood (induction proven).
In the case (i), since $\neg N$ was generated by A_i, A_i is interested in all its variables, and it will be announced by A_j of the modification by an **ok?** messages.
Case 2.b.i contradicts the assumption that the last **ok?** message was received by A_i at time t_o^i and the induction step is therefore proved for all alternative cases. The property can be attributed to an empty set of agents and it is therefore proved by induction for all agents. □

Proposition 1. *DMAC-ABT is correct, complete and terminates.*

Proof. **Completeness:** All the nogoods are generated by logical inference from existing constraints. Therefore, if a solution exists, no empty nogood can be generated.
No infinite loop: The result follows from Property 2.
Correctness: All valid proposals are sent to all interested agents and stored there. At quiescence all the agents know the valid interesting assignments of all predecessors. If quiescence is reached without detecting an empty nogood, then all the agents agree with their predecessors and their intersection is nonempty and correct. □

Proposition 3. *The minimum space an agent needs with DMAC-ABT for ensuring maintenance of the highest degree of consistency achievable with DC is O($v^2(v+d)$). With bound consistency, the required space is O(v^3).*

Proof. d-maximal domain size;v-number of variables. The space required for storing all valid assignments is O(v) for values and O(v) for the corresponding counters. The agents need to maintain at most v levels, each of them dealing with maximum v variables, for each of them having at most 1 last consistency nogood. Each consistency nogood refers at most v assignments in premise and stores at most d values in label. The stack of labels requires therefore O($v^2(v+d)$). The space required by the algorithm for solving the local problem depends on the corresponding technique (e.g. chronological backtracking requires O(v)). The stored explicit nogoods require O(dv) as mentioned in Property 1. In DMAC-ABT are also stored O(v^2) tags for consistency nogoods. □

Proposition 4. *The minimum space an agent needs with DMAC-ABT1 for ensuring maintenance of the highest degree of consistency achievable with DC is O($v^3(v+d)$). With bound consistency, the required space is O(v^4).*

Proof. The agents need to maintain at most v levels, each of them dealing with maximum v variables, for each of them having at most v last consistency nogoods. Each consistency nogood refers at most v assignments in premise and stores at most d values in label. The stack of labels requires therefore O($v^3(v+d)$). DMAC-ABT1 also stores O(v^3) tags for consistency nogoods. The other structures are identical as for DMAC-ABT. □

References

1. J.-F. Baget and Y.S. Tognetti. Backtracking through biconnected components of a constraint graph. In *Proc. of IJCAI-01*, pages 291–296, 2001.
2. B. Baudot and Y. Deville. Analysis of distributed arc-consistency algorithms. Technical Report RR-97-07, U. Catholique Louvain, 97.
3. C. Bessière, A. Maestre, and P. Meseguer. Distributed dynamic backtracking. In *Proc. IJCAI DCR Workshop*, pages 9–16, 2001.
4. Z. Collin, R. Dechter, and S. Katz. Self-stabilizing distributed constraint satisfaction. *Chicago Journal of Theoretical Computer Science*, 2000.
5. J. Denzinger. Tutorial on distributed knowledge based search. IJCAI-01, August 2001.
6. E.C. Freuder, M. Minca, and R.J. Wallace. Privacy/efficiency tradeoffs in distributed meeting scheduling by constraint-based agents. In *Proc. IJCAI DCR Workshop*, pages 63–72, 2001.
7. M. Hannebauer. On proving properties of concurrent algorithms for distributed csps. In *Proc. of CP-01 DisCS Workshop*. EPFL, 2000.
8. W. Havens. Nogood caching for multiagent backtrack search. In *Proc. AAAI'97 Constraints and Agents Workshop*, '97.
9. S. Kasif. On the Parallel Complexity of Discrete Relaxation in Constraint Satisfaction Networks. *Artificial Intelligence*, 45(3):275–286, October 90.
10. P. Meseguer and M. A. Jiménez. Distributed forward checking. In *Proceedings of the International Workshop on Distributed Constraint Satisfaction*. CP'00, 2000.
11. D. Sabin and E. C. Freuder. Contradicting conventional wisdom in constraint satisfaction. In *Proceedings ECAI-94*, pages 125–129, 94.
12. M.-C. Silaghi, Ş. Sabău, D. Sam-Haroud, and B.V. Faltings. Asynchronous search for numeric DisCSPs. In *Proc. of CP'2001*, Paphos,Cyprus, 2001.
13. M.-C. Silaghi, D. Sam-Haroud, and B. Faltings. ABT with Asynch. Reordering. In *IAT*, 01.
14. M.-C. Silaghi, D. Sam-Haroud, and B. Faltings. Asynchronous search with aggregations. In *Proc. of AAAI2000*, pages 917–922, 2000.
15. M.-C. Silaghi, D. Sam-Haroud, and B. Faltings. Maintaining hierarchical distributed consistency. In *Proc. of CP-00 Workshop on DisCS*, 2000.
16. M.-C. Silaghi, D. Sam-Haroud, and B. Faltings. Multiply asynchronous search with abstractions. In *IJCAI-01 DCR Workshop*, pages 17–32, Seattle, August 2001.
17. M.-C. Silaghi, D. Sam-Haroud, and B. Faltings. Search techniques for non-liniar constraint satisfaction problems with inequalities. In *Proc. of AI2001*, Otawa, June 2001.
18. M.-C. Silaghi, D. Sam-Haroud, and B.V. Faltings. Hybridyzing ABT and AWC into a polynomial space, complete protocol with reordering. Technical Report #364, EPFL, May 2001.
19. M.C. Silaghi and B. Faltings. Parallel proposals in asynchronous search. Technical Report #371, EPFL, August 2001.
20. G. Solotorevsky, E. Gudes, and A. Meisels. Distributed Constraint Satisfaction Problems - a model and application. Preprint: http://www.cs.bgu.ac.il/~am, 97.
21. G. Tel. *Multiagent Systems, A Modern Approach to Distributed AI*, chapter Distributed Control Algorithms for AI, pages 539–580. MIT Press, 99.
22. E. H. Turner and J. Phelps. Determining the usefulness of information from its use during problem solving. In *Proceedings of AA2000*, pages 207–208, 2000.
23. M. Yokoo, E. H. Durfee, T. Ishida, and K. Kuwabara. Distributed constraint satisfaction for formalizing distributed problem solving. In *ICDCS'92*, pages 614–621, June 92.
24. M. Yokoo, E. H. Durfee, T. Ishida, and K. Kuwabara. The Distributed CSP: Formalization and algorithms. *IEEE Trans. on KDE*, 10(5):673–685, 98.
25. Y. Zhang and A. K. Mackworth. Parallel and distributed algorithms for finite constraint satisfaction problems. In *Proc. of Third IEEE Symposium on Parallel and Distributed Processing*, pages 394–397, 91.

Constraint-Based Verification of Client-Server Protocols

Giorgio Delzanno[1] and Tevfik Bultan[2*]

[1] Dipartimento di Informatica e Scienze dell'Informazione
Università di Genova, via Dodecaneso 35, 16146 Italy
giorgio@disi.unige.it
[2] Department of Computer Science
University of California, Santa Barbara, CA 93106, USA
bultan@cs.ucsb.edu

Abstract. We show that existing constraint manipulation technology incorporated in the paradigm of *symbolic model checking with rich assertional languages* [KMM$^+$97], can be successfully applied to the verification of client-server protocols with a finite but unbounded number of clients. *Abstract interpretation* is the mathematical bridge between protocol specifications and the constraint-based verification method on heterogeneous data used in the Action Language Verifier, a model checker for CTL [BYK01]. The method we propose is incomplete but fully automatic and sound for *safety* and *liveness* properties. Sufficient conditions for termination of the resulting procedures can be derived by using the theory of [ACJT96]. As a case-study, we apply the method to check safety and liveness properties for a formal model of Steve German's directory-based consistency protocol [PRZ01].

1 Introduction

Formal verification of client-server protocols is an important and challenging problem. Client-server architectures are present at different levels of abstractions in modern computer systems. Consistency protocols for client-server architectures are used, e.g., in multiprocessor systems with shared memory and local caches, distributed file systems, distributed database systems, and web-based applications to ensure the coherency of distributed data. An important class of consistency protocols makes use of central servers to serialize the access to the data. This kind of protocols are often validated on test sets with a fixed number of clients. In many interesting examples, however, it is not possible to fix an a priori bound on the number of clients requesting access to the data. This assumption makes the application of automated (push-button) verification methods like BDD-based *symbolic model checking* [McM93], and state exploration [Hol88] problematic. State explosion limits de facto the applicability of

* The work by Tevfik Bultan is supported in part by NSF grant CCR-9970976 and NSF CAREER award CCR-9984822.

T. Walsh (Ed.): CP 2001, LNCS 2239, pp. 286–301, 2001.

finite-state techniques like symbolic model checking to concurrent systems with a relatively small number of components. Thus, although useful for debugging, in general symbolic model checking cannot help us in automatically proving a protocol correct for any possible number of clients.

In the last years many efforts have been spent in order to lift symbolic model checking from finite- to infinite-state applications. Following [KMM⁺97], this goal can be achieved by employing *rich assertional languages* to reason about potentially *infinite* collections of system states. This idea finds a natural counterpart in the paradigm of *constraint-based model checking*, see e.g. [BGP99,DP99, Fri00]. In this setting, the solutions of existentially quantified *constraint* formulas are used as denotations of an infinite collection of system states. Algorithmic verification procedures for temporal formulas are then defined on top of existing constraint-solvers such as a Presburger arithmetic solver as in [BGP99], and a real constraint solver as in [DP99].

In this paper we show that several verification problems of protocols designed for client-server architectures with a finite but potentially unbounded number of clients can be naturally solved using the *composite-constraint* approach proposed in [BGL00]. In this approach constraints over *heterogeneous* data are used as symbolic representation of states. The methodology we follow consists of the following steps.

We first specify the server and a generic client using finite-state communicating machines in the style of [BCR01,EN98,GS92,Del00]. In our model we allow synchronous and asynchronous communication mechanisms. Furthermore, we allow global variables with Boolean type. As main case-study, we present a formal model for the consistency protocol proposed by Steven German in [Ger00,PRZ01]. Many other examples can be modeled this way as shown, e.g., in [BCR01,Del00,EFM99]. The verification of the safety properties studied in [PRZ01] amounts to the following *parameterized reachability problem*: one has to show that for *any number of clients* unsafe states can never be reached.

Following the methodology proposed in [Del00], we apply a *counting abstraction* to reduce the family of communicating finite-state machines indexed on the number of clients to a transition system with *Boolean* and *integer variables*. Intuitively, the counting abstraction maps a *global state* (whose size depends on the number of clients) into a finite tuple of Boolean and integer values, in which we keep track of the current server state, the value of the global variables, and the number of clients in every possible local state. A formal model based on communicating finite-state machines can be compiled *automatically* into an abstract protocol using a set of rules mapping protocol transitions into guarded commands defined over Boolean, and integer variables. Via this abstraction, verification of safety properties can be reduced to a reachability problem in which initial and target states can be expressed as *composite constraints*, i.e., formulas over Boolean and integer variables. The Action Language Verifier [BYK01], a constraint-based CTL model checker, can then be used to attack this kind of verification problems. Action Language Verifier is built on top of the Composite Symbolic Library [YKTB01] which provides operations to manipulate composite constraints, by integrating a BDD library [CUDD], and a Presburger arithmetic manipulator [Pug92,KMP+95].

Using the theory proposed in [ACJT96], it is possible to prove the decidability of the resulting verification method for safety properties expressed via a special class of composite constraints in which the arithmetic part denotes *upward closed* sets of abstract states. Interestingly, the safety properties for the German's protocol considered in [PRZ01] can be expressed using this class of composite constraints.

As a practical result, we were able to automatically verify interesting safety properties like mutual exclusion for readers and writers for our case-study. Being a full-fledged model checker for temporal properties expressed in CTL, the Action Language Verifier also allowed us to automatically verify *liveness* properties. To our knowledge, this is the first time that constraint technology based on *composite symbolic representations* are used to verify formal models of client-server protocols for arbitrary number of clients.

Plan of the paper. In Section 2, we will informally describe our case-study. In Section 3, we will show how to formally specify it. In Section 4, we will introduce the *counting abstraction.* In Sections 5, 6, and 7 we will describe the tools we used to analyze the abstract protocol and the results we obtained. Finally, in Section 8, we will draw some conclusions and discuss related works.

2 A Consistency Protocol for Multi-client Systems

In this section we informally describe a *directory-based* consistency protocol for multi-client systems with sharing data (cache lines, memory pages, etc.) inspired by the protocol proposed by Steven German [Ger00] presented in [PRZ01]. The protocol is designed for a system consisting of a single *home node* and an arbitrary number of clients. The home node serializes requests for the data. A transaction begins when a client with *null* access rights sends a request either for *shared* or *exclusive* access to the home node. If the home node is not serving another request (it is *idle*), it can pick up a new request from one of the clients. The home node maintains the set of sharers identifiers, and the list of sharers that have to be invalidated before serving a given request. Furthermore, it uses an internal Boolean flag, we will call *ex*, to indicate whether or not *home granted exclusive access* to the data. When the home node is granting exclusive access, or granting shared access and there is a client with exclusive access right, the home node must invalidate all clients. The home node sends out invalidate messages to one client at a time. When a client in state *shared* or *exclusive* receives an invalidate message, it downgrades its access rights, and sends an acknowledgment back to the home node. The home node removes the client from the list of sharers when it gets the invalidate acknowledgment. When all necessary invalidations have been done, the home node sends a reply message to the client who made the request. A reply is either a grant of shared access or a grant of exclusive access.

The client updates its access when it receives a grant message from the home node. The protocol should ensure the following two *safety* properties (the first one is considered also in [PRZ01]): ($P1$) *at most* one process per time can obtain the *exclusive* access right; ($P2$) *exclusive* and *shared* access rights are mutually exclusive. The challenge here is to prove $P1$ and $P2$ for *any* number of clients. For this purpose, we will first turn the informal specification into a formal one.

3 Communicating Finite-State Machines

The specification language we propose is obtained by merging the asynchronous CCS-like model of [GS92] (one monitor, and many clients with asynchronous communication), the broadcast protocols of [EN98] (synchronous communication), the model used to specify cache coherence protocols of [Del00] (synchronous communication, conditions over the global state), and the global/local machines proposed in [BCR01] (asynchronous communication with global and local variables).

Global machines. A global machine is a tuple $\langle \mathcal{B}, Q_S, Q, \Sigma, \delta \rangle$, where: $\mathcal{B}$ is the tuple of *global Boolean variables*; Q_S is the finite set of states of the server; Q is the finite set of states of the local machines; and Σ is the set of synchronization labels used to build the set of possible actions $\mathcal{A}_\Sigma$ of a process. Specifically, let φ be a Boolean formula over $\mathcal{B}$ and $\mathcal{B}'$ (the primed version of the variables in $\mathcal{B}$). Then, an action has one of the following form:

- *Internal action:* $\ell : \varphi$ for $\ell \in \Sigma$.
- *Rendez-vous:* $!\ell : \varphi$ (send) and $?\ell$ (receive).
- *Broadcast:* $!!\ell : \varphi$ (send) and $??\ell$ (receive).

The Boolean formula φ is used to express pre-and post-conditions (using primed variables) on the global variables $\mathcal{B}$. In the rest of the paper, we will use ℓ to indicate the action ℓ : *true*. We will clarify the semantics of actions in the next paragraphs. The behavior of the server and of the clients is described via the transition relation $\delta : (Q_S \times \mathcal{A}_\Sigma \times Q_S) \cup (Q \times \mathcal{A}_\Sigma \times Q)$. In the following, we will use $s \xrightarrow{\alpha} s'$ to indicate that $\langle s, \alpha, s' \rangle \in \delta$, and we will restrict δ to be deterministic. In order to define an operational semantics we must fix the number of clients, say k, as shown next. A *global state* for k clients is a tuple $G = \langle s_0, \rho, \mathbf{s} \rangle$, where $s_0 \in Q_S$ (server state), ρ is an evaluation for the variables in $\mathcal{B}$, and $\mathbf{s} = \langle s_1, \ldots, s_k \rangle$ (local states) is such that $s_i \in Q$ for $i : 1, \ldots, k$. The execution of a protocol is formalized through the relation $\Rightarrow$ defined next. Let $G = \langle s_0, \rho, \mathbf{s} \rangle$, $\mathbf{s} = \langle s_1, \ldots, s_k \rangle$, $G' = \langle s'_0, \rho', \mathbf{s}' \rangle$, and $\mathbf{s}' = \langle s'_1, \ldots, s'_k \rangle$. Define $\gamma = \rho \cup \rho'$. Then, $G \stackrel{\ell}{\Longrightarrow} G'$ provided one of the following conditions holds:

- $\exists i$ s.t. $s_i \xrightarrow{\ell:\varphi} s'_i$, $\gamma(\varphi) = \mathit{true}$.
- $\exists i, j$ s.t. $s_i \xrightarrow{!\ell:\varphi} s'_i$, $\gamma(\varphi) = \mathit{true}$, and $s_j \xrightarrow{?\ell} s'_j$.
- $\exists i$ s.t. $s_i \xrightarrow{!!\ell:\varphi} s'_i$, $\gamma(\varphi) = \mathit{true}$, and $\forall j$ s.t. δ is defined on $??\ell$, $s_j \xrightarrow{??\ell} s'_j$.

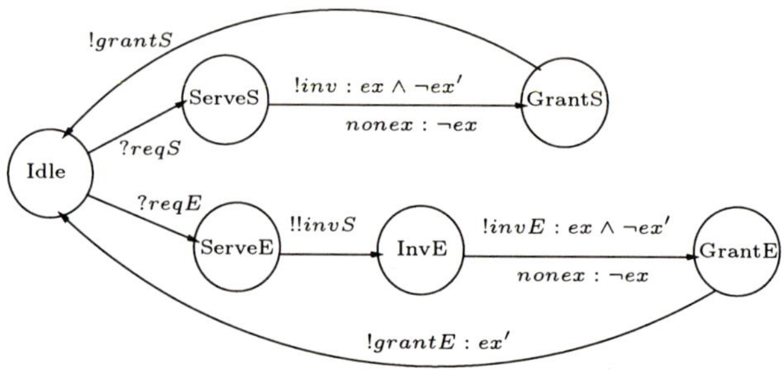

Fig. 1. Specification of the Home node.

In all the previous cases we assume that: $\rho'(b') = \rho(b)$ for any variable $b \in \mathcal{B}$ such that b' does not occur in the guard; and $s_i = s'_i$ if the i-th client is *not involved* in the action. A *run* of a global machine is a sequence of global states $G_0G_1\ldots$ such that $G_i \stackrel{\ell}{\Longrightarrow} G_{i+1}$ for $i \geq 0$. G_0 is the *initial* global state of the run. A global state G is reachable from G', written $G \stackrel{*}{\Rightarrow} G'$, if and only if there exists a run from G to G'.

3.1 A Formal Model for the Consistency Protocol

To specify our protocol, we use a Boolean variable *ex* (representing the flag *home granted exclusive right*), the machine for the home node described in Fig. 1, and the one for a generic client described in Fig. 2. Recall that the home node is supposed to serialize the requests and serve one client at a time. As in [Ger00, PRZ01], we consider message buffers of capacity at most one. Using synchronous communication, via the labels *reqE* and *reqS* we model the capability of the home node of storing the identifier of the client to be served: on reception of a request, home moves from *Idle* to one of the 'busy' states *ServeE*, *ServeS*. Differently from [Ger00,PRZ01], instead of handling invalidation via two global variables storing the identifiers of clients to be invalidated we use *broadcast* communication as explained below. Let us assume that the home node has to serve a request for *exclusive* access. Since all sharers must be invalidated, the server sends an *invalidation* broadcast to all clients in state *shared.* All sharers react to the broadcast downgrading their access rights. After having invalidated all sharers, home checks the flag *ex* to see if it still needs to invalidate clients with exclusive access. If the flag is on, instead of using broadcast, home assumes that only one process can be in *exclusive* state, and sends him the invalidation message *invE* using synchronous communication. The same situation repeats when the home node has to serve a request for *shared* access and the flag *ex* is on. On reception of the invalidation message, the client with exclusive access downgrades it to *null.* The flag *ex* is set to false (using the post-condition $\neg ex'$) after the invalidation process in state *ServeS* and *InvE*. The flag *ex* is set to true (using the post-condition ex') after granting exclusive access. When the home node is in state *ServeS* and *ex* is off, the server immediately grants shared access to the

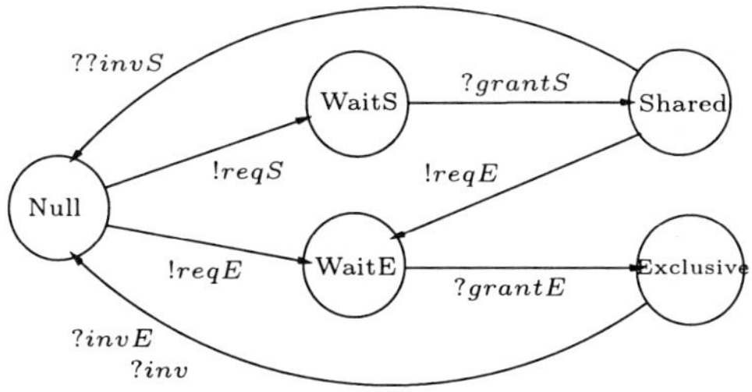

Fig. 2. Specification of a Client.

requesting client. In addition to the rule specified in [Ger00,PRZ01], we add the possibility for *sharers* to request an upgrade of their rights. This is accomplished via the transition $Shared \rightarrow ReqE$ labeled with $reqE$ in Fig. 2. The *initial global state* of the protocol with k clients is defined as $\langle Idle, \langle false \rangle, \mathbf{s} \rangle$, where $\mathbf{s}$ is the vector $\langle s_1, \ldots, s_k \rangle$ and $s_1 = \ldots = s_k = Null$.

Verification of Safety Properties. Let $G(k)$ denote a global state with k clients, and $\mathbb{B}_F(k)$ be the set of *unsafe* global states with k clients w.r.t. a given safety property F. Then, we say that the abstract protocol is k-safe if and only if there are no runs $G_o(k) \overset{*}{\rightarrow} G(k)$ such that $G(k) \in \mathbb{B}_F(k)$. In order to prove that a protocol is *safe* for all possible system configurations, it is necessary then to prove that it is k-safe for any $k \geq 1$. According to [EN98], we will call the reachability problem for arbitrary values of k a *parameterized reachability problem.* In our example $\mathbb{B}_{P1}$ and $\mathbb{B}_{P2}$ can be characterized as the sets of global states G *containing* the following *minimal violations*: $(P1)$ G contains one occurrence of *shared* and one of *exclusive*; $(P2)$ G contains two occurrences of *exclusive.* In other words, as often happens with safety properties, the set of unsafe states is *upward closed* (if a global state with k processes contains a violation generated by $k' < k$ processes, then it is unsafe). Furthermore, note that the description of unsafe states is independent from the *identifiers* of individual clients. In fact, we are not interested in proving that process 2 and process 6 are not violating mutual exclusion, we want to prove it for any pair of clients!

4 An Abstract Model

When trying to check safety properties that can be expressed independently from individual identifiers, it is often very useful to apply the following *counting abstraction.* The idea is to define an abstract state consisting of: (1) a *control* part obtained by merging the Boolean variables and the server control location; (2) a collection of counters to keep track of the number of clients in each local state $q \in Q$. Formally, let $G = \langle s, \rho, \mathbf{s} \rangle$ be a global state. The abstract state $G^{\#}$ is defined as: $G^{\#} = \langle s, \rho, \mathbf{c} \rangle$, where $\mathbf{c} = \langle c_1, \ldots, c_n \rangle$, and $c_i =$ *number of occurrences* of q_i in $\mathbf{s}$ for $i : 1, \ldots, n$, and $n = |Q|$. When applied to the transition relation δ, the counting abstraction returns the abstract protocol $M^{\#}$ that can be formally described as a transition system with Boolean and integer data paths. Formally, the abstract protocol consists of the control locations Q_S, the Boolean variables $\mathcal{B}$, and the *non-negative* integer variables $\mathbf{x} = \langle x_1, \ldots, x_n \rangle$; x_i represents the *counter* of the number of clients in state $q_i \in Q$. In the rest of the paper we will often use x_q to denote the counter associated to state $q \in Q$. Abstract transitions are *guarded commands* $s \to s' : C$, where $s, s' \in Q_S$, and C is a formula defined over the variables in $\mathcal{B} \cup \mathcal{B}' \cup \mathbf{x} \cup \mathbf{x}'$ as follows.

- The *internal* action $s \xrightarrow{\ell:\varphi} t$ is compiled into the formula $\varphi \wedge x_s \geq 1 \wedge x'_s = x_s - 1 \ \wedge \ x'_t = x_t + 1$.
- The *rendez-vous* $p \xrightarrow{!\ell:\varphi} q$, $r \xrightarrow{?\ell} s$ (all states distinct each other) is compiled into the formula $\varphi \wedge x_p \geq 1 \wedge x_r \geq 1 \wedge x'_p = x_p - 1 \ \wedge \ x'_q = x_q + 1 \ \wedge \ x'_r = x_r - 1 \ \wedge \ x'_s = x_s + 1$.
- Finally, consider the *broadcast* $p \xrightarrow{!!\ell:\varphi} q$, $s_i \xrightarrow{??\ell} s$ for $i : 1 \ldots m$ (all states distinct each other). Then, δ is compiled into the formula $\varphi \wedge x_p \geq 1 \wedge x'_p = x_p - 1 \wedge x'_q = x_q + 1 \ \wedge \ x'_s = x_s + x_{s_1} + \ldots + x_{s_m} \ \wedge \ x'_{s_1} = 0 \ \wedge \ldots \wedge \ x'_{s_m} = 0$.

In all above cases additional constraints of the form $x'_s = x_s$ and $b' = b$ are implicitly assumed for all integer and Boolean variables that are not involved in any action. The transition system resulting from the application of the counting abstraction is a Vector Addition System with state (server location and Boolean variables), a model underlying the usual operational semantics of Petri Nets, extended with special *transfer* arcs associated to broadcast operations [EN98, EFM99,Del00]. Given two abstract states $G_1^\# = \langle s, \rho, \mathbf{c} \rangle$ and $G_2^\# = \langle s', \rho', \mathbf{c}' \rangle$, we say that $G_1^\# \Rightarrow G_2^\#$ if and only if there exists a transition $s \to s' : C$ in $M^\#$ such that $C[\rho/\mathcal{B}, \rho'/\mathcal{B}', \mathbf{c}/\mathbf{x}, \mathbf{c}'/\mathbf{x}'] = true$. Given an abstract protocol $M^\#$ and an initial state $G_0^\#$, an abstract run is a sequence $G_0^\#, G_1^\#, \ldots$ of abstract states such that $G_i^\# \Rightarrow G_{i+1}^\#$ for $i \geq 0$. Then, we have the following proposition.

Proposition 1. *Let M be a global machine, and $M^\#$ be the corresponding abstract protocol. Then, $G_0 \stackrel{*}{\Rightarrow} G_1$ if and only if $G_0^\# \stackrel{*}{\Rightarrow} G_1^\#$ for any G_0, G_1.*

The abstract protocol for the example of Section 2 is described by the transitions of Fig. 3 defined over the control locations $Idle$, $ServeS$, $ServeE$, $GrantE$, $InvE$ and $GrantS$, the Boolean variables ex, and the integer variables x_N for the client state $Null$, x_{WE} for $WaitE$, x_{WS} for $WaitS$, x_S for $Shared$, and x_E for $Exclusive$. It is important to note that the representation of abstract global states is *independent* from the number of clients, and that it fully exploits the symmetries in their behavior. To check properties $P1$ and $P2$, it remains now to describe our approach to attack the reachability problem coming out from Proposition 1.

5 Composite Symbolic Representation

In order to analyze the behavior of a protocol for any possible number of *clients*, we need a finite representation for *infinite* collections of abstract states. One

$(reqS)$	$Idle \rightarrow ServeS :$	$x_N \geq 1 \wedge x'_N = x_N - 1 \wedge x'_{WS} = x_{WS} + 1$
$(reqE)$	$Idle \rightarrow ServeE :$	$x_N \geq 1 \wedge x'_N = x_N - 1 \wedge x'_{WE} = x_{WE} + 1$
$(reqE)$	$Idle \rightarrow ServeE :$	$x_S \geq 1 \wedge x'_S = x_S - 1 \wedge x'_{WE} = x_{WE} + 1$
(inv)	$ServeS \rightarrow GrantS :$	$ex \wedge \neg ex' \wedge x_E \geq 1 \wedge x'_E = x_E - 1 \wedge x'_N = x_N + 1$
$(nonex)$	$ServeS \rightarrow GrantS :$	$\neg ex$
$(invS)$	$ServeE \rightarrow InvE :$	$x'_N = x_N + x_S \ \wedge \ x'_S = 0$
$(invE)$	$InvE \rightarrow GrantE :$	$ex \ \wedge \ \neg ex' \ \wedge x_E \geq 1 \wedge x'_N = x_N + 1 \wedge x'_E = x_E - 1$
$(nonex)$	$InvE \rightarrow GrantE :$	$\neg ex$
$(grantS)$	$GrantS \rightarrow Idle :$	$x_{WS} \geq 1 \wedge x'_{WS} = x_{WS} - 1 \wedge x'_S = x_S + 1$
$(grantE)$	$GrantE \rightarrow Idle :$	$x_{WE} \geq 1 \wedge x'_{WE} = x_{WE} - 1 \wedge x'_E = x_E + 1 \wedge ex'$

Fig. 3. Abstract client-server protocol.

such representation could be obtained using linear constraints to encode sets tuples of integer and Boolean values. However, since manipulation of arithmetic constraints is expensive this strategy is not likely to scale. To solve this problem, we will use the *composite constraints* of [BGL00] as symbolic representation of infinite collections of global states. To explain this idea, let us first introduce a new set $\mathcal{L}$ of Boolean variables, which will be used to encode the control locations Q_S of the server; if $|Q_S| = m$, then we need $log_2 m$ variables. In our setting, a composite constraint is a formula $\varphi_{bool} \wedge \varphi_{int}$, where φ_{bool} is a Boolean formula over the Boolean variables $\mathcal{B} \cup \mathcal{L}$, and φ_{int} is a *disjunction* of linear arithmetic constraints over the variables $\mathbf{x}$ of the abstract protocol. The denotation of a composite constraint is defined as follows:

$$[\![\varphi_{bool} \wedge \varphi_{int}]\!] = \{\langle s, \rho, \mathbf{c} \rangle \mid \varphi_{bool} \text{ is true in } \rho_s \cup \rho, \text{ and } \ \varphi_{int} \text{ is satisfied in } \mathbf{c}\},$$

where ρ_s is the evaluation of variables $\mathcal{L}$ encoding location $s \in Q$. Composite constraints allow us to finitely and compactly represent *initial* and *unsafe states* for *parameterized* verification problems that can be formulated independently from client identifiers. As an example, the initial configuration of our protocol is described as the composite constraint Φ_0 defined as $\varphi_{Idle} \wedge \neg ex \wedge x_N \geq 1 \wedge x_S = 0 \wedge x_E = 0 \wedge x_{WE} = 0 \wedge x_{WS} = 0$, where φ_{Idle} is the Boolean formula over $\mathcal{L}$ representing location *Idle*. Furthermore, the set of potential violations of the *mutual exclusion* properties $P1$ and $P2$ can be represented as $\Phi_1 \vee \Phi_2$ where $\Phi_1 = x_S \geq 1 \wedge x_E \geq 1$, and $\Phi_2 = x_E \geq 2$. Based on this observation, it follows that we can reduce the verification problem for M and properties $P1$ and $P2$ to the following *reachability* problem for $M^{\#}$: *For any* $G_0^{\#} \in [\![\Phi_0]\!]$, *there are no runs* $G_0^{\#} \stackrel{*}{\Rightarrow} G^{\#}$ *of* $M^{\#}$, *such that* $G^{\#} \in [\![\Phi_1 \vee \Phi_2]\!]$.

Based on this idea, we encode collections of abstract states of the protocol using *composite symbolic representations* which are disjunctions of composite constraints [BGL00]. Formally, a composite symbolic representation Φ is in the form:

$$\Phi = \bigvee_i \Phi_i = \bigvee_i \varphi_{bool_i} \wedge \varphi_{int_i}$$

where each φ_{bool_i} is a Boolean formula, and each φ_{int_i} is a disjunction (set) of linear arithmetic constraints as mentioned above. Each φ_{int_i} can be represented in a disjunctive form as $\varphi_{int_i} = \bigvee_j \varphi_{int_{ij}}$ where $\varphi_{int_{ij}} = \bigwedge_k c_{ijk}$ and each c_{ijk} is an atomic linear constraint. Operations on arithmetic and Boolean constraints can be used to implement a symbolic *predecessor* operator **Pre** that computes the effect of firing the transition of an abstract protocol backwards on a composite symbolic representation. We first note that we can represent a guarded command t of $M^\#$ via the composite constraint φ_t defined over the variables $\mathcal{B}, \mathcal{L}, \mathbf{x}$ and their primed versions $\mathcal{B}', \mathcal{L}', \mathbf{x}'$ ($\mathcal{L}$ and $\mathcal{L}'$ are used to represent the old and the new control locations, respectively). Based on this observation, $Pre_t(\Phi)$ is defined as the existentially quantified formula (with variables in $\mathcal{L}, \mathcal{B}, \mathbf{x}$) defined as follows:

$$Pre_t(\Phi) \;\equiv\; \exists \mathcal{L}'.\exists \mathcal{B}'.\exists \mathbf{x}'.\; \varphi_t(\mathcal{L}, \mathcal{B}, \mathbf{x}, \mathcal{L}', \mathcal{B}', \mathbf{x}') \wedge (\bigvee_i \varphi_{bool_i}(\mathcal{L}', \mathcal{B}') \wedge \varphi_{int_i}(\mathbf{x}'))$$

Since existential quantification distributes over the disjunction we get

$$Pre_t(\Phi) \;\equiv\; \bigvee_i Pre_t(\Phi_i).$$

By hypothesis, Boolean and arithmetic constraints have no variables in common. Thus, the existential quantification also distributes over the conjunction to obtain

$$Pre_t(\Phi_i) \;\equiv\; (\exists \mathcal{L}'.\exists \mathcal{B}'.\; \varphi'_{bool_i}) \wedge (\exists \mathbf{x}'.\; \varphi'_{int_i}),$$

where φ'_{bool_i} and φ'_{int_i} are obtained collecting together, respectively, the Boolean and arithmetic constraints of $\varphi_t, \varphi_{bool_i}$, and φ_{int_i}. Furthermore, we can distribute the existential quantification over the set of linear arithmetic constraints in $\varphi'_{int_i} = \bigvee_j \varphi'_{int_{ij}}$ such that:

$$Pre_t(\Phi_i) \;\equiv\; (\exists \mathcal{L}'.\exists \mathcal{B}'.\; \varphi'_{bool_i}) \wedge (\bigvee_j (\exists \mathbf{x}'.\varphi'_{int_{ij}}))$$

Eliminating $\mathbf{x}'$ amounts to replacing every primed variable with its definition in φ_t. Hence, if $\varphi_{int_{ij}}$ is a set of linear constraints so is $\exists \mathbf{x}'.\varphi_{int_{ij}}$. The symbolic predecessor operator associated with $M^\#$ is defined then as:

$$\mathbf{Pre}(\Phi) = \bigvee_{t \in M^\#} Pre_t(\Phi).$$

The operator preserves our composite symbolic representation. Furthermore, it is easy to check that

$$[\![\mathbf{Pre}(\Phi)]\!] = \{G_1^\# \mid G_1^\# \Longrightarrow G_2^\#,\; G_2^\# \in [\![\Phi]\!]\}.$$

Symmetrically, it is possible to define a symbolic *successor* operator **Post** such that **Post**(Φ) returns the set of abstract states reachable from Φ (we omit its definition for brevity).

Symbolic forward and backward exploration procedures can be implemented then using the **Pre** and **Post** operators. The symbolic forward exploration procedure works on a composite symbolic representation $Current$. Given an initial set of composite constraints Φ_0, we first set $Current := \Phi_0$. Then, we apply **Post** to all the constraints in $Current$ to compute a new set of constraints New. If each composite constraint in New entails $Current$, we stop. Otherwise we add the composite constraints in New to $Current$ and continue. Symbolic backward exploration can be implemented similarly by starting from the composite constraints representing *unsafe* states, and using the **Pre** operator at each step.

In order to keep the *number of disjuncts* generated during a fixpoint computation small, it is possible to use simplification rules as the ones used in the Composite Symbolic Library described in the next section: for each composite constraint $\varphi_{bool_i} \wedge \varphi_{int_i}$ it checks if φ_{bool_i} is satisfiable, and removes the constraint if it is not; it looks for composite constraints $\varphi_{bool_i} \wedge \varphi_{int_i}$ and $\varphi_{bool_j} \wedge \varphi_{int_j}$ such that $[\![\varphi_{bool_i}]\!] = [\![\varphi_{bool_j}]\!]$, and merges them to form one composite constraint $\varphi_{bool_i} \wedge (\varphi_{int_i} \vee \varphi_{int_j})$. Since the boolean part of the composite constraint allows efficient equivalence and satisfiability checks (as is the case for BDDs) these simplification operations can be implemented efficiently and applied after each step in the symbolic forward and backward exploration procedures.

Interestingly, symbolic backward and forward exploration are not equivalent. As shown in [EFM99], symbolic forward exploration (enriched with acceleration operators *à la* Karp and Miller [EN98]) may not terminate for transition systems associated to *broadcast* protocols (a subclass of global machines). On the other hand, symbolic backward exploration is always guaranteed to terminate when the seed of the exploration is a constraint representing *upward-closed* set of abstract states. We will discussed this point in the next section.

Conditions for Termination. One interesting class of linear constraints that can be used to represent set of unsafe states with the special property of being *upward-closed* is that of *additive constraints* considered in [DEP99]. An additive constraint consists of a conjunction of atomic formulas of the form $a_1 \cdot y_1 + \ldots a_n \cdot y_n \geq c$, where a_i is a nonnegative integer constant, and y_i is a variable ranging over non-negative integers. As shown in [DEP99], the class of additive constraints equipped with the usual notion of entailment between linear constraints form a *well-quasi ordering*. This implies that there cannot be infinite chains of additive constraints whose elements are not comparable to each other with respect to the entailment relation. *Composite additive constraints* are obtained by restricting the linear arithmetic part of a composite constraint to be additive. Composite additive constraints are closed under application of the symbolic operator **Pre** associated to an abstract protocol. As a consequence, we have the following result.

Proposition 2. *Let Φ a* composite constraint representation. *Then, the symbolic backward exploration algorithm taking Φ as seed of the computation terminates and computes a symbolic representation of $Pre^*(\llbracket\Phi\rrbracket)$.*

Note that the composite constraints representing the unsafe states associated to property $P1$ and $P2$ of Section 3.1 are composite additive constraints. As a consequence, we have the following corollary.

Corollary 1. *The verification of properties $P1$ and $P2$ for the protocol of Section 3.1 is decidable.*

In the next section we will discuss the practical issues related to our methodology.

6 Tool Support for the Composite Constraint Method

The *Composite Symbolic Library* uses an object-oriented design to combine different assertional languages [YKTB01]. An abstract interface defines the operations used in symbolic verification: Boolean operations, equivalence and entailment tests, and image computations (for the **Pre** and **Post** operators). To define a new assertional language one simply has to implement the abstract interface with specialized operations. Currently, the Composite Symbolic Library provides two basic symbolic representations: BDDs via the Colorado University Decision Diagram Package (CUDD) [CUDD], and linear integer arithmetic constraints via the Omega Library [KMP+95]. Operations on composite symbolic representation are implemented using corresponding operations on these basic symbolic representations [BGL00]. The object-oriented design of the Composite Symbolic Library makes it possible to write polymorphic verification procedures, i.e. verification procedures that dynamically select symbolic representations based on the input specification. The input language of the Composite Symbolic Library is called the *Action Language* [Bul00]. Action Language is a specification language for reactive software systems which supports both synchronous and asynchronous compositions and hierarchical specifications; currently, it supports Boolean, enumerated, and integer types. In this setting, a specification consists of a set of modules and atomic actions. Modules can be defined by composing other modules or actions using synchronous or asynchronous compositions. Atomic actions are defined using formulas on primed and unprimed variables as in our abstract protocol example. In action formulas only Boolean logic and linear arithmetic operators are allowed. Given an input specification, the Action Language Verifier [BYK01] translates the input specification to a composite constraint representation and checks the verification conditions by computing forward or backward fixpoints using the Composite Symbolic Library. Verification conditions are specified in temporal logic CTL.

In general, for the class of systems that can be specified in the Action Language CTL model checking is undecidable. To achieve convergence, one can use conservative approximation techniques. Such operations have been successfully used for the verification of infinite-state systems using linear-arithmetic constraints (see e.g. [BGP99]). The Action Language Verifier extends these results to composite symbolic representations. Specifically, it implements a generalization of the widening operation on convex polyhedra to compute upper-bounds for fixpoints which do not converge. It also uses truncated fixpoint computations to compute lower-bounds. Using both these techniques, it is possible to compute both *lower* and *upper approximations* for any CTL property.

The Composite Symbolic Library and the Action Language Verifier are available at the URL `http://www.cs.ucsb.edu/~bultan/composite/`.

7 Experimental Results

In our experiments we focused on two kinds of CTL formulas: safety properties expressing *mutual exclusion* and liveness properties expressing *freedom from starvation*. In general, a *safety property*, expressed via the CTL formula $AG(\Phi)$, holds whenever all reachable states belong to the set of *safe* states Φ. Clearly, it can be proved by contraposition, by showing that there are no reachable states that belong the set of unsafe states $\neg\Phi$, in CTL this corresponds to the following equivalence $AG(\Phi) = \neg EF(\neg\Phi)$. Furthermore, one can show that $EF(\Psi) = Pre^*(\Psi)$ for any Ψ. This implies that AG-properties can be verified by first using symbolic backward reachability with seed $\neg\Phi$ to compute EF, and checking that the initial states are not in the resulting set of states. In CTL it is possible to express more complicated formulas like the liveness property $AG(\Phi_1 \rightarrow AF(\Phi_2))$. This formula can be read as follows: if Φ_1 holds at state s, then Φ_2 must eventually hold in all executions starting at s. Liveness properties can be checked algorithmically via nested *greatest* and *least fixpoint computations*. Verification of liveness for Vector Addition Systems with transfers arcs (or with test for zero in the guards) is *undecidable* [EFM99]. However, constraint-based model checkers can still be used as incomplete verification procedures using heuristics and approximation techniques to enforce termination [BGP99].

The table in Fig. 4 summarizes the practical results we obtained via the Action Language Verifier. We performed our experiments on two different models of the client-server protocol described in Section 2. The model 'B' of Fig. 4 is the abstract protocol of Fig. 3. The model 'I' is a refinement of model 'B' in which the atomic invalidation broadcast is replaced by the *invalidation loop* formulated at the abstract level as shown in Fig. 5. Note that this formulation needs *guards* with tests for zero. Tests for zero break the decidability of the verification of safety properties [Del00], i.e., approximations might be necessary in order to verify AG-formulas for the model 'I'. For both models, we considered the CTL properties listed in Fig. 6. The parameters of the experimental evaluation were the following: 'UA' denotes the use of approximations in the fixpoint computations; 'UF' denotes the use of approximate forward state exploration (see explanation below); 'Strategy' denotes the strategy used to check the properties, namely the sequence of steps (f=forward exploration, EF=least fixpoint, EG=greatest fixpoint) annotated with the number of iterations needed for each of them, e.g., $EF(4)$ means that the least fixpoint is reached in four iterations;

Property	Model	UA	UF	Strategy	Memory (Mbytes)	Time (secs.)
$P1-2$	B			$EF(4)$	10.2	0.60
$P1-2$	B		$\surd$	f(7), $EF(1)$	9.7	0.52
$P3$	B			$EG(3)$, $EF(5)$	14.1	2.37
$P3$	B		$\surd$	f(7), $EG(3)$, $EF(1)$	10.7	0.68
$P4$	B			$EG(3)$, $EF(8)$	25.6	9.34
$P4$	B		$\surd$	f(7), $EG(3)$, $EF(1)$	11.2	0.74
$P5$	B	$\surd$		$EG(4)$, $EF(11)$	14.1	3.01
$P5$	B	$\surd$	$\surd$	f(7), $EG(3)$, $EF(1)$	10.4	0.61
$P1-2$	I			$EF(4)$	10.4	0.59
$P1-2$	I		$\surd$	f(6), $EF(1)$	9.8	0.50
$P3$	I	$\surd$		$EG(3)$, $EF(5)$	11.9	2.01
$P3$	I		$\surd$	f(6), $EG(3)$, $EF(1)$	10.6	0.65
$P4$	I		$\surd$	f(6), $EG(3)$, $EF(1)$	11.6	0.81

Fig. 4. Experimental results obtained on a SUN ULTRA 10 workstation with 768 Mbytes of main memory, running SunOS 5.7.

$$ServeE \rightarrow GrantE : x_S = 0 \wedge x_E = 0$$
$$ServeE \rightarrow ServeE : x_S \geq 1 \wedge x'_N = x_N + 1 \wedge x'_S = x_S - 1$$
$$ServeE \rightarrow ServeE : x_E \geq \wedge x'_N = x_N + 1 \wedge x'_E = x_E - 1 \wedge \neg ex'$$

Fig. 5. The invalidation loop in state *ServeE*.

Property	Property specification in CTL
$P1-2$	$\neg EF((x_S \geq 1 \wedge x_E \geq 1) \ \vee \ x_E \geq 2)$
$P3$	$AG(x_{WS} \geq 1 \ \rightarrow \ AF(x_S \geq 1))$
$P4$	$AG(x_{WS} \geq N \ \rightarrow \ AF(x_S \geq N))$, $N \geq 1$
$P5$	$AG(x_{WE} \geq 1 \ \rightarrow \ AF(x_E \geq 1))$

Fig. 6. Specification of the properties for our case-study.

'Memory' and 'Time' denote the total resource consumption for the application of the corresponding strategy.

Some explanations for Fig. 4 are in order. Let us start from the model 'B'. As expected, we verified the safety properties $P1$ and $P2$ of Section 2, i.e., the CTL formula $P1-2$ of Fig. 6 without need of any approximation. We also verified the liveness properties $P3$ and $P4$ without using approximations. Since our method works on abstract models in which we forget identifiers of clients, the liveness property $P4$ must be read as *if more than k clients are waiting, then at least k clients will get the desired access*, i.e., a sort of freedom from *global deadlocks* for the original concrete protocol. Fixpoint computations for the liveness property $P5$ does not converge without approximation techniques. However, we were able to prove the property using truncated fixpoint computations and widening.

We also investigated the use of an a priori *forward* exploration of the abstract protocol reachable states (indicated as 'UF' in Fig. 4). Specifically, using widening techniques we first computed an *over-approximation* of the set of reachable states, and then used it to restrict the search-space during backward reachability. As an example, for model 'B' the approximate forward exploration (indicated as 'f' in Fig. 4) allowed us to verify all the properties faster, e.g., $P1-2$ in one iteration instead of four. By *caching* of the approximated reachable set, it should be possible to further improve the execution times of Fig. 4.

Let us consider now the model with invalidation loop. Again, to verify $P1-2$ we needed no approximations (however, note that termination is not guaranteed in this case). For property $P3$, the innermost fixpoint converged in three iterations, whereas the outermost fixpoint diverged without approximations. Using approximation techniques both fixpoints converged and we were able to verify the property. One interesting result is that we were able to verify property $P3$ without using approximations in the backward fixpoints when we combined them with the approximate forward exploration. The approximate forward exploration for model 'I' converges in six iterations and using it we can verify $P3$ more efficiently. For property $P4$, as with $P3$, the innermost fixpoint converged in three iterations, whereas the outermost fixpoint diverged without approximations. However, when we used approximation techniques although the fixpoint computations converged the results were not strong enough to verify the property. When we used approximate forward exploration backward fixpoint computations converged and we were able to verify the property. When we tried the to verify property $P5$ for model 'I', inner fixpoint computation did not converge. When we used approximations the results were not strong enough to verify the property. Even when we used approximate forward exploration, the results did not change. Hence, we were not able to verify or falsify the property $P5$ for model 'I'.

8 Conclusions and Related Works

In this paper we have shown that existing constraint technology can be successfully applied to the formal verification of protocols parametric on the number of participants. Abstract interpretation works as a bridge between protocol specifications and models that can be handled via constraint-based verification methods working on heterogeneous data like the Action Language Verifier of [BYK01]. The *counting abstraction* has been introduced in [GS92], where families of asynchronous CCS processes were verified via a reduction to Petri Nets. In [DEP99,Del00], a similar abstraction has been applied to the verification of cache coherence protocols (but not to directory-based as the protocol of [Ger00]), and concurrent systems specified as broadcast protocols [EN98]. The specification in [DEP99,Del00] allows synchronous communication but it does not admits heterogeneous data like global Boolean variables.

In [BCR01], the counting abstraction has been applied for the verification of *skeletons* of *multi-threaded* libraries. The resulting abstract models are basically Petri Nets with state. The authors analyze them using the Karp-Miller coverability construction, i.e., forward exploration with accelerations [EN98]. However, this procedure is not guaranteed to terminate in presence of broadcast communication [EFM99].

In [PRZ01], an alternative method based on deductive verification has been used to verify *safety properties* of parameterized systems like the German's protocol we considered in this paper. The method of [PRZ01] uses heuristics to discover invariants for parameterized systems, and to verify that the discovered invariants are *inductive.* The method is incomplete, but fully automatic (it is based on BDDs) and sound for *safety properties.* Differently from the previously mentioned approaches, constraint-based tools like the Action Language Verifier represents an incomplete but fully automatic sound tool for checking full *CTL formulas.* We exploited this feature to automatically verify *new* safety (property $P2$ has not been studied in [PRZ01]) and *liveness* properties for our case-study. On the other hand, the specification language used in [PRZ01] allows one to associate complex data structures, e.g. arrays storing process identifiers, to individual processes. Extending our approach in order to handle parameterized system with this kind of data structures seems an interesting direction of future research.

References

[ACJT96] P. A. Abdulla, K. Cerāns, B. Jonsson and Y.-K. Tsay. General Decidability Theorems for Infinite-State Systems. In *Proc. LICS '99*, pp. 313-321, 1996.

[BCR01] T. Ball, S. Chaki, S. K. Rajamani. Parameterized Verification of Multithreaded Software Libraries. In *Proc. TACAS '01*, LNCS 2031, pp. 158-173, 2001.

[BGP99] T. Bultan, R. Gerber, and W. Pugh. Model-checking concurrent systems with unbounded integer variables: Symbolic representations, approximations, and experimental results. *ACM TOPLAS*, 21(4):747–789, 1999.

[BGL00] T. Bultan, R. Gerber, C. League Composite model-checking: verification with type-specific symbolic representations. *ACM TOSEM*, 9(1): 3-50, 2000.

[Bul00] T. Bultan. Action Language: A specification language for model checking reactive systems. In *Proc. ICSE '00*, pp. 335–344, 2000.

[BYK01] T. Bultan and T. Yavuz-Kahveci. Action Language Verifier. In *Proc. ASE '01*, 2001.

[CC77] P. Cousot and R. Cousot. Abstract Interpretation: A Unified Lattice Model for Static Analysis of Programs by Construction or Approximation of Fixpoints. In *Proc. POPL '77* pp. 238-252, 1977.

[CGP99] E. M. Clarke, O. Grumberg, D. Peled. Model Checking. MIT Press, December 1999.

[CUDD] Fabio Somenzi. CUDD: the CU Decision Diagram Package, Release 2.3.1. `http://vlsi.colorado.edu/~fabio/cudd/`.

[Del00] G. Delzanno. Automatic Verification of Parameterized Cache Coherence Protocols. In *Proc. CAV '00*, LNCS 1855, pp. 53-68, 1996.

[DEP99] G. Delzanno, J. Esparza, and A. Podelski. Constraint-based Analysis of Broadcast Protocols. In *Proc. CSL '99*, LNCS 1683, pp. 50-66, 1999.

[DP99] G. Delzanno, A. Podelski. Model Checking in CLP. In *Proc. TACAS '99*, LNCS 1579, pp. 223-239, 1999.

[EN98] E. A. Emerson and K. S. Namjoshi. On Model Checking for Non-deterministic Infinite-state Systems. In *Proc. LICS '98*, pp. 70–80, 1998.

[EFM99] J. Esparza, A. Finkel, and R. Mayr. On the Verification of Broadcast Protocols. In *Proc. LICS '99*, pp. 352–359, 1999.

[Fri00] L. Fribourg. Constraint Logic Programming Applied to Model Checking. In *Proc. LOPSTR '99*, LNCS 1817, pp. 30–41, 1999.

[Ger00] S. M. German. Personal communication.

[GS92] S. M. German, A. P. Sistla. Reasoning about Systems with Many Processes. *JACM* 39(3): 675–735 (1992)

[Hal93] N. Halbwachs. Delay Analysis in Synchronous Programs. In *Proc. CAV '93*, LNCS 697, pp. 333–346, 1993.

[Hol88] G. Holzmann Algorithms for Automated Protocol Verification. AT&T Technical Journal 69(2):32-44, 1988.

[KMP+95] W. Kelly, V. Maslov, W. Pugh, E. Rosser, T. Shpeisman, and D. Wonnacott. The Omega library interface guide. Technical Report CS-TR-3445, Department of Computer Science, University of Maryland, College Park, March 1995. See also `http://www.cs.umd.edu/projects/omega/`.

[KMM+97] Y. Kesten, O. Maler, M. Marcus, A. Pnueli, E. Shahar. Symbolic Model Checking with Rich Assertional Languages. In *Proc. CAV '97*, pp. 424-435, 1997.

[McM93] K. L. McMillan. *Symbolic Model Checking: An Approach to the State Explosion Problem.* Kluwer Academic, 1993.

[PRZ01] A. Pnueli, S. Ruah, L. D. Zuck Automatic Deductive Verification with Invisible Invariants. In *Proc. TACAS '01*, LNCS 2031, pp. 82-97, 2001.

[Pug92] W. Pugh. The Omega Test: a Fast and Practical Integer Programming Algorithm for Dependence Analysis. *Communications of the ACM*, 8:102-114, 1992.

[YKTB01] T. Yavuz-Kahveci, M. Tuncer, and T. Bultan. A Library for Composite Symbolic Representations. In *Proc. TACAS '01*, LNCS 2031, pp. 52-66, 2001.

A Temporal Concurrent Constraint Programming Calculus

Catuscia Palamidessi[1] and Frank D. Valencia[2]

[1] Penn State University, USA
catuscia@cse.psu.edu
[2] **BRICS*****, University of Aarhus, Denmark
fvalenci@brics.dk

Abstract The tcc model is a formalism for reactive concurrent constraint programming. In this paper we propose a model of *temporal concurrent constraint programming* which adds to tcc the capability of modeling asynchronous and non-deterministic timed behavior. We call this tcc extension the *ntcc calculus.* The expressiveness of ntcc is illustrated by modeling cells, asynchronous bounded broadcasting and timed systems such as RCX controllers. We present a denotational semantics for the strongest-postcondition of ntcc processes and, based on this semantics, we develop a proof system for linear temporal properties of these processes.

1 Introduction

The tcc model [16] is a formalism for reactive ccp which combines deterministic ccp [18] with ideas from the Synchronous Languages [2]. Time is conceptually divided into *discrete intervals (or time-units).* In a particular time interval, a deterministic ccp process receives a stimulus (i.e. a constraint) from the environment, it executes with this stimulus as the initial store, and when it reaches its resting point, it responds to the environment with the resulting store. Also the resting point determines a residual process, which is then executed in the next time interval.

The tcc model is inherently deterministic and synchronous. Indeed, patterns of temporal behavior such as "the system must output c *within* the next t time units" or "the message must be delivered but *there is no bound* in the delivery time" cannot be expressed within the model. It also rules out the possibility of choosing one among several alternatives as an output to the environment. The task of *zigzagging* (see Section 4), in which a robot can unpredictably choose its next move, is an example where non-determinism is useful.

In general, a benefit of allowing the specification of non-deterministic behavior is to free programmers from the necessity of coping with issues that are irrelevant to the problem specification. Dijkstra's language of guarded commands, for example, uses a nondeterministic construction to help free the programmer from

*** Basic Research in Computer Science, Centre of the Danish National Research Foundation.

T. Walsh (Ed.): CP 2001, LNCS 2239, pp. 302–316, 2001.

over-specifying a method of solution. As pointed out in [21], a disciplined use of nondeterminism can lead to a more straightforward presentation of programs. This view is consistent with the declarative flavor of ccp: The programmer specifies by means of constraints the possible values that the program variables can take, without being required to provide a computational procedure to enforce the corresponding assignments.

Furthermore, a very important benefit of allowing the specification of non-deterministic and asynchronous behavior arises when modeling the interaction among several components running in parallel, in which one component is part of the environment of the others. These systems often need non-determinism and asynchrony to be modeled faithfully.

In this paper we propose an extension of tcc, which we call the *ntcc calculus*, for temporal ccp. The calculus is obtained by adding *guarded-choice* for modeling non-determinism and an *unbounded but finite delay* operator for asynchrony. Computation in ntcc progresses as in tcc, except for the non-determinism and asynchrony induced by the new constructs. The calculus allows for the specification of temporal properties, and for modeling and expressing constraints upon the environment both of which are useful in proving properties of timed systems. We shall illustrate the expressiveness of ntcc by modeling constructs such as cells, asynchronous bounded broadcasting and some applications involving RCX^{TM} controllers.

The declarative nature of ntcc comes to the surface when we consider the denotational characterization of the strongest postcondition of a process, as defined in [5] for ccp, and extend it to a timed setting. We show that the elegant model based on closure operators, developed in [18] for deterministic ccp, can be extended to a simple sound model for ntcc. We also obtain completeness for a fragment we shall call local-independent choice.

The logical nature of ntcc comes to the surface when we consider its relation with linear temporal logic: All the operators of ntcc correspond to temporal logic constructs. We develop a sound system for linear temporal properties of ntcc and show that the system is also (relatively) complete wrt local-independent choice processes. Our system is then complete for tcc as well, since every tcc process falls into the category of local-independent choice ntcc processes.

The main contributions of this paper can be summarized as follows: (1) a model of temporal ccp more expressive than tcc (2) a denotational semantics for the strongest postcondition of ntcc processes, and (3) a proof system for linear temporal properties of ntcc process.

2 The Calculus

In this section we present the syntax and an operational semantics of the ntcc calculus. First we recall the notion of constraint system.

Basically, a constraint system provides a signature from which syntactically denotable objects in language called *constraints* can be constructed, and an entailment relation specifying interdependencies between such constraints.

Definition 1 (Constraint Systems). *A constraint system is a pair (Σ, Δ) where Σ is a signature specifying functions and predicate symbols, and Δ is a consistent first order theory.*

Given a constraint system (Σ, Δ), let $\mathcal{L}$ be the underlying first-order language $(\Sigma, \mathcal{V}, \mathcal{S})$, where $\mathcal{V} = \{x, y, z, \dots\}$ is a countable set of variables and $\mathcal{S}$ is the set containing the symbols $\dot{\neg}, \dot{\wedge}, \dot{\Rightarrow}, \dot{\exists}$, $\mathtt{true}$ and $\mathtt{false}$ which denote logical negation, conjunction, implication, existential quantification, and the always true and always false predicates, respectively. *Constraints,* denoted by $c, d, \dots$ are first-order formulae over $\mathcal{L}$. We say that c *entails* d in Δ, written $c \vdash_\Delta d$ (or just $c \vdash d$ when no confusion arises), if $c \dot{\Rightarrow} d$ is true in all models of Δ. We write $c \approx d$ iff $c \vdash d$ and $d \vdash c$. We will consider constraints modulo $\approx$ and use $\mathcal{C}$ for the set of representants of equivalence classes of constraints. For operational reasons we shall require $\vdash$ to be decidable.

Process Syntax. Processes P, Q, $\dots \in$ *Proc* are built from constraints $c \in \mathcal{C}$ and variables $x \in \mathcal{V}$ in the underlying constraint system by the following syntax.

$$\begin{array}{rl} P, Q, \dots ::= & \mathbf{tell}(c) \;\mid \sum\limits_{i \in I} \mathbf{when}\, c_i\, \mathbf{do}\, P_i \mid P \parallel Q \;\mid \mathbf{local}\; x\; \mathbf{in}\, P \\ \mid & \mathbf{next}\, P \mid \mathbf{unless}\; c\; \mathbf{next}\, P \mid\, !P \quad \mid \star P \;. \end{array}$$

The only move or action of process $\mathbf{tell}(c)$ is to add the constraint c to the current store, thus making c available to other processes in the current time interval. The guarded-choice $\sum_{i \in I} \mathbf{when}\; c_i\; \mathbf{do}\; P_i$, where I is a finite set of indexes, represents a process that, in the current time interval, must non-deterministically choose one of the P_j $(j \in I)$ whose corresponding constraint c_j is entailed by the store. The chosen alternative, if any, precludes the others. If no choice is possible then the summation is precluded. We use $\sum_{i \in I} P_i$ as an abbreviation for the "blind-choice" process $\sum_{i \in I} \mathbf{when}\, (\mathtt{true})\, \mathbf{do}\, P_i$. We use **skip** as an abbreviation of the empty summation and "+" for binary summations.

Process $P \parallel Q$ represents the parallel composition of P and Q. In one time unit (or interval) P and Q operate concurrently, "communicating" via the common store. We use $\prod_{i \in I} P_i$, where I is finite, to denote the parallel composition of all P_i. Process **local** x **in** P behaves like P, except that all the information on x produced by P can only be seen by P and the information on x produced by other processes cannot be seen by P.

The process $\mathbf{next}\, P$ represents the activation of P in the next time interval. Hence, a move of $\mathbf{next}\, P$ is a unit-delay of P. The process $\mathbf{unless}\, c\, \mathbf{next}\, P$ is similar, but P will be activated only if c cannot be inferred from the current store. The "unless" processes add (weak) time-outs to the calculus, i.e., they wait one time unit for a piece of information c to be present and if it is not, they trigger activity in the next time interval. We use $\mathbf{next}^n(P)$ as an abbreviation for $\mathbf{next}(\mathbf{next}(\dots(\mathbf{next}\, P)\dots))$, where **next** is repeated n times.

The operator ! is a delayed version of the replication operator for the π–calculus ([14]): $!P$ represents $P \parallel \mathbf{next}\, P \parallel \mathbf{next}^2 P \parallel \dots$, i.e. unboundedly many copies of P but one at a time. The replication operator is the only way of defining infinite behavior through the time intervals.

The operator $\star$ corresponds to the unbounded but finite delay operator ϵ for synchronous CCS ([13]) and it allows us to express asynchronous behavior through the time intervals. The process $\star\, P$ represents an arbitrary long but finite delay for the activation of P. For example, $\star\, \mathbf{tell}(c)$ can be viewed as a message c that is eventually delivered but there is no upper bound on the delivery time. By using the $\star$ operator we can define a *fair asynchronous* parallel composition $P \mid Q$ as $(P \parallel \star\, Q) + (\star\, P \parallel Q)$ as described in [13]. A move of $P \mid Q$ is either one of P or one of Q (or both). Moreover, both P and Q are eventually executed (i.e. a fair execution of $P \mid Q$).

We shall use $!_I P$ and $\star_I P$, where I is an interval of the natural numbers, as an abbreviation for $\prod_{i \in I} \mathbf{next}^i P$ and $\sum_{i \in I} \mathbf{next}^i P$, respectively. For instance, $\star_{[m,n]} P$ means that P is eventually active between the next m and $m+n$ time units, while $!_{[m,n]} P$ means that P is always active between the next m and $m+n$ time units.

Operational Semantics. Operationally, the current information is represented as a constraint $c \in \mathcal{C}$, so-called *store*. Our operational semantics is given by considering transitions between *configurations* γ of the form $\langle P, c\rangle$. We define Γ as the set of all configurations. Following standard lines, we extend the syntax with a construct $\mathbf{local}\,(x, d)\,\mathbf{in}\,P$, which represents the evolution of a process of the form $\mathbf{local}\, x\, \mathbf{in}\, Q$, where d is the local information (or store) produced during this evolution. Initially d is "empty", so we regard $\mathbf{local}\, x\, \mathbf{in}\, P$ as $\mathbf{local}\ (x, \mathtt{true})\ \mathbf{in}\ P$

We need to introduce a notion of free variables that is invariant wrt the equivalence on constraints. We can do so by defining the "relevant" free variables of c as $fv(c) = \{x \in \mathcal{V} \,|\, \exists_x c \not\approx c\}$. For the bound variables, define $bv(c) = \{x \in \mathcal{V} \,|\, x \text{ occurs in } c\} - fv(c)$. Regarding processes, define $fv(\mathbf{tell}(c)) = fv(c)$, $fv(\sum_i \mathbf{when}\ c_i\ \mathbf{do}\ P_i) = \bigcup_i fv(c_i) \cup fv(P_i)$, $fv(\mathbf{local}\, x\, \mathbf{in}\, P) = fv(P) - \{x\}$. The bound variables and the other cases are defined analogously.

Definition 2 (Structural Congruence). *Let $\equiv$ be the smallest congruence over processes satisfying the following laws:*

1. $(Proc/_{\equiv}, \parallel, \mathbf{skip})$ *is a symmetric monoid.*
2. $P \equiv Q$ *if they only differ by a renaming of bound variables.*
3. $\mathbf{next}\,\mathbf{skip} \equiv \mathbf{skip}$ $\qquad \mathbf{next}(P \parallel Q) \equiv \mathbf{next}\, P \parallel \mathbf{next}\, Q$.
4. $\mathbf{local}\, x\, \mathbf{in}\, \mathbf{skip} \equiv \mathbf{skip}$ $\qquad \mathbf{local}\, x\, y\, \mathbf{in}\, P \equiv \mathbf{local}\, y\, x\, \mathbf{in}\, P$.
5. $\mathbf{local}\, x\, \mathbf{in}\, \mathbf{next}\, P \equiv \mathbf{next}(\mathbf{local}\, x\, \mathbf{in}\, P)$.
6. $\mathbf{local}\, x\, \mathbf{in}\, (P \parallel Q) \equiv P \parallel \mathbf{local}\, x\, \mathbf{in}\, Q$ *if* $x \notin fv(P)$.

We extend $\equiv$ to configurations by defining $\langle P, c\rangle \equiv \langle Q, c\rangle$ if $P \equiv Q$.

The reduction relations $\longrightarrow \subseteq \Gamma \times \Gamma$ and $\Longrightarrow \subseteq Proc \times \mathcal{C} \times \mathcal{C} \times Proc$ are the least relations satisfying the rules appearing in Table 1. The *internal transition* $\langle P, c\rangle \longrightarrow \langle Q, d\rangle$ should be read as "P with store c reduces, in one internal step, to Q with store d ". The *observable transition* $P \xRightarrow{(c,d)} Q$ should be read as "P on input c reduces, in one time unit, to Q with store d ". As in tcc, the store does not transfer automatically from one interval to another.

We now give a description of the operational rules. Rules TELL, CHOICE, PAR and LOC are standard [18]. Rule UNLESS says that if c is entailed by the current store, then the execution of the process P (in the next time interval) is precluded. Rule REPL specifies that the process $!\,P$ produces a copy P at the current time unit, and then persists in the next time unit. STAR says that $\star P$ triggers P in some time interval (either in the current one or in a future one). Rule STRUCT simply says that structurally congruent processes have the same reductions.

Rule OBS says that an observable transition from P labeled by (c, d) is obtained by performing a terminating sequence of internal transitions from $\langle P, c\rangle$ to $\langle Q, d\rangle$, for some Q. The process to be executed in the next time interval, $F(Q)$ ("future" of Q), is obtained by removing from Q what was meant to be executed only in the current time interval and any local information which has been stored in Q, and by "unfolding" the sub-terms within **next** R expressions. More precisely:

Definition 3 (Future Function). *The partial function $F : Proc \rightharpoonup Proc$ is defined as follows:*

$$F(P) = \begin{cases} Q & \textit{if } P = \textbf{next}\ Q \textit{ or } P = \textbf{unless}\ c\ \textbf{next}\ Q \\ F(P_1) \parallel F(P_2) & \textit{if } P = P_1 \parallel P_2 \\ \textbf{local}\ x\ \textbf{in}\ F(Q) & \textit{if } P = \textbf{local}\,(x, c)\ \textbf{in}\ Q \\ \textbf{skip} & \textit{if } P = \sum_{i \in I} \textbf{when}\ c_i\ \textbf{do}\ P_i \end{cases}$$

Remark 1. Function F does not need to be total since whenever we apply F to a process P (Rule OBS in Table 1), all replications and unbounded finite-delay operators in P occur within a next construction.

Interpreting Process Runs. Let us consider an infinite sequence of observable transitions

$$P \;=\; P_1 \xrightarrow{(c_1,c_1')} P_2 \xrightarrow{(c_2,c_2')} P_3 \xrightarrow{(c_3,c_3')} \ldots$$

This sequence can be interpreted as a *interaction* between the system P and an environment. At the time unit i, the environment provides a *stimulus* c_i and P_i produces c_i' as *response*. If $\alpha = c_1.c_2.c_3.\ldots$ and $\alpha' = c_1'.c_2'.c_3'\ldots$, we represent the above interaction as $P \xrightarrow{(\alpha,\alpha')}{}^{\omega}$.

Alternatively, if $\alpha = \texttt{true}^\omega$, we can interpret the run as an interaction among the parallel components in P without the influence of an external environment (i.e., each component is part of the environment of the others). In this case α is called the *empty* input sequence and α' is regarded as a *timed* observation of such an interaction in P.

3 Strongest Postcondition: Denotation and Logic

In this section we introduce the *strongest postcondition* of a process and investigate its denotational and logic. Henceforward, we use α, α' to represent elements

Table 1. An operational semantics for ntcc. The upper part defines the internal transitions while the lower part defines the observable transitions. The function F, used in OBS, is given in Definition 3

TELL $$\langle \mathbf{tell}(c), d\rangle \longrightarrow \langle \mathbf{skip}, d \dot\wedge c\rangle$$

CHOICE $$\langle \textstyle\sum_{i\in I} \mathbf{when}\ c_i\ \mathbf{do}\ P_i, d\rangle \longrightarrow \langle P_j, d\rangle \quad \text{if } d \vdash c_j, \text{ for } j \in I$$

PAR $$\frac{\langle P, c\rangle \longrightarrow \langle P', d\rangle}{\langle P \parallel Q, c\rangle \longrightarrow \langle P' \parallel Q, d\rangle}$$

LOC $$\frac{\left\langle P, c \dot\wedge \dot\exists_x d\right\rangle \longrightarrow \langle Q, c'\rangle}{\langle \mathbf{local}\ (x,c)\ \mathbf{in}\ P, d\rangle \longrightarrow \left\langle \mathbf{local}\ (x,c')\ \mathbf{in}\ Q, d \dot\wedge \dot\exists_x c'\right\rangle}$$

UNLESS $$\langle \mathbf{unless}\ c\ \mathbf{next}\ P, d\rangle \longrightarrow \langle \mathbf{skip}, d\rangle \quad \text{if } d \vdash c$$

REPL $$\langle !\, P, c\rangle \longrightarrow \langle P \parallel \mathbf{next}\, !\, P, c\rangle$$

STAR $$\langle \star\, P, c\rangle \longrightarrow \langle \mathbf{next}^n P, c\rangle \quad \text{for some } n \geq 0.$$

STRUCT $$\frac{\gamma_1 \equiv \gamma_1' \quad \gamma_1' \longrightarrow \gamma_2' \quad \gamma_2' \equiv \gamma_2}{\gamma_1 \longrightarrow \gamma_2}$$

OBS $$\frac{\langle P, c\rangle \longrightarrow^* \langle Q, d\rangle \not\longrightarrow}{P \xRightarrow{(c,d)} F(Q)}$$

of $\mathcal{C}^\omega$ and β to represent an element of $\mathcal{C}^*$. Given $c \in \mathcal{C}$, $c.\alpha$ represents the concatenation of c and α. Furthermore, $\beta.\alpha$ represents the concatenation of β and α. We use $\dot\exists_x \alpha$ to represent the sequence obtained by applying $\dot\exists_x$ to each constraint in α. Notation $\alpha(i)$ denotes the i-th element in α.

We define the *strongest postcondition* of P, $sp(P)$, as the set of all sequences P can possibly output. More precisely,

Definition 4 (Strongest Postcondition). *Let us define the set* $sp(P)$ *as* $\{\alpha' \mid P \xRightarrow{(\alpha,\alpha')}{}^{\omega}$ *for some* $\alpha\}$.

Denotational Semantics. We give now a denotational characterization of the strongest postcondition following ideas in [5] and [16] for the ccp and tcc case, respectively. The presence of non-determinism, however, presents a technical problem to deal with: The strongest postcondition for the hiding operator cannot be specified compositionally (see [5]). Therefore, we will have to identify a practical fragment for which the semantics is complete.

Table 2. Denotational Semantics of ntcc

D1	$[\![\mathbf{tell}(c)]\!]$	$= \{d.\alpha \mid d \vdash c, \alpha \in \mathcal{C}^\omega\}$
D2	$[\![\sum_{i\in I} \mathbf{when}\ c_i\ \mathbf{do}\ P_i]\!]$	$= \bigcup_{i\in I}\{d.\alpha \mid d \vdash c_i, d.\alpha \in [\![P_i]\!]\}$ $\cup$ $\bigcap_{i\in I}\{d.\alpha \mid d \not\vdash c_i, d.\alpha \in \mathcal{C}^\omega\}$
D3	$[\![P \parallel Q]\!]$	$= [\![P]\!] \cap [\![Q]\!]$
D4	$[\![\mathbf{local}\ x\ \mathbf{in}\ P]\!]$	$= \{\alpha \mid \text{there exists } \alpha' \in [\![P]\!] \text{ s.t. } \dot{\exists}_x\alpha = \dot{\exists}_x\alpha'\}$
D5	$[\![\mathbf{next}\ P]\!]$	$= \{d.\alpha \mid d \in \mathcal{C}, \alpha \in [\![P]\!]\}$
D6	$[\![\mathbf{unless}\ c\ \mathbf{next}\ P]\!]$	$= \{d.\alpha \mid d \vdash c, \alpha \in \mathcal{C}^\omega\} \cup \{d.\alpha \mid d \not\vdash c, \alpha \in [\![P]\!]\}$
D7	$[\![!\,P]\!]$	$= \{\alpha \mid \forall \beta \in \mathcal{C}^*, \alpha' \in \mathcal{C}^\omega \text{ s.t. } \alpha = \beta.\alpha', \text{ we have } \alpha' \in [\![P]\!]\}$
D8	$[\![\star\, P]\!]$	$= \{\beta.\alpha \mid \beta \in \mathcal{C}^*, \alpha \in [\![P]\!]\}$

The denotational semantics is defined as a function $[\![\cdot]\!]$ which associates to each process a set of infinite constraint sequences, namely $[\![\cdot]\!] : Proc \to \mathcal{P}(\mathcal{C}^\omega)$. The definition of this function is given in Table 2. Intuitively, $[\![P]\!]$ is meant to capture the set of all sequences P can possibly output. For instance, the sequences that **tell**(c) can output are those whose first element is stronger than c (D1). Process **next** P has not influence in the first element of a sequence, thus $d.\alpha$ can be output by it if α is can be output by P (D5). A sequence can be output by $!\,P$ if every suffix of it can be output by P (D7). The other rules can be explained analogously. The next theorems state the relation between the denotation of P and its strongest postcondition.

Theorem 1 (Soundness). *For every ntcc process P, $sp(P) \subseteq [\![P]\!]$.*

For the reasons mentioned at the beginning of this section, the converse of this theorem does not hold in general. Nevertheless, it holds for *local-independent choice* processes which we define next.

Definition 5 (Local-Independent Choice). *A process P is said to be* local-independent choice *iff for all* **local** x **in** Q *in P, for all* $\sum_{i\in I}$ **when** c_i **do** Q_i *in Q, the c_i's either are equivalent, mutually exclusive or do not have free occurrences of x.*

This is a substantial fragment of ntcc since every restricted-choice process is also local-independent choice and, unlike the restricted-choice fragment defined [7], its condition does not imply structural confluence. In fact, all the process examples in this paper are local-independent choice.

Theorem 2 (Completeness). *If P is a local-independent choice ntcc process, then $sp(P) = [\![P]\!]$.*

For deterministic processes such as tcc processes, namely those which contain neither the choice (except when the index set is a singleton) nor the $\star$ operator, we have an even stronger result: the semantics allows to retrieve the input-output relation (which for deterministic processes is a function). Let us use $\leq$ to denote the (partial) order relation $\{(\alpha, \alpha') \mid \forall i \geq 1 \ \ \alpha'(i) \vdash \alpha(i)\}$ and $min(S)$ to denote the minimal element of $S \subseteq \mathcal{C}^\omega$ in the complete lattice $(\mathcal{C}^\omega, \leq)$.

Theorem 3. *If P is a deterministic process, then $(\alpha, \alpha') \in io(P)$ iff $\alpha' = min([\![P]\!] \cap \uparrow \alpha)$, where $\uparrow \alpha = \{\alpha'' | \alpha \leq \alpha''\}$.*

Linear-Temporal Logic. Let us define a linear temporal logic for expressing properties of ntcc processes. The formulae $A, B, ... \in \mathcal{A}$ are defined by the grammar $A ::= c \mid A \Rightarrow A \mid \neg A \mid \exists_x A \mid \circ A \mid \Box A \mid \Diamond A$. The symbol c denotes an arbitrary constraint. The symbols $\Rightarrow$, $\neg$ and $\exists_x$ represent temporal logic implication, negation and existential quantification. These symbols are not to be confused with the logic symbols $\dot{\Rightarrow}$, $\dot{\neg}$ and $\dot{\exists}_x$ of the constraint system. The symbols $\circ$, $\Box$, and $\Diamond$ denote the temporal operators *next*, *always* and *sometime*. We use $A \vee B$ as an abbreviation of $\neg A \Rightarrow B$ and $A \wedge B$ as an abbreviation of $\neg(\neg A \vee \neg B)$.

The standard interpretation structures of linear temporal logic are infinite sequences of states [12]. In ntcc states are represented with constraints, thus we consider as interpretations the elements of $\mathcal{C}^\omega$. We say that $\alpha \in \mathcal{C}^\omega$ is a model of A, notation $\alpha \models A$, if $\langle \alpha, 1 \rangle \models A$, where:

$$
\begin{array}{lll}
\langle \alpha, i \rangle \models c & \text{iff} & \alpha(i) \vdash c \\
\langle \alpha, i \rangle \models \neg A & \text{iff} & \langle \alpha, i \rangle \not\models A \\
\langle \alpha, i \rangle \models A_1 \Rightarrow A_2 & \text{iff} & \langle \alpha, i \rangle \models A_1 \text{ implies } \langle \alpha, i \rangle \models A_2 \\
\langle \alpha, i \rangle \models \circ A & \text{iff} & \langle \alpha, i+1 \rangle \models A \\
\langle \alpha, i \rangle \models \Box A & \text{iff} & \text{for all } j \geq i \ \ \langle \alpha, j \rangle \models A \\
\langle \alpha, i \rangle \models \Diamond A & \text{iff} & \text{there exists } j \geq i \ \text{ s.t. } \langle \alpha, j \rangle \models A \\
\langle \alpha, i \rangle \models \exists_x A & \text{iff} & \text{there exists } \alpha' \in \mathcal{C}^\omega \text{ s.t. } \dot{\exists}_x \alpha = \dot{\exists}_x \alpha' \text{ and } \langle \alpha', i \rangle \models A.
\end{array}
$$

We define $[\![A]\!] = \{\alpha \mid \alpha \models A\}$, i.e., the collection of all models of A.

Proving Properties of Processes. We are interested in assertions of the form $P \vdash A$, whose intuitive meaning is that every sequence P can possibly output satisfies the property expressed by A – i.e., that every sequence in $sp(P)$ (Definition 4) is a model of A. An inference system for such assertions is presented in Table 3. We will say that $P \vdash A$ holds if the assertion $P \vdash A$ has a proof in this system.

The following theorem states the soundness and the relative completeness of the proof system.

Theorem 4 (Relative Completeness). *For every ntcc process P and every formula A, $P \vdash A$ holds iff $[\![P]\!] \subseteq [\![A]\!]$ holds.*

Table 3. A proof system for linear temporal properties of ntcc processes

$$\text{P1}\quad \mathbf{tell}(c) \vdash c \qquad\qquad \text{P3}\quad \frac{P \vdash A \quad Q \vdash B}{P \parallel Q \vdash A \wedge B}$$

$$\text{P2}\quad \frac{\forall i \in I \quad P_i \vdash A_i}{\sum_{i\in I} \mathbf{when}\ c_i\ \mathbf{do}\ P_i \vdash \bigvee_{i\in I}(c_i \wedge A_i) \vee \bigwedge_{i\in I} \neg c_i} \qquad \text{P4}\quad \frac{P \vdash A}{\mathbf{local}\ x\ \mathbf{in}\ P \vdash \exists_x A}$$

$$\text{P5}\quad \frac{P \vdash A}{\mathbf{next}\ P \vdash \bigcirc A} \qquad\qquad \text{P6}\quad \frac{P \vdash A}{\mathbf{unless}\ c\ \mathbf{next}\ P \vdash c \vee \bigcirc A}$$

$$\text{P7}\quad \frac{P \vdash A}{!P \vdash \Box A} \qquad\qquad \text{P8}\quad \frac{P \vdash A}{\star P \vdash \Diamond A}$$

$$\text{P9}\quad \frac{P \vdash A}{P \vdash B} \quad \text{if } A \Rightarrow B$$

The reason why this theorem is called "relative completeness" is because of the consequence rule P9 (consequence rule). Proving $A \Rightarrow B$ is known to be decidable for the quantifier-free fragment of linear time temporal formulae as well as for some other interesting first-order fragments (see [10]).

From Theorems 4, 1 and 2 we immediately derive the following:

Corollary 1. *1. For every ntcc process P and every formula A, if $P \vdash A$ holds then $sp(P) \subseteq [\![A]\!]$ holds.*

2. For every local-independent choice ntcc process P and every formula A, $P \vdash A$ holds iff $sp(P) \subseteq [\![A]\!]$ holds.

We shall see that the kind of recursion considered in [16] can be encoded in ntcc. Hence, tcc processes can be considered as a particular case of local-independent choice ntcc processes, and therefore the proof system is complete for tcc.

The following notion will be useful in the Section 4, for discussing properties of our examples.

Definition 6 (Strongest Derivable Formulae). *A formula A is the strongest temporal formula derivable for P if $P \vdash A$ and for all A' such that $P \vdash A'$, we have $A \Rightarrow A'$.*

Note that the strongest temporal formula of a process P is unique modulo logical equivalence. We give now a constructive definition of such formula.

Definition 7 (Strongest Temporal Formula Function). *Let the function* $stf : Proc \to \mathcal{A}$ *be defined as follows:*

$$\begin{array}{ll} stf(\mathbf{tell}(c)) & = c \\ stf(\sum_{i\in I} \mathbf{when}\,(c_i)\,\mathbf{do}\,P_i) & = (\bigvee_{i\in I} c_i \wedge stf(P_i)) \vee \bigwedge_{i\in I} \neg c_i \\ stf(P \parallel Q) & = stf(P) \wedge stf(Q) \\ stf(\mathbf{local}\,x\,P) & = \exists_x stf(P) \\ stf(\mathbf{next}\ P) & = \circ\, stf(P) \\ stf(\mathbf{unless}\ c\ \mathbf{next}\ P) & = c \vee \circ stf(P) \\ stf(!\,P) & = \Box\, stf(P) \\ stf(\star\, P) & = \Diamond\, stf(P). \end{array}$$

We can easily prove that $[\![stf(P)]\!] = [\![P]\!]$ and that $P \vdash stf(P)$. From these we have:

Proposition 1. *For every process* P, $stf(P)$ *is the strongest temporal formula derivable for* P.

Note that to prove that $P \vdash A$ is sufficient to prove that $stf(P) \Rightarrow A$. However, to prove such implication may not be always feasible or possible. The proof system provides the additional flexibility of proving $P \vdash A$ by using the consequence rule (P9) on subprocesses of P and on formulae different from A.

4 Applications

In this section we illustrate some ntcc examples. We first need to define an underlying constraint system.

Definition 8 (A Finite-Domain Constraint System). *Let max be a positive integer number. Define* $FD[max]$ *as the constraint system whose signature* Σ *includes symbols in* $\{0, \mathrm{succ}, +, \times, =\}$ *and the first-order theory* Δ *is the set of sentences valid in arithmetic modulo max.*

The intended meaning of $FD[max]$ is the natural numbers interpreted as in arithmetic modulo max. Henceforth, we assume that the signature is extended with two new unary predicate symbols call and change. We will designate Dom as the set $\{0, 1, ..., max - 1\}$ and use v and w to range over its elements.

Recursion. We can encode recursive definitions of the form $q(x) \stackrel{\text{def}}{=} P_q$, where q is the process name and P_q contains at most one occurrence of q which must be within the scope of a "**next**" and out of the scope of any "!". The reason for such a restriction is that we want to keep bounded the response time of the system.

We also want to consider the call-by-value. This may look unnatural since in constraint programming the natural parameter passing mechanism is through "logical variables", like in logic programming. Indeed, it is more difficult to encode in ntcc call-by-value than "call-by-logical-variable". However, for the kind of applications we have in mind (some of which are illustrated in the rest of this section), call-by-value is the mechanism we need. Note also that we mean call-by-value in the sense of value "persisting through the time intervals", and this would not be possible to achieve directly with the "call-by-logical-variable", because the values of variables are not maintained from one interval to the next. More precisely: The intended behavior of a call $q(t)$, where t is a term fixed to a value v (i.e. $t = v$ in the current store), is that of $P_q[v/x]$, where $[v/x]$ is the operation of (syntactical) replacement of every occurrence of x by v.

Given $q(x) \stackrel{\text{def}}{=} P_q$, we will use $q, qarg$ to denote any two variables not in $fv(P_q)$. Let $\ulcorner x := t \urcorner$ be defined as the process $\sum_v \mathbf{when}\, t = v\, \mathbf{do}\, !\, \mathbf{tell}(x = v)$, i.e., the persistent assignment of t's fixed value to x. Then the ntcc process corresponding to definition of $q(x)$, denoted as $\ulcorner q(x) \stackrel{\text{def}}{=} P_q \urcorner$, is :

$$!\ (\mathbf{when}\ \mathsf{call}(q)\ \mathbf{do}\ \mathbf{local}\, x\ \mathbf{in}\ (\ulcorner x := qarg \urcorner \parallel \ulcorner P_q \urcorner))\,,$$

where $\ulcorner P_q \urcorner$ denotes the process that results from replacing in P_q each $q(t)$ with $\mathbf{tell}(\mathsf{call}(q)) \parallel \mathbf{tell}(qarg = t)$ (thus telling that there is a call of q with argument t). Intuitively, whenever the process q is called with argument $qarg$, the local x is assigned the argument's value so it can be used by q's body $\ulcorner P_q \urcorner$.

We then consider the calls $q(t)$ in other processes. Each such a call is replaced by $\mathbf{local}\, q\, qarg\, \mathbf{in}\, (\ulcorner q(x) \stackrel{\text{def}}{=} P_q \urcorner \parallel \mathbf{tell}(\mathsf{call}(q)) \parallel \mathbf{tell}(qarg = t))$, which we shall denote by $\ulcorner q(t) \urcorner$. The local declarations are needed to avoid interference with other recursive calls.

The above encoding generalizes easily to stratified recursion and to the case of arbitrary number of parameters including the parameterless recursion of tcc considered in [16]. We now show some temporal properties satisfied by the encoding. Next theorem describes the strongest temporal formulae satisfied by $\ulcorner q(t) \urcorner$.

Proposition 2. *Given $\ulcorner q(x) \stackrel{\text{def}}{=} P_q \urcorner$, let B the strongest temporal formula derivable for $\ulcorner P_q \urcorner$. Then the temporal formula*

$$\exists_{q,qarg}(\mathsf{call}(q) \wedge qarg = t \wedge \Box(\mathsf{call}(q) \Rightarrow \exists_x(B \wedge \bigwedge_w (qarg = w \Rightarrow \Box x = w)))$$

is the strongest temporal formula derivable for $\ulcorner q(t) \urcorner$.

The above proposition gives us a proof principle for recursive definitions, i.e., in order to prove that $\ulcorner q(t) \urcorner \vdash A$ it is sufficient to prove that a strongest temporal formula of $\ulcorner q(t) \urcorner$ implies A. The next corollary states a property that one would expect of recursive calls, i.e., if B is satisfied by $q's$ body then $B[v/x]$ should be satisfied by $q(t)$ provided that $t = v$.

Corollary 2. *Given $\ulcorner q(x) \stackrel{\text{def}}{=} P_q \urcorner$, suppose that $q, qarg$ do not occur free in B and $\ulcorner P_q \urcorner \vdash B$. Then for all $v \in Dom$, $\ulcorner q(t) \urcorner \vdash t = v \Rightarrow B[v/x]$.*

Cells. Cells provide a basis for the specification and analysis of mutable and persistent data structures. A *cell* can be thought of as a structure that contains a value, and if tested, it yields this value. A *mutable cell* is a cell that can be assigned a new value[1]. We model mutable cells of the form $x\colon(v)$, which we interpret as a variable x currently fixed to some v.

$$\begin{array}{lcl} x\colon(z) & \stackrel{\text{def}}{=} & \mathbf{tell}(x=z) \parallel \mathbf{unless}\ \mathsf{change}(x)\ \mathbf{next}\ x\colon(z) \\ \mathit{exch}_f(x,y) & \stackrel{\text{def}}{=} & \sum_v \mathbf{when}\ (x=v)\ \mathbf{do}\ (\,\mathbf{tell}(\mathsf{change}(x)) \parallel \mathbf{tell}(\mathsf{change}(y)) \\ & & \qquad\qquad\qquad\qquad \parallel \mathbf{next}(\ulcorner x\colon(f(v))\urcorner \parallel \ulcorner y\colon(v)\urcorner)\ ). \end{array}$$

Definition $x\colon(z)$ represents a cell x whose current content is z. The current content of x will be the same in the next time interval unless it is to be changed next (i.e $\mathsf{change}(x)$). Definition $\mathit{exch}_f(x,y)$ represents an exchange operation between the contents of x and y. If v is x's current value then $f(v)$ and v will be the next x and $y's$ values, respectively. In the case of functions that always return the same value (i.e. constants), we will take the liberty of using that value as its symbol. For example, $\ulcorner x\colon(3)\urcorner \parallel \ulcorner y\colon(5)\urcorner \parallel \ulcorner \mathit{exch}_7(x,y)\urcorner$ gives us the cells $x\colon(7)$ and $y\colon(3)$ in the next time interval.

The following temporal property states the invariant behavior of a cell, i.e., if it satisfies A now, it will satisfy A next unless it is changed.

Proposition 3. *For all $v \in \mathit{Dom}$, $\ulcorner x\colon(v)\urcorner \vdash (A \wedge \neg\mathsf{change}(x)) \Rightarrow \circ A$.*

Zigzagging. An RCX is a programmable, microcontroller-based LEGO® brick used to create autonomous robotic devices (see e.g., [11]). Zigzagging [8] is a task in which an (RCX-based) robot can go either forward, left, or right but (1) it cannot go forward if its preceding action was to go forward, (2) it cannot turn right if its second-to-last action was to go right, and (3) it cannot turn left if its second-to-last action was to go left.

In order to model this problem, without over-specifying it, we use guarded choice and cells. We use cells act_1 and act_2 to be able to "look back" one and two time units, respectively. We use three distinct $\mathtt{f},\mathtt{r},\mathtt{l} \in \mathit{Dom} - \{0\}$ (standing for forward, right and left respectively) and three distinct $\mathtt{forward},\mathsf{right},\mathsf{left} \in \mathcal{C}$.

$$\begin{array}{lcl} \mathit{GoForward} & \stackrel{\text{def}}{=} & \ulcorner \mathit{exch}_{\mathtt{f}}(act_1, act_2)\urcorner \parallel \mathbf{tell}(\mathtt{forward}) \\ \mathit{GoRight} & \stackrel{\text{def}}{=} & \ulcorner \mathit{exch}_{\mathtt{r}}(act_1, act_2)\urcorner \parallel \mathbf{tell}(\mathsf{right}) \\ \mathit{GoLeft} & \stackrel{\text{def}}{=} & \ulcorner \mathit{exch}_{\mathtt{l}}(act_1, act_2)\urcorner \parallel \mathbf{tell}(\mathtt{left}) \\ \mathit{Zigzag} & \stackrel{\text{def}}{=} & (\ \mathbf{when}\,(act_1 \neq \mathtt{f})\,\mathbf{do}\,\ulcorner \mathit{GoForward}\urcorner \\ & & +\ \mathbf{when}\,(act_2 \neq \mathtt{r})\,\mathbf{do}\,\ulcorner \mathit{GoRight}\urcorner \\ & & +\ \mathbf{when}\,(act_2 \neq \mathtt{l})\,\mathbf{do}\,\ulcorner \mathit{GoLeft}\urcorner\ ) \\ & & \parallel\ \mathbf{next}\ \mathit{Zigzag} \\ \mathit{StartZigzag} & \stackrel{\text{def}}{=} & \ulcorner act_1\colon(0)\urcorner \parallel \ulcorner act_2\colon(0)\urcorner \parallel \ulcorner \mathit{Zigzag}\urcorner. \end{array}$$

---

[1] A richer notion of cell can be found in ccp based models such as the Oz calculus [19], the π^+ calculus [6], and PiCO [1].

Initially cells act_1 and act_2 contain neither f,r nor l. Just before a choice is made act_1 and act_2 contain the previous and the second-to-last taken actions (if any). After a choice is made according to (1), (2) and (3), the choice is recorded in act_1 and the previous choice moved to act_2. The definitions of the various processes are self-explanatory.

The next temporal property states that the robot chooses to go right and left infinitely often.

Proposition 4. $\ulcorner StartZigzag \urcorner \vdash \Box(\Diamond \texttt{right} \wedge \Diamond \texttt{left})$.

Other RCX examples modeled by ntcc includes a crane [20] and a wall-avoiding robot [20].

Value-passing Communication. Value passing plays an important role in several process calculi. Suppose that $x \uparrow (v)$ denotes the action of writing a value (or message) v in channel x which is then kept in the channel for one time unit. We assume that in the same time unit, two different values cannot be written in the same channel. The notation $x \downarrow_{P[y]}$ represents the action of reading, without consuming, the value (if any) in channel x which is then used in P. The variable y, which may occur free in P, is the placeholder for the read value. Several read actions can get the same value if they read the same channel in the same time interval. These basic actions can be defined as $x \uparrow (y) \stackrel{\text{def}}{=} \mathbf{tell}(x = y)$ and $x \downarrow_{P[y]} \stackrel{\text{def}}{=} \sum_v \mathbf{when}\ (x = v)\ \mathbf{do}\, \mathbf{local}\, y\, \mathbf{in}\, (!\, \mathbf{tell}(y = v) \parallel P)$.

Having defined the two basic actions, we can specify different behaviors, e.g., process $!\,(\star_{[0,1]}(x \downarrow_{P[y]}))$ checks "very often" for messages in channel x. Here we illustrate a form of asynchronous broadcasting communication.

$$\begin{aligned} SendAsyn_x(y) &\stackrel{\text{def}}{=} \star(\ulcorner x \uparrow (y) \urcorner) \\ Waiting_{Q,x} &\stackrel{\text{def}}{=} \mathbf{local}\, stop\, \mathbf{in}\, (\ \ulcorner x \downarrow_{(Q \parallel \mathbf{tell}(stop=1))[y]} \urcorner \\ &\qquad\qquad \parallel \mathbf{unless}\, stop = 1\, \mathbf{next}\ Waiting_{Q,x}). \end{aligned}$$

Process $SendAsyn_x(v)$ asynchronously sends value v in channel x. Process $Waiting_{Q,x}$ waits for a value in channel x. Note that, if a process is waiting at the time $SendAsyn_x(v)$ is executed, then it is guaranteed to get the value, while other processes may not get it. This property is expressed by the following result.

Proposition 5. *Suppose that* $Q \vdash B$ *and* $stop \notin fv(Q)$. *Then for all* $v \in Dom$,

$$\ulcorner SendAsyn_x(v) \urcorner \parallel \ulcorner Waiting_{Q,x} \urcorner \vdash \Diamond B[v/y].$$

5 Related and Future Work

Our proposal is a strict extension of tcc [16], in the sense that tcc can be encoded in (the restricted-choice subset of) ntcc, while the vice-versa is not possible because tcc does not have constructs to express non-determinism or unbounded finite-delay. In [16] the authors proposed also a proof system for tcc, based on an intuitionistic logic enriched with a next operator. The system, however, is complete only for hiding-free and recursion-free processes. In contrast our system is based on the standard classical temporal logic of [12] and is complete for local-independent choice ntcc processes, hence also for tcc processes. Other extension of tcc, which does not consider non-determinism or unbounded finite-delay, has been proposed in [17]. This extension adds strong pre-emption: the "unless" can trigger activity in the current time interval. In contrast, ntcc can only express weak pre-emption. As argued in [4], in the *specification* of (large) timed systems weak pre-emption often suffices (and non-determinism is crucial). Nevertheless, strong pre-emption is important for reactive systems. In principle, strong pre-emption could be incorporated in ntcc: Semantically one would have to consider assumptions about the future evolutions of the system. As for the logic, one would have to consider a temporal extension of Default Logic [15].

The tccp calculus [4] is the only other proposal for a non-deterministic timed extension of ccp that we know of. One major difference with our approach is that the information about the store is carried through the time units, so the semantic setting is rather different. The notion of time is also different; in tccp each time unit is identified with the time needed to ask and tell information to the store. As for the constructs, unlike ntcc, tccp provides for arbitrary recursion and does not have an operator for specifying (unbounded) finite-delay. A proof system for tccp processes was recently introduced in [3]. The underlying linear temporal logic in [3] can be used for describing input-output behavior while our logic can only be used for the strongest-postcondition. As such the temporal logic of ntcc processes is less expressive than that one underlying the proof system of tccp, but it is also semantically simpler and defined as the standard linear-temporal logic of [12]. This may come in handy when using the Consequence Rule which is also present in [3].

The plan for future research includes the extension of ntcc to a probabilistic model following ideas in [9]. This is justified by the existence of RCX program examples involving stochastic behavior which cannot be faithfully modeled with non-deterministic behavior. In a more practical setting we plan to define a programming language for RCX controllers based on ntcc.

Acknowledgments. We are indebted to Mogens Nielsen for having suggested and discussed this work. We thank Andrzej Filinski, Maurizio Gabbrielli, Camilo Rueda, Dale Miller, Vineet Gupta, Radha Jagadeesan and Kim Larsen for helpful comments on various aspects of this work. Thanks goes also to Paulo Oliva, Daniele Varacca, Oliver Moeller, Federico Crazzolara, Giuseppe Milicia and Pawel Sobocinski.

References

1. G. Alvarez, J.F. Diaz, L.O. Quesada, C. Rueda, G. Tamura, F. Valencia, and G. Assayag. Integrating constraints and concurrent objects in musical applications: A calculus and its visual language. *Constraints*, January 2001.

2. G. Berry and G. Gonthier. The ESTEREL synchronous programming language: design, semantics, implementation. *Science of Computer Programming*, 19(2):87–152, November 1992.
3. F. de Boer, M. Gabbrielli, and M. Chiara. A temporal logic for reasoning about timed concurrent constraint programs. In *TIME 01*. IEEE Press, 2001.
4. F. de Boer, M. Gabbrielli, and M. C. Meo. A timed concurrent constraint language. *Information and Computation*, 1999. To appear.
5. F. S. de Boer, M. Gabbrielli, E. Marchiori, and C. Palamidessi. Proving concurrent constraint programs correct. *ACM Transactions on Programming Languages and Systems*, 19(5):685–725, 1997.
6. J.F. Diaz, C. Rueda, and F. Valencia. A calculus for concurrent processes with constraints. *CLEI Electronic Journal*, 1(2), December 1998.
7. M. Falaschi, M. Gabbrielli, K. Marriott, and C. Palamidessi. Confluence in concurrent constraint programming. *Theoretical Computer Science*, 183(2):281–315, 1997.
8. J. Fredslund. The assumption architecture. Progress Report, Department of Computer Science, University of Aarhus, November 1999.
9. O. Herescu and C. Palamidessi. Probabilistic asynchronous pi-calculus. *FoSSaCS*, pages 146–160, 2000.
10. I. Hodkinson, F. Wolter, and M. Zakharyaschev. Decidable fragments of first-order temporal logics. In *Annals of Pure and Applied Logic*, 2000.
11. H. H. Lund and L. Pagliarini. Robot soccer with LEGO mindstorms. *Lecture Notes in Computer Science*, 1604, 1999.
12. Z. Manna and A. Pnueli. *The Temporal Logic of Reactive and Concurrent Systems, Specification.* Springer, 1991.
13. R. Milner. A finite delay operator in synchronous ccs. Technical Report CSR-116-82, University of Edinburgh, 1992.
14. R. Milner. *Communicating and Mobile Systems: the π-calculus.* Cambridge University Press, 1999.
15. R. Reiter. A logic for default reasoning. *Artificial Intelligence*, 13(1–2):81–132, April 1980.
16. V. Saraswat, R. Jagadeesan, and V. Gupta. Foundations of timed concurrent constraint programming. In *Proc. of the Ninth Annual IEEE Symposium on Logic in Computer Science*, pages 71–80, 4–7 July 1994.
17. V. Saraswat, R. Jagadeesan, and V. Gupta. Timed default concurrent constraint programming. *Journal of Symbolic Computation*, 22(5–6):475–520, November–December 1996.
18. V. Saraswat, M. Rinard, and P. Panangaden. The semantic foundations of concurrent constraint programming. In *POPL '91. Proceedings of the eighteenth annual ACM symposium on Principles of programming languages*, pages 333–352, 21–23 January 1991.
19. G. Smolka. The Oz programming model. In Jan van Leeuwen, editor, *Computer Science Today*, Lecture Notes in Computer Science, vol. 1000, pages 324–343. Springer-Verlag, Berlin, 1995.
20. F. Valencia. Reactive constraint programming. Progress Report, BRICS, June 2000. Availabe via http://www.brics.dk/~fvalenci/publications.html.
21. G. Winskel. *The Formal Semantics of Programming Languages.* The MIT Press, 1993.

Lower Bounds for Non-binary Constraint Optimization Problems*

Pedro Meseguer[1], Javier Larrosa[2], and Martì Sánchez[1]

[1] IIIA-CSIC, Campus UAB, 08193 Bellaterra, Spain
{pedro|marti}@iiia.csic.es
[2] Dep. LSI, UPC, Jordi Girona Salgado, 1-3, 08034 Barcelona, Spain
larrosa@lsi.upc.es

Abstract. The necessity of non-binary constraint satisfaction algorithms is increasing because many real problems are inherently non-binary. Considering overconstrained problems (and Partial Forward Checking as the solving algorithm), we analyze several lower bounds proposed in the binary case, extending them for the non-binary case. We show that techniques initially developed in the context of reversible DAC can be applied in the general case, to deal with constraints of any arity. We discuss some of the issues raised for non-binary lower bounds, and we study their computational complexity. We provide experimental results of the use of the new lower bounds on overconstrained random problems, including constraints with different weights.

1 Introduction

In the context of constraint satisfaction, increasing attention has been devoted to soft constraints in the last years. A constraint is *soft* when it can be violated by some solution, without making such solution unacceptable. A constraint is *hard* when it has to be satisfied by every solution. Soft constraints are used to express user preferences, which should be satisfied if possible but not necessarily, enhancing greatly the expressiveness of constraint programming. The inclusion of soft constraints has extended the CSP schema, which considers hard constraints only, into the VCSP [11] and Semiring CSP [3] schemas, able to model overconstrained problems for which a solution is the complete assignment that satisfies all hard constraints and best respects soft ones.

In parallel to these theoretical advances, new algorithms have appeared, able to solve with increasing efficiency different types of overconstrained CSPs. For simplicity reasons these algorithms assume binary constraints. However, beyond the theoretical equivalence between binary and non-binary formulations (see [8] for its applicability to overconstrained CSPs), nowadays is widely recognized the interest of solving directly non-binary constraints for real problems. As the CSP

* This work was supported by the IST Programme of the Commission of the European Union through the ECSPLAIN project (IST-1999-11969), and by the Spanish CICYT project TAP99-1086-C03.

T. Walsh (Ed.): CP 2001, LNCS 2239, pp. 317–331, 2001.

experience has shown, real problems are inherently non-binary and solving their natural formulation often causes significant improvements.

In this paper, we aim to bridge the gap between state-of-the-art algorithms and solving requirements of real problems, extending previously developed algorithms for binary soft constraints into the non-binary case. This is done for constrained optimization problems, a class of problems that includes those overconstrained CSPs that use the addition of costs of no satisfied constraints as the objective function to be minimized when searching for a solution. In particular, this class includes the Max-CSP problem, for which all constraints are soft with the same weight. Results presented here can be easily adapted to other kinds of problems including soft constraints.

The structure of the paper is as follows. In Section 2 we present some basic concepts. In Section 3 we study five binary lower bound formulations. In Section 4 we develop the corresponding non-binary lower bounds, analyzing their usage in the Partial Forward Checking algorithm. In Section 5 we provide experimental results using these lower bounds on overconstrained random 5-ary problems. Finally, Section 6 contains the conclusions and directions for further research.

2 Preliminaries

2.1 CSP and COP

A finite *constraint satisfaction problem* (CSP) is defined by a triple $(\mathcal{X}, \mathcal{D}, \mathcal{C})$,

- $\mathcal{X} = \{x_1, \ldots, x_n\}$ is a set of n variables;
- $\mathcal{D} = \{D_0(x_1), \ldots, D_0(x_n)\}$ is a collection of finite domains; $D_0(x_i)$ is the initial set of possible values for x_i, while $D(x_i)$ is the current set of possible values for x_i;
- $\mathcal{C}$ is a set of constraints among variables. A constraint c_i on the ordered set of variables $var(c_i) = (x_{i_1}, \ldots, x_{i_{r(i)}})$, called the scope of c_i, specifies the relation $rel_0(c_i)$ of the *allowed* combinations of values for the variables in $var(c_i)$. An element of $rel_0(c_i)$ is a tuple $(v_{i_1}, \ldots, v_{i_{r(i)}})$, $v_{i_k} \in D_0(x_{i_k})$. During search, valid tuples are reduced to $rel(c_i) \subseteq rel_0(c_i)$ formed by non-pruned values. An element of $rel(c_i)$ is a tuple $(v_{i_1}, \ldots, v_{i_{r(i)}})$, $v_{i_k} \in D(x_{i_k})$[1].

An assignment of values to variables is complete if it involves all variables, otherwise is partial. A *solution* is a complete assignment satisfying all constraints. Solving a CSP is an NP-*complete* problem.

The scope size of a constraint is its *arity*. The arity of a problem is the maximum arity of its constraints. In the sequel, n, d, m and r will denote the number of variables, the largest domain size, the number of constraints and the problem arity. Letters $i, j, k \ldots$ denote variable indexes (x_i is referred as variable i), $a, b, \ldots$ denote values, and a pair (i, a) denotes the value a of variable i.

[1] In this paper, we assume that constraints are expressed extensionally through relations. Constraints can also be expressed intentionally, by a mathematical formula or a procedure.

The join of two relations $rel_0(c_i)$ and $rel_0(c_j)$, denoted by $rel_0(c_i) \bowtie rel_0(c_j)$, is the set of tuples over $var(c_i) \cup var(c_j)$ satisfying the two constraints c_i and c_j. Accordingly, the join of two tuples is their union if they *match* in their common variables or the empty tuple otherwise. The subset of variables involved in tuple t is $var(t)$. The projection of a tuple t on a particular variable i is denoted by $t[i]$. The projection of set $\mathcal{X}$ over a subset Y is denoted by $\mathcal{X}[Y]$.

A finite *constraint optimization problem* (COP) is defined by a triple $(\mathcal{X}, \mathcal{D}, \mathcal{C})$, where $\mathcal{X}$ and $\mathcal{D}$ are as in the CSP case, and $\mathcal{C}$ is a set of *cost functions* $\mathcal{C} = \{f_1, \ldots, f_m\}$ which denote *preferences* among tuples. A cost function f_i is,

$$f_i : \prod_{x_j \in var(f_i)} D_0(x_j) \to R^+$$

where R^+ is the set of non-negative real numbers. Low values of $f_i(t)$ mean high preferences for tuple t, while high values of $f_i(t)$ mean low preferences for t. The extreme values for cost functions, namely 0 and ∞, represent the most and the least preferred tuples, respectively[2]. Tuple t is consistent with constraint f_i iif $f_i(t) = 0$; otherwise it is inconsistent. The objective function, also called the *global cost function*, is the sum of all individuals cost functions,

$$F^*(\mathcal{X}) = \sum_{i=1}^{m} f_i(\mathcal{X}[var(f_i)])$$

The *solution* is the complete assignment that minimizes $F^*(\mathcal{X})$. Solving a COP is an NP-*hard* problem.

Problems with soft constraints can naturally be formulated as COPs. Observe that, without loss of generality, hard constraints can also be expressed in this model as functions returning two values: 0 for allowed tuples and ∞ for disallowed ones. Also, the Max-CSP problem is formulated as a COP using constraints returning two values: 0 for allowed tuples and 1 for disallowed ones.

2.2 Solving COP

Partial Forward Checking (PFC) is a depth-first search algorithm used to solve COPs. It follows a *Branch and Bound* (BB) schema. At any point in search, P is the set of assigned or *past* variables, while F is the set of unassigned or *future* ones. The current partial assignment is the tuple τ over the set P. Regarding constraints, $\mathcal{C}_\mathcal{P}$ is the set of constraints having only past variables in their scope, $\mathcal{C}_\mathcal{F}$ is the set of constraints having only future variables in their scope, and $\mathcal{C}_{\mathcal{P}\mathcal{F}}$ is set of constraints having past and future variables in their scope.

BB traverses the search tree defined by the problem and it keeps the cost of the best solution found so far (complete assignment with minimum global cost in the explored part of the search tree). This cost is an *upper bound* (UB) of

[2] Alternatively, you could say that if $f_i(t) = 0$, tuple t satisfies completely the ith constraint, and if $f_i(t) = \infty$, tuple t violates completely the ith constraint.

the problem solution. At each node, BB computes an underestimation of the global cost of any leaf node descendant from the current one. This value is a *lower bound* (LB) of the best solution that can be found as long as the current search path is maintained. When $UB \leq LB$, the current best solution cannot be improved below the current node, so the current branch can be pruned.

Upon this schema, PFC performs lookahead at each node, assessing the impact of the current assignment into the set F. Lookahead allows to improve the quality of LB computed by BB. In addition, lookahead enables the computation of LB_{ia}, a specialization of LB for value a of future variable i. If $UB \leq LB_{ia}$, value a can be removed because it will not be present in any solution better than the current one. Removed values have to be restored when PFC backtracks above the node where they were eliminated.

3 Binary Case

For binary Max-CSP, the following types of inconsistency counters have been used when computing lower bounds.

- *Distance* [4]:

$$distance(\tau, \mathcal{C}_{\mathcal{P}}) = card\{c \in \mathcal{C}_{\mathcal{P}} | \tau \bowtie rel_0(c) = \emptyset\}$$

- *Inconsistency counts* [4]:

$$ic_{ia} = card\{c \in \mathcal{C}_{\mathcal{P}\mathcal{F}} | i \in var(c) \cap F, \tau \bowtie (i,a) \bowtie rel_0(c) = \emptyset\}$$

- *Directed arc-inconsistency counts* [16]: (static variable ordering)

$$dac_{ia} = card\{c \in \mathcal{C}_{\mathcal{F}} | var(c) = \{i,j\}, i < j, (i,a) \bowtie rel_0(c) = \emptyset\}$$

- *Reversible DAC* [7]: (G^F is a directed graph on $\mathcal{C}_{\mathcal{F}}$)

$$dac_{ia}(G^F) = card\{c \in \mathcal{C}_{\mathcal{F}} | var(c) = \{i,j\}, (j,i) \in \textsc{Edges}(G^F), (i,a) \bowtie rel_0(c) = \emptyset\}$$

- *Arc-inconsistency counts* [1]:

$$ac_{ia} = card\{c \in \mathcal{C}_{\mathcal{F}} | i \in var(c), (i,a) \bowtie rel_0(c) = \emptyset\}$$

- *Russian Doll Search* [15]:

$$RDS(F, \mathcal{C}_{\mathcal{F}}) = min_t\{distance(t, \mathcal{C}_{\mathcal{F}})\} \qquad t \in \prod_{j \in F} D_0(x_j)$$

Max-CSP assumes that every tuple unsatisfying any constraint has the same cost. This is a simplification that does not hold in general. Many real problems include constraints which can be unsatisfied with different costs. These problems can be formulated in terms of COPs, where constraints are represented by cost functions. We define the *initial cost* of value (i, a) in constraint f as,

$$icost(i, a, f) = min_{t[i]=a} f(t) \qquad t \in \prod_{j \in var(f)} D_0(x_j)$$

When search proceeds domains change. Every past variable has its domain reduced to its assigned value. Future domains may be reduced because value pruning. We define the *current cost* of value (i, a) in constraint f as,

$$ccost(i, a, f) = min_{t[i]=a} f(t) \qquad t \in \prod_{j \in var(f)} D(x_j)$$

Using these notions, previous counters can be easily generalized for COPs as,

- *Distance*:
$$distance(\tau, \mathcal{C_P}) = \sum_{f \in \mathcal{C_P}} f(\tau[var(f)])$$
- *Inconsistency counts*:
$$ic_{ia} = \sum_{f \in \mathcal{C_{PF}}} ccost(i, a, f)$$
- *Directed arc-inconsistency counts*: (static variable ordering)
$$dac_{ia} = \sum_{f \in \mathcal{C_F}, var(f)=\{i,j\}, i<j} icost(i, a, f)$$
- *Reversible DAC*: (G^F is a directed graph on $\mathcal{C_F}$)
$$dac_{ia}(G^F) = \sum_{f \in \mathcal{C_F}, var(f)=\{i,j\}, (j,i) \in \text{EDGES}(G^F)} icost(i, a, f)$$
- *Arc-inconsistency counts*:
$$ac_{ia} = \sum_{f \in \mathcal{C_F}} icost(i, a, f)$$
- *Russian Doll Search*:
$$RDS(F, \mathcal{C_F}) = min_t\{distance(t, \mathcal{C_F})\} \qquad t \in \prod_{j \in F} D_0(x_j)$$

These counters no longer record numbers of inconsistencies, but they aggregate costs caused by inconsistencies in COPs. We maintain their names as in the Max-CSP case for homogeneity reasons. From these elements, five lower bounds have been proposed. They appear in Figure 1. Lower bounds LB_2 and LB_3 require a static variable ordering.

Counters dac_{ia}, $dac_{ia}(G^F)$ and ac_{ia} are defined in terms of *icost*. They can equally be defined in terms of *ccost*. In that case, the word *maintained* is added to their names, to emphasize that those counters are maintained updated during search, taking into account value deletions in future domains. This requires the use of an arc-consistency algorithm. This approach was followed in [7].

$$LB_1(P,F) = distance(\tau, \mathcal{C_P}) + \sum_{i \in F} \min_a(ic_{ia}) \quad [4]$$

$$LB_2(P,F) = distance(\tau, \mathcal{C_P}) + \sum_{i \in F} \min_a(ic_{ia} + dac_{ia}) \quad [16,6]$$

$$LB_3(P,F) = distance(\tau, \mathcal{C_P}) + \sum_{i \in F} \min_a(ic_{ia}) + RDS(F, \mathcal{C_F}) \quad [15]$$

$$LB_4(P,F) = distance(\tau, \mathcal{C_P}) + \sum_{i \in F} \min_a(ic_{ia} + \frac{1}{2}ac_{ia}) \quad [1]$$

$$LB_5(P,F,G^F) = distance(\tau, \mathcal{C_P}) + \sum_{i \in F} \min_a(ic_{ia} + dac_{ia}(G^F)) \quad [7]$$

Fig. 1. Five lower bounds for binary COPs.

4 Non-binary Case

4.1 Lower Bounds

In the binary case, all constraints in $\mathcal{C_{PF}}$ have one future variable in their scope. This is no longer true in the non-binary case: a constraint $f \in \mathcal{C_{PF}}$ may have more than one future variable in its scope. If all extensions of τ are inconsistent with f and this is recorded in all its future variables, the lower bound cannot be added over the set F because the cost of the same inconsistency could be counted as many times as future variables are involved in the constraint. To prevent this, costs of inconsistencies of f have to be recorded in one of its future variables only. The same problem appears when considering a constraint $f' \in \mathcal{C_F}$: inconsistencies of f' have to be recorded in one of its future variables, in order to allow for a safe lower bound computation as the addition of contributions of future variables. Therefore, for each $f \in \mathcal{C_{PF}} \cup \mathcal{C_F}$ we select one of its future variables as the only variable recording the costs of f inconsistencies. This variable, denoted as var_f, may change during the solving process among the future variables of the constraint. An example of this problem appears in Figure 2. In the Max-CSP context, this idea was presented in [9] (Section 4.2), at the ECAI-00 workshop *Modelling and Solving Problems with Constraints.* A similar approach was presented in [10] (Section 4.1), as a poster at the CP-00 conference.

This problem occurs for ic_{ia} and dac_{ia} counters. From a graph point of view, the constraint hypergraph formed by $\mathcal{C_{PF}} \cup \mathcal{C_F}$ has to be directed, in the sense that each hyperedge points towards one of the nodes that it connects. The hyperedge representing constraint f points towards the node representing variable var_f. Denoting by G^{PF} the directed hypergraph formed by $\mathcal{C_{PF}}$, and by G^F the directed hypergraph formed by $\mathcal{C_F}$, we generalize binary ic_{ia} and dac_{ia} counters as follows.

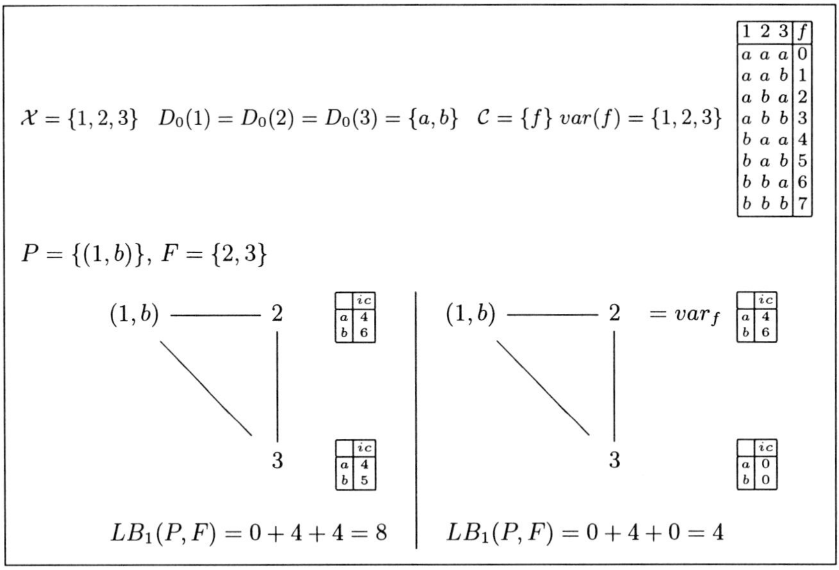

Fig. 2. A simple problem composed of three variables and one ternary constraint f. After assigning b to variable 1, all possible extensions of the current tuple are inconsistent with f. Recording the cost of these inconsistencies in every future variable of f causes to repeat the same cost in the computation of the lower bound, what renders it unsafe (left). The cost of inconsistencies is recorded in one future variable of f, var_f, causing a safe lower bound computation (right).

- *Inconsistency counts*: (G^{PF} is a directed hypergraph on $\mathcal{C}_{\mathcal{PF}}$)

$$ic_{ia}(G^{PF}) = \sum_{f \in \mathcal{C}_{\mathcal{PF}}, i = var_f} ccost(i, a, f)$$

- *Reversible DAC*: (G^F is a directed hypergraph on $\mathcal{C}_{\mathcal{F}}$)

$$dac_{ia}(G^F) = \sum_{f \in \mathcal{C}_{\mathcal{F}}, i = var_f} icost(i, a, f)$$

We maintain the IC and DAC names for pedagogical reasons, to keep a parallelism with the binary case. Observe, however, that in the non-binary case both counters record costs of directed inconsistencies, otherwise the cost of the same inconsistency could be recorded more than once. Keeping the meaning of $distance(\tau, \mathcal{C}_{\mathcal{P}})$, ac_{ia} and $RDS(F, \mathcal{C}_{\mathcal{F}})$ as in the binary case, we present the lower bounds for the non-binary COPs in Fig. 3. They correspond to the binary ones of Section 3 by using the same index, but for LB_2, which is now subsumed by LB_5. $LB_3(P, F, G^{PF})$ requires a static variable ordering.

As in the binary case, $dac_{ia}(G^F)$ are defined in terms of $icost$, but they can be defined in terms of $ccost$. In that case, $dac_{ia}(G^F)$ are maintained updated

$$LB_1(P,F,G^{PF}) = distance(\tau,\mathcal{C}_{\mathcal{P}}) + \sum_{i\in F} \min_a(ic_{ia}(G^{PF}))$$

$$LB_3(P,F,G^{PF}) = distance(\tau,\mathcal{C}_{\mathcal{P}}) + \sum_{i\in F} \min_a(ic_{ia}(G^{PF})) + RDS(F,\mathcal{C}_{\mathcal{F}})$$

$$LB_4(P,F,G^{PF}) = distance(\tau,\mathcal{C}_{\mathcal{P}}) + \sum_{i\in F} \min_a(ic_{ia}(G^{PF}) + \frac{1}{r}ac_{ia})$$

$$LB_5(P,F,G^{PF},G^{F}) = distance(\tau,\mathcal{C}_{\mathcal{P}}) + \sum_{i\in F} \min_a(ic_{ia}(G^{PF}) + dac_{ia}(G^{F}))$$

Fig. 3. Four lower bounds for non-binary COPs.

during search, taking into account value deletions. Any arc consistency strategy can be used for this purpose.

4.2 Partial Forward Checking

A PFC algorithm to be used with the proposed non-binary lower bounds is presented in Figure 4, where a generic lower bound is computed by the function LB. It follows the PFC algorithm of [7]. First, it checks if no more variables exists, then updates $BestS$ and $BestD$ (lines 1,2,3), the best solution and distance respectively. Otherwise, it selects a future variable i (line 5) and iterates on its feasible values (line 6). It assigns value a to variable i, it computes the new distance $newD$ (line 7), and it checks if the lower bound has reached the upper bound (line 8). If not, the lookahead is performed, returning new future domains $newFD$ (line 9). If no empty domain has been produced, a greedy optimization procedure is executed, redirecting the hypergraphs G^{PF} (for LB_1, LB_3, LB_4, LB_5) and G^F (for LB_5) in order to increase the lower bound (getting the optimum redirection of hypergraphs is a NP-hard problem [12], so we redirect hyperedges aiming at a *good* contribution to the lower bound). If the new lower bound does not reach the upper bound (line 12), it tries to remove value b in future variable j using the delete procedure (line 13). This is done redirecting the hypergraphs G^{PF} (for LB_1, LB_3, LB_4, LB_5) and G^F (for LB_5) in order to get the maximum contribution to LB_{jb}. If no empty domain has been produced (line 14), the process goes on with the recursive call (line 15).

This algorithm does not perform any maintenance of counters as values are pruned (which would imply redefining counters substituting *icost* by *ccost*). The inclusion of counter maintenance into the non-binary case is conceptually direct, although it can be computationally expensive.

```
procedure PFC(S, d, F, FD, G^PF, G^F)
if (F = ∅)
  BestD ← d;
  BestS ← S;
else
  i ← PopAVariable(F)
  for each (a ∈ FD_i)
    newD ← Distance(S ∪ {(i, a)});
    if (LB < BestD)
      newFD ← Lookahead(i, a, F, FD);
      if (¬ WipeOut(newFD))
        newG^PF, newG^F ← GreedyOpt(G^PF, G^F);
        if (LB < BestD)
          newFD ← Delete(F, newFD, newG^PF, newG^F);
          if (¬WipeOut(newFD))
            PFC(S ∪ {(i, a)}, newD, F, newFD, newG^PF, newG^F)
```

Fig. 4. Partial Forward Checking.

4.3 Complexity Analysis

In this subsection we discuss the time complexity of computing the proposed lower bounds. We begin with the complexity of each counter,

- $distance(\tau, \mathcal{C_P})$ requires to check whether the current assignment is consistent with every constraint in $\mathcal{C_P}$. Considering a consistency check a constant time operation, $distance(\tau, \mathcal{C_P})$ is time $O(e)$.

- $ic_{ia}(G^{PF})$ requires to explore constraints in $\mathcal{C_{PF}}$ having $i = var_c$ (there are at most e of these constraints). For them, one has to compute if $\tau \bowtie (i, a) \bowtie rel(c)$ is empty. There are at most $r - 2$ *free* variables among which to search for the right values, consequently it can be done with at most $exp(r - 2)$ consistency checks. Thus, the cost of computing ic_{ia} is $O(e \times exp(r - 2))$.

- $dac_{ia}(G^F)$ is also $O(e \times exp(r - 1))$. The exponential part (the individual contribution of each constraint) can be done prior search and recorded in an internal data structure.

- ac_{ia} is basically equivalent to compute dac_{ia} and has the same complexity.

- $RDS(F, \mathcal{C_F})$ amounts solving $n - 1$ problems with size (i.e. number of variables) $1, 2, \ldots, n - 1$. Clearly, this is time $O(exp(n - 1))$ and can be done as a pre-process, prior search.

Table 1. Complexity of computing the lower bounds of Figure 3

LB	pre-processing complexity	per node complexity
1	$O(1)$	$O(n \times d \times e \times exp(r-2))$
3	$O(exp(n-1))$	$O(n \times d \times e \times exp(r-2))$
4	$O(n \times d \times e \times exp(r-1))$	$O(n \times d \times e \times exp(r-2))$
5	$O(n \times d \times e \times exp(r-1))$	$O(n \times d \times e \times exp(r-2))$

Taking into account the previous complexities, is easy to see the complexity of computing each of the lower bounds considered in this paper. We differentiate between the work that has to be done at each node (and therefore, repeated a number of times exponential in the problem size) and the work that can be done prior search (and therefore, only one time). For the sake of clarity and easy comparison, these complexities are depicted in Table 1.

4.4 Limited Versions

The complexity per node of all lower bounds is exponential in the problem arity. As a consequence, they may be of no practical use in problems having large arity constraints. With a closer look, we see that complexity is exponential in $r-2$, while $r-1$ is the number of future variables that a constraint may have in its scope. If we limit the constraints to be processed to those having at most k future variables in their scope [3], we assure that the cost of the processing will be below some complexity threshold, having less accurate inconsistency counters. Controlled by parameter k, the new counters are defined as follows,

- *k-inconsistency counts*: (G^{PF} is a directed hypergraph on $\mathcal{C}_{\mathcal{PF}}$)

$$ic_{ia}(G^{PF}) = \sum_{f \in \mathcal{C}_{\mathcal{PF}}, |var_f \cap F| \leq k, i = var_f} ccost(i, a, f)$$

- *k-reversible DAC*: (G^F is a directed hypergraph on $\mathcal{C}_{\mathcal{F}}$)

$$dac_{ia}(G^F) = \sum_{f \in \mathcal{C}_{\mathcal{F}}, |var_f| \leq k, i = var_f} icost(i, a, f)$$

- *k-arc-inconsistency counts*:

$$ac_{ia} = \sum_{f \in \mathcal{C}_{\mathcal{F}}, |var_f| \leq k} icost(i, a, f)$$

Clearly, their time complexity is bounded by $O(exp(k-1))$ and the increment of k produces the detection of more inconsistencies. Thus, parameter k controls the trade-off between overhead and accuracy.

[3] The idea of only processing those constraints with at most k future variables was presented in [2], in the context of non-binary forward checking.

5 Experimental Results

We have evaluated the performance of our PFC algorithm using the proposed lower bounds on random COPs of arity 5. A random COP class of arity 5 is characterized by $\langle n, d, p_1, p_2, w_{min}, w_{max} \rangle$ where n is the number of variables, d the number of values per variable, p_1 the graph *connectivity* defined as the ratio of existing constraints over the total number of possible constraints $\binom{n}{5}$, and p_2 the constraint *tightness* defined as the ratio of value 5-tuples that are inconsistent with the constraint over the total number of possible 5-tuples d^5. The constrained variables and the inconsistent value tuples are randomly selected, as in the random CSP case [14]. Given a tuple t inconsistent with constraint f, the value of $f(t)$ is randomly selected from the integer interval $[w_{min}, w_{max}]$.

Using this model, we have experimented on the following problem classes: $\langle 10, 5, \frac{25}{252}, p2, 1, 1 \rangle$ and $\langle 10, 5, \frac{25}{252}, p2, 1, 100 \rangle$. The first class represents Max-CSP problems, because all inconsistent tuples have the same cost. The second class represents Weighted CSP, and the costs of inconsistent tuples are randomly distributed between 1 and 100. Connectivity is low because of the high constraint arity. Tightness varies from 0.6 to 1, to get overconstrained instances.

Each problem is solved by PFC using different lower bounds (including limited versions). When using LB_3, PFC uses a static variable ordering defined heuristically to decrease bandwidth. Otherwise, PFC uses *domain size* divided by *forward degree* as dynamic variable ordering. Values are selected randomly. The computation of different lower bounds shares code and data structures whenever it is possible. Experiments were performed on a Sun Ultra 60. Each point is averaged over 50 executions.

The first experiment aims at evaluating the performance of redirecting the directed hypergraph G^{PF} to increment the lower bound. This technique was introduced for binary DAC in [7]. Using the simplest lower bound, LB_1, problems are solved by PFC without optimizing the lower bound [4] (that is, removing lines 11, 12 and 13 of Figure 4) and by standard PFC. Results appear in Figure 5. We can see that optimizing the lower bound always implies a decrement in the number of visited nodes. For Max-CSP problems, this causes a decrement in CPU time as well. For Weighed CSP, the mean CPU time for both executions is practically equal: the optimization overhead compensates the optimized savings.

The second experiment tries to assess the quality of the different lower bounds. In random problems with constraints of arity 5, the probability of a value to be arc inconsistent is extremely low. Because of that, we do not consider LB_4 and LB_5, since the *dac* and *ac* counters will be practically zero for all instances (except those with p_2 very close to 1). In Figure 6 we provide results

[4] The hypergraph G^{PF} is randomly selected at the beginning. It not redirected for optimizing LB_1, but the following form of redirection is allowed. If the algorithm selects var_f as the next variable and constraint f has other future variables in its scope, one of these variables is randomly selected as new var_f. Otherwise, the contribution of constraint f in terms of ic would be lost.

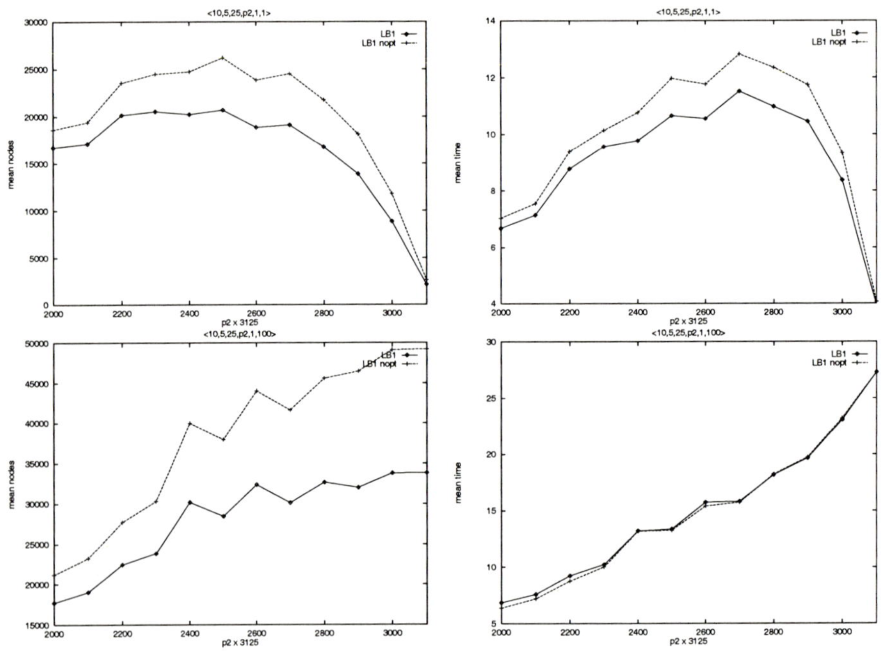

Fig. 5. Mean visited nodes and CPU time required by PFC using LB_1 with and without lower bound optimization, for the two problem classes tested.

for $LB1$, LB_3 and their limited versions for $k = 3, 2, 1$, that is, constraints in $\mathcal{C}_{\mathcal{PF}}$ are only propagated when they have up to 3, 2 and 1 future variables in their scope, respectively. We observe that LB_1 dominates LB_3 in both visited nodes and CPU time, for the two problem classes tested. This also happens for their limited versions. For Weighted CSP, there is no point in using LB_1 or LB_3 with $k > 2$ (there is no reduction in visited nodes when increasing k above 2).

Considering LB_1 in both problem classes, the mean number of visited nodes increases with p_2 faster for $k = 1$ than for $k = 2$. Given that the work per node is lower for $k = 1$ than for $k = 2$, there is a threshold in the number of visited nodes such that $k = 1$ dominates below it, and $k = 2$ dominates above. For Max-CSP, that threshold (around 40000 nodes) occurs at medium p_2, so $k = 2$ is the best trade-off between overhead and accuracy for the considered problems. For Weighted CSP, that threshold (around 90000 nodes) occurs at very high p_2, so $k = 1$ is the best trade-off for them. A similar analysis can be applied to LB_3.

The third experiment considers random problems with constraints of different arities. We generated instances of 10 variables and 5 values per variable, with 24 constraints distributed as follows: 6 constraints of arity 2, 6 of arity 3, 6 of arity 4, and 6 of arity 5. Constrained variables were selected randomly. All constraints shared the same tightness. As in the previous experiments, we considered two types of problems: Max-CSP, for which all inconsistent tuples have the same

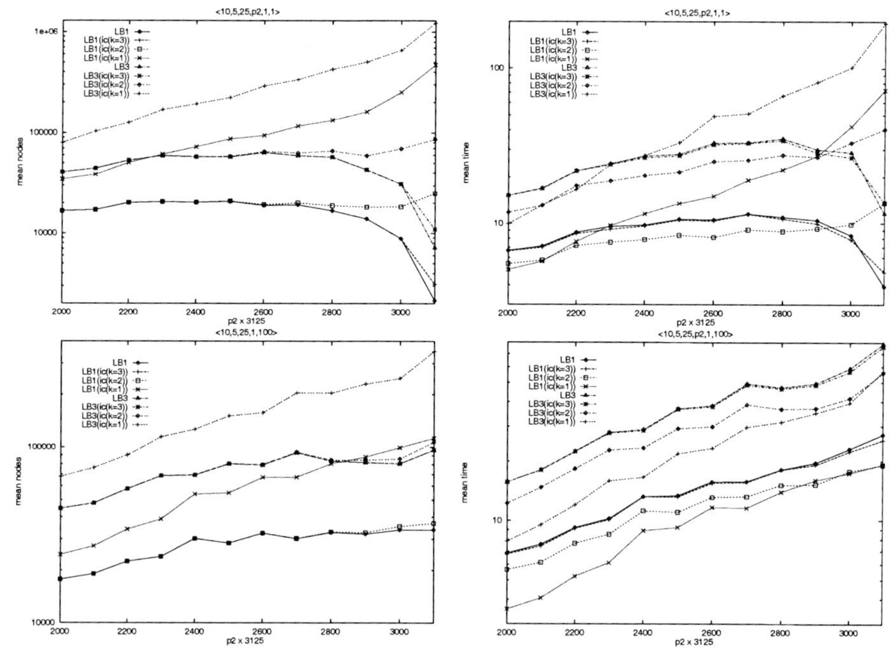

Fig. 6. Mean visited nodes and CPU time required by PFC using LB_1, LB_3 and their limited versions, for the two problem classes tested.

cost, and Weighted CSP, for which the cost of inconsistent tuples is randomly distributed between 1 and 100. We experimented with several limited versions of LB_1 and LB_5, with different k for *ic* and *dac* propagation. The best combinations are presented in Figure 7. We observed that the best limited versions of LB_5 are as follows: for Max-CSP, $k = 2$ for both *ic* and *dac*; for Weighted CSP, $k = 1$ for *ic* ($p_2 \leq 0.8$) and $k = 2$ for *ic* ($p_2 > 0.8$); $k = 2$ for *dac*. This is in agreement with the previous discussion of limited versions for LB_1, since *dac* contribution to LB_5 is limited to binary constraints (higher arities cause a very low probability for $dac > 0$ in random instances), playing a secondary role with respect to *ic* counters.

Therefore, according to these experimental results coming from random instances, the lower bounds of choice for non-binary PFC with low connectivity and medium to high tightness are the limited versions of LB_1 and LB_5. The main contribution to the lower bound comes from *ic* counters, for which a limited amount of propagation $k = 1, 2$ offers the best trade-off between the savings caused by propagation and its overhead. *dac* counters play a secondary role, limited to $k = 2$. By no means these experimental results prevent other bounds like LB_3 to be applicable to specific problem types. We also consider that LB_5 is applicable to real problems including arc-inconsistent values for some constraints.

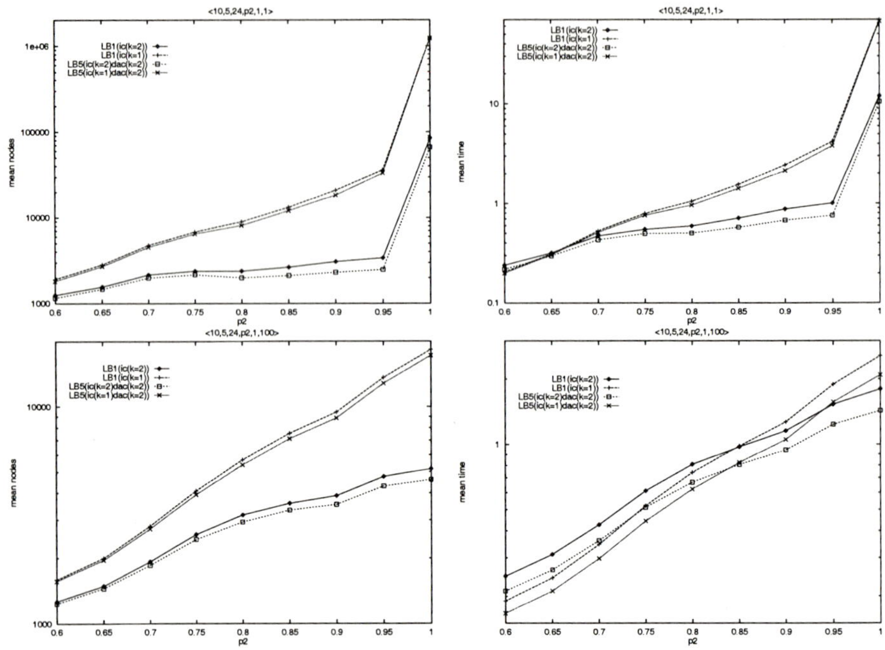

Fig. 7. Mean visited nodes and CPU time for two problem classes with constraints of different arities.

6 Conclusions and Further Work

In this paper, we have generalized binary lower bounds for the PFC algorithm developed for Max-CSP to COP, for which inconsistent tuples may have different costs. We have extended these lower bounds into the non-binary case. We have generalized the idea of directing the constraints (introduced in [7] for binary constraints between future variables) to any constraint with future variables in its scope. This means that there exists a variable per constraint where the cost of its inconsistencies is recorded. Also, we applied the idea of lower bound optimization by local search. Given the high complexity of lower bound computation, we presented the limited versions, where propagation is restricted to those constraints with a number of future variables in their scope below some limit. Experimental results on random instances show that these limited versions offer the best performance in terms of search effort.

More work, both practical and theoretical, is needed to fully understand the best way to solve COPs. On the practical side, the modelling and solving aspects of COPs present a number of issues to answer in the near future, in order to consolidate constraint technology on this type of problems. A more complete empirical evaluation is needed, including real problem instances. On the theoretical side, the development of new lower bounds based on specific local consistencies for soft constraints [13] will avoid the current limitation of counters which do not accumulate propagated inconsistencies. Also, the exploitation of the constraint graph topology [5] could speed up the resolution of COPs.

Acknowledgements. Authors thank anonymous reviewers for their constructive criticisms.

References

1. M. S. Affane and H. Bennaceur. A weighted arc consistency technique for Max-CSP. In *Proc. of the 13th ECAI*, 209–213, 1998.
2. C. Bessiere, P. Meseguer, E.C. Freuder, and J. Larrosa. On forward checking for non-binary constraint satisfaction. In *Non-binary constraints Workshop, IJCAI-99*, 1999.
3. S. Bistarelli, U. Montanari and F. Rossi. Constraint Solving over Semirings. In *Proc. of the 14th IJCAI*, 1995.
4. E.C. Freuder and R.J. Wallace. Partial constraint satisfaction. *Artificial Intelligence*, 58:21–70, 1992.
5. J. Larrosa. Boosting search with variable elimination. In *Proc. of the 6th CP*, 291–305, 2000.
6. J. Larrosa and P. Meseguer. Exploiting the use of DAC in Max-CSP. In *Proc. of the 2th CP*, 308–322, 1996.
7. J. Larrosa, P. Meseguer, and T. Schiex. Maintaining reversible dac for max-csp. *Artificial Intelligence*, 107:149–163, 1999.
8. J. Larrosa and R. Dechter. On the dual representation of non-binary semiring-based CSPs. In *Modelling and Solving Soft Constraints Workshop, CP-00*, 2000.
9. P. Meseguer. Lower bounds for non-binary Max-CSP. In *Modelling and Solving Constraint Problems Workshop, ECAI-00*, August 2000.
10. J.C. Régin, T. Petit, C. Bessière and J.F. Puget. An original constraint based approach for solving over constrained problems. In *Proc. of the 6th CP*, 543–548, September 2000.
11. T. Schiex, H. Fargier and G. Verfaillie. Valued Constraint Satisfaction Problems: hard and easy problems. In *Proc. of the 14th IJCAI*, 631–637, 1995.
12. T. Schiex. Maximizing the reversible DAC lower bound in Max-CSP is NP-hard. INRA Tec. Report 1998/02.
13. T. Schiex. Arc consistency for soft constraints In *Proc. of the 6th CP*, 411–424, 2000.
14. B. Smith. Phase transition and the mushy region in constraint satisfaction problems. In *Proc. of the 11th ECAI*, 100–104, 1994.
15. G. Verfaillie, M. Lemaître, and T. Schiex. Russian doll search. In *Proc. of the 13th AAAI*, 181–187, 1996.
16. R. Wallace. Directed arc consistency preprocessing. In M. Meyer, editor, *Selected papers from the ECAI-94 Workshop on Constraint Processing*, number 923 in LNCS, 121–137. Springer, Berlin, 1995.

New Lower Bounds of Constraint Violations for Over-Constrained Problems

Jean-Charles Régin[1], Thierry Petit[1,2], Christian Bessière[2], and Jean-François Puget[3]

[1] ILOG, 1681, route des Dolines, 06560 Valbonne, FRANCE
{regin, tpetit}@ilog.fr

[2] LIRMM (UMR 5506 CNRS), 161, rue Ada, 34392 Montpellier Cedex 5, FRANCE
{bessiere, tpetit}@lirmm.fr

[3] ILOG, 9, rue de Verdun, BP 85, 94253 Gentilly Cedex, FRANCE
puget@ilog.fr

Abstract. In recent years, many works have been carried out to solve over-constrained problems, and more specifically the Maximal Constraint Satisfaction Problem (Max-CSP), where the goal is to minimize the number of constraint violations. Some lower bounds on this number of violations have been proposed in the literature.

In this paper, we characterize the constraints that are ignored by the existing results, we propose new lower bounds which takes into account some of these ignored constraints and we show how these new bounds can be integrated into existing ones in order to improve the previous results.

Our work also generalize the previous studies by dealing with any kind of constraints, as non binary constraints, or constraints with specific filtering algorithms. Furthermore, in order to integrate these algorithms into any constraint solver, we suggest to represent a Max-CSP as a single global constraint. This constraint can be itself included into any set of constraint. In this way, an over-constrained part of a problem can be isolated from constraints that must be necessarily satisfied.

1 Introduction

A constraint network (CN) consists of a set of variables, each of them associated with a domain of possible values, and a set of constraints linking the variables and defining the set of allowed combinations of values. The search for an assignment of values to all variables that satisfies all the constraints is called the Constraint Satisfaction Problem (CSP). Such an assignment is a solution of the CSP.

Unfortunately, the CSP is an NP-Hard problem. Thus, many works have been carried out in order to try to reduce the time needed to solve a CSP. Some of the suggested methods turn the original CSP into a new one, which has the same set of solutions, but which is easier to solve. The modifications are done through filtering algorithms, that remove from domains values which cannot belong to any solution of the current CSP. If the cost of such an algorithm is less than

T. Walsh (Ed.): CP 2001, LNCS 2239, pp. 332–345, 2001.

the time required by the backtrack algorithm to discover many times the same inconsistency, then the solving will be accelerated.

It often happens that a CSP has no solution. In this case we say that the problem is over-constrained, and often the goal is then to find a good compromise. One of the most usual theoretical frameworks is called the Maximal Constraint Satisfaction Problem (Max-CSP). A solution of a Max-CSP is a total assignment that minimizes the number of constraint violations.

Most of existing algorithms for solving Max-CSPs are related to binary constraints and based on a branch and bound schema [2,8,4]. They perform successive assignments of values to variables through a depth-first traversal of the search tree, where internal nodes represent incomplete assignments and leaf nodes stand for complete ones. For any given node, the variables which have been instantiated are called past variables, whereas the other variables are called future variables (F). The *distance* of a node is the number of constraints violated by its assignment, UB is the distance of the best solution found so far, and LB is an underestimation of any leaf node descendant from the current one. When $LB \geq UB$, the current best solution cannot be improved below the current node. Thus it is not necessary to traverse the subtree rooted by the current node.

When filtering, the existing approaches combine generally LB with lower bounds local to each value, in order to remove values that cannot belong to a solution. These lower bounds are based on *direct violations of constraints by values.* A value a of a variable x directly violates a constraint C if C has no solution when $x = a$. In other words, (x, a) directly violates C if (x, a) is not consistent with C.

In the PFC-MRDAC algorithm [4], which can be considered as the best reference in the literature[1], two local lower bounds of violations are defined for every a in $D(x)$: $ic(x, a)$ which is related to constraints such that the other involved variable is a past variable, and $dac(x, a)$ which is related to constraints involving only future variables.

More precisely, $ic(x, a)$ is simply defined as the number of constraints involving x and a past variable that are directly violated if $x = a$. The definition of $dac(x, a)$ assumes that the constraint graph[2] is oriented. $dac(x, a)$ is equal to the number of constraints out-going x and involving only future variables that are violated if $x = a$. With these definitions LB is defined by:

(1) $LB = distance + \sum_{x \in F} inc(x)$,
where $inc(x) = min_{a \in D(x)}(ic(x, a) + dac(x, a))$.

When filtering future domains, PFC-MRDAC selects for each value the sum $ic(x, a) + dac(x, a)$. This sum is associated with LB, by removing $inc(x)$ from LB in order to guarantee that no violation of any constraint involving x is counted twice. Thus, a value a can be removed from $D(x)$ if:

[1] A variation of this algorithm has been suggested [5], based on a partitioning of the variable set.

[2] The vertex set of the constraint graph is the variable set and there is an edge between two vertices when there is a constraint involving these two variables.

(2) $ic(x,a) + dac(x,a) + LB - inc(x) \geq UB$.

Hence, the quality of the filtering algorithms depends on the value of *inc* counters, which depends on the value of *dac* counters.

However, some constraints which lead to inconsistencies are not taken into account in PFC-MRDAC. In particular, Equations (1) and (2) do not take into account inconsistencies involving constraints defined on variables such that the *inc* counter of each of them is equal to 0.

This drawback is quite important because the probability for having such constraints is huge in real-world applications especially when only few variables have been instantiated. It can be emphasized by the following example (Figure 2):

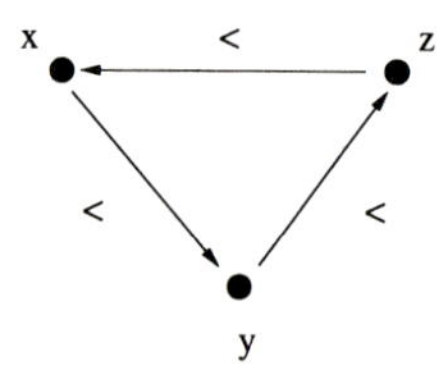

Fig. 1.

The problem involves three variables x, y, z with domains equal to $\{1, 2, 3\}$ and three constraints: $x < y$, $y < z$, and $z < x$. Value 2 of each variable does not directly violate any constraint. Thus, $inc(x) = inc(y) = inc(z) = 0$ whereas it is clear that any assignment of x, y, and z will lead to the violation of at least one constraint.

In this paper, we propose an original method for identifying constraints that are implicitly ignored by Equations (1) and (2). Then, we present a new way for computing a lower bound of the number of violations related to some of these constraints.

This lower bound can be computed by searching for disjoint conflicting sets of constraints. A *conflict set* is a set of constraints that cannot be simultaneously all satisfied. For instance, $\{x < y, y < z, z < x\}$ is a conflict set.

When a conflict set has been identified then in any solution at least one constraint of this conflict set will be violated. Thus, by finding disjoint conflict sets a non trivial lower bound of the number of violations holds. And this bound can be integrated to Equations (1) and (2).

The paper is organized as follows: first, we recall some notions about CNs. Then, we propose a new framework based on the representation of a Max-CSP as only one constraint called the Satisfiability Sum Constraint (ssc). Section 4 presents a generalization of the results proposed for binary Max-CSPs to the non binary case. Section 5 presents an original approach for computing a lower bound of the number of violations. This result is exploited in section 6 and leads to properties that improve the results of the previous studies. At last we recapitulate our results and conclude.

2 Background

A *constraint network* $\mathcal{N}$ is defined as a set of n *variables* $X = \{x_1, \ldots, x_n\}$, a set of *domains* $\mathcal{D} = \{D(x_1), \ldots, D(x_n)\}$ where $D(x_i)$ is the finite set of possible *values* for variable x_i, and a set $\mathcal{C}$ of *constraints* between variables. A *constraint* C on the ordered set of variables $X(C) = (x_{i_1}, \ldots, x_{i_r})$ is a subset $T(C)$ of the Cartesian product $D(x_{i_1}) \times \cdots \times D(x_{i_r})$ that specifies the *allowed* combinations of values for the variables $x_{i_1}, \ldots, x_{i_r}$. An element of $D(x_{i_1}) \times \cdots \times D(x_{i_r})$ is called a *tuple on* $X(C)$. $|X(C)|$ is the *arity* of C. A value a for a variable x is often denoted by (x, a). A tuple τ on $X(C)$ is *valid* if $\forall (x, a) \in \tau, a \in D(x)$. C is *consistent* iff there exists a tuple τ of $T(C)$ which is valid. A value $a \in D(x)$ is *consistent with* C iff $x \notin X(C)$ or there exists a valid tuple τ of $T(C)$ in which a is the value assigned to x. An Arc Consistency algorithm is an algorithm which guarantees that $\forall x \in X$, $\forall a \in D(x)$, $\forall C \in \mathcal{C}$, a is consistent with C. Given $\mathcal{K} \subseteq \mathcal{C}$, the subset of variables involved in constraints $\mathcal{K}$ is denoted by $X(\mathcal{K})$.

Some important results presented in the paper are based on the following definition:

Definition 1 *Let x be a variable, a be a value of $D(x)$, $\mathcal{C}$ be a set of constraints, $\#inc((x, a), \mathcal{C}) = |\{C \in \mathcal{C}$ s.t. (x, a) is not consistent with $C\}|$.*

3 Satisfiability Sum Constraint

Let $\mathcal{N} = (X, \mathcal{D}, \mathcal{C})$ be a constraint network. We suggest to integrate $\mathcal{C}$ into a single constraint, called the Satisfiability Sum Constraint (ssc):

Definition 2 *Let $\mathcal{C} = \{C_i, i \in \{1, \ldots, m\}\}$ be a set of constraints, and $S[\mathcal{C}] = \{s_i, i \in \{1, \ldots, m\}\}$ be a set of variables and unsat be a variable, such that a one-to-one mapping is defined between $\mathcal{C}$ and $S[\mathcal{C}]$. A* **Satisfiability Sum Constraint** *is the constraint $ssc(\mathcal{C}, S[\mathcal{C}], unsat)$ defined by:*

$$[unsat = \sum_{s_i=1}^{m} s_i] \wedge \bigwedge_{i=1}^{m} [(C_i \wedge (s_i = 0)) \vee (\neg C_i \wedge (s_i = 1))]$$

Notation 1 *Given a $ssc(\mathcal{C}, S[\mathcal{C}], unsat)$, a variable x, a value $a \in D(x)$ and $\mathcal{K} \subseteq \mathcal{C}$:*
- *$max(D(unsat))$ is the highest value of current domain of unsat;*
- *$min(D(unsat))$ is the lowest value of current domain of unsat;*
- *$minUnsat(\mathcal{C}, S[\mathcal{C}])$ is the minimum value of unsat consistent with $ssc(\mathcal{C}, S[\mathcal{C}], unsat)$;*
- *$minUnsat((x, a), \mathcal{C}, S[\mathcal{C}])$ is equal to $minUnsat(\mathcal{C}, S[\mathcal{C}])$ when $x = a$;*
- *$S[\mathcal{K}]$ is the subset of $S[\mathcal{C}]$ equals to the projection of variables $S[\mathcal{C}]$ on $\mathcal{K}$;*
- *$X(\mathcal{C})$ is the union of $X(C_i), C_i \in \mathcal{C}$.*

The variables $S[\mathcal{C}]$ are used in order to express which constraints of $\mathcal{C}$ must be violated or satisfied: value 0 assigned to $s \in S[\mathcal{C}]$ expresses that its corresponding constraint C is satisfied, whereas 1 expresses that C is violated[3]. Variable $unsat$ represents the objective, that is, the number of violations in $\mathcal{C}$, equal to the number of variables of $S[\mathcal{C}]$ whose value is 1.

Throughout this formulation, a solution of a Max-CSP is an assignment that satisfies the *ssc* with the minimal possible value of $unsat$. A lower bound of the objective of a Max-CSP corresponds to a necessary consistency condition of the ssc. The different domain reduction algorithms established for Max-CSP correspond to specific filtering algorithms associated with the ssc.

This point of view has some advantages in regards to the previous studies:
1. Any search algorithm can be used. Since we propose to define a constraint we can easily integrate our framework into existing solvers. This constraint can be associated with other ones, in order to separate soft constraints from hard ones.
2. No hypothesis is made on the arity of constraints $\mathcal{C}$.
3. If a value is assigned to $s_i \in S[\mathcal{C}]$, then a filtering algorithm associated with $C_i \in \mathcal{C}$ (resp. $\neg C_i$) can be used in a way similar to classical CSPs.

Moreover, properties are simplified: there is no longer references about past or future variables; $min(D(unsat))$ and $max(D(unsat))$ respectively correspond to the parameters *distance* and $UB - 1$ of PFC-MRDAC.

4 Related Work

The results presented in this section are a generalization to non binary constraints of the previous works for Max-CSP [2,9,4].

4.1 Simple Filtering Algorithm

Domains of variables of $S[\mathcal{C}]$ initially contain two values. Removing one of them amounts to saying that the other one is assigned to the variable. Let $s \in S[\mathcal{C}]$ and $C \in \mathcal{C}$, such that s is linked to C in a *ssc*:

Property 1 *If the value* 0 *(resp.* 1*) is assigned to* s *then values from domains of variables* $X(C)$ *which are not consistent with* C *(resp.* $\neg C$*) can be removed.*

Property 2 *Let* $x_i \in X(C)$*. If all values of* $D(x_i)$ *are not consistent with* C *(resp.* $\neg C$*) then* $s = 1$ *(resp.* 0*).*

4.2 Necessary Condition of Consistency

From the definition of $minUnsat(\mathcal{C}, S[\mathcal{C}])$ we have:

Property 3 *If* $minUnsat(\mathcal{C}, S[\mathcal{C}]) > max(D(unsat))$ *then* $ssc(\mathcal{C}, S[\mathcal{C}], unsat)$ *is not consistent.*

[3] An extension of the model can be performed [6], in order to deal with Valued CSPs [1]. Basically it consists of defining larger domains for variables in $S[\mathcal{C}]$.

A lower bound of $minUnsat(\mathcal{C}, S[\mathcal{C}])$ provides a necessary condition of consistency of a ssc. A possible way for computing it is to perform a sum of independent lower bounds of violations, one per variable. For each variable a lower bound can be defined by:

Definition 3 *Given a variable x and a constraint set $\mathcal{K}$,* $\#inc(x, \mathcal{K}) = min_{a \in D(x)}(\#inc((x, a), \mathcal{K}))$.

The sum of these minima with $\mathcal{K} = \mathcal{C}$ cannot lead to a lower bound of the total number of violations, because some constraints can be taken into account more than once. For instance, given a constraint C and two variables x and y involved in C, C can be counted in $\#inc(x, \mathcal{C})$ and also in $\#inc(y, \mathcal{C})$. In this case, the lower bound can be overestimated, and an inconsistency could be detected while the *ssc* is consistent. Consequently, for each variable, an independent set of constraints must be considered.

In the binary case, the constraint graph has been used in order to guarantee this independence [4]. Each edge is oriented and for each variable x only the constraints out-going x are taken into account.

This idea can be generalized to the non binary case, by associating with each constraint C one and only one variable x involved in the constraint: C is then taken into account only for computing the $\#inc$ counter of x. Therefore, the constraints are *partionned* w.r.t the variables that are associated with:

Definition 4 *Given a set of constraints $\mathcal{C}$, a* **var-partition** *of $\mathcal{C}$ is a partition $\mathcal{P}(\mathcal{C}) = \{P(x_1), ..., P(x_k)\}$ of $\mathcal{C}$ in $|X(\mathcal{C})|$ sets such that $\forall P(x_i) \in \mathcal{P}(\mathcal{C}) : \forall C \in P(x_i), x_i \in X(C)$.*

Given a var partition $\mathcal{P}(\mathcal{C})$, the sum of all $\#inc(x_i, P(x_i))$ is a lower bound of the total number of violations, because all sets belonging to $\mathcal{P}(\mathcal{C})$ are disjoint; thus we have:

Definition 5 $\forall \mathcal{P}(\mathcal{C}) = \{P(x_1), ..., P(x_k)\}$, $LB(\mathcal{P}(\mathcal{C})) = \sum_{x_i \in X(\mathcal{C})} \#inc(x_i, P(x_i))$.

Property 4 $\forall \mathcal{P}(\mathcal{C}) = \{P(x_1), ..., P(x_k)\}$, $LB(\mathcal{P}(\mathcal{C})) \leq minUnsat(\mathcal{C}, S[\mathcal{C}])$.

The necessary condition of consistency of a *ssc* is deduced from this property:

Corollary 1 $\forall \mathcal{P}(\mathcal{C}) = \{P(x_1), ..., P(x_k)\}$, *If* $LB(\mathcal{P}(\mathcal{C})) > max(D(unsat))$ *then* $ssc(\mathcal{C}, S[\mathcal{C}], unsat)$ *is not consistent.*

The quality of such a lower bound depends on the var-partition that is choosen. This property corresponds to Equation (1) given in Introduction.

4.3 Filtering Algorithm

From definition of $minUnsat((x,a),\mathcal{C},S[\mathcal{C}])$ we have the following theorem:

Theorem 1 *$\forall x \in X(\mathcal{C}), \forall a \in D(x)$: if $minUnsat((x,a),\mathcal{C},S[\mathcal{C}]) > max(D(unsat))$ then (x,a) is not consistent with $ssc(\mathcal{C},S[\mathcal{C}],unsat)$.*

Therefore, any lower bound of $minUnsat((x,a),\mathcal{C},S[\mathcal{C}])$ can be used to check the consistency of (x,a). An obvious lower bound is $\#inc((x,a),\mathcal{C})$:

Property 5 $\#inc((x,a),\mathcal{C}) \leq minUnsat((x,a),\mathcal{C},S[\mathcal{C}])$

From this property and theorem 1, we obtain a first filtering algorithm. This filtering algorithm can be achieved as a generalization of the constructive disjunction [7]: given $C_1 \vee C_2 ... \vee C_n$, the constructive disjunction removes a value from a domain when this value is not consistent with each constraint taken separately. The constructive disjunction corresponds to the particular case where $max(D(unsat)) = 1$.

This filtering algorithm can be improved, by including the lower bound of Property 4. In order to do so, we suggest to split $\mathcal{C}$ into two disjoint sets $P(x)$ and $\mathcal{C} - P(x)$, where $P(x)$ is the subset of constraints associated with x in a var-partition $P(\mathcal{C})$ of $\mathcal{C}$. Consider the following corollary of Theorem 1:

Corollary 2 *Let $P(\mathcal{C})$ be a var-partition of $\mathcal{C}$, x a variable and $a \in D(x)$, if $minUnsat((x,a),P(x),S[P(x)])$ $+minUnsat((x,a),\mathcal{C}-P(x),S[\mathcal{C}-P(x)]) > max(D(unsat))$ then (x,a) is not consistent with $ssc(\mathcal{C},S[\mathcal{C}],unsat)$.*

Proof: $\mathcal{C} - P(x)$ and $P(x)$ are disjoint and included in $\mathcal{C}$. Therefore, $minUnsat((x,a),P(x),S[P(x)]) + minUnsat((x,a),\mathcal{C}-P(x),S[\mathcal{C}-P(x)])$ $\leq minUnsat((x,a),\mathcal{C},S[\mathcal{C}])$. From theorem 1 the corollary holds.

Note that $minUnsat(\mathcal{C} - P(x),S[P(x)]) \leq minUnsat((x,a),\mathcal{C} - P(x),S[P(x)])$. From this remark and Properties 4 and 5 we deduce the following theorem, which corresponds to Equation (2) given in Introduction:

Theorem 2 *$\forall \mathcal{P}(\mathcal{C})$ a var-partition of $\mathcal{C}, \forall x \in X(\mathcal{C}), \forall a \in D(x)$, if $\#inc((x,a),P(x)) + LB(\mathcal{P}(\mathcal{C}-P(x))) > max(D(unsat))$ then a can be removed from its domain.*

5 Conflict Set Based Lower Bound

5.1 Intuitive Idea

Some inconsistencies are not taken into account by the previous lower bound, because it is based on counters of direct violations of constraints by values. This drawback is pointed out in the example of introduction.

In order to take more inconsistencies into account, we propose a new lower bound based on successive computations of disjoint conflict sets.

Definition 6 *A conflict set is a subset $\mathcal{K}$ of $\mathcal{C}$ which satisfies:* $minUnsat(\mathcal{K}, S[\mathcal{K}]) > 0$.

We know that a conflict set leads to at least one violation in $\mathcal{C}$. Consequently, if we are able to compute q disjoint conflict sets of $\mathcal{C}$ then q is a lower bound of $minUnsat(\mathcal{C}, S[\mathcal{C}])$. They must be disjoint to guarantee that all violations are independent.

For each $C_i \in \mathcal{C}$ such that $D(s_i) = 1$, the set $\{C_i\}$ is a conflict set. Moreover, constraints C_i of $\mathcal{C}$ with $D(s_i) = 0$ are not interesting in the determination of conflict sets. Hence we will focus on the set of constraints C_i of $\mathcal{C}$ with $D(s_i) = \{0, 1\}$.

5.2 Computation of Disjoint Conflict Sets

We will denote by ISACONFLICTSET($\mathcal{K}$) the function which returns true if $\mathcal{K}$ is a conflict set and false otherwise.

Determining if a set of constraints $\mathcal{K}$ satisfies the condition of definition 6 is a NP-complete problem. Indeed, it consists of checking the global consistency of the constraint network $\mathcal{N}[\mathcal{K}]$ defined by $\mathcal{K}$ and by the set of variables involved in the constraints of $\mathcal{K}$. However, for our purpose, the identification of some conflict sets is sufficient.

In lack of other algorithms ISACONFLICTSET($\mathcal{K}$) can be defined as follows: it returns true if the achievement of arc consistency on the constraint network $\mathcal{N}[\mathcal{K}]$ leads to a failure (i.e. the domain of one variable has been emptied), and false otherwise. Thus we can consider that we are provided with ISACONFLICTSET($\mathcal{K}$) function.

Let $\mathcal{C}$ be an identified conflict set, we are interested in finding subsets of $\mathcal{C}$ which are themselves conflict sets. Such a conflict set $\mathcal{K} \subseteq \mathcal{C}$ can be easily identified by defining an ordering on $\mathcal{C}$: the principle is to start with an empty set $\mathcal{K}$ and then successively add constraints of $\mathcal{C}$ to $\mathcal{K}$ until ISACONFLICTSET($\mathcal{K}$) returns true. This algorithm can be implemented thanks to OL, a data structure implementing a list of constraints ordered from 1 to *size*. The following basic functions are available:

- OL.$ct[i]$ returns the ith constraint of OL.
- OL.$size$ returns the number of constraints of OL.
- ADDFIRST(C,OL) adds C to OL at first position and shift all the other elements to the right.
- ADDLAST(C,OL) adds C to OL at last position.
- GETLAST(OL) returns the last constraint in OL.
- REMOVELAST(OL) removes from OL the last constraint in OL and returns it.
- REMOVE(OL, C) removes the constraint C from the OL.

For convenience, given a constraint set $\mathcal{C}$ stored in an OL ol, and $\mathcal{K} \subseteq \mathcal{C}$, $ol - \mathcal{K}$ denotes the OL obtained after calls of function REMOVE(ol,C) for all the constraints C of $\mathcal{K}$.

Given a conflict set $\mathcal{C}$ stored in an OL ol, a subset of $\mathcal{C}$ which is also a conflict set can be computed by calling the function COMPUTECONFLICTSET(ol) which is defined by:

```
COMPUTECONFLICTSET(OL ol) returns OL
  1: S ← emptyOL
  2: for i = 1 to ol.size
           ADDLAST(ol.ct[i],S);
           if ISACONFLICTSET(S) then return S;
  3: return emptyOL;
```

A set of disjoint conflict sets can be easily computed by calling function COMPUTECONFLICTSET(ol) with ol containing all constraint of $\mathcal{C}$ and by iteratively calling it with $ol \leftarrow ol - \mathcal{K}$ each time a conflict set $\mathcal{K}$ is detected in ol.

The lower bound we search for depends on the number of conflict sets, and, since they are disjoint, on the size of the conflict sets.

Definition 7 *Let $\mathcal{C}$ be a set of constraint. A minimal conflict set w.r.t.* COMPUTECONFLICTSET *is a subset $\mathcal{K}$ of $\mathcal{C}$ such that $\forall C \in \mathcal{K}$,* COMPUTECONFLICTSET($\mathcal{K} - \{C\}$) *detects no conflict set.*

A simple algorithm for finding a minimal conflict set from a conflict set was suggested by De Siqueira and Puget [3]. It requires only a monotonic propagation of constraints, that is, not dependent on the order in which constraints are added.

Is is implemented by the function COMPUTEMINCONFLICTSET(ol). The first step consists of computing an initial OL $firstOL$. This OL contains a subset of the constraint set given as parameter which forms a conflict set, if such a conflict set can be identified. Then, the algorithm repeatedly calls COMPUTECONFLICTSET with an OL which is the same OL than the previous one, except that the last constraint became the first one. This repetition is done until the last constraint of a new computed OL is the last constraint of $firstOL$. The latest computed OL contains the constraints of a minimal conflict set.

```
COMPUTEMINCONFLICTSET(OL ol) returns OL
  1: M ← COMPUTECONFLICTSET(OL);
  2: if M ≠ emptyOL then
           firstLast ← GETLAST(ol);
           do
              C ← REMOVELAST(M);
              ADDFIRST(C,M);
              M ← COMPUTECONFLICTSET(M);
           while GETLAST(M) ≠ firstLast
  3: return M;
```

5.3 Conflict Set Based Lower Bound

We can now propose an original algorithm for computing a lower bound of $minUnsat(\mathcal{C}, S[\mathcal{C}])$.

This algorithm is based on computation of disjoint conflict sets. Therefore, it performs successive calls of COMPUTEMINCONFLICTSET. This lower bound will be denoted by $LB_{DCS}(\mathcal{C})$:

```
COMPUTECONFLICTBASEDLB(C)
1: LB_DCS(C) ← min(D(unsat));
   create an OL ol and add all the constraints of C to it;
2: cs ←COMPUTEMINCONFLICTSET(ol);
   While cs ≠ emptyOL do
       LB_DCS(C) ← LB_DCS(C) + 1;
       ol ← ol − cs
       cs ← COMPUTEMINCONFLICTSET(ol);
3: return LB_DCS(C);
```

$LB_{DCS}(\mathcal{C})$ can be used to check the consistency of a *ssc*, as the variable-based lower bound $LB(\mathcal{P}(\mathcal{C}))$ described in section 4:

Corollary 3 *If $LB_{DCS}(\mathcal{C}) > max(D(unsat))$ then $ssc(\mathcal{C}, S[\mathcal{C}], unsat)$ is not consistent.*

6 Identification of Independent Set of Ignored Constraints w.r.t. a Var-Partition

In this section we show how to improve results presented in section 4, by integrating such a conflict set based lower bound of violations into Property 4 and Theorem 2. The idea is to identify ignored constraints, that is, constraints which are not taken into account in $LB(\mathcal{P}(\mathcal{C}))$. Then, it is possible to compute a conflict set based lower bound on a particular subset of these constraints, which can be added to $LB(\mathcal{P}(\mathcal{C}))$.

Definition 8 *Let $\mathcal{P}(\mathcal{C})$ be a var-partition. An ignored constraint w.r.t. $\mathcal{P}(\mathcal{C})$ is a constraint C such that $\forall x \in X(\mathcal{C}) : \#inc(x, P(x) - \{C\}) = \#inc(x, P(x))$.*

Thus, one ignored constraint can be removed from $\mathcal{C}$ without changing the value of $LB(\mathcal{P}(\mathcal{C}))$.

Definition 9 *Let $\mathcal{P}(\mathcal{C})$ be a var-partition. A set of constraints S satisfying $\forall x \in X(\mathcal{C}) : \#inc(x, P(x) - S) = \#inc(x, P(x))$ is called an independent set of ignored constraints w.r.t. the var-partition.*

If an independent set S is found then it is possible to improve Property 4 and Theorem 2, by adding $LB_{DCS}(S)$ to them. The identification of ignored constraints w.r.t var-partition is given by the following property:

Definition 10 *Let x be a variable, the set of ignored constraints w.r.t. $P(x)$ is the set $ignored(P(x)) = P(x) - \{C \in P(x), C$ is violated by $a \in D(x)$ with $\#inc((x,a), P(x)) = \#inc(x, P(x))\}$*

Unfortunately, the whole set $\mathcal{K}$ of ignored constraints w.r.t. $P(x)$ is not necessarily independent. Each constraint $C \in \mathcal{K}$ taken separately satisfies $\#inc(x, P(x) - \{C\}) = \#inc(x, P(x))$, but this fact does not guarantee that $\#inc(x, P(x) - \mathcal{K}) = \#inc(x, P(x))$.

For instance, consider a variable x with 3 values a, b and c and suppose that a is not consistent with C_1, b is not consistent with C_2 and c is not consistent with C_3 and C_4; Assume $P(x) = \{C_1, C_2, C_3, C_4\}$.

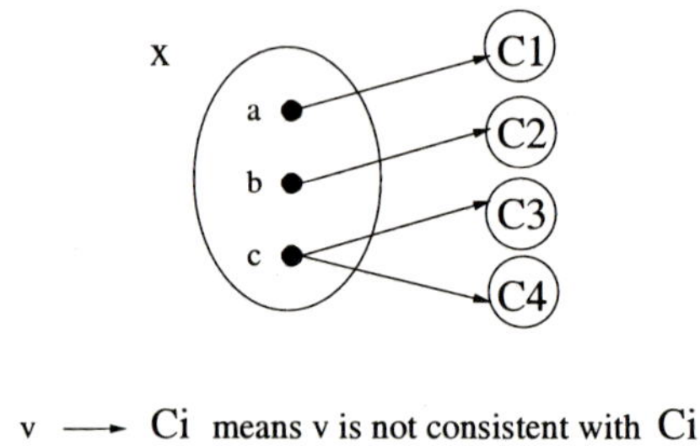

Fig. 2.

Then, $\#inc(x, P(x)) = 1 = \#inc((x, a), P(x)) = \#inc((x, b), P(x))$ and $ignored(P(x)) = \{C_3, C_4\}$. Unfortunately, $ignored(P(x))$ does not form an independent set of ignored constraints. That is, constraints C_3 and C_4 cannot be simultaneously removed from $P(x)$, because in this case: $\#inc(x, P(x) - \{C_3, C_4\}) = \#inc((x, c), P(x) - \{C_3, C_4\}) = 0$, which is less than $\#inc(x, P(x))$.

Nevertheless, a simple example of an independent set of ignored constraints is the set containing constraints involving only variables with $\#inc$ counters equal to 0. Now, we propose general method to identify such a set. Since $\mathcal{P}(\mathcal{C})$ is a partition, it is sufficient to identify *for each variable* x an independent subset of ignored constraints of $P(x)$. The union of these subsets will form an independent set.

Property 6 *Let $\mathcal{P}(\mathcal{C})$ be a var-partition, x be a variable of $X(\mathcal{C})$ and S be an independent set of ignored constraints included in $P(x)$. Then, $\cup_{x \in X(\mathcal{C})} S$ is an independent set of ignored constraints w.r.t. $\mathcal{P}(\mathcal{C})$.*

Thus, we can focus our attention to the determination of an independent set of ignored constraints included in a $P(x)$:

Property 7 *Let T be any subset of $P(x)$. If each value of $D(x)$ violate at least $\#inc(x, P(x))$ constraints of T, then $S = P(x) - T$ is an independent set of ignored constraints.*

Proof: $\forall a \in D(x)$ $\#inc((x, a), P(x) - S) = \#inc((x, a), T)$ which is greater than or equal to $\#inc(x, P(x))$. Therefore, by definition 9, S is an independent set of ignored constraints.

Such a set T can be found by solving a covering problem:

Proposition 1 *Let x be a variable, $G(x, P(x)) = (D(x), P(x), E)$ be the bipartite graph such that $(a, C) \in E$ iff $a \in D(x), C \in P(x)$ and (x, a) violates C. Let T be a subset of $P(x)$ such that $\forall a \in D(x)$ there are at least $\#inc(x, P(x))$ edges with an endpoint in T. Then, $S = P(x) - T$ is an independent set of ignored constraints w.r.t. $P(x)$.*

The proof of this proposition is straightforward. Finding a minimal set T is an NP-Complete problem, but it is not mandatory to search for a minimal set. From Property 7, we propose a greedy algorithm which returns an independent set of constraints from a set $P(x)$ of a var partition $\mathcal{P}(\mathcal{C})$ ($\#inc(x, K - \{C\})$ can be easily updated at each step):

COMPUTEINDEPENDENTSET($x, P(x)$)
1: $K \leftarrow P(x)$;
2: $S \leftarrow \emptyset$;
3: While $\exists C \in K$, $\#inc(x, K - \{C\}) \geq \#inc(x, P(x))$ **do**
$S \leftarrow S \cup \{C\}$;
$K \leftarrow K - \{C\}$;
4: return S;

$ISNC(\mathcal{P}(\mathcal{C})) = \cup_{x \in X(\mathcal{C})}$COMPUTEINDEPENDENTSET$(x, P(x))$ is an independent set of ignored constraints w.r.t. $\mathcal{P}(\mathcal{C})$. We can propose a new property which improve Property 4, and the corresponding necessary condition of consistency of a *ssc*:

Property 8 *$\forall \mathcal{P}(\mathcal{C})$ a var-partition of $\mathcal{C}$,*
$LB(\mathcal{P}(\mathcal{C})) + LB_{DCS}(ISNC(\mathcal{P}(\mathcal{C}))) \leq minUnsat(\mathcal{C}, S[\mathcal{C}])$

Corollary 4 *If $LB(\mathcal{P}(\mathcal{C})) + LB_{DCS}(ISNC(\mathcal{P}(\mathcal{C})))$ $> max(D(unsat))$ then $ssc(\mathcal{C}, S[\mathcal{C}], unsat)$ is not consistent.*

Note that if we compute these bounds in the example given in Introduction, we obtain the following result: at least one constraint among $x < y$, $y < z$ and $z < x$ is violated for any var-partition, since in all cases the independent set of ignored constraints contains the three constraints.

Moreover, Property 8 can be used in order to improve the filtering Theorem 2:

Theorem 3 *$\forall \mathcal{P}(\mathcal{C})$ a var-partition of $\mathcal{C}, \forall x \in X(\mathcal{C}, \forall a \in D(x)$, if $\#inc((x, a), P(x)) + LB(\mathcal{P}(\mathcal{C} - P(x)))$ $+ LB_{DCS}(ISNC(\mathcal{P}(\mathcal{C} - P(x))))$ $> max(D(unsat))$ then a can be removed from its domain.*

7 Summary

The two following tables recapitulate the results of this paper and compare them to the previous studies. Let $P(\mathcal{C})$ be a var-partition of $\mathcal{C}$:

1. Consistency:

Previous studies (binary constraints)
$LB(\mathcal{P}(\mathcal{C}))$ $> max(D(unsat))$
New Condition (any arity)
$LB_{DCS}(\mathcal{C})$ $> max(D(unsat))$
Improved Condition (any arity)
$LB(\mathcal{P}(\mathcal{C}))$ $+LB_{DCS}(ISNC(\mathcal{P}(\mathcal{C})))$ $> max(D(unsat))$

2. Filtering algorithm:

Previous studies (binary constraints)
$\#inc((x,a),P(x))$ $+LB(\mathcal{P}(\mathcal{C}-P(x)))$ $> max(D(unsat))$
New results (any arity)
$\#inc((x,a),P(x))$ $+LB(\mathcal{P}(\mathcal{C}-P(x)))$ $+LB_{DCS}(ISNC(\mathcal{P}(\mathcal{C}-P(x))))$ $> max(D(unsat))$

8 Conclusion

Some new properties improving existing results have been proposed. The lower bounds presented in this paper take into account some inconsistencies between constraints that are ignored by the previous studies. The constraints ignored by the existing algorithms for Max-CSP have been identified and an algorithm for computing a lower bound of the number of inconsistencies implied by these constraints have been proposed. One additional advantage of the framework we suggest is that the filtering algorithm associated with the constraints are used in a way similar to classical CSPs. Moreover, all the results make no assumption on the arity of constraints and generalize the previous studies which consider only binary Max-CSP.

Acknowledgements. The work of ILOG authors was partially supported by the IST Programme of the Commission of the European Union through the ECSPLAIN project (IST-1999-11969). We would like to thank Ulrich Junker and Olivier Lhomme for helpful comments they provided on the ideas of this paper.

References

1. S. Bistarelli, U. Montanari, F. Rossi, T. Schiex, G. Verfaillie, and H. Fargier. Semiring-based csps and valued csps: Frameworks, properties, and comparison. *Constraints*, 4:199–240, 1999.
2. E. Freuder and R. Wallace. Partial constraint satisfaction. *Artificial Intelligence*, 58:21–70, 1992.
3. J.L. de Siqueira N. and J. Puget. Explanation-based generalization of failures. *Proceedings ECAI*, pages 339–344, 1988.
4. J. Larrosa, P. Meseguer, and T. Schiex. Maintaining reversible dac for max-csp. *Artificial Intelligence*, 107:149–163, 1999.
5. J. Larrossa and P. Meseguer. Partition-based lower bound for max-csp. *Proceedings CP*, pages 303–315, 1999.
6. T. Petit, J. Régin, and C. Bessière. Meta constraints on violations for over constrained problems. *Proceedings ICTAI*, 2000.
7. P. Van Hentenryck. Constraint satisfaction in logic programming. *The MIT Press*, 1989.
8. G. Verfaillie, M. Lemaître, and T. Schiex. Russian doll search for solving constraint optimisation problems. *Proceedings AAAI*, pages 181–187, 1996.
9. R. Wallace. Directed arc consistency preprocessing as a strategy for maximal constraint satisfaction. *Proceedings ECAI*, pages 69–77, 1994.

A General Scheme for Multiple Lower Bound Computation in Constraint Optimization*

Rina Dechter[1], Kalev Kask[1], and Javier Larrosa[2]

[1] University of California at Irvine (UCI)
{dechter, kkask}@ics.uci.edu
[2] Universitat Politecnica de Catalunya (UPC)
larrosa@lsi.upc.es

Abstract. Computing lower bounds to the best-cost extension of a tuple is an ubiquous task in constraint optimization. A particular case of special interest is the computation of lower bounds to all singleton tuples, since it permits domain pruning in Branch and Bound algorithms. In this paper we introduce MCTE(z), a general algorithm which allows the computation of lower bounds to arbitrary sets of tasks. Its time and accuracy grows as a function of z allowing a controlled tradeoff between lower bound accuracy and time and space to fit available resources. Subsequently, a specialization of MCTE(z) called MBTE(z) is tailored to computing lower bounds to singleton tuples. Preliminary experiments on Max-CSP show that using MBTE(z) to guide dynamic variable and value orderings in branch and bound yields a dramatic reduction in the search space and, for some classes of problems, this reduction is highly cost-effective producing significant time savings and is competitive against specialized algorithms for Max-CSP.

1 Introduction

One of the main successes in constraint satisfaction is the development of *local consistency* properties and their corresponding *consistency enforcing algorithms* [19,11]. They allow to *infer* and make explicit constraints that are implicit in the problem. Most useful in practice are consistency enforcing algorithms that *filter out* values that cannot participate in a solution. Filtering algorithms can be embedded into a search-based solver, propagating the effect of the current assignment towards future variables by pruning infeasible values under the current assignment [20,3,6].

Several attempts have been made in recent years to extend the notion of local consistency to *constraint optimization* problems [4,5,21]. The main difficulty being that inferred soft constraints cannot be carelessly added to the problem, due to the non-idempotency of the operator used to aggregate costs. A whole line of research mitigates this problem by extending only directional local consistency to soft constraints and focuses on its most practical use: detecting *lower*

* This work was supported in part by NSF grant IIS-0086529, by MURI ONR award N00014-00-1-0617 and Spanish Cicyt project TAP1999-1086-C03-03

T. Walsh (Ed.): CP 2001, LNCS 2239, pp. 346–360, 2001.

bounds for the best extension of tuples[23,9,17,21,13,14]. When there is an upper bound on the maximum cost of a solution, tuples having a lower bound higher than this bound cannot participate in an optimal solution and can be viewed as infeasible (i.e., a *nogood*). As in the CSP context, lower bounds for values (singleton tuples) are of special interest, because they can be used to filter out infeasible values.

This paper, introduces MCTE(z), a general tree decomposition method for *multiple* lower bound computation, and MBTE(z), its specialization to tree that compute singleton tuples. Our scheme is built on top of *cluster-tree elimination* (CTE), a tree-based decomposition schema which unifies several approaches for automated reasoning tasks. Algorithm MCTE(z) approximates CTE using a partitioning idea similar to *mini-buckets* [9]. The parameter z controls its complexity (which is exponential in z) as well as its accuracy, and can therefore be tuned to best fit the available resources.

After describing CTE and introducing MCTE (sections 3 and 4), we describe MBTE(z) in Section 5. As we show in the empirical section, MBTE(z) facilitates a parameterized dynamic look-ahead method for variable and value ordering heuristics in branch and bound. The parameter controls its pruning power and overhead, and can therefore adjust branch and bound to different levels of problem hardness: while low accuracy suffices for easy problems, higher accuracy may be more cost-effective when problems grow harder and larger.

Lower bounds for singleton tuples can be obtained by n runs of the mini-bucket elimination MBE(z) [9] which we will call nMBE(z). We contrast MBTE(z) against this alternative nMBE(z). We argue that for the same level of accuracy (same parameter z), MBTE(z) is considerably more efficient (up to linear speed-up). Time efficiency is of the essence when the ultimate goal is to use these algorithms at every node of a branch and bound search. Indeed, our preliminary experiments on Max-CSP (Section 7) support theory-based expectations regarding MBTE(z)'s accuracy as a function of z as well as its speed-up relative to nMBE(z). Most significantly, however, we demonstrate the potential of embedding MBTE(z) in Branch and Bound, showing a dramatic pruning power in search space relative to competitive Branch and Bound algorithms, which, for some problem classes is highly cost-effective. For space considerations, some of the experiments and proofs can be found in the full paper in [15] appearing in http://www.ics.uci.edu/~ dechter/publications/.

2 Preliminaries

Definition 1 (sum of functions, variable elimination). *Let f and g be two functions defined over $var(f)$ and $var(g)$, respectively. Then,*

1. *The* sum *of f and g, denoted $f+g$, is a new function defined over $var(f) \cup var(g)$ which returns for each tuple the sum of values given by f and g, $(f+g)(t) = f(t) + g(t)$*

2. *The* elimination *of x_i from f by minimization, denoted* $\min_{x_i} f$*, is a new function defined over $var(f) - \{x_i\}$ which returns for each tuple the minimum cost extension to f, $(\min_{x_i} f)(t) = \min_{a \in D_i}\{f(t,a)\}$ where D_i denotes the domain of variable x_i and $f(t,a)$ denotes the value of f on the tuple t extended with value a assigned to x_i. We use* $(\min_S f)(t)$*, to denote the elimination of a set of variables $S \subseteq var(f)$.*

Definition 2 (lower bound function). *Let f and g be two functions defined over the same scope (same set of arguments). We say that g is a lower bound of f, denoted $g \leq f$, iff $g(t) \leq f(t)$, for all t.*

Definition 3 (constraint optimization problem (COP), constraint graph). *A* constraint optimization problem *(COP) is a triplet $P =< X, D, F >$, where $X = \{x_1, \ldots, x_n\}$ is a set of variables, $D = \{D_1, \ldots, D_n\}$ is a set of finite domains and $F = \{f_1, \ldots, f_m\}$ is a set of constraints. Constraints can be either* soft *(i.e., cost functions) or* hard *(i.e., sets of allowed tuples). Without loss of generality we assume that hard constraints are represented as (bi-valued) cost functions. Allowed and forbidden tuples have cost 0 and ∞, respectively. The* constraint graph *of a problem P has the variables as its nodes, and two nodes are connected if they appear in a scope of a function in F.*

Definition 4 (optimization tasks, global and singleton). *Given a COP instance P, a set of optimization tasks is defined by $Z = \{Z_i\}_{i=1}^k$, $Z_i \subseteq X$ where for each Z_i the task is to compute a function g_i over Z_i, such that $g_i(t)$ is the best cost attainable by extending t to X. Formally, $g_i(t) = \min_{X-Z_i}(\sum_{j=1}^m f_j)$. A* global optimization *is the task of finding the best global cost, namely $Z = \{\emptyset\}$.* Singleton optimization *is the task of finding the best-cost extension to every singleton tuple (x_i, a), namely $Z = \{\{x_1\}, \{x_2\}, \ldots, \{x_n\}\}$.*

Bucket elimination (BE) [7] is an algorithm for global optimization. Roughly, the algorithm starts by partitioning the set of constraints into n buckets, one per variable. Then variables are eliminated one by one. For each variable x_i, a new constraint h_i is computed using the functions in its bucket, summarizing the effect of x_i on the rest of the problem. h_i is then placed in the bucket of the last variable in its scope. After processing the last variable, only an empty-scope constraint (i.e., a constant function) containing the cost of the best solution remains in the problem. The bucket-elimination algorithm is time and space exponential in a graph parameter called induced-width (to be defined later).

Mini-bucket elimination (MBE) [9] is an approximation of BE that mitigates its high time and space complexity. When processing variable x_i, its bucket is partitioned into mini-buckets. Each mini-bucket is processed independently, producing bounded arity functions which are cheaper to compute and store. This paper extends the idea of mini-bucket elimination from variable-elimination algorithms to tree-decomposition schemes.

3 Cluster-Tree Elimination (CTE)

In this Section we present *cluster-tree elimination* (CTE), a general decomposition method for automated reasoning tasks. The algorithm is not new, it is a unifying description of variants of such algorithms appearing in the past 2 decades both in the constraints community and the probabilistic reasoning community [18,8,22,12]. We describe the scheme in some detail since it will allow presenting our approximation in the most general setting. We also provide refined complexity analysis (see [15] for additional details). CTE is based on the concept of *tree-decomposition.* We use notation borrowed from [12].

Definition 5 (tree-decomposition, separator, eliminator). *Given a COP instance P, a* tree-decomposition *is a triplet $< T, \chi, \psi >$, where $T = (V, E)$ is a tree, and χ and ψ are labeling functions which associate with each vertex $v \in V$ two sets, $\chi(v) \subseteq X$ and $\psi(v) \subseteq F$ that satisfy the following conditions:*

1. *For each function $f_i \in F$, there is* exactly *one vertex $v \in V$ such that $f_i \in \psi(v)$. Vertex v satisfies that $var(f_i) \subseteq \chi(v)$.*
2. *For each variable $x_i \in X$, the set $\{v \in V | x_i \in \chi(v)\}$ induces a connected subtree of T. This is called the* running intersection *property.*

Let (u, v) be an edge of a tree-decomposition, the separator *of u and v is defined as $sep(u, v) = \chi(u) \cap \chi(v)$; the* eliminator *of u and v is defined as $elim(u, v) = \chi(u) - sep(u, v)$.*

Definition 6 (tree-width, hyper-width, maximum separator size). *The tree-width of a tree-decomposition is $tw = \max_{v \in V} |\chi(v)| - 1$, its hyper-width is $hw = \max_{v \in V} |\psi(v)|$, and its maximum separator size is $s = \max_{(u,v) \in E} |sep(u, v)|$*

Definition 7 (valid tree-decomposition). *We say that the tree-decomposition $< T, \chi, \psi >$ is* valid *for a set of optimization tasks $Z = \{Z_i\}_{i=1}^k$ if for each Z_i there exists a vertex defined as $\{v \in V | \chi(v) = Z_i\}$. Such vertices are called* solution-vertices[1].

Example 1. Consider a constraint optimization problem P with six variables $\{x_1, \ldots, x_6\}$ and six constraints $\{f_1, \ldots, f_6\}$ with scopes: $var(f_1) = \{x_5, x_6\}$, $var(f_2) = \{x_1, x_6\}$, $var(f_3) = \{x_2, x_5\}$, $var(f_4) = \{x_1, x_4\}$, $var(f_5) = \{x_2, x_3\}$ and $var(f_6) = \{x_1, x_2\}$, respectively. Figure 2 depicts a tree-decomposition valid for $Z = \{\{x_1, x_5, x_6\}, \{x_1, x_2, x_5\}\}$ (v_1 and v_2 are solution-vertices for the first and second tasks, respectively).

[1] Normally, solution-vertices are only implicitly required. In our formulation we require them explicitly in order to simplify the algorithmic presentation.

Procedure CTE
Input: A COP instance P, a set of tasks $Z = \{Z_i\}_{i=1}^k$ and a valid tree-decomposition $< T, \chi, \psi >$.
Output: An augmented tree such that each solution-vertex for Z_i contains the solution to task Z_i.

Repeat

1. Select and edge (u, v) such that $m_{(u,v)}$ has not been computed and u has received messages from all adjacent vertices other than v
2. $m_{(u,v)} \leftarrow \min_{elim(u,v)} \sum_{g \in cluster(u), g \neq m_{(v,u)}} g$ (where $cluster(u) = \psi(u) \cup \{m_{(w,u)} | (w, u) \in T\}$)

Until all messages have been computed

Fig. 1. Algorithm cluster-tree elimination (CTE)

Algorithm CTE (Figure 1) computes the solution to a set of tasks by processing a valid tree-decomposition. It works by computing *messages* that are sent along edges in the tree. Message $m_{(u,v)}$ is a function computed at vertex u and sent to vertex v. For each edge, two messages are computed. One in each direction. Message $m_{(u,v)}$ can be computed as soon as all incoming messages to u other than $m_{(v,u)}$ have been received. Initially, only messages at leaves qualify. The set of functions associated with a vertex u augmented with the set of incoming messages is called a *cluster*, $cluster(u) = \psi(u) \cup_{(w,u) \in T} m_{(w,u)}$. A message $m_{(u,v)}$ is computed as the sum of all functions in $cluster(u)$ excluding $m_{(v,u)}$ and the subsequent elimination of variables in the eliminator of u and v. Formally, $m_{(u,v)} = \min_{elim(u,v)} (\sum_{g \in cluster(u), g \neq m_{(v,u)}} g)$. The algorithm terminates when all messages are computed. A solution to task Z_i is contained in any of its solution-vertices, as the sum of all functions in the cluster, $\sum_{g \in cluster(u)} g$.

Example 2. Figure 2 also shows the execution trace of CTE along the tree-decomposition, as the messages sent along the tree edges. Once messages are computed, solutions are contained in the solution-vertices. For instance, the solution to task $\{x_1, x_2, x_5\}$ is contained in $cluster(v_2)$ as $m_{(v_1,v_2)} + m_{(v_3,v_2)} + f_3 + f_6$. Similarly, the solution to task $\{x_1, x_5, x_6\}$ is contained in $cluster(v_1)$ as $f_1 + f_2 + m_{(v_2,v_1)}$.

Theorem 1 (correctness [18,8,22]). *Algorithm CTE is correct. Namely, for each solution-vertex v of Z_i, $\sum_{g \in cluster(v)} g = \min_{X - Z_i} (\sum_{j=1}^n f_j)$*

We can show that,

Theorem 2 (complexity). *The complexity of CTE is time $O(r \cdot (hw + dg) \cdot d^{tw+1})$ and space $O(r \cdot d^s)$, where r is the number of vertices in the tree-decomposition, hw is the hyper-width, dg is the maximum degree (i.e., number of adjacent vertices) in the graph, tw is the tree-width, d is the largest domain size in the problem and s is the maximum separator size.*

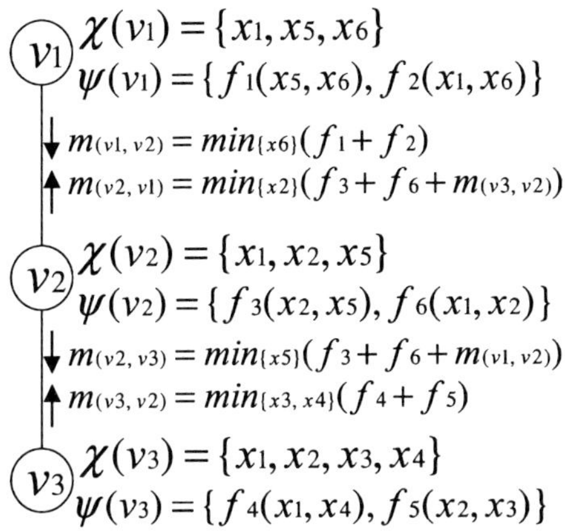

Fig. 2. Execution-trace of CTE along a tree-decomposition.

Since CTE is time and space exponential in tw and s, respectively, low width tree-decompositions are desirable (note that $tw+1 \geq s$). Finding the minimum width decomposition-tree is known to be NP-complete [1], but various approximation algorithms are available [2].

4 Mini-Cluster-Tree Elimination (MCTE)

The time and especially the space complexity of CTE renders the method infeasible for high-width tree-decompositions. One way to decrease the algorithm's complexity is to bound the size of the messages' arity to a predefined size z. This idea, called *mini-buckets*, was first introduced in the bucket elimination context [9]. Here we extend it from approximating bucket elimination to the more general setting of approximating CTE.

Let G be a set of functions having variable x_i in their scope. Suppose we want to compute a target function as the sum of functions in G and subsequently eliminate variable x_i (i.e., $\min_{x_i}(\sum_{g \in G} g)$). If exact computation is too costly, we can partition G into sets of functions $\mathcal{P}(G) = \{\mathcal{P}_j\}_{j=1}^{k}$ called mini-buckets, each one having a combined scope of size bounded by z. Such a partition is called a *z-partition*. If more than one partition is possible, any one is suitable. Subsequently, a bounded arity function h^j is computed at each mini-bucket $\mathcal{P}_j$ as the sum of all its included functions followed by the elimination of x_i (i.e., $h^j = \min_{x_i}(\sum_{g \in \mathcal{P}_j} g)$). The result is a set of functions $\{h^j\}_{j=1}^{k}$ which provides a lower bound to the target function. Namely, $\sum_j h^j \leq \min_{x_i} \sum_{g \in G} g$.

If more than one variable has to be eliminated, the process is repeated for each, according to a predefined ordering. Procedure $\mathsf{MiniBucketsApprox}(V, G, z)$

Procedure MiniBucketsApprox(V, G, z)
Input: a set of ordered variables V, a set of functions G, parameter z
Output: a set of functions $\{h^j\}_{j=1}^k$ that provide a lower bound as $\sum_{j=1}^k h^j \leq \min_V(\sum_{g \in G} g)$
for each $x_i \in V$ from last to first **do**
  $G' \leftarrow \{g \in G \mid x_i \in var(g)\}$
  compute $\mathcal{P}(G') = \{\mathcal{P}_j\}_{j=1}^k$ a z-partition of G'
  $h^j \leftarrow \min_{x_i}(\sum_{g \in \mathcal{P}_j} g)$, for $j = 1..k$
  $G \leftarrow (G - G') \cup \{h^j\}$
Return: G

Fig. 3. Procedure MiniBucketsApprox(V, G, z).

(Fig. 3) describes this process. Each iteration of the loop performs the elimination of one variable.[2]

Applying this idea to CTE yields a new algorithm called *mini-cluster-tree elimination* (MCTE(z)) The algorithm can be obtained by replacing line 2 in CTE by:

2. $M_{(u,v)} \leftarrow MiniBucketApprox(elim(u,v), cluster(u) - M_{(v,u)}, z)$
(where a message $M_{(u,v)}$ is a set of functions and
$cluster(u) = \psi(u) \cup \{M_{(w,u)} | (w,u) \in T\})$

It works similar to CTE except that each time that a message has to be computed, the set of functions required for the computation are partitioned into *mini-buckets*, producing a set of *mini-messages* that are transmitted along the corresponding edge. Thus, in MCTE(z), a message is a *set* of bounded arity functions, $M_{(u,v)} = \{m^j_{(u,v)}\}$ (note that we use upper-case to distinguish MCTE(z) messages from CTE messages). A cluster is now the union of all messages and all functions in a node, $cluster(u) = \psi(u) \cup_{(w,u) \in T} M_{(w,u)}$ The message $M_{(u,v)}$ is computed by calling MiniBucketsApprox(V, G, z) with $V = elim(u,v)$ and $G = cluster(u) - M_{(v,u)}$. When all messages have been computed, a lower bound to task Z_i is contained in its solution-vertex v as the sum of all the functions in its cluster, $\sum_{g \in cluster(v)} g$.

Example 3. Figure 4 shows the execution-trace of MCTE(2) with our running example and the tree-decomposition of Fig. 2. For instance, the computation of $M_{(v_3,v_2)}$ requires a 2-partition of $(cluster(v_3) - M_{(v_2,v_3)}) = \{f_4(x_1,x_4), f_5(x_2,x_3)\}$. The only 2-partition here is $\mathcal{P}_1 = \{f_4\}$ and $\mathcal{P}_2 = \{f_5\}$, which yields a two-functions message $M_{(v_3,v_2)} = \{\min_{x_4}(f_4), \min_{x_3}(f_5)\}$.

Theorem 3 (correctness). *Given a valid tree-decomposition, MCTE(z) computes a lower bound for each task Z_i. Specifically, if u is a solution-vertex of task Z_i then,* $\sum_{g \in cluster(u)} g \leq \min_{X - Z_i}(\sum_{j=1}^n f_j)$

[2] Another option is to eliminate all variables *at once* from each mini-bucket (i.e., $h^j = \min_V(\sum_{g \in \mathcal{P}_j} g)$). While correct, it will provide less accurate lower bounds.

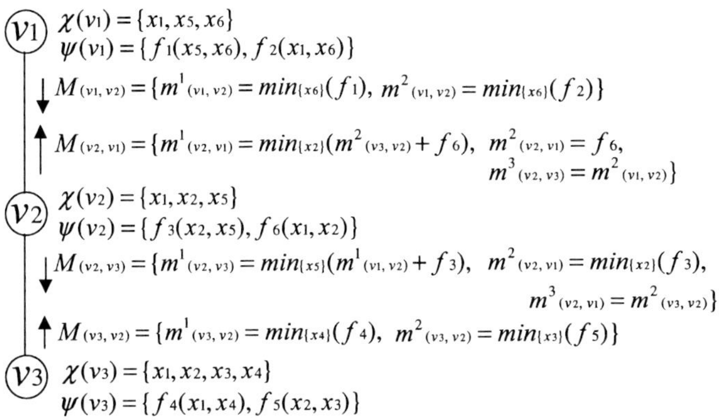

Fig. 4. An execution trace of MCTE(2).

In order to analyze the complexity of MCTE(z) we define a new labeling ψ^*, which depends on the tree-decomposition structure.

Definition 8 (ψ^*, induced hyper-width (hw^*)). *Let $P =< X, D, F >$ be a COP instance and $< T, \chi, \psi >$ be a tree-decomposition. We define a labeling function ψ^* over nodes in the tree as, $\psi^*(v) = \{f \in F| \; var(f) \cap \chi(v) \neq \emptyset\}$. The* induced hyper-width *of a tree-decomposition is $hw^* = \max_{v \in V} |\psi^*(v)|$*

Observe that $\psi^*(u)$ is a superset of $\psi(u)$ which includes those cost functions not in $\psi(u)$ that *may travel* to cluster u via message-passing. It can be shown that the *induced hyper-width* bounds the maximum number of functions that can be in a cluster, and therefore the number of mini-buckets in a cluster. Namely $hw^* \geq \max_{v \in V} |cluster(v)|$. Note that $hw \leq hw^* \leq m$, where hw is the hyper-width and m is the number of input functions.

Theorem 4 (complexity). *Given a problem P and a tree-decomposition T having induced hyper width hw^*, MCTE(z) is time and space $O(r \times hw^* \times d^z)$, where r is the number of nodes in T, and d bounds the domain size.*

Clearly, increasing z is likely to provide better lower bounds at a higher cost. Therefore, MCTE(z) allows trading lower bound accuracy for time and space complexity. There is no guaranteed improvement however.

5 MBTE(z): Computing Bounds to Singleton Tuples

There are a variety of ways in which valid tree-decompositions can be obtained. We analyze a special decomposition called bucket-trees, which is particularly suitable for the multiple singleton optimality task (def. 4). The concept of bucket-tree is inspired from viewing bucket-elimination algorithms as message-passing along a tree [7]. A *bucket-tree* can be defined over the *induced graph* relative to a variable ordering.

Definition 9 (induced graph, induced width [7]). *An* ordered constraint graph *is a pair (G, o), where G is a constraint graph and $o = x_1, ..., x_n$ is an ordering of its nodes. Its* induced graph $G^*(o)$ *is obtained by processing the nodes recursively, from last to first: when node x_i is processed, all its lower neighbors are connected. The* induced width $w^*(o)$ *is the maximum number of lower neighbors over all vertices of the induced graph.*

Definition 10 (bucket-tree). *Given the induced graph $G^*(o)$ of a problem P along ordering o, a* bucket-tree *is a tree-decomposition $< T, \chi, \psi >$ is defined as follows. (i) There is a vertex v_i associated with each variable x_i. The parent of v_i is v_j iff x_j is the closest lower neighbor of x_i in $G^*(o)$. (ii) $\chi(v_i)$ contains x_i and every lower neighbor of x_i in $G^*(o)$. (iii) $\psi(v_i)$ contains every constraint having x_i as the highest indexed variable in its scope.*

Notice that in a bucket-tree, vertex v_1, the root, is a solution-vertex for the task $\{x_1\}$. The bucket-tree can be augmented with solution-vertices for each singleton-optimality task. A vertex u_i with $\chi(u_i) = \{x_i\}$ and $\psi(u_i) = \emptyset$ is added for $i = 2..n$. Vertex v_i is the parent of u_i. Subsequently, we define algorithm *Bucket-tree elimination* (BTE) to be CTE applied to the augmented bucket-tree.

Example 4. Figure 5 shows the execution-trace of BTE on our running example. Observe that messages from u-nodes to v-nodes do not need to be sent because they are null functions ($\psi(u_i) = \emptyset$).

Observe that BTE computes the exact singleton optimality problem. Observe also that BTE can be viewed as a two-phases algorithm. The first phase (where messages from leaves to root are transmitted) is equivalent to *bucket elimination* (BE) [7]: Cluster v_i is the bucket of x_i. Incoming messages are new functions derived from higher buckets and added to the bucket of x_i. Computing message $m_{(v_i, p(v_i))}$, where $p(v_i)$ is the parent of v_i, performs the elimination of variable v_i and produces a new function (the message) that is sent to a lower bucket (the parent of v_i).

Next, *Mini bucket tree elimination* (MBTE(z)) is defined by approximating BTE via mini-buckets or, equivalently, by executing MCTE(z) over the augmented bucket-tree. BTE and MBTE(z) process the same tree-decomposition but in MBTE(z) clusters are z-partitioned, producing mini-bucket-based messages. From Theorem 4 we can conclude,

Theorem 5 (complexity). *Given a variable ordering, the complexity of MBTE(z) is $O(n \cdot hw^* \cdot d^z)$, when n is the number of variables and hw^* is the bucket-tree induced hyper-width.*

MBTE vs nMBE: It is easy to see that *mini-bucket elimination* MBE(z) [9] is equivalent to the first message-passing phase of MBTE(z). In particular, running MBE(z) n times, an algorithm that we call nMBE(z), each time having a different variable initiating the ordering, is an alternative for the singleton optimality

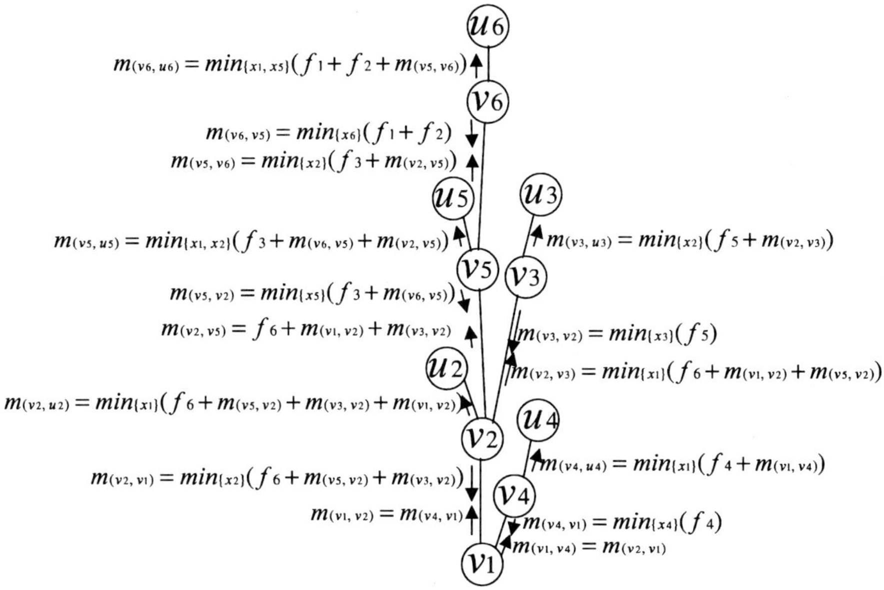

Fig. 5. An execution trace of BTE for the task of computing the best extension of all singleton tuples. If only top-down messages are considered, the algorithm is equivalent to BE

problem. MBTE and nMBE are closely related in terms of accuracy. Specifically, if MBE(z) is executed each time with the appropriate variable orderings, both approaches will produce exactly the same bounds, when using the same bucket-partitioning strategy. Clearly, however, MBTE(z) is always more efficient than multiple executions of MBE(z), since MBE(z) repeats message computation at different executions. The following Theorem summarizes these properties.

Theorem 6. *Let P be a constraint optimization problem and o a variable ordering. Lets consider the execution of MBTE(z) over the bucket-tree relative to o.*

- *(Accuracy) For each variable x_i, there is an ordering o_i initiated by x_i such that executing MBE(z) with o_i produces the same lower bound as MBTE(z) for task $\{x_i\}$, provided that both algorithms use the same criterion to select z-partitions.*
- *(time comparison) Let nMBE(z) be n executions of MBE(z) using the n previously defined o_i orderings. Then, every message computed by MBTE(z) is also computed by nMBE(z), and there are some messages that are computed multiple times (up to n) by nMBE(z).*

Thus, MBTE(z) is never worse than nMBE(z). Since the complexity of running MBE(z) n times is $O(n \cdot m \cdot d^z)$ and MBTE(z) is $O(n \cdot hw^* \cdot d^z)$, significant gains are expected when hw^* is smaller relative to m.

6 Comparison of MBTE with Soft Arc-Consistency

Soft arc-consistency (SAC) [21] is the most general of a sequence of bounds for singleton optimization. They are based in different forms of arc-consistency [17]. We consider the most general algorithm for SAC. Namely, the algorithm that after achieving soft arc-consistency, is allowed to iterate non-deterministically projecting and extending cost functions in order to increase, if possible, the available bounds ([21], Sec. 5).

In the following we briefly argue that there is no dominance relation between SAC and MBTE. Namely, there exist instances in which either approach computes better bounds than the other. In the full paper [15] we provide two examples illustrating this fact.

On the one hand, tree-decomposition based bounds such as MBTE need to transform the problem into an acyclic structure and each cost function has a single path to be propagated from one vertex to another. SAC works directly on the (possibly cyclic) constraint graph. Then the same function can be propagated simultaneously through different paths. As a result, information from a cost function may split and merge again. This fact allows SAC to outperform MBTE in some problem instances.

On the other hand, SAC algorithms can only project functions one by one, while MBTE can sum functions and project from the result. In a simplistic way, it is as if SAC is only allowed to compute bounds using $\sum_{f \in F} \min_V f$, while MBTE can perform $\min_V \sum_{f \in F} f$ as long as arities do not surpass value z. This fact allows MBTE to outperform SAC in some problem instances.

7 Empirical Results

We performed a preliminary experimental evaluation of the performance of MBTE(z) on solving the singleton optimality task. *i*) we have investigated the performance of MBTE(z) against its obvious brute-force alternative – nMBE(z), and showed that MBTE(z) achieves a significant speedup over nMBE(z). *ii*) we demonstrated that as expected, MBTE(z) accuracy grows as function of z, thus allowing a trade-off between accuracy and complexity. *iii*) we evaluated the effectiveness of MBTE(z) in improving Branch and Bound search. For space reasons we report only the search experiments. Details on experiments with speed-up and accuracy are available in the full paper [15].

All our experiments are done using the Max-CSP task as a sample domain. Max-CSP is an optimization version of Constraint Satisfaction and its task is to find an assignment that satisfies the most constraints. We use its formulation as a minimization problem where each constraint is a cost function that assigns a cost 1 to each nogood and cost 0 to each allowed tuple. We used the well known four parameter model, $< N, K, C, T >$, for random problem generation, where N is the number of variables, K is the domain size, C is the number of constraints, and T is the tightness of each constraint (see [16] for details).

Table 1. BBBT(z) vs. BBMB(z).

$N = 50$, $K = 5$, $C = 150$. $w^* = 17.6$. 10 instances. time = 600sec.							
T	BBMB z=2	BBMB z=3	BBMB z=4	BBMB z=5	BBMB z=6	BBBT z=2	PFC-MRDAC
	# solved time backtracks	# solved time backtracks	# solved time backtracks	# solved time backtracks	# solved time backtracks	# solved time backtracks	# solved time backtracks
5	6 45 1.11M	7 54 1.51M	6 6.2 177K	9 75 2.29M	10 6.2 123K	10 1.9 55	10 0.01 436
7	4 134 5.86M	5 150 4.62M	7 213 5.3M	8 208 5.14M	9 97 2.1M	10 2.5 94	10 1.7 15K
9	-	-	1 325 7.4M	3 227 4.97M	3 229 4.85M	10 14.3 2.1K	10 27.3 242K

Table 2. BBBT(z) vs. BBMB(z).

$N = 100$, $K = 5$, $C = 300$. $w^* = 33.9$. 10 instances. time = 600sec.								
T	BBMB z=2	BBMB z=3	BBMB z=4	BBMB z=5	BBMB z=6	BBMB z=7	BBBT z=2	PFC-MRDAC
	# solved time backtracks	# solved time backtracks	# solved time backtracks	# solved time backtracks	# solved time backtracks	# solved time backtracks	# solved time backtracks	# solved time backtracks
3	6 6 150K	6 6 150K	6 6 150K	6 5 115K	8 6.8 115K	8 15 8	10 7.73 60	10 0.03 750
5	2 36 980K	2 32 880K	2 24 650K	2 5.3 130K	3 38 870K	3 33 434K	10 14.3 114	10 0.06 1.5K
7	0	0	0	0	0	0	10 29 331	6 267 1.6M

7.1 BBBT: Branch and Bound with MBTE(z)

Since MBTE(z) computes lower bounds for each singleton-variable assignment, when incorporated within a Branch-and-Bound search, MBTE(z) can facilitate domain pruning and dynamic variable ordering. In this section we investigate the performance of such a new algorithm, called BBBT(z) (Branch-and-Bound with Bucket-Tree heuristics), and compare it against BBMB(z) [13].

BBMB(z) [13] is a Branch-and-Bound search algorithm that uses Mini-Bucket Elimination (MBE(z)) as a pre-processing step. MBE(z) generates intermediate functions that are used to compute a heuristic value for each node in the search space. Since these intermediate functions are pre-computed, before search starts, BBMB(z) uses the same fixed variable ordering as MBE(z). Unlike BBBT(z), BBMB(z) does not prune domains of variables. In the past [14] we showed that BBMB(z) was effective and competitive with alternative state-of-the-art algorithms for Max-CSP.

BBBT(z) is a Branch-and-Bound search algorithm that uses MBTE(z) at each node in the search space. Unlike BBMB(z), BBBT(z) has no pre-processing step. At each node in the search space, MBTE(z) is used to compute lower bounds for each variable-value assignment of future variables. These lower bounds are used for domain pruning – whenever a lower bound of a variable-value assignment is not less than the global upper bound, the value is deleted. BBBT(z) backtracks whenever an empty domain of a future variable is created.

Table 3. BBBT(z) vs. BBMB(z).

$N = 50$, $K = 5$, $C = 100$. $w^* = 10.6$. 10 instances. time = 600sec.							
T	BBMB z=4	BBMB z=6	BBMB z=8	BBBT z=2	BBBT z=5	BBBT z=8	PFC-MRDAC
	# solved time backtracks	# solved time backtracks	# solved time backtracks	# solved time backtracks	# solved time backtracks	# solved time backtracks	# solved time backtracks
15	8 184 13M	10 4.51 120K	10 12.4 24K	3 394 22K	9 190 565	8 91 30	9 108 1.0M

BBBT(z) also uses dynamic variable ordering – when picking the next variable to instantiate, it selects a variable with the smallest domain size. Ties are broken by picking a variable with the largest sum of lower bounds associated with each value. In addition, for value selection, BBBT(z) selects a value with the smallest lower bound.

In Tables 1-3 we have the results of experiments with three sets of Max-CSP problems: N=50, K=5, C=150, $5 \leq T \leq 9$, N=100, K=5, C=300, $3 \leq T \leq 7$, and N=50, K=5, C=100, T=15. On each problem instance we ran BBMB(z) for different values of z, as well as BBBT(2). We also ran BBBT(z) for larger values of z, but BBBT(2) was most cost effective on these problems. For comparison, we also report the results with PFC-MRDAC [17] that is currently one of the best algorithms for Max-CSP.

In column 1 we have the tightness, in the last two columns we report BBBT(2) and PFC-MRDAC, and in the middle columns we have BBMB(z). For each set of problems, we report the number of problems solved (within the time bound of 600 seconds), the average CPU time and number of deadends for solved problems. For example, we see from Table 1 (N=50, K=5, C=150), that when tightness T is 5, BBMB(6) solved all 10 problems, taking 6.2 seconds and 123 thousand backtracking steps, on the average, whereas BBBT(2) also solved all 10 problems, taking 1.9 seconds and 55 backtracking steps, on the average.

We see from Tables 1 and 2 that on these two sets of problems, BBBT(2) is vastly superior to BBMB(z), especially as the tightness increases. Average CPU time of BBBT(2) is as much as an order of magnitude less than BBMB(z). Sporadic experiments with 200 and 300 variable instances showed that BBBT(2) continues to scale up very nicely on these problems. BBBT(2) is also faster than PFC-MRDAC on tight constraints.

The experiments also demonstrate the pruning power of MBTE(z). The number of backtracking steps used by BBBT(2) is up to three orders of magnitude less than BBMB(z). For example, we see from Table 1 that when tightness T is 7, BBMB(6) solved 9 problems out of 10, taking 2.1 million backtracking steps in 97 seconds, whereas BBBT(2) solved all 10 problems, taking 94 backtracking steps in 2.5 seconds.

We observed a different behavior on problems having sparser constraint graphs and tight constraints. While still very effective in pruning the search space, BBBT was not as cost-effective as BBMB(z) (which invests in heuristic computation only once). Table 3 exhibits a typical performance (N=50,C=100,

K=5, T=15). We observe that here BBBT's performance exhibit a U-shape, improving with z up to an optimal z value. However, BBBT's slope of improvement is much more moderate as compared with BBMB.

8 Conclusions and Future Work

Since constraint optimization is NP-hard, approximation algorithms are of clear practical interest. In the paper we extend the mini-bucket scheme proposed for variable elimination to tree-decomposition. We have introduced a new algorithm for lower bound computation, MCTE(z), applicable to arbitrary sets of tasks. The parameter z allows trading accuracy for complexity and can be adjusted to best fit the available resources. MBTE(z) is a special case of MCTE(z) for the computation of lower bounds to singleton optimization, based on a bucket-tree. This task is relevant in the context of branch and bound solvers. Both algorithms have been derived to approximate CTE, a tree-decomposition schema for reasoning tasks which unifies a number of approaches appearing in the past 2 decades in the constraint satisfaction and probabilistic reasoning context.

We have shown that bounds obtained with MBTE(z) have the same accuracy as if computed with n runs of plain mini-buckets. The quality of such accuracy has already been demonstrated in a number of domains [9]. We have also shown that MBTE(z) can be up to n times faster than the alternative of running plain mini-buckets n times. This speed-up is essential if the algorithm is to be used at every node within a branch and bound solver. Our preliminary experiments suggest that MBTE(z) is very promising. It generates good quality bounds at a reasonable cost. When incorporated within branch and bound, it reduces dramatically the search space explored which sometimes translates into great time savings. Note that our implementation is general and has not yet been optimized.

Our approach leaves plenty of room for future improvement, which are likely to make it more cost effective in practice. For instance, it can be modified to treat separately hard and soft constraints, since hard constraints can be more efficiently processed and propagated [10]. As a matter of fact, even if the original problem has no hard constraints, our approach can be used to infer them (i.e., detect infeasible tuples). Also, currently our partitioning to mini-buckets was always random. Investigating heuristics for partitioning may increase the accuracy of the algorithms.

References

[1] S.A. Arnborg. Efficient algorithms for combinatorial problems on graphs with bounded decomposability - a survey. *BIT*, 25:2–23, 1985.

[2] A. Becker and D. Geiger. A sufficiently fast algorithm for finding close to optimal junction trees. In *Uncertainty in AI (UAI'96)*, pages 81–89, 1996.

[3] C. Bessiere and J.-C. Regin. MAC and combined heuristics: Two reasons to forsake FC (and CBJ?) on hard problems. *Lecture Notes in Computer Science*, 1118:61–75, 1996.

[4] S. Bistarelli, H. Fargier, U. Montanari, F. Rossi, T. Schiex, and G. Verfaillie. Semiring-based CSPs and valued CSPs: Frameworks, properties and comparison. *Constraints*, 4:199–240, 1999.

[5] S. Bistarelly, R. Gennari, and F. Rossi. Constraint propagation for soft constraints: Generalization and termination conditions. In *Proc. of the 6th CP*, pages 83–97, Singapore, 2000.

[6] R. Debruyne and C. Bessière. Some practicable filtering techniques for the constraint satisfaction problem. In *Proc. of the 16th IJCAI*, pages 412–417, Stockholm, Sweden, 1999.

[7] R. Dechter. Bucket elimination: A unifying framework for reasoning. *Artificial Intelligence*, 113:41–85, 1999.

[8] R. Dechter and J. Pearl. Tree clustering for constraint networks. *Artificial Intelligence*, 38:353–366, 1989.

[9] R. Dechter and I. Rish. A scheme for approximating probabilistic inference. In *Proceedings of the 13th UAI-97*, pages 132–141, San Francisco, 1997. Morgan Kaufmann Publishers.

[10] R. Dechter and P. van Beek. Local and global relational consistency. *Theoretical Computer Science*, 173(1):283–308, 20 February 1997.

[11] E. Freuder. A sufficient condition for backtrack-free search. *Journal of the ACM*, 29:24–32, March 1982.

[12] G. Gottlob, N. Leone, and F. Scarcello. A comparison of structural CSP decomposition methods. In Dean Thomas, editor, *Proceedings of the 16th International Joint Conference on Artificial Intelligence (IJCAI-99-Vol1)*, pages 394–399, S.F., July 31–August 6 1999. Morgan Kaufmann Publishers.

[13] K. Kask. new search heuristics for max-csp. In *Proc. of the 6th CP*, pages 262–277, Singapore, 2000.

[14] K. Kask and R. Dechter. A general scheme for automatic generation of search heuristics from specification dependencies. *Artificial Intelligence*, 129(1-2):91–131, 2001.

[15] K. Kask, J. Larrosa, and R. Dechter. A general scheme for multiple lower bound computation in constraint optimization. Technical report, University of California at Irvine, 2001.

[16] J. Larrosa and P. Meseguer. Partial lazy forward checking for max-csp. In *Proc. of the 13th ECAI*, pages 229–233, Brighton, United Kingdom, 1998.

[17] J. Larrosa, P. Meseguer, and T. Schiex. Maintaining reversible DAC for max-CSP. *Artificial Intelligence*, 107(1):149–163, 1999.

[18] S. L. Lauritzen and D. J. Spiegelhalter. Local computation with probabilities on graphical structures and their applications to expert systems. *Journal of the Royal Statistical Society, Series B*, 34:157–224, 1988.

[19] A. Mackworth. Consistency in networks of constraints. *Artificial Intelligence*, 8, 1977.

[20] B. Nudel. Tree search and arc consistency in constraint satisfaction algorithms. *Search in Artifical Intelligence*, 999:287–342, 1988.

[21] T. Schiex. Arc consistency for soft constraints. In *Proc. of the 6th CP*, pages 411–424, Singapore, 2000.

[22] P.P. Shenoy. Binary join-trees for computing marginals in the shenoy-shafer architecture. *International Journal of Approximate Reasoning*, 2-3:239–263, 1997.

[23] G. Verfaillie, M. Lemaître, and T. Schiex. Russian doll search. In *Proc. of the 13^{th}AAAI*, pages 181–187, Portland, OR, 1996.

Solving Disjunctive Constraints for Interactive Graphical Applications

Kim Marriott[1], Peter Moulder[1], Peter J. Stuckey[2], and Alan Borning[3]

[1] School of Comp. Science & Soft. Eng., Monash University, Australia
[2] Dept. of Comp. Science & Soft. Eng., University of Melbourne, Australia
[3] Dept. of Computer Science & Eng., University of Washington, Seattle, USA

Abstract. In interactive graphical applications we often require that objects do not overlap. Such non-overlap constraints can be modelled as disjunctions of arithmetic inequalities. Unfortunately, disjunctions are typically not handled by constraint solvers that support direct manipulation, in part because solving such problems is NP-hard. We show here that is in fact possible to (re-)solve systems of disjunctive constraints representing non-overlap constraints sufficiently fast to support direct manipulation in interactive graphical applications. The key insight behind our algorithms is that the disjuncts in a non-overlap constraint are not disjoint: during direct manipulation we need only move between disjuncts that are adjacent in the sense that they share the current solution. We give both a generic algorithm, and a version specialised for linear arithmetic constraints that makes use of the Cassowary constraint solving algorithm.

1 Introduction

In many constraint-based interactive graphical applications, we wish to declare that several objects should not overlap. When reduced to arithmetic inequality constraints, this becomes a disjunction. As a motivating example, consider the diagram in Figure 1(a) of a 4×3 box and a 2×2 right triangle. The positions of the box and right triangle are given by the coordinates of the lower left-hand corners ((x_B, y_B) and (x_T, y_T)). A user editing this diagram might well want to constrain the box and triangle to never overlap. We can model this using a disjunction of linear constraints that represent the five (linear) ways we can ensure that non-overlapping holds. These are illustrated in Figure 1(b), and depict the five constraints

$$\begin{array}{lcl} x_T \geq x_B + 4 \;\lor\; y_T \geq y_B + 3 \;\lor\; y_T \leq y_B - 2 \;\lor \\ x_T \leq x_B - 2 \quad \lor \quad x_T + y_T \leq x_B + y_B - 2 \end{array}$$

During direct manipulation of, say, the triangle, the solver is allowed to move it to any location that does not cause overlap. For instance, the triangle can be moved around the box. However, if it is moved directly to the left, then once it touches the box, the box (assuming it is unconstrained) will also be pushed left to ensure that overlap does not occur.

T. Walsh (Ed.): CP 2001, LNCS 2239, pp. 361–376, 2001.

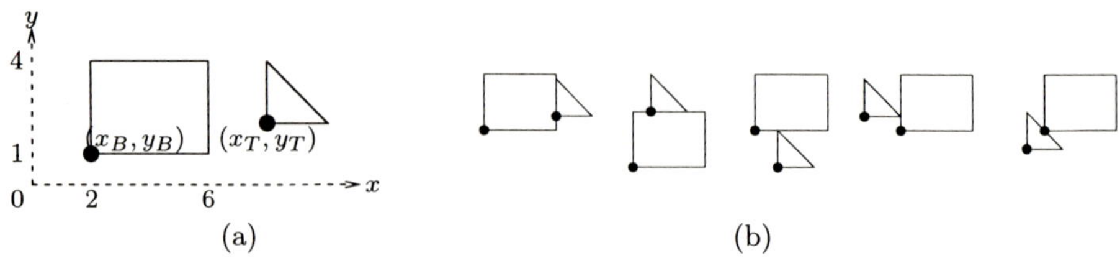

Fig. 1. Simple constrained picture, and five ways to ensure non-overlap.

Unfortunately, current constraint solving technology for interactive graphical applications cannot handle such disjunctive constraints. In part this is because solving such disjunctive systems is, in general, NP-hard. Thus, it seems very difficult to develop constraint solving algorithms that will be sufficiently fast for interactive applications and, in particular, support direct manipulation. An additional difficulty is that we wish to solve such disjunctive constraints in combination with the sort of constraints that are currently provided for interactive graphical applications. As an example, consider the state chart-like diagram shown in Figure 8(a).[1] In a constraint-based editor for such diagrams, we would like to combine non-overlap constraints with containment and connection constraints.

In this paper, we show that is in fact possible to (re-)solve systems of disjunctive constraints representing non-overlap constraints sufficiently fast to support direct manipulation in interactive graphical applications. The key insight behind our algorithms is that the disjuncts in a non-overlap constraint are not disjoint: during direct manipulation we need only move between adjacent disjuncts. At any given time one of the disjuncts will be active (and hence enforced by the solver). As we move to a new solution in which we must make one of the other disjuncts active instead, at the transition point the solution will satisfy both the current disjunct and the new one. This reflects that we want the graphical objects to behave sensibly and continuously during direct manipulation, and so we do not allow transitions through unsatisfiable regions, i.e., we do not allow objects to magically move through one another.

The paper includes three main technical contributions. The first is a general algorithm for solving such non-overlap constraint problems. The algorithm is generic in the choice of the underlying solver used to solve conjunctions of constraints. It is a true extension of the underlying solver, since it allows disjunctions in combination with whatever conjunctive constraints are provided by the underlying solver. We also show how the algorithm extends naturally to the case where the non-overlap constraints are preferred rather than required (Section 2). The second contribution is a specialisation of our generic algorithm to the case when the underlying solver is the Cassowary linear arithmetic constraint solver [3] (Sections 3 & 4). Cassowary is a simplex-based solver, and we can use

[1] State charts, introduced by David Harel [7], are now part of the Unified Modelling Language [12], rapidly becoming the industry standard for object-oriented design.

the information in the simplex tableau to guide the search between disjuncts. Our final contribution is an empirical evaluation of this algorithm (Section 5). We investigate both the speed of resolving and the expressiveness of disjunctions of linear constraints.

Starting with Sutherland [14], there has been considerable work on developing constraint solving algorithms for supporting direct manipulation in interactive graphical applications. These approaches fall into four main classes: propagation based (e.g. [13,15]); linear arithmetic solver based (e.g. [3]); geometric solver-based (e.g. [4,8]); and general non-linear optimisation methods such as Newton-Rapson iteration (e.g. [5]). However, none of these techniques support disjunctive constraints for modelling non-overlap. The only work that we know of that handles non-overlap constraints is that of Baraff [1], who uses a force based approach, modelling the non-overlap constraint between objects by a repulsion between them if they touch. Our approach differs in that it is generic and in that it handles non-overlap constraints in conjunction with other sorts of constraints. Subsequently, Harada, Witkin, and Baraff [6] extended the approach of [1] to support application-specific rules that allow temporary violation of non-overlap constraints in direct manipulation, so that the user can, if necessary, pass one object through another. Such application-specific rules could also be built on top of our algorithms.

2 A General Algorithm for Solving Disjunctions

We are interested in rapidly (re)-solving systems of constraints to support direct manipulation in interactive graphical applications. Graphical objects are displayed on the screen, with their geometric attributes represented by constrainable variables. Usually, the required constraints in such applications are not enough to uniquely fix a solution, i.e. the system of constraints is *underconstrained.* However, since we need to display a concrete diagram, the constraint solver must always determine an assignment θ to the variables that satisfies the constraints. Since we do not want objects to move unnecessarily over the screen, we prefer that the objects (and hence their attributes) stay where they are.

Such preferences can be formalised in terms of *constraint hierarchies* [2], one formalism for representing soft constraints. The idea is that constraints can have an associated strength that indicates to the solver how important it is to satisfy that constraint. There is a distinguished strength *required* which means that the constraint must be satisfied. By convention, constraints without an explicit strength are assumed to be required.

Given constraint hierarchies, it is simple to formalise the constraint solving required during direct manipulation. We have a conjunctive system of constraints C, some of which may be required, some of which may be not. We have some variables, typically one or two, say x and y, that correspond to the graphical attributes such as position that are being edited through direct manipulation. Let the remaining variables be $v_1, \ldots, v_n$ and let the current value of each v_i be

```
disj_solve(C,active[])
    let C be of form C0 ∧ D1 ∧ ··· ∧ Dn where
    C0 is a conjunction of constraints, and each Di is of form
    Di^1 ∨ ··· ∨ Di^ni
    repeat
        θ := csolv(C0 ∧ ⋀_{i=1}^n Di^{active[i]})
        finished := true
        for i := 1,...,n do
            current := active[i]
            active[i] := dchoose(Di^1 ∨ ··· ∨ Di^ni, current, θ)
            if active[i] ≠ current then
                finished := false
                break % Exit 'for' loop.
            endif
        endfor
    until finished
    return θ
```

Fig. 2. Generic algorithm for handling non-overlap constraints.

a_i. The constraint solver must repeatedly resolve a system of form

$$C \wedge v_1 =_{stay} a_1 \wedge \cdots \wedge v_n =_{stay} a_n \wedge x =_{edit} b_1 \wedge y =_{edit} b_2.$$

for different values of b_1 and b_2. The *stay constraints*, $v_1 =_{stay} a_1 \wedge \cdots \wedge v_n =_{stay} a_n$, indicate our preference that attributes are not changed unnecessarily, while the *edit constraints*, $x =_{edit} b_1 \wedge y =_{edit} b_2$, reflect our desire to give x and y the new values b_1 and b_2, respectively. Clearly the *edit* strength should be greater than the *stay* strength for editing to have the desired behaviour.

We can now describe our generic algorithm disj_solve for supporting direct manipulation in the presence of disjunctive constraints modelling non-overlap. It is given in Figure 2. It is designed to support rapid resolving during direct manipulation by being called repeatedly with different desired values for the edit variables. The algorithm is parametric in the choice of an underlying conjunctive constraint solver *csolv*. The solver takes a conjunction of constraints, including stay and edit constraints, and returns a new solution θ. The algorithm is also parametric in the choice of the function *dchoose* which chooses which disjunct in each disjunction is to be made active.

This algorithm is extremely simple. It takes a system of constraints C consisting of conjunctive constraints C_0 conjoined with disjunctive constraints $D_1, \ldots, D_n$, and an array *active* such that for each disjunction D_i, *active*$[i]$ is the index of the currently active disjunct in D_i. We require that the initial *active* value have a feasible solution. The algorithm uses *csolv* to compute the solution θ using the currently active disjunct in each disjunction. Then *dchoose* is called for each disjunction, to see if the active disjunct in that disjunction should be changed. If so, the process is repeated. If not, the algorithm terminates and returns θ. The algorithm is correct in that θ must be a solution of C since it is a solution of C_0 and one disjunct in each disjunction D_i. In practice, for efficiency *csolv* should use incremental constraint solving methods, since *csolv* is called repeatedly with a sequence of problems differing in only one constraint.

Clearly, the choice of *dchoose* is crucial to the efficiency and quality of solution found by disj_solve, since it guides the search through the various disjuncts. A bad choice of *dchoose* could even lead to looping and non-termination, unless some other provision is made. One simple choice for the definition of $dchoose(\mathcal{D}^1 \vee \cdots \vee \mathcal{D}^n, i, \theta)$ is to return j for some $j \neq i$ where θ is a solution of $\mathcal{D}^j$ and $\mathcal{D}^j$ has not been active before, or else i if no such j exists. A problem with this definition is that, even if a disjunction is irrelevant to the quality of solution, the algorithm may explore other disjuncts in the disjunction. We can improve this definition by only choosing a different disjunct from $\mathcal{D}^i$ if $\mathcal{D}^i$ is "active" in the sense that by removing it we could find a better solution. Another improvement is only to move to another disjunct if we can ensure that this leads to a better solution. Regardless, the key to the definition of *dchoose* is that it only chooses a j such that θ is a solution of $\mathcal{D}^j$. This greatly limits the search space and means that we use a hill-climbing strategy. Importantly, it means that we only move smoothly between disjuncts, giving rise to continuous, predictable behaviour during direct manipulation.

It is simple to modify the algorithm to handle the case of overlap constraints that are not required but rather are preferred with some strength w. We simply rewrite each such disjunction D_i to include an error variable for that disjunction e_i, and then conjoin the constraint $e_i =_w 0$ to C_0. For instance, if we prefer that the triangle and box from our motivating example do not overlap with strength *strong* then we can implement this using the constraints

$$\begin{array}{ll} & (e =_{strong} 0) \\ \wedge & (\quad x_T \geq x_B + 4 + e \;\vee\; y_T \geq y_B + 3 + e \;\vee\; y_T \leq y_B - 2 + e \\ & \;\vee\; x_T \leq x_B - 2 + e \;\vee\; x_T + y_T \leq x_B + y_B - 2 + e \;) \end{array}$$

The only difficulty is that we need to modify *dchoose* to allow disjuncts to be swapped as long as the associated error does not increase.

It is instructive to consider the limitations of our approach. First, there is no guarantee that it will find the globally best solution. In the context of interactive graphical applications, this is not as significant a defect as it might appear. As long as direct manipulation behaves predictably, the user can search for the best solution interactively. Second, there is an assumption that disjuncts in a disjunction are not disjoint. This means that we cannot directly handle a "snap to grid" constraint such as $x = 1 \vee x = 2 \vee \cdots \vee x = n$ in which we require that position attributes can take only a fixed number of values, since there is no way to move between these disjuncts. (One way of handling such constraints is using integer programming techniques; see e.g. [11].)

```
simplex(C, f, active[])
  repeat
    let f have form h + Σ_{j=1}^{m} d_j y_j and
    let C have form ∧_{i=1}^{n} x_i = k_i + Σ_{j=1}^{m} a_ij y_j
    % Choose variable y_J to become basic.
    if ∀[j ∈ {1,...,m}] (d_j ≥ 0 or ∃i.y_j ∈ active[i]) then
      return (C, f) % An optimal solution has been found.
    endif
    choose J ∈ {1,...,m} such that d_J < 0 and ∀i.y_j ∉ active[i]
    % Choose variable x_I to become non-basic
    choose I ∈ {1,...,n} such that
      -k_I/a_IJ = min {-k_i/a_iJ | i ∈ {1,...,n} and a_iJ < 0}
    e := (x_I - k_I - Σ_{j=1,j≠J}^{m} a_Ij y_j)/a_IJ
    C[I] := (y_J = e)
    replace y_J by e in f
    for each i ∈ {1,...,n}
      if i ≠ I then replace y_J by e in C[i] endif
    endfor
  endrepeat
```

Fig. 3. Simplex optimization.

3 Simplex Optimisation and the Cassowary Algorithm

We now give an instantiation of our generic algorithm for the case when the underlying solver is simplex based. We shall first review the simplex optimisation and the Cassowary Algorithm.

The simplex algorithm takes a conjunction of linear arithmetic constraints C and a linear arithmetic objective function f which is to be minimised. These must be in *basic feasible solved form*. More exactly, f should have form $h+\sum_{j=1}^{m} d_j y_j$ and C should have form $\bigwedge_{i=1}^{n} x_i = k_i + \sum_{j=1}^{m} a_{ij} y_j$. The variables $y_1, \ldots, y_m$ are called *parameters*, while the variables $x_1, \ldots, x_n$ are said to be *basic*. All variables are implicitly required to be non-negative, and the right-hand side constants (the k_i's) are required to be non-negative.[2] Although the constraints are equations, linear inequalities can be handled by adding a *slack* variable and transforming to an equation. Any set of constraints in basic feasible solved form has an associated variable assignment, which, because of the definition of basic feasible solved form, must be a solution of the constraints. In the case of C above it is

$$\{x_1 \mapsto k_1, \ \ldots, \ x_n \mapsto k_n, \ y_1 \mapsto 0, \ \ldots, \ y_m \mapsto 0\}.$$

The Simplex Algorithm is shown in Figure 3, and takes as inputs the simplex tableau C and the objective function f. The underlined text in the algorithm should be ignored for now. The algorithm repeatedly selects an entry variable

[2] See e.g. [3] for efficient handling of unrestricted-in-sign variables.

y_J such that $d_J < 0$. (An entry variable is one that will enter the basis, i.e., it is currently a parameter and we want to make it basic.) Pivoting on such a variable cannot increase the value of the objective function (and usually decreases it). If no such variable exists, the optimum has been reached. Next we determine the exit variable x_I. We must choose this variable so that it maintains basic feasible solved form by ensuring that the new k_i's are still positive after pivoting. That is, we must choose an I so that $-k_I/a_{IJ}$ is a minimum element of the set

$$\{-k_i/a_{iJ} \mid a_{iJ} < 0 \text{ and } 1 \leq i \leq n\}.$$

If there were no i for which $a_{iJ} < 0$ then we could stop since the optimization problem would be unbounded and so would not have a minimum: we could choose y_J to take an arbitrarily large value and thus make the objective function arbitrarily small. However, this is not an issue in our context since our optimization problems will always have a non-negative lower bound. We proceed to choose x_I, and pivot x_I out and replace it with y_J to obtain the new basic feasible solution. We continue this process until an optimum is reached.

One obvious issue is how we convert a system of equations into basic feasible solved form. Luckily the Simplex Algorithm itself can be used to do this. An incremental version of this algorithm is described in [10]. The only point to note is that adding a new constraint may require that simplex optimisation must be performed.

In the special case that we have constraints in a basic solved form which is infeasible in the sense that some right-hand side constants (the k_is) may be negative, but which is optimal in the sense that all coefficients in the objective function are non-negative, we can use the Dual Simplex Algorithm to restore feasibility. This is similar to the Simplex Algorithm, except that the role of the objective function and the right-hand side constants are reversed.

The Simplex Algorithm and the Dual Simplex Algorithm provide a good basis for fast incremental resolving of linear arithmetic constraints for interactive graphical applications. One simplex-based algorithm for solving direct manipulation constraints is Cassowary [3]. The key idea behind the approach is to rewrite non-required constraints (such as edit and stay constraints) of form $x =_w k$ into $x + \delta_x^+ - \delta_x^- = k$ and add the term $c_w \times \delta_x^+ + c_w \times \delta_x^-$ to the objective function, where δ_x^+ and δ_x^- are error variables, and c_w is a coefficient reflecting the strength w. The Dual Simplex Algorithm can now be used to solve the sequence of problems arising in direct manipulation, since only the right hand side constants are changing.

4 A Disjunctive Solver Based on the Cassowary Algorithm

We now describe how to embed the Cassowary Algorithm into the generic algorithm given earlier. We could embed it directly by simply using it as the constraint solver *csolv* referenced in Figure 2, but we can do better than this.

It is moderately expensive to incrementally add and delete constraints using the simplex method. For this reason, we keep all disjuncts in the solved form, rather than moving them in and out of the solved form whenever we switch disjuncts. Since we only want one disjunct from each disjunction to be active at any time, we represent each disjunction using linear constraints together with error variables representing the degree of violation of each disjunct. As long as one error variable in the disjunction has value zero, the disjunctive constraint is satisfied. (The other error variables can be disregarded.)

More formally, the *error form* of an equation $a_1x_1 + \ldots + a_nx_n = b$ is $a_1x_1 + \ldots + a_nx_n + e^- - e^+ = b$ where e^+ and e^- are two non-negative *error variables*, representing the degree to which the equation is satisfied, while the *error form* of an inequality $a_1x_1 + \ldots + a_nx_n \le b$ is $a_1x_1 + \ldots + a_nx_n + s - e = b$ where s is the slack variable and e is the *error variable*. Both s and e must be non-negative. Note that for any values of $x_1, \ldots, x_n$ there is a solution of the error form of each linear constraint. Note also that if we constrain the error variables for some linear constraint c to be zero, then the error form of c is equivalent to c.

The *conjunctive version* of a disjunctive constraint D is the conjunction of the error forms of the disjuncts $\mathcal{D}^1, \ldots, \mathcal{D}^n$ in D. The conjunctive version of a disjunctive constraint D does not ensure that D is satisfied. In order to ensure that the disjunctive constraint is satisfied we must ensure that, for some disjunct $\mathcal{D}^i$ in D, the error variable(s) of the error form of $\mathcal{D}^i$ take value 0.

The conjunctive version of our example disjunctive constraint is

$$\begin{array}{l} x_T + e_1 = x_B + 4 + s_1 \ \wedge \ y_T + e_2 = y_B + 3 + s_2 \ \wedge \ y_T + s_3 = y_B - 2 + e_3 \\ \wedge \quad x_T + s_4 = x_B - 2 + e_4 \quad \wedge \quad x_T + y_T + s_5 = x_B + y_B - 2 + e_5 \end{array}$$

where the error variables $e_1, \ldots, e_5$ and slack variables $s_1, \ldots, s_5$ are required to be non-negative. As long as one of the error variable takes value zero in a solution, then it is a solution of the original non-overlap constraint. A solution (corresponding to Figure 1(a)) is

$$\{x_B \mapsto 2,\ y_B \mapsto 1,\ x_T \mapsto 8,\ y_T \mapsto 2,\ s_1 \mapsto 2,\ s_2 \mapsto 0,\ s_3 \mapsto 0,\ s_4 \mapsto 0,\ s_5 \mapsto 0,\\ e_1 \mapsto 0,\ e_2 \mapsto 2,\ e_3 \mapsto 3,\ e_4 \mapsto 8,\ e_5 \mapsto 9\}$$

We must modify the Simplex Algorithm shown in Figure 3 to ensure that the error variable from the active disjunct in each disjunction is always kept zero. The changes are shown as underlined text in the figure. They are rather simple: we ensure that such *active error variables* are always kept as parameters and are never chosen to become basic. Thus, we must pass an extra argument to the Simplex Algorithm, namely *active*, the array of currently active error variables. For each disjunction D_i, *active*[i] is the set of active error variables in the error form of the the active disjunct in D_i. Note that *active*[i] will contain one variable if the disjunct is an inequality and two if it is an equation. When choosing the new basic variable y_J, we ignore any active error variables in the objective function: they cannot be chosen to become basic, and are allowed to have a negative coefficient in the objective function. We can modify the Dual Simplex Algorithm similarly.

```
disj_simplex_solve(C, f, active[])
   (C, f) := dual_simplex(C, f, active)
   tried := ∅
   repeat
      let θ be the solution corresponding to C
      prevf := θ(f)
      finished := true
      let C be of form C0 ∧ D1 ∧ ··· ∧ Dn where
      C0 is a conjunction of constraints and
      each Di is the conjunctive version of a disjunction
      for i := 1,...,n do
         current := active[i]
         active[i] := simplex_choose(Di, current, f, θ, tried)
         if active[i] ≠ current then
            tried := tried ∪ active[i]
            if some y ∈ active[i] is basic then make y a parameter endif
            finished := false
            (C, f) := simplex(C, f, active)
            if θ(f) < prevf then tried := ∅ endif
            break % Exit 'for' loop.
         endif
      endfor
   until finished = true
   return θ

simplex_choose(D, current, f, θ, tried)
   let D be of form c1 ∧ ··· ∧ cm
   if ∃y ∈ current s.t. y has a negative coefficient in f then
      for i := 1,...,m do
         let E be the error variables in ci
         if ∀[e ∈ E]. θ(e) = 0 and e ∉ tried and e ≠ current then
            return E
         endif
      endfor
   endif
   return current
```

Fig. 4. Algorithm for handling non-overlap constraints in the linear case.

The generic algorithm can be readily specialised to call the modified Simplex and Dual Simplex Algorithms. It is shown in Figure 4. The algorithm takes the current basic feasible solved form of the constraints C and objective function f as well as the active error variables. The main syntactic differences between the generic algorithm and this specialised algorithm result from the need to call the Dual Simplex Algorithm rather than the Simplex Algorithm when the algorithm is first entered. This is because we assume that only the right-hand side constants have been modified as the result of changing the desired values for the edit variables. (See [3] for further details.)

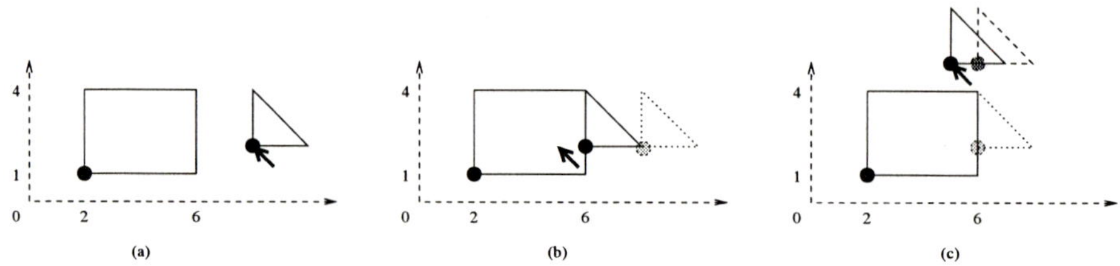

Fig. 5. Motion of the triangle during the mouse movement.

The function simplex_choose for switching between disjuncts uses information in the objective function in the solved form to assist in the choice of disjunct. The coefficient of an active error variable in the objective function provides a heuristic indication of whether it would be advantageous to switch away from that disjunct: we try to switch away only if the coefficient is negative, indicating that the objective function value can be decreased by making the variable basic (if it results in a non-zero value). When choosing which disjunct to switch to, the value of the error variables in the inactive disjuncts indicate which disjuncts are satisfied by the current solution. This is another advantage of keeping the error form of all disjuncts in the solved form.

If a newly chosen active variable is basic, we first make it a parameter before re-optimizing. If an error variable is basic and takes value 0 in the current solution, the right-hand side constant must be 0. This means that we can pivot on any parameter other than active error variables in the solved form, making that parameter basic. For example, if the disjunct is an inequality, it is always possible to pivot on the slack variable. The only difficult case is if the left hand side in the solved form consists entirely of active disjunctive error variables. The simplest way of handling this case is to split the equality into two inequalities, thus ensuring that each of the two rows has a slack variable that can be made basic.

The algorithm maintains a set of *tried* active error variables, which is reset to empty whenever we improve the objective function. This prevents us looping infinitely trying different combinations of active constraints without improving the solution.

To illustrate the operation of the algorithm consider our running example. For simplicity let us fix the position of the box at (2,1) and add constraints that the triangle attempt to follow the mouse position (x_M, y_M). Using the Cassowary encoding, we add the edit constraints

$$x_T = x_M + \delta_x^+ - \delta_x^- \qquad \wedge \qquad y_T = y_M + \delta_y^+ - \delta_y^-$$

where $\delta_x^+, \delta_x^-, \delta_y^+, \delta_y^- \geq 0$, and minimise the objective function $\delta_x^+ + \delta_x^- + \delta_y^+ + \delta_y^-$ where for simplicity we assume that the coefficient for the edit strength is 1.0. The motion of the triangle is illustrated in Figure 5, with the mouse pointer indicated by an arrow. When there is a change of active constraints, the intermediate point is shown as a dashed triangle.

$$\begin{array}{l} \text{minimize } \delta_x^+ + \delta_x^- + \delta_y^+ + \delta_y^- \\ x_T = 5 \ +\delta_x^+ \ -\delta_x^- \\ y_T = 2 \ +\delta_y^+ \ -\delta_y^- \\ s_1 = -1 \ +\delta_x^+ \ -\delta_x^- \ +e_1 \\ e_2 = 2 \ -\delta_y^+ \ +\delta_y^- \ +s_2 \\ e_3 = 3 \ +\delta_y^+ \ -\delta_y^- \ +s_3 \\ e_4 = 5 \ +\delta_x^+ \ -\delta_x^- \ +s_4 \\ e_5 = 6 \ +\delta_x^+ \ -\delta_x^- \ +\delta_y^+ \ -\delta_y^- \ +s_5 \\ \quad \textit{active}: \ e_1 \end{array}$$

(a)

$$\begin{array}{l} \text{minimize } 1 + s_1 - e_1 + 2\delta_x^- + \delta_y^+ + \delta_y^- \\ x_T = 6 \ +s_1 \ -e_1 \\ y_T = 2 \ +\delta_y^+ \ -\delta_y^- \\ \delta_x^+ = 1 \ +\delta_x^- \ +s_1 \ -e_1 \\ e_2 = 2 \ -\delta_y^+ \ +\delta_y^- \ +s_2 \\ e_3 = 3 \ +\delta_y^+ \ -\delta_y^- \ +s_3 \\ e_4 = 6 \ +s_1 \ -e_1 \ +s_4 \\ e_5 = 7 \ +s_1 \ -e_1 \ +\delta_y^+ \ -\delta_y^- \ +s_5 \\ \quad \textit{active}: \ e_1 \end{array}$$

(b)

$$\begin{array}{l} \text{minimize } 1 + s_1 - e_1 + 2\delta_x^- + \delta_y^+ + \delta_y^- \\ x_T = 6 \ +s_1 \ -e_1 \\ y_T = 5 \ +\delta_y^+ \ -\delta_y^- \\ \delta_x^+ = 1 \ -\delta_x^- \ +s_1 \ -e_1 \\ s_2 = 1 \ +\delta_y^+ \ -\delta_y^- \ +e_2 \\ e_3 = 6 \ +\delta_y^+ \ -\delta_y^- \ +s_3 \\ e_4 = 6 \ +s_1 \ -e_1 \ +s_4 \\ e_5 = 10 \ +s_1 \ -e_1 \ +\delta_y^+ \ -\delta_y^- \ +s_5 \\ \quad \textit{active}: \ e_1 \end{array}$$

(c)

$$\begin{array}{l} \text{minimize } \delta_x^+ + \delta_x^- + \delta_y^+ + \delta_y^- \\ x_T = 5 \ +\delta_x^+ \ -\delta_x^- \\ y_T = 5 \ +\delta_y^+ \ -\delta_y^- \\ e_1 = 1 \ -\delta_x^+ \ +\delta_x^- \ +s_1 \\ s_2 = 1 \ +\delta_y^+ \ -\delta_y^- \ +e_2 \\ e_3 = 6 \ +\delta_y^+ \ -\delta_y^- \ +s_3 \\ e_4 = 5 \ +\delta_x^+ \ -\delta_x^- \ +s_4 \\ e_5 = 9 \ +\delta_x^+ \ -\delta_x^- \ +\delta_y^+ \ -\delta_y^- \ +s_5 \\ \quad \textit{active}: \ e_2 \end{array}$$

(d)

Fig. 6. Tableaus resulting during the edits of Figure 5.

We assume the mouse begins at (8,2), the initial position of the triangle, and the initial basic feasible solved form is

$$\begin{array}{l} \text{minimize } \delta_x^+ + \delta_x^- + \delta_y^+ + \delta_y^- \\ x_T = 8 \ +\delta_x^+ \ -\delta_x^- \\ y_T = 2 \ +\delta_y^+ \ -\delta_y^- \\ s_1 = 2 \ +\delta_x^+ \ -\delta_x^- \ +e_1 \\ e_2 = 2 \ -\delta_y^+ \ +\delta_y^- \ +s_2 \\ e_3 = 3 \ +\delta_y^+ \ -\delta_y^- \ +s_3 \\ e_4 = 8 \ +\delta_x^+ \ -\delta_x^- \ +s_4 \\ e_5 = 9 \ +\delta_x^+ \ -\delta_x^- \ +\delta_y^+ \ -\delta_y^- \ +s_5 \\ \quad \textit{active}: \ e_1 \end{array}$$

This corresponds to the position in Figure 5(a). The special entry *active*: e_1 indicates that e_1 is an active error constraint and so is not allowed to enter the basis.

Suppose now we move the mouse to (5,2). The modified solved form is shown in Figure 6(a). We call disj_simplex_solve, which calls the dual_simplex algorithm. Since the solved form is no longer feasible, but still optimal, the Dual Simplex Algorithm recovers feasibility by performing a pivot that removes s_1 from the basis and enters δ_x^+ into the basis. This gives the tableau in Figure 6(b), whose corresponding solution gives position (6,2) for the triangle, illustrated in Figure 5(b). We now call simplex_choose for the single disjunction in the original constraint set. The appearance of $-e_1$ in the objective function means that a better solution could be found if we allowed e_1 to enter the basis, and so if possible we should switch disjuncts. However, since no other error variables are zero, we cannot switch disjuncts. Thus simplex_choose returns $\{e_1\}$, and, since the active error variables have not changed, disj_simplex_solve returns with this solved form.

Now the user moves the mouse to (5,5). The solved form is modified, giving a infeasible optimal solution. The call to disj_simplex_solve calls dual_simplex. This time we have e_2 as the exit variable and s_2 as the entry variable, resulting the tableau shown in Figure 6(c). Now we have a corresponding optimal solution positioning the triangle at (6,5) (the dashed triangle in Figure 5(c)) for this choice of active disjuncts. We call simplex_choose for the single disjunction in the constraint set. Again the appearance of $-e_1$ in the objective function means that a better solution could be found if we allowed e_1 to enter the basis, and so if possible we should switch disjuncts. This time, since e_2 is now a parameter, it takes value zero in the current solution, so we can make this disjunct active. Thus simplex_choose returns $\{e_2\}$. We therefore make this the active error variable and call simplex to optimise with respect to this new disjunct. It performs one pivot, with entry variable e_1 and exit variable δ_x^+, giving the tableau in Figure 6(d). Notice how we have moved to position (5,5) and changed which of the disjuncts is active (the final position in Figure 5(c)). Now, since there are no active error variables in the objective function, simplex_choose does not switch disjuncts and so disj_simplex_solve returns with the solution corresponding to the solved form.

5 Empirical Evaluation

In this section we provide a preliminary empirical evaluation of disj_simplex_solve. Our implementation is based on the C++ implementation of the Cassowary Algorithm in the QOCA toolkit [9]. All times are in milliseconds measured on a 333MHz Celeron-based computer. (Granularity of maximum re-solve times is 10ms.)

Our first experiment compares the overhead of disj_simplex_solve with the underlying Cassowary Algorithm. Figure 7(a) shows n boxes in a row with a small gap between them. Each box has a desired width but can be compressed to half of this width. The rightmost box has a fixed position. The others are free to move, but have stay constraints tending to keep them at their current location. For the disj_simplex_solve version of the problem we add a non-overlap constraint between each pair of boxes. In the Cassowary version of the experiment there is a constraint to preserve non-overlap of each pair of boxes by keeping their current relative position in the x direction. This corresponds to the active constraints chosen in the disj_simplex_solve version.

The experiment measures the average and maximum time required for a resolve during the direct manipulation scenario in which the leftmost box is moved as far right as possible, squashing the other boxes together until they all shrink to half width, and then moved back to its original position. The results shown in Table 1(a) gives the number n of boxes, for each version the number of

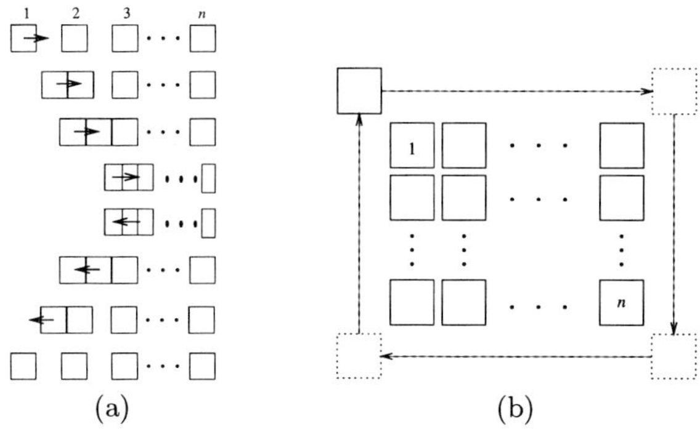

Fig. 7. Experiments for (a) overhead and (b) performance of disjunctive solving.

linear constraints (Cons) in the solver, the average time (AveR), and maximum time (MaxR) to resolve during the direct manipulation (in milliseconds). Note that in this experiment no disjuncts change status from active to inactive or vice versa. The results show that there is a surprising amount of overhead involved in keeping non-active disjuncts in the solved form. We are currently investigating why: even with the same number of constraints in the solved forms, the original Cassowary seems significantly faster.

Our second experiment gives a feel for the performance of disj_simplex_solve when disjunct swapping takes place. Figure 7(b) shows n fixed size boxes arranged in a rectangle and a single box on the left-hand side of this collection. There is a non-overlap constraint between this box and each box in the collection. The experiment measures the average and maximum time required for a resolve during the direct manipulation scenario in which the isolated box is moved around the rectangle of boxes, back to its original position. Table 1(b) gives the number n of boxes, the number of linear constraints in the solver, the average and maximum time for each resolve, and the average number of disjunct swaps in each resolve. The results here show that disj_simplex_solve is sufficiently

Table 1. Results for (a) overhead and (b) disjunctive swap speed.

	Cassowary			disj_simplex_solve		
n	Cons	AveR	MaxR	Cons	AveR	MaxR
20	190	1	10	760	6	20
40	780	3	10	3120	31	90
60	1770	7	20	7080	86	250
80	3160	12	30	12640	184	530

(a)

n	Cons	Swaps	AveR	MaxR
200	800	1.4	7	50
400	1600	2.6	18	90
600	2400	3.7	31	130
800	3200	4.7	47	170
1000	4000	5.5	66	230
1200	4800	6.3	85	260

(b)

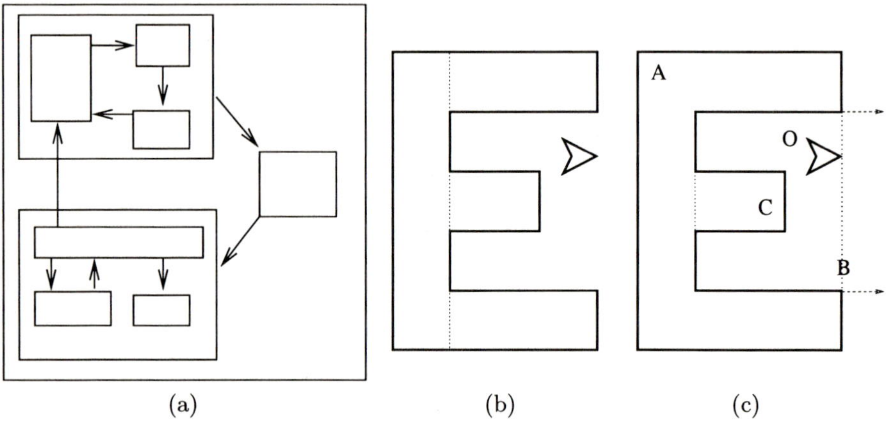

Fig. 8. Experiments to demonstrate expressiveness of disjunctive linear constraints.

fast for supporting direct manipulation for systems of up to 5000 constraints and disjuncts.

Our third and fourth experiments give a feel for the expressiveness of disjunctions of linear constraints. In the third experiment we use the solver to model the constraints in the state chart-like diagram shown in Figure 8(a). It has non-overlap constraints between boxes in the same box, and containment constraints between boxes and their surrounding box. This gives rise to 20 linear constraints. For such a small number of constraints, re-solve time is negligible (0.04ms average; the maximum is not accurately measurable).

In the fourth experiment we demonstrate non-overlap with non-convex polygons. One way of modelling this is as simple convex polygons whose sides are "glued" together using constraints. Dotted lines in the Figure 8(b) show a simple convex decomposition of the E, requiring 24 linear constraints plus 4 disjunctions. However, one can model the situation using fewer constraints by allowing disjuncts to be conjunctions, perhaps even containing other disjunctions. Figure 8(c) illustrates the embedded-conjunction approach, which uses 12 linear constraints plus 2 disjunctions, implicitly defining the relation between the small "chevron" object O and the three objects A (the bounding box of E), B (the open sided rectangular gap in the E) and C (the middle bar of E), modelling the non-overlap of the E and O as

$$nonoverlap(O, A) \vee (inside(O, B) \wedge nonoverlap(O, C)).$$

In the test case, we have 8 "E" shapes and one "chevron" shape, all constrained to lie within a screen rectangle and constrained not to overlap each other. This yields 226 linear constraints and 36 disjunctions. The test case movements were constructed by manually dragging the shapes about each other, bumping corners against each other as much as possible. There were on average 0.3 disjunct swaps per re-solve. The average re-solve time was 0.6ms; the maximum was 20ms.

6 Conclusions

We have described an algorithm for rapidly resolving disjunctions of constraints. The algorithm is designed to support direct manipulation in interactive graphical applications which contain non-overlap constraints between graphical objects. It is generic in the underlying (conjunctive) constraint solver. We also give a specialisation of this algorithm for the case when the underlying constraint solver is the simplex-based linear arithmetic constraint solver, Cassowary.

Empirical evaluation of the Cassowary-based disjunctive solver is very encouraging, suggesting that systems of up to five thousand constraints can be solved in less than 100 milliseconds. We have also demonstrated that the solver can support non-overlap of complex non-convex polygons, and complex diagrams such as State Charts that contain non-overlap as well as containment constraints.

However, our experimental results indicate that keeping inactive disjuncts in the solved form has significant overhead. Thus, we intend to investigate a "dynamic" version of the Cassowary-based disjunctive solver in which disjuncts are only placed in the solver when they become active. Preliminary investigation by Nathan Hurst is very promising.

Acknowledgements. This research has been funded in part by an Australian ARC Large Grant A49927003, and in part by U.S. National Science Foundation Grant No. IIS-9975990. We thank Nathan Hurst for his insightful comments and criticisms.

References

1. David Baraff. Fast contact force computation for nonpenetrating rigid bodies. In *SIGGRAPH '94 Conference Proceedings*, pages 23–32. ACM, 1994.
2. Alan Borning, Bjorn Freeman-Benson, and Molly Wilson. Constraint hierarchies. *Lisp and Symbolic Computation*, 5(3):223–270, September 1992.
3. Alan Borning, Kim Marriott, Peter Stuckey, and Yi Xiao. Solving linear arithmetic constraints for user interface applications. In *Proceedings of the 1997 ACM Symposium on User Interface Software and Technology*, October 1997.
4. Ioannis Fudos. *Geometric Constraint Solving.* PhD thesis, Purdue University, Department of Computer Sciences, 1995.
5. Michael Gleicher. *A Differential Approach to Constraint Satisfaction.* PhD thesis, School of Computer Science, Carnegie-Mellon University, 1994.
6. Mikako Harada, Andrew Witkin, and David Baraff. Interactive physically-based manipulation of discrete/continuous models. In *SIGGRAPH '95 Conference Proceedings*, pages 199–208, Los Angeles, August 1995. ACM.
7. David Harel. Statecharts: A visual formalism for complex systems. *Science of Computer Programming*, 8:231–274, 1987.
8. Glenn Kramer. A geometric constraint engine. *Artificial Intelligence*, 58(1–3):327–360, December 1992.
9. K. Marriott, S.S. Chok, and A. Finlay. A tableau based constraint solving toolkit for interactive graphical applications. In *International Conference on Principles and Practice of Constraint Programming (CP98)*, pages 340–354, 1998.

10. Kim Marriott and Peter Stuckey. *Programming with Constraints: An Introduction.* MIT Press, 1998.
11. George L. Nemhauser and Laurence A. Wolsey. *Integer and Combinatorial Optimization.* Wiley, New York, 1988.
12. James Rumbaugh, Ivar Jacobson, and Grady Booch. *The Unified Modeling Language Reference Manual.* Addison-Wesley, 1998.
13. Michael Sannella, John Maloney, Bjorn Freeman-Benson, and Alan Borning. Multi-way versus one-way constraints in user interfaces: Experience with the DeltaBlue algorithm. *Software—Practice and Experience*, 23(5):529–566, May 1993.
14. Ivan Sutherland. *Sketchpad: A Man-Machine Graphical Communication System.* PhD thesis, Department of Electrical Engineering, MIT, January 1963.
15. Brad Vander Zanden. An incremental algorithm for satisfying hierarchies of multi-way dataflow constraints. *ACM Transactions on Programming Languages and Systems*, 18(1):30–72, January 1996.

Sweep as a Generic Pruning Technique Applied to the Non-overlapping Rectangles Constraint

Nicolas Beldiceanu and Mats Carlsson

SICS, Lägerhyddsv. 18, SE-752 37 UPPSALA, Sweden
{nicolas,matsc}@sics.se

Abstract. We first present a generic pruning technique which aggregates several constraints sharing some variables. The method is derived from an idea called *sweep* which is extensively used in computational geometry. A first benefit of this technique comes from the fact that it can be applied to several families of global constraints. A second advantage is that it does not lead to any memory consumption problem since it only requires temporary memory which can be reclaimed after each invocation of the method.

We then specialize this technique to the non-overlapping rectangles constraint, describe several optimizations, and give an empirical evaluation based on six sets of test instances with different characteristics.

1 Introduction

The main contribution of this paper is to present a generic pruning technique for finite domain constraint solving[1]. As a second contribution, we specialize the technique to the non-overlapping rectangles constraints and evaluate its performance. Finally, we identify and evaluate four optimizations which should be applicable to many global constraints.

The technique is based on an idea which is widely used in computational geometry and which is called *sweep* [11, pp. 10–11]. Consider e.g. Fig. 1 which shows five constraints and their projections on two given variables X and Y. Assume that we want to find the smallest value of X so that the conjunction of the five constraints is feasible for some Y. By trying $X = 0, \ldots, 4$, we conclude that $X = 4$ is the only value that may be feasible. The sweep algorithm performs this search efficiently; see Sect. 3.2 for the details on this particular example.

In two dimensions, a plane sweep algorithm solves a problem by moving a vertical line from left to right[2]. The algorithm uses the two following data structures:

---

[1] A *domain variable* is a variable that ranges over a finite set of integers; $\min(X), \max(X)$ and $\mathrm{dom}(X)$ denote respectively the minimum value, the maximum value, and the set of possible values for X.

[2] In general, a plane sweep algorithm does not require neither the sweep-line to be vertical nor moving it from left to right.

T. Walsh (Ed.): CP 2001, LNCS 2239, pp. 377–391, 2001.

- a data structure called the *sweep-line status*, which contains some information related to the current position Δ of the sweep-line,
- a data structure named the *event point series*, which holds the events to process, ordered in increasing order wrt. the abscissa.

The algorithm initializes the sweep-line status for the initial value of Δ. Then the sweep-line jumps from event to event; each event is handled, updating the sweep-line status. A common application of the sweep algorithm is to solve the segments intersection problem [11, p. 278], with a time complexity that depends both on the number of segments and on the number of segment intersections.

In our case, the sweep-line scans the values of a domain variable X that we want to prune, and the sweep-line status contains a set of constraints that have to hold for $X = \Delta$. The generic pruning technique, which we call *value sweep pruning*, accumulates the values to be currently removed from the domain of a variable Y which is different from X. If, for some value of Δ, all values of Y have to be removed, then we will prune Δ from dom(X). The method is based on the aggregation of several constraints that have two variables in common. Let:

- X and Y be two distinct domain variables,
- $C_1(V_{11}, \ldots, V_{1n_1}), \ldots, C_m(V_{m1}, \ldots, V_{mn_m})$ be a set of m constraints such that $\forall i \in 1..m : \{X, Y\} \subseteq \{V_{i1}, \ldots, V_{in_i}\}$ (i.e. all constraints mention both variables X and Y).

The value sweep pruning algorithm will try to adjust the minimum[3] value of X wrt. the conjunction of the previous constraints by moving a sweep-line from the minimum value of X to its maximum value. In our case, the events to process correspond to the starts and ends of forbidden 2-dimensional regions wrt. constraints $C_1, \ldots, C_m$ and variables X and Y.

In this paper, we use the notation $(F_x^-..F_x^+, F_y^-..F_y^+)$ to denote an ordered pair F of intervals and their lower and upper bounds. rand(S) denotes a random integer in the set S.

The next section presents the notion of forbidden regions, which is a way to represent constraints that is suited for the value sweep algorithm. Sect. 3 describes the value sweep pruning algorithm and gives its worst-case complexity. Sect. 4 presents the specialization of this algorithm to the non-overlapping rectangles constraint, as well as several optimizations. Sect. 5 provides an empirical evaluation of six different variants of the algorithm according to several typical test patterns.

2 Forbidden Regions

We call F a *forbidden region of the constraint C_i wrt. the variables X and Y* if: $\forall x \in F_x^-..F_x^+, y \in F_y^-..F_y^+ : C_i(V_{i1}, \ldots, V_{in_i})$ has no solution in which $X = x$ and

[3] It can also be used in order to adjust the maximum value, or to prune completely the domain of a variable.

$Y = y$. Slightly abusing language, we say that $X = a$ *is feasible wrt.* $C_1, \dots, C_m$ if $a \in \mathrm{dom}(X) \wedge \exists b \in \mathrm{dom}(Y)$ such that (a, b) is not in any forbidden region of $C_1, \dots, C_m$ wrt. X and Y.

Fig. 1 shows five constraints and their respective forbidden regions (shaded) wrt. two given variables X and Y and their domains. The first constraint requires that X, Y and R be pairwise distinct. Constraints (B,C) are usual arithmetic constraints. Constraint (D) can be interpreted as requiring that two rectangles of respective origins (X, Y) and (T, U) and sizes $(2, 4)$ and $(3, 2)$ do not overlap. Finally, constraint (E) is a parity constraint of the sum of X and Y.

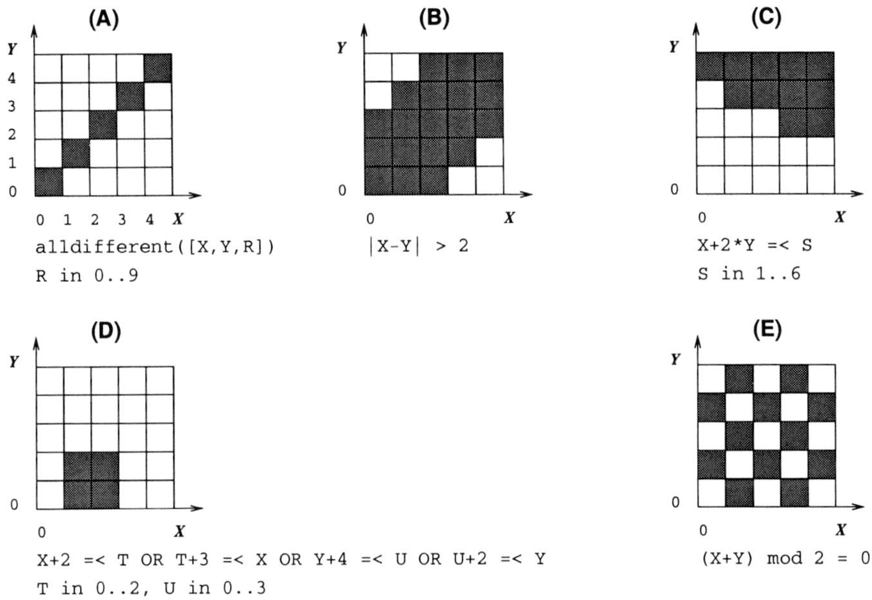

Fig. 1. Examples of forbidden regions. X in 0..4, Y in 0..4.

The value sweep pruning algorithm computes the forbidden regions on request, in a lazy evaluation fashion. The algorithm generates the forbidden regions of each constraint C_i gradually as a set of rectangles $R_{i1}, \dots, R_{in}$ such that:

- $R_{i1} \cup \dots \cup R_{in}$ represents all forbidden regions of constraint C_i wrt. variables X and Y.
- $R_{i1}, \dots, R_{in}$ are sorted by ascending start position on the X axis.

This will be handled by providing the following two functions[4] for each triple (X, Y, C_i) that we want to be used by the value sweep algorithm:

[4] An analogous function get_prev_forbidden_regions is also provided for the case where the sweep-line moves from the maximum to the minimum value.

- get_forbidden_regions(X, Y, C_i, x'_i), whose value is all the forbidden regions R_{C_i} of C_i such that:

$$\begin{cases} R_{C_i x}^{-} = next_{C_i} \\ R_{C_i y}^{+} \geq \min(Y) \wedge R_{C_i y}^{-} \leq \max(Y) \end{cases}$$

  where x'_i is the position of the previous start event of C_i and $next_{C_i}$ is the smallest value $> x'_i$ such that there exists such a forbidden region R_{C_i} of C_i.
- check_if_in_forbidden_regions(X, Y, x, y, C_i), which is true iff given values $x \in \text{dom}(X)$ and $y \in \text{dom}(Y)$ belong to a forbidden region of constraint C_i.

3 The Value Sweep Pruning Algorithm

3.1 Data Structures

The algorithm uses the following data structures:

The sweep-line status. Denoted P_{status}, this contains the current possible values for variable Y wrt. $X = \Delta$. More precisely, P_{status} can be viewed as an array which records for each possible value of Y the number of forbidden regions that currently intersect the sweep-line. The basic operations required on this data structure, and their worst-case complexity in an implementation that uses an (a, b)-tree [10] based data structure, are shown in Table 1.

The event point series. Denoted Q_{event}, this contains the start and the end+1 (+1 since the end is still forbidden whereas end+1 is not), on the X axis, of those forbidden regions of the constraints $C_1, \ldots, C_m$ wrt. variables X and Y that intersect the sweep line. These *start events* and *end events* are sorted in increasing order and recorded in a queue. The basic operations required, and their complexity e.g. in a heap, are also shown in Table 1. Checking if there is some start event in Q_{event} associated to a given constraint C_i can be implemented in $O(1)$ time with a reference counter. This last operation is the trigger which is used in order to gradually enqueue the start and end events associated to the forbidden regions of C_i when a start event associated to C_i is removed from the queue Q_{event}.

3.2 Principle of the Algorithm

In order to check if $X = \Delta$ is feasible wrt. $C_1, \ldots, C_m$, the sweep-line status records all forbidden regions that intersect the sweep-line. If, for $X = \Delta$, $\forall i \in \text{dom}(Y) : P_{status}[i] > 0$, Δ will move to the right.

Before going more into the detail of the sweep algorithm, let us illustrate how it works on a concrete example. Assume that we want to find out the minimum value of variable X wrt. the conjunction of the five constraints that were given in Fig. 1. Fig. 2 shows the contents of P_{status} for different values of Δ. The smallest feasible value of X is 4, since this is the first point where P_{status} contains an element with value 0. We now present the main procedure.

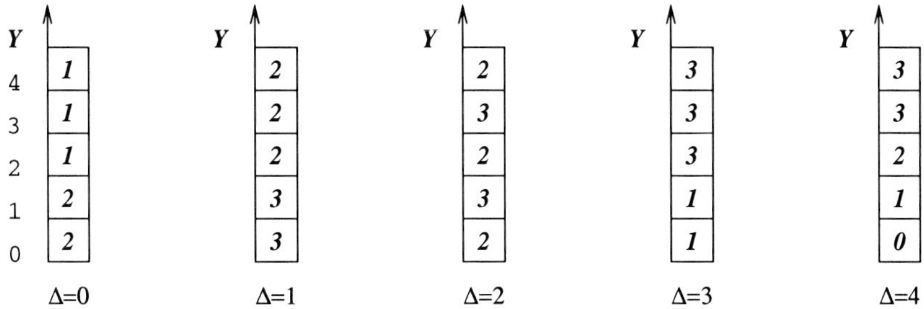

Fig. 2. Status of the sweep-line just after line 15 of Alg. 1. Values denote the number of forbidden regions per Y position.

3.3 The Main Procedure

The procedure FindMinimum[5] implements the value sweep pruning algorithm for adjusting the minimum value of a variable X, and finding a corresponding feasible value $\hat{y}$ of a variable Y, wrt. a set of constraints mentioning X and Y. The value $\hat{y}$ is called the *witness* of $\min(X)$ and is used in Alg. 3.

Holes in the domain of variable X are handled in the same way as constraints $C_1, \ldots, C_m$: an additional constraint which, for each interval of consecutive removed values, generates start and end event.

The next procedure, HandleEvent, specifies how to handle start and end event points.

3.4 Handling Start and End Events

Depending on whether we have a start or an end event E, we add 1 or -1 to $P_{status}[i], l \leq i \leq u$, where l and u are respectively the start and the end on the Y axis of the forbidden region that is associated to the event E. When E was the last start event of a given constraint C_E, we search for the next events of C_E and insert them in the event queue Q_{event}.

3.5 Discussion

The motivation for assigning a random value to $\hat{y}$ comes from the fact that, if we use the algorithm for pruning several variables, we don't want to get the same feasible solution for several variables, since a single future assignment could invalidate this feasible solution. This would result in reevaluating again the algorithm for several variables.

[5] The procedure can readily be transformed into an analogous procedure FindMaximum for adjusting the maximum value.

Input: A set of constraints $C_1, \ldots, C_m$ and two domain variables X and Y present in each constraint.
Output: An indication as to whether a solution exists, and values $\hat{x}, \hat{y}$.
Ensure: Either $\hat{x}$ is the smallest value of X such that $\hat{y} \in \text{dom}(Y)$ and $(\hat{x}, \hat{y})$ does not belong to any forbidden region of $C_1, \ldots, C_m$ wrt. variables X and Y, or no solution exists.

$Q_{event} \leftarrow$ an empty event queue
for all constraint $C_i (1 \leq i \leq m)$ **do**
  for all forbidden region $R_{C_i} \in$ get_forbidden_regions$(X, Y, C_i, min(X) - 1)$ **do**
    Insert $\max(R_{C_{i}}{}_x^-, \min(X))$ into Q_{event} as a start event
    if $R_{C_{i}}{}_x^+ + 1 \leq \max(X)$ **then**
      Insert $R_{C_{i}}{}_x^+ + 1$ into Q_{event} as an end event
if Q_{event} is empty
or the leftmost position of any event of Q_{event} is greater than $\min(X)$ **then**
  $\hat{x} \leftarrow \min(X)$, $\hat{y} \leftarrow \text{rand}(\text{dom}(Y))$
  return $(\textbf{true}, \hat{x}, \hat{y})$
$P_{status} \leftarrow$ an array ranging over $\min(Y)..\max(Y)$ with all zero elements
$P_{status}[i] \leftarrow 1$ **for** $i \in \min(Y)..\max(Y) \setminus \text{dom}(Y)$
while Q_{event} is not empty **do**
  $\Delta \leftarrow$ the leftmost position of any event of Q_{event}
  for all event E at Δ of Q_{event} **do**
    HandleEvent(E)
  if $P_{status}[i] = 0$ for some i **then**
    $\hat{x} \leftarrow \Delta$, $\hat{y} \leftarrow$ a random i such that $P_{status}[i] = 0$
    return $(\textbf{true}, \hat{x}, \hat{y})$
return $(\textbf{false}, 0, 0)$

Algorithm 1: FindMinimum$(C_1, \ldots, C_m, X, Y)$

Let f denote the total number of forbidden regions intersecting the initial domain of the variables X, Y under consideration, and m the number of constraints. For a complete sweep, Table 1 indicates the number of times each operation is

Extract E from Q_{event}
Get the corresponding forbidden region R_E and constraint C_E
Let $l = \max(R_{E}{}_y^-, \min(Y)), u = \min(R_{E}{}_y^+, \max(Y))$
if E is a start event **then**
  Add 1 to $P_{status}[i], l \leq i \leq u$
  if Q_{event} does not contain any start event associated to constraint C_E **then**
    $x'_E \leftarrow R_{E}{}_x^-$
    for all forbidden region $R_{C_i} \in$ get_forbidden_regions(X, Y, C_E, x'_E) **do**
      Insert $R_{C_E}{}_x^-$ into Q_{event} as a start event
      if $R_{C_E}{}_x^+ + 1 \leq \max(X)$ **then**
        Insert $R_{C_E}{}_x^+ + 1$ into Q_{event} as an end event
else
  Add -1 to $P_{status}[i], l \leq i \leq u$

Algorithm 2: HandleEvent(E)

performed, and its total worst case cost, assuming a reasonable implementation. Hence, the overall complexity of the algorithm is $O(m + f \log f)$.

Consider a given branch of the search tree and the total work spent by the algorithm pruning X on that branch. If we use complete pruning, many sweeps over $\mathrm{dom}(X)$ will be done. If we only adjust $\min(X)$ and $\max(X)$, however, the total work will amount to at most one total sweep over $\mathrm{dom}(X)$.

Table 1. Maximum no. of calls and total cost per basic operation in a sweep of FindMinimum

Operation	Max. times	Total cost (O)
Initialize to empty the queue	1	1
Compute the first forbidden regions of C_i	m	$m + f$
Add an event to the queue	$2 \times f$	$2 \times f \log f$
Extract the next event from the queue	$2 \times f$	$2 \times f$
Check if there exists some start event associated to C_i	f	f
Initialize to zero a range of array elements	1	1
Add 1 or -1 to a range of array elements	$2 \times f$	$2 \times f \log f$
Check if there exists an array element with value 0	$2 \times f$	$2 \times f \log f$
Compute the index of a random array element with value 0	1	$\log f$

Value sweep pruning can be seen as shaving [9] applied to constructive disjunction [13], where the main difference is that value sweep pruning does not try out each value one by one.

Value sweep pruning can be applied to any arbitrary set of constraints for which forbidden regions can be provided. In practice, however, the method is probably most suited for global constraints that can be defined in terms of a structured network [2] of elementary constraints over at least three variables. One suitable pattern is where the network has a clique structure and all elementary constraints have to hold. The non-overlapping rectangles constraint belongs to this class. Sliding constraints over consecutive variables form another pattern, e.g. among_seq and sliding_sum [2].

Finally, value sweep pruning can be readily generalized to $d \geq 2$ dimensions, given that we have:

- d distinct domain variables $X_1, \ldots, X_d$,
- a set of m constraints, each mentioning $X_1, \ldots, X_d$,
- d-dimensional forbidden regions for the constraints wrt. $X_1, \ldots, X_d$,
- a $(d-1)$-dimensional sweep-plane and sweep-plane status data structure, e.g. a quadtree or octtree [12], in the sweep algorithm.

4 Value Sweep for Non-overlapping Rectangles

Assume that we want to implement a constraint $\mathsf{NonOverlapping}(P_1, \ldots, P_m)$ over a set of rectangles, which should hold if no two rectangles $P_i, P_j, i \neq j$ overlap. This constraint is a 2-dimensional special case of the d-dimensional diffn constraint [3], and has been used to model a wide range of placement and scheduling problems [1]. In 2 dimensions, it is commonly used for modelling problems where one has to assign some activities to some resources, and schedule them so that no two activities on the same resource overlap in time. In [7], the constraint is used in more than 2 dimensions for modelling pipelining constraints.

The 2-dimensional constraint could be implemented by decomposition into a conjunction of $m(m-1)/2$ pairwise non-overlapping constraints:

$$\begin{array}{c} C_{ij}(\langle X_i, w_i, Y_i, h_i\rangle, \langle X_j, w_j, Y_j, h_j\rangle) \Leftrightarrow \\ X_i + w_i \leq X_j \vee X_j + w_j \leq X_i \vee Y_i + h_i \leq Y_j \vee Y_j + h_j \leq Y_i \end{array} \tag{1}$$

where we denote by the tuple $\langle X_i, w_i, Y_i, h_i\rangle$ a rectangle with origin coordinates (X_i, Y_i), width w_i and height h_i. Each pairwise constraint could in turn be implemented by cardinality or constructive disjunction [13]. This section shows how to instead specialize the value sweep scheme to the NonOverlapping constraint, thus avoiding decomposition.

Without loss of generality, we assume that w_i and h_i are fixed, and we only discuss how to adjust $\min(X_i)$.

4.1 The Basic Algorithm

It is straightforward to see that there can be at most one (non-empty) forbidden region $R_{ij} = (r_x^- .. r_x^+, r_y^- .. r_y^+)$ of C_{ij} wrt. (X_i, Y_i), where:

$$\begin{array}{ll} r_x^- = \max(X_j) - w_i + 1 & r_x^+ = \min(X_j) + w_j - 1 \\ r_y^- = \max(Y_j) - h_i + 1 & r_y^+ = \min(Y_j) + h_j - 1 \end{array} \tag{2}$$

Hence, we get the following definitions for the functions driving the algorithm:

$$\mathsf{get\_forbidden\_regions}(X_i, Y_i, C_{ij}, x') = \begin{cases} \{(r_x^- .. r_x^+, r_y^- .. r_y^+)\} & \text{if } x' < \min(X_1) \wedge r_x^- \leq r_x^+ \wedge r_y^- \leq r_y^+, \\ \emptyset & \text{otherwise} \end{cases}$$

$$\mathsf{check\_if\_in\_forbidden\_regions}(X_i, Y_i, x, y, C_{ij}) = r_x^- \leq x \leq r_x^+ \wedge r_y^- \leq y \leq r_y^+$$

where $r_x^-, r_x^+, r_y^-, r_y^+$ are defined in (2).

Given these definitions, we are now in a position to define Alg. 3 which adjusts $\min(X_i)$ for each rectangle so that a feasible origin is found for each rectangle. We also maintain for each rectangle P_i the value witness(X_i) to enable a quick check whether the origin point $(\min(X_i), \text{witness}(X_i))$ is feasible. From the complexity analysis of Sect. 3.5, we have that the worst case complexity of Alg. 3 is $O(m^2 + m \times f \log f)$ where f is the average number of rectangles that could overlap with the domain of placement of a given rectangle P_i.

Input: A set of rectangles $P_1, \ldots, P_m$.
Output: The number of lower bounds that were adjusted, or ∞ if no solution exists.
Ensure: Either $(\min(X_i), \text{witness}(X_i))$ is a feasible pair of coordinates for $1 \leq i \leq m$, or no solution exists.

1: $c \leftarrow 0$
2: **for all** rectangle $P_i (1 \leq i \leq m)$ **do**
3: Let $S = \{C_{ij} : 1 \leq j \leq m \wedge i \neq j\}$
4: **if** $\exists C \in S$: check_if_in_forbidden_regions$(X_i, Y_i, \min(X_i), \text{witness}(X_i), C)$ **then**
5: $(r, \hat{x}, \text{witness}(X_i)) \leftarrow$ FindMinimum(S, X_i, Y_i)
6: **if** $r =$ **false then**
7: **return** ∞
8: **else if** $\hat{x} \neq \min(X_i)$ **then**
9: $c \leftarrow c + 1, \min(X_i) \leftarrow \hat{x}$
10: **return** c

Algorithm 3: NonOverlapLeft$(P_1, \ldots, P_m)$

4.2 An Algorithm with a Shared Event Queue

The worst-case cost of NonOverlapLeft is dominated by the creation of the event queue, which is done from scratch for each successive call to FindMinimum. Hoping to reducing the complexity if $m \gg f$, we shall show how to instead create a single, *shared* event queue which is valid throughout the **for** loop.

Consider again $R_{ij} = (r_x^- .. r_x^+, r_y^- .. r_y^+)$ as defined by (2). We note that the only dependency of R_{ij} on P_i is r_x^- (r_y^-) which depends on w_i (h_i). Let $R_{\text{-}j} = (\max(X_j)+1 .. \min(X_j)+w_j-1, \max(Y_j)+1 .. \min(Y_j)+h_j-1)$ denote a *relative forbidden region associated to* P_j.

We then define a modified Q_{event} data structure consisting of two arrays of relative forbidden regions associated to P_j for $1 \leq j \leq m$, ordered by ascending $\max(X_j)$ and $\min(X_j) + w_j$ respectively. To use the shared event queue, the FindMinimum procedure needs to be modified as follows:

- Lines 1–6 are replaced by a search for the smallest $\Delta \geq \min(X)$.
- The **while** loop in line 12 should terminate when $\Delta > \max(X)$ or when Q_{event} is empty.
- The code must ignore events linked to forbidden regions that are empty.
- The event extraction operation must be modified according to the new data structure, and relative forbidden regions must be translated to absolute ones according to w_i and h_i of the current rectangle P_i.

The NonOverlapLeft procedure must be modified accordingly. Before line 2, the shared event queue must be built (takes $(O(m \log m))$ time) and passed in each call to Alg. 1. Thus compared to the worst-case complexity analysis in Sect. 4.1, we replace an $O(m^2)$ term by an $O(m \log m)$ term, an improvement especially if $m \gg f$.

4.3 A Filtering Algorithm

A simple filtering algorithm for NonOverlapping can be implemented as follows: Repeatedly call NonOverlapLeft (and similarly for the other three bounds) until failure or a fixpoint is reached. In the latter case, suspend if not all rectangles are fixed; succeed otherwise. The filtering algorithm should typically act as a coroutine which is resumed whenever one of the bounds is pruned by some other constraint. An implementation along these lines has been done for SICStus Prolog [4]. The implemented version provides optional extensions (variable width and height, wrap-around in either dimension, minimal margins between rectangles, global reasoning pruning), but these will not be discussed further.

4.4 Optimizations

Here, we will describe several optimizations which have been added to the basic filtering algorithm described above. The impact of these optimizations are empirically investigated in Sect. 5. Most of these optimizations are in fact generic to the family of value sweep pruning algorithms, and some could even be applied to most global constraints. Let $\mathcal{B}(P_i)$ denote the *bounding box of* P_i, i.e. the convex hull of all the feasible instances of a rectangle P_i and $\mathcal{C}(P_i)$ denote the *compulsory part [8] of* P_i, i.e. the intersection of all the feasible instances of a rectangle P_i:

$$\begin{array}{ll} \mathcal{B}(P_i)_x^- = \min(X_i) & \mathcal{C}(P_i)_x^- = \max(X_i) \\ \mathcal{B}(P_i)_x^+ = \max(X_i) + w_i - 1 & \mathcal{C}(P_i)_x^+ = \min(X_i) + w_i - 1 \\ \mathcal{B}(P_i)_y^- = \min(Y_i) & \mathcal{C}(P_i)_y^- = \max(Y_i) \\ \mathcal{B}(P_i)_y^+ = \max(Y_i) + h_i - 1 & \mathcal{C}(P_i)_y^+ = \min(Y_i) + h_i - 1 \end{array} \quad (3)$$

Sources and targets. Two properties are attached to each rectangle P_i: the *target* property, which is true if P_i can still be pruned or needs checking; and the *source* property, which is true of P_i can lead to some pruning.

The point is that substantially less work is needed for rectangles lacking one or both properties: the **for** loop of Alg. 3 only needs to iterate over the *targets*; when building the event queue, only *sources* need to be considered.

Consider a typical placement problem, in which most of the time spent searching for solutions will be spent in the lower parts of the search tree, where most rectangles are already fixed. Thus few rectangles will have *target* properties, and rectangles that can no longer interact with the non-fixed ones will lack both properties.

Initially, all rectangles have both properties. As the search progresses, the transitions $\{source, target\} \Rightarrow \{source\} \Rightarrow \emptyset$ take place.[6]

The first transition takes place whenever a rectangle is ground and has been checked (end of the **for** loop in Alg. 3). The second type of transition is done when a fixpoint is reached by means of the following linear algorithm:

[6] On backtracking, the converse transitions take place.

1. Compute the bounding box $\mathcal{B}$ of all *targets*.
2. For each *source* P_i, if the bounding box of P_i is disjoint from $\mathcal{B}$, then remove its *source* property.

Initial check of compulsory parts. A necessary condition for $\mathsf{NonOverlapping}(P_1, \ldots, P_m)$ is that the compulsory parts of P_i be pairwise disjoint. The following sweep algorithm verifies the necessary condition in $O(m \log m)$ time, and as a side effect, removes the *target* property from all ground rectangles. Thus it provides a quick initial test and avoids doing useless work later in the filtering algorithm:

1. Form a Q_{event} with start (end) events corresponding to $\mathcal{C}(P_i)^-_x$ $(\mathcal{C}(P_i)^+_x + 1)$ for $1 \leq i \leq m$ with non-empty $\mathcal{C}(P_i)$.
2. Let P_{status} record for each Y value the number of compulsory parts that currently intersect the sweep-line.
3. If after processing all events at Δ some element of P_{status} is greater than 1, the check fails.
4. When Q_{event} is empty, remove the *target* property from all ground P_i.

Domination. We say that *rectangle P_i dominates rectangle P_j* if the following relation holds between P_i and P_j for all $a \in \text{dom}(X_i)$:

$$\begin{array}{r} \textbf{if } X_i = a \text{ is feasible wrt. all constraints on } P_i \\ \textbf{then } X_j = a \text{ is also feasible wrt. all constraints on } P_j \end{array} \tag{4}$$

The point is to avoid useless work in line 4 of Alg. 3. We have come up with a domination check which runs in $O(1)$ time and finds many instances of domination. Roughly, throughout the **for** loop, we maintain a "most dominating rectangle" P_{dom} among the P_i for which the test in line 4 is found false. In line 4, we first check if P_{dom} dominates P_i, in which case we can ignore P_i in the loop. Similarly for the other three sweep directions.

Incrementality. When the filtering algorithm is resumed, typically very few (usually one) rectangles have been pruned by some other constraint since the last time the algorithm suspended. We would like to avoid running a complete check of all rectangles vs. all rectangles, and instead focus on the subset of rectangles that could be affected by the external events. This idea is captured by the following steps, and is valid if we still are on the same branch of the search tree as at the previous call to the filtering algorithm.

1. Compute the bounding box $\mathcal{B}$ of the *targets* that were pruned since the last time. This takes $O(m)$ time.
2. In Alg. 3 and in the initial check, ignore any rectangles that do not intersect $\mathcal{B}$, but if Alg. 3 adjusts some bound, $\mathcal{B}$ must be updated to include the newly pruned rectangle.

5 Performance Evaluation

From a deductive point of view, the value sweep pruning algorithm is similar to the work done by du Verdier [5]. Competing with specialized methods for specific placement problems [6] was not a goal for this work. Wanting to measure the speed rather than the pruning power of the sweep algorithm, and the speedups of the optimizations, we generated six sets of problem instances, each consisting of three instances of m rectangles, $m \in \{100, 200, 400\}$; see Table 2. The sets were selected to represent typical usages of the constraint. E.g., Set 2 is a loosely constrained problem; Set 3 and 4 use rectangles of different sizes; in Set 5, the rectangles are all the same; Set 6 is 95% ground: it was computed by taking a solved instance of Set 4 and resetting the origin variables of 5% of the rectangles to their initial domains.

Table 2. Rectangle P_i for the different sets

	$\min(X_i)$	$\max(X_i)$	w_i	$\min(Y_i)$	$\max(Y_i)$	h_i
Set 1	1	10000	rand(1..20)	1	$101 - h_i$	rand(1..20)
Set 2	rand(1..200)	10000	rand(1..20)	rand(1..90)	$101 - h_i$	rand(1..20)
Set 3	1	10000	i	1	$1.05\sqrt{\sum_{j=1}^{m} j^2} - h_i$	i
Set 4	1	10000	$w_i^{(4)}$	1	$1.05\sqrt{\sum_{j=1}^{m} w_i * h_i} - h_i$	$h_i^{(4)}$
Set 5	1	10000	1000	1	10000	1000

$$\text{where } (w_i^{(4)}, h_i^{(4)}) = \begin{cases} ((m+3-i)/2, (m+1+i)/2), & \text{for odd i} \\ ((m+2+i)/2, (m+2-i)/2), & \text{otherwise} \end{cases}$$

Each of the 18 instances was run by setting up the constraint and fixing the origins of each $P_i, 1 \leq i \leq m$, to its lower bound using NonOverlapping (see Sect. 4.3). Each instance was run six times with different parameters controlling the algorithm (see Sect. 4.4):

s The sweep algorithm with shared event queue.
sp The sweep algorithm plus *sources* and *targets*.
sc The sweep algorithm plus the initial check.
sd The sweep algorithm plus domination.
si The sweep algorithm plus incrementality.
s∗ All optimizations switched on.

Fig. 3 summarizes the benchmark results. There is one graph per set, each with six plots comparing the different settings. Each legend is ordered by decreasing runtime, in milliseconds. The benchmarks were run in SICStus Prolog compiled with `gcc -O2` version 2.95.2 on a 248 MHz UltraSPARC-II processor, running Solaris 7. The results tell us the following:

- Set 4 was the most difficult instance, while Set 6 was the fastest to solve by at least an order of magnitude.
- The *sources* and *targets* was by far the most effective optimization. Incrementality was also generally effective. Both can be generalized to a large class of global constraints.
- Domination alone was not effective. We conjecture that it does contribute to the performance of s*, at least on Set 5.
- The initial check optimization was not effective on any of the problem sets. We applied it each time the filtering algorithm was resumed. If used more judiciously, it might prove effective in some cases.
- There is a synergetic effect when several optimizations are combined.

Finally, we have compared the sweep (s*) algorithm with implementations of the same constraint based on decomposition, cardinality and constructive disjunction as well as with diffn [3] in CHIP V5. The results for 100 rectangles are shown in Table 3. For each set, the memory usage was measured after searching for the first solution, retaining all choice points, garbage collecting, then counting all working memory in use. For cardinality, runtimes became prohibitive for larger instances.

6 Conclusion

We have presented a value sweep pruning algorithm which performs global constraint propagation by aggregating several constraints that share $d \geq 2$ variables. This method is quite general and can be applied on a wide range of constraints. The usual way to handle finite domain constraints is to accumulate forbidden one-dimensional regions in the domain of the variables of the problem. However, this is inefficient for constraints that do not initially have any one-dimensional forbidden regions since they have to be handled in a generate-and-test way (i.e. forbidden values appear only after fixing some variables). Value sweep pruning is an alternative which allows to accumulate forbidden regions much earlier in time.

A key point is that we do not represent explicitly all forbidden regions but rather compute them lazily in order to perform specific pruning. Neither does the method lead to any memory consumption problem since it only requires temporary memory which can be reclaimed after each invocation of the method.

The main weak point of the algorithm is in line 2 of Alg. 1. We would like to efficiently filter out the constraints C_i that do not generate any forbidden regions wrt. the variables X and Y under consideration.

We have shown how the value sweep algorithm can be used in a filtering algorithm for the non-overlapping rectangles constraint, first by simple specialization, and then by a modified sweep algorithm that uses a shared event queue corresponding to relative forbidden regions. Again, the weak point is in the search for relevant, non-empty forbidden regions in the event queue. Some combination of interval and range trees [11] could be appropriate.

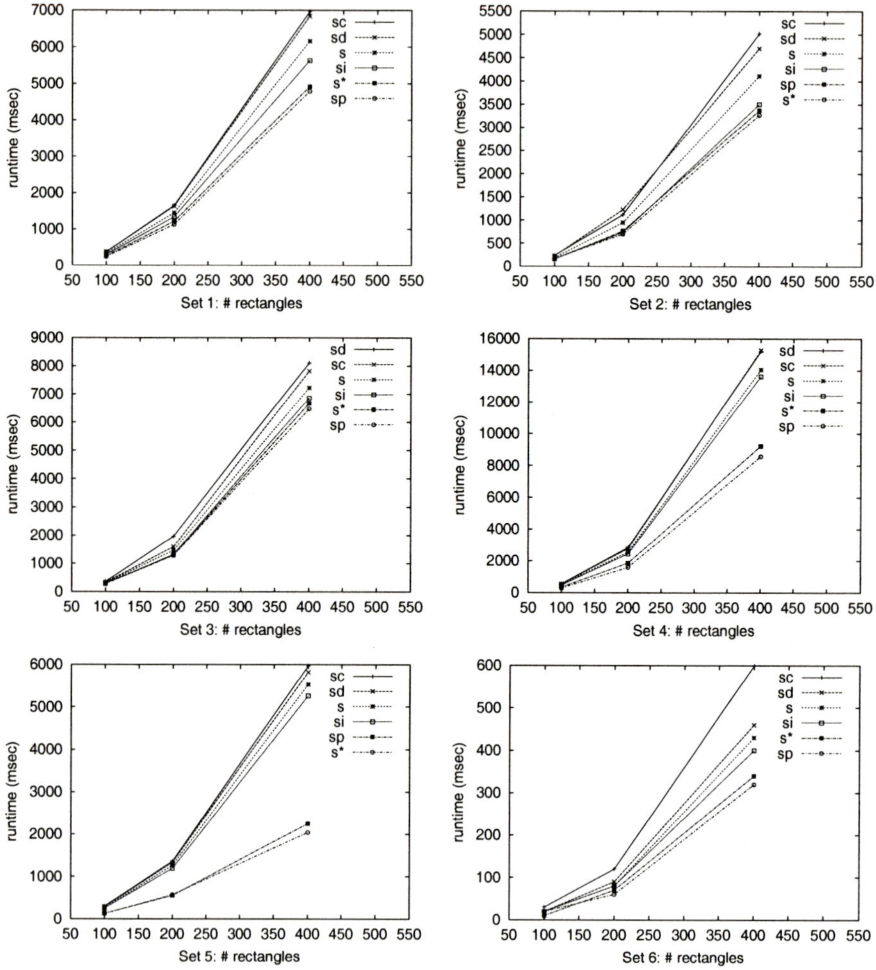

Fig. 3. Benchmark results

Table 3. Runtime (memory) in msec (kb) for 100 rectangles

	Set 1	Set 2	Set 3	Set 4	Set 5	Set 6
card	113830 (29295)	5110 (27784)	508150 (29187)	382870 (30056)	9751490 (29178)	1940 (2595)
cd	5300 (2935)	210 (2810)	44190 (2966)	16330 (2975)	590890 (2904)	10 (309)
diffn	600 (693)	140 (468)	690 (713)	1030 (920)	520 (835)	10 (220)
sweep	260 (141)	170 (100)	300 (151)	350 (189)	120 (122)	10 (54)

We have described four optimizations to the filtering algorithm. The algorithm and the optimizations have been implemented, and a performance evaluation and some indication to their generality are given. The evaluation shows an improvement by several orders of magnitude overs implementations based on decomposition into binary constraints.

Acknowledgements. The research reported herein was supported by NUTEK (the Swedish National Board for Industrial and Technical Development). The idea of a shared event queue is due in part to Sven Thiel.

References

1. A. Aggoun and N. Beldiceanu. Extending CHIP in order to solve complex scheduling and placement problems. *Mathl. Comput. Modelling*, 17(7):57–73, 1993.
2. N. Beldiceanu. Global constraints as graph properties on structured network of elementary constraints of the same type. SICS Technical Report T2000/01, Swedish Institute of Computer Science, 2000.
3. N. Beldiceanu and E. Contejean. Introducing global constraints in CHIP. *Mathl. Comput. Modelling*, 20(12):97–123, 1994.
4. M. Carlsson, G. Ottosson, and B. Carlson. An open-ended finite domain constraint solver. In H. Glaser, P. Hartel, and H. Kucken, editors, *Programming Languages: Implementations, Logics, and Programming*, volume 1292 of *LNCS*, pages 191–206. Springer, 1997.
5. F.R. du Verdier. *Résolution de problèmes d'aménagement spatial fondée sur la satisfaction de contraintes. Validation sur l'implantation d'équipements électroniques hyperfréquences.* PhD thesis, Université Claude Bernard-Lyon I, July 1992.
6. I. Gambini. A method for cutting squares into distinct squares. *Discrete Applied Mathematics*, 98(1–2):65–80, 1999.
7. K. Kuchciński. Synthesis of distributed embedded systems. In *Proc. 25th Euromicro Conference, Workshop on Digital System Design*, Milan, Italy, 1999.
8. A. Lahrichi. Scheduling: the notions of hump, compulsory parts and their use in cumulative problems. *C. R. Acad. Sci., Paris*, 1982.
9. P. Martin and D.B. Shmoys. A new approach to computing optimal schedules for the job-shop scheduling problem. In *Proc. of the 5th International IPCO Conference*, pages 389–403, 1996.
10. K. Mehlhorn. *Data Structures and Algorithms 1: Sorting and Searching.* EATCS Monographs. Springer, Berlin, 1984.
11. F.P. Preparata and M.I. Shamos. *Computational Geometry. An Introduction.* Springer, 1985.
12. H. Samet. *The Design and Analysis of Spatial Data Structures.* Addison-Wesley, 1989.
13. P. Van Hentenryck, V. Saraswat, and Y. Deville. Design, implementation and evaluation of the constraint language cc(FD). In A. Podelski, editor, *Constraints: Basics and Trends*, volume 910 of *LNCS*. Springer, 1995.

Non-overlapping Constraints between Convex Polytopes*

Nicolas Beldiceanu[1], Qi Guo[2**], and Sven Thiel[3]

[1]SICS, Lägerhyddsvägen 18, SE-75237 Uppsala, Sweden
nicolas@sics.se
[2]Department of Mathematics, Harbin Institute of Technology, 150006 Harbin, China
guo@math.uu.se
[3]MPI für Informatik, Stuhlsatzenhausweg 85, 66123 Saarbrücken, Germany
sthiel@mpi-sb.mpg.de

Abstract. This paper deals with *non-overlapping* constraints between convex polytopes. Non-overlapping detection between fixed objects is a fundamental geometric primitive that arises in many applications. However from a constraint perspective it is natural to extend the previous problem to a non-overlapping constraint between two objects for which both positions are not yet fixed. A first contribution is to present theorems for convex polytopes which allow coming up with general necessary conditions for non-overlapping. These theorems can be seen as a generalization of the notion of *compulsory part* which was introduced in 1984 by Lahrichi and Gondran [7] for managing non-overlapping constraint between rectangles. Finally, a second contribution is to derive from the previous theorems efficient filtering algorithms for two special cases: the non-overlapping constraint between two convex polygons as well as the non-overlapping constraint between *d*-dimensional boxes.

1 Introduction

The first part of this paper introduces necessary conditions for the *non-overlapping* constraint between convex polytopes. A convex polytope[1] [4] is defined by the convex hull of a finite number of points. Non-overlapping detection between fixed objects is a fundamental geometric primitive that arises in many applications. However from a constraint perspective it is natural to extend the previous problem to a non-overlapping constraint between objects for which the positions are not yet fixed. Concretely this means that we first want to detect as soon as possible before fixing completely two polytopes whether they will overlap or not. Secondly, we would like to find out the portion of space where placing a polytope will necessarily cause it to overlap with another not yet completely fixed polytope. For instance consider the illustrative example given in Fig. 1. We have a rectangle R_1 of length 3 and height 1 which must be included within box B and which should not overlap the

* Partly supported by the IST Program of the EU under contract number IST-1999-14186, (ALCOM-FT).

** Currently at: Department of Mathematics, Uppsala University, SE-75237 Uppsala, Sweden.

[1] From now on, the term *polytope* will refer to a convex polytope.

T. Walsh (Ed.): CP 2001, LNCS 2239, pp. 392-407, 2001.

rectangle R_2 of length 2 and height 4. We want to find out that the origin of R_2 (i.e. the leftmost lower corner of R_2) can't be put within box F.

(A) Rectangles to place (B) Domain of R_1 and forbidden domain F for the origin of R_2

Fig. 1. An illustrative example of a forbidden domain

Within constraint programming [10], elaborate shapes are currently approximated [6] by a set of rectangles, where the origin of each rectangle is linked to the origin of another rectangle by an external equality constraint. Since a huge number of rectangles may be required in order to approximate a specific shape, this increases the problem's size. This also leads to poor constraint propagation since each small rectangle is considered separately from the other rectangles to which it is linked by an external equality constraint. Practical motivations for having more than two dimensions are as follows. First it allows modelling both the geographical location and the time location of objects that should not be at the same location at the same instant. Secondly introducing a third dimension for a two-dimensional placement problem is also valuable for including relaxation directly within the constraint: in this third dimension, the coordinates of the origin of the objects which could be placed (respectively not placed) will be set to 0 (respectively to a value greater than 0).

The second part of this paper presents efficient filtering algorithms for two special cases of the non-overlapping constraints: the non-overlapping constraint between 2 convex polygons as well as the non-overlapping constraint between 2 d-dimensional boxes.

The next section introduces gradually the different definitions needed for describing the objects we consider, as well as the notion of *intersection* between these objects. Sect. 3 defines the concept of *overlapping polytope*, which is a portion of space where placing the origin of one polytope will lead it to overlap with another not yet fixed polytope. This extends the concept of *compulsory part* (i.e. the intersection of all the feasible instances of an object to place) which was presented for the case of rectangles in [7]. Finally based on the theorems of Sect. 3, we respectively derive in Sect. 4 and 5 two efficient filtering algorithms for the case of convex polygons and for the case of d-dimensional boxes.

2 Background, Definitions, and Notation

The purpose of this section is twofold. First, it describes the objects we consider for our placement problem. Second, it introduces the notion of intersection between these objects.

Definition 1 *domain variable*

A domain variable is a variable that ranges over a finite set of integers; $\underline{V}$ and $\overline{V}$ respectively denote the minimum and maximum values of variable V.

Definition 2 *fixed polytope*
A fixed polytope in IR^d is a polytope defined by k vertices and their respective integer coordinates, such that all points of the polytope belong to the convex hull of the k vertices.

Definition 3 *shape polytope*
A shape polytope in IR^d is a polytope defined by its k vertices and their respective integer coordinates, such that all points of the polytope belong to the convex hull of the k vertices, and such that one of its vertices has only zero coordinates. This specific vertex is called the origin of the shape polytope.

The shape polytope describes the shape of the objects we have to place, while a fixed polytope gives the possible positions for the origin of a shape.

(A) Fixed polytope (B) Shape polytope

Fig. 2. Examples of polytopes

Part (A) of Fig. 2 gives an example of a fixed polytope, while part (B) describes a shape polytope. The next four definitions are introduced in order to define the notion of *intersection* between two fixed polytopes.

Definition 4 *interior point*
A point X of a fixed polytope P is called an interior point if there is an $r>0$ such that $Ball(X,r)\subset P$, where $Ball(X,r)=\{Y: dist(Y,X)<r\}$, and $dist(Y,X)$ is the Euclidean distance between points X and Y.

Definition 5 *k-dimensional hyperplane*
$H\subset IR^d$ is called a k-dimensional hyperplane if $H=x+R_k$, where $x\in IR^d$ is a fixed point and R_k is a k-dimensional subspace of IR^d.

Definition 6 *dimension of a fixed polytope*
If there is a k-dimensional hyperplane that contains a fixed polytope P and no any $k-1$-dimensional hyperplane contains P then k is called the dimension of P.

Definition 7 *relative interior point*
Let P be a fixed polytope of dimension k. Then there exists a k-dimensional hyperplane H such that $P\subseteq H$. If a point X of P is an interior point of P considered only in H, then X is called a relative interior point of P.

In order to illustrate the previous definitions let us consider a fixed polytope P of IR^2 that corresponds to a line-segment between points $X1$ and $X2$. P has no interior points, but the dimension of P is 1 and all points of P that are distinct from $X1$ and $X2$ are relative interior points of P.

Definition 8 *intersection of fixed polytopes*
Two fixed polytopes P and Q intersect (i.e. overlap) if P and Q have a common relative interior point.

Part (A) of Fig. 3 gives three pairs (P_1,P_2), (P_3,P_4) and (P_5,P_6) of intersecting polytopes, while part (B) shows seven pairwise non-intersecting polytopes. Note that, according to Definition 8, point P_{13} does not overlap rectangle P_9 since P_{13} has no relative interior points.

(A) Intersecting polytopes (B) Non-intersecting polytopes

Fig. 3. Illustration of the definition of intersection

Throughout the paper we use the following notations:
- $|P|$ designates the *number of vertices* of a fixed or of a shape polytope P,
- $\min_i(P)$ (respectively $\max_i(P)$) is the *minimum* (respectively *maximum*) *value* of the coordinates on the i axis of the vertices of a fixed polytope P,
- $P^\bullet$ designates the set of *relative interior points* of P,
- $bd(P)$ denotes the set of points of P which do not belong to $P^\bullet$ (i.e. the boundary of P),
- $conv(X_1,X_2,\ldots,X_n)$ denotes the *convex hull* of a given set of points $X_1,X_2,\ldots,X_n$,
- Finally, $box(O_1,O_2,\ldots,O_d)$, where $O_1,O_2,\ldots,O_d$ are domain variables, is the fixed polytope defined as the points of $[\underline{O_1},\overline{O_1}] \times [\underline{O_2},\overline{O_2}] \times \ldots \times [\underline{O_d},\overline{O_d}]$.

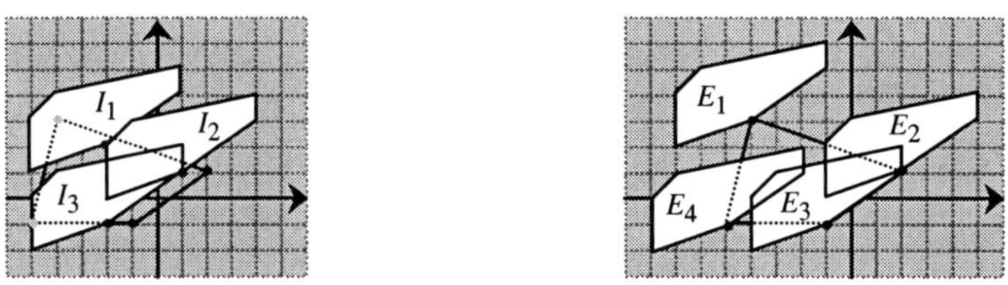

(A) Three instances of a family (B) Extremum polytopes of a family

Fig. 4. A family of polytopes

Definition 9 *family of polytopes*
A family F of polytopes in IR^d is a set of fixed polytopes defined by:
- A shape polytope $P_{shape}(F)$ in IR^d that describes the shape of the polytopes of the family,
- A fixed polytope $P_{origin}(F)$ in IR^d that gives the initial possible placements for the origin of the polytope $P_{shape}(F)$,

- A tuple $\langle O_1, O_2, \ldots, O_d \rangle$ of d domain variables that further restricts the possible placements for the origin of the polytope $P_{shape}(F)$ to the polytope $P_o(F)$ defined by $box(O_1, O_2, \ldots, O_d)$.

The members of F are fixed polytopes that are obtained by fixing the origin of $P_{shape}(F)$ to any integer point that is not located outside $P_{origin}(F) \cap P_o(F)$. The tuple $\langle O_1, O_2, \ldots, O_d \rangle$ is called the *origin* of the family F. From now on, the polytope $P_{origin}(F) \cap P_o(F)$[2] will be denoted by $P_{dom}(F)$. Within the context of the non-overlapping constraint, we associate to each object to place a given family of polytopes F, where each polytope corresponds to one possible positioning of the object. As the ranges of the variables of $\langle O_1, O_2, \ldots, O_d \rangle$ get more and more restricted, the number of distinct elements of F will decrease until it becomes a single fixed polytope, which is associated to the final positioning of the shape $P_{shape}(F)$.

Definition 10 *extremum polytopes of a family of polytopes*
The *extremum polytopes* of a family F of polytopes is a set of fixed polytopes generated by fixing the origin of $P_{shape}(F)$ to one of the vertices $X_1, \ldots, X_k$ of $P_{dom}(F)$. The *i*-th extremum polytope of F is $X_i + P_{shape}(F)$, it is denoted $\text{Extremum}_i(F)$.

Fig. 4 provides an example of a family F of polytopes described by the shape polytope $P_{shape}(F)$ of vertices $\begin{pmatrix}0\\0\end{pmatrix}, \begin{pmatrix}3\\2\end{pmatrix}, \begin{pmatrix}3\\3\end{pmatrix}, \begin{pmatrix}-3\\2\end{pmatrix}, \begin{pmatrix}-4\\1\end{pmatrix}, \begin{pmatrix}-4\\-1\end{pmatrix}$, by the fixed polytope $P_{origin}(F)$ of vertices $\begin{pmatrix}-5\\-1\end{pmatrix}, \begin{pmatrix}-1\\-1\end{pmatrix}, \begin{pmatrix}2\\1\end{pmatrix}, \begin{pmatrix}-4\\3\end{pmatrix}$ and by the tuple of domain variables $\langle O_1, O_2 \rangle$ such that $\underline{O_1} = -6$, $\overline{O_1} = 6$, $\underline{O_2} = -3$, $\overline{O_2} = 7$. Part (A) gives 3 feasible instances I_1, I_2, I_3 of the family, while part (B) presents the 4 extremum polytopes E_1, E_2, E_3, E_4 associated to F.

3 The Overlapping Polytope

The purpose of this section is to characterize the portion of the placement space, called the *overlapping polytope*, where positioning the origin of a polytope will necessarily cause it to intersect with another not yet completely fixed polytope.

Theorem 1

Let F be a family of polytopes of a IR^d defined by $P_{dom}(F)$ and $P_{shape}(F)$, and let P be a fixed polytope of IR^d. If P overlaps[3] all the extremum polytopes of the family F, then P overlaps all the members of F.

---

[2] Since $P_{origin}(F) \cap P_o(F)$ is the intersection of two polytopes it is also a polytope.

[3] Overlap refers to the definition of *intersection of fixed polytopes* introduced by Definition 8.

The proof of Theorem 1 is given in [3]. When the intersection of all extremum polytopes of a family F is not empty, then one can observe that this intersection coincides with the notion of *compulsory part* introduced in [7]. The *compulsory part* is the portion of space that is covered by all the members of the family F.

Definition 11 *shadow polytope*

The *shadow polytope* of a fixed polytope P_1 of IR^d according to a shape polytope P_2 of IR^d is a fixed polytope P_{12} of IR^d defined as follows. We consider all the fixed instances I_{12} of P_2 such that one vertex of P_2 coincides with one vertex of P_1. The *shadow polytope*[4] is the convex hull of the origin vertices of all the fixed instances of I_{12}. It is denoted $\text{Shadow}(P_1, P_2)$.

One can notice that the shadow polytope of a fixed polytope P_1 according to a shape polytope P_2 is actually the Minkowski sum [5, pp. 272-279] of P_1 and $-P_2$[5].

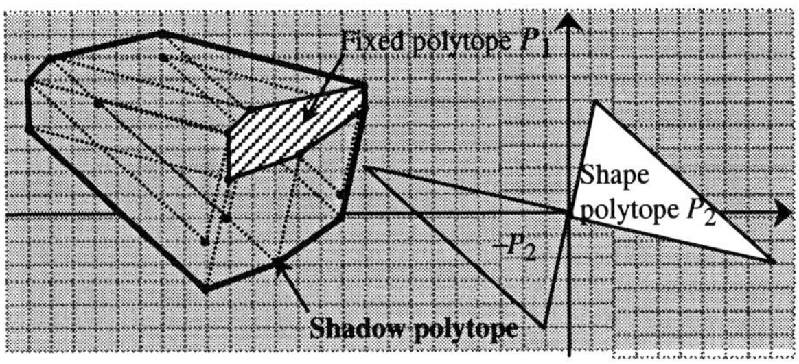

Fig. 5. Shadow polytope of P_1 according to P_2

Fig. 5 shows with a bold line the shadow polytope of the fixed polytope P_1 according to the shape polytope P_2. It consists of the convex hull of the 18 points that are obtained by making one of the 3 vertices of P_2 to coincide with one of the 6 vertices P_1.

Theorem 2

Let P_{12} be the shadow polytope of a fixed polytope P_1 of IR^d according to a shape polytope P_2 of IR^d.

1° If the origin of P_2 is a relative interior point of P_{12}, then P_2 and P_1 overlap.

2° If the origin of P_2 is not a relative interior point of P_{12}, then P_2 and P_1 do not overlap.

Proof of Theorem 2

Part 1° Suppose $x \in P_{12}^{\bullet}$ then $x \in \left(x^* + (-P_2)\right)^{\bullet}$ for some $x^* \in P_1$.

So $x = x^* + x_2$ where $x_2 \in (-P_2)^{\bullet}$,

hence $x - x_2 \in x + P_2^{\bullet} = (x + P_2)^{\bullet}$ and $x - x_2 = x^* \in P_1$, i.e. $x - x_2 = x^* \in (x + P_2)^{\bullet} \cap P_1$.

---

[4] We call it "shadow" since the shadow polytope is partially looking like the fixed polytope from which it is derived.

[5] We get $-P_2$ by reflecting P_2 about its origin.

Now choose $r > 0$ such that $Ball(x^*, r) \subset (x + P_2)^\bullet$ and notice that $x^* \in P_1$, hence $Ball(x^*, r) \cap P_1^\bullet \neq \emptyset$, so $(x + P_2)^\bullet \cap P_1^\bullet \neq \emptyset$.

Part 2° Suppose $P_1^\bullet \cap (x + P_2)^\bullet \neq \emptyset$ where $x \in bd(P_{12})$,

then there exists an $x_1 \in P_1^\bullet \cap (x + P_2)^\bullet$.

So $x_1 = x + x_2$ where $x_2 \in P_2^\bullet$,

therefore $x = x_1 - x_2 \in P_1^\bullet - P_2^\bullet \subset (P_{12})^\bullet$ which is a contradiction. □

Definition 12 *overlapping polytope*

The *overlapping polytope* of a family of polytopes F of IR^d according to a given shape polytope P_{shape} of IR^d is the polytope (it may be an empty set) defined as follows: $\text{Overlapping}(F, P_{shape}) = \bigcap_{i=1}^{|P_{dom}(F)|} \text{Shadow}(\text{Extremum}_i(F), P_{shape})$.

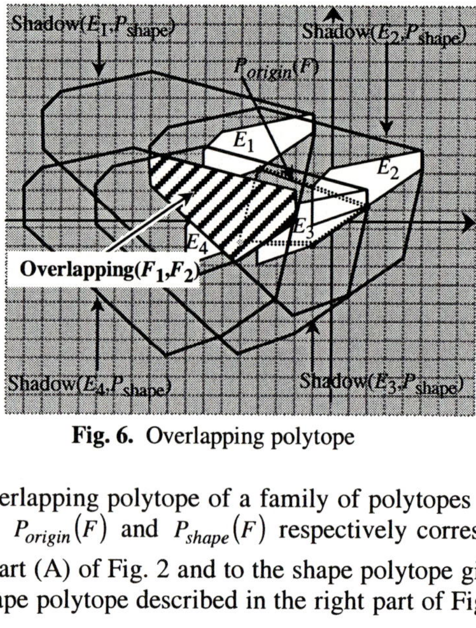

Fig. 6. Overlapping polytope

Fig. 6 shows the overlapping polytope of a family of polytopes F according to a shape polytope P_{shape}. $P_{origin}(F)$ and $P_{shape}(F)$ respectively correspond to the fixed polytope specified in part (A) of Fig. 2 and to the shape polytope given in part (B) of Fig. 2. P_{shape} is the shape polytope described in the right part of Fig. 5 (i.e. the shape polytope P_2). Since F has 4 extremum polytopes E_1, E_2, E_3 and E_4, the overlapping polytope is the intersection of the corresponding 4 shadow polytopes. As an easy corollary of Theorems 1 and 2, we have the following theorem.

Theorem 3

Let F be a family of polytopes of IR^d and P_{shape} a shape polytope of IR^d. For any point $X \in \text{Overlapping}(F, P_{shape})^\bullet$ the fixed polytope $X + P_{shape}$ will overlap any fixed polytope of the family F.

Proof of Theorem 3

From the definition of an overlapping polytope and from Theorem 2, we have that all fixed polytopes $X + P_{shape}\ \left(X \in \text{Overlapping}\left(F, P_{shape}\right)^{\bullet}\right)$ overlap all extremum polytopes of F. From Theorem 1, we generalize to the fact that they overlap all fixed polytopes of F. □

The overlapping polytope is related to the notion of forbidden region which was introduced in [2]. It is a forbidden portion of the space according to the binary non-overlapping constraint between two families of polytopes. However unlike the forbidden region, it is multi-dimensional and it has a more general shape than a rectangle. In Sect. 4 and 5 we will prune the origin of a polytope in order to avoid that it is a relative interior point of a given overlapping polytope.

4 A Filtering Algorithm for the Non-overlapping Constraint between Two Convex Polygons

This section first presents a linear algorithm for computing the overlapping polytope. It then gives a filtering algorithm which exploits the previous overlapping polytope in order to prune the origin variables of a polygon.

4.1 Computing the Overlapping Polytope in Two Dimensions

Suppose we want to compute the overlapping polytope for a shape polytope P_{shape} according to a family F of polygons.

Computing the shadow polytope. Let Q denote the domain polytope $P_{dom}(F)$ and let $w_1,\ldots,w_m$ be the vertices of Q in counter-clockwise order. Since the shadow polytope $P = \text{Shadow}\left(P_{shape}(F), P_{shape}\right)$ is the Minkowski sum of $P_{shape}(F)$ and $-P_{shape}$ it can be computed in linear time in the number of vertices of $P_{shape}(F)$ and P_{shape} by using the algorithm given in [5, page 277] for computing the Minkowski sum in two dimensions.

Extracting the relevant halfspaces. If we denote the overlapping polytope by O, we have $O = \cap_{j=1}^{m} w_j + P$. If P has n edges, then P is the intersection of n halfspaces $H_1,\ldots,H_n$, where the boundary of H_i contains the ith edge (see Fig. 7). And hence, $O = \cap_{i=1}^{n} \cap_{j=1}^{m} w_j + H_i$. If we look at Fig. 7, we observe that the halfspace $w_2 + H_2$ is contained in the halfspaces $w_1 + H_2$ and $w_3 + H_2$. Thus of the three halfspaces only $w_2 + H_2$ has to be considered in the computation of O. This observation holds in general: for every $i\ (1 \le i \le n)$ there is a $j(i)$ such that $w_{j(i)} + H_i \subseteq w_j + H_i$ for $j = 1,\ldots,m$.

We call $w_{j(i)}$ an *extremal vertex* of Q with respect to H_i. We have just seen that $O = \cap_{i=1}^{n} w_{j(i)} + H_i$.

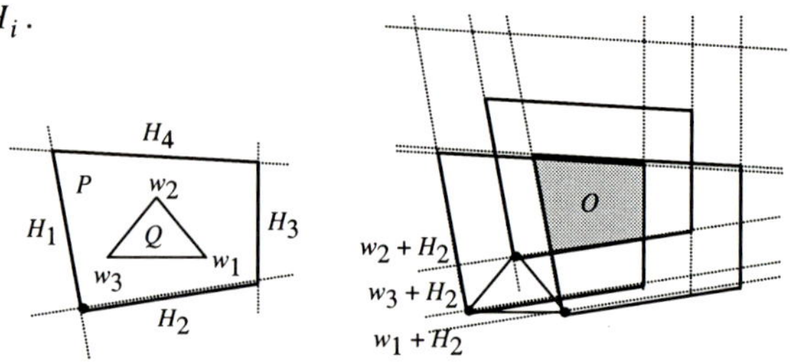

Fig. 7. Computing the overlapping polytope O according to the domain polytope Q and the shadow polytope P (the origin of P is the intersection of H_1 and H_2)

How do we find these extremal vertices efficiently? In two dimensions this is quite easy. Let us look at Fig. 8 and suppose we want to find the extremal vertex for H_2. Let $n(H_2)$ denote the normal vector of the edge induced by H_2. In two dimensions we define the normal vector of the edge induced by two vertices u and v (given in counter-clockwise ordering) as $n(u,v) = \begin{pmatrix} v_y - u_y \\ u_x - v_x \end{pmatrix}$, i.e. we suppose that normal vectors point to the outside. In order to find an extremal vertex for H_2, we perform a parallel slide of H_2 in direction $-n(H_2)$; the boundary of H_2 hits the vertices of Q in the order w_1, w_3, w_2. And since w_2 is the last vertex to be hit, it is the extremal vertex. When is w_2 extremal with respect to some halfspace H_i? Let e, f denote the edges incident to w_2. Obviously, w_2 is extremal when $-n(H_i)$ lies in the cone spanned by the normal vectors $n(e), n(f)$, as shown on the right hand side of Fig. 8.

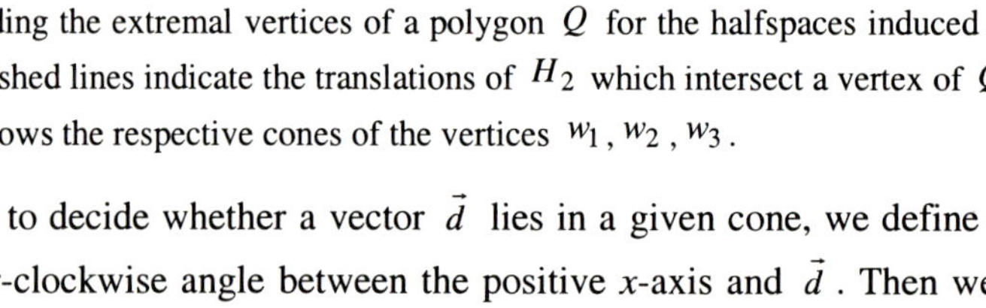

Fig. 8. Finding the extremal vertices of a polygon Q for the halfspaces induced by the edges of P (the dashed lines indicate the translations of H_2 which intersect a vertex of Q). The right hand side shows the respective cones of the vertices w_1, w_2, w_3.

In order to decide whether a vector $\vec{d}$ lies in a given cone, we define $angle(\vec{d})$ as the counter-clockwise angle between the positive x-axis and $\vec{d}$. Then we can easily perform the *in-cone-test* by comparing the angles of $\vec{d}$ and the vectors that are spanning the cone. Suppose that w_1 is the vertex of Q with largest x-coordinate and, in case of tie, smallest y-coordinate. If we start in w_1 and visit the edges of Q in counter-clockwise ordering the angles of the normal vectors increase monotonously in the interval $[0;2\pi[$. A similar observation can be made for the negative normal vectors for the edges (or halfspaces) of P. And hence determining the extremal points for the halfspaces of P amounts to a merging of angles. This leads to Algorithm 1 for which the runtime is clearly in $O(n+m)$.

We want to point out that it is not necessary to compute the angles explicitly in order to do the comparison. Suppose we want to compare the angle between two directions $\vec{d} = \begin{pmatrix} d_1 \\ d_2 \end{pmatrix}$ and $\vec{e} = \begin{pmatrix} e_1 \\ e_2 \end{pmatrix}$. First we compare the quadrants, where $quadrant(\vec{d})$ is 1 if $d_1 \geq 0 \wedge d_2 \geq 0$, 2 if $d_1 < 0 \wedge d_2 \geq 0$, 3 if $d_1 < 0 \wedge d_2 < 0$, 4 if $d_1 \geq 0 \wedge d_2 < 0$. If the quadrant of $\vec{d}$ is greater (smaller) than the quadrant of $\vec{e}$ then the angle is also greater (smaller). If the quadrants are equal we know that there is an acute angle between the two directions. And hence we can consider the third component of the cross product $\vec{d} \times \vec{e}$, which is $d_1 e_2 - d_2 e_1$. When the quadrants are equal, this component is negative iff $angle(\vec{d}) > angle(\vec{e})$.

Input : Polygons $P=(v_1,\ldots,v_n)$ and $Q=(w_1,\ldots,w_m)$.
Require: The vertices are in counter-clockwise ordering. The vertex v_1 has smallest x-coordinate and, in case of ties, largest y-coordinate; vertex w_1 has largest x-coordinate and, in case of ties, smallest y-coordinate.

$v_{n+1} \leftarrow v_1$; $w_{m+1} \leftarrow w_1$; $i \leftarrow 1$; $j \leftarrow 1$;
repeat
  while $angle(-n(v_i, v_{i+1})) > angle(n(w_j, w_{j+1}))$ **do** $j \leftarrow j+1$;
  store w_j as an extremal vertex of H_i;
  $i \leftarrow i+1$;
until $i = n+1$;

Alg. 1. Computing extremal vertices

Computing the intersection of the relevant halfspaces. Now we can compute $O = \cap_{i=1}^{n} w_{j(i)} + H_i$. It is well known that this can be done in time $O(n \log n)$ [5, page 71]. But we can provide an $O(n)$ algorithm since we recognize that $angle(H_i) < angle(H_{i+1})$ for $i = 1,\ldots,n-1$. Our algorithm computes the intersection of the halfspaces iteratively; in the i-th iteration $(i \geq 2)$ we compute $O_i = \cap_{k=1}^{i} w_{j(k)} + H_k$. We represent O_i with a data structure B_i describing its boundary. The boundary of the halfspace $w_{j(k)} + H_k$ is the line $L_k = \{(w_{j(k)} + v_k) + \lambda(v_{k+1} - v_k); \lambda \in IR\}$. The boundary of O_i may be infinite, and then it consists of two rays and of zero or more line segments. If it is finite, it consists only of line segments. We call such a ray or a line segment a *boundary element* and B_i will be a list of boundary elements.

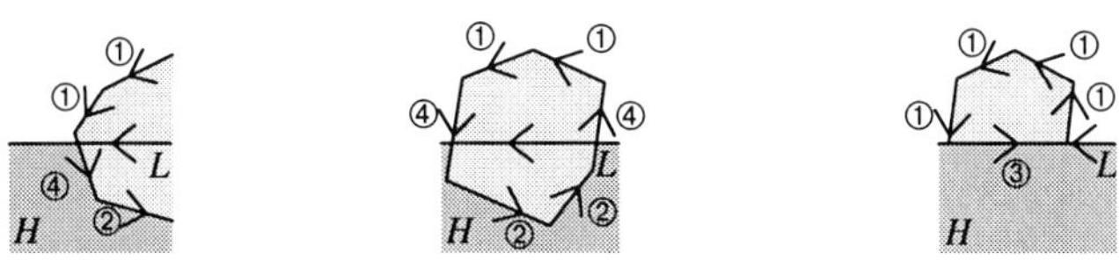

Fig. 9. Intersection of the halfspace H (with the bounding line L) with an infinite or a finite boundary

Now suppose that O_{i-1} is not empty and we have computed the list B_{i-1}. In order to compute B_i we have to determine how the boundary changes if we add the halfspace $H = w_{j(i)} + H_i$ to the intersection. It is clear that the halfspace can contribute at most one new boundary element, but some of the old elements may have to be updated or discarded. Let us consider an old element B from B_{i-1} and distinguish four possible cases (In Fig. 9 the respective case is marked beside every element):

1. B lies to the right of L_i: then $B \cap L_i = \varnothing$ and we can discard B.
2. B lies to the left of L_i: then $B \subset H$ and we keep B unchanged.
3. B lies on L_i: this means that the normal vector of H and of the halfspace form which B originates are anti-parallel. And hence the interior of O_i is empty and B_i only consists of B.
4. B and L_i properly intersect in a point x: then we have to update B; we discard the part of B which lies to right of L_i.

It is easy to find the contribution B_H of H to the boundary. Since the boundary is convex there can be at most two proper intersection points. If there are two intersection points x and x' then B_H is the line segment between x and x'. In case there is only one point x, B_H is a ray starting in x. If all elements of B_{i-1} lie to the right of L_i, then the intersection is empty and we can terminate. If all old boundary elements lie to the left of L_i then H is redundant, i.e. it does not contribute to the boundary.

In the *i*-th iteration we first update B_{i-1} as just discussed and append the contribution of $w_{j(i)} + H_i$ to the end of the list, if there is any. Thus we obtain the new list B_i. In order to obtain the desired time bound we cannot afford to test L_i against all old boundary elements. Suppose $\mathsf{B}_{i-1} = \langle B_1, \ldots, B_l \rangle$ and that B_λ originates from $H_{h(\lambda)}$. From the construction of B_{i-1} it is easy to see that $h(1) < \ldots < h(l)$. And hence the angles of the negative normal vectors of $B_1, \ldots, B_l$ increase monotonously and are smaller than the angle of $-n(H_i)$. Thus we can do the test in the following way. First we process the list from left to right and discard elements lying to the right of L_i until we find an element that does not lie to the left of L_i, then we process the list from right to left and do the same. If the list becomes empty, we know that the intersection is also empty. Due to the order of the elements in B_{i-1} we can be sure that all elements that we do not test lie to the left of L_i and hence need no update.

Our algorithm performs only $O(n)$ tests altogether. This can be seen as follows. Assume we test a boundary element B and a line L_i. If B lies to the right of L_i we charge the test to B, otherwise we charge it to L_i. Every line L_i is charged at most twice, and every boundary element is charged at most once, because it is immediately discarded after being charged. This gives us the desired bound.

4.2 Pruning in Two Dimensions

Suppose we want to prune the origin of a family F_1 with respect to a family F_2. We describe the algorithm for the domain variable O_x which denotes the x-coordinate of the origin of F_1. In the previous section we have seen how to compute $O = \text{Overlapping}(F_2, P_{shape}(F_1))$. We know that we have to place the origin of F_1 into $P_{dom}(F_1) \setminus O^\bullet$. Let L_{x_0} denote the vertical line given by the equation $x = x_0$. We can prune a value x_0 from O_x if the set $I(x_0) = (P_{dom}(F_1) \setminus O^\bullet) \cap L_{x_0}$ contains no point with integer coordinates. The line L_{x_0} can intersect the boundary of the polygon $P_{dom}(F_1)$ in at most two points. Let $p_l(x_0)/p_u(x_0)$ denote the y-coordinate of the lower/upper intersection point (see part (A) of Fig. 10), if there is no intersection set $p_l(x_0)$ to ∞ and $p_u(x_0)$ to $-\infty$. And define $o_l(x_0)/o_u(x_0)$ in an analogous way for O. Suppose $\min_x(P_{dom}(F_1)) \leq x \leq \max_x(P_{dom}(F_1))$. Then $I(x_0)$ is empty iff $o_l(x_0) < p_l(x_0)$ and $p_u(x_0) < o_u(x_0)$. And for integral x_0 the set $I(x_0)$ contains a point with integer coordinates iff there is an integer k with $p_l(x_0) \leq k \leq p_u(x_0)$ and $k \leq o_l(x_0) \vee k \geq o_u(x_0)$. This observation leads to the following algorithm. We (conceptually) move a sweep-line [8, pp. 10-11] L from left to right: we start in $\underline{O}_x$ and stop in $\overline{O}_x$.

A. Pruning in the continuous case. We first describe an algorithm which does not achieve maximum pruning, because it does not remove x_0 from O_x if $I(x_0)$ contains no integer point, but only if $I(x_0)$ is empty. In order to do so it suffices to find the x-coordinates where one of the differences $o_l(x_0) - p_l(x_0)$ and $p_u(x_0) - o_u(x_0)$ changes its sign. This can only happen if there is a *proper intersection*[6] between two lower edges or two upper edges of the two polygons (see transitions $x_1 \to x_2 \to x_3$ in part (A) of Fig. 10) or a vertex of one polygon lies on the boundary of the other one (see sweep-line at x_4 in part (A) of Fig. 10).

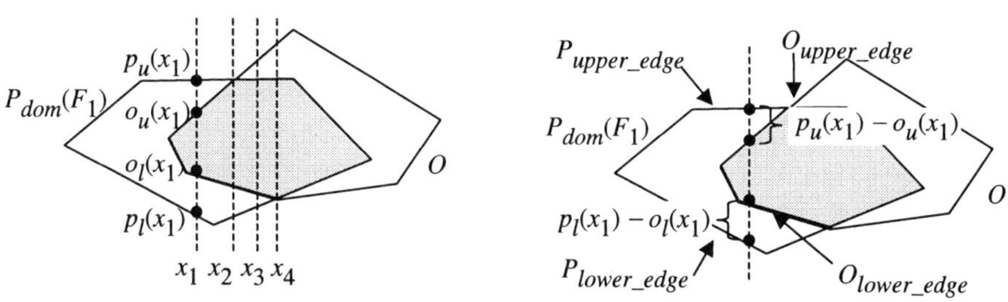

(A) Different positions of the sweep-line (B) Sweep-line status

Fig. 10. Illustration of the sweep

[6] We call an intersection between two edges *proper* if they intersect in a single point which is not an endpoint of either edge.

Sweep-line status. We restrict our attention to the case where $\min_x(P_{dom}(F_1)) < x_0 < \max_x(P_{dom}(F_1))$ and $\min_x(O) < x_0 < \max_x(O)$. Then the sweep-line intersects both polygons in two points and it does not intersect a vertical edge. The data structure representing the sweep-line status [5 page 68] stores its current position x_0, the signs of the differences $o_l(x_0) - p_l(x_0)$ and $p_u(x_0) - o_u(x_0)$ and the four edges which are intersected by it: P_{lower_edge}, P_{upper_edge}, O_{lower_edge}, O_{upper_edge} (see part B of Fig. 10). If the sweep-line intersects a vertex v of a polygon, we store the edge starting at v, i.e. the edge where the opposite vertex lies to the right of L_{x_0}.

Events. An event is an *x*-coordinate where the sweep-line status has to be updated. As we said before, this is the case whenever the sweep-line hits a vertex or a proper intersection point between lower or upper edges. Since the sweep-line intersects only 4 edges, we can always determine the next event in constant time without maintaining any additional data structure. Processing an event can also be done in constant time. Note that there may be several updates to the sweep-line status at a single event. For every edge of either polygon there can be at most two proper intersection points. Hence every edge gives rise to a constant number of events. If n denotes the number of edges of O and m the number of edges of $P_{dom}(F_1)$, the overall sweep can be done in time $O(n+m)$. The additional time needed for pruning depends on the representation of a domain variable.

B. Additional pruning in the discrete case. Now suppose that we want to achieve some stronger pruning, taking into account the fact that O_y will be an integer. We can prune a value $x_0 \in O_x$ not only if $I(x_0)$ is empty but also if $I(x_0)$ does not contain a vertex with integer coordinates. One way to do this is to generate *check events* which make the sweep-line stop at every x_0 in O_x (in addition to the *regular events* generated in the continuous case) and to check in constant time whether x_0 can be pruned. This increases the running time by $O(|O_x|)$.

One does not have to generate all check events. If $I(x_0)$ is empty at some regular event, then there is no need to generate check events until the next regular event occurs. And if at least one of the differences $p_u(x_0) - o_u(x_0)$ or $o_l(x_0) - p_l(x_0)$ is greater than or equal to 1 at some event x_0 and will not go below 1 until the next regular event x_1, then we know that $I(x)$ contains an integer point for every integer x in $[x_0, x_1]$, and hence we do not have to generate check events. So check events are only necessary if both upper and both lower edges are close together.

4.3 Summary of the Filtering Algorithm

We are given two families F_1 and F_2 of polygons. Let n_i and m_i denote the number of vertices of the shape and origin polygon of family F_i respectively. We do the following to prune the origin variables $O_{1,x}$ and $O_{1,y}$ of F_1 according to F_2:

- Compute $P_{dom}(F_1) = P_{origin}(F_1) \cap P_o(F_1)$. This can be done in time $O(m_1)$ using the algorithm given in [9] and yields a polygon with at most $m_1 + 4$ vertices,

- Compute the overlapping polytope $O = \text{Overlapping}(F_2, P_{shape}(F_1))$. This involves the following three substeps:
  - compute P as the Minkowski sum of $P_{shape}(F_2)$ and $-P_{shape}(F_1)$ in time $O(n_1+n_2)$,
  - find for every facet of P an extremal vertex of $P_{dom}(F_2)$, which requires time $O(n_1+n_2+m_2)$,
  - compute O as the intersection of n_1+n_2 halfspaces in linear time.
- Prune $O_{1,x}$ and $O_{1,y}$ with the sweep algorithm described previously in time $O(n_1+n_2+m_1)$ or $O(n_1+n_2+m_1+|O_{1,x}|+|O_{1,y}|)$ if we want to take into account the fact that the coordinates are integer.

5 A Filtering Algorithm for the Non-overlapping Constraint between Two *d*-dimensional Boxes

This section develops an efficient filtering algorithm for the special case where we have *d-dimensional boxes*. A *d*-dimensional box of origin $\langle O_1, O_2, \ldots, O_d \rangle$ and size $\langle S_1, S_2, \ldots, S_d \rangle$ where $O_1, O_2, \ldots, O_d$ are domain variables and $S_1, S_2, \ldots, S_d$ are strictly positive integers is a family of polytopes such that:

- the shape of the family is defined as the convex hull of the following 2^d vertices of coordinates $s_1, s_2, \ldots, s_d$ where s_i $(i = 1,2,..,d)$ stands for 0 or for S_i,
- the initial possible placement for the origin of the previous shape is defined by $box(O_1, O_2, \ldots, O_d)$,
- $\langle O_1, O_2, \ldots, O_d \rangle$ is the origin of the family of polytopes.

Consider now two *d*-dimensional boxes B_1, B_2 of respective origins $\langle O_{11}, O_{21}, \ldots, O_{d1} \rangle$, $\langle O_{12}, O_{22}, \ldots, O_{d2} \rangle$ and respective sizes $\langle S_{11}, S_{21}, \ldots, S_{d1} \rangle$, $\langle S_{12}, S_{22}, \ldots, S_{d2} \rangle$. We describe how to prune the origin of B_2 according to B_1. The overlapping polytope of B_1 according to $\langle S_{12}, S_{22}, \ldots, S_{d2} \rangle$ is defined by all the points of coordinates $p_1, p_2, \ldots, p_d$ such that, for all $i \in 1..d$ we have $\overline{O_{i1}} - S_{i2} \le p_i \le \underline{O_{i1}} + S_{i1}$. Pruning the origin of B_2 according to B_1 consists preventing the origin of B_2 from being a relative interior point of the previous overlapping polytope. For this purpose we count the number of times the condition $\overline{O_{i1}} - S_{i2} + 1 \le \underline{O_{i2}} \wedge \overline{O_{i2}} \le \underline{O_{i1}} + S_{i1} - 1$ $(1 \le i \le d)$ holds. The non-overlapping constraint fails if the previous condition holds d times. If it holds for all dimensions except one dimension j, then we remove the interval of values that starts at $\overline{O_{j1}} - S_{j2} + 1$ and ends at $\underline{O_{j1}} + S_{j1} - 1$ from the domain variable O_{j2}. This leads to an algorithm for which the runtime is clearly in $O(d)$.

6 Discussion and Conclusion

Note that it should be easy to apply the results of this paper for handling other binary geometrical constraints for which the forbidden set of points is convex. As an example, consider the case of the non-inclusion constraint which enforces a first given polytope to not be completely included within a second given polytope. The only change is to provide an algorithm that computes the shadow polytope according to this new type of constraint. Fig. 11 shows the shadow polytope S (see part B) associated to the non-inclusion constraint between polytope P_1 (see part A) and polytope P_2 (see part B). This indicates that vertex O of polytope P_1 should not be located within polytope S (see parts C and D), if P_1 should not be completely included within P_2.

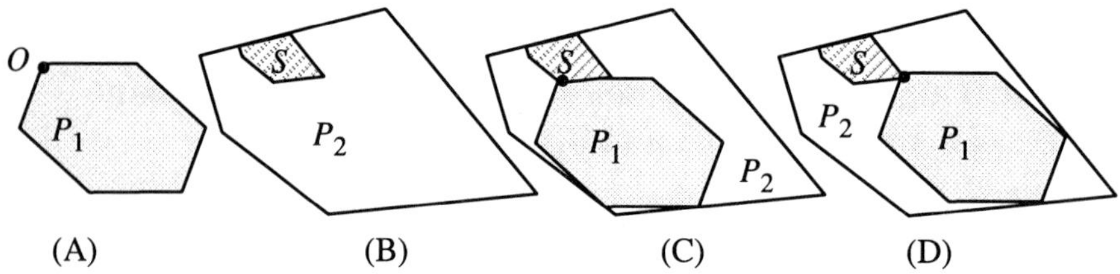

Fig. 11. Example of another convex constraint: the non-inclusion constraint

We have introduced necessary conditions for the non-overlapping constraint between polytopes. The key idea that leads to the propagation algorithm is that one can derive the overlapping polytope by considering only a very restricted number of instances of a family, namely the extremum polytopes. From these necessary conditions, we have derived efficient filtering algorithms for the non-overlapping constraint between two convex polygons as well as the non-overlapping constraint between two *d*-dimensional boxes [1]. However if we would like to come up with a more efficient propagation algorithm for the case of a clique of non-overlapping constraints, the following question remains open. One would get much more propagation by aggregating the different overlapping polytopes, but it is not clear how to efficiently generalize the algorithm presented in [2] to this situation.

References

1. Beldiceanu, N., Contejean, E.: Introducing global constraint in CHIP. *Mathl. Comput. Modelling* Vol. 20, No. 12, 97-123, 1994.
2. Beldiceanu, N.: Sweep as a generic pruning technique. In *TRICS: Technique foR Implementing Constraint programming*, CP2000, Singapore, 2000.
3. Beldiceanu, N., Guo, Q., Thiel, S.: Non-overlapping Constraint between Convex Polytopes. SICS technical report T2001-12, (May 2001).
4. Berger, M.: *Geometry II*, Chapter 12. Springer-Verlag, 1980.
5. de Berg, M., van Kreveld, M., Overmars, M., Schwarzkopf, O.: *Computational Geometry – Algorithms and Applications*. Springer, 1997.
6. Chamard, A., Deces, F., Fischler, A.: A Workshop Scheduler System written in CHIP. *2nd Conf Practical Applications of Prolog*, London, April 1994.

7. Lahrichi, A., Gondran, M.: Théorie des parties obligatoires et découpes à deux dimensions. Research report HI/4762-02 from EDF (Électricité de France), (23 pages), 1984. In French.
8. Preparata F.P., Shamos M.I.: *Computational Geometry. An Introduction.* Springer-Verlag, 1985.
9. Sutherland, I.E., Hodgman, G.W.: Reentrant Polygon Clipping, *CACM*, 17(1), 32-42, 1974.
10. Van Hentenryck, P.: *Constraint Satisfaction in Logic Programming.* The MIT Press, 1989.

Formal Models of Heavy-Tailed Behavior in Combinatorial Search

Hubie Chen, Carla Gomes, and Bart Selman

Department of Computer Science, Cornell University, Ithaca, NY 14853, USA
{hubes,gomes,selman}@cs.cornell.edu

Abstract. Recently, it has been found that the cost distributions of randomized backtrack search in combinatorial domains are often heavy-tailed. Such heavy-tailed distributions explain the high variability observed when using backtrack-style procedures. A good understanding of this phenomenon can lead to better search techniques. For example, restart strategies provide a good mechanism for eliminating the heavy-tailed behavior and boosting the overall search performance. Several state-of-the-art SAT solvers now incorporate such restart mechanisms. The study of heavy-tailed phenomena in combinatorial search has so far been been largely based on empirical data. We introduce several abstract tree search models, and show formally how heavy-tailed cost distribution can arise in backtrack search. We also discuss how these insights may facilitate the development of better combinatorial search methods.

1 Introduction

Recently there have been a series of new insights into the high variability observed in the run time of backtrack search procedures. Empirical work has shown that the run time distributions of backtrack style algorithms often exhibit so-called *heavy-tailed* behavior [5]. Heavy-tailed probability distributions are highly non-standard distributions that capture unusually erratic behavior and large variations in random phenomena. The understanding of such phenomena in backtrack search has provided new insights into the design of search algorithms and led to new search strategies, in particular, restart strategies. Such strategies avoid the long tails in the run time distributions and take advantage of the probability mass at the beginning of the distributions. Randomization and restart strategies are now an integral part of several state-of-the-art SAT solvers, for example, Chaff [12], GRASP [11], Relsat [1], and Satz-rand [9,4].

Research on heavy-tailed distributions and restart strategies in combinatorial search has been largely based on empirical studies of run time distributions. However, so far, a detailed rigorous understanding of such phenomena has been lacking. In this paper, we provide a formal characterization of several tree search models and show under what conditions heavy-tailed distributions can arise.

Intuitively, heavy-tailed behavior in backtrack style search arises from the fact that wrong branching decisions may lead the procedure to explore an exponentially large subtree of the search space that contains no solutions. Depending

T. Walsh (Ed.): CP 2001, LNCS 2239, pp. 408–421, 2001.

on the number of such "bad" branching choices, one can expect a large variability in the time to find a solution on different runs. Our analysis will make this intuition precise by providing a search tree model, for which we can formally prove that the run time distribution is heavy-tailed. A key component of our model is that it allows for highly irregular and imbalanced trees, which produce search times that differ radically from run to run. We also analyze a tree search model that leads to fully balanced search trees. The balanced tree model does not exhibit heavy-tailed behavior, and restart strategies are provably ineffective in this model. The contrast between the balanced and imbalanced models shows that heavy-tailedness is not inherent to backtrack search in general but rather emerges from backtrack searches through highly irregular search spaces.

Whether search trees encountered in practice correspond more closely to balanced or imbalanced trees is determined by the combination of the characteristics of the underlying problem instance and the search heuristics, pruning, and propagation methods employed. Balanced trees occur when such techniques are relatively ineffective in the problem domain under consideration. For example, certain problem instances, such as the parity formulas [2], are specifically designed to "fool" any clever search technique. (The parity problems were derived using ideas from cryptography.) On such problem instances backtrack search tends to degrade to a form of exhaustive search, and backtrack search trees correspond to nearly fully balanced trees with a depth equal to the number of independent variables in the problem. In this case, our balanced search tree model captures the statistical properties of such search spaces.

Fortunately, most CSP or SAT problems from real-world applications have much more structure, and branching heuristics, dynamic variable ordering, and pruning techniques can be quite effective. When observing backtrack search on such instances, one often observes highly imbalanced search trees. That is, there can be very short subtrees, where the heuristics (combined with propagation) quickly discover contradictions; or, at other times, the search procedure branches deeply into large subtrees, making relatively little progress in exploring the overall search space. As a result, the overall search tree becomes highly irregular, and, as our imbalanced search tree model shows, exhibits heavy-tailed behavior, often making random restarts effective.

Before proceeding with the technical details of our analysis, we now give a brief summary of our main technical results. For our balanced model, we will show that the expected run time (measured in leaf nodes visited) scales exponentially in the height of the search tree, which corresponds to the number of independent variables in the problem instance. The underlying run time distribution is not heavy-tailed, and a restart strategy will not improve the search performance.

For our imbalanced search tree model, we will show that the run time of a randomized backtrack search method is heavy-tailed, for a range of values of the model parameter p, which characterizes the effectiveness of the branching heuristics and pruning techniques. The heavy-tailedness leads to an infinite variance and sometimes an infinite mean of the run time. In this model, a restart strategy will lead to a polynomial mean and a polynomial variance.

We subsequently refine our imbalanced model by taking into account that in general we are dealing with finite-size search trees of size at most b^n, where b is the branching factor. As an immediate consequence, the run time distribution of a backtrack search is bounded and therefore cannot, strictly speaking, be heavy-tailed (which requires infinitely long "fat" tails). Our analysis shows, however, that a so-called "bounded heavy-tailed" model provides a good framework for studying the search behavior on such trees. The bounded distributions share many properties with true heavy-tailed distributions. We will show how the model gives rise to searches whose mean scales exponentially. Nevertheless, short runs have sufficient probability mass to allow for an effective restart strategy, with a mean run time that scales polynomially. These results closely mimic the properties of empirically determined run time distributions on certain classes of structured instances, and explain the practical effectiveness of restarts, as well as the large observed variability between different backtrack runs.

The key components that lead to heavy-tailed behavior in backtrack search are (1) an exponential search space and (2) effective branching heuristics with propagation mechanisms. The second criteria is necessary to create a reasonable probability mass for finding a solution early on in the search. Interestingly, our analysis suggests that heuristics that create a large variability between runs may be more effective than more uniform heuristics because a restart strategy can take advantage of some of the short, but possibly relatively rare, runs.[1]

We should stress that although our imbalanced tree model results in heavy-tailed behavior, we do not mean to suggest that this is the only such model that would do so. In fact, our imbalanced model is just one possible search tree model, and it is a topic for future research to explore other search models that may also result in heavy-tailed behavior.

The paper is structured as follows. In section 2, we present our balanced tree model. In section 3, we introduce the imbalanced search tree model, followed by the bounded version in section 4. Section 5 gives the conclusions and discusses directions for future work.

2 Balanced Trees

We first consider the case of a backtrack search on a balanced tree. To obtain the base-case for our analysis, we consider the most basic form of backtrack search. We will subsequently relax our assumptions and move on to more practical forms of backtrack search. In our base model, we assume chronological backtracking, fixed variable ordering, and random child selection with no propagation or prun-

[1] In an interesting study, Chu Min Li (1999) [8] argues that asymmetric heuristics may indeed be quite powerful. The study shows that heuristics that lead to "skinny" but deep search trees can be more effective that heuristics that uniformly try to minimize the overall depth of the trees, thereby creating relative short but dense trees.

ing. We consider a branching factor of two, although the analysis easily extends to any constant branching factor.

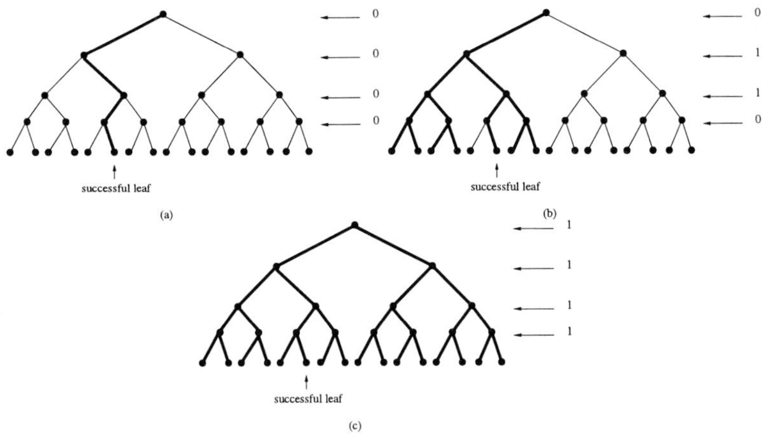

Fig. 1. Balanced tree model.

Figure 1 shows three examples of our basic setup. The full search space is a complete binary tree of depth n with 2^n leaf nodes at the bottom. We assume that there is exactly a single successful leaf.[2] The bold-faced subtrees show the nodes visited before the successful leaf is found. The figure is still only an abstraction of the actual search process: there are still different ways to traverse the bold-faced subtrees, referred to as "abstract search subtrees". An abstract search tree corresponds to the tree of all visited nodes, without specification of the order in which the nodes are visited. Two different runs of a backtrack search can have the same abstract tree but different concrete search trees in which the same nodes are visited but in different order.

2.1 Probabilistic Characterization of the Balanced Tree Model

Our balanced tree search model has a number of interesting properties. For example, each abstract search subtree is characterized by a unique number of visited leaf nodes, ranging from 1 to 2^n. Moreover, once the successful leaf is fixed, each abstract subtree occurs with probability $(1/2)^n$. The number of leaf nodes visited up to and including the successful leaf node is a discrete uniformly distributed random variable: denoting this random variable by $T(n)$, we have $P[T(n) = i] = (1/2)^n$, when $i = 1, \ldots, 2^n$.

As noted above, several runs of a backtrack search method can yield the same abstract tree, because the runs may visit the same set of nodes, but in a

[2] Having multiple solutions does not qualitatively change our results. In the full version of this paper, we will discuss this issue in more detail.

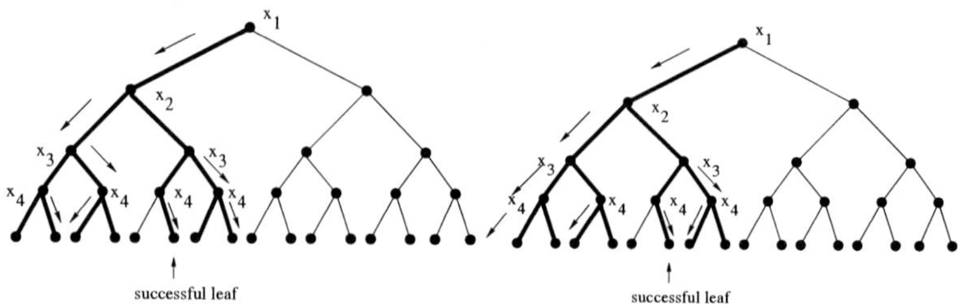

Fig. 2. Balanced tree model (detailed view).

different order. It is useful, to also consider such actual traversals (or searches) of an abstract subtree. See Figure 2. The figure shows two possible traversals for the subtree from Figure 1(b). At each node, the figure gives the name of the branching variable selected at the node, and the arrow indicates the first visited child. The only possible variation in our search model is the order in which the children of a node are visited. To obtain the bold-faced subtree in Figure 1(b), we see that, at the top two nodes, we first need to branch to the left. Then we reach a complete subtree below node x_3, where we have a total of 4 possible ways of traversing the subtree. In total, we have 6 possible searches that correspond to the abstract subtree in Figure 1(b).

Note that the abstract subtree in Figures 1(a) has only one possible corresponding traversal. Each possible traversal of a abstract search tree is equally likely. Therefore, the probability of an actual search traversal is given by $(1/2)^n(1/K)$, where K is the number of distinct traversals of the corresponding abstract subtree.

We now give a brief derivation of the properties of our balanced tree search. Consider the abstract binary search trees in Figure 1. Let "good" nodes be those which are ancestors of the satisfying leaf, and let "bad" nodes be all others. Our backtrack search starts at the root node; with probability 1/2, it descends to the "bad" node at depth one, and incurs time 2^{n-1} exploring all leaves below this "bad" node. After all of these leaves have been explored, a random choice will take place at the "good" node of depth one. At this node, there is again probability 1/2 of descending to a "good" node, and probability 1/2 of descending to a "bad" node; in the latter case, all 2^{n-2} leaves below the "bad" node will be explored. If we continue to reason in this manner, we see that the cost of the search is

$$T(n) = X_1 2^{n-1} + \ldots + X_j 2^{n-j} + \ldots + X_{n-1} 2^1 + X_n 2^0 + 1$$

where each X_j is an indicator random variable, taking on the value 1 if the "bad" node at depth j was selected, and the value 0 otherwise. For each $i = 1, \ldots, 2^n$, there is exactly one choice of zero-one assignments to the variables X_j so that i is equal to the above cost expression; any such assignment has probability 2^{-n} of occurring, and so this is the probability that the cost is i.

Stated differently, once the satisfying leaf is fixed, the abstract subtree is determined completely by the random variables X_j: all descendants of the "bad" sibling of the unique "good" node at depth j are explored if and only if $X_j = 1$. In Figure 1, we give the X_j settings alongside each tree. A good choice at a level gets label "0" and a bad choice gets label "1". Each possible binary setting uniquely defines an abstract search tree and its number of leaf nodes. Hence, there are 2^n abstract subtrees, each occurring with probability $1/2^n$. The overall search cost distribution is therefore the uniform distribution over the range $i = 1, \ldots, 2^n$.

This allows us to calculate the expectation and variance of the search cost in terms of the number of visited leaves, denoted by $T(n)$. The expected value is given by $E[T(n)] = \sum_{i=1}^{2^n} iP[T(n) = i]$, which with $P[T(n) = i] = 2^{-n}$ gives us $E[T(n)] = (1 + 2^n)/2$.

We also have $E[T^2(n)] = \sum_{i=1}^{2^n} i^2 P[T = i]$, which equals $(2^{2n+1} + 3.2^n + 1)/(6)$. So, for the variance we obtain $\mathrm{Var}[T] = E[T^2(n)] - E[T(n)]^2$, which equals $(2^{2n} - 1)/(12)$.

These results show that both the expected run time and the variance of chronological backtrack search on a complete balanced tree scale exponentially in n. Of course, given that we assume that the leaf is located somewhere uniformly at random on the fringe of the tree, it makes intuitive sense that the expected search time is of the order of half of the size of the fringe. However, we have given a much more detailed analysis of the search process to provide a better understanding of the full probability distribution over the search trees and abstract search trees.

2.2 The Effect of Restarts

We conclude our analysis of the balanced case by considering whether a randomized restart strategy can be beneficial in this setting. As discussed earlier, restart strategies for randomized backtrack search have shown to be quite effective in practice [4]. However, in the balanced search tree model, a restart strategy is not effective in reducing the run time to a polynomial.

In our analysis, we slightly relax the assumptions made about our search model. We assume a branching factor of $b \geq 2$, and we make no assumptions about the order in which the algorithm visits the children of an internal node, other than that the first child is picked randomly. Indeed, our analysis applies even if an arbitrarily intelligent heuristic is used to select among the remaining unvisited children at a node. However, for the case of $b = 2$, this model is identical to our previous model. As we will see, the mean of $T(n)$ is still exponential.

Our first observation gives the probability that the number of visited leaf nodes $T(n)$ does not exceed a power of b.

Lemma 1. *For any integers n, k such that $0 \leq k \leq n$ and $1 \leq n$, $P[T(n) \leq b^{n-k}] = b^{-k}$.*

Proof. Observe that $T(n) \leq b^{n-k}$ if and only if at least the first k guesses are correct. The probability that the first k guesses are correct is b^{-k}. □

It follows that the expected run time is exponential, as one would expect.

Theorem 1. *The expectation of the run time, $E[T(n)]$, for a balanced tree model is exponential in n.*

Proof. By Lemma 1, $P[T(n) \leq b^{n-1}] = b^{-1}$. Thus, $E[T(n)]$ is bounded below by $b^{n-1}(1-b^{-1})$, which is exponential in n.

We now refine Lemma 1 to obtain an upper bound on the probability that $T(n)$ is below $f(n)$.[3]

Lemma 2. *If $f : \mathbb{N}^+ \to \mathbb{N}^+$ is a function such that $f(n) \leq b^n$ (for all $n \geq 1$), then $P[T(n) \leq f(n)] \leq f(n)/b^{n-1}$ (for all $n \geq 1$).*

Proof. We have that $0 \leq \log_b f(n) \leq n$. Set $k(n) = n - \log_b f(n)$, so that $\log_b f(n) = n - k(n)$. Then, $0 \leq n - k(n) \leq n$, implying that $0 \leq k(n) \leq n$. Since $0 \leq \lfloor k(n) \rfloor \leq n$, we can apply Lemma 1 to $\lfloor k(n) \rfloor$ to obtain $P[T(n) \leq b^{n-\lfloor k(n) \rfloor}] = 1/b^{\lfloor k(n) \rfloor}$. So, we have $P[T(n) \leq f(n)] = P[T(n) \leq b^{\log_b f(n)}] \leq P[T(n) \leq b^{n-\lfloor k(n) \rfloor}] = 1/b^{\lfloor k(n) \rfloor} \leq 1/b^{n-\log_b f(n)-1} \leq f(n)/b^{n-1}$. □

This theorem implies that the probability of the search terminating in polynomial time is exponentially small in n, as $f(n)/b^{n-1}$ is exponentially small in n for any polynomial f. Using this observation, we can now show that there does not exist a restart strategy that leads to expected polynomial time performance.

Formally, a restart strategy is a sequence of times $t_1(n), t_2(n), t_3(n), \ldots$. Given a randomized algorithm A and a problem instance I of size n, we can run A under the restart strategy by first executing A on I for time $t_1(n)$, followed by restarting A and running for time $t_2(n)$, and so on until a solution is found. The expected time of A running under a restart strategy can be substantially different from the expected time of running A without restarts. In particular, if the run time distribution of A is "heavy-tailed", there is a good chance of having very long runs. In this case, a restart strategy can be used to cut off the long runs and dramatically reduce the expected run time and its variance.

Luby *et al.* [10] show that optimal performance can be obtained by using a purely *uniform* restart strategy. In a uniform strategy, each restart interval is the same, *i.e.*, $t(n) = t_1(n) = t_2(n) = t_3(n) = \ldots$, where $t(n)$ is the "uniform restart time".

Theorem 2. *Backtrack search on the balanced tree model has no uniform restart strategy with expected polynomial time.*

Proof. We prove this by contradiction. Let $t(n)$ be a uniform restart time yielding expected polynomial time. Using a lemma proved in the long version of this paper, we can assume $t(n)$ to be a polynomial. If we let the algorithm run for time $t(n)$, the probability that the algorithm finds a solution is $P[T(n) \leq t(n)]$, which by Lemma 2 is bounded above by $t(n)/b^{n-1}$. Thus, the expected time of the uniform restart strategy $t(n)$ is bounded below by $t(n)[t(n)/b^{n-1}]^{-1} = b^{n-1}$, a contradiction. □

[3] Note on notation: We let $\mathbb{N}^+$ denote the set of positive integers, *i.e.*, $\{1, 2, 3, \ldots\}$. We say that a function $f : \mathbb{N}^+ \to \mathbb{N}^+$ is exponential if there exist constants $c > 0$ and $b > 1$ such that $f(n) > cb^n$ for all $n \in \mathbb{N}^+$.

3 The Imbalanced Tree Model: Heavy-Tails and Restarts

Before we present a tree search model where a restart strategy does work, it is useful to understand intuitively why restarts do not enhance the search on a balanced tree: When we consider the cumulative run time distribution, there is simply not enough probability mass for small search trees to obtain a polynomial expected run time when using restarts. In other words, the probability of encountering a small successful search tree is too low. This is of course a direct consequence of the balanced nature of our trees, which means that in the search all branches reach down to the maximum possible depth. This means that if one follows a path down from the top, as soon as a branching decision is made that deviates from a path to a solution, say at depth i, a full subtree of depth $n - i$ needs to be explored.

Assume that in our balanced model, our branching heuristics make an error with probability p (for random branching, we have $p = 1/2$). The probability of making the first incorrect branching choice at the ith level from the top is $p(1-p)^{i-1}$. As a consequence, with probability p, we need to explore half of the full search tree, which leads directly to an exponential expected search cost. There are only two ways to fix this problem. One way would be to have very clever heuristics ($p << 1$) that manage to eliminate almost all branching errors and have a reasonable chance of making the first wrong choice close to the fringe of the search tree. However, it appears unlikely that such heuristics would exist for any interesting search problem. (Such heuristics in effect almost need to solve the problem.)

Another way to remedy the situation is by having a combination of non-chronological backtracking, dynamic variable ordering, pruning, propagation, clause or constraint learning, and variable selection that terminate branches early on in a "bad subtree".[4] Such techniques can substantially shrink the unsuccessful subtrees. (Below, we will refer to the collection of such techniques as "CSP techniques".) The resulting search method will be allowed to make branching mistakes but the effect of those errors will not necessarily lead to subtrees exponential in the full problem size. Of course, the resulting overall search trees will be highly irregular and may vary dramatically from run to run. As noted in the introduction, such large variations between runs have been observed in practice for a range of state-of-the-art randomized backtrack search methods. The underlying distributions are often "heavy-tailed", and in addition, restart strategies can be highly effective.

Heavy-tailed probability distributions are formally characterized by tails that have a *power-law* (polynomial) decay, *i.e.*, distributions which asymptotically have "heavy tails" — also called tails of the Pareto-Lévy form:

$$P[X > x] \sim Cx^{-\alpha}, \quad x > 0 \qquad (\star)$$

[4] A particularly exciting recent development is the Chaff [12] SAT solver. In a variety of structured domains, such as protocol verification, Chaff substantially extends the range of solvable instances. Chaff combines a rapid restart strategy with clause learning. The learned clauses help in pruning branches and subtrees on future restarts.

where $0 < \alpha < 2$ and $C > 0$ are constants. Some of the moments of heavy-tailed distributions are infinite. In particular, if $0 < \alpha \leq 1$, the distribution has infinite mean and infinite variance; with $1 < \alpha < 2$, the mean is finite but the variance is infinite.

We now introduce an abstract probability model for the search tree size that, depending on the choice of its characteristic parameter setting, leads to heavy-tailed behavior with an effective restart strategy. Our model was inspired by the analysis of methods for sequential decoding by Jacobs and Berlekamp [7].

Our imbalanced tree model assumes that the CSP techniques lead to an overall probability of $1-p$ of guiding the search directly to a solution.[5] With probability $p(1-p)$, a search space of size b, with $b \geq 2$, needs to be explored. In general, with probability $p^i(1-p)$, a search space of b^i nodes needs to be explored. Intuitively, p provides a probability that the overall amount of backtracking increases geometrically by a factor of b. This increase in backtracking is modeled as a global phenomenon.

More formally, our generative model leads to the following distribution. Let p be a probability ($0 < p < 1$), and $b \geq 2$ be an integer. Let T be a random variable taking on the value b^i with probability $(1-p)p^i$, for all integers $i \geq 0$. Note that for all $\sum_{i \geq 0}(1-p)p^i = 1$ for $0 < p < 1$, so this is indeed a well-specified probability distribution.

We will see that the larger b and p are, the "heavier" the tail. Indeed, when b and p are sufficiently large, so that their product is greater than one, the expectation of T is infinite. However, if the product of b and p is below one, then the expectation of T is finite. Similarly, if the product of b^2 and p is greater than one, the variance of T is infinite, otherwise it is finite. We now state these results formally.

The expected run time can be calculated as $E[T] = \sum_{i \geq 0} P[T = b^i]b^i = \sum_{i \geq 0}(1-p)p^i b^i = (1-p)\sum_{i \geq 0}(pb)^i$.

Therefore, when p, the probability of the size of the search space increasing by a factor of b, is sufficiently large, that is, $p \geq 1/b$, we get an infinite expected search time: $E[T] \rightarrow \infty$. For $p < 1/b$ ("better search control"), we obtain a finite mean of $E[T] = (1-p)/(1-pb)$.

To compute the variance of the run time, we first compute $E[T^2] = \sum_{i \geq 0} P[T = b^i](b^i)^2 = \sum_{i \geq 0}(1-p)p^i(b^i)^2 = (1-p)\sum_{i \geq 0}(pb^2)^i$.

Then, it can be derived from $\mathrm{Var}[T] = E[T^2] - (E[T])^2$ that (1) for $p > 1/b^2$, the variance becomes infinite, and (2) for smaller values of p, $p \leq 1/b^2$, the variance is finite with $\mathrm{Var}[T] = \frac{1-p}{1-pb^2} - (\frac{1-p}{1-pb})^2$.

Finally, we describe the asymptotics of the survival function of T.

[5] Of course, the probability $1-p$ can be close to zero. Moreover, in a straightforward generalization, one can assume an additional polynomial number of backtracks, $q(n)$, before reaching a successful leaf. This generalization is given later for the bounded case.

Lemma 3. *For all integers $k \geq 0$, $P[T > b^k] = p^{k+1}$.*

Proof. We have $P[T > b^k] = \sum_{i=k+1}^{\infty} P[T = b^i] = \sum_{i=k+1}^{\infty}(1-p)p^i = (1-p)p^{k+1}\sum_{i=k+1}^{\infty} p^{i-(k+1)} = (1-p)p^{k+1}\sum_{j=0}^{\infty} p^j = p^{k+1}$. □

Theorem 3. *Let p be fixed. For all real numbers $L \in (0,\infty)$, $P[T > L]$ is $\Theta(L^{\log_b p})$. In particular, for $L \in (0,\infty)$, $p^2 L^{\log_b p} < P[T > L] < L^{\log_b p}$.*

Proof. We prove the second statement, which implies the first. To obtain the lower bound, observe that $P[T > L] = P[T > b^{\log_b L}] \geq P[T > b^{\lceil \log_b L \rceil}] = p^{\lceil \log_b L \rceil + 1}$, where the last equality follows from Lemma 3. Moreover, $p^{\lceil \log_b L \rceil + 1} > p^{\log_b L + 2} = p^2 p^{\log_b L} = p^2 L^{\log_b p}$. We can upper bound the tail in a similar manner: $P[T > L] \leq P[T > b^{\lfloor \log_b L \rfloor}] = p^{\lfloor \log_b L \rfloor + 1} < p^{\log_b L} = L^{\log_b p}$. □

Theorem 3 shows that our imbalanced tree search model leads to a heavy-tailed run time distribution whenever $p > 1/b^2$. For such a p, the α of equation ($\star$) is less than 2.

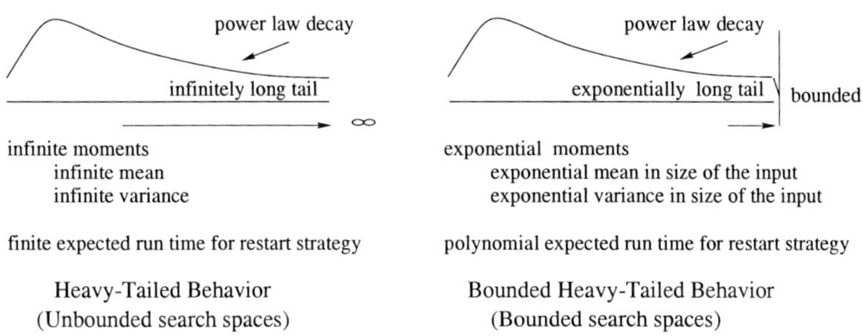

Fig. 3. Correspondence of concepts for heavy-tailed distributions and bounded heavy-tailed distributions.

4 Bounded Heavy-Tailed Behavior for Finite Distributions

Our generative model for imbalanced tree search induces a single run time distribution, and does not put an apriori bound on the size of the search space. However, in practice, there is a different run time distribution for each combinatorial problem instance, and the run time of a backtrack search procedure on a problem instance is generally bounded above by some exponential function in the size of the instance. We can adjust our model by considering heavy-tailed distributions with bounded support or so-called "bounded heavy-tailed distributions", for short [6]. Analogous to standard heavy-tailed distributions, the bounded version has power-law decay of the tail of the distribution (see equation ($\star$) over a finite, but exponential range of values. Our analysis of the bounded search space case shows that the main properties of the run time distribution observed for the unbounded imbalanced search model have natural analogues when dealing with finite but exponential size search spaces.

Figure 3 highlights the correspondence of concepts between the (unbounded) heavy-tailed model and the bounded heavy-tailed model. The key issues are: heavy-tailed distributions have infinitely long tails with power-law decay, while bounded heavy-tailed distributions have exponentially long tails with power-law decay; the concept of infinite mean in the context of a heavy-tailed distribution translates into an exponential mean in the size of the input, when considering bounded heavy-tailed distributions; a restart strategy applied to a backtrack search procedure with heavy-tailed behavior has a finite expected run time, while, in the case of bounded search spaces, we are interested in restart strategies that lead to a polynomial expected run time, whereas the original search algorithm (without restarts) exhibits bounded heavy-tailed behavior with an exponential expected run time. Furthermore, we should point out that exactly the same phenomena that lead to heavy-tailed behavior in the imbalanced generative model — the conjugation of an exponentially decreasing probability of a series of "mistakes" with an exponentially increasing penalty in the size of the space to search — cause bounded heavy-tailed behavior with an exponential mean in the bounded case.

To make this discussion more concrete, we now consider the bounded version of our imbalanced tree model. We put a bound of n on the depth of the generative model and normalize the probabilities accordingly. The run time $T(n)$ for our search model can take on values $b^i q(n)$ with probability $P[T(n) = b^i q(n)] = Cp^i$, for $i = 0, 1, 2, \ldots, n$. We renormalize this distribution using a sequence of constants C_n, which is set equal to $\frac{1-p}{1-p^{n+1}}$. This guarantees that we obtain a valid probability distribution, since $\sum_{i=0}^{n} C_n p^i = 1$. Note that $C_n < 1$ for all $n \geq 1$. We assume $b > 1$ and that $q(n)$ is a polynomial in n.
For the expected run time we have $E[T] = \sum_{i=0}^{n} P[T = b^i q(n)](b^i q(n)) = \sum_{i=0}^{n} (C_n p^i)(b^i q(n)) = C_n q(n) \sum_{i=0}^{n} (pb)^i$.

We can distinguish two cases.

(1) For $p \leq 1/b$, we have $E[T] \leq C_n q(n)(n+1)$.

(2) For $p > 1/b$, we obtain a mean that is exponential in n, because we have $E[T] \geq C_n q(n)(pb)^n$.

We compute the variance as follows. First, we have $E[T^2] = \sum_{i=0}^{n} P[T = b^i q(n)](b^i q(n))^2 = \sum_{i=0}^{n} C_n p^i (b^{2i} q^2(n)) = C_n q^2(n) \sum_{i=0}^{n} (pb^2)^i$. From $\text{Var}[T] = E[T^2] - (E[T])^2$, we can now derive the following.

(1) If $p \leq 1/b^2$, we obtain polynomial scaling for the variance, as $\text{Var}[T] \leq E[T^2] \leq C_n q^2(n)(n+1)$.

(2) For $p > 1/b^2$, the variance scales exponentially in n. To prove this, we establish a lower bound for $\text{Var}[T]$. $\text{Var}[T] \geq C_n q^2(n)(pb^2)^n - C_n^2 q^2(n)[\sum_{i=0}^{n} (pb)^i]^2 = C_n q^2(n)[(pb^2)^n - C_n[\sum_{i=0}^{n} (pb)^i]^2] \geq C_n q^2(n)[(pb^2)^n - C_n(n+1)^2 M_n^2] = C_n q^2(n)(pb^2)^n[1 - C_n(n+1)^2 M_n^2/(pb^2)^n]$, where M_n is the max-

imum term in the summation $\sum_{i=0}^{n}(pb)^i$. There are two cases: if $p > 1/b$, $M_n = (pb)^n$, and if $1/b^2 < p \leq 1/b$, $M_n = 1$. In either case, $[1 - C_n(n+1)^2 M_n^2/(pb^2)^n]$ goes to 1 in the limit $n \to \infty$, and $\mathrm{Var}[T]$ is bounded below by $(pb^2)^n$ times a polynomial (for sufficiently large n). Since $p > 1/b^2$ by assumption, we have an exponential lower bound.

Next, we establish that the probability distribution is bounded heavy-tailed when $p > 1/b$. That is, the distribution exhibits power-law decay up to run time values of b^n. Set $\epsilon = (1-p)/b$. Then, $C_n p^i \geq \epsilon/b^{i-1}$, since $(1-p) \leq C_n$ for all n and $bp > 1$ by assumption. Now consider $P[T(n) \geq L]$, where L is a value such that $b^{i-1} \leq L < b^i$ for some $i = 1, \ldots, n$. It follows that $P[T(n) \geq L] \geq P[T(n) = b^i q(n)] = C_n p^i \geq \epsilon/L$. Thus, we again have power-law decay up to $L < b^n$.

Finally, we observe that we can obtain an expected polytime restart strategy. This can be seen by considering a uniform restart strategy with restart time $q(n)$. We have $P[T(n) = q(n)] = C_n$, so the expected run time is $q(n)/C_n$. In the limit $n \to \infty$, $C_n = 1 - p$; so, the expected run time is polynomial in n.

5 Conclusions

Heavy-tailed phenomena in backtrack style combinatorial search provide a series of useful insights into the overall behavior of search methods. In particular, such phenomena provide an explanation for the effectiveness of random restart strategies in combinatorial search [3,5,13]. Rapid restart strategies are now incorporated in a range of state-of-the-art SAT/CSP solvers [12,11,1,9]. So far, the study of such phenomena in combinatorial search has been largely based on the analysis of empirical data. In order to obtain a more rigorous understanding of heavy-tailed phenomena in backtrack search, we have provided a formal analysis of the statistical properties of a series of randomized backtrack search models: the balanced tree search model, the imbalanced tree model, and the bounded imbalanced tree model. We also studied the effect of restart strategies.

Our analysis for the balanced tree model shows that a randomized backtrack search leads to a uniform distribution of run times (*i.e.*, not heavy-tailed), requiring a search of half of the fringe of the tree on average. Random restarts are not effective in this setting. For the (bounded) imbalanced model, we identified (bounded) heavy-tailed behavior for a certain range of the model parameter, p. The parameter p models "the (in)effectiveness" of the pruning power of the search procedure. More specifically, with probability p, a branching or pruning "mistake" occurs, thereby increasing the size of the subtree that requires traversal by a constant factor, $b > 1$. When $p > 1/b^2$, heavy-tailed behavior occurs. In general, heavy-tailedness arises from a conjugation of two factors: exponentially growing subtrees occurring with an exponentially decreasing probability.

Figure 4 illustrates and contrasts the distributions for the various models. We used a log-log plot of $P(T > L)$, *i.e.*, the tail of the distribution, to highlight the differences between the distributions. The linear behavior over several orders of magnitude for the imbalanced models is characteristic of heavy-tailed behavior [5]. The drop-off at the end of the tail of the distribution for the bounded

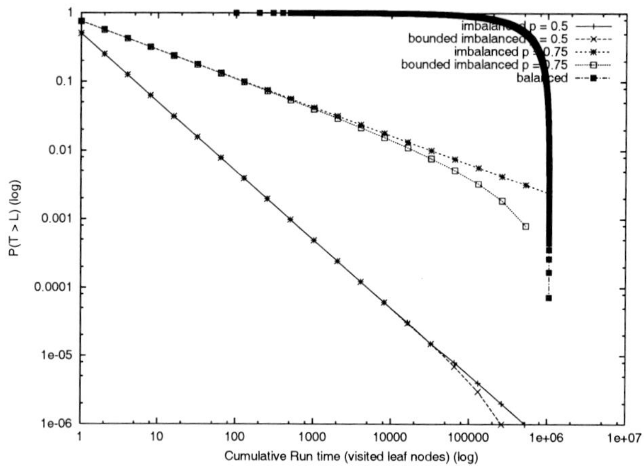

Fig. 4. Example distributions for the balanced, imbalanced and bounded imbalanced models. Parameters: $b = 2, n = 20, p = 0.5$ and 0.75.

case illustrates the effect of the boundedness of the search space. However, given the relatively small deviation from the unbounded model (except for the end of the distribution), we see that the boundary effect is relatively minor. The sharp drop-off for the balanced model indicates the absence of heavy-tailedness.

Our bounded imbalanced model provides a good match to heavy-tailed behavior as observed in practice on a range of problems. In particular, depending on the model parameter settings, the model captures the phenomenon of an exponential mean and variance combined with a polynomial expected time restart strategy. The underlying distribution is bounded heavy-tailed.

The imbalanced model can give rise to an effective restart strategy. This suggests some possible directions for future search methods. In particular, it suggests that pruning and heuristic search guidance may be more effective when behaving in a rather asymmetrical manner. The effectiveness of such asymmetric methods would vary widely between different regions of the search space. This would create highly imbalanced search tree, and restarts could be used to eliminate those runs on which the heuristic or pruning methods are relatively ineffective. In other words, instead of trying to shift the overall run time distribution downwards, it may be better to create opportunities for some short runs, even if this significantly increases the risk of additional longer runs.

As noted in the introduction, our imbalanced model is just one particular search tree model leading to heavy-tailed behavior. An interesting direction for future research is to explore other tree search models that exhibit heavy-tailed phenomena.

In our current work, we are also exploring a set of general conditions under which restarts are effective in randomized backtrack search. The long version of the paper, gives a formal statement of such results.

We hope our analysis has shed some light on the intriguing heavy-tailed phenomenon of backtrack search procedures, and may lead to further improvements in the design of search methods.

References

1. R. Bayardo and R.Schrag. Using csp look-back techniques to solve real-world sat instances. In *Proc. of the 14th Natl. Conf. on Artificial Intelligence (AAAI-97)*, pages 203–208, New Providence, RI, 1997. AAAI Press.
2. J. M. Crawford, M. J. Kearns, and R. E. Schapire. The minimal disagreement parity problem as a hard satisfiability problem. Technical report (also in dimacs sat benchmark), CIRL, 1994.
3. C. Gomes, B. Selman, and N. Crato. Heavy-tailed Distributions in Combinatorial Search. In G. Smolka, editor, *Princp. and practice of Constraint Programming (CP97). Lect. Notes in Comp. Sci.*, pages 121–135. Springer-Verlag, 1997.
4. C. Gomes, B. Selman, and H. Kautz. Boosting Combinatorial Search Through Randomization. In *Proceedings of the Fifteenth National Conference on Artificial Intelligence (AAAI-98)*, pages 431–438, New Providence, RI, 1998. AAAI Press.
5. C. P. Gomes, B. Selman, N. Crato, and H. Kautz. Heavy-tailed phenomena in satisfiability and constraint satisfaction problems. *J. of Automated Reasoning*, 24(1–2):67–100, 2000.
6. M. Harchol-Balter, M. Crovella, and C. Murta. On choosing a task assignment policy for a distributed server system. In *Proceedings of Performance Tools '98*, pages 231–242. Springer-Verlag, 1998.
7. I. Jacobs and E. Berlekamp. A lower bound to the distribution of computation for sequential decoding. *IEEE Trans. Inform. Theory*, pages 167–174, 1963.
8. C. M. Li. A constrained-based approach to narrow search trees for satisfiability. *Information processing letters*, 71:75–80, 1999.
9. C. M. Li and Anbulagan. Heuristics based on unit propagation for satisfiability problems. In *Proceedings of the International Joint Conference on Artificial Intelligence*, pages 366–371. AAAI Pess, 1997.
10. M. Luby, A. Sinclair, and D. Zuckerman. Optimal speedup of las vegas algorithms. *Information Process. Letters*, pages 173–180, 1993.
11. J. P. Marques-Silva and K. A. Sakallah. Grasp - a search algorithm for propositional satisfiability. *IEEE Transactions on Computers*, 48(5):506–521, 1999.
12. M. Moskewicz, C. Madigan, Y. Zhao, L. Zhang, and S. Malik. Chaff: Engineering an efficient sat solver. In *Proc. of the 39th Design Automation Conf.*, 2001.
13. T. Walsh. Search in a small world. In *IJCAI-99*, 1999.

The Phase Transition of the Linear Inequalities Problem

Alessandro Armando[1], Felice Peccia[1], and Silvio Ranise[1,2]

[1] DIST–Università degli Studi di Genova,
via all'Opera Pia 13, 16145, Genova, Italy,
{armando, peck, silvio}@dist.unige.it
[2] LORIA-INRIA-Lorraine, 615, rue du Jardin Botanique, BP 101,
54602 Villers les Nancy Cedex, France
ranise@loria.fr

Abstract. One of the most important problems in the polynomial class is checking the satisfiability of systems of linear inequalities over the rationals. In this paper, we investigate the phase-transition behavior of this problem by adopting a methodology which has been proved very successful on NP-complete problems. The methodology is based on the concept of *constrainedness*, which characterizes an ensemble of randomly generated problems and allows to predict the location of the phase transition in solving such problems. Our work complements and confirms previous results obtained for other polynomial problems. The approach provides a new characterization of the performance of the Phase I of the Simplex algorithm and allows us to predict its behavior on very large instances by exploiting the technique of finite size scaling.

1 Introduction

Many types of problems exhibit a phase transition phenomenon as a control parameter varies from a region in which almost all problems have many solutions, and hence it is relatively easy to guess one of them, to a region where almost all problems have no solutions, and it is usually easy to show this. In between—i.e. where the phase transition occurs—problems are "critically constrained" and it is difficult to determine whether their are solvable or not. Moreover it has been observed that the phase transition occurs more rapidly as problem size increases.

Research into phase transition phenomenon in NP-complete problems has led to many interesting results: problems from the phase transition are now used to benchmark a wide variety of algorithms; the phase transition phenomenon has shed new light on previously proposed heuristics and has even provided new ones; and although an ensemble of problems usually depends on a wide variety of parameters, problems can often be characterized simply by their size and their constrainedness.

The investigation of the phase transition phenomenon on problems in polynomial class is more recent. The studies carried out in [GS96,GMPS97] confirm the existence of the phase transition phenomenon in the problem of establishing

T. Walsh (Ed.): CP 2001, LNCS 2239, pp. 422–432, 2001.

arc consistency (AC) in constraint satisfaction problems and indicate that most of the results initially obtained for the class of NP-complete problems carry over to AC. A thorough theoretical investigation of the 2-SAT transition is carried out in [BBC+99].

We have applied the same methodology to the problem of checking the satisfiability of systems of linear inequalities over the rationals, LI for short. LI is one of the most important problems in P and it is virtually ubiquitous in Computer Science. As a matter of fact LI lies at the core of a wide variety of tools and techniques such as optimization (Linear Programming [Chv83], LP for short, can be readily reduced to LI), constraint solving, constraint logic programming [JMSY92], automated deduction [BM88], and automated verification [HHWT97].

The contributions of our work are manyfold:

- We show that *(i)* LI exhibits a phase transition as the ratio $r = m/n$ between the number of constraints m and the number of variables n increases, that *(ii)* the phase transition occurs for $r \approx 2$, and that *(iii)* it occurs more rapidly as problem size grows. Moreover, computer experiments carried out with a state-of-the-art procedure based on the Simplex method confirm the existence of the easy-hard-easy pattern.
- While r models the constrainedness of LI when regarded as a constraint satisfaction problem, it does not apparently take into account the combinatorial nature of the problem. We therefore propose a new parameter κ to measure the constrainedness of the problems in LI following the methodology presented in [GMPW96]. Computer experiments show that the phase transition occurs for $\kappa \approx 1$ and that the qualitative behavior of the phase transition is similar to that obtained using r. This seems to suggest that also r somehow succeeds in taking into account the combinatorial nature of the problem.
- Using the technique of *finite size scaling* [GMPW95] we provide a simple and accurate model of the computational cost of the Phase I of the Simplex algorithm in the easy and in the hard regions. This gives asymptotic linear growths in the easy under- and over-constrained regions respectively, and a cubic growth at the phase transition as the size of the problems increases.

These contributions pave the way to a new and elegant approach to benchmarking decision procedures for LI based on a concise characterization of problem instances in terms of their size and their constrainedness.

The paper is organized in the following way. Section 2 introduces the LI problem, the experimental methodology we used as well as the experimental results which show the phase transition and the easy-hard-easy pattern of the computational cost using r to plot the data. In Section 3 we introduce the κ parameter and replot our experimental data using κ in place of r. In Section 4 we rescale our experimental data using the technique of finite size scaling and use the results to deduce the asymptotic behaviors of the Simplex in the easy and in the hard regions. We conclude in Section 5 with some final remarks.

2 The Linear Inequalities Problem and Its Phase Transition

The Linear Inequalities problem is formally defined as follows.

Problem 1 (The Linear Inequalities problem). Let a_{ij} and b_i be integers for $i = 1, \ldots, m$ and $j = 1, \ldots, n$ where $m \geq 1$ and $n \geq 1$. Do there exist rational numbers $x_1, \ldots, x_n$ such that $\sum_{j=1}^{n} a_{ij}x_j \leq b_i$ holds for $i = 1, \ldots, m$?

Notice that the assumption that the coefficients a_{ij} and b_i ($i = 1, \ldots, m$ and $j = 1, \ldots, n$) are integers is without loss of generality, rational coefficients in each inequality can always be turned into integers by standard arithmetic manipulations.

It is also worth pointing out that the Linear Programming problem is no more difficult than LI (in the sense that there is a polynomial-time algorithm for LP if and only if there is a polynomial-time algorithm for LI). In particular, the problem of checking the satisfiability of $\sum_{j=1}^{n} a_{ij}x_j \leq b_i$ for $i = 1, \ldots, m$ can be reduced to the LP problem of minimizing z subject to $-z + \sum_{j=1}^{n} a_{ij}x_j \leq b_i$ (for $i = 1, \ldots, m$) and $z \geq 0$. Indeed this is the *auxiliary problem* generated and tackled by the Phase I of the Simplex algorithm to determine the initial basic feasible solution (see, e.g., [Chv83] for the details).

In order to study the phase transition, we generated instances of LI by randomly selecting the coefficients a_{ij} and b_i $i = 1, \ldots, m$ and $j = 1, \ldots, n$ with uniform distribution over the interval $[-1,000; +1,000]$. Hence, the number of variables n and the number of inequalities m uniquely characterize a set of instances of LI.

As a first step of our study, we experimentally determined the probability that our randomly generated instances of LI are satisfiable by using `LP_Solve` [Ber], a standard implementation of the Simplex algorithm. The results are reported in Figure 1 where curves for $n = 50, 100, 150, 200, 250$ are shown. Along the horizontal axis is the number of linear inequalities in the generated instances of LI normalized through division by the number of variables (i.e. the ratio r). Each data point gives the probability of satisfiability for a sample size of 100 problem instances. Figure 1 shows a clear phase transition in the satisfiability of the randomly generated instances of LI. Moreover the phase transition is more and more evident as the number n of variables grows. The 50% satisfiability point is located around the ratio $r = 2$, i.e. when the number of linear inequalities in the system doubles the number of variables.

The next step of our study is to consider the performance of the Simplex algorithm on the randomly generated instances of LI. Figure 2 shows the number of pivoting operations performed by `LP_Solve` to check the satisfiability of the same set of instances of LI as in Figure 1. Again, we have curves for $n = 50, 100, 150, 200, 250$ plotted against r. Each data point gives the median number of pivoting operations for a sample size of 100 problem instances. A familiar easy-hard-easy pattern is displayed and it is more evident as the number n of variables grows. For r much smaller than 2, instances of LI are under-constrained and it is easy to establish the existence of a solution. For r much bigger than 2, instances of LI are over-constrained and it is easy to establish

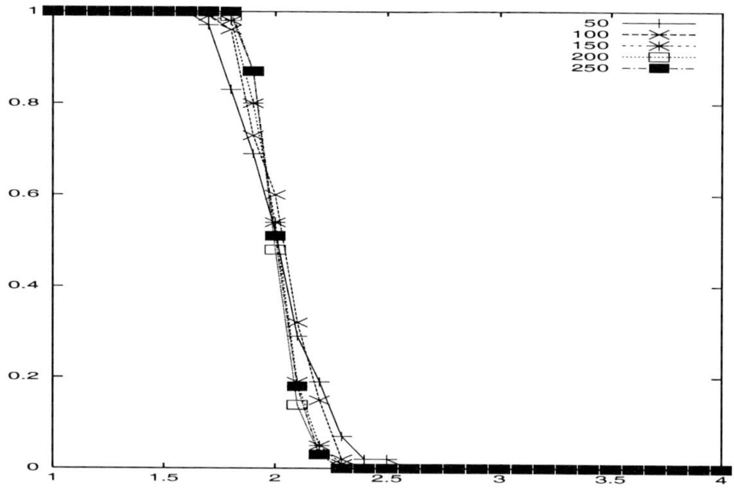

Fig. 1. Probability of establishing the satisfiability of LI (y-axis) against r (x-axis) for varying n

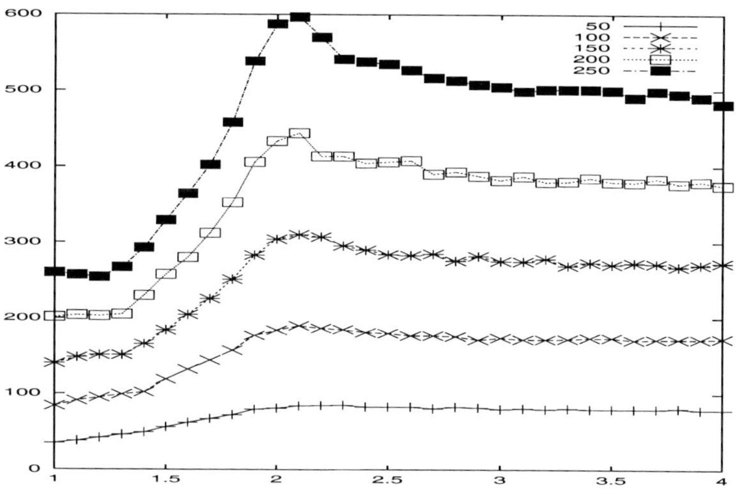

Fig. 2. Median number of pivoting operations used by `LP_Solve` (y-axis) against r (x-axis) for varying n

that there is no solution. The most difficult instances of LI are clustered around a value of 2 for r. As with NP-complete problems, the complexity peak for the cost of establishing the satisfiability of LI is associated with the 50% satisfiability point, i.e. the probability phase transition.

It must be noted that while the problems in the over-constrained regions are easier than those in the phase transition, they are apparently not as easy as those in the under-constrained region. However, the analysis reported in Section 4 indicates that the number of pivot operations grows linearly both in the under-constrained and in the over-constrained regions (albeit with a bigger constant factor in the over-constrained region) whereas it has a cubic growth in the phase transition.

It is worth pointing out that the number of pivoting operations are a good measure of the performance of the Simplex algorithm only under the assumption that the basic arithmetic operations can be done in constant time. The problem is that the number of digits required to represent the integer coefficients a_{ij} and b_i resulting from pivoting is (in the worst case) the sum of digits in all the integers coefficients before pivoting. This can be shown by generalizing Cramer's rule. Given a solvable system of n linear equalities in n variables with integer coefficients, the solutions of such a system can be expressed as the ratios of $n+1$ integers. The digits required to store the $n+1$ integers are at most the total number of digits in the $n(n+1)$ integers representing the coefficients of the system. Hence, in our case, we need $3n(n+1)$ digits in the worst case. Since exact integer arithmetic is computationally more expensive as the number of digits in the coefficients grows, measuring the performance of the Simplex algorithm by counting the number of pivoting operations can be an underestimate. In our computer experiments, `LP_Solve` uses floating-point arithmetic. Arithmetic operations are therefore performed in constant time.

3 The Constrainedness of the Linear Inequalities Problem

While r models the constrainedness of LI when regarded as a constraint satisfaction problem, it does not apparently take into account the combinatorial nature of the problem. To determine a new measure that takes into account this fundamental feature of the problem we employ the definition of constrainedness proposed in [GMPW96]:

$$\kappa := 1 - \frac{\log_2 \langle Sol \rangle}{N}. \tag{1}$$

Here N is the number of bits required to represent one state of the space where we search for the solutions of the problem under consideration and $\langle Sol \rangle$ is the expected number of such solutions. Notice that in doing this we cannot possibly employ the constraint satisfaction formulation of the problem as LI has an infinite state space.

Our solution to the problem is based on the following well-known result (see, e.g., [Chv83]). (The reverse implication is trivial.)

Fact 1 *Let S be a system of linear inequalities of the form*

$$\sum_{j=1}^{n} a_{ij} x_j \leq b_i \quad i = 1, \ldots, m. \tag{2}$$

If S is solvable, then there exist two sets of subscripts $I \subseteq \{1,\ldots,m\}$ and $J \subseteq \{1,\ldots,n\}$ s.t. the system of linear equations

$$\sum_{j\in J} a_{ij}x_j = b_i \quad i \in I \tag{3}$$

has a unique solution x_j^* for $j \in J$ and

$$\sum_{j\in J} a_{ij}x_j^* \leq b_i \quad i = 1,\ldots,m. \tag{4}$$

The above fact guarantees that LI can be reduced to the combinatorial problem of finding two sets of subscripts $I \subseteq \{1,\ldots,m\}$ and $J \subseteq \{1,\ldots,n\}$ such that (3) has a unique solution and (4) holds.

If the coefficients are randomly selected with uniform distribution over the interval $[-1,000;+1,000]$ (as we assumed in Section 3), then the probability that (3) has a unique solution is close to 1 if I and J have the same cardinality and is negligible in all other cases (see page 273 of [Chv83]). We can therefore restrict the state space to the sets of subscripts I and J such that $|I| = |J|$. Under the same assumptions on the coefficients, if $|I| = |J|$ and (4) holds, then for all $I' \subseteq I$ and $J' \subseteq J$ such that $|I'| = |J'|$ we have that also (3) has a unique solution with probability close to 1 and (4) holds. This allows us to further restrict the state space to the set of maximal (w.r.t. set inclusion) sets of subscripts I and J such that $|I| = |J| = n$. This amounts to considering the state space consisting of all sets of subscripts $J = \{1,\ldots,n\}$, $I \subseteq \{1,\ldots,m\}$ such that $|I| = n$ (obviously also $|J| = n$). It is immediate to conclude that the size of the state space is $\binom{m}{n}$. The solutions to our problem are the states, i.e. the set of subscripts I and J with $|I| = |J| = n$, such that (3) has a unique solution and (4) holds.

We are now in the position to compute the number of expected solutions in the ensemble of randomly generated LI problems we introduced in Section 3. Let I and J be sets of subscripts such that $|I| = |J| = n$. As we said before the probability that (3) has a unique solution x_j^* for $j \in J$ is close (and hence can be approximated) to 1. For the state to be a solution $x_1^*,\ldots,x_n^*$ must also be a solution of (4). Under our assumption on the distribution of the coefficients the probability that each of the inequalities in (4) is satisfied by $x_1^*,\ldots,x_n^*$ has probability (close to) $\frac{1}{2}$ and therefore the probability that $x_1^*,\ldots,x_n^*$ satisfy all the $m-n$ inequalities in (4) is $(\frac{1}{2})^{m-n}$. Thus, the expected number of solutions to our randomly generated LI problems is

$$\langle Sol \rangle = \binom{m}{n} 2^{n-m}.$$

By substitution in (1) and simple algebraic simplifications, we obtain the following value of the constrainedness of our randomly generated instances of LI:

$$\kappa = \frac{m-n}{\log_2 \binom{m}{n}}. \tag{5}$$

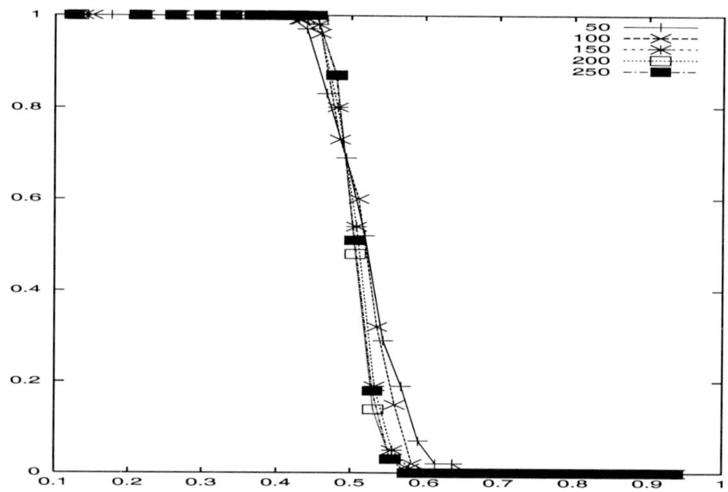

Fig. 3. Probability of establishing the satisfiability of LI (y-axis) against κ (x-axis) for varying n

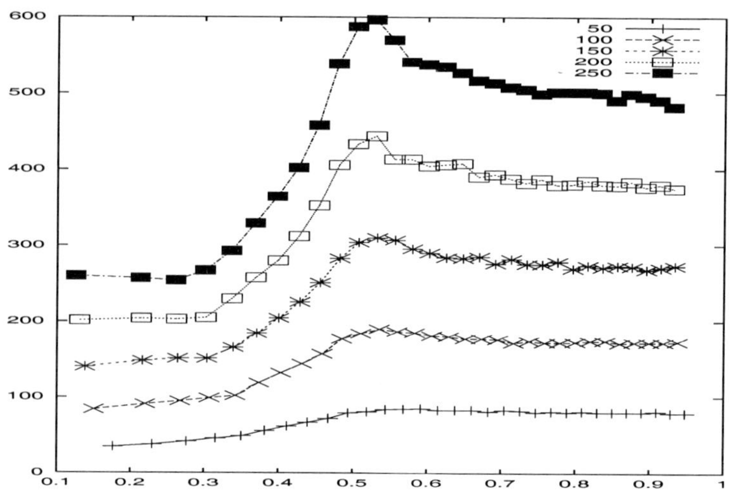

Fig. 4. Median number of pivoting operations used by `LP_Solve` (y-axis) against κ (x-axis) for varying n

Figures 3 and 4 plot the same data as Figures 1 and 2 respectively by plotting against κ in place of r. The phase transition occurs for $\kappa \approx 1$ and the qualitative behavior of the phase transition is similar to that obtained using r thereby indicating that r somehow captures the combinatorial nature of the problem.

It is interesting to observe that the Phase I of the Simplex algorithm (which amounts to searching for a basic feasible solution, bfs for short, that makes the value of the auxiliary variable 0) can be seen as a greedy (and usually very effective) search through the above state space. To see this it suffices to observe that each bsf of the auxiliary problem corresponds to a system of the form (3) with $|I| = |J| = n$ and that any bfs that makes the value of the auxiliary variable 0 corresponds to a system of the form (3) with $|I| = |J| = n$ whose unique solution satisfies (4).

4 Finite Size Scaling

Finite size scaling is a technique developed in statistical mechanics which predicts that values of a property of a complex system are indistinguishable around the phase transition of a given parameter except for a change of scale. The key insight is that the values of the variables in the system become strongly correlated at the phase transition since there is only one expected state towards which the system evolves. In our case, finite size scaling predicts that the probability of satisfiability is indistinguishable except for a simple power law scaling in the size of the instances of LI. As in [GMPW95], we consider the rescaled parameter

$$\gamma := \frac{\kappa - \kappa_c}{\kappa_c} N^{1/\nu} \tag{6}$$

where κ_c is the critical value of the constrainedness κ of LI at the phase transition and $N^{1/\nu}$ gives the change of scale.

Analysis of the experimental data based on a simple trial and error methodology suggests values of 0.5 for κ_c and 2.9 for ν. Figure 5 reports the data shown in Figure 3 replotted against the rescaled parameter γ. As predicted, finite size scaling models the probability of establishing the satisfiability of instances of LI since the curves of Figure 3 do line up when plotted against γ. Next, we consider the median number of pivoting operations performed by `LP_Solve` depending on the rescaled parameter γ. The behavior is depicted in Figure 6.

To estimate the asymptotical computational cost of the Phase I of the Simplex algorithm in the easy and hard regions we proceeded in the following way. We performed linear regression on the median number of pivoting operations performed by `LP_Solve` for a value of γ in the easy under-constrained region corresponding to a ratio $r = 1.5$ and found that such a number varies linearly in n with a coefficient of 1.5. We then performed linear regression on the median number of pivoting operations performed by `LP_Solve` for a value of γ in the easy over-constrained region corresponding to a ratio $r = 4$ and found that such a number varies linearly in n with a coefficient of 2.2. Finally, we performed non-linear regression on the median number of pivoting operations performed by `LP_Solve` for a value of γ corresponding to the ratio $r = 2$ (namely $\gamma = 0$) and found a cubic growth in n. Figure 7 summarizes the situation in for $r = 1.5$, $r = 2$, and $r = 4$.

It is worth pointing out that the cost of a pivoting operation of the Simplex algorithm cannot be considered constant as n varies in this case. In fact, the

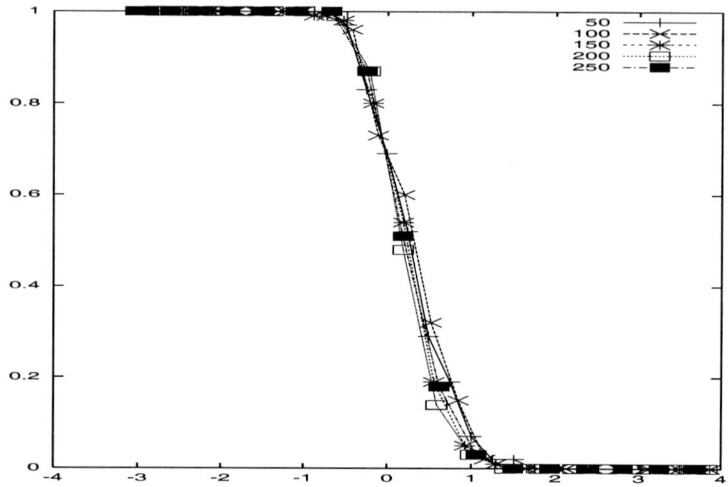

Fig. 5. Probability of establishing the satisfiability of LI (y-axis) against γ (x-axis) for varying n

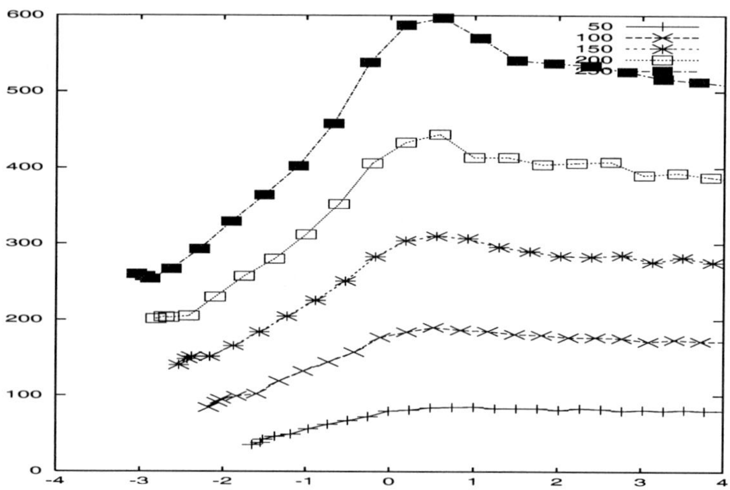

Fig. 6. Median number of pivoting operations (y-axis) against γ (x-axis) for varying n

number of arithmetic operations required to perform each pivot is in $O(mn)$ or, equivalently in our hypotheses, in $O(n^2)$. However, the CPU time spent by `LP_Solve` to solve our randomly generate problems seems to confirm the cubic growth.

The rescaled parameter γ has been used to model growth of search cost as size increases for problems both in NP [KS94] as well as in P [GMPS97]. As

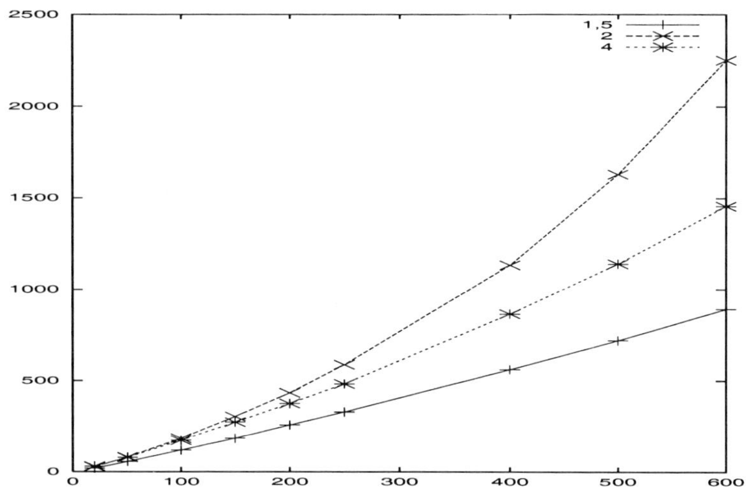

Fig. 7. Median number of pivoting operations against n (x-axis) for $r = 1.5$, $r = 2$, and $r = 4$

shown in Figure 7, rescaling of the number of pivoting operations performed by the Simplex algorithm gives a simple model of its practical performances across the phase transition. More precisely, our study confirms and refines well-known results about the practical efficiency of the Simplex algorithm. In a seminal work by Dantzig [Dan63], it is reported the number of pivoting operations to be cm where c is a constant between 1.5 and 3 when $m < 50$ and $m + n < 200$. This is in accordance with the results obtained for values of γ characterizing over- and under-constrained instances of LI. Finally, we extended these known results by highlighting a cubic behavior of the Simplex algorithm on hard instances (i.e. for $\gamma = 0$) of our randomly generated instances of LI.

5 Conclusions

We have shown that the methodology used to study phase transition behavior in NP-complete problems works with the P-complete problem of checking the satisfiability of systems of linear inequalities over the rationals, thereby confirming previous results obtained for the arc consistency problem. A new measure, κ, capturing the combinatorial nature of the LI problem is given. Computer experiments show the existence of the phase transition as well as of a familiar easy-hard-easy pattern in the computational cost needed to solve the problem. Finite size scaling of the κ parameter models both the scaling of the probability transition and of the search cost of LI in the easy and in the hard regions as the size of the problems increases: asymptotic linear growths are obtained both in the under-constrained and in the over-constrained regions, whereas a cubic growth is obtained at the phase transition.

In the future work we plan to extend our study to systems of linear inequalities with sparse coefficients. It is common knowledge the fact that most of the coefficients in problems arising in practical applications are equal to 0. A look ahead into the problem indicates that it might be necessary to change the definition of κ so to reflect the likely change of the number of expected solutions in the ensemble of randomly generated LI problems.

Further experimental results and the Prolog code used to generate the random problems used to carry out the experiments described in this paper are publicly available at the URL `http://www.mrg.dist.unige.it/~peck`.

References

[BBC+99] B. Bollobas, C. Borgs, J. Chayes, J. Kim, and D. Wilson. The scaling window of the 2-sat transition. Technical report, Microsoft Research, 1999.

[Ber] Michel Berkelaar. `LP_Solve` *3.2*. Available at the URL: `ftp://ftp.es.ele.tue.nl/pub/lp_solve/`.

[BM88] R.S. Boyer and J S. Moore. Integrating Decision Procedures into Heuristic Theorem Provers: A Case Study of Linear Arithmetic. *Machine Intelligence*, 11:83–124, 1988.

[Chv83] Vašek Chvátal. *Linear Programming.* W. H. Freeman and Company, New York, 1983.

[Dan63] G. B. Dantzig. *Linear Programming and Extensions.* Princeton University Press, Princeton, New Jersey, 1963.

[GMPS97] I. P. Gent, E. MacIntyre, P. Prosser, and P. Shaw. The constrainedness of arc consistency. *Lecture Notes in Computer Science*, 1330:327–340, 1997.

[GMPW95] I. P. Gent, E. MacIntyre, P. Prosser, and T. Walsh. Scaling effects in the CSP phase transition. *Lecture Notes in Computer Science*, 976:70–87, 1995.

[GMPW96] Ian P. Gent, Ewan MacIntyre, Patrick Prosser, and Toby Walsh. The constrainedness of search. In *Proceedings of the Thirteenth National Conference on Artificial Intelligence and the Eighth Innovative Applications of Artificial Intelligence Conference*, pages 246–252, Menlo Park, August 4–8 1996. AAAI Press / MIT Press.

[GS96] S. A. Grant and B. M. Smith. The arc and path consistency phase transitions. *Lecture Notes in Computer Science*, 1118:541–542, 1996.

[HHWT97] T. A. Henzinger, P-H. Ho, and H. Wong-Toi. HYTECH: A model checker for hybrid systems. In *Proc. 9th International Computer Aided Verification Conference*, pages 460–463, 1997.

[JMSY92] Joxan Jaffar, Spiro Michaylov, Peter J. Stuckey, and Roland H. C. Yap. The CLP($\mathcal{R}$) language and system. *TOPLAS*, 14(3):339–395, July 1992.

[KS94] S. Kirkpatrick and B. Selman. Critical behavior in the satisfiability of random boolean expressions. *Science*, 264:1297–1301, 1994.

In Search of a Phase Transition in the AC-Matching Problem*

Phokion G. Kolaitis and Thomas Raffill

Computer Science Department
University of California Santa Cruz
{kolaitis, raff}@cse.ucsc.edu

Abstract. AC-matching is the problem of deciding whether an equation involving a binary associative-commutative function symbol, formal variables and formal constants has a solution. This problem is known to be strong NP-complete and to play a fundamental role in equational unification and automated deduction. We initiate an investigation of the existence of a phase transition in random AC-matching and its relationship to the performance of AC-matching solvers. We identify a parameter that captures the "constrainedness" of AC-matching, carry out large-scale experiments, and then apply finite-size scaling methods to draw conclusions from the experimental data gathered. Our findings suggest that there is a critical value of the parameter at which the asymptotic probability of solvability of random AC-matching changes from 1 to 0. Unlike other NP-complete problems, however, the phase transition in random AC-matching seems to emerge very slowly, as evidenced by the experimental data and also by the rather small value of the scaling exponent in the power law of the derived finite-size scaling transformation.

1 Introduction

During the past decade there has been an extensive investigation of phase-transition phenomena in various NP-complete problems, including Boolean satisfiability [SML96], constraint satisfaction [SD96], and number partitioning [GW98]. The goal of this investigation is to bring out the finer structure of NP-complete problems and to explore the relationship between phase transition phenomena and the average-case performance of algorithms for the problem at hand.

In this paper, we initiate an investigation of the existence of a phase transition in the (elementary) AC-matching problem, which is the problem of solving equations involving an associative-commutative function symbol, formal variables, and formal constants. AC-matching is a strong NP-complete problem, i.e., it remains NP-complete even when the coefficients of the formal variables and constants are given in unary. Moreover, AC-matching is a fundamental problem in equational unification (see [BS94]) and has found many applications in

* Research partially supported by NSF Grants CCR-9732041 and IIS-9907419

T. Walsh (Ed.): CP 2001, LNCS 2239, pp. 433–450, 2001.

automated deduction, where it is a key component of many systems. In particular, McCune's solution of Robbins' conjecture [McC97] made essential use of an improved AC-matching algorithm in an extension of the theorem prover EQP.

We carried out a large-scale experimental investigation in search of a phase transition in the AC-matching problem. Although this investigation proceeded along the general lines of similar investigations for other NP-complete problems, in the process we discovered that AC-matching possesses certain characteristics that make it quite different from other NP-complete problems studied earlier. The first difference arises in identifying the parameter that measures the "constrainedness" of an instance. While for many NP-complete problems the choice of this parameter is rather clear, in the case of AC-matching the state of affairs is more complicated as several different quantities seem to affect how constrained a given instance is. A second difference has to do with the generation of random AC-matching instances, which turns out to be a much more involved algorithmic task than, say, generating random 3CNF-formulas, as it entails the generation of random partitions of positive integers. Finally, the most striking difference is that, unlike 3SAT, number partitioning and other NP-complete problems, the phase transition in the asymptotic probability of solvability of random AC-matching instances appears to emerge very slowly, even on instances of size as large as 1600 and on samples of size as large as 30000 (typical experiments for other NP-complete problems used instances of smaller sizes and samples of size around 1200).

The balance of this paper is organized as follows. In Section 2, we give the basic definitions, present the parametrization of AC-matching, define the probability spaces of random AC-matching, and introduce the phase transition conjecture for the asymptotic probability of solvability of random AC-matching. In Section 3, we describe our experimental setup and present three widely different algorithms we used in our study: a direct AC-matching solver, an algorithm based on an integer linear programming solver, and an algorithm based on a SAT solver. Finally, in Section 4 we report our experimental findings, describe the application of the finite-size scaling methods to the data gathered, and present the evidence for a phase transition in random AC-matching. Our findings suggest that the asymptotic probability of solvability of AC-matching changes from 1 to 0 around the critical value 0.73 of the "constrainedness" parameter. This phase transition, however, emerges very slowly as evidenced by the experimental data and also supported by the application of finite-size scaling methods. Indeed, these methods suggest that a power law $r' = \frac{r-0.73}{0.73}s^{\nu}$ governs the scaling of the probability of solvability, but the scaling exponent in this law is rather small, since $\nu \approx 0.171$; in contrast, the scaling exponent in 3SAT has been estimated to be between $1/1.6 = 0.625$ and $1/1.4 = 0.714$ (see [KS94]), and in number partitioning at least $1/1.3 = 0.769$ (see [GW98]). We also compare the three algorithms and present findings to the effect that on average the SAT-solver-based algorithm reaches its peak in the vicinity of the critical value 0.73.

2 The AC-Matching Problem

Let $\mathcal{X}$ be a countable set of formal variable symbols X_n, $n \geq 1$, and let $\mathcal{F}$ be a signature consisting of an associative and commutative binary function symbol $+$ and a countable set of constant symbols C_n, $n \geq 1$. We write $\mathcal{T}(\mathcal{X}, \mathcal{F})$ to denote the set of all terms built using the symbols in $\mathcal{F}$ and the variables in $\mathcal{X}$; as usual, a *ground term* is a variable-free term.

The AC-*matching problem* is the following decision problem: given a term s in and a ground term t in $\mathcal{T}(\mathcal{F}, \mathcal{X})$, is there a substitution ρ such that $s\rho =_{\mathrm{AC}} t$? Using the associativity and commutativity of $+$, an instance of the AC-matching problem can, without loss of generality, be viewed as a formal equation:

$$\alpha_1 X_1 + \cdots + \alpha_m X_m \doteq_{\mathrm{AC}} \beta_1 C_1 + \cdots \beta_n C_n,$$

where the X_i's are variable symbols in $\mathcal{X}$, the C_j's are constant symbols in $\mathcal{F}$, and the α_i's and β_j's are positive integer coefficients representing the multiplicities of the variable and constant symbols. The question is to decide whether this equation has at least one solution, i.e., an assignment

$$X_1 \leftarrow \sum_{j=1}^{n} \gamma_{1,j} C_j, \quad \ldots, \quad X_m \leftarrow \sum_{j=1}^{n} \gamma_{m,j} C_j$$

such that the following hold: (1) each $\gamma_{i,j}$ is a nonnegative integer; (2) no X_i is given an assignment with all its $\gamma_{i,j}$'s set to 0; (3) after making the above substitutions and using the associativity and commutativity of $+$, the left hand side becomes identical to the right hand side. An instance of the AC-matching problem is *positive* if it has at least one solution; otherwise, it is *negative*. For example, the instance $X_1 + 2X_2 \doteq_{\mathrm{AC}} 3C_1 + 4C_2 + 5C_3$ is positive, since the assignment $X_1 \leftarrow C_1 + C_3$, $X_2 \leftarrow C_1 + 2C_2 + 2C_3$ is a solution. In contrast, it is easy to see that the instance $3X_1 + 4X_2 \doteq_{\mathrm{AC}} 8C_1$ is negative. This instance would have a solution if we were allowed to make an all-zero assignment to X_1, for then we could assign $2C_1$ to X_2. This, however, is disallowed, since we have not assumed that $+$ has a unit element (a zero). Note that if $+$ has a unit element, then we are in the case of the ACU-matching problem.

It is known that AC-matching is a strong NP-complete problem, which means that it remains NP-complete even when all integer coefficients occurring in an instance are given in unary (see [Eke93,HK99]). The assumption that the instances are given in unary makes sense in the context of equational matching and unification, since the inputs are strings of formal symbols and thus the integer coefficients have no other interpretation than duplicating the formal variable and constant symbols for the given number of times. In contrast, ACU-matching is solvable in polynomial time using dynamic programming (see [Eke93,HK99]).

2.1 Parametrizing Instances of the AC-Matching Problem

A phase transition phenomenon in a problem is an abrupt change in the typical behavior of instances generated randomly from spaces of instances determined by the value of a parameter. This parameter should measure the "constrainedness" of the instance, so that "small" values of the parameter, should be associated with underconstrained (hence, mostly positive) instances, while "large" values should be associated with overconstrained (hence, mostly negative) instances. Phase transition phenomena may occur at values of the parameter that give rise to spaces containing for the greater part "critically constrained" instances.

For most NP-complete problems studied to date from the perspective of phase transition phenomena, identifying a parameter that measures "constrainedness" has been relatively straightforward. In particular, this holds true for k-SAT, $k \geq 3$, where this parameter is the ratio of the number of clauses to the number of variables in a k-CNF formula. In contrast, selecting a suitable parameter for the AC-matching problem is a more challenging task, because several different quantities (and the interaction between them) appear to affect the "constrainedness" of an instance, including the number of variables, the number of constants, the maximum variable coefficient, and the maximum constant coefficient. Gent et al. [GMW96] have introduced a general concept of a parameter that captures the "constrainedness" of a set (an *ensemble* in their terminology) of instances of decision problems. Unfortunately, their approach does not seem to be directly applicable to the AC-matching problem for the following reasons. First, in their framework it is essentially assumed that a parametrization of the problem has already been obtained, so that their parameter measures the "constrainedness" of different ensembles of instances and not individual instances. Second, the computation of the "constrainedness" parameter of an ensemble entails the computation of the expected number of solutions in that ensemble; while this task is easy for k-SAT, it appears to be highly non-trivial for AC-matching and to involve difficult results from the theory of partitions (see also Section 3.1).

After considerable reflection, we chose the ratio of the sum of the variables' coefficients to the sum of the constants' coefficients as a "constrainedness" parameter for the AC-matching problem. More precisely, with every instance of AC-matching of the form $\sum_{i=1}^{m} \alpha_i X_i \doteq_{\mathrm{AC}} \sum_{j=1}^{n} \beta_j C_j$, we associate the ratio $r = (\sum_{i=1}^{m} \alpha_i)/(\sum_{j=1}^{n} \beta_j)$ as the "constrainedness" parameter of that instance. Thus, the numerator is the total number of occurrences of variable symbols and the denominator is the total number of occurrences of constant symbols. Since each instance is given in unary, the numerator is essentially the size of the left-hand side of the instance, while the denominator is essentially the size of the right-hand side of the instance. We now discuss the justification that we will provide in this paper in support of our choice of this ratio as the "constrainedness" parameter of the AC-matching problem.

For every positive rational number r, let AC(r)-matching be the space consisting of all AC-matching instances of ratio r. The first observation is that if $r > 1$, then *every* instance of AC(r)-matching is negative. This is because each occurrence of a variable must be assigned at least one occurrence of some constant, but there are not enough occurrences of constants to assign to all of them. Consequently, we will focus on the spaces AC(r), where r is a rational number such that $0 < r \leq 1$, and will carry out an extensive experimental study of the asymptotic probability of positive instances in these spaces. We will give evidence that the asymptotic probability of positive instances is high when the ratio r is "low", while on the contrary this asymptotic probability is low when the ratio r is "high". Before proceeding with the description of our experiments, however, we address and resolve an important complexity-theoretic issue that will provide additional justification for the choice of our parametrization.

2.2 NP-Completeness of AC(r)-Matching

We just observed that AC(r)-matching is trivial for every ratio $r > 1$. This leads us to consider what happens when $0 < r \leq 1$. It turns out that AC-matching restricted to any fixed ratio in this range is as hard as the full problem.

Theorem 1 *For every rational number r such that $0 < r \leq 1$, the* AC(r)-*matching problem is strong* NP-*complete.*

Proof Outline: In what follows, we assume that instances of AC-matching are of the form $\sum_{i=1}^{m} \alpha_i X_i \doteq_{\mathrm{AC}} \sum_{j=1}^{n} \beta_j C_j$, i.e., α_i is the ith variable coefficient, $1 \leq i \leq m$, and β_j is the jth constant coefficient, $1 \leq j \leq n$. We will frequently have recourse to a fact which allows us to multiply all coefficients of an instance by a constant factor. Specifically, it is easy to verify that for every positive integer k the instances $\sum_{i=1}^{m} \alpha_i X_i \doteq_{\mathrm{AC}} \sum_{j=1}^{n} \beta_j C_j$ and $\sum_{i=1}^{n} k\alpha_i X_i \doteq_{\mathrm{AC}} \sum_{j=1}^{m} k\beta_j C_j$ have identical solution sets.

Let r be a rational number between 0 and 1. We will show that AC(r)-matching is strong NP-complete in a series of reductions that reveal that certain restricted cases of AC-matching are strong NP-complete. Here, we outline the main steps; full details are given in [Raf00].

Step 1: AC(1)-matching is strong NP-complete.

Eker [Eke93] showed that AC-matching is strong NP-complete via a reduction from 3-PARTITION (see also [HK99]). As a matter of fact, this reduction reduces instances of 3-PARTITION to instances of AC(1)-matching. Specifically, an instance of 3-PARTITION consists of a set $S = \{a_1, \ldots a_{3m}\}$, an integer γ, and positive integer weights $s(a_i)$ for $a_i \in S$ such that $\gamma/4 < s(a_i) < \gamma/2$ and $\sum_{i=1}^{3m} s(a_i) = m\gamma$; the question is whether S can be partitioned into m disjoint sets $S_1, \ldots, S_m$ with $\sum_{a \in S_j} s(a) = \gamma$ for $1 \leq j \leq m$. Eker's reduction takes such an instance to an AC-matching instance of the form $\sum_{i=1}^{3m} s(a_i) X_i \doteq_{\mathrm{AC}} \sum_{j=1}^{m} \gamma C_j$, which is an AC(1)-matching instance, since $\sum_{i=1}^{3m} s(a_i) = m\gamma$.

Step 2: The restriction of AC(1)-matching to instances where $\sum_{i=1}^{m} \alpha_i = \sum_{j=1}^{n} \beta_j$ is an odd number and $\frac{\max_{1 \leq j \leq n}(\beta_j)}{\sum_{j=1}^{n} \beta_j} < 1/2$ is strong NP-complete.

We describe a reduction of AC(1)-matching to this restricted case of AC(1)-matching. Given an instance $\sum_{i=1}^{m} \alpha_i X_i \doteq_{\mathrm{AC}} \sum_{j=1}^{n} \beta_j C_j$ of AC(1)-matching, let $t = \sum_{i=1}^{m} \alpha_i = \sum_{j=1}^{n} \beta_j$. Multiply all coefficients by 2, add to the left-hand side three new variables, and add to the right-hand side three new constants all of coefficient $2t+1$. Note that in any solution, the new constants can and must be assigned to the new variables (their multiplicities are too large to assign them to any of the original constants), so no solutions are added or taken away by this transformation. The sum of coefficients on either side of the new instance is $2t + 3(2t + 1) = 8t + 3$, which is an odd number. The new maximum constant coefficient is $2t + 1$; moreover, since $t \geq 1$, the ratio $\frac{2t+1}{8t+3}$ of this coefficient to the sum of the constant coefficients is at most $3/11$.

Step 3: For every rational number r such that $0 < r < 1$, the AC(r)-matching problem is strong NP-complete.

This time, we start with an instance of AC(1)-matching as in Step 2, i.e., the sum of constant coefficients is odd and more than twice the maximum constant coefficient. Given a rational r between 0 and 1, choose positive integers $u \geq 2$ and $v \geq 2$ such that $u/v = r$. Let $t = \sum_{i=1}^{m} \alpha_i = \sum_{j=1}^{n} \beta_j$ and let $b = \max_{1 \leq j \leq m}(\beta_j)$; thus, $2b < t$. Multiply all coefficients by 6, then add $2(u-1)$ variables to the left-hand side and $2(v-1)$ constants to the right-hand side, all of coefficient $3t$. The new variables have coefficients higher than those of any old constants now have, because $6b < 3t$. Thus no new variable can ever be assigned to an old constant. Also, no combination of the old variables can cover the new constants, because the old variables now have coefficients that are multiples of 6 but the new constant coefficients are multiples of $3t$, which is an odd number. Thus, any solution must take the form that new variables are assigned to new constants, and no old variables are assigned to new constants. To assign the new variables to the new constants, we can pair off each new variable with each new constant until the last new variable, which can be assigned to all the remaining new constants. This is always possible because $u < v$ (since $r < 1$), so we have at least as many new constants as new variables. The resulting ratio of the sum of variable coefficients over the sum of constant coefficients is $\frac{6t+2(u-1)3t}{6t+2(v-1)3t} = \frac{6t[1+(u-1)]}{6t[1+(v-1)]} = u/v = r$. ▮

We note that Dunne, Gibbons and Zito [DGZ00] have argued that, when phase transitions in an NP-complete problem are investigated, it is important to determine for which values of the parameter the resulting restrictions of the problem remain NP-complete. In particular, [DGZ00] have shown that, for every $r > 0$, 3SAT is NP-complete when restricted to instances in which the ratio of the number of clauses to the number of variables is equal to r (this fact has also been pointed out in [CDS$^+$00]).

2.3 Random AC-Matching

An instance $\sum_{i=1}^{m} \alpha_i X_i \doteq_{\mathrm{AC}} \sum_{j=1}^{n} \beta_j C_j$ of the AC-matching problem can be specified by presenting the set of variable coefficients α_i, $1 \leq i \leq m$, and the set of constant coefficients β_j, $1 \leq j \leq n$. Note that this suffices to specify the instance because of the associativity and commutativity of the binary function symbol $+$. Given such an instance, we let $\alpha = \sum_{i=1}^{m} \alpha_i$ be the sum of all variable coefficients and we let $\beta = \sum_{j=1}^{n} \beta_j$ be the sum of all constant coefficients. We also let $r = \alpha/\beta$ be the ratio of the sum of variable coefficients to the sum of constant coefficients and we let $s = \alpha + \beta$ be the sum of all variable and constant coefficients. We call s the *size* of the given instance of AC-matching.

Assume that r is a rational number and s is a positive integer having the following properties: (i) $0 < r \leq 1$ and $s \geq 2$; (ii) the unique solution (α, β) to the system of equations $x/y = r$ and $x + y = s$ is an integer solution. For every such pair (r, s), we let AC(r, s)-matching be the space of all instances of AC(r)-matching of size s. We now describe what a random instance of AC(r, s)-matching is. Since specifying an instance of AC(r, s)-matching amounts to producing a set of variable coefficients adding up to α and a set of constant coefficients adding up to β, a random instance of AC(r, s)-matching consists of a randomly generated set of positive integers adding up to α and a randomly generated set of positive integers adding up to β. In other words, a random instance of AC(r, s)-matching is a uniformly chosen random *partition* of the integer α and a uniformly chosen random *partition* of the integer β. These partitions are *unlabeled*, i.e., the order of parts within partitions is not distinguished. This is entirely consistent with the specification of AC-matching instances in terms of the sets of variable coefficients and constant coefficients, which, as explained above, is justified by the associativity and commutativity of +.

Let Pr(r, s) be the probability that a random instance of AC(r, s)-matching is a positive instance. We now formally introduce the phase-transition conjecture for AC(r)-Matching, $0 < r \leq 1$.

Conjecture 1 *There is a critical value r_c with $0 < r_c < 1$ such that the following hold for every rational number r with $0 < r \leq 1$:*

- *if $r < r_c$, then $\lim_{s \to \infty} \Pr(r, s) = 1$;*
- *if $r > r_c$, then $\lim_{s \to \infty} \Pr(r, s) = 0$.*

The rest of the paper is devoted to a description of the experimental study we carried out to investigate this conjecture.

3 The Experiments

In this section, we describe the procedure used for generating random instances of AC-matching, provide information of the size of instances and number of samples used in the experiments, and describe the three algorithms used to solve randomly generated instances of AC-matching.

3.1 Generating Random Instances of AC(r, s)-Matching

A random instance of AC(r, s) consists of a random partition of the integer α and a random partition of the integer β, where (α, β) is the unique solution to the system of equations $x/y = r$ and $x + y = s$. The partition of α becomes the set of variable coefficients, while the partition of β becomes the set of constant coefficients. Thus, the ability to generate random instances of AC(r, s)-matching boils down to the ability to generate random partitions of integers.

At first, we used Maple's built-in random integer partition generator to generate the partitions needed in our experiments. We soon realized, however, that this generator became biased in favor of partitions whose largest part became smaller when generating partitions of integers around 300 or higher. In view of this, we gave up on this random integer partition generator and, instead, searched the literature for algorithms on random integer partition generation. We then implemented ourselves the following algorithm, which is generally considered to be the best algorithm for this purpose (see Nijenhuis and Wilf [NW78]). Let n be the number we wish to partition randomly. We choose a pair of integers (d, j) randomly with the joint probability distribution $\Pr(d, j) = \frac{dp(n-jd)}{np(n)}$, where $p(k)$ is the *partition function*, i.e., the function that gives the number of partitions of k. We then add d copies of j to our partition and recursively generate a random partition of $n - dj$. The recursion bottoms out when $n - dj = 0$.

It should be pointed out that the study of integer partitions is a mature research area in the interface between number theory and combinatorics (see Andrews [And84]). Several deep results are known about the properties of the partition function $p(n)$. In particular, the work of Hardy, Ramanujan and Rademacher produced an exact formula for $p(n)$ in terms of an infinite series that involves π, roots of unity, and hyperbolic functions (see [And84]). A corollary of this exact formula is the following simpler asymptotic formula for $p(n)$, as $n \to \infty$:

$$p(n) \approx \frac{1}{4n\sqrt{3}} e^{\pi\sqrt{(2n)/3}}.$$

The values of $p(n)$ increase very rapidly with n. For instance, $p(40) = 37338$, $p(60) = 966467$, $p(80) = 15796476$, and $p(100) = 190569292$. To implement the above random partition generating algorithm, we cached the actual values of $p(n)$ needed and used large-integer routines to handle these values.

3.2 Size of Instances and Size of Samples

For most NP-complete problems studied thus far, phase transition phenomena emerge quite clearly even on random instances of small size. In particular, in the case of 3-SAT the probability of satisfiability exhibits a clear phase transition on random instances with as few as 20 variables and 100 clauses [SML96]. When we embarked on the experimental investigation of random AC-matching, we were naively anticipating a similar rapidly emerging phase transition phenomenon. Since preliminary experiments on instances of size 50 and below failed to show a sharp transition from the underconstrained to overconstrained regions, we decided to work with somewhat larger sizes, taking 100, 200, 300 and 400 as the problem sizes s for our experiments.

Concerning the choice of ratios $r \leq 1$, we decided to experiment at every available ratio for size 100, i.e., every ratio $r \leq 1$ for which the system $x/y = r$ and $x + y = 100$ has integer solutions; consequently, we worked with the ratios $1 : 99$, $2 : 98$, $\ldots$, $50 : 50$. We then used the same ratios for sizes 200, 300, and 400, to see how things changed as size increased by a constant amount.

For the size of samples, in our initial set of experiments we used 1200 random instances for each ratio r and each size s as above. Standard results in statistics imply that this sample size guarantees a 95% confidence interval with a margin of error well under 4%. Sample sizes between 1000 and 1200 have been used in most other experimental studies of phase transitions in NP-complete problems.

This initial set of experiments did provide sufficient data to make meaningful comparisons between the different algorithms we used to solve the AC-matching problem. The experimental results, however, did not provide strong evidence for the existence of a phase transition, although they suggested a possible crossover in the vicinity of the 42:58 ratio (see Figure 1). There were two difficulties with the experimental findings: first, any phase transition appeared to be emerging very slowly; and, second, the variation in behavior with problem size was of the same order as the margin of error of the experiments. Consequently, to reach a stronger conclusion about the existence of a phase transition, we carried out a new set of large-scale experiments in which we increased both the size of instances and the size of samples. We staggered the instance sizes geometrically, taking sizes 100, 200, 400, 800 and 1600, in the hope that the resulting curves would be far enough apart to show a clear trend. For this series of experiments, we focused on an interval of ratios around 42:58, since the earlier experiments had suggested a possible crossover near 42:58. Specifically, we stepped from ratio 30:70 to ratio 50:50, taking every available ratio at size 100 as before. Finally, to significantly reduce the margin of error, this time we used 30000 random instances for each data point; this sample size gives a margin of error of well under eight tenths of one percent (in fact, about 0.742%).

3.3 Algorithms for AC-Matching

We used three widely disparate algorithms: a direct AC-Matching solver; an industrial-strength integer linear programming solver in conjunction with a reduction from AC-Matching to Integer Linear Programming; and a Boolean satisfiability solver in conjunction with a reduction from AC-Matching to SAT. The first two algorithms were used for both the initial experiments (instance size up to 400, sample size 1200) and the large-scale experiments (instance size up to 1600, sample size 30000). Since we quickly determined that the third algorithm performed poorly in comparison to the other two, we only ran the third algorithm on instances of size 100 and on samples of size 1200.

Direct Solving with Maude. Maude is a powerful programming tool for equational logic and rewriting; it has been developed at SRI International and is freely available for research purposes [CDE+99]. Maude features a fast AC-matching solver, which has been designed and implemented by Steven Eker. In a private communication [Eke00], we were provided with the following information about this solver: a given instance of an equational matching problem is "decomposed in sets of subproblems; any variables that can be uniquely bound in some branch are eliminated in that branch and then a backtracking search is used on the reduced subproblems in a carefully chosen order. A number of theory specific optimizations are also used such as a very sophisticated Diophantine equation solver in the AC/ACU cases." A published comparison of several AC-Matching systems against a benchmark problem set showed that Maude is one of the fastest AC-Matching solvers [MK98].

In our experiments, we used Maude as the direct AC-matching algorithm.

CPLEX and Reduction to Integer Linear Programming. There is a direct and well known reduction from AC-Matching to Integer Linear Programming (ILP), which we present here without any further explanation (additional information can be found in [Eke93,HK99]). Given an instance of AC-matching $\sum_{i=1}^{m} \alpha_i X_i \doteq_{\mathrm{AC}} \sum_{j=1}^{n} \beta_j C_j$, we generate the following system of linear equations and inequalities for which we seek integer solutions:

$$\begin{aligned} \alpha_1\gamma_{1,j} + \cdots + \alpha_m\gamma_{m,j} &= \beta_j, \quad \text{for } 1 \leq j \leq n; \\ \gamma_{i,1} + \cdots + \gamma_{i,n} &> 0, \quad \text{for } 1 \leq i \leq m. \end{aligned}$$

Consequently, a given instance of AC-matching can first be transformed to an instance of ILP using the above reduction and then solved using any integer linear programming solver. In our experiments, we used the integer linear programming solver CPLEX, which is a commercially available optimization package widely used in industry today. CPLEX solves integer linear programming problems using a sophisticated set of strategies at the base of which is a branch-and-cut search method that first searches for solutions to the relaxation of the problem to general linear programming. If the resulting solution is not all-integer, it branches around variables with non-integer assignments and cuts parts of the feasible region to seek integer solutions. It should be pointed out that CPLEX, in conjunction with a reduction of SAT to ILP, has also been used as one of the algorithms for studying phase transitions in Boolean satisfiability [CDS+00].

Grasp and Reduction to SAT. Our reduction from AC-matching to SAT is essentially the composition of the earlier reduction from AC-matching to Integer Linear Programming with a reduction from Integer Linear Programming to SAT. The detailed steps of this reduction will be spelled out in the full paper.

We used Grasp, one of the main Boolean satisfiability solvers, to solve the SAT instances generated by the above reduction when applied to random AC-matching instances. Admittedly, this method for solving AC-matching problems is rather indirect; moreover, the SAT instances produced by the above reduction are quite large, since their size is $O(s^4)$, where s is the size of the AC-matching instance. As mentioned earlier, this algorithm turned out to be vastly inferior than the other two and, as a result, we only used it on instances of size 100 and on samples of size 1200.

4 Experimental Results

In this section, we present our experimental results and discuss their implications for the phase transition conjecture and the performance of the three algorithms.

4.1 Evidence for the Phase Transition Conjecture

We begin by presenting the results for the probability of solvability of random AC(r, s)-matching against the parameter r for various instance sizes s. Figure 1

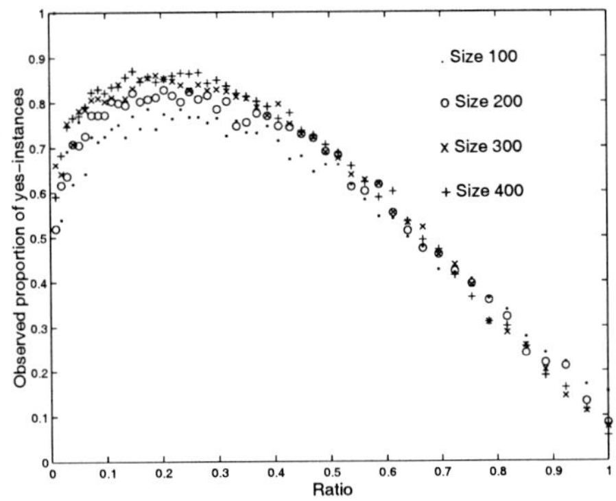

Fig. 1. Prob. of positive AC(r, s)-matching as function of r based on 1200 samples

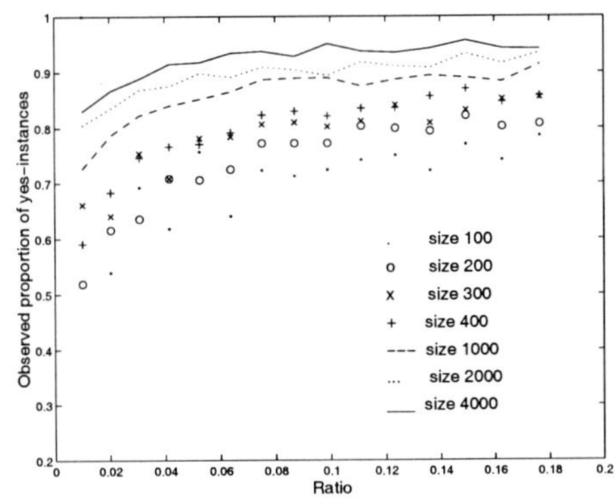

Fig. 2. Prob. of positive AC(r, s)-matching for small r based on 1200 samples

depicts the results of our initial set of experiments. Each data point is based on a sample of 1200 randomly generated AC(r, s)-matching instances; every ratio available at instance size 100 (i.e., 1:99, 2:98, ..., 50:50) was used for the instance sizes 100, 200, 300, 400. As anticipated, when r approaches 1, the probability of solvability gets close to 0. As r approaches 0, the probability dips down again, for reasons that we need to explain before proceeding further. First, this does not contradict our phase-transition conjecture, because this conjecture only asserts that, for each $r < r_c$, the limit of the probability as size goes to infinity is 1 (and not that the probability is necessarily a monotonic function of r for every fixed instance size). Second, the decrease in probability as r approaches 0 is due to the small size of the sum of the variables' coefficients for the instance sizes depicted in Figure 1. We note that random partitions of large integers have at least one part equal to 1 with overwhelmingly high probability, so we expect to see constants with coefficient 1 in all our random instances. But the same is not true of random partitions of small integers; moreover, if there is a constant of coefficient 1 but no variable of coefficient 1, the instance will be trivially unsolvable. The jumping and dip in the value of the value of the probability as r approaches 0 starts to fade away if experiments with instances of larger sizes are carried out, as depicted in Figure 2.

More importantly, in Figure 1, we also see a crossover region between mostly positive to mostly negative instances somewhere between $r = 0.3$ and $r = 0.8$. This crossover appears to be getting increasingly sharp as size increases; this transition, however, is not as sharp and pronounced as the transition observed in k-SAT, $k \geq 3$. Figure 3 depicts the results of our follow-up large scale experiments with focus on this crossover region. Each data point is based on a sample of 30000 randomly generated AC(r, s)-matching instances; since the focus was on the crossover region identified in the initial experiments, all ratios available at size 100 from 30:70 and higher are considered (i.e., 30:70, 31:69, ..., 50:50). The instance sizes are 100, 200, 400, 800, 1600.

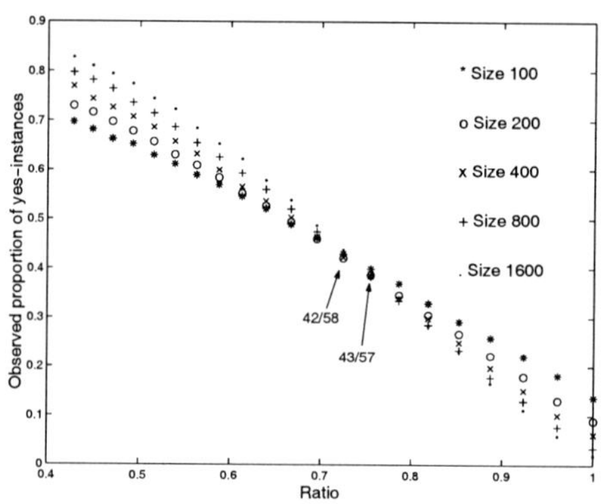

Fig. 3. Prob. of positive AC(r, s)-matching as function of r based on 30000 samples

Finite-Size Scaling. Finite-size scaling is a technique from statistical mechanics which, when applied to experimental data, may provide support for a phase transition phenomenon (such as the one we conjectured in Section 2.3). It has been used in the study of phase transitions in several different NP-complete problems, including k-SAT and number partitioning [KS94,GW98]. We now give a brief discussion of the technique and its relevance to our investigation.

The basic purpose of finite-size scaling is to support extrapolation toward the limit of a theoretically infinitely large system from data sets of systems of finite size. With this end in view, it takes curves relating to systems of various sizes and attempts to account for the size effects by a rescaling of the x-axis such that the curves collapse into a single *universal* curve. The standard finite-size scaling transformation takes the form of a *power law* $r' = \frac{r-r_c}{r_c} s^\nu$, where r is the original abscissa, r' is the abscissa on the rescaled x-axis, r_c is the critical value, s is the system size, and ν is the scaling exponent. This transforms a function $f(r,s)$ depending on the parameter r and the size s to a hypothesized universal function $f(r')$ of a single variable r'. If $f(r')$ is a monotonic function with range between p and q and with $\lim_{r' \to -\infty} f(r') = p$ and $\lim_{r' \to \infty} f(r') = q$, establishing such a scaling law would imply that in the limit, as $s \to \infty$, there is a jump discontinuity in the system from p for $r < r_c$ to q for $r > r_c$. In our case, we would be looking for $p = 1$ and $q = 0$ to support the phase transition conjecture introduced in Section 2.3.

We applied finite-size scaling to AC-matching using the data gathered in the large-scale experiments depicted in Figure 3. We now describe the procedures we used to estimate the critical value r_c and the scaling exponent ν, and we report our findings. First, we estimated the critical ratio r_c by linear interpolation on either side of the region where the curves cross over, finding the least-squares solution of the simultaneous equations of the five lines determined by the data points on both sides of the crossover. In our case, the crossover appeared to be between the ratios 42:58 and 43:57. The result of this procedure was that the crossover was estimated to be $(0.73, 0.42)$, so that we used 0.73 for the critical ratio r_c in the further computations.

After this, we proceeded to estimate the scaling exponent ν. The first step was to use linear interpolation to find two horizontal lines cutting across the curves, one above and one below the crossover point and approximately equally spaced. Fortunately, we found nearly collinear points in the actual data. Above the line, the data for sizes 100, 200, 400, 800, and 1600 line up approximately at the respective ratios 33:37, 34:66, 35:65, 36:64 and 37:63, where the ordinates all are around 0.655; below the line, they lined up approximately at the ratios 49:51, 48:42, 47:53, 47:53 and 47:53, where the ordinates all are around 0.18. We found these sets of nearly collinear points by inspection, and we took the average of their ordinates to find the level for the horizontal lines. Then we interpolated along each curve for $f(r) = 0.655$ and $f(r) = 0.18$ to find the corresponding values of r in the curves for every size. This procedure gave us two sets of pairs of abscissae assumed to come together into one point under the rescaling. We then solved for ν simultaneously for all pairs in each set of abscissae. We had equations of the form: $((r_i - r_c)/r_c)s_i^\nu = ((r_j - r_c)/r_c)s_j^\nu$, in which ν is the only unknown. By taking logarithms on both sides, we obtained the matrix equation

$$[\log s_i - \log s_j]\,[\nu] = [\log(r_j - r_c) - \log(r_i - r_c)]$$

where the first element on the left side is a column vector with s_i and s_j as all pairs of sizes, the second element is a 1x1 vector consisting of ν, and the right side is a column vector with r_i and r_j as all pairs of abscissae to be matched together. Then we calculated the least-squares solution to this matrix equation. Taking all pairs our from five collinear data points gave 10 pairs, so with two horizontal lines we obtained 20 simultaneous equations. This procedure gave $\nu \approx 0.171$ as the value of the scaling exponent. Thus, putting everything together, we obtained the following finite-size scaling transformation:

$$r' = \frac{r - 0.73}{0.73} s^{0.171}.$$

To test the validity of the finite-size scaling transformation, we superimposed the curves in Figure 3 rescaled by the above transformation. This means that every data point (r, p) on a curve of size s in Figure 3 was transformed to the point $(\frac{r-0.73}{0.73} s^{0.171}, p)$, and all such transformed points were plotted in a single graph. The resulting graph is depicted in Figure 4. It appears that the fit is indeed quite good, as the different curves appear to collapse to a universal curve. Moreover, this universal curve satisfies the conditions of monotonicity with the values at the limits $\lim_{r' \to -\infty} f(r') = 1$ and $\lim_{r' \to \infty} f(r') = 0$, lending evidence for the phase-transition conjecture in random AC-matching. The estimation of

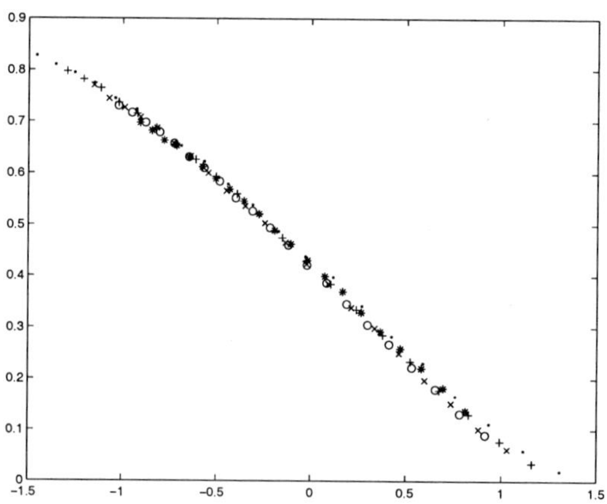

Fig. 4. Data sets of various sizes superimposed with finite-size scaling

the parameters in the finite-size scaling transformation were based on data set of instance size $s \leq 1600$ and sample size 30000. As a further validation, we used the universal curve and scaling transformation above to predict a curve for size $s = 5000$. We then compared this predicted curve with actual data from experiments with size 5000 and sample size 1200. The results of this comparison are depicted in the left side of Figure 5. As can be seen, the curve from the actual data varies a little bit around the predicted curve. But these variations are within the margin of error for the 1200 samples per data point, leaving open the possibility that the variations may decrease with samples of larger size. It should be noted that the scaling exponent $\nu = 0.171$ is rather small.

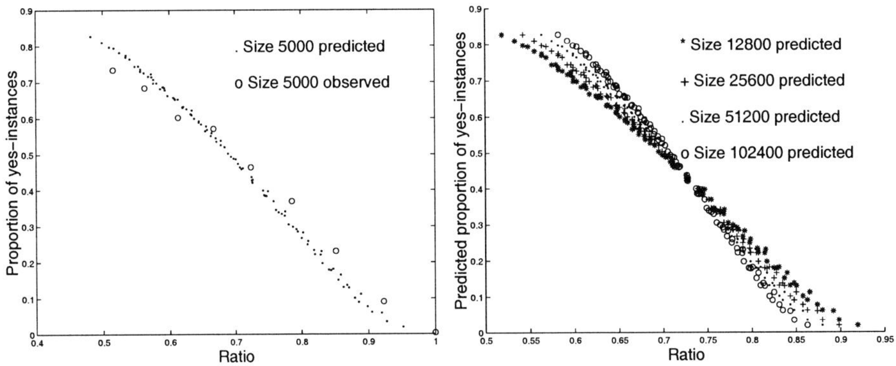

Fig. 5. Predicted & actual values for $s = 5000$; Extrapolation to very large sizes

This implies that any phase transition would be slow to emerge as the instance size s increases (which is quite consistent with the experimental findings). To illustrate this point, in the right side of Figure 5 we show the shape of the curve for very large values of s as predicted by this finite-size scaling transformation. Note that the predicted curve is still not very steep even for the enormous instance size of $s = 102400 = 2^{10} \cdot 100$, i.e., ten doublings of size 100. Thus, it is unlikely that larger-scale experiments will make a more convincing case for the existence of a phase transition in random AC-matching. Consequently, any further progress will hinge on analytical results, which, however, seem to require the use of sophisticated techniques from the theory of integer partitions.

4.2 Comparison of Solvers and Average-Case Performance

We ran our experiments on three Sun Spark Ultra 5/10 workstations with 512 MB of main memory, 1.8 GB of virtual memory, and a 300 MHz CPU. The output of each experiment was sent to a log file stamped with the machine name, the result of the solver on the instance, and the time taken (each solver provided its own timing information in terms of CPU time). We then analyzed the timing results with two aims in mind: first, to compare the performance of the three solvers used; second, to determine whether a relationship exists between the value of the parameter and the computational effort of each solver.

Our experiments showed conclusively that using the SAT-solver Grasp in conjunction with our reduction to SAT is vastly inferior to using a direct AC-Matching solver or a fast ILP solver with a reduction to ILP. Typically, Grasp took minutes to solve instances solved by Maude and CPLEX in under a millisecond. As mentioned earlier, we had to abandon Grasp on instances of size higher than 100. It should be pointed out that Kautz and Selman [KS92] have reported that SAT solvers can be used to efficiently solve planning problems, after these problems have been reduced to SAT. It is an interesting problem to determine if an improved reduction from AC-matching to SAT combined with a different SAT solver can give rise to an algorithm for AC-matching that perform as well as the other two algorithms we used.

For Maude, the median time to solve an instance at any ratio and for sizes 100, 200, 300 and 400 was under 1 millisecond. For CPLEX with the reduction to ILP, the median time at any ratio was under 1 millisecond for sizes 100 and 200, rose to 1 millisecond for size 300 at most ratios ($r \geq 5 : 95$) and to 2 milliseconds for size 400 at most ratios ($12 : 88 \leq r \leq 47 : 53$). The median times for Maude and CPLEX were close at all ratios for the sizes considered. Maude appeared to be superior to CPLEX when we looked at the harder instances. For size 400, for example, if we look at the 90th percentile of times instead of the median times, we find that Maude is still 10 milliseconds at all ratios, while CPLEX requires up to 60 milliseconds at certain ratios. However, we sent a few samples of the instances we found to be hardest for CPLEX to a CPLEX benchmarking team and they were able to make CPLEX solve them quickly by using an upgraded version of the program and tuning the solver's strategy parameters appropriately. In view of this, we cannot make any conclusive comparisons between Maude and CPLEX other than that they are close.

We now turn to our second aim, which was to determine whether a relationship exists between the critical value of the parameter and the computational effort of the solver used. In the case of Grasp, the evidence is quite striking: even for our size 100 experiments, there is a steep increase in solving time around the critical ratio 0.73. Figure 6 contains plots for the median time and for the 70th percentile time against the ratio. The plots show that the peak becomes sharper as we look at higher percentiles. This reflects the existence of a relatively small set of very-hard-to-solve instances heavily concentrated around the critical ratio.

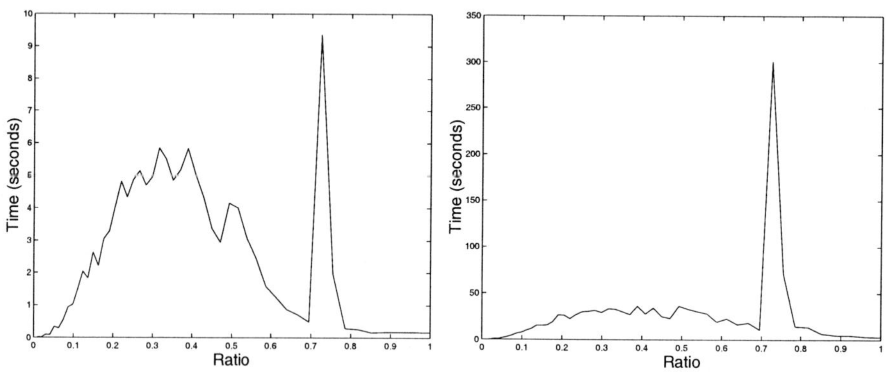

Fig. 6. Median (l.) and 70th percentile (r.) of Grasp's time to solve for size 100

With Maude and CPLEX, the results were much less conclusive. At the median level, both solvers were very fast consistently at all ratios and for all sizes. In the size 400 experiments, Maude's median was under 1 millisecond and that of CPLEX varied from under 1 millisecond to 2 milliseconds. Even in the size 1600 experiments, Maude's median time ranged from 10 milliseconds to 20 milliseconds. Thus, it appears that it will take experiments of considerably larger scale to detect a pattern for these two solvers, assuming one exists.

Acknowledgments. Our work benefited from numerous discussions and exchanges with V. Dalmau, S. Eker, M. Hermann, S. Kalyanaraman, L.M. Kirousis, U. Martin, M. Palassini, A.P. Young, M.Y. Vardi, and R. Wheeler. In addition, S. Kalyanaraman provided invaluable help with the optimization of the random partition generator program. We are particularly grateful to A.P. Young for generously sharing with us his expertise on finite-size scaling and also for suggesting to run experiments with samples of very large size, so that the margin of error would be significantly reduced. Finally, we thank the reviewers of CP '01 for their useful suggestions, constructive criticisms, and pointers to the literature.

References

[And84] G. E. Andrews. *The Theory of Partitions.* Cambridge U. Press, 1984.

[BS94] F. Baader and J. H. Siekmann. Unification theory. In *Handbook of Logic in AI and Logic Programming*, volume 2, pages 41–125. Oxford U. Press, 1994.

[CDE+99] M. Clavel, F. Duran, S. Eker, J. Meseguer, and M. Stehr. Maude as a formal meta-tool. In *The World Congress On Formal Methods In The Development Of Computing Systems*, pages 1684–1703, 1999.

[CDS+00] C. Coarfa, D. D. Demopoulos, A. San Miguel Aguirre, D. Subramanian, and M. Y. Vardi. Random 3-SAT: The plot thickens. In *Constraint Programming 2000*, pages 143–159, 2000.

[DGZ00] P.E. Dunne, A. Gibbons, and M. Zito. Complexity-theoretic models of phase transitions in search problems. *Theor. Comp. Sci.*, 249:243–263, 2000.

[Eke93] S. Eker. Improving the efficiency of AC-matching and unification. Technical Report, INRIA-Lorraine, 1993.

[Eke00] S. Eker. Personal communication, 2000.

[GMW96] I.P. Gent, E. MacIntyre, and P. Prosser T. Walsh. The constrainedness of search. In *Proceedings of AAAI '96*, pages 246–252, 1996.

[GW98] I. Gent and T. Walsh. Analysis of heuristics for number partitioning. *Computational Intelligence*, 14(3):430–451, 1998.

[HK99] M. Hermann and P. G. Kolaitis. Computational complexity of simultaneous elementary matching problems. *J. Autom. Reasoning*, 23(2):107–136, 1999.

[KS92] H. Kautz and B. Selman. Planning as satisfiability. In *Proceedings of ECAI*, pages 359–379, 1992.

[KS94] S. Kirkpatrick and Bart Selman. Critical behavior in the satisfiability of random boolean expressions. *Science*, 264:1297–1301, 1994.

[McC97] W. McCune. Solution of the Robbins problem. *J. Autom. Reasoning*, 19(3):263–276, 1997.

[MK98] P. Moreau and H. Kirchner. A compiler for rewrite programs in associative-commutative theories. In *ALP/PLILP: Principles of Declarative Programming*, volume 1490 of *LNCS*, pages 230–249. Springer-Verlag, 1998.

[NW78] A. Nijenhuis and H. S. Wilf. *Combinatorial Algorithms for Computers and Calculators*, chapter 10. Academic Press, 2nd edition, 1978.

[Raf00] T. Raffill. On the search for a phase transition in AC-matching. Master's thesis, UC Santa Cruz, 2000.

[SD96] B.M. Smith and M.E. Dyer. Locating the phase transition in binary constraint satisfaction problems. *Artificial Intelligence J.*, 8(1–2):155–181, 1996.

[SML96] B. Selman, D. G. Mitchell, and H. J. Levesque. Generating hard satisfiability problems. *Artificial Intelligence*, 81(1-2):17–29, 1996.

Specific Filtering Algorithms for Over-Constrained Problems

Thierry Petit[1,2], Jean-Charles Régin[1], and Christian Bessière[2]

[1] ILOG, 1681, route des Dolines, 06560 Valbonne, FRANCE
{tpetit, regin}@ilog.fr
[2] LIRMM (UMR 5506 CNRS), 161, rue Ada, 34392 Montpellier Cedex 5, FRANCE
{bessiere, tpetit}@lirmm.fr

Abstract. In recent years, many constraint-specific filtering algorithms have been introduced. Such algorithms use the semantics of the constraint to perform filtering more efficiently than a generic algorithm. The usefulness of such methods has been widely proven for solving constraint satisfaction problems. In this paper, we extend this concept to over-constrained problems by associating specific filtering algorithms with constraints that may be violated. We present a paradigm that places no restrictions on the constraint filtering algorithms used. We illustrate our method with a complete study of the All-different constraint.

1 Introduction

A problem is over-constrained when no assignment of values to variables satisfies all constraints. In this situation, the goal is to find a compromise. Violations are allowed in solutions, providing that such solutions retain a practical interest. Therefore, it is mandatory to respect some rules and acceptance criteria defined by the user. A *cost* is generally associated with each constraint in order to quantify its violation [3]. Then, costs can be bounded from above. For instance, consider a cost associated with the violation of a temporal constraint imposing that a person should stop working before a given date: this cost should be proportional to the additional amount of working time she performs, and this amount should not be excessive.

A global objective related to the whole set of costs is usually defined. For instance, the goal can be to minimize the total sum of costs. In some applications it is necessary to express more complex rules on violations, which involve several costs independently from the objective. Such rules can be defined through meta-constraints [9]. In this paper, we are interested in solving such problems.

Existing algorithms dedicated to over-constrained problems [6,15,8,14,13] are generic. However, the use of constraint-specific filtering algorithms is generally required to solve real-world applications (e.g., [10,2,12]), as their efficiency can be much higher.

Regarding over-constrained problems, existing constraint-specific filtering algorithms can be used only in the particular case where the constraint must be

T. Walsh (Ed.): CP 2001, LNCS 2239, pp. 451–463, 2001.

satisfied. Indeed, they removes values which are not consistent with the constraint: the deletion condition is linked to the fact that it is mandatory to satisfy the constraint. This condition is not applicable when the violation is allowed.

However, domains can be reduced from the objective and from the costs associated with violations of constraints. The main idea of this paper is to perform this kind of filtering specifically, that is, to take advantage from the semantics of a constraint and from the semantics of its violation to efficiently reduce the domains of the variables it constrains.

The deletion condition will be linked to the necessity of having an acceptable cost, instead of being related to the satisfaction requirement. For instance, consider the constraint $C : x \leq y$, such that $D(x) = [0, 3]$ and $D(y) = [0, 1]$. Assume that, when C is violated, the cost is defined as the difference between x and y. If the cost of C has to be less than or equal to 1, then the value 3 can be removed from $D(x)$. Note that the domain of allowed values of the cost of a given constraint can be reduced during the search, by propagation of the objective and of the other costs.

We present a model such that the costs are expressed by variables directly integrated into the problem. Roughly, the principle is to turn an over-constrained problem into a classical optimization problem. Then, as any other variable, a cost can be constrained. In this way, the violation of a constraint C can be controled through a constraint $\bar{C}$ linking C and the cost. In terms of efficiency, the main interest of this approach is the possibility to associate a specific filtering algorithm with $\bar{C}$, which exploits the semantics.

We discuss how a violation can be quantified. For a given constraint, several possible definitions of the cost can be considered. They correspond to different filtering algorithms. We propose two general definitions for non-binary constraints.

We provide a complete study of the All-different Constraint [10]: we present two algorithms based on flow theory, related to the two definitions of the cost.

2 Background

CSP. A *constraint network* $\mathcal{N}$ is defined as a set of n *variables* $X = \{x_1, \ldots, x_n\}$, a set of *domains* $\mathcal{D} = \{D(x_1), \ldots, D(x_n)\}$ where $D(x_i)$ is the finite set of possible *values* for variable x_i, and a set $\mathcal{C}$ of *constraints* between variables. A *constraint* C on the ordered set of variables $var(C) = (x_{i_1}, \ldots, x_{i_r})$ (also denoted by $C(x_{i_1}, \ldots, x_{i_r})$) is a subset $rel(C)$ of the Cartesian product $D(x_{i_1}) \times \cdots \times D(x_{i_r})$ that specifies the *allowed* combinations of values for the variables $x_{i_1}, \ldots, x_{i_r}$. $D(var(C)) = \cup_{x \in var(C)} D(x)$. An element of $D(x_{i_1}) \times \cdots \times D(x_{i_r})$ is called a *tuple on* $var(C)$. $|var(C)|$ is the *arity* of C. C is *binary* iff $|var(C)| = 2$. A value a for a variable x is denoted by (x, a). A tuple τ on $var(C)$ is *valid* if $\forall (x, a) \in \tau, a \in D(x)$. C is *consistent* iff there exists a tuple τ of $rel(C)$ which is valid. A value $a \in D(x)$ is *consistent with* C iff $x \notin var(C)$ or there exists a valid tuple τ of $rel(C)$ in which a is the value assigned to x. Given $Y \subseteq X$, an *instantiation* I of Y is an assignment of values to variables Y such that $\forall x \in Y$, the value a assigned to x belongs to $D(x)$. Given $Y \subseteq X$ and $C \in \mathcal{C}$ such that

$var(C) \subseteq Y$, an instantiation I of Y *satisfies* a constraint C iff the projection of I on $var(C)$ belongs to $rel(C)$. If I does not satisfy C, then I *violates* C. The *Constraint Satisfaction Problem* (CSP) consists of finding an instantiation I of X such that $\forall C \in \mathcal{C}$, I satisfies C.

Over-Constrained Problem. When a CSP has no solution, we say that the problem is *over-constrained.* $\mathcal{C}_h \subseteq \mathcal{C}_s$ is the set of *hard* constraints, that is, the constraints that must necessarily be satisfied. $\mathcal{C}_s = \mathcal{C} \setminus \mathcal{C}_h$ is the set of *soft* constraints. Let I be an instantiation of X. If I is a solution of an over-constrained problem then $\forall C \in \mathcal{C}_h$, I satisfies C. The Maximal Constraint Satisfaction Problem (Max-CSP) is the problem where all the constraints are soft; the goal is to minimize the number of violated constraints.

All-different Constraint. The All-different constraint, called *AllDiff*, is the constraint C stating that the variables in $var(C) = \{x_{i_1}, \ldots, x_{i_k}\}$ must take values different from each other: it is defined by the set of tuples $rel(C) = \{(d_1, \ldots, d_k) \in D(x_{i_1}), \ldots, D(x_{i_k})$ s.t. $\forall u, v$: $d_u \neq d_v\}$.

Graphs. A *graph* $G = (X, E)$ consists of a set X of vertices and a set of edges E, where every edge is a pair of distinct vertices. $G' = (X', E')$ is a *subgraph* of G iff $X' \subseteq X$ and $E' \subseteq E$. A *clique* of G is a subgraph $G' = (X', E')$ of G such that $\forall u \in X', \forall v \in X'$, $(u, v) \in E'$. A *directed graph* $G = (X, U)$ consists of a vertex set X and a set of arcs U, where every arc (u, v) is a directed pair of distinct vertices. An arc (u, v) *leaves* u and *enters* v. $\Gamma^-(v)$ is the set of edges entering a vertex v. $\Gamma^+(v)$ is the set of edges leaving v. $\Gamma(v) = \Gamma^- \cup \Gamma^+$.

– **Matchings:** Given a graph $G = (X, E)$, a *matching* $M \subseteq E$ is a subset of edges such that no two edges have a vertex in common. The *cardinality* of a matching is the number of edges it contains. A matching of maximum cardinality is called a *maximum matching.* Given a matching M, every edge of E which does not belong to M is *free*. Every vertex v in X which is not an endpoint of an edge of M is *free*; for convenience, if v is not free then we say that $v \in M$.

– **Flows:** Flow theory was originally introduced by Ford and Flukerson [5]. Let $G = (X, U)$ be a directed graph such that each arc (u, v) is associated with two positive integers $lb(u, v)$ and $ub(u, v)$. $ub(u, v)$ is called the *upper bound capacity* of (u, v) and $lb(u, v)$ the *lower bound capacity.* A *flow* in G is a function f satisfying the following two conditions:

1. For any arc (u, v), $f(u, v)$ represents the amount of commodity which flows along the arc. Such a flow is allowed only in the direction of the arc (u, v), that is, from u to v.
2. A *conservation law* is observed at each of the vertices: $\forall v \in X$:
$\sum_{u \in \Gamma^-(v)} f(u, v) = \sum_{w \in \Gamma^+(v)} f(v, w)$.

The *feasible flow problem* is the problem of the existence of a flow in G which satisfies the *capacity constraint*, that is: $\forall (u, v) \in U : lb(u, v) \leq f(u, v) \leq ub(u, v)$.

3 Propagating Costs

3.1 Preliminary Example

Let C be the constraint $x \leq y$. In order to quantify its violation, a *cost* is associated with C. The semantics are the following:

– if C is satisfied then $cost = 0$.

– if C is violated then $cost > 0$ and its value is proportional to the gap between x and y, that is, $cost = x - y$.

Assume that $D(x) = [90001, 100000]$ and $D(y) = [0, 200000]$, and that the cost is contrained to be less than 5. We deduce[1] that $x - y \leq 5$, and, by propagation, $D(y) = [89996, 200000]$.

Such a deduction is made directly by propagating *bounds* of the variables x, y and *cost*. Inequality constraints admit such propagation on bounds without consideration of the domain values which lie between. Such propagation, which depends on the semantics of the inequality constraint, is fundamentally more efficient than the consideration for deletion of each domain value in turn. If we ignore the semantics in the example, the only way to filter a value is to study the cost of each tuple in which this value is involved. Performing the reduction of $D(y)$ in the example above is costly: at least $|D(x)| * 89996 = 899960000$ checks are necessary. This demonstrates the gain to achieved by directly integrating constraints on costs into the problem and employing constraint-specific filtering algorithms.

Following this idea, our goal is to allow the *same* modelling flexibility with respect to violation costs as with any other constrained variable. The most natural way to achieve this is to include these violation costs as variables in a new constraint network[2].

3.2 New Model

The model we present in this section is well suited to use specific algorithms, for any kind of constraints. For sake of clarity, we consider that the values of the cost associated with a constraint C are positive integers. 0 expresses the fact that C is satisfied, and strict positive values are proportional to the importance of a violation. This assumption is not a strong restriction; it just implies that values of cost belong to a totally ordered set.

We suggest solving a new optimization problem derived from the initial problem. It involves the same set of hard constraints $\mathcal{C}_h$, but a set of disjunctive constraints replaces $\mathcal{C}_s$. This set of disjunctive constraints is denoted by $\mathcal{C}_{disj}$ and a one-to-one correspondance is defined between $\mathcal{C}_s$ and $\mathcal{C}_{disj}$. Each disjunction involves a new variable $cost \in X_{costs}$, which is used to express the cost

[1] Either C is satisfied: $x - y \leq 0$, or C is violated: $x - y = cost$ and $cost \leq 5$, which implies $x - y \leq 5$.

[2] In existing frameworks [3] the variable set is not extended. The costs are not included into the problem through variables.

of $C \in \mathcal{C}_s$. A one-to-one correspondance is also defined between $\mathcal{C}_s$ and X_{costs}. Given $C \in \mathcal{C}_s$, the disjunction is the following:

$$[C \wedge [cost = 0]] \vee [\bar{C} \wedge [cost > 0]]$$

$\bar{C}$ is the constraint including the variable $cost$ that expresses the violation[3]. A specific filtering algorithm can be associated with it. Regarding the preliminary example, the constraints C and $\bar{C}$ are respectively $x \leq y$ and $cost = x - y$:

$$[[x \leq y] \wedge [cost = 0]] \vee [[cost = x - y] \wedge [cost > 0]]$$

The new defined problem is not over-constrained: it consists of satisfying the constraints $\mathcal{C}_h \cup \mathcal{C}_{disj}$, while optimizing an objective defined over all the variables X_{costs} (we deal with a classical optimization problem); constraints on a variable $cost$ can be propagated.

Such a model can be used for encoding directly over-constrained problems with exisiting solvers [13]. Moreover, additional constraints on cost variables can be defined in order to select solutions which are acceptable for the user [9].

3.3 Consistency and Domain Reduction

In this section we formalize our motivations. Assume that the objective is to minimize the sum obj of m costs $\{cost_1, ..., cost_m\}$, corresponding to constraints $\mathcal{C}_s = \{C_1, ..., C_m\}$. Let C_i be a constraint in $\mathcal{C}_s$, and $cost_i$ be its cost variable. We are interested in computing a lower bound lb_i of the minimal value of $cost_i$ consistent with $\bar{C}_i$. This lower bound can be used to check the consistency of $\bar{C}_i$. If $lb_i > max(D(cost_i))$, or if $lb_i + \sum_{k \in \{1,\dots,m\}} min(D(cost_k)) - min(D(cost_i)) > max(obj)$, then $\bar{C}_i$ is not consistent.

Moreover, the same kind of lower bound can be computed in order to reduce domains of variables constrained by C_i. Let x be a variable of C_i, and a be a value of $D(x)$. Let $lb_{i(x,a)}$ be the minimal value of $cost_i$ consistent with $\bar{C}_i \wedge (x = a)$. If $lb_{i(x,a)} > max(D(cost_i))$, or if $lb_{i(x,a)} + \sum_{k \in \{1,\dots,m\}} min(D(cost_k)) - min(D(cost_i)) > max(obj)$, then a can be removed from $D(x)$.

Note that, when studying the consistency with respect to $max(obj)$, some algorithms have been proposed to compute a global lower bound greater than the sum of minima of costs in the left part of the equations above. Even if it is not the main topic of this paper, we point out that our model does not impose any restriction about using such algorithms. For instance, the best existing algorithm for binary Max-CSPs (e.g., PFC-MRDAC [8]) has been extended to the non-binary case and adapted to this model [13].

Similar reasoning can be performed with objectives different from a minimization of the sum of costs, providing that there is a way of infering how a change to local costs affects the objective. For some problems, the costs should be normalized in order to make them comparable and to integrate them into the global objective. They can also be weighted in order to favor the satisfaction of some constraints rather than others.

[3] It is possible to define any constraint $\bar{C}$, and even a constraint that does not constrain $cost$.

3.4 General Definitions of Cost

When natural semantics can be associated with the violation of a constraint, we use them (for instance, the constraint of the preliminary example $C : x \leq y$). However, it is not necessarily the case. When there are no natural semantics associated with the violation of a constraint, different definitions of the cost can be considered, depending on the problem.

The Alldiff example. Let C be an Alldiff defined on variables $var(C) = \{x_1, x_2, x_3, x_4\}$, such that $\forall i \in [1,4], D(x_i) = \{a, b, c, d\}$. If we ignore the symmetric cases by considering that no value (resp. no variable) has more importance than another, we have the following possible assignments: (1) a, b, c, d, (2) a, a, c, d, (3) a, a, c, c, (4) a, a, a, c, (5) a, a, a, a.

Intuitively, it is straightforward that the violation of case (5) is more serious than the one of case (2). This fact has to be expressed through the cost.

We propose two general definitions of the cost associated with the violation of a non-binary constraint.

Definition 1 Variable Based Violation Cost *Let C be a constraint. The cost of its violation can be defined as the number of assigned values that should change in order to make C satisfied.*

The advantage of this definition is that it can be applied to any (non-binary) constraint. However, depending on the application, it can be inconvenient. In the Alldiff example above, a possible problem is that assignments (3) and (4) have the same cost according to definition 1. For an Alldiff involving more than four variables, a lot of different assignments have the same cost.

Therefore, we propose another definition of the cost, which is well suited to constraints that are representable through a primal graph [4,7]:

Definition 2 *The* **primal graph** *$Primal(C) = (var(C), E_p)$ of a constraint C is the graph such that each edge represents a binary constraint, and the set of solutions of the CSP defined by $\mathcal{N} = (var(C), D(var(C)), E_p)$ is the set of allowed tuples of C.*

For an Alldiff C, $Primal(C)$ is a complete graph where each edge represents a binary inequality.

Definition 3 Primal Graph Based Violation Cost *Let C be a constraint representable by a primal graph. The cost of its violation can be defined as the number of binary constraints violated in the CSP defined by $Primal(C)$.*

In the Alldiff case, the user may aim at controlling the number of binary inequalities implicitely violated. The advantage of this definition is that the granularity of the quantification is more accurate (in the example, costs of assignments (3) and (4) are different). Unfortunately, some constraints are not representable through a primal graph (for instance the constraint $C : p = q + r$).

4 Algorithms for the AllDiff

Let $C \in \mathcal{C}_s$ be an Alldiff, and *cost* its cost variable. In the following, we use two bipartite graphs. A bipartite graph is a graph $G = ((X_1, X_2), E)$ such that the vertex set $X_1 \cup X_2$ is partitioned in two disjoint sets X_1 and X_2, and such that there is no edge between any two vertices of the same set.

Definition 4 Value Graph *Let C be an AllDiff.*
$VG(C) = (var(C), D(var(C)), E)$ is the graph such that $(x, a) \in E$ iff $a \in D(x)$.

Note that an instantiation of $var(C)$ corresponds to a graph where for each variable $x \in var(C)$ there is exactly one edge leaving x. If such a graph is a matching, C is satisfied.

Definition 5 Value Graph with x=a *Let C be an AllDiff. Let $x \in var(C)$ and $a \in D(x)$. $VG_{(x,a)}(C) = (var(C), D(var(C)), F \cup \{(x, a)\})$ is the graph such that $(y, b) \in F$ iff $y \neq x$ and $b \in D(y)$.*

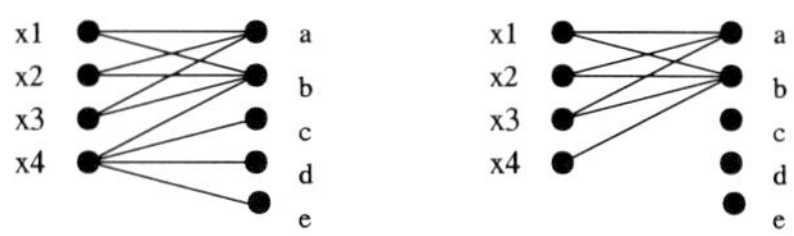

Fig. 1. $D(x_1) = \{a, b\}, D(x_2) = \{a, b\}, D(x_3) = \{a, b\}, D(x_4) = \{b, c, d, e\}$. The left graph is $VG(C)$, the right graph is $VG_{(x4,b)}(C)$.

Notation 1 *$\mu(G)$ is the cardinality of a maximum matching of a graph G.*

4.1 Variable Based Violation Cost

$\bar{C}$ is a constraint of arity $|var(C)| + 1$, where the additional variable is *cost*. According to definition 1, the *cost* is equal to the number of variables that should change their value in order to satisfy the property of having no value of $D(var(C))$ assigned to more than one variable in $var(C)$.

Firstly, we aim at computing a lower bound of *cost* in order to check the consistency of $\bar{C}$:

Property 1 *Let C be an AllDiff, $cost \in X_{costs}$ be the cost associated with C. $lb = |var(C)| - \mu(VG(C))$ is a lower bound of cost. (if $lb > max(D(cost))$ then $\bar{C}$ is not consistent).*

Proof: The existence of an instantiation of $var(C)$ such that C can become satisfied by changing the value of p variables implies the existence of a matching of size $|var(C)| - p$. By definition of $\mu(VG(C))$, $|var(C)| - p \leq \mu(VG(C))$, and $p \geq |var(C)| - \mu(VG(C))$.

The maximum size of a matching in a bipartite graph can be polynomially computed [1] in $O(\sqrt{|var(C)|} * K)$, where $K = \sum |D(x)|, x \in var(C)$.

Secondly, the same principle can be applied to reduce domains of variables in $var(C)$. Let $x \in var(C)$ and $a \in D(x)$. From Property 1 we have:

Theorem 1 *Let $x \in var(C)$ and $a \in D(x)$. Let $lb_{(x,a)} = |var(C)| - \mu(VG_{(x,a)}(C))$. If $lb_{(x,a)} > max(D(cost))$ then a can be removed from $D(x)$.*

The complexity of this filtering algorithm can be improved:

Property 2 *Let $lb = |var(C)| - \mu(VG(C))$. If $lb < max(D(cost))$ then all the values of domains of variables in $var(C)$ are consistent with $\bar{C}$.*

Proof: See Régin's Ph.D. Dissertation [11]

Therefore, the only case to study is $lb = max(D(cost))$:

Property 3 *Given $\bar{C}$, values of the domains of $var(C)$ which are not arc-consistent can be removed in $O(K)$ where $K = \sum |D(x)|, x \in var(C)$.*

Proof: e.g. Régin [10,11].

4.2 Primal Graph Based Violation Cost

$\bar{C}$ is a constraint of arity $|var(C)| + 1$, where the additional variable is *cost*. According to definition 3, the *cost* is equal to the number of binary inequalities violated in the CSP corresponding to the primal graph of C.

Necessary Condition of Consistency of $\bar{C}$.

Notation 2 *Let C be an Alldiff, and I an instantiation of $var(C)$.*
- *$\#(a, I)$ is the number of time the value a is assigned to variables in I.*
- *$max\#(I) = max(\#(a, I), a \in D(var(C)))$ is the maximum value of $\#(a, I)$ among all the values.*

Vertices of the primal graph $Primal(C)$ can be colored w.r.t. I, and *cost* is the sum of number of edges of cliques of each color.

The problem we have to solve is: "Among all the possible instantiations of $var(C)$, which is the one which has the lowest cost?"

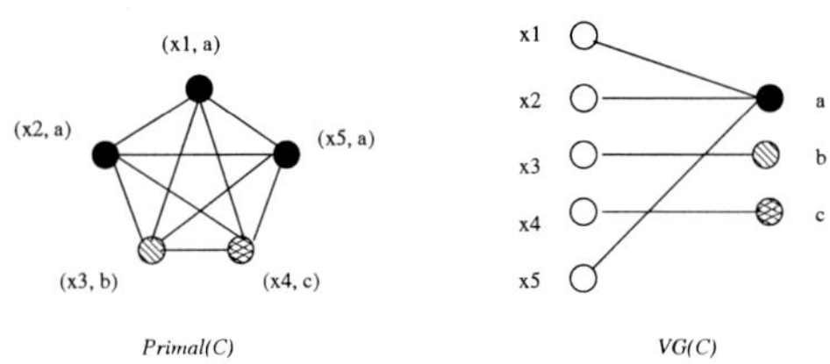

Fig. 2. *cliques* $= \{\{x_1, x_2, x_5\}, \{x_3\}, \{x_4\}\}$. *cost* $= (3 * 2)/2 + 0 + 0 = 3$.

Consider I any instantiation of $var(C)$. If the number of different values involved in I is equal to $|var(C)| - 1$, then we know that we will have one value assigned to two variables (i.e., $max\#(I) = 2$). Thus, we know that $cost = 1$; if the number of different values involved in I is equal to $|var(C)| - 2$, then we will have two possibilities: either there are two values a and b such that $\#(a, I) = \#(b, I) = 2$ (corresponding to a cost equal to 2), or one value c with $\#(c, I) = 3$ (corresponding to a cost of 3). This means that the cost depends on the number of different values involved in I and also on the maximum number of times a value is taken.

In the following table, all cases up to symmetry are presented for an AllDiff C defined on $var(C) = \{x_1, ..., x_8\}$. "$p$ of q" means p cliques of q variables in the primal graph, and *cost* represents the cost of violation. For instance, the cost value for 5 values and $max\#(I) = 4$ is equal to 6 which is greater than 4, the cost value for 4 values and $max\#(I) = 2$, but which is lower than 7 the cost value for 4 values and $max\#(I) = 4$.

Number of values	$max\#(I)$	Cliques in $Primal(C)$	Cost	Example
1	8	1 of 8	28	(a,a,a,a,a,a,a,a)
2	4	2 of 4	12	(a,a,a,a,b,b,b,b)
	5	1 of 5 + 1 of 3	13	(a,a,a,a,a,b,b,b)
	6	1 of 6 + 1 of 2	16	(a,a,a,a,a,a,b,b)
	7	1 of 7 + 1 of 1	21	(a,a,a,a,a,a,a,b)
3	3	2 of 3 + 1 of 2	7	(a,a,a,b,b,b,c,c)
	4	1 of 4 + 2 of 2	8	(a,a,a,a,b,b,c,c)
	4	1 of 4 + 1 of 3 + 1 of 1	9	(a,a,a,a,b,b,b,c)
	5	1 of 5 + 1 of 2 + 1 of 1	11	(a,a,a,a,a,b,b,c)
	6	1 of 6 + 2 of 1	15	(a,a,a,a,a,a,b,c)
4	2	4 of 2	4	(a,a,b,b,c,c,d,d)
	3	1 of 3 + 2 of 2 + 1 of 1	5	(a,a,a,b,b,c,c,d)
	3	2 of 3 + 2 of 1	6	(a,a,a,b,b,b,c,d)
	4	1 of 4 + 1 of 2 + 2 of 1	7	(a,a,a,a,b,b,c,d)
	5	1 of 5 + 3 of 1	10	(a,a,a,a,a,b,c,d)
5	2	3 of 2 + 2 of 1	3	(a,a,b,b,c,c,d,e)
	3	1 of 3 + 1 of 2 + 3 of 1	4	(a,a,a,b,b,c,d,e)
	4	1 of 4 + 4 of 1	6	(a,a,a,a,b,c,d,e)
6	2	2 of 2 + 4 of 1	2	(a,a,b,b,c,d,e,f)
	3	1 of 3 + 5 of 1	3	(a,a,a,b,c,d,e,f)
7	2	1 of 2 + 6 of 1	1	(a,a,b,c,d,e,f,g)
8	1	8 of 1	0	(a,b,c,d,e,f,g,h)

We aim at proving that:

- There is an instantiation I with a minimum cost which involves the highest number of values and which has the minimum value for $\#max(I)$.
- We can identify I' an instantiation with a minimum value of $max\#(I)$.

Notation 3 *Let I be a instantiation of $var(C)$, V be the set of values involved in I, and $VGI(C) = (var(C) \cup V, E)$ the graph of the instantiation I defined by $E = \{(x, a)$ s.t. a is assigned to $x\}$.*
– matching(I) denotes a matching of $VGI(C)$ such that each value of I is an extremity of an edge of this matching.
– cost(I) is the sum of edges of cliques in the graph $Primal(C)$ colored w.r.t I.

Note that if a value is involved in I then it belongs to $matching(I)$. By construction this matching is necessarily of matching of maximum size in $VGI(C)$ because it covers V. The following theorem greatly helps us to compute a lower bound of *cost*:

Theorem 2 *For each instantiation I of $var(C)$ there exists an intantiation I' of $var(C)$ such that $max\#(I') \leq max\#(I)$, $|matching(I')| = \mu(VG(C))$ and $cost(I') \leq cost(I)$.*

This theorem is proved by successively applying the following lemma:

Lemma 1 *For each instantiation I of $var(C)$ such that $|matching(I)| = s-1 < \mu(VG(C))$ there exists an instantiation I' of $var(C)$ such that $|matching(I')| = s$, $max\#(I') \leq max\#(I)$ and $cost(I') \leq cost(I)$.*

Proof: Let $M = matching(I)$. Then $|M| = s - 1 < \mu(VG(C))$, which means that M is not maximum; thus, from the matching theory, there is an alternating path P (i.e. a path those arcs are alternately in M and not in M) from $x \notin M$ to $v \notin M$. Consider M' be the matching obtained by augmenting M along P. Let I' be the instantiation of $var(C)$ defined as follows: a is assigned to y iff $(y, a) \in M'$ or ($y \notin M'$ and a is assigned to y in I). Value v is taken by one variable in I' whereas it is not involved in I. Let z be the variable which immediately preceeds v in P, and w the value assigned to z in I'. Then, $\#(w, I') = \#(w, I) - 1$. And $\forall u \in (D(var(C)) \setminus \{v, w\})$ $\#(u, I') = \#(u, I)$. Therefore $max\#(I') \leq max\#(I)$. Moreover, the constraints violated by the variables which take their values in $D(var(C)) \setminus \{v, w\}$ are the same for I and I'; v is taken by only one variable in I' thus no violation is induced; there are less variables in I' which take the value w than in I. Hence, $cost(I') \leq cost(I)$.

The algorithm we propose for computing the minimum possible value of $max\#(I)$ for an instantiation I of $var(C)$, denoted by $minMax\#(C)$, is based on the search of feasible flows on the following graph:

Definition 6 Value Assignment Graph
Let C be an AllDiff and $VG(C)$ its value graph. The **Value Assignment Graph** *of C is the directed graph $VAG(C) = (var(C) \cup D(var(C)) \cup \{s, t\}, E')$ such that E' is defined by:*
– s is a vertex such that $\forall x \in var(C)$, $(s, x) \in E'$.
– t is a vertex such that $\forall v \in D(var(C))$, $(v, t) \in E'$.
– $(t, s) \in E'$.
– $\forall (x, v) \in E$, $(x, v) \in E'$.

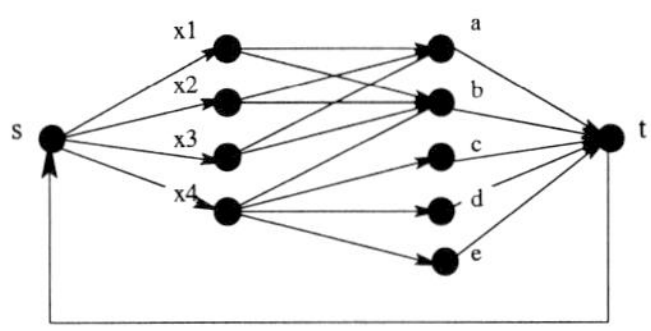

Fig. 3. Example of a Value Assignment Graph. $D(x_1) = \{a, b\}, D(x_2) = \{a, b\}, D(x_3) = \{ab\}, D(x_4) = \{b, c, d, e\}$.

The lower-bounds and upper-bound capacities in E' are:
– $\forall(s, x)$, $x \in var(C)$, $lb(s, x) = ub(s, x) = 1$.
– $\forall(x, v)$, $x \in var(C)$, $v \in D(var(C))$, $lb(x, v) = 0$ *and* $ub(x, v) = 1$.
– $\forall(v, t)$, $v \in D(var(C))$, $lb(v, t) = 0$ *and* $ub(v, t) = max\#$ *where* $max\#$ *is an integer such that* $1 \leq max\# \leq |var(C)|$.
– $lb(t, s) = ub(t, s) = |var(C)|$.

The link between $VAG(C)$ and an instantiation is a flow satisfying the following condition: if a value v is assigned to a variable x then $f(x, v) = 1$, otherwise $f(x, v) = 0$. The idea is to search for a first feasible flow problem on $VAG(C)$ with $max\#$ equal to 1. If there is none, a new feasible problem is run with $max\#$ equal to 2, and so on, until a feasible flow is found in $VAG(C)$.

Given $minMax(C)$, $|var(C)|$ and a matching size s, the COMPUTEMINCOST function returns the corresponding minimum *cost*. This function can be run before search in order to compute all the possible costs.

```
isTooLow(size, #vars, #vals)
    return size * #vals < #vars;

isTooHigh(size, #vars, #vals)
    return #vars − size < #vals − 1;

existsSize(size, #vars, #vals)
    return ¬ isTooLow(size, #vars, #vals)
              ∧ ¬ isTooHigh(size, #vars, #vals);

computeMinCost(minMax(C), |var(C)|, s)
    if ¬ existsSize(minMax(C), |var(C)|, s)) then return -1;
    if minMax(C) ≠ 1 then cost ← minMax(C) * (minMax(C) − 1)/2;
    #vars ← |var(C)| − minMax(C);
    #takenVals ← 1;
    while #vars > 0 do
            while ¬ isTooLow (minMax(C) − 1, #vars, s − #takenVals) do
                    minMax(C) − −;
            if minMax(C) ≠ 1 then cost ← cost+minMax(C)*(minMax(C)−1)/2;
            #takenVals + +;
            #vars ← #vars − minMax(C);
    return cost;
```

Now, we can compute the lower bound. It is equal to the smallest possible cost according to the values of $minMax\#(C)$ and $\mu(VG(C))$).

It is not optimal because for a given cardinality of a maximum matching $\mu(VG(C))$ and a given value of $minMax\#(C)$, more than one value of cost may be possible.

For instance, if $|var(C)| = 8$, $\mu(VG(C)) = 4$ and $minMax\# = 3$ then the *cost* can be 5 or 6; but since many matchings of maximum size exist, improving more this lower bound would probably be too costly.

The following algorithm returns true if $\bar{C}$ is consistent according to the domain of the variable *cost*:

```
isConsistent(C̄, cost)
    μ(VG(C)) ← size of a maximum matching of VG(C);
    max# ← 2;
    while max# ≤ |var(C)|
        if there exists a feasible flow on (VAG(C), max#) then
            return computeMinCost(max#, var(C), μ(VG(C))) ≤ max(D(cost));
        else max# ← max# + 1;
```

The complexity of this algorithm is $O(|var(C)| * \sqrt{|var(C)|} * K)$, where $K = \sum |D(x)|, x \in var(C)$.

Based on the same principle, we propose the follwing filtering algorithm:

Let $x \in var(C)$ and $a \in D(x)$. Let $VAG_{(x,a)}(C) = (var(C) \cup D(var(C)) \cup \{s,t\}, E'')$ be the subgraph of $VAG(C) = (var(C) \cup D(var(C)) \cup \{s,t\}, E')$ such that $E'' = E' \setminus \Gamma^{+}(x) \cup \{(x,a)\}$. In the algorithm, we use the graphs $VG_{(x,a)}(C)$ and $VAG_{(x,a)}(C)$:

```
Filter(C̄, cost)
    for all x ∈ var(C)
        for all a ∈ D(x)
            μ(VG_(x,a)(C)) ← size of a maximum matching of VG_(x,a)(C);
            max# ← 2;
            while max# ≤ |var(C)|
                if there exists a feasible flow on (VAG_(x,a)(C), max#) then
                    if computeMinCost(max#, var(C), μ(VG_(x,a)(C)))
                    > max(D(cost)) then
                        D(x) ← D(x) \ {a};
                    max# = |var(C)| + 1;
                else max# ← max# + 1;
```

The complexity of this algorithm is $O(|var(C)|^2 * \sqrt{|var(C)|} * K * d)$, where $K = \sum |D(x)|, x \in var(C)$ and $d = max(|D(x)|), x \in var(C)$.

5 Conclusion

This paper introduces a new approach for solving over-constrained problems as classical constraint problems, such that filtering algorithms specific to violated constraints can be used. Two definitions of the cost associated with the violation of a constraint are proposed. A complete study of the All-different constraint is provided: two specific filtering algorithms based on flow theory are presented, related to the two definitions of the cost.

Acknowledgements. We thank Paul Shaw for the helpful comments he provided. This work also profited from discussions with Olivier Lhomme and Jean-Francois Puget. It was partially supported by the IST Programme of the European Commission through the ECSPLAIN project (project IST-1999-11969).

References

1. R. Ahuja, T. Magnanti, and J. Orlin. Networks flows: theory, algorithms, and applications. *Prentice Hall, Inc.*, 1993.
2. N. Beldiceanu and E. Contejean. Introducing global constraints in chip. *Journal of Mathematical and Computer Modelling*, 20(12):97–123, 1994.
3. S. Bistarelli, U. Montanari, F. Rossi, T. Schiex, G. Verfaillie, and H. Fargier. Semiring-based CSPs and valued CSPs: Frameworks, properties, and comparison. *Constraints*, 4:199–240, 1999.
4. R. Dechter. Constraint networks. *Encyclopedia of Artificial Intelligence*, pages 276–285, 1992.
5. L. Ford and D. Flukerson. Flows in networks. *Princeton University Press*, 1962.
6. E. Freuder and R. Wallace. Partial constraint satisfaction. *Artificial Intelligence*, 58:21–70, 1992.
7. I. Gent, K. Stergiou, and T. Walsh. Decomposable constraints. *Artificial Intelligence*, 123:133–156, 2000.
8. J. Larrosa, P. Meseguer, and T. Schiex. Maintaining reversible DAC for MAX-CSP. *Artificial Intelligence*, 107:149–163, 1999.
9. T. Petit, J.-C. Régin, and C. Bessière. Meta constraints on violations for over constrained problems. *Proceedings ICTAI*, pages 358–365, 2000.
10. J.-C. Régin. A filtering algorithm for constraints of difference in CSPs. *Proceedings AAAI*, pages 362–367, 1994.
11. J.-C. Régin. Développement d'outils algorithmiques pour l'Intelligence Artificielle. Application à la Chimie Organique. *Ph.D. Dissertation, Université Montpellier II*, 1995.
12. J.-C. Régin. Generalized arc consistency for global cardinality constraint. *Proceedings AAAI*, pages 209–215, 1996.
13. J.-C. Régin, T. Petit, C. Bessière, and J.-F. Puget. An original constraint based approach for solving over constrained prolems. *Proceedings CP*, pages 543–548, 2000.
14. T. Schiex. Arc consistency for soft constraints. *Proceedings CP*, pages 411–424, 2000.
15. G. Verfaillie, M. Lemaître, and T. Schiex. Russian doll search for solving constraint optimisation problems. *Proceedings AAAI*, pages 181–187, 1996.

Specializing Russian Doll Search*

Pedro Meseguer and Martì Sánchez

IIIA-CSIC, Campus UAB, 08193 Bellaterra, Spain
{pedro, marti}@iiia.csic.es

Abstract. Russian Doll Search (RDS) is a clever procedure to solve overconstrained problems. RDS solves a sequence of nested subproblems, where two consecutive subproblems differ in one variable only. We present the Specialized RDS (SRDS) algorithm, which solves the current subproblem for each value of the new variable with respect to the previous subproblem. The SRDS lower bound is superior to the RDS lower bound, which allows for a higher level of value pruning, although more work per node is required. Experimental results on random and real problems show that this extra work is often beneficial, providing substantial savings in the global computational effort.

1 Introduction

When solving a Constraint Satisfaction Problem (CSP), one has to assign values to variables satisfying a set of constraints. In real applications it often happens that problems are over-constrained and do not have any solution. In this situation, it is desirable to find the assignment that *best respects* the constraints under some preference criterion. Under this view, over-constrained CSPs are optimization problems for which *branch and bound* is a suitable solving strategy. The efficiency of branch and bound-based algorithms greatly depends on the lower bound used to detect deadends and to avoid the exploration of large regions in the search space. This lower bound should be both as large and as cheap to compute as possible.

An approach [4,11,7,1,8] for lower bound computation aggregates two main elements: (i) the global contribution of assigned variables, and (ii) the addition of individual contributions of unassigned variables. Another approach [10] keeps (i) but substitutes (ii) by a global contribution of unassigned variables. This is done by the Russian Doll Search (RDS) method, which requires n successive searches on nested subproblems to finally solve a problem of n variables.

Two consecutive subproblems differ in one variable only. RDS computes the cost of including that variable in the previously solved subproblem, getting the cost of the next subproblem. In this paper, we extend the RDS approach by computing the cost of including each value of that variable in the previously

* This work was supported by the IST Programme of the Commission of the European Union through the ECSPLAIN project (IST-1999-11969), and by the Spanish CICYT project TAP99-1086-C03-02.

T. Walsh (Ed.): CP 2001, LNCS 2239, pp. 464–478, 2001.

solved subproblem. Given that this new approach performs RDS specialized per value, we call it *Specialized Russian Doll Search* (SRDS).

While RDS performs n searches, SRDS requires up to $n \times d$ independent searches (where d is the domain size) because it solves each subproblem for each feasible value of the new variable. This extra effort permits to compute a lower bound greater than (or equal to in the worst case) RDS lower bound, and allows the user to adjust good upper bounds when solving each subproblem. In addition, some searches can be skipped, under some conditions. Experimental results show that SRDS strategy is often superior to RDS, because its extra pruning causes substantial savings in global search effort.

In this paper we consider the Max-CSP model where all constraints are considered equally important, and the Weighted CSP model where constraints can be assigned different weights and the goal is to find the assignment that minimizes the accumulated weight of unsatisfied constraints. These two models are tested in the experimental results with the Random Problems and Celar Frequency Assignment Problems respectively. Our approach can also be applied to other frameworks.

This paper is structured as follows. In Section 2 we introduce notation and briefly review previous approaches to Max-CSP lower bound. In Section 3 we introduce our approach, analising the different lower bounds that can be calculated. Section 4 presents the SRDS algorithm. In Section 5 we discuss some experimental results. Finally, Section 6 contains some conclusions and directions of further work.

2 Preliminaries

A discrete binary constraint satisfaction problem (CSP) is defined by a finite set of variables $X = \{1, \ldots, n\}$, a set of finite domains $\{D_i\}_{i=1}^n$ and a set of binary constraints $\{R_{ij}\}$. Each variable i takes values in its corresponding domain D_i. A constraint R_{ij} is a subset of $D_i \times D_j$ which only contains the allowed value pairs for variables i, j [1]. An assignment of values to variables is complete if it includes every variable in X, otherwise it is partial. A *solution* for a CSP is a complete assignment satisfying every constraint. The problem is called over-constrained if such an assignment does not exist. It may be of interest to find a complete assignment that best respects all constraints [2,9]. We consider the Max-CSP problem, for which the solution of an over-constrained CSP is a complete assignment satisfying the maximal number of constraints. The number of variables is n, the maximum cardinality of domains is d and the number of constraints is e. Letters $i, j, k \ldots$ denote variables, $a, b, c \ldots$ denote values, and a pair (i, a) denotes the value a of variable i.

Most exact algorithms for solving Max-CSP follow a *branch and bound* schema. These algorithms perform a depth-first traversal on the search tree defined by the problem, where internal nodes represent incomplete assignments and

[1] We assume that for each pair of variables i, j there is only one constraint $R_{i,j}$

leaf nodes stand for complete ones. Assigned variables are called *past* (P), while unassigned variables are called *future* (F). The *distance* of a node is the number of constraints violated by its assignment. At each node, branch and bound computes the *upper bound* (UB) as the distance of the best solution found so far, (complete assignment with minimum distance in the explored part of the search tree), and the *lower bound* (LB) as an underestimation of the distance of any leaf node descendant from the current one. When $UB \leq LB$, we know that the current best solution cannot be improved below the current node. In that case, the algorithm prunes all its successors and performs backtracking.

Partial forward checking (PFC) [4], is a branch and bound based algorithm whose lower bound has been improved by lookahead. When a variable is assigned, PFC performs lookahead on future variables and its effects are recorded in *inconsistency counts* (IC). The inconsistency count of value a of a future variable i, ic_{ia}, is the number of past variables inconsistent with (i, a). PFC lower bound is $dist(P) + \sum_{i \in F} \min_a(ic_{ia})$, where $dist(P)$ is the number of inconsistencies among past variables. This lower bound can be improved by adding inconsistencies among future variables in several ways,

- Directed arc inconsistency counts: constraints among future variables must be directed, either by a static variable ordering [11] or by a directed constraint graph [8]. Arc inconsistencies are recorded in the variable where the constraint points to, using directed arc inconsistency counts (DAC), which can be combined with IC to produce a new lower bound [11,7,8].
- Arc inconsistency counts: constraints among future variables are not directed. Arc inconsistencies are recorded using arc inconsistency counts (AC), a fraction of which can be combined with IC to produce a new lower bound [1].
- Russian doll search (RDS): at a point in search, the subproblem formed by future variables and constraints among them has been previously solved to optimality. The distance of the optimal solution of the subproblem is added to the PFC lower bound producing a new lower bound [10].

In this paper, we focus on RDS [10]. Its central idea is to replace one search by n successive searches on nested subproblems. Given a static variable ordering, the first subproblem involves the nth variable only, the ith subproblem involves all variables from the $(n - i + 1)$th to the nth, and the nth subproblem involves all variables. Each subproblem is optimally solved using the RDS algorithm, following an increasing variable order: the first variable has the lowest number in the static ordering, and the last is always n. The central point in this technique is that, when solving the whole problem, subproblem solutions obtained before can be used in the lower bound in the following form,

$$LB(P, F) = dist(P) + \sum_{j \in F} min_b(ic_{jb}) + rds(F)$$

where $rds(F)$ is the distance of the optimal solution of the subproblem restricted to the variables in F. Let us suppose that we are solving the whole problem and

P involves the first $n - i$ variables. The set F involves from $n - i + 1$ to n variables, that is, F is composed by the variables of the ith subproblem. The distance of the best solution found in that subproblem can be safely added to the contribution of P plus ic counters to form the lower bound, because each term counts different inconsistencies. This strategy is also used when solving the subproblem sequence. Solving the ith subproblem involves reusing all solutions from previously solved subproblems.

3 Specializing RDS

The motivation for specializing the RDS contribution for every value of the new variable, instead of a unique RDS contribution for that variable is as follows. In general, the cost of including the values of one variable in the previously solved subproblem is not necessarily homogeneous, that is, *good* values (with low cost) and *bad* values (with high cost) may be present in the variable domain. Standard RDS only takes into account the minimum cost of all values of the variable. Using this specialized contribution, SRDS is able to develop pruning conditions stronger than RDS ones.

In addition, for one future variable we can combine their ic and rds contributions for each value, and take the minimum in the lower bound.

The central idea of the algorithm is to replace the n successive searches on nested subproblems of RDS by $n \times d$ searches: one for including every value of every new variable. Given a static variable ordering, the $n - i + 1$th subproblem considers the subset of variables $\{i, \ldots, n\}$. SRDS performs d independent searches for each value of variable i. The optimal cost of assigning value a to variable i in the $n-i+1$th subproblem is called rds_{ia}. After solving the $n-i+1$th subproblem for each value of variable i, counters recording rds_{ia} are updated and remain unchanged during the rest of the process. It is worth noting that,

$$rds(\{i, \ldots, n\}) = min_a rds_{ia}$$

3.1 A New Lower Bound

Let us consider the last iteration of SRDS, when the sets of past and future variables are $P = \{1, \ldots, i - 1\}$ and $F = \{i, \ldots, n\}$. For every $k \in F$ and $a \in D_k$, rds_{ka} contains the optimal cost of solving the subproblem $n - k + 1$ defined by the variables $(k, \ldots, n)$ with value a for variable k. From these new elements, a new family of lower bounds can be defined as follows,

$$\widehat{LB}^S(P, F, j) = dist(P) + min_a(ic_{ja} + rds_{ja}) + \sum_{k \in F, k \neq j} min_a ic_{ka} \quad j \in F$$

Property 1. $\widehat{LB}^S(P, F, j)$ is a safe lower bound for any variable $j \in F$.

Proof. The distance of any complete assignment including the partial assignment of P will include $dist(P)$. Given an arbitrary variable $j \in F$, $min_a(ic_{ja}+rds_{ja})$ is the minimum number of inconsistencies that j will have with any other variable of the problem when completing the current partial assignment, no matter which value is assigned to j. These inconsistencies are different from the ones recorded in $dist(P)$, so they can safely added. For any other variable $k \in F, k \neq j$, $\sum_{k \in F, k \neq j} min_a ic_{ka}$ is the minimum number of inconsistencies that all other future variables will have with past variables when completing the current partial assignment, no matter which value is assigned to them. This third term records different inconsistencies from the other two, $dist(P)$ and $min_a(ic_{ja}+rds_{ja})$, so they can be safely added. Only true inconsistencies are recorded, and no true inconsistency is recorded more than once. Therefore, $\widehat{LB}^S(P,F,j)$ is a safe lower bound. □

The SRDS lower bound, $LB^S(P,F)$, is the best lower bound of this family,

$$LB^S(P,F) = max_j \widehat{LB}^S(P,F,j)$$

Obviously, $LB^S(P,F)$ is a safe lower bound. In addition, it improves the standard lower bound of RDS.

Property 2. Using the same static variable ordering $LB^S(P,F) \geq LB(P,F)$

Proof.

$$\begin{aligned}
LB^S*(P,F) &= max_j \widehat{LB}^S*(P,F,j) \\
&\geq \widehat{LB}^S*(P,F,i) \\
&= dist(P) + min_a(ic_{ia}+rds_{ia}) + \sum_{k \in F, k \neq i} min_a ic_{ka} \\
&\geq dist(P) + min_a(ic_{ia}) + min_a(rds_{ia}) + \sum_{k \in F, k \neq i} min_a ic_{ka} \\
&= dist(P) + \sum_{k \in F} min_a ic_{ka} + min_a(rds_{ia}) \\
&= dist(P) + \sum_{k \in F} min_a ic_{ka} + rds(F) \\
&= LB(P,F)
\end{aligned}$$

Realizing that $min_a(rds_{ia})$ is referred to the first variable in F, it is clear that $min_a(rds_{ia}) = rds(F)$. □

Note that the expression,

$$distance(P) + \sum_{k \in F} min_a(ic_{ka}+rds_{ka})$$

is not a safe lower bound because the same inconsistency may be counted more than once. In Figure 1 we provide an example of this.

$P = \{(1,a)\},\ \ F = \{2,3,4\},\ \ D_1 = D_2 = D_3 = D_4 = \{a,b,c\}$
$R_{12} = \{ac,bb,bc,cc\},\ \ R_{13} = \{ab,bb,bc,cb\},\ \ R_{14} = \{ab,ac,ba,cc\}$
$R_{23} = \{aa,ac,ba,cb\},\ \ R_{24} = \{aa,ab,ac,cb\},\ \ R_{34} = \{aa,ab,ac,cb\}$

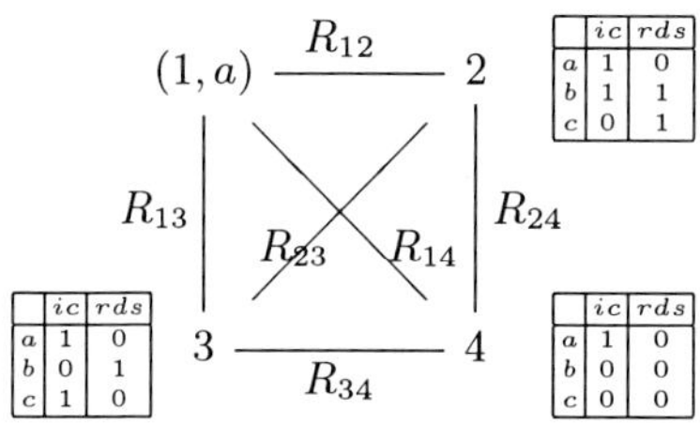

$distance(P) + \sum_{k\in F} min_a(ic_{ka} + rds_{ka}) = 0 + 1 + 1 + 0 = 2$
$BestSolution = ((1,a)(2,c)(3,b)(4,b)),\ \ distance(BestSolution) = 1$

Fig. 1. This example shows that rds_{ka} cannot be added over F without risk of repeating inconsistencies. After $(1,a)$, you count 2 inconsistencies, although only one exists (inconsistency on R_{34}).

3.2 Future Value Pruning

A value b of a future variable l can be pruned when the lower bound specialized for that value is greater than or equal to the current UB. For standard RDS, the specialized lower bound is,

$$LB_{lb}(P,F) = dist(P) + ic_{lb} + \sum_{k\in F, k\neq l} min_a ic_{ka} + rds(F)$$

In SRDS there is a family of lower bounds, $LB^S(P,F,j)$, which can be specialized for value b of future variable l as follows,

$$\widehat{LB}^S_{lb}(P,F,j) = \begin{cases} dist(P) + ic_{lb} + min_a(ic_{ja} + rds_{ja}) + \sum_{k\in F, k\neq j,l} min_a ic_{ka} & j \neq l \\ dist(P) + ic_{lb} + rds_{lb} + \sum_{k\in F, k\neq l} min_a ic_{ka} & j = l \end{cases}$$

The SRDS lower bound specialized for value b of future variable l is,

$$LB^S_{lb}(P,F) = max_j(\widehat{LB}^S_{lb}(P,F,j))$$

which is always better than the specialized lower bound of RDS.

Property 3. Using the same static variable ordering $LB^S_{lb}(P,F) \geq LB_{lb}(P,F)$.

Proof. Assuming that $F = \{i, \ldots, n\}$ and $l \neq i$, we have,

$$\begin{aligned}
LB^S_{lb}(P,F) &= max_j \widehat{LB}^S_{lb}(P,F,j) \\
&\geq \widehat{LB}^S_{lb}(P,F,i) \\
&= dist(P) + ic_{lb} + min_a(ic_{ia} + rds_{ia}) + \sum_{k \in F, k \neq i,l} min_a ic_{ka} \\
&\geq dist(P) + ic_{lb} + min_a ic_{ia} + min_a rds_{ia} + \sum_{k \in F, k \neq i,l} min_a ic_{ka} \\
&= dist(P) + ic_{lb} + \sum_{k \in F, k \neq l} min_a ic_{ka} + min_a rds_{ia} \\
&= LB_{lb}
\end{aligned}$$

If $l = i$, we have,

$$\begin{aligned}
LB^S_{lb}(P,F) &= max_j \widehat{LB}^S_{lb}(P,F,j) \\
&\geq \widehat{LB}^S_{lb}(P,F,i) \\
&= dist(P) + ic_{lb} + rds_{lb} + \sum_{k \in F, k \neq l} min_a ic_{ka} \\
&\geq dist(P) + ic_{lb} + \sum_{k \in F, k \neq l} min_a ic_{ka} + min_a rds_{la} \\
&= LB_{lb}
\end{aligned}$$

□

3.3 Initial Adjustment of UB

When solving subproblem $\{i, \ldots, n\}$ for every value of variable i, it is very important to start with a good UB, instead of taking $UB = \infty$ by default. In this way, pruning is optimized from the very beginning. Two initial adjustments of UB are considered, as follows,

1. When solving the subproblem composed by the variables $\{i+1, \ldots, n\}$, and a better solution is found, the current UB is decreased. Then, this new solution is extended to value a of variable i, and the distance of the extended solution is taken as a candidate UB for the subproblem to be solved with (i, a). This strategy is performed for all feasible a of variable i.
2. When solving the subproblem composed by the variables $\{i, \ldots, n\}$ with (i, a) and a better solution is found, the current UB is decreased. This new solution is modified, substituting a by b in variable i, if b is still unsolved in i. The distance of the modified solution is taken as a candidate UB for the subproblem to be solved with (i, b). This strategy is performed for all feasible b unsolved of variable i.

Candidates UB for subproblem with (i, a) are compared and the minimum is recorded as UB_{ia}. If $UB_{ia} = rds_{i+1,b}$, the resolution of the subproblem $\{i, \ldots, n\}$ with (i, a) is skipped, taking $rds_{ia} = UB_{ia}$.

4 The SRDS Algorithm

The SRDS algorithm appears in Figure 2. The *specializedRDS* procedure is called with the problem variables and their domains, and it executes n times the *PFC_SRDS* procedure, following the RDS subproblem sequence. The *PFC_SRDS* procedure is called on a particular subproblem, with a set P of past variables, a set F of future variables and their current domains FD. If the set F is empty (line 1), it means that a solution better than the current one has been found, and this is recorded in *Sol* and UB (lines 2 and 3). Also the *adjustUB* procedure is executed, following the description given in Section 3.3. If the set F is not empty, the first variable i of F is extracted (line 6) and all its values are processed as follows. Considering a as the current value, if i is the first variable of the current subproblem the upper bound is initialized (line 8). If the pruning condition is not satisfied (line 10), the *lookahead* procedure is executed updating the ic counters (line 11). Again, the pruning condition is checked (line 12) and if it not satisfied, the *prune* function is executed on future domains (line 13), producing new future domains. If again the pruning condition is not satisfied (line 14), a recursive call is performed where the set P is incremented with (i, a) and new future domains are passed (line 15). When all possible combinations of values for F variables have been tried, the rds contribution for the current value of the first variable of the current subproblem is updated (line 16). Procedure *lookahead* and functions *prune* and LB^S_{jb} present no difficulty.

In line 12 of *PFC_SRDS*, a safe approximation of the lower bound LB^S is computed. Instead of computing the variable $j \in F$ that provides the highest contribution, $i+1$ the first variable of F is taken. Something similar occurs in function LB^S_{jb}, where no complete maximization is performed on the set F. Instead, the best specialized lower bound for (j, b) is selected from two candidates, which differ in the variable that provides the rds contribution, $i+1$ or j. These approximations have been done to reduce overhead without causing a serious decrement in the lower bound.

The fundamental difference between the RDS and the SRDS algorithms is as follows. When SRDS starts assigning a new value for the first variable of the subproblem, it reinitializes the upper bound (line 8). This is not performed by RDS, which reinitializes the upper bound for the first value only. In this way, RDS computes the minimum contribution of the whole subproblem, while SRDS specializes that contribution of each value of the first variable of the subproblem.

Removing line 8 of *PFC_SRDS* in Figure 2, we obtain an algorithm which is in between RDS and SRDS. We call it *limited SRDS*. It computes the rds contribution for each value of the first subproblem variable until it finds the minimum for that variable. This minimum will be stored as the rds contribution for the values which were not processed when that minimum was found. Limited SRDS requires the same search effort as RDS (both compute the minimum rds contribution of a subproblem), but SRDS lower bounds allow for a better usage of this information. $LB^S(P, F)$ combines ic and rds counters in one future variable, while $LB(P, F)$ always takes the rds contribution in isolation. Because of that, limited SRDS has a higher pruning capacity than RDS, with the same effort.

procedure $specializedRDS(\{1,\ldots,n\},\{FD_1,\ldots,FD_n\})$
for i **from** n **downto** 1 **do**
  $PFC\_SRDS(\{\},\{i,\ldots,n\},\{FD_i,\ldots,FD_n\})$;

procedure $PFC\_SRDS(P,F,FD)$
if $(F=\emptyset)$ **then**
  $Sol \leftarrow assignment(P)$;
  $UB \leftarrow distance(P)$;
  $adjustUB()$;
else
  $i \leftarrow PopAVariable(F)$;
  for all $a \in FD_i$ **do**
    if $P=\emptyset$ **then** $UB \leftarrow UB_{ia}^{start}$;
    $newD \leftarrow distance(P)+ic_{ia}$;
    if $(newD + rds_{ia} + \sum_{k\in F} min_b ic_{kb} < UB)$ **then**
      $lookahead(i,a,F,FD)$;
      if $(newD + min_b(ic_{i+1,b} + rds_{i+1,b}) + \sum_{k\in F,k\neq i+1} min_b ic_{kb} < UB)$ **then**
        $newFD \leftarrow prune(F,FD)$;
        if $(newD + max_{j\in F}(min_b(ic_{jb}+rds_{jb}) + \sum_{k\in F,k\neq j} min_b ic_{kb}) < UB)$ **then**
          $PFC\_SRDS(P\cup\{(i,a)\},F,NewFD)$;
    if $P=\emptyset$ **then** $rds_{ia} \leftarrow UB$

procedure $lookahead(i,a,F,FD)$
for all $j \in F$ **do**
  for all $b \in FD_j$ **do**
    if $(inconsistent(i,a,j,b))$ **then** $ic_{jb} \leftarrow ic_{jb}+1$;

function $prune(F,FD)$
for all $j \in F$ **do**
  for all $b \in FD_j$ **do**
    if $(LB_{jb}^{S}(newD,F) \geq UB)$ **then** $FD_j \leftarrow FD_j - \{b\}$;
return FD;

function $LB_{jb}^{S}(newD,F)$
$lb_1 \leftarrow newD + ic_{jb} + \sum_{k\in F,k\neq j,i+1} min_c ic_{kc} + min_c(ic_{i+1,c}+rds_{i+1,c})$;
$lb_2 \leftarrow newD + ic_{jb} + rds_{jb} + \sum_{k\in F,k\neq j} min_c ic_{kc}$;
if $(lb_1 > lb_2)$ **return** lb_1;
else return lb_2;

Fig. 2. Specialized Russian Doll Search algorithm

5 Experimental Results

Experimental results in [10] show that RDS performs better than Depth First Branch and Bound on high problem connectivity. This is observed also in SRDS but in a sort of way that extremes are exaggerated: very connected problems give very good results and low connected problems (for example combined with high constraint tightness) can give very poor results. This is because the increase in the number of subproblems to solve up to $n * m$.

5.1 Random Problems

We give results on 6 classes of binary random problems. A binary random problem class is defined by the tuple $\langle n, m, p_1, p_2 \rangle$, where n is the number of variables, m is the number of values per variable, p_1 is the problem connectivity and p_2 is the constraint tightness. We tested the following six classes $\langle 10, 10, 1, p_2 \rangle$, $\langle 15, 5, 1, p_2 \rangle$, $\langle 15, 10, 50/105, p_2 \rangle$, $\langle 20, 5, 100/190, p_2 \rangle$, $\langle 25, 10, 37/300, p_2 \rangle$, $\langle 40, 5, 55/780, p_2 \rangle$, increasing the number of variables and decreasing connectivity. Results are presented in Figure 3, showing mean CPU time versus tightness. Each point is averaged over 50 executions. The graphics show the good behaviour of SRDS algorithm for complete graphs. For low connected problems the algorithm starts performing badly; this can be seen in the last random class $\langle 40, 5, 55/780, p_2 \rangle$, where SRDS performs as bad as RDS for high constraint tightness.

Random problems should not show the entire advantages of specializing RDS for every value. All values of a same variable have the same expected cost, this is because the homogeneity of the constraint tightness in the whole problem.

We have experimented also in the effect of adding values one by one to every variable of a highly connected problem. The results are very interesting because contradicting intuition, more values cause to increase the algorithm performance even if, theoretically, more subproblems are solved. This result can be visualized in Figure 4. This is only the case for high connected problems. For low connected problems solving every value to optimality can be computationally expensive. This will be explained in the next subsection for CELAR problems.

5.2 Frequency Assignment Problems

The Frequency Assignment Problem from CELAR [3] is a widely used binary overconstrained CSP benchmark. It consists of 11 instances to which different optimization criteria can be applied. We have centered our efforts in instance number 6 one of the hardest, which has 200 variables and the optimization criteria consists of minimizing the accumulated cost of the violated constraints. Constraints have violation costs that vary from 1 to 1000.

A simplification exists pointed out by Thomas Schiex for eliminating all the hard equality constraints of the problem and reducing the number of variables by two (because of the bijective property of the equality). From now we will assume this simplification.

Instance number 6 was first optimaly solved [5] in 32 days with a Sparc 5 workstation using a RDS technique. Five subinstances of the total instance number 6 were extracted, and the total accumulated cost of the subinstances was proven equal to best upperbound found at that moment for the global instance,

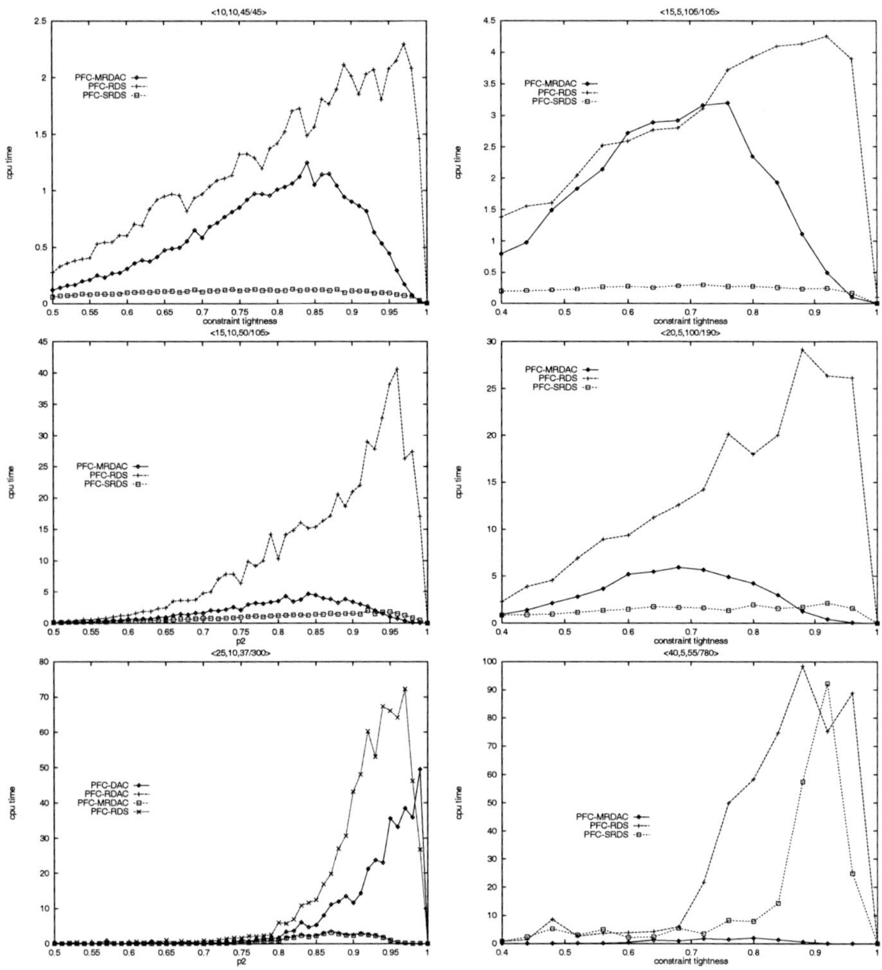

Fig. 3. Average CPU versus tightness for six classes of binary random problems.

so it was directly proven optimal. The subinstances all together induce a total cost of 3389 which is the optimal cost of instance 6.

Four subinstances are solved using directed arconsistency techniques in [8]. The CPU time given correspond to the time to prove optimality, that means the DAC algorithm is initialized with the optimal cost as upperbound.

Recently in [6] the whole instance 6 is solved to optimality in no more than 3 hours using graph decomposition techniques combined with a dynamic programing algorithm.

We have focussed solving the five subinstances and our results show a substantial decrement in CPU time, with respect to results reported in [5] and [8].

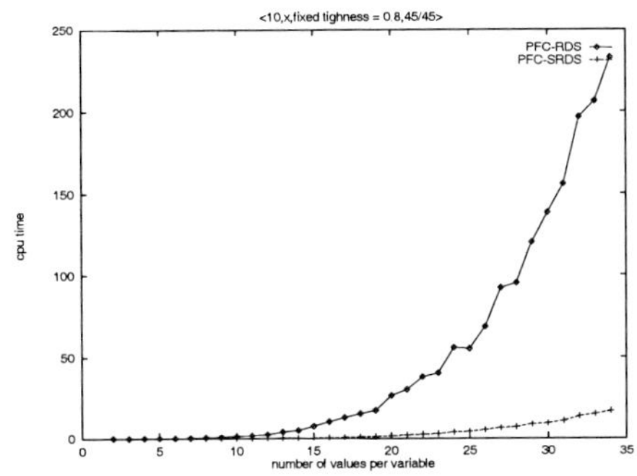

Fig. 4. Mean CPU time versus the number of values per variable on the $\langle 10, m, 1, 0.8 \rangle$ binary random problem class (complete graph). As the number of values per variable increases, the RDS lower bound loses quality and becomes less efficient

Experiments show that the SRDS algorithm is very sensitive to problem connectivity. When problems became less connected our algorithm performance decreases. An alternative for this problem is to solve with SRDS the first n' variables, $n' < n$, while the $n - n'$ last variables are solved with Limited SRDS. A study of the effect of this parameter n' in the CELAR-6 subinstance 2 can be visualized in Figure 5.

Table 1 shows results for the 5 CELAR-6 subinstances. The subinstances are solved using the SRDS until a certain number of variables per subproblem is reached (this parameter is indicated in the column *limitedto*). For example, subinstance SUB_4 is solved using SRDS up to a 18 variables subproblem, for the following subproblems 19, 20, 21, and 22 variables, the limited version of SRDS is used instead. In Table 2 the detailed execution for solving subinstance SUB_4 is presented.

We have observed that CELAR-6 subinstances are a perfect example of poor homogeneity within the specialized lower bounds for every value rds_{ia} for the same variable i (in the same variable, values with high cost can coexist with consistent values with cost 0) and also it can happen that the mean value cost of a variable is high and the following (respect to the static order) is low; suggesting that the variable where to combine rds and ic that gives the best lower bound contribution is not necessary the previous variable in the static ordering. So, our algorithm could aport advantages in comparison with standard RDS.

We have also noticed the extreme sensitivity of the algorithm to the static order of SRDS resolution. In a particular subproblem of CELAR-6 involving only 8 variables, different static orders gave CPU solving time from 0.3 to 513 seconds. For RDS it is known that orders that give best results are those with minimum bandwidth, that is the maximum distance (in terms of number of variables) between two connected variables. This results need to be adapted for taking in account the cost associated to constraints.

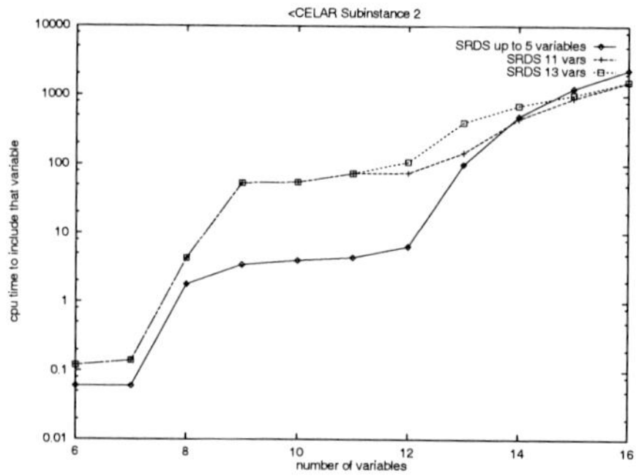

Fig. 5. CPU time for including each variable of subinstance 2 for different values of the limited version of SRDS, that is SRDS (to optimaly solve every value of a variable) is used up to different problem sizes. Plot in logarithmic scale.

Table 1. Results on CELAR-6 subinstances. The subinstances are solved using SRDS until a certain number of variables is reached (column 'limited to'). For the subproblems bigger than 'limited to' variables the limited version is used instead. CPU time corresponds to a Sun Ultra60 machine with SUN CC C++ compiler.

instance	variables	connectivity	optimal cost	limited to	cpu time
SUB_0	16	0.47	159	all vars	89s
SUB_1	14	0.82	2669	10 vars	711s
SUB_2	16	0.74	2746	13 vars	1573s
SUB_3	18	0.69	3079	16 vars	34671s
SUB_4	22	0.56	3230	18 vars	206314s

6 Conclusions

We have presented the SRDS algorithm that specializes the RDS approach solving each nested subproblem for each value of the new variable. This new approach requires more effort to solve completely each subproblem, but it provides a family of lower bounds, from which the best one is selected. This SRDS lower bound is superior to RDS lower bound. The main point in this new lower bound is the combination in one future variable of *ic* and *rds* contribution, taking the minimum of their sum, instead of adding both minimums as performed by RDS. The new lower bound can be specialized for future values, resulting in a value pruning condition better than the RDS one. Additionally, this allows for a better adjustment of initial upper bounds. We provided the SRDS algorithm and the approximations used to compute the lower bound in practice. This algorithm can be reduced to limited SRDS, an algorithm that requires the same search effort as RDS but offering a better performance. Empirical results show that this new approach provides substantial savings in computational effort.

For RDS-based approaches, the cost of solving a subproblem increases exponentially with the subproblem size. RDS is able to solve quickly small subprob-

Table 2. Subproblem results of subinstance SUB_4 with the algorithm SRDS limited to 18 variables. Each subproblem is build from the previous one including a new variable. The columns are: number of variables of the subproblem, time for optimally solving the subproblem in seconds, optimal cost of the subproblem (that is $min_a rds_{ia}$ being i the variable included in this particular subproblem), maximum cost of all the values of the variable included (that is $max_a rds_{ia}$), and the mean of the costs of the values of the new variable.

number of variables	cpu time	optimal cost	maximum cost	mean cost
2	0.00	0	0	0.00
3	0.00	0	0	0.00
4	0.01	0	0	0.00
5	0.01	0	0	0.00
6	0.01	0	100	47.32
7	0.02	100	113	102.82
8	0.04	202	304	237.55
9	0.26	323	3611	2294.68
10	0.30	347	1457	619.56
11	9.10	350	664	469.05
12	19.69	435	1639	849.68
13	101.63	1115	1981	1362.00
14	337.39	1632	2731	1871.09
15	1072.77	2271	3435	2698.14
16	10702.25	2746	4246	3277.23
17	16012.65	2858	4081	3339.32
18	64744.13	3079	4293	3565.27
19	67852.85	3109	3109	3109.00
20	67852.85	3109	3109	3109.00
21	206314.41	3230	3420	3240.56
22	206314.41	3230	3230	3230.00

lems, but it slows down dramatically when subproblems increase to reasonable size. SRDS performance is worse than RDS on small subproblems, but its superior lower bound allows for a better performance with increasing size. Above some size, is the limited SRDS algorithm the one that offers the best performance. More work, both theoretical and experimental, is needed to fully understand these empirical results. The final goal would be to capture the subproblem information that offers the best cost/benefit trade-off in global terms.

Acknowledgements. Authors thank anonymous reviewers for their constructive criticisms.

References

1. M. S. Affane and H. Bennaceur. A weighted arc consistency technique for Max-CSP. In *Proc. of the 13th ECAI*, 209–213, 1998.
2. S. Bistarelli, U. Montanari and F. Rossi. Constraint Solving over Semirings. In *Proc. of the 14th IJCAI*, 1995.
3. B.Cabon, S. De Givry, L.Lobjois, T.Schiex and J.P.Warners Radio Link Frequency Assignment *Constraints*, February 1999, Vol 4, Number 1.
4. E.C. Freuder and R.J. Wallace. Partial constraint satisfaction. *Artificial Intelligence*, 58:21–70, 1992.
5. S. Givry, G. Verfaillie and T. Schiex. Bounding the optimum of constraint optimization problems. In *Proc. of the 3th CP* 1997.
6. A.M. Koster, C. P. Hoesel and A. W. Kolen. Optimal solutions for a frequency assignment problem via tree-decomposition. In Lecture Notes in Computer Science, , 1665:338-349, 1999.
7. J. Larrosa and P. Meseguer. Exploiting the use of DAC in Max-CSP. In *Proc. of the 2th CP*, 308–322, 1996.
8. J. Larrosa, P. Meseguer, and T. Schiex. Maintaining reversible dac for max-csp. *Artificial Intelligence*, 107:149–163, 1999.
9. T. Schiex, H. Fargier and G. Verfaillie. Valued Constraint Satisfaction Problems: hard and easy problems. In *Proc. of the 14th IJCAI*, 631–637, 1995.
10. G. Verfaillie, M. Lemaître, and T. Schiex. Russian doll search. In *Proc. of the 13th AAAI*, 181–187, 1996.
11. R. Wallace. Directed arc consistency preprocessing. In M. Meyer, editor, *Selected papers from the ECAI-94 Workshop on Constraint Processing*, number 923 in LNCS, 121–137. Springer, Berlin, 1995.

A CLP Approach to the Protein Side-Chain Placement Problem

Martin T. Swain and Graham J.L. Kemp

Department of Computing Science, University of Aberdeen,
King's College, Aberdeen, Scotland, AB24 3UE
{mswain,gjlk}@csd.abdn.ac.uk

Abstract. Selecting conformations for side-chains is an important subtask in building three-dimensional protein models. Side-chain placement is a difficult problem because of the large search space that has to be explored. We show that the side-chain placement problem can be expressed as a CLP program in which rotamer conformations are used as values for finite domain variables, and bad atomic clashes involving rotamers are represented as constraints. We present a new side-chain placement method that uses a series of automatically generated CLP programs to represent successively tighter side-chain packing constraints. By using these programs iteratively our method produces side-chain conformation predictions whose accuracy is comparable with that of other methods. The resulting system provides a testbed for evaluating the quality of protein models obtained using different domain enumeration heuristics and side-chain rotamer libraries.

1 Introduction

Proteins are large biomolecules that are found in all living organisms where they perform a variety of biochemical functions. For example, proteins are essential for growth, metabolism, the immune and nervous systems, and for catalysing chemical reactions. Knowing the three-dimensional structure of a protein is vital to having a full understanding of its function. Since the experimental determination of a protein's structure can be a slow and difficult process, there is a demand to be able to generate hypothetical 3D protein models.

A significant sub-task in constructing a 3D model of a protein, and the focus of this paper, is *side-chain placement*. In the following section we describe the protein side-chain placement problem, and introduce relevant biochemical concepts and terminology. In section 4 we show how the protein side-chain placement problem can be modelled as a CLP problem. In section 5 we present the results of using our method to model several proteins, and we compare results obtained with several "rotamer libraries" (see section 3) and domain enumeration heuristics. Finally we summarise the main features of our approach, and the main conclusions that can be drawn from our results.

T. Walsh (Ed.): CP 2001, LNCS 2239, pp. 479–493, 2001.

2 Proteins and Side-Chain Modelling

Each protein contains at least one polypeptide chain, which is typically made up of hundreds of amino-acid residues; two such *residues* are shown in Figure 1. All residues have a common configuration of atoms in their *backbone* (or *main-chain*) part with a nitrogen atom (N), a central carbon atom (the alpha-carbon, or Cα) and a carboxyl group (atoms C and O). Attached to the Cα of each residue is a *side-chain.* There are twenty different side-chain types (listed in Table 1) in natural proteins, and these differ from one another in size, charge, and various other properties.

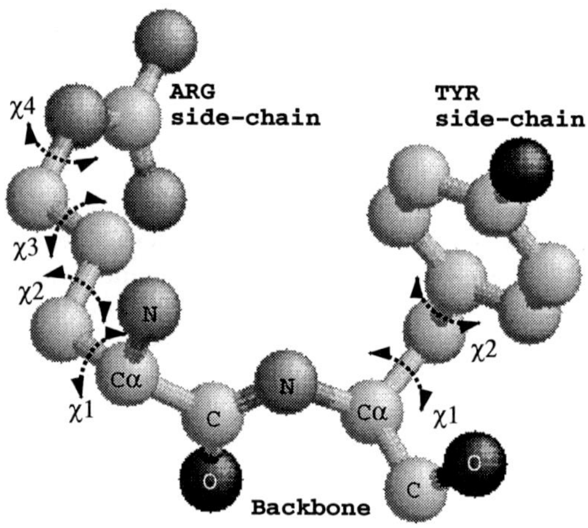

Fig. 1. The backbone and the side-chains of two residues are shown. The amino group consists of the nitrogen atom labelled N, and the carboxyl group consists of atoms C and O. The side-chains are attached to the main-chain at the Cα atoms. The χ angles are a measurement of the "twist" around rotatable side-chain bonds (as defined in [14]). These angles define the conformation of each rotamer.

Proteins that have evolved from a common ancestor will have similar (or *homologous*) amino acid sequences. The sequence of amino acid residues in a protein chain, which is always listed from the *N-terminus* to the *C-terminus* of the protein chain, can be determined relatively easily. If two protein chains have a similar sequence of amino acid residues in their chains, then these will generally have very similar 3D structures, with amino acid residues common to both sequences usually expected to occupy the same positions in the model and the known structure. The process of constructing a model of a protein based on predicted similarity to a protein whose structure has been determined previously is called *homology modelling* [5,12,18]. Early protein modelling studies were done using physical wire models (e.g. [3]), however today protein models are usually constructed by computer.

In homology modelling it is common to first construct a model of the entire protein backbone, and then to add side-chains to this backbone, adjusting the conformations of the side-chain by rotating their internal chemical bonds (labelled $\chi 1$, $\chi 2$, etc. outward along the side-chain, away from the Cα atom) so that no side-chain clashes with either the protein backbone or with any other side-chain. To achieve this we consider each atom to be a sphere with a radius (the *van der Waals* radius) determined by the atom's type, and we require that the centres of two atoms that are not covalently bonded to one another should be further apart than the sum of their van der Waals radii. The van der Waals radius of each atom is approximately 2.5 times larger than the radius of the spheres in ball-and-stick representation in Figure 1, and the resulting protein model is usually extremely well packed with atoms entirely filling the internal volume of the protein. Indeed, side-chain placement has been compared to a complex 3D jigsaw puzzle [27].

3 Side-Chain Rotamers

The principal problem encountered when modelling side-chains is the extremely large number of possible combinations of side-chain conformations — infinite if we consider side-chain bonds to be continuously variable. For practical purposes the search space can be discretised by considering a finite set of possible torsion angles for each side-chain. However, this can still result in an enormous search space: if we were to consider a rotational step size of 10°, then a protein with 100 amino acid residues, with 2 rotatable bonds per residue would yield a search space of $(36 \times 36)^{100}$ possible side-chain combinations [19].

The discovery that the distribution of side-chain conformations fell into statistically significant clusters [23], known as *rotamers*, has brought notable advances in side-chain modelling [24,7,10]. Rather than considering regular torsion angle increments for each rotatable bond, one can instead choose from a much smaller set of torsion angles representing the most common side-chain conformations observed in experimentally determined protein structures. Thus the vast combinatorial search space can be greatly reduced.

Rotamer libraries [23,28,8,7,21] typically contain up to 30-50 rotamers for side-chains with four rotatable bonds like Lys and Arg, and about three rotamers for side-chains with only one rotatable bond like Ser, Cys and Thr. An exception is the very extensive rotamer library developed by Dunbrack *et al.* [8,7] which has separate rotamer conformations listed for different backbone configurations. This reflects observations that have shown a correlation between residues' main-chain and side-chain conformations. The backbone dependent library (BBDEP) is based on Bayesian statistics and typically contains three angular conformations per rotatable side-chain bond, resulting in 81 rotamers for Lys and Arg.

Side-chain modelling methods typically consist of a potential energy function to describe the interactions of the side-chains represented by rotamers. This energy function plays an important role in discriminating between possible side-chain combinations since it is generally accepted that as the potential energy is lowered the protein model becomes more accurate. In a review of side-chain modelling [30], Vasquez states that most side-chain modelling algorithms use comparatively simple energy functions. These functions, based mainly on van der Waals interactions, can give excellent results for residues in hydrophobic cores, however the results for surface and buried polar residues can be poor, and very little difference is made by adding terms for electrostatics and hydrogen bonding [30].

Various algorithms have been used to search through the energy landscape generated by the potential energy function's description of different rotamer combinations [31,11,16,9,15]. Optimisation methods include Monte Carlo algorithms [11,12], genetic algorithms [29] and dead end elimination (DEE) [6,17].

4 Expressing Side-Chain Placement as a CLP Problem

Side-chain modelling is essentially the task of searching through a large combinatorial space of possible side-chain conformations to find a mutually consistent set — a problem for which CLP is well suited. In the modelling method presented here the main determinants of side-chain conformation are:

1. avoiding atomic clashes;
2. using the most common rotamer conformation whenever possible.

Our method starts by placing the complete set of rotamers from a rotamer library onto the protein backbone as shown in Figure 2. We assume that we already have a modelled backbone, and in testing our method we consider the extreme situation in which all side-chains have to be placed.

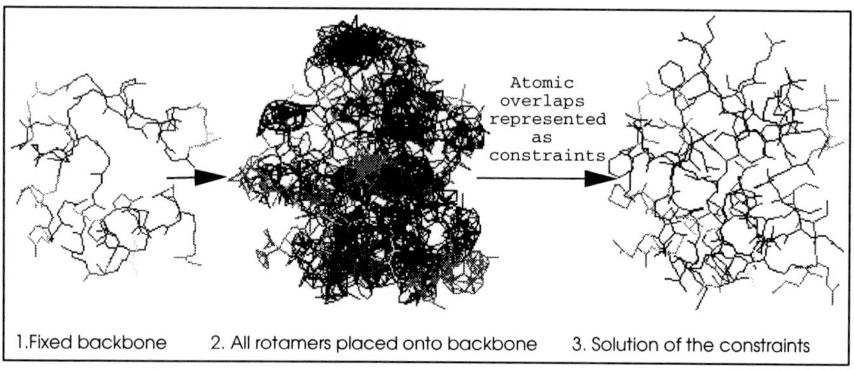

Fig. 2. The CLP method begins with a given backbone. For every residue, all rotamers in the library are placed onto the backbone. CLP selects a single rotamer for each residue.

4.1 Domain Variables

CLP domain variables are used to represent amino acid residue positions along the folded protein chain. A variable's finite domain is the set of rotamers corresponding to possible conformations of that residue's side-chain.

In the rotamer libraries used in this paper, each rotamer has a stored probability value indicating how common the conformation is for that type of residue. We have ordered the each variable's domain so that the most common rotamer conformations are at the start of the domain i.e. value 1 is the most common rotamer. Thus, the CLP solver will initially try to assign the most common rotamer to a residue.

4.2 Constraints

A C program is used to generate a constraint-based description of atomic packing by calculating clashes between rotamers and the backbone, and between rotamers of different residues. These constraints model the physical forces that prevent any clashes (or *steric overlap*) occurring between atoms i.e. no two atoms can occupy the same space. This need to avoid atomic clashes can be expressed using two types of constraint:

1. rotamers cannot be involved in any steric overlaps with the fixed backbone;
2. rotamers cannot be involved in any steric overlaps with rotamers from other residues.

Rotamers that overlap with the fixed backbone will be eliminated from their residue's finite domain. Two rotamers that overlap with each other cannot both be part of the solution, and so if one of the pair is part of the solution, then the other must be eliminated from its residue's finite domain.

To illustrate how the domain variables and constraints are expressed in SICStus Prolog syntax [4], Figure 3 shows a mini-example CLP program for a chain containing the amino acid residues Val-Lys-Tyr-Gln-Gly-Ser. When modelling full proteins, the CLP programs generated are much larger than this.

If $\mathbf{r_1}$ and $\mathbf{r_2}$ are the position vectors of the centres of two atoms, then the C program uses the following rule to decide whether those atoms overlap:

$$|\mathbf{r_1} - \mathbf{r_2}| \times \left(1 + \frac{\triangle\text{radius}}{2.5}\right) < \text{ConDist}$$

Here, ConDist is the minimum allowed interatomic distance, and $\triangle$radius is the difference in the atomic radii of the atoms being considered: all carbon and sulphur atoms are assumed to have the same radius, nitrogen atoms are 0.2Å smaller, and oxygen atoms are another 0.2Å smaller. Thus if a carbon and an oxygen atom are being considered, $\triangle\text{radius} = (0.0 + 0.4)$.

```
%
% Predicate to solve the constraints using
% the most constrained [ffc] heuristic.
%
solve_constraints :-
        constraints(ResiduePositions),
        labeling([ffc], ResiduePositions).



%
% SICStus Prolog CLP syntax for
% constraints on side-chain placement
%
constraints([VAL1, LYS2, TYR3, GLN4, GLY5, SER6]) :-

        % Finite domains for variables, e.g.
        % VAL1 has 3 rotamers, LYS2 has 81 rotamers
        %
        VAL1 in 1..3,
        LYS2 in 1..81,
        TYR3 in 1..4,
        GLN4 in 1..10,
        GLY5 in 1..1,
        SER6 in 1..3,

        % Clashes with the backbone, e.g.
        % VAL1 cannot be rotamer 2
        %
        VAL1 #\= 2,
        TYR3 #\= 3,
        TYR3 #\= 4,
        GLN4 #\= 1,
        GLN4 #\= 5,

        % Clashes between rotamers, e.g.
        % if VAL1 is rotamer 1 then TYR3 cannot be rotamer 1
        %
        VAL1 #= 1 #=> TYR3 #\= 1,
        VAL1 #= 1 #=> LYS2 #\= 1,
        VAL1 #= 1 #=> LYS2 #\= 2,
        SER6 #= 1 #=> LYS2 #\= 2,
        SER6 #= 1 #=> GLN4 #\= 2,
        SER6 #= 1 #=> GLN4 #\= 8,
        true.
```

Fig. 3. SICStus Prolog syntax for declaring CLP variables, finite domains and constraints. Programs like this are generated automatically by our system; the typical size of such programs is from 3000 to 8000 lines.

4.3 Search Strategy Used by the CLP Solver

The SICStus Prolog `labeling` predicate shown in Figure 3 has search options to control the order in which variables are selected and assigned a rotamer. When the variables are listed in the order in which the residues occur in the protein chain, the biological interpretations of the five alternative `labeling` options are as follows:

leftmost: residues are selected in order from the N-terminus towards the C-terminus.
min: the residue closest to N-terminus with the smallest lower bound, i.e. with a constraint on its most probable rotamer, is selected first.
max: the residue closest to N-terminus with the greatest upper bound, i.e. with a constraint on its most improbable rotamer, is selected first.
ff: the residue closest to N-terminus with the least number of rotamers is selected first.
ffc: the residue closest to N-terminus with the least number rotamers and with the most constraints suspended on it is selected first.

A comparison of these different enumeration heuristics is given in section 5.1.

4.4 Problems with Unsatisfiable CLP Programs

An unfortunate characteristic of a single CLP side-chain placement program is that it either works, or it doesn't — if the value of ConDist is too high, variables will be over-constrained, and a model cannot be produced. This failure to find even a poor solution for an over-constrained system is a disadvantage of using CLP to model side-chains, since even a poor solution with known weaknesses can still provide scientists with useful information about a protein's structure, and can serve as a starting point for further structural refinement.

The advantage of using the ConDist parameter when calculating steric overlaps is that it can be varied easily, tightening or loosening the constraints, in order to achieve a solution. The largest value of ConDist that produces a solution can vary greatly between proteins. Typically, small proteins, with less than 100 residues, can be modelled with a ConDist of about 2.4 Å. Larger proteins, with over 200 residues, can be modelled with a ConDist of only 1.6 Å — a value that represents some very severe steric overlaps.

The severe steric overlaps present in the models created using CLP highlight some of the problems experienced by approximating continuous side-chain conformations by fixed rotamers. In side-chain modelling methods that use explicit energy functions such close contacts lead to very high van der Waals terms that approach infinity as the distance shrinks to zero. This has led some researchers to fix the van der Waals term to a certain value for small interatomic distances [19,12,15,13].

When ConDist is at a value small enough to produce a solution, the constraints on many residues will be so weak that they will be poorly modelled. To achieve greater modelling accuracy high values of ConDist are needed to place constraints on loosely packed residues, while low values of ConDist are needed for residues that are more tightly packed. A method embracing these apparently conflicting requirements is described in section 4.6.

4.5 Null Rotamers

One method of identifying variables that are likely to be over-constrained is to use *null values* (or *null rotamers*). In doing this, we add an extra value to the end of each variable's finite domain, after the least common rotamer, that corresponds to "no (real) value found". When this value is part of the solution it means that no rotamer can be placed for the corresponding residue. Because the null rotamer has no physical representation, no constraints can be placed upon it. No matter how tight the constraints on a variable may be, there will always be a solution that contains the null rotamer. Thus, under very tightly constrained conditions, the residues in the core of the protein may be over constrained and allocated null rotamers, whereas those under-constrained residues found towards the surface of the protein will be allocated real rotamers.

4.6 An Iterative Implementation of the CLP Method

The simple CLP method for side-chain placement described above has been modified to make use of null rotamers. The basic idea is that ConDist is increased iteratively from zero to around 3.2 Å in steps of 0.4 Å so that at each iteration a CLP program is created with successively tighter packing constraints.

When ConDist is low a solution will be found easily, and this solution is stored for later use. As ConDist is increased to relatively high values, residues will become over-constrained and cause the CLP solver to fail. When this happens the CLP program is rewritten automatically, with null rotamers in the domains of all residue variables. The solution to this program will allocate null rotamers to some of the over-constrained residues. These over-constrained residues are set to the rotamer that was part of the solution solved (and stored) under the previous iteration. They are now considered to be fixed like the backbone, and do not take part in any constraints. Now another CLP program is created without null rotamers. If this program fails then null rotamers are used again, and the process repeated, until a solution is found for a program that does not use null rotamers. When this occurs the rotamers chosen are stored, and ConDist is increased.

The CLP solver will not backtrack when null rotamers are used. This is not a serious problem because our method only uses null rotamers to identify over-constrained residues. Once all the residues causing the CLP solver to fail have been identified, null rotamers are no longer used and the CLP solver is once more able to backtrack.

An outline of the improved CLP side-chain placement algorithm is shown in Figure 4.

```
find close inter-atomic distances between rotamers
ConDist = 0

while ConDist < 3.2 Angstroms

      turn off null rotamers
      automatically write CLP program for current value of ConDist
      try to solve constraints with CLP

      if no solution exists

            turn on null rotamers
            automatically write CLP program for current value of ConDist
            solve constraints with CLP (success guaranteed)
            relace any null rotamers previously recorded solution

      else CLP found a solution

            store the set of rotamers that is the solution
            evaluate model
            ConDist := ConDist + 0.4

      end else

end while
```

Fig. 4. Pseudo-code description of the iterative CLP side-chain placement algorithm.

5 Results and Discussion

We have used the iterative CLP method described in section 4.6 to investigate the accuracy of models constructed using different enumeration options and rotamer libraries, and we have compared the accuracy of our CLP method with other side-chain placement algorithms. In this study we have modelled a set of forty-three proteins [1] collated from those modelled by Keohl and Delarue [15], Shenkin *et al.* [25], and Holm and Sander [12]. All of these structures are high quality, with a resolution value less than or equal to 2.0 Å. Comparing side-chain modelling methods is complicated by the different criteria used by authors to assess the accuracy of their predictions [25,26]. Predicted side-chain conformations are commonly compared to the X-ray structures obtained from the Protein Data

[1] The Protein Data Bank [1] codes of the proteins are: 1BP2, 1CA2, 1CCR, 1CRN, 1CTF, 1HOE, 1LZ1, 1MBA, 1PAZ, 1PPD, 1PPT, 1R69, 1RDG, 1UBQ, 256B 2CAB, 2CDV, 2CGA, 2CI2, 2CTS, 2I1B, 2LYZ, 2LZT, 2MLT, 2OVO, 2RHE, 2UTG, 3APP, 3GRS, 3LZM, 4HHB, 4LYZ, 4PEP, 4PTI, 4TNC, 5CYT, 5PCY, 5PTI, 5RXN, 6LDH, 6LYZ, 7RSA, 8DFR. The number of amino acid residues in these proteins ranges from 36 to 574, with an average of 165.

Bank [1] by calculating the root mean square distance (RMSD) of the side-chain atoms (excluding hydrogens), or by comparing side-chain dihedral (χ) angles (as defined in [14]).

5.1 Enumeration Option Comparison

Figure 5 shows the accuracy of the modelling method when using the different CLP variable enumeration heuristics. Both the `ffc` and `ff` search options perform very similarly. The `leftmost` and `min` options also give similar predictions to each other, and the `max` is the least successful. We have used the `ffc` heuristic to obtain the results given in this paper.

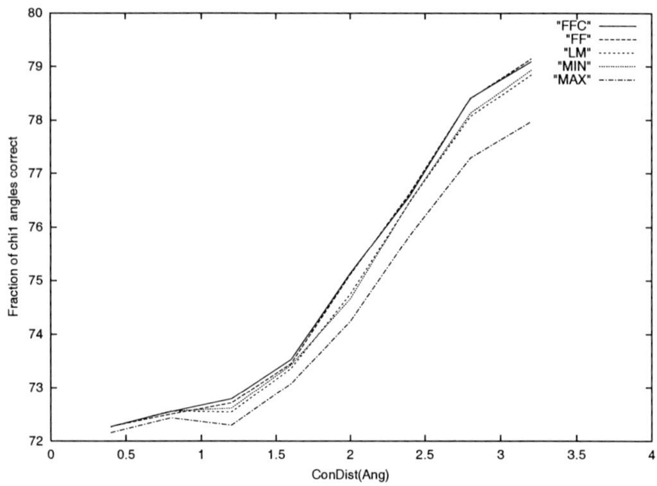

Fig. 5. The average side-chain atom RMSD, including Cβ atoms, of forty-three models built using the CLP method, with five different enumeration heuristics, and ConDist parameter increasing from 0.4 Å to 3.2 Å.

We believe that the first fail options options place the smaller side-chains first and, having determined those conformations, they propagate constraints onto the larger, more flexible side-chains. Thus the larger side-chains are packed around the smaller ones. This is the opposite to what happens when the `max` option is used: more flexible side-chains are placed first, and propagated constraints eliminate the most common conformations for small side chains with fewer rotamers.

The results presented in Figure 5 were obtained using the CULL2 library, described in Section 5.2. Tests with other rotamer libraries give similar results.

5.2 Reducing the Variables' Domain Sizes

Since each variable's domain has been ordered with the most common rotamers first, the CLP solver will try to find a solution with these rotamers before it tries the less common rotamers. In the BBDEP library rotamers are included for every region of backbone torsion space [7]. Some of these rotamers are very uncommon, have large internal clashes, and are unlikely to be genuinely observed [21]. When the rotamers of two residues are involved in a clash, the CLP solver will backtrack through the least probable rotamers of the first residue before trying a different, more common conformation of the second residue. By culling very improbable rotamers from the rotamer library we build models with only the most common rotamers. Although the maximum theoretical accuracy of the rotamer libraries has decreased because they contain fewer side-chain conformations (the complete BBDEP library covers 97% of $\chi 1$ conformations, whereas the CULL1 version covers 93%), the accuracy of the models created tends to increase, as is shown in Figures 6 and 7.

In Figures 6 and 7 we compare the accuracy of the CLP method when used with different rotamer libraries, and show that reducing the size of the rotamer library can lead to more accurate side-chain placement. These libraries have been created by removing all rotamers with probabilities less than a certain minimum value.[2] In addition we added some extra rotamers to CULL1 and CULL2. For these libraries, CULL1X and CULL2X, rotamers with $\chi 2$ angles differing by $\pm 10°$ were added. These extra rotamers are intended to alleviate the slight steric overlaps that the most common rotamers may be involved in although, as can be seen in Figures 6 and 7, the gain in accuracy is relatively small.

5.3 Comparisons with Other Side-Chain Prediction Methods

In Table 1 we show the modelling predictions for all residues with one or more rotatable side-chain bond in the set of 43 proteins, and compare our results with those obtained using SCWRL [2] and confmat [15]. Implementations of SCWRL and confmat were obtained via the web, and were tested using the same set of proteins and evaluation methods as our CLP method. Our method compares favourably with the other methods; with the CULL2 library it predicts just over 79% of $\chi 1$ angles correctly, an improvement of about 1% over SCWRL, and 6% over confmat. The method presented here, which has not been optimised for speed, took about 60 minutes to model the set of 43 proteins — 30 minutes longer than SCWRL.

[2] For the smallest library, CULL1, the amino acids Cys, Pro, Ser, Thr, Val had minimum probabilities of 0.1, Asp, Asn, Ile and Leu had minimum probabilities of 0.075, Arg, Gln, Glu, Lys, Met had minimum probabilities of 0.05, and Phe, Tyr, Trp, His had minimum probabilities of 0.025. For CULL2 the minimum probabilities were 0.075, 0.05, 0.025 and 0.125 for each of the groups, and for CULL3 the minimum probabilities were 0.05, 0.025, 0.0125 and 0. The rotamers in the BBDEP library cover 97% of the $\chi 1$ angles in our set of 43 proteins; this decreases to 96%, 95% and 93% for the CULL3, CULL2 and CULL1 libraries.

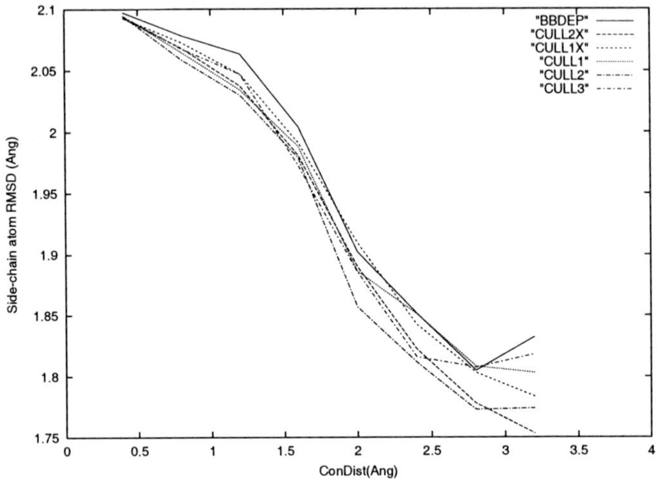

Fig. 6. The average side-chain atom RMSD, including Cβ atoms, of forty-three models built using the CLP method, with ConDist parameter increasing from 0.4 Å to 3.2 Å. Each curve represents a modification, described in the main text, to the BBDEP library [7].

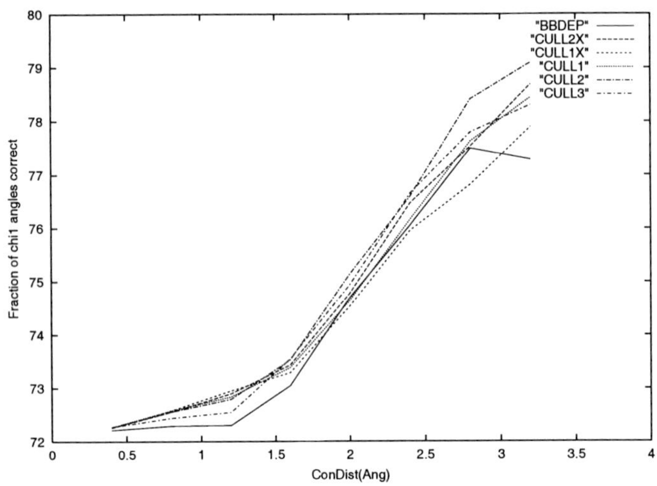

Fig. 7. The average percentage of modelled side-chains with $\chi 1$ angles within 40° of those in the forty-three X-ray structures. The models were built using the CLP method, with ConDist parameter increasing from 0.4 Å to 3.2 Å. Each curve represents a modification, described in the main text, to the BBDEP library [7].

The theoretical limit of side-chain prediction accuracy is set by the differences in X-ray structures crystallised by different laboratories [20]. More recent side-chain prediction algorithms approach this theoretical limit, modelling up to 85%

of $\chi 1$ conformations correctly [22,32], improving on the results of the SCWRL algorithm by up to 4%. However, these recent approachs are time-consuming, taking hours rather than minutes to model a single protein.

Table 1. The percentage of $\chi 1$ angles correct, are shown for each residue when modelled by the CLP side-chain method using the `ffc` enumeration heuristic and different rotamer libraries. These values were taken when ConDist was equal to 2.8Å for the BBDEP library, and 3.2Å for CULL2, and CULL2X.

Residue	No. χ Angles	Number	CLP BBDEP	CLP CULL2	CLP CULL2X	SCWRL [2]	confmat [15]
Ala	0	-	-	-	-	-	-
Arg	4	226	64	68	67	69	67
Asn	2	333	76	75	75	74	71
Asp	2	379	80	77	77	75	66
Cys	1	170	80	84	85	76	58
Gln	3	228	70	73	74	71	73
Glu	3	306	62	60	61	62	63
Gly	0	-	-	-	-	-	-
His	2	127	78	80	81	83	84
Ile	2	303	86	91	90	88	85
Leu	2	490	81	85	85	84	84
Lys	4	432	67	67	68	67	67
Met	3	126	76	80	80	78	74
Phe	2	222	88	93	91	91	92
Pro	2	275	89	89	81	90	83
Ser	1	483	60	62	62	60	38
Thr	1	362	82	84	84	83	74
Trp	2	103	90	91	90	91	90
Tyr	2	219	92	94	94	89	93
Val	1	437	86	86	86	89	84
Overall			77.5	79.1	78.7	78.3	73.3

6 Conclusions

The side-chain placement problem can be expressed as a CLP program in which rotamer conformations are used as values for finite domain variables, and bad steric contacts involving rotamers are represented as constraints. We have described an initial CLP method of side-chain placement that is fast and accurate. Our method uses a series of automatically generated CLP programs to represent successively tighter side-chain packing constraints. By using these programs iteratively our method predicts 79% of $\chi 1$ angles correctly.

We have presented results obtained using several different domain enumeration heuristics, and have found those based on "first fail" to be the most successful for this application. We have constructed several rotamer libraries based on the backbone independent library of Dunbrack *et al.* [7] and our results indicate that discarding the least common rotamers from this library both improves the accuracy of the predicted side-chain conformations, and reduces the size of the combinatorial search space.

Acknowledgements. M.T.S. is supported by a BBSRC CASE award with Biovation Ltd.

References

1. F. C. Bernstein, T. F. Koetzle, G. J. B. Williams, E. F. Mayer, M. D. Bruce, J. R. Rodgers, O. Kennard, T. Shimanouchi, and M. Tasumi. The Protein Data Bank: a Computer-Based Archival File for Macromolecular Structures. *J. Mol. Biol.*, 112:535–542, 1977.
2. M. J. Bower, F. E. Cohen, and R. L. Dunbrack. Prediction of protein side-chain rotamers from a backbone-dependent rotamer library: A new homology modeling tool. *J. Mol. Biol.*, 267:1268–1282, 1997.
3. W.J. Browne, A.C.T. North, D.C. Phillips, K. Brew, T.C. Vanman, and R.L. Hill. A Possible Three-dimensional Structure of Bovine α-Lactalbumin based on that of Hen's Egg-White Lysozyme. *J. Mol. Biol.*, 42:65–86, 1969.
4. M. Carlsson, G. Ottosson, and B. Carlson. An open-ended finite domain constraint solver. *Proc. Programming Languages: Implementations, Logics, and Programs*, 1997.
5. G. Chinea, G. Padron, R. W. W. Hooft, C. Sander, and G. Vriend. The use of position specific rotamers in model building by homology. *Prot. Struct. Funct. Genet.*, 23(415–421), 1995.
6. J. Desmet, M. De Maeyer, B. Hazes, and I. Lasters. The dead-end elimination theorem and its use in protein side-chain positioning. *Nature*, 356:539–542, 1992.
7. R. L. Dunbrack and F. E. Cohen. Bayesian statistical analysis of side-chain rotamer preferences. *Protein Science*, 6:1661–1681, 1997.
8. R. L. Dunbrack and M. Karplus. Backbone-dependent rotamer library for proteins: application to side-chain prediction. *J. Mol. Biol.*, 230:543–574, 1993.
9. D. B. Gordon and S. L. Mayo. Branch-and-terminate: a combinatorial optimization algorithm for protein design. *Structure*, 7:1089–1098, 1999.
10. J. Heringa and P. Argos. Strain in protein structures as viewed through nonrotameric side-chain: I. their positions and interaction. *Prot. Struct. Funct. Genet.*, 37:30–43, 1999.
11. L. Holm and C. Sander. Database Algorithm for Generating Protein backbone and Side-chain Co-ordinates from a Cα Trace. *J. Mol. Biol.*, 218:183–194, 1991.
12. L. Holm and C. Sander. Fast and Simple Monte Carlo Algorithm for Side Chain Optimization in Proteins: Application to Model building by Homology. *Prot. Struct. Funct. Genet.*, 14:213–233, 1992.
13. J. K. Hwang and W. F. Liao. Side-chain prediction by neural networks and simulated annealing optimization. *Prot. Eng.*, 8:363–370, 1995.
14. IUPAC-IUB Commission on Biochemical Nomenclature. Abbreviations and Symbols for the Description of the Conformation of Polypeptide Chains. *Eur. J. Biochem.*, 17:193–201, 1970.

15. P. Koehl and M. Delarue. Application of a self-consistent mean field theory to predict protein side-chains conformation and estimate their conformational entropy. *J. Mol. Biol.*, 239:249–275, 1994.
16. H. Kono and J. Doi. A new method for side-chain conformation prediction using a hopfield network and reproduced rotamers. *J. Comp. Chem.*, 17:1667–1683, 1996.
17. I. Lasters, M. De Maeyer, and J. Desmet. Enhanced dead-end elimination in the search for the global minimum energy conformation of a collection of protein side chains. *Prot. Eng.*, 8:815–822, 1995.
18. C. A. Laughton. Prediction of Protein Side-chain Conformations from Local Three-dimensional Homology Relationships. *J. Mol. Biol.*, 235:1088–1097, 1994.
19. C. Lee and S. Subbiah. Prediction of protein side-chain conformation by packing optimization. *J. Mol. Biol.*, 217:373–388, 1991.
20. M. Levitt, M. Gerstein, E. Huang, S. Subbiah, and J. Tsai. Protein folding: The endgame. *Annu. Rev. Biochem.*, 1997.
21. S. C. Lovell, M. Word, J. S. Richardson, and D. C. Richardson. The Penultimate Rotamer Library. *Prot. Struct. Funct. Genet.*, 40:389–408, 2000.
22. J. Mendes, A.M. Baptista, M.A. Carrondo, and C.M. Soares. Improved modeling of side-chains in proteins with rotamer-based methods: A flexible rotamer model. *Prot. Struct. Funct. Genet.*, 37:530–543, 1999.
23. J. W. Ponder and F. M. Richards. Tertiary templates for proteins. *J. Mol. Biol.*, 193:775–791, 1987.
24. H. Schrauber. Rotamers: to be or not to be? *J. Mol. Biol.*, 230:592–612, 1993.
25. P.S. Shenkin, H. Farid, and J.S. Fetrow. Prediction and evaluation of side-chain conformations for protein backbone structures. *Prot. Struct. Funct. Genet.*, 26:323–352, 1996.
26. M.T. Swain and G.J.L. Kemp. Modelling protein side-chain conformations using constraint logic programming. *Computers Chem.*, in press.
27. W. Taylor. New paths from dead ends. *Nature*, 356:748–479, 1992.
28. P. Tuffery, C. Etchebest, and S. Hazout. Prediction of protein side chain conformations: a study on the influence of backbone accuracy on conformation stability in the rotamer space. *Prot. Eng.*, 10:361–372, 1997.
29. P. Tuffery, C. Etchebest, S. Hazout, and R. Lavery. A new approach to the rapid determination of protein side-chain conformations. *J. Biomol. Struct. Dynam.*, 8:1267–1289, 1991.
30. M. Vasquez. Modeling side-chain conformations. *Curr. Opin. Struct. Biol.*, 6:217–221, 1996.
31. C. Wilson, L. M. Gregoret, and D. A. Agard. Modeling side-chain conformation for homologous proteins using an energy-based rotamer search. *J. Mol. Biol.*, 229:996–1006, 1993.
32. Z. Xiang and B. Honig. Extending the accuracy limits of prediction for side-chain conformations. *J. Mol. Biol.*, 2001.

Fast, Constraint-Based Threading of HP-Sequences to Hydrophobic Cores

Rolf Backofen and Sebastian Will*

Institut für Informatik, LMU München
Oettingenstraße 67, D-80538 München
{backofen,wills}@informatik.uni-muenchen.de

Abstract. Lattice protein models are used for hierarchical approaches to protein structure prediction, as well as for investigating principles of protein folding. So far, one has the problem that there exists no lattice that can model real protein conformations with good quality *and* for which an efficient method to find native conformations is known.
We present the first method for the FCC-HP-Model [3] that is capable of finding native conformations for real-sized HP-sequences. It has been shown [23] that the FCC lattice can model real protein conformations with coordinate root mean square deviation below 2 Å.
Our method uses a constraint-based approach. It works by first calculating maximally compact sets of points (hydrophobic cores), and then threading the given HP-sequence to the hydrophobic cores such that the core is occupied by H-monomers.

1 Introduction

The protein structure prediction is one of the most important unsolved problems of computational biology. It can be specified as follows: Given a protein by its sequence of amino acids (more generally monomers), what is its native structure? NP-completeness of the problem has been proven for many different models (including lattice and off-lattice models) [10,12]. These results strongly suggest that the protein folding problem is NP-hard in general. Therefore, it is unlikely that a general, efficient algorithm for solving this problem can be given. Actually, the situation is even worse, since the general principles how natural proteins fold into a native structure are unknown. This is cumbersome since rational design is commonly viewed to be of paramount importance e.g. for drug design, where one faces the difficulty to design proteins that have a unique and stable native structure.

To tackle structure prediction and related problems, simplified models have been introduced. They are used in hierarchical approaches for protein folding (e.g., [29], see also the meeting review of CASP3 [18], where several groups have successfully used lattice models). Furthermore, they have became a major tool for investigating general properties of protein folding.

* Supported by the PhD programme "Graduiertenkolleg Logik in der Informatik" (GKLI) of the "Deutsche Forschungsgemeinschaft" (DFG).

T. Walsh (Ed.): CP 2001, LNCS 2239, pp. 494–508, 2001.

Most important are the so-called lattice models. The simplifications commonly used in this class of models are: 1) monomers (or residues) are represented using a unified size 2) bond length is unified 3) the positions of the monomers are restricted to lattice positions and 4) a simplified energy function. Native conformations are those having minimal energy.

In the literature, many different lattice models (i.e., lattices and energy functions) have been used. Examples of how such models can be used for predicting the native structure or for investigating principles of protein folding are given in [28,1,15,27,17,2,20,29]. Of course, the question arises which lattice and energy function have to be preferred. There are two (somewhat conflicting) aspects that have to be evaluated when choosing a model: 1) the accuracy of the lattice in approximating real protein conformations and the ability of the energy function to discriminate native from non-native conformations, and 2) the availability and quality of search algorithm for finding minimal (or nearly minimal) energy conformations.
While the first aspect is well-investigated in the literature (e.g., [23,13]), the second aspect is underrepresented. By and large, there are mainly two different heuristic search approaches used in the literature: 1) Ad hoc restriction of the search space to compact or quasi-compact conformations (a good example is [28], where the search space is restricted to conformations forming an $n \times n \times n$-cube). The main drawback here is that the restriction to compact conformation is not motivated biologically for a complete amino acid sequence (as done in these approaches), but only for the hydrophobic amino acids. In consequence, the restriction either has to be relaxed and then leads to an inefficient algorithm or is chosen too strong and thus may exclude optimal conformations. 2) Stochastic sampling like Monte Carlo methods with simulated annealing, genetic algorithms etc. Here, the degree of (sub)optimality for the best conformations and the quality of the sampling cannot be determined by state of the art methods.[1]

In this paper, we follow the proposal by [3] to use a lattice model with a simple energy function, namely the HP (hydrophobic-polar) model (which has been introduced in [19] using cubic lattice), but on a better suited lattice, namely the face-centered cubic lattice (*FCC*). In the FCC, every point has 12 neighbors (instead of 6 as in the cubic lattice). The resulting model is called the *FCC-HP-model*. In the HP-model, the 20 letter alphabet of amino acids is reduced to a two letter alphabet, namely H and P. H represents *hydrophobic* amino acids, whereas P represent *polar* or hydrophilic amino acids. The energy function for the HP-model is given by the matrix as shown in Figure 1(a). It simply states that the energy contribution of a contact between two monomers is -1 if both are H-monomers, and 0 otherwise. Two monomers form a *contact* in some specific conformation if they are not connected via a bond, and occupied positions are nearest neighbors. A conformation with *minimal energy* (called

[1] Despite that there are mathematical treatments of Monte Carlo methods with simulated annealing, the partition function of the ensemble (which is needed for a precise statement) is in general unknown.

(a)

	H	P
H	-1	0
P	0	0

(b) 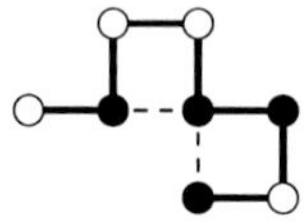

Fig. 1. Energy matrix and sample conformation for the HP-model

native conformation) is just a conformation with the maximal number of contacts between H-monomers. Just recently, the structure prediction problem has been shown to be NP-complete even for the HP-model [10,12].

A sample conformation for the sequence PHPPHHPH in the two-dimensional cubic lattice with energy −2 is shown in Figure 1(b). The white beads represent P, the black ones H monomers. The two contacts are indicated via dashed lines.

There are two reasons for using the FCC-HP-Model:
1) The FCC can model real protein conformations with good quality (see [23], where it was shown that FCC can model protein conformations with coordinate root mean square deviation below 2 Å)
2) The HP-model models the important aspect of hydrophobicity. Essentially, it is a polymer chain representation (on a lattice) with one stabilizing interaction each time two hydrophobic residues have unit distance. This enforces compactification while polar residues and solvent is not explicitly regarded. The idea of the model is the assumption that the hydrophobic effect determines the overall configuration of a protein (for a definition of the HP-model, see [19,13]).

Once a search algorithm for minimal energy conformations is established for this FCC-HP-model, one can employ it as a filter step in a hierarchical approach. This way, one can improve the energy function to achieve better biological relevance and go on to resemble amino acid positions more accurately.

Related Work and Contribution. In this paper, we describe a successful application of constraint-programming for finding native conformations in the FCC-HP-model. In this respect, the situation as given in the literature was not very promising. Although the FCC-HP-model is known to be an important lattice model, no exact algorithm was known for finding native conformations in any model different from the cubic lattice. Even for the cubic lattice, there are only three exact algorithms known [30,4,7], which are able to enumerate minimal (or nearly minimal) energy conformations, all for the cubic lattice. However, the ability of this lattice to approximate real protein conformations is poor. For example, [3] pointed out especially the parity problem in the cubic lattice. This drawback of the cubic lattice is that every two monomers with chain positions of the same parity cannot form a contact.

So far, beside heuristic approaches (e.g., the hydrophobic zipper [14], the genetic algorithm by Unger and Moult [26], the chain growth algorithm by Bornberg-Bauer [11], or [8], which is a method applicable for any regular lattice), there is only one approximation algorithm [3] for the FCC. It finds conformations whose number of contacts is guaranteed to be 60% of the number of contacts of the native conformation (which is far from being useful, since, even if the algorithm yields far better results, the information on the quality of the outcome is still too fuzzy). The situation was even worse, since the main ingredient needed for an exact method, namely bounds on the number of HH-contacts given some partial information about the conformation, was missing. This changed with [5, 6], where such a bound is introduced and applied to the problem of finding maximally compact hydrophobic cores. Given a conformation of an HP-sequence, the *hydrophobic core* of this sequence is the set of all points occupied by H-monomers. A hydrophobic core of n-points is *maximally compact* if there is no packing of n-points in the FCC which has more contacts. In this paper, we show how we can efficiently thread a given HP-sequence to a maximally compact hydrophobic core[2]. We have implemented our method in the constraint language Oz [25] with extensions in C++.

2 Preliminaries

Given vectors $\boldsymbol{v_1}, \ldots, \boldsymbol{v_n}$, the lattice generated by $\boldsymbol{v_1}, \ldots, \boldsymbol{v_n}$ is the minimal set of points L such that $\forall \boldsymbol{u}, \boldsymbol{v} \in L$, both $\boldsymbol{u}+\boldsymbol{v} \in L$ and $\boldsymbol{u}-\boldsymbol{v} \in L$. The *face-centered cubic lattice* (FCC) is defined as the lattice

$$D_3 = \{ \left(\begin{smallmatrix} x \\ y \\ z \end{smallmatrix}\right) \mid \left(\begin{smallmatrix} x \\ y \\ z \end{smallmatrix}\right) \in \mathbb{Z}^3 \text{ and } x+y+z \text{ is even} \}.$$

We use $\uplus$ to denote disjoint union. The set N_{D_3} of *minimal vectors* connecting so-called *neighbors* in D_3 is given by

$$N_{D_3} = \left\{ \left(\begin{smallmatrix} 0 \\ \pm 1 \\ \pm 1 \end{smallmatrix}\right) \right\} \uplus \left\{ \left(\begin{smallmatrix} \pm 1 \\ 0 \\ \pm 1 \end{smallmatrix}\right) \right\} \uplus \left\{ \left(\begin{smallmatrix} \pm 1 \\ \pm 1 \\ 0 \end{smallmatrix}\right) \right\}.$$

Thus, every point in the FCC has 12 neighbors. A *hydrophobic core* is is a function $f : D_3 \rightarrow \{0,1\}$, where $f^{-1}(1) \neq \emptyset$. The purpose of a hydrophobic core is to characterize the set of positions occupied by H-monomers. We will identify a hydrophobic core f with the set of all *points occupied by* f, i.e. $\{\boldsymbol{p} \mid f(\boldsymbol{p}) = 1\}$. Hence, for hydrophobic cores f_1, f_2 we will use standard set notation for size $|f_1|$, union $f_1 \cup f_2$, disjoint union $f_1 \uplus f_2$, and intersection $f_1 \cap f_2$. Given a hydrophobic core f, we define the *number of contacts of* f by $\mathrm{con}(f) := \frac{1}{2} |\{(\boldsymbol{p}, \boldsymbol{p}') \mid f(\boldsymbol{p}) \wedge f(\boldsymbol{p}') \wedge (\boldsymbol{p} - \boldsymbol{p}') \in N_{D_3}\}|$. A hydrophobic core f is *maximally compact* if $\mathrm{con}(f) = \max\{\mathrm{con}(f') \mid |f| = |f'|\}$.

An *HP-sequence* is an element in $\{H,P\}^*$. With s_i we denote the ith element of a sequence s. A *conformation* c of a sequence s is a function $c : \{1, \ldots, |s|\} \rightarrow D_3$ such that 1) $\forall 1 \leq i < |s| : c(i) - c(i+1) \in N_{D_3}$, and 2) $\forall i \neq j : c(i) \neq c(j)$. The hydrophobic core associated with a conformation c is defined as the set of positions occupied by an H-monomer in c. The *number of contacts* $\mathrm{con}(c)$ of a conformation c is defined to be $\mathrm{con}(f)$, where f is the hydrophobic core associated with c. A conformation c is called *native for* s if it has maximal number of contacts.

A *finite CSP (constraint satisfaction problem)* $P = (\mathcal{X}, \mathcal{D}, \mathcal{C})$ is defined by

[2] Of course, the methods described in this paper can also be applied to hydrophobic cores that are not maximally compact.

- a set of *variables* $\mathcal{X}$,
- a set of finite domains $\mathcal{D}$, where the domain of $x \in \mathcal{X}$ is $\mathrm{dom}(x) \in \mathcal{D}$.
- a set of constraints $\mathcal{C}$ between the variables.

A constraint C on the tuple $X(C) = (x_1, \ldots, x_n)$ of variables is interpreted as a subset $\mathrm{T}(C)$ of the Cartesian product $\mathrm{dom}(x_1) \times \cdots \times \mathrm{dom}(x_n)$ which specifies allowed combinations of values for the variables. A constraint C, where $X(C) = (x_1, \ldots, x_n)$, is called *n-ary*.

$a \in \mathrm{dom}(x)$ is *consistent* with a constraint C, if either $x \notin X(C)$ or x is the $i-th$ variable of C and $\exists \tau \in \mathrm{T}(C) : a = \tau_i$. A constraint C is *(hyper-)arc consistent* iff for all $x_i \in X(C)$, $\mathrm{dom}(x_i) \neq \emptyset$ and for all $a \in \mathrm{dom}(x_i)$ holds a is consistent with C.

2.1 Enumerating Hydrophobic Cores

We are interested in maximally compact hydrophobic cores, since a conformation with a maximally compact hydrophobic core is already native.[3] We recall the main principles for calculating maximally compact hydrophobic cores as described in [5,6].

To determine maximally compact hydrophobic cores, we partition a hydrophobic core f into cores $f_1, \ldots, f_k$ of the layers $x = 1, \ldots, x = k$. For searching a maximal hydrophobic core f, we do a branch-and-bound search on k and $f_1 \ldots f_k$. Of course, the problem is to give good bounds that allow us to cut off many k and $f_1 \ldots f_k$ that will not maximize $\mathrm{con}(f_1 \uplus \ldots \uplus f_k)$. For this purpose, we distinguish between contacts in a single layer ($= \mathrm{con}(f_i)$ for $1 \leq i \leq k$), and interlayer contacts $\mathrm{IC}_{f_i}^{f_{i+1}}$ for $1 \leq i < k$ between two successive layers. Interlayer contacts are pairs $(\boldsymbol{p}, \boldsymbol{p}')$ such that $\boldsymbol{p}$ and $\boldsymbol{p}'$ are neighbors, $\boldsymbol{p} \in f_i$ and $\boldsymbol{p}' \in f_{i+1}$. The hard part is to bound the number of contacts between two successive layers, since a simple but tight bound for the number of (intra)layer contacts can be taken from the literature [30].

For defining the bound on the number of contacts between two successive layers, we introduce the notion of an i-point, where $i = 1, 2, 3, 4$. Any point in $x = c+1$ can have at most 4 neighbors in the plane $x = c$. Let f be a hydrophobic core of the plane $x = c$. Call a point $\boldsymbol{p}$ in plane $x = c+1$ an *i-point for f* if it has i neighbors in plane $x = c$ that are contained in f (where $i \leq 4$). Of course, if one occupies an i-point in plane $x = c+1$, then this point generates i contacts between layer $x = c$ and $x = c+1$. In the following, we will restrict ourself to the case where $c = 1$ for simplicity. Of course, the calculation is independent of the choice of c.

Consider as an example the two hydrophobic cores f_1 of plane $x = 1$ and f_2 of plane $x = 2$ as shown in Figure 2. f_1 contains 5 points, and f_2 contains 3 points. Since f_2 contains one 4-point, one 3-point and one 2-point of f_1, there are 9 contacts between these two layers. It is easy to see that we generate the most contacts between layers $x = 1$ and $x = 2$ by first occupying the 4-points,

[3] Of course, there can be the rare case that there is a native conformation whose hydrophobic core is *not* maximally compact.

then the 3 points and so on until we reach the number of points to be occupied in layer $x = 2$.[4]

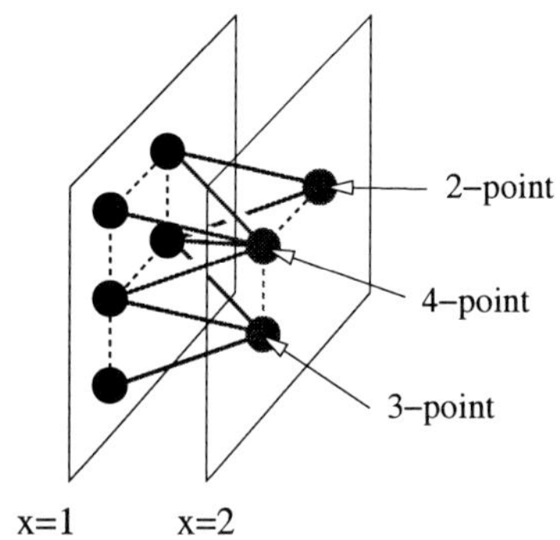

Fig. 2. H-Positions in FCC

For this reason, we are interested in calculating the maximal number of i-points (for $i = 1, 2, 3, 4$), given only the number of colored points n in layer $x = 1$. But this would overestimate the number of possible contacts, since we would maximize the number of 4-, 3-, 2- and 1- points independently from each other. We have found a dependency between these numbers, which requires to fix the side length (a, b) of the minimal rectangle around all colored points in layer $x = 1$ (called the *frame*). In our example, the frame is $(3, 2)$.

Denote with $max_i(n, a, b)$ the maximal number of i-points in layer $x = 2$ for any hydrophobic core of layer $x = 1$ with n points and frame (a, b). Then we have found that

$$max_4(n,a,b) = n + 1 - a - b \qquad max_2(n,a,b) = 2a + 2b - 2\ell - 4$$
$$max_3(n,a,b) = \ell \qquad max_1(n,a,b) = \ell + 4.$$

The remaining part is to find $\ell = max_3(n, a, b)$, which is described in detail in [5,6]. This calculation involves several special cases to treat layers that are not sufficiently filled with H-monomers. Using these $max_i(n, a, b)$, we can define a bound

$$B^{n_{i+1}}_{n_i,a_i,b_i} \geq \max \left\{ \mathrm{IC}^{f_{i+1}}_{f_i} \middle| \begin{array}{c} \#f_i = n_i,\ f_i \text{ has frame } (a_i, b_i), \\ \text{and } \#f_{i+1} = n_{i+1}, \end{array} \right\}$$

where $1 \leq i \leq k-1$ and $\#X$ denotes the cardinality of a set X. This bound can be calculated in polynomial time using dynamic programming [5,6].

This bound is used in searching for a maximally compact core for n H-monomers as follows. Instead of directly enumerating k and all possible cores $f_1 \uplus \ldots \uplus f_k$, we search through all possible sequences $((n_1, a_1, b_1) \ldots (n_k, a_k, b_k))$ of parameters with the property that $n = \sum_i n_i$. By using the $B^{n_{i+1}}_{n_i,a_i,b_i}$, only a few layer sequences have to be considered further. For these optimal layer sequences, we search for all admissible cores $f_1 \uplus \ldots \uplus f_k$ using again a constraint-based approach. Our implementation is able to find maximally hydrophobic cores for n upto 100 within seconds.

3 Threading an HP-Sequence to a Hydrophobic Core

3.1 Problem Description and Modeling

Since we are able to determine maximally hydrophobic cores, it remains to thread an HP-sequence to such an optimal core in order to get HP-optimally

[4] Note that this strategy might not result necessarily in the coloring with the maximal number of contacts, since we might loose contacts within the layer $x = 2$.

folded structures for the sequence. We tackle the problem by a constraint based approach.

For this reason, let a hydrophobic core be given as a set of lattice points **C**. The sequence is given as a word s in $\{\mathrm{H},\mathrm{P}\}^*$. For correct input, the size of **C** equals the number of H's occurrences in the sequence.

The protein structure is modeled by a set of variables $x_1,\ldots,x_{|s|}$, whose finite domains are sets of lattice points, resp. more generally nodes of a graph, where a graph G is a tuple (V,E) of the finite set of nodes V and the set of edges $E \subseteq V \times V$. The problem is now to find a solution, i.e. an assignment of the monomers to nodes, satisfying the following constraints

1. the nodes x_i, where $s_i = \mathrm{H}$ and $1 \leq i \leq |s|$, are elements of **C**.
2. all the x_i, where $1 \leq i \leq |s|$, are different
3. the nodes $x_1,\ldots,x_{|s|}$ form a path

Note that for correct input, the first constraint implies that P monomers are not in the core. However, due to the finite chain length we can determine finite domains for the P-representing variables. The second constraint tells that a protein structure has to be self avoiding. Finally, the last constraint tells that chain bonds between monomers are to be preserved in a protein structure, such that the monomer positions form a path through the lattice.

Some attention has to be paid to the fact that many constraint systems do only support integer finite domain variables, whereas in our formulation domains are lattice nodes. Since depending on the input only a finite set of nodes can be assigned in solutions, we straightforwardly solve this by assigning unique integers to these nodes.

3.2 Path Constraints

The treatment of the first constraint of the preceeding section involves the computation of domains and the assignment of domains to the variables. Both of the remaining constraints can be handled globally. The global treatment of the so called all-different constraint is well described in [24]. Thus, we will focus on the treatment of the path constraint. We will further discuss how one gets further propagation by combining the two constraints.

For generality, we discuss the constraints on arbitrary finite graphs. Clearly, we can use the results for the FCC lattice afterwards. There, the set of graph nodes is a subset of the lattice nodes and the edges are all pairs of graph nodes in minimal lattice distance.

In the following, we fix a graph $G = (V,E)$. A *path of length* n is a word $p = p_1 \ldots p_n$ of length n of alphabet V, such that

$$\forall 1 \leq i \leq n-1 : (p_i, p_{i+1}) \in E.$$

Denote the set of paths of length n by $\mathrm{paths}(n)$. Note that intentionally paths are allowed to contain cycles due to the definition.

We define a path constraint to state that the nodes assigned to the argument variables form a path.

Definition 1 (Path Constraint). *Let $x_1, \ldots, x_n$ be variables. We call a path $p \in \mathrm{paths}(n)$* consistent *for $x_1, \ldots, x_n$, iff $\forall 1 \leq i \leq n : p_i \in \mathrm{dom}(x_i)$ holds.*
The path constraint *$C = \mathrm{Path}(x_1, \ldots, x_n)$ is defined by the tuples*

$$\mathrm{T}(C) = \{p \in \mathrm{paths}(n) | p \text{ is consistent for } x_1, \ldots, x_n\}.$$

Hyper-arc consistency of this path constraint is a local property in the following sense. By a general result of Freuder [16], arc consistency amounts to global consistency in a tree-structured network of binary constraints. The next lemma is an instance of this result.

Lemma 1. *Let $x_1, \ldots, x_n$ be variables.* $\mathrm{Path}(x_1, \ldots, x_n)$ *is hyper-arc consistent, iff for $1 \leq i \leq n-1$ all constraints* $\mathrm{Path}(x_i, x_{i+1})$ *are arc consistent.*

Due to this lemma, the hyper-arc consistency of the n-ary path constraint is reduced to the arc consistency of the set of all 2-ary path constraints.

3.3 Combining Path and All-Different Constraint

The combination of the path constraint with the all-different constraint yields a new constraint which allows only self avoiding paths. Formally, let $x_1, \ldots, x_n$ be variables, define the *all-different constraint* $C = \mathrm{AllDiff}(x_1, \ldots, x_n)$ by

$$\mathrm{T}(C) = \left\{ (\tau_1, \ldots, \tau_n) \in \mathrm{dom}(x_1) \times \cdots \times \mathrm{dom}(x_n) \middle| \forall 1 \leq i < j \leq n : \tau_i \neq \tau_j \right\}.$$

We define the *self avoiding path constraint* $\mathrm{SAPath}(x_1, \ldots, x_n)$ by

$$\mathrm{T}(\mathrm{SAPath}(x_1, \ldots, x_n)) = \mathrm{T}(\mathrm{AllDiff}(x_1, \ldots, x_n)) \cap \mathrm{T}(\mathrm{Path}(x_1, \ldots, x_n)).$$

Unfortunately, we are not aware of any efficient arc consistency algorithm for this combined constraint in the literature. Furthermore, it is unlikely that there exists one. It is well known that many problems involving self-avoiding walks (we use the term path here), especially counting of such walks, are intrinsically hard and there are no efficient algorithms to solve them [21].

On the other hand, the treatment of self avoiding paths promises much better propagation in practice. Therefore, we propose a relaxation of the intractable self-avoiding path arc consistency in the following. An efficiently tractable relaxation one may think of first, is to constrain the paths to be non-reversing. Non-reversing paths are paths which do not turn back immediately, hence their class lies between general paths and self-avoiding paths. Here, we choose a more general approach and define the following sets of paths.

Definition 2. *Let $1 \leq k \leq n$. A k*-avoiding path *$p = p_1 \ldots p_n$* of length *n is a path $p \in \mathrm{paths}(n)$, where for all $1 \leq i \leq n-k+1$, the $p_i \ldots p_{i+k-1}$ are all different. We define that for $k > n$, k-avoiding is equivalent to n-avoiding. Denote the set of k-avoiding paths of length n by* $\mathrm{paths}[k](n)$.

Note that obviously, general paths (resp. self-avoiding paths) of length n are special cases of k-avoiding paths namely 1-avoiding paths (resp. n-avoiding paths) of length n. For graphs with symmetric and non-reflexive edges, the property non-reversing is equivalent to 3-avoiding. Obviously by definition, $\text{paths}[k'](n) \subseteq \text{paths}[k](n)$ holds for all $1 \leq k \leq k' \leq n$.

Let $x_1, \ldots, x_n$ be variables. Define the *set of k-avoiding paths consistent with* $x_1, \ldots, x_n$ as $\text{cpaths}[k](x_1, \ldots, x_n)$. We define corresponding constraints, which constrain their variables to form k-avoiding paths. Define the *k-avoiding path constraint* $\text{Path}[k](x_1, \ldots, x_n)$ by

$$\mathrm{T}(\text{Path}[k](x_1, \ldots, x_n)) = \text{cpaths}[k](x_1, \ldots, x_n).$$

Analogously to the general path constraint the k-avoiding path constraints possess locality, i.e. we get arc consistency of an n-ary k-avoiding path constraint by the arc consistency of the k-ary k-avoiding path constraints on every length k subsequences of variables.

Since the k-ary constraints have to be computed independently by searching for self-avoiding paths, the reduction to local arc consistency leads to unnecessary inefficiency. To avoid this, we propose a global algorithm in the following. This will be rewarded by even stronger propagation possibilities.

The key to our algorithm is the counting of paths. For arc consistency, we need to know, whenever there is no path left, where a i-th monomer is positioned on a node v. It is a good starting point to count the number of all (consistent) k-avoiding paths.

Denote the cardinality of a set X by $\#X$. For computing the number of paths $\#\,\text{cpaths}[k](x_1, \ldots, x_n)$, we will first define the *set of k-avoiding paths consistent with $x = x_1, \ldots, x_n$ with suffix (path) $q = q_1 \ldots q_m$* for $n \geq m$ as

$$\text{scpaths}[k](x)[q] = \left\{ p \in \text{cpaths}[k](x) \middle| \forall 1 \leq i \leq m : p_{n-m+i} = q_i \right\}$$

To resemble an efficient implementation more closely, we define $\text{sp}[k+1](x)[q]$ analogous to $\text{scpaths}[k](x)[q]$ with the only difference that $\text{sp}[k+1](x)[q]$ is only defined when q is consistent with $x_{n-k+1}, \ldots, x_n$. Note that for all practical purposes, we will consider only $\text{scpaths}[k](x)[q]$ where $|q| = k-1$. The idea is that one has to remember a suffix (or later a prefix) of length $k-1$ in order to check k-avoiding.

Lemma 2. *Let $x = x_1, \ldots, x_n$ be variables, $0 < k \leq n$.*

The number of paths $\#\,\text{cpaths}[k+1](x)$ is equal to the sum

$$\sum_{q \in \text{paths}(k)} \#\,\text{scpaths}[k+1](x)[q].$$

For $q = q_1 \ldots q_k \in \text{paths}(k)$, the following number of paths can be computed recursively.

$$\#\,\text{scpaths}[k+1](x)[q] = \begin{cases} \#\,\text{sp}[k+1](x)[q] & q \in \text{cpaths}[k](x_{n-k+1}, \ldots, x_n) \\ 0 & \textit{otherwise}, \end{cases}$$

where for $q \in \text{cpaths}[k](x_{n-k+1}, \ldots, x_n)$,

$$\#\text{sp}[k+1](x)[q] = \begin{cases} 1 & n = k \\ \sum\limits_{\substack{(q_0,q_1)\in E,\\ q_0 \notin \{q_1,\ldots,q_k\},\\ q_0 \in \text{dom}(x_{n-k})}} \#\text{sp}[k+1](x_1,\ldots,x_{n-1})[q_0 \ldots q_{k-1}] & n > k. \end{cases}$$

Clearly, the numbers of paths with suffixes can be computed efficiently by a dynamic programming algorithm furnished by the recursive definition.

This algorithm to compute the numbers of k-avoiding paths of maximal length n, where $2 \leq k \leq n$, has a polynomial complexity in n and the number of nodes $|V|$.

Note that the lemma handles only the case of k-avoiding paths, where $k \geq 2$. The reason is that for the path property itself we have to remember a history of minimal length 1. Hence, the number of 1-avoiding paths can not be computed more efficiently than the number of 2-avoiding paths. Obviously the lemma could be slightly modified (by dropping the condition $q_0 \notin \{q_1, \ldots, q_k\}$ in the sum of the recursion step) to compute the number of 1-avoiding, i.e. general paths.

Analogously to paths with suffixes, we can treat paths with prefixes. Hence, define the *set of* k*-avoiding paths consistent with* $x = x_1, \ldots, x_n$ *with prefix* $q = q_1 \ldots q_m$ as

$$\text{pcpaths}[k][q](x) = \left\{ p \in \text{cpaths}[k](x) \middle| \forall 1 \leq i \leq \min(m,n) : p_i = q_i \right\}.$$

It is easy to see (by symmetry), that the paths with prefixes can be treated analogously to paths with suffixes.

We can now express the number of k-avoiding paths consistent with $x = x_1, \ldots, x_n$, where the i-th monomer occupies the position v, in terms of suffix and prefix path numbers.

For preparation, define the set of these paths as $\text{cpaths}[k](x|i \mapsto v)$. In the case of usual paths, the number of walks that map x_i to position v is the number of prefixes of length i that end in v times the number of suffixes of length $n-i$ starting in v. For k-avoiding paths, this does not suffice, since the composition of a k-avoiding prefix and suffix will not generate a k-avoiding path in general. To guarantee this, the prefix and suffix has to overlap at least by $k-1$ positions. Note that the i can be located arbitrarily in this overlapping region. These considerations are summarized by the next lemma.

Lemma 3. *Let* $x = x_1, \ldots, x_n$ *be variables,* $1 \leq i \leq n$*, and* $v \in V$*. Let* j *be such that* $1 \leq k+1 \leq n$*,* $1 \leq j \leq i \leq j+k-1 \leq n$*.*

$$\#\text{cpaths}[k+1](x|i \mapsto v) = \sum_{\substack{q \in \text{paths}[k](k)\\ q_{i-j+1}=v}} \begin{pmatrix} \#\text{scpaths}[k+1](x_1,\ldots,x_{j+k-1})[q] \cdot \\ \#\text{pcpaths}[k+1][q](x_j,\ldots,x_n) \end{pmatrix}.$$

Based on the computation of these numbers we develop an arc consistency algorithm for the k-avoiding path constraints.

Theorem 1. *Let $x = x_1, \ldots, x_n$ be variables with non-empty domains. The constraint $C = \mathrm{Path}[k](x)$ is arc consistent, iff for every $1 \leq i \leq n$ and $v \in V$, where $\#\,\mathrm{cpaths}[k](x|i \mapsto v) = 0$, it holds that $v \notin \mathrm{dom}(x_i)$.*

Proof. Let x and C be defined as in the theorem.

First, let C be arc consistent. Let $1 \leq i \leq n$ and $v \in V$, such that the set $\mathrm{cpaths}[k](x|i \mapsto v)$ is empty. Then, there is no path $p \in \mathrm{paths}(k)x$, where $p_i = v$. Hence there is no such path in $\mathrm{T}(C)$. We get $v \notin \mathrm{dom}(x_i)$, due to the arc consistency of C.

Second, let C be not arc consistent. We show that there is a $1 \leq i \leq n$ and $v \in V$, such that $v \in \mathrm{dom}(x_i)$ and $\#\,\mathrm{cpaths}[k](x|i \mapsto v) = 0$. The arc consistency of C has to be violated by at least one pair $1 \leq i \leq n$ and $v \in V$, where $v \in \mathrm{dom}(x_i)$. Choose such i and v. Since consequently there is no path in $\mathrm{T}(C)$, where $p_i = k$, there is no such path in $\mathrm{cpaths}[k](x)$. This implies $\mathrm{cpaths}[k](x|i \mapsto v) = \emptyset$.

Assume that the variables in a set X are constrained as all different. If we can derive, that in every solution one of the variables in $Y \subseteq X$ is assigned to a node v, we may introduce the basic constraints $v \notin \mathrm{dom}(x)$ for all $x \in X - Y$. The following theorem tells how to derive this.

Theorem 2. *Let $x = x_1, \ldots, x_n$ be variables, $1 \leq k \leq n$, and $\tau \in \mathrm{T}(\mathrm{Path}[k](x))$. Further, $S \subseteq \{1, \ldots, n\}$, such that $\max S - \min S \leq k$, and $v \in V$.*

Then, $\sum_{j \in S} \#\,\mathrm{cpaths}[k](x|j \mapsto v) = \#\,\mathrm{cpaths}[k](x)$ implies that $\tau_j = v$ for exactly one $j \in S$.

Proof. Let n, x, k, τ, S, and v be defined as in the theorem.

Let $j \in S$ and $p \in \mathrm{cpaths}[k](y|j \mapsto v)$. Since $\max S - \min S \leq k$, we know that $p_{j'} = v$ if and only if $j = j'$ for all $j' \in S$. Hence, the sets $\mathrm{cpaths}[k](y|j \mapsto v)$ are disjoint for $j \in S$. Thus, $\sum_{j \in S} \#\,\mathrm{cpaths}[k](y|j \mapsto v) = \#\,\mathrm{cpaths}[k](y)$ implies $\biguplus_{j \in S} \mathrm{cpaths}[k](y|j \mapsto v) = \mathrm{cpaths}[k](y)$, i.e., for every path $p \in \mathrm{cpaths}[k](y)$, $p_j = v$ for exactly one $j \in S$.

Finally, since $\tau_r \ldots \tau_{r+m-1} \in \mathrm{cpaths}[k](y)$, we get $\tau_j = v$ for exactly one $j \in S$.

In the following, we discuss in more detail how to avoid unnecessary large values for k, since the consistency and propagation algorithms are due to our recursion equations still exponential in k.

For $s, t \in V$, define a *path from s to t* as a path $p = p_1 \ldots p_n$, where $p_1 = s$ and $p_n = t$. Further, define a distance on nodes by

$$\mathrm{dist}(s,t) = \min \left\{ n > 0 \middle| p \in \mathrm{paths}(n), s = p_1, p_n = t \right\}.$$

Since V is finite, the defined distance can be computed by Dijkstra's shortest path algorithm. Note that $\mathrm{dist}(s,t)$ is neither a metric nor total.

Depending on the distance of first and last nodes of a path, k-avoidingness might be already guaranteed by k'-avoidingness for $k' < k$. This is stated by the next theorem.

Theorem 3. *Let $s,t \in V$, such that $d = \mathrm{dist}(s,t)$ is defined. Let $n > 0$, $1 \leq k', k \leq n$, such that $d + k' - n = n - k$. For every path $p \in \mathrm{paths}[k'](n)$ from s to t, it holds $p \in \mathrm{paths}[k](n)$.*

Proof. Fix $s,t \in V$, such that $d = \mathrm{dist}(s,t)$ is defined. Let $1 \leq k' \leq k \leq n$, where $d + k' - n = n - k$. Let $p \in \mathrm{paths}[k'](n)$ be a path from s to t. Assume $p \notin \mathrm{paths}[k](n)$. Then exists $1 \leq i \leq j \leq n$, where $j - i > k$ and $p_i = p_j$. Then, $p_1 \dots p_i p_j + 1 \dots p_n$ is a path of length $n - (j - i)$ from s to t. Now, by the minimality of d, $n - (j - i) \geq d$ holds. This implies $n - k > d$. By assumption $k = 2n - d - k'$. Hence, $n - (2n - d - k') > d$ and thus $k' - n > 0$ in contradiction to $k' \leq n$.

In a constraint search, the theorem allows to replace k-avoiding path constraints by more efficiently computed, but semantically equivalent k'-avoiding path constraints, whenever the conditions of the theorem are derived. Inversely, if we derive that k'-avoiding paths are in fact k-avoiding this allows stronger propagation due to theorem 2.

3.4 A Propagator for the Path Constraint

Based on the considerations of the previous subsections we sketch an implementation of the k-avoiding path constraint propagator.

Let $x = x_1, \dots, x_n$ be finite domain variables. The general strategy of the propagator for $\mathrm{Path}[k](x)$ is as follows

1. For all $q \in \mathrm{paths}[k](k)$ and $k \leq i \leq n$, compute $\#\,\mathrm{scpaths}[k](x_1, \dots, x_i)[q]$ and $\#\,\mathrm{pcpaths}[k][q](x_{n-i+1}, \dots, x_n)$.
2. Compute from this the numbers $\#\,\mathrm{cpaths}[k](x|i \mapsto v)$ for all $1 \leq i \leq n$ and $v \in V$. Whenever such a value is 0, remove v from the domain of x_i.
3. If at least one domain of the $x_1, \dots, x_n$ changes repeat from step 1.

Even since we have presented efficient algorithms to compute the above numbers and thus get arc consistency of the path constraint, there are some remaining problems. Most demanding are incremental computation and the saving of copying time.

At the first invocation, the computation of the path numbers can be done by dynamic programming algorithms. If domains are narrowed, the previously computed path numbers can be updated. For this aim, there exists an efficient update algorithm, which works destructively on the data structures. However, the incremental computation comes at the price of copying the data structures, whenever the tree branches.

Since for our purpose, the k-avoiding path propagator always works in presence of an all-different constraints, the k-avoiding path propagator should be able to handle further propagation due to the combination with this constraint. The justification to do this is given by Theorem 2. We use that for the arc consistency of a k-avoiding path constraint, the numbers $\#\,\mathrm{cpaths}[k'](x|i \mapsto v)$ are already computed for all $k' \leq k$. For tractability one has to restrict the subsets S, e.g. to all subsets of successive numbers up to size k.

Finally, one can simplify a k-avoiding path propagator by a more efficient k'-avoiding one, in situation described by Theorem 3, while preserving semantical equivalence.

3.5 Results

Exact structure prediction in the HP-model on the cubic lattice was previously possible up to chain lengths of 88 [30]. Yue and Dill report to find a native conformation for those chains in times ranging from minutes to hours. Our own algorithm for exact structure prediction on the cubic lattice regularly folds proteins with a length of 30 – 40 monomers [4,7]. Note that structure prediction in the cubic lattice is not necessarily easier for inexact, heuristic methods. For example, in [9] a heuristic stochastic approach is reported to fail on all but one of the investigated 48-mers.

We implemented two threading algorithms. For the first algorithm, we implemented a propagator to handle general paths by reduction to binary path constraint propagators. For the second algorithm, an experimental, non-optimized version of a propagator for 3-avoiding pathes is implemented. The propagators are implemented as extension to Mozart (Oz 3) [25]. Mozart provides a convenient interface for extension by C++-constraint-propagators [22].

For benchmarking of the two threading algorithms, the following experiment was performed. Random HP-sequences were threaded to cores of sizes n =25, 50, and 75. Therefore, for each core 50 sequences were randomly generated with n H-monomers and $0.8 \cdot n$ P-monomers, which is a rather high ratio of P-monomers to H-monomers and is chosen to challenge the algorithm. Additionally, we threaded 50 random sequences of length 160 to a core of size 100. We also managed to thread some random sequences of length 180 to this core. For each sequence, the threading is performed by both algorithms.

Table 1. Threading of random sequences to cores of four different sizes. The table shows size of the core, the length of the sequences, the percentage of sequences which could not be threaded successfully within the given time limit by the two algorithms, and the average number of nodes in successfull runs by both algorithms. We choose a time limit of 5 minutes for the first algorithm. The second algorithm is given a longer time limit of 15 minutes, since the path propagator is experimental and non-optimized.

core size	seq. length	fails alg. 1	fails alg. 2	avg. nodes alg. 1	avg. nodes alg. 2
25	45	0%	0%	36	36
50	90	12%	2%	970	103
75	135	20%	8%	586	513
100	160	60%	50%	1468	598

Both algorithms thread the very majority of the test sequences successfully. The results show that the combination of the path constraint with the all-different constraint yields significantly better propagation even for the strong relaxation of only 3-avoiding paths. Both algorithms successfully threaded all of the 50 sequences to the core of size 25 (which means a sequence length of 45). For longer sequences, the second algorithm succeeds for significantly more sequences than the first one. Furthermore, it often finds a solution in less search nodes (up to a factor of 303). The results are summarized in Table 1.

References

1. V. I. Abkevich, A. M. Gutin, and E. I. Shakhnovich. Impact of local and non-local interactions on thermodynamics and kinetics of protein folding. *Journal of Molecular Biology*, 252:460–471, 1995.
2. V.I. Abkevich, A.M. Gutin, and E.I. Shakhnovich. Computer simulations of prebiotic evolution. In Russ B. Altman, A. Keith Dunker, Lawrence Hunter, and Teri E. Klein, editors, *PSB'97*, pages 27–38, 1997.
3. Richa Agarwala, Serafim Batzoglou, Vlado Dancik, Scott E. Decatur, Martin Farach, Sridhar Hannenhalli, S. Muthukrishnan, and Steven Skiena. Local rules for protein folding on a triangular lattice and generalized hydrophobicity in the HP-model. *Journal of Computational Biology*, 4(2):275–296, 1997.
4. Rolf Backofen. Constraint techniques for solving the protein structure prediction problem. In Michael Maher and Jean-Francois Puget, editors, *Proceedings of* 4th *International Conference on Principle and Practice of Constraint Programming (CP'98)*, volume 1520 of *Lecture Notes in Computer Science*, pages 72–86. Springer Verlag, 1998.
5. Rolf Backofen. An upper bound for number of contacts in the HP-model on the face-centered-cubic lattice (FCC). In Raffaele Giancarlo and David Sankoff, editors, *Proc. of the 11th Annual Symposium on Combinatorial Pattern Matching (CPM2000)*, volume 1848 of *Lecture Notes in Computer Science*, pages 277–292, Berlin, 2000. Springer–Verlag.
6. Rolf Backofen and Sebastian Will. Optimally compact finite sphere packings — hydrophobic cores in the FCC. In Amihood Amir and Gad Landau, editors, *Proc. of the 12th Annual Symposium on Combinatorial Pattern Matching (CPM2001)*, volume 2089 of *Lecture Notes in Computer Science*, pages 257–271, Berlin, 2001. Springer–Verlag.
7. Rolf Backofen, Sebastian Will, and Erich Bornberg-Bauer. Application of constraint programming techniques for structure prediction of lattice proteins with extended alphabets. *J. Bioinformatics*, 15(3):234–242, 1999.
8. Rolf Backofen, Sebastian Will, and Peter Clote. Algorithmic approach to quantifying the hydrophobic force contribution in protein folding. In Russ B. Altman, A. Keith Dunker, Lawrence Hunter, and Teri E. Klein, editors, *Pacific Symposium on Biocomputing (PSB 2000)*, volume 5, pages 92–103, 2000.
9. U Bastolla, H Frauenkron, E Gerstner, P Grassberger, and W Nadler. Testing a new monte carlo algorithm for protein folding. *Proteins*, 32(1):52–66, 1998.
10. B. Berger and T. Leighton. Protein folding in the hydrophobic-hydrophilic (HP) modell is NP-complete. In *Proc. of the Second Annual International Conferences on Compututational Molecular Biology (RECOMB98)*, pages 30–39, New York, 1998.

11. Erich Bornberg-Bauer. Chain growth algorithms for HP-type lattice proteins. In *Proc. of the* 1st *Annual International Conference on Computational Molecular Biology (RECOMB)*, pages 47 – 55. ACM Press, 1997.
12. P. Crescenzi, D. Goldman, C. Papadimitriou, A. Piccolboni, and M. Yannakakis. On the complexity of protein folding. In *Proc. of STOC*, pages 597–603, 1998. Short version in *Proc. of RECOMB'98*, pages 61–62.
13. K.A. Dill, S. Bromberg, K. Yue, K.M. Fiebig, D.P. Yee, P.D. Thomas, and H.S. Chan. Principles of protein folding – a perspective of simple exact models. *Protein Science*, 4:561–602, 1995.
14. Ken A. Dill, Klaus M. Fiebig, and Hue Sun Chan. Cooperativity in protein-folding kinetics. *Proc. Natl. Acad. Sci. USA*, 90:1942 – 1946, 1993.
15. Aaron R. Dinner, Andreaj Šali, and Martin Karplus. The folding mechanism of larger model proteins: Role of native structure. *Proc. Natl. Acad. Sci. USA*, 93:8356–8361, 1996.
16. Eugene C. Freuder. A sufficient condition for backtrack-free search. *Journal of the Association for Computing Machinery*, 29(1):24–32, 1982.
17. S. Govindarajan and R. A. Goldstein. The foldability landscape of model proteins. *Biopolymers*, 42(4):427–438, 1997.
18. Patrice Koehl and Michael Levitt. A brighter future for protein structure prediction. *Nature Structural Biology*, 6:108–111, 1999.
19. Kit Fun Lau and Ken A. Dill. A lattice statistical mechanics model of the conformational and sequence spaces of proteins. *Macromolecules*, 22:3986 – 3997, 1989.
20. Hao Li, Robert Helling, Chao Tnag, and Ned Wingreen. Emergence of preferred structures in a simple model of protein folding. *Science*, 273:666–669, 1996.
21. Neil Madras and Gordon Slade. *The Self-Avoiding Walk.* Probability and Its Applications. Springer, 1996.
22. Tobias Müller and Jörg Würtz. Interfacing propagators with a concurrent constraint language. In *JICSLP96 Post-conference workshop and Compulog Net Meeting on Parallelism and Implementation Technology for (Constraint) Logic Programming Languages*, pages 195–206, 1996.
23. Britt H. Park and Michael Levitt. The complexity and accuracy of discrete state models of protein structure. *Journal of Molecular Biology*, 249:493–507, 1995.
24. J.-C. Regin. A filtering algorithm for constraints of difference in CSPs. In *Proc. 12th Conf. American Assoc. Artificial Intelligence*, volume 1, pages 362–367. Amer. Assoc. Artificial Intelligence, 1994.
25. Gert Smolka. The Oz programming model. In Jan van Leeuwen, editor, *Computer Science Today*, Lecture Notes in Computer Science, vol. 1000, pages 324–343. Springer-Verlag, Berlin, 1995.
26. R. Unger and J. Moult. Genetic algorithms for protein folding simulations. *Journal of Molecular Biology*, 231:75–81, 1993.
27. Ron Unger and John Moult. Local interactions dominate folding in a simple protein model. *Journal of Molecular Biology*, 259:988–994, 1996.
28. A. Šali, E. Shakhnovich, and M. Karplus. Kinetics of protein folding. *Journal of Molecular Biology*, 235:1614–1636, 1994.
29. Yu Xia, Enoch S. Huang, Michael Levitt, and Ram Samudrala. Ab initio construction of protein tertiary structures using a hierarchical approach. *Journal of Molecular Biology*, 300:171 – 185, 2000.
30. Kaizhi Yue and Ken A. Dill. Forces of tertiary structural organization in globular proteins. *Proc. Natl. Acad. Sci. USA*, 92:146 – 150, 1995.

One Flip per Clock Cycle

Martin Henz, Edgar Tan, and Roland Yap

School of Computing
National University of Singapore
Singapore
{henz,tanedgar,ryap}@comp.nus.edu.sg

Abstract. Stochastic Local Search (SLS) methods have proven to be successful for solving propositional satisfiability problems (SAT). In this paper, we show a hardware implementation of the greedy local search procedure GSAT. With the use of field programmable gate arrays (FPGAs), our implementation achieves one flip per clock cycle by exploiting maximal parallelism and at the same time avoiding excessive hardware cost. Experimental evaluation of our prototype design shows a speedup of two orders of magnitude over optimized software implementations and at least one order of magnitude over existing hardware schemes. As far as we are aware, this is the fastest known implementation of GSAT. We also introduce a high level algorithmic notation which is convenient for describing the implementation of such algorithms in hardware, as well as an appropriate performance measure for SLS implementations in hardware.

1 Introduction

Local search has been used successfully for finding models for propositional satisfiability problems given in conjunctive normal form (*cnf*), after seminal work by Selman, Levesque, and Mitchell [SLM92] and Gu [Gu92]. A family of algorithms has been studied extensively over the last 10 years, all of which are instances of the algorithm scheme given in Program 1.

The algorithm repeatedly tries to turn an initial assignment of variables occurring in the given set of clauses *cnf* into a satisfying assignment by performing flips, which inverts the truth value of a chosen variable. The instances of GenSAT differ in their choice of `INIT_ASSIGN` and `CHOOSE_FLIP`. Note that `INIT_ASSIGN` and `CHOOSE_FLIP` are place-holders for code in the sense of macros, which will be explained later. In all instances of GenSAT, the concept of the score for a variable plays a crucial role. The function $score(i, cnf, V)$ returns the number of clauses in *cnf* that are satisfied by the assignment V modified by inverting the truth value of variable i. For simplicity of discussion, we concentrate on the most basic variant, GSAT [SLM92], where `INIT_ASSIGN` randomly assigns truth values to the components of V and `CHOOSE_FLIP` assigns to f a randomly chosen variable i that produces maximal $score(i, cnf, V)$. Variants of this algorithm, random walk [SKC94], history and tabu mechanisms [MSK97], are presented systematically in [HS00].

T. Walsh (Ed.): CP 2001, LNCS 2239, pp. 509–523, 2001.

Program 1 The GenSAT Algorithm Family

```
procedure GenSAT(cnf, maxtries, maxflips)
    output: satisfying assignment satisfying cnf
    for i = 1 to maxtries do /* outer loop */
        INIT_ASSIGN(V);
        for j = 1 to maxflips do /* inner loop */
            if V satisfies cnf then return V
            else
                CHOOSE_FLIP(f);
                V := V with variable f flipped;
end end end end
```

The speed of GSAT is determined by the cost of checking and flipping a variable. Its time complexity is $\mathcal{O}(\mathit{maxtries}\ \mathit{maxflips}\ m\ n)$, where m is the number of clauses and n is the number of variables. In this paper, our goal is to make this flipping step as fast as possible. Given the simplicity of the GSAT algorithm and that boolean formulae can be directly represented as digital logic, the best way of meeting this objective is an implementation of GSAT in hardware. The advantage of hardware is of course speed and fine-grained parallelism which is to be balanced against the difficulty and complexity of realization in hardware. For maximum flexibility and ease of implementation, we use the Xilinx Virtex family of Field Programmable Gate Arrays (FPGAs).

The potential of FPGAs for solving SAT was realized by Hamadi and Merceron [HM97] and Yung, Seung, Lee and Leong [YSLL99]. Hamadi and Merceron describe an implementation of GSAT on FPGAs where the inner loop is done in hardware with n cycles per flip, hence the time complexity for GSAT is $\mathcal{O}(\mathit{maxtries}\ \mathit{maxflips}\ n)$ since the clause checking and the computation of the score is done within one cycle. However, the results in Hamadi and Merceron are sketchy and appear to be estimates based on cycle time rather than results of actual implementation and measurement. Hamadi and Merceron claim a speedup over software of two orders of magnitude, but the software timings which are presented seem to be particularly slow and appear to be using an unoptimized implementation of GSAT. In the work by Yung et al., the implementation in FPGAs is similar, but their results are slower than GSAT in pure software. We shall show in Section 3, why this is not surprising.

Hardware implementation and FPGAs have been used for solving SAT problems using other techniques than SLS. Abramovici and de Sousa [Ad00] present a recent approach based on the Davis-Putnam-Loveland-Logemann procedure, and give a thorough overview of earlier work on solving SAT problems using hardware.

After introducing a notation for parallel programs in Section 2 that allows for asymptotic complexity analysis, we state and discuss existing hardware-based GSAT implementations in Section 3, and suggest several improvements. Section 4 further optimizes the algorithm through aggressive parallelization. The details for our GSAT implementation are given in Section 5. Section 6 reports the results of an initial experimental evaluation of the described approach.

2 Notation

In order to analyze the parallel complexity of SLS algorithms, we adapt the notation used in [BM99], which in turn adopts central constructs of the parallel functional language NESL [BHSZ95]. We adapt the work-depth model of [BM99] so that we can asymptotically determine the two factors that determine the cost of running a program on an FPGA. The number of gates needed for running the program P is denoted by $g(P)$, which reflects the total size of the FPGA. The depth of a program P is the number of time units required to execute it, and is denoted by $d(P)$ which contributes both to the maximum gate delay within a clock cycle as well as the total number of clock cycles required for execution.

The most basic construct is an assignment such as $P : x := y + z$, where x, y and z are integers. As usual, we assume that integers are represented by a constant number of bits, and thus a constant number of gates suffices to perform integer arithmetic and logical operations, and such operations require only constant time. Thus, $g(P) = \mathcal{O}(1)$ and $d(P) = \mathcal{O}(1)$. Sequential composition $P; Q$ of programs P and Q has the obvious depth $d(P; Q) = d(P) + d(Q)$. The number of gates accumulates in a similar way $g(P; Q) = g(P) + g(Q)$. Note that in some cases the number of gates could be reduced by reusing P's gates for Q. For a sequential loop P : **for** $i = 1$ **to** n **do** Q **end** , we have $g(P) = g(Q)$, since the gates are reused by sequential runs, and $d(P) = n \cdot d(Q)$.

A central feature of the notation is support for sequences (one-dimensional arrays of integers). For example, the assignment $V := [0, 1, 0, 0, 1]$ assigns the sequence of boolean values $[0, 1, 0, 0, 1]$ to a variable V, which can represent an assignment of boolean variables $V_1, \dots, V_5$. Such sequences are accessed using the usual array notation ($V[3]$ returns 0). Assignment of a field in a sequence is done by $V[3] := 1$, which updates V to $[0, 1, 1, 0, 1]$. A non-destructive substitution expression of the form $V[i \leftarrow x]$ denotes a new sequence that is different by one slot where index i in the sequence has x substituted without affecting V, for example $V[3 \leftarrow 1]$. These sequences can be implemented in hardware by arrays of flip-flops. Thus, the depth of both sequence assignments and substitution is $\mathcal{O}(1)$ and the number of gates needed is $O(n)$, where n is the size of the sequence. Note that the implementation of sequences requires that their size must be a compile time constant, which is the case for all programs given in this paper.

Since we are constructing a gate array to solve an individual SAT problem, we can encode a clause directly in circuitry. For example, if the third clause of the SAT problem has the form $v_2 \vee \neg v_3 \vee v_5$, the circuit $\texttt{EVAL}_3(V)$ depicted to the right can be used to evaluate the clause. Since the OR-gates can be arranged into a binary tree structure, for clauses of size n, we have $d(\texttt{EVAL}_i(V)) = \mathcal{O}(\log n)$ and $g(\texttt{EVAL}_i(V)) = \mathcal{O}(n)$. Throughout the paper, log denotes the logarithm function with the base of 2.

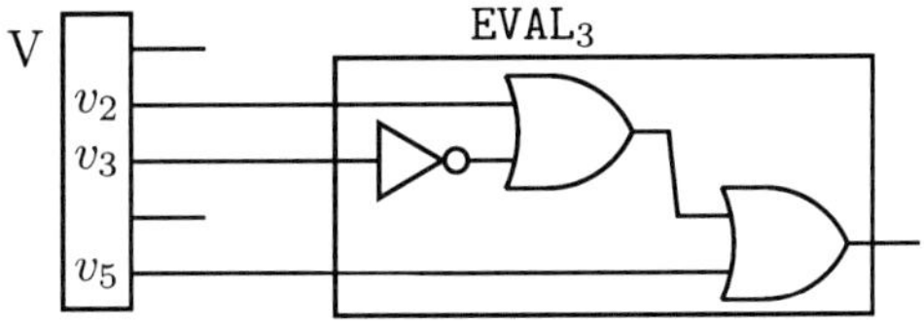

The most interesting feature of the notation is with the parallel processing of sequences. This is done using a set like notation. The following expression P evaluates all m clauses of a given SAT problem with n variables in parallel with respect to a given assignment V, $P : \{\texttt{EVAL}_i(V) : i \in [1..m]\}$. The depth of such a parallel construct is the maximal depth of its parallel components and the number of gates is the sum of the numbers of all component gates. Thus, under the assumptions above, we have $g(P) = \mathcal{O}(mn)$ and $d(P) = \mathcal{O}(\log n)$. Usually there are more variables than clauses in SAT problems, therefore we set $n < m$ for complexity analysis.

The sum of all integers in a given sequence of statically known length n can be computed with the following divide-and-conquer SUM program. For simplicity, we assume that n is a power of 2.

macro SUM(S, n):
  if $n = 1$ **then** $S[0]$
  else SUM($\{A[2i] + A[2i+1] : i \in [0..n/2-1]\}, n/2$)

Note that we call SUM a macro. We refrain from using runtime functions or procedures in this paper in order to avoid issues regarding parallel calls in the FPGA implementation, which cannot in general map directly to gates. Such macros can be recursive, as long as static macro expansion terminates. This is the case for SUM, since the size n of the sequence S is statically known. Consequently, the macro SUM creates a binary tree of adders. Thus for a given sequence S of size n, we have $g(\texttt{SUM}(S, n)) = \mathcal{O}(n)$ and $d(\texttt{SUM}(S, n)) = \mathcal{O}(\log n)$.

3 Naive GSAT in Hardware

Current Implementations of GSAT

In this section, we will review the implementation of GSAT given in Hamadi and Merceron [HM97]. The work in Yung et al. [YSLL99], is essentially the same but allows clauses with a fixed number of variables to be reconfigured on the FPGA without the need for re-synthesis. This is possible because the particular FPGA used, Xilinx XC6216, documents the configuration file for reconfiguring the FPGA. This is not the case with the FPGAs we are using, where changing the design requires re-synthesis of the FPGA. The issue of reconfiguration is beyond the scope of this paper, but briefly discussed in Section 6.

As we will be describing both parallel algorithms and the associated hardware, we will in this paper interchangeably use the terms design, implementation, circuit and algorithm where appropriate.

Here, we describe the algorithm sketched in [HM97] in more detail using our notation. This allows for a complexity analysis and comparison. For reasons which we will see later, we will refer to this algorithm as Naive GSAT. In Naive GSAT, the inner loop from Figure 1 is implemented in hardware. Meanwhile, the outer loop is implemented in software which is used to make the initial assignment (INIT_ASSIGN) and for communication and control to and from the FPGA. The design for CHOOSE_FLIP is given in Program 2.

In Program 2, the gate size is primarily bounded by the clause evaluation EVAL, therefore, $g(\texttt{CHOOSE\_FLIP}) = \mathcal{O}(nm)$. The rationale in the design for both [HM97,YSLL99] is to make use of the data independence of all calls to EVAL

Program 2 CHOOSE_FLIP of Naive GSAT

```
macro CHOOSE_FLIP(f):
    max := −1; f := RANDOM_VARIABLE(n);
    for i = 1 to n do
        score := SUM({EVAL_j(V[i ← ¬V[i]]) : j ∈ [1...m]});
        if (score > max) ∨ (score = max ∧ RANDOM_BIT()) then
            max := score; f := i
        end
    end
```

for checking the clauses. This observation and the use of SUM for counting the satisfied clauses yields a depth of $d(\text{CHOOSE\_FLIP}) = n * (\mathcal{O}(\log m) + \mathcal{O}(\log n)) = \mathcal{O}(n \ \log m)$. The overall depth of Naive GSAT is $\mathcal{O}(\mathit{maxtries}\ \mathit{maxflips}\ n\ \log m)$.

The experimental results from [YSLL99] show the hardware implementation to be slower than the pure software implementation of GSAT. GSAT version 41 from Selman and Kautz, which we refer to as GSAT41, is an optimized software implementation, which usually serves as a reference benchmark implementation. The results from [HM97] are unclear as they appear to be estimates. The software results seem to stem from an unoptimized implementation of GSAT rather than GSAT41, because the flip rate (flips/s) is relatively low. It is however not surprising that neither hardware implementations in [HM97,YSLL99] are particularly fast, as both are based in the GSAT algorithm as given in the paper [SLM92] as opposed to the implementation GSAT41. Furthermore, they assume the bottleneck is in clause evaluation and only parallelize that portion of the algorithm.

Optimized software implementations such as GSAT41 recognize that the basic algorithm of [SLM92] can be greatly improved in practice given two observations: (i) the maximum number of variables in a clause is typically bounded, as in 3-SAT; and (ii) the maximum number of clauses where a variable occurs in is also bounded. While this does not improve the worst case time complexity in general, it does mean a substantial improvement for many benchmarks and examples occurring in practice, where either one or both of these observations hold. As an example, for a 3-SAT problem, the time complexity of EVAL becomes $\mathcal{O}(1)$.

This is the reason why we refer to the implementation from [HM97,YSLL99] as Naive GSAT. A detailed description of GSAT41 together with a complexity analysis is given in [Hoo96]. We conclude that it is necessary to parallelize GSAT more aggressively in order to significantly improve over GSAT41 running on fast CPUs.

Improving Naive GSAT

A problem of Naive GSAT is that the selection process for the selection of moves is not fair. Sequential calls to the macro RANDOM_BIT generate a bias towards variables that appear earlier in the variable sequence V. Since RANDOM_BIT only produces a stream of 0/1s without knowledge of the underlying V, it is impossible

Program 3 CHOOSE_FLIP for Naive GSAT with random selection

macro CHOOSE_FLIP(f):
    $max := -1$; $f :=$ RANDOM_VARIABLE(n);
    $MaxV := \{0 : k \in [1 \ldots n]\}$;
    for $i := 1$ **to** n **do**
        $score :=$ SUM($\{$EVAL$_j(V[i \leftarrow \neg V[i]]) : j \in [1 \ldots m]\}$);
        if $score > max$ **then**
            $max := score$;
            $MaxV := \{0 : k \in [1 \ldots n]\}[i \leftarrow 1]$
        else if $score = max$ **then**
            $MaxV := MaxV[i \leftarrow 1]$
        end
    end
    $f :=$ CHOOSE_ONE($MaxV$)

to make a fair variable selection. An improved version of Naive GSAT that avoids this problem is given in Program 3, which also allows the implementation of various variable choice strategies. This version uses a macro CHOOSE_ONE for randomly choosing a value out of a given sequence. This macro is discussed in detail in Section 5. The complexity of gates and depth is unchanged, considering a depth d(CHOOSE_ONE) $= \mathcal{O}(log\ n)$ and number of gates g(CHOOSE_ONE) $= \mathcal{O}(n)$.

Parallelism can be increased by using the classical hardware technique of pipelining. The block diagrams in [HM97] show a pipelined implementation, as opposed to [YSLL99] which uses a sequential design. Pipelining can be applied to parallelize operations that multiplies performance with only a minimal increase in the circuit size. The use of pipelining is restricted by data dependencies between operations. In Programs 2 and 3, we can see that only the comparison with max is dependent on the results of the previous loop iteration. By making use of an additional queue that ensures data consistency, these designs can be pipelined. Note that while pipelining does not change the asymptotic depth, it can reduce the depth by a constant factor s, where s is the number of stages in the pipeline.

4 A Fully Parallel Design

The speed of the Naive GSAT implementation in the previous section is limited, because only clause evaluation is parallelized and not the variable scoring, hence the minimal depth of CHOOSE_FLIP after applying pipelining is still $\mathcal{O}(n)$.

In Program 2, there is no data dependency between the score computations for the variables. Program 4 improves over Program 2 by exploiting this obvious parallelization opportunity using parallel score computation.

The depth of Program 4 is $\mathcal{O}(\log m)$, since the *Scores* computation is bounded by $\mathcal{O}(\log m + \log n)$ and the CHOOSE_MAX computation is bounded by $\mathcal{O}(\log n)$ (see Section 5), and we assumed $n < m$. While this design comes closer to our goal, its drawback lies in an increase of the circuit size by a factor of n to $\mathcal{O}(mn^2)$. With the exception of small problems, this design is not practical.

Program 4 Basic CHOOSE_FLIP Design with Parallelized Variable Scoring

```
macro CHOOSE_FLIP(f):
    Scores := {SUM({EVAL_j(V[i ← ¬V[i]]) : j ∈ [1...m]}) : i ∈ [1...n]};
    f := CHOOSE_MAX(Scores);
```

Selective Parallel Score Computation

To alleviate this problem, we turn to an alternative hardware design. The idea is related to the software optimizations in GSAT41, but here the rationale is to decrease the circuit size while keeping parallel score evaluation. The key observations are:

- The selection of the flip variable can be done on the basis of relative contribution to the score of that variable when flipped.
- The number of clauses which will be affected by a change to one variable is small and typically bounded.

The new optimized design is given in Program 5. As we need to refer to only the affected clauses, we will use the notation $\mathtt{EVAL}_j^{\mathcal{C}(i)}$ to denote the j-th clause from the set of clauses which contain variable i and can be thought of as a fixed boolean function for a particular SAT problem. $NCl[i]$ is a constant and denotes the number of clauses containing variable i.

The total number of $\mathtt{EVAL}_j^{\mathcal{C}(i)}$ needed for Program 5 is bounded by the number of instances of variable i for all clauses. We will denote the bound on the maximal number of clauses per variable as *MaxClauses*. In practice, most problems have also a bound on the number of variables per clause, which we denote by *MaxVars*. For example, for 3-SAT, *MaxVars* is 3. Thus, the number of gates for Program 5 is $\mathcal{O}(MaxVars\ MaxClauses\ n)$. The depth for Program 5 is $\mathcal{O}(\log MaxClauses + \log MaxVars)$, which for practical SAT problems is much smaller than $\mathcal{O}(\log m)$. We remark that one more advantage of this design is that the circuit for SUM is smaller now, because the numbers to be added require fewer bits.

Hoos [Hoo96] discusses the time complexity of a parallel implementation of GSAT41 using bounds on variable dependencies, but does not give the actual parallel implementation, and an analysis in terms of number of gates is outside the scope of his analysis.

Program 5 Parallel CHOOSE_FLIP with relative scoring

```
macro CHOOSE_FLIP(f):
s1: NewS := {SUM({EVAL_j^C(i)(V[i ← ¬ V[i]]) : j ∈ [1... NCl[i]}) : i ∈ [1... n]};
s1: OldS := {SUM({EVAL_j^C(i)(V) : j ∈ [1... NCl[i]}) : i ∈ [1... n]};
s2: Diff := {NewS[i] − OldS[i] : i ∈ [1... n]};
s3: MaxDiff := OBTAIN_MAX(Diff);
s4: MaxVars := {Diff[i] = MaxDiff : i ∈ [1... n]};
s5: f := CHOOSE_ONE(MaxVars);
```

Multi-try Pipelining

The last step taken for achieving one flip per clock cycle is to push pipelining to its limits. With Program 5 the innermost loop of GSAT is now operating over each flip. Unfortunately, it is not possible to pipeline the different flip iterations of `CHOOSE_FLIP`, since each iteration is data dependent on the flip of the previous iteration. Instead, we look at the outer loop of Program 1. Since there is no data dependency between different tries in GSAT, multiple tries can be run in parallel as observed by Hoos [Hoo96]. Pipelining then optimizes the circuit consumption for this parallelization. Each pipeline stage deals in parallel with the work of a different try. For simplicity, *maxtries* should be a multiple of the number of stages in the pipeline. We call the resulting approach multi-try pipelining.

In practice, for the actual implementation it is feasible in one clock cycle to accommodate the evaluation of every $\texttt{EVAL}_j^{\mathcal{C}(i)}$ and the computation of `SUM`. Therefore, we only need to allocate each design block in Program 5 to a pipeline of five stages. The five stages, list as *s1* to *s5*, can be found in Program 5 is illustrated below.

Tries	Time1	Time2	Time3	Time4	Time5	Time6	Time7	Time8	...
Try1	*s1*	*s2*	*s3*	*s4*	*s5*	*s1*	*s2*	*s3*	...
Try2		*s1*	*s2*	*s3*	*s4*	*s5*	*s1*	*s2*	...
Try3			*s1*	*s2*	*s3*	*s4*	*s5*	*s1*	...
Try4				*s1*	*s2*	*s3*	*s4*	*s5*	...
Try5					*s1*	*s2*	*s3*	*s4*	...

5 GSAT on FPGA Implementation

In this section, we describe further refinements of the design, which result in our final implementation of GSAT on an FPGA. Specific implementation details are discussed for each stage of the design.

In Program 5 stage *s1*, the relative contribution of a variable to the score is computed twice; once for the current value of the variable and once for the flipped value. The corresponding circuits for clause evaluation and summation are essentially duplicated. In a sequential implementation one could reuse the clause evaluation and summation. However given either the use of pipelining or parallel evaluation of the two sequences, reuse of the circuits is prohibited by resource dependency, and duplication of the circuits is necessary.

We therefore propose a refinement to the circuits for clause evaluation and summation that reduces the overall circuit size. We first introduce some notation. Instead of working with the original form of the clauses, we use a reduced form. Let $\mathcal{C}(v^+)$ denote the a new set of clauses where variable v occurs positively in the original clauses, and where in each clause, v itself has been deleted. Similarly, $\mathcal{C}(v^-)$ contains those clauses where variable v occurs negated, and where in each clause, v has been deleted. These new clauses are smaller by one variable. We use the term $\texttt{EVAL}_i^{\mathcal{C}(v^+)}$ to denote the evaluation circuit for clause i in the clause set $\mathcal{C}(v^+)$, and similarly $\texttt{EVAL}_i^{\mathcal{C}(v^-)}$. The idea in the previous section was that it was sufficient to consider the relative effect on the score on a per variable basis.

We use the term $rscore(v)$ to denote the relative score for the clauses defined on v with respect to the current assignment. We know that when $v = 1$, all the clauses in $\mathcal{C}(v^+)$, but not necessarily all clauses in $\mathcal{C}(v^-)$, are satisfied, which results in:

$$rscore(v) = \begin{cases} \texttt{SUM}(\{\texttt{EVAL}_i^{\mathcal{C}(v^-)} : i \in [1 \dots |\mathcal{C}(v^-)|]\}) + |\mathcal{C}(v^+)| & \text{if } v = 1 \\ \texttt{SUM}(\{\texttt{EVAL}_j^{\mathcal{C}(v^+)} : j \in [1 \dots |\mathcal{C}(v^+)|]\}) + |\mathcal{C}(v^-)| & \text{if } v = 0 \end{cases}$$

To simplify the discussion and program, we define

$$\begin{aligned} Dyn1[v] &= \texttt{SUM}(\{\texttt{EVAL}_i^{\mathcal{C}(v^-)} : i \in [1 \dots |\mathcal{C}(v^-)|]\}) \\ Dyn0[v] &= \texttt{SUM}(\{\texttt{EVAL}_j^{\mathcal{C}(v^+)} : j \in [1 \dots |\mathcal{C}(v^+)|]\}) \end{aligned}$$

These refer to the evaluation of the reduced two new clauses where v occurs positively and negatively only. Note that v itself is not used in the circuit. Furthermore, we define the constant values

$$Static[v] = |\mathcal{C}(v^+)| \; - |\mathcal{C}(v^-)|$$

The relative change to the score when a variable v is flipped from 0 to 1 is the difference in $rscore$ for both values of v, which is:

$$Diff'[v] = Dyn1[v] - Dyn0[v] + Static[v]$$

Note that this is not the same as $Diff'[v]$ in Program 5 since the sign depends on the direction in which v is flipped.

We illustrate the computation with the following example where $n = 4$ and $m = 8$. A clause $v_1 \vee v_2 \vee \neg v_3$ is written in the form (1 2 − 3). The current assignment of the variables v_1, v_2, v_3, v_4 is the sequence $[1, 1, 1, 0]$.

All clauses	Clauses with variable 1^+	1^-
(1 2 3)	(1 2 3)	(-1 -2 -3)
(1 2 4)	(1 2 4)	(-1 -2 3)
(-1 -2 -3)	(1 3 4)	
(-1 -2 3)	(1 -3 -4)	
(1 3 4)	Simplified clauses	
(-2 3 -4)	$\mathcal{C}(1^+)$	$\mathcal{C}(1^-)$
(1 -3 -4)	(2 3)	(-2 -3)
(2 3 4)	(2 4)	(-2 3)
	(3 4)	
	(-3 -4)	

$Static[1] = 2$
$Dyn1[1] = 1$
$Dyn0[1] = 4$

flip $0 \to 1$ gives:
$Diff'[1] = 1 - 4 + 2 = -1$
flip $1 \to 0$ is $-Diff'[1]$

Program 6 shows the complete algorithm. Our final implementation on the FPGA is a five staged multi-try pipeline, labelled in Program 6 by *s1* to *s5*. Each stage is executed in one cycle, thus we assume that the circuit for each stage can execute within the time constraints of one cycle. RECEIVE_INITIAL_ASSIGNMENT() and SEND_ASSIGNMENT() perform the data

Program 6 Final implementation

MAIN():
    $V :=$ RECEIVE_INITIAL_ASSIGNMENT();
    for $i := 1$ **to** *maxflips* **do**
s1   **if** SATISFIED(V) **then BREAK** ;
s1 $Dyn0 := \{\mathtt{SUM}(\{\mathtt{EVAL}_j^{\mathcal{C}(i^+)} : j \in [1 \ldots |\mathcal{C}(i^+)|]\}) : i \in [1 \ldots n]\}$;
s1 $Dyn1 := \{\mathtt{SUM}(\{\mathtt{EVAL}_j^{\mathcal{C}(i^-)} : j \in [1 \ldots |\mathcal{C}(i^-)|]\}) : i \in [1 \ldots n]\}$;
s2 $Diff' := \{Dyn1[i] - Dyn0[i] + Static[i] : i \in [1 \ldots n]\}$;
s3 $MaxDiff :=$ OBTAIN_MAX($Diff'$);
s4 $MaxVars := \{Diff'[i] = MaxDiff : i \in [1 \ldots n]\}$;
s5 $v :=$ CHOOSE_ONE($MaxVars$);
s5 $V[v] := \neg V[v]$;
    end ;
    SEND_ASSIGNMENT(V);

transfer from and to the software in that order. The SATISFIED(V) macro (discussed later) exits the loop, when a satisfying assignment is found. Both the *Dyn0* and *Dyn1* are computed in parallel at stage *s1*, and are used to compute *Diff'* at stage *s2*. At stage *s3*, the OBTAIN_MAX macro retrieves the maximum relative score difference for all variables stored in the sequence *Diff'*. Upon knowing the value of the maximum change in the score, stage *s4* finds and selects all variables that correspond to the highest increase in score. In the last stage *s5*, we integrate both the CHOOSE_ONE and the actual flipping of the variable into a single stage. The CHOOSE_ONE makes a fair selection of one variable from a list of variables in *MaxVars*. After we flip the variable, the flip counter i is incremented and all stages are repeated.

The multi-try pipeline that parallelizes five tries corresponding to the five pipeline stages is realized using an additional scheduling queue to switch between multiple tries. Separate queues are added for the results of each stage in the pipeline. Due to the constant overhead for pipelining, the resulting design has an asymptotic performance of one-flip per clock cycle as *maxflips* increases.

Support Macros

The SATISFIED Macro. This macro represents the entire *cnf* formula. Due to the optimization for the clause evaluation based on the relative scores of variables, the information that all clauses are satisfied is lost, and thus this macro is needed. The macro implements an conjunction of disjunctions, each representing a clause. Thus we get $d(\mathtt{SATISFIED}) = \mathcal{O}(\log m \ \log MaxVars)$ and $g(\mathtt{SATISFIED}) = \mathcal{O}(m \ MaxVars)$.

The OBTAIN_MAX Macro. This macro returns the maximum value from a sequence. We use comparators structured in a binary tree, similar to the SUM macro in Section 2. The complexities are $d(\texttt{OBTAIN\_MAX}) = \mathcal{O}(\log n)$ and $g(\texttt{OBTAIN\_MAX}) = \mathcal{O}(n)$.

The CHOOSE_ONE Macro. This macro selects one variable at random from the input set of variables. To make the variable selection fair, we implement a shift-register-based pseudo random number generator where $g(\texttt{RANDOM}) = \mathcal{O}(1)$ and $d(\texttt{RANDOM}) = \mathcal{O}(1)$. While it is possible to use mod, to simplify the circuit, we use instead a binary decision tree where a random bit selects between the left and right branches. This gives $d(\texttt{CHOOSE\_ONE}) = \mathcal{O}(\log n)$ and $g(\texttt{CHOOSE\_ONE}) = \mathcal{O}(n)$.

6 Experimental Evaluation

For the FPGA implementation of Program 6 we have used a C-like design language, Handel-C [Pag96,APR+96] which compiles the program to a gate level description. Handel-C was chosen, because it has a simple timing model which fits well to the analysis of gates and depth used here. Handel-C does not have the sequences used here but has a parallel construct which can be used to implement the parallel evaluation of sequences. Individual statements execute in one clock cycle and thus sequencing and loops fit the model here. Expressions and variables can be declared on arbitrary bit sizes, which is consistent with the $\mathcal{O}(1)$ assumptions for operations on integers. Handel-C is convenient for rapid prototyping and we observed a shorter development cycle than with traditional hardware design languages such as VHDL or Verilog. While VHDL and Verilog give finer control and possibly better performance, the Handel-C implementation used in the experimental evaluation is sufficient to demonstrate the efficiency and efficacy of our GSAT designs.

The hardware used with Handel-C is their supplied prototyping board, RC-1000PP. The RC-1000PP board includes an XCV1000 FPGA from Xilinx, and allows a maximum clock rate of 33MHz when using the 4 Mbytes of on-board RAM. The XCV1000 itself is capable of running at clock speeds of up to 300MHz and includes 1Mbits of distributed RAM. The XCV1000 chip contains 6144 CLBs (configurable logic blocks), which roughly amounts to 1M system gates. Each CLB in the Virtex series is divided into 2 slices, and thus the we are capable of programming 12,288 slices.

Our Handel-C programs are compiled into a net list using a Handel-C compiler by Celoxica. We compiled the net list into a bitmap that can be loaded onto the FPGA, using Xilinx software. The latter step typically involves routing optimization and is very time (often several hours of processor time) and memory consuming. Obviously, the resulting process is not practical for solving individual SAT formulae. In typical applications of boolean satisfiability, the structure of formulae is rather fixed. For a practically useful SAT solver based on FPGA technology, this property would have to be exploited, and the algorithm described in this paper would have to be implemented in a way that the FPGA bitmap with tolerable gate delays could be generated quickly. Given the regular parallel structure of the algorithm, we see this process as an engineering task, which is beyond the scope of this paper. Yung et al. [YSLL99] show how this can be done for Naive GSAT on the Xilinx XC6216 family of FPGAs.

Table 1. Speed Comparison of Different GSAT Implementations

SAT Problems Name	Var (n)	Clause (m)	*Software* (GSAT 41) K *fps*	*Naive* @20MHZ K *fps*	*Multi-Try* @20MHZ K *fps*	*Speed-Up Ratio* vs. SW	vs. Naive
uf20-01	20	91	47.7	962.9	20610	432	21
uf50-01	50	218	74.4	383.6	20670	278	54
uf100-01	100	430	72.7	194.9	20620	284	106
uf200-01	200	860	70.8	98.6	20480	289	208
aim-50-1_6-yes1-1	50	80	129.8	383.4	20678	159	54
aim-50-2_0-yes1-1	50	100	111.1	383.4	20688	186	54
aim-50-3_4-yes1-1	50	170	75.4	383.7	20662	274	54
aim-50-6_0-yes1-1	50	300	40.5	383.5	20674	510	54
aim-100-1_6-yes1-1	100	160	140.1	194.9	20645	147	106
aim-100-2_0-yes1-1	100	200	111.0	194.9	20627	186	106
aim-100-3_4-yes1-1	100	340	71.8	194.9	20644	288	106
aim-100-6_0-yes1-1	100	600	39.6	194.9	20613	521	106
aim-200-1_6-yes1-1	200	320	121.4	98.6	20579	170	209
aim-200-2_0-yes1-1	200	400	98.5	98.6	20570	209	209
aim-200-3_4-yes1-1	200	680	67.5	98.6	20570	305	209
aim-200-6_0-yes1-1	200	1200	38.9	98.6	20427	525	207
flat30-1	90	300	94.4	216.0	20678	219	96
flat50-1	150	545	92.7	130.9	20588	222	157
rti_k3_n100_m429_0	100	429	72.5	195.0	20630	285	106
bms_k3_n100_m429_0	100	429	117.3	195.0	20645	176	106

The preliminary experimental results reported in Table 1 compare the flip rate per second between:

- the software implementation of GSAT41 by Selman and Kautz run on a Pentium II-400MHZ machine with 256Mbytes of memory (Software),
- the FPGA implementation of Program 2 with pipelining (Naive), and
- the FPGA implementation of Program 6 (Multi-Try).

Our implementations for both Naive and Multi-Try use software for the outer loop and the FPGA for the entire inner loop. The measurements are the average times from measuring the time used for the FPGA itself, and is subject to some experimental timing variation. The theoretical flip rate for Multi-Try is approximately equal to the clock rate since it achieves one flip per clock cycle. For uniform comparison, we always ran the FPGA with a clock rate of 20MHZ. We attribute the actual measurement of more than 20 million fps in Table 1 to inaccuracies in our time measurements. We discuss the effect of the design on the clock rate later in this section.

The results in Table 1 shows the disadvantage of the naive implementation. Its speed in flips per second (fps) is inversely proportional to the number of variables in the problem. As the number of variables increases, the fps of Multi-Try only decreases by a small amount. We see that due to the subsumption of the cost of `SUM` within a clock cycle the flip rate is not affected by the number of

Table 2. Performance Comparison of FPGA-based Implementations

Problem	*Naive*			*Multi-Try*			
	Delay (ns)	Size (slice)	Flip Density (fps/slice)	Delay (ns)	Size (slice)	Flip Density (fps/slice)	Improv.
uf20-01	11	511	1884	14	1490	13832	7
uf50-01	16	1006	381	18	3170	6521	17
uf100-01	24	1825	107	21	5918	3484	33
uf200-01	21	3481	28	32	11848	1729	62
aim-50-1_6-yes1-1	12	650	590	14	1818	11374	19
aim-50-2_0-yes1-1	14	705	544	12	1824	11342	21
aim-50-3_4-yes1-1	15	889	432	12	2464	8386	19
aim-50-6_0-yes1-1	15	1219	315	18	3506	5897	19
aim-100-1_6-yes1-1	18	1136	172	14	3480	5932	34
aim-100-2_0-yes1-1	17	1242	157	17	3194	6458	41
aim-100-3_4-yes1-1	17	1559	125	22	4712	4381	35
aim-100-6_0-yes1-1	19	2271	86	17	6690	3081	36
aim-200-1_6-yes1-1	22	2100	47	22	6452	3190	68
aim-200-2_0-yes1-1	17	2304	43	18	6307	3261	76
aim-200-3_4-yes1-1	23	3019	33	24	9106	2259	68
aim-200-6_0-yes1-1	26	4328	23	31	12286	1663	72
flat30-1	18	1440	150	17	3515	5883	39
flat50-1	20	2409	54	21	6066	3394	63
rti_k3_n100_m429_0	19	1824	107	22	5904	3494	33
bms_k3_n100_m429_0	16	1463	133	17	4766	4332	33

clauses. The speed-up for Multi-Try versus Naive is at least one order of magnitude and increases with the problem size. When compared with the optimized software implementation, Multi-Try exhibits a speed-up of two orders of magnitude. Note that the software is running on a machine with a clock rate, which is one order of magnitude higher.

Due to the absence of data dependencies, the parallelism to be extracted from the outer loop is unlimited. Such algorithms are often called "embarrassingly parallel". The cost of exploiting this parallelism lies in the hardware needed. A performance measure for computing devices that takes this hardware cost into account is called computational density [DeH96] and measures bit operations per second per micron square. We propose to apply this cost measure to SLS algorithms running on FPGAs. We define flip density to be the number of flips per second per slice of the FPGA. For a given FPGA architecture (here the Xilinx Virtex family), the flip density adequately measures the performance of a GSAT implementation.

In Table 2, the size of the circuits for both designs are listed in terms of slices. The minimal gate delay—as reported by the Xilinx synthesis tools—for these examples lies between 11 and 31 nanoseconds, but does not vary significantly between the two implementations. By cross referencing the fps from the first table, the results are shown in terms of flip density. The last column compares the two algorithms with respect to flip density, and shows an improvement of factors between 7 and 76. The improvement factor increases with the problem size.

We remark that we are limited by the maximum clock speed of the RC-1000-PP board due to the interaction between external RAM and the simple Handel-C timing model, even though the XCV1000 FPGA is itself capable of being clocked at higher speeds. This does not diminish our results as it is possible to implement our design and algorithms in VHDL or Verilog, which would incur a slower development cycle.

7 Conclusion

We have shown that previous work on implementing the GSAT family of algorithms using FPGAs leave considerable room for improvement. From an implementation of the algorithms described by Hamadi and Merceron [HM97] and Yung et al. [YSLL99], we proceeded in three stages:

- We achieved a uniform random selection of candidate flips by storing the candidate flips in a vector and employing a binary decision tree (`CHOOSE_ONE`).
- We parallelized the score computation and still avoided excessive use of gates.
- We exploited the absence of data dependencies by using multi-try pipelining.

The resulting algorithm achieves an improvement of the depth by at least a factor of n, where n is the number of variables. Its implementation on an FPGA achieves one flip per clock cycle. Preliminary experimental evaluation shows that formulae of realistic size can be solved using the presented algorithm with current FPGA technology running at reasonably high clock speed. The improvement over an optimized sequential implementation is more than two orders of magnitude. We analyzed the combined effect of increased flip rate and increased space consumption using the cost measure of flip density, which showed an improvement of more than one order of magnitude compared to existing FPGA-based implementations.

The main design ideas presented in this paper can be applied to FPGA implementations of other SLS algorithms. Current work in progress is investigating the WalkSat algorithm family.

Acknowledgements. We thank the company Celoxica for providing technical support and an educational license for Handel-C. The National University of Singapore supported this research with the ARF grant R-252-000-084-112.

References

[Ad00] Miron Abramovici and Jose T. de Sousa. A SAT solver using reconfigurable hardware and virtual logic. *Journal of Automated Reasoning*, 24(1–2):37–65, February 2000.

[APR+96] M. Aubury, I. Page, G. Randall, J. Saul, and R. Watts. Handel-C language reference guide. Technical report, Oxford University Computing Laboratory, Oxford, UK, 1996.

[BHSZ95] Guy Blelloch, Jonathan Hardwick, Jay Sipelstein, and Marco Zagha. NESL user's manual, version 3.1. Technical Report CMU-CS-95-169, Carnegie Mellon University, Pittsburgh, PA, 1995.

[BM99] Guy Blelloch and Bruce Maggs. Parallel algorithms. In *Algorithms and Theory of Computation Handbook*. CRC Press, Boca Raton, Florida, 1999.

[DeH96] A. DeHon. *Reconfigurable Architectures for General-Purpose Computing*. PhD thesis, The MIT Press, Cambridge, MA, September 1996.

[Gu92] J. Gu. Efficient local search for very large-scale satisifiability problems. *SIGART Bulletin*, (3):8–12, 1992.

[HM97] Youssef Hamadi and David Merceron. Reconfigurable architectures: A new vision for optimization problems. In Gert Smolka, editor, *Principles and Practice of Constraint Programming - CP97, Proceedings of the 3rd International Conference*, Lecture Notes in Computer Science 1330, pages 209–221, Linz, Austria, 1997. Springer-Verlag, Berlin.

[Hoo96] Holger Hoos. Aussagenlogische SAT-Verfahren und ihre Anwendung bei der Lösung des HC-Problems in gerichteten Graphen. Diplomarbeit. Fachbereich Informatik, Technische Hochschule Darmstadt, Germany, March 1996.

[HS00] Holger H. Hoos and Thomas Stützle. Local search algorithms for SAT: An empirical evaluation. *Journal of Automated Reasoning*, 24(4):421–481, 2000.

[MSK97] David McAllester, Bart Selman, and Henry Kautz. Evidence for invariants in local search. In *Proceedings Fourteenth National Conference on Artificial Intelligence (AAAI-97)*, 1997.

[Pag96] I. Page. Constructing hardware-software systems from a single description. *Journal of VLSI Signal Processing*, (12):87–107, 1996.

[SKC94] B. Selman, H. Kautz, and B. Cohen. Noise strategies for improving local search. In *Proceedings of AAAI-94*, pages 337–343, 1994.

[SLM92] B. Selman, Hector Levesque, and David Mitchell. A new method for solving hard satisfiability problems. In *Proceedings of AAAI-92*, pages 440–446, 1992.

[YSLL99] Wong Hiu Yung, Yuen Wing Seung, Kin Hong Lee, and Philip Heng Wai Leong. A runtime reconfigurable implementation of the GSAT algorithm. In Patrick Lysaght, James Irvine, and Reiner W. Hartenstein, editors, *Field-Programmable Logic and Applications*, pages 526–531. Springer-Verlag, Berlin, / 1999.

Solving Constraints over Floating-Point Numbers*

Claude Michel[1], Michel Rueher[1], and Yahia Lebbah[2]

[1] Université de Nice–Sophia Antipolis, I3S–CNRS, 930 route des Colles
B.P. 145, 06903 Sophia Antipolis Cedex, France
{cpjm, rueher}@unice.fr

[2] Université d'Oran Es-Senia, Faculté des Sciences, Département d'Informatique
B.P. 1524 El-M'Naouar, Oran, Algeria
ylebbah@algeriecom.com

Abstract. This paper introduces a new framework for tackling constraints over the floating-point numbers. An important application area where such solvers are required is program analysis (e.g., structural test case generation, correctness proof of numeric operations). Albeit the floating-point numbers are a finite subset of the real numbers, classical CSP techniques are ineffective due to the huge size of the domains. Relations that hold over the real numbers may not hold over the floating-point numbers. Moreover, constraints that have no solutions over the reals may hold over the floats. Thus, interval-narrowing techniques, which are used in numeric CSP, cannot safely solve constraints systems over the floats. We analyse here the specific properties of the relations over the floats. A CSP over the floats is formally defined. We show how local-consistency filtering algorithms used in interval solvers can be adapted to achieve a safe pruning of such CSP. Finally, we illustrate the capabilities of a CSP over the floats for the generation of test data.

1 Introduction

This paper introduces a new framework for tackling constraints over the floating-point numbers. Due to the specific properties of the floating-point numbers, neither classical CSP techniques nor interval-narrowing techniques are effective to handle them. The tricky point is that constraints that have no solutions over the reals may hold over the floats. Moreover, relations that hold over the real numbers may not hold over the floating-point numbers. For instance, Equation $16.0 + x = 16.0$ with $x > 0$ has solutions over the floats with a rounding mode set to *near* whereas there is no solution over $\mathbb{R}$. Equation $x^2 = 2$ has no solution over the floats with the usual rounding mode (round to nearest) whereas the solution over $\mathbb{R}$ is $\sqrt{2}$.

An important application area where such solvers are required is program analysis (e.g., structural test case generation, correctness proof of numeric operations). For instance, structural test techniques are widely used in the unit

* This work was partially supported by the RNTL project INKA

T. Walsh (Ed.): CP 2001, LNCS 2239, pp. 524–538, 2001.

testing process of software. A major challenge of this process consists in generating test data automatically, i.e., in finding input values for which a selected point in a procedure is executed. We have shown in [Got00,GBK98] that the later problem can be handled efficiently by translating a non-trivial imperative program into a CSP over finite domains. However, when these programs contain arithmetic operations that involve floating-point numbers, the challenge is to compute test data that are valid even when the arithmetic operations performed by the program to be tested are unsafe. In other word, the constraint solver should not compute the smallest interval that contains the solution in $\mathbb{R}$, but a solution over the floats that complies with the arithmetic evaluation process in imperative language like C or C++.

Thus, when generating test data for programs with numeric operations over the floats, the critical issue is to guaranty that the input data derived from the constraint system are safe, i.e., that the selected instruction will actually be executed when the program to be tested is called with that data (see Section 5). So, what we need is a safe solver over the floats.

In the remainder of this section we first detail our motivations before providing a brief summary of our framework.

1.1 Motivations

Like any constraint over finite domains, a constraint over the floats is a subset of the Cartesian product of the domains, which specifies the allowed combinations of values for the variables. However constraints systems over the floats have some very specific properties:

- The size of the domains is very large: they are more than 10^{18} floating-point numbers in the interval $[-1,1]$. So, classical CSP techniques are ineffective to handle these constraint systems.
- The evaluation of a constraint is not a trivial task: the result of the evaluation of constraint $c(x_1,\dots,x_n)$ for an n-uplet of floating-point numbers depends on various parameters (e.g., rounding mode, mathematical library, floating-point unit processor, sequence of evaluation).

Since constraints over the floats are defined by arithmetic expressions, a question which naturally arises is that of the ability of interval solvers –like `PROLOG IV`[Col94], `Numerica`[VHMD97] or `DeClic` [Gua00]– to handle them. Using interval solvers to tackle constraints over the floats yields two major problems:

- *Interval solvers are not conservative over the floats*, i.e., they may remove solutions over the floats, which are not solutions over the reals. For instance, any floating-point value in $[-1.776356839400250 46e-15, 1.77635683940025046e-15]$ is a solution of the relation $16.1 = 16.1 + x$ over the floats whereas `PROLOG IV` reduces the domain of x to 0 (with a rounding mode set to near). Likewise, the relation $cos(x) = 1$ holds for any floating-point value in the interval $[-1.05367121277235798e-08, 1.05367121277235798e-08]$[1] while

[1] With $x \in [-\frac{\pi}{2}, \frac{\pi}{2}]$ on a SPARC processor (with the *libm* library and a rounding mode set to near).

`PROLOG IV` and `DeClic` respectively reduce the domain of x to 0 and to $[-4.9406564584124655e-324, +4.9406564584124655e-324]$.
Of course, these problems are amplified by the symbolic transformations that some solvers perform to prune the intervals better.
- Solutions provided by interval solvers are tight intervals that may contain a solution over the reals whereas the solutions we are looking for are n-uplet of floating-point values.

That is why we introduce here a new solver based on a conservative filtering algorithm, i.e., an algorithm that does not remove any solutions over the floats. Roughly speaking, this algorithm takes advantages of the local consistency algorithms used in the interval solvers to identify a subpart of the search space which may not contain any solution. An evaluation process that complies with the arithmetic computations performed in imperative language like C or C++, is used to verify that these subparts do not contain any solution.

1.2 Outline of the Paper

The next section introduces the notations, recalls some basic definitions, and states the working hypothesis (e.g., compliance with IEEE 754 norm [ANS85]). A CSP over the floats is formally defined in Section 3. Filtering algorithms for CSP over the floats are detailed in Section 4. Section 5 illustrates the capabilities of a CSP over the floats for test data generation. The last section discusses some extensions of our framework.

2 Notations and Basic Definitions

This section introduces the notations and recalls some basic definitions that are required in the rest of the paper. Note that the definition of the intervals differs from the classical definition of intervals over the reals.

2.1 Notations

We mainly use the notations suggested by Kearfott [Kea96]. Thus, throughout, boldface will denote intervals, lower case will denote scalar quantities, and upper case will denote vectors and sets. Brackets "[.]" will delimit intervals while parentheses "(.)" will delimit vectors. Underscores will denote lower bounds of intervals and overscores will denote upper bounds of intervals.

We will also use the following notations, which are slightly non-standard :

- $\mathbb{R} = \mathcal{R} \cup \{-\infty, +\infty\}$ denotes the set of real numbers augmented with the two infinity symbols. $\mathbb{F}$ denotes a finite subset of $\mathbb{R}$ containing $\{-\infty, +\infty\}$. Practically speaking, $\mathbb{F}$ corresponds to the set of floating-point numbers;
- v stands for a constant in $\mathbb{F}$, v^+ (resp. v^-) corresponds to the smallest (resp. largest) number of $\mathbb{F}$ strictly greater (resp. lower) than v;
- f, g denote functions over the floats; $c \ : \mathbb{F}^n \rightarrow \mathcal{B}ool$ denotes a constraint over the floats; $X(c)$ denotes the variables occurring in constraint c.

2.2 Intervals

Definition 1 (Intervals).
An interval $\mathbf{x} = [\underline{x}, \overline{x}]$, *with* $\underline{x}$ *and* $\overline{x} \in \mathbb{F}$, *is the set of floating-point values* $\{v \in \mathbb{F} \mid \underline{x} \leq v \leq \overline{x}\}$. $\mathcal{I}$ *denotes the set of intervals and is ordered by set inclusion.*

We draw the attention of the reader to the fact that an interval represents here a finite subset of the reals.

2.3 Representation of Floating-Point Numbers

Floating-point numbers provide a discrete representation of the real numbers. This discretisation is needed due to the limited memory resources of the computers. It results in approximations and tricky properties.

The IEEE 754 standard [ANS85] for binary floating-point arithmetic[2] is now widely accepted and most of the available floating-point units comply with it. This section recalls the main features of the IEEE 754 standard that are required to understand the rest of this paper.

IEEE 754 defines two primary representations of floating-point numbers, *simple* and *double*, and offers the possibility to handle two others representations *simple extended* and *double extended.* If the two first representations are well defined and always available within the IEEE 754 compliant floating-point units, the latter may vary among the different implementations[3].

Differences between representations could be captured by two parameters: the size t (in bits) of the exponent e and the size p (in bits) of the significant m. Thus a set of floating-point numbers is well defined by $\mathbb{F}_{(t,p)}$.

Each floating-point number is fully defined by a 3-uples $\langle s, m, e\rangle$ where s is a bit which denotes the sign, m is the represented part of the significant and e is the biased exponent[4].

The standard distinguishes different classes of floating-point numbers. Assuming e_{max} is the maximal value an exponent could take in $\mathbb{F}_{(t,p)}$ (i.e., with all its t-bits set to 1), the standard defines the following classes of numbers:

- *normalized* numbers defined by $0 < e < e_{max}$. This class of numbers represent the following real number $(-1)^s \times 1.m \times 2^{(e-bias)}$.
- *denormalized* numbers defined by $m \neq 0$ and $e = 0$. Denormalized numbers are used to fill regularly the gaps between zero and the first normalized numbers. Their value is $(-1)^s \times 0.m \times 2^{(-bias+1)}$.

[2] IEEE 854 extends floating-point number representation by allowing the use of decimal instead of binary numbers. In this paper we restrict ourselves to the binary format.

[3] The standard just fixes some minimal requirement over the precision offered by the representation

[4] Exponents in IEEE 754 follow a quite unusual convention to represent negative values: a *bias* is subtracted from the stored value in order to get its real value.

- *infinites* defined by $m = 0$ and $e = e_{max}$ and represented by the two symbols $+\infty$ and $-\infty$.
- *signed zero* defined by $m = 0$ and $e = 0$. The IEEE 754 standard has chosen to sign the zero to handle cases where a signed zero is required to get a correct result.
- *Not-a-Number (NaN's)* defined by $m \neq 0, e = e_{max}$. The `NaN's` allows to handle exceptional cases —like a division by zero— without stopping the computation.

2.4 Floating-Point Arithmetic: Rounding Modes and Exceptions

Rounding is necessary to close the operations over $\mathbb{F}$. The usual result of the evaluation of an expression over floating-point numbers is not a floating-point number. The rounding function maps the result of evaluations to available floating-point numbers. Four rounding modes are available:

- to $+\infty$ which maps x to the least floating-point number x_k such that $x \leq x_k$.
- to $-\infty$ which maps x to the greatest floating-point number x_k such that $x \geq x_k$.
- to *0* which is equivalent to rounding to $-\infty$ if $x \geq 0$ and to rounding to $+\infty$ if $x < 0$. This rounding mode has to be compared with truncation.
- to *the nearest even* which maps x to the nearest floating point number. When x is equidistant from two floating-point numbers, then x is mapped to the one that has a 0 as its least significant bit in its mantissa.

To provide a better accuracy, the standard requires exact rounding of the basic operations. Exactly rounded means that the computation of the result must be done exactly before rounding. More formally, let $\odot \in \{\oplus, \ominus, \otimes, \oslash\}$ be a binary operator, $x \in \mathbb{F}$, $y \in \mathbb{F}$, two floating-point numbers, and *Round* a rounding function, then, if $\odot$ is exactly rounded: $x \odot y =_{def} Round(x \cdot y)$. The square root also belongs to exactly rounded functions. Functions which do not work with the exactly rounded mode may yield significant round off error (e.g., Intel 387 provides transcendental functions with up to 4.5 *ulps*[5] error).

IEEE 754 also defines *exceptions* and exceptions flags. They denote events which might occur during the computation. Such events are *underflow*, *overflow*, *inexact result*, etc. The handling of these exceptions is out of the range of this paper.

Almost none of the nice algebraic properties of the reals is preserved by floating-point arithmetic. For example, the basic operations do not have an inverse operation.

[5] Roughly speaking, an *ulps* corresponds to the size of the gap between two consecutive floating-point numbers.

2.5 Working Hypothesis

In the rest of this paper we assume that all computations are done with the same rounding mode and comply with the IEEE 754 recommendations.
Floating-point numbers will be understood as *double* (i.e. $\mathbb{F}_{(11,52)}$), and neither NaN's nor exceptions flags will be handled. That's to say, the set $\mathbb{F}$ is defined by the union of the set *normalized* numbers, the set of the *denormalized* numbers, the *infinites* and the *signed zero*.
The level of reasoning is that of the FPU (Floating Point Unit). So, when source code is considered, we assume that the compiler complies both with the ANSI C and IEEE754 standard, and that the compiler does not perform any optimization.

3 Constraint Systems over Floating-Point Numbers

In this section we formally define constraint systems over floating-point numbers (named FCSP in the rest of the paper). We investigate the capabilities of local consistencies —like $2B$–consistency and Box–consistency— for pruning the search space. We show that the filtering algorithms that achieves these consistencies require a relaxation of the projection functions that prevents them to ensure that all solutions of the FCSP are preserved.

3.1 Floating-Point Number CSPs

A **FCSP** (floating-point constraint system) $P = (\mathcal{X}, \mathcal{D}, \mathcal{C})$ is defined by:

- a set of *variables* $\mathcal{X} = \{x_1, ..., x_n\}$;
- a set $\mathcal{D} = \{D_1, ..., D_n\}$ of current *domains* where D_i is a finite set of possible floating-point values for variable x_i;
- a set $\mathcal{C}$ of constraints between the variables.

$|\mathcal{C}|$ denotes the number of constraints while $|\mathcal{X}|$ denotes the number of variables. A **constraint** c on the ordered set of variables $X(c) = (x_1, ..., x_r)$ is a subset $T(c)$ of the Cartesian product $(D_1 \times ... \times D_r)$ that specifies the *allowed* combinations of values for variables $(x_1, ..., x_r)$.

The syntactical expression of a constraint $c_j : \mathbb{F}^k \rightarrow Bool$ is denoted by $f_j(x_1, ..., x_n) \quad \diamond \quad 0$ where $\diamond \in \{=, \ \leq, \ \geq\}$ and $f_j : \mathbb{F}^k \rightarrow \mathbb{F}$. Note that any expression of the form $f_j(x_1, ..., x_n) \ \diamond \ g_j(x_1, ..., x_m)$ can be rewritten in $f_j(x_1, ..., x_n) - g_j(x_1, ..., x_m) \ \diamond \ 0$ since the following property : $x = y \leftrightarrow x - y = 0$ over the set of considered floating point numbers [Gol91].

Let $eval(f(v_1, \ldots, v_n), r)$ be the arithmetic evaluation of expression f over the n-uplet of floating-point numbers $< v_1, \ldots, v_n >$ with a rounding mode $r \in \{+\infty, -\infty, 0, near\}$.

A constraint c holds for a n-uplet $< v_1, \ldots, v_n >$ if $eval(f(v_1, ..., v_n), r) \ \diamond \ 0$ is true. A solution of a $FCSP$ defined by the 3-uplet $\langle \mathcal{X}, \mathcal{D}, \mathcal{C} \rangle$ is a n-uplet $<$

$v_1, \ldots, v_n >$ of floating-point values such that $\forall c_j \in \mathcal{C}$, $eval(f_j(v_1, ..., v_n), r) \diamond 0$ is true.

Next section outlines the limit of standard local consistency algorithms for a safe pruning of the search space of an FCSP.

3.2 Limits of Local Consistencies

Local filtering algorithms over reals are based upon $2B$-consistency and *Box*-consistency. Formal definitions of $2B$-consistency and *Box*-consistency can be found in [CDR98]. We will just recall here the basic idea of these local consistencies.

$2B$-consistency [Lho93] states a local property on the bounds of the domains of a variable at a single constraint level. Roughly speaking, a constraint c is $2B$-consistent if, for any variable x, there exist values in the domains of all other variables which satisfy c when x is fixed to $\underline{x}$ and $\overline{x}$.

Algorithms achieving $2B$-filtering work by narrowing domains and, thus, need to compute the projection of a constraint c_j over the variable x_i in the space delimited by the domains of all variables but x_i occurring in c_j. Exact projection functions cannot be computed in the general case [CDR98]. Thus, $2B$-filtering decomposes the initial constraints in ternary basic constraints for which it is trivial to compute the projection [Dav87,Lho93].

Unfortunately, the inverse projection functions introduced by the $2B$-filtering are not conservative. For example, the equation $16.0 = 16.0 + x$, is handled by the solver as $x = 16.0 - 16.0$, which results in $x = 0$, whereas the floating-point solutions is any float belonging to $[-8.88178419700125232e-16, 1.776356839400250 46e-15]$.

Box-consistency [BMVH94,HS94] is a coarser relaxation of *Arc*-consistency than $2B$-consistency. It generates univariate relations by replacing all existentially quantified variables but one with their intervals in the initial constraints. Contrary to $2B$-filtering, *Box*-filtering does not require any constraint decomposition of the initial constrain systems.

Effective implementations of *Box*-consistency (e.g., `Numerica`[VHMD97], `De- Clic` [Gua00]) use the interval Newton method to compute the leftmost and the rightmost 0 of the generated univariate relations. Again, some solutions over the floats may be lost due to the Taylor manipulation introduced by the interval Newton method. For example, consider the equation $f(x, y, z) = x + y + z = 0$, with $x \in X = [-1, 1], y \in Y = [16.0, 16.0], z \in Z = [-16.0, -16.0]$. Interval Newton iteration $X := X \cap (m(X) - \frac{f(m(X),Y,Z)}{\frac{\partial f}{\partial x}(X,Y,Z)})$ immediately yields $X = [0, 0]$, whereas on floating-point numbers the solution is much more wider.

However, the definition of the *Box*-consistency does not mention the interval Newton method. Next section shows how the definition of the *Box*-consistency can be extended to handle interval of floating point numbers.

4 Solving FCSP

This section shows that interval analysis provides a decision procedure for checking whether a given interval contain no solution of an FCSP. We also introduce a new algorithm, which exploit local consistency algorithms as heuristics. Roughly speaking, local consistency algorithms are very helpful to identify a part of the search space which may not contain any solution; Interval analysis being used to verify that these spaces do actually contain no solution.

4.1 A Decision Procedure Based upon Interval Analysis

The basic property that a filtering algorithm of an FCSP must satisfy is the conservation of all the solutions. So, to reduce interval $\mathbf{x} = [\underline{x}, \overline{x}]$ to $\mathbf{x} = [x_m, \overline{x}]$ we must check that there exists no solution for some constraint $f_j(x, x_1, ..., x_n) \diamond 0$ when $\mathbf{x}$ is set to $[\underline{x}, x_m]$. This job can be done by using interval analysis techniques to evaluate $f_j(x, x_1, ..., x_n)$ over $[\underline{x}, x_m]$ when all computations comply with the IEEE 754 recommendations.

To establish this nice property let us recall some basics on interval analysis over reals.

Let $\mathbf{x} = [\underline{x}, \overline{x}]$, with $\underline{x}$ and $\overline{x} \in I\!\!F$, be an interval of $\mathcal{I}$. We note $\mathbf{X} = [\underline{x}, \overline{x}]$ the corresponding interval over $I\!\!R$, i.e., $\mathbf{X}$ is the set of reals $\{v \in I\!\!R \mid \underline{x} \leq v \leq \overline{x}\}$. $\mathcal{I}_{\mathcal{R}}$ denotes the set of intervals over the reals. Functions defined over $I\!\!R$ will be subscripted by $\mathcal{R}$.

Definition 2 (Interval Extension [Moo66,Han92]).
Let $\tilde{x}$ denotes any value in interval $\mathbf{X}$.
• $\mathbf{f} : \mathcal{I}_{\mathcal{R}}{}^n \to \mathcal{I}_{\mathcal{R}}$ *is an interval extension of* $f_{\mathcal{R}} : \mathcal{R}^n \to \mathcal{R}$ *iff* $\forall\ \mathbf{X_1}, \ldots, \mathbf{X_n} \in \mathcal{I}_{\mathcal{R}} : f_{\mathcal{R}}(\tilde{x}_1, \ldots, \tilde{x}_n) \in \mathbf{f}(\mathbf{X_1}, \ldots, \mathbf{X_n})$.
• $\mathbf{c} : \mathcal{I}_{\mathcal{R}}{}^n \to \mathcal{B}ool$ *is an interval extension of* $c : \mathcal{R}^n \to \mathcal{B}ool$ *iff* $\forall\ \mathbf{X_1}, \ldots, \mathbf{X_n} \in \mathcal{I}_{\mathcal{R}} : c(\tilde{x}_1, \ldots, \tilde{x}_n) \Rightarrow \mathbf{c}(\mathbf{X_1}, \ldots, \mathbf{X_n})$

Definition 3 (Set Extension).
Let S be a subset of $\mathcal{R}$. The Hull *of S —denoted $\Box S$— is the smallest interval* $\mathbf{I}$ *such that* $S \subseteq \mathbf{I}$.

The term "smallest subset" (w.r.t. inclusion) must be understood according to the precision of floating-point operations. We consider that results of floating-point operations are outward-rounded when a function is evaluated over an interval.

Similarly, $\mathbf{f}$ is the *natural* interval extension of $f_{\mathcal{R}}$ (see [Moo66]) if $\mathbf{f}$ is obtained by replacing in $f_{\mathcal{R}}$ each constant k with the smallest interval containing k, each variable x with an interval variable $\mathbf{X}$, and each arithmetic operation with its optimal interval extension [Moo66]. $\mathbf{c}$ denotes the natural interval extension of c.

Now, let us recall a fundamental result of interval analysis :

Proposition 1. *[Moo66]*
Let $\mathbf{f}\colon \mathcal{I_R}^n \to \mathcal{I_R}$ *be the natural interval extension of* $f_{\mathcal{R}} : \mathcal{R}^n \to \mathcal{R}$, *then* $\Box\{f_{\mathcal{R}}(\tilde{x}_1, \ldots, \tilde{x}_n)\} \subseteq \mathbf{f}(\mathbf{X_1}, \ldots, \mathbf{X_n})$ *where* $\tilde{x}_i$ *denotes any value in* $\mathbf{X}_i$.

Proposition 1 states that $\mathbf{f}(\mathbf{X_1}, \ldots, \mathbf{X_n})$ contains at least all solutions in $\mathcal{R}$.

Proposition 2.
Let $\mathbf{f}\colon \mathcal{I_R}^n \to \mathcal{I_R}$ *be the natural interval extension of* $f_{\mathcal{R}} : \mathcal{R}^n \to \mathcal{R}$, *then* $\Box\{f(\tilde{v}_1, \ldots, \tilde{v}_n)\} \subseteq \mathbf{f}(\mathbf{X_1}, \ldots, \mathbf{X_n})$ *where* $\tilde{v}_i$ *denotes any value in* $\mathbf{x}_i$.

Sketch of the proof: It is trivial to show that $\mathbf{f}(\mathbf{X_1}, \ldots, \mathbf{X_n})$ contains all solutions over the floats when f is a basic operation, i.e., operations for which an optimal interval exists [Moo66]. Indeed, if f is a basic operation, the bounds of $\mathbf{f}(\mathbf{X_1}, \ldots, \mathbf{X_n})$ correspond respectively to $\min(eval(f(x_1, ..., x_n), -\infty)$ and $\max(eval(f(x_1, ..., x_n), +\infty))$ for $x_i \in \mathbf{x}_i$ and $i \in \{1, n\}$.

So, it results from the properties of the rounding operations[6] that

$$\underline{\mathbf{f}(\mathbf{X_1}, \ldots, \mathbf{X_n})} \leq eval(f(x_1, ..., x_n), r) \leq \overline{\mathbf{f}(\mathbf{X_1}, \ldots, \mathbf{X_n})}$$

for $r \in \{+\infty, -\infty, 0, near\}$, $x_i \in \mathbf{x}_i$ and $i \in \{1, n\}$. That is to say, whatever rounding mode is used, there exist no floating-point value $v_x \in \mathbf{x}$ such that $eval(f(v_x, v_1, \ldots, v_k), r) \notin \mathbf{f}(\mathbf{X}, \mathbf{X_1}, \ldots, \mathbf{X_k})$.

It is straightforward to show by induction that this property still holds when $f(x_1, \ldots, x_n)$ is a composition of basic operations. The essential observation is that the computation of $eval(f_j(x_1, ..., x_n), r)$ and of $\mathbf{f}(\mathbf{X_1}, \ldots, \mathbf{X_n})$ are performed by evaluating the same sequence of basic operations (based on the same abstract tree). □

Thus, interval analysis based evaluation provides a safe procedure to check whether a constraint c may contain a solution in some interval.

Now, we are in position to introduce a "conservative" local consistency for interval of floating point numbers.

Definition 4 (FP-Box–Consistency). *Let* $(\mathcal{X}, \mathcal{D}, \mathcal{C})$ *be an FCSP and* $c \in \mathcal{C}$ *a k-ary constraint c is FB-Box–Consistent if, for all* x_i *in* $X(c)$ *such that* $D_{x_i} = [a, b]$, *the following relations hold :*
1. $\mathbf{c}(\mathbf{D}_{x_1}, \ldots, \mathbf{D}_{x_{i-1}}, [a, a], \mathbf{D}_{x_{i+1}}, \ldots, \mathbf{D}_{x_k})$,
2. $\mathbf{c}(\mathbf{D}_{x_1}, \ldots, \mathbf{D}_{x_{i-1}}, [b, b], \mathbf{D}_{x_{i+1}}, \ldots, \mathbf{D}_{x_k})$.

Next section describes a filtering algorithm which enforces FP-Box–Consistency.

[6] It follows from the definition of rounding [ANS85] that: $Round_{-\infty}(x \,.\, y) \leq Round_r(x \,.\, y) \leq Round_{+\infty}(x \,.\, y)$ where $Round_r$ is rounding toward r, for all $r \in \{-\infty, 0, near, +\infty\}$.

4.2 A New Filtering Algorithm

In the following, we introduce a new algorithm for pruning the domain of an FCSP. This algorithm is adapted from the "Branch and Prune Algorithm Newton" algorithm introduced in [VMK97]

Algorithm 1 prunes the domain of a variable by increasing the lower bound. The function that computes the upper bound can be written down in a similar way.

The function $\texttt{guess}(c_j, \mathbf{x})$ searches for the left most 0 of the constraint c_j. The simplest way to implement $\texttt{guess}(c_j, \mathbf{x})$ consists in using a dichotomy algorithm to split the domain. Of course, such a process would be very inefficient. That is why we suggest to use 2B or Box–consistency to implement function $\texttt{guess}(c_j, \mathbf{x})$. Of course, different heuristics may be used to choose x_m. For instance, a value closer from $\overline{x}$ than the midpoint could be selected.

Algorithm 1 Computing Lower bound

```
Function Lower-bound(IN: c_j, x) return Lower bound of x
% ε: minimal reduction

    x̄ ←guess(c_j, x)
    if c_j([x̲, x̄], X_1, ... , X_n) & x̲ < x̄
    then
        x_m ← (x̲+x̄)/2
        if c_j([x̲, x_m], X_1, ... , X_n)
        then return  Lower-bound(c_j, [x̲, x_m])
        else  return  Lower-bound (c_j, [x_m, x̄])
        endif
    else return  x̄
    endif

end Lower-bound
```

The scheme of the standard narrowing algorithm —derived from AC3 [Mac77]–is given by algorithm 2. $narrow(c, \mathbf{X})$ is a function which prunes the domains of all the variables occurring in c. Implementation of $narrow(c, \mathbf{X})$ consists just in a call of the functions `Lower_bound` and `Upper_bound` for each variable. FB–Filtering achieves FP–Box consistency. An approximation of FP–Box consistency can be computed by replacing the test $\underline{x} < \overline{x}$ by $|\underline{x} - \overline{x}| > \epsilon$ where ϵ is an arbitrary value.

Algorithms that achieve stronger consistency filtering can be derived from algorithm 2 in the same way as 3B–consistency [Lho93] (resp. Bound–consistency [VHMD97,PVH98]) algorithms have been derived from the 2B–consistency (resp. Box-consistency) algorithms.

Algorithm 2 FB–Filtering

```
Procedure FB--Filtering(IN C, INOUT X)

    Queue ← C
    while Queue ≠ ∅
        c ← POP(Queue)
        X' ← narrow(c, X)
        if X' ≠ X then
            X ← X'
            Queue ←Queue ∪ {c' ∈ C | X(c) ∩ X(c') ≠ ∅}
        endif

end FB--Filtering
```

4.3 Labelling and Search

Solving a constraint system requires to alternate filtering steps and search steps. In the applications where constraints over the floats occur, we often have to deal with very different types of problems:

- Problems without solutions, e.g. , the point to reach correspond to so-called dead code[7] in the test case generation application;
- Problems with a huge number of solutions, e.g. , the point to reach correspond to a standard instruction;
- Problems with very few solutions, e.g. , the point to reach correspond to very specific exceptions handling.

Stronger consistencies are a key issue to prove that a problem has no solution. Although we could define a complete labelling and filtering process, practically we may fail to prove that some problems do not have any solution. Since in most cases numerous solutions exists, we suggest to start by a labelling process which "fairly" selects values in the domain of a variable (see section 5.2).

5 Experimentations and Applications

We have implemented the `FB-filtering` algorithm and various labelling strategies in a solver named FPics (which stands for floating-point numbers interval constraint solver). In the first subsection, we compare the results of `FB-filtering`, `DeClic` and `PROLOG IV` on several small examples. In the second subsection, we compare these different solvers on a small test case generation problem. The labelling strategy developed for that application is also described. Unless otherwise specified, the constraints are solved with a rounding mode set to *near*.

[7] Dead code is a piece of code in a program, which can never be executed [Kor90].

5.1 Naive Examples

A simple example already given to argue for floating-point CSP is the following equation : $x + y = y$ where y is a constant. This equation was used to show that solvers over $\mathbb{R}$ do not take into account addition cancellation.

Consider the equation $x+16.1 = 16.1$. Table 1 and table 2 show the computation results of `DeClic`, `PROLOG IV`, and `FB-filtering` on two different instances of such an equation.

Table 1. Computing results for $x + 16.1 = 16.1$

results	$[\underline{x}, \overline{x}]$
DeClic	$[-7.10542735760100186e-15,\ +7.10542735760100186e-15]$
PROLOG IV	$[0, 0]$
FB-filtering	$[-3.55271367880050053e-15,\ 3.55271367880050053e-15]$

Table 2. Computing results for $x + 16.0 = 16.0$

result	$[\underline{x},\ \overline{x}]$
DeClic	$[0,\ 0]$
PROLOG IV	$[0,\ 0]$
FB-filtering	$[-1.77635683940025027e-15,\ 3.55271367880050053e-15]$

The two different constants used in these examples illustrate well the behaviours of solvers over $\mathbb{R}$. `FB-filtering` preserve all the solutions over $\mathbb{F}$ in both cases. Note that the second result provided by the `FB-filtering` is not symmetric around 0. This is due to the fact that the exponent of the first floating-point number strictly smaller than 16 and the exponent of 16 are different.

`DeClic` converts decimal numbers to binary floating-point numbers whenever an interval contains only one float. This conversion extends the interval to up to three floats unless the float maps an integer. That is why it yields a larger interval for the first example.

The reader can easily check that numerous solutions exist in the intervals yield by `FB-filtering`. Consider for instance the subpart $X = [1.0e-200, 1.0e-15]$ of the interval computed by `FB-filtering`. The evaluation of $(16.0 - x) - 16.0$ yields an interval which actually contains 0. The following lines of C code compute that interval R :

```
round_down();
R.low = (16.0 + X.low) - 16.0;
round_up();
R.high = (16.0 + X.high) - 16.0;
```

5.2 Application to Automatic Data Test Generation

In this subsection we investigate a small test case generation example. In automatic test case generation applications, a problem is defined by the set of constraints that represent all the executable path that goes through some point or instruction[8]. Before going into the details of the example, let us first introduce the labelling process.

Labelling

The labelling process is based on an uniform exploration of the whole domain. It is parameterised by a *depth* which defines the number p of levels of exploration. Figure 1 illustrates the different steps of this enumeration process on one variable. The number correspond to the levels.

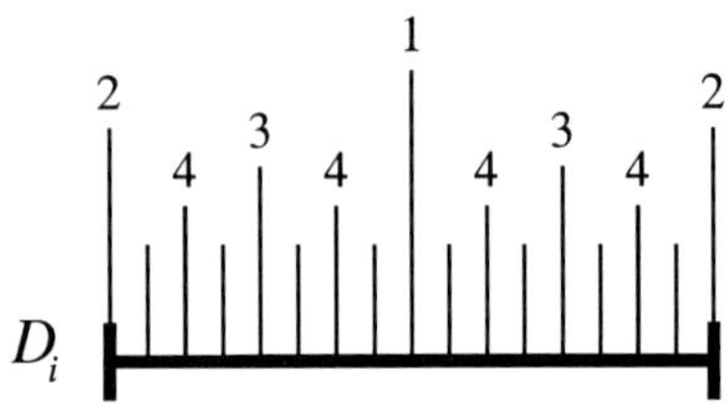

Fig. 1. Barycentric enumeration schema

Such an enumeration process is applied in a round robin fashion to all variables; each labelling step being followed with a filtering step.

The solver `FPics` is based on such a labelling process and on the `FB-filtering` algorithm. It also propagates the constant values after each labelling step.

The Cubic Example

Consider the piece of `C` code in figure 2, which is extracted from a program that computes the cubic roots of a number.

Here is the constraint system that defines the path going through `point 1`:

$$\begin{aligned}
&Q = (3.0 \times B - A \times A)/3.0 \\
\wedge\ &R = (2.0 \times A \times A \times A - 9.0 \times A \times B + 27.0 \times C)/27.0 \\
\wedge\ &DELTA = (Q \times Q \times Q/27.0 + R \times R/4.0) \\
\wedge\ &abs(DELTA) < 1.0e - 40
\end{aligned}$$

where *abs* stands for the function that returns the absolute value of a number.

[8] The generation of this constraint system is not always possible: it is undecidable in the general case since it can be reduced to the halting problem.

```
int solve(double a, double b, double c) {
   double q, r, delta;
   ...

   q = (3.0*b - a*a)/3.0;
   r = (2.*a*a*a - 9.0*a*b + 27.0*c)/27.0;
   delta = q*q*q/27.0 + r*r/4.0;
   if(fabs(delta) < 1.0e-40) {
      /** point 1 **/
      ...
   } else {
      ...
   }
   ...
}
```

Fig. 2. Code of cubic-roots example

We have generated test data which satisfy these constraints with `DeClic` and `FPics`. For both solvers, we have used the same labelling process with a depth of 6.

DeClic could generate 35 sets of input values, 10 of them were wrong. The problems mainly came from the combination of outward rounding and the constraint $abs(DELTA) < 1.0e - 40$: outward rounding transforms floating-point values in intervals and the constraints $DELTA = (Q \times Q \times Q/27.0 + R \times R/4.0)$ holds as long as $DELTA$ contains values in $(-1.0e - 40, 1.0e - 40)$, even if the evaluation of C expression is out of range.

`FPics` did generate 337 sets of input values. `FPics` could generate much more test data because it preserves all floating-point solutions. However the point is that, for all of them, the `C` program did reach '`point 1`'. Moreover, both the `C` program and `FPics` generate the sames values for the local variables.

6 Conclusion

This paper has introduced a new framework for tackling constraint systems over the floating-point numbers, which are required to model imperative programs. After a detailed analysis of the specificity of constraints systems over the floats, we have introduced algorithms that achieve a safe filtering of the domains of floating point valued variables. Experimentations with the FPics solver are promising and provide a first validation of the proposed approach.

Further works concerns the improvement of the guess function of algorithm 1, the handling of specific values like NaNs or exception flags as well as efficiency issues. It would also be worthwhile to investigate the problems that raise implementations where functions are not exactly rounded.

Acknowledgements. Many thanks to Bernard Bottela and Arnaud Gotlieb for numerous and enriching discussions on this work. We also gratefully thank an anonymous reviewer for his constructive remarks, and Gilles Trombettoni for his careful reading of this paper.

References

[ANS85] ANSI/IEEE, New York. *IEEE Standard for Binary Floating Point Arithmetic*, Std 754-1985 edition, 1985.

[BMVH94] F. Benhamou, D. McAllester, and P. Van-Hentenryck. Clp(intervals) revisited. In *Proceedings of the International Symposium on Logic Programming*, pages 124–138, 1994.

[CDR98] H. Collavizza, F. Delobel, and M. Rueher. A note on partial consistencies over continuous domains solving techniques. In *Proc. CP98 (Fourth International Conference on Principles and Practice of Constraint Programming), Pisa, Italy, October 26-30*, 1998.

[Col94] A. Colmerauer. Spécifications de prolog iv. Technical report, GIA, Faculté des Sciences de Luminy,163, Avenue de Luminy 13288 Marseille cedex 9 (France), 1994.

[Dav87] E. Davis. Constraint propagation with interval labels. *Journal of Artificial Intelligence*, pages 32:281–331, 1987.

[GBK98] A. Gotlieb, B. Botella, and Rueher K. A clp framework for computing structural test data. In *Proc. ISSTA 98 (Symposium on Software Testing and Analysis)*,. ACM SIGSOFT, vol. 2, pp. 53-62, 1998.

[Gol91] David Goldberg. What every computer scientist should know about floating-point arithmetic. *ACM Computing Surveys*, 23(1):5–48, March 1991.

[Got00] A. Gotlieb. *Automatic Test Data Generation using Constraint Logic Programming.* PhD thesis, Université de Nice — Sophia Antipolis, France, 2000.

[Gua00] F. Gualard. *Langages et environnements en programmation par contraintes d'intervalles.* PhD thesis, Université de Nantes — 2, rue de la Houssinière, F-44322 NANTES CEDEX 3, France, 2000.

[Han92] E. Hansen, editor. *Global optimization using interval analysis.* Marcel Dekker, 1992.

[HS94] H. Hong and V. Stahl. Safe starting regions by fixed points and tightening. *Computing*, pages 53:323–335, 1994.

[Kea96] R. Baker Kearfott. *Rigorous Global Search: Continuous Problems.* Number 13 in Nonconvex optimization and its applications. Kluwer Academic Publishers Group, Norwell, MA, USA, and Dordrecht, The Netherlands, 1996.

[Kor90] Bogdan Korel. Automated Software Test Data Generation. *IEEE Transactions on Software Engineering*, 16(8):870–879, august 1990.

[Lho93] O. Lhomme. Consistency techniques for numeric csps. In *Proceedings of IJ-CAI'93*, pages 232–238, 1993.

[Mac77] A. Mackworth. Consistency in networks of relations. *Journal of Artificial Intelligence*, pages 8(1):99–118, 1977.

[Moo66] R. Moore. *Interval Analysis.* Prentice Hall, 1966.

[PVH98] J.F. Puget and P. Van-Hentenryck. A constraints satisfaction approach to a circuit design problem. *Journal of global optimization*, pages 13(1):75–93, 1998.

[VHMD97] P. Van-Hentenryck, L. Michel, and Y. Deville. *Numerica : a Modeling Languge for Global Optimization.* MIT press, 1997.

[VMK97] P. Van Hentenryck, D. McAllester, and D. Kapur. Solving polynomial systems using a branch and prune aprroach. *SIAM Journal*, 34(2), 1997.

Optimal Pruning in Parametric Differential Equations

Micha Janssen[1], Pascal Van Hentenryck[2], and Yves Deville[1]

[1] UCL, Place Sainte-Barbe, 2, B-1348 Louvain-La-Neuve, Belgium
[2] Brown University, Box 1910, Providence, RI 02912

Abstract. Initial value problems for parametric ordinary differential equations (ODEs) arise in many areas of science and engineering. Since some of the data is uncertain, traditional numerical methods do not apply. This paper considers a constraint satisfaction approach that enhances traditional interval methods with a pruning component which uses a relaxation of the ODE and Hermite interpolation polynomials. It solves the main theoretical and practical open issue left in this approach: the choice of an optimal evaluation time for the relaxation. As a consequence, the constraint satisfaction approach is shown to provide a quadratic (asymptotical) improvement in accuracy over the best interval methods, while improving their running times. Experimental results confirm the theoretical results.

1 Introduction

Initial value problems (IVPs) for ordinary differential equations (ODEs) arise naturally in many applications in science and engineering, including chemistry, physics, molecular biology, and mechanics to name only a few. In vector notation, an *ordinary differential equation* $\mathcal{O}$ is a system of the form $u'(t) = f(t, u(t))$ or $u' = f(t, u)$. An *initial value problem* is an ODE with an initial condition $u(t_0) = u_0$. In addition, in practice, it is often the case that the parameters and/or the initial values are not known with certainty but are given as intervals. Hence traditional methods do not apply to the resulting parametric ordinary differential equations since they would have to solve infinitely many systems. Interval methods, pioneered by Moore [Moo66], provide an approach to tackle parametric ODEs. These methods return enclosures of the exact solution at different points in time, i.e., they are guaranteed to return intervals containing the exact solution. In addition, they accommodate easily uncertainty in the parameters or initial values by using intervals instead of floating-point numbers. Interval methods typically apply a one-step Taylor interval method and make extensive use of automatic differentiation to obtain the Taylor coefficients [Eij81,Kru69,Moo66]. Their major problem however is the explosion of the size of the boxes at successive points as they often accumulate errors from point to point and lose accuracy by enclosing the solution by a box (this is called the *wrapping effect*). Lohner's AWA system [Loh87] was an important step in interval methods which features efficient coordinate transformations to tackle the wrapping effect. More recently, Nedialkov and Jackson's IHO method [NJ99] improved on AWA by extending a Hermite-Obreschkoff's approach (which can be viewed as a generalized Taylor method) to intervals (see also [Ber98]).

This research takes a constraint satisfaction approach to ODEs [DJVH98]. Its basic idea is to view the solving of ODEs as the iteration of three processes: (1) a *bounding*

T. Walsh (Ed.): CP 2001, LNCS 2239, pp. 539–553, 2001.

box process that computes bounding boxes for the current step and proves (numerically) the existence and uniqueness of the solution, (2) a *predictor* process that computes initial enclosures at given times from enclosures at previous times and bounding boxes and (3) a *pruning* process that reduces the initial enclosures without removing solutions. The real novelty in our approach is the pruning component. Pruning in ODEs however generates significant challenges since ODEs contain unknown functions. The main contribution of our research is to show that an effective pruning technique can be derived from a relaxation of the ODE, importing a fundamental principle from constraint satisfaction into the field of differential equations. Four main steps are necessary to derive an effective pruning algorithm. The first step consists in obtaining a relaxation of the ODE by enclosing its solution using, e.g., Hermite interpolation polynomials. The second step consists in using the mean-value form of this relaxation to prune the boxes accurately and efficiently. Unfortunately, these two steps, which were skeched in [JDVH99], are not sufficient and the resulting pruning algorithm still suffers from traditional problems of interval methods. The third fundamental step, which was presented in [JVHD01a], consists in globalizing the pruning by considering several successive relaxations together. This idea of generating a global constraint from a set of more primitive constraints is also at the heart of constraint satisfaction. It makes it possible, in this new context, to address the problem of dependencies and the wrapping effect simultaneously.[1] *The fourth step, which is the main contribution of this paper, consists of choosing an evaluation time for the relaxation that maximizes pruning.* Indeed, the global constraint generated in the third step, being a relaxation of the ODE itself, is parametrized by an evaluation time. In [JVHD01a], the evaluation time was chosen heuristically and its choice was left as the main open issue in the constraint satisfaction approach to parametric ODEs.

The main contribution of this paper is to close this last open problem and to show that, for global filters based on Hermite interpolation polynomials, the optimal evaluation time is independent from the ODE itself and can be precomputed before starting the integration steps at negligible cost. This result has fundamental theoretical and practical consequences. From a theoretical standpoint, it can be shown that the constraint satisfaction approach provides a quadratic improvement in accuracy (asymptotically) over the best interval methods we know of while decreasing their computation costs as well. This result also implies that our approach should be significantly faster when the function f is very complex. Experimental results confirm the theory. They show that the constraint satisfaction approach often produces a quadratic improvement in accuracy over existing methods while decreasing computation times. Alternatively, at similar accuracy, other approaches are significantly slower. The rest of the paper is organized as follows. Section 2 introduces the main definitions and notations. Section 3 gives a high-level overview of the constraint satisfaction approach to parametric ODEs. Section 4 is the core of the paper. It describes how to choose an evaluation time to maximize pruning. Sections 5 and 6 report the theoretical and experimental analyses. The appendix contains the proofs of the main results. A comprehensive presentation of all results and algorithms is available in the technical report version of this paper (TR CS-05-04, Brown University, April 2001).

[1] Global constraints in ordinary differential equations have also been found useful in [CB99]. The problem and the techniques in [CB99] are however fundamentally different.

2 Background and Definitions

Small letters denote real values, vectors and functions of real values. Capital letters denote matrices, sets, intervals, vectors and functions of intervals. $\mathbb{IR}$ denotes the set of all *closed* intervals $\subseteq \mathbb{R}$. A vector of intervals $D \in \mathbb{IR}^n$ is called a *box*. If $r \in \mathbb{R}$, then $\overline{r}$ denotes the smallest interval $I \in \mathbb{IR}$ such that $r \in I$. If $r \in \mathbb{R}^n$, then $\overline{r} = (\overline{r_1}, \dots, \overline{r_n})$. We often use r instead of $\overline{r}$ for simplicity. If $A \subseteq \mathbb{R}^n$, then $\Box A$ denotes the smallest box $D \in \mathbb{IR}^n$ such that $A \subseteq D$ and $g(A)$ denotes the set $\{g(x) \mid x \in A\}$. We also assume that a, b, t_i, t_e and t are reals, $I_i \in \mathbb{IR}$, u_i is in $\mathbb{R}^n$, and D_i and B_i are in $\mathbb{IR}^n$ $(i \in \mathbb{N})$. We use $m(D)$ to denote the midpoint of D and $s(D)$ to denote $D - m(D)$. Observe that $m(D) + s(D) = D$. We use $D_x g$ to denote the Jacobian of g wrt x and $\omega(D)$ to denote the width of a box. More precisely, $\omega([a, b]) = b - a$ and $\omega((I_1, \dots, I_n)) = (\omega(I_1), \dots, \omega(I_n))$.

Notation 1 *Let A be a set and $a_i \in A$ where $i \in \mathbb{N}$. We use the bold face notations:* $\mathbf{a} = (a_0, \dots, a_k) \in A^{k+1}$, $\mathbf{a}_i = (a_{ik}, a_{ik+1}, \dots, a_{(i+1)k-1}) \in A^k$, *and* $\mathbf{a}_{i..i+j} = (a_i, \dots, a_{i+j}) \in A^{j+1}$

Observe that $\mathbf{a}_0 = (a_0, \dots, a_{k-1})$, $\mathbf{a}_1 = (a_k, \dots, a_{2k-1})$, and $\mathbf{a} = (a_0, \dots, a_k)$. In the theoretical parts, we assume that the underlying interval arithmetic is exact. As traditional, we restrict attention to ODEs that have a unique solution for a given initial value and where $f \in C^\infty$. Techniques to verify this hypothesis numerically are well-known. Moreover, in practice, the objective is to produce (an approximation of) the values of the solution of $\mathcal{O}$ at different points $t_0, t_1, \dots, t_m$. This motivates the following definition of solutions and its generalization to multistep solutions.

Definition 1 (Solution of an ODE). *The* solution *of an ODE $\mathcal{O}$ on $I \in \mathbb{IR}$ is the function $s : \mathbb{R} \times \mathbb{R}^n \times \mathbb{R} \to \mathbb{R}^n$ such that $\forall t \in I : \frac{\partial s}{\partial t}(t_0, u_0, t) = f(t, s(t_0, u_0, t))$ for an initial condition $s(t_0, u_0, t_0) = u_0$.*

Definition 2 (Multistep solution of an ODE). *The* multistep solution *of an ODE $\mathcal{O}$ is the* partial *function $ms : A \subseteq \mathbb{R}^{k+1} \times (\mathbb{R}^n)^{k+1} \times \mathbb{R} \to \mathbb{R}^n$ defined as $ms(\mathbf{t}, \mathbf{u}, t) = s(t_0, u_0, t)$ if $u_i = s(t_0, u_0, t_i)$ $(1 \leq i \leq k)$ where s is the solution of $\mathcal{O}$ and is undefined otherwise.*

We generalize interval extensions of functions (e.g., [VHMD97]) to partial functions.

Definition 3 (Interval Extension of a Partial Function). *The interval function $G : \mathbb{IR}^n \to \mathbb{IR}^m$ is an* interval extension *of the partial function $g : E \subseteq \mathbb{R}^n \to \mathbb{R}^m$ if $\forall D \in \mathbb{IR}^n : g(E \cap D) \subseteq G(D)$.*

Finally, we generalize the concept of bounding boxes to multistep methods. Intuitively, a bounding box encloses all solutions of an ODE going through certain boxes at given times over a given time interval. Bounding boxes are often used to enclose error terms in ODEs.

Definition 4 (Bounding Box). *Let $\mathcal{O}$ be an ODE system, ms be the multistep solution of $\mathcal{O}$, and $\{t_0, \dots, t_k\} \subseteq T \in \mathbb{IR}$. A box B is a* bounding box *of $\mathcal{O}$ over T wrt $(\mathbf{t}, \mathbf{D})$ if, for all $t \in T$, $ms(\mathbf{t}, \mathbf{D}, t) \subseteq B$.*

3 The Constraint Satisfaction Approach

The constraint satisfaction approach for ODEs consists of a generic algorithm that iterates three processes: (1) a *bounding box* process that computes bounding boxes for the current step and proves (numerically) the existence and uniqueness of the solution, (2) a *predictor* process that computes initial enclosures at given times from enclosures at previous times and bounding boxes and (3) a *pruning* process that reduces the initial enclosures without removing solutions. The bounding box and predictor components are standard in interval methods for ODEs. This paper thus focuses on the pruning process, the main novelty of the approach. *Our pruning component is based on relaxations of the ODE.* To our knowledge, no other approach uses relaxations of the ODE to derive pruning operators and the only other approaches using a pruning component [NJ99,Rih98] were developed independently. Note also that, in the following, predicted boxes are generally superscripted with the symbol $-$ (e.g., D_1^-), while pruned boxes are generally superscripted with the symbol $*$ (e.g., D_1^*).

The pruning component uses *safe approximations* of the ODE to shrink the boxes computed by the predictor process. To understand this idea, it is useful to contrast the constraint satisfaction approach to nonlinear programming [VHMD97] and to ordinary differential equations. In nonlinear programming, a constraint $c(x_1, \ldots, x_n)$ can be used almost directly for pruning the search space (i.e., the Cartesian product of the intervals I_i associated with the variables x_i). It suffices to take an interval extension $C(X_1, \ldots, X_n)$ of the constraint. Now if $C(I'_1, \ldots, I'_n)$ does not hold, it follows, by definition of interval extensions, that no solution of c lies in $I'_1 \times \ldots \times I'_n$. The interval extension can be seen as a filter that can be used for pruning the search space in many ways. For instance, Numerica uses box(k)-consistency on these interval constraints [VHMD97]. Ordinary differential equations raise new challenges. In an ODE $\forall\, t:\ u' = f(t, u)$, functions u and u' are, of course, unknown. Hence it is not obvious how to obtain a filter to prune boxes.

One of the main contributions of our approach is to show how to derive effective pruning operators for parametric ODEs. The first step consists in rewriting the ODE in terms of its multistep solution *ms* to obtain

$$\forall\, t:\ \frac{\partial ms}{\partial t}(\mathbf{t}, \mathbf{u}, t) = f(t, ms(\mathbf{t}, \mathbf{u}, t)).$$

Let us denote this formula $\forall\, t: fl(\mathbf{t}, \mathbf{u}, t)$. This rewriting may not appear useful since *ms* is still an unknown function. However it suggests a way to approximate the ODE. Indeed, we show in Section 3.3 how to obtain interval extensions of *ms* and $\frac{\partial ms}{\partial t}$ by using polynomial interpolations together with their error terms. This simply requires a bounding box for the considered time interval and safe approximations of *ms* at successive times, both of which are available from the bounding box and predictor processes. Once these interval extensions are available, it is possible to obtain an interval formula of the form $\forall\, t: FL(\mathbf{t}, \mathbf{D}, t)$ which approximates the original ODE. The above formula is still not ready to be used as a filter because t is universally quantified. The solution here is simpler and consists of restricting attention to a finite set T of times (possibly a singleton) to obtain the relation $\forall\, t \in T: FL(\mathbf{t}, \mathbf{D}, t)$ which produces a computable filter. Indeed, if the relation $FL(\mathbf{t}, \mathbf{D}, t)$ does not hold for a time t, it follows that no solution of $u' = f(t, u)$ can go through boxes $D_0, \ldots, D_k$ at times $t_0, \ldots, t_k$. The following definition and proposition capture these concepts more formally.

Definition 5 (Multistep Filter). *Let $\mathcal{O}$ be an ODE and s its solution. A* multistep filter *for $\mathcal{O}$ is an interval relation $FL : \mathbb{R}^{k+1} \times (\mathbb{IR}^n)^{k+1} \times \mathbb{R} \rightarrow Bool$ satisfying*

$$u_i \in D_i \;\&s(t_0, u_0, t_i) = u_i \; (0 \leq i \leq k) \;\; \Rightarrow \;\; \forall t: \; FL(\mathbf{t}, \mathbf{D}, t).$$

How can we use this filter to obtain tighter enclosures of the solution? A simple technique consists of pruning the last box computed by the predictor process. Assume that D_i^* is a box enclosing the solution at time t_i $(0 \leq i < k)$ and that we are interested in pruning the last predicted box D_k^-. A subbox $D \subseteq D_k^-$ can be pruned away if the condition $FL(\mathbf{t}, (D_0^*, \dots, D_{k-1}^*, D), t_e)$ does not hold for some evaluation point t_e. Let us explain briefly the geometric intuition behind this formula by considering what we call *natural filters*. Given interval extensions *MS* and *DMS* of *ms* and $\frac{\partial ms}{\partial t}$, it is possible to approximate the ODE $u' = f(t, u)$ by the formula

$$DMS(\mathbf{t}, \mathbf{D}, t) = F(t, MS(\mathbf{t}, \mathbf{D}, t)).$$

In this formula, the left-hand side of the equation represents *the approximation of the slope of u* while the right-hand represents *the slope of the approximation of u*. Since the approximations are conservative, these two sides must intersect on boxes containing a solution. Hence an empty intersection means that the boxes used in the formula do not contain the solution to the ODE system. Traditional consistency techniques and algorithms based on this filter can now be applied. For instance, one may be interested in updating the last box computed by the predictor process using the operator $D_k^* = \Box\{r \in D_k^- \mid FL(\mathbf{t}, (D_0^*, \dots, D_{k-1}^*, r), t_e)\}$. *Observe that this operator uses an evaluation time t_e and the main result of this paper consists in showing that t_e can be chosen optimally to maximize pruning.* The following definition is a novel notion of consistency for ODEs to capture pruning of the last r boxes.

Definition 6 (Backward Consistency of Multistep Filters). *A multistep filter $FL(\mathbf{t}, \mathbf{D}, e)$ is backward-consistent in $(\mathbf{t}, \mathbf{D})$ for time e if $\mathbf{D} = \Box\{u_k \in D_k \mid \exists \mathbf{u}_0 \in \mathbf{D}_0 : FL(\mathbf{t}, \mathbf{u}, e)\}$. A system of r successive multistep filters $\{FL_i(\mathbf{t}_{i..k+i}, \mathbf{D}_{i..k+i}, e_i)\}_{0 \leq i < r}$ is* backward(r)-consistent *in $(\mathbf{t}_{0..k+r-1}, \mathbf{D}_{0..k+r-1})$ for times e_i $(0 \leq i < r)$ if $\mathbf{D}_{k..k+r-1}$ is*

$$\Box\{\mathbf{u}_{k..k+r-1} \in \mathbf{D}_{k..k+r-1} \mid \exists \mathbf{u}_0 \in \mathbf{D}_0 : \forall\, 0 \leq i < r : FL_i(\mathbf{t}_{i..k+i}, \mathbf{u}_{i..k+i}, e_i)\}.$$

3.1 Multistep Filters

Filters rely on interval extensions of the multistep solution and of its derivative wrt t. These extensions are, in general, based on decomposing the (unknown) multistep solution into the sum of a computable approximation p and an (unknown) error term e, i.e., $ms(\mathbf{t}, \mathbf{u}, t) = p(\mathbf{t}, \mathbf{u}, t) + e(\mathbf{t}, \mathbf{u}, t)$. There exist standard techniques to build p and $\frac{\partial p}{\partial t}$ and to bound e and $\frac{\partial e}{\partial t}$. Section 3.3 reviews how they can be derived from Hermite interpolation polynomials. Here we simply assume that they are available and we show how to use them to build filters. The presentation so far showed how natural multistep filters can be obtained by simply replacing the multistep solution and its derivative wrt t by their interval extensions to obtain $DMS(\mathbf{t}, \mathbf{D}, t) = F(t, MS(\mathbf{t}, \mathbf{D}, t))$. It is not easy however to enforce backward consistency on a natural filter since the variables may occur in complex nonlinear expressions. This problem is addressed by mean-value filters that we now briefly explain.

Mean-value forms (MVFs) play a fundamental role in interval computations and are derived from the mean-value theorem. They correspond to problem linearizations around a point and result in filters that are systems of linear equations with interval coefficients and whose solutions can be enclosed reasonably efficiently. Mean-value forms are effective when the sizes of the boxes are sufficiently small, which is the case in ODEs. In addition, being linear equations, they allow for an easier treatment of the so-called *wrapping effect*, a crucial problem in interval methods for ODEs. As a consequence, mean-value forms are especially appropriate in our context and will produce filters which are efficiently amenable to backward consistency. The rest of this section describes how to obtain mean-value filters. Mean-value filters are presented in detail in [JVHD01a] and in the technical report version of this paper. For the purpose of this paper, it is sufficient to observe that they lead to a system of linear equations with interval coefficients. More precisely, let $\mathbf{D}^- \in \mathbb{IR}^{n(k+1)}$ be the predicted box of variable $\mathbf{u}$ and define $\mathbf{X}$ as $\mathbf{D} - m(\mathbf{D}^-)$. A mean-value filter is a system of equations of the form $\sum_{i=0}^{k} A_i(t)X_i = K(t)$ where $A_i(t) \in \mathbb{R}^{n\times n}$, $i = 0,\ldots,k$ and $K(t) \in \mathbb{IR}^n$. In general, for initial value problems, we will be interested in pruning the last predicted box D_k^-. Hence it is convenient to derive a mean-value filter which is explicit in D_k by isolating X_k to obtain $X_k = A_k(t)^{-1}K(t) - \sum_{i=0}^{k-1} \left(A_k(t)^{-1}A_i(t)\right) X_i$. which is an explicit mean-value filter ($A_k(t)^{-1}$ denotes an enclosure of the inverse of $A_k(t)$). It is easy to use an explicit mean-value filter to prune the predicted box D_k^- at time t_k given the boxes $D_0^*,\ldots,D_{k-1}^*$ from the previous integration steps, since X_k (and thus D_k) has been isolated. The filter simply becomes

$$D_k = m(D_k^-) + A_k(t)^{-1}K(t) - \sum_{i=0}^{k-1} \left(A_k(t)^{-1}A_i(t)\right)\left(D_i^* - m(D_i^*)\right)$$

and the pruned box D_k^* at time t_k is given by $D_k^* = D_k \cap D_k^-$. It follows directly that the explicit mean-value filter is backward-consistent in $\mathbf{D}^*$.

3.2 Global Filters

Mean-value filters may produce significant pruning of the boxes computed by the predictor process. However, they suffer from two limitations: the *wrapping effect* which is inherent in interval analysis and a *variable dependency* problem since the same boxes are used indirectly several times in a multistep method, possibly inducing a significant loss of precision. These two problems were addressed in [JVHD01a] through global filters. The main idea underlying global filters is to cluster several mean-value filters together so that they do not overlap. The intuition is illustrated in Figure 1 for $k = 3$. It can be seen that the global filter prunes the 3 predicted boxes D_3^-, D_4^-, and D_5^- for times t_3, t_4, and t_5 using the boxes D_0^*, D_1^*, and D_2^* computed for times t_0, t_1, and t_2. Observe also that global filters do not overlap, i.e., the boxes D_0^*, D_1^*, and D_2^* will not be used in subsequent filters. More precisely, a global filter is a system of k successive explicit mean-value filters. It can be transformed into an explicit form $\mathbf{X}_1 = C(\mathbf{e}_0)\mathbf{X}_0 + R(\mathbf{e}_0)$ where $C(\mathbf{e}_0) \in \mathbb{IR}^{nk\times nk}$ and $R(\mathbf{e}_0) \in \mathbb{IR}^{nk}$. An interesting property of global filters is

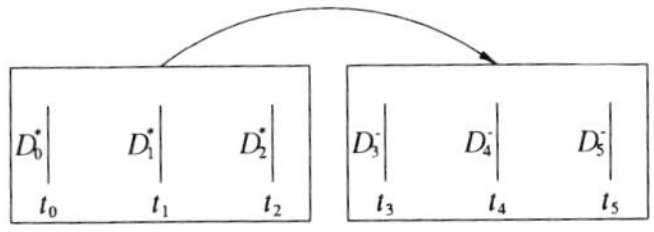

Fig. 1. Intuition of the Globalization Process ($k = 3$).

that each pruned box at times t_3, t_4, or t_5 can be computed only in terms of the predicted boxes and the boxes at times t_0, t_1, and t_2 by using Gaussian elimination. The resulting filter is backward(k)-consistent with respect to the resulting boxes. Finally, observe that global filters not only remove the variable dependency problem by globalizing the pruning process. They also produce square systems which makes it possible to apply standard techniques from one-step methods (e.g., local coordinate transformations and QR factorizations [Loh87]) to address the wrapping effect.

3.3 Hermite Filters

So far, we assumed the existence of interval extensions of p and $\partial p/\partial t$ and bounds on the error terms e and $\partial e/\partial t$. We now show how to use Hermite interpolation polynomials for this purpose. Informally speaking, a Hermite interpolation polynomial approximates a function $f \in C^\infty$ which is known implicitly by its values and the values of its successive derivatives at various points. A Hermite interpolation polynomial is specified by imposing that its values and the values of its successive derivatives at some given points be equal to the values of f and of its derivatives at the same points. Note that the number of conditions (i.e., the number of successive derivatives that are considered) may vary at the different points.

Definition 7 (Hermite(σ) Interpolation Polynomial). *Consider the ODE* $u' = f(t,u)$ *and let* $\sigma = (\sigma_0, \dots, \sigma_k) \in \mathbb{N}^{k+1}$ *and* $\sigma_i \neq 0$ $(0 \leq i \leq k)$. *Let* $\sigma_s = \sum_{i=0}^{k} \sigma_i$, $u_i^{(0)} = u_i$, *and* $u_i^{(j)} = f^{(j-1)}(t_i, u_i)$ $(0 \leq i \leq k \;\&\; 0 \leq j \leq \sigma_i - 1)$. *The* Hermite($\sigma$) interpolation polynomial *wrt* f *and* $(\mathbf{t}, \mathbf{u})$ *is the unique polynomial* q *of degree* $\leq \sigma_s - 1$ *satisfying* $q^{(j)}(t_i) = u_i^{(j)}$ $\quad (0 \leq j \leq \sigma_i - 1 \;\&\; 0 \leq i \leq k)$.

Proposition 1 (Hermite Interpolation Polynomial). *The polynomial* q *satisfying conditions of definition 7 is given by* $q(t) = \sum_{i=0}^{k} \sum_{j=0}^{\sigma_i - 1} u_i^{(j)} L_{ij}(t)$ *where* $L_{i,\sigma_i-1}(t) = l_{i,\sigma_i-1}(t)$ $(0 \leq i \leq k)$, $L_{ij}(t) = l_{ij}(t) - \sum_{\nu=j+1}^{\sigma_i-1} l_{ij}^{(\nu)}(t_i) L_{i\nu}(t)$ $(0 \leq i \leq k, 0 \leq j \leq \sigma_i - 2)$, *and* $l_{ij}(t) = \frac{(t-t_i)^j}{j!} \prod_{\substack{\nu=0 \\ \nu \neq i}}^{k} \left(\frac{t-t_\nu}{t_i - t_\nu}\right)^{\sigma_\nu}$ $\quad (0 \leq i \leq k, 0 \leq j \leq \sigma_i - 1)$.

It is easy to take interval extensions of a Hermite interpolation polynomial and of its derivatives. The only remaining issue is to bound the error terms. The following standard theorem (e.g., [SB80], [Atk88]) provides the necessary theoretical basis.

Proposition 2 (Hermite Error Term). *Let* $p(\mathbf{t}, \mathbf{u}, t)$ *be the Hermite(σ) interpolation polynomial in* t *wrt* f *and* $(\mathbf{t}, \mathbf{u})$. *Let* $u(t) \equiv ms(\mathbf{t}, \mathbf{u}, t)$, $T = \square\{t_0, \dots, t_k, t\}$, $\sigma_s = \sum_{i=0}^{k} \sigma_i$ *and* $w(t) = \prod_{i=0}^{k} (t - t_i)^{\sigma_i}$. *We have* $(1 \leq i \leq n)$

- $\exists\, \xi_i \in T : e_i(\mathbf{t}, \mathbf{u}, t) = \frac{1}{\sigma_s!} f_i^{(\sigma_s - 1)}(\xi_i, u(\xi_i)) w(t)$;
- $\exists\, \xi_{1,i}, \xi_{2,i} \in T : \frac{\partial e_i}{\partial t}(\mathbf{t}, \mathbf{u}, t) = \frac{1}{\sigma_s!} f_i^{(\sigma_s - 1)}(\xi_{1,i}, u(\xi_{1,i})) w'(t) + \frac{1}{(\sigma_s + 1)!} f_i^{(\sigma_s)}(\xi_{2,i}, u(\xi_{2,i})) w(t)$.

How to use this proposition to bound the error terms? It suffices to take interval extensions of the formula given in the proposition and to replace $\xi_i, \xi_{1,i}, \xi_{2,i}$ by T and $u(\xi_i), u(\xi_{1,i}), u(\xi_{2,i})$ by a bounding box for the ODE over T. As a consequence, we can compute an effective relaxation of the ODE by specializing global filters with a Hermite interpolation and its error bound. Filters based on these interpolations are called *Hermite(σ) filters* and a global Hermite(σ) filter is denoted by GHF(σ).

4 Optimal Pruning in Hermite Filters

Let us summarize what we have achieved so far. The basic idea of our approach is to approximate the ODE $\forall\, t : u' = f(t, u)$ by a filter $\forall\, t : FL(\mathbf{t}, \mathbf{D}, t)$. We have shown that a global filter prunes the last k boxes by using k successive mean-value filters and it addresses the wrapping effect and the variable dependency problem. We have also shown that a global filter can be obtained by using Hermite interpolation polynomials together with their error bounds. As a consequence, we obtain a filter $\forall\, \mathbf{e_0} : GHF(\sigma)(\mathbf{t}, \mathbf{D}, \mathbf{e_0})$ which can be used to prune the last k predicted boxes. The main remaining issue is to find an *evaluation time vector* $\mathbf{e_0}$ which maximizes pruning or, alternatively, which miminizes the sizes of the solution boxes in $GHF(\sigma)(\mathbf{t}, \mathbf{D}, \mathbf{e_0})$. More precisely, our main goal in choosing an evaluation time vector is to minimize the *local error* of the filter, i.e., the sizes of the boxes produced by the filter.

Definition 8 (Local Error of a Filter). *Let FL be a filter for ODE $u' = f(t, u)$. The local error $e_{loc}(FL, \mathbf{t_0}, \mathbf{u_0}, t)$ of FL wrt $(\mathbf{t_0}, \mathbf{u_0}, t)$ is* $\omega\left(\square\{u_k \in \mathbb{R}^n \mid FL(\mathbf{t}, \mathbf{u}, t)\}\right)$.

Observe that a global filter is obtained from several mean-value filters. Hence minimizing its local error amounts to minimizing the local error of individual mean-value filters. Moreover, since the local error is defined by evaluating the filter on real numbers, we can restrict attention, without loss of generality, to natural Hermite filters and do not need to consider their mean-value forms. To find an optimal evaluation time, we first derive the local error (Section 4.1). From the local error, we can then characterize the optimal evaluation time (Section 4.2). Two of the main results of this section are:

1. For a sufficiently small stepsize $h = t_k - t_0$, the relative distance between the optimal evaluation time and the point t_k in a natural or mean-value Hermite filter depends only on the relative distances between the interpolation points $t_0, \ldots, t_k$ and on σ. It does not depend on the ODE itself.
2. From a practical standpoint, the optimal evaluation time can be precomputed once for all for a given step size and σ. This computation does not induce any significant overhead of the method.

The third main result is concerned with the order of a natural Hermite filter which is shown to be $O(h^{\sigma_s+1})$ where $\sigma_s = \sum_{i=0}^{k} \sigma_i$ when the evaluation point is chosen carefully (but not necessarily optimally!).

4.1 Local Error of a Natural Hermite Filter

To analyze the local error and determine the optimal evaluation time, we use standard asymptotical notations from numerical analysis. Note that these notations characterize the behaviour of a function when h is sufficiently small. Asymptotic notations in computer science characterize, in general, the behaviour of algorithms when the size n of the problem becomes larger. These notations are simply obtained by substituting h by $1/n$. We also make a number of assumptions in this section. (Additional, more technical, assumptions are given in the appendix.) We assume that the step size h is given by $t_k - t_0$ and that the integration times are increasing, i.e., $t_0 < \ldots < t_k$. Moreover, we assume that the multistep solution ms is defined at $(\mathbf{t}_0, \mathbf{u}_0)$ or, in other words, that $\mathcal{O}$ has a solution going through $u_0, \ldots, u_{k-1}$ at times $t_0, \ldots, t_{k-1}$. We also use the notations $\sigma = (\sigma_0, \ldots, \sigma_k)$, $\sigma_s = \sum_{i=0}^{k} \sigma_i$, and $w(t) = \prod_{i=0}^{k}(t-t_i)^{\sigma_i}$. To characterize the local error of a natural Hermite filter, we first need a technical lemma which characterizes the behavior of the derivatives of the filter.

Lemma 1. *Consider an ODE $u' = f(t,u)$, let $p(\mathbf{t},\mathbf{u},t)$ be the Hermite(σ) interpolation polynomial in t wrt f and $(\mathbf{t},\mathbf{u})$ and let $\Phi(t) = D_{u_k}\frac{\partial p}{\partial t}(\mathbf{t},\mathbf{u},t) - D_u f(t, p(\mathbf{t},\mathbf{u},t) + e) D_{u_k} p(\mathbf{t},\mathbf{u},t)$, $e \in \mathbb{R}^n$. Then, when $t - t_k = O(h)$ and h is sufficiently small, we have*

1. $\Phi(t) \approx I\lambda(t)$; 2. $\lambda(t) = \Theta(h^{-1})$ if $\lambda(t) \neq 0$; 3. $\lambda(t) \neq 0$ for $t_{k-1} < t < t_k$

where $\lambda(t)$ is defined by the formula

$$\begin{aligned}
&\lambda(t) = \left(\left(\sum_{j=0}^{\sigma_k-2} \beta_{j+1}\frac{(t-t_k)^j}{j!}\right) + \left(\sum_{j=0}^{\sigma_k-1} \beta_j \frac{(t-t_k)^j}{j!}\right) \sum_{\nu=0}^{k-1} \frac{\sigma_\nu}{t_k - t_\nu}\right)\pi(t);\\
&\beta_0 = 1, \beta_j = -\pi^{(j)}(t_k),\ j = 1, \ldots, \sigma_k - 1;\\
&\pi(t) = \prod_{\nu=0}^{k-1}\left(\frac{t-t_\nu}{t_k-t_\nu}\right)^{\sigma_\nu}.
\end{aligned} \tag{1}$$

This lemma shows that $\Phi(t)$ is a $\Theta(h^{-1})$ almost diagonal matrix for $t_{k-1} < t < t_k$. Its proof is given in the appendix. We are now in position to characterize the local error of a natural Hermite filter.

Theorem 1 (Local Error of a Natural Hermite Filter). *Let FL be a natural Hermite(σ) filter for $u' = f(t,u)$ and assume that $t - t_k = O(h)$. With the notations of Lemma 1, we have*

1. *if $\Phi(t)$ is not singular, $e_{loc}(FL, \mathbf{t}_0, \mathbf{u}_0, t) = |\Phi^{-1}(t)|\,(\Theta(h)|w(t)| + \Theta(h)|w'(t)|)$;*
2. *if $\Phi(t)$ is not singular, then $\Phi(t) = \Theta(h^{-1})$;*
3. *if $t_{k-1} < t < t_k$ and if h is sufficiently small, then $\Phi(t)$ is not singular;*

We are now ready to show how to find an optimal evaluation time.

4.2 Optimal Evaluation Time for a Natural Hermite Filter

Our first result is fundamental and characterizes the order of a natural Hermite filter. It also hints on how to obtain an optimal evaluation time. Recall that the order of a method is the order of the local error minus 1.

Theorem 2 (Order of a Natural Hermite Filter). *Assume that $t - t_k = O(h)$ and let FL be a natural Hermite(σ) filter. With the notations of Lemma 1, we have*

1. *There exists t such that $t_{k-1} < t < t_k$ and $w'(t) = 0$;*

2. *If* $t_{k-1} < t < t_k$*,* $w'(t) = 0$*, and* h *is sufficiently small, then* $e_{loc}(FL, \mathbf{t}_0, \mathbf{u}_0, t) = O(h^{\sigma_s+2})$*;*
3. *If* $w'(t) \neq 0$ *and* $\Phi(t)$ *is not singular, then* $e_{loc}(FL, \mathbf{t}_0, \mathbf{u}_0, t) = \Theta(h^{\sigma_s+1})$*.*

Observe that the above theorem indicates that *the zeros of* w' *are evaluation times which lead to a method of a higher order for natural and mean-value Hermite filters* (provided that the matrix $\Phi(t)$ be non-singular at these points). This is the basis of our next result which describes a necessary condition for optimality.

Theorem 3 (Necessary Condition for Optimal Natural Hermite Filters). *Let* FL *be a natural Hermite(*σ*) filter and let* $t_e \in \mathbb{R}$ *be such that* $e_{loc}(FL, \mathbf{t}_0, \mathbf{u}_0, t_e) = \min_{t-t_k=O(h)}\{e_{loc}(FL, \mathbf{t}_0, \mathbf{u}_0, t)\}$*. We have that, for* h *sufficiently small,* t_e *is a zero of the function* $\gamma(t) = \sum_{i=0}^{k} \frac{\sigma_i}{t-t_i}$

Our next result specifies the number of zeros of the function γ as well as their locations.

Theorem 4. *The function* γ *in Theorem 3 has exactly* k *zeros* $s_0, \ldots, s_{k-1}$ *satisfying* $t_i < s_i < t_{i+1}$*.*

We now characterize precisely the optimal evaluation time for a natural Hermite filter.

Theorem 5 (Optimal Evaluation Time). *Let* FL *be a natural Hermite(*σ*) filter, let* $t_e \in \mathbb{R}$ *be such that* $e_{loc}(FL, \mathbf{t}_0, \mathbf{u}_0, t_e) = \min_{t-t_k=O(h)}\{e_{loc}(FL, \mathbf{t}_0, \mathbf{u}_0, t)\}$*, let* λ *and* γ *be the functions defined in Lemma 1 and Theorem 3 respectively, and let* $s_0, \ldots, s_{k-1}$ *be the zeros of* γ*. Then, for* h *sufficiently small,*

$$|(w/\lambda)(t_e)| = \min_{s \in \{s_0, \ldots, s_{k-1}\}} \{|(w/\lambda)(s)|\} \tag{2}$$

It is important to discuss the consequences of Theorem 3 in some detail. First observe that the *relative distance* between the optimal evaluation time t_e and the point t_k depends *only* on the *relative distances* between the interpolation points $t_0, \ldots, t_k$ and on the vector σ. In particular, it is independent from the ODE itself. For instance, for $k = 1$, we have $\gamma(t) = \frac{\sigma_0}{t-t_0} + \frac{\sigma_1}{t-t_1}$ and γ has a single zero given by $t_e = \frac{\sigma_1 t_0 + \sigma_0 t_1}{\sigma_0 + \sigma_1}$. In addition, if $\sigma_0 = \ldots = \sigma_k$, then the zeros of γ are independent from σ. In particular, for $k = 1$, we have $t_e = (t_0 + t_1)/2$. As a consequence, for a given σ and step size h, the relative distance between t_k and an optimal evaluation time t_e can be computed once at the beginning of the integration. In addition, since it does not depend on the ODE itself, this relative distance can be precomputed and stored for a variety of step sizes and vectors σ. The overhead of choosing an optimal evaluation time is thus negligible. Finally, it is worth stressing that any zero of function γ in Theorem 3 gives an $O(h^{\sigma_s+1})$ order for the Hermite filter (provided that the matrix $\Phi(t)$ be non-singular at that zero). Hence any such zero is in fact an appropriate evaluation time, although it is not necessarily optimal. In our experiments, the right-most zero was always the optimal evaluation time, although we have not been able to prove this result theoretically.

We now illustrate the theoretical results experimentally. Figure 2 gives approximative values of the relative distance between the rightmost zero of the function γ and the point t_k $(1 \leq k \leq 6)$, for $\sigma_0 = \ldots = \sigma_k$, and $h = t_k - t_0$. Observe that, for two interpolation points, t_e is in the middle of t_0 and t_1. It then moves closer and closer to t_k for larger values

k	1	2	3	4	5	6
$(t_e - t_k)/h$	-0.5000	-0.2113	-0.1273	-0.0889	-0.0673	-0.0537

Fig. 2. Relative Distance between the Rightmost Zero t_e of γ and t_k when $\sigma_0 = \ldots = \sigma_k$.

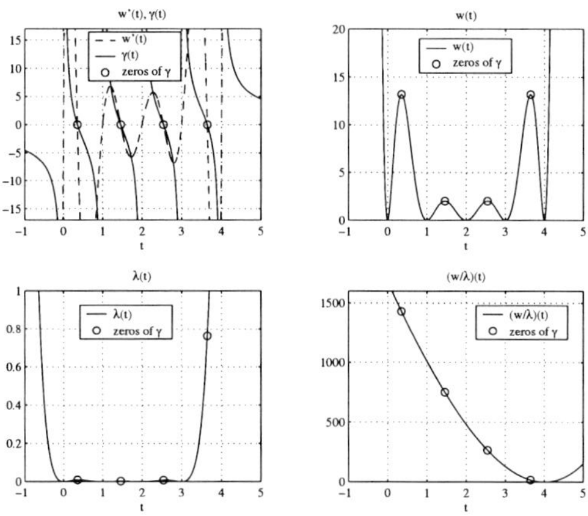

Fig. 3. The functions γ, w, w', λ and w/λ for the case $k = 4, \sigma = (2, 2, 2, 2, 2)$.

of k. Figure 3 illustrates the functions γ, w, w', λ, and w/λ for $k = 4, \sigma = (2, 2, 2, 2, 2)$ and their sometimes complex interactions. The top-left figure shows the function w' and γ, as well as the zeros of γ. The top-right figure shows the function w with the zeros of γ in superposition. The bottom-left figure shows function λ with the zeros of γ in superposition. The bottom-right picture shows the function w/λ and the zeros of γ. It can be seen that the right-most zero minimizes the local error in this example. Figure 4 illustrates our theoretical results experimentally on a specific ODE. It plots the local error of several global Hermite filters (GHF) as a function of the evaluation time for the Lorenz system (e.g., [HNW87]). It is assumed that $t_{i+1} - t_i$ is constant ($0 \le i \le 2k-2$). In addition, we assume that, in each mean-value filter composing the GHF, the distance between the evaluation time and the rightmost interpolation point is constant. In the graphs, $[t_0, t_k] = [0, 0.01]$ and $h = t_k - t_0 = 0.01$. The figure also shows the rightmost zero of the function γ as obtained from Figure 2. As can be seen, the rightmost zero of γ is a very good approximation of the optimal evaluation time of the filter for all the cases displayed.

5 Theoretical Analysis

We analyze the cost of our algorithm based on the global Hermite filter method GHF(σ) and compare it to Nedialkov's IHO(p, q) method [NJ99], the best interval method we know of. Nedialkov shows that the IHO method outperforms interval Taylor series methods (e.g. Lohner's AWA [Loh87]). The step size is given by $h = t_k - t_0$ and we use the same step size in GHF(σ) and IHO(p, q). Let $\sigma_m = \max(\sigma)$ and $\sigma_s = \sigma_0 + \ldots + \sigma_k$. At each step i, we use the following assumptions when comparing GHF(σ) and IHO(p, q): (1) The bounding box process uses a Taylor series method ([CR96]) of order σ_s. Moreover, we assume that $B_{ik} = \ldots = B_{(i+1)k-1}$, i.e., the function computes a single

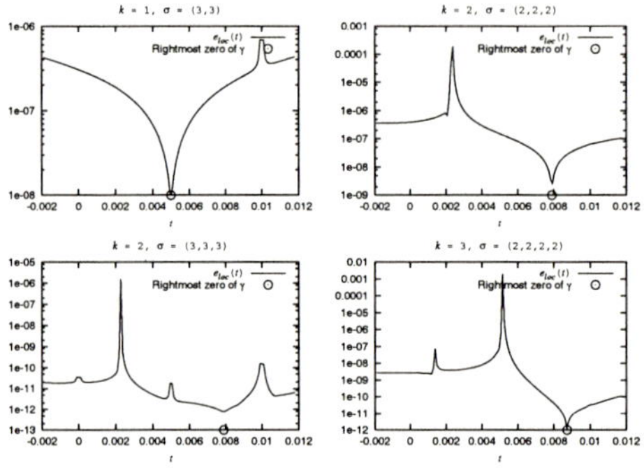

Fig. 4. Local Error of Global Filters as a Function of the Evaluation Time (Lorentz System).

	Cost-1	Cost-2
IHO	–	$2\lceil \frac{\sigma_s}{2} \rceil^2 nN_1 + O(\sigma_s nN_2)$
GHF	$7k^3n^3$	$((\sigma_m - 1)^2 + 1)knN_1 + \sigma_m knN_2$
GHF-1	–	$(\lfloor \frac{\sigma_s - 1}{2} \rfloor^2 + 1)nN_1 + O(\sigma_s nN_2)$
GHF-2	$(\frac{7}{8}\sigma_s - \frac{21}{4})\sigma_s^2 n^3$	$(\sigma_s - 2)nN$

Fig. 5. Cost Analysis : Methods of the Same Order.

	Cost-2
IHO	$2\lfloor \frac{\sigma_s - 1}{2} \rfloor^2 nN_1 + O(\sigma_s nN_2)$
GHF-1	$(\lfloor \frac{\sigma_s - 1}{2} \rfloor^2 + 1)nN_1 + O(\sigma_s nN_2)$

Fig. 6. Cost Analysis : Methods of Different Orders.

bounding box over $[t_{ik-1}, t_{(i+1)k-1}]$; (2) The predictor process uses Moore's Taylor method [Moo66] of order $q+1$ (same order as the predictor used in IHO(p, q)) to compute the boxes $\mathbf{D}_i^-$; (3) We choose the rightmost zero of function γ as an evaluation time in the Hermite filters. Consequently, the GHF(σ) method is of order $\sigma_s + 1$.

Methods of the Same Order: We first compare the costs of the GHF(σ) and IHO(p, q) methods when we assume that $p + q = \sigma_s$ and $q \in \{p, p+1\}$. The methods GHF and IHO are thus of the same order ($\sigma_s + 1$). Figure 5 reports the *main* cost of a step in the IHO method and our GHF method. It also shows the complexity of two particular cases of GHF. The first case (GHF-1) corresponds to a polynomial with only two interpolation points ($k = 1$) and $|\sigma_1 - \sigma_0| \leq 1$, while the second case (GHF-2) corresponds to a polynomial imposing two conditions on every interpolation points ($\sigma_0 = \ldots = \sigma_k = 2$). The first main result is that GHF-1 *is always cheaper than* IHO, which means that our method can always be made to run faster by choosing only two interpolation points. (The next section will show that improvement in accuracy is also obtained in this case). GHF-2 is more expensive than GHF-1 and IHO when f is simple because in this case the Jacobians are cheap to compute and the fixed cost Cost-1 becomes large wrt Cost-2. However, *when f contains many operations (which is the case in many practical applications),* GHF-2 *can become substantially faster* because Cost-1 in GHF-2 is independent of f and Cost-2 is substantially smaller in GHF-2 than in GHF-1 and IHO. It also shows the versatility of the approach that can be taylored to the application.

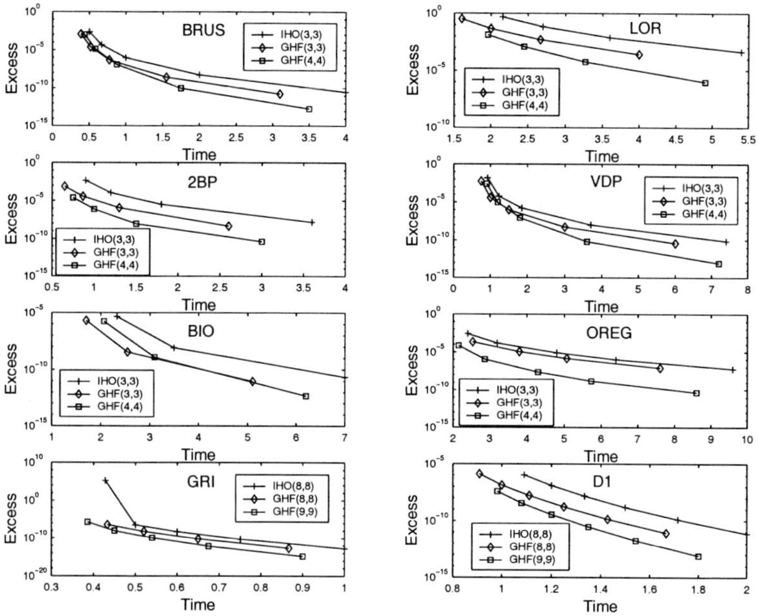

Fig. 7. Experimental Comparison of the Methods IHO(p, p), GHF(p, p) and GHF($p + 1, p + 1$).

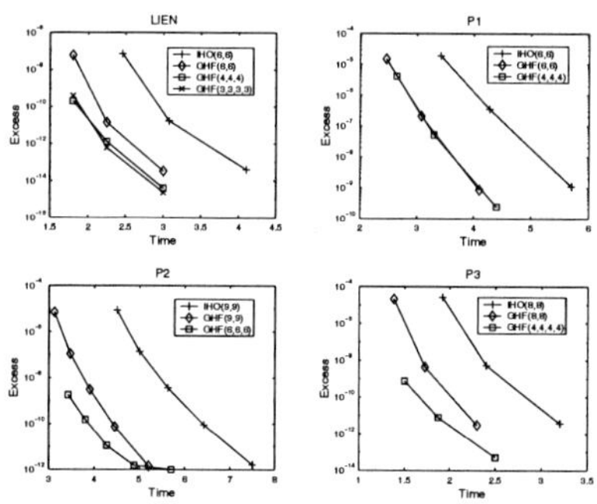

Fig. 8. Experimental Comparison of Multistep and One-Step Methods.

One-Step Methods of Different Orders: Our approach can be made both asymptotically more precise and faster. Consider the costs of the IHO(p, q) and GHF(σ_0, σ_1) methods when we assume that $|\sigma_1 - \sigma_0| \leq 1, p + q = \sigma_s - 2$ and $q \in \{p, p + 1\}$. Under these conditions, IHO is a method of order $\sigma_s - 1$, while GHF is a method of order $\sigma_s + 1$. Figure 6 reports the main cost of a step in IHO and GHF. As can be seen from the figure, GHF is always cheaper than IHO. *The* GHF *method is thus both asymptotically more precise (by two orders of magnitude) and faster than the* IHO *method.*

6 Experimental Analysis

We now report experimental results of a C++ implementation of our approach on a Sun Ultra 10 workstation with a 333 MHz UltraSparc CPU. The underlying interval arithmetic and automatic differentiation packages are PROFIL/BIAS [Knu94] and FADBAD/TADIFF [BS97] respectively. Many of the tested examples are classical benchmarks for ODE solvers. These problems are taken from various domains, including chemistry, biology, mechanics, physics and electricity. Note that, although we could use interval initial conditions, we consider only point initial conditions to compare the different methods. The "full Brusselator" (BRUS) and the "Oregonator" (OREG), a stiff problem, model famous chemical reactions, the Lorenz system (LOR) is an example of the so-called "strange attractors", the Two-Body problem (2BP) comes from mechanics, and the van der Pol (VDP) equation describes an electrical circuit. All these problems are described in detail in [HNW87]. We also consider a problem from molecular biology (BIO), the Stiff DETEST problem D1 [Enr75], and another stiff problem (GRI) from [Gri72]. Finally, we consider four problems (LIEN, P1, P2, P3) where the ODE has a more complex expression (i.e. the function f contains many operations). They are taken from [Per00]. The experimental results follow the same assumptions as in the theoretical analysis section and we make three types of comparisons: (1) one-step methods of the same order; (2) one-step methods of different orders, but of similar cost; and (3) multistep versus one-step methods of the same order. The figures report the global excess (where the global excess at point t_i is given by the infinite norm of the width of the enclosure D_i at t_i, i.e., the quantity $\|\omega(D_i)\|_\infty$) at the end of the interval of integration of the compared IHO and GHF methods.

One-Step Methods: Figure 7 plots the excess as a function of the execution time in the methods IHO(p, p), GHF(p, p) and GHF($p + 1, p + 1$). We take $p = 8$ for GRI and D1 and $p = 3$ for the other problems. As can been seen, the curve of IHO is always above the curves of the GHF methods, showing that IHO is less precise than the GHF methods for a given execution time or, alternatively, IHO is slower than the GHF methods for a given precision. Thus, although GHF(p, p) may sometimes be less precise than IHO(p, p) for a given step size in the stiff problems OREG, GRI and D1, GHF(p, p) still performs better than IHO(p, p) because the cost of a step is less in GHF(p, p) than in IHO(p, p). The figure also shows that GHF($p + 1, p + 1$) performs better than GHF(p, p) in all cases. Furthermore, our results confirm that IHO(p, p) and GHF(p, p) are methods of the same order, and that GHF($p + 1, p + 1$) is a method of higher order.

Multistep Versus One-Step Methods: We now compare multistep GHF methods versus IHO and one-step GHF methods of the same order in problems where the ODE has a more complex expression (i.e., f contains many operations). Figure 8 plots the excess as a function of the execution time in several methods. Again, the curve of IHO is always above the curves of the GHF methods, showing that the latter perform better on these problems. Furthermore, we observe that the curves of the one-step GHF methods are above those of the multistep GHF methods. Multistep GHF methods perform thus better in these cases.

Summary. The results indicate that our method produces orders of magnitude improvements in accuracy and runs faster than the best known method. The theoretical results are also confirmed by the experiments. When f contains many operations, using many interpolation points is particularly effective. For very complex functions, the gain in computation time could become substantial. When f is simple, using few interpolation points becomes more interesting.

References

[Atk88] K. E. Atkinson. *An introduction to Numerical Analysis*. John Wiley & Sons, 1988.

[Ber98] Berz, M. and Makino, K. Verified Integration of ODEs and Flows Using Differential Algebraic Methods on High-Order Taylor Models. *Reliable Computing*, 4:361-369, 1998.

[BS97] C. Bendsten and O. Stauning. *TADIFF, a Flexible C++ Package for Automatic Differentiation Using Taylor Series*. Technical Report 1997-x5-94, Technical University of Denmark, April 1997.

[CB99] J. Cruz, and P. Barahona. An Interval Constraint Approach to Handle Parametric Ordinary Differential Equations for Decision Support. *EKBD-99*, 93-108, 1999.

[CR96] G. F. Corliss and R. Rihm. Validating an a Priori Enclosure Using High-Order Taylor Series. In *Scientific Computing, Computer Arithmetic, and Validated Numerics*, 1996.

[DJVH98] Y. Deville, M. Janssen, and P. Van Hentenryck. Consistency Techniques in Ordinary Differential Equations. In *CP'98*, Pisa, Italy, October 1998.

[Eij81] Eijgenraam, P. *The Solution of Initial Value Problems Using Interval Arithmetic*. Mathematical Centre Tracts No. 144. Stichting Mathematisch Centrum, Amsterdam, 1981.

[Enr75] W. H. Enright, T. E. Hull, and B. Lindberg. Comparing Numerical Methods for Stiff Systems of ODEs. *BIT*, 15:10-48, 1975.

[Gri72] R. D. Grigorieff. *Numerik gewöhnlicher Differentialgleichungen 1*. Teubner, 1972.

[HNW87] E. Hairer, S.P. Nørsett, G. Wanner. *Solving Ordinary Differential Equations I*. Springer-Verlag, Berlin, 1987.

[JDVH99] M. Janssen, Y. Deville, and P. Van Hentenryck. Multistep Filtering Operators for Ordinary Differential Equations. In *CP'99*, Alexandria, VA, October 1999.

[JVHD01a] M. Janssen, P. Van Hentenryck, and Y. Deville A Constraint Satisfaction Approach to Parametric Differential Equations In *IJCAI-2001*, Seattle, WA, August 2001.

[Knu94] O. Knüppel. PROFIL/BIAS - A Fast Interval Library. *Computing*, 53(3-4), 1994.

[Kru69] Krueckeberg, F. Ordinary Differential Equations. In E. Hansen, editor, *Topics in Interval Analysis*, page 91-97. Clarendon Press, Oxford, 1969.

[Loh87] Lohner R. J. Enclosing the Solutions of Ordinary Initial and Boundary Value Problems. In *Computer Arithmetic*, Wiley, 1987.

[Moo66] R.E. Moore. *Interval Analysis*. Prentice-Hall, Englewood Cliffs, N.J., 1966.

[Ned99] N. S. Nedialkov. Computing Rigorous Bounds on the Solution of an Initial Value Problem for an Ordinary Differential Equation, Ph.D. Thesis, Univ. of Toronto, 1999.

[NJ99] N.S. Nedialkov and K.R. Jackson. An Interval Hermite-Obreschkoff Method for Computing Rigorous Bounds on the Solution of an Initial Value Problem for an ODE, *Developments in Reliable Computing*, Kluwer, 1999.

[Per00] L. Perko. *Differential Equations and Dynamical Systems*. Springer-Verlag, 2000.

[Rih98] R. Rihm. Implicit Methods for Enclosing Solutions of ODEs. *J. of Universal Computer Science*, 4(2), 1998.

[SB80] J. Stoer and R. Bulirsch. *Introduction to Numerical Analysis*. Springer-Verlag, 1980.

[VHMD97] P. Van Hentenryck, L. Michel, and Y. Deville. *Numerica: a Modeling Language for Global Optimization*. The MIT Press, Cambridge, Mass., 1997.

Interaction of Constraint Programming and Local Search for Optimisation Problems

Francisco Azevedo* and Pedro Barahona

Departamento de Informática, Universidade Nova de Lisboa
2829-516 Caparica — Portugal
{fa,pb}@di.fct.unl.pt

Abstract. In this paper we show, for the specific problem of test pattern optimisation, that adapting constraint propagation with results obtained from local search outperforms the use of each of these techniques alone. We show that a tool we developed to solve this problem using such approach with multi-valued logics achieves better results than those obtained with a highly efficient tool based on an integer linear programming formulation over a SAT model.

1 Introduction

In circuit design, a *test pattern* is a vector of primary inputs (PI) that detects a fault in a circuit, i.e. for which some output of the circuit (PO) takes a different value if the circuit is faulty. An efficient Constraint Programming (CP) solution for the problem of test pattern generation (TG) extends the Boolean domain with two values that denote dependency on the faulty state of some gate [1]. Test pattern optimisation (TGO) consists in finding test patterns with the maximum number of unspecified PIs. This problem was addressed in [2] by using a completely heuristic approach, and Flores *et al.* [3,4] proposed the first *formal* model for TGO, and implemented a tool (MTP) based on an integer linear programming formulation over a SAT model for TG.

A search procedure that produces all the solutions to a problem may be adapted to an optimisation algorithm, by using a branch and bound (B&B) algorithm, available in most CLP systems [5,6]. Unfortunately it is not easy to apply B&B in the above mentioned CP approach to TG since the function to optimise is the number of unspecified PIs, and these are all instantiated in the test patterns generated.

Hence we adopted and developed multi-valued logics that explicitly consider an unspecified input as an extra value of the logic, making it possible to count the number of such values in the input patterns.

---

* Financially supported by "Sub-Programa Ciência e Tecnologia do 2º Quadro Comunitário de Apoio"

T. Walsh (Ed.): CP 2001, LNCS 2239, pp. 554-559, 2001.

More interestingly, in the tool that we developed (*Maxx*) and which outperforms MTP, a "weaker" logic was used to construct solutions and a more complex logic to improve the solutions found by local search. Despite its stronger expressive power, a specialised constraint solver for the latter logic would not be efficient. However, it does pay off to use it in local search to obtain better solutions near those already found, circumventing the inefficiency of changing, by backtracking in chronological order, the earlier choices made in PI bits.

This paper is organised as follows. Section 2 presents the multi-valued logics we have used, section 3 presents the results obtained with our tool and compares them with those obtained by MTP, and section 4 presents the concluding remarks.

2 Multi-valued Logics

To implement a specialised constraint solver for the constructive phase of B&B we adopted a multi-valued logic that encodes the behaviour of a normal and faulty circuit, in whose lines one may consider 3 values – the usual 0/1 Boolean values plus the unspecified value *u*. The combination of these 3 values in 2 circuits defines a 9-valued logic (Fig. 1). Since values 1/0 and 0/1 guarantee different behaviour of a normal and faulty circuit, a test pattern must yield one such value at some PO. Although slightly less expressive, we used a simplified 5-valued logic, for which a more efficient specialised solver could be developed, allowing a CP tool to find solutions for the TG problem with explicit *u* values in the input vectors.

Normal	0	1	u	0	1	u	0	1	u
Faulty	0	0	0	1	1	1	u	u	u
9-value	**0/0**	**1/0**	**u/0**	**0/1**	**1/1**	**u/1**	**0/u**	**1/u**	**u/u**
5-Value	**0**	**d-1**	**u**	**d-0**	**1**	**u**	**u**	**u**	**u**

Fig. 1. 5- and 9-valued logic codifications for normal and faulty circuits

The model is not complete as shown in Fig. 2 for PI *b* stuck-at-1: 5-valued logic does not yield a *d*-0 output and 9-valued logic does not yield a 0/1 output. Rather than implementing an inefficient solver for a more expressive logic, better solutions may be found by local search (LS) near solutions found by 5-valued logic. The advantages are twofold. Firstly, by using a more expressive logic, LS may find more solutions. Secondly, even solutions detected with 5-valued logic can be found more efficiently, as LS may avoid the inefficiency of chronological backtracking earlier choices.

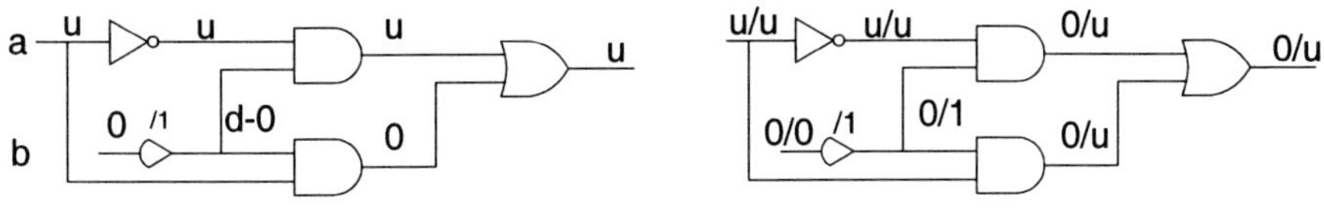

Fig. 2. Circuit modelling with 5- and 9-valued logic

2.1 Extended Logic for Local Search

In LS we do not construct a solution as in CP, but simply test whether a complete input pattern is a solution. Hence, rather than adopting a logic that encodes two circuits (normal and faulty), and where some values (e.g. *d*-0 and *d*-1) in a PO denote dependency on a fault, we may simply test the two circuit models and check whether a PO takes value 0 in one of the circuits and value 1 in the other.

To detect that two unspecified values come from the same source but have opposite values (i.e. different inversion parities), unspecified bits are represented by a pair *id-p*, where *id* denotes the source of the unspecified bit and p denotes the parity of the signal, i.e. whether the unspecified bit has been subject to an even (0) or odd (1) number of inversions. With this interpretation, the basic logic operations can be described, as shown in Fig. 3 for the *not*- and *and*-gates (the others are similar).

NOT	0	1	*id*-0	*id*-1
	1	0	*id*-1	*id*-0

A	0	1	*Arg*	*id*-0	id_A-p_A
B	*Arg*	*Arg*	*Arg*	*id*-1	id_B-p_B
Z=A.B	0	*Arg*	*Arg*	0	id_Z-0

Fig. 3. Extended logic considering the inversion parity of an unspecified value

When two unspecified values coming from different sources id_A and id_B, meet at an and-gate, its output Z is also unspecified. Since it depends on both inputs, we code the output as id_Z–0, i.e. having source Z and inversion parity 0. Notice that even when there is only one source of uncertainty (e.g. one PI) this logic applied to the two circuits is more complete than the 9-valued logic applied to a single circuit (Fig. 4).

Fig. 4 represents the previously shown normal and faulty circuits with input vector *t*=*u*0, modelled with this logic. The normal circuit outputs value 0, while in the faulty circuit (with PI *b* buffer stuck-at-1) the output is value 1 due to the conflicting unspecified values at the or-gate. Hence, *t* indeed detects fault *f* = *b* stuck-at-1, since the output values for the two circuits are different and specified.

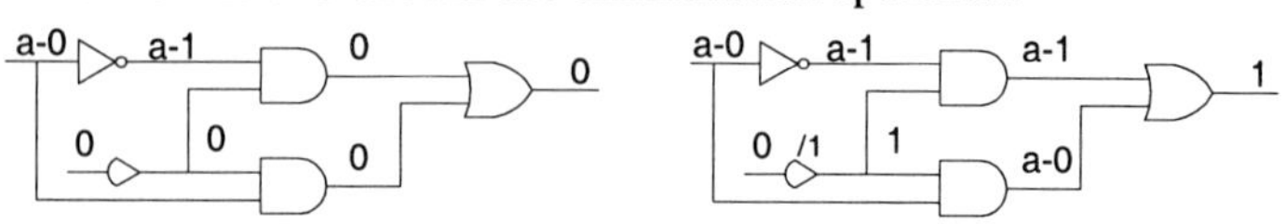

Fig. 4. Normal and faulty circuits with extended logic

This extended logic just presented, though still unable to detect some (rarely occurring) input patterns, does detect more cases than the 5-valued logic, and even the 9-valued logic. However, a constraint solver over this logic would deal with large finite domains, making constraint reasoning very inefficient. Instead, it is very simple to use this logic to test alternative solutions, namely those obtained by unspecifying one bit of some already known solution.

2.2 Keeping Dependencies

Despite the expressive power of the extended logic, its efficient use on LS depends on an efficient method to find which PIs in a solution can be made unspecified. To denote dependency on specified PI values, we code circuit signals as *Set:Value* pairs, where *Value* is, as before, either a Boolean value or an unspecified value in the form *id-p*. *Set* is a set of *id/V* pairs, denoting that turning PI *id* unspecified makes the signal to take a *different* value *V* (either Boolean or unspecified). Conversely, if for some PI *id*, there is no member *id/V* in *Set*, then making *id* unspecified does not affect the signal.

Due to space limitations, we show in Fig. 5, how dependencies are propagated in an *and*-gate. If both inputs are 0, the output remains 0 even if one input alone becomes unspecified. For a 01 input combination, if the 0 input becomes unspecified so does the output. When both inputs are 1, the output is 1 and depends on both inputs since if any become unspecified so would the output (as either *x*-0 or y-0).

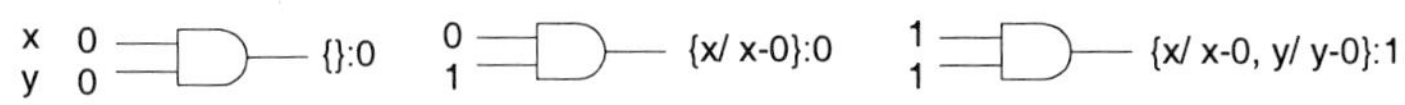

Fig. 5. Sets of dependencies on 0, 1 and 2 specified values

In Fig. 6, we show the result of keeping dependencies on the circuit previously shown. The values for the normal and faulty circuits are placed, respectively, above and under each line. Since the output of the circuit takes values 0 and 1 for the normal and faulty circuit, the fault is indeed detected with input pattern *ab*=00. Moreover, since a pair *a/V* is not present in any of the dependency sets, PI *a* may safely be made unspecified, and the output of the improved input pattern *ab*=*u*0 would still be 0/1.

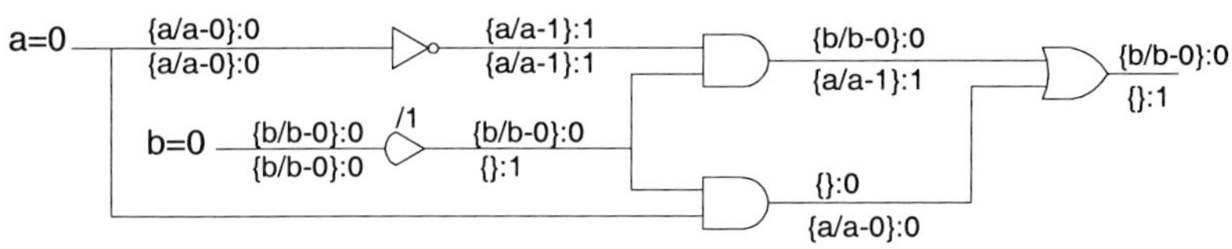

Fig. 6. Local search logic: PI *a* may be unspecified

3 Experimental Results

The method just described was tested with the standard ISCAS benchmark circuits [7]. Table 1 shows the results obtained by using as starting point the solutions provided by **Atalanta** [8], a widely used special purpose tool for solving the TG problem. Since this tool does not primarily aim at maximising the unspecified bits of the test patterns, both MTP (allowing 100 backtracks per fault) and our tool, *Maxx* (allowing a 7 seconds limit for each B&B try), significantly increase the number of unspecified bits.

Table 1. MTP and *Maxx* improvements on *Atalanta*

	PI	F	Atalanta %U	MTP %U	MTP Gain	MTP t/f	*Maxx* %U	*Maxx* Gain	*Maxx* t/f	Diff
c432	36	524	56.2	60.8	10.5	3.21	71.4	34.7	7.16	24.2
c499	41	758	17.1	18.7	1.9	4.35	25.6	10.3	7.95	8.3
c880	60	942	82.2	83.8	9.0	2.54	85.2	16.9	6.08	7.9
c1355	41	1574	13.3	13.7	0.5	9.12	20.0	7.7	7.93	7.3
c1908	33	1879	44.7	48.4	6.7	9.61	52.8	14.6	7.51	8.0
c2670	233	2747	92.0	92.4	5.0	10.99	94.1	26.2	5.90	21.2
c3540	50	3428	74.6	77.3	10.6	16.81	79.2	18.1	7.07	7.5
c5315	178	5350	92.6	92.9	4.1	9.34	93.6	13.5	7.53	9.5
c6288	32	7744	22.2	22.2	0.0	36.65	28.4	8.0	12.51	8.0
c7552	207	7550	86.9	86.9	0.0	17.46	90.9	30.5	10.17	30.5

In this table, *F* represents the number of faults to test, *%U* the number of PIs that are left unspecified, as a fraction of the total number *PI*F*. Assuming that resources spent in testing the circuit are proportional to the number of *specified* bits, we show the *Gain* (in %) for MTP and *Maxx* wrt *Atalanta*, i.e. the saving of resources that can be achieved with the solutions provided by these tools, as well as their difference, *Diff*. The average time (in seconds) spent per fault in each tool, *t/f*, is also shown.

The results show that the *Gain* obtained with *Maxx* is always significantly better than those obtained with MTP, with similar time spent per fault (MTP in a SUN Sparc, 166MHz / 384 Mb, *Maxx* in a Pentium III, 500MHz / 256Mb).

To test the ability of MTP and *Maxx* to improve the previous MTP solutions for the same benchmarks, we used such solutions as starting points for *Maxx* and increased the number of backtracks per fault to 1000 in MTP. In these experiments, *Maxx* always achieved better improvements than MTP, with gain difference ranging from 2 to 18 (average: 12). Moreover, they were obtained significantly faster, as *Maxx* always took around 7 secs per fault, whereas MTP took from 20s in the smaller circuits to 72s in c2670 (for larger circuits MTP produced no results).

Finally we analysed the sources of our improvements in these last experiments for the two larger circuits. In the table below INIT shows the initial number of unspecified bits. An important increase in the number of unspecified bits in the test patterns is obtained purely by LS on the initial solutions (LS_1). A significant improvement is still obtained by restarting a CP search, with the bound updated to that obtained in the LS phase (CP_1). Solutions still improved with a subsequent LS (LS_2) and in circuit c7552, additional CP and LS steps still improve the previous solutions.

	INIT	LS_1	CP_1	LS_2	CP_2	LS_3	CP_3	LS_4	CP_4	LS_5
c6288	52,874	10,749	2,126	303						
c7552	1,334,794	56,052	5,630	628	22	29	26	8	2	2

These results show that the model used in the CP step, although less complete than that used in the LS step, was often able to provide a different starting point that enabled LS to escape from local optima. Moreover, the extended logic used for LS proved quite useful to improve a solution found by constraint propagation.

4 Conclusions and Further Research

This paper has shown that using both constraint propagation and LS to solve constraint satisfaction and optimisation problems may outperform the use of each of these techniques alone. Although the tool we developed does not fully integrate constraint propagation with LS, we believe that integrating these two techniques is an important improvement in CP and should be further exploited and such ability should be made available by the CP tools themselves, enabling their B&B primitives to be parameterised with some LS procedure.

For the particular problem of test pattern optimisation, other improvements are envisaged, namely extending our dependency encoding to multiple input bits.

References

[1] H. Simonis. *Test Generation using the Constraint Logic Programming Language CHIP*, 6th Int. Conf. on Logic Programming , MIT Press, 101-112, 1989.

[2] S. Hellebrand, B. Reeb, S. Tarnick and H.-J. Wunderlich. *Pattern Generation for a Deterministic BIST Scheme*, Int. Conf. on Computer-Aided Design, 1995.

[3] Paulo F. Flores, Horácio C. Neto, Krishnendu Chakrabarty and João P. Marques-Silva. *A Model and Algorithm for Computing Minimum-Size Test Patterns*, in IEEE European Test Workshop (ETW), 147-148, May 1998.

[4] Paulo F. Flores, Horácio C. Neto and João P. Marques-Silva. *An Exact Solution to the Minimum-Size Test Pattern Problem*, in IEEE/ACM Int. Ws on Logic Synthesis (IWLS), 452-470, 1998.

[5] ECRC, *ECLiPSe user manual and extensions*, Technical Report, ECRC, 1994.

[6] Programming Systems Group of the Swedish Institute of Computer Science. *SICStus Prolog User's Manual*, 1995.

[7] ISCAS. *Special Session on ATPG*, IEEE Symp. Circuits and Systems, 1985.

[8] H. K. Lee and D. S. Ha, *On the Generation of Test Patterns for Combinational Circuits*, Technical Report No. 12_93, Department of Electrical Engineering, Virginia Polytechnic Institute and State University, 1993.

Partition-k-AC: An Efficient Filtering Technique Combining Domain Partition and Arc Consistency

Hachemi Bennaceur and Mohamed-Salah Affane

Laboratoire d'informatique de Paris-Nord, Institut Galilée,
Avenue Jean-Baptiste Clément, F-93430 Villetaneuse.
{bennaceu,msa@lipn.univ-paris13.fr

Abstract. The constraint propagation process is a powerful tool for solving constraint satisfaction problems (CSPs). We propose a filtering technique which exploits at best this tool in order to improve the pruning efficiency. This technique, combining domain partition and arc consistency, generalizes and improves the pruning efficiency of the arc consistency, and the singleton arc consistency filtering techniques. The presented empirical results show the gain brought by this technique.

1 Introduction

Constraint Satisfaction Problems (CSPs) involve the assignment of values to variables which are subject to a set of constraints. Filtering techniques are important for solving CSPs. Arc consistency (AC) filtering is widely used in practice because of its simplicity and its low space and time complexities. In the last years some classes of filtering techniques have been proposed in order to improve the pruning efficiency of AC, such as the Singleton Arc Consistency (SAC) [Debruyne and Bessière 1997], the Neighborhood Inverse Consistency (NIC) [Freuder and Elfe 1996], the Restricted Path Consistency (RPC) [Berlandier 1995], the Circuit Consistency (CC) [Bennaceur 1994]. The objective of all these techniques is to improve the search solutions by filtering more values than AC while still keeping the advantages of AC. An experimental comparison between these techniques is given in [Debruyne and Bessière 1997]. We propose, in this paper, a new filtering technique called k-Partition-Arc Consistency (k-Partition-AC) having the same objective as the above techniques and improving the pruning efficiency. Given an arc consistent CSP, our filtering technique divides the variable domains into disjoint sub-domains in order to build a set of arc inconsistent CSPs. The filtering of these CSPs by arc consistency may remove a common set of values from each CSP. We show that these values are inconsistent in the original CSP (see property 2).

We illustrate this technique on the following simple example. Figure 1 shows a CSP P, with five variables and five constraints, represented by its constraint graph. We can easily verify that P is arc consistent. By partitionning the domain D_1 into $D_1^1 = \{v_1, v_2\}$ and $D_1^2 = \{v_3, v_4\}$, P is decomposed into two CSPs P_1^1 and P_1^2 such that P has a solution if and only if P_1^1 or P_1^2 has one. Note that

T. Walsh (Ed.): CP 2001, LNCS 2239, pp. 560–564, 2001.

both P_1^1 and P_1^2 can be filtered by arc consistency. The value v_1 of X_4 is arc inconsistent both in P_1^1 and P_1^2, so using property 2 of section 3, we deduce that this value is also inconsistent in P.

This example shows how our method exploits the advantages of the constraint propagation process. We remark that, both in P_1^1 and P_1^2, the value v_1 is detected arc inconsistent after using the constraint propagation process. k-Partition-AC is based on the main idea in order to increase the pruning efficiency of arc consistency: any common inconsistent value of the CSPs obtained by the domain partition is also inconsistent in the original CSP.

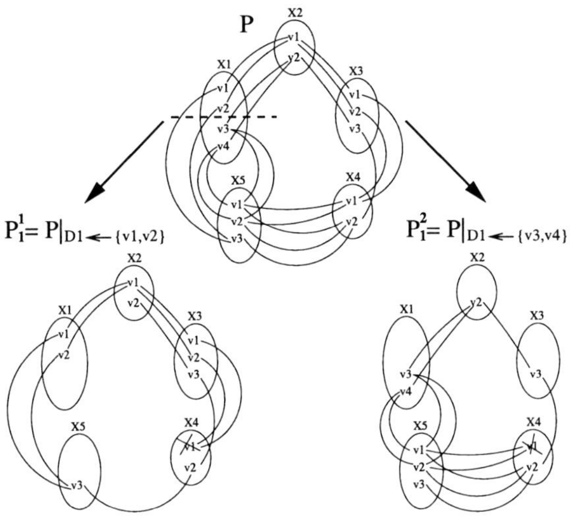

Fig. 1. Example

2 Combining Domain Partition and Arc Consistency

We denote by $P|_{D_i \leftarrow D_i^j}$, $(D_i^j \subset D_i)$, the CSP obtained by restricting the domain D_i to D_i^j in P. Let $P = (\mathcal{X}, \mathcal{D}, \mathcal{C}, \mathcal{R})$ be an arc consistent CSP and X_i be a variable of P. Given a partition $(D_i^1, D_i^2, \ldots, D_i^h)$ of D_i $(h \leq d_i)$, P can be decomposed into h CSPs $P_i^1, P_i^2, \ldots, P_i^h$, $h \leq d_i$, where each CSP P_i^j $1 \leq j \leq h$ is defined by

- $P_i^j = (\mathcal{X}^j, \mathcal{D}^j, \mathcal{C}^j, \mathcal{R}^j)$
- $\mathcal{X}^j \leftarrow \mathcal{X}$
- $\mathcal{C}^j \leftarrow \mathcal{C}$
- $\mathcal{D}^j \leftarrow \{D_r^j,\ 1 \leq r \leq n\}$ where $D_r^j = \begin{cases} D_r \ if\ r \neq i \\ D_i^j\ (D_i^j \subset D_i)\ otherwise. \end{cases}$
- $\mathcal{R}^j \leftarrow \{R_{rs}^j,\ 1 \leq r < s \leq n\}$ with $R_{rs}^j = \begin{cases} R_{rs}\ if\ r \neq i\ and\ s \neq i \\ R_{rs}^j \bigcap (D_r^j \times D_s^j) otherwise. \end{cases}$

Note that: $\bigcup_{j=1}^{h} D_i^j = D_i$ *and* $D_i^{j_1} \bigcap D_i^{j_2} = \emptyset$, $1 \leq j_1 < j_2 \leq h$. It is clear that the CSPs P_i^1, P_i^2, ..., P_i^h may be arc inconsistent. The following results supply a sufficient condition for a value to be inconsistent in P.

Property 1. Let $v \in D_i^j$, $1 \leq j \leq h$. If v is an arc inconsistent value in P_i^j, then v is an inconsistent value in P.

Property 2. Let $v \in D_r$ $(r \neq i)$. If v is arc inconsistent in each CSP P_i^j, $j = 1, \ldots, h$, then v is an inconsistent value in the original CSP P.

Given a partition P in k_i $(k_i \leq d_i)$ sub-domains $\{D_i^1, D_i^2, \ldots, D_i^{k_i}\}$ of each D_i $(1 \leq i \leq n)$ such that the size of each $\{D_i^j\}$ is bounded by a constant $k \leq d_i$, we have:

Definition 1. *A binary CSP is P-k-arc consistent if and only if* $\forall X_i \in X$, $i = 1, \ldots, n$:

- $D_i \neq \emptyset$;
- $\forall D_i^j \subset D_i$, $1 \leq j \leq k_i$, *the CSP* $P_i^j = (P|_{D_i \leftarrow D_i^j})$ *is arc consistent* [1]. ;
- $\forall v \in D_r$, $r = 1, \ldots, n$ $r \neq i$, $\exists P_i^j = (P|_{D_i \leftarrow D_i^j})$ *in which the value* v *is arc consistent.*

2.1 Analysis

The technique k-Partition-AC divides a variable domain into disjoint domains, each of them contains at most k elements. The simple way is to divide a domain into singleton sub-domains. Otherwise, many questions can be set here, as what is the size of each sub-domain ? if the size of a sub-domain is known, what are the values that we put in ?. For the moment our aim here is to show that the domain partition combined with a filtering technique as arc consistency can increase the efficiency of these techniques by performing a few more of consistency checks. k-Partition-AC removes a maximum number of values when all the domains are divided into singleton sub-domains. In this particular case, $k = 1$, (all the sub-domains D_i^j are singleton), property 3 shows that 1-Partition-AC removes at least the set of values suppressed by SAC[2].

Property 3. Let P be a binary CSP. If P is 1-arc consistent then P is singleton arc consistent. Conversely if P is singleton arc consistent, P is not necessary 1-arc consistent.

Proof. According to the definition 1, in the particular case, $k = 1$, (all the sub-domains D_i^j are singleton), any 1-arc consistent value is singleton arc consistent. But the reciprocal is not true, see the example in Figure 2 providing a SAC

[1] The definition is here restricted to arc consistency. Naturally, the domain partition may be combined with any filtering concept as the restricted path consistency for instance.

[2] A binary CSP is singleton arc consistent iff $\forall X_i \in X$, $D_i \neq \emptyset$ and $\forall v_r \in D_i$ $P|_{D_i \leftarrow \{v_r\}}$ is arc consistent.

and not 1-Partition-AC CSP. Let us consider the following CSP P where: $X = \{X_1, X_2, X_3, X_4\}$, $D_1 = \{v_1, v_2, v_3\}$, $D_2 = \{v_1, v_2\}$, $D_3 = \{v_1, v_2, v_3\}$ and $D_4 = \{v_1, v_2\}$. The constraints are defined by the relations of Figure 2. Note that there is no constraint between X_2 and X_4:

We can verify that P is singleton arc consistent, since except the value v_1 of D_4, all other values of D_1, D_2, D_3 and D_4 participate in a solution of P. Moreover $P|_{D_4 \leftarrow \{v_1\}}$ is arc consistent. On the contrary, P is not domain arc consistent, since by partitionning the domain D_1 into singleton sub-domains $D_1^1 = \{v_1\}$, $D_1^2 = \{v_2\}$ and $D_1^3 = \{v_3\}$, P is decomposed into three CSPs P_1^1, P_1^2 and P_1^3. The value v_1 of X_4 is arc inconsistent in P_1^1, P_1^2 and P_1^3, then we deduce that this value is 1-arc inconsistent in P.

R_{12}

X_1	X_2
v_1	v_1
v_2	v_2
v_3	v_1
v_3	v_2

R_{13}

X_1	X_3
v_1	v_1
v_1	v_3
v_2	v_2
v_2	v_3
v_3	v_1
v_3	v_2
v_3	v_3

R_{14}

X_1	X_4
v_1	v_1
v_1	v_2
v_2	v_1
v_2	v_2
v_3	v_2

R_{23}

X_2	X_3
v_1	v_2
v_1	v_3
v_2	v_1
v_2	v_3

R_{34}

X_3	X_4
v_1	v_1
v_1	v_2
v_2	v_1
v_2	v_2
v_3	v_2

Fig. 2. Table of relations

3 Computational Experiments

This section provides experimental tests on the performances of the k-Partition-AC filtering technique. We have implemented the particular case 1-Partition-AC, using the AC6 algorithm [Bessière 1994], the algorithm k-Partition-AC and detailled experiments are described in [?].

The experiments were performed over randomly generated problems using the random model proposed in [Hubbe and Freuder 1992]. We have randomly generated a list of problems according to the following values of the parameters: the number of variables n=100, the domain size d=10, the constraints tightness (the proportion of forbidden value pairs between two constrained variables) $pu = 0.5$ and the graph connectivity (the proportion of the existing constraints) pc varying in $[0, 1]$. The performance measure is the ratio $R = \frac{number\ of\ consistency\ checks}{number\ of\ removed\ values}$. For each problem type (pc fixed) 50 instances were tested. Results reported so far represent the average of the ratio R over the 50 problems for each of the algorithms.

We first compare the behavior of k-Partition-AC relatively to the basic arc consistency filtering AC6 in order to show the impact of k-Partition-AC on arc consistent CSPs (Figure 3). The figures 3 and 4 provide comparing results of our filtering technique and the singleton arc consistency technique.

The experimental results comparing 1-Partition-Arc Consistency with the Arc Consistency and the Singleton Arc Consistency show that the pruning effect

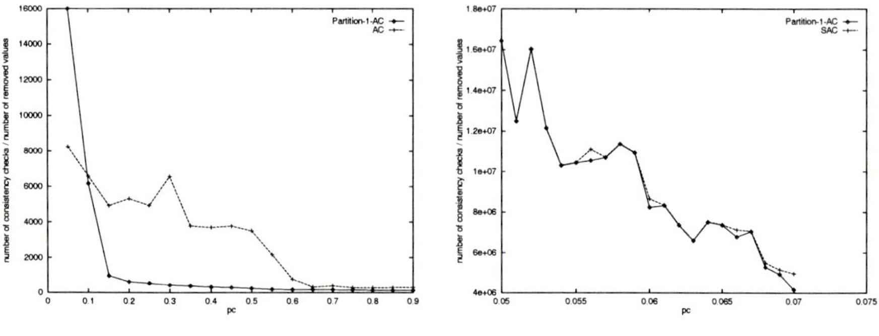

Fig. 3.

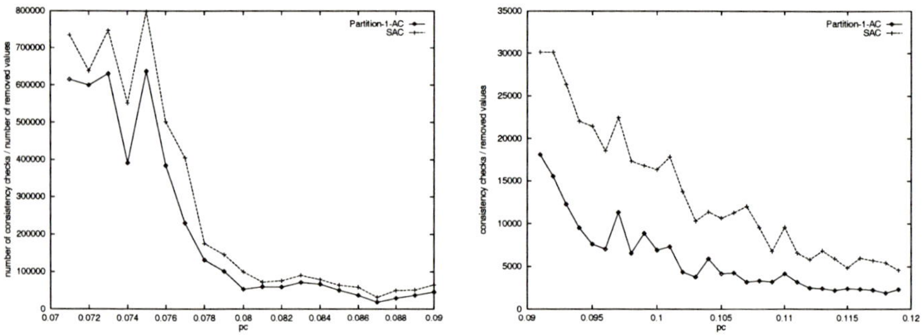

Fig. 4.

is considerably improved and that 1-Partition-AC outperforms SAC on all tested problems.

References

[Bennaceur and Affane 2001] Bennaceur2001 H. Bennaceur and M-S. Affane. Combining Domain Partition and Local Consistencies : An efficient filtering technique. *LIPN report*, 2001.

[Bennaceur 1994] H. Bennaceur. Partial Consistency for Constraint Satisfaction Problems. In *Proc. of the ECAI*, pages 120–125, Amesterdam, Netherlands, 1994.

[Berlandier 1995] P. Berlandier. Improving Domain Filtering Using Restricted Path Consistency. In *Proc. of the IEEE CAIA*, Los Angeles, CA, USA, 1995.

[Bessière 1994] C. Bessière. Arc-consistency and arc-consistency again. *Artificial Intelligence Journal*, 65 (1):179–190, 1994.

[Debruyne and Bessière 1997] R. Debruyne and C. Bessière. Some Practicable Filtering Techniques for the Constraint Satisfaction Problem. In *Proc. of IJCAI*, Nagoya, Japan, 1997.

[Freuder and Elfe 1996] E.C. Freuder and D. Elfe. Neighborhood Inverse Consistency Preprocessing. In *Proc. of the AAAI*, pages 202–208, Portland, OR, USA, 1996.

Neighborhood-Based Variable Ordering Heuristics for the Constraint Satisfaction Problem*

Christian Bessière[1], Assef Chmeiss[2], and Lakhdar Saïs[2]

[1] Member of the Coconut group
LIRMM-CNRS (UMR 5506), 161, rue Ada, 34392 Montpellier Cedex 5, France
bessiere@lirmm.fr
[2] CRIL - Université d'Artois - IUT de Lens
Rue de l'université - SP 16, 62307 LENS Cedex, France
{chmeiss, sais}@cril.univ-artois.fr

Abstract. One of the key factors in the efficiency of backtracking algorithms is the rule they use to decide on which variable to branch next (namely, the variable ordering heuristics). In this paper, we give a formulation of dynamic variable ordering heuristics that takes into account the properties of the neighborhood of the variable.

1 Introduction

Constraint satisfaction problems (*CSPs*) are widely used to solve combinatorial problems appearing in a variety of application domains. They involve finding solution in a *constraint network*, i.e., finding *values* for network *variables* subject to *constraints* on which combinations are acceptable.

The usual technique to solve CSPs is systematic backtracking. But if we want to tackle highly combinatorial problems, we need to enhance this basic search procedure with clever improvements. An improvement that has shown to be of major importance is the ordering of the variables, namely, the criterion under which we decide which variable will be the next to be instantiated. Many variable ordering heuristics for solving CSPs have been proposed over the years. However, the criteria used in those heuristics to order the variables are often quite simple, and concentrate on characteristics inherent to the variable to be ordered, and not too much on the influence its neighborhood could have. Those that use more complex criteria, essentially based on the constrainedness or the solution density of the remaining subproblem, need to evaluate the tightness of the constraints, and so, need to perform many constraint checks.

The goal of this paper is to propose heuristics that take into account properties of the neighborhood in the criterion of choice of a variable, while remaining free of any constraint check.

* This work was partially supported by the IUT of Lens, the Nord/PasdeCalais region, and the European community.

T. Walsh (Ed.): CP 2001, LNCS 2239, pp. 565–569, 2001.

2 Preamble

Numerous criteria have been proposed to find good variable orderings for backtrack search procedures. Among them, dynamic[1] variable orderings (DVOs) have always shown better average performances than static ones. In [4], Haralick and Elliott introduced `dom`, the DVO choosing as next variable the one with the smallest remaining domain.

Since `dom` can be completely fooled by the structure, especially at the beginning of the search, when domains have more chances to be of equal size, other heuristics have been proposed. `dom+futdeg` is the one derived from the Brélaz heuristic (proposed for graph coloring) [3]. It breaks ties in `dom` by preferring the variable with highest future degree [6]. Smith also improved `dom+futdeg` by adding to it a second and a third tie breakers, namely, the size of the smallest neighbor, and the number of triangles in which the first chosen variable is involved. She called this DVO `BZ3`.

However, both `dom+futdeg` and `BZ3` use the domain size as the main criterion. The degree of the variables is considered only in case of ties, which can again fool the heuristic. Combined heuristics [2] do not give priority to the domain size or degree of variables, but use them equally in the criterion. `DD` chooses as the next variable, the variable X_i minimizing the ratio "size of domain/degree". `DD` has extensively been studied in [5].

To give an insight into the state of the art, we performed experiments with some of these well-known heuristics: `dom`, the oldest and most well known DVO, `DD` and `BZ3`, the best current VOs for CSPs [5,6]. On random problems with 10 values per domain, an average degree of 5 (i.e., 5/2 times more constraints than variables), and the tightness fixed at the cross-over point (which is stable at 55 forbidden tuples per constraint), we increased the number N of variables by steps of 10, and could see the following:[2]

- when $N = 110$, `DD` needs less than 1 sec., `BZ3` less than 10 sec., and `dom` less than 100 sec.,
- when $N = 120$, `dom` goes above 100 sec.,
- when $N = 150$, `DD` needs less than 10 sec., and `BZ3` less than 100 sec.,
- when $N = 160$, `BZ3` goes above 100 sec.,
- when $N = 210$, `DD` goes above 100 sec.

3 Multi-level DVOs

One of the key features for the efficiency of a backtrack search method lies in its branching strategy. At each step of the search process, a problem P is reduced into a finite number of sub-problems $(P_1, P_2, \ldots, P_{|D(X_i)|})$, where X_i is

[1] A variable ordering is dynamic when it can change the order of the variables from one branch to the other.

[2] These experiments have been run on a PC Pentium III 667 MHz under Linux. 100 instances for each value of the parameters.

the chosen variable. Following ideas developed for the DP procedure on SAT, we think that a good DVO should reduce both the *number* and the *difficulty* of such subproblems.

We propose a general formulation of DVOs which integrates in the selection function a measure of the constrainedness of the given variable. The constrainedness of a variable can be defined as a function of the constraints involving the variable. One could choose semantical constraints-based measures (e.g., number of allowed tuples) or syntactical ones (e.g., size of the Cartesian product of the domains). Choosing the most constrained variable should have a great impact on the search space, leading the search to the most constrained parts of the CSP, and thus provoking early detection of local inconsistencies.

3.1 A General Criterion Free of Constraint Checks

From now on, we will denote by $\Gamma(X_i)$ the set of variables sharing a constraint with the variable X_i. Let us first define $W(R_{ij})$ as the weight of the constraint R_{ij} and,

(1) $W(X_i) = \frac{\sum_{X_j \in \Gamma(X_i)} W(R_{ij})}{|\Gamma(X_i)|}$

as the mean weight of the constraints involving X_i. In order to maximize the number of constraints involving a given variable and to minimize the mean weight of such constraints, the next variable to branch on should be chosen according to the minimum value of

(2) $H(X_i) = \frac{W(X_i)}{|\Gamma(X_i)|}$

over all uninstantiated variables (numerator to minimize the weight, and denominator to maximize the number of constraints).

For reasons of efficiency of computation, the weight we will associate to a constraint must be something cheap to compute (e.g., free of constraint checks). It can be defined by $W(R_{ij}) = \alpha(X_i) \circledcirc \alpha(X_j)$, where $\alpha(X_i)$ is instantiated to a simple syntactical property of the variable such as $|D(X_i)|$ or $\frac{|D(X_i)|}{|\Gamma(X_i)|}$, and $\circledcirc \in \{+, \times\}$. For $\alpha(X_i) = |D(X_i)|$, and $\circledcirc = \times$, the weight associated to a given constraint R_{ij} represents an upper bound of the number of tuples allowed by R_{ij}.

We obtain the new formulation of (2):

(3) $H_\alpha^\circledcirc(X_i) = \frac{\sum_{X_j \in \Gamma(X_i)} (\alpha(X_i) \circledcirc \alpha(X_j))}{|\Gamma(X_i)|^2}$

3.2 Multi-level Generalization

In the formulation of the DVOs presented above, the evaluation function $H(X_i)$ considers only the variables at distance one from X_i (first level or neighborhood). However, when arc consistency is maintained (MAC), the instantiation of a value to a given variable X_i could have an immediate effect not only on the variables of the first level, but also on those at distance greater than one.

To maximize the effect of such a propagation process on the CSP, and consequently to reduce the difficulty of the subproblems, we propose a generalization of the DVO $H_\alpha^\circledcirc$ such that variables at distance k from X_i are taken into account. This gives what we call a "multi-level DVO", $H_{(k,\alpha)}^\circledcirc$. To obtain this multi-level DVO, we simply replace $\alpha(X_j)$ in formula (3) by a recursive call to $H_{(k-1,\alpha)}^\circledcirc(X_j)$. This means that to compute $H_{(k,\alpha)}^\circledcirc$ on a given variable, we need to compute $H_{(k-1,\alpha)}^\circledcirc$ on all its neighbors, and so on. The recursion terminates with $H_{(0,\alpha)}^\circledcirc$, equal to α. This is formally stated as follows:

(4) $H_{(0,\alpha)}^\circledcirc(X_i) = \alpha(X_i)$

(5) $H_{(k,\alpha)}^\circledcirc(X_i) = \dfrac{\sum_{X_j \in \Gamma(X_i)} (\alpha(X_i) \circledcirc H_{(k-1,\alpha)}^\circledcirc(X_j))}{|\Gamma(X_i)|^2}$

In the following, $H_{(0,dom)}^\circledcirc$ and $H_{(0,DD)}^\circledcirc$ are denoted by their classical name, dom and DD, respectively. $H_{(k,dom)}^\circledcirc$ and $H_{(k,DD)}^\circledcirc$ are denoted by H_k_dom_◎ and H_k_DD_◎ respectively.

4 Experiments

We have compared experimentally the behavior of the new DVOs defined above (and others) on several classes of random CSPs and on real instances from the FullRLFAP archive[3]. We give here a brief snapshot of the results. Extensive experiments can be found in [1]. In all our experiments, we stopped search after the first solution is found. The search procedure used maintains arc consistency (MAC).

We ran the H_1_DD_◎ (◎ ∈ {+, ×}) on the experiment described in Section 2. The gap between H_1_DD_◎ and DD grows with N. At $N = 230$, H_1_DD_× is more than 5 times faster than DD, which was by far the best DVO known so far. We performed other experiments, fixing the number of variables to 100, and increasing the number of constraints in the network. H_1_DD_× becomes better and better when density grows. (As opposed to H_1_DD_+ which was even better than H_1_DD_× on sparse problems, but which becomes slower on denser problems.)

If we increase the number of variables or the domain size, the gain of the $H_{(1,\alpha)}^\circledcirc$ heuristics continues to grow compared to DD.

As a synthesis of the results on different classes of random CSPs, we can say that, except H_1_dom_×, the first level DVOs improve significantly DD. Furthermore, in general, H_1_DD_◎ are better than H_1_dom_◎. This is not surprising because the former take into account the connectivity of the neighborhood of the chosen variable.

[3] We thank the Centre d'Electronique de l'Armement (France).

We also compared the behavior of these DVOs on the real instances of the FullRLFAP archive. Since these are optimization problems, we built a series of satisfaction problems for each instance of optimization problem. In the table below, we report results for all instances on which a significant difference has been observed among the DVOs tested. The cpu time limit was put to one hour on a PC Pentium II 300MHz.

	scen11-01234 (sat)		scen06-012 (unsat)		scen02-24 (sat)		scen02-25 (unsat)	
	#nodes	time (sec.)	#nodes	time (sec.)	#nodes	time (sec.)	#nodes	time (sec.)
DD	6,019	8.43	—	> 1 h.	31,308,876	2,296.61	—	> 1 h.
H_1_dom_+	21,156	29.68	41	0.40	663	0.32	—	> 1 h.
H_1_DD_+	—	> 1 h.	41	0.41	—	> 1 h.	11,668	10.18
H_1_dom_×	12,517	16.99	—	> 1 h.	677	0.32	—	> 1 h.
H_1_DD_×	226,011	337.55	41	0.41	—	> 1 h.	8,529	6.99

No conclusion can be drawn on a so small number of pertinent instances. However, it seems that H_1_DD_◎ are better on inconsistent problems, and H_1_dom_◎ on satisfiable ones. But, more extensive tests should be run to draw definite conclusions.

5 Conclusion

In this paper, a general formulation of dynamic variable ordering heuristics has been proposed. It admits numerous advantages,

- the constrainedness of a given variable is computed without any constraint check, thanks to simple syntactical properties,
- it takes advantage of the neighborhood of the variable, with the notion of distance as a parameter,
- it can be instantiated to different known variable ordering heuristics,
- it is possible to use other functions to measure the weight of a given constraint.

References

1. C. Bessière, A. Chmeiss, and L. Saïs. Neighborhood-based variable ordering heuristics for the constraint satisfaction problem. Technical Report 01002, LIRMM – University of Montpelllier II, Montpellier, France, January 2001. (available at http://www.lirmm.fr/~bessiere/).
2. C. Bessière and J.C. Régin. MAC and combined heuristics: two reasons to forsake FC (and CBJ?) on hard problems. In *Proceedings CP'96*, pages 61–75, Cambridge MA, 1996.
3. D. Brélaz. New methods to color the vertices of a graph. *Communications of the ACM*, 22:251–256, 1979.
4. R.M. Haralick and G.L. Elliott. Increasing tree seach efficiency for constraint satisfaction problems. *Artificial Intelligence*, 14:263–313, 1980.
5. B. Smith and S.A. Grant. Trying harder to fail first. In *Proceedings ECAI'98*, pages 249–253, Brighton, UK, 1998.
6. B.M. Smith. The Brélaz heuristic and optimal static orderings. In *Proceedings CP'99*, pages 405–418, Alexandria VA, 1999.

The Expressive Power of Binary Linear Programming

Marco Cadoli

Dipartimento di Informatica e Sistemistica
Università di Roma "La Sapienza"
Via Salaria 113, I-00198 Roma, Italy
cadoli@dis.uniroma1.it

Abstract. Very efficient solvers for Integer Programming exist, when the constraints and the objective function are linear. In this paper we tackle a fundamental question: what is the expressive power of Integer Linear Programming? We are able to prove that ILP, more precisely *Binary* LP, expresses the complexity class NP. As a consequence, in principle all specifications of combinatorial problems in NP formulated in constraint languages can be translated as BLP models.

1 Introduction

In this paper we tackle a fundamental question: what is the *expressive power* of Integer Linear Programming (ILP)? We are able to prove that ILP expresses the complexity class NP, i.e., that for each problem ψ in NP there is an ILP model π such that for all instances i, ψ and π are equivalent. As a consequence, in principle all specifications of combinatorial problems in NP formulated in constraint programming (CP) can be translated as ILP models. Actually, we need only integer variables taking values in $\{0, 1\}$, hence the result holds for *Binary* Linear Programming (BLP).

Expressive power must not be confused with computational complexity. The latter refers to the difficulty to solve an *instance* of a problem, while the former refers to the capability of a language to *describe problems*, i.e., functions. In fact, the expressive power of a language is not necessarily the same as its complexity: for examples of languages with this property, cf., e.g., [1]. Separating data from problem description, called *model* in the terminology of operations research, is a fundamental idea in database theory, and is enforced also by mathematical programming modeling languages such as AMPL [3]. Using database terminology, it is obvious that the *data complexity* of BLP, i.e., the complexity wrt the size of data and disregarding the model, is NP-hard. On the other hand, to the best of our knowledge, the question of whether all problems in NP can be stated as BLP models has not been addressed so far.

Our research is motivated by two facts. First of all, there have been recent efforts in finding suitable translations in IP of specifications formulated in CP. As an example, in [6] the main effort is in trying to translate CP specifications into

T. Walsh (Ed.): CP 2001, LNCS 2239, pp. 570–574, 2001.

linear constraints, because this allows to use a solver for ILP for solving a CP problem without having to give a linear formulation, which is sometimes far from natural. Secondly, non-linear IP solvers are relatively rare: for example, ILOG's CPLEX solver [4] handles only linear integer constraints (plus non-linear, non-integer constraints). Our result proves that imposing the syntactic constraint of linearity does not rule out the possibility of modeling problems of interest.

2 The Expressive Power of Binary Linear Programming

Logical specification of problems. We refer to the data of a problem, i.e., the representation of an instance, with the term *database*. All constants appearing in a database are *uninterpreted*, i.e., they don't have a specific meaning.

In the following, σ denotes a fixed set of relational symbols not including equality "=" and $S_1, \ldots, S_h$ denote variables ranging over relational symbols distinct from those in $\sigma \cup \{=\}$. By Fagin's theorem [2] any collection $\mathbf{D}$ of finite databases over σ recognizable in NP time is defined by an existential second-order (ESO) formula of the kind:

$$(\exists S_1, \ldots, S_h)\ \phi, \tag{1}$$

where $S_1, \ldots, S_h$ are relational variables of various arities and ϕ is a function-free first-order formula containing occurrences of relational symbols from $\sigma \cup \{S_1, \ldots, S_h\} \cup \{=\}$. The symbol "=" is always interpreted in the obvious way, i.e., as "identity".

A database D is in $\mathbf{D}$ if and only if there is a list of relations $\Sigma_1, \ldots, \Sigma_h$ (matching the list of relational variables $S_1, \ldots, S_h$) which, along with D, satisfies formula (1), i.e., such that $(D, \Sigma_1, \ldots, \Sigma_h) \models \phi$. The tuples of $\Sigma_1, \ldots, \Sigma_h$ must take elements from the *Herbrand universe* of D, i.e., the set of constant symbols occurring in it.

Example 1 ([5]). In the propositional satisfiability problem the input is a set V of propositional variables, a set C of names of propositional clauses, and two sets N, P of pairs $\langle c, v\rangle$ ($c \in C, v \in V$) encoding the clauses, i.e., $N(c,v)$ $[P(c,v)]$ holds iff v occurs negatively [positively] in clause c. The question is whether there is an assignment S of truth values to variables in V such that each clause in C is satisfied. The question can be specified as an ESO formula as follows:

$$\begin{array}{ll}(\exists S)\ (\forall x)(\exists y) & [S(x) \rightarrow V(x)] \wedge \\ & [\neg V(x) \rightarrow (P(x,y) \wedge S(y)) \vee (N(x,y) \wedge \neg S(y))]\end{array} \tag{2}$$

Normalization of ESO formulae. As explained in [5], instead of the general formula (1), we can restrict our attention to second-order formulae in the following form:

$$(\exists S_1, \ldots, S_h)(\forall \mathbf{X})(\exists \mathbf{Y})\ \psi(\mathbf{X}, \mathbf{Y}), \tag{3}$$

where $\mathbf{X}$ and $\mathbf{Y}$ are lists of first-order variables and $\psi(\mathbf{X}, \mathbf{Y})$ is a quantifier-free first-order formula involving relational symbols which belong to the set $\sigma \cup$

$\{S_1,\ldots,S_h\}\cup\{=\}$. Since $\psi(\mathbf{X},\mathbf{Y})$ can be put in Disjunctive Normal Form, i.e., disjunctions of conjunctions, in what follows we refer to the following form:

$$(\exists S_1,\ldots,S_h)(\forall \mathbf{X})(\exists \mathbf{Y})(\theta_1(\mathbf{X},\mathbf{Y}) \vee \cdots \vee \theta_k(\mathbf{X},\mathbf{Y})), \tag{4}$$

where $\theta_1,\ldots,\theta_k$ are conjunctions of literals, and each conjunction θ_i contains the occurrence of some variables among $\mathbf{X},\mathbf{Y}$.

A conjunction $\theta_i(\mathbf{X},\mathbf{Y})$ $(1 \le i \le k)$ of the kind occurring in formula (4) will be denoted as $\alpha_i(\mathbf{X},\mathbf{Y}) \wedge \delta_i(\mathbf{X},\mathbf{Y})$, where $\delta_i(\mathbf{X},\mathbf{Y})$ is a conjunction of literals whose relational symbol are in $\{S_1,\ldots,S_h\}$, while $\alpha_i(\mathbf{X},\mathbf{Y})$ is a conjunction of literals whose relational symbols are not from that set.

The first step of a method that transforms a formula of the kind (4) into a BLP model is the introduction of a modified ESO formula:

$$\begin{array}{ll} (\exists S_1,\ldots,S_h,D_1,\ldots,D_k) & \\ \quad (\forall \mathbf{X})(\exists \mathbf{Y})\ (\alpha_1(\mathbf{X},\mathbf{Y}) \wedge D_1(\mathbf{X},\mathbf{Y})) \vee \cdots \vee (\alpha_k(\mathbf{X},\mathbf{Y}) \wedge D_k(\mathbf{X},\mathbf{Y})) \wedge & \\ \quad\quad (\forall \mathbf{X},\mathbf{Y})\ D_1(\mathbf{X},\mathbf{Y}) \equiv \delta_1(\mathbf{X},\mathbf{Y}) \hfill \wedge & \\ \quad\quad \cdots \hfill \wedge & \\ \quad\quad (\forall \mathbf{X},\mathbf{Y})\ D_k(\mathbf{X},\mathbf{Y}) \equiv \delta_k(\mathbf{X},\mathbf{Y}) & \end{array} \tag{5}$$

in which there are k new relational symbols $D_1,\ldots,D_k$ which are existentially quantified. Each symbol $D_i(\mathbf{X},\mathbf{Y})$ $(1 \le i \le k)$ is defined as the conjunction $\delta_i(\mathbf{X},\mathbf{Y})$. The advantage of formula (5) over formula (4) is that the former generates *linear* constraints, while the latter generates *non-linear* constraints. The following lemma (proofs are omitted for lack of space) clarifies that the satisfiability problem for the two formulae is equivalent.

Lemma 1. *Given a database D, formula (4) is satisfiable if and only if formula (5) is satisfiable.*

Example 1 (cont.) The ESO formula for satisfiability in the form (4) is:

$$\begin{array}{l} (\exists S)\ (\forall x)(\exists y)\ V(x) \vee [P(x,y) \wedge \neg S(x) \wedge S(y)] \quad \vee \\ \qquad\qquad\qquad\qquad [N(x,y) \wedge \neg S(x) \wedge \neg S(y)] \end{array} \tag{6}$$

For obtaining the form (5) we need two more relational variables D_1 and D_2 of arity 2, as follows:

$$\begin{array}{lr} (\exists S,D_1,D_2) & \\ \quad (\forall x)(\exists y)\ \ V(x) \vee [P(x,y) \wedge D_1(x,y)] \vee [N(x,y) \wedge D_2(x,y)] \wedge & (a) \\ \quad\quad (\forall x\ y)\ \ D_1(x,y) \equiv \neg S(x) \wedge S(y) \hfill \wedge & (b) \\ \quad\quad (\forall x\ y)\ \ D_2(x,y) \equiv \neg S(x) \wedge \neg S(y) & (c) \end{array} \tag{7}$$

Translation of ESO formulae in BLP models. The second step is to prove that every ESO formula of the form (5) can be translated into an equivalent BLP model. Since such formulae contain quantifications of several kinds and various propositional connectives, we have to take into account several aspects. The most important thing we have to remember is that, in linear constraints, products of variables are not allowed. Instead, products of variables and non-variables are allowed. In what follows, we use the terminology of [3]. The translation rules are the following:

- Unquantified relational symbols, i.e., those in the database, correspond to *sets*, i.e., collections of uninterpreted symbols.
- Existentially quantified relational symbols, i.e., those representing the search space in which solutions are to be found, correspond to collection of binary *variables*.
- Literals such as $P(x, y)$ and $S(x)$ can be directly mapped into binary terms.
- As for quantifier-free formulae, the general idea is to translate disjunctions ($\vee$) into sums, conjunctions ($\wedge$) into products, and negations ($\neg$) into difference from 1.
- First-order existential quantification can be modeled taking into account that the existential quantifier is an iterated disjunction. As a consequence, we obviously translate it into a sum over all elements of the Cartesian product of the Herbrand universe, provided that terms not depending on the quantified variable are taken out of the sum.
- First-order universal quantification can be easily modeled declaring constraints for each element of the Cartesian product of the Herbrand universe, with the appropriate arity.
- Finally, a constraint is true iff the corresponding integer expression is assigned a value greater than or equal to 1.

Example 1 (cont.) The translation in a BLP model of formula (7) using the AMPL syntax is the following:

```
set V;                  # names of propositional variables
set C;                  # names of propositional clauses
set U := V union C;     # Herbrand universe
set N within {C,V};     # negative occurrences of variables in clauses
set P within {C,V};     # positive occurrences of variables in clauses

var S {U} binary;       # satisfying assignment
var D1 {U,U} binary;    # auxiliary guessed relation
var D2 {U,U} binary;    # auxiliary guessed relation

s.t. A {x in U}:                # translation of constraint (7a)
        (if x in V then 1) +
         sum {y in U} ((D1[x,y] * if (x,y) in P then 1) +
                       (D2[x,y] * if (x,y) in N then 1)) >= 1;

s.t. D1_1 {x in U, y in U}:  # translation of constraint (7b)
        1 - S[x] >= D1[x,y];              # D1[x,y] IMPLIES !S[x]
s.t. D1_2 {x in U, y in U}:
        S[y] >= D1[x,y];                  # D1[x,y] IMPLIES S[y]
s.t. D1_3 {x in U, y in U}:
        S[x] + 1 - S[y] + D1[x,y] >= 1; # !S[x]&&S[y] IMPLIES D1[x,y]
```

```
s.t. D2_1 {x in U, y in U}:  # translation of constraint (7c)
          1 - S[x] >= D2[x,y];              # D2[x,y] IMPLIES !S[x]
s.t. D2_2 {x in U, y in U}:
          1 - S[y] >= D2[x,y];              # D2[x,y] IMPLIES !S[y]
s.t. D2_3 {x in U, y in U}:
          S[x] + S[y] + D2[x,y] >= 1;       # !S[x]&&!S[y] IMPLIES D2[x,y]
```

Database literals such as $V(x)$ and non-database ones such as $S(x)$ have different translations: the former must be translated as `if x in V then 1`, while the latter is translated as `S[x]`. Apart from such minor syntactic peculiarities of AMPL, formula (7) is translated in a modular way.

We note that all constraints are linear, since there are no products among variables, i.e., terms originating from the translation of existentially quantified relations. The reason of introducing normal form (5) is that the same translation applied to formulae of the form (4) may introduce non-linear constraints. As an example, the same translation applied to the second disjunct of non-normalized formula (6) would yield the integer expression:

```
(if (x,y) in P then 1) * (1 - S[x]) * S[y]
```

which is clearly non-linear. For the same reason, an equivalence such as (7b) which involves non-database literals, is split into several implications, all of them admitting a linear translation.

3 Conclusions

The transformation shown in Section 2 shows that the language of BLP models is a notational variant of ESO. This implies that it is in principle possible to model all problems in the complexity class NP by means of BLP. It is important to remark that the translation from ESO to BLP is done at the intensional level, i.e., not considering data, but just problem specifications.

Practical considerations about the best way to perform the translation deserve further research. In particular, it would be interesting to consider more realistic CP languages, which allow integer, and not just binary, variables.

References

1. S. Abiteboul, R. Hull, and V. Vianu. *Foundations of Databases.* Addison Wesley Publ. Co., Reading, Massachussetts, 1995.
2. R. Fagin. Generalized First-Order Spectra and Polynomial-Time Recognizable Sets. In R. M. Karp, editor, *Complexity of Computation*, pages 43–74. AMS, 1974.
3. Robert Fourer, David M. Gay, and Brian W. Kernigham. *AMPL: A Modeling Language for Mathematical Programming.* International Thomson Publishing, 1993.
4. ILOG AMPL CPLEX system version 7.0 user's guide. Available at `www.ilog.com`, 2001.
5. P. G. Kolaitis and C. H. Papadimitriou. Why not negation by fixpoint? *J. of Computer and System Sciences*, 43:125–144, 1991.
6. Philippe Refalo. Linear formulation of constraint programming models and hybrid solvers. In *Proc. of CP 2000*, LNCS, pages 369–383. Springer-Verlag, 2000.

Constraint Generation via Automated Theory Formation

Simon Colton[1] and Ian Miguel[2]

[1] Division of Informatics, University of Edinburgh
80 South Bridge, Edinburgh EH1 1HN, UK
simonco@dai.ed.ac.uk

[2] Department of Computer Science, University of York
Heslington, York YO10 5DD, UK
ianm@cs.york.ac.uk

1 Introduction

Adding constraints to a basic CSP model can significantly reduce search, e.g. for Golomb rulers [6]. The generation process is usually performed by hand, although some recent work has focused on automatically generating symmetry breaking constraints [4] and (less so) on generating implied constraints [5]. We describe an approach to generating implied, symmetry breaking and specialisation constraints and apply this technique to quasigroup construction [10].

Given a problem class parameterised by size, we use a basic model to solve small instances with the Choco constraint programming language [7]. We then give these solutions to the HR automated theory formation program [1] which detects implied constraints (proved to follow from the specifications) and induced constraints (true of a subset of solutions). Interpreting HR's results to reformulate the model can lead to a reduction in search on larger instances. It is often more efficient to run HR, interpret the results and solve the CSP, than to solve the problem with the basic model alone.

2 System Architecture

The HR program [1] [2] performs theory formation in domains of pure mathematics. When used in finite algebraic domains such as quasigroup theory, given some examples of the algebra, HR invents new concepts and makes and proves theorems using the Otter theorem prover [8]. Given a basic model of a family of quasigroup CSPs, we employ the following 5-stage approach:

[1] We use Choco to produces solutions for small instances.

[2] HR is employed to form a theory around the examples supplied by Choco.

[3] We interpret HR's results as implied and induced constraints for the CSP.

[4] We remodel the problem using the additional constraints and see which, if any, reformulations increase efficiency for the small instances.

T. Walsh (Ed.): CP 2001, LNCS 2239, pp. 575–579, 2001.

[5] We add any constraints which improve efficiency to the CSP model and look for solutions to larger problem instances.

We look for both concepts and theorems in HR's output. Theorems can potentially be added as implied constraints to a basic CSP model. Any concept which specialises the notion of quasigroup can be used in two ways. Firstly, it can be used as a case split: we remodel the CSP twice to specify the quasigroups with and without the specialised property. Performing both searches covers the space, but splitting it in this fashion can introduce symmetry breaking constraints, thus reducing overall search. Secondly, if we are only interested in finding an example, rather than exhausting the search space, we can choose to look for solutions to the specialised CSP only (which will be solutions to the original problem).

3 Quasigroup Generation Experiments

Quasigroups are finite algebras where every element appears in every row and column, i.e. Latin squares. Quasigroups of every size exist, but for certain specialised classes of quasigroups, there are open questions about the existence of examples. Such classes include those termed QG3-QG7, which are quasigroups with these additional axioms: QG3: $(a*b)*(b*a) = a$, QG4: $(b*a)*(a*b) = a$, QG5: $((b*a)*b)*b = a$, QG6: $(a*b)*b = a*(a*b)$, QG7: $(b*a)*b = a*(b*a)$. Constraint satisfaction approaches to existence questions have been very successful, e.g. size 12 QG3 quasigroups, settled by Slaney [10].

To find a quasigroup of size n, we used n^2 variables, $x_{(ij)}$, with domain $\{1, 2, \ldots, n\}$. The quasigroup constraint imposed an all-different on each row and column, and the constraints imposed by the quasigroup type were implemented via sets of implication constraints. For each quasigroup class, we ran Choco for increasing sizes until 10 million backtracks were reached. For small orders, Choco constructed all solutions of each size and HR removed isomorphic copies.

For each class, we ran HR with full functionality for 45 minutes with the examples from Choco. Then, for a further 15 minutes, we turned off the theorem proving abilities, so that HR performed a best first search for concepts only (using the coverage heuristic measure discussed in [3]). On average, after each theory was formed, there were around 150 prime implicates (implication theorems where no proper subset of the premises implies the goal) and 100 concepts of which around 10 were specialisations suitable for case splits. The reformulations we made for each class are summarised below.

For QG3, Choco produced 4 non-isomorphic quasigroups from which HR formed a theory. We noticed this prime implicate: $a \in Q \rightarrow \exists\, b \in Q$ s.t. $b*b = a$, meaning that every element must appear on the diagonal of the multiplication table, i.e. an all-different constraint on the diagonal (constraint $C_{3.1}$). Next we noticed this theorem: $\forall\, a, b, \in Q\ (\exists\, c \in Q$ s.t. $a*c = c*a = b \rightarrow a*a = b)$. Since $a*c = b$ and $a*a = b$ and it is a quasigroup, $a = c$. Hence, for all elements a, the only other element a commutes with is itself, i.e. QG3 quasigroups are anti-Abelian: no pair of distinct elements commute, which we interpreted as constraint $C_{3.2}$: $\forall i, j\ (i \neq j \rightarrow x_{(i,j)} \neq x_{(j,i)})$. HR also found this

Table 1. Quasigroup class 3 and 4 results. Dash: no solutions found after 10^6 backtracks

QG3 results for lexicographic column-wise variable ordering

Size	reformulation:	B	$R_{3.1}$ $C_{3.1}$	$R_{3.2}$ $C_{3.2}$	$R_{3.3}$ $C_{3.3}$	$R_{3.4}$ $C_{3.1}, C_{3.2}$	$R_{3.5}$ $C_{3.1}, C_{3.3}$	$R_{3.6}$ $C_{3.2}, C_{3.3}$	$R_{3.7}$ $C_{3.1}, C_{3.2}$ $C_{3.3}$	$R_{3.8}$ $C_{3.1}, C_{3.2}$ $C_{3.3}, C_{3.4}$
Size 6	backtracks	79790	24187	60312	17080	19791	10838	13489	8876	
	nodes	34278	10177	28758	7167	9358	4636	6407	4314	
	time(s)	39.7	16.2	33.4	9.4	13.8	7.1	8.1	6.4	
Size 7	backtracks	-	3868973	-	1988844	3170536	1286951	1560592	1049433	
	nodes		1430498		771719	1305952	503660	671361	453885	
	time(s)		4143.9		1743.5	3526.5	1302.5	1521.5	1156.0	
Size 8	backtracks	-	-	-	8562552	9760235	5693438	6953252	4746356	
	nodes				3604043	4217717	2431697	3037033	2070629	
	time(s)				11868.8	16576.9	9456.2	10476.0	3197.7	

QG3 results for smallest-domain variable ordering

Size	reformulation:	B	$R_{3.1}$	$R_{3.2}$	$R_{3.3}$	$R_{3.4}$	$R_{3.5}$	$R_{3.6}$	$R_{3.7}$	$R_{3.8}$
Size 6	backtracks	133587	112785	1387	26306	54408	13581	2468	6853	n/a
	nodes	77154	75828	847	16746	35909	9084	1595	4514	
	time(s)	57.9	42.6	0.8	12.8	24.2	5.7	1.3	3.4	
Size 7	backtracks	-	-	104422	3459554	-	3156515	246642	920531	n/a
	nodes			65050	2174882		2075222	157386	593561	
	time(s)			72.7	2467.2		1912.3	182.7	654.9	
Size 8	backtracks	-	-	7944	1845922	-	3895653	750418	955368	n/a
	nodes			5245	1091624		2538539	449061	627981	
	time(s)			7.6	1838.2		3730.6	865.0	991.3	
Size 9	backtracks	-	-	-	-	-	-	-	-	8993
	nodes									5886
	time(s)									19.6

QG4 results for lexicographic column-wise variable ordering

Size	reformulation:	B	$R_{4.1}$	$R_{4.2}$	$R_{4.3}$	$R_{4.4}$	$R_{4.5}$	$R_{4.6}$	$R_{4.7}$	
Size 6	backtracks	99782	28364	67760	24001	21684	13263	17015	10164	
	nodes	44581	12623	32812	10700	10579	6027	8275	5036	
	time(s)	52.0	20.3	41.3	13.6	16.5	10.1	11.4	8.2	
Size 7	backtracks	-	5323512	-	3481163	4117108	1982834	2447659	1535644	
	nodes		2097639		1453990	1776126	819581	1120053	696060	
	time(s)		5948.2		3005.7	4690.9	2112.2	2430.9	1848.6	
Size 8	backtracks	-	-	-	-	-	6992701	-	5835174	
	nodes						2927378		2609254	
	time(s)						13126.0		11521.3	

QG4 results for smallest-domain variable ordering

Size	reformulation:	B	$R_{4.1}$	$R_{4.2}$	$R_{4.3}$	$R_{4.4}$	$R_{4.5}$	$R_{4.6}$	$R_{4.7}$	$R_{4.9}$ $C_{4.2}, C_{4.5}$
Size 6	backtracks	134737	108104	4292	30187	54306	13223	3180	6852	n/a
	nodes	82930	71954	2761	19215	35805	8776	2066	4512	
	time(s)	61.4	43.0	3.0	16.5	25.3	5.8	2.3	8.2	
Size 7	backtracks	-	-	278106	5021932	-	3243714	222411	958003	n/a
	nodes			173172	3133722		2115918	140388	613611	
	time(s)			274.8	3718.4		2058.8	213.1	750.6	
Size 8	backtracks	-	-	144393	-	-	-	2906628	3271140	n/a
	nodes			95325				1827743	2130288	
	time(s)			173.1				3624.0	34644.1	
Size 9	backtracks	-	-	-	-	-	-	-	-	508657
	nodes									324236
	time(s)									901.7

prime implicate: $a * a = b \rightarrow b * b = a$, which highlights a symmetry on the diagonal, i.e. if $x_{(a,a)} = b$, then $x_{(b,b)} = a$, (constraint $C_{3.3}$). HR also made some specialisations, including quasigroups with symmetry of left identities, i.e. $\forall\, a, b\ (a * b = b \rightarrow b * a = a)$, interpreted as constraint $C_{3.4}$. We used the specialisation constraints to specialise the model.

As shown in table 1, using combinations of constraints $C_{3.1}$ to $C_{3.4}$, we reformulated the problem in 8 additional ways. We tested whether the reformulations reduced (a) the number of backtracks (b) the number of nodes and (c) the CPU time to solve the CSPs. In order to test the relative effectiveness of the reformulations with different search strategies, we ran Choco with both a lexicographic column-wise variable ordering beginning in the top left-hand corner, and the smallest-domain first heuristic. Results are presented in table 1. For QG4, HR found a similar theory to that for QG3 and all the same theorems held. As we found no better results, we used the same reformulations for QG4 as for QG3, with the results also presented in table 1. For QG4, in reformulation $R_{4.9}$, we also used specialisation constraint $C_{4.5}$, idempotent quasigroups: $\forall\, a\, (a * a = a)$.

The implied constraints are clearly beneficial to the solver. Choco did not solve any instance above order 6 using the basic model, but with the implied constraints, Choco solved instances of orders 7 and 8 for both QG3 and QG4. Variable ordering is also important when using the implied constraints, because, while $R_{3.2}$ and $R_{4.2}$ (anti-Abelian) were the least effective reformulations using the lexicographic ordering, they were the most effective when using the smallest domain heuristic. The heuristic forces Choco to jump around the quasigroup table, using the extra pruning given by the anti-Abelian constraint.

None of the reformulated models containing implied constraints only solved the order 9 problem within the specified limits. However, some of the induced models did solve this problem quickly. For QG3, reformulation $R_{3.8}$ (symmetry of left identities) allowed an instance of order 9 to be found in 20 seconds. Similarly, reformulation $R_{4.9}$ (idempotency) found an instance of QG4, size 9. This shows the value of induced constraints: searching for specific quasigroup types reduces the effort required so that a solution is obtained relatively easily.

As discussed in [3], for classes QG5-QG7 we did less analysis of HR's output, making one reformulation for each. For QG5, we used this result from HR: $\forall\, a, b \in Q\ (a * b = a \leftrightarrow b * a = a)$ to reformulate the problem. This significantly outperformed the basic model by all measures, finding an instance of order 9 which the basic model could not. When the basic model did solve the problem, it was much slower than the reformulated model. This trend increased with problem size, and easily justified the time spent on reformulation. The smallest domain heuristic was always beneficial to this model, taking advantage of its extra pruning power, but was of limited value to the basic model.

For QG6 and 7, HR re-discovered the theorem stated in [10] that both quasigroup types are idempotent (i.e. $\forall\, a,\ (a * a = a)$). We added this constraint to produce two reformulations (see [3]). Using the smallest domain heuristic with the basic model, QG6 and QG7 were solvable up to orders 9 and 10 respectively, matching the abilities of the reformulated idempotent models. As with QG5, however, the decrease in search offered by the reformulated models was significant and increased with problem size. For both QG6 and QG7, the smallest domain heuristic made a substantial saving, suggesting that the structure of these problem classes is such that the solver must be allowed to focus on the most constrained areas of the quasigroup table to be most efficient.

4 Conclusions and Further Work

A more complete account of this work with additional applications to group theory and Balanced Incomplete Block Designs is presented in [3]. We have demonstrated that HR can find implied and induced constraints for CSPs and that reformulating the model to include these additional constraints gives a clear improvement in efficiency, even considering the time taken to run HR, interpret the results and re-formulate the CSP. The implied constraints produced a consistent, significant, speedup, yet only with both implied and induced constraints were we able to find solutions to the larger problems.

So far, our approach has been interactive, whereby we interpret HR's results and use them to reformulate the CSP. We intend to automate the interaction between HR and the solver, eventually using them in a cycle whereby the examples found by solver feed HR's theory formation, which in turn generates constraints to improve the solver's performance. This may be problematic, as some implied constraints may not improve the search at all, and combining implied constraints may reduce efficiency, because one constraint subsumes another. It is therefore likely that the pruning phase will be important for a fully automated approach.

The question of how to reformulate CSPs automatically in general needs much more research. The system we have described could be applied to other problem classes, such as tournament scheduling [9], to shed further light on automating this process. We hope to have added to the evidence that reformulating CSPs, in particular by adding implied and induced constraints, can dramatically increase efficiency, and to have shown that automating certain aspects of this process is certainly possible and a worthy area for future research.

Acknowledgments. The first author is also affiliated to the Department of Computer Science, University of York. We thank Toby Walsh and Alan Bundy for their continued input. This work is supported by EPSRC grants GR/M98012 and GR/N16129.

References

1. S Colton. *Automated Theory Formation in Pure Mathematics.* PhD thesis, Division of Informatics, University of Edinburgh, 2001.
2. S Colton, A Bundy, and T Walsh. HR: Automatic concept formation in pure mathematics. In *Proceddings of the 16th IJCAI*, pages 786–791, 1999.
3. S Colton and I Miguel. Automatic generation of implied and induced constraints. Technical Report APES-32-2001, APES Research Group, 2001. Available from http://www.dcs.st-and.ac.uk/~apes/apesreports.html.
4. J Crawford. A theoretical analysis of reasoning by symmetry in first-order logic. In *Proceedings of the Workshop on Tractable Reasoning, AAAI*, 1992.
5. A Frisch, I Miguel, and T Walsh. Extensions to proof planning for generating implied constraints. In *Proceedings of the 9th Symposium on the Integration of Symbolic Computation and Mechanized Reasoning*, 2001.
6. P Galinier, B Jaumard, R Morales, and G Pesant. A constraint-based approach to the Golomb ruler problem. In *Proceedings of the 3rd International Workshop on Integration of AI and OR Techniques (CPAIOR-01)*, 2001.
7. F Laburthe and the OCRE group. Choco: implementing a CP kernel. In *Proceedings of the CP00 Post Conference Workshop on Techniques for Implementing Constraint programming Systems (TRICS)*, 2000.
8. W McCune. The OTTER user's guide. Technical Report ANL/90/9, Argonne National Laboratories, 1990.
9. A Schaerf. Scheduling sport tournaments using constraint logic programming. *Constraints*, 4(1):43–65, 1999.
10. J Slaney, M Fujita, and M Stickel. Automated reasoning and exhaustive search: Quasigroup existence problems. *Computers and Mathematics with Applications*, 29:115–132, 1995.

The Traveling Tournament Problem Description and Benchmarks

Kelly Easton[1], George Nemhauser[1], and Michael Trick[2]

[1] School of Industrial and Systems Engineering
Georgia Institute of Technology, Atlanta, Georgia USA, 30332
{keaston,george.nemhauser}@isye.gatech.edu
[2] Graduate School of Industrial Administration
Carnegie Mellon, Pittsburgh, PA USA, 15213
trick@cmu.edu

Abstract. The *Traveling Tournament Problem* is a sports timetabling problem that abstracts two issues in creating timetables: home/away pattern feasibility and team travel. Instances of this problem seem to be very difficult even for a very small number of teams, making it an interesting challenge for combinatorial optimization techniques such as integer programming and constraint programming. We introduce the problem, describe one way of modeling it, and give some interesting classes of instances with base computational results.

1 Introduction

This research was inspired by work done for Major League Baseball (MLB) in North America. Creating a reasonable MLB schedule is a daunting task, since thirty teams play 162 games each over a 180 day season that stretches from early April to the end of September. While creating a playable schedule involves juggling hundreds of requests and requirements, the key issues for a schedule revolve around travel distance and "flow", the pattern of home and away games in the schedule.

While teams wish to limit the total amount they travel, teams are also concerned with more traditional issues with respect to their home and away patterns. No team likes to be away more than two weeks or so (corresponding to visiting 3 or 4 teams since teams play multiple games before moving on), nor do teams want to be home for longer than that period.

The conflict between travel and flow is not unique to MLB. Any time teams travel from one opponent to another leads to issues of distance and flow. In college basketball, some leagues work on a Friday-Sunday schedule where teams travel from their Friday game to their Sunday game directly. This has been explored by Campbell and Chen [4] where the goal was to minimize the distance traveled over such weekend pairs. Russell and Leung [7] had a similar travel objective in their work for scheduling minor league baseball. In both of these cases, the limit on the number of consecutive away games was set to two, leading to

T. Walsh (Ed.): CP 2001, LNCS 2239, pp. 580–584, 2001.

interesting bounds based on variants of the matching problem. Many other references to sports scheduling problems can be found in Nemhauser and Trick [6].

We propose a problem class called the *Traveling Tournament Problem (TTP)* which abstracts the key issues in creating a schedule that combines travel and home/away pattern issues. While it seems that either insights from sports scheduling problems that involve complex home/away pattern constraints or from the Traveling Salesman Problem (which the distance issues seem to mimic) would make this problem reasonably easy to solve, the combination makes this problem very difficult. Even instances with as few as eight teams are intractable relative to the state-of-the-art. This makes the problem attractive as a benchmark: it is easy to state and the data requirements are minimal. The fact that neither the integer programming nor the constraint programming community has studied this type of problem contributes to its interest. The TTP seems a good medium for contrasting approaches and for exploring combinations of methods.

2 The Traveling Tournament Problem

Given n teams with n even, a double round robin tournament is a set of games in which every team plays every other team exactly once at home and once away. A game is specified by and ordered pair of opponents. Exactly $2(n-1)$ slots or time periods are required to play a double round robin tournament. Distances between team sites are given by an n by n distance matrix D. Each team begins at its home site and travels to play its games at the chosen venues. Each team then returns (if necessary) to its home base at the end of the schedule.

Consecutive away games for a team constitute a road trip; consecutive home games are a home stand. The length of a road trip or home stand is the number of opponents played (not the travel distance).

The TTP is defined as follows.

Input: n, the number of teams; D an n by n integer distance matrix; L, U integer parameters.

Output: A double round robin tournament on the n teams such that

- The length of every home stand and road trip is between L and U inclusive, and
- The total distance traveled by the teams is minimized.

The parameters L and U define the tradeoff between distance and pattern considerations. For $L = 1$ and $U = n - 1$, a team may take a trip equivalent to a traveling salesman tour. For small U, teams must return home often, so the distance traveled will increase.

3 Modeling

The TTP is an intriguing problem not just for its modeling of issues of interest to real sports leagues. First, the problem combines issues of feasibility (the home/away patterns) and optimality (the distance traveled). Roughly, constraint programming excels at the former (see, for instance, Henz [5]) while integer programming does better at the latter (as in Applegate et al. [1]). This combination seems to be difficult for both methods, making the TTP a good problem for exploring combinations of methods. Even small instances seem to be difficult. While $n = 4$ leads to easy instances, $n = 6$ is a challenging problem, and $n = 8$ is still unsolved for our sample distance matrices.

The generation of tight lower bounds is fundamental to proving optimality. A simple lower bound is obtained by determining the minimal amount of travel for each team independent of any other team constraint. This problem, while formally difficult (it can easily be seen to be equivalent to a capacitated vehicle routing problem), can be solved easily for the problem sizes of interest. The sum of the team bounds gives a lower bound (the Independent Lower Bound or ILB) on the TTP. We can then use this lower bound to attack the TTP.

A straightforward constraint programming formulation of this problem, even armed with the ILB, cannot solve instances larger than $n = 4$. Instances with $n = 6$ require some interesting search techniques. We first find a good upper bound, then we work to increase the lower bound from ILB.

The key to our search is to order solutions by the number of trips taken by the the teams. In general, fewer trips means less distance traveled because a team does not have to return home too often. Let a pattern be a vector of home and away designations, one for each slot. Let a pattern set be a collection of patterns, one for each team. It is easy generate pattern sets in increasing order of the number of trips. For a given pattern set, forcing a solution to match that set is a much easier problem, and is the basis of a large part of the sports scheduling literature (see [6] for references). We can therefore generate pattern sets by increasing number of trips and find the minimum length distance for each pattern set. Once we have a feasible solution, we can add a constraint that we only want better solutions, which will further speed the computation.

We do not want, however, to work with all the pattern sets: there are far too many even for $n = 6$. Instead, we can modify ILB to include a minimum total number of trips constraint. Once the ILB with this constraint is above our feasible solution, we know that we do not need to consider any pattern with more trips.

This method generally finds very good solutions quickly and can prove optimality for small instances. For larger instances, we have worked on a combination of integer and constraint programming methods involving column generation approaches [2]. In these models, the variables correspond to higher level structures, including road trips, homestands, and even complete team schedules. Constraint programming methods are used to generate variables that are then combined using integer programming techniques. Success depends heavily on the initial set of variables and on the branching rules used. For more detail on this, see the longer version of this paper, available from the web page http://mat.gsia.cmu.edu/TTP.

4 Instance Classes and Computational Results

We propose two problem classes for algorithmic experiments of the TTP. The first is an artificial set of instances designed to determine the effect of the TSP aspects of the TTP. The second is a series of instances from Major League Baseball which provided the original inspiration for this work.

Circle instances. Arguments for the complexity of TTP revolve around the embedded traveling salesman problem. It is not clear, however, that the TTP is easy even if the TSP is trivial. We explore this with this instance class where the TSP is easily solved (and for which the solution is unique) but the TTP still seems to be challenging.

The n node circle instance (denoted CIRCn) has distances generated by the n node circle graph with unit distances. In this graph, the nodes are labeled $0, 1, \ldots n-1$; there is an edge from i to $i+1$ and from $n-1$ to node 0, each with length 1. The distance from i to j (with $i > j$) is the length of the shortest path in this graph, and equals the minimum of $i-j$ and $j-i+n$.

In this graph, $0, 1, \ldots, n-1$ gives the optimal TSP tour. Does this make the TTP easy?

National League Instances. As stated in the introduction, the primary impetus for this work was an effort to find schedules for Major League Baseball. Unfortunately, MLB has far too many teams for the current state-of-the-art for finding optimal solutions. MLB is divided into two leagues: the National League and the American League. Almost all of the games each team plays are against teams in its own league, so it is reasonable to limit analysis to an individual league.

We have generated the National League distance matrices by using "air distance" from the city centers. To generate smaller instances, we simply take subsets of the teams. In doing so, we create instances NL4, NL6, NL8, NL10, NL12, NL14, and NL16, where the number gives the number of teams in the instance. All of these instances are on the challenge page associated with this work: `http://mat.gsia.cmu.edu/TOURN`.

Computational Results. We have attempted to solve the benchmark instances using a wide variety of techniques, including those given in Section 3. In general, size 4 instances are trivial, size 6 instances are difficult, and size 8 and larger instances are unsolved. In Table 1, we give bound values for some of the instances. Computation time seems less interesting for these instances at this stage due to their difficulty. In short, size 4 problems take at most a couple of seconds, size 6 solutions are found in between 1 and 2 hours, and we have spent days of computation time on the size 8 instances without proving optimality (the results in the table are the best bounds from all of our efforts).

5 Conclusions and Future Directions

We propose the TTP as a benchmark problem for two primary reasons:

1. The problem has practical importance in modeling important issues from real sport schedules

Table 1. Some Benchmark Results for Challenge Instances

Name	U	IB	LB	UB	Optimal?
NL4	3		8276	8276	Y
NL6	3	22969	23916	23916	Y
NL8	3	38670	38870	41113	
NL16	3	248,852	248,852	312,623	
CIRC4	3	16	20	20	Y
CIRC6	3	60	64	64	Y
CIRC8	3	128	128	148	

2. The mix of feasibility and optimality, together with no long history in either field, make the problem interesting to both the operations research and constraint programming communities.

The proposed instances seem to be unusually difficult for either constraint programming or integer programming alone. One interesting study of some of these instances has been given by Benoist, Laburthe, and Rottembourgh [3] who propose an algorithm combining lagrangean relaxation and constraint programming. While their results to date have not been competitive with the techniques in this work, their paper does exactly what we hoped would happen with these instances: spurring research in combining different methods to solve hard combinatorial problems.

References

1. Applegate, D. R. Bixby, V. Chvatal, and W. Cook. 1998. "On the solution of traveling salesman problems", Documenta Mathematica Journal der Deutschen Mathematiker-Verinigung International Congress of Mathemeticians, 645-656.
2. Barnhart, C., E.L. Johnson, G.L. Nemhauser, M.W.P. Savelsbergh, and P.H.Vance. 1998. "Branch-and-Price: Column Generation for Huge Integer Programs", Operations Research **46:** 3, 316- 329.
3. Benoist, T., F. Laburthe, and B. Rottembourg, 2001. "Lagrange relaxation and constraint programming collaborative schemes for traveling tournament problems", CPAI-OR, Wye College, UK, 15-26.
4. Campbell, R.T., and D.S. Chen, 1976. "A Minimum Distances Basketball Scheduling Problem", in *Optimal Strategies in Sports*, S.P. Ladany and R.E Machol (eds.), North-Holland, Amsterdam, 32-41.
5. Henz, M. 2001. "Scheduling a Major College Basketball Conference: Revisted", Operations Research, 49:1,.
6. Nemhauser, G.L. and M.A. Trick. 1998. "Scheduling a Major College Basketball Conference", Operations Research, 46, 1-8.
7. Russell, R.A. and J.M Leung. 1994. "Devising a cost effective schedule for a baseball league", Operations Research 42, 614-625.

Deriving Explanations and Implications for Constraint Satisfaction Problems*

Eugene C. Freuder, Chavalit Likitvivatanavong, and Richard J. Wallace

Cork Constraint Computation Centre, University College Cork
Cork, Ireland

Abstract. We explore the problem of deriving explanations and implications for constraint satisfaction problems (CSPs). We show that consistency methods can be used to generate inferences that support both functions. Explanations take the form of trees that show the basis for assignments and deletions in terms of previous selections. These ideas are illustrated by dynamic, interactive testbeds.

1 Introduction

Solving a problem is not always sufficient. Users like to have an *explanation* for a result, and they want to know the *implications* of their choices. These issues are especially difficult for constraint based systems because such systems generally rely on combinatorial search. An obvious response to the need for explanation or implication information - tracing the solution process - does not work well for search. Pruning away "dead ends" in a search tree simply results in the solution itself.

However, the consistency processing that distinguishes the AI approach to constraint solving is an inference process. In this case, inferences lead to domain restrictions, and in the extreme case the inference process limits us to assigning a specific value or shows us that the previous assignments produce a non-solution. This means that solution search can provide at least partial explanations for why an assignment was made or why a solution is not possible under the circumstances.

The present work builds upon this insight, and is concerned with automating the process of providing information about explanation and implication. With respect to providing explanations, our goal is to help the user understand the following situations:

- why did we get this as a solution?
- why did this choice of labels lead to a conflict?
- why was this value chosen for this variable during processing?

Knowing about implications of current choices will help the user make intelligent choices during the subsequent course of problem solving. For implications our goal is to provide the user with information about the following:

- is there a basis for choosing among values in a future domain?

* This work was supported in part by Calico Commerce, and was carried out at the Department of Computer Science, University of New Hampshire,Durham, NH 03824 USA.

T. Walsh (Ed.): CP 2001, LNCS 2239, pp. 585–589, 2001.

- are there values whose choice will lead to conflict, even though they are consistent with the present domains?

For the problem of explanation generation, we consider the properties that explanations should have in this context and propose a generic structure, the *explanation tree* that appears to meet these specifications. We also consider the question of "goodness" of an explanation; here the criterion is explanation size, assuming that, other things being equal, smaller is better.

In this work we can distinguish the logical structure of explanation and implication from the manner in which critical information is presented to the user, especially in an interactive setting. Although our focus is on the first area, the rationale for the logical structures we have developed depends on their suitability for interactive use. To handle to this problem, we have created a series of testbeds, implemented in Java, that illustrate strategies for presentation and allow us to evaluate our overall approach.

2 Deriving Explanations

We define an explanation as a set of problem features which, for a given problem, entails the result to be explained. Given such features, we must still present them in a way that makes the entailment clear to the user. We proceed as follows. When a label is assigned, this means that all values in a domain except one have been eliminated because of selections already made during search. From the set of earlier assignments we can obtain an *immediate explanation* for a new assignment that meets the entailment requirement. But the elements in the immediate explanation may have their own explanations (unless they were either chosen by the user or given in the original problem description), and this process can be iterated. This means that explanatory elements can be linked to form a network of elements or an *extended explanation*, which in its fully extended form, where all elements are either themselves explained or givens, is a complete explanation of the assignment in question.

There are several ways to avoid incorporating cycles into our extended explanations. In the first place, whenever a value is deleted, information about the assignment that led to the deletion can be stored in connection with the deleted value. Similarly, whenever an assignment is deduced, we can use this stored information to derive a set of existing assignments that form a sufficient basis for assigning this new value. Since the process of storage follows the order of search, and at any time during search there is a current, acyclic search path, then in forming an extended explanation from this information we are guaranteed not to encounter cycles. Because the explanations formed in this way are acyclic, we call such explanations *explanation trees*.

Of course, there is a cost for updating: in particular, if an assignment is retracted (and possible altered) by the user, information must be discarded from that point in the current search path, and at least partly regenerated. In practice, doing this has proven to be roughly as efficient as the processing required after a new assignment.

Explanation trees are related to truth maintenance systems (TMS's, [2]) and other nogood recording schemes [4], in that they provide a form of justification for particular facts such as variable assignments. In fact, a full explanation tree for an assignment is a transitive closure of explanatory elements, which corresponds directly to this feature in justification truth maintenance systems. The major difference pertains to selectivity: for explanation trees, justifications are directly tied to search paths. As a result they are always enlarged in a certain order, one that guarantees a tree structure.

3 Testbeds

Our first testbed, the 9-puzzle [1], can be solved by inference alone. It consists of a 9 X 9 array of cells, 36 of which contain numbers from 1 to 9. The goal is to place a number in each empty cell so that each row, each column, and each adjacent 9-cell block in the array contains all the numbers 1 through 9. We can represent this type of puzzle as a CSP, where each cell is a variable whose domain consists of the numbers 1 to 9. The constraints are all binary inequality constraints, holding between each pair of cells in each row, column and 9-cell block.

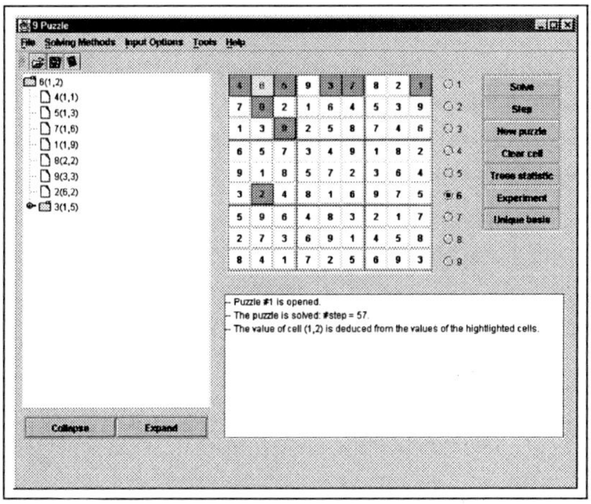

Fig. 1. A 9-puzzle problem with solution and immediate explanation for label 6 in cell (1,2). Explanatory elements are highlighted on puzzle board, and the tree in lefthand panel can be expanded.

We used two methods of inference. "Method 1" is based directly on the constraints: if cell (x,y) is labeled with the number n, then other cells in the same row, column, and block as (x,y) cannot be n. This is implemented by taking each labeled cell in turn and deleting its number from the domains of other cells in the same row, column and block. If a cell's domain is reduced to one number, this is its label. "Method 2" is more indirect: for each unlabeled cell, determine whether a number in its domain can be excluded from every other unlabeled cell in the same block; if so, then the former cell must be given this number. (For more details on both methods, consult [3].)

In the 9-puzzle testbed a puzzle board is shown at the center of the display (Figure 1). The user can click on any labeled cell to evoke an explanation for that labeling. This appears in the form of a set of highlighted cells on the puzzle board and, simultaneously in a panel to the left of the board.

The second testbed is based on the n-queens problem, which cannot be solved by inference alone. In this problem, n queens must be placed on an n by n chessboard in such a way that no queen can attack another. We represent the problem in the conventional manner, where rows are variables and the domain values are in different columns.

Here, we solve the problem using arc consistency. This is a simple form of inference in which the domains of each pair of variables linked by a constraint are made fully consistent. Since arc consistency by itself cannot solve the n-queens problem, it must be interspersed with user selections.

4 Finding Better Explanations

Two quantitative properties that can be used as criteria for goodness are average number of nodes in a tree and average number of levels in the tree. For demonstration purposes, we use the 9-puzzle. For method 1 we compared three ordering heuristics, a default row-and-column ordering, a most-cells-deleted (greedy) ordering, and a method that chooses cells with the fewest nodes in their explanation trees. The results are shown in Table 1, together with number of solution steps. Both the greedy and smallest-tree heuristics improve on the default ordering. Times to find a solution are uniformly low.

Table 1. Characteristics of Explanation Trees Built with Method 1 and Different Heuristics

ordering	solution steps	average nodes	average height	avg. time(s)
default	73	272	7.2	.02
greedy	56	58	3.8	.03
smallest tree	74	29	2.8	.03

Table 2. Characteristics of Explanation Trees with Method 2 and Different Selection Criteria

criterion	average nodes	average height	avg. time(s)
default	558	7.5	1.9
smallest set	44	4.6	4.9
smallest tree	19	2.9	5.1

With method 2 explanations can be chosen according to different criteria, after a cell is discovered that must be given a certain number. “Default" explanations were obtained by choosing cells in a row-and-column order. This was compared with the choice of the smallest set of cells for an explanation, and the set of cells with the smallest average explanation tree size (cf. Table 2; "solution steps" is always 45).

5 Deriving Implications

Each successive value assignment alters the status of values in the rest of the problem in various ways that are often not obvious. With the queens problem, using arc consistency we can determine many of these implications of user choice. In the first place, we can run arc consistency with each future value selected for assignment to determine the reduction in domains that will ensue. In the course of doing this, we can sometimes determine that a given value if selected will lead to a solution in the next round of arc consistency or, conversely, that it will lead to failure in the form of a situation in which all the values in some domain have been deleted.

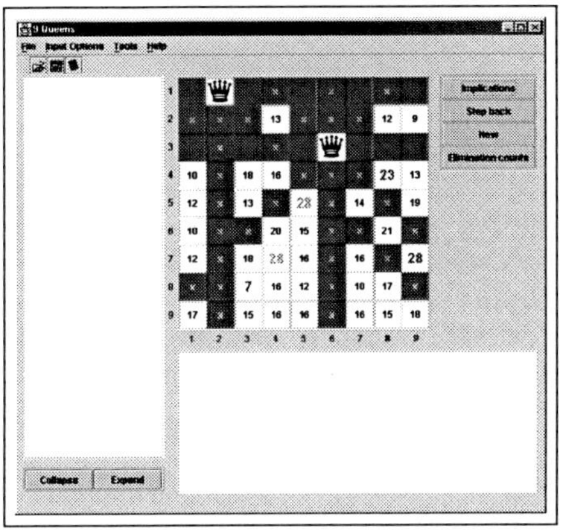

Fig. 2. n-queens interface. Greyed-out cells have been eliminated by the two queens placed on the board. White cells indicate remaining values. Other features are described in the text.

These capacities are illustrated with the queens problem (Figure 2). Each empty cell is labeled with the number of cells deleted if a queen is placed there and full arc consistency performed. In carrying out arc consistency with one of these presumptive assignments, it may be found that there is no solution; in this case the count is given in red. (Examples are cells (4,8) and (7,9).) If the problem is solved when the prospective problem is made arc consistent, by deducing positions for the remaining queens, the count is given in green ((5,5) and (7,4)).

References

[1] Dell. *Dell Math Puzzles and Logic Problems*. Dell Magazines, 2000.

[2] K. D. Forbus and J. deKleer. *Building Problem Solvers*. MIT, Cambridge, MA, 1993.

[3] E. C. Freuder, C. Likitvivatanavong, and R. J. Wallace. A case study in explanation and implication. In *CP2000 Workshop on Analysis and Visualization of Constraint Programs and Solvers*, 2000.

[4] T Schiex and G. Verfaillie. Nogood recording for static and dynamic constraint satisfaction problems. *Inter. J. Artific. Intell. Tools*, 3:187–207, 1994.

Generating Tradeoffs for Interactive Constraint-Based Configuration

Eugene C. Freuder[1]* and Barry O'Sullivan[2]

[1] Cork Constraint Computation Centre
University College Cork, Ireland
e.freuder@4c.ucc.ie

[2] Department of Computer Science
University College Cork, Ireland
b.osullivan@cs.ucc.ie

Abstract. In this paper we have modeled tradeoffs in constraint-based configuration as additional constraints, and begun to study the issues involved in generating and evaluating such tradeoffs. We describe our basic approach in the context of a "toy" configuration problem based on the classic N-Queens problem. Initial experiments compare "proposal strategies" for generating tradeoffs. We demonstrate that arc-consistency can be used as an effective trigger for generating tradeoff proposals in interactive configuration.

1 Introduction

Configuration is becoming a well studied design activity [5]. While there has been a growing interest in issues such as diagnosis of knowledge-bases for configuration [2], advice generation for design [1] and explanation generation [3], there is still a need for work on techniques which learn user's preferences and use these to assist users achieve satisfactory configurations. This paper presents initial steps towards the development of such techniques.

During an interactive configuration session we may reach a point where our desires cannot be met. At this point we can consider "tradeoffs". For example, in configuring a camera, we find that it is impossible to get one weighing less that 10 ounces with a zoom lens of 10X or more, so we consider a tradeoff: "I will increase my weight limit to 14 ounces if I can have a zoom lens of 10X or more." Ideally, we would like the configurator to suggest appropriate tradeoffs to us.

We have modeled tradeoffs in constraint-based configuration as additional constraints, and begun to study the issues involved in generating and evaluating such tradeoffs [4]. In Section 2, we describe our basic approach in the context of a "toy" configuration problem. We utilize the classic N-Queens problem, with the addition of user-generated "preference constraints" and system-generated "tradeoff constraints". Initial experiments compare "proposal strategies" for generating tradeoffs. Our results can be summarized as follows. Firstly, users who

* This work was performed while this author was at the University of New Hampshire.

T. Walsh (Ed.): CP 2001, LNCS 2239, pp. 590–594, 2001.

have strong preferences can be more successfully assisted in finding acceptable solutions to a configuration problem. Secondly, when users have strong preferences, arc-consistency is a sufficient trigger for proposing tradeoffs to the user to successfully overcome inconsistency. This is a particularly interesting result since techniques based on arc-consistency are extremely useful in industry-based configurators. Finally, a number of concluding remarks are made in Section 3.

2 A Case Study

The configuration problem that will be studied here is based on the N-Queens problem. The user attempts to solve the configuration problem by interactively specifying a series of preference constraints to a constraint-based configurator. We assume that the user prefers higher column values. Thus, when the user proposes a preference constraint we will assume it to be of the form $row \geq column$, where *row* corresponds to a row number in the N-Queens problem and *column* corresponds to the column value for that row. For example, the constraint $4 \geq 6$ means that the queen on row 4 should be placed in a column whose value is at least 6.

During an interactive session with the configurator, the user may specify a constraint which causes the set of preference constraints to become "over-constrained", identified using some measure of consistency (e.g the problem becomes arc-inconsistent). At this point our configurator attempts to recommend a set of appropriate "tradeoff" constraints to the user which she can accept before continuing to develop a solution for the configuration problem.

User-specified preference constraints are modeled as unary constraints. On the other hand, tradeoffs are modeled as binary constraints. During an interactive session with our configurator, when a tradeoff constraint, involving row x and y, is accepted, it replaces the unary preference constraints involving these variables.

2.1 Tradeoff Proposal Strategies

We have considered a number of tradeoff proposal strategies. These will be briefly outlined below:

- *Maximum Sum of Column Values* – this strategy proposes a set of tradeoff constraints, each of whose sum of column values is maximal and is *arc-consistent.*
- *Maximum Sum of Viable Column Values* – this strategy generates a set of tradeoff constraints, each of whose sum of column values is maximal and could yield a *solution* to the configuration problem.
- *Maximum Viability* – this strategy generates a set of tradeoff constraints which have the potential to yield the greatest number of solutions (maximally viable) to the configuration problem.
- *Minimum Viability* – this strategy generates a set of tradeoff constraints which could yield at least one solution (minimally viable) to the configuration problem.

– *Pareto optimality* – this strategy generates a set of tradeoff constraints which could yield a Pareto optimal solution to the configuration problem.

2.2 Evaluation of Proposal Strategies

Experiments were made on the 8-Queens problem. The experiments involved simulating the interaction between a human user and a configurator.

We simulated the human user on a combination of two axes. Firstly, we considered the set of solutions to the problem which the user would find acceptable as an experimental axis. Different points on this axis were chosen and solutions were generated at random for each point. Our simulated user would accept a tradeoff if it permitted a solution in the "set of acceptable solutions".

Secondly, we modeled the "strength" (greediness) of the user's preference constraints. Therefore, we considered the strength (m) of the simulated user's constraints as an experimental axis. Based on this axis our simulated user proposes new preference constraint bounds randomly chosen between m and N (for N-Queens) for different values of m. In our experiments we chose points along this axis from the set $\{2, 4, 6\}$. Thus, if we were simulating a user whose preference constraints had strength 4, a new constraint on row x would be of the form $x \geq y$, where y would be randomly chosen from the set of integers between 4 and 8 (for 8-Queens).

We simulated an interactive configurator. The configurator accepted user-specified preference constraints and incorporated these into the "built-in" model of the Queens problem. Preference constraints were accepted from the simulated user while they were consistent. If the simulated user managed to solve the problem without encountering an inconsistency, tradeoffs were never proposed. When the user proposed a preference constraint, $x \geq i$, which had the effect of introducing an inconsistency into the model, the configurator proposed a set of tradeoffs to the user. We used two different measures of consistency to trigger the proposal of tradeoffs: arc-consistency and full viability checking. If the user accepted one of the proposed tradeoff constraints, $C_{(x,y)}$, the unary constraints on x and y in the user's set of preference constraints were replaced with a single binary constraint representing the accepted tradeoff. If the set of tradeoff constraints proposed to the user was empty, or none was acceptable to the user, this was regarded as a failure. In the experiments presented here we assumed that the user could not "backup" by retracting a previous preference constraint or tradeoff. We are currently addressing the issue of revisiting previous decisions.

2.3 Most Significant Results

Of the five tradeoff proposal strategies evaluated, two are of particular interest: maximum sum of viable column values and minimum viability. The results for these will be discussed below.

The "maximum sum of viable column values" strategy only recommends tradeoffs which it knows could lead to a full solution to the problem. Thus,

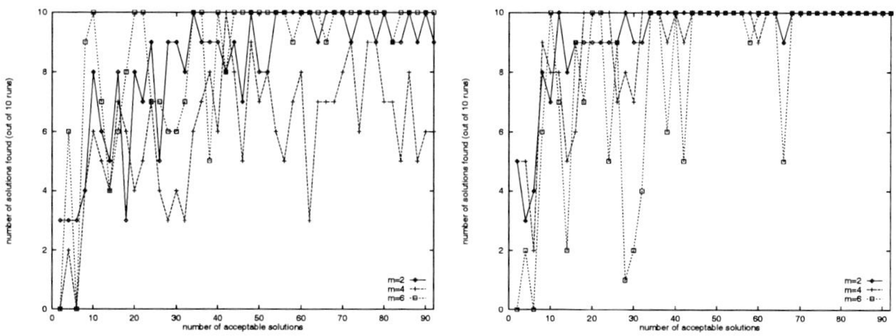

(a) Generating tradeoffs when arc-inconsistent

(b) Generating tradeoffs when viability check fails

Fig. 1. The performance of the "maximum sum of column values with full viability checking" strategy.

while greedy, it attempts to work with the distributions found in the solutions to the N-Queens problem. The performance of this strategy is presented in Figure 1. One of the most interesting aspects of the performance of this strategy is that its performance is quite volatile for smaller sets of acceptable solutions. This can be seen quite clearly in Figure 1(b), but is also evident in Figure 1(a) for user preference strengths of 2 (m=2) and 6 (m=6). The fact that either high strength (m=6) and low strength (m=2) preferences are more successful at finding solutions (Figure 1(a)) is a consequence of the tradeoffs working with both the distribution of solutions in the Queens problem and their symmetries. It should also be noted that for high strength preferences (m=6), solutions are found consistently regardless of the type of consistency check used to trigger tradeoff proposals. This is significant since it implies that arc-consistency can be used to generate good tradeoff proposals to the user. Arc-consistency is of much more practical use than full viability checking.

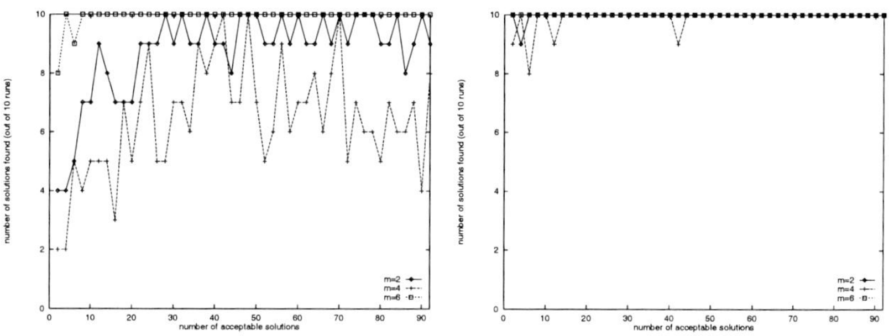

(a) Generating tradeoffs when arc-inconsistent

(b) Generating tradeoffs when viability check fails

Fig. 2. The performance of the "minimum viability" strategy.

The "minimum viability" strategy found acceptable solutions for almost every point along the axis of number of acceptable solution when using a high preference strength Figure 2). However, since this strategy generates tradeoffs which are minimally viable there is a disadvantage associated with it, namely, that a large number of tradeoffs are proposed. In an interactive environment this could cause a certain amount of information overload from the perspective of the user. However, it may be possible to alleviate the problems associated with this by using an anytime approach to generating tradeoffs based on "minimum viability".

3 Conclusion

The ability of configurators to generate tradeoffs to users during interactive configuration is valuable. In this paper we have modeled tradeoffs in constraint-based configuration as additional constraints, and begun to study the issues involved in generating and evaluating such tradeoffs. We have found that users who have strong preferences can be more successfully assisted in finding acceptable solutions to a configuration problem. In addition, when users have strong preferences, arc-consistency is a sufficient trigger for proposing tradeoffs to the user to successfully overcome inconsistency. This is a particularly interesting result since techniques based on arc-consistency are extremely useful in industry-based configurators.

Acknowledgments. This work was supported in part by Trilogy. Professor Freuder is supported by a Principal Investigator Award from Science Foundation Ireland.

References

1. James Bowen. Using dependency records to generate design coordination advice in a constraint-based approach to Concurrent Engineering. *Computers in Industry*, 33(2–3):191–199, 1997.
2. Alexander Felfernig, Gerhard Friedrich, Dietmar Jannach, and Markus Stumpter. Consistency-based diagnosis of configuration knowledge-bases. In *Proceedings of the 14h European Conference on Artificial Intelligence*, pages 146–150, 2000.
3. Eugene C. Freuder, Chavalit Likitvivatanavong, and Richard J. Wallace. A case-study in explanation and implication. In *In CP2000 Workshop on Analysis and Visualization of Constraint Programs and Solvers*, 2000.
4. Eugene C. Freuder and Barry O'Sullivan. Generating tradeoffs for constraint-based configuration. In *Working Notes of the CP-2001 Workshop on User-Interaction in Constraint Satisfaction*, December 2001.
5. Daniel Sabin and Rainer Weigel. Product configuration frameworks – a survey. *IEEE Intelligent Systems and their applications*, 13(4):42–49, July–August 1998. Special Issue on Configuration.

Structural Constraint-Based Modeling and Reasoning with Basic Configuration Cells

Rafael M. Gasca, Juan A. Ortega, and Miguel Toro

Department of Languages and Computer Systems
University of Sevilla
Avda. Reina Mercedes s/n 41012 Sevilla (Spain)
{gasca, ortega, miguel.toro}@lsi.us.es

Abstract. Configuration tasks are an important application area in engineering design. The proposed solving techniques use either a constraint-based framework or a logic-based approach. We propose a methodology to obtains desired configuration using basic configuration cells(*BCC*). They are built by means of the predefined components and connections of the given configuration problem.

In practical applications of configuration tasks the *BCCs* and configuration goals are represented according to object-oriented programming paradigm. They are mapped into a numeric constraint satisfaction problem. The transformation of a basic configuration cell into a new one generates a sequence of numeric constraint satisfaction problems. We propose an algorithm that solves this sequence of problems in order to obtain a configuration solution according to the desired requirements or that detects inconsistencies in the requirements. The integration of object-oriented and constraint programming paradigms allows us to achieve a synergy that produces results that could not be obtained if each one were working individually.

1 Introduction

The goal of a lot of scientific and engineering activities has long been regarded the discovery of structural configuration. The design tasks in engineering sometimes need to combine the predefined components in order to obtain a desired configuration in a realistic time. A predefined component is described by a set of properties, by a set of ports for connecting it to other components and by structural constraints . The configuration tasks select and arrange combinations of predefined components that satisfy all the requirements.

The configuration problems have been studied in Artificial Intelligence area for the last years. A survey about the configuration frameworks has been recently published[13]. The proposed solving techniques use a constraint-based framework [12], [8] or a logic-based approach [6][10]. We propose a new structural constraint-based methodology. The modeling and search of possible configurations take into account object-oriented and constraint programming paradigms. The main motivation for integrating both paradigms is to achieve a synergy that produces results that could not be obtained if each mode were working individually.

T. Walsh (Ed.): CP 2001, LNCS 2239, pp. 595–599, 2001.

Our work allows us to describe easily how to select and arrange components in a configuration problem. These tasks can be carried out through the series or parallel connection of components such as capacitors, resistors, chemical reactors, etc. in order to satisfy given goals. The properties of these components may be constrained between real upper and lower bounds. It takes us to consider a configuration task as a numeric constraint satisfaction problem($NCSP$). These problems can be efficiently solved by combining local consistency methods, such as approximations of arc-consistency, together with a backtracking search. Different techniques have been proposed in the bibliography [7], [1], [9],[14],[4]. The search space in numeric constraint problems is too wide and a lot of these techniques have a major drawback since they introduce choice points and they are exponential. The efficiency of some previous algorithms has been analyzed in a recent work [2].

We use abstractions named basic configuration cells(BCC) for solving previous configuration problems. These $BCCs$ allow us to model the configuration task as a set of structural constraints expressed in the form of equations, inequalities over integer or/and real variables. The model is enriched by means of the addition of symmetry-breaking constraints to avoid the inherent symmetry of the different configurations and to reduce its complexity. It is the major issue in CSP, specially when there is a large number of constraints and/or wide domains of the variables. In the last years, it has been an active research area [11], [3], [5].

The article is organized as follows: We show modeling of configuration problems in Section 2. Section 3 presents the structural constraint-based reasoning. In the last Section our conclusions and future works are presented.

2 Modeling of Configuration Problems

In the same way as the animal tissue contains cells, we consider that the solution of a configuration problem is to build something similar to a set of cells put on a determined way. These cells are the $BCCs$ and they must cover all the possible combinations of the components and their connections.

We will first show some simple configuration problem. We would like to know the series-parallel combination of predefined resistors to obtain a new resistor that has a given real resistance value R_{goal} and a set of constraints related to its cost and volume. The construction of $BCCs$ must take into account the domain knowledge and the constructs of the configurations(Components, Connections and Goals). $BBCs$ are the entities that reflect in a minimal way the possible connections of the basic components. They must allow the pure connection of the components. It will indicate the absence of some component in the $BCCs$. In the proposed problem we may add a null Resistor instance whose attributes are $R_{null}.r = 0, R_{null}.Vol = 0, R_{null}.Cost = 0$. A grammatical description of a BCC can be :

$$\begin{aligned} BCC_0 : & \; BCC_1 \| (BCC_2; BCC_3) \\ & \mid R \end{aligned}$$

The associated attributes and constraints of these $BCCs$ are the following:

BCC
Attributes:$\{Name, R, Cost, Vol, \{Components : BCC_1, BCC_2, BCC_3\}$
Constraints: $\{BCC_1.Cost + BCC_2.Cost + BCC_3.Cost = Cost,$
$BCC_1.Vol + BCC_2.Vol + BCC_3.Vol = Vol,$
$BCC_3.R > 0 \Rightarrow$
$(BCC_1.R + BCC_2.R) * BCC_3.R = (BCC_1.R + BCC_2.R + BCC_3.R) * R,$
$BCC_3.R = 0 \Rightarrow (BCC_1.R + BCC_2.R) = R\}$

In these $BCCs$, the modeler can add redundant symmetry-breaking constraints to remove the symmetries of the configuration problems. The object-oriented paradigm allows us to specify a BCC easily. In a similar way we specify the goals of a configuration problem as

---

Goals
Attributes: $\{Name\}$
Constraints: $\{BCC.Cost \leq MaxCost, BCC.Vol \leq MaxVol,$
$(BCC).R = R_{Goal}\}$

---

3 Methodology of Structural Constraint-Based Reasoning

This reasoning must search the *structural constraints* that satisfy the requirements of the configuration problem. Some attributes of Components Objects are numeric variables. It forces the structural constraint-based reasoning to treat numeric constraint satisfaction problems.These variables, their continuous domains and the constraints determine a $NCSP$. A $NCSP$ instance is defined by a triple (X, D, C), where $X = \{x_1, ..., x_n\}$ is a set of variables, $D = \{d_1, ..., d_n\}$ is a set of continuous domains for the variables, and C is a set of constraints. A constraint is defined by a subset of variables $X_c \subseteq X$ on which it holds, and a numeric relation linking them [7]. A solution of an instance is an assignment of values for all constrained variables, which satisfy all constraints.

A solving algorithm obtains the desired configuration. The attributes and constrainst of the BCC Objects can be mapped into Variables, Domains and Constraints Objects and their conjunction generates a $NCSP$. We have named the methodology of reasoning in these configuration problems as *Structural Constraint-based Reasoning*. The solution of the reasoning is a set of "*structural constraints*" that satisfies all the specified goals. The abstraction of the $BCCs$ allows us the performance of this task. A structural constraint-based reasoning is modeled by means of the following steps: Generation of the $NCSP$ by means of BCC Objects and application of a constraint solver with the corresponding heuristic. In this point, we want to highlight the sharp separation between the configuration problem specification and solving method. It allows the easy modification of the configuration problem specification.

3.1 Generation of the Numeric Constraint Satisfaction Problems

In this step, we generate a $NCSP$ using the BCC Objects. The variables are the attributes related to the constraints of the goals. The domains are the types of these variables and the constraints are $C_{goals} \cup C_{BCC}$. These problems may have multiple solutions or may have none. Our goal is to obtain the "*structural constraint*", such that a $NCSP$ is satisfied. If the desired requirements of the configuration problem are not satisfied in a certain $NCSP$, then we must consider a new $NCSP$.

3.2 Configuration Problem Solving

Every $NCSP$ is solved according to the exact topology of the previous $BCCs$. If they do not hold the requirements of the desired configuration, then we will build a new $NCSP$. It will have equivalent constraints, variables and the domains of the $BCCs$ Objects will increase. Then we will have a configuration problem mapped into a sequence of $NCSP$. The mechanism that obtains this sequence is a recurrent task.

Many constraint solvers are designed to tackle $NCSP$. Constraint solvers are systems that implement data structures and algorithms to perform consistency and entailment checks very efficiently. In our case we must tackle a sequence of $NCSP$ that only varies the domains of the constrained variables. We propose an algorithm that begins the construction of the initial $NCSP$. If the requirements are satisfied, then it will return the solutions that are the associated "*structural constraints*" to the BCC, but if the requirements are not satisfied, then we will build a new $NCSP$ with different BCC Objects instances. The pseudocode of the algorithm is as follows:

```
program Configuration Solving (in p:Configuration Problem)
                            out Sol:BCC
      begin
         Sol := ∅
         ncsp:= Generate an initial NCSP of p
         while ( time < MaxTime and DepthCell <= MaxDepth)
            Sol := Solve(ncsp)
            if Sol ≠ ∅
               Return Sol
            else
               ncsp:= Generate a new NCSP
            endif
         endwhile
      end
```

The *Solve* function is a numeric constraint solver that searches possible solutions, it creates new $BCCs$ in order to build a new $NCSP$ and it avoids the recalculation of nogood $BCCs$.The condition of termination of this algorithm may depend on the maximum Time($MaxTime$) of computation or the depth($MaxDepth$) of the $BCCs$ used.

4 Conclusions and Future Works

We have defined a novel methodology for configuration tasks that use *structural constraint-based reasoning*. Our methodology uses the advantages of object-orientation paradigm for the abstraction of components and the constraint programming paradigm that allows us an easy declaration of the constraints and a search of the structural constraints. The main entities of this methodology are basic configuration cells that permit a recursive effect in the configuration tasks. A constraint solver treats the sequence of generated $NCSPs$ efficiently.

A future work will consider other more complex configuration problems, where the components have more ports. Other interesting problems are the obtaining of configuration with different types of connections and components at the same time.

References

1. Benhamou F. and Granvilliers L.: Combining Local Consistency, Symbolic Rewriting and Interval Methods in Proceedings of AISMC-3 volume 1138 of LNCS, Springer-Verlag. (1996) 44-159
2. Collavizza H., Delobel F. and Rueher M.: Extending consistent domains of numeric CSP Proceecings of Sixteenth IJCAI'99, Stockholm, (1999) 406-411
3. Fox M. and Long D.: The Detection and Explotation of Symmetry in Planning Problems IJCAI'99 (1999), 956-961
4. Gasca, R. M. Razonamiento y simulación en sistemas que integran conocimiento cualitativo y cuantitativo Ph. D. dissertation Seville University, (1998)
5. Gent I.P. and Barbara M. Smith Symmetry Breaking in Constraint Programming. In ECAI'2000 14th European Conference on Artificial Intelligence. (2000)
6. Klein R., Buchheit M. and Nutt W. Configuration as model construction: The constructive problem solving approach. In Proc. of the 3rd Int. Conference on AI in Design (1994)
7. Lhomme O.: Consistency Techniques for Numeric CSPs Proceedings IJCAI'93, (1993) 232-238
8. D. Mailharro, A Classification and constraint-based framework for configuration. Artificial Intelligence for Engineering Design, Analysis and Manufacturing, 12(4) (1998)
9. Marti P., Rueher M.: Concurrent Cooperating Solvers over Reals. Reliable Computing 3 (1997) 325-333
10. McGuiness D.L. and Wright J. R.: Conceptual Modelling for Configuration: A description Logic-based Approach. Artificial Intelligence for Engineering Design, Analysis and Manufacturing, 12(4) (1998)
11. Meseguer P. and Torras C. Solving Strategies for Highly Symmetric CSPs. In IJCAI'99 (1999) 400-411
12. Sabin, D. and Freuder F. Configuration as Composite Constraint Satisfaction. In Workshop Notes of AAAI Fall Symposium on Configuration AAAI Press. Menlo Park, CA (1996) 28-36
13. Sabin D. and Weigel R. Product Configuration Frameworks-A survey. In IEEE Intelligent Systems (1998) 42-49
14. Van Hentenryck P., (1998) 42-49 Michel L. and Deville Y. Numerica. A modeling language for global optimization The MIT Press (1997)

Composition Operators for Constraint Propagation: An Application to Choco*

Laurent Granvilliers and Eric Monfroy

IRIN – University of Nantes
2, rue de la Houssinière – B.P. 92208 – 44322 Nantes cedex 3 – France
{granvilliers,monfroy}@irin.univ-nantes.fr

1 Introduction

A constraint satisfaction problem is defined by a set of variables associated to domains, and a set of constraints on these variables. Solving a constraint satisfaction problem consists in finding assignments of all variables that satisfy all constraints. Since this problem is NP-hard, constraint propagation has been designed to struggle against the combinatorial explosion of brute-force search by pruning domains before enumeration. Filtering algorithms enforcing consistency properties [8] are the most well-known techniques for constraint propagation.

Recently, K. R. Apt [1] has proposed a unified framework for constraint propagation. The reduction process is defined as a chaotic iteration: an iteration of *reduction functions* over domains. Iteration-based algorithms are shown to be finite and confluent under well-chosen properties of domains (e.g., partial ordering, well-foundedness) and functions (e.g., monotonicity, contractance). In [2], further refinements are proposed for tackling strategies based on additional properties of reduction functions. Hence, specificities of reduction functions are used to tune orders for applying functions in the generic iteration algorithm.

In this paper, we are concerned with specific strategies for filtering algorithms: the main goals are to take into account dynamic behaviours of reduction processes, to tackle parallel computations, and to lay foundations of generic "dynamic strategy-based" filtering algorithms. To this end, we introduce the notion of *composition operator* to dynamically order reduction functions: basically, a composition operator is a dynamic and local strategy for applying functions. Using composition operators and properties of reduction functions, we have already easily modeled several strategies and heuristics of well-known propagation-based constraint solvers: priorities of constraints in the finite domain solver `Choco` [6], described in Section 3, slow convergence arising in interval narrowing [7], efficient heuristics for interval narrowing [3], and finally, parallel computations [4]. The generic iteration algorithm for compound functions (`COGI`) is similar to the generic iteration algorithm of [1], where reduction functions are replaced with compound functions. The semantics of iterations of [1] is preserved (termination and confluence properties).

* This work is supported by the COCONUT IST european project.

T. Walsh (Ed.): CP 2001, LNCS 2239, pp. 600–604, 2001.

2 Constraint Propagation with Compound Functions

2.1 Reduction Functions

We first introduce the notion of *reduction function* over a domain. For our purpose, we are less general than in [2], and we directly consider contracting and monotonic functions on a finite semilattice ordered by set inclusion. Such a domain is used to address the decoupling of reductions arising in parallel computations. Note that the results given here hold under these assumptions.

More formally, the *computation domain* is a finite semilattice $(\mathcal{D}, \subseteq, \cap)$, that is a partially ordered set $(\mathcal{D}, \subseteq)$ in which every nonempty finite subset has a greatest lower bound. The ordering $\subseteq$ corresponds to set inclusion. The meet operation is set intersection, and the bottom element is the empty set.

Definition 1 (Reduction function). *Consider a function f on $\mathcal{D}$.*

- *f is contracting if $\forall x \in \mathcal{D},\ f(x) \subseteq x$;*
- *f is monotonic if $\forall x, y \in \mathcal{D},\ x \subseteq y \Rightarrow f(x) \subseteq f(y)$.*

A reduction function on *$\mathcal{D}$ is a contracting and monotonic function on $\mathcal{D}$.*

2.2 Compound Functions

Consider a sequence of reduction functions $F = (f_1, \ldots, f_k)$ on $\mathcal{D}$. We introduce a set of composition operators on F as follows:

Sequence:	F°	denotes the function	$x \mapsto f_1 f_2 \ldots f_k(x)$
Closure:	F^*	"	$x \mapsto (\cap_{i=1}^k f_i)^*(x)$
Decoupling:	$F^\cap$	"	$x \mapsto f_1(x) \cap \cdots \cap f_k(x)$

where $(\cap_{i=1}^k f_i)^*(x)$ denotes the greatest common fixed-point of f_i, $1 \leqslant i \leqslant n$, included in x (see [2] for more details).

The notion of *compound function* models strategies of application of reduction functions using composition operators.

Definition 2 (Compound function). *Let $F = (f_1, \ldots, f_k)$ be a finite sequence of reduction functions. A* compound function on *F is a function $\mathcal{D} \to \mathcal{D}$ defined by induction as follows:*

Atomic: *f_i is a compound function for $i = 1, \ldots, k$.*

Given a sequence Φ of compound functions on F,

Sequence: *Φ° is a compound function;*
Closure: *Φ^* is a compound function;*
Decoupling: *$\Phi^\cap$ is a compound function.*

Lemma 1. *Consider a finite set of reduction functions $F = \{f_1, \ldots, f_k\}$. Then, every compound function on F is contracting and monotonic, and thus is a reduction function.*

In the COGI iteration algorithm described in Section 2.3, a compound function g is applied at each loop. However, the update function depends on the reduction functions that are the basic bricks of g. We thus need the notion of *generator* of a compound function.

Definition 3 (Generator). *The* generator $\texttt{Gen}(\phi)$ *of a compound function* ϕ *on* F *is the subset of functions from* F *that are "involved" in* ϕ*. It is defined inductively by:*

- $\texttt{Gen}(\phi) = \{\phi\}$ *if* $\phi \in F$*;*
- $\texttt{Gen}(\phi) = \texttt{Gen}(\phi_1) \cup \cdots \cup \texttt{Gen}(\phi_k)$ *if* $\phi = (\phi_1, \ldots, \phi_k)^\star$ *for* $\star \in \{\circ, \omega, \cap\}$.

Lemma 2 states that a fixed-point of a compound function is also a common fixed-point of all the functions from its generator. The key idea is that an application of a compound function implies that each reduction function from its generator is applied at least once.

Lemma 2. *Consider a finite set of reduction functions* F *and a compound function* ϕ *on* F*. Then,* e *is a fixed-point of* ϕ *iff* e *is a common fixed-point of all the functions from* $\texttt{Gen}(\phi)$*.*

2.3 Iteration of Compound Functions

The notion of iteration of [2] is extended to deal with compound functions.

Definition 4 (Iteration). *Consider a finite sequence of reduction functions* F*, and a finite set* $\Phi = \{\phi_1, \ldots, \phi_k\}$ *of compound functions on* F*. Given an element* $d \in \mathcal{D}$*, an iteration of* Φ *over* d *is an infinite sequence of values* $d_0, d_1, \ldots$ *defined inductively by:*

$$
\begin{aligned}
d_0 &:= d \\
d_i &:= \phi_{j_i}(d_{i-1}) \quad i \geqslant 1
\end{aligned}
$$

where j_i *is an element of* $[1, k]$*.*

Lemma 3. *Consider a finite sequence of reduction functions* F*, and a finite set* $\Phi = \{\phi_1, \ldots, \phi_k\}$ *of compound functions on* F*. Suppose that an iteration of* Φ *over* d *stabilizes at a common fixed-point* e *of the functions from* Φ*. Then,*

$$e = \texttt{Gen}(\Phi)^*(d)$$

We describe now the generic iteration algorithm COGI based on compound functions on a finite set of reduction functions F (see Table 1). The set of compound functions is not fixed at the beginning of the algorithm, since each function is dynamically created from the set G of active reduction functions, and it is applied only once. Thus, G is still a set of reduction functions to be applied, and the update function still depends on reduction functions (i.e., the functions to be applied, or the generators of the compound function that is currently being applied). Theorem 1 proves the correctness of COGI w.r.t. F.

Theorem 1. *Every execution* $\texttt{COGI}(F, d)$ *terminates and computes in* d *the greatest common fixed-point of the functions from* F*.*

Table 1. Generic Iteration Algorithm based on Compound Functions.

```
COGI (F: set of reduction functions on 𝒟 ; d: element of 𝒟): 𝒟
begin
   G := F
   while G ≠ ∅ do
      ϕ := create a compound function on G
      G := G − Gen(ϕ)
      G := G ∪ update (G, ϕ, d)
      d := ϕ(d)
   od
   return d
end
```

where for all G, ϕ, d the set of functions $\texttt{update}\,(G, \phi, d)$ is such that

A. $\{f \in F - G \mid f(d) = d \ \wedge \ f\phi(d) \neq \phi(d)\} \subseteq \texttt{update}\,(G, \phi, d)$

B. $\phi(d) = d$ implies that $\texttt{update}\,(G, \phi, d) = \varnothing$

C. $\{f \in \texttt{Gen}(\phi) \mid f\phi(d) \neq \phi(d)\} \subseteq \texttt{update}\,(G, \phi, d)$

3 An Application to Choco

`Choco` is a constraint programming system for finite domains that has been developed by F. Laburthe et al. [6]. Different kinds of constraints are processed by constraint propagation, such as primitive constraints, and global constraints with linear or quadratic complexity. The strategy implemented in the solver consists in computing successive fixed-points for subsets of constraints: primitive constraints are first considered, then, global constraints with linear complexity, and so on until a global fixed-point is reached. In other words the computation is a sequence of application of closures, each closure handling all active constraints from one category. Moreover, propagation events (modification of domains) are generated between applications of closures.

The propagation engine of `Choco` can be described with our generic algorithm `COGI` by considering priorities associated to reduction functions. At each iteration, the created compound function is as follows:

$$\phi := \{g \in G \mid priority(g) = \alpha\}^* \text{ s.t. } \alpha = \min(\{priority(g) \mid g \in G\})$$

This implements a closure of the set of active reduction functions from the propagation list G with the greatest priority (i.e., the computationally less expensive functions). This is a model of `Choco` in the sense that only functions with greatest priority are applied at a time.

Our model allows one not only to describe existing strategies, but also to design new strategies. In particular, costs for updating propagation structures can be decreased if updates are realized after long periods of application of functions. The following strategy is a model of `Choco` that takes into account this feature.

$$\phi := (G_1^*, \ldots, G_p^*)^\circ \text{ s.t. } G_1, \ldots, G_p \text{ is a partition of } G \text{ and } \forall i \in [1, \ldots, p], \forall g \in G_i, \text{priority}(g) = \alpha_i \text{ with } \alpha_p < \alpha_{p-1} < \cdots < \alpha_1.$$

The coumpound function is a sequence of closures, each closure processing the set of functions of a given priority. The main difference w.r.t. the first method is that no propagation step is performed between the application of two closures.

4 Conclusion and Perspectives

A set of composition operators of reduction functions is introduced to design dynamic constraint propagation strategies. K. R. Apt's iteration model is slightly modified while preserving the semantics. Modeling of well-known strategies are described in a long version of this paper [5].

The set of composition operators is (intentionally) reduced to sequence, closure, and decoupling operators. One may desire additional operators to model sequences of fixed length, quasi closures with a notion of precision, or conditional strategies w.r.t. dynamic criteria. We believe that their integration in our framework is feasible, and should be carried out the same way as the operators presented in this paper.

Acknowledgements. We are grateful to Frédéric Benhamou for interesting discussions on these topics.

References

1. Krzysztof R. Apt. The Essence of Constraint Propagation. *Theoretical Computer Science*, 221(1-2):179–210, 1999.
2. Krzysztof R. Apt. The Role of Commutativity in Constraint Propagation Algorithms. *ACM Transactions on Programming Languages and Systems*, 22(6):1002–1036, 2000.
3. Laurent Granvilliers. On the Combination of Interval Constraint Solvers. *Reliable Computing*, 7(6):467–483, 2001.
4. Laurent Granvilliers and Gaétan Hains. A Conservative Scheme for Parallel Interval Narrowing. *Information Processing Letters*, 74:141–146, 2000.
5. Laurent Granvilliers and Eric Monfroy. Enhancing constraint propagation with composition operators. In *Proceedings of the ERCIM/CompulogNet Workshop on Constraints*, Prague, Czech Republic, 2001.
6. François Laburthe and the OCRE project team. CHOCO: implementing a CP kernel. In *Proceedings of the CP'2000 workshop on techniques for implementing constraint programming systems*, Singapore, 2000.
7. Olivier Lhomme, Arnaud Gotlieb, and Michel Rueher. Dynamic Optimization of Interval Narrowing Algorithms. *Journal of Logic Programming*, 37(1–2):165–183, 1998.
8. Alan K. Mackworth. Consistency in Networks of Relations. *Artificial Intelligence*, 8(1):99–118, 1977.

Solving Boolean Satisfiability Using Local Search Guided by Unit Clause Elimination

Edward A. Hirsch[1]* and Arist Kojevnikov[2]

[1] Steklov Institute of Mathematics at St.Petersburg, 27 Fontanka 191011 St.Petersburg, Russia, `http://logic.pdmi.ras.ru/~hirsch`
[2] St. Petersburg State University, Department of Mathematics and Mechanics St.Petersburg, Russia, `http://logic.pdmi.ras.ru/~arist`

Abstract. In this paper we present a new randomized algorithm for SAT combining unit clause elimination and local search. The algorithm is inspired by two randomized algorithms having the best current worst-case upper bounds ([9] and [11,12]). Despite its simplicity, our algorithm performs well on many common benchmarks (we present results of its empirical evaluation). It is also probabilistically approximately complete.

Keywords: Boolean satisfiability, local search, empirical evaluation.

1 Introduction

Under the hypothesis of $\mathcal{P} \neq \mathcal{NP}$, designing a polynomial-time algorithm for SAT is a hopeless task. During the past decade, this obstacle has been attacked in two main directions: proving "weakly exponential" worst-case upper bounds on the running time of SAT algorithms (see [1] for survey), and designing more practical "heuristic" algorithms (see [2,6] for survey). Unfortunately, the worst-case upper bounds currently known for SAT algorithms are still too large for practical purposes. On the contrary, "heuristic" algorithms, though very hard for theoretical study, show good performance in practice both on randomly generated instances and on structured instances encoding various practical problems.

In this paper, we suggest a new SAT algorithm UnitWalk. Similarly to good practical algorithms (e.g. WalkSAT family [8]) and good theoretical algorithms [11,12], our algorithm uses local search, i.e., it chooses an initial assignment at random and modifies it step by step. However, the heuristic for flipping a variable is motivated by the randomized unit clause elimination algorithm of [9].

This short version of the paper is organized as follows. In Sect. 2 we give definitions and describe notation related to SAT algorithms. Our algorithm is described in Sect. 3. In Sect. 4 we formulate the result on PAC property of our algorithm. Section 5 contains experimental data describing the execution of our algorithm on various benchmarks. A full version of this paper will appear in PDMI preprint series (`http://www.pdmi.ras.ru/preprint/`). The C source code for UnitWalk is available from `http://logic.pdmi.ras.ru/~arist/`.

* Supported by INTAS YSF 99-4044, RFBR 99-01-00113 and RAS Young Scientists Project #1 of the 6th competition (1999).

T. Walsh (Ed.): CP 2001, LNCS 2239, pp. 605–609, 2001.

We leave the following directions for further research:

1. Design an *efficient* implementation of UnitWalk.
2. Experiment with various formula transformation rules (in addition to unit clause elimination) and with changing the distributions of initial assignments (cf. [12]) and permutations.
3. Design a complete algorithm based on UnitWalk. (See [1] for survey of related derandomization issues).
4. Prove upper and lower bounds on the running time of UnitWalk.

2 Preliminaries

We denote by $F[v \leftarrow t]$ the formula obtained from a formula F in CNF by substituting of a truth value t to a variable v. Namely, we remove all clauses containing the satisfied literal (v or $\neg v$), and remove the opposite literal from the remaining clauses. The value of v in an assignment A is denoted by $A[v]$.

An *incomplete randomized SAT algorithm* either finds a (correct) satisfying assignment for the input formula, or gives the answer "Not found". In the latter case the formula may be either unsatisfiable or satisfiable. Most incomplete algorithms for SAT are *local search* algorithms. A local search algorithm chooses an initial assignment at random. At each step, it changes (at most) one value in it, trying to get closer to a satisfying assignment. If an algorithm changes the value of a variable, we say that the algorithm *flips* it. This procedure (as well as the whole algorithm) is called *probabilistically approximately complete* (*PAC*) [3] if for every satisfiable formula and *every* initial assignment the procedure finds a satisfying assignment with probability one.

3 Description of the Algorithm

As a typical local search algorithm, UnitWalk generates an initial assignment at random and then modifies it step by step. The main difference from other local search algorithms is that during this walk our algorithm modifies also the input formula.

The random walk is divided into *periods*. During one period at least one (usually, much more) flip is made. A period starts with choosing a random permutation of variables. Then algorithm takes the input formula and modifies it step by step, sometimes also modifying the current assignment. At each step, the algorithm substitutes the value of one variable in the current formula, i.e., replaces a formula G by $G[v \leftarrow t]$ for a variable v and a truth value t. If there are unit clauses, then v is taken from one of them; if the value of v does not satisfy the unit clause and satisfies no other unit clause, it is flipped before substitution. If there are no unit clauses, the algorithm substitutes the value to the next variable in the chosen permutation (taking the value from the current assignment).

Input: A formula F in CNF containing n variables $x_1, \ldots, x_n$.
Output: A satisfying assignment for F, or "Not found".
Method:

```
For t := 1 to MAX_TRIES(F) do
    A := random truth assignment for n variables;
    For p := 1 to MAX_PERIODS(F) do
        π := random permutation of 1..n;
        G := F;
        f := 0;
        For i := 1 to n do
            While G contains a unit clause, repeat
            • Pick a unit clause {x_j} or {¬x_j} from G at random;
            • If this clause is not satisfied by A, and G does not contain the
              opposite unit clause, then flip A[j] and set f := 1;
            • G := G[x_j←A[j]];
            If variable x_π[i] still appears in G, then G := G[x_π[i]←A[π[i]]].
        If G contains no clauses, then output A and exit;
        If f = 0, choose j at random from 1..n and flip A[j].
Output "Not found".
```

Fig. 1. Algorithm UnitWalk

If a period finishes (i.e., all variables are processed), but no variable was flipped during it, the algorithm chooses a variable at random and flips it (in fact, this is a very rare situation). After period finishes, the algorithm chooses a new random permutation, replaces the current formula (which is trivial now) by the input formula, and starts a new period. The number of periods is limited to MAX_PERIODS(F) which may be a function of certain syntactic characteristics of the input formula, e.g., of the number of variables. After the last period finishes, the random walk is restarted from another random initial assignment. If a satisfying assignment is not found after taking MAX_TRIES(F) initial assignments, the algorithm outputs the answer "Not found".

4 Probabilistic Approximate Completeness

Some of the known local search algorithms *need* restarts because there are initial assignments such that the probability that the random walk (if allowed to run infinitely long) hits a satisfying assignment is strictly less than one (e.g., GSAT, WalkSAT/TABU, Novelty, R-Novelty [3,4]). Other algorithms have the PAC property (e.g., GWSAT with strictly positive noise parameter [3,4]). The following theorem shows that our algorithm also is PAC, i.e., if we set MAX_PERIODS(F) to $+\infty$ and MAX_TRIES(F) to 1, then for every satisfiable formula and *every* initial assignment, UnitWalk finds a satisfying assignment with probability one.

Theorem 1. *Algorithm UnitWalk is probabilistically approximately complete.*

Table 1. The data for IDB is taken from [10] where the experiments were made on a 400 MHz Intel Pentium II. All other experiments were made on a 466MHz Intel Celeron Pentium II running under Linux; each experiment was repeated 100 times, the table contains the average number. The DIMACS hardware bencmark program *dfmax r500.5* [7] takes 43.71 seconds on the machine. The implementations of WalkSat, Novelty and R-Novelty were taken from http://www.cs.washington.edu/homes/kautz/walksat/, GSAT and SDF from http://logos.uwaterloo.ca/~dale/ and UnitWalk from http://logic.pdmi.ras.ru/~arist. The limits that we have used for all algorithms were: `MAX_TRIES`$(F) = 1$; `MAX_PERIODS`$(F) = +\infty$ for UnitWalk, and `MAX_FLIPS`$(F) = 1,000,000$ for other algorithms on all formulas except par-8, par-16-c and ais12. For those formulas we have used `MAX_FLIPS`$(F) = 10,000,000$.

	UnitWalk		GSAT	WalkSAT	Novelty	R-Novelty	SDF	IDB
	substitutions	flips(time)	flips(time)	flips(time)	flips(time)	flips(time)	flips(time)	time
uf100-430	13,500	2,547(0.029)	*	3,652(0.009)	15,699(0.047)	1,536(0.005)	876(0.013)	
par8-5-c	5,311	863(0.011)	*21,859(0.160)	*19,182(0.056)	4,318(0.012)	2,640(0.007)	3,691(0.033)	
par8-5	13,078	1,022(0.022)	*	*	*$2.0 \cdot 10^6$(3.875)	*271,632(0.577)	$1.0 \cdot 10^6$(19.11)	
par16-5-c	$12,7 \cdot 10^6$	$3.1 \cdot 10^6$(33.85)	*	*	$85.8 \cdot 10^6$(236.6)	$49.9 \cdot 10^6$(145.2)	*	
flat50-115	1,521	261(0.002)	*16,857(0.100)	3,896(0.008)	*24,421(0.027)	*9,373(0.019)	773(0.010)	
flat100-239	18,833	3,500(0.051)	*752,775(4.631)	44,900(0.164)	17,893(0.036)	12,345(0.027)	6,983(0.154)	
flat150-360	208,719	46,096(0.499)	*	254,188(0.562)	130,359(0.296)	*731,825(1.429)	39,156(0.863)	
aim100	24,059	4,020(0.048)	*	*251,618(0.445)	*269,700(0.453)	*265,862(0.456)	*116,467(1.889)	
ii8	1,468	203(0.021)	*169,366(7.095)	495(0.021)	5,593(0.180)	*3,166(0.010)	3,946(0.804)	
ii16	9,093	1,086(0.273)	*	6,201(0.769)	*91,031(10.07)	*85,742(4.036)	7,180(1.346)	0.305
ii32	5,989	854(0.227)	*	2,284(1.040)	*88,779(6.775)	*77,589(3.736)	*	1.17
jnh	3,625	484(0.026)	*291,729(2.585)	5,449(0.049)	3,329(0.031)	1,943(0.020)	732(0.039)	
ssa	6,992	707(0.023)	*	45,181(0.171)	*650,156(7.024)	*1,374,403(13.76)	27,238(2.146)	0.31
logistics.d	103,686	4,120(0.942)	*	472,513(3.013)	136,938(1.187)	1,115,760(12.63)	74,090(56.72)	
ais6	2,780	204(0.007)	*	1,192(0.005)	*	7,412(0.032)	430(0.008)	
ais8	56,370	2,875(0.229)	*	28,528(0.152)	*	*$1.2 \cdot 10^6$(6.529)	4,645(0.169)	
ais10	432,191	18,405(6.077)	*	173,422(1.978)	*	*	20,870(1.521)	
ais12	$6.0 \cdot 10^6$	222,967(142.5)	*	*$2.9 \cdot 10^6$(34.28)	*	*	*154,249(18.64)	
bw_large.a	15,174	1,215(0.159)	*	19,158(0.093)	9,699(0.050)	6,911(0.039)	2,917(0.184)	0.425
bw_large.b	215,889	11,848(3.562)	*	480,187(3.793)	203,813(2.005)	347,827(4.443)	38,927(6.440)	7.75
2bitadd_11	6,804	292(0.011)	32,517(0.558)	1,174(0.005)	*99,489(0.35)	*139,062(0.498)	166,089(11.07)	0.026
2bitadd_12	4,620	249(0.009)	23,554(0.443)	751(0.004)	*99,478(0.411)	*53,076(0.194)	111,328(8.074)	0.028
2bitcomp_5	382	48($4.7 \cdot 10^{-5}$)	1,537(0.007)	156($5.1 \cdot 10^{-5}$)	*99,838(0.250)	441(0.001)	69(0.001)	0.002
2bitmax_6	941	106(0.001)	12,163(0.103)	400(0.001)	230(0.001)	173($9.2 \cdot 10^{-5}$)	871(0.030)	
3bitadd_31	725,152	5,105(7.946)	*	28,511(1.090)	*	210,907(19.54)	*	11.0
3bitadd_32	435,200	3,825(4.853)	*	14,209(0.628)	*	*	*	8.6
3blocks	100,153	2,839(4.959)	*	33,256(0.643)	13,696(0.270)	8,304(0.179)	10,561(2.602)	

* `MAX_FLIPS`(F) has been reached in one or more runs; if no data present, all runs were unsuccessful.

5 Experimental Data

It is a difficult task to compare algorithms empirically. To a large extent, the running time spent by an algorithm corresponds to a specific implementation, and may also vary as environment conditions change. For local search algorithms, a more uniform complexity measure is the number of flips, since it corresponds to the essential exponential factor of the running time (cf., e.g., [6,11]). However, while the time spent per flip is usually polynomial, it is not a constant and may vary during the execution. It also heavily depends on the implementation and therefore the number of flips does not allow to compare implementations.

In Table 1 we present the number of flips made by UnitWalk on various benchmarks from [5], and its running time. We also present the number of *substitutions* made, which characterizes the current implementation better. For the comparision, we present the data for several other algorithms: GSAT [15], WalkSAT [14], Novelty, R-Novelty [8], SDF [13], IDB (aka CLS) [10].

References

1. E. Dantsin, E. A. Hirsch, S. Ivanov, and M. Vsemirnov. Algorithms for SAT and upper bounds on their complexity. ECCC Technical Report 01-012, ftp://ftp.eccc.uni-trier.de/pub/eccc/reports/2001/TR01-012/index.html.
2. J. Gu, P. W. Purdom, J. Franco, and B. W. Wah. Algorithms for satisfiability (SAT) problem: A survey. DIMACS Ser. in DM and TCS 35, 1997, pages 19–152.
3. H. H. Hoos. On the run-time behaviour of stochastic local search algorithms for SAT. In *Proc. AAAI'99*, pages 661–666.
4. H. H. Hoos. *Stochastic Local Search — Method, Models, Applications.* PhD thesis, Department of Computer Science, Darmstadt University of Technology, 1998.
5. H. H. Hoos and T. Stützle. SATLIB. `http://www.satlib.org/`.
6. H. H. Hoos and T. Stützle. Local search algorithms for SAT: An empirical evaluation. *Journal of Automated Reasoning*, 24(4):421–481, 2000.
7. D. S. Johnson and M. A. Tricks, editors. *Cliques, Coloring and Satisfiability*, volume 26 of *DIMACS Ser. in DM and TCS.* AMS, 1996.
8. D. McAllester, B. Selman, and H. Kautz. Evidence in invariants for local search. In *Proc. AAAI'97*, pages 321–326.
9. R. Paturi, P. Pudlák, M. E. Saks, and F. Zane. An improved exponential-time algorithm for k-SAT. In *Proc. FOCS'98*, pages 628–637.
10. S. D. Prestwich. Local search and backtracking vs non-systematic backtracking. In *AAAI 2001 Fall Symposium on Using Uncertainty within Computation.* To appear.
11. U. Schöning. A probabilistic algorithm for k-SAT and constraint satisfaction problems. In *Proc. FOCS'99*, pages 410–414.
12. R. Schuler, U. Schöning, and O. Watanabe. An improved randomized algorithm for 3-SAT. Technical Report TR-C146, Dept. of Math. and Comp. Sci., Tokyo Inst. of Tech., 2001.
13. D. Schuurmans and F. Southey. Local search characteristics of incomplete SAT procedures. In *Proc. of AAAI'2000*, pages 297–302.
14. B. Selman, H. A. Kautz, and B. Cohen. Noise strategies for improving local search. In *Proc. AAAI'94*, pages 337–343.
15. B. Selman, H. Levesque, and D. Mitchell. A new method for solving hard satisfiability problems. In *Proc. AAAI'92*, pages 440–446.

GAC on Conjunctions of Constraints

George Katsirelos[1] and Fahiem Bacchus[1]

Department of Computer Science, University Of Toronto*
Toronto, Ontario, Canada
{gkatsi,fbacchus}@cs.toronto.edu

Abstract. Applying GAC on conjunctions of constraints can lead to more powerful pruning [1]. We show that there exists a simple heuristic for deciding which constraints might be useful to conjoin. The result is a useful *automatic* way of improving a CSP model for GAC solving.

1 Introduction

Generalized arc consistency (GAC) [2] is arc consistency generalized to the non-binary case. GAC can be used as a mechanism for constraint propagation to reduce the complexity of a CSP. GAC can also be embedded in a backtracking search algorithm to provide constraint propagation dynamically (cf. the binary MAC algorithm [3,4]).

Bessière and Régin have pointed out that GAC can also be applied to conjunctions of constraints [1], and they provide an algorithm for enforcing GAC on conjunctions. In this paper we make some further observations on this idea. Specifically, we show that there is a simple heuristic that can be used to determine whether or not it might be worthwhile grouping a collection of constraints into a conjunction and performing GAC on this conjunction.

This provides a method for achieving a potential improvement of any given CSP model automatically: using the heuristic we simply group together collections of constraints and then perform GAC on these conjunctions instead of on the individual constraints. The model with conjoined constraints can then be tested to determine if in fact an improvement has been achieved. Importantly, performing GAC on a conjunction of constraints does not require modifying the original model: the original representation of the constraints in each conjunction can be used directly by the GAC algorithm. It simply requires identifying the sets of constraints that might be worth conjoining. Since CSP modeling is a complex and potentially costly task, any improvements to a model that can be achieved automatically can help reduce the cost of finding a sufficiently efficient model. We demonstrate that this idea can be effective in two different CSP models.

2 Background and Notation

A CSP $(\mathcal{V},\mathcal{C})$ consists of a set of variables $\mathcal{V} = \{V_1,\ldots,V_n\}$ and a set of constraints $\mathcal{C} = \{C_1,\ldots,C_m\}$. Each variable V has a finite domain of values $\mathit{Dom}[V]$, and can be assigned a value v, indicated by $V \leftarrow v$, if and only if $v \in \mathit{Dom}[V]$. Let $\mathcal{A}$ be any

* This research was supported by the Canadian Government through their NSERC program.

T. Walsh (Ed.): CP 2001, LNCS 2239, pp. 610–614, 2001.

set of assignments. No variable can be assigned more than one value, so $\|\mathcal{A}\| \leq n$ (i.e., the cardinality of this set is at most n). When $\|\mathcal{A}\| = n$ we call $\mathcal{A}$ a *complete* set of assignments. Associated with $\mathcal{A}$ is a set of variables $VarsOf(\mathcal{A})$: the set of variables assigned values in $\mathcal{A}$.

Each constraint C is over some set of variables $VarsOf(C)$, and has an arity equal to $\|VarsOf(C)\|$. A constraint is a set of sets of assignments: if the arity of C is k, then each element of C is a set of k assignments, one for each of the variables in $VarsOf(C)$. We say that a set of assignments $\mathcal{A}$ *satisfies* a constraint C if $VarsOf(C) \subseteq VarsOf(\mathcal{A})$ and there exists an element of C that is a subset of $\mathcal{A}$.

$\mathcal{A}$ is said to be *consistent* if it satisfies all constraints C such that $VarsOf(C) \subseteq VarsOf(\mathcal{A})$, i.e., it satisfies all constraints it fully instantiates. Otherwise it is inconsistent. A *solution* to a CSP is a complete and consistent set of assignments.

Definition 1 (Generalized Arc Consistency). *Given a constraint C and a variable $V \in VarsOf(C)$, a value $a \in Dom[V]$ is **supported** in C if there is a set of assignments $\mathcal{A} \in C$, such that $V \leftarrow a \in \mathcal{A}$. $\mathcal{A}$ is called a **support** for $\{V \leftarrow a\}$ in C. C is **(generalized) arc consistent** iff each value a of each variable $V \in VarsOf(C)$ is supported in C. The entire CSP is **arc consistent** iff each of its constraints is arc consistent.*

Definition 2 (Conjunctive Consistency (Bessière and Régin)). *Let $\mathcal{C} = \{C_1, \ldots, C_k\}$ be a set of constraints and $VarsOf(\mathcal{C}) = \cup_i VarsOf(C_i)$ be the set of variables these constraints are over. $\mathcal{C}$ is conjunctively GAC iff for each value a of each variable $V \in VarsOf(\mathcal{C})$ there exists a set of assignments $\mathcal{A}$ such that (1) $V \leftarrow a \in \mathcal{A}$, (2) $VarsOf(\mathcal{A}) \supseteq VarsOf(\mathcal{C})$, and (3) $\mathcal{A}$ satisfies each constraint $C \in \mathcal{C}$. We call such an $\mathcal{A}$ a **support** for $\{V \leftarrow a\}$ on the conjunction $\mathcal{C}$.*

This definition says that there exists an assignment extending $V \leftarrow a$ that *simultaneously* satisfies all of the constraints in $\mathcal{C}$. This is equivalent to asserting that the (natural) join of all of the constraints in $\mathcal{C}$ is arc consistent (when viewed as being a new constraint relation).

As shown in [1], conjunctive GAC can be achieved in time upper bounded by $O(d^{\|\cup_i VarsOf(C_i)\|})$ where d is the maximum domain size of any of the variables in $VarsOf(\mathcal{C})$. Furthermore, their method does not require computing an explicit representation of the conjunction. That is, the representation of the individual constraints contained in the original model can be used directly.

Consider a CSP model containing the two constraints C_1 and C_2. If GAC is going to be used to solve the CSP, we would have to perform GAC(C_1) and GAC(C_2), a task that would require time $O(d^{\|VarsOf(C_1)\|})$ plus $O(d^{\|VarsOf(C_2)\|})$ [5]. If we choose to perform GAC on their conjunction instead, GAC($C_1 \wedge C_2$), we would need time $O(d^{\|VarsOf(C_1) \cup VarsOf(C_2)\|})$. That is, the increased time required decreases as the number of variables shared by C_1 and C_2 increases. In the extreme case where $VarsOf(C_1) \subseteq VarsOf(C_2)$ performing GAC on the conjunction instead of over each constraint individually has the same order of complexity. In fact, for the GAC-schema algorithm of [1] it would be faster to compute GAC($C_1 \wedge C_2$) than computing both GAC(C_1) and GAC(C_2) in this case—each of these computations would require approximately the same amount of time, so we reduce the number of separate GAC computations by doing GAC on the conjunction.

From the definition it can be seen that GAC($C_1 \wedge C_2$) is a stronger consistency condition than individually enforcing GAC(C_1) and GAC(C_2). For the separate application of GAC to the two constraints, we would require only that there exists two sets of assignments $\mathcal{A}_1$ and $\mathcal{A}_2$ both extending $V \leftarrow a$, with $\mathcal{A}_1$ satisfying C_1 and $\mathcal{A}_2$ satisfying C_2. GAC on the conjunction requires that there exist a set of assignments $\mathcal{A}_\wedge$ extending $V \leftarrow a$ that satisfies C_1 and C_2 simultaneously. Hence, GAC($C_1 \wedge C_2$) has the potential to prune more values.

What is also interesting, but was not as well highlighted in [1], is that the relative strength of GAC on the conjunction increases as the number of shared variables between C_1 and C_2 increases. If these two constraints share no variables, then we can find the required set of assignments $\mathcal{A}_\wedge$ satisfying the conjunction, by simply unioning the two sets of assignments $\mathcal{A}_1$ and $\mathcal{A}_2$. That is, in this case GAC on the conjunction is identical to GAC on each constraint separately. On the other hand if these two constraints share i variables, then the required set of assignments $\mathcal{A}_\wedge$ only exists if we can find an $\mathcal{A}_1$ satisfying C_1 and $\mathcal{A}_2$ satisfying C_2 that agree on their assignments to all i shared variables (and then $\mathcal{A}_\wedge$ can again be $\mathcal{A}_1 \cup \mathcal{A}_2$). Clearly, this constraint on the individually satisfying assignments becomes stronger as the number of shared variables, i, grows.

Hence, the optimal case is when $\mathit{VarsOf}(C_1) \subseteq \mathit{VarsOf}(C_2)$: GAC($C_1 \wedge C_2$) is faster and it yields the maximal improved strength over doing GAC on each constraint separately.

In general, a simple heuristic for grouping constraints into conjunctive sets is as follows.

1. Initialize CS, the set of conjunctive sets, to contain m conjunctive sets each containing the single constraint C_i.
2. If there exist two conjunctive sets $\mathcal{C}_1, \mathcal{C}_2 \in CS$ such that (1) $\mathcal{C}_1$ and $\mathcal{C}_2$ share some variables, (2) the number of variables constrained by $\mathcal{C}_1 \cup \mathcal{C}_2$ is less than $\max(\|\mathit{VarsOf}(\mathcal{C}_1)\|, \|\mathit{VarsOf}(\mathcal{C}_2)\|) + M$, and (3) also less than N, then remove $\mathcal{C}_1$ and $\mathcal{C}_2$ from CS and add $\mathcal{C}_1 \cup \mathcal{C}_2$.
3. Repeat 2 until no more such pairs exist.

In this algorithm M places a limit on the increase in arity we are willing to allow, while N places an absolute limit on the arity of the conjoined constraints we are willing to allow. An optimal value for M will be problem dependent. For example, if $M = 0$ the algorithm will only conjoin constraints satisfying $\mathit{VarsOf}(C_1) \subseteq \mathit{VarsOf}(C_2)$.

3 Empirical Results

We report on experiments we performed with two different CSP models. The first is a model for the Golomb ruler problem containing quaternary constraints developed in [6]. In this model, there is a quaternary constraint $|x_i - x_j| \neq |x_k - x_l|$ for all marks $x_1, \ldots, x_m, j < i, l < k$. Hence, over every set of four marks there will be 7 different constraints posted over these variables, 4 quaternary constraints and 3 ternary constraints. We consider finding optimal solutions and proving them to be optimal using a backtracking search that maintains GAC. For this model we set $M = 0$, thus we only conjoin constraints whose variables are a subset of another.

The results are shown in Table 1. We used a 500MHz PIII machine, and the same underlying implementation for GAC on all of our tests. The first column shows the

Problem size	goal	Quat ∪ Tern		(∧ Quat) ∪ Tern		∧ (Quat ∪ Tern)	
7	F	95	0.14	95	0.07	90	0.06
7	P	988	1.62	988	0.81	894	0.51
8	F	574	1.33	574	0.64	492	0.45
8	P	7791	27.51	7791	13.35	7131	7.99
9	F	5581	26.51	5581	12.53	4920	7.75
9	P	57545	403.28	57545	190.16	52868	117.16
10	F	40141	360.64	40141	167.45	36666	107.24
10	P	-	-	-	-	-	-

Fig. 1. Backtracks and cpu time to find (F) a golomb ruler of a given size or prove (P) its optimality. "-" indicates that the solver was unable to find a solution after reaching 10^5 backtracks.

number of branches explored (and time required in CPU seconds) using the constraints without any conjunctions. The second column shows what happens when we conjoin together only the 3 quaternary constraints, and the final column show what happens when we conjoin all 7 constraints (for each set of 4 variables). The results show that a useful improvement in speed is obtained and a moderate improvement in the number of branches explored. The improvement in speed is greater than the improvement in branches due to the efficiency gained by performing GAC over conjunctions (see Section 2 for a discussion of this point). The middle column demonstrates that our technique is heuristic—improved pruning is not always obtained through conjunctions. In particular, it turns out that the three quaternary constraints all logically entail each other, so enforcing one is as powerful as enforcing all three or as enforcing the conjunction. Thus, we see no improvement in number of branches. The improvement in speed arises from the fact that with conjunctions we have fewer constraints over which GAC has to be enforced.

In the second model we experiment with random 3-sat problems. These problems are converted from a set of clauses into a CSP containing a set of binary variables and a ternary constraint for each clause. In this case, we set $M = 1$ and $N = 4$, thus generating conjunctions over 4 variables. The results are shown in Table 2.

It is worthwhile noting in this case that there were instances where the solver actually performed more backtracks when using conjoined constraints than it did in the original

		avg leafs		avg time		
# Variables	# Instances	original	w/conjunctions	original	w/conjunctions	perc
60	100	674.33	522.71	0.9951	0.8485	71
70	100	1637.36	1300.21	2.8882	2.4676	74
80	100	3504.36	2888.33	7.204	6.3182	74
90	100	9204.49	7085.21	21.7589	17.8116	75
100	100	19573.2	14434.2	52.5704	40.7247	83

Fig. 2. Average number of backtracks and cpu time to prove whether a problem is satisfiable or not. The last column indicates the percentage of instances where the solver performed better if constraints were conjoined.

# Variables	# Instances	avg leafs original	avg leafs w/conjunctions	avg time original	avg time w/conjunctions	perc
60	79	1602.62	540.81	2.35886	0.879747	88.6076
70	78	3890.79	1322.47	6.84756	2.50756	93.5897
80	82	7829.66	2706.33	16.0824	5.94561	90.2439
90	79	21926.1	7214.34	51.7696	18.1687	94.9367
100	85	44843.2	15398.1	120.359	43.482	97.6471

Fig. 3. The same data Table 2 but only instances for which conjoining constraints did not interfere with the behavior of the DVO heuristic are counted.

problem. This anomaly can be attributed to the fact that 3-SAT has a special structure, which is not accounted for by the minimal remaining values-break ties by degree heuristic used. Therefore, even though the conjunctive constraints cause more pruning, they end up making the search slower by fooling the heuristic. This anomaly could probably be eliminated by using one of the heuristics that have been developed specifically for SAT problems.

If we factor out these instances, and look only at those instances where the solver performed fewer backtracks with conjunctive constraints, we find that the cpu time used is at worst only 10% more than the time used to solve the problem using the original model. This shows that despite the fact that we are generating constraints of higher arity in this case (and hence the complexity of enforcing GAC on the conjunction is higher than enforcing GAC on the individual constraints separately) the overhead of performing GAC on the conjoined constraints is alleviated by the extra pruning it generates. More specifically, Table 3 show the same results as Table 2 except that the instances where the heuristic performed poorly have been removed. The results show a useful improvement is achieved by using conjunctions.

References

1. C. Bessière and J.-C. Régin. Local consistency on conjunctions of constraints. In *Proceedings of the ECAI'98 Workshop on Non-binary constraints*, pages 53–59, Brighton, UK, 1998.
2. A. K. Mackworth. On reading sketch maps. In *Proceedings of the Fifth International Joint Conference on Artificial Intelligence*, pages 598–606, Cambridge, Mass., 1977.
3. J. Gaschnig. Experimental case studies of backtrack vs. Waltz-type vs. new algorithms for satisficing assignment problems. In *Proceedings of the Second Canadian Conference on Artificial Intelligence*, pages 268–277, Toronto, Ont., 1978.
4. D. Sabin and E. C. Freuder. Contradicting conventional wisdom in constraint satisfaction. In *Proceedings of the 11th European Conference on Artificial Intelligence*, pages 125–129, Amsterdam, 1994.
5. C. Bessière and J.-C. Régin. Arc consistency for general constraint networks: Preliminary results. In *Proceedings of the Sixteenth International Joint Conference on Artificial Intelligence*, pages 398–404, Nagoya, Japan, 1997.
6. B. Smith, K. Stergiou, and T. Walsh. Using auxilliary variables and implied constraints to model non-binary problems. In *Proceedings of the Seventeenth National Conference on Artificial Intelligence*, Austin, Texas, 2000.

Dual Models of Permutation Problems

Barbara M. Smith

School of Computing & Mathematics
University of Huddersfield
Huddersfield HD1 3DH, U.K.
b.m.smith@hud.ac.uk

Abstract. A constraint satisfaction problem is a permutation problem if it has the same number of values as variables, all variables have the same domain and any solution assigns a permutation of the values to the variables. The dual CSP interchanges the variables and values; the effects of combining both sets of variables in a single CSP are discussed.

1 Introduction

A constraint satisfaction problem is a permutation problem if it has the same number of values as variables, all variables have the same domain and any solution assigns a permutation of the values to the variables. Other constraints in the problem determine the acceptable permutations. Many rostering, routing and sequencing problems can be modelled in this way.

Each possible value is assigned to exactly one variable and each variable is assigned exactly one value. The *dual* CSP, also a permutation problem, interchanges the variables and values. For instance, if there are n people to do n tasks, we can either assign tasks to people or people to tasks.

We can include both sets of variables, linked by *channelling constraints* [1], in a single CSP. If the primal variables are p_i, $1 \leq i \leq n$, and the dual variables are d_j, $1 \leq j \leq n$, the required channelling constraints are $p_i = j$ iff $d_j = i$, for all pairs $1 \leq i, j \leq n$. ILOG Solver provides an *inverse* constraint to link two arrays of variables in this way. The inverse constraint gives the same constraint propagation as the set of binary constraints, but a shorter running time.

When CSP models representing different views of a problem can be linked, Cheng, Choi, Lee and Wu [1] propose that the constraints of both models should be used, hence their term 'redundant modelling'. They mention that using all the constraints of both models may be unnecessary, and experience suggests that redundancy is often wasteful. We can instead use the constraints of the primal model and just the variables of the dual, with the channelling constraints.

The primal CSP has either binary $\neq$ constraints between all pairs of variables or a single allDifferent constraint on the n variables, to ensure that any solution is a permutation of the values. Maintaining generalized arc consistency on the allDifferent constraint, using the algorithm in [3], achieves more domain pruning than maintaining arc consistency on the $\neq$ constraints, but is time-consuming.

T. Walsh (Ed.): CP 2001, LNCS 2239, pp. 615–619, 2001.

Hence, even if a smaller search tree is explored in solving the CSP, there may not be a reduction in running time.

As observed in [4], the channelling constraints are sufficient to ensure that the values assigned to the p_i variables must all be different, since each must correspond to a unique d_j variable. Maintaining arc consistency on the channelling constraints gives more domain pruning than the $\neq$ constraints, though less than the allDifferent constraint. With the $\neq$ constraints, domain reduction occurs only when there is a variable whose domain is a single value: that value is removed from every other domain. The channelling constraints have the same effect as $\neq$ constraints on both primal and dual variables: in terms of the primal variables, if a value appears in the domain of only one variable, every other value is removed from that domain. Maintaining GAC on the allDifferent constraint detects cases where k of the variables have just k values between them and removes those values from all other domains.

Walsh [6] confirms this observation and shows that adding $\neq$ constraints on the primal or the dual variables to the channelling constraints will not give more domain pruning than the channelling constraints alone. If there is an allDifferent constraint on the primal variables, channelling constraints or an allDifferent constraint on the dual variables will give no additional domain pruning. Hence, we should consider three possible ways of ensuring that any solution is a permutation: the single model with $\neq$ constraints; the single model with an allDifferent constraint; the combined model, with its channelling constraints.

These arguments lead to a *minimal combined model* of a permutation problem: it has constraints on the primal variables defining acceptable permutations, but neither $\neq$ constraints nor an allDifferent constraint. There are no constraints on the dual variables other than the channelling constraints. This is the smallest CSP model of the problem which uses both primal and dual variables. It is also easy to define: for a permutation problem with n variables, it is only necessary to specify n new variables, each with domain 1 to n, and channelling constraints.

2 The n-Queens Problem and Langford's Problem

Two problems which can be modelled as permutation problems are considered here: more details of the models are given in [4,5]. The first is the n-queens problem (placing n queens on an $n \times n$ chessboard so that no two queens are in the same row, column or diagonal). The variable r_i, $1 \leq i \leq n$, represents the queen on row i; the value assigned is the column on which this queen is placed. A solution assigns a permutation of the columns to the rows: the acceptable permutations are those with no two queens on the same diagonal. The dual variable c_j, $1 \leq i \leq n$, represents the queen in column j. The dual and primal models are identical, with $c_1, ..., c_n$ substituted for $r_1, ..., r_n$.

By contrast, in Langford's problem (Problem 24 of CSPLib), the constraints are much easier to express in terms of one set of variables than their dual. The (3,9) instance of this problem requires a sequence, consisting of the digits 1 to 9, each used 3 times, such that there is just one digit between the first two 1s, and one digit between the last two 1s; there are just two digits between the first two 2s and two digits between the last two 2s, and so on.

This instance can be modelled as a permutation problem with 27 variables, $p_1, p_2, ..., p_{27}$ corresponding to $1_1, 1_2, 1_3, 2_1, ..., 9_2, 9_3$, where 1_1 represents the first 1 in the sequence, 1_2 the second 1, etc. The value assigned to a variable gives the position in the sequence of the corresponding digit. *Separation constraints* ensuring the correct spacing between the digits, e.g. $p_2 = p_1 + 2$, $p_5 = p_4 + 3$, specify the acceptable permutations.

This model finds the place in the sequence for each digit. The dual model finds the digit to go in each place in the sequence. The (3,9) instance has dual variables d_j, $1 \leq j \leq 27$, whose possible values correspond to the three 1s, the three 2s, and so on. It is hard to express the separation constraints in Solver in terms of the d_j variables, in a form that can propagate well. However, we can still build a minimal combined model: we then define the separation constraints on only one set of variables, and the p_i variables are the obvious choice.

3 Results

The models were implemented in ILOG Solver and all solutions found for several instances of both problems. If just one solution is found, a different model or search strategy can lead to a different solution, whereas finding all solutions allows a fairer comparison. The symmetry in the n-queens problem was eliminated using SBDS (Symmetry Breaking During Search) [2]. Any solution to Langford's problem can be reversed to give another: constraints were added to break this symmetry. Smallest domain variable ordering was used for both problems.

Tables 1 (first 3 rows) and 2 compare the three models described in section 1, which use different constraints to ensure that a solution is a permutation. Table 1 shows the number of backtracks (fails) and approximate running time, on a dual processor 666MHz PIII, in finding all non-symmetric solutions to the n-queens problems with $10 \leq n \leq 15$. Table 2 gives the same data for finding all solutions to Langford's problem (or proving that there is no solution, for the (3,11) and (3,12) instances) on a 166MHz Pentium PC.

The 'combined' model in each table is the minimal combined model. As expected, the number of fails is greatest for the single model with $\neq$ constraints and least for the single model with an allDifferent constraint. In both cases, the channelling constraints of the combined model lead to far fewer fails than the $\neq$ constraints, and not many more than the allDifferent constraint. All three models give similar running times for the n-queens problem: the reduced search given by the channelling constraints or the allDifferent constraint is balanced by the additional overhead. In Langford's problem, however, there is a clear difference in running time: the channelling constraints give the shortest time and the $\neq$ constraints the longest.

As noted by Cheng *et al.*, when there are two sets of variables the search variables can be either set, or both sets at once. With a smallest domain ordering, the latter possibility allows the search to choose either the primal variable which

Table 1. Finding all non-symmetric solutions to the n-queens problem. Search variables in the combined model are (a) r_i variables or (b) both r_i and c_j variables.

n	10		11		12		13		14		15	
	fails	sec.	fails	sec.	fails	sec.	fails	sec.	fails	sec.	fails	sec.
Single model, $\neq$	888	0.07	3839	0.29	17940	1.43	90512	7.04	487948	38.4	2804307	225
Single model, allDiff	635	0.07	2719	0.32	12204	1.44	58800	7.26	308706	38.1	1718862	223
Combined model (a)	643	0.08	2758	0.33	12391	1.53	59833	7.51	315914	40.1	1755260	229
Combined model (b)	711	0.08	2736	0.32	12431	1.48	58946	7.15	307525	37.6	1670747	211

Table 2. Finding all solutions to Langford's problem.

Model	(3,9)		(3,10)		(3,11)		(3,12)	
	fails	sec.	fails	sec.	fails	sec.	fails	sec.
Single, $\neq$	469	0.64	1557	2.42	7256	10.8	31008	47.8
Single, allDiff	208	0.57	658	1.88	2553	8.34	10421	33.5
Combined	213	0.55	666	1.70	2618	6.83	10597	28.9

Table 3. Finding all solutions to Langford's problem, using a minimal combined model.

Search vars	allDiff constr.?	(3,9)		(3,10)		(3,11)		(3,12)	
		fails	sec.	fails	sec.	fails	sec.	fails	sec.
p_i	no	213	0.55	666	1.70	2618	6.83	10597	28.9
p_i	yes	208	0.66	658	2.36	2553	9.11	10421	38.6
d_j	no	178	0.50	549	1.54	2120	6.00	7926	23.0
d_j	yes	170	0.64	517	1.83	2023	7.14	7527	27.3
both	no	120	0.36	433	1.22	1550	4.34	6240	18.0
both	yes	114	0.46	419	1.50	1514	5.31	6153	22.2

has fewest values or the primal value which can be assigned to fewest variables. In the n-queens problem, searching on the c_j variables rather than the r_i variables makes no difference since the primal and dual models are identical, but the final row of Table 1 shows that searching on both sets of variables is slightly quicker for the larger problems.

Table 3 shows the results of using the p_i variables, the d_j variables or both, as the search variables in Langford's problem. The number of fails in the second row is the same as in the last row of Table 2: as shown in [6], adding the channelling constraints to an allDifferent constraint gives no benefit, and the additional overhead leads to increased running time. Clearly, if the dual variables are used as search variables, the channelling constraints are needed to link the two sets of variables, even with the allDifferent constraint. For this problem, the d_j variables are a better choice of search variable than the p_i variables, even though the constraints are defined only in terms of the latter; searching on both sets of variables gives still better results. The allDifferent constraint reduces the number of fails slightly, but the running time is consistently longer.

Cheng *et al.* proposed using all the constraints of both models. If this is done, rather than using the minimal combined model, there is no reduction in search in either problem. Hence, the constraints of the dual model do not themselves give any further constraint propagation. The running time using both complete models is, of course, much longer than with the minimal combined model, since there are far more constraints to handle.

4 Conclusions

When a problem can be modelled as a CSP from two different viewpoints, the potential benefit of combining both viewpoints, linked by channelling constraints, into a single CSP is ease of modelling. Each problem constraint can be expressed in whichever viewpoint is most natural. Furthermore, the CSP can be solved by using either set of variables as the search variables: hence to some extent modelling decisions can be divorced from decisions about the search strategy.

In the special case of permutation problems, we have shown that there are two additional benefits. Firstly, the channelling constraints linking the primal and dual variables are sufficient to ensure that any solution is a permutation, so that $\neq$ constraints or an allDifferent constraint are unnecessary. In the examples considered, the channelling constraints lead to only slightly more backtracks than an allDifferent constraint, and can reduce the running time. Secondly, both sets of variables can be used as search variables, with an ordering heuristic such as smallest domain, allowing the search to swap between primal and dual variables. For Langford's problem, this gives a much shorter running time, with a minimal combined model, than using a single model. However, there is little benefit in a combined model of the n-queens problem, perhaps because the primal and dual models are identical in this case. Building a minimal combined model requires little more effort than building a single model and is worth trying, along with searching on both primal and dual variables, for any permutation problem.

References

1. B. M. W. Cheng, K. M. F. Choi, J. H. M. Lee, and J. C. K. Wu. Increasing constraint propagation by redundant modeling: an experience report. *Constraints*, 4:167–192, 1999.
2. I. P. Gent and B. M. Smith. Symmetry Breaking During Search in Constraint Programming. In W. Horn, editor, *Proceedings ECAI'2000*, pages 599–603, 2000.
3. J.-C. Régin. A filtering algorithm for constraints of difference in CSPs. In *Proceedings AAAI'94*, volume 1, pages 362–367, 1994.
4. B. M. Smith. Modelling a Permutation Problem. Research Report 2000.18, School of Computer Studies, University of Leeds, June 2000. Presented at the ECAI'2000 Workshop on Modelling and Solving Problems with Constraints.
5. B. M. Smith. Dual Models in Constraint Programming. Research Report 2001.02, School of Computing, University of Leeds, Jan. 2001.
6. T. Walsh. Permutation problems and channelling constraints. Technical Report APES-26-2001, January 2001. (From `www.dcs.st-and.ac.uk/~apes/`).

Boosting Local Search with Artificial Ants

Christine Solnon

LISI - University Lyon 1 - 43 bd du 11 novembre
69 622 Villeurbanne cedex, France
csolnon@bat710.univ-lyon1.fr

Local Search: Incomplete approaches for solving CSPs are usually based on local search —or neighborhood search— techniques [4]: the idea is to start from an inconsistent complete assignment of values to the variables, and then gradually and iteratively repair it by changing some variable-value assignments, preferably towards better ones. One of the main problems with local search is that it may get stuck in local optima, i.e., complete assignments that cannot be locally improved by changing one conflicting variable/value assignment, and that are not globally optimal. Therefore, local search has been combined with different meta-heuristics in order to help it escape from local optima, e.g., simulated annealing or tabu search [2]. Local search has proved to be effective and efficient to solve very large CSPs. However, like complete search, it often has more difficulties in solving problems that are within the phase transition region —where the solvable probability is around 50%. Indeed, before the phase transition region, problems are weakly constrained and have many solutions so that local search can usually easily find one. On the other side, beyond the phase transition region, problems are hardly constrained and only have few solutions, but they also have much less local optima so that local search can more easily reach a solution without being trapped in local optima [7]. Between these two "easy" regions, search space landscapes of problems contain more local minima so that local search is more often trapped in these local minima and, even when using some meta-heuristics for escaping from them, local search often "walks" from a local minimum to another without finding a global minimum.

Motivations: A main motivation of the work presented in this paper is to provide a way of taking benefit of the different local minima found by local search in order to guide it towards the most promising states of the search space. Indeed, a study of the shape of the search space of many combinatorial optimization problems has shown a high correlation between the quality of a local minimum and its distance to the closest global minimum, i.e., the better the local minimum, the closer to a global minimum [3]. To perform this task, we use the Ant Colony Optimization (ACO) metaheuristics [1]. The main idea of ACO is to model the problem as the search of a best path in a graph that represents the states of the problem. Artificial ants walk through this graph, looking for good paths. They communicate by laying pheromone trails on edges of the graph, and they choose their path with respect to probabilities that depend on the amount of pheromone previously left. In our context of CSP solving, we

T. Walsh (Ed.): CP 2001, LNCS 2239, pp. 620–624, 2001.

propose to use pheromone to keep track of the best local minima found, in order to guide the search when constructing new assignments to be repaired, as heuristics for choosing values to be assigned to variables. One should remark that this approach is complementary to other meta-heuristics, such as simulated annealing or tabu search, that aim at helping local search to escape from local optima.

Definitions and notations: A *CSP* is defined by a triple (X, D, C) such that X is a finite set of variables, D is a function which maps every variable to its finite domain and C is a set of constraints. A *label*, denoted by $<X_i, v_i>$, is a variable-value pair which represents the assignment of value v_i to variable X_i. A *compound label*, denoted by $\mathcal{A} = \{<X_1, v_1>, \ldots, <X_k, v_k>\}$, is a set of labels and corresponds to the simultaneous assignment of values $v_1, \ldots, v_k$ to variables $X_1, \ldots, X_k$ respectively. A *complete compound label* is a compound label that contains a label for each variable of the CSP. The *valuation* of a compound label $\mathcal{A}$ is defined by the number of violated constraints in $\mathcal{A}$. A *solution of a CSP* is a complete compound label the valuation of which is 0.

Many real-life CSPs are over-constrained, so that no solution exists. Hence, the general CSP framework has been generalized to the partial or maximal constraint satisfaction problem —*max-CSP*. In this case, the goal is no longer to find a consistent solution, but to find a complete assignment which maximizes the number of satisfied constraints. In this paper, we implicitely solve max-CSPs.

Overall description of Ant-solver. We propose to use the ACO meta-heuristics for guiding local search —when constructing a new complete assignment to be repaired— towards the most promising areas of the search space. The algorithm, called Ant-solver, is sketched in figure 1.

```
procedure Ant-solver(X, D, C)
    τ ← InitializePheromoneTrails()
    repeat
        for k in 1..nbAnts do
            A_k ← ∅
            while | A_k |<| X | do
                X_j ← SelectVariable(X, A_k)
                v ← ChooseValue(τ, X_j, D(X_j), A_k)
                A_k ← A_k ∪ {<X_j, v>}
            end while
            A_k ← ApplyLocalSearch(A_k)
        end for
        τ ← UpdatePheromoneTrails(τ, {A_1, ..., A_nbAnts})
    until valuation(A_i) = 0 for some i ∈ {1..nbAnts} or max cycles reached
```

Fig. 1. Ant-solver algorithmic scheme

At each cycle of this algorithm, every ant constructs a complete assignment $\mathcal{A}_k$, i.e., it iteratively selects a variable X_j and chooses a value v for this variable. Then, the constructed assignment is improved by applying some local search techniques. Finally, pheromone trails are updated with respect to the different local minima computed during the current cycle. We shall now briefly describe the pheromone graph on which artificial ants lay pheromone trails, and the different functions used in Ant-solver. More details can be found in [6].

Pheromone graph: The pheromone graph associates a vertex with each variable/value pair $<X_i, v>$ such that $X_i \in X$ and $v \in D(X_i)$. There is a non oriented edge between any pair of vertices corresponding to two different variables. The amount of pheromone laying on an edge $(<X_i, v>, <X_j, w>)$ is noted $\tau(<X_i, v>, <X_j, w>)$. Intuitively, this amount of pheromone represents the learned desirability of assigning simultaneously value v to variable X_i and value w to variable X_j.

SelectVariable($X, \mathcal{A}_k$): This function returns a variable $X_j \in X$ that is not yet assigned in $\mathcal{A}_k$. This choice can be performed randomly, or with respect to some commonly used variable ordering, such as the *smallest-domain ordering*, which selects a variable that has the smallest number of consistant values with respect to some given partial consistency.

ChooseValue($\tau, X_j, D(X_j), \mathcal{A}_k$): This function returns a value $v \in D(X_j)$ to be assigned to X_j. The choice of v is done with respect to a probability $p(v, \tau, X_j, D(X_j), \mathcal{A}_k)$ which depends on two factors: the pheromone factor $\mathcal{P}$ — which evaluates the learned desirability of v— and the quality factor $\mathcal{Q}$ —which evaluates the number of conflicts of v with the already assigned variables:

$$p(v, \tau, X_j, D(X_j), \mathcal{A}_k) = \frac{[\mathcal{P}(\tau, \mathcal{A}_k, X_j, v)]^\alpha [\mathcal{Q}(\mathcal{A}_k, X_j, v)]^\beta}{\sum_{w \in D(X_j)} [\mathcal{P}(\tau, \mathcal{A}_k, X_j, w)]^\alpha [\mathcal{Q}(\mathcal{A}_k, X_j, w)]^\beta}$$

where α and β are two parameters which determine the relative importance of pheromone and quality factors; the pheromone factor $\mathcal{P}(\tau, \mathcal{A}_k, X_j, v)$ corresponds to the sum of all pheromone trails laid on all edges between $<X_j, v>$ and the labels in $\mathcal{A}_k$, i.e., $\mathcal{P}(\tau, \mathcal{A}_k, X_j, v) = \sum_{<X_l, m> \in \mathcal{A}_k} \tau(<X_l, m>, <X_j, v>)$; and the quality factor $\mathcal{Q}(\mathcal{A}_k, X_j, v)$ is inversely proportional to the number of new violated constraints when assigning value v to variable X_j, i.e., $\mathcal{Q}(\mathcal{A}_k, X_j, v) = 1/(1 + valuation(\{<X_j, v>\} \cup \mathcal{A}_k) - valuation(\mathcal{A}_k))$.

ApplyLocalSearch($\mathcal{A}_k$): This function allows one to improve the constructed assignment $\mathcal{A}_k$ by performing some local search, i.e., by iteratively changing some variable-value assignments. Different heuristics can be used to choose the variable to be repaired and the new value to be assigned to this variable (see, e.g., [2] for an experimental comparison of some of these heuristics). The approach proposed in this paper can be applied to any local search algorithm for solving CSP and is independant from heuristics used to select the repair to be performed.

UpdatePheromoneTrails(τ, $\{\mathcal{A}_1, \ldots, \mathcal{A}_{nbAnts}\}$): This function updates the amount of pheromone laying on each edge according to the ACO meta-heuristics, i.e., all pheromone trails are uniformely decreased —in order to simulate some kind of evaporation that allows ants to progressively forget worse paths— and then pheromone is added on edges participating to the construction of the best local minimum —in order to further attract ants towards the corresponding area of the search space. Hence, at the end of each cycle, the quantity of pheromone laying on each edge (i, j) is updated as follows:

$\tau(i,j) \leftarrow \rho * \tau(i,j)$
if $i \in \mathcal{A}_{Best}$ and $j \in \mathcal{A}_{Best}$ then $\tau(i,j) \leftarrow \tau(i,j) + \frac{1}{valuation(\mathcal{A}_{Best})}$
if $\tau(i,j) < \tau_{min}$ then $\tau(i,j) \leftarrow \tau_{min}$
if $\tau(i,j) > \tau_{max}$ then $\tau(i,j) \leftarrow \tau_{max}$

where ρ is the trail persistence parameter such that $0 \leq \rho \leq 1$, $\mathcal{A}_{Best}$ is the best assignment of $\{\mathcal{A}_1, \ldots, \mathcal{A}_{nbAnts}\}$, and τ_{min} and τ_{max} are bounds, such that $0 \leq \tau_{min} \leq \tau_{max}$.

InitializePheromoneTrails(): Pheromone trails can be initialized to a constant value, e.g., $\tau_{\max}$, as proposed in [5]. However, Ant-solver can be boosted by introducing a preprocessing step. The idea is to collect a significant number of local minima by performing "classical" local search, i.e., by iteratively constructing complete compound labels —without using pheromone— and repairing them. For easy problems, that are far enough from the phase transition region, local search usually quickly find solutions, so that this preprocessing step stops iterating on a success, and the whole algorithm terminates. However, for harder problems within the phase transition region, local search may be successively trapped in local minima without finding a solution. In this case, the goal of the preprocessing step is to collect a representative set of local minima, thus constituting a kind of sampling of the search space. Then, we select from this sample set the best local minima and we use them to initialize pheromone trails.

Experiments on Random Binary CSPs: Ant-solver has been implemented in C++. For all experiments reported below, we have used the smallest-domain ordering as the variable selection rule, and the min-conflict heuristics [4] for the local search procedure. Parameters have been setted to $\tau_{min} = 0.01$, $\tau_{max} = 4$, $\alpha = 3$, $\beta = 10$, $\rho = 0.98$ and $nbAnts = 8$. Figure 2 reports experimental results for solving random binary CSPs with 100 variables, 8 values in each variable domain, a connectivity (p_1) successively equals to 0.05 and 0.14 and different tightness values (p_2) around the phase transition. For each tightness, we report average results on 100 feasible problem instances. We successively display, for Local Search (LS) and Ant-Solver (AS), the success rate within a same limit of time (300s for $p_1 = 0.05$ and 1000s for $p_1 = 0.14$), the CPU time (in seconds) spent to find a solution and the corresponding number of repairs (in thousands of repairs).

Problems with connectivity $p_1 = 0.05$							Problems with connectivity $p_1 = 0.14$						
	Succ rate		CPU Time		Nb of repairs			Succ rate		CPU Time		Nb of repairs	
p_2	LS	AS	LS	AS	LS	AS	p_2	LS	AS	LS	AS	LS	AS
0.38	100	100	0.1	0.1	9K	11K	0.19	100	100	0.7	0.8	20K	24K
0.40	100	100	2.5	2.2	123K	102K	0.20	100	100	17.6	14.6	424K	291K
0.42	100	100	4.0	4.9	177K	170K	0.21	86	100	41.5	17.9	926K	309K
0.44	88	100	39.9	9.6	1 824K	313K	0.22	54	99	107.3	40.5	2 566K	491K
0.46	57	100	55.7	14.1	2 604K	402K	0.23	28	97	183.5	62.1	4 060K	665K
0.48	50	100	43.0	10.8	2 044K	376K	0.24	34	98	141.3	63.8	3 593K	661K
0.50	82	100	38.8	9.6	1 948K	419K	0.25	40	99	117.4	37.1	2 681K	513K
0.52	87	100	20.4	8.4	989K	412K	0.26	47	100	69.4	22.4	1 621K	414K
0.54	94	100	14.7	3.9	789K	216K	0.27	69	100	30.5	12.2	746K	290K

Fig. 2. Experimental results on $< 100, 8, p_1, p_2 >$ binary random CSPs

One can remark that, on the easiest problems, that are far enough from the phase transition region Ant-solver and local search have comparable results: for these problems, solutions are nearly always found during the preprocessing step, after the computation of very few complete compound labels. However, on the hardest problems that are within the phase transition region, Ant-solver is always much more successful and efficient than local search, showing that ACO actually allows one to boost the resolution.

References

1. M. Dorigo, G. Di Caro and L. M. Gambardella. Ant Algorithms for Discrete Optimization. *Artificial Life*, 5(2):137–172, 1999
2. J.K. Hao and R. Dorne. Empirical studies of heuristic local search for constraint solving. In *Proceedings of CP'96, LNCS 1118, Springer Verlag*, pages 194–208, 1996
3. P. Merz and B. Freisleben. Fitness landscapes and memetic algorithm design. In D. Corne and M. Dorigo and F. Glover, editors, *New Ideas in Optimization*, pages 245–260. McGraw Hill, UK, 1999
4. S. Minton, M.D. Johnston, A.B. Philips and P. Laird. Minimizing Conflicts: a Heuristic Repair Method for Constraint Satistaction and Scheduling Problems. *Artificial Intelligence*, 58:161–205, 1992
5. T. Stutzle and H.H. Hoos. MAX-MIN Ant System. *Journal of Future Generation Computer Systems*, 16:889–914, 2000
6. C. Solnon. Boosting Local Search with Artificial Ants (long paper). Research Report, LISI, 15 pages, 2001
7. M. Yokoo. Why adding more constraints makes a problem easier for hill-climbing algorithms: analyzing landscapes of CSPs. In *Proceedings of CP'97, LNCS 1330, Springer Verlag*, pages 356–370, 1997

Fast Optimal Instruction Scheduling for Single-Issue Processors with Arbitrary Latencies

Peter van Beek[1] and Kent Wilken[2]

[1] Department of Computer Science
University of Waterloo
Waterloo, ON, Canada N2L 3G1
vanbeek@uwaterloo.ca

[2] Department of Electrical and Computer Engineering
University of California
Davis, CA, USA 95616
wilken@ece.ucdavis.edu

Abstract. Instruction scheduling is one of the most important steps for improving the performance of object code produced by a compiler. The local instruction scheduling problem is to find a minimum length instruction schedule for a basic block subject to precedence, latency, and resource constraints. In this paper we consider local instruction scheduling for single-issue processors with arbitrary latencies. The problem is considered intractable, and heuristic approaches are currently used in production compilers. In contrast, we present a relatively simple approach to instruction scheduling based on constraint programming which is fast and optimal. The proposed approach uses an improved constraint model which allows it to scale up to very large, real problems. We describe powerful redundant constraints that allow a standard constraint solver to solve these scheduling problems in an almost backtrack-free manner. The redundant constraints are lower bounds on selected sub-problems which take advantage of the structure inherent in the problems. Under specified conditions, these constraints are sometimes further improved by testing the consistency of a sub-problem using a fast test. We experimentally evaluated our approach by integrating it into the Gnu Compiler Collection (GCC) and then applying it to the SPEC95 floating point benchmarks. All 7402 of the benchmarks' basic-blocks were optimally scheduled, including basic-blocks with up to 1000 instructions. Our results compare favorably to the best previous approach which is based on integer linear programming (Wilken et al., 2000): Across the same benchmarks, the total optimal scheduling time for their approach is 98 seconds while the total time for our approach is less than 5 seconds.

1 Introduction

Instruction scheduling is one of the most important steps for improving the performance of object code produced by a compiler. The local instruction scheduling problem is to find a minimum length instruction schedule for a basic block—a

T. Walsh (Ed.): CP 2001, LNCS 2239, pp. 625–639, 2001.

straight-line sequence of code with a single entry point and a single exit point—subject to precedence, latency, and resource constraints. In this paper we consider local instruction scheduling for single-issue processors with arbitrary latencies. This is a classic problem which has received a lot of attention in the literature and remains important as single-issue RISC processors are increasingly being used in embedded systems such as automobile brake systems and air-bag controllers.

Instruction scheduling for a single-issue processor is NP-complete if there is no fixed bound on the maximum latency [8,18]. Such negative results have led to the belief that in production compilers one must take a heuristic or approximation algorithm approach, rather than an exact approach to basic-block scheduling (e.g., see [17]). Recently, however, Wilken et al. [21] showed that through various modeling and algorithmic techniques, integer linear programming could be used to produce optimal instruction schedules for large basic blocks in a reasonable amount of time.

In this paper, we present a relatively simple constraint programming approach to instruction scheduling which is fast and optimal. The key to scaling up to very large, real problems is an improved constraint model. We describe powerful redundant constraints that allow a standard constraint solver to solve these scheduling problems in an almost backtrack-free manner. The redundant constraints are lower bounds on selected sub-problems which take advantage of the structure inherent in the problems. Under specified conditions, these constraints are sometimes further improved by testing the consistency of a sub-problem using a fast test.

We experimentally evaluated our approach by integrating it into the Gnu Compiler Collection (GCC) and then applying it to the SPEC95 floating point benchmarks. All 7402 of the benchmarks' basic-blocks were optimally scheduled, including basic-blocks with up to 1000 instructions. Our results compare favorably to the best previous approach which is based on integer linear programming (Wilken et al., 2000): Across the same benchmarks, the total optimal scheduling time for their approach is 98 seconds while the total time for our approach is less than 5 seconds.

2 Background and Definitions

We first define the instruction scheduling problem studied in this paper followed by a brief review of the needed background from constraint programming (for more background on these topics see, for example, [9,15,17]).

Throughout the paper, the number of elements in a set U is denoted by $|U|$, the minimum and maximum values in a finite set U of integers are denoted by $\min(U)$ and $\max(U)$, respectively, and the interval notation $[a, b]$ is used as a shorthand for the set of integers $\{a, a+1, \ldots, b\}$.

We consider single-issue pipelined processors (see [9]). On such processors a single instruction can be issued (begin execution) each clock cycle, but for some instructions there is a delay or *latency* between when the instruction is issued and when the result is available for other instructions which use the result.

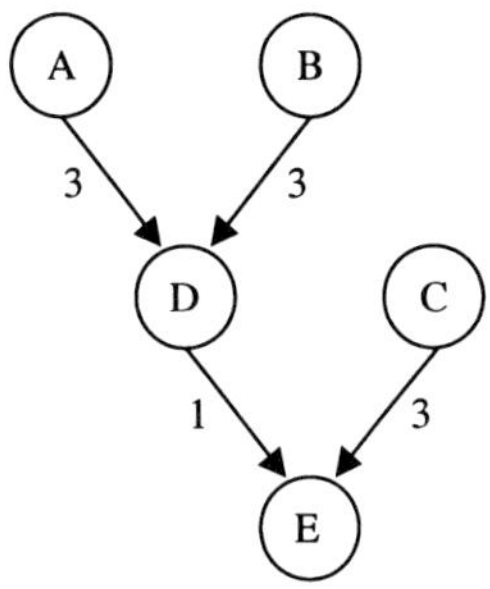

(a)

```
A r1 ← a
B r2 ← b
  NOP
  NOP
D r1 ← r1 + r2
C r3 ← c
  NOP
  NOP
E r1 ← r1 + r3
```

(b)

```
A r1 ← a
B r2 ← b
C r3 ← c
  NOP
D r1 ← r1 + r2
E r1 ← r1 + r3
```

(c)

Fig. 1. (a) Dependency DAG associated with the instructions to evaluate $(a+b)+c$ on a processor where loads from memory have a latency of 3 cycles and integer operations have a latency of 1 cycle; (b) non-optimal schedule; (c) optimal schedule.

We use the standard labeled directed acyclic graph (DAG) representation of a basic-block, where each node corresponds to an instruction (see [17]). There is an edge from i to j labeled with a positive integer $l(i,j)$ if j must not be issued until i has executed for $l(i,j)$ cycles. In particular, if $l(i,j) = 1$, j can be issued in the next cycle after i has been issued and if $l(i,j) > 1$, there must be some intervening cycles between when i is issued and when j is subsequently issued. These cycles can possibly be filled by other instructions. The *critical path distance* from a node i to a node j in a DAG is the length of the longest path from i to j, if there exists a path from i to j; $-\infty$ otherwise.

Definition 1. (Local Instruction Scheduling Problem) *Given a labeled dependency DAG* $G = (N, E)$ *for a basic-block, a* schedule S *for a single-issue processor specifies an issue or start time* $S(i)$ *for each instruction or node such that* $S(i) \neq S(j)$, $i, j \in N, i \neq j$ *(no two instructions are issued simultaneously), and* $S(j) \geq S(i) + l(i,j), (i,j) \in E$ *(the issue or start time of an instruction depends upon the issue times and latencies of its predecessors) The* local instruction scheduling problem *is to construct a schedule with minimum length; i.e.,* $\max\{S(i) \mid i \in N\}$ *is minimized.*

Example 1. Figure 1 shows a simple dependency DAG and two possible schedules for the DAG. The non-optimal schedule requires four NOP instructions (null operations) because the values loaded are used by the following instructions. The optimal schedule requires one NOP and completes in three fewer cycles.

Constraint programming is a methodology for solving combinatorial problems. A problem is modeled by specifying constraints on an acceptable solution, where a constraint is simply a relation among several unknowns or variables, each taking a value in a given domain. Such a model is often referred to as a constraint satisfaction problem or CSP model.

Definition 2 (Constraint Satisfaction Problem (CSP)). *A* constraint satisfaction problem *consists of a set of* n variables, $\{x_1, \ldots, x_n\}$*; a finite domain* $dom(x_i)$ *of possible* values *for each variable* x_i, $1 \leq i \leq n$*; and a collection of* r constraints, $\{C_1, \ldots, C_r\}$. *Each constraint* C_i, $1 \leq i \leq r$, *is a constraint over some set of variables, denoted by* $vars(C)$*, that specifies the allowed combinations of values for the variables in* $vars(C)$. *A* solution *to a CSP is an assignment of a value to each variable that satisfies all of the constraints.*

CSPs are often solved using a backtracking algorithm. At every stage of the backtracking search, there is some current partial solution which the algorithm attempts to extend to a full solution by assigning a value to an uninstantiated variable. One of the keys behind the success of constraint programming is the idea of constraint propagation. During the backtracking search when a variable is assigned a value, the constraints are used to reduce the domains of the uninstantiated variables by ensuring that the values in their domains are "consistent" with the constraints. The form of consistency we use in our approach to the instruction scheduling problem is bounds consistency.

Definition 3 (Bounds Consistency). *Given a constraint* C, *a value* $d \in dom(x)$ *for a variable* $x \in vars(C)$ *is said to have a* support *in* C *if there exist values for each of the other variables in* $vars(C) - \{x\}$ *such that* C *is satisfied. A constraint* C *is* bounds consistent *if for each* $x \in vars(C)$, *the value* $\min(dom(x))$ *has a support in* C *and the value* $\max(dom(x))$ *has a support in* C.

A CSP can be made bounds consistent by repeatedly removing unsupported values from the domains of its variables.

Example 2. Consider the CSP model of the small instruction scheduling problem in Example 1 with variables A, ..., E, each with domain $\{1, \ldots, 6\}$, and the following constraints,

C_1: $\mathrm{D} \geq \mathrm{A} + 3$, C_3: $\mathrm{E} \geq \mathrm{C} + 3$, C_5: all-different(A, B, C, D, E),
C_2: $\mathrm{D} \geq \mathrm{B} + 3$, C_4: $\mathrm{E} \geq \mathrm{D} + 1$,

where constraint C_5 enforces that its arguments are pair-wise different. The constraints are not bounds consistent. For example, the minimum value 1 in the domain of D does not have a support in constraint C_1 as there is no corresponding value for A that satisfies the constraint. Enforcing bounds consistency using constraints C_1 through C_4 reduces the domains of the variables as follows: $dom(\mathrm{A}) = \{1, 2\}$, $dom(\mathrm{B}) = \{1, 2\}$, $dom(\mathrm{C}) = \{1, 2, 3\}$, $dom(\mathrm{D}) = \{4, 5\}$, and $dom(\mathrm{E}) = \{5, 6\}$. Subsequently enforcing bounds consistency using constraint C_5 further reduces the domain of C to be $dom(\mathrm{C}) = \{3\}$. Now constraint C_3 is no longer bounds consistent. Re-establishing bounds consistency causes $dom(\mathrm{E}) = \{6\}$.

3 Previous Work

Instruction scheduling for a single-issue processor is NP-complete if there is no fixed bound on the maximum latency d [8,18].

Previous work has identified polynomial algorithms for the special case when $d \leq 2$. These algorithms can also be used as approximation algorithms for the general problem. Bernstein and Gertner [2] give a polynomial time algorithm based on list scheduling when $d \leq 2$. The algorithm can be used as an approximation algorithm when $d > 2$ and is guaranteed to give a schedule whose length is no more than a factor of $2 - 2/d$ times that of an optimal schedule [3]. Palem and Simons [18] extend this work by allowing timing constraints in the form of release times (the earliest time at which an instruction can start) and deadlines (the latest time by which an instruction must complete). Such constraints can be important in embedded systems[1]. Recently, Wu et al. [22] gave an improved algorithm for the case when $d \leq 2$ and timing constraints are allowed. It is a long-standing open problem whether there exists a polynomial time algorithm for any fixed $d > 2$.

Previous work has also developed optimal algorithms for the general problem when $d > 2$. The approaches taken include dynamic programming [10], integer linear programming [1,5,14,21], and constraint programming [7]. However, with the exception of [21] (to which we do a detailed comparison later in the paper), these previous approaches have only been evaluated on a few problems with the sizes of the problems ranging between 10 and 40 instructions. Further, their experimental results suggest that none of them would scale up beyond problems of this size. For example, Ertl and Krall [7] present a constraint programming approach which solves the problem optimally. Their CSP model has latency constraints and an all-different constraint. As our experiments confirm (see Table 3 and the discussion at the end of Section 5), such a model does not scale beyond 50 instructions. However, real problems can contain a thousand or more instructions.

4 CSP Model

In this section, we present our CSP model of the local instruction scheduling problem. In the constraint programming methodology we cast the problem as a CSP in terms of variables, values, and constraints. The choice of variables defines the search space and the choice of constraints defines how the search space can be reduced so that it can be effectively searched using backtracking search. Each constraint can be classified as to whether it is redundant or non-redundant. A constraint is redundant if its removal from the CSP does not change the set of solutions.

We model each instruction by a variable with names $1, \ldots, n$ (we use i to refer interchangeably to variable i, instruction i, and node i in the DAG). Each

[1] Note that timing constraints can be viewed as just a special case of latency constraints. Thus, any approach that solves the general problem by allowing arbitrary latencies (such as the one in this paper), can also handle timing constraints.

Table 1. Notation used in specifying the constraints.

lower(i)	lower bound of domain of variable i
upper(i)	upper bound of domain of variable i
pred(i)	set of immediate predecessors of node i in DAG
succ(i)	set of immediate successors of node i in DAG
between(i, j)	set of nodes between nodes i and j
$l(i, j)$	latency on edge between nodes i and j
$cp(i, j)$	critical path distance between nodes i and j
$d(i, j)$	lower bound on distance between nodes i and j

variable takes a value from the domain $\{1, \ldots, m\}$ which are the available time cycles. Assigning a value $t \in dom(i)$ to a variable i has the intended meaning that instruction i will be issued at time cycle t.

We now specify the five types of constraints in the model: latency, all-different, distance, predecessor and successor constraints. The notation we use is summarized in Table 1. As is clear, for a minimal correct model of the instruction scheduling problem all that is needed are the latency and all-different constraints. The distance, predecessor, and successor constraints are therefore redundant. However, they were found to be essential in improving the efficiency of the search for a schedule.

Latency constraints. Given a labeled dependency DAG $G = (N, E)$, for each pair of variables i and j such that $(i, j) \in E$, a latency constraint of the form $j \geq i + l(i, j)$ is considered for addition to the constraint model. A latency constraint is added if it is not redundant. A latency constraint between i and j is redundant if there exists a $k < j$ such that, $l(i, j) \leq l(i, k) + cp(k, j)$. In other words, the constraint is redundant if there is a path from i to j that goes through k that is equal to or longer than the direct path $l(i, j)$. (If the constraint is redundant, adding it will have no effect as the remaining latency constraints will derive a stronger result.) Since we are enforcing bounds consistency, the actual form of the constraints added to the constraint model are,

$$\text{lower}(j) \geq \text{lower}(i) + l(i, j)$$

and its symmetric version,

$$\text{upper}(i) \leq \text{upper}(j) - l(i, j).$$

The latency constraints are easy to propagate when establishing lower and upper bounds for the variables, and easy to propagate incrementally during the backtracking search.

All-different constraints. A single all-different constraint over all n of the variables is needed to ensure that at most one instruction is issued each cycle. Fast algorithms for enforcing bounds consistency on an all-different constraint have been proposed. In our implementation, we used the $O(n^2)$ propagator described in [20] and included the optimization suggested by Puget [20] of first removing any fixed values (time cycles that have already been assigned to variables) from the lower and upper bounds of the uninstantiated variables, and the techniques suggested by Leconte [12] for taking advantage of the fact that, when propagating the all-different constraint during the backtracking search, we are *re*-establishing bounds consistency; i.e., the constraint was previously bounds consistent[2].

Distance constraints. Dependency DAGs that arise from real instruction scheduling problems appear to contain much structure, no doubt because they arise from high-level programming languages. In what follows, we are interested in sub-DAGS called regions [21] which are induced from a given dependency DAG. Real problems typically contain many such regions embedded within them, with larger problems containing many thousands.

Definition 4. (Region [21]) *Given a labeled dependency DAG $G = (N, E)$, a pair of nodes $i, j \in N$ define a* region *in G if there is more than one path between i and j and there does not exist a node k distinct from i and j such that every path between i and j goes through k. A node h distinct from i and j that lies on a path from i to j is said to be between i and j and the set of all such nodes is denoted by* $\text{between}(i, j)$.

For each pair of nodes i and j which define a region, a distance constraint of the form $j \geq i + d(i, j)$ is considered for addition to the constraint model. A distance constraint is added if it is an improvement over the critical path distance; i.e., $d(i, j) > cp(i, j)$. (If the distance is not greater than the critical path distance, adding the constraint will have no effect as the latency constraints will derive a stronger result.) The distance constraints are lower bounds on the number of cycles that must elapse between when i is scheduled and j is scheduled. Although syntactically identical to latency constraints and hence propagated in the same manner, they are conceptually distinct and are key to effectively reducing the size of the search space.

An initial estimate of $d(i, j)$ is given by the following.

$$\begin{aligned} d(i,j) = {} & \min\{l(i,k) \mid k \in (\text{succ}(i) \cap \text{between}(i,j))\} - 1 \\ & + \mid \text{between}(i,j) \mid \\ & + \min\{l(h,j) \mid h \in (\text{pred}(j) \cap \text{between}(i,j))\} - 1 \\ & + 1 \end{aligned}$$

To explain, the nodes in $\text{between}(i, j)$ must all be scheduled after node i and before node j. We do not know which node in $\text{between}(i, j)$ will be or must be

[2] Propagators with better worst case complexity are known: $O(n \log n)$ [20] and $O(n)$ [16]. Since the all-different propagator is a bottle-neck in our current implementation, it would be interesting to investigate whether these algorithms would work better in practice on instruction scheduling problems.

scheduled first. However, it can be seen that any successor of node i that is in between(i,j) can only be scheduled once the minimum latency among those successors has been satisfied. As well, once all of the nodes in between(i,j) have been scheduled, node j can only be scheduled once the minimum latency of its predecessors in between(i,j) has been satisfied. The number of nodes that are between node i and node j can quickly be determined given the critical path distances between all pairs of nodes, since a node k is on a path from i to j if $cp(i,k) > 0$ and $cp(k,j) > 0$. The initial estimate of $d(i,j)$ can be viewed as a generalization of rules which were proposed for bounding the range of values for variables in integer programming formulations of instruction scheduling [5,21], although in that work it was not applied to regions.

Example 3. Consider the dependency DAG shown in Figure 2 (ignore for now the lower and upper bounds associated with the nodes). For the region defined by A and H, $d(\mathrm{A},\mathrm{H}) = (\min\{l(\mathrm{A},\mathrm{B}), l(\mathrm{A},\mathrm{C})\} - 1) + |\mathrm{between}(\mathrm{A},\mathrm{H})| + (\min\{l(\mathrm{F},\mathrm{H}), l(\mathrm{G},\mathrm{H})\} - 1) + 1 = 0 + 6 + 2 + 1 = 9$. Similarly, $d(\mathrm{A},\mathrm{F}) = 5$ and $d(\mathrm{E},\mathrm{H}) = 5$. The distance constraint $\mathrm{H} \geq \mathrm{E} + 5$ would be added to the constraint model and the distance constraint $\mathrm{F} \geq \mathrm{A} + 5$ would not be added (as it is not an improvement over the critical path distance between A and F). The distance constraint between A and H is taken up again in Example 4.

An attempt is made to improve the initial estimate of $d(i,j)$ for the distance constraints if the number of nodes between i and j is sufficiently small. We found that a value of 50 was robust on real problems. This was determined empirically using a set of five instruction scheduling examples of varying size and then verified on an additional set of ten examples.

The method for improvement works as follows. Given an initial estimate of $d(i,j)$, the region defined by i and j is (conceptually) extracted from the DAG and considered in isolation. We test whether scheduling node i at time 1 and node j at time $d(i,j) + 1$ is consistent. The test for consistency is done by propagating the relevant latency constraints and any previously added distance constraints, and an all-different constraint over the variables in the region. If the constraints are inconsistent, the value of $d(i,j)$ is incremented and the test is repeated, stopping when a value is found for $d(i,j)$ such that the constraints over the region are found to be consistent. Note that we are determining lower bounds, not solving the region exactly, as the idea is to test the consistency of the constraints quickly and approximately. The regions in the DAG are examined in an "inside-out" manner so that distance constraints for inner regions can be used in the consistency tests of the larger outer regions.

Example 4. Consider again the dependency DAG shown in Figure 2 and previously discussed in Example 3. The initial estimate of $d(\mathrm{A},\mathrm{H}) = 9$ can be improved. Figure 2a shows the bounds on the variables after propagating the latency and previously added distance constraints. Propagating the all-different constraint determines that the constraints are inconsistent, because four instructions (D, E, F and G) must be issued in the three-cycle interval [5,7]. Figure 2b shows the bounds on the variables after propagating all the constraints for the

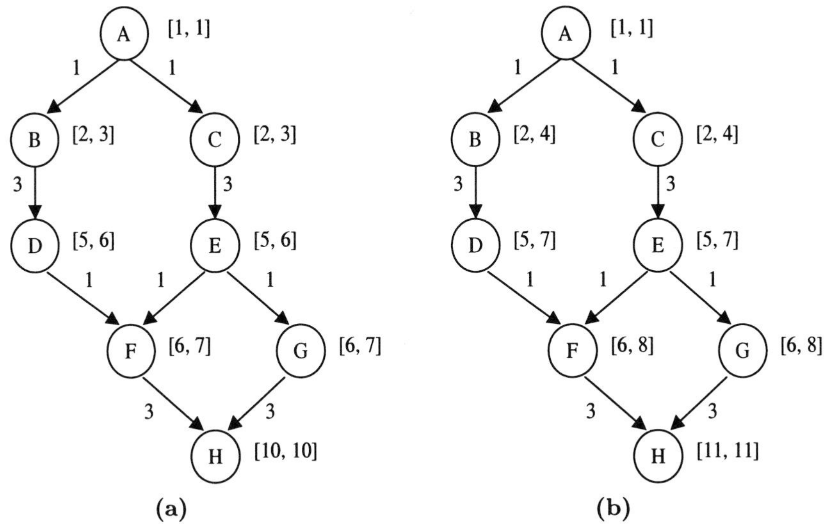

Fig. 2. Example of improving the lower bound estimate for the distance constraint for the region defined by A and H.

improved estimate $d(\mathrm{A},\mathrm{H}) = 10$. The constraints are consistent, so the constraint $\mathrm{H} \geq \mathrm{A} + 10$ is added to the constraint model.

Predecessor and successor constraints. For each node i which has more than one immediate predecessor, a single predecessor constraint of the following form is added.

$$\begin{aligned} \mathrm{lower}(i) \geq\ & \min\{\mathrm{lower}(k) \mid k \in P\} \\ & + \ |P| - 1 \\ & + \ \min\{l(k,i) \mid k \in P\}, \end{aligned}$$

$$\text{for every subset } P \text{ of } \mathrm{pred}(i) \text{ where } |P| > 1.$$

The predecessor constraints can be viewed as both a generalization of the latency constraints and as an adaptation of edge finding rules [4,11]. It can be seen that a predecessor constraint can be propagated in $O(|\mathrm{pred}(i)|^2)$ time by first sorting the predecessors of i by increasing lower bounds and then stepping through the lower bounds, each time finding the minimum latency among the remaining predecessors. A symmetric version, called successor constraints, for the immediate successors of a node is given by the following.

$$\begin{aligned} \mathrm{upper}(i) \leq\ & \max\{\mathrm{upper}(k) \mid k \in P\} \\ & - \ |P| + 1 \\ & - \ \min\{l(i,k) \mid k \in P\}, \end{aligned}$$

$$\text{for every subset } P \text{ of } \mathrm{succ}(i) \text{ where } |P| > 1.$$

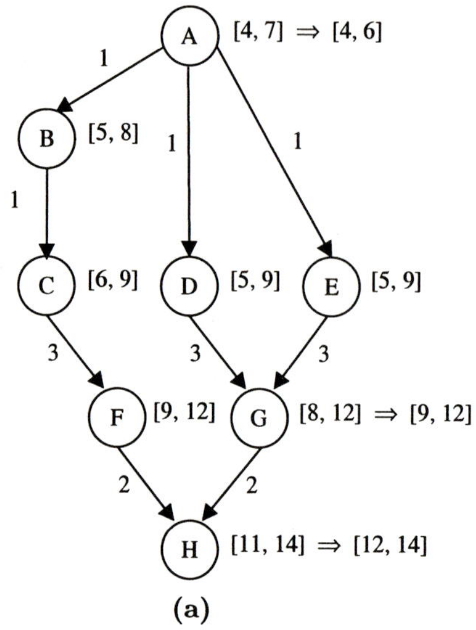

Fig. 3. Examples of improving the lower and upper bounds of variables using the predecessor and successor constraints.

Example 5. Suppose that the sub-DAG shown in Figure 3a is embedded in a larger dependency DAG and that it has been determined that lower(A) $= 4$ and upper(H) $= 14$. Propagating the latency constraints results in the domains shown closest to the associated node. Propagating the predecessor and successor constraints improves the bounds of A, G, and H. The earliest that one of the predecessors of node G can be scheduled is cycle 5 and therefore cycle 6 is the earliest that the last of its predecessors could be scheduled. Therefore, because the minimum latency between G and its predecessors is 3, the earliest that G can be scheduled is cycle 9. Once the lower bound of G has been raised, in a similar manner the lower bound of H can be raised. As well, the latest that one of the successors of node A can be scheduled is cycle 9 and therefore cycle 7 is the latest that the last of its successors could be scheduled. Therefore, the latest that A can be scheduled is cycle 6. Figure 3b shows an example of a predecessor constraint that initially has no effect but could become effective during the backtracking search as, if either lower(A) or lower(B) are raised during the search, lower(D) can also be raised.

To solve an instance of an instruction scheduling problem, we start by using the constraints to establish the lower bounds of the variables and a lower bound on the length m of an optimal schedule. Given m, the upper bounds of the variables are similarly established and the CSP is passed to the backtracking algorithm. If no solution is found, a length m schedule does not exist and the value of m is incremented, the upper bounds of the variables are re-established using the new value of m, and the new CSP is passed to the backtracking algorithm. This is repeated, each time incrementing m until a solution is found. The backtracking search interleaves constraint propagation with branching on variables. A dynamic variable ordering is used which selects as the next variable to instantiate the variable with the least number of values remaining in its domain, breaking ties by choosing the variable that participates in the most constraints. Given a selected variable x, the backtracking search first branches on x assigned to lower(x), then on x assigned to lower(x) + 1, and so on, until either a solution is found or the domain of x is exhausted.

Before turning to our experimental results, it is worthwhile summarizing three of the ideas that did not make it into the final version with which we did our full scale experimentation. Our goal was to design an approach that was as simple as possible while maintaining robustness and while the following ideas proved promising when evaluated in isolation on a set of test examples, they appeared to become unnecessary when combined with the improved constraint model we described above. The first technique was identifying cycle cutsets [6] and thereby decomposing a problem into independent subproblems. We found that most of the larger problems in our test suite (not the full benchmark set, but a small subset consisting of some of the harder problems) had small cutsets ranging from two to 20 nodes that approximately evenly decomposed the problem. The second technique was a variation on singleton consistency (see, e.g., [19]) where one temporarily instantiates a variable to a single value and tests the consistency of a subproblem that includes that variable. If the consistency test fails, the value can be removed from the domain of the variable. Wilken et al. [21] showed that a related technique called probing in the context of integer linear programming worked well on the instruction scheduling problem. We found that singleton consistency could sometimes dramatically reduce the domains of the variables prior to search. The third technique was the inclusion of symmetry-breaking constraints which rule out symmetric (non) schedules. Although each of these techniques was not included in our final prototype, it is possible of course that they may still prove important should we encounter harder problems in practice than we have yet seen.

5 Experimental Results

The CSP model was implemented and was embedded inside the Gnu Compiler Collection (GCC) [http://gnu.gcc.org], version 2.8.0. The CSP model was compared experimentally with critical-path list scheduling and with the integer linear programming (ILP) formulation proposed in [21]. The SPEC95 floating point benchmarks [http://www.specbench.org] were compiled by GCC using GCC's native instruction scheduler, which uses critical-path list scheduling, the most popular heuristic scheduling method [17]. The same benchmarks were also compiled using the CSP scheduler. The compilations were done using GCC's highest level of optimization (−O3) and were targeted to a single-issue processor with a maximum latency of three cycles. The target processor has a latency of 3 cycles for loads, 2 cycles for all floating point operations and 1 cycle for all integer operations. The SPEC95 integer benchmarks are not included in this experiment

Table 2. Experimental results for the CSP instruction scheduler.

Total Basic Blocks (BB)	7,402
BB Passed to CSP Scheduler	517
BB Solved Optimally by CSP Scheduler	517
BB with Improved Schedule	29
Cycles Improved	66
Total Benchmark Cycles	107,245
CSP Scheduling Time (sec.)	4.5
Baseline Compile Time (sec.)	708

because for this processor model there would be no instructions with a 2-cycle latency, which makes the scheduling problems easier to solve. The SPEC95 floating point benchmarks were chosen rather than the more recent SPEC2000 benchmarks to allow a direct comparison with the ILP optimal scheduling results in [21]. The optimal schedule length produced by the CSP scheduler was compared with that from the ILP scheduler from [21] for each basic block to verify the correctness of both formulations. The experiments were run on an HP C3000 workstation with a 400MHz PA-8500 processor and 512MB of main memory, the same processor that produced the results in [21].

The filter used in [21] was applied prior to the CSP scheduler to eliminate the trivial scheduling problems, and so that the CSP scheduler solved the same set of problems solved by the ILP scheduler in [21]. The GCC list scheduler is first run to produce an initial feasible schedule of length u, which is an upper bound on the length of an optimal schedule. A lower bound on the schedule length m is determined by the maximum of the critical path from a root node to a leaf node and the node count. If $u = m$ the list schedule is optimal and the CSP scheduler is not called. Also, for each node i the initial domain is tightened using latency constraints for a schedule length of $u - 1$. If the domain of any i is empty, the length u list schedule is optimal and the CSP scheduler is not called. A summary of the results for the CSP scheduler is shown in Table 2 and more detailed results for the CSP scheduler and the ILP scheduler are shown in Figure 4.

The results in Table 2 are identical with the results in [21] with the notable exception that the ILP scheduler uses 98.3 seconds to optimally schedule these benchmarks (a noticeable 14% compile-time increase), whereas the CSP scheduler is 22 times faster, using only 4.5 seconds (a negligible 0.6% compile-time increase). As a point of reference, the GCC list scheduler takes 0.5 seconds to schedule these benchmarks. The cycles measured in Table 2 are static cycles, one cycle for each clock cycle in each schedule. On average static cycles are reduced by 0.06% using the CSP scheduler versus the list schedule. The dynamic cycle savings will tend to be higher because the more complex basic blocks tend to appear in loops where the execution counts are higher (the improvement can be as high as several percent should an improved basic block appear within an application's critical inner loop). Also performance improvement is expected to

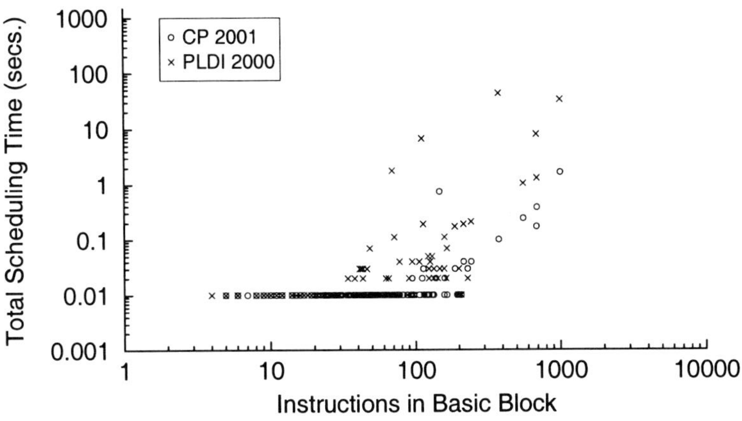

Fig. 4. Scattergram of basic block size versus optimal scheduling time for the CSP and ILP schedulers.

be much higher for processors that issue multiple instructions per clock cycle, a harder scheduling problem which will be considered in future work.

Figure 4 shows a scattergram of scheduling time versus basic block size which includes a point for each of the 517 basic blocks scheduled by the CSP scheduler in the present experiment. The scattergram also shows corresponding points for the ILP scheduler from the experiment in [21]. The system timer used in both experiments has a resolution of 0.01 seconds and rounds up to the nearest 0.01 second increment. Most of these basic blocks are scheduled within the minimum timer resolution for both schedulers. The CSP scheduler takes more than 0.01 second for only 15 basic blocks while the ILP scheduler takes more than 0.01 second for 42 basic blocks. The maximum time the CSP scheduler takes to schedule an individual basic block is 1.6 seconds (for a 1006-instruction block) and the maximum time for the ILP scheduler is 43.5 seconds (for a 377-instruction block). For the basic blocks which take more than 0.01 second for either scheduler (44 basic blocks), the CSP scheduler is faster in 40 cases and the ILP scheduler is faster in only 4 cases.

Besides being faster and more robust than the ILP scheduler, the code for the CSP scheduler is significantly smaller, which implies it would be easier to implement and maintain in a production compiler. The CSP solver is also self contained, whereas the ILP scheduler uses an external (potentially expensive) commercial ILP solver.

Table 3 shows the results from a set of experiments which were run to quantify the contributions of the three CSP model improvements. The experiments used various of levels of model improvement run at various time limits, applied to fifteen representative hard problems ranging in size from 69 to 1006 instructions that were taken from the SPEC95 floating point, SPEC2000 floating point and MediaBench [13] benchmarks. The results show that the minimal constraint

Table 3. Hard problems out of 15 *not* solved within specified time limit (seconds) using: (a) minimal constraint model (only latency and all-different constraints); (b) minimal model plus predecessor and successor constraints; (c) minimal model plus distance constraints based only on initial estimate, no consistency testing; (d) minimal model plus complete distance constraints; and (e) full constraint model (minimal model plus complete distance constraints and predecessor and successor constraints).

Time Limit	(a)	(b)	(c)	(d)	(e)
10	14	14	4	3	0
100	14	13	4	2	0
1000	14	13	4	2	0

model proposed by Ertl and Krall [7] has poor scaling behavior (see column (a) in Table 3) and that together the three improvements dramatically improve the scaling behavior of a constraint programming approach.

6 Conclusions

We presented a constraint programming approach to instruction scheduling for single-issue processors with arbitrary latencies. The problem is considered intractable, yet our approach is optimal and fast on very large, real problems. The key to scaling up to very large, real problems was in the development of an improved constraint model by identifying techniques for generating powerful redundant constraints. These techniques allow a standard constraint solver to solve these scheduling problems in an almost backtrack-free manner. We performed an extensive experimental evaluation and demonstrated that our approach has the advantage over other previous approaches in terms of the robustness and speed with which optimal schedules can be found.

References

1. S. Arya. An optimal instruction-scheduling model for a class of vector processors. *IEEE Transactions on Computers*, C-34(11):981–995, 1985.
2. D. Bernstein and I. Gertner. Scheduling expressions on a pipelined processor with a maximal delay of one cycle. *ACM Transactions on Programming Languages and Systems*, 11(1):57–66, 1989.
3. D. Bernstein, M. Rodeh, and I. Gertner. On the complexity of scheduling problems for parallel/pipelined machines. *IEEE Transactions on Computers*, 38(9):1308–1313, 1989.
4. J. Carlier and E. Pinson. Adjustment of heads and tails for the job-shop problem. *European Journal of Operational Research*, 78:146–161, 1994.
5. C.-M. Chang, C.-M. Chen, and C.-T. King. Using integer programming for instruction scheduling and register allocation in multi-issue processors. *Computers and Mathematics with Applications*, 34(9):1–14, 1997.
6. R. Dechter. Enhancement schemes for constraint processing: Backjumping, learning, and cutset decomposition. *Artificial Intelligence*, 41:273–312, 1990.

7. M. A. Ertl and A. Krall. Optimal instruction scheduling using constraint logic programming. In *Programming Language Implementation and Logic Programming (PLILP)*, 1991.
8. J. Hennessy and T. Gross. Postpass code optimization of pipeline constraints. *ACM Transactions on Programming Languages and Systems*, 5(3):422–448, 1983.
9. J. Hennessy and D. Patterson. *Computer Architecture: A Quantitative Approach.* Morgan Kaufmann, second edition, 1996.
10. C. W. Kessler. Scheduling expression DAGs for minimal register need. *Computer Languages*, 24(1):33–53, 1998.
11. C. Le Pape and P. Baptiste. Constraint-based scheduling: A theoretical comparison of resource constraint propagation rules. In *Proceedings of the ECAI Workshop on Non-Binary Constraints*, Brighton, UK, August 1998.
12. M. Leconte. A bounds-based reduction scheme for constraints of difference. In *Proceedings of the Constraint-96 International Workshop on Constraint-Based Reasoning*, pages 19–28, Key West, Florida, May 1996.
13. C. Lee, M. Potkonjak, and W. Manginoe-Smith. MediaBench: A tool for evaluating and synthesizing multimedia and communications. In *Proceedings of International Symposium on Microarchitecture*, pages 330–335, December 1997.
14. R. Leupers and P. Marwedel. Time-constrained code compaction for DSPs. *IEEE Trans. VLSI Systems*, 5(1):112–122, 1997.
15. K. Marriott and P. J. Stuckey. *Programming with Constraints.* The MIT Press, 1998.
16. K. Mehlhorn and S. Thiel. Faster algorithms for bound-consistency of the sortedness and alldifferent constraint. In *Proceedings of the Sixth International Conference on Principles and Practice of Constraint Programming*, pages 306–319, Singapore, September 2000.
17. S. Muchnick. *Advanced Compiler Design and Implementation.* Morgan Kaufmann, 1997.
18. K. Palem and B. Simons. Scheduling time-critical instructions on RISC machines. *ACM Transactions on Programming Languages and Systems*, 15(4):632–658, 1993.
19. P. Prosser, K. Stergiou, and T. Walsh. Singleton consistencies. In *Proceedings of the Sixth International Conference on Principles and Practice of Constraint Programming*, pages 353–368, Singapore, September 2000.
20. J.-F. Puget. A fast algorithm for the bound consistency of alldiff constraints. In *Proceedings of the Fifteenth National Conference on Artificial Intelligence*, pages 359–366, Madison, WI, July 1998.
21. K. Wilken, J. Liu, and M. Heffernan. Optimal instruction scheduling using integer programming. In *Proceedings of the SIGPLAN 2000 Conference on Programming Language Design and Implementation (PLDI)*, pages 121–133, Vancouver, BC, June 2000.
22. H. Wu, J. Jaffar, and R. Yap. Instruction scheduling with timing constraints on a single RISC processor with 0/1 latencies. In *Proceedings of the Sixth International Conference on Principles and Practice of Constraint Programming*, pages 457–469, Singapore, September 2000.

Evaluation of Search Heuristics for Embedded System Scheduling Problems

Cecilia Ekelin and Jan Jonsson

Department of Computer Engineering
Chalmers University of Technology
SE–412 96 Göteborg, Sweden
{cekelin,janjo}@ce.chalmers.se

Abstract. In this paper we consider the problem of optimal task allocation and scheduling in embedded real-time systems. This problem is far from trivial due to the wide range of complex constraints that typically appear in this type of systems. We therefore address this problem using constraint programming due to its expressive, yet powerful features. Our work includes an evaluation of different search heuristics, such as variable-value orderings and symmetry exclusion, for this particular problem domain. It is shown that by using search configurations appropriate for the problem, the average search complexity can be reduced by as much as an order of magnitude.

1 Introduction

A real-time system is a system where the correctness of an action depends on the operational result as well as the time the result is produced. In particular, this holds for *embedded* systems which interact with a dynamic environment in safety-critical applications. For such systems, correct behavior must be guaranteed as a result of the system design, that is, off-line. The design of an embedded system is often regarded as being extra complicated due to certain design restrictions that stem from the application-specific nature of such systems. In the context of real-time allocation and scheduling, this manifests itself in two areas. First, finding an optimal solution to the allocation and scheduling problem is in general NP-hard [4]. To make matters worse, the problem is also known to be impeded from a modeling point of view. There exists a large set of constraint constructs that can potentially appear in embedded real-time applications [7], for example system constraints (processors, resources), intra/inter-task timing constraints (period, deadline, jitter, distance, harmonicity) and intra/inter-task execution constraints (preemption, locality, precedence, clustering). The sheer amount, and special features, of these constraints makes it difficult to design an scheduling algorithm that handles them all. Second, the specification of an embedded system includes requirements on cost, performance, and functionality which affect the choice of implementation. For example, applications in embedded systems are often parallel in nature, making distributed systems a common design. As a result, network communication becomes an additional design issue. Furthermore, since

T. Walsh (Ed.): CP 2001, LNCS 2239, pp. 640–654, 2001.

embedded systems must frequently be cost-effective, the scheduling algorithm must maximize resource utilization, which implies the need for an optimization approach, often with support for multiple (sometimes conflicting) objectives.

It is clear that any optimization algorithm to be used in practice requires efficient (that is, polynomial-time on the average) heuristics to guide the search. To that end, there are several aspects of the design of an optimization algorithm that can be targeted. Primarily, it is important that the search starting point is likely to quickly lead to an optimal solution. For real-time systems, this is addressed using task allocation heuristics that attempts to maximize the likelihood of successful subsequent scheduling. Furthermore, search directions leading to inferior solutions should be detected in order to avoid unnecessary computations. This in particularly relevant when the associated search problem contains symmetries. Real-time applications often contain symmetries such as task allocation to equivalent processors or task execution order of equivalent tasks.

The *constraint programming* paradigm has recently been demonstrated to be a viable candidate for solving problems in the real-time systems domain. In fact, the modeling simplicity and level of abstraction provided by constraint programming and the problem-specific information in heuristics for real-time allocation and scheduling seems to be a powerful combination. To investigate this, we have implemented a scheduling framework based on constraint programming which combines various task allocation heuristics and processor symmetry exclusion with general constraint programming heuristics. In this paper, we show how these techniques should be combined to yield good algorithm performance for the real-time allocation and scheduling problem.

We begin with a problem description and a discussion on related work. Then we move on to present our constraint model and explain the search heuristics we have looked into. Finally, we describe our evaluation studies and discuss their results.

2 Preliminaries

2.1 Problem Description

The general allocation and scheduling problem considers the assignment of *tasks* to processing *nodes* and the execution of these tasks in a timely fashion. These actions are restricted by a set of *constraints* that must be satisfied and *objectives* that measure the quality of a solution. The constraints and objectives that we consider will be described in Section 3.

Our model of the hardware architecture (see Fig. 1(a)) has been chosen to reflect a typical embedded system. It consists of m nodes $\eta_1, ..., \eta_m$, which are connected via a *communication bus*, and each node contains one *processor*. Each node also has a number of *resources* that can be used locally by tasks at that node, or globally by all tasks in the system. The application (see Fig. 1(b)) includes n periodic tasks $\tau_1, ..., \tau_n$, that execute on the processors and possibly communicate by *message passing*. The worst-case execution time of task τ_i on processor η_p is $execution\_time(i,p)$ and the size of a message from τ_i to τ_j is

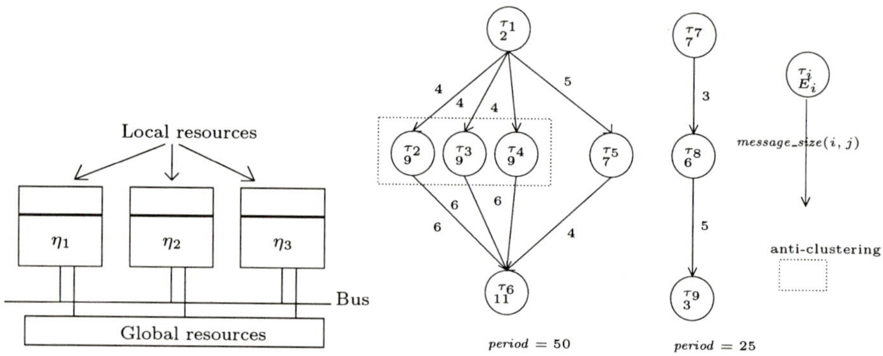

(a) Hardware architecture (b) Safety-critical application

Fig. 1. Models

message_size(i, j). Each periodic task is invoked at regular intervals of length *period*(i); we use τ_i^k to denote the kth invocation of τ_i. Each task invocation must complete its execution within a time interval of length *deadline*(i).

The dependability demand on an embedded system requires that its behavior is predictable. This implies that the allocation and scheduling must be analyzed off-line before the system is started. The analysis either involves (i) generating a time-table for the tasks (on each processor) or (ii) verifying the correctness of an online algorithm such as priority-based scheduling [10]. In this paper we focus on approach (i) because it has the nice property to translate directly into a constraint satisfaction problem, thus being well suited for our solution paradigm. Note that, because tasks are periodic, it is possible to have a time-table of finite length even if the system is supposed to run forever. To that end, the time-table size equals the least common multiple of all task periods, referred to as the *lcp*.

The specific problem we address is then the following. For each node, we first want to determine which tasks that should execute on it and then generate a feasible schedule in the form of a (cyclic) time-table. By 'feasible' we mean that the execution of each task instance is scheduled in such a way that all constraints are satisfied. A similar time-table should be constructed for the messages sent on the bus. This resulting solution should be optimal regarding given objectives.

2.2 Related Work

A great deal of research efforts have been spent on off-line task allocation and scheduling in distributed real-time systems. Unfortunately, commonly-used approaches in embedded systems scheduling, such as heuristic algorithms [11], branch-and-bound [18,8] and simulated annealing [16], suffer from two major drawbacks. First, task allocation and scheduling are often considered in isolation which means that important information resulting from one of these actions is missed when performing the other. Second, the system and task models used do not consider all the various constraint constructs that typically appear in embedded systems scheduling problems.

Recently, constraint programming has been found to be a promising approach for solving allocation and scheduling problems. To that end, a significant contribution was made by Schild and Würtz [12]. That work consider the timely scheduling of tasks that have been pre-assigned, but does not support allocation or optimization. Another relevant contribution was made by Szymanek, Gruian and Kuchcinski in [15] where they present a constraint programming approach for embedded system hardware/software synthesis. However, the considered optimization objectives are mainly aimed at finding a good balance between components in software and hardware, and less useful for real-time systems where the hardware architecture is already fixed.

3 Constraint Programming Framework

Basically, constraint programming involves two steps, namely (i) formulate the problem in variables and constraints and (ii) find an assignment of the variables such that the constraints are satisfied. This process is aided by a constraint solver that includes constraint propagation techniques for problem reduction. We have previously developed a scheduling framework for real-time systems that is based on constraint programming [6]. The tool that we have based our framework on is SICStus Prolog [9] and its associated constraint solver for finite domains [5]. In this section we describe how the allocation and scheduling problem is expressed as a constraint satisfaction optimization problem within this framework.

In the constraint expressions, we use the following notation. Variables are denoted with capital letters, symbolic constraints available in SICStus Prolog[1] are written in `type-writer` font and constants as *name*(*indices*).

3.1 Assumptions

In the following, we will make some assumptions that are representative of embedded distributed real-time systems. First, it is assumed that task execution and message transmission are *non-preemptive*, that is, they can not be interrupted. Second, we assume that all invocations of a task execute on the same node, that is, *no migration* is possible. Third, we assume that each task has an individual deadline and that *the deadline equals the period* of the task.

3.2 Variables

Recall that we have three types of variables that represent initially unknown problem properties, namely, the start time, S_i^k, of each task instance, the allocated execution node, N_i, of each task, and the transmission start time, SM_{ij}^{kl},

[1] These constraints also exist in other constraint systems (albeit under other names).

of a message sent from task τ_i^k to τ_j^l. In addition, we use the following set of support variables: the (worst-case) execution time, E_i, of a task (which depends on the allocated node) and the actual communication delay of a message EM_{ij} (which differs for inter- and intra-node communication).

Since the tasks are periodic, their start time of each task is restricted to fall within certain intervals, that is, $S_i^k \in [(k-1) \cdot \mathit{period}(i), k \cdot \mathit{period}(i)]$. For the allocation we have $N_i \in [1, m]$, while for the messages we use $SM_{ij}^{kl} \in [0, lcp]$.

3.3 Constraints

The constraints used in this paper is a small but representative subset of the potential constraint constructs found in embedded real-time applications.

In the framework, the actual execution time of a task τ_i^k is expressed as `element`$(N_i, [\mathit{execution\_time}(i,1), ..., \mathit{execution\_time}(i,m)], E_i)$. Task deadlines impose $S_i^k + E_i \leq \mathit{deadline}(i,k)$ where $\mathit{deadline}(i,k) = k \cdot \mathit{period}(i)$ because of our special constraint on task deadlines.

The fact that tasks execute non-preemptively can be modeled using the constraint `disjoint2`$([(S_i^k, E_i, N_i, 1)])$ which means that the tasks are regarded as non-overlapping rectangles. That is, the x-dimension corresponds to time and the y-dimension to the nodes. Message transmission is also non-preemptive; however, we do not know which messages will actually be sent on the bus since this depends on the task allocation. If the communicating tasks are located on the same node, the message passing is instantaneous and does not involve the bus. Hence, the communication delay[2] $EM_{ij} = c_{speed} \cdot \mathit{message\_size}(i,j) \cdot B_{ij}$ where $B_{ij} \Leftrightarrow N_i \neq N_j$. In order to avoid scheduling non-existent bus communication, we use $SM_{ij}^{kl} = B_{ij} \cdot (S_i^k + E_i + X_{ij}^{kl})$, where X_{ij}^{kl} is a support variable that is constrained by $0 \leq X_{ij}^{kl} \leq S_j^l - (S_i^k + E_i) - EM_{ij}$. Unlike task execution, message transmissions cannot be modeled using the `disjoint2` constraint, since some of the corresponding rectangles $(SM_{ij}^{kl}, EM_{ij}, 0, 1)$ will be transformed into "lines" $(0, 0, 0, 1)$. For the addressed allocation and scheduling problem, such "lines" are allowed to overlap. Unfortunately, such overlapping rectangles are not permitted by the `disjoint2` constraint. Instead, we use the constraint `serialized`$([SM_{ij}^{kl}], [EM_{ij}])$, which is a special case of the `cumulative` constraint. Finally, to account for the message transmission in the scheduling of tasks, the communication imposes the following constraint on the minimum distance between the tasks: $S_i^k + E_i + EM_{ij} \leq S_j^l$.

As mentioned, tasks may require other resources than processors for their execution Now, these resources may only be available on some of the nodes and also have varying capacities. Hence, we must constrain both the allocation of the tasks and the resource usage. That is, $N_i \in \{\eta_p\}$, where η_p is a node that has the requested resource. To ensure that a task is allocated to a node with enough static resource capacity, our framework uses the constraint
`cumulative`$([S_i^k \cdot B_i], [E_i \cdot B_i], [\mathit{amount\_used}(i, \rho) \cdot B_i], \mathit{capacity}(\eta_p, \rho))$, where

[2] Without loss of generality, we assume a normalized bus data rate, $c_{speed} = 1$.

$B_i \Leftrightarrow N_i = \eta_p$. Here, $amount\_used(i, \rho)$ is the amount of resource ρ that is required by task τ_i and $capacity(\eta_p, \rho)$ is the amount that is available at η_p.

To represent systems where some tasks are not allowed to execute on the same processor (e.g., due to fault-tolerant replication), tasks may be subject to *anti-clustering* constraints. This requirement is modeled using the constraint `all_different`($[N_i]$) for all tasks τ_i for which the anti-clustering apply. An example of anti-clustering was found in the application in Fig. 1(b).

3.4 Objectives

Because of requirements on various aspects of system design (timeliness, low cost, low power consumption, etc) the allocation and scheduling of embedded systems is driven by a number of, often contradicting, objectives.

One such objective is to minimize the inter-node *communication*. This is relevant since a low bus utilization may (i) allow for the use of a slower but cheaper bus and (ii) reduce the amount of cabling which decreases the cost as well as the weight. We model this objective as $f_{communication} = \sum_{i=1}^{n} \sum_{j=1}^{n} EM_{ij}$. Another common objective is to *load balance*, that is, to evenly distribute the tasks between the nodes to leave as much slack as possible in the schedule. This is useful in fault-tolerant systems where dynamic reexecution of tasks is needed in case of faults. We model this objective by first defining $LOAD_p = \sum_{i=1}^{n} E_i \cdot B_i$ for each node η_p where $B_i \Leftrightarrow N_i = \eta_p$. The objective function is then modeled as $f_{load\_balance} \geq LOAD_p$. Another objective that can provide slack in the schedule is to minimize the *maximum lateness*. Unlike load balancing, this objective attempts to force tasks to complete their execution as early as possible. To model this objective, we define $LAT_i^k = S_i^k + E_i - deadline(i, k)$ for each task and then strive for $f_{max\_lateness} \geq LAT_i^k$.

3.5 Optimization Algorithm

An optimization algorithm defines an objective function $f(x)$ that represents the value of a solution x. A solution x^* is then optimal (assuming minimization) if $\forall x : f(x) \geq f(x^*)$. Using our framework, the objective function can be modeled as yet another problem constraint. An optimal solution can then be found by iteratively solving the same problem with increasingly tighter bounds on the objective function. Although the finite domain solver in SICStus Prolog features a built-in branch-and-bound algorithm for this purpose we have chosen to use the approach outlined above by exploiting SICStus Prolog's exception mechanism. The reason is that this enables us to (i) keep track of the currently best solution in case we want to abort the search prematurely, (ii) change the behavior of the algorithm during search, and (iii) handle several objective functions simultaneously which is useful in multi-objective optimization.

4 Search Heuristics

In constraint programming, two important heuristics are essential for the performance of the problem solving, namely how to decide which variable to assign next and which value to assign to this variable. In the embedded system allocation and scheduling problem we have two different groups of variables, one for allocation ($\{N_i\}$) and one for scheduling ($\{S_i\}, \{SM_{ij}\}$). It therefore seems natural to use different variable-value ordering heuristics for these groups.

For optimization using a constraint-programming framework, it has been argued that the variable order is more important than the value order [17], since to ensure optimality (infeasibility) all values have to be tried anyway. However, as we will demonstrate, this is not necessarily always the case since it is possible to discard many values values by detecting symmetries in the search tree.

In the following sections we describe suitable variable-value ordering heuristics for allocation and scheduling and also explain how it is possible to exclude symmetries in these problems. Furthermore, we propose how these various heuristics can be combined to yield even better performance.

4.1 Allocation

It is quite natural to perform allocation before scheduling since knowledge about the location of a task determines many potentially unknown properties — for example message transmission time and resource contention — resulting in a reduction of the search space. However, a poor allocation might make it hard or even impossible to find a feasible schedule. Hence, an important objective of the allocation is to increase the likelihood of successful subsequent scheduling.

Allocation in our constraint programming approach concerns assigning values to the N_i variables. The simplest value ordering heuristic is to step through the domains of the variables. However, the end result of this strategy is that all tasks become allocated to the same node and more nodes are only used as a last resort. It seems obvious that this *depth-first* value heuristic will often result in an unschedulable system since the utilization between the processors easily becomes skewed, that is, poorly load balanced. A better approach would therefore be to attempt to divide the tasks between the nodes. This can be achieved by using a *round-robin* value selection order. That is, a counter modulo m is used to determine the next value to assign. Although this heuristic is likely to improve over the previous one, it can actually be refined further as in the *load-balancing* approach [3]. In this heuristic the tasks (variables) are first ordered according to their largest[3] total[4] possible execution times. Starting with the task with the largest total execution time, each task is then allocated to the processor with the currently least utilization (load). The same effect is sought in the *period-based* approach [1], where tasks are grouped according to how harmonic their periods are. That is, when a task τ_i is to be allocated its period is compared with the periods of all other tasks τ_j according to the formula:

$$coef(i,j) = \begin{cases} \frac{max(period(i),period(j))}{min(period(i),period(j))} & \text{if } period(i) \text{ and } period(j) \text{ are harmonic} \\ \frac{lcp(i,j)}{period(i)} \cdot \frac{lcp(i,j)}{period(j)} & \text{otherwise} \end{cases}$$

[3] We make this pessimistic assumption because tasks have not yet been allocated.

[4] The total execution time of a task is the time for all invocations in the *lcp* to execute.

If the task τ_j that yields the smallest $coef(i,j)$ has already been allocated, the present task τ_i is allocated to the same node. Otherwise, τ_i is allocated to the next node in a round-robin value order. The idea behind this heuristic is to reduce the execution interference between tasks and also reflect the fact that communicating tasks usually operate at the same frequency (or at least at even multiples). Note that, in general, increasing the amount of communication results in that the scheduling problem becomes tighter. If this should become a problem, it may be more appropriate to use a *communication-clustering* heuristic [11], which attempts to allocate highly communicating tasks to the same processor thus reducing the overall bus usage. Hence, tasks are first ordered according to their potential amount of communication (taken over all invocations). A task is then allocated to the same processor as the one it communicates with the most.

Note that, for the communication-clustering and load-balancing heuristics, information about the variable order already exists. For the other heuristics, no specific order is explicitly defined. In our framework implementation of these heuristics, the variables are dynamically ordered based on increasing domain size and decreasing degree according to the *fail-first most-constrained* heuristic [17].

4.2 Scheduling

Scheduling concerns assigning values to the S_i and SM_i variables. While the depth-first value heuristic (trying increasing values from a range) may not be the best for allocation it should work reasonably well for scheduling. This is because the domains of S_i and SM_i are more likely to be disjoint due to the separation of invocations and also the presence of communication constraints that somewhat restricts the order of the tasks. In addition, selecting the least value in the domain corresponds to scheduling the tasks and messages as soon as possible, increasing the room for succeeding tasks (thereby increasing the likelihood of meeting deadlines). Note that the performance of this heuristic also depends on how we select the variables. Clearly, variables with low least values in their domains should be selected first. However, it is still likely that several variables have the same least domain value so we need to know how to break ties. This is done by having the variables statically ordered according to the fail-first most-constrained heuristic. Since this is a second order heuristic, a dynamic ordering is not likely to be superior.

In [12] it is claimed that finding a consistent ordering between the tasks and also between the messages on the bus, before assigning actual start times, has a positive effect on the performance. Furthermore, it is claimed that the so called edge-finder algorithm[5] provides no improvement in relation to its overhead. Contrary to that belief, however, we will show (in our evaluation section) that these claims are not necessarily true for real-time allocation and scheduling. With respect to our constraint-programming framework, the resource-ordering strategy is available in SICStus Prolog through `order_resource`. The edge-finder algo-

[5] The edge-finder algorithm allows us to identify sets of messages/tasks that have to precede other messages/tasks, thereby offering a reduction of search space.

rithm is in SICStus Prolog possible to use in combination with the `serialized` constraint which we use for the messages.

4.3 Symmetry Exclusion

Symmetries can appear in both allocation and scheduling due to equality properties. Assume that there are two equal nodes, η_1 and η_2, and two tasks, τ_1 and τ_2. Due to the equality property, $N_1 = \eta_1$ and $N_2 = \eta_2$ give an equal solution as $N_1 = \eta_2$ and $N_2 = \eta_1$. Similarly, $N_1 = \eta_1$ and $N_2 = \eta_1$ give an equal solution as $N_1 = \eta_2$ and $N_2 = \eta_2$. Another symmetry can be seen if the two tasks are equal (subject to the same constraints), because then $S_1 = t_1$ and $S_2 = t_2$ give an equal solution as $S_1 = t_2$ and $S_2 = t_1$. In an embedded system, task scheduling symmetries typically arise due to task replication. However, the majority of tasks can be expected to be distinct, thereby making it less necessary to exclude these symmetries. Task allocation symmetries, on the other hand, occur more often and are also more likely to reduce the search space if excluded. This is because the location of a task controls more scheduling aspects than the scheduled start time does. In the most basic case where the nodes are homogeneous, task allocation can be viewed as an instance of the graph coloring problem. In this problem the nodes of a graph are supposed to be colored (using a minimum number of colors) such that no node has the same color as any of its neighbors. A constraint programming heuristic for excluding symmetries for this problem has been proposed in [14]. The same heuristic applied to real-time allocation and scheduling is presented in [2]. The basic idea is as follows. Assume that a task is allocated to a previously unused node, η_1. If this allocation turns out to be invalid and has to be redone (upon backtracking), there is no point in selecting another unused node η_2. The outcome will be the same since η_1 is equal to η_2. However, since our model allows processors to have different speed and varying amounts of resources attached, the above heuristic must be extended. Instead of just keeping track of the set containing the unused nodes, we must keep track of several sets containing the unused nodes within each group of equal processors (same speed and equal resources). When using the heuristic, we only have to try one node from each set to get a full coverage. This means that, in the worst case, when all nodes are distinct, we get no exclusion at all. However, in such a system task allocation is more likely to be restricted by resource constraints, making symmetry exclusion less crucial. On the other hand, in a homogeneous system where tasks can be allocated more freely, symmetry exclusion will be more desired and the impact of the heuristic is also larger. In order to make this symmetry exclusion as effective as possible we should only use new nodes when absolutely necessary. Since this property is already present in the depth-first value heuristic, described in Section 4.1, we incorporate our symmetry exclusion scheme into this heuristic. The complete allocation algorithm is described in Fig. 2. The symmetry exclusion is handled by the underlined part, which upon backtracking is not re-executed unless another Ω_q set has been selected. In order to get the tasks to spread out a little bit more than in the original depth-first heuristic, the nodes (values) in the set Θ are selected in a last-in-first-out order.

- Θ is the set of already assigned nodes
- Ω_q is a set of equal unused nodes
- Ω is the super set containing the Ω_q sets

(1) Select N_i to assign (or finished)
(2) Select $\eta_p \in \Theta$ such that $N_i := \eta_p$ is ok
(3) **If** (2) is possible **then** go to (1)
(4) Select $\Omega_q \in \Omega$ and $\eta_n \in \Omega_q$ such that $N_i := \eta_p$ is ok
(5) **If** (4) is possible **then** $\Omega_q := \Omega_q \setminus \{\eta_p\}$, $\Theta := \Theta \cup \{\eta_p\}$, go to (1)

Fig. 2. Allocation algorithm with symmetry exclusion

4.4 Algorithm Configuration

We have implemented the following allocation heuristics in our framework: round-robin (RR), communication-clustering (CC), load-balancing (LB), period-based (PB) and depth-first with symmetry exclusion (DF). The heuristics are used in three different algorithm setups. In Setup 1, the chosen heuristic is used throughout the search. We use this setup to evaluate the basic strengths of each heuristic, without using symmetry exclusion (except in DF). In Setup 2, the chosen heuristic is only used to find a feasible solution. The optimal solution is then generated using DF (and symmetry exclusion). The motivation for this setup is that we want to see whether the chosen heuristic can produce a good initial solution that results in a significant reduction of the problem to be solved by DF. In Setup 3, the chosen heuristic is always used, but it is not allowed to backtrack. That is, the heuristic is allowed to try another value on the current variable, but it is not allowed to change the value of a previously assigned variable. If the heuristic cannot find a feasible allocation on its first attempt, DF (and symmetry exclusion) is run instead. This setup allows us to observe the performance when "intelligent" search is used and "unintelligent" backtracking is avoided. Note that, for the DF heuristics, all three setups will be identical.

5 Evaluation

The purpose of this section is to investigate how well the search heuristics in Section 4 operate on different types of problems. Since it is difficult to get access to a sufficiently large set of real-world real-time scheduling problems, we have to base our evaluation on simulations. In the following, we describe how these simulations were performed and discuss their results. We will use X-Y to denote algorithm setup Y with task allocation heuristic X.

5.1 Experimental Setup

To illustrate the behavior of the heuristics we use an example from [11]. The application is a safety-critical application which includes 3 homogeneous nodes and 9 tasks with communication and anti-clustering constraints. The task graph of that application was shown in Fig. 1(b).

Table 1. Configuration parameters for the task sets

Parameter	Study		
	A	B	C
Number of tasks	16	8	8
Execution times	10–20	20–30	20–30
Communication probability	0.25	0	0.5
Message sizes	5–15	-	5–15
Number of processors	8	8	2,3,4,5,6,7,8
Resource probability	0.5	0.25,0.5,0.75	0
Resource capacity	1–3	1–5	-
Task resource usage probability	0.2	0.5	0
Task resource usage amount	1–2	1–3	-

In addition to this example, we have conducted 100 experiments, using randomly generated task sets. A new task set was generated for each experiment using the parameters displayed in Table 1. Values indicated using ranges were chosen randomly from a uniform distribution. The task periods in each experiment were drawn (with uniform probability) from the set $\{100, 150, 300\}$ to avoid a too large *lcp* and to get a small deviation in the total number of task invocations for each experiment. Cyclic or mutual communication was avoided by only allowing a task τ_i to communicate with a task τ_j if $j < i$. To discredit communication between tasks with non-harmonic periods, the probability for communication between two tasks, τ_i and τ_j, decreased with increasing $coef(i, j)$. The processors had the same speed and a probability of having a resource attached which, with another probability, was required by a task.

The generated task sets were used in three different studies labeled A, B and C (see Table 1). The purpose of study A was to examine whether the edge-finder and resource-ordering algorithms mentioned in Section 4.2 are useful for a typical real-time application. Study B addressed performance versus resource availability while optimizing the load balance. The experiments in this study did not have any communication constraints in order to avoid their influence on the performance. Study C investigated performance versus system size while minimizing bus communication. Here we wanted to vary the number of processors without changing any other properties (i.e., no resources can be used).

The performance of our evaluations was measured in terms of *average run times* of the search algorithm to find the optimal solution, taken over the 100 experiments. It should be noted that, with the given parameter setup, there was no guarantee that a generated problem was feasible. In our evaluation, we found that only about 5% were infeasible. Furthermore, runs that did not finish within one hour were terminated and excluded in the result analysis. Unless stated, the fraction of such runs were less than 5%.

5.2 Application Study

Table 2 displays the results of allocating and scheduling the safety-critical application from [11]. Similar to the experiments reported in [11], the optimization criterion used was to minimize bus communication.

The best results are obtained with PB-2/3 followed by CC-2/3. In this application, communication is indeed only present between tasks with the same period, making PB a suitable choice. CC can also expected to be a good choice but obviously has a slightly larger overhead in our implementation. The importance of symmetry exclusion is obvious when comparing the results for Setup 1 and Setup 2/3. In fact, for some cases (such as PB), a performance improvement in the order of one magnitude is obtained when symmetry exclusion is used.

Table 2. Safety-critical application (secs/#backtracks)

Allocation	Setup		
	1	2	3
RR	1.3/587	0.28/63	0.31/70
LB	2.5/1734	0.26/63	0.33/66
PB	3.6/4127	0.15/63	0.17/81
CC	1.1/530	0.21/54	0.23/63
DF	0.26/63	-	-

Table 3. Study A (secs/#time outs)

Algorithm	Objective		
	lateness	load balance	communication
CC-3	180/49	324/52	82/11
CC-3+or	332/53	145/87	241/25
CC-3-ef	153/51	367/55	78/11

5.3 Study A: Effects of Resource-Ordering and Edge-Finder

Table 3 shows the results from allocating and scheduling the randomly-generated application using the CC heuristic with Setup 3 under three different optimization objectives. As indicated in the table, CC has been used in the standard way with edge-finder (CC-3), in combination with the resource-ordering heuristic (CC-3+or), and without edge-finder (CC-3-ef). The results indicate that, on average, it does not pay off to explicitly order the tasks and messages. The explanation for this is most likely that finding an order does not directly contribute to the value of the objective function. In the case of load balance and communication, the value only depends on the allocation. In the case of lateness, the value depends on the start times which still are unknown after the ordering. On the other hand, the edge-finder algorithm can be useful in the case of optimizing lateness and load-balance. Since we use the edge-finder algorithm only for the messages, it is likely to have more impact if the number of messages is large (load-balancing) or the order of the messages are important (lateness). Thus, the claims made in [12] about the usefulness of the resource-ordering and edge-finder heuristics are not necessarily true for embedded real-time applications.

5.4 Study B: Effects of Resource Availability on Performance

Fig. 3 shows the results from allocating and scheduling the randomly-generated application while optimizing the load balance. In this study we varied the number of available resources in the system. Since the tasks in this study do not communicate, CC is reverted to (static) RR but with an arbitrary variable order. When comparing the results for CC and RR, it is clear that the variable order has a significant impact, particularly in Setup 1. However, when symmetry exclusion is used (Setup 2 and 3), CC performs comparable to RR (and, in fact, better than DF). The results for LB are perhaps the most surprising in this study. The reason for LB's contradicting plots for Setup 1 and 3 is that the use

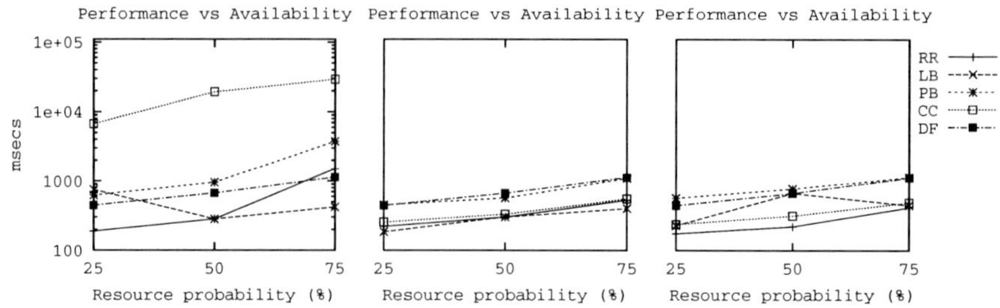

(a) Setup 1 (b) Setup 2 (c) Setup 3

Fig. 3. Study B ($f_{load\_balance}$)

of DF has two advantages. If there are few available resources, LB will be forced to backtrack a lot. This "unintelligent" backtracking is prevented by using DF. On the other hand, since the load balance is optimized, LB otherwise has the potential to produce near-optimal solutions. DF then reduces the time to ensure optimality. Hence, in the "middle" LB performs neither good nor bad and the plots for Setup 1 and 2 suggest that in this region some backtracking can be beneficial after all.

5.5 Study C: Effects of System Size on Performance

Fig. 4 shows the results from allocating and scheduling the randomly-generated application while minimizing the bus communication. In this study we varied the number of processors in the system. From this study it is clearly seen that the allocation strategy has an important role even when symmetry exclusion is used. In fact, the performance of CC and LB differ with almost an order of magnitude. Based on the results from Setup 2, it is clear that PB, LB and RR have difficulties just finding a first solution whereas CC quickly finds a good one. It can also be seen that Setup 3 is less sensitive of the choice of allocation heuristic. The relative performance among the heuristics is perhaps not that surprising considering that we try to minimize communication. For instance, LB and RR rather tend to increase the communication. However, additional simulations show that CC-2/3 outperforms the other configurations also when optimizing lateness and load balance. This is most probably because a reduction in the number of messages decreases the number of (unassigned) variables and also relax the problem constraints.

6 Discussion and Future Work

The purpose of our work was to get a better understanding of how different problem properties affect the search complexity and how this relates to the algorithm configuration. Although our studies have given some insights regarding this issue,

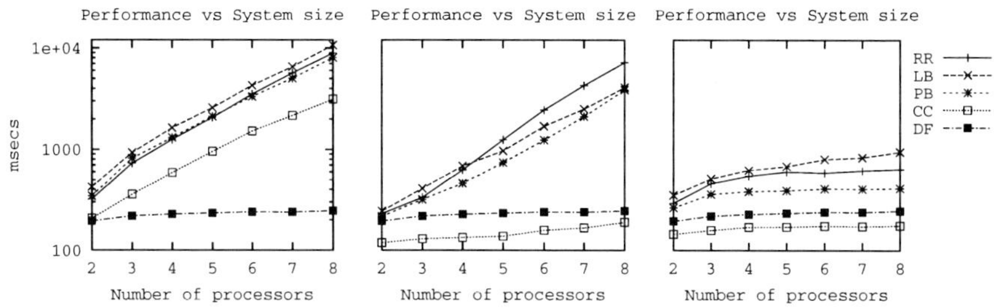

(a) Setup 1 (b) Setup 2 (c) Setup 3

Fig. 4. Study C ($f_{communication}$)

there are still problem and algorithm combinations that would be interesting to examine. For example, in study B communication-clustering is not really tested since there is no communication. In general, CC provides no information on how to order tasks with no communication. Instead of an arbitrary order maybe it would be beneficial to use (static) RR. Another observation is that the presence of resources degrades the performance of the heuristics (particularly LB) since none of them actively considers resource usage. A resource aware heuristic, similar to the one presented in [15], could therefore be an interesting alternative.

An important part in optimization is to have a tight lower bound on the object function. So far, we have not really considered this factor in our approach. However, finding better estimations of the optimum is indeed a subject for future research. A commonly-used approach in operations research is to solve a relaxed variant of the problem. The opposite approach is to over-constrain the problem, regarding the value of the object function, to be close to some estimated optimum. The estimated hardness of solving such problems could be used to give a better location of the actual optimum [13].

7 Conclusions

Optimal allocation and scheduling of embedded real-time systems is a problem that not only suffers from high computational complexity but also from complicated modeling. In this paper, we have shown that constraint programming, equipped with problem specific search heuristics like processor symmetry exclusion and suitable task allocation, is a viable approach for this problem. Our simulation studies show that the performance in many cases could be reduced by orders of magnitude by configuring the algorithm according to the problem. In fact, the symmetry exclusion mechanism in combination with a communication-clustering heuristic often lead to an average polynomial-time complexity.

References

1. T. F. Abdelzaher and K. G. Shin. Period-based load partitioning and assignment for large real-time applications. *IEEE Trans. on Computers*, 49(1):81–87, 2000.
2. I. Ahmad and Y.-K. Kwok. Optimal and near-optimal allocation of precedence-constrained tasks to parallel processors: Defying the high complexity using effective search techniques. In *Proc. of the Int'l Conf. on Parallel Processing*, pp. 424–431, Minneapolis, Minnesota, August 10–14, 1998.
3. J. A. Bannister and K. S. Trivedi. Task allocation in fault-tolerant distributed systems. *Acta Informatica*, 20:261–281, 1983.
4. P. Brucker, M. R. Garey, and D. S. Johnson. Scheduling equal-length tasks under treelike precedence constraints to minimize maximum lateness. *Mathematics of Operations Research*, 2(3):275–284, August 1977.
5. M. Carlsson, G. Ottosson, and B. Carlson. An open-ended finite domain constraint solver. In H. Glaser et al., editors, *Proc. of the Int'l Symposium on Programming Languages: Implementations, Logics, and Programs*, volume 1292 of *Lecture Notes in Computer Science*, pp. 191–206, Southampton, UK, September 3–5, 1997.
6. C. Ekelin and J. Jonsson. A modeling framework for constraints in real-time systems. Tech. Rep. 00-9, Dept. of Computer Engineering, Chalmers University of Technology, S-412 96 Göteborg, Sweden, May 2000.
7. C. Ekelin and J. Jonsson. Solving embedded system scheduling problems using constraint programming. Tech. Rep. 00-12, Dept. of Computer Engineering, Chalmers University of Technology, S-412 96 Göteborg, Sweden, April 2000.
8. J. Jonsson and K. G. Shin. A parametrized branch-and-bound strategy for scheduling precedence-constrained tasks on a multiprocessor system. In *Proc. of the Int'l Conf. on Parallel Processing*, pp. 158–165, Bloomingdale, Illinois, 1997.
9. Intelligent Systems Laboratory. *SICStus Prolog User's Manual.* Swedish Institute of Computer Science, 1995. http://www.sics.se/isl/sicstus/
10. C. L. Liu and J. W. Layland. Scheduling algorithms for multiprogramming in a hard-real-time environment. *Journal of the ACM*, 20(1):46–61, January 1973.
11. K. Ramamritham. Allocation and scheduling of precedence-related periodic tasks. *IEEE Trans. on Parallel and Distributed Systems*, 6(4):412–420, April 1995.
12. K. Schild and J. Würtz. Scheduling of time-triggered real-time systems. *Constraints*, 5(4):335–357, October 2000.
13. J. Slaney and S. Thiébaux. On the hardness of decision and optimisation problems. In *Proc. of ECAI*, pp. 244–248, Brighton, UK, 1998.
14. B. M. Smith and I. P. Gent. Symmetry breaking during search in constraint programming. In *Proc. of ECAI*, pp. 599–603, Berlin, Germany, 2000.
15. R. Szymanek, F. Gruian, and K. Kuchcinski. Digital systems design using constraint logic programming. In *Proc. of the Practical Application of Constraint Tec hnology and Logic Programming*, Manchester, England, April 10–12, 2000.
16. K. W. Tindell, A. Burns, and A. J. Wellings. Allocating hard real-time tasks: An NP-hard problem made easy. *Real-Time Systems*, 4(2):145–165, June 1992.
17. E. Tsang. *Foundations of Constraint Satisfaction.* Academic Press, 1993.
18. J. Xu. Multiprocessor scheduling of processes with release times, deadlines, precedence, and exclusion relations. *IEEE Trans. on Software Engineering*, 19(2):139–154, February 1993.

Interpreting Sloppy Stick Figures with Constraint-Based Subgraph Matching

Markus P.J. Fromherz and James V. Mahoney

Xerox PARC, 3333 Coyote Hill Road, Palo Alto, CA 94304, USA
{fromherz,mahoney}@parc.xerox.com

Abstract. Machine systems for understanding hand-drawn sketches must reliably interpret common but sloppy curvilinear configurations. The task is commonly expressed as finding an image model in the image data, but few approaches exist for recognizing drawings with missing model parts and noisy data. In this paper, we propose a two-stage structural modeling approach that combines computer vision techniques with constraint-based recognition. The first stage produces a data graph through standard image analysis techniques augmented by rectification operations that account for common forms of drawing variability and noise. The second stage combines CLP(FD) with concurrent constraint programming for efficient and optimal matching of attributed model and data graphs. This approach offers considerable ease in stating model constraints and objectives, and also leads to an efficient algorithm that scales well with increasing image complexity.

1 Introduction

Sketching plays an important role in many common tasks, where it is often used to record and communicate informal ideas for human consumption. Sketching is used to draw maps for directions, organizational charts, plans and flow charts, drawings for presentation slides, story books for movies, and countless other illustrations in often task-specific notations. Today, sketches are then often redrawn on a computer for use in documentation and presentation. This is the step we aim to support with our work.

Machine systems for understanding such hand-drawn sketches must reliably interpret common curvilinear configurations, such as geometric shapes, arrows, and conventional signs and symbols. Sketches are often sloppily drawn and highly variable from one instance to the next (cf. Fig. 1). Typical sketches also contain multiple instances of one or several prototypical elements as well as noise or spurious elements.

In this work, we examine how a recognition system may allow great variability in form while also providing efficient matching and easy extensibility to new configurations, focusing on the domain of human stick figures in arbitrary poses. This domain is intermediate in the range of structural complexity we want the recognition system to handle, yet complex enough to discourage an approach in which specialized and detailed matching routines must be written for each new configuration. The goal of such a system is to find the set of all optimal sketch interpretations, where the optimality criteria are designed to be consistent with human perceptual experience.

T. Walsh (Ed.): CP 2001, LNCS 2239, pp. 655-669, 2001.

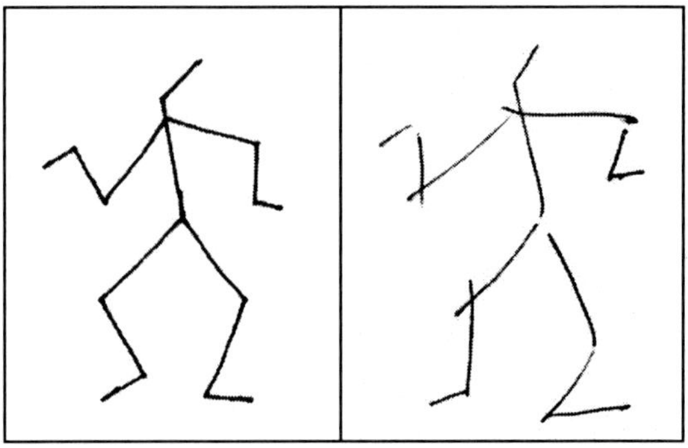

Fig. 1. Neat and sloppy stick figures

We adopt a structural modeling approach, suitable for highly articulated or abstract configurations. The configuration model and the input scene are represented as graphs, with nodes representing figure *parts* (e.g., lines), and edges representing part *relations* (e.g., line connections). Recognition is cast as subgraph matching of the *model graph* to the *data graph*, to allow for irrelevant parts or relations in the input. This paper describes contributions in three areas: the *constraint-based description* of model and data sketches for ease of specification and transformation to an *attributed graph representation*; the formulation of the attributed subgraph matching problem as a *constrained optimization problem*; and a *generic matching algorithm* to solve this constraint problem that makes effective use of local and global constraints during search.

There is a long history of work in rigid geometric matching, mostly focused on finding close-to-exact replicas of model images in data images under translation, rotation, and scaling [2]. Formulating the recognition problem as subgraph matching [12] (also called subgraph isomorphism detection) allows for more variability at the semantic level of the image, including finding model images that are geometrically different but topologically similar (cf. Fig. 2).

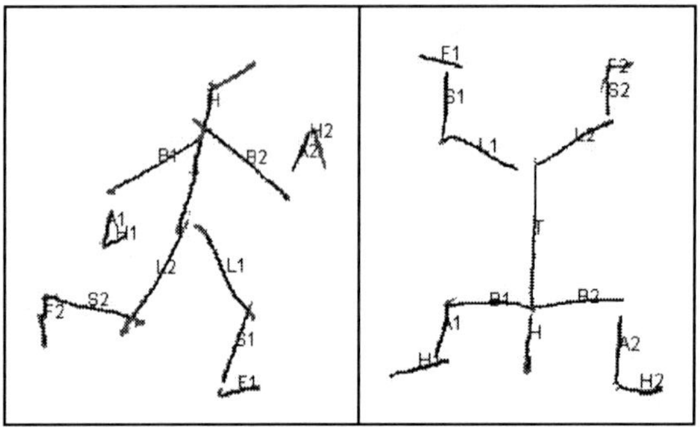

Fig. 2. Example matching results for different instances of the same model

Constraint-based matching is attractive for several reasons. Primary among them is the ease of describing the model, which consists not only of the graph (parts and relations), but also part and relation attributes such as length and orientation, as well as constraints and objectives on these attributes. A constraint-based formulation exploits the natural structure of the problem ("the thigh bone is connected to the hip-bone") and thus provides a declarative programming scheme. Furthermore, this allows us to extend subgraph matching to optimal attributed subgraph matching, where the result is a match that optimizes objectives such as minimal limb distances and "anatomically correct" limb proportions. Finally, constraint propagation and branch-and-bound optimizing search make effective use of the natural constraints of this application.

Constraint-based pattern recognition approaches have been used primarily in domains with strong (visual) grammars, such as musical notation [6,1] and state-transition diagrams [5]. The former two references extend Definite Clause Grammars (e.g., with bags instead of lists) to allow for the nonlinear composition of the graphical elements; the latter work uses Constraint Multiset Grammars for similar reasons. Despite these extensions, grammar-based approaches still rely on the relatively linear structure of data such as a musical score. Since sketches typically don't have such a linear structure, a grammar-based approach is not well suited for sketch interpretation. Other work has proposed dedicated forward checking and full lookahead search algorithms for subgraph matching [12,8]. In these cases, special-purpose algorithms were developed that cannot be extended easily to user-provided constraints and objectives. (Constraint-based subgraph matching should not be confused with constraint-based 3-D line labeling as pioneered by Waltz [15], which finds consistent 3-D interpretations of lines in line drawings.)

The rest of this paper is organized as follows. Data and model representations are introduced and discussed in the next section. Section 3 formalizes the subgraph-matching problem as a constrained optimization problem and describes the search algorithm. Section 4 presents and discusses a variety of experiments on the accuracy and scaling of our approach. Section 5 closes with conclusions and future work.

2 Data and Model Specifications

As mentioned, both the configuration model (the "model") and the description of the input scene (the "data") are represented as graph structures, the nodes representing figure parts and the edges representing part relations.

Matching Complexity

Graph generation and representation have important implications for matching complexity. Due to drawing variability and noise in the sketch domain, a data graph would rarely contain a verbatim instance of the model as a subgraph. One solution is to use error-tolerant subgraph matching to explicitly allow and account for structural or attribute discrepancies [11]. However, this increases matching complexity, e.g., from $O(dm)$ to $O(dm^2)$ in the best case, and from $O(d^m m^2)$ to $O(d^{m+1} m^2)$ in the worst case, d and m being the node counts of the data and model graphs respectively.

In the alternative we propose, variability is characterized in terms of the possible ways that each constituent local relation of a configuration can be perturbed from its ideal form (cf. Fig. 3). The data graph is explicitly corrected for these deviations in a prior perceptual organization stage, termed *graph rectification,* so as to greatly increase the chance that the model will find a direct match in the data.

Subgraph isomorphism is exponential in the general case, and although an algorithm linear in the size of the data graph is known for planar graphs and a fixed model [7], this algorithm is still exponential in the model size. Therefore, it is essential either to focus and guide the search for a match based on cues in the data, or to restrict the size of the problem, or both. Our results so far indicate that, with careful design, a constraint-based matching scheme can provide very good performance for inputs within a useful size range, containing a few target figures.

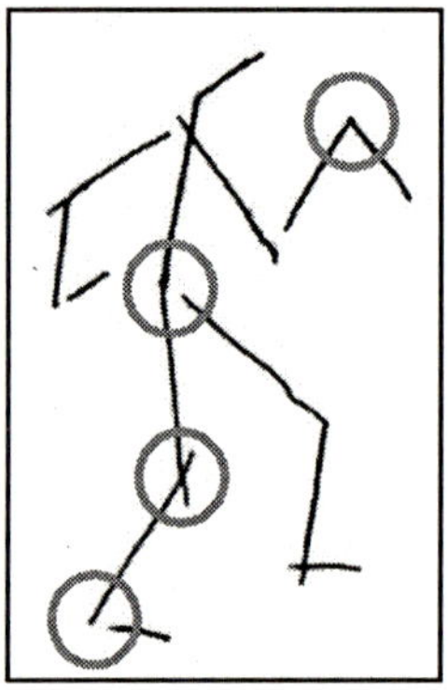

Fig. 3. This figure requires (circles, top to bottom) corner detection, virtual junction detection, junction detection and spurious segment elimination, and proximity linking

Data Specification

Consider an initial *data graph*, created from an image of a line drawing like Fig. 1. The initial data graph represents the curve segments and co-termination relations that result from applying standard computer vision techniques, such as binarization, thinning, junction detection, corner detection, and curve tracing operations. Subsequent graph rectification operations (augmentation, reduction, and elaboration) apply general perceptual organization principles, such as good continuation and co-termination, to the specific goal of producing a suitable data graph for matching. Figs. 3 and 4 show examples for some of these operations. However, a thorough discussion of this process is beyond the scope of this paper; see [9,10] for more details.

The resulting data graph is attributed in both its nodes and edges. Typical attributes include length, orientation, end-point locations, and angles.

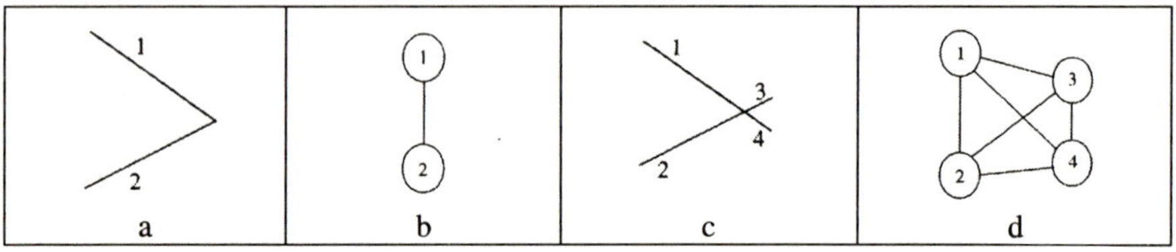

Fig. 4. Two lines just meeting at a corner (a) give data graph (b), but overshoot (c) results in graph (d). Graph rectification operation applied to (c, d) produce a graph identical to (b)

Model Specification

A stick figure configuration *model* is expressed in a simple syntax, illustrated below. Each `limb` statement defines a part of the figure. The `optional` modifier allows a part to be missing in the data. The `linked` statement asserts an end-to-end connection between two curvilinear parts. Two optional integer arguments allow the modeler to specify with which end of each part the link is associated. For example, the (default) values (2,1) indicate that the link goes from the second end of the first named part to the first end of the second (where "first" and "second" can be arbitrary but must be consistent).

```
model stick_figure {
  limb head, torso, biceps1, ...;
  optional limb hand1, hand2, ...;
  link(head, torso);
  link(torso, biceps1, 1, 1);
  ...
  minimize (torso.len-2*head.len)^2
         + (2*torso.len-3*biceps1.len)^2
         + ...;
  ...
} // end model stick_figure
```

Like the data graph, the model graph allows for attributes such as length (e.g., `torso.len`) and the `optional` flag. (In a typical model, we allow only end limbs to be missing, i.e., here the hands and feet.) Finally, the modeler can specify constraints and objectives on these attributes. For example, the `minimize` objectives above specify optimal relative limb lengths. For the most part, this modeling language only provides syntactic sugar over constraint logic programming (CLP). It should be obvious how the model can be translated to and represented in a standard CLP language.

3 Constraint-Based Formulation of Subgraph Matching

3.1 The Subgraph Matching Problem

We first formalize data and model graphs and then define the subgraph-matching problem. Given are a data graph $G_D = \langle V_D, E_D \rangle$ and a model graph $G_M = \langle V_M, E_M \rangle$, each with nodes V_D and V_M, respectively, and edges E_D and E_M, respectively. V_D represents the d data parts labeled from 1 through d, i.e., $V_D = \{1,\ldots,d\}$. E_D is the set of links $c_D(i,j,e_i,e_j)$ between end e_i of line i and end e_j of line j ($i,j \in V_D$, $e_i,e_j \in \{1,2\}$). Similarly, V_M represents the m model parts, each denoted by a variable x_i, i.e., $V_M = \{x_1,\ldots,x_m\}$, and E_M is the set of expected links $c_M(i,j,e_i,e_j)$ between parts x_i and x_j. (Note that edges are bi-directional, e.g., $c_M(i,j,e_i,e_j)$ implies $c_M(j,i,e_j,e_i)$.)

In addition, the data and model graphs are augmented by attributes on nodes and edges. For clarity, we use a functional notation to denote these attributes, with cursive font indicating variables. For example, $\mathrm{opt}_M(i)$ is a Boolean attribute of node i in the model graph, indicating whether or not part i is optional, and $len_M(i)$ is an integer attribute of node i in the model graph, representing the length of part i (which is initially unknown). Other common attributes are the length $\mathrm{len}_D(i)$ of data part i, the length $\mathrm{len}_D(i,j,e_i,e_j)$ of data link $c_D(i,j,e_i,e_j)$, the length $len_M(i,j,e_i,e_j)$ of expected model link $c_M(i,j,e_i,e_j)$, the coordinates of the end points of data and model parts, etc.

According to the sketch interpretation task outlined above, the goal of the matching process is to find a labeling of all model parts x_i in V_M with values from V_D such that the model instance found in the data is as close to the "ideal model" as possible. Formally, the subgraph-matching problem can be defined as follows:

$$\begin{array}{lll} \text{find a solution} & \langle x_1,\ldots,x_m\rangle = \langle v_1,\ldots,v_m\rangle & \\ \text{with minimal} & h(v_1,\ldots,v_m) & \\ \text{subject to} & v_i \in D_i & i = 1,\ldots,m \\ & c_j(v_1,\ldots,v_m) & j = 1,\ldots,n \end{array} \tag{1}$$

where h and c_j encode the objectives and constraints that define the ideal model instance in the data, and $D_i = V_D \cup \{0\}$ if $\text{opt}_M(i)$ and $D_i = V_D$ otherwise, i.e., optional parts are labeled with 0 if they can't be found in the data.

This formulation can be extended easily to finding multiple instances of the model, or multiple models, in the data, for example by repeatedly searching for model instances and removing found instances from the data graph.

Constraints

The subgraph-matching problem has two topological constraints defined as follows.

Unique label constraint. Except for optional nodes labeled 0, all variables x_i require a unique value, i.e., $\forall i,j\ .\ x_i \neq x_j \vee x_i = 0 \wedge x_j = 0$. Because multiple variables can be labeled with 0, we use the cardinality constraint $\#(l,[c_1,\ldots,c_n],u)$ [13], which states that at least l and at most u of the n constraints c_i are satisfied. In this paper, we will repeatedly use a special version varcard(l,V,v,u) that restricts the variables assignments $x_i = v$ in $V = \{x_1,\ldots,x_n\}$, i.e., varcard$(l,V,v,u) \Leftrightarrow \#(l,[x_1{=}v,\ldots,x_n{=}v],u)$. Unique labeling is then defined as

$$\forall i \in V_D\ .\ \text{varcard}(0,V_M,i,1) \tag{2}$$

Link support constraint. For all data nodes assigned to a model node, the data node has to have at least the links expected by the model part. Formally,

$$\begin{aligned} \forall x_i \in V_M\ .\ x_i \neq 0\ \rightarrow (&\forall \text{c}_M(i,j,e_i,e_j) \in E_M\ .\ x_j \neq 0 \rightarrow \text{c}_D(x_i,x_j,e_i,e_j) \in E_D\ \vee \\ &\forall \text{c}_M(i,j,e_i,e_j) \in E_M\ .\ x_j \neq 0 \rightarrow \text{c}_D(x_i,x_j,3-e_i,3-e_j) \in E_D) \end{aligned} \tag{3}$$

where the reversal of the ends in c_D (which are either 1 or 2) is the only difference between the two disjuncts (cf. Fig. 5a for sample data and model graphs).

The disjunction in (3) is required because of our choice to represent lines as a single extended part instead of as two separate points with a link between them. This choice has efficiency advantages over the latter, more generic version (e.g., the graph has only half the node count), but we may change this in the future to generalize our algorithm. Notably, if parts were simply points, constraint (3) would be

$$\forall x_i \in V_M\ .\ x_i \neq 0 \rightarrow (\forall \text{c}_M(i,j)\ .\ x_j \neq 0 \rightarrow \text{c}_D(x_i,x_j) \in E_D) \tag{4}$$

While the formulation in (3) and (4) is easy to understand, the following alternative better shows how the domains of connected variables x_j can be constrained with help of the data graph, once a variable x_i has been determined:

$$\begin{aligned} &\forall x_i \in V_M\ .\ x_i \neq 0\ \rightarrow (\ \forall \text{c}_M(i,j,e_i,e_j) \in E_M\ .\ x_j \in D_{xi}(e_i) \cup O_j\ \vee \\ &\qquad\qquad\qquad\qquad\quad \forall \text{c}_M(i,j,e_i,e_j) \in E_M\ .\ x_j \in D_{xi}(3-e_i) \cup O_j) \\ &D_{xi}(e_i) = \{\ v \mid \exists e_j\ .\ \text{c}_D(x_i,v,e_i,e_j) \in E_D\ \} \\ &O_j = \{0\} \text{ if } \text{opt}_M(j) \text{ and } \{\,\} \text{ otherwise} \end{aligned} \tag{5}$$

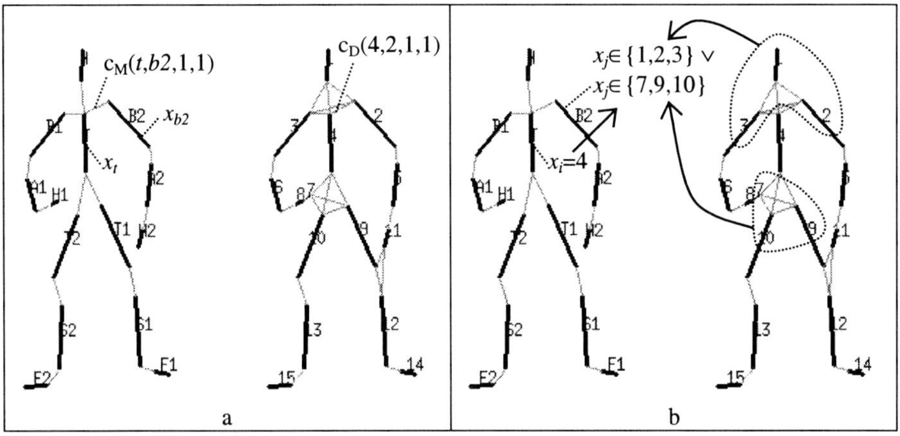

Fig. 5. Model and data graphs side by side: a) examples for nodes x_i and edges $c_M(x_i,x_j,e_i,e_j)$; b) effect of the link support constraint on the variable for biceps 2 as the torso's variable becomes instantiated with data node 4

Note that for a given x_i, D_{xi} depends only on e_i, and thus there are only two different sets D_{xi}, one for each end of line x_i. In fact, these domains can be precomputed for all nodes in the data graph. It can further be inferred that the size of D_{xi} has to be at least as large as the number of non-optional parts linked to model part *i*. Fig. 5b shows an example where x_i is the torso's variable, labeled 4, and biceps 2 is an example for a linked variable x_j constrained by data node 4's neighbors.

Again, if parts were simply points, constraint (5) would simplify to

$$\begin{aligned} &\forall x_i \in V_M \,.\, x_i \neq 0 \rightarrow \forall c_M(i,j) \in E_M \,.\, x_j \in D_{xi} \cup O_j \\ &D_{xi} = \{ v \mid c_D(x_i,v) \in E_D \} \\ &O_j = \{0\} \text{ if } \mathrm{opt}_M(j) \text{ and } \{\} \text{ otherwise} \end{aligned} \tag{6}$$

The link support constraint may be the most important constraint during search, as it rapidly narrows the search tree once a few variables have been instantiated.

Further constraints are possible. The following is one example.

Missing parts limit constraint. In all our experiments we are allowing no more than two model parts to be missing in the data, expressed as

$$\mathrm{varcard}(0,V_M,0,2) \tag{7}$$

Objectives

The constraints so far describe a purely topological match of the model graph against the data graph. This usually is sufficient for matching against isolated figures, but sketches with multiple model instances or even just a few additional lines often lead to several possible matches. To identify "good" matches in such cases, geometric information and a formulation of preferences are required. The objectives we define are designed to be consistent with human perceptual experience. For example, we expect that limbs to be linked are drawn close to each other (the phenomenon of proximity grouping) and that the various limbs have the proper proportions (visual similarity). The reason for adopting human perceptual criteria is that the system should classify shapes in a manner consistent with its human users — we want a "shared interpretation" between man and machine.

In order to allow for variability, we formalize these expectations as objectives instead of constraints and combine them in a weighted sum:

$$h(v_1,\ldots,v_m) = \Sigma_i\, w_i\, h_i(v_1,\ldots,v_m) \quad (8)$$

Weights w_i are chosen such that individual objectives are optimized according to their priorities.

The individual objectives we have been using so far are defined as follows.

Minimal missing part count objective. This objective can be defined easily using a cardinality constraint as in

$$h_1(V_M) = k \text{ such that varcard}(k, V_M, 0, k) \quad (9)$$

which instantiates k with the number of variables labeled 0.

Minimal link length objective. This objective can be defined as minimizing the sum of squares of the instantiated link lengths:

$$h_2(V_M) = \Sigma_{i,j}\, l_{i,j}$$
$$l_{i,j} = \begin{cases} 0 & (x_i = 0 \vee x_j = 0) \\ len_M^2(i,j,e_i,e_j) & \text{(otherwise)} \end{cases} \quad (10)$$

where of course len_M is assigned from len_D as x_i and x_j become instantiated.

Optimal part proportion objective. This objective prefers model instances with the right proportions. In contrast to the previous two objectives, this objective is model-specific and therefore defined with the model (cf. Section 2). As an example, a typical desired proportion may be $len_M(x_{torso}) = 2\ len_M(x_{head})$, where *torso* and *head* are the indices of the nodes in V_M corresponding to the head and torso, respectively. In the model, this desired proportion is defined as objective $p_{torso,head} = (len_M(x_{torso}) - 2\ len_M(x_{head}))^2$, and – given these functions $p_{i,j}$ – this component of the objective function is defined as

$$h_3(V_M) = \Sigma_{i,j}\, p_{i,j} \quad (11)$$

Without going into further detail, we note that experiments with individual objectives turned off have shown this objective to be the most important factor in successful matching. Still, all objectives are required for robust matching against noisy data.

3.2 Matching Algorithm

The matching process takes as input the attributed data and model graphs and assigns to each node in the model graph either a node in the data graph or the missing-node identifier 0. We have considered three algorithms for solving the constrained optimization problem (1). The major difference between these algorithms is in how they make use of the link support constraint (5).

A first, straightforward algorithm is *depth-first search*, which labels the variables in a fixed order given by the model, using constraint (5) to dynamically build the search tree. This approach seems quite effective for small data graphs and without objectives to be optimized, but doesn't scale well and is difficult to extend to optimal search. Worse, it partly implements a propagation scheme that should really be handled by a constraint system and its solver.

Another approach is to completely *extensionalize the link support constraint* as stated in (5). Taking the version in (6) as the simpler example, this leads, for each x_i in V_M, to propositional constraints of the form

$$\begin{aligned} &x_i = 1 \rightarrow |R_i| \leq |D_1| \wedge v_1 \in D_1 \cup O_1 \wedge \ldots \wedge v_n \in D_1 \cup O_n \vee \\ &x_i = 2 \rightarrow |R_i| \leq |D_2| \wedge v_1 \in D_2 \cup O_1 \wedge \ldots \wedge v_n \in D_2 \cup O_n \vee \\ &\ldots \\ &x_i = d \rightarrow |R_i| \leq |D_d| \wedge v_1 \in D_d \cup O_1 \wedge \ldots \wedge v_n \in D_d \cup O_n \end{aligned} \tag{12}$$

where $R_i = \{v_1,\ldots,v_n\}$ is the set of variables in V_M that are linked to node i in the model, D_v is the set of nodes in V_D that are linked to node v in the data, and O_j is $\{0\}$ if $\text{opt}_M(i)$ and $\{\}$ otherwise. Although this disjunction can be partially evaluated before a search because the sizes of R_i and D_v are known, this partial evaluation noticeably reduces the disjunction only for nodes with many links (such as the torso in a stick figure). This extensional constraint can be implemented with propositonal constraints in SICStus Prolog clp(FD) [4] and posted with all other constraints before labeling search. However, our experience is that the overhead far outweighs any gains, and that this approach is more than an order of magnitude slower than our third approach. Furthermore, this approach wouldn't scale well with increasing data size. (Space doesn't allows us to include further details on these alternative implementations, but the differences in performance are quite significant.)

As our current approach, we have chosen a *concurrent constraint programming* formulation instead (implemented with coroutining in SICStus Prolog, but akin to cc(FD) [14]). In this version, all constraints and objectives except for the link support constraint are posted before labeling as usual in CLP(FD), while the link support constraint is encoded in a set of concurrent processes, one per model node. Each process waits until its node label x_i is determined and then constrains those nodes that are linked to it in the model graph to the corresponding linked nodes D_{xi} in the data graph as defined in constraint (5). The support sets D_{xi} are precomputed and then looked up when x_i is known. (Disjunction with backtracking chooses between the two alternative interpretations of ends e_i.) From a different point of view, this implements a task-specific constraint with its own propagation scheme in the context of CLP(FD).

The remaining constraints are straightforward to implement in a CLP(FD) language. (With SICStus Prolog clp(FD), the cardinality constraint is implemented using constraint reification and Boolean variables [4].)

Thus, following problem definition (1), our algorithm for subgraph matching has the following operational structure.

```
match(GM, GD, VM) ←
  precompute all Dxi from GD,
  spawn link support constraint processes for VM,
  post other constraints on VM,
  define objective function h(VM) from GM,
  labeling([ff,minimize(h(VM)], VM)
```

As already indicated, we believe that the link support constraint plays a crucial role in reducing the search tree: as soon as a node is labeled, its neighbors in the model graph are restricted to the small number of neighbors in the data graph, no matter how large the data graph. When used together with the "fail-first" (ff) heuristic, this leads to search trees that are broad at the top level but very narrow at lower levels. (With the "fail-first" heuristic, variables are labeled in order of increasing domain size.)

The processes for the link support constraints play an additional role in this approach: whenever a model node is labeled with a data node label, the corresponding attributes in the model graph are set from the corresponding attributes in the data graph. This concerns in particular length and coordinate attributes, which are used in constraints and objectives as shown, for example, in (10).

This is the algorithm used in the experiments of Section 4. We have also implemented a variant of this algorithm with a portion of (12) added as additional constraints, namely the upfront restriction of variables x_i to those values v where $|R_i| \leq |D_v|$. We have found that this reduces runtimes by an average of 30%.

4 Experiments and Results

Multiple Models and Distractors

We consider two primary scenarios for sketch interpretation: the data typically contains *multiple instances of multiple models*, and the data often contains *noise* such as spurious lines ("distractors"). In either case, the data will grow in the best case. In the worst case, new relations and thus often possible but senseless configurations are introduced. For example, Fig. 6a shows a figure with a distractor line that could be interpreted as an alternative head, as shown with the graph of Fig. 6b. Fig. 7a demonstrates even more dramatically that finding the original stick figure can be difficult even for the human eye if many distractor lines compete for interpretation. In general, such data can easily lead to missed solutions or false positives.

The matching algorithm typically has no problem correctly interpreting an isolated stick figure, even without the objective function (i.e., with all objective weights at 0). In order to correctly identify a stick figure in a noisy sketch environment as shown in Fig. 7a, the optimization is absolutely essential. For example, Fig. 8 displays the model instances found in Fig. 7a when no or only some of the objectives are turned on. All instances "make sense" as they match the model structure, but they wouldn't ordinarily be accepted as stick figures. Consequently, all objectives are turned on in our experiments, with objective weights set such that the minimal missing part count objective is the primary objective and the other two have about equal weight.

Implementation

The subgraph-matching algorithm described in Section 3 has been implemented in SICStus Prolog [3], using the clp(FD) library for constraint representation and search. The computer vision algorithms of the first stage of our approach are implemented in Java. All runtimes were recorded on a 600 MHz Pentium III PC and consist of the runtime of the subgraph matching algorithm plus the data conversion between Java and Prolog through the Jasper interface, but not the first stage (image analysis) execution nor any display routines.

Experiments

We have conducted a series of experiments to measure how the algorithm scales with an increasing number of distractor lines and with multiple model instances. The base group of drawings is a set of twenty stick figure drawings (as shown in the various figures of this paper), which cover a good range of variations in posture. In the first set of experiments, we added from 0 to 29 random, non-overlapping lines, each combination of drawing and random-line count repeated ten times. (Note that the data graph is increased from 14 to 43 nodes if no parts are missing, i.e., with 29 distractor lines, the number of nodes in the data graph is triple that of the model graph.) This resulted in a total of 300 runs per drawing, or 200 runs per random-line count, for a total of 6000 runs.

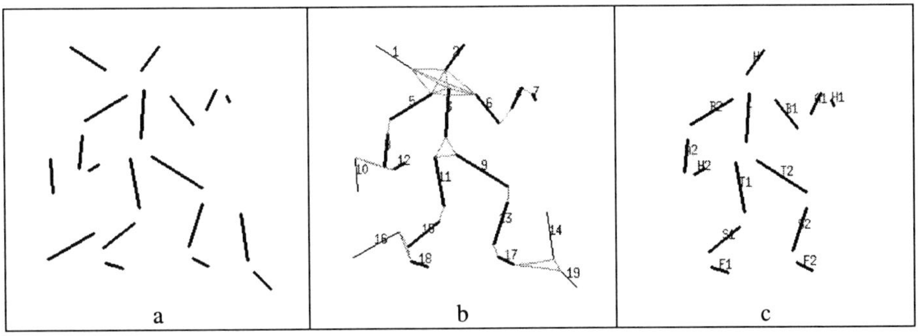

Fig. 6. A stick figure with five distractor lines (a), the corresponding graph with labels and links produced by the image analysis stage (b), and the interpretation found by the matching process (c), where labels in c are given by the model and denote Head, Torso, Biceps1, Arm1, Hand1, Thigh1, Shin1, Foot1, Biceps2, etc. Unlabeled lines are shown thinner in b) for illustrative purposes

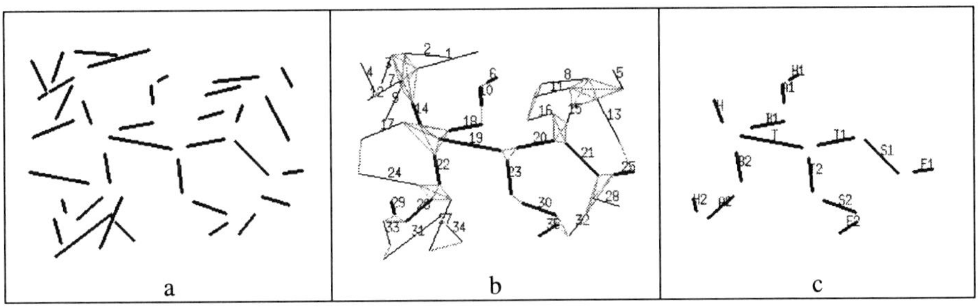

Fig. 7. A stick figure with 20 distractor lines (a), the corresponding graph with labels and links produced by the image analysis stage (b), and the interpretation found by the matching process (c), using the same notations as in Fig. 6

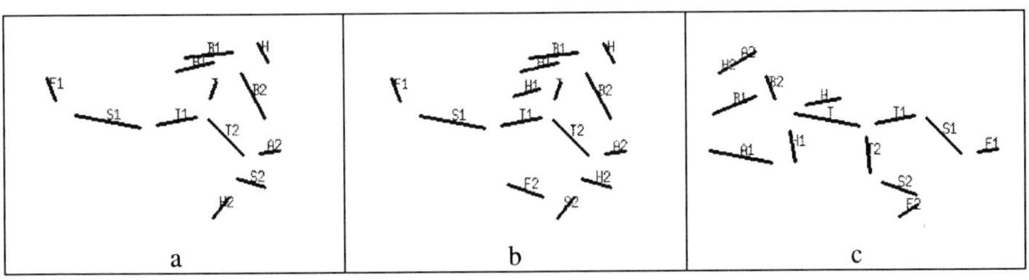

Fig. 8. Three stick figure instances found in the data of Fig. 7a with different objectives: a) without optimization, b) with minimal missing part count objective, c) with minimal missing part count and optimal part proportion objectives (all labels are the same as in Fig. 6)

Fig. 9a shows the runtimes of these experiments for an increasing number of random lines, averaged over the 20 drawings and 10 runs per drawing. (All times are in milliseconds.) Fig. 9b shows the corresponding average error rate. The unit of error is the number of line interpretations that mismatch with the base case (0 distractors).

For no or few distractors, runtimes are typically around 0.5 to 1 s. While an average of 20 s (for 27+ distractors) is long, the overall curve shows very slow growth in runtime, attesting to the effect of constraint propagation on search. Furthermore, realistic sketches contain no more than five to ten nearby distractors, for which the increases in runtime are barely noticeable. Note however the large standard deviation. Distractors sometimes lead to almost correct stick figures in the data, literally distracting the search algorithm from the real stick figure.

Similarly, it is not surprising that the number of errors increases with the number of distractors. Sometimes, a distractor line makes a "better" limb than one in the original drawing. Still, according to the data in Fig. 9b, the error rate appears to increase only linearly with the number of distractors for these experiments.

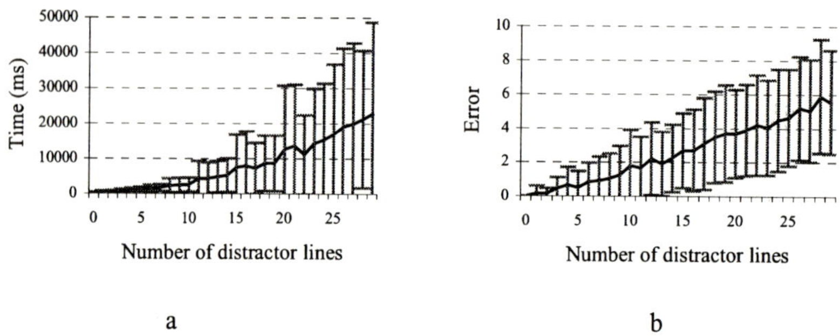

Fig. 9. a) Average runtimes to identify the stick figure in sketches with increasing numbers of random lines (0 through 29). b) Average errors in identifying the stick figure in the same runs. For each random-line-count, the standard deviation over 200 runs is shown as an error bar

We conducted a second series of experiments to measure how the algorithm scales with multiple model instances (and occasional distractors). Fig. 10 shows a sample sketch with three stick figures, its graph, and the identified model instances.

Fig. 11a shows the runtimes of these experiments for an increasing number of model instances, averaged over 10 cases. Fig. 11b shows the corresponding average error rate. The unit of error is the number of line interpretations that mismatch with the base case (component image by itself).

The runtimes appear to show exponential runtime growth in the data size. However, the average runtime for 5 instances (about 70 data nodes) is still only about as much as the average runtime for one instance plus 29 distractors in the previous experiment (about 43 data nodes). This is probably due to the fact that the model instances tend to have few interconnections with each other. Also, the error curve seems to follow a similar trend as in the first experiment. Above five instances, runtimes are unacceptable. Overall, these results show that our approach should give reasonable performance for data graphs of moderate size. For large data graphs, however, there clearly is a need for additional steps to focus the matching process on appropriate subsets of a scene.

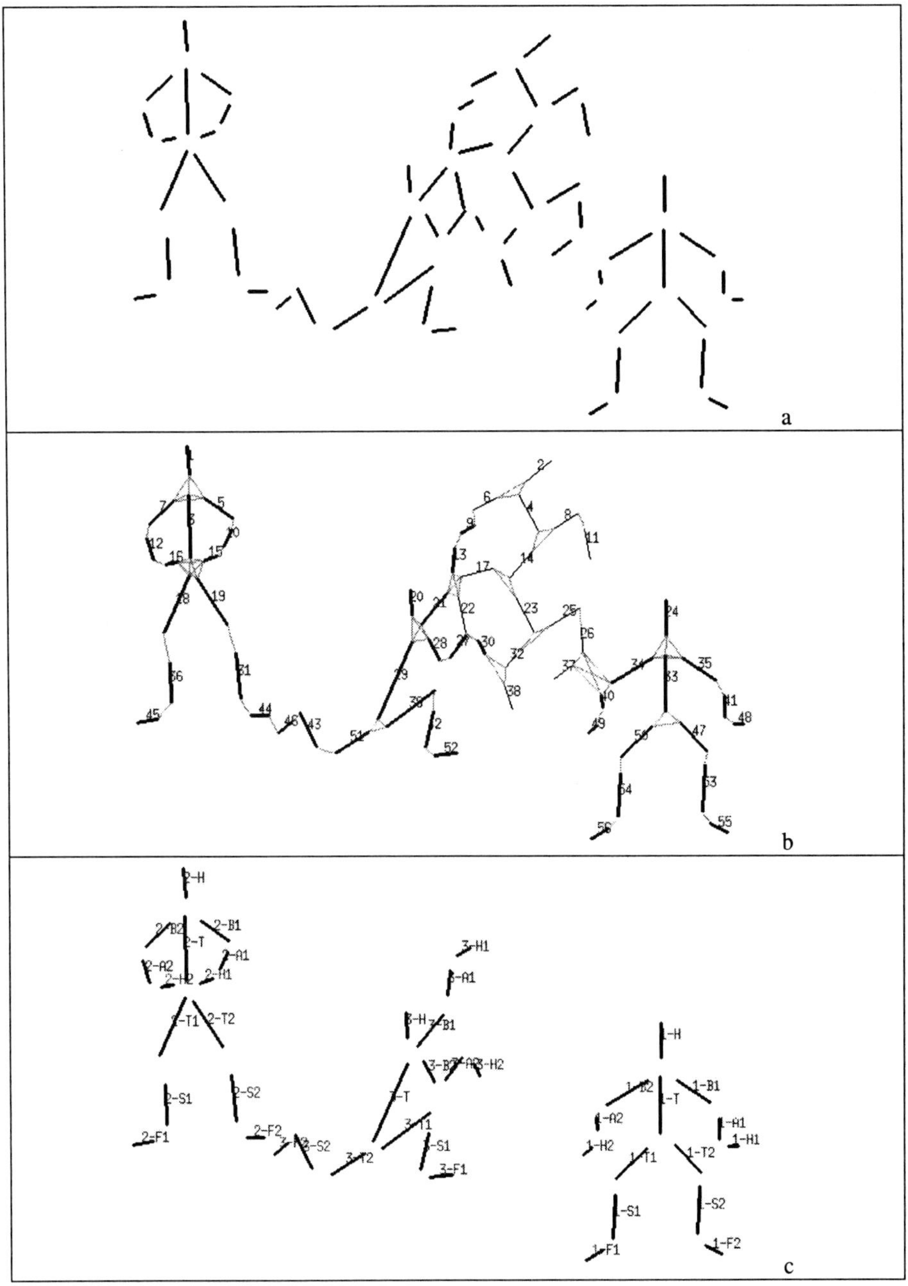

Fig. 10. Sketch with three stick figures and a distractor figure (a), the corresponding graph with labels and links produced by the image analysis stage (b), and the interpretation found by the matching process (c), using the same notations as in Fig. 6 (with labels preceded by an index)

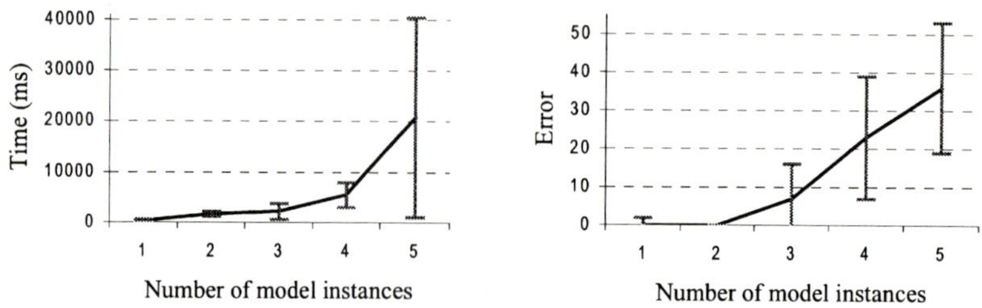

a b

Fig. 11. a) Average runtimes to find stick figures in sketches with increasing numbers of model instances (1 through 5). b) Average errors in finding the stick figure in the same runs. For each random-line-count, the standard deviation over 10 runs is shown as an error bar

5 Conclusions

We have described a two-stage approach to sketch interpretation that synergistically combines computer vision and optimal subgraph matching techniques. The subgraph-matching algorithm makes use of a generic constraint-based representation of the matching problem that takes into account generic graph-matching constraints as well as domain-specific and model-specific objectives. This approach enables a comprehensive way of modeling data and models for sketch interpretation by providing graph representation, graph attributes, and the specification of attribute constraints and objectives in a single environment. This enables a reliable identification of model image even in noisy and larger data images.

The implementation of the subgraph-matching algorithm uses a combination of built-in and special-purpose constraints linked into standard constraint-based search. Our experiments indicate that this combination is very effective and scales reasonably well with increasing numbers of distractors and model instances in the data image. The link support constraints, the fail-first heuristic, and the optimization of part proportions appear to be the most important factors in efficient and robust matching.

A promising but unexplored next step in this work is to use constraints such as the link support constraint not only in propagation, but also as a heuristic in variable value enumeration. Longer term, our work will focus on making the approach more reliable and efficient for sketches with multiple model instances, and we will extend this work to matching with multiple models.

References

1. D. Bainbridge and T. Bell, "An extensible optical music recognition system." In *Proc. Nineteenth Australasian Computer Science Conf.*, 1996.
2. J. R. Beverdige and E. M. Riseman, "How easy is matching 2D line models using local search?" In *IEEE Transactions on Pattern Analysis and Machine Intelligence*, vol. 19, no. 6, June 1997, pp. 564-579.
3. M. Carlsson et al., *SICStus Prolog User's Manual*. Swedish Institute of Computer Science, SICStus Prolog version 3.8.6, 2001.

4. M. Carlsson, G. Ottosson, and B. Carlson, "An open-ended finite domain constraint solver". In *Proc. Programming Languages: Implementations, Logics, and Programs*, 1997.
5. S. S. Chok and K. Marriott, "Parsing visual languages." In Proc. Eighteenth Australasian Computer Science Conf., vol. 27, no. 1, 1995, pp. 90-98.
6. B. Coüasnon, P. Brisset, and I. Stéphan, "Using logic programming languages for optical music recognition." In *Proc. Third Int. Conf. on the Practical Application of Prolog*, Paris, April 1995.
7. D. Eppstein, "Subgraph isomorphism in planar graphs and related problems." In *Journal of Graph Algorithms and Applications*, vol. 3, no. 3, 1999, pp. 1-27.
8. J. Larrosa and G. Valiente, "Constraint satisfaction algorithms for graph pattern matching." Under consideration for publication in *J. Math. Struct. in Computer Science*, 2001.
9. J. V. Mahoney and M. P.J. Fromherz, "Interpreting sloppy stick figures by graph normalization and constraint-based matching." In *Proc. Fourth IAPR Int. Workshop on Graphics Recognition*, Kingston, Ontario, Canada, Sept. 2001.
10. J. V. Mahoney and M. P.J. Fromherz, "Perceptual organization as graph rectification in a constraint-based scheme for interpreting sloppy stick figures." In *Proc. Third Workshop on Perceptual Organization in Computer Vision*, Vancouver, Canada, July 2001.
11. B. Messmer, *Efficient graph matching algorithms for preprocessed model graphs*. PhD Thesis, Univ. of Bern, Switzerland, 1995.
12. L. G. Shapiro and R. M. Haralick, "Structural descriptions and inexact matching." In *IEEE Transactions on Pattern Analysis and Machine Intelligence*, vol. PAMI-3, no. 5, Sept. 1981, pp. 504-519.
13. P. van Hentenryck and Y. Deville, "The cardinality operator: A new logical connective and its application to constraint logic programming." In *Proc. Int. Conf. on Logic Programming*, 1991, pp. 745-759.
14. P. van Hentenryck, V. A. Saraswat, and Y. Deville, "Design, implementation, and evaluation of the constraint language cc(FD)." In A. Podelski (ed.), *Constraint Programming: Basic and Trends*, LNCS 910, Springer Verlag, 1995, pp. 293-316.
15. D. Waltz, "Understanding Line Drawings of Scenes with Shadows." In P. H. Winston (ed.), *Psychology of Computer Vision*, MIP Press, 1975, pp. 19-91.

Selecting and Scheduling Observations for Agile Satellites: Some Lessons from the Constraint Reasoning Community Point of View

Gérard Verfaillie and Michel Lemaître

ONERA, Center of Toulouse
2 avenue Édouard Belin, BP 4025, 31055 Toulouse Cedex 4, France
{Gerard.Verfaillie,Michel.Lemaitre}@cert.fr
http://www.cert.fr/dcsd/cd/THEMES/oc.html

Abstract. This paper presents some lessons that can be drawn, from the point of view of the *constraint reasoning* and *constraint programming* community, from trying to model and to solve as best as possible the *mission management* problem for the new generation of *agile* Earth observation satellites, that is the *selection* and the *scheduling* of observations performed by the satellite.

1 Introduction

The mission management problem for the current generation of Earth observation satellites, like those of the French *Spot* family, has been already presented [3]. Various methods, able to solve it either optimally or approximately, have been proposed and compared [4,3,14].

This paper is devoted to the mission management problem for the new generation of *agile* Earth observation satellites, like the already operational American *Ikonos* satellite and those of the future French *Pléiades* family.

The main difference between both these generations of satellites lies on the *degrees of freedom* that are available for image acquisition. Whereas the non-agile *Spot* satellites have only *one* degree of freedom, along the roll axis, provided by a mobile mirror in front of each instrument, the agile *Pléiades* satellites will have *three* degrees of freedom, along the roll, pitch, and yaw axes, provided by the attitude control system of the whole satellite. Whereas there is, with the *Spot* satellites, only *one* way of acquiring an image of a given area on the Earth surface from a satellite revolution, there will be, with the *Pléiades* satellites, an *infinite* number of ways of acquiring it from a satellite revolution, because the *starting time* and the *azimuth* of image acquisition will be free.

The first consequence of this greater freedom is an expected better *efficiency* of the whole imaging system. The second one is a far larger *space* (in fact infinite) of imaging opportunities, and consequently a far greater *complexity* of the management problem.

In this paper, we describe the *mission management* problem for agile Earth observation satellites, as it has been stated by the *CNES*[1] managers of the

[1] French space agency: http://www.cnes.fr.

T. Walsh (Ed.): CP 2001, LNCS 2239, pp. 670–684, 2001.

Pléiades project (Section 2). Then, we describe the *simplifications* we had to do in order to get a manageable problem (Section 3). We show how this simplified problem can be *mathematically* stated (Section 4) and describe the four *algorithms* or *approaches* we designed, implemented and experimented for solving it (Section 5). We show and discuss the *experimental* results that have been obtained on training instances provided by the *CNES* (Section 6). We conclude with some *lessons* that we drew from this study and that deserve, in our opinion, discussion in the *constraint reasoning* and *constraint programming* community (Section 7).

2 Problem Description

Satellite orbit. Earth observation satellites use specific orbits that are:

- *quasi polar*: the satellite orbital plane passes nearly through the Earth north and south poles; the conjunction of a quasi polar orbit with the natural Earth movement around its polar axis allows the whole Earth surface to be flown by the satellite each day (see Figure 1);
- *circular*; this implies a constant image acquisition altitude;
- *heliosynchronous*: the angle between the satellite orbital plane and the Earth-Sun axis remains constant during the whole year; this implies constant Earth illumination conditions for image acquisition; note that the satellite can only acquire images during the illuminated part of each revolution;
- *phased*: after a given number of revolutions, the satellite goes back exactly at the same position with respect to Earth.

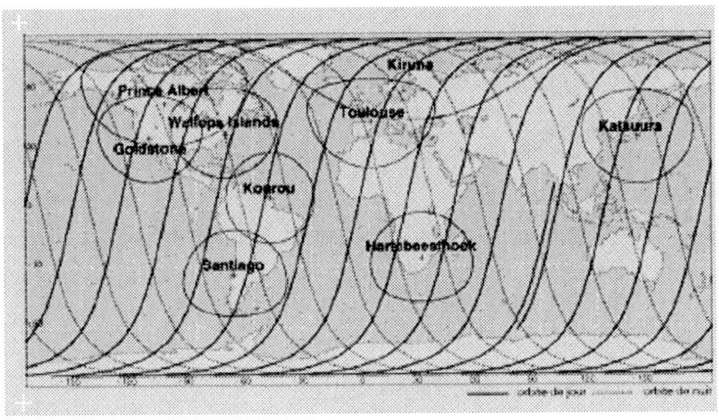

Fig. 1. The track of the satellite on the Earth surface during one day.

Image acquisition degrees of freedom. The satellite is compactly built around one *optical instrument*. At any time, it is moving on its orbit and can simultaneously move around its roll, pitch and yaw axes, thanks to its *attitude control* system.

The core of the instrument is made up of a set of aligned photo-diodes that allow at any time a *segment* on the Earth surface to be acquired as a set of aligned pixels. The combined translation and rotation movements of the satellite allow then an *image* to be acquired as a set of contiguous segments (see Figure 2).

To simplify their processing, these images are constrained to be rectangular *strips*. Although the *width* of these strips actually depends on the acquisition angle, we consider that it is fixed and equal to its minimum value (obtained exactly under the satellite orbit). Their *length* and their *direction* (from 0 to 180 degrees) are however free.

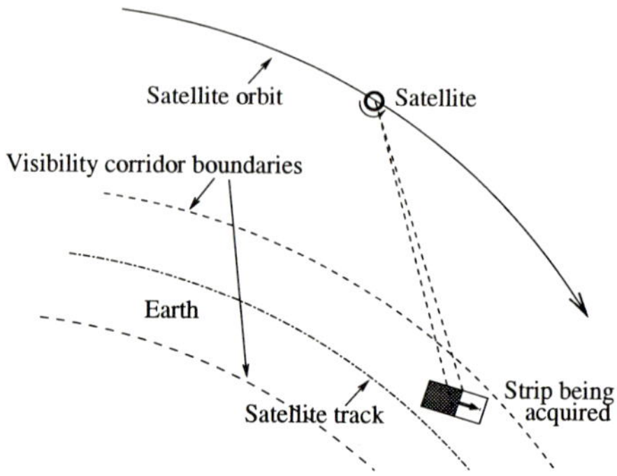

Fig. 2. Acquisition of a rectangular strip.

User requests. Observation requests can be submitted by users at any time. Each of these requests is defined by:

- a *target area*, which can be, either a *spot* (a small circular area), or a *polygon* (a large polygonal area);
- a *validity period*, outside of which its acquisition has no utility (usually specified in days);
- a set of *acquisition angular constraints* (minimum and maximum roll and pitch angles);
- a *type*, which can be either *mono* or *stereo*; in case of a *stereoscopic* request, an associated selected strip must be acquired twice during the same illuminated half-revolution, by satisfying specified acquisition angular constraints and by using the same azimuth;
- a *weight*, which expresses its importance.

From requests to images. A *spot* can be covered by one strip of any direction. It is not the case with *polygons* that generally need several strips to be covered. The strips associated with a polygon can be acquired from several successive illuminated half-revolutions.

Note that any strip can be acquired using either of the two associated opposite *azimuths* (azimuths range from 0 to 360 degrees). We call an *image* the association between a strip and an acquisition azimuth. Two potential images are thus associated with any strip.

Acquisition and transition constraints. For each illuminated half-revolution h and for each candidate image i, the acquisition angular constraints allows us to determine whether or not i can be acquired from h and, in case of positive answer, the *earliest* and *latest* acquisition *starting time* of i. As the acquisition *speed* is constant, the acquisition *duration* of any image is proportional to its length.

For each illuminated half-revolution h and for each pair of candidate images i and j, a minimum *transition time* between the end of the acquisition of i and the beginning of the acquisition of j can be computed, taking into account the movement of the satellite on its orbit and its attitude manoeuvering capabilities. Note that this transition time depends on the time at which the transition begins, that is on the time at which the acquisition of i begins. Note also that the computation of this transition time implies itself to solve a complex *continuous* constrained optimization problem, that has no analytical solution and may be very time consuming, since the best algorithms in terms of solution quality may need a half hour of computing.

Energy consumption. As satellite attitude manoeuvres are *energy* consuming and as this energy is limited on board, this limitation must be taken into account. Note that, because solar panels are firmly attached to the satellite, in order to limit vibrations and to increase agility, energy production and image acquisition may be conflicting tasks (the attitude positions needed for image acquisition may imply that the solar panels are no more well oriented towards the sun).

Data recording and downloading. Images must be not only acquired. The resulting data must be *recorded* on board and *downloaded* to any appropriate station on the ground. Consequently, the limitation of the *on board recorders*, the *visibility windows* between the satellite and the stations on the ground, and the limitation of the *data flow* between the satellite and the ground must be taken into account too. Note also a possible conflict between data downloading and image acquisition.

Acquisition uncertainties. Because of the optical nature of the instrument, the presence of *clouds* can decrease the quality of an acquired image and even invalidate it. As an absence of clouds over a given area cannot be guaranteed a long time in advance, it is never sure that a planned image acquisition will be successful.

Optimization criterion. Although other criteria could be meaningful, the chosen criterion is the *sum* (or the *expected sum* to take into account uncertainties) of the *gains* associated with the *satisfied requests*, that is an *utilitarist* criterion. In a first time, it can be considered that the gain associated with a satisfied request equals its *weight*. But, whereas *spot* acquisition requests are either satisfied or not, *polygon* acquisition requests may be only partially satisfied. Consequently, two criteria have been considered:

- a first, called *linear*, where the gain associated with a completely satisfied request equals its weight and where the one associated with a partially satisfied request is proportional to the useful acquired surface;

- a second, called *non linear*, where the gain associated with a completely satisfied request is the same, but the one associated with a partially satisfied request is the result of the application of a *convex* function to the useful acquired surface.

The advantage of the non linear criterion is to favour the *termination* of already partially acquired polygons.

Mission management organization. It is assumed that the selection and the scheduling of the images that will be acquired by the satellite is done *each day* for the following day, taking into account the current *set of user requests*, the current *state of the satellite*, and the currently available *meteorological forecasts.*

As each illuminated half-revolution defines a nearly independent subproblem, we consider that the basic problem to solve is a selection and scheduling problem on *one illuminated half-revolution.*

Selection and scheduling are done *on the ground*, under the supervision of human operators. When an acquisition plan has been built, the associated set of commands is uploaded to the satellite. When this plan has been executed, the associated data are analyzed by human operators and the strips associated with validated images are withdrawn from the set of user requests.

This kind of organization can be characterized as a regular *off-line on the ground* mission management organization. Others *on-line*, eventually *on board*, more *reactive* organizations could be considered, but are out of the scope of this paper.

3 Problem Simplifications

In order to get a manageable problem, we must simplify substantially the previously described problem. The successive simplifications we did are the following.

Image acquisition degrees of freedom. In addition to the assumption of a fixed strip *width*, we made the assumption of a fixed *direction*. Such an assumption may seem strange in the context of an agile satellite, because it removes in fact one of the three degrees of freedom. Is is however justified by the results of simulations which showed that the satellite attitude movements around the yaw axis, required to vary the acquisition direction, are very costly in terms of transition time and are not compensated by a greater freedom of acquisition of either spots or polygons. This fixed direction can be however freely chosen.

From requests to images. As a consequence of the previous assumption of a fixed acquisition direction, all the *spots* are acquired using this direction and all the *polygons* are cut up along the same direction. For each polygon, this cutting up is performed once and for all before selection and scheduling and an *offset* is chosen such that the useless acquired surface is minimized.

Acquisition and transition constraints. We assume that the transition time between two image acquisitions does not depend on the time at which the transition begins. Moreover, in order to bypass the complexity of the computing of this minimum transition time, we pre-compute a *table* of minimum transition times using a reasonable discretization of the parameter space, that we exploit using simple *linear interpolations.*

Energy consumption, data recording, and downloading. For the moment, we do not consider the constraints related to the energy, memory, visibility, and data flow limitations.

Acquisition uncertainties. In order to take into account the acquisition uncertainties, as well as the remaining acquisition opportunities from other satellite revolutions, we use an approach inspired from [15], which defines a rational way of modifying the weight that is associated with each request and used by the selection and scheduling process. Roughly speaking, this modification favours the requests the acquisition certainty of which is high from this revolution and the number of remaining acquisition opportunities from other revolutions is low.

Optimization criterion. For the *non linear* criterion, we use a *piecewise linear* convex function.

4 Problem Mathematical Statement

The problem resulting from these simplifications, we call *SRSS* for *Satellite Revolution Selection and Scheduling*, can be mathematically stated as follows.

Data. Let R be the set of *requests* that can be acquired, at least partially, from the considered illuminated half-revolution. For each $r \in R$, let W_r be its weight and A_r be its surface (multiplied by two in case of a stereoscopic request).

Let I be the set of potential *images*, associated with R. For each $i \in I$, let r_i be its associated request, E_i be its earliest starting time, L_i be its latest starting time, D_i be its duration, A_i be its useful surface, and $W_i = W_{r_i} \cdot \frac{A_i}{A_{r_i}}$ be its weight.

For each pair of images $(i, j) \in I \times I$, let M_{ij} be the minimum transition time between i and j. Let $B \subseteq I \times I$ be the set of *pairs of images* (i, j), such that i and j are images of the same strip, using opposite azimuths. Let $S \subseteq I \times I$ be the set of *pairs of images* (i, j), such that i and j are the two elements of a *stereoscopic* image of the same strip, using thus the same azimuth.

Decision variables. We need three sets of *decision variables*: the first for the *selection*, the second for the *scheduling* of the selected images, and the third for the acquisition *starting times* of the selected images.

For each $i \in I$, let x_i be equal to 1 if the image i is selected, and to 0 otherwise. For each pair $(i, j) \in I \times I$, let f_{ij} be equal to 1 if the image i is followed by the image j in the chosen sequence, and to 0 otherwise. For each $i \in I$, let t_i be the starting time of the the image i, if it is selected.

Constraints. Let o be a fictitious image, used to begin and end the chosen sequence, and $I^+ = I \cup \{o\}$.

The constraints that define the feasible selections and sequences are the following:

$$\forall i \in I : (x_i = 1) \Rightarrow (E_i \leq t_i \leq L_i) \tag{1}$$
$$\forall (i,j) \in I \times I : (f_{ij} = 1) \Rightarrow (t_i + D_i + M_{ij} \leq t_j) \tag{2}$$
$$\forall (i,j) \in B : x_i + x_j \leq 1 \tag{3}$$
$$\forall (i,j) \in S : x_i = x_j \tag{4}$$
$$x_o = 1 \tag{5}$$
$$\forall i \in I^+ : \sum_{j \in I+} f_{ij} = \sum_{j \in I+} f_{ji} = x_i \tag{6}$$

The constraints 1 and 2 are *temporal constraints*, associated with the acquisition angular constraints and the minimum transition time constraints. The constraints 3 state that only one image per strip is needed. The constraints 4 state that the two elements of a stereoscopic image are needed. The constraints 6 state that the variables x_i and f_{ij} actually define a sequence of selected images.

Criterion. Whereas the *linear* criterion Q_l can be defined as follows:

$$Q_l = \sum_{i \in I} W_i \cdot x_i = \sum_{i \in I} W_{r_i} \cdot \frac{A_i}{A_{r_i}} \cdot x_i \tag{7}$$

the *non linear* criterion Q_{nl} can be defined as follows:

$$Q_{nl} = \sum_{r \in R} W_r \cdot P(\sum_{i \in I | r_i = r} \frac{A_i}{A_r} \cdot x_i) \tag{8}$$

where P is a *piecewise linear* convex function, defined on $[0,1]$ and such that $P(0) = 0$ and $P(1) = 1$. Note that both criteria are equivalent when $\forall x \in [0,1], P(x) = x$.

Problem analysis. Apart from the constraints 3 and 4, and the non linear criterion, *SRSS* has the classic form of a *selection* and *scheduling* problem. In fact, it is close to well known problems like:

- the *Traveling Salesman* problem [6,10], at which temporal constraints would be added and where the goal would be no more to visit all the cities by minimizing the travel distance, but to maximize the sum of the weights of the visited cities;
- the *Job Shop* and *Open Shop Scheduling* problems [6], where the goal would be no more to complete all the jobs in a minimum time, but to maximize the sum of the weights of the completed jobs;
- the *Knapsack* problem [6], where the usual linear capacity constraints would be replaced by temporal constraints.

It can be established that, like these problems, *SRSS* is *NP-hard.* This implies in practice that any algorithm able to solve it to optimality may need in the worst case a computation time that grows exponentially with the size of the instance to be solved.

It may be interesting to look at it as the combination of three subproblems: *selection*, *scheduling*, and *temporal assignment.* Indeed, whereas the *selection* and *scheduling* subproblems are hard, the *temporal assignment* subproblem, that is the problem of deciding if a specified sequence of images can be achieved or not, is *polynomial* and can be solved by a simple *propagation* on the earliest and latest starting times associated with each image (in fact, by enforcing *arc consistency*). This observation will be used by the *local search* algorithm (see Section 5.4). Note also that the optimization criterion only depends on the *selection* choices, and does not depend on the *scheduling* and *temporal assignment* choices.

It can be also noted that, provided that the *time* has been *discretized*, a *weighted acyclic directed graph* can be associated with any instance of *SRSS.* In this graph, a *vertex* is associated with any pair (i, t), where $i \in I$ is a candidate image and t a possible acquisition starting time for i ($E_i \leq t \leq L_i$, equations 1). A *directed edge* exists between two vertices (i, t) and (j, t') iff $i \neq j$ and the acquisition of i starting at time t can be followed by the acquisition of j starting at time t' ($t + D_i + M_{ij} \leq t'$, equations 2). This temporal constraint prevents the presence of cycles. The *weight* associated with each directed edge is the weight W_i of the image i associated with its origin. Assuming a *linear* optimization criterion (equation 7), looking for an optimal solution for an *SRSS* instance is equivalent to looking for a *longest path* in the associated graph, that does not involve two vertices associated with the same image (equations 3), and that involves the two vertices associated with the two elements of a stereoscopic image each time it involves one of them (equations 4). This observation will be used by the *dynamic programming* algorithm (see Section 5.2).

5 Four Solving Algorithms

First, it can be observed that, in case of a *linear* optimization criterion, the problem mathematical statement presented in the previous section defines a *mixed integer programming* problem, that suggests the use of dedicated tools. Unfortunately the use of *CPLEX*, one of the most powerful *Integer Programming* tools, provided us with poor results : only very small instances (no more than twenty candidate images) could be deal with. So, this way has been given up. Four other ways have been then explored :

- a *greedy* algorithm (*GA*);
- a *dynamic programming* algorithm (*DPA*);
- a *constraint programming* approach (*CPA*);
- a *local search* algorithm (*LSA*).

The first two (*GA* and *DPA*) are limited to a *linear* optimization criterion (equation 7) and do not take into account the *stereoscopic* acquisition constraints (equations 4). The last two (*CPA* and *LSA*) are not limited and take into account the whole set of constraints.

5.1 A Greedy Algorithm

The *greedy* algorithm we considered imitates the behavior of an on-line mission management system that, in parallel with image acquisition, would be wondering what next image to acquire. It starts with an empty sequence of images. At each step, it chooses an image to be added at the end of the current sequence and repeats this until no image can be added.

At each step, the chosen image is one of the images that is not present in the current sequence yet, can follow the last image of the current sequence, and maximizes a criterion that is an *approximation* of the gain that is possible to get by making this choice. When the chosen image is added at the end of the current sequence, the temporal constraints are propagated.

If $\hat{G}$ is an approximation of the problem optimum, $E = min_{i \in I} E_i$ and $L = max_{i \in I} L_i$, and T_i is the earliest ending time of i, if it would be added at the end of the current sequence, the chosen criterion is:

$$W_i + \hat{G} \cdot \frac{L - T_i}{L - E} \tag{9}$$

The first part of the criterion measures the immediate gain resulting of the choice of i. The second part is approximation of the gain that it would be possible to obtain later. This later gain is assumed to be proportional to the remaining time. As the problem optimum is not known, it is possible to start with any approximation, to run the greedy algorithm, to use its result as a better approximation, and so on.

A non linear optimization criterion (equation 8), as well as stereoscopic acquisition constraints (equations 4), which both link images that are set anywhere in the sequence, cannot be easily taken into account by such a sequential decision process.

5.2 A Dynamic Programming Algorithm

The *dynamic programming* algorithm uses the observation, done in Section 4, of the possible transformation of *SRSS* into a *longest path* problem in a *weighted acyclic directed graph*, obtained thanks to a *time discretization* and under the assumption of a *linear* optimization criterion. But, to obtain a purely longest path problem, *polynomially* solvable, it is necessary to remove the constraints 3 and 4.

Assuming that the stereoscopic acquisition constraints 4 have been anyway removed, a way of removing the constraints 3 consists in *ordering* the set of candidate images and in imposing that the chosen sequence respects this order, which comes down to deciding about the *scheduling* subproblem. Indeed, if we remove now from the graph all the edges the destination vertex of which precedes its origin vertex in the chosen order, the constraints 3 will be necessarily met by any path.

In the general case, it may be difficult to find a pertinent order. But, *natural* orders may be exhibited in our specific problem: either a *temporal* order according to the middle of the temporal window associated with any image, or a *geographical* order according to the latitude of the middle of the strip associated with any image. In both cases, the idea is to prevent the satellite to turn its instrument backwards thanks to its attitude control system while going forwards on its orbit, because this kind of movement may be considered to be generally inefficient.

The *dynamic programming* algorithm we designed is only an efficient way of looking for such a longest path. It explores the images in the inverse order of the chosen order, and the possible starting times in the inverse order of the natural order. For each pair (i, t), it computes the maximum gain $G^*(i, t)$ that it is possible to obtain by acquiring i and starting this acquisition at time t. For that, it uses the following equation [2]:

$$G^*(i,t) = max_{(j,t')|c(i,t,j,t')}[W_i + G^*(j,t')] \qquad (10)$$

where $c(i, t, j, t')$ holds iff there is an edge between (i, t) and (j, t'), that is iff $i \neq j$ and the acquisition of i starting at time t can be followed by the acquisition of j starting at time t' ($t + D_i + M_{ij} \leq t'$, equations 2). Doing that, it records the pair (j, t') (in fact, one of these) associated with $G^*(i, t)$. Moreover, it takes advantage of the following monotonicity property:

$$\forall i, t, t' : t < t' \Rightarrow G^*(i,t') \leq G^*(i,t) \qquad (11)$$

which states that starting later cannot improve the gain.

As the *greedy* algorithm and for the same reasons, this *dynamic programming* algorithm can easily take into account, neither the non linear optimization criterion (equation 8), nor the stereoscopic acquisition constraints (equations 4). For example, taking into account stereoscopic acquisition constraints would induce time and memory requirements growing exponentially with the number of stereoscopic images.

5.3 A Constraint Programming Approach

Constraint programming is neither an algorithm nor a family of algorithms. It is first a *modelling framework*, which uses the basic notions of *variables* and *constraints* and to which many various generic algorithms can be applied.

For solving our problem, we could have used any basic *constraint reasoning* or *constraint programming* tool, provided by software companies, research centers, or academic teams, like our own tools[2]. We decided to use *OPL* [8], firstly because it is a nice high level *modelling* tool, and secondly because it can call and combine *constraint programming* and *integer linear programming*.

OPL allowed us to build various models of *SRSS*, all of them more compact than the linear one described in Section 4. The model we finally chose deals with a restriction of *SRSS*, which consists in finding a feasible optimal sequence of images of a *fixed length*. We start with a length equal to 2 and increase this

[2] See ftp://ftp.cert.fr/pub/lemaitre/LVCSP/.

length at each step, until no feasible sequence can be found. The largest optimal found sequence is an optimal solution of *SRSS*.

Unfortunately, even with this approach, the first results, obtained within a limited time, were very poor in terms of quality. Neither the use of pertinent heuristics for the variable and value orderings, nor the use of non standard search strategies like *Limited Discrepancy* [7], improve them significantly.

The only way we found to obtain better results with this approach was to add *constraints* that are not redundant, and thus may decrease the problem optimum, but are chosen in such a way that we can hope that the loss in terms of quality will not be too high. The constraints we added are the following :

- images the *weight* of which is too low are removed from the set of candidate images;
- each image is constrained to appear only in a specified *sub-sequence* of the whole sequence; for example, an image the associated strip of which is located near the equator will not appear at the beginning of the sequence;
- although the considered sequences can follow an *order* that is different from the natural temporal or geographical order (discussed in Section 5.2 and used by the *dynamic programming* algorithm), the amplitude of a *backtrack* with respect to this order is limited;
- at each step of the algorithm, the considered sequences are constrained to involve all the images that are involved in the sequence that has been chosen at the previous step (not necessarily in the same order).

Adding these constraints allows us to obtain reasonable quality results on all the instances whatever their size.

5.4 A Local Search Algorithm

Local search algorithms, like *hill-climbing search*, *simulated annealing*, *tabu search*, or *genetic algorithms* [1], are known to be applicable each time one wants to find within a limited time reasonable quality solutions to large constrained optimization problems.

Rather than using generic algorithms, we designed a simple *specific* algorithm dedicated to our problem. This algorithm defines a local search through the set of the *feasible* sequences of images. It starts with an empty sequence and stops when a specified time limit is reached.

At each step, it chooses one action among two possible ones: either to *add* an image to the current sequence, or to *remove* an image from it. The choice between both these actions is random and made according to a dynamically evolving probability. The result of an image adding may be either a success or a failure. In case of success (resp. failure), the adding probability is increased (resp. decreased). On the other hand, an image removal is always successful and does not modify the adding probability.

In both cases (adding or removal), an image is chosen to be added or removed. This choice is random, with a probability to be added (resp. removed) that is proportional (resp. inversely proportional) to its *weight*. In case of image adding, the choice of the position in the sequence is random, with a uniform probability among all the alternatives.

To determine if adding an image at a specified position is possible or not, and to update the time windows associated with each image in the current sequence when adding or removing an image, temporal constraint propagation mechanisms are used (see Section 4).

6 Experimental Results

We compared the performances of these four approaches, by running the associated algorithms on six instances we chose among a set of training instances provided by the *CNES*, as being representative of this set.

For each instance and each algorithm, the computation time was limited to two minutes, expect for *LSA* that was running one hundred times, two minutes each time, because of its stochastic behavior. Within this time, *GA* and *DPA* terminated, *CPA* was stopped before termination, and *LSA*, which cannot terminate naturally, simply stopped after two minutes. Results were compared in terms of quality (quality of the best solution found after two minutes).

A first experiment, involving the four algorithms (*GA*, *DPA*, *CPA*, and *LSA*), was carried out. In this experiment, the optimization criterion was linear and the stereoscopic requests dealt with as if they were unrelated (the stereoscopic constraints 4 were ignored). Results are presented in Table 1. Despite of its restriction to a predefined image sequencing, *DPA* produces systematically the best results.

Unfortunately, the best two algorithms from this first experiment (*DPA* and *GA*) cannot deal with a non linear optimization criterion and with stereoscopic constraints.

A second experiment, involving only the two other algorithms (*CPA* and *LSA*), was carried out. In this experiment, the optimization criterion was non linear and the stereoscopic requests correctly dealt with. Results are presented in Table 2. *LSA* produces systematically the best results.

In both tables, a row is associated with each instance. The instance number appears in the first column, the number of involved strips in the second column, the results, in terms of quality, provided by *GA*, *DPA*, *CPA*, and *LSA*, in the last four columns. For *LSA*, average and maximum results over the hundred trials are provided. For each instance, the best results are displayed in bold.

7 Lessons

We conclude with some lessons we drew from this study and choose to present along the four considered algorithms. It is however important to stress that, because many mistakes may be done while modelling a problem, designing and implementing an algorithm, using a tool, carrying out experiments ... these lessons cannot be considered as being universal and definitive truths. They are presented here to stimulate discussions in the *constraint reasoning* and *constraint programming* community.

Table 1. First experiment: linear optimization criterion, stereoscopic constraints ignored.

instance id	# strips	GA	DPA	CPA	LSA av. (max.)
2:13_111	106	532	**603**	442	574 (587)
2:15_170	295	707	**843**	527	723 (779)
2:26_96	483	831	**1022**	782	826 (877)
2:27_22	534	895	**1028**	777	800 (861)
3:25_22	342	436	**482**	253	345 (375)
4:17_186	147	188	**204**	177	192 (196)

Table 2. Second experiment: non linear optimization criterion, stereoscopic constraints dealt with.

instance id	# strips	CPA	LSA av. (max.)
2:13_111	106	241	**414** (490)
2:15_170	295	350	**446** (490)
2:26_96	483	439	**516** (592)
2:27_22	534	410	**455** (561)
3:25_22	342	149	**255** (298)
4:17_186	147	125	**145** (156)

Greedy algorithm. It is confirmed that *greedy* algorithms are always the first available solution when facing a large complex constrained optimization problem. They are easy to implement, generally require little computation time, and produce reasonable quality solutions. The one we considered can be seen as a degraded version of the *dynamic programming* algorithm. But other greedy algorithms could have been considered, based on other *variable* and *value heuristics.*

Dynamic programming algorithm. When applicable, that is when the number p of subproblems to consider is not too high, *dynamic programming* is clearly the best solution. It is easy to implement, requires a computation time and a memory that are proportional to p, and produces optimal solutions. As shown in [5], its applicability depends widely on the structure of a graph associated with each problem instance (the *induced width* of the *macro-structure* graph in the *CSP* framework). Is is however important to note that, if p grows exponentially with the problem size, both computation time and memory requirements of *dynamic programming* grow the same way. To bypass this difficulty, hybridizations between *dynamic programming* and *tree search*, as it is for example proposed in [9], deserve certainly more attention in the *constraint reasoning* community.

Constraint programming approach. *Constraint programming* offers clearly very nice modelling frameworks: various types of constraints can be expressed in an elegant way, various models of a problem can be explored by adding or removing constraints. Difficulties arise with the solving methods, that are currently limited to *constraint propagation* and *tree search.*

For our problem, *local constraint propagation* mechanisms are clearly not powerful enough. We think that there are at least two reasons for that: firstly, although powerful specific propagation rules are available for *scheduling* problems, these rules are not applicable as long as *selection* decisions have not been made; the same phenomenon occurs when one goes from the *CSP* framework to the *Max-CSP* framework: basic *arc consistency* algorithms do not work anymore [12]; secondly, even when these *selection* decisions have been made, the time windows associated with each image are too large with regard to the duration of each image to allow propagation mechanisms to deduce any *scheduling* constraint. As it is well known, *depth-first tree search* mechanisms do not succeed to improve quickly the first *greedy* solution and exhibit a poor *anytime* behavior.

On the other hand, adding constraints to the problem statement, allowed us to obtain reasonable quality results. It is known in the constraint community, that adding *redundant* constraints, that is constraints that are satisfied in all the problem solutions, helps the search (this is what is done by the *constraint propagation* mechanisms). In constrained optimization problems, an interesting way of helping the search consists in adding *non redundant* constraints, that is constraints that are not satisfied in all the problem solutions, but in all the optimal solutions, or at least in some of them, and thus do not decrease the problem optimum, or decrease it at least as possible. It is in fact what has been done with success with the *dynamic programming* algorithm: discretizing the time and adding sequencing constraints result in that case in a *polynomial* problem, solvable by a *dynamic programming* approach.

Local search algorithm. *Local search* mechanisms are widely applicable, because they only require the ability to evaluate any complete solution. The results we obtained with a very simple search strategy confirm the significance of a search through the set of the feasible solutions and of a combination between heuristic and random movements. The stochastic behavior of the resulting algorithms is always irritating and the numerous parameters difficult to tune. Hybridizations between *local search*, *limited tree search* and *constraint propagation*, as it has been for example proposed in [13,11], is certainly one of the currently most promising ways of research.

These lessons may seen to be negative for the constraint programming approach, because the basic constraint programming tools we used did not provide us with actually satisfactory results. It is true if constraint programming is seen as limited to the combination between constraint propagation and tree search. But it is not true if it is seen as a powerful modelling framework, as well as a modular software architecture, to which many either specialized or generic algorithms, coming from the *Constraint Reasoning*, *Interval Analysis*, *Graph Theory*, *Artificial Intelligence*, or *Operations Research* communities, can be connected.

Acknowlegments. We thank Jean-Michel Lachiver and Nicolas Bataille from CNES for their confidence, and Frank Jouhaud, Roger Mampey, Jérôme Guyon, and Mathieu Derrey from ONERA for their participation in this study.

References

1. E. Aarts and J. Lenstra, editors. *Local Search in Combinatorial Optimization.* John Wiley & Sons, 1997.
2. R. Bellman. *Dynamic Programming.* Princeton University Press, 1957.
3. E. Bensana, M. Lemaître, and G. Verfaillie. Earth Observation Satellite Management. *Constraints : An International Journal*, 4(3):293–299, 1999.
4. E. Bensana, G. Verfaillie, J.C. Agnèse, N. Bataille, and D. Blumstein. Exact and Approximate Methods for the Daily Management of an Earth Observation Satellite. In *Proc. of SpaceOps-96*, Münich, Germany, 1996.
5. R. Dechter. Bucket Elimination: a Unifying Framework for Reasoning. *Artificial Intelligence*, 113:41–85, 1999.
6. M. Garey and D. Johnson. *Computers and Intractability : A Guide to the Theory of NP-completeness.* W.H. Freeman and Company, New York, 1979.
7. W. Harvey and M. Ginsberg. Limited Discrepancy Search. In *Proc. of IJCAI-95*, pages 607–613, Montréal, Canada, 1995.
8. P. Van Hentenryck. *The OPL Optimization Programming Language.* MIT Press, 1999.
9. J. Larrosa. Boosting Search with Variable Elimination. In *Proc. of CP-00*, Singapore, 2000.
10. E. Lawler, J. Lenstra, A. Rinnooy Kan, and D. Shmoys, editors. *The Traveling Salesman Problem: A Guided Tour of Combinatorial Optimization.* John Wiley & Sons, 1985.
11. L. Lobjois, M. Lemaître, and G. Verfaillie. Large Neighbourhood Search using Constraint Propagation and Greedy Reconstruction for Valued CSP Resolution. In *Proc. of the ECAI-00 Workshop on "Modelling and Solving with Constraints"*, Berlin, Germany, 2000.
12. T. Schiex. Arc Consistency for Soft Constraints. In *Proc. of CP-00*, Singapore, 2000.
13. P. Shaw. Using Constraint Programming and Local Search Methods to Solve Vehicle Routing Problems. In *Proc. of CP-98*, pages 417–431, Pisa, Italia, 1998.
14. M. Vasquez and J.K. Hao. A Logic-constrained Knapsack Formulation and a Tabu Algorithm for the Daily Photograph Scheduling of an Earth Observation Satellite. *To appear in the Journal of Computational Optimization and Applications*, 2001.
15. G. Verfaillie, E. Bensana, C. Michelon-Edery, and N. Bataille. Dealing with Uncertainty when Managing an Earth Observation Satellite. In *Proc. of i-SAIRAS-99*, pages 205–207, Noordwijk, The Netherlands, 1999.

A Dynamic Distributed Constraint Satisfaction Approach to Resource Allocation

Pragnesh Jay Modi, Hyuckchul Jung, Milind Tambe, Wei-Min Shen, and Shriniwas Kulkarni

University of Southern California/Information Sciences Institute
4676 Admiralty Way, Marina del Rey, CA 90292, USA
{modi,jungh,tambe,shen,kulkarni}@isi.edu

Abstract. In distributed resource allocation a set of agents must assign their resources to a set of tasks. This problem arises in many real-world domains such as disaster rescue, hospital scheduling and the domain described in this paper: distributed sensor networks. Despite the variety of approaches proposed for distributed resource allocation, a systematic formalization of the problem and a general solution strategy are missing. This paper takes a step towards this goal by proposing a formalization of distributed resource allocation that represents both dynamic and distributed aspects of the problem and a general solution strategy that uses distributed constraint satisfaction techniques. This paper defines the notion of Dynamic Distributed Constraint Satisfaction Problem (DyDCSP) and proposes two generalized mappings from distributed resource allocation to DyDCSP, each proven to correctly perform resource allocation problems of specific difficulty and this theoretical result is verified in practice by an implementation on a real-world distributed sensor network.

1 Introduction

Distributed resource allocation is a general problem in which a set of agents must intelligently perform operations and assign their resources to a set of tasks such that all tasks are performed. This problem arises in many real-world domains such as distributed sensor networks [7], disaster rescue[4], hospital scheduling[2], and others. Resource allocation problems of this type are difficult because they are both *distributed* and *dynamic*. A key implication of the distributed nature of this problem is that the control is distributed in multiple agents; yet these multiple agents must collaborate to accomplish the tasks at hand. Another implication is that the multiple agents each obtain only local information, and face global ambiguity — an agent may know the results of its local operations but it may not know which other collaborators must be involved to fulfill the global task and which operations these collaborators must perform for success. Finally, the situation is dynamic so a solution to the resource allocation problem at one time may become obsolete when the underlying tasks have changed. This means that once a solution is obtained, the agents must continuously monitor it for changes and must have a way to express such changes in the problem. In this paper, we first propose a formalization of distributed resource allocation that is expressive enough to represent both dynamic and distributed aspects of the problem. This formalization allows us to understand the complexity of

T. Walsh (Ed.): CP 2001, LNCS 2239, pp. 685–700, 2001.

different types of resource allocation problems. Second, in order to address this type of resource allocation problem, we define the notion of a Dynamic Distributed Constraint Satisfaction Problem (DyDCSP). DyDCSP is a generalization of DCSP (Distributed Constraint Satisfaction Problem) [8] that allows constraints to be added or removed from the problem as external environmental conditions change. Third, we present two reusable, generalized mappings from distributed resource allocation to DyDCSP, each proven to correctly perform resource allocation problems of specific difficulty and experimentally verified through implementation in a real-world application. In summary, our central contribution is 1) a formalization that may enable researchers to understand the difficulty of their resource allocation problem and 2) generalized mappings to DyDCSP which provide automatic guarantees for correctness of the solution.

There is significant research in the area of distributed resource allocation; for instance, Liu and Sycara's work[5] extends dispatch scheduling to improve resource allocation. Chia et al's work on distributed vehicle monitoring and general scheduling (e.g. airport ground service scheduling) is well known but space limits preclude us from a detailed discussion [1]. However, a formalization of the general problem in distributed settings is yet to be forthcoming. Some researchers have focused on formalizing resource allocation as a centralized CSP, where the issue of ambiguity does not arise[3]. The fact that resource allocation is distributed means that ambiguity must be dealt with. Dynamic Constraint Satisfaction Problem has been studied in the centralized case by [6]. However, there is no distribution or ambiguity during the problem solving process.

The paper is structured as follows: Section 2 describes the application domain of our resource allocation problem and Section 3 presents a formal model and defines subclasses of the resource allocation problem. Section 4 introduces Dynamic Distributed Constraint Satisfaction Problems. Then, Sections 5 and 6 describe solutions to subclasses of resource allocation problems of increasing difficulty, by mapping them to DyDCSP. Section 7 describes empirical results and Section 8 concludes.

2 Application Domain

The domain in which this work has been applied is a distributed sensor domain. This domain consists of multiple stationary sensors, each controlled by an independent agent, and targets moving through their sensing range (Figure 1.a) illustrates the real hardware and simulator screen, respectively). Each sensor is equipped with a Doppler radar with three sectors. An agent may activate at most one sector of a sensor at a given time or switch the sensor off. While all of the sensor agents must act as a team to cooperatively track the targets, there are some key difficulties in such tracking. First, in order for a target to be tracked accurately, at least three agents must collaborate — concurrently activating overlapping sectors. For example, in Figure 1.b which corresponds to the simulator in Figure 1.a, if an agent A1 detects a target 1 in its sector 0, it must coordinate with neighboring agents, A2 and A4 say, so that they activate their respective sectors that overlap with A1's sector 0. Activating a sector is an agent's operation. Since there are three sectors of 120 degrees, each agent has three operations. Since target 1 exists in the range of a sector for all agents, any combination of operations from three agents or all four agents can achieve the task of tracking target 1.

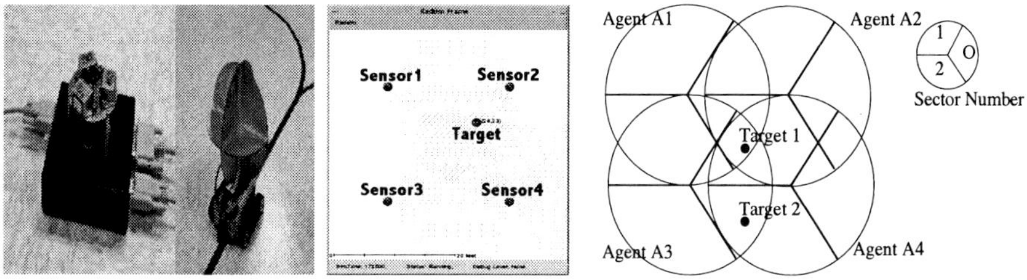

(a) hardware and simulator (b) sensor sectors

Fig. 1. A distributed sensor domain

Second, there is ambiguity in selecting a sector to find a target. Since each sensor agent can detect only the distance and speed of a target, an agent that detects a target cannot tell other agents which sectors to activate. When there is only target 1 in Figure 1.b and agent A1 detects the target first, A1 can tell A4 to activate sector 1. However, A1 cannot tell A2 which of the two sectors (sector 1 or sector 2) to activate since it only knows that there is a target in its sector 0. That is, agents don't know which task is to be performed. Identifying a task to perform depends on the result of other related agents' operations.

Third, if there are multiple targets, that introduces resource contention — an agent may be required to activate more than one sector, which it can not! For instance, in Figure 1.b, A4 needs to decide whether to perform either a task for target 1 or a task for target 2. Since at most one sector can be activated at a given time, A4 should decide which task to perform. Thus, the relationship among tasks will affect the difficulty of the resource allocation problem.

Fourth, the situation is dynamic as targets move through the sensing range. The dynamic property of the domain makes problems even harder. Since target moves over time, after agents activate overlapping sectors and track a target, they may have to find different overlapping sectors.

The above application illustrates the difficulty of resource allocation among distributed agents in dynamic environment. Lack of a formalism for dynamic distributed resource allocation problem can lead to ad-hoc methods which cannot be easily reused. On the other hand, adopting a formal model allows our problem and its solution to be stated in a more general way, possibly increasing our solution's usefulness. More importantly, a formal treatment of the problem also allows us to study its complexity and provide other researchers with some insights into the difficulty of their own resource allocation problems. Finally, a formal model allows us to provide guarantees of soundness and completeness of our results. The next section presents our general, formal model of resource allocation.

3 Formalization of Resource Allocation

A Distributed Resource Allocation Problem consists of 1) a set of agents that can each perform some set of operations, and 2) a set of tasks to be completed. In order to be completed, a task requires some subset of agents to perform the necessary operations. Thus, we can define a task by the operations that agents must perform in order to complete it. The problem to be solved is an allocation of agents to tasks such that all tasks are performed. This problem is formalized next.

A Distributed Resource Allocation Problem is a structure $<\mathcal{A}g, \Omega, \Theta>$ where

- $\mathcal{A}g$ is a set of agents, $\mathcal{A}g = \{A_1, A_2, ..., A_n\}$.
- $\Omega = \{O_1^1, O_2^1, ..., O_p^i, ..., O_q^n\}$ is a set of operations, where operation O_p^i denotes the p'th operation of agent A_i. An operation can either succeed or fail. Let $Op(A_i)$ denote the set of operations of A_i. Operations in $Op(A_i)$ are *mutually exclusive*; an agent can only perform one operation at a time.
- Θ is a set of tasks, where a task is a collection of sets of operations that satisfy the following properties: $\forall T \in \Theta$,
  (i) $T \subseteq P(\Omega)$ (Power set of Ω)
  (ii) T is nonempty and, $\forall t \in T$, t is nonempty;
  (iii) $\forall t_r, t_s \in T, t_r \not\subseteq t_s$ and $t_s \not\subseteq t_r$. t_r and t_s are called *minimal sets*. Two minimal sets *conflict* if they contain operations belonging to the same agent.

Notice that there may be alternative sets of operations that can complete a given task. Each such set is a minimal set. (Property (iii) above requires that each set of operations in a task should be minimal in the sense that no other set is a subset of it.) A *solution* to a resource allocation problem then, involves choosing a minimal set for each task such that the minimal sets do not conflict. In this way, when the agents perform the operations in those minimal sets, all tasks are successfully completed.

To illustrate this formalism in the distributed sensor network domain, we cast each sensor as an agent and activating one of its (three) sectors as an operation. We will use O_p^i to denote the operation of agent A_i activating sector p. For example, in Figure 1.b, we have four agents, so $\mathcal{A}g = \{A_1, A_2, A_3, A_4\}$. Each agent can perform one of three operations, so $\Omega = \bigcup_{A_i \in \mathcal{A}g} Op(A_i)$, where $Op(A_i) = \{ O_0^i, O_1^i, O_2^i \}$.

Now we only have left to define our task set Θ. We will define a separate task for each target in a particular location, where a location corresponds to an area of overlap of sectors. In the situation illustrated in Figure 1.b, we have two targets shown, so we define two tasks: $\Theta = \{T_1, T_2\}$. Since a target requires three agents to track it so that its position can be triangulated, Task T_1 requires any three of the four possible agents to activate their correct sector, so we define a minimal set corresponding to the all (4 choose 3) combinations. Thus, $T_1 = \{\{O_0^1, O_2^2, O_0^3\}, \{O_2^2, O_0^3, O_1^4\}, \{O_0^1, O_0^3, O_1^4\}, \{O_0^1, O_2^2, O_1^4\}\}$. Note that the subscript of the operation denotes the number of the sector the agent must activate. Task T_2 can only be tracked by two agents, both of which are needed, so $T_2 = \{\{O_0^3, O_2^4\}\}$.

For each task, we use $\Upsilon(T_r)$ to denote the union of all the minimal sets of T_r, and for each operation, we use $T(O_p^i)$ to denote the set of tasks that include O_p^i. For instance, $\Upsilon(T_1) = \{O_0^1, O_2^2, O_0^3, O_1^4\}$ and $T(O_0^3) = \{ T_1, T_2 \}$. We will also require that every operation should serve some task, i.e. $\forall\, O_p^i \in \Omega, \mid T(O_p^i) \mid \neq 0$. Formal definitions for Υ and T are as follows:

- $\forall\, T_r \in \Theta, \Upsilon(T_r) = \bigcup_{t_r \in T_r} t_r$

– $\forall\, O_p^i \in \Omega, T(O_p^i) = \{T_r \mid O_p^i \in \Upsilon(T_r)\}$

All the tasks in Θ may not always be present. We use $\Theta_{current}$ ($\subseteq \Theta$) to denote the set of tasks that are currently present. This set is determined by the environment. We call a resource allocation problem *static* if $\Theta_{current}$ is constant over time and *dynamic* otherwise. So in our distributed sensor network example, a moving target represents a dynamic problem. Agents can execute their operations at any time, but the success of an operation is determined by the set of tasks that are currently present. The following two definitions formalize this interface with the environment.

Definition 1: $\forall\, O_p^i \in \Omega$, if O_p^i is executed and $\exists\, T_r \in \Theta_{current}$ such that $O_p^i \in \Upsilon(T_r)$, then O_p^i is said to *succeed.*

So in our example, if agent A_1 executes operation O_0^1 and if $T_1 \in \Theta_{current}$, then O_0^1 will succeed, otherwise it will fail. Next, a task is performed when all the operations in some minimal set succeed. More formally,

Definition 2: $\forall T_r \in \Theta$, T_r is *performed* iff $\exists t_r \in T_r$ such that all the operations in t_r succeed. All tasks that satisfy this definition are contained in $\Theta_{current}$.

Agents must somehow be informed of the set of current tasks. The notification procedure is outside of this formalism. Thus, the following assumption states that at least one agent is notified that a task is present by the success of one of its operations. (This assumption can be satisfied in the distributed sensor domain by agents "scanning" for targets by rotating sectors when they are currently not tracking a target.)

Notification assumption: $\forall T_r \in \Theta$, if $T_r \in \Theta_{current}$, then $\exists\, O_p^i \in \Upsilon(T_r)$ such that $\forall T_s (\neq T_r) \in \Theta_{current}$, $O_p^i \notin T_s$ and O_p^i succeeds.

We now state some definitions that will allow us to categorize a given resource allocation problem and analyze its complexity. In many resource allocation problems, tasks have the property that they require at least k agents from a pool of n ($n > k$) available agents. That is, the task contains a minimal set for each of the $\binom{n}{k}$ combinations. The following definition formalizes this notion.

Definition 3: $\forall\, T_r \in \Theta$, T_r is **task-$\binom{n}{k}$-exact** iff T_r has exactly $\binom{n}{k}$ minimal sets of size k, where $n = \mid \Upsilon(T_r) \mid$.

For example, the task T_1 (corresponding to target 1 in Figure 1.b) is task-$\binom{4}{3}$-exact. The following just defines the class of resource allocation problems where all tasks satisfy the above definition.

Definition 4 : $\binom{n}{k}$**-exact** denotes the class of resource allocation problems <$\mathcal{A}g$, Ω, Θ> such that $\forall\, T_r \in \Theta$, T_r is task-$\binom{n}{k_r}$-exact for some k_r.

We find it useful to define a special case of $\binom{n}{k}$-exact resource allocation problems, namely those when $k = n$. In other words, the task contains only one minimal set.

Definition 5: $\binom{n}{n}$**-exact** denotes the class of resource allocation problems <$\mathcal{A}g$, Ω, Θ> such that $\forall\, T_r \in \Theta$, T_r is task-$\binom{n_r}{k_r}$-exact, where $n_r = k_r = \mid \Upsilon(T_r) \mid$.

For example,the task T_2 (corresponding to target 2 in Figure 1.b) is task-$\binom{2}{2}$-exact.

Definition 6: **Unrestricted** denotes the class of resource allocation problems <$\mathcal{A}g$, Ω, Θ> with no restrictions on tasks.

The following definitions refer to relations between tasks. We define two types of *conflict-free* to denote tasks that can be performed concurrently. The **strongly conflict free** condition implies that all choices of minimal sets from the tasks are non-conflicting.

The **weakly conflict free** condition implies that there exists a choice of minimal sets from the tasks that are non-conflicting or in other words, there exists some solution.

Definition 7: A resource allocation problem is called **strongly conflict free (SCF)** if $\forall\, T_r, T_s \in \Theta$, the following statement is true:

– if $T_r \neq T_s$, then $\forall\, t_r \in T_r, \forall\, t_s \in T_s, \forall\, A_i \in \mathcal{A}g, \mid t_r \cap Op(A_i) \mid + \mid t_s \cap Op(A_i) \mid \leq 1$.

Definition 8: A resource allocation problem is called **weakly conflict free (WCF)** if $\forall\, T_r, T_s \in \Theta$, the following statement is true:

– if $T_r \neq T_s$, then $\exists\, t_r \in T_r, \exists\, t_s \in T_s$ s.t. $\forall\, A_i \in \mathcal{A}g, \mid t_r \cap Op(A_i) \mid + \mid t_s \cap Op(A_i) \mid \leq 1$.

4 Dynamic DCSP

In order to solve general resource allocation problems that conform to our formalized model, we will use distributed constraint satisfaction techniques. Existing approaches to distributed constraint satisfaction fall short for our purposes however because they cannot capture the dynamic aspects of the problem. In dynamic problems, a solution to the resource allocation problem at one time may become obsolete when the underlying tasks have changed. This means that once a solution is obtained, the agents must continuously monitor it for changes and must have a way to express such changes in the problem. In order to address this shortcoming, the following section defines the notion of a Dynamic Distributed Constraint Satisfaction Problem (DyDCSP). A Constraint Satisfaction Problem (CSP) is commonly defined by a set of variables, each associated with a finite domain, and a set of constraints on the values of the variables. A solution is the value assignment for the variables which satisfies all the constraints. A distributed CSP is a CSP in which variables and constraints are distributed among multiple agents. Each variable belongs to an agent. A constraint defined only on the variable belonging to a single agent is called a *local constraint*. In contrast, an *external constraint* involves variables of different agents. Solving a DCSP requires that agents not only solve their local constraints, but also communicate with other agents to satisfy external constraints.

DCSP assumes that the set of constraints are fixed in advance. This assumption is problematic when we attempt to apply DCSP to domains where features of the environment are not known in advance and must be sensed at run-time. For example, in distributed sensor networks, agents do not know where the targets will appear. This makes it difficult to specify the DCSP constraints in advance. Rather, we desire agents to sense the environment and then activate or deactivate constraints depending on the result of the sensing action. We formalize this idea next.

We take the definition of DCSP one step further by defining Dynamic DCSP (DyDCSP). DyDCSP allows constraints to be conditional on some predicate P. More specifically, a *dynamic* constraint is given by a tuple (P, C), where P is an arbitrary predicate that is continuously evaluated by an agent and C is a familiar constraint in DCSP. When P is true, C must be satisfied in any DCSP solution. When P is false, C may be violated. An important consequence of dynamic DCSP is that agents no longer terminate when they reach a stable state. They must continue to monitor P, waiting to see if it changes. If its value changes, they may be required to search for a new solution. Note that a solution when P is true is also a solution when P is false, so the deletion of a constraint does not require any extra computation. However, the converse does not hold. When a constraint is added to the problem, agents may be forced to compute a new solution. In this work, we only need to address a restricted form of DyDCSP i.e. it is only necessary that *local constraints* be dynamic.

AWC [8] is a sound and complete algorithm for solving DCSPs. An agent with local variable A_i, chooses a value v_i for A_i and sends this value to agents with whom it has external constraints. It then waits for and responds to messages. When the agent receives a variable value ($A_j = v_j$) from another agent, this value is stored in an AgentView. Therefore, an AgentView is a set of pairs $\{(A_j, v_j), (A_k, v_k), ...\}$. Intuitively, the AgentView stores the current value of non-local variables. A subset of an AgentView is a NoGood if an agent cannot find a value for its local variable that satisfies all constraints. For example, an agent with variable A_i may find that the set $\{(A_j, v_j), (A_k, v_k)\}$ is a NoGood because, given these values for A_j and A_k, it cannot find a value for A_i that satisfies all of its constraints. This means that these value assignments cannot be part of any solution. In this case, the agent will request that the others change their variable value and a search for a solution continues. To guarantee completeness, a discovered NoGood is stored so that that assignment is not considered in the future.

The most straightforward way to attempt to deal with dynamism in DCSP is to consider AWC as a subroutine that is invoked anew everytime a constraint is added. Unfortunately, in many domains such as ours, where the problem is dynamic but does not change drastically, starting from scratch may be prohibitively inefficient. Another option, and the one that we adopt, is for agents to continue their computation even as local constraints change asynchronously. The potential problem with this approach is that when constraints are removed, a stored NoGood may now become part of a solution. We solve this problem by requiring agents to store their own variable values as part of non-empty NoGoods. For example, if an agent with variable A_i finds that a value v_i does not satisfy all constraints given the AgentView $\{(A_j, v_j), (A_k, v_k)\}$, it will store the set $\{(A_i, v_i), (A_j, v_j), (A_k, v_k)\}$ as a NoGood. With this modification to AWC, NoGoods remain "no good" even as local constraints change. Let us call this modified algorithm Locally-Dynamic AWC (LD-AWC) and the modified NoGoods "LD-NoGoods" in order to distinguish them from the original AWC NoGoods.

Lemma I: LD-AWC is sound and complete.

The soundness of LD-AWC follows from the soundness of AWC. The completeness of AWC is guaranteed by the recording of NoGoods. A NoGood logically represents a set of assignments that leads to a contradiction. We need to show that this invariant is maintained in LD-NoGoods. An LD-NoGood is a superset of some non-empty AWC NoGood and since every superset of an AWC NoGood is no good, the invariant is true when a LD-NoGood is first recorded. The only problem that remains is the possibility that an LD-NoGood may later become good due to the dynamism of local constraints. A LD-NoGood contains a specific value of the local variable that is no good but never contains a local variable exclusively. Therefore, it logically holds information about external constraints only. Since external constraints are not allowed to be dynamic in LD-AWC, LD-NoGoods remain valid even in the face of dynamic local constraints. Thus the completeness of LD-AWC is guaranteed.

5 Solving SCF Problems via DyDCSP

In this section, we state the complexity of SCF resource allocation problems and map our formal model of the resource allocation problem onto DyDCSP. Our goal is to provide a general mapping so that any unrestricted SCF resource allocation problem can be solved in a distributed manner by a set of agents by applying this mapping.

Our complexity analysis (not the DyDCSP mapping, but just the complexity analysis) here assumes a static problem. This is because a dynamic resource allocation problem can be cast as solving a sequence of static problems, so a dynamic problem is at least as hard as a static one. Furthermore, our results are based on a centralized problem solver. We conjecture that distributed problem solving is no easier due to ambiguity, which requires more search.

Theorem I: Unrestricted Strongly Conflict Free resource allocation problems can be solved in time linear in the number of tasks.

proof: Greedily choose any minimal set for each task. They are guaranteed not to conflict by the Strongly Conflict Free condition. □

We now describe a solution to this subclass of resource allocation problems by mapping onto DyDCSP. Mapping I is motivated by the following idea. The goal in DCSP is for agents to choose values for their variables so all constraints are satisfied. Similarly, the goal in resource allocation is for the agents to choose operations so all tasks are performed. Therefore, in our first attempt we map variables to agents and values of variables to operations of agents. So for example, if an agent A_i has three operations it can perform, $\{O_1^i, O_2^i, O_3^i\}$, then the variable corresponding to this agent will have three values in its domain. However, this simple mapping attempt fails due to the dynamic nature of the problem; operations of an agent may not always succeed. Therefore, we define two values for every operation, one for success and the other for failure. In our example, this would result in six values.

It turns out that even this mapping is inadequate due to ambiguity. Ambiguity arises when an operation can be required for more than one task. We desire agents to be able to not only choose which operation to perform, but also to choose for which task they will perform the operation. For example in Figure 1.b, Agent A3 is required to active the same sector for both targets 1 and 2. We want A3 to be able to distinguish between the two targets, so that it does not unnecessarily require A2 to activate sector 2 when target 2 is present. So, for each of the values defined so far, we will define new values corresponding to each task that an operation may serve.

Mapping I: Given a Resource Allocation Problem $\langle \mathcal{A}g, \Omega, \Theta \rangle$, the corresponding DyDCSP is defined over a set of n variables,

- $A = \{A_1, A_2, \ldots, A_n\}$, one variable for each $A_i \in$ Ag. We will use the notation A_i to interchangeably refer to an agent or its variable.

The domain of each variable is given by:

- $\forall A_i \in \mathcal{A}g, \text{Dom}(A_i) = \bigcup_{O_p^i \in \Omega} O_p^i \text{x} T(O_p^i) \text{x} \{\text{yes,no}\}$.

In this way, we have a value for every combination of operations an agent can perform, a task for which this operation is required, and whether the operation succeeds or fails.

For example in Figure 1.b, Agent A3 has two operations (sector 1 and 2) with only one possible task (target) and one operation (sector 0) with two possible tasks (target 1 and 2). This means it would have 8 values in its domain.

A word about notation: $\forall\, O_p^i \in \Omega$, the set of values in O_p^ix$T(O_p^i)$x$\{$yes$\}$ will be abbreviated by the term O_p^i*yes and the assignment $A_i = O_p^i$*yes denotes that $\exists v \in O_p^i$*yes s.t. $A_i = v$. Intuitively, the notation is used when an agent detects that an operation is succeeding, but it is not known which task is being performed. This analogous to the situation in the distributed sensor network domain where an agent may detect a target in a sector, but not know its exact location. Finally, when a variable A_i is assigned a value, we assume the corresponding agent is required to execute the corresponding operation.

Next, we must constrain agents to assign "yes" values to variables only when an operation has succeeded. However, in dynamic problems, an operation may succeed at some time and fail at another time since tasks are dynamically added and removed from the current set of tasks to be performed. Thus, every variable is constrained by the following dynamic local constraints.

- **Dynamic Local Constraint 1 (LC1)**: $\forall T_r \in \Theta, \forall O_p^i \in \Upsilon T_r)$, we have
  LC1(A_i) = (P, C), where P: O_p^i succeeds.
  C: $A_i = O_p^i$*yes
- **Dynamic Local Constraint 2 (LC2)**: $\forall T_r \in \Theta, \forall O_p^i \in \Upsilon(T_r)$, we have
  LC2(A_i) = (P, C), where P: O_p^i does not succeed.
  C: $A_i \neq O_p^i$*yes

The truth value of P is not known in advance. Agents must execute their operations, and based on the result, locally determine if C needs to be satisfied. In dynamic problems, where the set of current tasks is changing over time, the truth value of P will change, and hence the corresponding DyDCSP will also be dynamic.

We now define the external constraint (EC) between variables of two different agents. EC is a normal static constraint and is always present.

- **External Constraint**: $\forall T_r \in \Theta, \forall O_p^i \in \Upsilon(T_r), \forall A_j \in A$,

  EC(A_i, A_j): (1) $A_i = O_p^i T_r$yes, and
  (2) $\forall t_r \in T_r$ s.t. $O_p^i \in t_r$, $\exists q$ s.t. $O_q^j \in t_r$.
  $\Rightarrow A_j = O_q^j T_r$yes

The EC constraint requires some explanation. Condition (1) states that an agent A_i has found an operation that succeeds for task T_r. Condition (2) quantifies the other agents whose operations are also required for T_r. If A_j is one of those agents, the consequent requires it to choose its respective operation for the T_r. If A_j is not required for T_r, condition (2) is false and EC is trivially satisfied. Finally, note that every pair of variables A_i and A_j, have two EC constraints between them: one from A_i to A_j and another from A_j to A_i. The conjunction of the two unidirectional constraints can be considered one bidirectional constraint.

The following theorems state that our mapping can be used to solve any given SCF Resource Allocation Problem. The first theorem states that our DyDCSP always has a solution, and the second theorem states that if agents reach a solution, all current tasks are performed. It is interesting to note that the converse of the second theorem does not hold, i.e. it is possible for agents to be performing all tasks *before* a solution state is reached. This is due to the fact that when all current tasks are being performed, agents whose operations are not necessary for the current tasks could still be violating constraints.

Theorem II: Given an unrestricted SCF Resource Allocation Problem $\langle Ag, \Omega, \Theta \rangle$, $\Theta_{current} \subseteq \Theta$, a solution always exists for the DyDCSP obtained from Mapping I.

proof: We proceed by presenting a variable assignment and showing that it is a solution.

Let $B = \{A_i \in A \mid \exists T_r \in \Theta_{current}, \exists O_p^i \in \Upsilon(T_r)\}$. We will first assign values to variables in B, then assign values to variables that are not in B. If $A_i \in B$, then $\exists T_r \in \Theta_{current}, \exists O_p^i \in \Upsilon(T_r)$. In our solution, we assign $A_i = O_p^i T_r yes$. If $A_i \notin B$, we may choose any $O_p^i T_r no \in$ Dom(A_i) and assign $A_i = O_p^i T_r no$.

To show that this assignment is a solution, we first show that it satisfies the EC constraint. We arbitrarily choose two variables, A_i and A_j, and show that EC(A_i, A_j) is satisfied. We proceed by cases. Let $A_i, A_j \in A$ be given.

- *case 1:* $A_i \notin B$
  Since $A_i = O_p^i T_r no$, condition (1) of EC constraint is false and thus EC is trivially satisfied.
- *case 2:* $A_i \in B, A_j \notin B$
  $A_i = O_p^i T_r yes$ in our solution. Let $t_r \in T_r$ s.t. $O_p^i \in t_r$. We know that $T_r \in \Theta_{current}$ and since $A_j \notin B$, we conclude that $\nexists O_q^j \in t_r$. So condition (2) of the EC constraint is false and thus EC is trivially satisfied.
- *case 3:* $A_i \in B, A_j \in B$
  $A_i = O_p^i T_r yes$ and $A_j = O_q^j T_s yes$ in our solution. Let $t_r \in T_r$ s.t. $O_p^i \in t_r$. T_s and T_r must be strongly conflict free since both are in $\Theta_{current}$. If $T_s \neq T_r$, then $\nexists$ $O_n^j \in \Omega$ s.t. $O_n^j \in t_r$. So condition (2) of EC(A_i,A_j) is false and thus EC is trivially satisfied. If $T_s = T_r$, then EC is satisfied since A_j is helping A_i perform T_r.

Next, we show that our assignment satisfies the LC constraints. If $A_i \in B$ then $A_i = O_p^i T_r yes$, and LC1, regardless of the truth value of P, is clearly not violated. Furthermore, it is the case that O_p^i succeeds, since T_r is present. Then the precondition P of LC2 is not satisfied and thus LC2 is not present. If $A_i \notin B$ and $A_i = O_p^i T_r no$, it is the case that O_p^i is executed and, by definition, does not succeed. Then the precondition P of LC1 is not satisfied and thus LC1 is not present. LC2, regardless of the truth value of P, is clearly not violated. Thus, the LC constraints are satisfied by all variables. We can conclude that all constraints are satisfied and our value assignment is a solution to the DyDCSP. □

Theorem III: Given an unrestricted SCF Resource Allocation Problem $\langle Ag, \Omega, \Theta \rangle$, $\Theta_{current} \subseteq \Theta$ and the DyDCSP obtained from Mapping I, if an assignment of values to variables in the DyDCSP is a solution, then all tasks in $\Theta_{current}$ are performed.

proof: Let a solution to the DyDCSP be given. We want to show that all tasks in $\Theta_{current}$ are performed. We proceed by choosing a task $T_r \in \Theta_{current}$. Since our choice is arbitrary and tasks are strongly conflict free, if we can show that it is indeed performed, we can conclude that all members of $\Theta_{current}$ are performed.

Let $T_r \in \Theta_{current}$. By the **Notification Assumption**, some operation O_p^i, required by T_r will be executed. However, the corresponding agent A_i, will be unsure as to which task it is performing when O_p^i succeeds. This is due to the fact that O_p^i may be required for many different tasks. It may randomly choose a task, $T_s \in T(O_p^i)$, and LC1 requires it to assign the value $O_p^i T_s$yes. The EC constraint will then require that all other agents A_j, whose operations are required for T_s also execute those operations and assign $A_j = O_q^j T_s yes$. We are in solution, so LC2 cannot be present for A_j. Thus, O_q^j succeeds. Since all operations required for T_s succeed, T_s is performed. By definition, $T_s \in \Theta_{current}$. But since we already know that T_s and T_r have an operation in common, the Strongly Conflict Free condition requires that $T_s = T_r$. Therefore, T_r is indeed performed. □

6 Solving WCF Problems via DyDCSP

In this section, we state the complexity of $\binom{n}{k}$-exact WCF resource allocation problems and that of unrestricted WCF resource allocation problems. The following complexity results are based on a centralized problem solver, but as mentioned we conjecture that distributed problem solving is no easier. We also present a second mapping for WCF problems onto DyDCSP (Section 6.1).

Theorem IV: $\binom{n}{n}$-exact WCF resource allocation problems can be solved in time linear in the number of tasks.

proof: Greedily choose the single minimal set for each task.

Theorem V: $\binom{n}{k}$-exact WCF resource allocation problems can be solved in time polynomial in the number of tasks and operations.

proof: To prove this theorem, we convert a given $\binom{n}{k}$-exact resource allocation problem to a network-flow problem which is known to be polynomial. See Appendix.

Theorem VI: Determining whether an unrestricted resource allocation problem is Weakly Conflict Free is NP-Complete.

proof-sketch: We reduce from 3 coloring problem. For reduction, let an arbitrary instance of 3-color with colors c_1, c_2, c_3, vertices V and edges E, be given. We construct the RAP as follows:

- For each vertex $v \in V$, add a task T_v to Θ.
- For each task $T_v \in \Theta$, for each color c_k, add a minimal set $t_v^{c_k}$ to T_v.
- For each edge $v_i, v_j \in E$, for each color c_k, add an operator $O_{v_i,v_j}^{c_k}$ to Ω and add this operator to minimal sets $t_{v_i}^{c_k}$ and $t_{v_j}^{c_k}$.
- Assign each operator to a unique agent $A_{O_{v_i,v_j}^{c_k}}$ in $\mathcal{A}g$.

Figure 2 illustrates the mapping from a 3 node graph to a resource allocation problem. With the mapping above, it is somewhat easy to show that the 3-color problem has a solution if and only if the constructed RAP is weakly conflict free. (We preclude a detailed proof due to space limits)

6.1 Mapping II

Our first mapping has allowed us to solve any SCF resource allocation problem. However, when we attempt to solve WCF resource allocation problems with this mapping, it fails

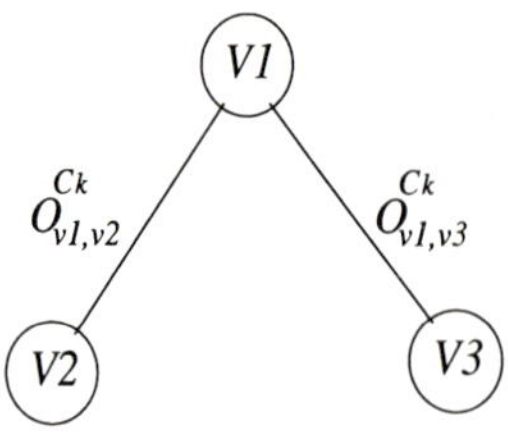

Color = {R, G, B}

$T_{V1} = \{\{O^R_{v1,v2}, O^R_{v1,v3}\}, \{O^G_{v1,v2}, O^G_{v1,v3}\}, \{O^B_{v1,v2}, O^B_{v1,v3}\}\}$

$T_{V2} = \{\{O^R_{v1,v2}\}, \{O^G_{v1,v2}\}, \{O^B_{v1,v2}\}\}$

$T_{V3} = \{\{O^R_{v1,v3}\}, \{O^G_{v1,v3}\}, \{O^B_{v1,v3}\}\}$

Fig. 2. Reduction of graph 3-coloring to Resource Allocation Problems

because the DyDCSP becomes overconstrained. This is due to the fact that the mapping requires all agents who can possibly help perform a task to do so. In some sense, this results in an overallocation of resources to some tasks. This in turn leaves other tasks without sufficient resources to be performed. One way to solve this problem is to modify the constraints in the mapping to allow agents to reason about relationships among tasks. However, this requires adding non-binary external constraints to the mapping. This is problematic in a distributed situation because there are no efficient algorithms for non-binary distributed CSPs. Instead, create a new mapping that has only binary external constraints. This mapping is similar to the dual of a version of mapping I with non-binary external constraints. This new mapping allocates only minimal resources to each task, allowing WCF problems to be solved. This mapping is described next and proven correct. Here, each agent has a variable for each task in which its operations are included.

Mapping II: Given a Resource Allocation Problem $\langle \mathcal{A}g, \Omega, \Theta \rangle$, the corresponding DyDCSP is defined as follows:

- **Variables:** $\forall T_r \in \Theta, \forall O^i_p \in \Upsilon(T_r)$, create a DyDCSP variable $T_{r,i}$ and assign it to agent A_i.
- **Domain:** For each variable $T_{r,i}$, create a value $t_{r,i}$ for each minimal set in T_r, plus a "NP" value (not present). The NP value allows agents to avoid assigning resources to tasks that are not present and thus do not need to be performed.

Next, we must constrain agents to assign non-NP values to variables only when an operation has succeeded, which indicates the presence of the corresponding task. However, in dynamic problems, an operation may succeed at some time and fail at another time since tasks are dynamically added and removed from the current set of tasks to be performed. Thus, every variable is constrained by the following dynamic local constraints.

- **Dynamic Local (Non-Binary) Constraint (LC1):**
  $\forall A_i \in \mathcal{A}g, \forall O^i_p \in Op(A_i)$, let B = $\{ T_{r,i} \mid O^i_p \in T_r \}$. Then let the constraint be defined as a non-binary constraint over the variables in B as follows:
  P: O^i_p succeeds
  C: $\exists T_{r,i} \in$ B s.t. $T_{r,i} \neq$ NP.
- **Dynamic Local Constraint (LC2):** $\forall T_r \in \Theta, \forall O^i_p \in \Upsilon(T_r)$, let the constraint be defined on $T_{r,i}$ as follows:
  P: O^i_p does not succeed
  C: $T_{r,i}$ = NP

We now define the constraint that defines a valid allocation of resources and the external constraints that require agents to agree on a particular allocation.

- **Static Local Constraint (LC3)**: $\forall T_{r,i}, T_{s,i}$, if $T_{r,i} = t_{r,i}$, then the value of $T_{s,i}$ cannot conflict with the minimal set $t_{r,i}$. NP does not conflict with anything.
- **External Constraint (EC)**: $\forall i, j, r\ T_{r,i} = T_{r,j}$

We will now prove that Mapping II can also be used to solve any given WCF Resource Allocation Problem. The first theorem shows that our DyDCSP always has a solution, and the second theorem shows that if agents reach a solution, all current tasks are performed.

Theorem VII: Given a WCF Resource Allocation Problem $\langle \mathcal{A}g,\Omega,\Theta \rangle$, $\Theta_{current} \subseteq \Theta$, there exists a solution to DyDCSP obtained from Mapping II.

proof: For all variables corresponding to tasks that are not present, we can assign the value "NP". This value satisfies all constraints except possibly LC1. But the P condition must be false since the task is not present, so LC1 cannot be violated. We are guaranteed that there is a choice of non-conflicting minimal sets for the remaining tasks (by the WCF condition). We can assign the values corresponding to these minimal sets to those tasks and be assured that LC3 is satisfied. Since all variable corresponding to a particular task get assigned the same value, the external constraint is satisfied. So we have a solution to the DyDCSP. □

Theorem VIII: Given a WCF Resource Allocation Problem $\langle \mathcal{A}g,\Omega,\Theta \rangle$, $\Theta_{current} \subseteq \Theta$ and the DyDCSP obtained from Mapping II, if an assignment of values to variables in the DyDCSP is a solution, then all tasks in $\Theta_{current}$ are performed.

proof Let a solution to the DyDCSP be given. We want to show that all tasks in $\Theta_{current}$ are performed. We proceed by randomly choosing a task from $\Theta_{current}$ and showing that it is performed. Since we are in a solution state, LC3 allows us to repeat this argument for every task in $\Theta_{current}$.

Let $T_r \in \Theta_{current}$. By the **Notification Assumption**, some operation O_p^i, required by T_r will be executed and (by definition) succeed. LC1 requires the corresponding agent A_i, to assign a minimal set, say t_r to the variable $T_{r,i}$. The EC constraint will then require that all other agents A_j, whose operation O_q^j is in the minimal set t_r, to assign $T_{r,j} = t_r$ and execute that operation. LC2 requires that it succeeds. Since all operations required for T_r succeed, T_r is performed. □

7 Experiments in a Real-World Domain

We have successfully applied the DyDCSP approach to the distributed sensor network problem, using the mapping introduced in Section 6. In the last evaluation trials conducted in government labs in August and September 2000, this DyDCSP implementation was successfully tested on four actual hardware sensor nodes (see Figure 1.a), where agents collaboratively tracked a moving target. This target tracking requires addressing noise, communication failures, and other real-world problems; although this was done outside the DyDCSP framework and hence not reported here. The unavailability of the hardware in our lab precludes extensive hardware tests; but instead, a detailed simulator that very faithfully mirrors the hardware has been made available to us. We have done extensive tests using this simulator to further validate the DyDCSP formalization: indeed a single implementation runs on both the hardware and the simulator. One key evaluation criteria for this implementation is how accurately it is able to track targets, e.g., if agents do not switch on overlapping sectors at the right time, the target tracking has poor accuracy. Here, the accuracy of a track is measured in terms of the *RMS* (root mean square) error in the distance between the real position of a target and the target's position as estimated by a team of sensor agents. Domain experts termed the RMS error of upto 3 units as acceptable.

Table 1 presents our results from the implementation with the Mapping II in Section 6. Experiments were conducted in different dynamic situations varying the type of resource allocation problem, the number of nodes/targets, and the configuration. RMS error, message number, and sector change are averaged over the number of involved agents. In the "node number" column, the number in parentheses indicates the number of rows and columns of the grid configuration where sensor agents are located. For instance, the last row represents the result of the WCF resource allocation problem with 12 sensor nodes (in 3x4 grid) and 4 four targets: the RMS of 3.24 units with average 30 messages and 2 sector changes per node.

The results show that our mapping works, and agents are able to accurately track targets, with average RMS around 3 units as the experts require. This proves the usefulness of the DyDCSP approach to this resource allocation problem. Furthermore, scaling up the number of nodes and targets does not degrade the tracking accuracy. Some interesting differences between WCF and SCF arise: WCF resource allocation problems require more number of messages and sector changes than SCF problems. These are due to the fact that, given WCF problems, agents need to reason about possible minimal sets of the current tasks to be performed.

Table 1. Results from sensor network domain for dynamic resource allocation problems.

RAP type	node number	target number	avg RMS	avg message number	avg sector changes
WCF/SCF	4 (2x2)	1	2.58	14	0.5
SCF	8 (2x4)	2	3.21	17.08	0.5
SCF	9 (3x3)	2	3.21	21.89	0.2
SCF	16 (4x4)	4	2.58	23.13	0.5
WCF	6 (2x3)	2	2.50	45.17	1.6
WCF	12 (3x4)	4	3.24	30	2.0

8 Summary

In this paper, we proposed a formalization of distributed resource allocation that is expressive enough to represent both dynamic and distributed aspects of the problem. We define different categories of difficulties of the problem and present complexity results for them. Table 2 summarizes these complexity results. To address these formalized problems, we define the notion of Dynamic Distributed Constraint Satisfaction Problem

Table 2. Complexity Classes of Resource Allocation, n = size of task set Θ, m = size of operation set Ω

	SCF	WCF
$\binom{n}{n}$-exact	O(n)	O(n)
$\binom{n}{k}$-exact	O(n)	O($(n+m)^3$)
unrestricted	O(n)	NP-Complete

(DyDCSP) and present a generalized mapping from distributed resource allocation to DyDCSP. Through both theoretical analysis and experimental verifications, we have shown that this approach to dynamic and distributed resource allocation is powerful and unique, and can be applied to real-problems such as the Distributed Sensor Network Domain. Indeed, in the future, our formalization may enable researchers to understand the difficulty of their resource allocation problem, choose a suitable mapping using DyDCSP, with automatic guarantees for correctness of the solution.

Acknowledgements. This research is sponsored in part by DARPA/ITO under contract number F30602-99-2-0507, and in part by AFOSR under grant number F49620-01-1-0020.

References

1. M. Chia, D. Neiman, and V. Lesser. Poaching and distraction in asynchronous agent activities. In *ICMAS*, 1998.
2. K. Decker and J. Li. Coordinated hospital patient scheduling. In *ICMAS*, 1998.
3. C. Frei and B. Faltings. Resource allocation in networks using abstraction and constraint satisfaction techniques. In *Proc of Constraint Programming*, 1999.
4. Hiroaki Kitano. Robocup rescue: A grand challenge for multi-agent systems. In *ICMAS*, 2000.
5. J. Liu and K. Sycara. Multiagent coordination in tightly coupled task scheduling. In *ICMAS*, 1996.
6. S. Mittal and B. Falkenhainer. Dynamic constraint satisfaction problems. In *AAAI*, 1990.
7. Sanders. Ecm challenge problem, http://www.sanders.com/ants/ecm.htm. 2001.
8. M. Yokoo and K. Hirayama. Distributed constraint satisfaction algorithm for complex local problems. In *ICMAS*, July 1998.

Appendix

Theorem V: $\binom{n}{k}$-exact WCF resource allocation problems can be solved in time polynomial in the number of tasks and operations.

proof: We can convert a given $\binom{n}{k}$-exact resource allocation problem to a network-flow problem known to be polynomial. Let such a resource allocation problem be given. We first construct a tripartite graph and then convert it to a network-flow problem.

- Create three empty sets of vertices, U, V, and W and an empty edge set E.
- For each task $T_r \in \Theta$, add a vertex u_r to U.

- For each agent $A_i \in \mathcal{A}g$, add a vertex v_i to V.
- For each agent A_i, for each operation $O_p^i \in Op(A_i)$, add a vertex w_p^i to W.
- For each agent A_i, for each operation $O_p^i \in Op(A_i)$, add an edge between vertices v_i, w_p^i to E.
- For each task T_r, for each operation $O_p^i \in \Upsilon(T_r)$, add an edge between vertices u_r, w_p^i to E.

We convert this tripartite graph into a network-flow graph in the usual way. Add two new vertices, a supersource s, and supersink t. Connect s to all vertices in V and assign a max-flow of 1. For all edges among V, W, and U, assign a max-flow of 1. Now, connect t to all vertices in U and for each edge (u_r, t), assign a max-flow of k_r. We now have a network flow graph with an upper limit on flow of $\sum_{i=1}^{|\theta|} k_i$.

We show that the resource allocation problem has a solution if and only if the max-flow is equal to $\sum_{i=1}^{|\theta|} k_i$.

$\Rightarrow$ Let a solution to the resource allocation problem be given. We will now construct a flow equal to $\sum_{i=1}^{|\theta|} k_i$. This means, for each edge between vertex u_r in U and t, we must assign a flow of k_r. It is required that the in-flow to u_r equal k_r. Since each edge between W and U has capacity 1, we must choose k_r vertices from W that have an edge into u_r and fill them to capacity. Let T_r be the task corresponding to vertex u_r, and $t_r \in T_r$ be the minimal set chosen in the given solution. We will assign a flow of 1 to all edges (w_p^i, u_r) such that w_p^i corresponds to the operation O_p^i that is required in t_r. There are exactly k_r of these. Furthermore, since no operation is required for two different tasks, when we assign flows through vertices in U, we will never choose w_p^i again. For vertex w_p^i such that the edge (w_p^i, u_r) is filled to its capacity, assign a flow of 1 to the edge (v_i, w_p^i). Here, when a flow is assigned through a vertex w_p^i, no other flow is assigned through $w_q^i \in Op(A_i)$ $(p \neq q)$ because all operations in $Op(A_i)$ are mutually exclusive. Therefore, v_i's outflow cannot be greater than 1. Finally, the assignment of flows from s to V is straightforward. Thus, we will always have a valid flow (inflow=outflow). Since all edges from U to t are filled to capacity, the max-flow is equal to $\sum_{i=1}^{|\theta|} k_i$.

$\Leftarrow$ Assume we have a max-flow equal to $\sum_{i=1}^{|\theta|} k_i$. Then for each vertex u_r in U, there are k_r incoming edges filled to capacity 1. By construction, the set of vertices in W matched to u_r corresponds to a minimal set in T_r. We choose this minimal set for the solution to the resource allocation problem. For each such edge (w_p^i, u_r), w_p^i has an in-capacity of 1, so every other edge out of w_p^i must be empty. That is, no operation is required by multiple tasks. Furthermore, since outgoing flow thorough v_i is 1, no more than one operation in $Op(A_i)$ is required. Therefore, we will not have any conflicts between minimal sets in our solution. □

A Constraint Optimization Framework for Mapping a Digital Signal Processing Application onto a Parallel Architecture

Juliette Mattioli, Nicolas Museux, J. Jourdan, Pierre Savéant, and Simon de Givry

THALES, Corporate Research Laboratory
Domaine de Corbeville, 91404 Orsay Cedex
juliette.mattioli@thalesgroup.com

Abstract. In this paper, we present a domain specific optimization framework based on a concurrent model-based approach for handling the complete problem of mapping a DSP application on a parallel architecture. The implementation is based on Constraint Programming and the model is described in details. Our concurrent resolution approach undertaking linear and non linear constraints takes advantage of the special features of signal processing applications. Finally, our mapping tool developped with the ECLAIR solver is evaluated and compared to a classical approach.

1 Introduction

In order to reduce development costs, a major trend in Software Engineering is to follow a strategy of capitalization built on the reuse of software components. This strategy has been adopted in Thales for the development of the planning/optimization functions of Defence and Aeronautics systems. The concrete side of this approach is the design of applicative frameworks dedicated to specific domains and built on the expertise of the company. Such a framework provides an abstract model together with a generic resolution procedure. The development of a specific application is then reduced to a simple customization. The objective of the paper is to describe how this approach was applied to the automatic parallelization of Digital Signal Processing (DSP) applications.

Taking advantage of a multi-processor architecture to speed up a processing which has a potential of parallelization is natural but can become a huge challenge. In the context of Digital Signal Processing (DSP) applications running on a parallel machine with distributed memory, the *mapping problem* can be seen as a scheduling problem with multiple resource allocation where typical objective functions aim at the minimization of:

- the memory capacity,
- the number of processors,
- the response time of the application,
- the bandwith used for communication between processes.

T. Walsh (Ed.): CP 2001, LNCS 2239, pp. 701–715, 2001.

Running an application on such an architecture implies both distributing the code and data on the processors, and scheduling computations and communications. Real life DSP applications run in open loop with a time unit in the order of magnitude of the millisecond, a volume of data in the order of magnitude of the mega byte and consist of thousands of elementary tasks.

The mapping problem has been proved to be NP-complete [10,21] and is usually decomposed into sub-problems which are solved separately by dedicated algorithms [5] making global optimization impossible. Work based on Integer Programming with Boolean variables led to a combinatorial explosion [21]. A lot of work has been done to optimise local criteria such as data and/or computation distribution locality [15,6,13], parallelism level, number of communications [2, 24]. In [11], the scheduling is computed w.r.t. a given partitioning.

Since a few years, THALES in collaboration with Ecole des Mines de Paris open a radically new way by bringing up a concurrent model-based approach to handle the problem as a whole [1,12,16]. Since then, this model has been implemented with contraints in finite domains using ECLAIR ©, the THALES constraint solver. Today an application framework dedicated to the mapping of a DSP application onto a "parallel" machine is available where the target architecture can be specified as well as the type of outputs for code generation.

Our objective has been to provide specialists with an interactive tool for application domains that involve signal processing: radar[27], sonar[12] or telecom[3].

The framework can be specialized for different types of:

- architecture: SIMD, MultiSPMD, MIMD,
- processors network topology: fully connected, ring based,
- memory: simple, multiple level,
- computer: mainframe (100 processors) [12], on-board [27], system-on-chip [3].

All this flexibility supposes a high degree of modularity and we will try to show in this paper how this goal is met with Constraint Programming.

Several tools that aim at mapping applications onto a multi-processor architecture are presently available as research prototypes or commercial off the shelf products. CASCH, FX, GEDAE [23], PTOLEMY [35], SYNDEX [33], TRAPPER [30] are tools of this type. Each tool has its own features but none of them allows to simultaneously take into account all the architecture and applicative constraints in a global optimization process.

Mapping in a deterministic way a DSP application with specific signal requirements [17,34] have been widely investigated. The representative PTOLEMY framework [22,32,25] brings some solutions but at a coarse grain level.

2 Architectural and Application Features

A DSP application is decomposed in tasks and computational dependencies are stated by a data flow graph.

The control structure of a task is restricted to a set of perfect nested loops (like russian dolls). Each "loop nest" encapsulates a call to a procedure such as for instance a Fast Fourier Transform. These procedures work on arrays and are the elementary tasks w.r.t. parallelization and are thus considered as black boxes.

The source of parallelism comes from the following properties of the procedures:

- single-assignment form: only one writing operation in an array can occur,
- each loop index is associated to a unique dimension of an array,
- there are no read/write dependencies [4].

Therefore all permutations of loops in a nest are equivalent. Note that parallelization is maximal since any elementary iteration can be done separately.

Finally, a DSP application is a system in open loop which is fed periodically. This is captured by introducing an infinite dimension.

A toy example composed of three tasks is given in Figure 1. Tasks are described in a pseudo-language which supposes infinite loops and arrays with infinite dimensions. Tasks precedences can be inferred by the fact that the Sum Task needs TAB23 which is computed by Diff Task. Diff Task needs TAB12 computed by Square Task.

Square Task: C

```
DO I=0,INFINITE
  DO J=0,7
    TAB12[I,J]=
        TAB1[I,J]*TAB1[I,J]
  ENDDO
ENDDO
```

Diff Task: D

```
DO I=0,INFINITE
  DO J=0,3
    TAB23[I,J]=
        TAB12[2*I,J]-TAB12[2*I+1,J]
  ENDDO
ENDDO
```

Sum Task: I

```
DO I=0,INFINITE
  S=0
    DO J=0,3
      S=S+TAB23[I,J]
    ENDDO
  TAB3[I]=S
ENDDO
```

Fig. 1. A simple DSP application defined by a sequence of 3 loop nests

The target architecture considered here is an abstract Single Program Multiple Data (SPMD) distributed memory machine. In such an architecture, all processors are executing the same elementary task on different data at the same time. The architecture is defined by:

- the network topology,
- the number of processors,
- the memory capacity of each processor,
- the type of memory (hierarchical, circular buffering)
- the clock rate of each processor,

- the communication bandwith,
- the type of communication (point to point, pipeline, block by block)

In the following we have chosen a fully connected topology where all processors are connected to each other in order that communication duration depends only on the size of the data, and not on the position of the processors. Under this assumption explicit processor assignment can be ignored. In addition it is assumed that a communication and a computation can be done simultaneously on one processor.

3 The Mapping Model

The mapping problem is decomposed in a set of concurrent models as shown in Figure 2:

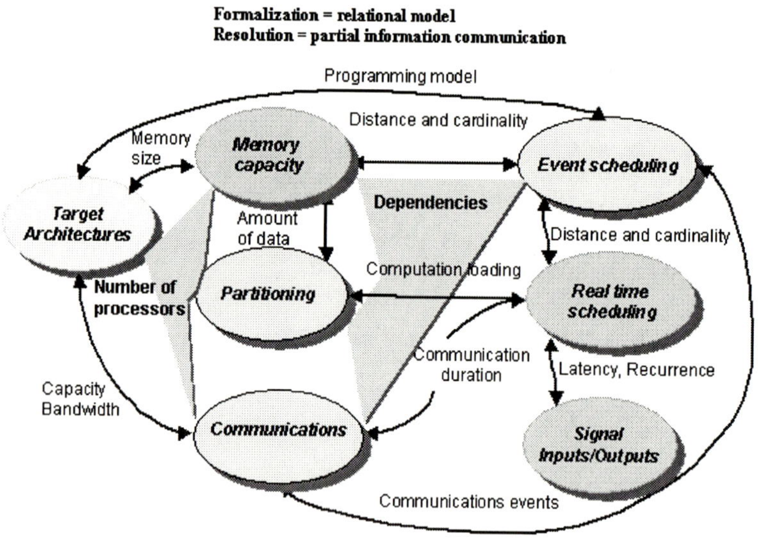

Fig. 2. The concurrent modeling view of the mapping problem

A model has to be viewed semantically as the set of formal specifications [19, 20] of the behaviors of the (functional or physical) sub-problem components. In the mapping context, we have the following models:

memory capacity: ensures the application executability under a memory constraint. A capacitive memory model is used. It evaluates the memory required for each computational block mapped onto a processor.
partitioning: controls the distribution of data onto processors.
communications: schedules the communications between processors.

event scheduling: associates to each computational block a logical execution event on a processor.

real time scheduling: schedules tasks and communications taking into account computation and communication duration and their overlapping.

signal inputs/outputs: the signal is characterized by two values: the input signal *recurrence*, i.e. the time between two consecutive input signals and the *latency*, i.e. an upper time bound for the production of the results on an input signal.

dependencies: express that a piece of data of loop nest cannot be read before being updated by the corresponding written piece of loop nest.

number of processors: defines the available processors.

target architecture: defines the class of which the target architecture belongs: SIMD, MIMD,...

A model, represented in fig. 2 by a bubble, is viewed as a set of variables and a set of constraints over them. All the constraints of each model have been defined separately. The relations between models are either constraints or defined predicates, and are represented by arcs or hyper-arcs in fig. 2.

The modeling phase consists in axiomatizing the behavior using the properties and relations of all the different components. Consequently a model is identified to the set of relations defined on its interface variables. The relations are either predefined constraints or user defined predicates. The variables have to be considered as *access ports* to the model. Thus, model coordinations can be achieved either by unifying some ports of several models together or by involving ports of different models in a relation. Each variable takes part in a global cross-model composite solving, such that only relevant information is exchanged between models. A global resolution mechanism (search) looks for partial solutions in the different concurrent models. For instance, the set of scheduling and target machine variables are partially instantiated by inter-model relations during the resolution. The search relies on the semantic of the different variables involved in each model and their importance according to other different models as well as in regards of the goal to achieve (e.g. resources minimization). Model-specific or more global heuristics are used to improve the resolution. For instance, computing the shortest path in the data-flow graph drives good schedule choices.

The concurrent model based approach matches directly the constraint programming paradigm which provides a concurrent model of solving.

Due to space limitation, only the partitioning, scheduling and memory models[16] are presented in the following sub-sections. But the communication, latency, architectural and applicative models obviously influence the resolution.

3.1 The Data-Partitioning Model

The data-partitioning controls the application parallelism level, memory location requirement and event scheduling parameters. Its model is designed to distribute elementary tasks onto the target architecture without resource and real time scheduling considerations. Since DSP applications are sequences of parallel loop nests, the partitioning problem results in a nest by nest partitioning [1].

[1] Here, we use the word *partitioning* in the mathematical sense.

Due to DSP application features (presented in §2), only the multidimensional iteration domain $\mathcal{I}$ is partitioned. This domain is defined by the Cartesian product of each iteration domain of the loop.

In the example given in fig. 1, the iteration domain of the Square Task, is given by: $\mathcal{I} = dom(I) \times dom(J) = [0..\infty[\times[0..7]$.

The iteration domain is projected on a three-dimension space. For that, the iteration domain is decomposed in 3 vector parameters: c, p, l where c represents the cyclic recurrence, p a processor and l a local memory area. This projection gives a hierarchical definition of the partioning model: at one time c, p processors are used and each of them uses a local memory area l. This implies that all vectors of iterations $i \in \mathcal{I}$ is constrained by

$$i = LPc + Lp + l \tag{1}$$

where P and L are variable diagonal square integer matrices involving respectively processor distribution and memory data location. Diagonal matrices L and P (resp. vectors c, l, p) are lists of variables defined in ECLAIR by

```
DMATRIX :: list[Var]
VECTOR  :: list[Var]
VECTOR+ :: (list[Var U {infinity}])
```

Equation (1) induces $i_{up} = L.P.c_{up}$ if the target machine is in a SIMD programming mode and $c_{up} = \left\lceil \frac{i_{up}}{L.P} \right\rceil$ if the target machine is in a SPMD programming mode. Then we have, in the SIMD case, the following constraints:

```
let lb  := (if (lpartition[NbTache].upC[1] = infinity) 2 else 1)
in  (for i in (1 .. lb - 1) LP[i] = L[i] * P[i],
       for i in (lb .. length(UpI))
         (LP[i] = L[i] * P[i],
          LP[i] <= UpI[i],
          UpI[i] = UpC[i] * LP[i])
```

Vector l (resp. p) is constrained by $\forall l, 0 \leq L^{-1}l < 1$ (resp. $\forall p, 0 \leq P^{-1}p < 1$) which means that there is no computation replication on the processors (resp. over the time). One iteration on memory is modeled [2] by $det(L) \neq 0$ and $det(P) \neq 0$ which means that there is at least one processor. At least, since matrices L and P are diagonal, new constraints are induced:

- $\prod_i L_{ii}$ which is the number of local iterations executed by one processor at each cycle c (each local iteration execute a procedure call);
- $\prod_i P_{ii}$ which gives the maximum number of processors and
- the following variable max(c) represents the maximum number of synchronization (cycles) necessary for the loop nest completion.

[2] The determinant of a m by m matrix A equals the volume of a parallelepiped K in m-dimensional space, provided the edges of K come from the rows of A, or the edges could form the columns of A, giving an entirely different parallelepiped with the same volume.

For example, a partitionning for application defined on fig.1 could be:

Square: $P = \begin{pmatrix} 1 & 0 \\ 0 & 4 \end{pmatrix}$ and $L = \begin{pmatrix} 1 & 0 \\ 0 & 1 \end{pmatrix}$
Which means that the finite dimension J is mapped onto 4 processors, and only one data element is distributed at each cycle c.

Diff: $P = \begin{pmatrix} 1 & 0 \\ 0 & 4 \end{pmatrix}$ and $L = \begin{pmatrix} 1 & 0 \\ 0 & 1 \end{pmatrix}$ **Sum:** $P = \begin{pmatrix} 1 \end{pmatrix}$ and $L = \begin{pmatrix} 1 \end{pmatrix}$

3.2 The Scheduling Model

The scheduling model is designed to associate each partitioned subset of elementary tasks, a logical execution event on a processor. This schedule is an event schedule, that defines only a total order between tasks.

Since we are in a cyclic applicative context, an affine scheduling approach, used in parallelization techniques [14], has been applied. In terms of constraints, we post:

$$d^k(c^k) = \alpha^k \cdot c^k + \beta^k \tag{2}$$

Thanks to the SPMD architecture, all processors work on the same volume of data at each time unit. That is why the link with the partioning model is its cyclic recurrence c.

Variables are indexed by the loop nest number k. d^k is the scheduling event date of the kth-loop nest; α^k and β^k are the scheduling affine variables, where α^k is a line vector, and β^k is scalar. (2) is implemented in ECLAIR by:

```
[d(alpha:VECTOR, beta:Var, C:VECTOR) : Var
-> scalar(alpha /+ list(beta), C /+ list(ONE))]
```

For example, an event schedule for the example defined on fig. 1 could be the one of fig. 3.2:

Square: $\alpha^1 = (1,1)$, $\beta^1 = 0$
Diff: $\alpha^2 = (2,1)$, $\beta^2 = 2$
Sum: $\alpha^3 = (2)$, $\beta^3 = 3$

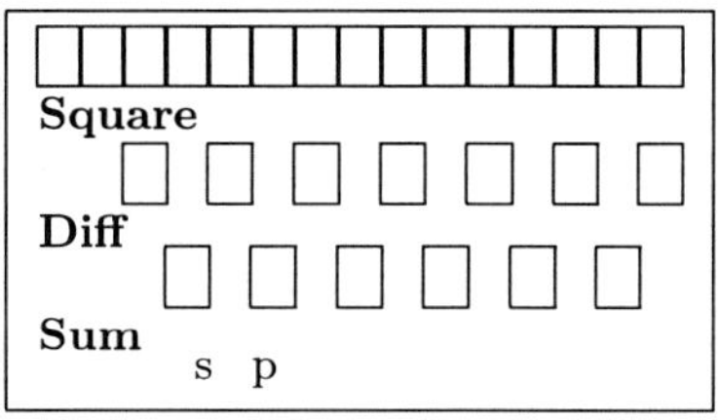

Symbol s denotes the start-up and p represents the beginning of periodic schedule.

Fig. 3. Bi-dimentionnal Chronogram on the application defined in fig. 2

3.3 The Data Flow Dependencies Model

The relation (represented by an hyper-arc on fig. 2) that links the partitioning and scheduling models is the *data flow dependencies*. It expresses that a piece of data of the loop nest N^r cannot be read before being updated by written loop nest N^w. These dependencies between two cycles c^w (written cycle) of loop nest N^w and c^r (readen cycle) of N^r imply that:

$$\forall(c^w, c^r)\ Dependencies(c^w, c^r) \Rightarrow d^w(c^w) + 1 \leq d^r(c^r) \tag{3}$$

d^w (respectively d^r) is the schedule associated to N^r (resp. N^w). These dependencies enforce a partial order on parallel program instructions for guarantying the same result to the sequential program. Note that these dependencies are computed between iterations of *different* loop nests. All the dependency relationship between blocks of computation can not be stated in the original constraint (3) due to the universal quantifier over the data flow dependency universal predicate: $\forall(c^w, c^r), Dependencies(c^w, c^r)$.

Due to DSP characteristics, data flow dependencies universal predicate is characterized by a set of integer points belonging to a Cartesian product of polygons called the dependency polygon. Furthermore, thanks to the convexity property of this polygon [31], the data flow dependency constraint (3) has been encoded as constraint (4):

$$\forall(c_s^w, c_s^r)\ \ d^w(c_s^w) + 1 \leq d^r(c_s^r) \tag{4}$$

where (c_s^w, c_s^r) are the vertices components of the integer convex hull of the dependency polygon, that have been computed symbolically. Hence, the scope of this $\forall$ is *narrower* than in constraint (3). Unfortunately, these vertices are rational and data flow dependencies are approximated by their *integer* convex hull representation. Since the coordinates of the convex hull vertices are given by constraints, we can't use the Harvey convex hull algorithm [18].

This approximation allow us to obtain the same set of valid schedules as with the exact representation but with an impact [3] in the parallel generated code. For reducing the impact, the data flow dependencies are characterized by the smallest convex hull which vertices are integer. This convex hull is defined through a gcd constraint [26].

3.4 The Target SMPD Architecture Model

Let N is be the number of loop nests. It is used over the scheduling constraint (2) with the offset $+k$ in order to avoid the execution at the same date of two computations belonging to different loop nests. Then the scheduling model is transformed for taking into account the SPMD architectural feature, and we obtain a SPMD specific schedule:

$$d^k(c^k) = N(\alpha^k \cdot c^k + \beta^k) + k$$

In the same way, two computational blocks of a single loop nest cannot be executed at the same date. Let c_i^k and c_j^k with $i < j$ be two cyclic components of the partitioned loop nest N^k. Then, the execution period of cycle c_i^k must be greater than the execution time of all cycles c_j^k. Hence, constraints: $\alpha_i^k > \sum_{j>i} \alpha_j^k \max(c_j^k)$ with $\alpha_n^k \geq 1$ must be verified.

[3] In some case, the generated code is not optimal in sense of number of lines.

3.5 The Memory Capacity Model

The memory model ensures the application executability under a memory constraint. Since the capacity of the memory on each processor is limited, it is necessary to make sure that the memory used by the data partitioning do not exceed its resources [12]. A capacitive memory model is used and this model is based on a kind of producer/consumer constraint closely related to a capacity constraint. It evaluates the memory required for each partitioned elementary tasks block mapped onto a processor by analyzing the data dependencies. The number of data needed to execute an elementary tasks block is computed. Due to the partitioning model all elementary tasks blocks have the same simple structure and the same size. Data dependencies are used to determine the data block lifetime. For each block, the schedule and data dependencies give the maximum lifetime of involving data and the number of data creations during one cycle. This gives the required memory capacity per elementary tasks block and cycle.

4 APOTRES: A Mapping Framework

In order to assist specialists on parallel machines with distributed and hierarchical memory levels for DSP applications, a mapping framework called APOTRES[4] for rapid DSP prototyping has been developed. Thanks to the concurrent model-based approach, each model defines a modular component of the mapping framework. For example, if an architectural feature is required, a new model will be designed and relations with the other models will be refined.

4.1 Eclair Solver

ECLAIR © is a finite domain constraint solver over integers written in the CLAIRE functional programming language [9,8]. The current release includes arithmetic constraints, global constraints and boolean combinations.

ECLAIR [7,28] provides a standard labeling procedure for solving problems and a branch-and-bound algorithm for combinatorial optimization problems. Programmers can also design easily their own non-deterministic procedures thanks to the dramatically efficient trailing mechanism available in CLAIRE.

ECLAIR can be embedded in a real time system. A package has been developed to take into account time management and memory allocation with the introduction of interrupt points.

ECLAIR has been used mainly in the domain of weapon allocation, weapon/sensor deployment and the parallelization of DSP applications (the topic of this paper).

An open source version is available at:

http://www.lcr.thomson-csf.com/projects/openeclair

[4] APOTRES is the french acronym of "Aide au Placement Optimisé pour application de Traitement Radar Et Sonar" which means "Computer-assisted mapping framework for Radar and Sonar applications" and is protected by a patent.

The non-linear constraints appearing in the partitioning model and in the scheduling model rely on the *type reduction* implementation scheme presented in [29]. This approach makes effective the reduction of complex constraints into simpler ones.

4.2 Search Procedure

The optimization procedure is a classical Branch-and-Bound algorithm. An enumeration is performed for each model according to its decision variables and for which there are specific strategies and heuristics. In our context, two enumerations are required to find a solution of the whole problem. The first one concerns the partitionning and consists in trying all possible mappings for the data. The second one is related to scheduling where the goal is to order the tasks.

4.3 The User Interface

After loading the DSP application, the user specifies through a graphical interface (cf. fig. 4):

- the target machine through the parametrization of the number of processors, the bound of memory capacity, the bandwith and the frequency clock;
- the optimization criteria, if the user wants to use the system in order to get for example the smallest number of processors, the smallest amount of memory, the smallest latency and/or the cheapest architecture.

Several use modes are possible:

- The system finds automatically an optimal mapping or a mapping near a percentage of the optimum. (In this case, a complete algorithm is used.)

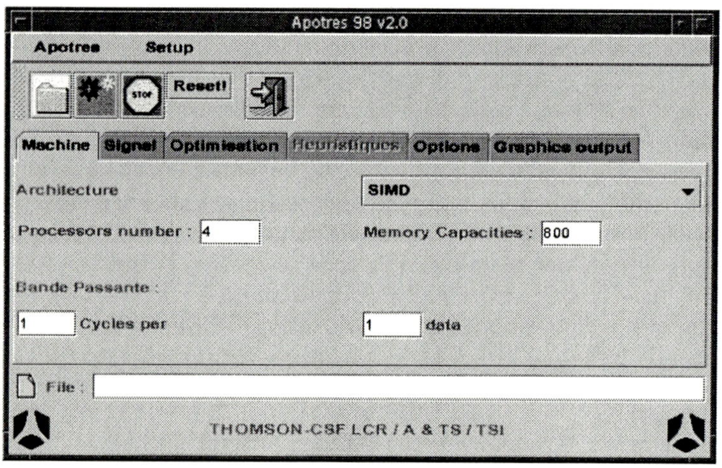

Fig. 4. The user graphical interface

- Another possibility is to find (if it is possible) a solution of a given partial mapping, that allow to enforce a specific schedule or a specific data partitioning. The search stops after finding the first solution.
- It is also a mapping verification system. The user can instantiate all the mapping variables and the result will be a "yes/no"-answer.

There are graphical user interfaces for visualizing the data partitionning, the schedule, the task/communication overlapping, and finally the tool can generate a LaTeX report (or html report), in order to get all the mapping directives that allow the target machine compiler to generate the parallel code.

5 An Industrial Validation

Our tool has been evaluated successfully on several THALES DSP benchmarks.

5.1 A Simple Example of a Mapping Solution

We present in this section the results on the application described in Fig.1. In this example, the optimizing cost function is the *latency minimization*. The target machine has 4 processors. The capacity memory constraint is set to 200 memory elements (8,16,32 or 64 bits).

The latency optimum is reached (and proved by the completeness of the search algorithm). Its value is 4 cycles for a memory capacity of 64 memory elements. The table of fig.5 gives latency and memory values at each step of the search. The diagram of fig.5 describes partitioning and event scheduling of the optimal solution, and arrrows represent the data flow dependencies.

Optimization criteria latency minimization			
no	# proc.	memory element	Latency cycle
0	4	200	12
1	4	80	8
2	4	64	7
3	4	64	4

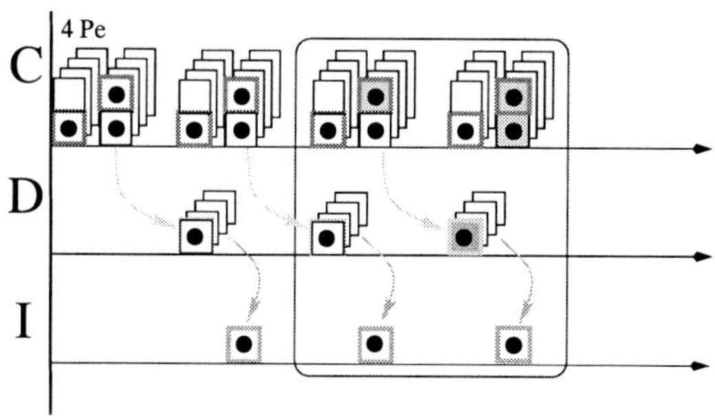

Fig. 5. The optimal latency mapping on the application defined in fig.1

5.2 Validation on Real DSP Applications

To evaluate the approach, we have compared the solutions found with Apotres to solutions found by experts on real DSP applications [12]. We present in this

```
doall r,c
  call FFT(r,c)
enddo
doall r,f,v
  call BeamForming(r,f,v)
enddo
doall r,f,v
  call Energy(r,f,v)
enddo
doall r,v
  call ShortIntegration(r,v)
enddo
doall r,v
  call AzimutStabilization(r,v)
enddo
doall r,v
  call LongIntegration(r,v)
enddo
```

Fig. 6. *Panoramic Analysis* application

```
do r=0,infinity
 do c=0,511

  c    Read Region:
  c          SENSOR(c,512*r:512*r+511)
  c    Write Region:
  c          TABFFT(c,0:255,r)

  call FFTDbl(SENSOR(c,512*r:512*r+511),
              TABFFT(c,0:255,r))

 enddo
enddo
```

Fig. 7. FFT Loop nest

section the results on the Panoramic Analysis application described in fig. 6 and fig. 7.

In this application, the optimizing cost function is the *memory size minimization.* The target machine has 8 processors. The latency constraint is set to 4.10^8 processor clock cycles and the memory is unbounded. Figure 8 describes the partitioning and the schedule found by Apotres.

The partitioning characteristics follow. (1) Only finite dimensions are mapped onto the 8 processors. (2) The write region of the second loop nest is identical to the read region of the third loop nest. So the system fuses these loop nests in order to reduce memory allocation. (3) The access analysis of the second and third loop nests presents read region overlaps between successive iteration execution. This overlap is detected. The system parallelizes according to another dimension to avoid data replication.

According to the different partitions, only the time dimension is globally scheduled. From the α and β scheduling parameters in Figure 8, the schedule can be expressed using the regular expression:

$$(((FFT, [BF, E], BB)^8, SI, SA)^8, LI)^\infty$$

The system provides a fine grain schedule at the procedural level using the dependence graph shortest-path. This enables the use of data as soon as possible, avoids buffer allocation, and produces output results at the earliest. Eight iterations of Tasks `FFT,BF-E,BB` (executed every $\alpha_1^1 = 6$ steps) are performed before one iteration of `SI,SA` (executed every 48 = 6*8 steps). The last task `LongInteg` cannot be executed before 8 iterations of the precedent tasks. So it is executed every 384 (=8*48) steps.

Partitionning	*FFT*	*Beam Forming Energy*	*BroadBand*	*Sht Integ*	*Azimut*	*LongInteg*
Parallelism, $P =$	$\begin{pmatrix}1&0\\0&8\end{pmatrix}$	$\begin{pmatrix}1&0&0\\0&1&0\\0&0&8\end{pmatrix}$	$\begin{pmatrix}1&0\\0&8\end{pmatrix}$	$\begin{pmatrix}1&0\\0&8\end{pmatrix}$	$\begin{pmatrix}1&0\\0&8\end{pmatrix}$	$\begin{pmatrix}1&0\\0&8\end{pmatrix}$
Locality, $L =$	$\begin{pmatrix}1&0\\0&64\end{pmatrix}$	$\begin{pmatrix}1&0&0\\0&128&0\\0&0&25\end{pmatrix}$	$\begin{pmatrix}1&0\\0&16\end{pmatrix}$	$\begin{pmatrix}1&0\\0&16\end{pmatrix}$	$\begin{pmatrix}1&0\\0&16\end{pmatrix}$	$\begin{pmatrix}1&0\\0&16\end{pmatrix}$
Scheduling	*FFT*	*Beam Forming Energy*	*Broad Band*	*Sht Integ*	*Azimut*	*Long Integ*
α	$\begin{pmatrix}6\\1\end{pmatrix}$	$\begin{pmatrix}6\\1\\1\end{pmatrix}$	$\begin{pmatrix}6\\1\end{pmatrix}$	$\begin{pmatrix}48\\1\end{pmatrix}$	$\begin{pmatrix}48\\1\end{pmatrix}$	$\begin{pmatrix}384\\1\end{pmatrix}$
β	0	1	2	45	46	383

Fig. 8. Partitioning and Scheduling matrices for Panoramic Analysis

Manual mappings of DSP applications are very difficult because finding an effective mapping imperatively requires to take into account both architectural resources constraints and real time constraints and of course the resulted mapping program must return the same result as the sequential program. We have compared our solution to two different manual solutions. The first one is based on loop transformation techniques. The second one uses the maximization of the processor usage as economic function. Our result is equivalent to the one suggested by parallelization techniques. It is better than the second one which requires more memory allocation.

6 Conclusions

This work illustrates the applicability of the concurrent model-based approach to the resolution of problems of multi-function and multi-component systems through a domain specific framework. This approach transforms the difficulty of dealing with the whole system into the advantage of considering several models concurrently. It also allows the design of a mapping framework dedicated to parallel architectures and DSP applications. The relevance of using CP languages for solving the complex problem of automatic application mapping on parallel architectures has been shown.

In this paper, we focused on SPMD architecture, but our system is currently being extended in order to remove different restrictions such as considering more complex mapping functions[27,3], considering other architectures (Multi-SPMD, MIMD machines).

Moreover, we give a new alternative for the automatic determination of array alignment and task scheduling on parallel machines opening a radically new way to tackle parallelization problems. For some complex DSP application such as Radar applications, a manual mapping which preserves all constraints, costs about 6 months of effort. The major benefit of our system is that it gives a first solution in few minutes and thus reduces the development time cost.

Acknowledgments. We are very grateful to Pr. F. Irigoin and Dr. C. Ancourt for their permanent help on the modeling phase and to P. Gérard for its fruitful comments.

References

1. C. Ancourt, D. Barthou, C. Guettier, F. Irigoin, B. Jeannet, J. Jourdan, and J. Mattioli. Automatic mapping of signal processing applications onto parallel computers. In *Proc. ASAP 97*, Zurich, july 1997.
2. J.M. Anderson and M.S. Lam. Global optimizations for parallelism and locality on scalable parallel machines. In *SIGPLAN Conf. on Programming Language Design and Implementation*, pages 112–125, Albuquerque, NM, June 1993. ACM Press.
3. M. Barreteau, J. Mattioli, T. Granpierre, Y. Sorel C. Lavarenne and, P. Bonnot, P. Kajifasz, F. Irigoin, C. Ancourt, and B. Dion. Prompt: A mapping environnment for telecom applications on *System-On-a-Chip*. In *Compilers, Architecture, and synthesis for embedded systems*, pages 41–48, november 2000.
4. A. J. Bernstein. Analysis of programs for parallel processing. *IEEE Trans. on El. Computers*, EC-15, 1966.
5. S. S. Bhattacharyya, S. Sriram, and E. A. Lee. Latency-Constrained Resynchronisation For Multiprocessor DSP Implementation. In *Proceedings of ASAP'96*, 1996.
6. E. Bixby, K. Kennedy, and U. Kremer. Automatic Data Layout Using 0-1 Integer Programming. In *Proc. of the International Conference on Parallel Architectures and Compilation Techniques*, August 1994.
7. Y. Caseau, F. Josset, F. Laburthe, B. Rottembourg, S. de Givry, J. Jourdan, J. Mattioli, and P. Savéant. Eclair at a glance. Tsi / 99-876, Thomson-CSF/LCR, 1999.
8. Yves Caseau, François-Xavier Josset, and François Laburthe. CLAIRE: Combining Sets, Search and Rules to better express algorithms. In *Proc. of ICLP'99*, pages 245–259, Las Cruces, New Mexico, USA, November 29, December 4 1999.
9. Yves Caseau and François Laburthe. *Introduction to the* CLAIRE *programming language - Version 2.4.0.* Ecole Normale Supérieure - DMI, www.ens.fr/~caseau/claire.html, 1996-1999.
10. A. Darte. On the complexity of loop fusion. *Parallel Coomputing*, 26(9):1175–1193, August 2000.
11. A. Darte, C. Diderich, M. Gengler, and F. Vivien. Scheduling the computations of a loop nest with respect to a given mapping. In *Eighth International Workshop on Compilers for Parallel Computers*, CPC2000, pages 135–150, january 2000.
12. A. Demeure, B. Marchand, J. Jourdan, J. Mattioli, F. Irigoin, C. Ancourt, and all. Placement automatique optimisé d'applications de traitement du signal. Technical report, Rappport Final DRET 913060009, 1996.
13. M. Dion. *Alignement et distribution en parallélisation automatique.* Thèse informatique, ENS,LYON, 1996. 136 P.
14. P. Feautrier. Some efficient solutions to the affine scheduling problem, part ii: mutidimensional time. *International Journal of Parallel Programming*, 21(6):389–420, december 1992.
15. P. Feautrier. Toward Automatic Distribution. *Parallel Processing Letters*, 4(3):233–244, 1994.

16. Ch. Guettier. *Optimisation globale et placement d'applications de traitement de signal sur architectures parallèles utilisant la programmation logique avec contraintes.* PhD thesis, Ecole des Mines de Paris, 1997.
17. C. Han, K.-J. Lin, and C.-J. Hou. Distance Constrained Scheduling and its Applications to Real-Time Systems. *IEEE Transactions On Computers*, 45(7):814–825, Jul 1996.
18. W. Harvey. Computing two-dimensional integer hulls. *Society for Industrial and Applied Mathematics*, 28(6):2285–2299, 1999.
19. J. Jourdan. *Concurrence et coopération de modèles multiples dans les langages de contraintes CLP et CC: Vers une méthodologie de programmation par modélisation.* PhD thesis, Université Denis Diderot, Paris VII, février 1995.
20. J. Jourdan. Concurrent constraint multiple models in clp and cc languages: Toward a programming methodology by modelling. In *Proc. INFORMS conference*, New Orleans, USA, October 1995.
21. U. Kremer. NP–completeness of Dynamic Remapping. In *Workshop on Compilers for Parallel Computers, Delft*, pages 135–141, December 1993.
22. E. A. Lee and D. G. Messerschmitt. Synchronous Dataflow. In *Proceedings of the IEEE*, September 1987.
23. Lockheed Martin. *GEDAE Users' Manual / GEDAE Training Course Lectures.*
24. B. Meister. Localité des données dans les opérations stencil. In *Treizième Rencontres Francophones du Parallélisme des Architectures et des Systèmes*, Compilation et Parallélisation automatique, pages 37–42, avril 2001.
25. P. Murthy, S. S. Bhattacharyya, and E. A. Lee. Minimising Memory Requirements for Chain-Structured Synchronous Dataflow Programs. In *Proceedings of the International Conference on Acoustics, Speech and Signal Processing, April 1994.*, 1996.
26. N. Museux. De la sur-approximation des dépendances. Technical Report E/227/CRI, ENSMP/CRI, 2000.
27. N. Museux, F. Irigoin, M. Barreteau, and J. Mattioli. Parallélisation automatique d'applications de traittement du signal sur machines parallèles. In *Treizième Rencontres Francophones du Parallélisme des Architectures et des Systèmes*, Compilation et Parallélisation automatique, pages 55–60, avril 2001.
28. Platon Team. Eclair reference manual. Technical report, THALES/LCR, 2001.
29. P. Saveant. Constraint reduction at the type level. In *Proceedings of TRICS: Techniques foR Implementing Constraint programming Systems, a post-conference workshop of CP 2000*, Singapore, 2000.
30. L. Schäfers and C. Scheidler. trapper: A graphical programming environment for embedded mimd computers. In IOS Press, editor, *1993 World Transputer Congress*, Transputer Applications and Systems'93, pages 1023–1034, 1993.
31. M. Schmitt and J. Mattioli. Strong and weak convex hulls in non-Euclidean metric: Theory and Application. *Pattern recognition letters*, 15:943–947, 1994.
32. Gilbert C. Sih and Edward A. Lee. Declustering: A New Multiprocessor Scheduling Technique. *IEEE Transaction on Parallel and Distributed Systems*, 4(6):625–637, June 1993.
33. Y. Sorel and C. Lavarenne. http://www-rocq.inria.fr/Syndex/pub.htm.
34. J. Subhlok and G. Vondran. Optimal latency-troughput tradeoffs for data parallel pipelines. In *Proc. SPAA'96*, Padua, Italy, 1996.
35. E. A. Lee team. http://ptolemy.eecs.berkeley.edu/papers.

iOpt: A Software Toolkit for Heuristic Search Methods

Christos Voudouris, Raphael Dorne, David Lesaint, and Anne Liret

BTexact Technologies, Intelligent Systems Lab,
B62 Orion Building, pp MLB1/12,
Martlesham Heath, Ipswich IP5 3RE, Suffolk, United Kingdom
{chris.voudouris, raphael.dorne, david.lesaint,
anne.liret}@bt.com

Abstract. Heuristic Search techniques are known for their efficiency and effectiveness in solving NP-Hard problems. However, there has been limited success so far in constructing a software toolkit which is dedicated to these methods and can fully support all the stages and aspects of researching and developing a system based on these techniques. Some of the reasons for that include the lack of problem modelling facilities and domain specific frameworks which specifically suit the operations of heuristic search, tedious code optimisations which are often required to achieve efficient implementations of these methods, and the large number of available algorithms - both local search and population-based - which make it difficult to implement and evaluate a range of techniques to find the most efficient one for the problem at hand. The iOpt Toolkit, presented in this article, attempts to address these issues by providing problem modelling facilities well-matched to heuristic search operations, a generic framework for developing scheduling applications, and a logically structured heuristic search framework allowing the synthesis and evaluation of a variety of algorithms. In addition to these, the toolkit incorporates interactive graphical components for the visualisation of problem and scheduling models, and also for monitoring the run-time behaviour and configuring the parameters of heuristic search algorithms.

1 Introduction

The iOpt Toolkit research project at BTexact Technologies was motivated by the lack of appropriate tools to support the development of real-world applications, which are based on heuristic search methods. The goal, originally set, was to develop a set of software frameworks and libraries dedicated to heuristic search to address this problem.

Following contemporary thinking in software engineering, iOpt allows code reuse and various extensions to reduce as much as possible the fresh source code required to be written for each new application. Furthermore, application development is additive in the sense that the toolkit is enhanced by each new application, reducing further the effort in developing similar applications to those already included.

iOpt is fully written in the Java programming language with all the acknowledged benefits associated with that, including:

- easier deployment in different operating systems and environments,

T. Walsh (Ed.): CP 2001, LNCS 2239, pp. 716-729, 2001.

- stricter object oriented programming,
- compatibility with 3-tier application servers based on J2EE, and also
- better integration with visualisation code in Web browsers and stand alone applications.

Up to recently, Java was considered too inefficient (e.g. compared to C++) for developing optimisation applications. This situation has significantly improved with the introduction of new compilation technologies such as Sun's HotSpot and the ever improving performance of PCs. iOpt has taken advantage of these two developments using Java as a promising alternative to C++; at least from the software engineer's point of view who is sometimes willing to sacrifice ultimate performance for ease of use and better integration.

iOpt incorporates many libraries and frameworks such as a constraint library, a problem modelling framework, a generic framework for modelling scheduling applications, a heuristic search framework, as well as interactive visualisation facilities for constraint networks, scheduling applications, algorithm configuration and monitoring.

In this paper, due to space limitations, we only provide a general description of the different parts of the toolkit while focusing on the software engineering aspects and design choices. For a more detailed technical description and computational results on the problem solving modules (i.e. constraint library and heuristic search framework) the reader may refer to [18] and also [3].

2 One-Way Constraints

The iOpt Toolkit, to facilitate problem modelling, provides declarative programming capabilities within the Java programming language. The paradigm followed is similar to C++ libraries for constraint programming such as ILOG Solver [15], consisting of a number of built-in relations which are available to the user to state its problem. A constraint satisfaction algorithm is used to transparently maintain these relations. In contrast to constraint programming tools, relations available in iOpt are based exclusively on one-way dataflow constraints [19, 20].

A one-way dataflow constraint is an equation (also called) formula, in which the value of the variable in the left-hand side is determined by the value of the expression in the right-hand side. For example, a programmer could use the equation $y = x + 10$ to constrain the value of y to be always equal to the value of x plus 10. More formally, a one-way constraint is an equation of the form [19]:

$$u = C(p_0, p_1, p_2, \ldots, p_n) \tag{1}$$

where each p_i is a variable that serves as a parameter to the function C. Arbitrary code can be associated with C that uses the values of the parameters to compute a value. This value is assigned to variable u. If the value of any p_i is changed during the program's execution, u's value is automatically recomputed (or incrementally updated in constant time). Note that u has no influence on any p_i as far as this constraint is concerned; hence, it is called one-way.

2.1 Constraint Satisfaction Algorithms for One-Way Constraints

The two most common constraint satisfaction schemes for one-way constraints are the mark/sweep strategy [7, 20] and the topological ordering strategy [6, 20]. A mark/sweep algorithm has two phases. In the mark phase, constraints that depend on changed variables are marked out-of-date. In the sweep phase, constraints whose values are requested are evaluated and the constraints are marked as up-to-date. If constraints are only evaluated when their values are requested, then the sweep phase is called a *lazy* evaluator. If all the out-of-date constraints are evaluated as soon as the mark phase is complete, then the sweep phase is called an *eager* evaluator.

A topological ordering algorithm is one, which assigns numbers to constraints that indicate their position in topological order. Like the mark/sweep strategy, the topological ordering strategy has two phases. A numbering phase that brings the topological numbers up-to-date and a sweep phase that evaluates the constraints. The numbering phase is invoked whenever an edge in the constraint dataflow graph changes. The sweep phase can either be invoked as soon as a variable changes value or it can be delayed to allow several variables to be changed. The sweep phase uses a priority queue to keep track of the next constraint to evaluate. Initially all constraints that depend on a changed variable are added to the priority queue. The constraint solver removes the lowest numbered constraint from the queue and evaluates it. If the constraint's value changes, all constraints that depend on the variable determined by this constraint are added to the priority queue. This process continues until the priority queue is exhausted.

For the purposes of this project, we evaluated both topological ordering and mark/sweep algorithms. Although, theory suggests that topological algorithms should be faster at least for basic constraint types [19], our experience (with both approaches implemented in the Java language) showed that topological algorithms were slower something, which is in agreement with the findings in [19]. This is primarily because mark/sweep methods are simple and therefore subject to faster implementations compared to the queue-based topological ordering methods. When cycles and dynamic relations are added then mark/sweep algorithms also become theoretically faster [20].

One-way constraints have been used extensively by the GUI community in building interactive user interfaces [13, 14], and also in circuits [1] and spreadsheet programming [12]. Localizer, a scripting language for implementing local search algorithms also uses this approach for modelling combinatorial optimization problems [10, 11]. A specialized topological ordering algorithm is deployed there [10].

In Localizer, one-way functional constraints are called invariants. We will also use the same term to refer to one-way constraints when used in the context of Heuristic Search. This would help distinguish them from multi-way relational constraints as they are traditionally defined and used in Constraint Programming and also from the problem's constraints as they are given in its mathematical formulation.

2.2 Invariant Library

The Invariant Library (IL) of iOpt, as the name suggests, is solely based on invariants (i.e. one-way constraints). IL provides a number of built-in data types such as Integer, Real, Boolean, String and Object and also set versions of these types (except for

Boolean). Arithmetic, logical, string, object, set and other operators are available to the user to state its problem (i.e. decision variables, parameters, constraints and objective function). Being a library of Java, IL brings a number of advantages such as integration with visualisation components, ability for the user to extend the operators available by defining its own, facilities to work on language data structures such as Java Object and String (useful for producing on-the-fly constraint explanations) and also easier embedding into other Java programs. IL incorporates many optimisations such as incremental updates for aggregate types (e.g. sum, prod, min, max), lazy and eager evaluation modes, constraint priorities, cycle detection facilities, propagation stopping and the ability to work with undefined parts of the dataflow graph (e.g. when some of the decision variables are yet unassigned). In addition to these, it is more geared towards computationally demanding applications compared to other Java libraries and applications. This is achieved by avoiding some of the built-in but inefficient Java data structures and also by trying to avoid the constant creation and garbage collection of objects, something very common in a strict object oriented environment such as Java's.

Arbitrary dataflow graphs can be configured to model optimisation problems by mapping the decision variables representing a solution to the objective and constraints as they are given by the problem's mathematical formulation.

The reason for selecting invariants for supporting Heuristic Search, over relational constraints (as used in CP), is that invariants are particularly suited for heuristic search. Heuristic search techniques require an efficient way to access the impact of incremental solution changes to the problem's constraints (i.e. constraint checks) and also the value of the objective function. Invariants are particularly adept at this task since they can incorporate specialized incremental update mechanisms for the different operators implemented, in addition to the general algorithms available for restricting the parts of the constraint graph that need to be updated after a change in the input variables (decision variables in this case).

Small solution changes (often called moves) are the foundation of Heuristic Search (Local Search to be more precise). They are iteratively used to improve a starting solution for the problem. Devising an efficient move evaluation mechanism normally requires a person with significant expertise in the area. This hinders the widespread use of Heuristic Search. The invariant library addresses this problem by utilising the generic mark/sweep algorithm mentioned above which can achieve relatively efficient move evaluations in an automated way and that without any particular expertise or special programming skills required by the user. The library also supports dynamic changes such as the addition and deletion of variables and constraints always bringing the network of invariants in a consistent state after each modification.

3 Problem Modelling Framework

A Problem Modelling Framework (PMF) is part of the toolkit. The role of the framework is to provide an ontology for combinatorial optimisation problems something which is not explicit in the invariant library which is general in its nature. PMF includes foundation classes for Problem and Solution and also for the various types of decision variables. In addition, it incorporates solution management facilities by keeping the best solution, current solution or a population of solutions, which can be used by local search or population-based techniques. It can also be instructed to detect constraint violations and stop the evaluation algorithm at an early stage. As with the invariant library, arbitrary dynamic changes to the objectives/constraints or decision variables are allowed with the problem model always ending up in a consistent state.

In Figure 1, we provide an annotated code sample demonstrating the use of invariants in conjunction with the problem modelling framework to model a simple optimisation problem. We also include operations, which change the problem model.

```
/* Create a simple problem model using invariants */
Problem p = new Problem();
p.beginModelChanges();                  // start changes to the problem model
RealVar x = new RealVar(10.0);          // create a real variable x and set its initial value to 10.0
p.addDecisionVar(x);                    // set x to be a decision variable
p.addObjective(Inv.plus(x, 5.0));       // add the term x + 5.0 to the objective initially undefined
p.addConstraint(Inv.gt(x, 5.0));        // set the constraint x > 5.0
p.endModelChanges();                    // end changes to the problem model

/* Change to the value of the decision variable */
/* Similar operations are performed when local search is evaluating a move
   or the user modifies the solution through a GUI */
p.beginValueChanges();                  // start changes to the values of the decision variables
x.setValue(100.0);                      // set x to the new value of 100.00
p.endValueChanges();                    // end changes to the values of the decision variables
p.propagateValueChanges();              // the mark/sweep algorithm is updating the invariants
p.saveValueChanges();                   // we commit the changes, we may undo them instead
                                        // in case of constraint violations or inferior cost

/* Dynamic addition of decision variable/objective to the problem model */
RealVar y = new RealVar(15.0);
p.addDecisionVar(y);
p.addObjective(Inv.plus(y, 10.0));      // the overall objective is now (x + 5.0) + (y + 10.0)
p.endModelChanges();
```

Fig. 1. Sample source code demonstrating the use of invariants and PMF.

The above example is a very simple one and only for illustration purposes. In fact, the problem modelling framework usually serves as the basis for domain specific frameworks such as the Scheduling Framework explained next. It has also been extended to model specific problems such as the Graph Colouring, Car Sequencing, Set Partitioning, Frequency Assignment as well as a real-world BT application related to field resource planning.

4 Scheduling Framework

Scheduling problems can be found in diverse sections of the economy (e.g. Manufacturing, Transportation/Logistics, Utilities). To assist non-expert users to develop applications in these areas, we developed a framework of Java classes for specifically modelling scheduling problems with unary resources. These classes hide the complexity of invariant-based decision models from the user, who instead focuses on describing his/her problem using domain-specific entities (e.g. Activity, Resource, Break, etc.).

There is a class hierarchy included for activities to capture the different types found in applications. Depending on the type of the activity, the user can state resource and/or time constraints (e.g. task A before/after task B, multiple time windows, "same"/"different" resource constraints and others).

For modelling the resources, the framework includes different types of timelines such as state, capacity and capability timelines. The interactions of activities with these timelines capture all the necessary constraints related to the execution of activities on resources.

The scheduling framework also supports user-defined models for resource setup(travel)/service times. These are sub-models, which can be implemented by external systems such as GIS (in the case of travel times), to offer realistic duration estimates for activities and also for resource transitions between activities.

One or more of several built-in objectives can be selected and used. These are listed below:

- unallocated costs for activities,
- resource usage costs,
- time window/lateness penalties,
- overtime costs,
- setup and service duration costs and also
- resource-activity compatibility preferences.

The scheduling framework internally uses the problem modelling framework mentioned in section 3. This makes it possible to extend it to capture the different variations of scheduling problems in terms of additional decision variables, constraints or costs.

In contrast to CP-based scheduling libraries, the framework solely uses invariants for both constraint checking and also for the computation of the objective function. The move operators *relocate* and *swap* are readily available so that heuristic search methods or interactive graphical components such as a Gantt Chart can operate on the schedule.

Using the Scheduling Framework, we have experimented building models for well-known problems such as the Vehicle Routing Problem, Job Shop Scheduling Problem and also a Workforce Scheduling Problem.

As with PMF and the invariant library, dynamic changes are allowed such as adding/removing activities/resources, resource/temporal constraints and also time windows. These operations internally use the facilities of PMF and of the invariant library to implement changes in a consistent and transparent manner.

5 Heuristic Search Framework

The Heuristic Search Framework (HSF) was created to be a generic framework for the family of optimisation techniques known as Heuristic Search. It covers single solution methods such as Local Search, population-based methods such as Genetic Algorithms as well as hybrids combining one or more different algorithms. Heuristic Search methods are known to be efficient on a large range of optimisation problems but they remain difficult to design, tune, and compare. Furthermore, they tend to be problem specific often-requiring re-implementation to address a new problem.

HSF proposes a new way to design a Heuristic Search method whereby the functionality of common HS algorithms is broken down into components (i.e. parts) for which component categories are defined. Component categories are represented by Java interfaces while specific components are defined as Java classes implementing these interfaces. The designer has the capability to build a complete and complex algorithm by assembling these components which are either build-in or user extensions to the framework. In particular, three main concepts are the basis of HSF: Search Component, Heuristic Solution and Heuristic Problem.

- *Search Component* as explained above is the basic entity that is used to build an optimisation method. Most often a Search Component represents a basic concept that could be encountered in an HS method. For example, the concept of Neighbourhood in a Local Search. A complete algorithm is a valid tree of search components[1].
- *Heuristic Solution* is the solution representation of an optimisation problem manipulated inside HSF. At the present moment, a *Vector of Variables* and a *Set of Sequences* are readily available. These representations are commonly used in modelling combinatorial optimisation problems. For example a vector of variables can model CSPs while a set of sequences can model various scheduling applications with unary resources.
- *Heuristic Problem* is only an interface between an optimisation problem model implemented by IL (or my other means[2]) and HSF. This interface allows using the same algorithm for a family of optimisation problems without re-implementing any separate functionality. The following theoretical problems and real applications are already implemented using the Invariant Library (and also higher-level frameworks such as the Problem Modelling Framework and the Scheduling Framework) and used by HSF using that concept: Graph Colouring, Set Partitioning, Frequency Assignment, Job Shop Scheduling, Workforce Scheduling, Vehicle Routing, Car Sequencing, and Field Resource Planning.

In the current version of HSF, the Search Component categories group many basic concepts encountered in *Single Solution Heuristic Search* such as *Initial Solution Generation, Local Search, Move, Neighbourhood, Neighbourhood Search, Aspiration Criterion, Taboo* mechanism, *Dynamic Objective Function* and others, and in *Population-based Heuristic Search* such as *Initial Population Generation, Crossover, Mutation, Selection, Mutation Population Method, Crossover Population Method, Selection Population Method, Restart Population Method*, and others.

Furthermore, many popular meta-heuristics such as Simulated Annealing (SA), Tabu Search (TS), and Guided Local Search (GLS) are implemented. Methods such as Tabu Search and Guided Local Search can become observers of other search components such as *Neighbourhood Search* and receive notifications for certain events, which require them to intervene (e.g. move performed, local minimum reached, population converged and others). Invariants are often used to model parts of these methods such as the acceptance criterion in SA, tabu restrictions in TS or features and their penalties in GLS.

---

[1] A valid tree is a tree of search components that can be executed.

[2] HSF is generic like the Invariant Library and it can be used independently from it. For example, it can be used in conjunction with a hard-coded procedural problem model.

Using the available set of search components and the other facilities explained briefly above, even the most complex hybrid methods can be modelled as the next example shows where a population-based method for Graph Colouring is composed using a local search method as the mutation, IUS crossover specialised to the Graph Colouring, *Selection*, and various other search components (see Figure 2).

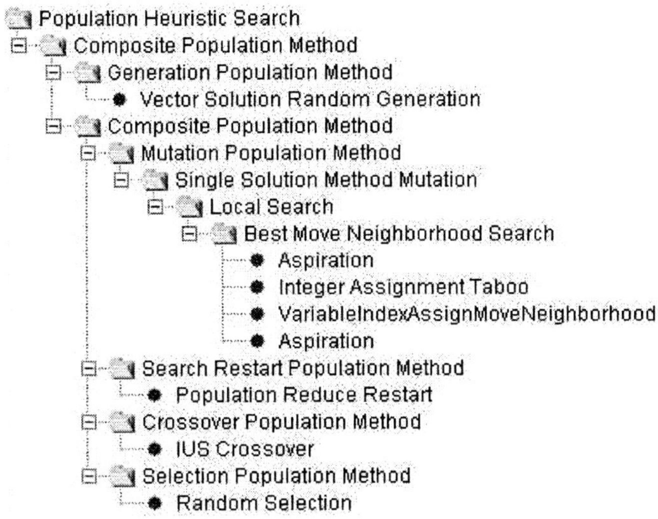

Fig. 2. Hybrid Algorithm for Graph Colouring using Local Search as a mutation.

As it becomes obvious, designing a heuristic search is simplified to a great extend through assembling a set of components even for a sophisticated method such as the hybrid algorithm in Figure 2. The framework further allows the possibility to specialise an algorithm to an optimisation problem as we did above by adding a Graph Colouring specific crossover IUS. Thus for the development of a problem-specific algorithm, we have only to implement the specialised problem-specific components not included in HSF. These can be incorporated in the framework and possibly re-used in similar applications.

Another benefit is that we can conduct easily and fairly comparisons between different algorithms or between different components of the same category (e.g. various Neighbourhood Search methods, currently fifteen of them incorporated in HSF). Since any new component can be directly plugged into the algorithmic tree replacing an old one, we can quickly determine the real benefit of different components to the search process. This is particularly useful when we are trying to determine what is the best variant of a method based on a particular philosophy (e.g. Tabu Search, Genetic Algorithms).

An additional functionality included in HSF is that any heuristic search algorithm composed by the user can be saved in XML (a commonly-used Internet format for exchanging information). An efficient algorithm is never lost, instead can be kept in a simple text file. A build-in software generator can recreate the method at a later time from its XML specification.

Since problem models are declarative and implemented by the Invariant Library, performing moves (in Local Search) or evaluating new solutions (in Population Methods) is transparent to the user. The user can then focus on the more important task of choosing and tuning the right algorithm instead of getting involved in low-level tasks such as trying to devise hard-coded efficient move evaluation mechanisms or implementing problem-specific methods to compute a complex fitness function.

6 Interactive Visualisation

For optimisation systems to unlock their potential, they require not only sound algorithmic frameworks but also intuitive visualisation facilities to enable the user to participate in the problem solving process. For addressing this issue, the toolkit incorporates visualisation components (and also add-ons to third-party visualisation components), which can be connected to the various algorithmic/modelling frameworks, included in the toolkit. This facilitates the development of interactive optimisation systems, which allow what-if scenario testing along with intelligent manual interventions. In particular, three areas of visualisation are addressed.

6.1 Invariant Visualisation

Software components have been developed to visualise invariant networks. The Model-View-Controller (MVC) approach is followed and the visual components use the Observer-Observable pattern (supported by the Invariant Library) to connect to the constraint network. The user may modify the values of variables or read the value of invariants in a table format or use a graph view to visualise the structure of the invariant network. This is particularly useful in the early stages of development for debugging parts of the problem model and also understanding the mechanism of invariant evaluation. Figure 3 provides an example of a simple invariant network as visualised by the system.

6.2 Schedule Visualisation

Similarly to invariant visualisation, a number of interactive components have been developed to visualise the entities in a schedule model amongst them a schedule tree representation, a Gantt Chart, a Capacity Chart, and a Map Viewer, along with several table views for the schedule entities (e.g. Resources, Activities, Breaks, etc.). The visual components are directly connected to a schedule model using again the MVC architecture and the Observer/Observable pattern. The user may drag and drop activities or change parameters and immediately see the impact they have on the problem's constraints and objectives as the underlying invariant network propagates changes and updates only the affected parts of the visual display. Essentially, this approach implements an interesting form of interactive constraint satisfaction/optimisation, engaging the user in the problem solving process. It has also been useful to demonstrate to non-optimisation people the complexity of scheduling problems so that they appreciate more the usefulness of Heuristic Search methods.

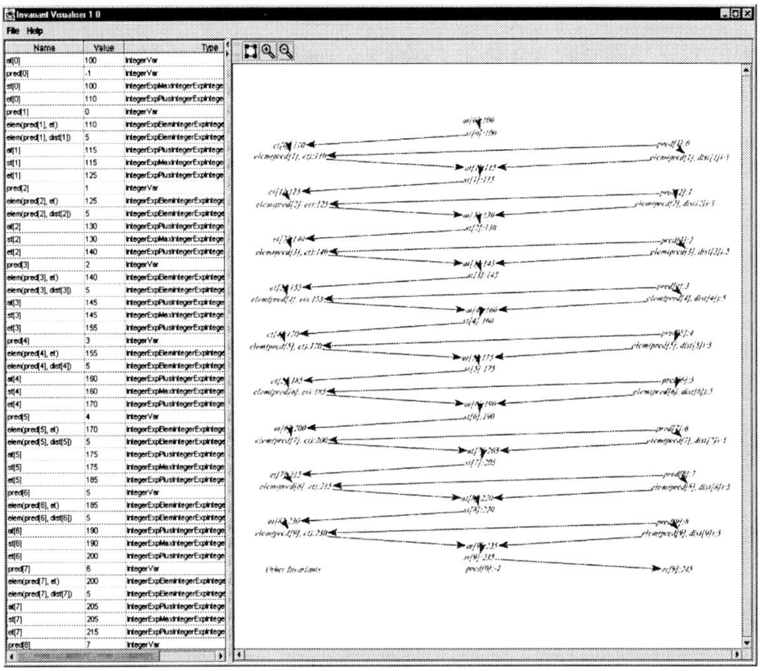

Fig. 3. Invariant visualisation example.

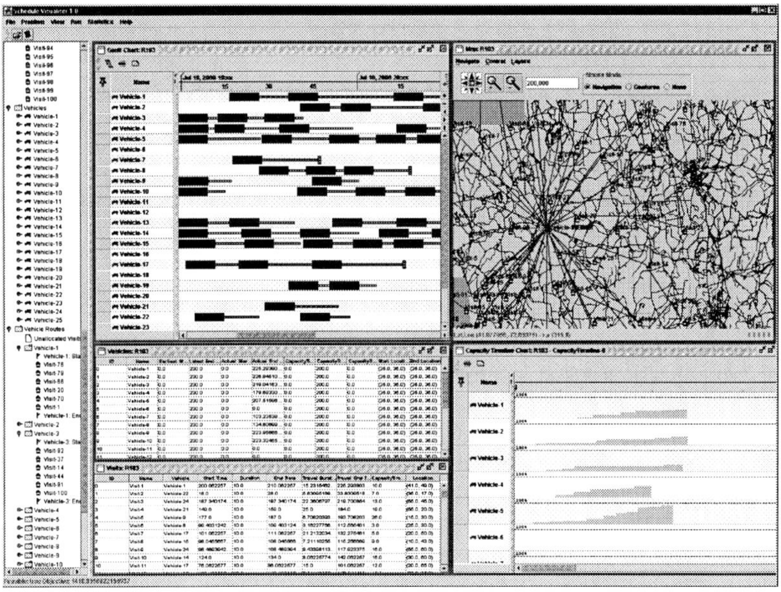

Fig. 4. Schedule visualisation example.

The visual components because they are Java-based can be incorporated inside a Web browser interface significantly reducing lead times otherwise needed to connect to the constraint engine on the server in order to assess the impact of changes to the solution. Figure 4 shows a screen shot from a fully assembled system utilising the different components.

6.3 Algorithm Visualisation

To visualise heuristic search algorithms, a special Java software package has been implemented with the focus being on allowing the user to understand and control the structure and behaviour of the methods. The facilities provided in the library include the visualisation of the tree of search components comprising an algorithm alongside with information on the parameters used by these search components.

The user can walk through the tree of search components for any heuristic search method built using the toolkit. As shown in Figure 5, the UI is divided into two panels. On the left, the tree of search components for the method selected is available and on the right appears a panel with all parameters of the currently selected component that can be adjusted by the user. Changes to these parameters can be done before commencing the search process or during the search process.

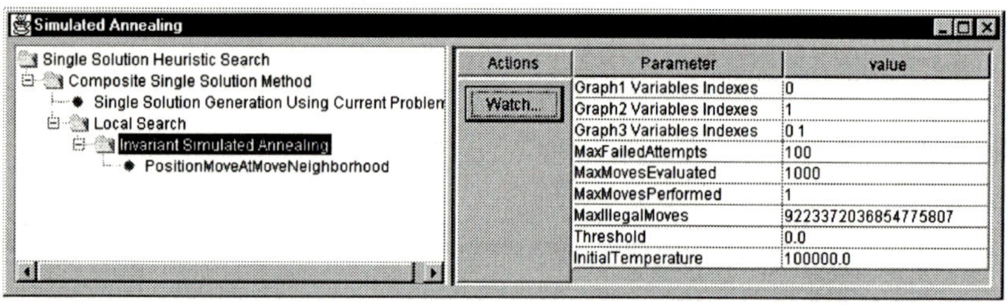

Fig. 5. Component visualisation and settings for a Simulated Annealing method.

This latter facility allows the user to have interactive control over the algorithm. For example, if a tabu search method is trapped in a local optimum then we may want to increase (even temporarily) the size of the tabu tenure to allow the search to escape from it.

As it can be seen in Figure 5, on the right panel there is a "Watch" button. When pressed, this button activates a monitoring facility for the particular search component. Watching a search component means displaying its different major variables. For example, watching a Simulated Annealing search component will display the objective value of the current/best solution, its current temperature, acceptance probability etc. (see Figure 6).

This last facility allows the possibility to visualise the workings of the whole algorithm as well as of separate search components during a search process and then exploit this information to make further changes to their parameters.

This can be seen as a form of heuristic search behaviour "trouble-shooter". After having designed a heuristic search method using the HSF framework, the user can get a better understanding of the method by watching, setting or dynamically modifying critical parameters. This could be used to make a better design resulting into a better-tuned and more efficient system.

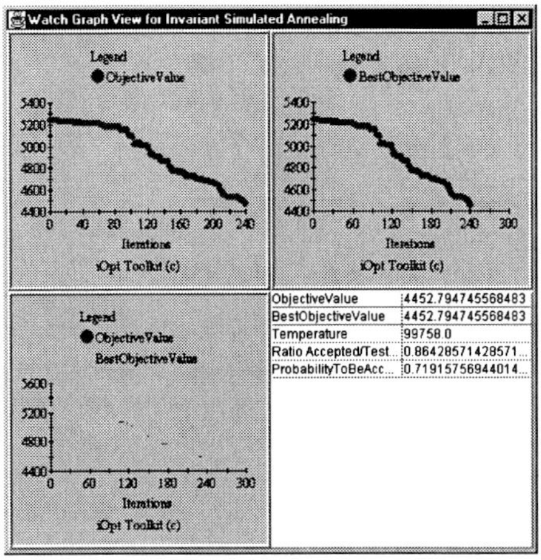

Fig. 6. Watching a Simulated Annealing search component.

8 Related Work and Discussion

In terms of the Invariant Library, the system uses algorithms initially explored in the areas of Computer Graphics [19, 20]. Related work on using one-way constraints for heuristic optimisation is the Localizer language described in [10, 11] also mentioned earlier in this paper. Differences between the IL and Localizer include the algorithms used for propagation (mark/sweep and topological-ordering respectively), the ability to model dynamic problems in IL, but most importantly the fact that Localizer is a language on its own, whereas IL uses the Java programming language by providing a declarative environment within it.

In the area of Scheduling, different frameworks have been developed such as DITOPS/OZONE[17], ASPEN[5], ILOG Schedule[9], with varying degrees of modelling capabilities. iOpt's scheduling framework is solely based on invariants, which is unique among the published work in the above mentioned systems since most of them use relational constraints or a combination of functional and relational constraints as in the case of ASPEN. Secondly, the model provided is suited for the variety of Heuristic Search methods included in HSF with the addition of dynamic problem modelling capabilities. Systems such as ILOG Schedule are primarily based on exact search methods while DITOPS/OZONE and ASPEN support only a limited set of customised heuristic methods that have been built specifically for these libraries.

In the case of the HSF, most of the frameworks proposed in the literature are either Local Search based or Genetic Algorithm based. In the case of Local Search examples of frameworks include HotFrame [4], Templar [8], LOCAL++ [16], SCOOP (http://www.oslo.sintef.no/SCOOP/), and also the work of Andreatta et al. [2]. These tend to provide templates with the user having to define the problem model rather than use a constraint-based problem modelling paradigm. The same applies for move operators.

CP toolkits such as Eclipse and ILOG Solver in their latest versions also have integrated certain basic Heuristic Search methods such as Tabu Search and Simulated

Annealing. Finally, almost all of the related works mentioned in this section, are either C/C++-based or rely on specialized scripting languages.

9 Conclusions

The iOpt toolkit presented in this article represents a research effort to integrate a number of technologies to offer a complete set of tools for developing optimisation applications based on Heuristic Search. At its present stage of development, it plays the role of a prototype platform for experimenting with the integration of a number of technologies such as constraint satisfaction, domain-specific frameworks, heuristic search and interactive visualisation whilst utilising the capabilities of the much promising Java language in doing so.

In this article, we examined parts comprising the toolkit and in particular:

- a lightweight constraint library for modelling combinatorial optimisation problems,
- a problem modelling framework providing an ontology for combinatorial optimisation problems,
- a scheduling framework which can be customized to model applications in areas such as manufacturing, transportation, workforce management,
- a heuristic search framework for synthesising local search and population based algorithms and
- various visualisation components which integrate with the above algorithmic modules.

We described how these can work in synergy allowing a developer to focus on the high level task of algorithm design, automating in an efficient way large parts of his/her work in developing a real-world optimisation system. Current research is focused on incorporating as part of iOpt a relational constraint library and an exact search framework developed in-house. Relational constraints and invariants and also exact and heuristic search methods can work collaboratively in many different ways and at present we are trying to identify the most promising ones. This is analogous to the link between MP and CP. Hopefully, a successful link of HS with CP in iOpt can lead to an environment which not only supports CP and HS but also guides the user how to exploit the best combinations of these techniques.

On the industrialisation front, iOpt is presently being validated on internal BT applications and an enterprise system based on the toolkit will be deployed later in the year. First results are promising both in terms of reducing development times and also with regard to use of the system by non-expert software developers. Experience gained from in-house development is utilised to rationalise the system and also improve its robustness and performance.

References

1. Alpern, B., Hoover, R., Rosen, B.K., Sweeney, P. F., and Zadeck, F.K., Incremental evaluation of computational circuits. In ACM SIGACT-SIAM'89 Conference on Discrete Algorithms, pp. 32–42, 1990.

2. Andreatta, A., Carvalho, S., and Ribeiro, C., An Object-Oriented Framework for Local Search Heuristics, 26th Conference on Technology of Object-Oriented Languages and Systems (TOOLS USA'98), IEEE Press, 33-45, 1998.
3. Dorne, R, and Voudouris, C., HSF: A generic framework to easily design Meta-Heuristic methods, 4th Metaheuristics International Conference (MIC' 2001), Porto, Portugal, 423-428, 2001.
4. Fink, A., Voß, S., Woodruff, D., Building Reusable Software Components for Heuristic Search, In: P. Kall, H.-J. Lüthi (Eds.), Operations Research Proceedings 1998, Springer, Berlin, 210-219, 1999.
5. Fukunaga, A., Rabideau, G., Chien, S., and Yan, D., Toward an Application Framework for Automated Planning and Scheduling, Proceedings of the 1997 International Symposium on Artificial Intelligence, Robotics and Automation for Space, Tokyo, Japan, July 1997.
6. Hoover, R., Incremental Graph Evaluation. PhD thesis, Department of Computer Science, Cornell University, Ithaca, NY, 1987.
7. Hudson, S., Incremental Attribute Evaluation: A Flexible Algorithm for Lazy Update, ACM Transactions on Programming Languages and Systems, Vol.13, No. 3, pp. 315-341, July 1991.
8. Jones, M., McKeown, G, Raywar-Smith, V., Templar: An Object Oriented Framework for Distributed Combinatorial Optimization, UNICOM Seminar on Modern Heuristics for Decision Support, London, 7 December, 1998.
9. Le Pape, C., Implementation of Resource Constraints in ILOG SCHEDULE: A Library for the Development of Constraint-Based Scheduling Systems, Intelligent Systems Engineering, 3(2):55-66, 1994.
10. Michel, L. and Van Hentenryck, P., Localizer, Tech Report CS-98-02, Brown University, March 1998.
11. Michel, L. and Van Hentenryck, P., Localizer: A Modeling Language for Local Search, INFORMS Journal of Computing 11(1): 1-14, 1999.
12. Microsoft Corporation, Microsoft Excel.
13. Myers B.A., McDaniel, R.G., Miller, R.C., Ferrency, A., Faulring, A., Kyle, B.D., Mickish, A., Klimovitski, A., and Doane, P., The Amulet Environment: New Models for Effective User Interface Software Development, IEEE Transactions on Software Engineering, Vol. 23, No. 6, pp. 347-365, 1997.
14. Myers, B.A., Giuse D., Dannenberg, R.B., Zanden, B.V., Kosbie, D.S., Pervin E., Mickish, A., and Marchal, P., Garnet: Comprehensive Support for Graphical, Highly-Interactive User Interfaces, IEEE Computer, Vol. 23, No. 11., pp. 71-85, 1990.
15. Puget, J-F., Applications of constraint programming, in Montanari, U. & Rossi, F. (ed.), Proceedings, Principles and Practice of Constraint Programming (CP'95), Lecture Notes in Computer Science, Springer Verlag, Berlin, Heidelberg & New York, 647-650,1995.
16. Schaerf, A., Lenzerini, M., Cadoli, M, LOCAL++: a C++ framework for local search algorithms, Proc. of TOOLS Europe '99: Technology of Object Oriented Languages and Systems. 29th Int. Conf. 7-10 June, IEEE Comput. Soc, pp. 152-61, 1999.
17. Smith, S.F., and Becker, M., An Ontology for Constructing Scheduling Systems, Working Notes of 1997 AAAI Symposium on Ontological Engineering, Stanford, CA, March, 1997 (AAAI Press).
18. Voudouris, C., and Dorne, R., Heuristic search and one-way constraints for combinatorial optimisation, Proceedings of CP-AI-OR'01, Wye College (Imperial College), Asford, Kent UK, pp. 257 – 269, April 2001.
19. Zanden, B.V., Halterman, R., Myers, B.A., McDaniel, R., Miller, R., Szekely, P., Giuse, D., and Kosbie, D., Lessons Learned About One-Way, Dataflow Constraints in the Garnet and Amulet Graphical Toolkits, manuscript in preperation, 1999.
20. Zanden, B.V., Myers, B.A., Giuse, D. and Szekely, P., Integrating Pointer Variables into One-Way Constraint Models, ACM Transactions on Computer-Human Interaction. Vol. 1, No. 2, pp. 161-213, June, 1994.

AbsCon: A Prototype to Solve CSPs with Abstraction*

Sylvain Merchez[1,2], Christophe Lecoutre[1], and Frederic Boussemart[1]

[1] Université d'Artois, Centre de Recherche en Informatique de Lens, Rue de l'université, 62307 Lens, France
{merchez,lecoutre,boussemart}@univ-artois.fr
[2] Université d'Artois, Laboratoire en Organisation et Gestion de la Production, Technoparc Futura, 62408 Béthune, France

Abstract. In this paper, we present a Java constraint programming prototype called *AbsCon* which has been conceived to deal with CSP abstraction. *AbsCon* considers n-ary constraints and implements different value and variable ordering heuristics as well as different propagation methods. As *AbsCon* exploits object technology, it is easy to extend its functionalities.

1 Introduction

Abstraction techniques concern many fields of computer science including planning, theorem proving, program analysis and, more recently, constraint satisfaction. In general, solving a Constraint Satisfaction Problem (CSP) is NP-complete. To cope with larger and larger problem instances, many methods based on propagation and abstraction principles, have been developed.

Generally speaking, a CSP abstraction consists of approximating a concrete (or ground) problem by an abstract one which can be defined by clustering values and variables, and by simplifying or removing constraints. Solving an abstract problem can then be seen as a guiding method to solve a concrete problem since it is possible to use abstract solutions in order to look for concrete solutions [10]. As a rule, CSP abstraction involves fewer variables and smaller domains. Therefore, in some cases, solving a concrete problem through abstraction is eventually far more efficient than directly solving it.

In this paper, we propose the description of a prototype, so-called *AbsCon* [1], which can be used to deal with CSP abstraction. *AbsCon* is fully implemented in Java, and, consequently, it can be run on different platforms. One requirement about the development was to make *AbsCon* as clear and flexible as possible. This is the reason why we have exploited as much as possible object-oriented principles such as encapsulation, inheritance and polymorphism.

The main features of *AbsCon* can be summarized in three points. First, following the growing interest in the constraint community with respect to n-ary

* This paper has been supported in part by a "contrat de plan Etat-Région Nord/Pas-de-Calais" and by the "IUT de Lens".

T. Walsh (Ed.): CP 2001, LNCS 2239, pp. 730–744, 2001.

constraints (see e.g. [2]), *AbsCon* has been conceived to take them into consideration. Second, different value and variable ordering heuristics as well as different propagation techniques have been integrated in *AbsCon*. Third, *AbsCon* offers two forms of resolution: a classical one and a hybrid one (using abstraction).

2 Preliminaries

Let S be a set, $|S|$ denotes the number of elements in S and $\wp(S)$ denotes the power-set of S, i.e., the set $\{A \mid A \subseteq S\}$. Any subset R of a Cartesian product $S_1 \times ... \times S_n$ is called a n-ary relation. We will note $def(R)$ the Cartesian product from which a relation R is defined. Let f be a mapping defined from a set E to a set F, then E and F are respectively called domain and co-domain of f. Let D_s be a set of domains, $\prod(D_s)$ denotes the Cartesian product established from elements of D_s (by assuming an implicit total order). A covering Q of S is a subset of $\wp(S)$ such that the union of elements of Q gives S. A partition P of S is a covering such that any pair of elements of P is disjoint.

3 CSP Abstraction Framework

Lecoutre et al. [16] have proposed a framework which allows to define CSP abstraction from approximation relations rather than abstraction mappings [12, 10] or Galois connection [9,6,5]. As a result, classical and original forms of abstraction can be taken into account. Classical forms correspond to simple value and variable clustering where "simple" means that the clustering represents a partition of the set of concrete elements. Original forms correspond to general clustering where "general" means that the clusters of concrete elements corresponding to two different abstract elements may overlap. This section is a summary of [16,18].

3.1 Constraint Satisfaction Problems

Definition 1. *A constraint satisfaction problem is a 4-tuple* $(\mathcal{V}, \mathcal{D}, \mathcal{C}, \mathcal{R})$ *where:*

- $\mathcal{V} = \{V_1, ..., V_n\}$ *is a finite set of variables,*
- $\mathcal{D} = \{D_1, ..., D_n\}$ *is a finite set of domains where* D_i *denotes the set of values allowed for the variable* V_i*,*
- $\mathcal{C} = \{C_1, ..., C_m\}$ *is a finite set of constraints,*
- $\mathcal{R} = \{R_1, ..., R_m\}$ *is a finite set of relations where* R_j *denotes the set of tuples allowed for the variables involved in the constraint* C_j*.*

A solution is an assignment of values to all the variables such that all the constraints are satisfied. The set of solutions of a CSP P will be denoted by $sol(P)$. If $R\uparrow$ denotes the extension of the relation R with respect to all domains of P then $sol(P) = \cap\{R\uparrow \mid R \in \mathcal{R}\}$. Below, we present a problem, the abstraction of which will be studied later in the paper.

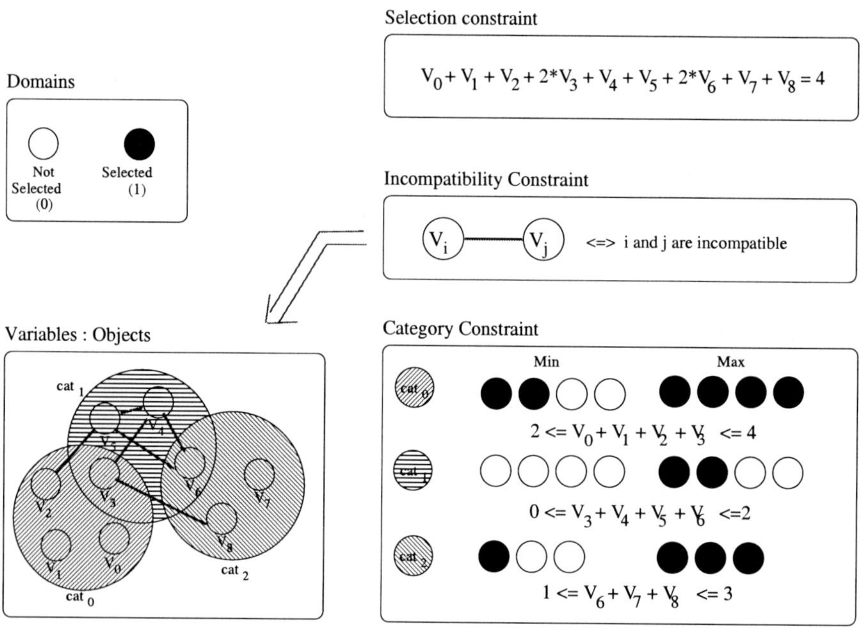

Fig. 1. Selection problem

Example: selection problem

Given a set of p objects structured in q categories, the problem consists of determining which objects can be selected when considering the following n-ary constraints:

- selection constraint: the weighted[1] sum of selected objects must be equal to a fixed value.
- incompatibility constraints: some objects can not be selected together.
- category constraints: a lower bound and an upper bound fix the limits of selection for each category.

As an instance of this problem, let us consider $p = 9$ and $q = 3$. This instance, illustrated in Figure 1, is clearly a CSP with 9 variables. Each domain is given by the set $\{0, 1\}$ where 1 (resp. 0) denotes that the object is (resp. not) selected. Note that some objects belong to several categories.

3.2 Approximation Relations

Before defining CSP abstraction, we need to introduce some basic definitions about approximation relations. Let us consider a mapping g (denoting a concrete

[1] The weight of an object is given by the number of categories where it appears in.

calculation) and a mapping g' (denoting an abstract calculation). For instance, g and g' can be viewed as mappings which associate with a given CSP its set of solutions. In order to establish a correspondence between g and g', domains and co-domains of g and g' must be linked. Notice that domains and co-domains can be complex structures, i.e., structures that are established from elementary sets and extension operators. This is the reason why we introduce a set $\Xi = \{\xi_1, ..., \xi_n\}$ of binary relations defined from a set of elementary sets. A relation ξ of Ξ will be called an approximation relation. For any pair (d, d') of elements of $def(\xi)$, $\xi(d, d')$ means that d' is an approximation of d, or in other words, that d is approximated by d'. From Ξ, it is possible to define the set Ξ^{ext} by induction, including all approximation relations obtained by considering powerset and Cartesian product extensions [18].

3.3 Abstraction Base

The idea of CSP abstraction is to establish a correspondence between two CSPs (called concrete and abstract CSPs) from basic links defined on domains. More precisely, the set of domains of both CSPs are first structured into subsets. The result of this operation can be seen as a partition but more generally as a covering. Then, a correspondence via a bijective mapping must be established between elements of the concrete and abstract coverings, expressing basic links between concrete and abstract problems. Finally, an approximation relation must be associated with each such link. All these elements form the abstraction base.

Definition 2. *An abstraction base B is a 6-tuple $(\mathcal{D}, \mathcal{D}', \mathcal{K}, \mathcal{K}', \varphi, \Xi)$ where:*

- *$\mathcal{D}$ is a set of (concrete) domains,*
- *$\mathcal{D}'$ is a set of (abstract) domains,*
- *$\mathcal{K}$ is a covering of $\mathcal{D}$,*
- *$\mathcal{K}'$ is a covering of $\mathcal{D}'$ with $|\mathcal{K}'| = |\mathcal{K}|$,*
- *φ is a bijective mapping from $\mathcal{K}$ to $\mathcal{K}'$,*
- *$\Xi = \{\xi_i \mid c_i \in \mathcal{K}\}$ where ξ_i is an approximation relation associated with c_i such that $def(\xi_i) = \prod(c_i) \times \prod(\varphi(c_i))$. Note that $|\Xi| = |\mathcal{K}| = |\mathcal{K}'|$.*

Example: selection problem
The principle of the abstraction that we propose is to reason about categories instead of objects. The abstraction base is given by Figure 2 (only the approximation relation ξ_2 defined between $D_6 \times D_7 \times D_8$ and D'_2 is depicted). An abstract domain corresponds to one category and is associated with the concrete domains corresponding to the objects of this category. The values of the abstract domains represent the number of objects which can be selected in each category. Each approximation relation corresponds to a simple value clustering and $\mathcal{K}$ corresponds to a general variable clustering[2].

[2] You can read variable or domain (clustering) since domains and variables are intrinsically linked.

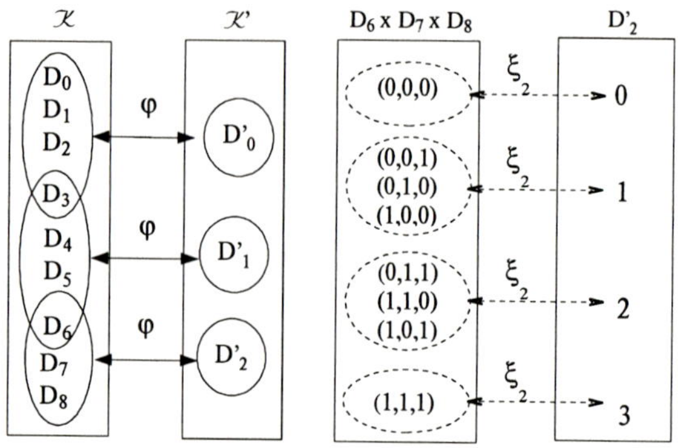

Fig. 2. Selection problem abstraction base

3.4 CSP Abstraction

A CSP abstraction consists of two CSPs and an abstraction base which expresses the links between these two problems.

Definition 3. *A CSP abstraction is a 3-tuple* (P, P', B) *where* $P = (\mathcal{V}, \mathcal{D}, \mathcal{C}, \mathcal{R})$ *and* $P' = (\mathcal{V}', \mathcal{D}', \mathcal{C}', \mathcal{R}')$ *are two CSPs and* $B = (\mathcal{D}, \mathcal{D}', \mathcal{K}, \mathcal{K}', \varphi, \Xi)$ *is an abstraction base.*

It is possible to classify a CSP abstraction as below [16,18].

Definition 4. *A CSP abstraction* (P, P', B) *is*

- *a SD abstraction if and only if* $\forall s' \in sol(P'), \exists s \in sol(P) \mid \xi(s, s')$,
- *a SI abstraction if and only if* $\forall s \in sol(P), \exists s' \in sol(P') \mid \xi(s, s')$,

where "S" stands for "Solution", "D" for "Decreasing" and "I" for "Increasing", and where $\xi \in \Xi^{ext}$ *such that* $def(\xi) = \prod(\mathcal{D}) \times \prod(\mathcal{D}')^3$.

In other words, if (P, P', B) is a SD abstraction then any abstract solution approximates a concrete one. Therefore, if an abstract solution exists, the concrete problem is proved to be consistent. However, using a SD abstraction implies the possibility of missing solutions in the concrete space. Likewise, if (P, P', B) is a SI abstraction then any concrete solution is approximated by an abstract one. Therefore, if no abstract solution exists, the concrete problem is proved to be inconsistent. However, using a SI abstraction implies the possibility of finding abstract solutions corresponding to parts of the concrete space whithout solutions.

[3] It can be shown [18] that this relation exists.

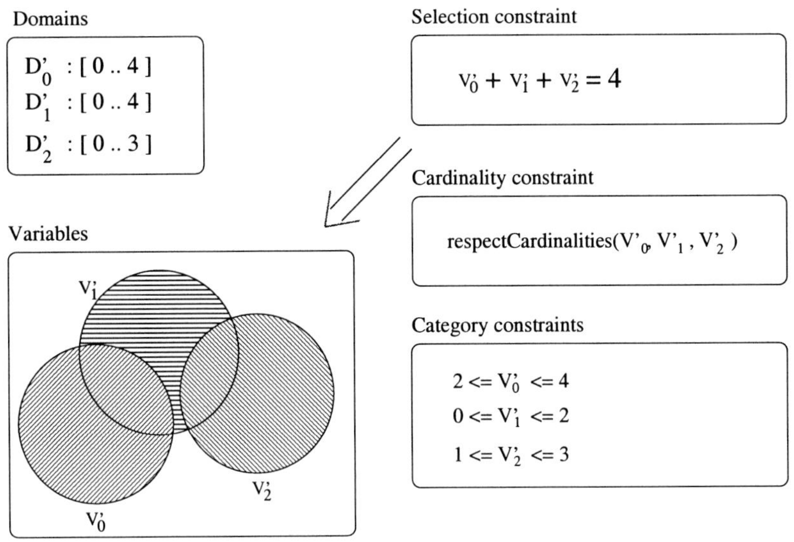

Fig. 3. Abstract selection problem

Notice that one can pass from a SD abstraction to a SI abstraction by simply inverting concrete and abstract problems [18]. In practice, SI abstractions are mainly used (e.g. [6,10,19,16]).

Example: selection problem
After describing an abstraction base (section 3.3), we propose to introduce an abstraction of the selection problem, i.e. to define an abstract problem. Figure 3 depicts this one. First, we can remark that we get a SI abstraction (a proof is given in [18]). Second, the selection and category constraints can be fully preserved in the abstract problem. Third, as expected, some information is lost when defining the abstract problem since incompatibility constraints can be only partially represented in the abstract problem by considering the cardinality of the different categories.

4 AbsCon

In this section, we present a prototype called *AbsCon* which allows to represent and to solve any binary or n-ary CSP. *AbsCon* offers the user two solving methods: a classical one and a hybrid one. The classical method is based on a backtracking search algorithm using a filtering (propagation) technique at each step. The hybrid method which is employed in order to solve CSPs with abstraction is composed of two solvers which cooperate during the resolution.

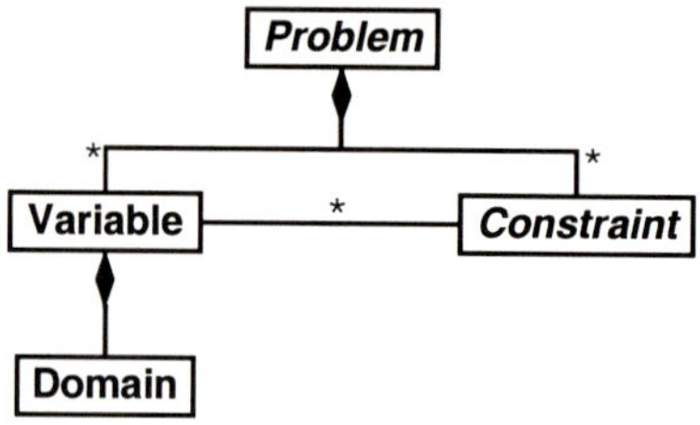

Fig. 4. CSP representation

4.1 Representing a CSP

In this subsection, we present the different classes occurring in the representation of any CSP. These are the so-called *Problem*, *Variable*, *Domain* and *Constraint* classes. A UML class diagram is given by Figure 4. We have chosen to express the bijection between variables and domains by an inheritance link and to use predicates (defined in the *Constraint* class) instead of exhaustively defining relations.

In *AbsCon*, a problem is characterized by two arrays specifying a set of variables and a set of constraints. The *Problem* class is an abstract class from which it is possible to derive a class representing a specific problem. Then, the user has just to override two methods (*addVariables()*, *addConstraints()*) to specify variables and constraints. A variable is characterized by a domain and by an array specifying the set of constraints in which it occurs. Note that in the *Variable* class, there is also a reference on a *ValueChooser* object which implements a value ordering heuristic. This aspect will be discussed in section 4.2. A domain is associated with a variable and is characterized by an array specifying the set of values that can be assigned. A constraint is characterized by an array specifying the set of variables which it binds and by a set of methods (denoting predicates) which may be called during constraint propagation.

4.2 Solving a CSP

In this subsection, we present the different classes used when solving a CSP. These are the so-called *Solver*, *ValueChooser*, *VariableChooser* and *Propagator* classes. A UML class diagram is given by Figure 5.

The *Solver* class implements a depth first search algorithm with backtracking. When a *Solver* object is created, a specific CSP instance is associated with it. A *Solver* object deals with a current set of assignments and try, at each step, to make a new variable assignment. The next variable to be assigned is chosen by a *VariableChooser* object and the next value to assign is chosen by a *ValueChooser* object. After each new assignment, a constraint propagation is performed by a *Propagator* object. The resolution stops when one (or n) solution is found or when the search space has been fully covered.

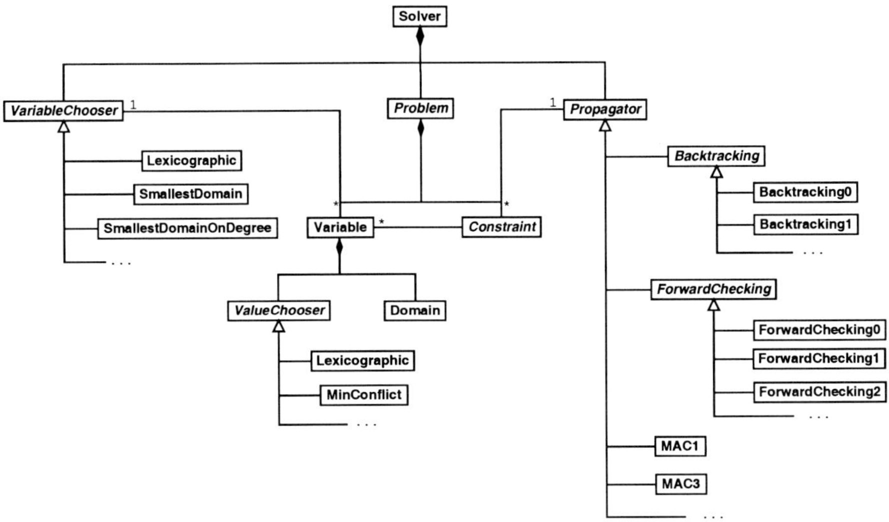

Fig. 5. CSP resolution

The abstract *ValueChooser* class represents a value ordering heuristic attached to a given variable. Currently, two heuristics are implemented: *Lexicographic* and *MinConflicts* (*mc* [11]).

The abstract *VariableChooser* class represents a variable ordering heuristic. The following heuristics are implemented: *Lexicographic*, *SmallestDomain* (*dom* [13]) and *SmallestDomainOnDegree* (*dom/deg* [4]).

The abstract *Propagator* class represents a constraint propagation method. Currently, some derived classes implement different constraint propagation algorithms and correspond to different forms of consistency: backtracking, forward-checking and arc-consistency. According to the type of the *Propagator* object, "checking a constraint" consists of using a specific predicate (i.e. of calling a specific method defined in the *Constraint* class). The Table 1 summarizes the correspondence between *Propagator* types and predicates. As n-ary constraints are taken into consideration in *AbsCon*, we have to adapt binary backtracking, forward-checking and maintening arc-consistency algorithms. There are several alternatives. First, we propose two generalizations of backtracking: a *Backtracking0* object applies checks on constraints involving the current variable and no future (not assigned) variables whereas a *Backtracking1* object applies checks on constraint projections involving the current and past (assigned) variables. Second, we propose three generalizations of forward-checking: the *ForwardChecking0*, *ForwardChecking1* and *ForwardChecking2* classes respectively correspond to the implementation of the nFC0, nFC1 and nFC2 algorithms as defined by [3]. Finally, the AC1 [23] and AC3 [17] algorithms have been generalized and implemented by the *MAC1* and *MAC3* classes.

Table 1. Propagators and Predicates

Propagator	Predicate
GenerateAndTest	isCoherent()
Backtracking0 Backtracking1	isCoherent() isBT1Coherent()
ForwardChecking0 ForwardChecking1 ForwardChecking2	isAssignmentCoherent(variable,value) isFC1Coherent(variable,value) isAssignmentCoherent(variable,value)
MAC1 MAC3	isAssignmentCoherent(variable,value) isAssignmentCoherent(variable,value)

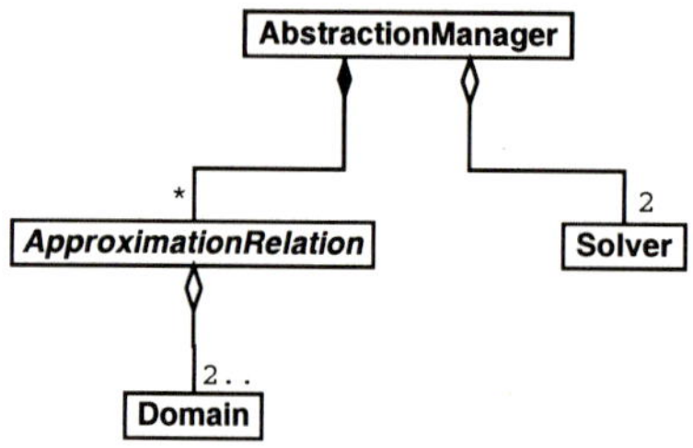

Fig. 6. CSP abstraction

4.3 Abstracting a CSP

As given by Definition 3, a CSP abstraction is described by two CSPs and an abstraction base. In this section, we present the *AbstractionManager* and *ApproximationRelation* classes and we examine the mechanism of hybrid resolution (i.e. resolution with abstraction). A UML class diagram is given by Figure 6.

The *AbstractionManager* class contains all elements occurring in the definition of a CSP abstraction. More precisely, an *AbstractionManager* object holds references on two solvers (a concrete and an abstract one) and a set of approximation relations. The abstract *ApproximationRelation* class describes in a general way an approximation relation defined between some concrete domains and some abstract domains. An *ApproximationRelation* object identifies some links between concrete tuples and abstract tuples, i.e. which concrete tuples are approximated by abstract ones or which abstract tuples are the approximation of concrete ones.

Solving a CSP using an abstraction mechanism consists of solving the abstract problem such that for any abstract solution, the concrete solver is run with respect to the portion of the search space corresponding to the "concretisation" of this solution. All steps of this process are described by Figure 7 where it clearly appears that a cooperation between the abstract and concrete solvers is necessary. An *AbstractionManager* object allows to establish the communication between both solvers (steps 2 and 5). More precisely, it manages abstraction

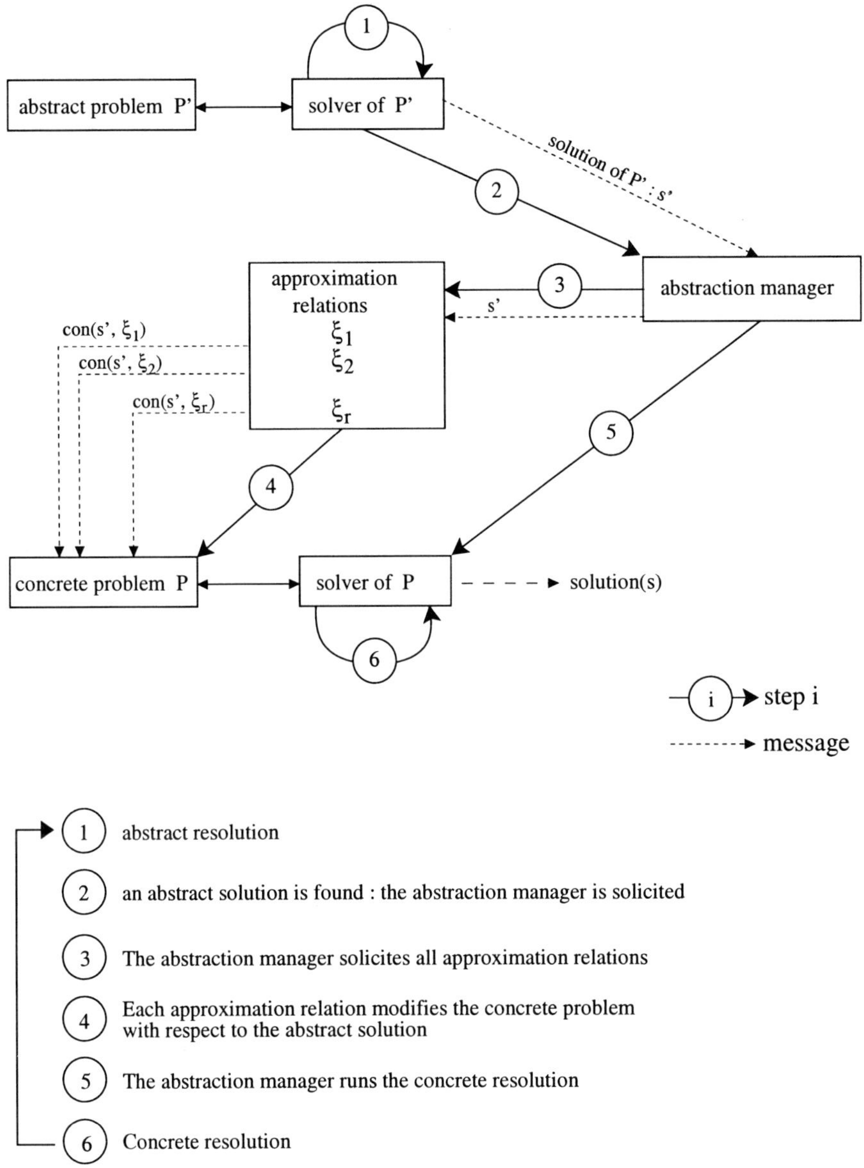

Fig. 7. Resolution process

that it is to say, for any found abstract solution s' (steps 1 and 2), it modifies the concrete search space (steps 3 and 4) and runs the concrete solver on this modified search space (steps 5 and 6). This modification (denoted by $con(s', \xi_i)$) is obtained by asking each approximation relation ξ_i to concretise the abstract

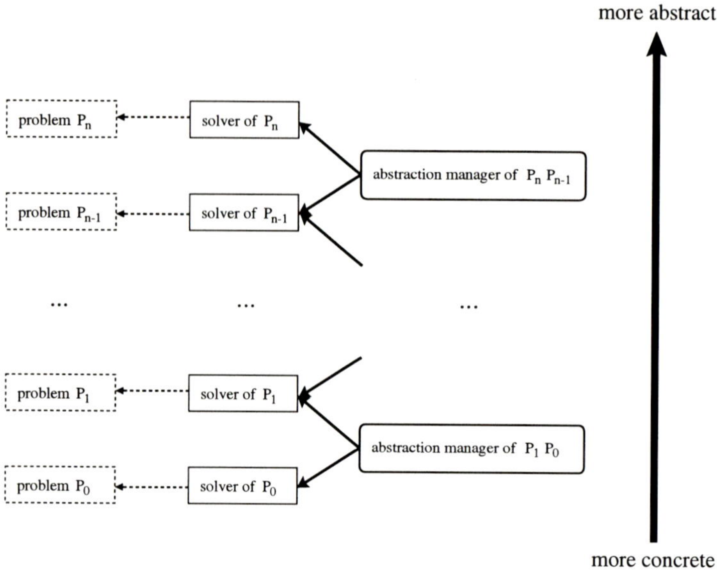

Fig. 8. Abstraction hierarchy

solution (step 3). In practice, when the abstraction corresponds to a value clustering, concrete domains are reduced and when the abstraction corresponds to a variable clustering, some concrete constraints are modified or added (step 4). As a result, the concrete resolution is guided by the abstract solution.

Notice that it is possible to solve a CSP by using abstractions in succession. Then, solvers which are associated with more and more abstract problems can cooperate through different abstraction managers. An illustration is given by Figure 8.

We illustrate the resolution process with respect to the selection problem presented above. Let us assume that the abstract solution $s' = (V_0' \leftarrow 2, V_1' \leftarrow 1, V_2' \leftarrow 1)$ has been found (steps 1 and 2). As the proposed abstraction corresponds to a variable clustering, some concrete constraints are modified (steps 3 and 4). More precisely, the category constraints are transformed as follows:

- $2 \leq V_0 + V_1 + V_2 + V_3 \leq 2$
- $1 \leq V_3 + V_4 + V_5 + V_6 \leq 1$
- $1 \leq V_6 + V_7 + V_8 \leq 1$

Finally, the concrete solver yields many solutions (steps 5 and 6), one of which is $s = (V_0 \leftarrow 0, V_1 \leftarrow 0, V_2 \leftarrow 1, V_3 \leftarrow 1, V_4 \leftarrow 0, V_5 \leftarrow 0, V_6 \leftarrow 0, V_7 \leftarrow 1, V_8 \leftarrow 0)$.

5 Experiments

In this section, some representative results of experiments that we have run are presented. With respect to the selection problem described in previous sections, we have compared the respective efficiency of the classical (CS) and hybrid (HS) solvers.

Classical sets of instances are characterized by a 4-tuple (n, m, p_1, p_2) where n is the number of variables, m the number of values in each domain, p_1 the constraint density and p_2 the constraint tightness. Solving an instance consists of either finding a solution or determining inconsistency. A phase transition from under-constrained to over-constrained problems has been observed (e.g. [19,21]) on random binary CSPs as p_2 varies while n, m, p_1 are kept fixed.

With respect to the selection problem (described above), n corresponds to p whereas m corresponds to 2 (selected or not). p_1 is entirely determined from p and p_2 is determined from the number i of incompatibilities. Our sets of instances will be referred to by the tuple $(p, 2, s, i)$ where s denotes the number of objects which belong to more than one category. For example, the problem instance of Figure 1 belongs to the class $(9, 2, 2, 6)$. Note that the number of categories has been fixed to $\sqrt{p}$.

We have run a series of experiments by considering different sets of instances, heuristics and propagation methods. At each settings of the sets $(p, 2, s, i)$, 100 instances were randomly generated. The results[4] that are presented below have been obtained with the *dom/deg* variable ordering heuristic, *mc* value ordering heuristic and *nFC*1 propagation method. These results concern the set $(36, 2, 6, i)$ where i is varied from 0 to 200. Figure 9 shows the satisfiability curve (including the phase transition) when considering this variation. Figure 10 shows the mean and median behavior of the classical (CS) and hybrid (HS) solvers whereas Figure 11 shows the min and max behavior. It clearly appears that the hybrid solver outperforms the classical one. The difference between the efficiency of both solvers is significant around the crossover point (where 50% of problems are satisfiable) and still more important when moving away from this point.

6 Conclusion

This paper describes a free constraint programming prototype called *AbsCon* [1]. As it has been developed in Java by exploiting object technology, we think that its architecture is sufficiently open to easily extend its functionalities.

To our best knowledge, JCL (Java Constraint Library) [22] is the first proposal of Java constraint programming class library. The main limitation of JCL is the fact that n-ary constraint can not be considered. More recently, *Laburthe et al.* [15], *Hon Wai Chun* [7] and *Roy et al.* [20] have proposed more advanced free object libraries, *CHOCO*, *JSolver* and *BackTalk* respectively, allowing to consider n-ary constraints. On the one hand, *CHOCO* and *BackTalk*[5] essentially differ from *AbsCon* by the choice of the implementation language (*CLAIRE* and

[4] Other heuristics and propagation methods have been tested. In all cases, the hybrid approach outperforms the classical one.

[5] A (unavailable) Java version of *BackTalk* is currently implemented by Sony CSL Lab.

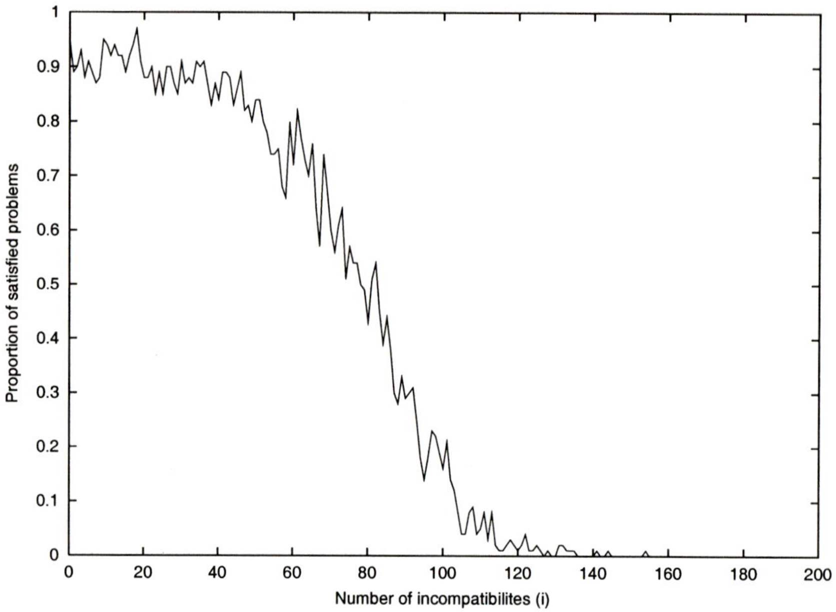

Fig. 9. Satisfiability for $(36, 2, 6, i)$

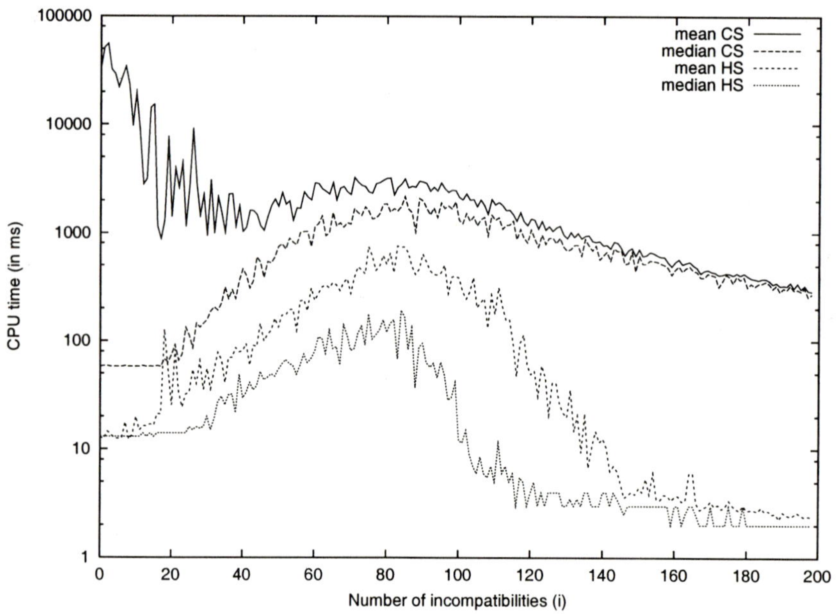

Fig. 10. Mean and median of search effort for $(36, 2, 6, i)$

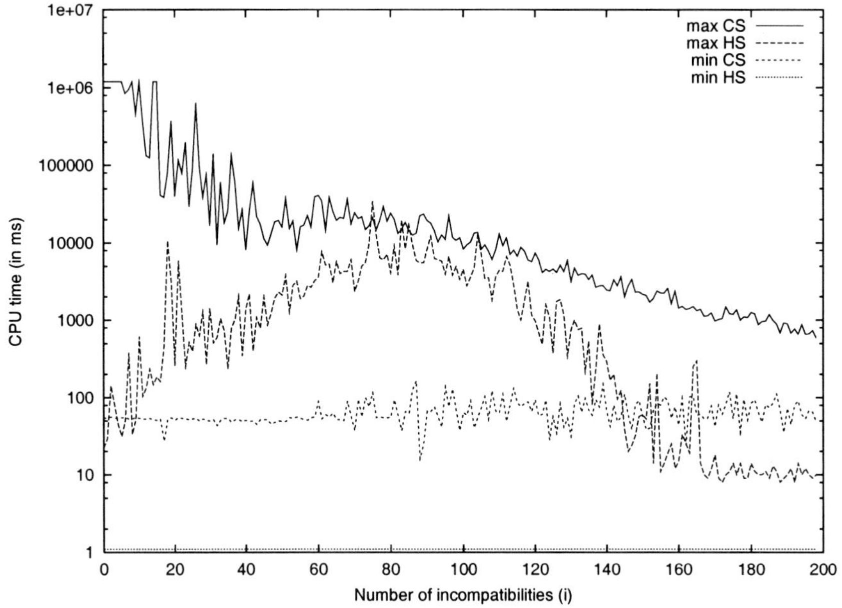

Fig. 11. Min and max of search effort for $(36, 2, 6, i)$

SmallTalk respectively). On the other hand, *JSolver*[6] considers the Waltz filtering algorithm [8] whereas *AbsCon* integrates various propagation methods.

Despite of some similarities between *AbsCon* and the above mentioned libraries, our main contribution with *AbsCon* is to propose a prototype which can be used to build and solve CSP abstractions. To show the interest of such an approach, we have presented some experimental results about an original form of CSP abstraction corresponding to general variable clustering.

One perspective of this work is to offer the user some guidelines in order to build efficient abstractions. Another one is to study the pratical interest of SD abstractions with *AbsCon*. Finally, we project to extend *AbsCon* in order to deal with optimization problems.

References

1. AbsCon, Université d'Artois. *http://www.cril.univ-artois.fr/~lecoutre*. AbsCon (about 5000 lines of code) is currently maintained by S. Merchez and C. Lecoutre.
2. C. Bessiere. Non-binary constraints. In *Proc. of CP'99*, pages 24–27, Alexandria, VA, USA, October 11-14 1999.

[6] *JSolver* is now integrated in the commercial ILOG software [14] as a part of the *JConfigurator* product.

3. C. Bessiere, P. Meseguer, E.C. Freuder, and J. Larrosa. On forward checking for non-binary constraint satisfaction. In *Proc. of CP'99*, pages 88–102, Alexandra, VA, 1999.
4. C. Bessiere and J.C. Regin. Mac and combined heuristics: two reasons to forsake fc (and cbj?) on hard problems. In *Proc. of CP'96*, Cambridge MA, 1996.
5. S. Bistarelli, P. Codognet, and F. Rossi. An abstraction framework for soft constraints and its relationship with constraint propagation. In *Proc. of SARA'2000*, pages 71–86, 2000.
6. Y. Caseau. Abstract interpretation of constraints on order-sorted domains. In *Proc. of the International Symposium on Logic Programming*, pages 435–452, 1991.
7. A. Hon Wai Chun. Constraint programming in Java with JSolver 2.0. Technical report, City university of Hong Kong, 1999.
8. A. Hon Wai Chun. Waltz filtering in Java with JSolver. In *PA Java'99*, London, April 1999.
9. P. Cousot and R. Cousot. Abstract interpretation frameworks. *Logic and Computation*, 2(4):447–511, August 1992.
10. Thomas Ellman. Abstraction via approximate symmetry. In *Proc. of IJCAI'93*, pages 916–921, Chambéry, France, 1993.
11. D. Frost and R. Dechter. Look-ahead value ordering for constraint satisfaction problems. In *Proc. of IJCAI'95*, pages 572–578, 1995.
12. F. Giunchiglia and T. Walsh. A theory of abstraction. *Artificial Intelligence*, 56(2-3):323–390, October 1992.
13. A. Haralick and G.L. Elliot. Increasing tree search efficienciy for constraint satisfaction problems. *Artificial Intelligence*, 14:263–313, 1980.
14. ILOG. *http://www.ilog.com.*
15. F. Laburthe and the OCRE project team. Choco: implementing a cp kernel. In *Actes des* 6ème *Journées Nationales pour la résolution des Problèmes NP-Complets*, 2000.
16. C. Lecoutre, S. Merchez, F. Boussemart, and E. Grégoire. A csp abstraction framework. In *Proc. of SARA'2000*, pages 164–184, Lake LBJ, Texas, July 26-29 2000. Springer Verlag. Lecture Notes in Artificial Intelligence (LNAI), volume 1864.
17. A.K. Mackworh. Consistency in networks of relations. *Artificial Intelligence*, 8:99–118, 1977.
18. S. Merchez. *Constraint Satisfaction Problems: a study of abstraction and hierarchy mecanisms.* PhD thesis, Université d'Artois, 2000. In French.
19. P. Prosser. An empirical study of phase transition in binary constraint satisfaction problems. *Artificial Intelligence*, 81, 1996.
20. P. Roy, A. Liret, and F. Pachet. *Implementing Application frameworks: Object-Oriented Frameworks at Work*, volume 2(4), chapter Constraint Satisfaction Problems Framework. Wiley & sons, 1999.
21. B. Smith and M. Dyer. Locating the phase transition in binary constraint satisfaction problems. *Artificial Intelligence*, 81, 1996.
22. M. Torrens, R. Weigel, and B. Faltings. Distributing problem solving on the web using constraint technology. In *Proc. of ICTAI'98*, pages 42–49, Taipei, Taiwan (ROC), 1998.
23. D. Waltz. *Understanding line drawings of scenes with shadows*, chapter The psychology of computer vision, pages 19–91. Winston (Ed), Mac-Graw Hill, New York, 1975.

A Constraint Engine for Manufacturing Process Planning

József Váncza and András Márkus

Computer and Automation Institute, Hungarian Academy of Sciences
H-1518 Budapest P.O.B. 63, Hungary
{vancza,markus}@sztaki.hu

Abstract. We present a constraint-based model and planning engine for manufacturing process planning. By exploiting the expressive power of constraint programming (CP), all relevant, sometimes conflicting pieces of domain knowledge are represented. The planner applies standard propagation techniques and customized search to find cost-optimal solutions in presence of hard, soft and conditional constraints. The planning engine was built on an existing general-purpose CP system and was validated in the domains of machining and of sheet metal bending.

1 Introduction

Manufacturing process planning (PP) is the bridge between design and production: it generates plans of discrete manufacturing operations that are executed in a given production environment. *Computer-aided process planning* (CAPP) holds the promises of better designs, lower production costs, larger flexibility, and improved quality. There have been many research initiatives to develop appropriate methods and architectures for CAPP systems [15]. Recent work in CAPP is dominated by artificial intelligence approaches, but the industrial impact of these efforts has been embarrassingly small. While in other areas of manufacturing – in design and scheduling – AI methods, and constraint-based techniques in particular, are indeed successful, PP puts up a stout resistance to automation. Hence, CAPP is considered now the weakest link in manufacturing automation.

The PP problem is complex because it has to include aspects of both design and production. A process planner has to cover geometry and tolerances, material properties, manufacturing processes and tools, holding devices, machines and other equipments used in production. Consequently, planning expertise is typically a collection of fragmentary, context-dependent, often conflicting pieces of advice. The actual planning problems vary with technologies (machining, sheet metal bending, inspection, (dis)assembly), with part and resource models, as well as with the requirements toward the plans. Solutions of any CAPP problem should comply – as far as possible – with available domain knowledge and approach complex, production-related optimization objective.

Our goal was to develop a *generic planning engine* for process planning that meets the following requirements:

T. Walsh (Ed.): CP 2001, LNCS 2239, pp. 745–759, 2001.

- Support the representation of the relevant pieces of PP knowledge from several manufacturing domains, no matter whether generated by human experts or by program modules.
- Consolidate conflicting pieces of knowledge and generate plans that approach given optimization criteria.
- Operate in mixed-initiative, exploratory modes. Support not only generative, but also similarity-based planning, typical in real-life engineering work.

While *general purpose planning* methods are infiltrated with causal reasoning, in PP reasoning can be isolated into specific tasks, and the problem could be seen as solving a kind of *scheduling* problem as well. In order to avoid confusion due to the different vocabularies, this paper adheres word usage accepted in the application area.

Below, after presenting the CAPP problem, we give an account of how the first two requirements have been met by a novel model and a planning engine based on *constraints* [21] and the methods of *constraint programming* [25]. Lessons of experiments suggest that the approach can be extended to meet the third main requirement as well.

2 The Process Planning Problem

The problem can be stated as follows: *given* (1) the descriptions of the blank and the finished part (material, dimensions, tolerances, surface quality), (2) the available production resources, and (3) the technological knowledge and optimization objectives, *find* an executable and close-to-optimal plan. Main phases of solving a CAPP problem [8,18] are as follows (see Fig. 1):

1. **Analysis** of the part, technological processes and resources yields a technological interpretation of the design specification. It determines the entities to be produced – the so-called *features* – and the alternatives of producing them with using the available resources.
2. **High-level planning** specifies the operations by selecting from among the alternative resources (sets of tools, holding device and machines), determines the sequence of operations and makes groups of operations – so-called *setups* – that will be performed together, by using the same resource(s).
3. **Low-level planning** generates paths for moving the tools and other equipments, and determines the parameters of operations (e.g., cutting speed). Results are numerical control programs for the machines.

We are interested in *high-level planning*, where the complexity of the problem is concentrated. In this phase, planning is a "wicked" problem because the tasks mutually interact: there is no evident ordering of the decisions, and partial solutions can not be simply combined into a final one. For instance, tool selection requires knowledge of holding and machine (and *vice versa*); both operation sequencing and setup planning determine the order of operations. Selection of resources has an impact on setup planning, but setup requirements restrict the sets of applicable resources. Decisions should be changed in order to fulfill a

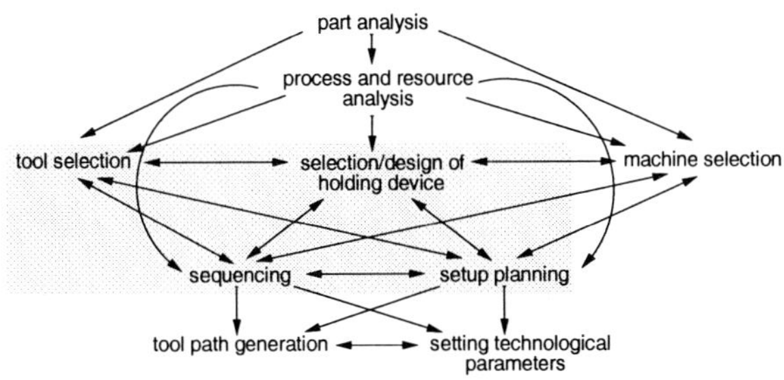

Fig. 1. The tasks of CAPP. Tasks included in our current model are within the gray area.

constraint that arose due to a earlier decision, but this may lead to spurious cycles in reasoning. All in all, the problem can be decomposed only at the price of substantial simplifying assumptions.

In this study we assume that a single, standard machine is used, so we do not deal with machine selection. This omission makes the problem more tractable without changing its tangled structure.

Having validated the approach in the domains of *machining prismatic parts* and in *bending sheet-metal parts*, first we describe these domains.

2.1 The Machining Domain

Machining is the classical domain of CAPP [6,16,28,29]. Here part analysis produces a feature-based model [18]. *Features* (like holes, slots, pockets, etc.) tie frequently occurring geometrical and functional groups of surfaces to their production patterns. Each operation produces just the next *state* of a feature; reaching the finished state usually needs 3-5 operations.

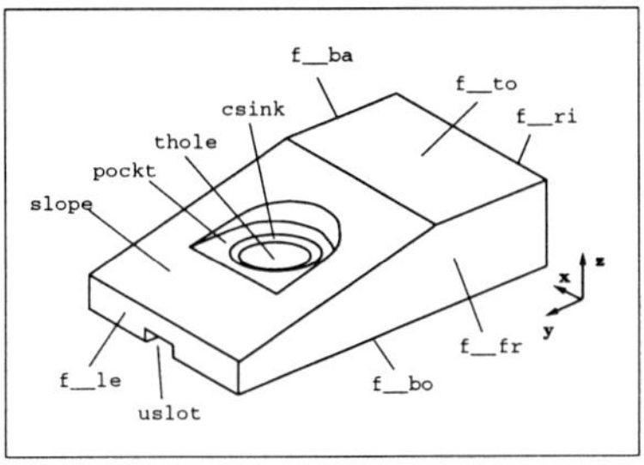

- *Centering the through-hole must be done before drilling it.*
- *In this orientation, the top face can be made by a face-milling tool.*
- *Make large faces first.*
- *Make all the states of strictly toleranced features in one setup.*
- *If the through-hole is made from the bottom face, make it before u-slot.*

Fig. 2. An example workpiece and some typical constraints. The initial state is a blank part (e.g., die cast) with unmachined surfaces.

Since most of the resources are multi-purpose and the ordering of the operations on different features is only partially constrained, there are many plan variants. Constraints arise due to the applied technology (e.g., heat treatment should be made before super-finishing; strictly toleranced features should be produced in one setup), to the shape of the part (e.g., accessibility of the features), and resource compatibility (e.g., a tool needs a specific orientation of the part).

By their very definition, features have local nature and the pieces of advice concerning their production are local, too. Hence, having added up these pieces of advice, there is no guarantee of getting a consistent body of information. It is the *high-level planning* phase that has to find an appropriate selection, combination and ordering of the partial solutions. The final plans have to comply – as far as possible – with the domain knowledge and to approach a cost optimum. Fig. 2 shows a sample machining problem and some of the relevant constraints.

2.2 The Bending Domain

Sheet-metal bending operations involve bending of parts on a V-shaped die with a punch, operated by a bending machine [5,7,26]. During the operation the whole part is moving, hence it is held by a robotic gripper. In this domain features are *bends*, and the operations produce them with appropriate tools (die and punch), holding device (gripper), and machine (press brake). Tools are of different profile and length; usually, a tool can make shorter bends, too. Operation selection and sequencing is based, first of all, on geometrical considerations: the part-tool and part-part interferences must be avoided. Further on, the planner has to strive to use a small set of tools and to minimize the repositionings of the sheet. Here again, since the features are local, the aim is to find a consolidated set of advice for making the complete sheet metal part. Fig. 3 shows a problem instance and typical planning advice.

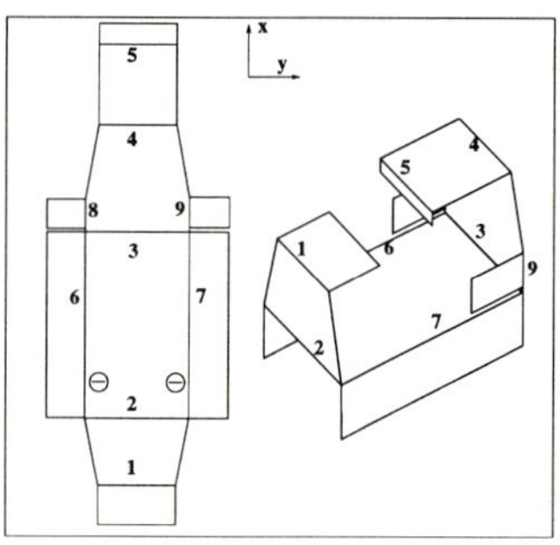

- *Make small tabs first.*
- *Make outside bends before inside bends.*
- *Make internal tabs first.*
- *If bends 6 and 7 have been made prior 2 and 3, then bends 2 and 3 need exact length tool.*
- *If possible, perform two collinear bends in one operation.*

Fig. 3. A bending problem and some constraints.

2.3 Related Work

One of the first approaches to planning with conflicting pieces of advice was a constraint-based CAPP system [4]: the GARI planner generated plans by trying to maximize the weights attached to the technological constraints fulfilled. The idea of a planning engine to synthesize the results of several domain-specific reasoning modules appeared in [12]: this process planner worked with a hierarchical task network (HTN). (HTN-planners are still considered the most appropriate vehicles for solving real-world planning problems [27].) However, the HTN engine could only work with consistent and coherent domain knowledge and did not concern – as most logic-based planners did not either – optimization. A similar, modular architecture appeared in [20], while [28] suggested a blackboard-based platform for integrating the results of various modules.

Most CAPP methods take a hierarchical approach to planning and optimization: the planners first try to form optimal setups, then sequence the operations relative to this so-called setup plan [2,16,29].

Some recent planners cover also part analysis and do not commit themselves to a particular feature-based part model [3,6]. Since planning with alternative part models requires powerful geometric reasoning and ample computing resources, such planners work in limited planning domains. Even so, as [6] notes, in manufacturing domains the search spaces can be as large as in chess.

Process planning was modeled in [1] as a temporal constraint satisfaction problem. However, this method could handle neither inconsistent bodies of domain knowledge nor cost-related optimization criteria. Constraint solving techniques were applied in [5] for solving sheet metal bending problems. Here conflicting pieces of engineering advice were handled by a special penalty system.

Since our first work in CAPP [10] we have tried to reconcile the reasoning and optimization aspects of the problem. Later on, we defined a three-stage framework where (1) the search space was built up (implicitly) by knowledge-based reasoning, (2) conflicting constraint sets were relaxed, and (3) close-to-optimal plans were extracted by genetic algorithms [11,22] or by case-based reasoning [23]. One of the goals of the recent work is to merge the last two planning phases by using constraint programming. To the best of our knowledge no approach to CAPP applied this computing paradigm yet.

3 The Constraint-Based CAPP Model

Our basic approach was that we should develop an *expressive and efficient* constraint-based PP model to be used with a professional constraint engine. The available PP tools (and, in the last resort, user interaction) generate a description of the planning problem at hand, we automatically translate it to a constraint model, and then the engine solves the problem. Obviously, we had to find the proper balance between generality and detail of the constraint-based model *versus* the efficiency of generating and solving such a system of constraints.

3.1 Operations and Resources

There is a set of n *operations*. The place of operation i, $i \in [1, \ldots, n]$ in the plan is represented by the variable o_i. The operations are irreversible, and all of them have to be executed in sequence. Hence, the o_i-s are a permutation of $\{1, \ldots, n\}$.

Two resource types are modeled: each operation needs some *holding device* and some *tool*. Usually, operations can be executed with several resource combinations. Let H denote the set of the possible holding devices, and T the set of the available tools. Each operation i needs an appropriate holding h_i and a tool t_i where these variables take values from the domains $H_i \subseteq H$, and $T_i \subseteq T$, respectively.

3.2 Constraints

Constraint types. The types of technological constraints defined in our CAPP model are as follows:

A) Operation precedence and neighborhood
- *Operation precedence:* $o_i < o_j$, i.e., operation i has to be made before j.
- *Immediate operation precedence:* $o_j = o_i + 1$, i.e., operation i has to be made immediately before j.
- *Neighborhood:* operation j has to be made immediately either before or after i. Expressed by a disjunctive constraint: $o_j = o_i + 1 \lor o_j = o_i - 1$.

B) Setup formation
- *Common resource:* The operations i and j, no matter where they are in the plan, must have the same holding/tool. For holding: $h_i = h_j$.
- *Shared resource within a plan segment:* All operations in the plan segment between operations i and j $(o_i < o_j)$ must use the same holding/tool. For holding: $\forall k$ such that $o_i < o_k < o_j, h_i = h_k = h_j$.

C) Resource compatibility

For each operation i, a *resource compatibility* constraint specifies the compatible (h_i, t_i) pairs, i.e., the applicable combinations from $H_i \times T_i$.

D) Conditional constraints on precedences and resources
- *Operation precedence conditioned by resource*: If the selected resource of operation i belongs to the set given in the constraint R_i, then a given operation j has to precede another, given operation k. For holding: $h_i \in R_i \subseteq H_i \Rightarrow o_j < o_k$.
- *Resource conditioned by operation precedence*: If the given operation precedences are present in the plan, then the resource set of a given operation m is restricted. For holding: $(o_i < o_j) \land, \ldots, \land (o_k < o_l) \Rightarrow h_m \in R_m$.
- *Operation precedence conditioned by operation precedence*: If one or more given operation precedences are present in the plan, then another given precedence is to be satisfied. $(o_i < o_j) \land, \ldots, \land (o_k < o_l) \Rightarrow o_a < o_b$.

Hard and soft constraints. There are hard and soft constraints in our model. *Hard constraints* express technological requirements that must be satisfied by any solution: a plan cannot be executed if it violates any of the hard constraints. Hard constraints can be defined in all of the above types.

Soft constraints are defined as follows: A *base predicate* is a Boolean expression made of constraints and evaluated over a plan. A base predicate evaluated to true/false yields a binary value 1/0. Base predicates can be only of type A) and B) defined above. Each base predicate has an attached fixed *weight*. This weight reflects the importance of the property described by the base predicate.

A *predicate group* is a set of base predicates. Its *evaluation* yields the weighed sum of the satisfied base predicates. The same base predicate may be used in more than one predicate groups.

A *soft constraint* is an expression in the form $e_G \geq l_G$ where e_G is the evaluation of a predicate group G and $l_G \in \{0, 1, 2, \ldots\}$ is a given constant value, called the *threshold* of the constraint. Hence, each soft constraint captures a *set of properties* of the plan.

Soft constraints are needed (1) to express *best practice* by formulating complex, global properties that the domain experts expect to find in "good" (i.e., not only feasible but close-to-optimal, good looking) plans – although there might be no proof that good plans must have these properties; and (2) to deal with *over-constrained* problem formulations. For more details, see Section 4.

Examples. As for the examples of the various types of constraints defined above, consider Figures 2 and 3:

A) On the machined part, centering (*h_cen*) of the through-hole should be made before twist-drilling (*h_drl*). The right face (*f__ri*) has to be made before the slope, because after making the slope the left face (*f__le*) becomes too small as a positioning surface when making the right face. These precedence constraints are hard. On the bending example, the first three pieces of advice can be captured together by a soft constraint consisting of precedences.

B) On the machined part, centering and twist-drilling of the through-hole have to be made from the same direction. This makes a hard constraint on the applicable holdings. Further on, if the hole has strict position tolerance, then no re-fixturing is allowed in-between the two operations; hence the holding of the part must not be changed between centering and twist-drilling.

C) For each specific tool allowed in an operation, there can be specified the set of compatible holdings. E.g., Table 1 gives the resource pairs that satisfy the resource compatibility constraint for the operation *uslot.* (Under the assumption that the operations are executed on a vertical, 3-axis machine tool, holding is given in terms of the orientation of the part.)

D) On the machined part, if the through-hole is drilled from the top face (*f__to*), then this operation has to be executed before making the slope to avoid slip of the drill. Alternatively, if the hole is made from the bottom face (*f__bo*), then the hole must be drilled before milling the u-slot, so as to avoid breakage of the drill. In the bending example, the fourth advice on Fig. 3 can be captured as a resource constraint conditioned by operation precedence.

Table 1. Compatible resource combinations for the operation producing *uslot.*

Operation	Tool	Holding	Tool	Holding
uslot	e_mill	+x−y−z	s_mill	−z−y−x
		−y−x−z		+y−z−x
		−x+y−z		−z+y+x
		+y+x−z		−y−z+x

Interactions of constraints. Different instances of the constraints may interact and even get in conflict with each other. Cycles in the graph of precedences are typical examples of conflicts in PP (see e.g., [11,22]). For a more subtle, though simple example of interaction consider Fig. 4 with operations i, j and k. Suppose the constraints $o_i < o_j$ and $o_j < o_k$. Now, a setup segment constraint introduced for operations i and k is satisfiable only if all the three operations have overlapping sets of holding resources, i.e., if $H_i \cap H_j \cap H_k \neq \emptyset$.

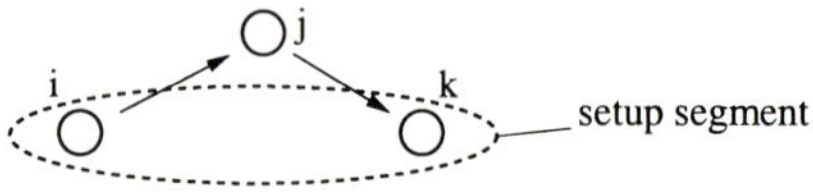

Fig. 4. An interaction of basic constraints.

If the above system of constraints has no solution and the constraints are soft, then the problem can be relaxed in the following ways: (1) If $H_i \cap H_k = \emptyset$ then the setup constraint has to be neglected. (2) If H_j does not have a common subset with H_i and H_k, then either the setup constraint or one of the precedence constraints should be passed by.

3.3 The Evaluation of Plans

A process plan is determined by the values of the o_i, h_i and t_i variables. The variable assignment has to satisfy all the hard constraints; hence, the plan determines a permutation of the operations, with single resources assigned. Such plans are called *feasible*. The *cost* of a plan has two components:

- The *cost of operations*. The cost of each individual operation, c_i depends on the assigned resources.
- The *change-over cost* of resources. The cost of changing the holding device between two subsequent operations i and j is calculated as follows:

$$change\_holding_i = \begin{cases} change\_holding & \text{if } h_i \neq h_j, \\ 0 & \text{otherwise.} \end{cases}$$

The same applies for changing the tools with the constant change-over cost *change_tool*.

Hence, the total cost of a plan is:

$$\sum_{i=1}^{n} c_i(h_i, t_i) + \sum_{i=1}^{n-1} (change\_holding_i + change\_tool_i)$$

Note that resource changes impose usually far higher costs than the operations because re-positioning and re-fixturing takes considerable time and deteriorates the accuracy of the manufacturing operations. However, in the machining domain changing the holding device used to be more expensive than changing the tool, while in the bending domain it is just the other way around.

4 Solving CAPP Problems by CP

Our planning system was built by using an advanced constraint programming environment, the Mozart (Oz) system, that is freely available for research purposes from `http://www.mozart-oz.org/`. Below we use its terminology.

The domains of variables are either finite sets of non-negative integers (FD) or finite sets with no specific structure (FS). Some types of the constraints can be checked efficiently and their implications are easy to find. These, so-called *basic constraints* are stored in the *constraint store*. Further, so called *non-basic constraints* cannot be checked in an efficient way (e.g., (in)equalities over the sum of several FD variables). The mutual satisfiability of these constraints is handled by *propagators* that automatically trigger each other while running in quasi-parallel threads. Since the propagation machinery is incomplete, the solution space must be searched: so-called *distribution* introduces a new, artificial constraint c and divides the original problem by adding c and $\neg c$ to the copies of the store. If the constraint store becomes inconsistent, work continues on the other copy; in the last resort, the system backtracks. For finding a useful constraint c a number of built-in distribution strategies are available, such as the *first-fail*. Customized distributors can be programmed, too.

The search may run for a *single solution* and for *all solutions*. By default, the system enumerates solutions in a depth-first manner. Satisfiability and optimization can be coupled by *branch-and-bound*: here the cost of the best solution found imposes a new constraint on the cost of further solutions.

Table 2. Basic constraint programming techniques applied.

operations	finite domain variables
precedence constraints	$I < J$; $I + 1 = J$; $I + 1 = J$ *or* $J + 1 = I$
resource alternatives	finite set variables
setup constraints	$A \subseteq B$ *and* $B \subseteq A$
conditional constraints	reified constraints ($c \Rightarrow B$)
soft constraints	reified constraints

Table 2 shows how key elements of the PP model have been mapped to CP concepts (for more details, see [14,24]). We have defined a domain description language and compiled the domain model into the language of the Mozart engine. The planner was constructed by using the built-in propagation, distribution and branch-and-bound search methods of Mozart. However, to solve the problem we had to develop specific solution methods. Below we analyze the role of the elements of the model and describe the solution strategy.

4.1 Key Characteristics of the Optimization Objective

The most relevant characteristic of the cost function we found by experimentation is that useful lower cost estimates cannot be made by considering either relaxed problems (e.g., plans with some resource constraints discarded) or partially specified solutions (e.g., plans with undefined ordering of some operations, with resources left free). Without such estimates, the only *optimization constraint* available is the cost of the best solution found earlier.

Since the engineering meanings of various kinds soft constraints are different, there is of no use to sum up their evaluations: the *total weight* of the satisfied base predicates would be an inappropriate optimization objective. Hence, our proposition contrasts with present techniques of dealing with soft (or valued) constraints [17].

Due to the role of possible user interaction in further, subjective evaluation of the solutions, the ability of getting a small relative improvement in the cost value is far less important then having a handy environment for exploratory problem solving. The other extreme, an approach without optimization would be contradictory to the engineering requirements: offering the user a large bundle of all the feasible solutions, with no ordering among them, would waste precious resources since best solution(s) at the current level of abstraction are usually the input(s) to the next, finer level of engineering problem solving.

4.2 The Roles of the Soft Constraints

In our approach soft constraints have a role in a variety of techniques, that are used for different purposes. Each soft constraint can be used in two modes:

- In *query mode* the evaluation of the soft constraint is freely used in the constraint script (e.g., as read-only control information that helps the engine to point out the good distribution step).
- In *cutting mode*, the soft constraint has to be fulfilled just as a hard one. Different settings of the constraint's *threshold value* lead to different solutions.

Soft constraints are suitable tools for a variety of search control purposes. In *cutting mode*, soft constraints can be used for the following purposes:

- When dealing with *over-constrained* problem formulations, by replacing a conflicting set of hard constraints G with a single soft constraint. Using the predicate group G and an appropriate threshold l_G the problem may become satisfiable.
- For finding a *maximal subset* of conflicting pieces of advice by replacing a conflicting set of hard constraints with a soft one. It will work as an optimization constraint.
- Dealing with *under-constrained* problem formulations: by introducing soft constraint(s) the size of the search space can be decreased. If the space became too small (e.g., a known, good solution was not generated), then the threshold(s) should be relaxed. However, it is hard to tune these settings so that the best solutions should not go lost again. In PP, setup constraints are extensively applied for this purpose. Another opportunity is to implode the search space by breaking symmetries. This technique can be applied to a wide range of CAPP problems, since 95% of the machined parts possess some degree of symmetry (see [19]).
- By using the l_G threshold values as aspiration levels, plan evaluation could find a *balance among the various aspects* given by the soft constraints.

In the query mode combined with the cutting mode, soft constraints can be used for *learning* by incorporating *lessons of earlier runs* into similar problem instances. E.g., having got an idea of the proper order of exploring the decision alternatives at a distribution point, with using soft constraints in the query mode, it is straightforward to use limited discrepancy search (i.e., iterated depth-first search with increasing difference in the exploration order of the alternatives, as suggested by best-first node-ordering [9]).

4.3 The Constraint Solver Engine

We have built a soft constraint solver applicable to the above purposes. It works both in query and cutting mode with using the constraint satisfaction mechanism of the available (hard) constraint engine. The solver runs the problem instances with the following control elements:

- the search mode is one of $SearchOne$, $SearchNext$, $SearchAll$, $SearchBest$;
- a cost function f for evaluating and ordering the solutions;
- an upper limit C of the acceptable cost;
- a vector $\overline{L}$ for the thresholds of the soft constraints.

Returned is a set of solutions generated according to the above control data. If no solution is found within the given computing limits, then the empty set is returned. To each solution further information is attached: (1) the computing cost of getting the solution; (2) relative improvement in the cost value; and (3) a vector that indicates which soft constraints are active in the solution (i.e., which thresholds are touched).

The engine can be used in a number of ways:

- First of all, one may use it in the strong cutting mode, by setting the thresholds in the soft constraints so high that they become hard constraints and then searching for the cost-optimal solution in this restricted solution space. This approach strives to maximize the applied domain knowledge, but rarely gives a solution because most of the problem instances are inherently over-constrained.
- Another basic strategy is when the engine increases the thresholds of soft constraints as high as possible. This is a kind of multi-objective optimization strategy for various aspects of plan quality, and it may be combined with the objective of minimal cost. Unfortunately, the computational burden makes the application of this strategy prohibitive for all but the simplest problem instances (c.f., [17]). Hence, we have not applied it. Planning problems with specified aspiration levels and a cost function could be solved, provided the aspiration levels were high enough. However, finding a strategy for setting the threshold values is an open problem.

All in all, we had to combine the strategies into an approximating search method, aimed at finding maximal thresholds of the soft constraints *and* cheapest plan together. The resulting strategy (Fig. 5) performs multiple resolution search and produces a series of solutions where new solutions Pareto-dominate the

```
CONSOLIDATE-AND-OPTIMIZE(objective,solution)
loop do
   new-solution ← SEARCH-NEXT(objective,solution)
   if new-solution is null then return solution
   if DOMINATES(new-solution,solution)
      then objective ← ALTERNATE(objective)
           return CONSOLIDATE-AND-OPTIMIZE(objective,new-solution)
end
```

Fig. 5. The search strategy CONSOLIDATE-AND-OPTIMIZE.

earlier ones. The strategy uses the most recent solution s for constraining the next search pass: its cost $C(s)$ is used as an optimization constraint, and the values of the satisfied soft constraints are fed back in the threshold vector $\overline{L}$. A search pass is stopped when a new solution dominates the result of the previous pass. For the purpose of guiding the search (but not for comparing solutions) we use also an evaluation function v that calculates the total value of the satisfied soft constraints. In subsequent passes the strategy alternates the f cost function between the "real" cost c and v.

5 Experiments

We have conducted experiments with several instances of process planning problems. These investigations have been focused on the representation power of the planning model and the performance of the solver.

The constraint-based planning model has been validated both in the machining and bending domains. The problems were hand-coded into our domain description language that handles the constraint types introduced here. We did our best to cover all aspects of process planning and to build models as detailed as possible, no matter whether some constraints contradict each other or not. The representation power of the model proved to be sufficient enough in both domains. On the other hand, all facilities of the model have been used – though never in the same problem instance.

Figures 6 and 7 show solutions and performance statistics for the two example problems. The problems – like the domains – are rather different: while machining needed much more search, in bending the key issue was finding a maximal subset of soft constraints. Note that on the level of the CP mechanism the planner needs much more variables than on the domain level.

In every case, the search engine coped with the complexity of the problem and gave acceptable results within reasonable response time. The solution of the machining example is optimal (and in this problem instance all soft constraints could be satisfied), the bending problem may have a slightly better plan, however only at lower thresholds.

Problem

operations:	13
holdings:	20
tools:	7
hard constraints:	126
predicates in soft consts.:	10

Performance statistics

variables created:	1.5×10^5
propagators invoked:	3×10^6
number of nodes:	5×10^4
depth:	26
solution time (s):	80

Solution

op	holding	tool
f__to	−x−y+z	f_mill
f__fr		e_mill
f__ri		e_mill
f__bo	+y+x−z	f_mill
f__ba		e_mill
f__le		e_mill
h_cen		c_drl
h_drl		t_drl
uslot		e_mill
slope	+x+y+z	f_mill
pockt		e_mill
csink		c_sink
h_thr		thr_ml

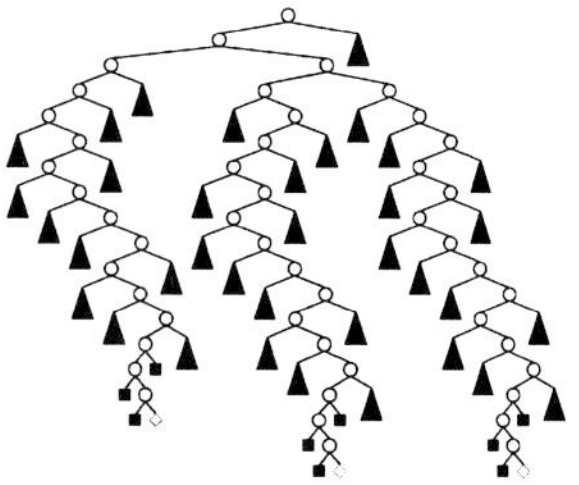

Fig. 6. Solution of the machining example, with the tree of the last search pass.

Problem

operations:	9
holdings:	6
tools:	4
hard constraints:	45
predicates in soft consts.:	36

Performance statistics

variables created:	6×10^2
propagators invoked:	2×10^5
number of nodes:	2×10^3
depth:	32
solution time (s):	6,6

Solution

op	holding	tool
b8	up+y	t4
b9	up−y	
b1	up−x	
b5	up+x	
b4	up+x	
b6	dn+y	
b7	dn−y	
b2	up−x	t3
b3	up+x	

Soft constraint weights

precedences:	70	(83)
neighbors:	20	(20)
setupequs1:	10	(10)
setupequs2:	30	(30)
total:	130	(143)

Fig. 7. Solution of the bending example, with satisfied thresholds and maximal weights of soft constraints.

6 Conclusions and Further Work

This research aimed at developing a generic constraint-based model and planning method for CAPP, a practical planning problem. The central claims are that:

- The constraint-based representation has enough expressive power to capture relevant pieces of domain knowledge, even if they are inconsistent.
- Cost functions, hard and soft constraints form a minimal set of concepts that, if used together in a proper way, do offer an efficient and extendible framework for dealing with CAPP problems. In our framework we can deal with several planning tasks, including setup planning, resource assignment and operation sequencing.
- Clear-cut separation should be made between the domain-level description of the actual planning problem and the dedicated problem solver. It is, however, advisable to drive the solver by a general-purpose, powerful constraint engine. This separation enables the consolidation of data and knowledge

coming from a variety of sources, and helps to shift the attention between the logical and optimization aspects of planning in a smooth and principled way.

In the future we intend to improve the performance of the solver by the application of customized distribution strategies and by learning from lessons of earlier sessions. Such improvements will certainly be needed when scaling up the model by including also the machine dimension. We need also interactive solution strategies to support the user in exploring the space of plans.

Acknowledgments. Special thanks are due to the creators of the Mozart system for making it freely available. Partial support of this research came from the NRDP grant No. 2/040/2001.

References

1. Balaban, M., Braha, D.: Temporal Reasoning in Process Planning. *Artificial Intelligence for Engineering Design, Analysis and Manufacturing*, **13**, 91–104, (1999)
2. Birtanik, J., Marefat, M.: Hierarchical Plan Merging with Application to Process Planning. In: *Proc. of the IJCAI'95*, Montreal, 1677–11683, (1995)
3. Brown, K.N., Cagan, J.: Optimized Process Planning by Generative Simulated Annealing. *Artificial Intelligence for Engineering Design, Analysis and Manufacturing*, **11**, 219–235, (1997)
4. Descotte, Y., Latombe, J.-C.: Making Compromises among Antagonist Constraints in a Planner. *Artificial Intelligence*, **27**, 183–217, (1985)
5. Duflou, J.R., Van Oudheusden, D., Kruth, J.-P., Cattrysse, D.: Methods for the Sequencing of Sheet Metal Bending Operations. *Int. J. of Production Research*, **37**(14), 3185–3202, (1999)
6. Gupta, S.K., Nau, D.S., Regli, W.C.: IMACS: A Case Study in Real-World Planning. *IEEE Intelligent Systems*, **13**(3), 49–60, (1998)
7. Gupta, S.K.: Sheet Metal Bending Operation Planning: Using Virtual Node Generation to Improve Search Efficiency. *Journal of Manufacturing Systems*, **18**(2), 127–139, (1999)
8. Halevi, G., Weill, R.D.: *Principles of Process Planning.* Chapman & Hall, 1995.
9. Harvey, W.D., Ginsberg, M.L.: Limited Discrepancy Search. In: *Proc. of the IJCAI'95*, Montreal, 607–613, (1995)
10. Horváth, M., Márkus, A.: Operation Sequence Planning Using Optimization Concepts and Logic Programming. In: *Proceedings of IFAC 9th World Congress*, Budapest, Vol. VI. 153–156 (1984)
11. Horváth, M., Márkus, A., Váncza, J.: Process Planning with Genetic Algorithms on Results of Knowledge-Based Reasoning. *Int. J. of Computer Integrated Manufacturing*, **9**, 145–166, (1996)
12. Kambhampati, S., Cutkosky, M.R., Tenenbaum, J.M., Lee, S.H.: Integrating General Purpose Planners and Specialized Reasoners: Case Study of a Hybrid Planning Architecture. *IEEE Trans. on Systems, Man, and Cybernetics*, **23**(6), 1503–1518, (1993)
13. Kis, T., Váncza, J.: Computational Complexity of Manufacturing Process Planning. In: Ghallab, M. and Milani, A. (eds.), *New Directions in AI Planning*, IOS Press, 299–311, 1996.

14. Márkus A., Váncza J.: Process Planning with Conditional and Conflicting Advice. *Annals of the CIRP*, **50**(1), 327–330, (2001)
15. Marri, H.B., Gunasekaran, A., Grieve, R.J.: Computer-Aided Process Planning: A State of the Art. *Int. J. of Advanced Manufacturing Technology*, **14**, 261–268, (1998)
16. Sarma, S.E., Wright, P.K.: Algorithms for the Minimization of Setups and Tool Changes in "Simply Fixturable" Components in Milling. *Journal of Manufacturing Systems*, **15**(2), 95–112, (1996)
17. Schiex, T.: Valued constraints networks. *CP'2000 Workshop on Modelling and Solving Soft Constraints*, Singapore, (2000). `http://www.math.unipd.it/~frossi/cp2000-soft/`
18. Shah, J.J., Mäntylä, M.: *Parametric and Feature-Based CAD/CAM*. Wiley, 1995.
19. Tate, S.J., Jared, G.E.M., Swift, K.G.: Detecting of Symmetry and Primary Axes in Support of Proactive Design for Assembly. In: Bronsvoort, W.F., Anderson, D.C. (eds.), *Proc. of the Fifth Symposium on Solid Modeling and Applications*, Ann Arbor, MI, ACM Press, 151–158, 1999.
20. Teramoto, K., Onosato, M., Iwata, K.: Coordinative Generation of Machining and Fixturing Plans by a Modularized Problem Solver. *Annals of the CIRP*, **47**(1), 437–440, (1998)
21. Tsang, E.P.K.: *Foundations of Constraint Satisfaction*, Academic Press, 1993.
22. Váncza J., Márkus A.: Genetic Algorithms in Process Planning. *Computers in Industry*, **17**, 181–194, (1991)
23. Váncza, J., Horváth, M., Stankóczi, Z.: Robotic Inspection Plan Optimization by Case-Based Reasoning. *Journal of Intelligent Manufacturing*, **9**(2), 181-188, (1998)
24. Váncza, J., Márkus, A.: Solving Conditional and Conflicting Constraints in Manufacturing Process Planning. In: *Proc. of the CP-AI-OR'2001 Workshop*, Wye, (2001) `http://www.icparc.ic.ac.uk/cpAIOR01/`
25. Wallace, M.G.: Constraint Programming. In: Liebowitz, J. (ed.), *The Handbook of Applied Expert Systems*, CRC Press, 1998.
26. Wang, Ch.-H., Bourne, D.A.: Design and Manufacturing of Sheet-Metal Parts: Using Features to Aid Process Planning and Resolve Manufacturability Problems. *Robotics and Computer Integrated Manufacturing*, **13**(3), 281–294, (1997)
27. Wilkins, D.E., desJardins, M.: A Call for Knowledge-Based Planning. *AI Magazine*, **22**(1), 99–115, (2001).
28. Zeir, G. van, Kruth, J.-P., Detand, J.: A Conceptual Framework for Interactive and Blackboard-Based CAPP. *Int. J. of Production Research*, **36**(6), 1453–1473, (1998)
29. Zhang, H.-C., Lin, E.: A Hybrid-Graph Approach for Automated Setup Planning in CAPP. *Robotics and Computer-Integrated Manufacturing*, **15**, 89–100, (1999)

On the Dynamic Detection of Interchangeability in Finite Constraint Satisfaction Problems

Amy M. Beckwith and Berthe Y. Choueiry

Department of Computer Science and Engineering
University of Nebraska-Lincoln
{abeckwit,choueiry}@cse.unl.edu

We investigate techniques that detect, dynamically during search, *undeclared* symmetries in the form of interchangeability (Freuder'91) in Constraint Satisfaction Problems, with the long-term goal of drawing a compact landscape of the solution space of a given CSP instance. As a first step towards our goal, we propose a new algorithm for dynamically computing interchangeability during backtrack search and demonstrate how it enhances the performance of search.

A technique for exploiting interchangeability during search, which we call FC-NI_C (i.e., forward checking with neighborhood interchangeability according to one constraint), is described by Haselböck (1993). NI_C sets are computed in a pre-processing step prior to search and yield a *static* bundling of the solution space. Since Freuder noted that the *dynamic* computation of interchangeability sets during search yields more opportunities for interchangeability, it is natural to suspect that it also yields better bundling. We design, implement and test a new *dynamic* bundling strategy that we call FC-DNPI. While it was so far believed that the dynamic computation of interchangeability would be too costly to implement during search, we prove that FC-DNPI (i.e., forward checking with dynamic neighborhood partial interchangeability) requires *no more constraint checks than those necessary for performing forward checking.* This strategy computes the DNPI sets using the Joint Discrimination Tree (JDT) of Choueiry and Noubir (1998), which is a generalization of the discrimination tree (DT) of Freuder (1991). Further, we uncover the never-stated relation between interchangeability and the Cross Product Representation (CPR) of Hubbe and Freuder (1992) as being almost equivalent: Search with CPR (FC-CPR) and FC-DNPI yield exactly the same bundles and constraint checks while visiting more nodes in the tree.

We provide theoretical guarantees for the performance of FC-DNPI by comparing it with FC, FC-NI_C, and FC-CPR in terms of the numbers of nodes visited, constraint checks, and generated bundles. Then we provide empirical evidence of the advantages of FC-DNPI in terms of these criteria and also CPU time in the following settings: finding all solutions or the first solution (bundle) to the CSP under static, dynamic variable, and dynamic variable-value orderings. Our tests are performed in the most adversary conditions, i.e. randomly generated problems whose degree of embedded interchangeability is finely controlled over a complete range. We establish that dynamic bundling is orthogonal to, and can only benefit from, traditional enhancements to backtrack search such as strategies for dynamic ordering and for maintaining-arc consistency.

T. Walsh (Ed.): CP 2001, LNCS 2239, p. 760, 2001.

Automatic Generation of Implied Clauses for SAT

Lyndon Drake

Artificial Intelligence Group, Department of Computer Science
University of York, York YO10 5DD, United Kingdom,
lyndon@cs.york.ac.uk,
http://www.cs.york.ac.uk/~lyndon

Davis-Putnam (DP) [3] was the first practical complete algorithm for solving propositional satisfiability (SAT) problems. DP uses resolution to determine whether a SAT problem instance is satisfiable. However, resolution is generally impractical, as it can use exponential space and time. The most important refinement to DP was DLL [2], which replaced the resolution in DP with backtracking search. Backtracking search still uses exponential time in the worst case, but only needs linear space. As time is more readily available than space, the change to search was a big improvement.

Since then, the DLL algorithm has been used almost exclusively in complete SAT solvers [4]. However, Rish and Dechter [5] recently showed that a hybrid complete solver which used ordered resolution along with backtracking search often outperformed pure DLL. Cha and Iwama [1] separately described a local search algorithm that used resolution between similar (or neighbouring) clauses to improve performance. We have investigated the use of this neighbourhood resolution in a complete SAT solver.

Preliminary results show that on certain problems, using neighbourhood resolution in conjunction with search can provide substantial improvements in performance over pure DLL, both in the number of search nodes explored and in the runtime used. Further work on neighbourhood resolution is planned to improve its performance and to identify suitable problem classes.

References

1. Byungki Cha and Kazuo Iwama. Adding new clauses for faster local search. In *Proceedings of AAAI-96*, pages 332–337, 1996.
2. Martin Davis, George Logemann, and Donald Loveland. A machine program for theorem-proving. *Communications of the ACM*, 5:394–397, 1962.
3. Martin Davis and Hilary Putnam. A computing procedure for quantification theory. *Journal of the ACM*, 7:201–215, 1960.
4. Jun Gu, Paul W. Purdon, John Franco, and Benjamin W. Wah. Algorithms for the satisfiability (SAT) problem: A survey. In *Satisfiability Problem: Theory and Applications*, DIMACS Series in Discrete Mathematics and Theoretical Computer Science, pages 19–152. American Mathematical Society, 1997.
5. Irina Rish and Rina Dechter. Resolution versus search: Two strategies for SAT. In Ian Gent, Hans van Maaren, and Toby Walsh, editors, *SAT2000: Highlights of Satisfiability Research in the Year 2000*, volume 63 of *Frontiers in Artificial Intelligence and Applications*, pages 215–259. IOS Press, 2000.

T. Walsh (Ed.): CP 2001, LNCS 2239, p. 761, 2001.

Verification of Infinite-State Systems by Specialization of CLP Programs

Fabio Fioravanti

IASI-CNR and Università di Roma "La Sapienza"
fioravanti@iasi.rm.cnr.it

The goal of automated verification is the definition of a logical framework where hardware or software systems can be formally specified and formal proofs about their properties can be given in a fully automatic way. This involves defining formalisms for encoding the systems and properties of interest.

This paper reports on some results of the application of techniques developed for specializing constraint logic programs to the verification of properties of systems with a possibly infinite number of states. The properties of interest are expressed by formulas of the Computational Tree Logic (CTL, for short). Our method is applicable to a large class of concurrent systems and properties.

Program specialization is a program transformation technique whose goal is the automatic adaptation of a program to the context where it is used. We develop a general framework for the automatic specialization of constraint logic programs with locally stratified negation. Our specialization technique is *correct* w.r.t. the perfect model semantics in the sense that, given a locally stratified CLP program P_1 and an atom A whose predicate is defined in P_1, and given a program P_2 which is a specialization of P_1 w.r.t. A, for every ground instance A_g of A,

$$A_g \in M(P_1) \quad \text{iff} \quad A_g \in M(P_2) \tag{1}$$

where, for any program P, $M(P)$ denotes the perfect model of P.

Our verification method consists of the following two steps.

Step 1. Given a system S with initial state s_0, and a CTL property φ, we introduce a CLP program P_S which defines a binary predicate *sat* such that $s_0 \models \varphi$ iff $sat(s_0, \varphi) \in M(P_S)$.

Step 2. We introduce a new 0-ary predicate f defined by the clause $f \leftarrow sat(s_0, \varphi)$ and thus, $sat(s_0, \varphi) \in M(P_S)$ iff $f \in M(P_S \cup \{f \leftarrow sat(s_0, \varphi)\})$. We then apply our program specialization technique and transform $P_S \cup \{f \leftarrow sat(s_0, \varphi)\}$ into a specialized program P_f. By the correctness of program specialization, stated by the equivalence (1) above, we have that $f \in M(P_S \cup \{f \leftarrow sat(s_0, \varphi)\})$ iff $f \in M(P_f)$. Thus, $s_0 \models \varphi$ iff $f \in M(P_f)$. Finally, we check whether or not $s_0 \models \varphi$ as follows: (i) if the unit clause $f \leftarrow$ occurs in P_f then $s_0 \models \varphi$, and (ii) if no clause with head f occurs in P_f (that is, f has an empty definition in P_f) then $s_0 \not\models \varphi$.

We performed some experiments on two infinite state protocols for mutual exclusion between two processes, the *bakery* algorithm and the *ticket* algorithm, and, by using our verification method, we automatically proved that they both guarantee mutual exclusion and starvation freedom.

T. Walsh (Ed.): CP 2001, LNCS 2239, p. 762, 2001.

Partially Ordered Constraint Optimization Problems*

Marco Gavanelli

Dip. di Ingegneria - University of Ferrara
Via Saragat, 1 - 44100 Ferrara, Italy.
mgavanelli@ing.unife.it

In Constraint Optimization Problems (COP) the objective function induces a total order on the solution set. However, in many real-life applications, more functions, possibly conflicting, should be optimized at the same time, and solutions are ranked by means of a Partial Order.

We propose the model of Partially-Ordered COP, along with a solving algorithm for it:

Definition 1. *A* Partially-ordered COP *(PCOP) is a couple* $R = \langle P, f \rangle$, *where* $P = \langle \{X_1, \ldots, X_n\}, \{D_1, \ldots, D_n\}, C \rangle$ *is a CSP and* $f : D_1 \times \ldots \times D_n \mapsto S_p$, *(where* $\langle S_p, \preceq \rangle$ *is a partially-ordered set) is a function. A* Solution *of a PCOP is a solution* S *of* P *such that* $\nexists S'$ *solution of* P *and* $f(S) \prec f(S')$.

The PCOP generalizes many real-life problems, like the Multi-Objective Problem (MOP) or CSPs that embed the concept of partial order on the solution space. E.g., in a MOP, a solution is non-dominated if a better solution (i.e., such that all the objective functions are better) does not exist. In general, there are many non-dominated solutions in a MOP.

A PCOP can be solved in a variety of ways, the most trivial is finding all the solutions of the CSP and a posteriori select only the non-dominated ones. A more efficient approach is an extension of Branch and Bound (B&B). B&B is an efficient, widely used method for solving COPs; it could be described as follows: first find a solution (typically using tree search), then add a further *unbacktrackable* constraint saying that "new solutions must be *better* than the current best". We have extended B&B by considering, instead of a single additional constraint, a set of unbacktrackable constraints that limit the next solutions to be better (in the $\preceq$ sense) than the already achieved ones. In other words, to solve a PCOP, we have to store all the solutions of the CSP that are currently believed to be non-dominated.

For example, in the MOP case, the constraints added in the B&B are $not(\overline{f(X)} \prec \overline{f(S)})$; i.e., a (tentative) possible solution X will be pruned off if an already obtained solution S is better in all the objective functions: $\forall_{i=1}^{m} f_i(X) \leq f_i(S)$.

We are currently studying very efficient methods for the propagation of the unbacktrackable constraint store. Experimental results show that our B&B extension takes about 40-50% of the time of standard methods providing the whole non-dominated frontier.

* This work was partially supported by CNR

T. Walsh (Ed.): CP 2001, LNCS 2239, p. 763, 2001.

Translations for Comparing Soft Frameworks

Rosella Gennari

Computational and Applied Logic Group, CWI* & ILLC
*Kruislaan 413, 1098 SJ Amsterdam, The Netherlands
Rosella.Gennari@cwi.nl

There are various formalizations of soft constraints in the literature; so far, we have analyzed the semiring-based approach of [BMR97], the fuzzy ones in [Rut94] and the Max-CSP's from [FW92]. If we abstract the common features from those frameworks, we can define soft constraints and frameworks via a restricted collection: a finite set of variables, a finite variable domain, a universal algebra. The latest is composed by a set, called universe, and functions to combine universe elements. A *universe* collects the values (for instance, only 0 and 1 in the hard constraint case) that a constraint can assign to variable domain elements. An *algebra function* combines universe elements; hence an algebra function can be used to derive constraints from input ones, as it can be applied to the universe values in the input constraints' range. We can generalize all the soft constraint operations of [BMR97,Rut94,FW92] via universal algebra functions; and we can construct all solution sets of [BMR97,Rut94] by means of such operations. So, bingo!, all aforementioned soft frameworks are *instances* of ours: i.e., constraints, constraint operations and solution sets of those frameworks are instances of ours.

Yet, this generalization per se is not interesting to us. In fact, we aim to formally define *translations for comparing soft frameworks* and so give a formal version to expressions like "to model a soft framework into another", "this framework is most general because it computes most solutions" etc. First, we define an encoding as a map of an algebra into another; given constraint systems over the two algebras, the encoding is a translation if it preserves solution set computations. Hence we study which properties characterize translations and prove that *algebra homomorphisms* are encodings that satisfy them. Finally, we compare the aforementioned soft frameworks by means of translations and precisely prove which translation can/cannot preserve solution set computations.

References

[BMR97] S. Bistarelli, U. Montanari, and F. Rossi. Semiring-based Constraint Satisfaction and Optimization. *Journal of ACM*, 44(2):201–236, 1997.

[DFP93] D. Dubois, H. Fargier, and H. Prade. The Calculus of Fuzzy Restrictions as a Basis for Flexible Constraint Satisfaction. In *Proc. of the 2nd IEEE International Conference on Fuzzy Systems (IEEE)*, pages 1131–1136, 1993.

[FW92] E.C. Freuder and R.J. Wallace. Partial Constraint Satisfaction. *Artificial Intelligence*, 58:21–70, 1992.

[Rut94] Zs. Ruttkay. Fuzzy Constraint Satisfaction. In *Proceedings of the 3rd IEEE International Conference on Fuzzy Systems*, pages 1263–1268, 1994.

T. Walsh (Ed.): CP 2001, LNCS 2239, p. 764, 2001.

Counting Satisfiable k-CNF Formulas

Mitchell A. Harris

Department of Computer Science
University of Illinois at Urbana-Champaign
1304 W. Springfield Avenue
Urbana, Illinois 61801, USA
maharri@cs.uiuc.edu

We use basic combinatorial techniques to count the number of satisfiable boolean formulas given in conjunctive normal form. The intention is to provide information about the relative frequency of boolean functions with respect to statements of a given size. This in turn will provide information about algorithms attempting to decide problems such as satisfiability and validity. The method we use is an explicit counting of those formulas that are satisfiable. We count the number for any boolean function over v variables, k literals per clause and c clauses. First, we describe a correspondence between the syntax of propositions to the semantics of functions using a system of equations. Then we show how to solve such a system.

The method of creating a system of equations to count the functions can be applied to any formula syntax using any set of logical operators. In the case of k-CNF, regular syntax and the dual behavior of the operators 'and' and 'or' simplify the analysis considerably.

Simply counting combinatorial objects is interesting enough of itself but the method and the result can be used for other things. The general method can be applied to other families of formulas, especially those with a simple syntax and those with other logical operators. For non-linear grammars, that is non-regular grammars, the results will involve the Catalan numbers and its analogues. The result for k-CNF formulas can also be used to derive analytically the 'phase-transition' threshold for satisfiability which has only been approximated experimentally.

T. Walsh (Ed.): CP 2001, LNCS 2239, p. 765, 2001.

High-Level Modelling and Reformulation of Constraint Satisfaction Problems

Brahim Hnich

Computer Science Division, Department of Information Science
Uppsala University, Box 513, S – 751 20 Uppsala, Sweden
Brahim.Hnich@dis.uu.se

The modelling process of constraint satisfaction problems as constraint programs requires sophisticated reasoning skills and involves crucial decisions on which *variable representations* to choose, on which *constraint formulation* to state, and on which *solution methods* to employ. Furthermore, the tight interaction between representation, constraint formulation, and solution methods adds another degree of complexity to the modelling task. For instance, the choice of the constraint formulation is strongly affected by the choice of the representation of variables and values, and by the choice of the solution methods. In addition, the performance of solution methods is sensitive to the problem instances. Thus, modelling combinatorial optimisation problems so as to solve them in more efficient ways is a major challenge for constraint programming.

To address the problem of *decreasing the modelling time*, ever more expressive and declarative constraint programming languages are being designed, providing traditional algebraic notations (such as sums and products over indexed expressions) and useful datatypes (such as sets, arrays, and enumerations) to enable a more natural expression of the variables and constraints, freeing the programmer thus more and more from traditional and often low-level computing obligations, such as the writing of iterative/recursive code or the encoding of concepts as numbers.

To address the *solver's efficiency problem*, alternate models can be tried, the default behaviour of the solver can be modified, implied constraints can be posted so as to reduce the search space, variable and value ordering heuristics can be designed, symmetry-breaking constraints can be added, etc. Such optional, but often necessary, procedural practice is however a concession that fully declarative constraint programming is still far away.

Starting from the very expressive (and fast) OPL (Optimisation Programming Language), we design an even more expressive (and equally fast) language, called ESRA, and show how it can be compiled into OPL. Like OPL, the ESRA language is strongly typed, and a sugared version of what is essentially a first-order logic language. Unlike OPL, the ESRA language supports more advanced types, such as mappings, and allows variables of these types as well as of type set, making it a set constraint language. Furthermore, we propose a set of high-level ESRA reformulation rules that achieve models that switch from a pure constraint program to an integer linear program, or integrate different models of the problem (such as primal and dual models) and add appropriate channelling constraints.

T. Walsh (Ed.): CP 2001, LNCS 2239, p. 766, 2001.

Distributed Constraint Satisfaction as a Computational Model of Negotiation via Argumentation*

Hyuckchul Jung

Dept. of Computer Science, University of Southern California
Henri Salvatori Computer Center, Los Angeles, CA 90089-0781, USA
jungh@usc.edu

Distributed and collaborative agents are promising to play an important role in large-scale multi-agent applications where such collaborative agents may enter into conflicts over their shared resources. Negotiation via argumentation (NVA), where agents provide explicit arguments or justifications for their proposals for resolving conflicts, is a promising approach to collaborative conflict resolution[1]. While previous implemented argumentation systems have performed well in small-size applications, no systematic investigation in large scale has been done. Thus, several questions about computational performance of argumentation remain unaddressed; such as understanding if (and when) argumentation actually speeds up conflict resolution convergence and formulating different collaborative NVA strategies to understand their impact on convergence. Answering these questions requires an abstract, well-understood *computational model of argumentation*, suitable for large-scale experimental investigations.

In this research, we proposed distributed constraint satisfaction problem (DCSP) as a novel computational model of NVA. Here, externally constrained variables (negotiation variables) represent the issues over which agents negotiate. Argument is local constraint that justify the values of the negotiation variables. We modeled argumentation as local constraint communication and propagation in DCSP framework. Argumentation essentially enables DCSP search algorithm to interleave constraint propagation in its normal execution. Using this extended DCSP as our computational model, we formulated different NVA strategies as value ordering heuristics in DCSP, varying the level of cooperativeness towards others. Specially we incorporated argumentation and those NVA strategies into AWC algorithm[3]. This mapping enabled us to investigate the impact of argumentation and different NVA strategies in large-scale. One surprising result from our experiments is that the most cooperative strategy is not the most dominant strategy. This research illustrates the usefulness of these results in applying NVA to multi-agent systems, as well as to DCSP systems in general.

References

1. S. Parsons and N. R. Jennings, Negotiation through argumentation - a preliminary report, *Proc. of Intl. Conf. on Multi-agent Systems*, 1996.
2. H. Jung, M. Tambe, and S. Kulkarni, Argumentation as distributed constraint satisfaction problems, *Proc. of Intl. Conf. on Autonomous Agents*, 2001.
3. M. Yokoo and K. Hirayama, Distributed constraint satisfaction algorithm for complex local problems, *Proc. of the Intl. Conf. on Multi-Agent Systems*, 1998.

* Key parts of this research have been published in the Proceedings of the International Conference on Autonomous Agents Conference, 2001[2].

T. Walsh (Ed.): CP 2001, LNCS 2239, p. 767, 2001.

Aircraft Assignment Using Constraint Programming

Erik Kilborn

Computing Science, Chalmers University of Technology,
SE-412 96 Göteborg, Sweden
ek@cs.chalmers.se
http://www.cs.chalmers.se/~ek/

The aircraft assignment (or tail assignment) problem is to determine the routes flown by each aircraft in a given fleet, such that each flight is included in exactly one route and the aircraft visit maintenance stations according to regulations. Before this problem is solved, an airline has to: i) construct the timetable of flights, and ii) decide the aircraft type of each flight (fleet assignment). The aircraft assignment problem, thus, is a vehicle scheduling problem for a homogeneous fleet where all flight activities are fixed in time.

Simple vehicle scheduling problems are known to be straightforward network flow problems, and can be formulated as bipartite matching. The complicating constraints here are the maintenance regulations (without these we would have had a polynomial problem). A typical OR approach in these situations is to apply column generation. But we should note that this means that the original network problem gets split up in two: a set partitioning problem and a (constrained) shortest path problem. A CP approach lets us keep the entire network flow problem as the core subproblem; allowing us a global view and exploitation of highly efficient network flow algorithms.

The network structure is expressed by finite domain variables, *next*-variables, denoting the successor of each activity. An *alldifferent* constraint is applied over all the *next*-variables, guaranteeing that each activity belongs to exactly one route (i.e. our core subproblem). In a first prototype, the maintenance regulations have been expressed in the simplest possible way: in terms of fixed time maintenance checks locked to certain aircraft. A path constraint was constructed to guarantee that these locked assignments are respected. The prototype is built as a construction heuristic, stopping as soon as a feasible solution is found. An important property of the solver is that it always assigns all flights if possible. Cost-wise this is the dominating aspect. Costs of different connections are considered in the search heuristic.

Tests have been run on different fleets from two commercial passenger airlines. For these problems, the solver provides solutions of good quality very quickly (the latter since the degree of backtracking is minimal). A one-month problem of 17 aircraft and over 3000 flights was solved in 20 seconds (the solver backtracked only 5 times). All encountered over-constrained problems have been identified as such in a matter of seconds.

Work in progress includes constructing a branch-and-bound solver based on the model, and an aircraft re-scheduler for day-of-operation problems.

T. Walsh (Ed.): CP 2001, LNCS 2239, p. 768, 2001.

Labelling Heuristics for CSP Application Domains

Zeynep Kızıltan

Computer Science Division, Department of Information Science
Uppsala University, Box 513, S – 751 20 Uppsala, Sweden
Zeynep.Kiziltan@dis.uu.se

Many real-life problems are *constraint satisfaction problems* (CSPs), which can be programmed as constraint models and then be solved using constraint solvers. *Constraint solvers* are equipped with a *search algorithm*, such as forward-checking, and *labelling heuristics*, one of which is the default. To enhance the performance of constraint models, a lot of research has been made in recent years to develop new labelling heuristics, which concern the choice of the next variable to branch on during the search and the choice of the value to be assigned to that variable. These heuristics significantly reduce the search space.

However, little is said about the application domains of these heuristics, so modellers find it difficult to decide when to apply a particular heuristic, and when not. Indeed, it is not a trivial task to infer the application domains of heuristics because the performance of heuristics is not only model-dependent but also instance-dependent, i.e., for a given constraint model, a heuristic can perform well for some (distributions on the) instances, but very poorly on others; this is taken into account by some generators of model-specific solvers.

Instead of inferring the application domains of heuristics, we advocate inferring heuristics for application domains. If a mapping between application domains and heuristics is known to the solver, then modellers can — if they wish so — be relieved from the procedural aspect of modelling, namely figuring out which heuristic to indicate or implement. Forcing modellers to deal with this procedural aspect may not only add a challenging step but also has the disadvantage that they must commit — at modelling time — to a *single* heuristic and thus expose their models to the instance sensitivity of heuristics.

Towards inferring labelling heuristics for application domains, our three-step approach is to first formalise an application domain as a family of CSP models, so as to exhibit the generic constraint store for all models in that family. Second, the interaction — for a given search algorithm — between the constraints in this generic store and the domain propagation during search is analysed, so as to infer — before modelling any CSP — suitable heuristics for any model in that family. Due to the instance sensitivity of heuristics, the outcome of this process usually is a *set* of heuristics, rather than a single one. The final step of our approach is to address the issue of selecting or switching — at solving time — among the inferred family-specific heuristics, according to the instance to be solved.

Our ultimate aim is thus a new generation of more intelligent solvers that allow CSP modellers to concentrate on the declarative aspect of modelling, without compromising (much) on efficiency.

T. Walsh (Ed.): CP 2001, LNCS 2239, p. 769, 2001.

Improving SAT Algorithms by Using Search Pruning Techniques

Inês Lynce and João Marques-Silva

Technical University of Lisbon, IST/INESC/CEL, Portugal
{ines,jpms}@sat.inesc.pt

Propositional Satisfiability (SAT) is fundamental in solving many application problems in Artificial Intelligence and in other fields of Computer Science and Engineering. In the recent past, intelligent backtrack search algorithms for SAT have empirically been shown to be highly effective in pruning the amount of search, by applying strategies for non-chronological backtracking and procedures for clause recording. Apart from the commonly used pruning techniques, these algorithms can be augmented with other different techniques, namely identification of necessary assignments, randomized strategies and simplification techniques.

Necessary assignments can be obtained by using different forms of *value probing*. The idea of probing consists in identifying assignments that are deemed necessary, usually called *implied necessary assignments*. In SAT algorithms, the most used procedure for identifying necessary assignments consists in the iterated application of the unit clause rule. Moreover, the identification of necessary assignments can be augmented with value probing techniques. For example, *Recursive Learning* recursively evaluates clause satisfiability requirements for identifying common assignments to variables, whereas *Stålmark's Method* also identifies common assignments to variables, despite being based on variables.

The utilization of different forms of randomization in SAT algorithms has seen increasing acceptance in recent years. Randomization is also a key aspect of restart strategies, ensuring that different sub-trees are searched each time the search algorithm is restarted. More recently, the utilization of randomization has been used in the backtrack step of a complete backtrack search algorithm, where we randomly pick the backtracking point from the set of literals in the recorded conflict clause.

Resolution is probably the most well-known from the existing simplification techniques. Two-variable equivalence is another well-known formula simplification procedure. Whenever a two-variable equivalence is detected, the number of variables in the formula decreases by 1. In addition, the inference of binary clauses using selective resolution, i.e. based on specific clause patterns, can contribute to finding more equivalent variables. We should note that the inference of clauses always contributes to adding more information to the problem specification, and therefore can potentially simplify the search.

With this work we propose improving backtrack search algorithms by integrating new and more effective search pruning techniques. Some interesting results have already been obtained. In the future, we expect to further pursue this work and conduct a more comprehensive experimental evaluation and categorization of the proposed techniques.

T. Walsh (Ed.): CP 2001, LNCS 2239, p. 770, 2001.

Optimum Symmetry Breaking in CSPs Using Group Theory

Iain McDonald*

University of St Andrews, Fife, Scotland,
iain@dcs.st-and.ac.uk

There has been a lot of interest in breaking symmetries in CSPs over the past ten years. The research carried out has detailed how to exploit the symmetries in CSPs so that we only search for unique solutions i.e. we will count two symmetrically equivalent solutions as one solution. In doing so we hope to take less time finding solutions.

There are many already implemented methods of breaking symmetries but there are none yet that can cope with $n!$ symmetries where n is the number of constrained variables. My current research is a first step in making a system that can deal with a very large number of symmetries.

This first step is to break unique symmetries. Given a set of symmetries S, of a CSP, a partial assignment A can be taken to another partial assignment A', using symmetry $g \in S$. It is possible for another symmetry $h \in S$ to take A to A'. Thus we only need to break g or h but not both. By doing this we perform unique symmetry breaking.

The way we find unique symmetries is by using techniques from group theory, a field of pure maths. Hundreds of years of work has gone into group theory and so its methods are very efficient and well researched. A group can be described using a set of generators, and we can represent a group with millions of elements (in this case symmetries) with only a few generators. We can use the orbit finding algorithm which runs in linear time and whose output are the unique symmetries.

I have used an encoding of the orbit finding algorithm to perform symmetry breaking and I have solved a 4 by 4 alien tiles grid problem (with $2n!^2 = 1152$ symmetries where n is 4) in 125 seconds. With no symmetry breaking this takes 1293 seconds.

There are other methods that are more efficient such as those that do not perform symmetry breaking on symmetries that have already been broken. Using group theory techniques though I can expand my current method to include the advantages of previous research making a system which should hopefully be able to cope with $n!$ symmetries.

---

* I would like to thank my supervisor Ian Gent and also Steve Linton and Barbara Smith for their help and encouragement. I would also like to thank the EPSRC for funding my research.

T. Walsh (Ed.): CP 2001, LNCS 2239, p. 771, 2001.

Distributed Dynamic Backtracking

Christian Bessière[1], Arnold Maestre[1], and Pedro Meseguer[2]

[1] Member of the COCONUT group
LIRMM-CNRS (UMR 5506), 161 rue Ada, 34392 Montpellier Cedex 5, France
{bessiere, maestre}@lirmm.fr
[2] IIIA-CSIC, Campus UAB, 08193 Bellaterra, Spain
pedro@iiia.csic.es

Abstract. In the scope of distributed constraint reasoning, the main algorithms presented so far have a feature in common: the addition of links between previously unrelated agents, before or during search. Our work presents a new search procedure for finding a solution in a distributed constraint satisfaction problem. This algorithm makes use of some of the good properties of centralized dynamic backtracking. It is sound, complete and allows a high level of asynchronism by sidestepping the unnecessary addition of links.

In the last years, several works have considered constraint satisfaction in a distributed form, where a CSP is shared between several agents located on different sites. Each agent owning only a part of the data, they have to collaborate by exchanging messages in order to solve the global problem (see [2] for an introduction). These works are motivated by the existence of naturally distributed constraint problems for which it is impossible or undesirable to gather the whole problem knowledge into a single agent and to solve it using centralized methods.

The main complete and asynchronous algorithms for solving distributed CSPs add communication links between agents that were not connected in the initial problem, to ensure the consistency of the information stored during search. We show that the number of such links added may be very significant, and thus may lead to a lot of extra message passing. We then propose a polynomial-space asynchronous search algorithm which remains sound and complete without performing any link addition, and we check it against ABT on random distributed problems of various size and tightness. A more in-depth description of the algorithm, as well as experimental results, may be found in [1].

References

1. C. Bessière, A. Maestre, and P. Meseguer. Distributed dynamic backtracking. In *http://www.lirmm.fr/~bessiere/stock/ddb01.ps.gz*, 2001.
2. M. Yokoo and T. Ishida. Search algorithms for agents. In G. Weiss, editor, *Multiagent Systems*, pages 165–199. MIT Press, 1999.

T. Walsh (Ed.): CP 2001, LNCS 2239, p. 772, 2001.

Constraint Programming for Distributed Resource Allocation

Pragnesh Jay Modi

University of Southern California/Information Sciences Institute
4676 Admiralty Way, Marina del Rey, CA 90292, USA
modi@isi.edu

Constraint based techniques offer a promising approach to coordinating a set of agents in solving a distributed resource allocation problem. Distributed resource allocation is a general problem in which a set of agents must intelligently assign their resources to a set of tasks such that all tasks are performed with respect to certain criteria. This problem arises in many real-world domains such as distributed sensor networks [4], disaster rescue[2], hospital scheduling[1], and others.

This work proposes a formalization of distributed resource allocation that is expressive enough to represent both dynamic and distributed aspects of the problem [3]. These two aspects present some key difficulties. First, a distributed situation results in agents obtaining only local information, but facing global *ambiguity* — an agent may know the results of its local operations but it may not know the global task and hence may not know what operations others should perform. Second, the situation is dynamic so a solution to the resource allocation problem at one time may become unsuccessful when the underlying tasks have changed. So the agents must continuously monitor the quality of the solution and must have a way to express such changes in the problem.

In order to address this type of resource allocation problem, the work presented here extends and applies constraint based techniques, in particular the Dynamic Distributed Constraint Satisfaction Problem (DyDCSP), to the distributed resource allocation problem. The central contribution is a reusable, generalized mapping from distributed resource allocation to DyDCSP. This mapping is proven to correctly perform resource allocation problems of specific difficulty. Ideally, the formalization and mapping may enable researchers to understand the difficulty of their resource allocation problem, choose a suitable DyDCSP problem using the presented mapping, with automatic guarantees for correctness of the solution.

References

1. K. Decker and J. Li. Coordinated hospital patient scheduling. In *ICMAS*, 1998.
2. Hiroaki Kitano. Robocup rescue: A grand challenge for multi-agent systems. In *ICMAS*, 2000.
3. PJ. Modi, H. Jung, Tambe M., Shen W., and S. Kulkarni. A dynamic distributed constraint satisfaction approach to resource allocation. In *Proc of Constraint Programming*, 2001.
4. Sanders. Ecm challenge problem, http://www.sanders.com/ants/ecm.htm. 2001.

T. Walsh (Ed.): CP 2001, LNCS 2239, p. 773, 2001.

Exploiting the CSP Structure by Interchangeability

Nicoleta Neagu

Artificial Intelligence Laboratory (LIA),
Computer Science Department, Swiss Federal Institute of Technology (EPFL)
CH-1015 Ecublens, Switzerland
neagu@lia.di.epfl.ch http://liawww.epfl.ch/

Abstract. While there are many AI algorithms designed for finding solutions in a *Constraint Satisfaction Problems*, finding similar solutions of a CSP requires entirely new and different methods. The method we propose here is based on the *interchangeability* concept first introduced by Freuder [1].

Keywords: constraint satisfaction problem, interchangeability.

Till now days there are methods for abstraction and reformulation of CSPs which facilitate easier and faster solving of CSPs but there are not yet methods for organising and structuring the solution space.

This work is primely motivated by the need for an method which can find relations between the solutions and then, classify them. Usual approaches are searching CSP solutions without watching relations between them and thus they are deficient in structuring the solution space. The solutions are usually listed, without describing the similarities or differences between them. Here we propose a method based on interchangeability which can determine limits within which the effect of change in a solution stays local and thus, other close solutions can be found.

In [1], Freuder defined for the first time the notion of interchangeability and its different types. The concept of interchangeability capture the equivalence among values of the variables in a CSP.

Further, the procedure for computing local interchangeability proposed by Freuder, neighbourhood interchangeability (NI), was extended by Choueiry and Noubir [2] for computing a weaker form of interchangeability: neighbourhood partial interchangeability (NPI).

Depending on the CSP structure, we studied the occurrence of NPI, see [3]. It has been notice that since NPI is weaker than NI, it necessarily occurs more frequently and the resulting benefits should be at least as good.

An important issue is to localise minimal and minimum changes in the CSP solutions. We proposed an algorithm for computing minimal NPI sets in [3]. It determines how changes propagates in a solution set and generates a minimal set of choices which can be changed in order to stay solution. The algorithm applies for an input which specifies which variables want to be changed and the corresponding changes. In the further work we intend to improve the heuristics for a faster and efficient searching and to reduce complexity.

T. Walsh (Ed.): CP 2001, LNCS 2239, pp. 774–775, 2001.

For a specific change there are more minimal NPI sets, but only few minimum ones; where a minimal set means that by changing the value of one variable all the variables from the set have to change.

In our further work, we propose to study how to find the minimum set of changes, thus even more similar solutions.

References

1. Eugene C. Freuder. Eliminating Interchangeable Values in Constraint Satisfaction Problems. In *In Proc. of AAAI-91*, pages 227–233, Anaheim, CA, 1991.
2. Berthe Y. Choueiry and Guevara Noubir. On the Computation of Local Interchangeability in Discrete Constraint Satisfaction Problems. In *Proc. of AAAI-98*, pages 326–333, Madison, Wiscowsin, 1998.
3. Nicoleta Neagu and Boi Faltings. Exploiting Interchangeabilities for Case Adaptation. In *In Proc. of the 4th ICCBR-01*, pages 422–437, Vancouver, CA, 2001.

Constraint Processing Techniques for Model-Based Reasoning about Dynamic Systems

Andrea Panati

Dipartimento di Informatica – Università di Torino
Corso Svizzera 185, 10149 Torino, Italy

In recent years, there is an increasing interest in modeling and reasoning about complex dynamic systems for tasks such as design, configuration, simulation and diagnosis of technical devices. These tasks, however, require expensive reasoning methods, therefore one of the main issues in real applications is how to reduce the computational cost of reasoning about dynamic models.

In our work, we propose the application of qualitative abstractions (such as Qualitative Deviations Equations implemented as CSPs on finite domains) for qualitative simulation of dynamic systems, in particular for the task of model-based diagnosis. Qualitative simulation requires the ability to reason on sets of instantaneous equations (i.e. constraints) as well as reasoning across time in order to compute the dynamics of the system. We call these sub-tasks intra-state and inter-state reasoning, respectively.

Given that, in our applications, constraint-based models are derived from equations, the resulting CSPs are usually structured. The structure is captured by a bipartite graph, those edges connect variables and equations, and allows for a convenient decomposition, e.g. into acyclic clusters of constraints. To improve the efficiency of intra-state reasoning, we propose a feedback vertex set decomposition technique applied to bipartite graphs in order to exploit the structure of such CSPs.[1] In particular, we present an exact (or anytime) algorithm for solving the One Side Minimum Feedback Vertex Set on Bipartite Graphs problem. The algorithm is based on a branch and bound approach, in which bounds are efficiently computed by solving maximum spanning forest problems on the bipartite graph.[2]

To improve reasoning across time in qualitative simulation applications (i.e. reasoning on temporal constraints between different states of the system), a different approach based on causal information has been proposed. Given a causal semantics for the constraints appearing in our models, we have shown how this causal structure can be used for efficiently compute a solution for the CSP, as well as for computing all possible successor states of the system (i.e. behaviors).

A causal simulation algorithm has been developed and implemented within a constraint-based diagnostic engine.[3] The techniques discussed here have been applied to real case studies in the automotive field, such as the Common Rail fuel injection system, a guiding application of the VMBD project.[4]

[1] [http://link.springer.de/link/service/series/0558/bibs/1792/17920166.htm]
[2] [http://www.di.unito.it/~panati/papers/mfvs.ps]
[3] [http://www.di.unito.it/~panati/papers/ecai-00.ps]
[4] [http://dblp.uni-trier.de/db/journals/aicom/aicom12.html#CascioCOPSD99]

T. Walsh (Ed.): CP 2001, LNCS 2239, p. 776, 2001.

Distributed Constraint Satisfaction with Cooperating Asynchronous Solvers

Georg Ringwelski

GMD FIRST, German National Research Center for Information Technology
Kekuléstraße 7, 12489 Berlin, Germany, georg.ringwelski@gmd.de

A Constraint Satisfaction Problem (CSP) is to find an assignment to a set of variables that is consistent wrt. a set of constraints over these variables. CSPs frequently arise in applications of distributed artificial intelligence [3] and may often not be solved by a centralized constraint solver for privacy or security reasons. In this distributed case (DCSP) constraints and variables are distributed among multiple automated agents.

To solve a CSP it has turned out to be effective to provide information gained from constraints to other constraints via common variables as soon as it is available. With this constraint propagation large parts of the search space are cut very early. Constraint propagation defines a confluent transition system if the constraints are interpreted as inflationary and monotonic functions reducing the variables' domains [1]. In Asynchronous Constraint Solving (ACS) [2] we make use of this fact by invoking the propagation algorithms of posted constraints from a buffer with an internal scheduling. In addition we offer the possibility to asynchronously retract constraints. If a previously posted constraint is retracted, all variables and constraints will have the same state as if it had never been posted. Using the asynchronously executed methods 'post' and 'retract' on variable assignments (that *constrain* a variable to have a certain value) search algorithms can be defined to solve any CSP if implementations for all used constraints are provided.

ACS is well suited for the use in DCSP because no global information is necessary for history management or other CSP tasks. Constraint postings and retractions are buffered in the priority-queue of their corresponding solver such that no synchronization has to be made. In our current Java implementation every agent holds a solver, where constraints over any physically reachable variable can be posted or retracted from any other agent or local application. As application we implement a distributed time schedulung tool where appointments can be organized and reorganized automatically with constraint satisfaction.

References

[1] Krzysztof R. Apt. The essence of constraint propagation. *Theoretical Computer Science*, 221(1-2):179–210, 1998.
[2] Georg Ringwelski. A new execution model for constraint processing in object-oriented software. In *Proceedings of the WFLP01*, 2001.
[3] Makoto Yokoo and Edmund H. Durfee. The distributed constraint satisfaction problem: Formalization and algorithms. *IEEE Transactions on Knowledge and Data Engineering*, 10(5), 1998.

T. Walsh (Ed.): CP 2001, LNCS 2239, p. 777, 2001.

Building Negative Reduced Cost Paths Using Constraint Programming

Louis-Martin Rousseau[1], Gilles Pesant[1], and Michel Gendreau[1]

Centre for Research on Transportation
Universite de Montreal, C.P. 6128, succursale Centre-ville
Montreal, CANADA, H3C 3J7
{louism,pesant,michelg}@crt.umontreal.ca
http://www.crt.umontreal.ca

Column Generation is a powerful method used to solve Constrained Set Partitioning problems. This method can be decomposed in two parts: the master problem and the sub-problem. The Master Problem that should be solved in Column Generation is derived from a simple Set Partitioning problem. Depending on the context the subproblem may become a variant of the simple Shortest-Path Problem; applications in scheduling generally present an acyclic graph (since one dimension of the graph is time) as opposed to routing problems that are cyclic by nature. However, most real life applications present resource constrained subproblems, typical resources being time, capacity, money, etc.

In this paper we will consider the routing domain of application and thus concentrate our studies on the Cyclic Resource Constrained Shortest Path Problems. These problems are also referred to as Profitable Tour Problems (PTP) in the literature, since the objective is to construct a tour that minimizes the distance traveled, while maximizing the total amount of prize (here dual values) collected.

Most of the methods that address the cyclic cases do so by first rendering the associated graph acyclic. This transformation enables the use of dynamic programming to solve the shortest path problem given that the resources are discrete. This method is very efficient, however the size of the graph generated is usually quite impressive, and, since the problem allows negative weight on the arcs, the shortest paths produced are not elementary.

It is hoped that the use of Constraint Programming in combination with Operations Research methods will allow us to solve Elementary Shortest Path Problem instances by working on the smaller original cyclic graph.

The paper presents the model we have chosen to represent the Profitable Tour Problem, introduces some redundant constraints and discusses the transformation of a PTP into an Asymmetric Traveling Salesman Problem (ATSP) in order to use known lower bounds. We also propose arc elimination techniques and a novel way to compute dual values that could be use in the more traditional Dynamic Programming based column generation scheme.

T. Walsh (Ed.): CP 2001, LNCS 2239, p. 778, 2001.

An Incremental and Non-binary CSP Solver: The Hyperpolyhedron Search Algorithm

Miguel A. Salido and Federico Barber

Dpto. Sistemas Informáticos y Computación
Universidad Politécnica de Valencia
Camino de Vera s/n 46071
Valencia, Spain
{msalido, fbarber}@dsic.upv.es

Nowadays, many real problems can be efficiently modelled as Constraint Satisfaction Problems (CSP's). Most of these problems can be naturally modeled using non-binary constraints. However, researchers traditionally had focused on binary constraints, due to the simplicity of dealing with binary constraints and the fact that any non-binary CSP can be transformed into an equivalent binary one. Moreover, this transformation may not be practical in some problems, because the binarized CSP produces a significant increase in the problems size and the translation process generates new variables, which may have very large domains. Thus, it becomes necessary to manage problems with non-binary constraints directly. In this work, we propose an algorithm called "Hyperpolyhedron Search Algorithm (HSA)" that solves non-binary constraint satisfaction problems in a natural way as an incremental and non-binary CSP solver. HSA is a constraint propagation algorithm that carries out the search through a hyperpolyhedron that maintains in its vertices those solutions that satisfy all non-binary constraints. In HSA, the handling of the non-binary constraints (linear inequations) can be seen as a global hyperpolyhedron constraint. Initially, the hyperpolyhedron is created by the Cartesian Product of the domain bounds of variables. For each constraint, HSA checks the consistency, updating the hyperpolyhedron (if the constraint is consistent), by means of LP techniques. This constraint is a hyperplane that is intersected to obtain the new hyperpolyhedron vertices. The resulting hyperpolyhedron is a convex set of solutions to the CSP.

Traditional CSP techniques obtain the solution by searching systematically through the possible assignments of values to variables. The complexity of these techniques increases exponentially with the number of variables, number of constraints and domain length. However, HSA only increases exponentially with the number of variables, and has constant cost respect to domain length.

To reduce this exponential complexity, some heuristics can be used. They carried out the search through an incomplete hyperpolyhedron that is generated by the Cartesian Product of the some domain bounds of variables. Some algorithms are OFHH [1] and NFHH [2]. Their complexities are linear and quadratic respectively. The more appointment algorithm will be a mixture of these algorithms, which it is configured depending on the problem topology and the user requirement.

T. Walsh (Ed.): CP 2001, LNCS 2239, pp. 779–780, 2001.

References

[1] Salido, M.A., Giret, A., Barber, F.: A Non-binary Constraint Satisfaction Solver: The One-face Hyperpolyhedron Heuristic. In Proceeding of ES2001. (Ed. Springer Verlag). (2001)

[2] Salido, M.A., Giret, A., Barber, F.: Realizing a Global Hyperpolyhedron Constraint via LP Techniques. In Proceedings of KI-2001 Workshop (Ed. Jügen Sauer) (78-88) (2001)

Partial Stable Generated Models of Generalized Logic Programs with Constraints

Sibylle Schwarz

Institut für Informatik, Universität Leipzig
Augustusplatz 10–11, 04109 Leipzig, Germany
schwarz@informatik.uni-leipzig.de

Generalized logic programs. (GLP) are sets of rules with arbitrary quantifier free formulas in their bodies and heads. Well-known program classes, such as definite, normal and disjunctive programs, are syntactically restricted special cases of GLP. Combining this program class with the advantages of the additional use of constraints in the bodies of the rules results in the very expressive language $\mathcal{C}$-GLP, appropriate to solve complex knowledge representation tasks.

Stable generated models. provide a declarative semantics for GLP and $\mathcal{C}$-GLP. Two-valued stable generated models (SGM) were introduced and studied by Herre and Wagner in [4]. Recently Herre [3] defined partial stable generated models (SGM_3) and compared them to Przymusinski's partial stable models [5].

A (partial) interpretation is a (partial) stable model of a GLP-program, if it can be reached by a *stable chain* of (partial) interpretations starting from the truth-minimal (partial) interpretation of the program. Succeeding stages of a stable chain are connected by a special relation, that guarantees monotonicity inside the chain and the groundedness of the achieved stable generated model.

SGM and SGM_3 are the only declarative semantics for the whole class GLP defined so far and can be naturally extended to programs with constraints. The author presented a definition of SGM for $\mathcal{C}$-GLP in [6] and is now studying the more interesting case of partial stable generated models and their properties.

Some other ideas. of declarative and operational semantics for restricted program classes with constraints have been published (for instance in [2], [1]). Comparisons of these approaches to our semantics will help to develop a proof theoretical characterization of stable generated models and a query answering mechanism.

References

[1] J. Dix and F. Stolzenburg. A framework to incorporate non-monotonic reasoning into constraint logic programming. *JLP*, 37(1-3), 1998.

[2] F. Fages and R. Gori. A hierarchy of semantics for normal constraint logic programs. In *Algebraic and Logic Programming ALP'96, lncs 1139*, 1996.

[3] H. Herre. Regular partial models and wellfounded semantics for generalized logic programs. *unpublished*, 2000.

T. Walsh (Ed.): CP 2001, LNCS 2239, pp. 781–782, 2001.

[4] H. Herre and G. Wagner. Stable models are generated by a stable chain. *Journal of Logic Programming*, 30(2), 1997.

[5] T. Przymusinski. Well-founded and stationary models of logic programs. *Annals of Mathematics and Artificial Intelligence 12 (1994), 141-187.*, 1994.

[6] S. Schwarz. Stable generated models of generalized constraint logic programs. (to appear in) *Proc. WFLP 2001.* Universität Kiel, 2001.

Heterogeneous Constraint Problems
An Outline of the Field of Work

Frank Seelisch

DaimlerChrysler AG - Research & Technology
Knowledge-Based Engineering
Alt-Moabit 96a, 10559 Berlin, Germany
phone: +49 (0)30 39982-391, fax: -107
Frank.Seelisch@DaimlerChrysler.com

Nowadays, constraint processing has become a mayor issue in engineering applications based on digital product models. A modern product naturally decomposes into numerous subcomponents, the physical behaviour of which can be mathematically described by constraints. By collecting all components's constraints we obtain a rich mathematical description of the entire product. A surprisingly small number of services implemented on such constraint problems (*consistency check*; finding *solutions* resp. *conflicts; explanations*) can provide engineers with a great deal of useful information and help them solve their problems.

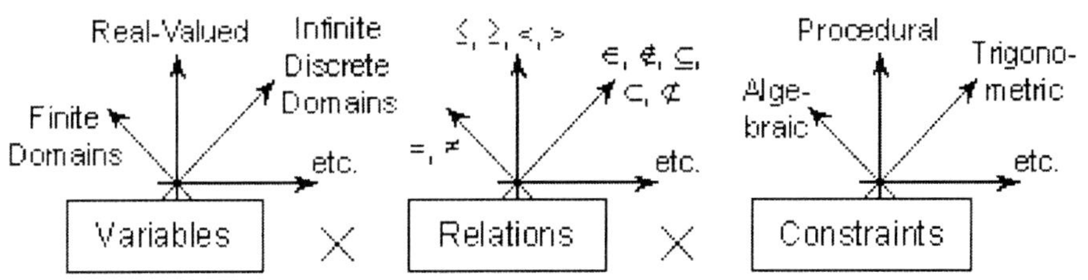

Fig. 1. Heterogeneous Constraints in Engineering

The crucial observation is that a mathematical formulation of physical behaviour will, in general, involve all imaginable types of constraints. Figure 1 illustrates the complex problem space in engineering applications. Apart from a possibly great variety of variables's domains, we are usually confronted with linear, non-linear, trigonometric and other types of equations, inequations, inequalities, etc. Also, procedural, i.e. directed and not explicitely available constraints modelling the behaviour of control units, often join in the problem.

In my work, I attempt to define and implement a framework in which an *automatic analysis of constraint problems typical for engineering tasks*, and especially providing the above services, become possible and tractable. In order to gain workable performance, trading off computational completeness is a realistic option. Inherent properties, like e.g. rather small widths of associated constraint hypergraphs, can and must be utilized.

T. Walsh (Ed.): CP 2001, LNCS 2239, p. 783, 2001.

Comparing SAT Encodings for Model Checking

Daniel Sheridan

Artificial Intelligence Group
Department of Computer Science
University of York
York, England
djs@cs.york.ac.uk

Bounded model checking (BMC) [1] was proposed as a solution to some of the problems (*e.g.* space explosion) of conventional BDD-based symbolic model checking by introducing a temporal bound. The problem can then be encoded as a Boolean formula and used as input to a SAT checker: the output of a BMC tool is a conjunction of state transition functions and state verification functions.

Our work has focused on improving encodings for BMC by using a normal form for temporal logic [2]. With a variety of encodings available, it has become necessary to perform a comparison between them so that the best encoding can be chosen. By making available a method of comparison that is not based on benchmarks, we can develop systems which are able to chose the best encoding for a given input. In addition, a comparison that is not based on benchmarks is less time consuming to perform and can yield more detailed results; for example, the pathological cases for each encoding can easily be found.

Initial work in this area has been based on the method in [3] for predicting the number of clauses produced by the encoding. This analysis has been extended to allow for other clause form conversions, and we have developed new metrics allowing for the consideration of, for example, clause size. We use a variety of different benchmarks in comparing the time taken by a SAT checker running on clauses sets generated by BMC with the predictions based on the number of clauses, size of clauses, and other metrics. We show how these comparisons indicate the strengths of the various encodings, and suggest ways in which the choice of encoding might be made based on these predictions.

References

1. Armin Biere, Alessandro Cimatti, Edmund Clarke, and Yunshan Zhu. Symbolic model checking without BDDs. In W.R. Cleaveland, editor, *Tools and Algorithms for the Construction and Analysis of Systems. 5th International Conference, TACAS'99*, volume 1579 of *Lecture Notes in Computer Science*, pages 193–207. Springer-Verlag Inc., July 1999.
2. Alexander Bolotov and Michael Fisher. A resolution method for CTL branching-time temporal logic. In *Proceedings of the Fourth International Workshop on Temporal Representation and Reasoning (TIME)*. IEEE Press, 1997.
3. Andreas Nonnengart, Georg Rock, and Christoph Weidenbach. On generating small clause normal forms. In Claude Kirchner and Hélène Kirchner, editors, *Fifteenth International Conference on Automated Deduction*, volume 1421 of *Lecture Notes in Artificial Intelligence*, pages 397–411. Springer-Verlag, 1998.

T. Walsh (Ed.): CP 2001, LNCS 2239, p. 784, 2001.

Asynchronous Search for Numeric DisCSPs

Marius-Călin Silaghi[1], Ştefan Sabău[2], Djamila Sam-Haroud[1], and Boi Faltings[1]

[1] Artificial Intelligence Lab (LIA), EPF-Lausanne, CH-1015, Switzerland;
[2] Inspectorat Şcolar, Baia-Mare, 4800, Romania

In Distributed CSPs (DisCSPs), agents may want to keep parts of their problem secret but accept to cooperate by exchanging proposals. Asynchronism in solving DisCSPs [1] increases flexibility, parallelism, and robustness. Enumerative algorithms apply for discrete problems with small domains. Our goal is to develop asynchronous algorithms that can deal with numeric constraints. Centralized techniques for CSPs with continuous domains interleave (dichotomous) splitting of the search space with forms of bound consistency. Consecutive numerical values are aggregated into intervals. As a first step towards our goal, we have developed Asynchronous Aggregation Search (AAS) [1], allowing agents to asynchronously propose subspaces of their search space. Agents propose splits of domains that ensure the feasibility of their subproblem. Then we have proposed DMAC, allowing to maintain bound (or arc) consistency in AAS [1]. Dichotomous splits are generally only partially sound splits since the agent proposing them does not necessarily have its constraints fully satisfied by them. The simplest and most widely used strategy for partially sound splits is the dichotomous one, but the technique we propose next can similarly deal with more complex splitting strategies.

We propose a framework called Replicas-based DisCSP (RDisCSP) where each initial agent is represented by a set of *abstract agents*. Except for the last positioned abstract agent of an initial agent A_j (called *checking replica*), its other abstract agents in a RDisCSP do not intend to satisfy the whole problem of A_j, but a relaxation of it or even a totally feasible constraint. For achieving Asynchronous Dichotomous search Maintaining Bound-consistency (ADMB) using DMAC over RDisCSPs, each abstract agent behaves according to complete splitting operators. They propose search spaces that are half of the size of their allowed search space (within a relative tolerance k). Each initial agent A_j has constraints over the external variables V_j and any $x_i, x_i \in V_j$ can take values from a domain D_i. With ADMB, the upper-bound of the number of abstract agents for A_j required to reach solutions with resolution ε is $\sum_{x_i \in V_j} \log_{2/(1+k)} (|D_i|/\varepsilon)$. ADMB can be used for solving RDisCSPs with numerical constraints. All abstract agents of any initial agent can be represented in ADMB by the same physical agent and all messages sent to them are then sent in only one message. The structures of abstract agents required for maintaining consistency at different splitting levels are shared in the physical agent. The consistency nogoods for a level are generated only once for an initial agent (by its *checking replica*). The checking replica has to ensure that the subproblem it proposes is feasible with the resolution ε. ADMB is the first asynchronous algorithm for dealing with private constraints over mixed and *continuous* domains.

References

1. M.-C. Silaghi, D. Sam-Haroud, and B. Faltings. Multiply asynchronous search with abstractions. In *IJCAI-01 DCR Workshop*, pages 17–32, Seattle, August 2001.

T. Walsh (Ed.): CP 2001, LNCS 2239, p. 785, 2001.

Temporal Concurrent Constraint Programming

Frank D. Valencia

BRICS[*], University of Aarhus, Denmark
fvalenci@brics.dk

The temporal ccp model *tcc* [3] is aimed at specifying timed systems. Time is conceptually divided into discrete intervals. In a particular time interval, a ccp process receives a stimulus (i.e. a constraint) from the environment, it executes with this stimulus as the initial store, and when it reaches its resting point, it responds to the environment with the resulting store. Also the resting point determines a residual process, which is then executed in the next time interval. This temporal ccp model is inherently deterministic and synchronous.

The *ntcc calculus* [2] is a nondeterministic version of tcc which also allows asynchronous behavior. The motivation for this extension was partly the desire to be able to specify natural temporal behaviors like "the system must output c *within* the next t time intervals", which is not possible in tcc. Also, the extension is argued to be consistent with the declarative flavor of ccp, i.e. to free the programmer from over-specifying a deterministic solution, when a non-deterministic simple solution is more appropriate (following the arguments behind Dijkstra's language of guarded commands). Furthermore, it is argued that a very important benefit of allowing the specification of non-deterministic and asynchronous behavior arises when modeling the interaction among several components running in parallel. These systems often need non-determinism to be modeled faithfully.

In [2] a relative complete proof system for linear-time properties of ntcc processes is studied. In [1] various notions of behavior for the ntcc calculus are introduced: the input-output and the language equivalence and their congruences, all motivated operationally and/or logically. The notions are related, and proved to be decidable for a substantial fragment of the calculus. The expressive power of ntcc has been illustrated by modeling bounded response and invariance specifications, constructs such as cells, bounded broadcasting, some applications involving the programming of RCX™ controllers [2] and a version of a Predator/Prey (Pursuit) game [1].

References

1. M. Nielsen and F. Valencia. Temporal concurrent constraint programming: Applications and behavior. Technical report, BRICS, August 2001.
2. C. Palamidessi and F. Valencia. A temporal concurrent constraint programming calculus. In *Proc. of the Seventh International Conference on Principles and Practice of Constraint Programming*, 26 November 2001.
3. V. Saraswat, R. Jagadeesan, and V. Gupta. Foundations of timed concurrent constraint programming. In *Proc. of the Ninth Annual IEEE Symposium on Logic in Computer Science*, pages 71–80, 4–7 July 1994.

[*] Basic Research in Computer Science, Centre of the Danish National Research Foundation.

T. Walsh (Ed.): CP 2001, LNCS 2239, p. 786, 2001.

Author Index

Lecture Notes in Computer Science

For information about Vols. 1–2144
please contact your bookseller or Springer-Verlag

Vol. 2122: H. Alt (Ed.), Computational Discrete Mathematics. VII, 173 pages. 2001.

Vol. 2145: M. Leyton, A Generative Theory of Shape. XVI, 554 pages. 2001.

Vol. 2146: J.H. Silverman (Eds.), Cryptography and Lattices. Proceedings, 2001. VII, 219 pages. 2001.

Vol. 2147: G. Brebner, R. Woods (Eds.), Field-Programmable Logic and Applications. Proceedings, 2001. XV, 665 pages. 2001.

Vol. 2149: O. Gascuel, B.M.E. Moret (Eds.), Algorithms in Bioinformatics. Proceedings, 2001. X, 307 pages. 2001.

Vol. 2150: R. Sakellariou, J. Keane, J. Gurd, L. Freeman (Eds.), Euro-Par 2001 Parallel Processing. Proceedings, 2001. XXX, 943 pages. 2001.

Vol. 2151: A. Caplinskas, J. Eder (Eds.), Advances in Databases and Information Systems. Proceedings, 2001. XIII, 381 pages. 2001.

Vol. 2152: R.J. Boulton, P.B. Jackson (Eds.), Theorem Proving in Higher Order Logics. Proceedings, 2001. X, 395 pages. 2001.

Vol. 2153: A.L. Buchsbaum, J. Snoeyink (Eds.), Algorithm Engineering and Experimentation. Proceedings, 2001. VIII, 231 pages. 2001.

Vol. 2154: K.G. Larsen, M. Nielsen (Eds.), CONCUR 2001 – Concurrency Theory. Proceedings, 2001. XI, 583 pages. 2001.

Vol. 2155: H. Bunt, R.-J. Beun (Eds.), Cooperative Multimodal Communication. Proceedings, 1998. VIII, 251 pages. 2001. (Subseries LNAI).

Vol. 2156: M.I. Smirnov, J. Crowcroft, J. Roberts, F.Boavida (Eds.), Quality of Future Internet Services. Proceedings, 2001. XI, 333 pages. 2001.

Vol. 2157: C. Rouveirol, M. Sebag (Eds.), Inductive Logic Programming. Proceedings, 2001. X, 261 pages. 2001. (Subseries LNAI).

Vol. 2158: D. Shepherd, J. Finney, L. Mathy, N. Race (Eds.), Interactive Distributed Multimedia Systems. Proceedings, 2001. XIII, 258 pages. 2001.

Vol. 2159: J. Kelemen, P. Sosík (Eds.), Advances in Artificial Life. Proceedings, 2001. XIX, 724 pages. 2001. (Subseries LNAI).

Vol. 2161: F. Meyer auf der Heide (Ed.), Algorithms – ESA 2001. Proceedings, 2001. XII, 538 pages. 2001.

Vol. 2162: Ç. K. Koç, D. Naccache, C. Paar (Eds.), Cryptographic Hardware and Embedded Systems – CHES 2001. Proceedings, 2001. XIV, 411 pages. 2001.

Vol. 2163: P. Constantopoulos, I.T. Sølvberg (Eds.), Research and Advanced Technology for Digital Libraries. Proceedings, 2001. XII, 462 pages. 2001.

Vol. 2164: S. Pierre, R. Glitho (Eds.), Mobile Agents for Telecommunication Applications. Proceedings, 2001. XI, 292 pages. 2001.

Vol. 2165: L. de Alfaro, S. Gilmore (Eds.), Process Algebra and Probabilistic Methods. Proceedings, 2001. XII, 217 pages. 2001.

Vol. 2166: V. Matoušek, P. Mautner, R. Mouček, K. Taušer (Eds.), Text, Speech and Dialogue. Proceedings, 2001. XIII, 452 pages. 2001. (Subseries LNAI).

Vol. 2167: L. De Raedt, P. Flach (Eds.), Machine Learning: ECML 2001. Proceedings, 2001. XVII, 618 pages. 2001. (Subseries LNAI).

Vol. 2168: L. De Raedt, A. Siebes (Eds.), Principles of Data Mining and Knowledge Discovery. Proceedings, 2001. XVII, 510 pages. 2001. (Subseries LNAI).

Vol. 2169: M. Jaedicke, New Concepts for Parallel Object-Relational Query Processing. XI, 161 pages. 2001.

Vol. 2170: S. Palazzo (Ed.), Evolutionary Trends of the Internet. Proceedings, 2001. XIII, 722 pages. 2001.

Vol. 2171: R. Focardi, R. Gorrieri (Eds.), Foundations of Security Analysis and Design. VII, 397 pages. 2001.

Vol. 2172: C. Batini, F. Giunchiglia, P. Giorgini, M. Mecella (Eds.), Cooperative Information Systems. Proceedings, 2001. XI, 450 pages. 2001.

Vol. 2173: T. Eiter, W. Faber, M. Truszczynski (Eds.), Logic Programming and Nonmonotonic Reasoning. Proceedings, 2001. XI, 444 pages. 2001. (Subseries LNAI).

Vol. 2174: F. Baader, G. Brewka, T. Eiter (Eds.), KI 2001: Advances in Artificial Intelligence. Proceedings, 2001. XIII, 471 pages. 2001. (Subseries LNAI).

Vol. 2175: F. Esposito (Ed.), AI*IA 2001: Advances in Artificial Intelligence. Proceedings, 2001. XII, 396 pages. 2001. (Subseries LNAI).

Vol. 2176: K.-D. Althoff, R.L. Feldmann, W. Müller (Eds.), Advances in Learning Software Organizations. Proceedings, 2001. XI, 241 pages. 2001.

Vol. 2177: G. Butler, S. Jarzabek (Eds.), Generative and Component-Based Software Engineering. Proceedings, 2001. X, 203 pages. 2001.

Vol. 2180: J. Welch (Ed.), Distributed Computing. Proceedings, 2001. X, 343 pages. 2001.

Vol. 2181: C. Y. Westort (Ed.), Digital Earth Moving. Proceedings, 2001. XII, 117 pages. 2001.

Vol. 2182: M. Klusch, F. Zambonelli (Eds.), Cooperative Information Agents V. Proceedings, 2001. XII, 288 pages. 2001. (Subseries LNAI).

Vol. 2183: R. Kahle, P. Schroeder-Heister, R. Stärk (Eds.), Proof Theory in Computer Science. Proceedings, 2001. IX, 239 pages. 2001.

Vol. 2184: M. Tucci (Ed.), Multimedia Databases and Image Communication. Proceedings, 2001. X, 225 pages. 2001.

Vol. 2185: M. Gogolla, C. Kobryn (Eds.), «UML» 2001 – The Unified Modeling Language. Proceedings, 2001. XIV, 510 pages. 2001.

Vol. 2186: J. Bosch (Ed.), Generative and Component-Based Software Engineering. Proceedings, 2001. VIII, 177 pages. 2001.

Vol. 2187: U. Voges (Ed.), Computer Safety, Reliability and Security. Proceedings, 2001. XVI, 249 pages. 2001.

Vol. 2188: F. Bomarius, S. Komi-Sirviö (Eds.), Product Focused Software Process Improvement. Proceedings, 2001. XI, 382 pages. 2001.

Vol. 2189: F. Hoffmann, D.J. Hand, N. Adams, D. Fisher, G. Guimaraes (Eds.), Advances in Intelligent Data Analysis. Proceedings, 2001. XII, 384 pages. 2001.

Vol. 2190: A. de Antonio, R. Aylett, D. Ballin (Eds.), Intelligent Virtual Agents. Proceedings, 2001. VIII, 245 pages. 2001. (Subseries LNAI).

Vol. 2191: B. Radig, S. Florczyk (Eds.), Pattern Recognition. Proceedings, 2001. XVI, 452 pages. 2001.

Vol. 2192: A. Yonezawa, S. Matsuoka (Eds.), Metalevel Architectures and Separation of Crosscutting Concerns. Proceedings, 2001. XI, 283 pages. 2001.

Vol. 2193: F. Casati, D. Georgakopoulos, M.-C. Shan (Eds.), Technologies for E-Services. Proceedings, 2001. X, 213 pages. 2001.

Vol. 2194: A.K. Datta, T. Herman (Eds.), Self-Stabilizing Systems. Proceedings, 2001. VII, 229 pages. 2001.

Vol. 2195: H.-Y. Shum, M. Liao, S.-F. Chang (Eds.), Advances in Multimedia Information Processing – PCM 2001. Proceedings, 2001. XX, 1149 pages. 2001.

Vol. 2196: W. Taha (Ed.), Semantics, Applications, and Implementation of Program Generation. Proceedings, 2001. X, 219 pages. 2001.

Vol. 2197: O. Balet, G. Subsol, P. Torguet (Eds.), Virtual Storytelling. Proceedings, 2001. XI, 213 pages. 2001.

Vol. 2198: N. Zhong, Y. Yao, J. Liu, S. Ohsuga (Eds.), Web Intelligence: Research and Development. Proceedings, 2001. XVI, 615 pages. 2001. (Subseries LNAI).

Vol. 2199: J. Crespo, V. Maojo, F. Martin (Eds.), Medical Data Analysis. Proceedings, 2001. X, 311 pages. 2001.

Vol. 2200: G.I. Davida, Y. Frankel (Eds.), Information Security. Proceedings, 2001. XIII, 554 pages. 2001.

Vol. 2201: G.D. Abowd, B. Brumitt, S. Shafer (Eds.), Ubicomp 2001: Ubiquitous Computing. Proceedings, 2001. XIII, 372 pages. 2001.

Vol. 2202: A. Restivo, S. Ronchi Della Rocca, L. Roversi (Eds.), Theoretical Computer Science. Proceedings, 2001. XI, 440 pages. 2001.

Vol. 2204: A. Brandstädt, V.B. Le (Eds.), Graph-Theoretic Concepts in Computer Science. Proceedings, 2001. X, 329 pages. 2001.

Vol. 2205: D.R. Montello (Ed.), Spatial Information Theory. Proceedings, 2001. XIV, 503 pages. 2001.

Vol. 2206: B. Reusch (Ed.), Computational Intelligence. Proceedings, 2001. XVII, 1003 pages. 2001.

Vol. 2207: I.W. Marshall, S. Nettles, N. Wakamiya (Eds.), Active Networks. Proceedings, 2001. IX, 165 pages. 2001.

Vol. 2208: W.J. Niessen, M.A. Viergever (Eds.), Medical Image Computing and Computer-Assisted Intervention – MICCAI 2001. Proceedings, 2001. XXXV, 1446 pages. 2001.

Vol. 2209: W. Jonker (Ed.), Databases in Telecommunications II. Proceedings, 2001. VII, 179 pages. 2001.

Vol. 2210: Y. Liu, K. Tanaka, M. Iwata, T. Higuchi, M. Yasunaga (Eds.), Evolvable Systems: From Biology to Hardware. Proceedings, 2001. XI, 341 pages. 2001.

Vol. 2211: T.A. Henzinger, C.M. Kirsch (Eds.), Embedded Software. Proceedings, 2001. IX, 504 pages. 2001.

Vol. 2212: W. Lee, L. Mé, A. Wespi (Eds.), Recent Advances in Intrusion Detection. Proceedings, 2001. X, 205 pages. 2001.

Vol. 2213: M.J. van Sinderen, L.J.M. Nieuwenhuis (Eds.), Protocols for Multimedia Systems. Proceedings, 2001. XII, 239 pages. 2001.

Vol. 2214: O. Boldt, H. Jürgensen (Eds.), Automata Implementation. Proceedings, 1999. VIII, 183 pages. 2001.

Vol. 2215: N. Kobayashi, B.C. Pierce (Eds.), Theoretical Aspects of Computer Software. Proceedings, 2001. XV, 561 pages. 2001.

Vol. 2216: E.S. Al-Shaer, G. Pacifici (Eds.), Management of Multimedia on the Internet. Proceedings, 2001. XIV, 373 pages. 2001.

Vol. 2217: T. Gomi (Ed.), Evolutionary Robotics. Proceedings, 2001. XI, 139 pages. 2001.

Vol. 2218: R. Guerraoui (Ed.), Middleware 2001. Proceedings, 2001. XIII, 395 pages. 2001.

Vol. 2220: C. Johnson (Ed.), Interactive Systems. Proceedings, 2001. XII, 219 pages. 2001.

Vol. 2221: D.G. Feitelson, L. Rudolph (Eds.), Job Scheduling Strategies for Parallel Processing. Proceedings, 2001. VII, 207 pages. 2001.

Vol. 2224: H.S. Kunii, S. Jajodia, A. Sølvberg (Eds.), Conceptual Modeling – ER 2001. Proceedings, 2001. XIX, 614 pages. 2001.

Vol. 2225: N. Abe, R. Khardon, T. Zeugmann (Eds.), Algorithmic Learning Theory. Proceedings, 2001. XI, 379 pages. 2001. (Subseries LNAI).

Vol. 2229: S. Qing, T. Okamoto, J. Zhou (Eds.), Information and Communications Security. Proceedings, 2001. XIV, 504 pages. 2001.

Vol. 2230: T. Katila, I.E. Magnin, P. Clarysse, J. Montagnat, J. Nenonen (Eds.), Functional Imaging and Modeling of the Heart. Proceedings, 2001. XI, 158 pages. 2001.

Vol. 2232: L. Fiege, G. Mühl, U. Wilhelm (Eds.), Electronic Commerce. Proceedings, 2001. X, 233 pages. 2001.

Vol. 2233: J. Crowcroft, M. Hofmann (Eds.), Networked Group Communication. Proceedings, 2001. X, 205 pages. 2001.

Vol. 2239: T. Walsh (Ed.), Principles and Practice of Constraint Programming – CP 2001. Proceedings, 2001. XIV, 788 pages. 2001.

Vol. 2241: M. Jünger, D. Naddef (Eds.), Computational Combinatorial Optimization. IX, 305 pages. 2001.